Children and Youth in America

Children and Youth in America

A Documentary History

VOLUME I: 1600-1865

EDITOR

Robert H. Bremner

ASSOCIATE EDITORS

John Barnard

Tamara K. Hareven

Robert M. Mennel

Harvard University Press

Cambridge, Massachusetts   1970

© 1970 by The American Public Health Association

All rights reserved

Distributed in Great Britain by Oxford University
Press, London

Library of Congress Catalog Card Number 74-115473

SBN 674–11610–0

Printed in the United States of America

Foreword

By Martha M. Eliot, M.D. and William M. Schmidt, M.D.

This and the two succeeding volumes of *Children and Youth in America* have been prepared by the staff of the Child and the State Project under the auspices of the American Public Health Association and with the financial support of the Children's Bureau of the Department of Health, Education, and Welfare. The project took its name and derived its inspiration from the work of Grace Abbott (1878–1939), Chief of the Children's Bureau from 1921 to 1934, and from 1934 to 1939 professor of public welfare administration in the School of Social Service Administration of the University of Chicago. In the latter position Miss Abbott undertook the preparation of a two-volume documentary history of legislative, judicial, and administrative actions affecting apprenticeship and child labor, child welfare, delinquency, and the legal relations of children to parents and other adults in the American community. Published as *The Child and the State* in 1938 by the University of Chicago Press, this work was put to good use in the training of students in schools of social work and public health and as a reference for historians and administrators of voluntary and government programs for children. *The Child and the State* remains a useful source book whose value is enhanced by Miss Abbott's informative introductory essays on the development of public care for dependent children, the mothers' aid movement, and the development of state and federal child labor legislation. Miss Abbott herself regretted the omission of materials on child health from the study and once proposed the preparation of a supplementary volume on community action for the health care of mothers and children and related social services.

Convinced that an enlargement and revision of the work would serve the needs of scholars and professionals in work with children in many fields, we undertook in 1964 the initial planning of the Child and the State Project. Our point of view has been expressed in this way: "Children, because of their ever changing, gradually merging patterns of growth and development, and because of their constantly shifting response to environmental influences require for the solution of their problems the attention of closely integrated health and social services and a variety of educational opportunities in their homes, their communities, their schools, and in many cultural settings." [1] We first thought to supply a volume on child health to accompany Grace Abbott's work on child welfare, delinquency, labor, and legal status. As we discussed the idea further, however, we became convinced that it would not suffice merely to add a volume on health and bring the subjects of the two earlier volumes down to date. In particular, the topics of education and of the treatment of children of minority racial and ethnic groups seemed so intimately related to the development of public policy for children that those subjects could not be ignored. A thorough restudy and expansion of the material was called for if we were to do justice to the

1. Martha M. Eliot, "Howland Award Address," *American Journal of the Diseases of Children,* CXIV (1967), 567.

range and complexity of the involvement of the American public with its children.

Since many of the additional documents would come in the field of child health, it was appropriate to approach the American Public Health Association and its Program Area Committee on Child Health in seeking a sponsor for the project. At the October 1964 meeting of the committee a proposal for the preparation of a new edition of *The Child and the State* was considered. The committee's membership, drawn from a broad spectrum of those concerned with maintaining children's health, endorsed the proposal with enthusiasm and authorized a search for funds. From the beginning the committee intended that the work should be so broadly conceived that it would appeal to professional schools and scholars in medicine and the health professions, social work, law, education, public administration, and the clergy. The committee expected that many who are actively engaged in organizing and directing services for children would also find interest in the work and would profit from its breadth.

The members of the committee during the life of the project have been:

Paul F. Wehrle, M.D. (chairman 1967–1969)
David B. Ast, D.D.S.
Virginia A. Beal, M.P.H.
Sidney S. Chipman, M.D.
Mildred E. Doster, M.D. (acting chairman 1968–1969)
Agnes L. Fuller, R.N.
Enrique L. Matta, Jr., M.D.
Sam Shapiro
William Schmidt, M.D. (chairman 1964–1966)
Elizabeth Watkins, D. Sci. Hyg.
Staff: Thomas R. Hood, M.D.
Susan V. Baker

A statement requesting financial support was submitted to the Children's Bureau in April 1965. It was prepared by Dr. Eliot, who accepted the committee's invitation to become project director. The approval of the application on June 24, 1965, assured generous backing. The American Public Health Association, the recipient of the grant, its staff, and especially its deputy executive director, Thomas Hood, were prepared to supply administrative services and guidance. Oscar Handlin, director of the Charles Warren Center for Studies in American History, Harvard University, kindly offered the splendid facilities of the center for use by the project's editors and their staff. This gave the project a congenial home and access to the great library resources of Harvard University. When Robert H. Bremner of the Department of History, Ohio State University, assumed responsibility as executive research editor in April 1966, and a policy committee consisting of Dr. Eliot as chairman, Professor Handlin, Dr. Hood, Dr. Schmidt, Dr. Wehrle, and Professor Bremner had been formed, the project was ready to begin work. Professors Barnard and Hareven, and Mr. Mennel, joined the project later in the year.

The collection and editing of the documents and the interpretive introductions are the work of Mr. Bremner and his staff. In this first volume of the series, Mr. Bremner, in addition to supervising the preparation of the entire work, assumed responsibility for the materials on dependency and, with Mr. Barnard, collected and edited the documents which form the introductory sections on family and child life at the beginning of each of the three parts of the volume. Mr. Barnard prepared the sections on education and on Negro and Indian children. Miss Hareven contributed the documents and introductions on child labor and on immigrant children. Mr. Mennel supplied the materials on the history of delinquency, and assisted all the members of the staff in a variety of research tasks. Manfred Waserman assisted Mr. Bremner and Mr. Mennel in the collection of documents on the history of child health.

Harvard School of Public Health
Boston, Massachusetts

Editor's Preface

This is the first of three volumes dealing with the history of public policy toward children and youth in America from the colonial period to the present. "Public policy" as used here includes the activities of governmental and voluntary agencies at the local, state, and national levels for the promotion and protection of the welfare of children and youth. The volumes do not comprise a history of childhood and family life in America. Many of the documents, however, illustrate various conditions of family life because, as far as children are concerned, the necessity for public action is in large measure determined by conditions within the family.

Volume I covers a period of 265 years — the span of four lifetimes — extending from the founding of the early English settlements to the end of the Civil War. Volume II includes events occurring within the space of a single life, the years between 1866 and 1932; and Volume III deals with policies adopted and developed since 1933. The briefer time period covered in Volume II and the still briefer period dealt with in Volume III reflect the great expansion of interest in, and concern for, the rights and problems of children and youth during the past century. Richard Titmuss, commenting on the appearance of the same phenomenon in Great Britain, speaks of "the rise in esteem of children in our society" and of "the revolution in standards of child care since the nineteenth century." [1] In the United States as in Great Britain, growing sensitivity to the needs of children and the importance of youth has led to multiplication and elaboration of governmental and voluntary programs for their benefit.

1. *Essays on "The Welfare State"* (New Haven, 1959), pp. 30, 32.

This volume deals with nine or more generations of children who lived in America before the revolution of which Titmuss speaks. It examines the status of children and youth in American society in the seventeenth, eighteenth, and first two-thirds of the nineteenth centuries. The major topics treated are education, labor, dependency, delinquency, child health, and the special problems of slave, Indian, immigrant, and free black children.

In format the book is a collection of documents arranged topically within chronological periods and linked by interpretive introductions. Although we recognize that documentary history is no more authentic or objective than narrative history, we have adopted the documentary approach because it offers the breadth and flexibility required for examining the ramifications of our subject. Finding, selecting, and organizing the documents into meaningful patterns has proved almost as challenging and rewarding as the writing of narrative history. It has been impossible to avoid overlap between topics because education, child labor, health, dependency, and delinquency are closely related subjects. Instead of attempting to maintain rigid topical distinctions we have tried to present similar problems from different viewpoints. We have also crossed chronological lines when subject matter indicated.

For the sake of clarity, especially in seventeenth- and eighteenth-century documents, we have modernized some spelling and punctuation. In editing statutes we have sought to eliminate legal verbiage. All omissions within documents are indicated by ellipsis points. Since, in numerous documents, large sections have been excised, readers who require complete transcriptions will find it necessary to refer to the sources. Our objective has not been to enshrine the documents but to use them to illustrate the course of events and the development of policies. Footnotes not supplied by the editors are followed by bracketed explanations of source.

In a work covering a span of more than two and a half centuries it is necessary to adopt some chronological subdivisions. We have divided the work into three units or parts with the following dates: 1600–1735; 1735–1820; 1820–1865. Although we have assigned dates to each of the three parts, we do not ask or expect readers to accept the divisions as distinct historical periods precisely delimited and widely different from each other. In history, continuity is sometimes more apparent than change. But change is what makes a year, a decade, or a century different, in some degree, from the past. Our purpose in dividing the book into chronological units has been to identify trends and shifts, sometimes barely perceptible, in the directions of public attitudes and community responsibility for children.

The three subdivisions of the book represent stages in the development of public policies toward children. These stages can be presented in interrogative form. The question raised by the first stage is: What is the function of government or the public authority when the child is a subject, not a citizen, of private family government? In the second: How does the public sector respond when children, although still officially subject to family or familial authority, practice the doctrines of self-help, independence, and self-interest? Third: How did the state and the adult public regard children in a society marked by political and social change, population mobility, and rapid economic growth? What was expected of children? What was done for them? What was denied them?

The editors have followed common law and statute in using twenty-one as the age of ma-

jority or the end of childhood. The bulk of documents in this volume, however, refer to boys and girls under sixteen, the age group which, in the first federal census of 1790, constituted 49 per cent of the total white population.[2] Youth, the period immediately preceding maturity, is difficult to define in terms of age because its onset and close are governed by physical, cultural, and economic factors that vary from time to time. Before 1865 Americans could not support the luxury of prolonged youth. Youth problems existed, and there was concern about them; but young people had to assume many of the responsibilities, if not the rights, of adulthood at an early age. In Volume I, therefore, more than in the succeeding volumes, public provision for children looms larger than provision for youth.

The editors share the hope of Dr. Eliot and Dr. Schmidt that *Children and Youth in America* will prove useful to students in the humanities, social sciences, and professional schools of law, medicine, public health, education, and social work. We hope that this particular volume will contribute background information and perspective on later developments and issues in the social welfare history of children. Finally, we hope that the book and the two succeeding volumes will provide a new perspective on American history. It is possible to read political, constitutional, military, diplomatic, and some social and intellectual history without being aware of children. It is impossible, however, to study the development of public policies for children without becoming conscious of adults and their world, and without seeing that world from a new and different point of view.

R.H.B.

Columbus, Ohio
November 1969

2. W. S. Rossiter, *A Century of Population Growth from the First Census of the United States, to the Twelfth, 1790–1900* (Washington, D.C., 1909), p. 103.

Acknowledgments

Publication of the first volume of *Children and Youth in America* offers the editors a welcome opportunity to express gratitude to all those who made the Child and the State Project possible. Martha M. Eliot and William M. Schmidt of the Harvard School of Public Health initiated and directed the project; Berwyn F. Mattison, Thomas R. Hood, and Carroll E. Cary of the American Public Health Association supervised its administration; and Charles Gershenson, Hyman Goldstein, and Gloria Wackernah of the Children's Bureau superintended the funding of the several grants which financed the project. The editors deem it a privilege to have been associated in this undertaking with Drs. Eliot and Schmidt and with officers of the American Public Health Association and the Children's Bureau. While benefiting from their counsel and encouragement we have enjoyed the widest freedom in developing the organization and content of this work.

From June 1967 to September 1969 the Child and State Project was housed at the Charles Warren Center for Studies in American History, Harvard University. Oscar Handlin, his administrative assistants, Katharine E. Top and Alicia Zintl, and the administrative committee of the Charles Warren Center provided the editorial staff with a hospitable base and stimulating atmosphere for scholarly research. Widener Library and the Countway Library of Medicine, in addition to many other courtesies, furnished valuable study space to the editors and their assistants. In the academic year 1969–1970, when headquarters of the project moved to Ohio State University, Harry L. Coles and Charles Morley of the department of history arranged for a generous assignment of space and liberal research and clerical assistance. Deans and chairmen of departments of history at Ohio State, Oakland, and Dalhousie Universities granted the editors leave and reduced teaching schedules to permit work on the study. The editors wish to express their deep appreciation to all of the above for their help in the conduct and completion of the work. We are also indebted to the librarians and archivists whose interest and knowledge facilitated research on the project.

At the outset an advisory panel of experts in many fields of work with children was appointed. The editors extend thanks to the several members of the panel who offered advice in the fields of their specialties. The editors have also benefited from the constructive criticism of a number of eminent scholars who served the project as consultants. We have enjoyed the companionship of a large, enthusiastic, and capable group of co-workers. It is a particular pleasure to acknowledge the contributions made by research, editorial, and secretarial assistants. A complete listing of the staff and consultants of the Child and State Project is appended to this volume. Several members of the staff deserve special recognition: Manfred Waserman prepared the original drafts of the chapters and sections on child health; Susanna Adams and Leslie Rosenfeld contributed invaluable research and editorial help in chapters on education, child labor, and administration of child welfare services; Paula Cronin maintained editorial conformity throughout the volume and also took responsibility for obtaining permissions. Claudia Crispin, Gisela Mennel, and Marie-Dolores Solano performed responsible and demanding secretarial and administrative assignments with unfailing competence and good humor.

ix

Contents

Illustrations

Works Cited in Shortened Form

The Burlington Court Book: H. Clay Reed and G. C. Miller, eds. *The Burlington Court Book: A Record of Quaker Jurisprudence in West New Jersey, 1680–1709.* Washington, D.C.: American Historical Association, 1944.

Conn. Records: J. Hammond Trumbull and C. J. Hoadley, eds. *Public Records of the Colony of Connecticut (1636–1776).* 15 volumes. Hartford: Case, Lockwood & Brainard Company, etc., 1850–1890.

CSM *Publications: Publications* of the Colonial Society of Massachusetts. 43 volumes. Boston: The Colonial Society of Massachusetts, 1895–1966.

Documents of the Slave Trade: Elizabeth Donnan, ed. *Documents Illustrative of the History of the Slave Trade to America.* 4 volumes. Washington, D.C.: Carnegie Institution of Washington, 1930–1935.

Documents Relative to the Colonial History of New York: E. B. O'Callaghan and Berthold Fernow, comps. *Documents Relative to the Colonial History of the State of New York.* 15 volumes. Albany: Weed, Parsons & Company, Printers, 1856–1887.

Ga. Colonial Records: Allen D. Candler, comp. *The Colonial Records of the State of Georgia (1732–1782).* 26 volumes. Atlanta: C. P. Byrd, 1904–1916.

Mass. Records: Nathaniel Shurtleff, ed. *Records of the Governor and Company of Massachusetts Bay, 1628–1686.* 5 volumes. Boston: W. White, 1853–1854.

Md. Archives: W. H. Browne et al., eds. *Archives of Maryland.* 65 volumes. Baltimore: Maryland Historical Society, 1883–1952.

MHS *Collections: Collections* of the Massachusetts Historical Society. Cambridge, Mass.: The Massachusetts Historical Society, etc., 1792——.

MHS *Proceedings: Proceedings* of the Massachusetts Historical Society. Boston: The Society, 1859——.

MSR: Middlesex Sessions Rolls. Greater London Record Office, London.

No. Car. Records: William L. Saunders, ed. *The Colonial Records of North Carolina (1662–1776).* 10 volumes. Raleigh: P. M. Hale, etc., 1886–1890.

N.Y.C. Council Minutes: Minutes of the Common Council of the City of New York, 1675–1776. 8 volumes. New York: Dodd, Mead and Company, 1905. *1784–1831.* 21 volumes. New York: M. B. Brown Printing and Binding Company, 1917–1930.

Penna. Statutes at Large: James T. Mitchell and Henry Flanders, comps. *The Statutes at Large of Pennsylvania from 1682 to 1801.* 17 volumes. Harrisburg: C. M. Bush, etc., 1896–1908.

PRO: Great Britain. Public Record Office. London.

Records of the Moravians: Adelaide L. Fries, ed. *Records of the Moravians in North Carolina.* 9 volumes. Raleigh: Edwards & Broughton Printing Company, etc., 1922–1964.

So. Car. Statutes at Large: Thomas Cooper and D. J. McCord, eds. *Statutes at Large of South Carolina.* 10 volumes. Columbia: State Printers, 1836–1841.

Va. Co. Records: Susan M. Kingsbury, ed. *The Records of the Virginia Company of London: The Court Book, from the Manuscript in the Library of Congress.* 4 volumes. Washington, D.C.: Government Printing Office, 1906–1935.

Va. Statutes at Large: W. W. Hening, ed. *Statutes at Large of Virginia (1619–1782).* 13 volumes. Richmond: Samuel Pleasants, 1809–1823.

Part One   Children and Youth in Colonial
                America, 1600–1735

I The New World as Refuge and Bridewell: Children in the Colonizing Process

After 1500 the nations of Europe sought wealth and strength through exploration and empire. As an infant rejuvenates the spirits of its parents, ancient Europe expected a renewal of life through the birth and nurture of colonial dependencies. Naturally, the planning and execution of imperial projects were duties for the mature, but children figured in the calculations as instruments and beneficiaries of colonization. In England especially, children were expected to play an important part in the creation of empire.

Motives and expectations differed from one promoter of colonization to another. Richard Hakluyt of London, an enthusiast for empire, thought children's labor would be beneficial for all concerned. Even boys and girls of "twelve or fourteene yeeres of age, or under," he wrote, "may bee kept from idlenesse, in making of a thousand kindes of trifling things, which wil be good merchandize for that country." [1] His new world would be a workshop of busy children, with employment, profits, and social harmony the inevitable results. New England Puritans, on the other hand, often spoke of migration to the New World as a movement for the benefit of their children's souls. "It was for your sakes especially, that your Fathers ventured their lives upon the rude waves of the vast Ocean," Increase Mather told his congregation. "Was

it not with respect unto Posterity that our Fathers came into this Wilderness, that they might train up a Generation for Christ?" [2]

Englishmen's visions of America as a setting for childhood were about as varied as Englishmen themselves. Since the Reformation they had been divided. In the upper reaches of society, factions in church and state revolved around the crown in a ceaseless rivalry for influence and office. At the bottom of the social hierarchy, great numbers moved about the countryside or were absorbed into London, looking for work or hoping to avoid it, seeking pleasure, fleeing unhappiness, or simply trying to survive. English national life was a spectacle of contrasts: wealth and poverty, power and dependence, faith and heresy contended and coexisted. In these circumstances even a wilderness might bear a hopeful aspect.

And what of childhood in this boisterous world? Certainly its beginnings were hazardous for both mother and infant regardless of their station in society. When John Chamberlain, a London gentleman, wrote in 1601 to a friend: "My niece Stukeley was lately brought abed of a son, but the joy lasted not longe, for they both vanished soone thereafter," he told a tale common in the households of the time. [3] Epidemics, malnutrition, the ordinary diseases of

---

1. Richard Hakluyt, *Hakluyt's Collection of the Early Voyages, Travels, and Discoveries of the English Nation* (London, 1810), III, 219.

2. Increase Mather, *A Call from Heaven* (Boston, 1685), p. 42.
3. Norman E. McClure, ed., *The Letters of John Chamberlain* (Philadelphia, 1939), I, 133.

A In *Adam's* Fall
   We Sinned all.

B Thy Life to Mend
   This *Book* Attend.

C The *Cat* doth play
   And after flay.

D A *Dog* will bite
   A *Thief* at night.

E An *Eagles* flight
   Is out of fight.

F The Idle *Fool*
   Is whipt at School.

N *Nightingales* fing
   In Time of Spring.

O The *Royal Oak*
   it was the Tree
   That fav'd His
   Royal Majeftie.

P *Peter* denies
   His Lord and cries

Q Queen *Efther* comes
   in Royal State
   To Save the JEWS
   from difmal Fate

R *Rachol* doth mour.
   For her firft born.

S *Samuel* anoints
   Whom God appoint:

G As runs the *Glafs*
   Mans life doth pafs.

H My *Book* and *Heart*
   Shall never part.

J *Job* feels the Rod
   Yet bleffes GOD.

K Our *KING* the
   good
   No man of blood.

L The *Lion* bold
   The *Lamb* doth hold.

M The *Moon* gives light
   In time of night.

T *Time* cuts down all
   Both great and fmall.

U *Uriah's* beauteous Wife
   Made *David* feek his
   Life.

W *Whales* in the Sea
   God's Voice obey.

X *Xerxes* the great did
   die,
   And fo muft you & I,

Y *Youth* forward flips
   Death fooneft nips.

Z *Zacheus* he
   Did climb the Tree
   His Lord to fee,

Illustrated Alphabet

childhood and those contracted from mothers, especially tuberculosis, carried off hundreds in the earliest stage of life. Perhaps as many as two-thirds of all children died before they reached the age of four.[4] Despite this rate of mortality, English families tended to be large. The admonition to "be ye fruitful, multiply, and replenish the earth," like some other biblical teachings, was held in serious regard. Families were further enlarged by extending over several generations and by including unrelated members as well. The young, the mature, and the elderly, other relations, apprentices, workmen, and servants, were often to be found within a single household. Consequently, families of a dozen or more were common in the villages and the countryside, and eight to a household was near the average in towns and cities.[5] Many people, however, lived outside of families. Losses at sea and work accidents made widows of wives and orphans of children. A large floating lower-class population, including numerous children and young people, only irregularly participated in family life.

Social conditions were a propelling force, persuading people to leave the kingdom and venture into the New World. Shifts in occupational and social structure, uneasiness over the course of politics under the Stuarts, and, perhaps more than anything else, the failure of the Church of England to satisfy religious longings, created a sense of rootlessness and drift that led men whose ancestors had lived in England for countless generations to consider migration. Although the situation was not entirely novel, the presence of an alternative to acquiescence was. The New World as a lure, a refuge from care and anxiety, figured in the calculations of emigrants.

The early middle-Atlantic colonies, for a variety of reasons, were settled mainly by individuals instead of families. Organized groups came to Virginia and Maryland, but rarely entire families. Individual indentured servants,

artisans, or farmers usually made up the passenger lists. The municipal authorities of England, who had responsibility under the Poor Law for the care of orphans and abandoned children, were a source of supply. The usual way to care for these unfortunates was to bind them out in families at home, but often there were more than could be accommodated, especially in London and some of the larger towns. Colonial officers sought dependent children for the settlements. A portion of the business of collecting young people for shipment was in the hands of "spirits," commission agents of merchants, and shipowners, who signed up young men, women, and even children. The spirit, with his persuasive powers strengthened by promises of food, drink, and a small bounty for the enlistee, beguiled his prospect with the wonders of America. Spirits were sometimes charged with kidnapping, particularly of children. Most whom they attracted, however, went of their own accord. Those enlisted by agents were usually unable to pay for their passage and had little or nothing in the way of supplies. Their needs were met through indentures, a contract with which all Englishmen were familiar. The emigrant agreed with the ship's captain, a merchant, or perhaps even another emigrant, to work a stipulated term, usually four years, to repay the sum or service advanced. Indentures were freely sold or assigned to others. Probably the majority of seventeenth-century colonists reached the Chesapeake region in this way.

The Puritans characteristically came to America in families. Passenger lists of vessels bound for New England chiefly consisted of entire families or of a portion leading the way for others temporarily left behind. Frequently families banded together, as, for example, when a dissenting minister departed from England with his flock. The interests of posterity, even the presence of a child, sometimes determined a family's decision to migrate. Thomas Shepard, a minister in both old and New England, decided to leave because the anticipated birth and christening of his child would force him to

4. Carl Bridenbaugh, *Vexed and Troubled Englishmen* (New York, 1968), pp. 25–27.
5. *Ibid.,* pp. 140–141.

reveal his Puritan sympathies to the authorities and thus jeopardize the security of his family.[6] As a variation on the theme, John Dane, a young man estranged from his parents after his father "toke a stick and basted me . . . [when] I went to a dansing scoll to larne to dans," left for New England.[7] Eventually he was joined by his parents and reconciled to them. The New England environment helped

6. "The Autobiography of Thomas Shepard," *Publications* of the Colonial Society of Massachusetts, XXVII (1930), 352–353; hereafter cited as CSM *Publications.*

7. Quoted in Bridenbaugh, *Vexed and Troubled Englishmen,* pp. 461–462.

both to bring and to keep families together.

Although no complete figures for the total emigration from England in the first half of the seventeenth century exist, it has recently been estimated that about 80,000, or 2 per cent, of all Englishmen left Britain between 1620 and 1642, with 58,000 of them crossing the Atlantic to North America.[8] Since most English imigrants expected their colonies to be permanent residences and settled communities, children were rightfully accorded full and essential participation in this movement.

8. *Ibid.,* p. 395.

A. SOUTHERN COLONIES

Child colonists of Portugal, 1609

Hugh Lee to Thomas Wilson from Lisbon, Portugal, March 26, 1609, Great Britain, Public Record Office, SP/89/3, folio 118; hereafter cited as PRO.

This report is from an English diplomatic correspondent on Portugal's transportation of children to colonies in the East Indies.

Here departed hence on Sunday last being the 22nd hereof, five carracks laden with merchandizes for the East Indies who carried in the place of soldiers many children and youths from the age of 10 years upwards, to the number of 1500 persons and upwards as the common report goeth here; their policy is given out to be in sending such youth, that in few years they will be able to perform good service and so much the better in regard their bodies will be well acquainted with the climates of those countries, which were no evil course to be followed in England for the planting of

inhabitants in Virginia. But this policy here is forced by necessity, wanting men to supply their rooms, for if the peace with Holland take not effect, they may lose their Indies before these children shall be able to do any service to the saving thereof.

Transportation of poor children from London to Virginia, 1619–1620

Transportation of idle and needy children from crowded England to labor-starved Virginia was regarded not only as a boon to the Virginia planters but as a service to king and country and a kindness to the children. From the early days of the colony, children were sent to Virginia as servants or apprentices. In 1619, the year of the landing of the first Negroes and the arrival of the "tobacco brides," efforts were made to put the importation of children on a systematic basis.

---

1. The Virginia Company requests the mayor, aldermen, and council of the City of London to send one hundred children to Virginia, 1619

Susan M. Kingsbury, ed., *The Records of the Virginia Company of London. The Court Book, from the Manuscript in the Library of Congress,* I (Washington, 1906), 270–271; hereafter cited as *Va. Co. Records.*

The Treasurer, Council, and Company of Virginia assembled in their great and general Court the 17th of November 1619 have taken into consideration the continual great forwardness of his honorable City in advancing the plantation of Virginia and particularly in furnishing out one hundred children this last year, which by the goodness of God there safely arrived (save such as died in the way), and are well pleased we doubt not for their benefit, for which your bountiful assistance, we in the name of the whole plantation do yield unto you due and deserved thanks.

And forasmuch as we have now resolved to send this next spring very large supplies for the strength and increasing of the Colony . . . and find that the sending of those children to be apprentices hath been very grateful to the people: we pray your Lordship and the rest in pursuit of your former so pious actions to renew your like favors and furnish us again with one hundred more for the next spring. Our desire is that we may have them of twelve years old and upward with allowance of three pounds apiece for their transportation and forty shillings apiece for their apparel as was formerly granted. They shall be apprentices the boys till they come to twenty-one years of age the girls till the like age or till they be mar-

ried, and afterwards they shall be placed as tenants upon the public land with best conditions where they shall have houses with stock of corn and cattle to begin with, and afterward the moiety of all increase and profit whatsoever. And so we leave this motion to your honorable and grave consideration.

---

2. The Company requests authority to coerce children of London to go to Virginia, 1620

Sir Edwin Sandys to Sir Robert Naunton, principal secretary of James I, Jan. 28, 1620, in *Va. Co. Records,* III (1933), 259.

Right Honorable:

Being unable to give my personal attendance upon the Lords, I have presumed to address my suit in these few lines unto your Honor. The City of London have by act of their Common Council, appointed one hundred children out of their superfluous multitude to be transported to Virginia; there to be bound apprentices for certain years, and afterward with very beneficial conditions for the children. And have granted moreover a levy of five hundred pounds among themselves for the appareling of those children, and toward their charges of transportation. Now it falleth out that among those children, sundry being ill disposed, and fitter for any remote place than for this City, declare their unwillingness to go to Virginia, of whom the City is especially desirious to be disburdened, and in Virginia under severe masters they may be brought to goodness. But this City wanting authority to deliver, and the Virginia Company to transport, these persons against their wills, the burden is laid upon me, by humble suit unto the Lords to procure higher authority for the warranting thereof. May it please your Honor therefore, to vouchsafe unto us of the Company here, and to the whole plantation in Virginia, that noble favor, as to be a means unto their Lordships out of their accustomed goodness, and by their higher authority, to discharge both the City and our Company of this difficulty, as their Lordships and your Honors in your wisdom shall find most expedient. For whose health and prosperity our Company will always pray . . .

---

3. The Privy Council grants the Virginia Company authority to coerce children, 1620

Great Britain, Privy Council, *Acts of the Privy Council of England, 1619–1621* (London, 1930), p. 118.

January 31, 1620.

Whereas we are informed that the City of London hath, by an act of the Common Council, appointed one hundred children, out of the multitudes that swarm in that place, to be sent to Virginia, there to be bound apprentices for certain years with very beneficial conditions for them afterwards, and have moreover yielded to a levy of five hundred pounds for the appareling of those children and towards the charge of their transportation; wherein, as the City deserveth thanks and commendations for redeeming so many poor souls from misery and ruin and putting them in a condition of use and service to the State; so forasmuch as information is likewise made that among that number there are divers unwilling to be carried thither and that it is conceived that both the City wanteth authority to deliver and the Virginia Company to receive and carry out these persons against their wills, we have thought meet, for the better furtherance of so good a work, hereby to authorize and require as well such of the City as take charge of that service as the Virginia Company, or any of them, to deliver, receive, and transport into Virginia all and every the foresaid children as shall be

most expedient. And if any of them shall be found obstinate to resist or otherwise to disobey such directions as shall be given in this behalf, we do likewise hereby authorize such as shall have the charge of this service to imprison, punish, and dispose any of those children, upon any disorder by them or any of them committed, as cause shall require, and so to ship them out for Virginia with as much expedition as may stand with conveniency. For which this shall be unto all persons whom the same may any way concern a sufficient warrant.

John Donne praises the Virginia Company plantation, 1622

John Donne, "Sermon CLVI Preached to the Virginia Company, 1622," *Works, 1621–1631*, ed. Henry Alford (London, 1839), VI, 232–233.

John Donne (1572–1631), dean of St. Paul's Cathedral, expounded Virginia's "great uses" just when the colonists were suffering from disease and an Indian massacre, and the Company was verging on bankruptcy.

. . . God says to you, No kingdom, not ease, not abundance; nay nothing at all yet; the plantation shall not discharge the charges, not defray itself yet; but yet already, now at first, it shall conduce to great uses. It shall redeem many a wretch from the jaws of death, from the hands of the executioner, upon whom, perchance a small fault or perchance a first fault, or perchance a fault heartily and sincerely repented, perchance no fault, but malice, had otherwise cast a present, and ignominious death. It shall sweep your streets, and wash your doors, from idle persons, and the children of idle persons, and employ them: and truly, if the whole country were but such a Bridewell, to force idle persons to work, it had a good use. But it is already, not only a spleen, to drain the ill humours of the body, but a liver, to breed good blood; already the employment breeds mariners; already the place gives essays, nay freights of merchantable commodities; already it is a mark for the envy, and for the ambition of our enemies; I speak but of our doctrinal, not national enemies; as they are papists, they are sorry we have this country; and surely, twenty lectures in matter of controversy, do not so much vex them, as one ship that goes, and strengthens that plantation. Neither can I recommend it to you by any better rhetoric, than their malice. They would gladly have it, and therefore let us be glad to hold it.

Children and youth "spirited" from England to America, 1638–1668

1. Memorial of the Lord Mayor and Court of Aldermen, London, to the Privy Council, ca. 1638

PRO, SP 16/408, no. 117.

The Lord Mayor and Court of Aldermen humbly represent to their Lordships that usually for the supply of soldiers into divers parts, and sending of men to the several plantations beyond seas, without lawful press, certain persons called spirits, do inveigle and by lewd subtilties entice away youth, against the consent either of their parents, friends, or masters; whereby oftimes great tumults and uproars are raised within the city, to the breach of the peace, and the hazard of men's lives, which being of dangerous consequence, that their Lordships will be pleased to take it into consideration and to direct some course for the suppressing of them, either by proclamation or otherwise as so their Lordships in their wisdom shall be thought requisite.

2. Recognizances taken before Thomas Swalow esq. J.P., of William Graves and Godfrey Vale

Greater London Record Office, Middlesex Sessions Rolls, MJ/SR 1165/54; hereafter cited as MSR.

May 4, 1657.

That the said Sarah Sharp shall personally appear at the next Session of the Peace to be holden for the County of Middlesex then and there to answer all such matters that shall be objected against her by Katheren Wall, for violently assaulting her, tearing her by the hair of the head, and biting of the arm, as also for that she is a common taker up of children into ships and a setter to betray young men and maidens to be conveyed into ships, and as it hath been proved upon oath before me, that she confessed to one Mr. Guy that she hath at this time four persons aboard a ship whereof one is a child about eleven years of age, all to be transported to foreign parts as the Barbadoes and Virginia. And in the meantime she is to be of good behavior, and not to depart the Court without license.

3. Recognizances taken before Thomas Swalow esq. J.P., of Richard Wills and William Ritch and William Stone all of Stepney

MSR, MJ/SR 1236/170.

August 6, 1661.

That the said William Stone shall personally appear at the next Sessions of the Peace to be held for the County of Middlesex then and there to answer all such matters as on his Majesty's behalf shall be objected against him by Edward Baylay, Nathanel Smyth, and Frances Creech, for that he by flattering and great promises made unto George Creech and Thomas Riddle, did so obtain this desire, as that he got them to yield and go with him to a ship, where he left them to be transported to Virginia, the one being an apprentice, and the other without the consent of his parents, to their great loss and grief. And in the meantime, he is to be of good behavior and not to depart the Court without license.

---

4. Petition of the Mayor of Bristol to Charles II, July 16, 1662

PRO, SP 29/57, no. 71, p. 195.

The humble petition of the Mayor of Bristol humbly sheweth that your petitioner having the honor to serve your Majesty as Mayor of the City of Bristol, has thought it not the least part of his duty to represent unto your Majesty that in the administration of his office, many things have occurred, which he humbly conceives, may not be unworthy your Majesty's notice, and which if not redressed may prove very prejudicial to your service and government. Amongst which it is a common practice for persons who repair to the said City, from all parts, to be transported for servants unto your Majesty's plantation beyond the seas, some of which prove to be husbands that upon discontent and humor have foresaken their wives and children, and thereby exposed them to misery or parish mercy . . . wives out of a peevish passion have abandoned their husbands and houses; children and apprentices that run away from their parents and masters, and oftentimes unwary and credulous persons, have been tempted and betrayed on shipboard by man-stealers, commonly called spirits, and many also which have been pursued

by hue and cries, either for robberies, burglaries or breaking prison, do thereby escape the prosecution of law and justice to all which inconveniences your petitioner according to his ability hath given check, and remedy, but finds that all his endeavors do come short of curing the disease from the want of lawful powers to countenance and warrant him therein.

May it therefore please your Majesty for the future prevention and redress of those mischiefs, with the consequences that attend them, and that your Majesty may have an account of your subjects from time to time, to grant your petitioner power, either by letters patent, under your great seal of England, or otherwise as so your Majesty shall seem meet, for the examining of all masters of ships belonging unto the port of Bristol, bound for your Majesty's plantations, of and concerning such servants and passengers as they have on board, and also that the said servants and passengers, themselves from whence they came, whether they be free and at their own disposal, with power likewise to stop all such passengers who cannot give a fair account of themselves, and also for the keeping of a register, by himself, or a sufficient person, to be appointed by and under your petitioner of all passengers bound for those plantations, and of all such other matters from time to time as may concern your service.

---

5. Lady Yarborough to Joseph Williamson, under secretary of state

PRO, SP 29/109, no. 23.

---

ca. 1664.

I am ashamed to give you this trouble. It is to beg a very great favor from you which is this: A poor boy that I had a care of about a fortnight ago was taken away by spirits, they call them, which they say convey them to ships, and from thence to New England or Barbadoes.

So my humble request to you is that you will be so [kind] to procure this bearer, whose apprentice he was, a warrant to search in all the ships that go out for such a boy, in which you will do a great charity and forever oblige your most humble servant

Yarborough

---

6. Petition of merchants, planters, and masters of ships trading to the plantations to the King, July 12, 1664

PRO, CO 1/15, no. 31, p. 16.

To the King's most excellent Majesty, the humble petition of divers merchants, planters and masters of ships in the behalf of themselves and others of your Majesty's loyal subjects trading to your Majesty's plantations in America.

Sheweth that whereas it is generally believed that there is a wicked custom to seduce or spirit away young people, to go as servants to your Majesty's plantations, that yet your petitioners are so far from that practice or knowledge that they abominate the very thought thereof. However, this gives the opportunity to many evil-minded people to enlist themselves voluntarily to go the said voyage; and having received money, clothes, diet and other conveniencies from your petitioners, and coming to be cleared at Gravesend, or in the Downs, or put into some other ports, they pretend they were betrayed or carried away without their consents, not only to the scandal and great vexation of your petitioners and others [of] your Majesty's good subjects, but oftentimes to the loss of their charge on the said evil persons, and retarding if not the absolute hindering of their voyage, to the great discouragement of your petitioners and obstruction of that so important trade.

Wherefore your petitioners, having a most dutiful sense of your Majesty's gracious indul-gence to trade in general and particularly to your said plantations, and desiring . . . to carry on the improvement and interest thereof (which is of so great advantage and benefit to this kingdom), but being discouraged by the abusive practice of the said evil-minded people, and of the scandal, trouble, loss, and other ill consequences that attend it, do in all humility supplicate your Majesty (in consideration of the premises) to appoint and commission some person residing in or near the city, under your great seal, before whom such persons as desire to go to the said plantations may declare that they go voluntary without compulsion, or any deceitful or sinister practice whatsoever, who may also enter the names, age, quality, place of birth, and last residence of the said parties so desiring to go to the said plantations. And these will not only be a means to prevent the betraying and spiriting away of people, but the certificate under the hand and seal of the said officer will be a sufficient testimony of the fair and open dealing of the respective merchants, planters, and masters of ships in their behalf, and also full authority to transport the said persons, so voluntarily listing themselves for the said voyage, without the disturbance or interruption of any of your Majesty's officers at land or sea, they submitting to the established customs and paying the duty of the ports.[1]

---

7. Referral of the petition of merchants, planters, and masters of ships by Charles II to Sir Heneage Finch, the attorney-general, with the latter's recommendations

PRO, CO 1/15, no. 31, p. 17.

July 12, 1664.

His Majesty is graciously pleased to refer

1. On September 7, 1664, the Council for Foreign Plantations recommended the Privy Council approve the plan outlined in the petition. PRO, SP 29/102, no. 27.

this petition to Master Attorney and Master Solicitor General, or either of them, to consider what may be done by law and what may be convenient to be done in this case; also to call some of the petitioners before them, if they think fit, and to hear what they can say in the business. And then to make report of all to his Majesty who will thereupon declare his further pleasure.

July 18, 1664.

May it please your Majesty:

1. I have called some of the petitioners before me and do find upon examination that the mischiefs complained of in the petition are very frequent, there being scarce any voyage to the plantations but some persons are carried away against their wills or pretend to be so after they have contracted with the merchants and so run away.

2. A registry of passengers to the plantations, who go by contract with the merchant would be a proper remedy.

3. Your Majesty may by law erect such an office with a small fee annexed, but it will never be effectually executed without Act of Parliament imposing a fee sufficient to recompense the pains.

8. George C. [*torn away*] to Sir Anthony Ashley Cooper, April [?], 1668

PRO, CO 1/22, no. 56.

I have inquired after the child that was lost, and have spoken with the parents. His name was John Brookes. The last night he was after much trouble and charge freed again, and he relates that there are divers other children in the ship crying, that were enticed away from their parents, that are kept and detained in the

ship. The name of the ship is the Seven Brothers and as I hear bound for Virginia; and she is now fallen down to Gravesend, and, if a speedy course be not taken to stop her she will be gone. I heard of two other ships in the river that are at the same work, although the parents of the children see their children in the ship, yet without money they will not let them have them. The woman and child will wait on you, where you approach and when to give you this relation and 'tis believed there are divers people and others carried away that are strangers come from other parts, so that it were good to get the ships searched, and to see who are against their wills carried away. Pray you move it in the House to have a law to make it death.[1] I am confident your mercy to these innocent children will ground a blessing on yourself your own. Pray let not your great affairs put this good work out of your head to stop the ships and discharge the children.

Your most humble servant
George

Colonial legislation to encourage immigration

1. The headright system in Maryland, 1636

Proclamation in Council of Cecelius Calvert, Lord Baltimore, in W. H. Browne, ed., *Archives of Maryland,* III (Baltimore, 1885), 47; hereafter cited as *Md. Archives.*

. . . These are, therefore, to will and authorise you, that presently upon receipt hereof, you

1. Although such a bill was introduced and debated in Parliament in 1670/71, it was not passed. Abbot E. Smith, *Colonists in Bondage* (Chapel Hill, 1947), p. 74.

make or cause to be made under our Great Seal of that our said province, unto every first adventuror, for every five men aged between sixteen and fifty years, which such adventuror did bring into our said province to inhabit and plant there in the year of our Lord 1633, and unto his heirs forever, a grant of 2000 acres of land of English measure, for the yearly rent of 400 lbs. weight of good wheat; and to every adventuror which in that year did bring a less number then five men into that our said province of the ages aforesaid to inhabit and plant there, and unto his heirs forever, a grant of 100 acres of land (of like measure) for himself and 100 acres more for his wife (if he brought any), and for and in respect of every servant, and fifty acres for every child under the age of sixteen years for the rent of 10 lbs. of wheat, yearly for every fifty acres . . .

2. Carolina promises land to freemen and their families, 1664

Robert Horne, "A Brief Description of the Province of Carolina . . ." [1666] in William L. Saunders, ed., *The Colonial Records of North Carolina*, I (Raleigh, 1886), 155–156; hereafter cited as *No. Car. Records.*

Every free man and free woman that transport themselves and servants by the 25th of March next, being 1667, shall have for himself, wife, children, and men-servants, for each, one hundred acres of land for him and his heirs forever, and for every woman-servant and slave fifty acres, paying at most 1/2 d. per acre per annum, in lieu of all demands, to the lords proprietors: Provided always that every man be armed with a good musket, full bore, ten pounds of powder, and twenty pounds of bullet, and six months' provision for all, to serve them whilst they raise provision in that country.

3. "An Act for the Encouragement of the Importation of White Servants," South Carolina, 1698

Thomas Cooper, ed., *Statutes at Large of South Carolina*, II (Columbia, 1837), 153–154.

Whereas, the great number of Negroes which of late have been imported into this Colony may endanger the safety thereof if speedy care be not taken and encouragement given for the importation of white servants,

Be it enacted . . . that every merchant, owner or master of any ship or vessel, or any other person not intending to settle and plant here, which shall bring any white male servants, Irish only excepted, into Ashley river, above sixteen years of age and under forty, and the same shall deliver to the Receiver General, shall receive and be paid by the said Receiver . . . the sum of thirteen pounds for every servant so delivered, and for every boy of twelve years and under sixteen, imported and delivered to the Receiver as aforesaid, the sum of twelve pounds, as aforesaid; Provided, that every servant, as aforesaid, hath not less than four years to serve from and after the day of his arrival in Ashley River, and every boy aforesaid, not less than seven years. And if any person shall deliver to the Receiver aforesaid, any servant or boy, as aforesaid, which hath less time to serve than the respective times before appointed, the Receiver shall pay such person proportionably to the rates and times aforesaid, for so long time as such servant or boy hath to serve.

. . . . . .

Every owner of every plantation to which doth belong six men Negro slaves above sixteen years old, shall take from the Receiver one servant, when it shall happen to be his lot to have one, and shall within three months pay the said Receiver so much money for the said servant as the Receiver gave to the person from whom he received the same; and the owner of every plantation to which doth belong twelve Negro men, as aforesaid, shall when it shall be his lot, take two servants as aforesaid; and every master of every plantation proportionably . . .

---

4. Georgia Trustees offer assistance to needy settlers, 1735

"Rules for the year 1735," in Francis Moore, *A Voyage to Georgia Begun in the Year 1735* (London, 1744), in *Collections* of the Georgia Historical Society, I (1840), 80–81, 83–84.

The Trustees for establishing the Colony of Georgia, in America, ordered a new town to be built in that colony, and an embarkation to be made for that purpose. They were pleased to appoint me to be keeper of the stores.

The following rules were given for the embarkation, viz.:

.   .   .   .   .

. . . To every person of the age of 12 years and upwards, the following [annual] allowance . . . : 260 lbs. of beef or pork; 104 lbs. of rice; 104 lbs. of Indian corn or peas; 104 lbs. of flour; 52 quarts of molasses for brewing beer; 16 lbs. of cheese; 12 lbs. of butter; 8 oz. of spice; 12 lbs. of sugar; 4 gallons of vinegar; 24 lbs. of salt; 6 quarts of lamp oil; half lb. of spun cotton; 12 lbs. of soap.

For every person above the age of seven, and under the age of twelve, half the said allowance, being esteemed half a head.

And for every person above the age of two, and under the age of seven, one third of said allowance, being esteemed one third of a head.

The trustees pay their passage from England to Georgia; and in the voyage they will have in every week four beef days, two pork days, and one fish day.

.   .   .   .   .

[Assistance is limited to]

1. Such as are in decayed circumstances, and thereby disabled from following any business in England; and who, if in debt, must have leave from their creditors to go.

2. Such as have numerous families of children, if assisted by their respective parishes and recommended by the minister, churchwardens and overseers thereof.

The Trustees do expect to have a good character of the said persons given; because no drunkards, or other notoriously vicious persons will be taken.

And for the better enabling the said persons to build the new town, and clear their lands, the Trustees will give leave to every freeholder to take over with him one male servant, or apprentice of the age of eighteen years and upwards, to be bound for not less than four years; and will, by way of loan to such freeholder, advance the charges of passage for such servant or apprentice, and of furnishing him with . . . clothing and provision.

.   .   .   .   .

And to each man servant, and the heirs male of his body forever, after the expiration of his service, upon a certificate from his master of his having served well, will be granted twenty acres of land, under such rents and agreements as shall have been then last granted to any other men-servants in like circumstances.

Children in the African slave trade

---

1. Agents of the Royal African Company object to the purchase of young children, 1681, 1683

Elizabeth Donnan, ed., *Documents Illustrative of the History of the Slave Trade to America* (New York, 1965), I, 275, 289.

Henry Carpenter and Robert Helmes to the Royal African Company, 1681:

On the 3rd instant in the evening, Captain Cope in the *George and Betty* arrived in this road with 415 Negroes, most women, amongst which [were] about forty children under the ages of eight years to our best judgment, which we told him was contrary to his charter party, who answered that they could not buy so many men and women without [also taking] that number of children, but we believe something else in it which we hope in little time to discover . . .

Edwin Stede and Stephen Gascoigne to the Royal African Company, 1683:

And about one third part of those he did bring were very small, most of them no better than sucking children, nay many of them did suck their mothers that were on board . . . some of [the] mothers we believe died on board of ship, and the most part of those small ones [were] not worth above £5 per head. We told Agent White we wondered to see so many small children brought by him, for that they were not worth their freight, to which he replied they cost not much, and the ship as good bring them as nothing, she being paid by the month . . .

---

2. African family reunited on slave ship

John Barbot, "A Description of the Coasts of North and South Guinea . . . [1682]," in *Documents of the Slave Trade*, I, 306–307.

I also remember that I once, among my several runs along that coast, happened to have aboard a whole family, man, wife, three young boys, and a girl, bought here one after another at several places; and cannot but observe here what mighty satisfaction those poor creatures expressed to be so come together again, though in bondage. For several days successively they could not forbear shedding tears of joy, and continually embracing and caressing one another; which moving me to compassion, I ordered they should be better treated aboard than commonly we can afford to do it, where there are four or five hundred in a ship. And at Martinico, I sold them all together to a considerable planter, at a cheaper rate than I might have expected had they been disposed of severally, being informed of that gentleman's good nature, and having taken his word that he would use that family as well as their circumstances would permit, and settle them in some part by themselves.

---

3. Childstealing on the coast of Africa

Thomas Clarkson, "Essay on the Efficiency of Regulation or Abolition [1789]," in *Documents of the Slave Trade*, II, 571–572.

Inquiring today of a Negro lad, how he came into the situation of a slave, he informed me that he had been stolen from his parents in the interior country above Cape Rouge; that the inhabitants of the shore usually came up in bodies for this purpose, and that they unfortunately met with him, and brought him to Goree in company with others, whom they had taken in the same manner . . .

Since our arrival here, the king of Barbasin has twice sent out his military to attack his own villages in the night. They have been very unsuccessful, having taken but three children. They had no better fortune last night, having brought in but one girl.

4. Prices offered for Negro boys and girls, Virginia, 1683

William Fitzhugh to Mr. Jackson, February 11, 1682/83, in *Documents of the Slave Trade*, IV, 57.

I will deal with them . . . under the condition and at these ages and prices following, to say—to give 3000 lbs. tobacco for every Negro boy or girl, that shall be between the ages of seven and eleven years old; to give 4000 lbs. tobacco for every youth or girl that shall be between the age of eleven to fifteen and to give 5000 lbs. tobacco for every young man or woman that shall be above fifteen years of age and not exceed twenty-four.

B. NEW ENGLAND

"Here by their labor may live exceeding well"

John Smith, *A Description of New England* . . . (London, 1616), p. 40.

Captain John Smith (1579/80–1631), best remembered for the part he played in the settlement and governance of Virginia, explored the New England coast and issued this forecast of opportunity and riches for future colonists in 1616.

My purpose is not to persuade children from their parents, men from their wives, nor servants from their masters; only such as with free consent may be spared. But that each parish or village, in city or country, that will but apparel their fatherless children of thirteen or fourteen years of age, or young married people that have small wealth to live on, here by their labor may live exceeding well; provided always, that first there be a sufficient power to command them, houses to receive them, means to defend them, and meet provisions for them. For any place may be overlain, and it is most necessary to have a fortress (ere this grow to practice) and sufficient masters (as carpenters, masons, fishers, fowlers, gardeners, husbandmen, sawyers, smiths, spinsters, tailors, weavers and such like) to take ten, twelve or twenty, or as there is occasion, for apprentices. The masters by this may quickly grow rich; these may learn their trades themselves to do the like, to a general and an incredible benefit for king and country, master and servant.

The Pilgrim Fathers and the children of Plymouth

1. William Bradford (1589/90–1657), who shared the Pilgrims' exile in Holland, gives the reasons for their immigration to America, 1620

William Bradford, *History of Plymouth Plantation, 1620–1647* (Boston, 1912), I, 54–55.

As necessity was a taskmaster over them, so they were forced to be such, not only to their servants (but in a sort) to their dearest children; the which as it did not a little wound the tender hearts of many a loving father and mother, so it produced likewise sundry sad and sorrowful effects. For many of their children that were of best dispositions and gracious inclinations (having learned to bear the yoke in their youth) and willing to bear part of their parents burden, were (often times) so oppressed with their heavy labors, that though their minds were free and willing, yet their bodies bowed under the weight of the same, and became decrepit in their early youth, the vigor of nature being consumed in the very bud as it were. But that which was more lamentable, and of all sorrows most heavy to be borne, was that many of their children, by these occasions, and the great licentiousness of youth in that country, and the manifold temptations of the place, were drawn away by evil examples into extravagant and dangerous courses, getting the reins off their necks and departing from their parents. Some became soldiers, others took upon them far voyages by sea, and others some worse courses, tending to dissoluteness and the danger of their souls, to the great grief of their parents and dishonor of God. So that they saw their posterity would be in danger to degenerate and be corrupted.

Lastly, (and which was not least) a great hope, and inward zeal they had of laying some good foundation, (or at least to make some way thereunto) for the propagating and advancing the gospel of the kingdom of Christ in those remote parts of the world; yea, though they should be but even as stepping-stones unto others for the performing of so great a work.

---

2. Approximately one-third of the founders of Plymouth were children and youths

William T. Davis, ed., *Bradford's History of Plymouth Plantation, 1606–1646* (New York, 1908), pp. 407–409.

The names of those which came over first, in the year 1620, and were by the blessing of God the first beginers and (in a sort) the foundation of all the Plantations and Colonies in New-England; and their families.

Mr. John Carver; Kathrine, his wife; Desire Minter; and 2. man-servants, John Howland, Roger Wilder; William Latham, a boy; and a maid servant, and a child that was put to him, called Jasper More.

Mr. William Brewster; Mary, his wife; with 2. sones, whose names were Love and Wrasling; and a boy was put to him called Richard More; and another of his brothers. The rest of his children were left behind, and came over afterwards.

Mr. Edward Winslow; Elizabeth, his wife; and 2. men servants, caled Georg Sowle and Elias Story; also a litle girle was put to him, caled Ellen, the sister of Richard More.

William Bradford, and Dorothy, his wife; having but one child, a sone, left behind, who came afterward.

Mr. Isaack Allerton, and Mary, his wife; with 3. children, Bartholmew, Remember, and Mary; and a servant boy, John Hooke.

Mr. Samuell Fuller, and a servant, caled William Butten. His wife was behind, and a child, which came afterwards.

John Crakston, and his sone, John Crakston.

Captain Myles Standish, and Rose, his wife.

Mr. Christopher Martin, and his wife, and 2. servants, Salamon Prower and John Langemore.

Mr. William Mullines, and his wife, and 2. children, Joseph and Priscila; and a servant, Robart Carter.

Mr. William White, and Susana, his wife, and one sone, caled Resolved, and one borne a ship-bord, caled Peregriene; and 2. servants, named William Holbeck and Edward Thomson.

Mr. Steven Hopkins, and Elizabeth, his wife, and 2. children, caled Giles, and Constanta, a doughter, both by a former wife; and 2. more by this wife, caled Damaris and Oceanus; the last was borne at sea; and 2. servants, called Edward Doty and Edward Litster.

Mr. Richard Warren; but his wife and children were lefte behind, and came afterwards.

John Billinton, and Elen, his wife; and 2. sones, John and Francis.

Edward Tillie, and Ann, his wife; and 2. children that were their cossens, Henery Samson and Humillity Coper.

John Tillie, and his wife; and Eelizabeth, their doughter.

Francis Cooke, and his sone John. But his wife and other children came afterwards.

Thomas Rogers, and Joseph, his sone. His other children came afterwards.

Thomas Tinker, and his wife, and a sone.

John Rigdale, and Alice, his wife.

James Chilton, and his wife, and Mary, their dougter. They had an other doughter, that was maried, came afterward.

Edward Fuller, and his wife, and Samuell, their sonne.

John Turner, and 2. sones. He had a doughter came some years after to Salem, wher she is now living.

Francis Eaton, and Sarah, his wife, and Samuell, their sone, a yong child.

Moyses Fletcher, John Goodman, Thomas Williams, Digerie Preist, Edmond Margeson, Peter Browne, Richard Britterige, Richard Clarke, Richard Gardenar, Gilbart Winslow.

John Alden was hired for a cooper, at South-Hampton, wher the ship victuled; and being a hopfull yong man, was much desired, but left to his owne liking to go or stay when he came here; but he stayed, and maryed here.

John Allerton and Thomas Enlish were both hired, the later to goe m^r of a shalop here, and the other was reputed as one of the company, but was to go back (being a seaman) for the help of others behind. But they both dyed here, before the shipe returned.

There were allso other 2. seamen hired to stay a year here in the country, William Trevore, and one Ely. But when their time was out, they both returned.

These, being aboute a hundred sowls, came over in this first ship; and began this worke, which God of his goodnes hath hithertoo blesed; let his holy name have the praise.

Puritan children in the great migration to Massachusetts Bay, 1629–1630

1. Children as burdens or blessings

Stewart Mitchell, ed., *Winthrop Papers,* II (Boston, 1931), 114–115.

John Winthrop (1587/88–1649), first governor of the Bay Colony, drew up this list of "General Observations" to justify migration.

1. It will be a service to the Church of great consequence to carry the Gospel into those parts of the world, and to raise a bulwark against the kingdom of Antichrist which the Jesuits labor to rear up in all places of the world.

2. All other Churches of Europe are brought to desolation, and it cannot be but the like judgment is coming upon us. And who knows, but that God hath provided this place to be a refuge for many, whom he means to save out of the general destruction?

3. This land grows weary of her inhabitants so as man, which is the most precious of all creatures, is here more vile and base than the earth they tread upon; so as children, neighbors, and friends (especially if they be poor) are rated the greatest burdens which, if things were right, would be the chiefest earthly blessings.

4. We are grown to that height of intemperance in all excess of riot as no mans estate almost will suffice to keep sail with his equals; and he that fails in it must live in scorn and contempt. Hence it comes, that all arts and trades are carried in that deceitful and unrighteous course, as it is almost impossible for a good and upright man to maintain his charge and live comfortably in any of them.

5. The fountains of learning and religion are so corrupted as (besides the unsupportable

charge of their education) most children, even the best wits and of fairest hopes, are perverted, corrupted, and utterly overthrown by the multitude of evil examples and the licentious government of those seminaries.

6. The whole earth is the Lords garden and he hath given it to the sons of men to be tilled and improved by them. Why then should we stand striving here for places of habitation etc. (many men spending as much labor and cost to recover or keep sometime an acre or two of land, as would procure him many hundred acres as good or better in another place) and in the meantime suffer whole countries as fruitful and convenient for the use of man to lie waste without any improvement?

at, and difficulties they broke through, but only this? And if this were the portion they thought worth so much that they might have it to leave them, it concerns you to mind and regard it. It was their love to your souls that embarked them in this design, and it will be horrible ingratitude in you to slight it. You cannot neglect God's Covenant, but you do withal cast reflections upon, and greatly undervalue, yea, and despise that work, which will be *New England's* glory, and was so signally owned and abetted by God's providence in the day of it; and will be unworthy heirs of your father's estates, if you do not prosecute their begun designs.

---

2. A half-century later, amid fears of a decline in New England piety, Samuel Willard (1639/40–1707), an eminent divine and vice-president of Harvard College, recalls the purpose that moved the founders

Samuel Willard, *Covenant-Keeping the Way to Blessedness* (Boston, 1682), pp. 117–118.

The main errand which brought your fathers into this Wilderness was not only that they might themselves enjoy, but that they might settle for their children, and leave them in full possession of the free, pure, and uncorrupted liberties of the Covenant of Grace. They have made this profession openly to the world. Yea, let reason speak and say what else was there which could have tempted them to come into a land which was not sown, leaving the pleasant enjoyments of a good land, and of which many of them had a good share, running through so many hazards, wrestling with so many hardships, not expecting (and it would have seemed vain and presumptuous to have expected) any worldly advantage, or likelihood of any other compensation for such expenses as they were

A young Irish immigrant to Puritan Massachusetts, 1633

Edward Howes in London to John Winthrop, Jr., in Massachusetts, Aug. 5, 1633, in *Winthrop Papers,* III (1943), 133–134.

You shall also receive in this ship three wolf dogs and a bitch with an Irish boy to tend them. For the dogs my master hath writ sufficiently, but for the boy thus much. You have been in Ireland, know partly the Irish condition. This is a very tractable fellow, and yet of a hardy and stout courage. I am persuaded he is very honest, especially he makes great conscience of his promise and vow. I could wish (for as much as I have seen by him) you would take him to be your servant, although he be bound to your father for five years. At his first coming over he would not go to church nor come to prayers; but first we got him up to prayers and then on the Lords Day to catechize, and afterwards very willingly he hath been at church four or five times. He as yet makes conscience of Fridays fast from flesh; and doth not love to hear the Romish religion spoken against, but I hope with gods grace he will become a good convert. . . . The fellow can read and write reasonable well which is somewhat rare for one of his condition and makes me hope the more of him.

Transportation of poor children to New England, 1639–1643

1. A London merchant's bequest

Will of John Parker, in Henry F. Waters, *Geneological Gleanings in England* (Boston, 1901), I, 578–579.

John Parker of London, haberdasher, and of the parish of St. Pancras, Soper Lane, London, 7th and 14th May 1639, proved 27 August 1639.

Item I do give and bequeath three hundred pounds to be employed in the taking up out of the street or out of the Bridewell twelve fatherless and motherless boys and eight girls from seven years old and upwards and for the furnishing them with necessaries and paying for their passage to New England and for their being bound apprentices to some such as will be careful to bring them up in the fear of God and to maintain themselves another day. And my will is that my brother James should take his choice out of these, of three of them if he need so many for his own use.

2. A plea for philanthropic assistance: the Weld-Peter mission to England, 1641–1645

New Englands First Fruits . . . (London, 1643), p. 23, in Samuel E. Morison, *The Founding of Harvard College* (Cambridge, Mass., 1935), p. 443.

In 1641 three Massachusetts clergymen, Hugh Peter, Thomas Weld, and William Hibben, were sent to England to raise money for Harvard College, for missionaries to the Indians, and for the transportation of poor children. Their solicitation resulted in funds for the Reverend John Eliot, the apostle to the Indians, several gifts to Harvard College, notably that of £100 for a scholarship from Lady Mowlson, née Radcliffe, and a large sum for the poor children. A promotional tract of uncertain authorship publicized the enterprise.

[Among other helps, Providence would assist New England] by stirring up some well-minded to clothe and transport over poor children, boys and girls, which may be a great mercy to their bodies and souls and a help to us, they being super abundant [in London], and we wanting hands to carry on our trades, manufacture, and husbandry there.

3. Gifts for transporting poor children

"Thomas Weld's Receipts and Disbursements," CSM *Publications,* XIV (1913), 124.

Parliament authorized collecting alms in London churches; country parishes with New England affiliations and individuals gave the rest. Mismanagement, as Weld confessed, diminished the effectiveness of the mission. Much of the money was spent for chartering and provisioning the ships. Many children died of disease in camp before leaving England; others ran away; some returned to their parents. Twenty children arrived in Boston in June 1643. What became of them there is unknown. Morison, *Founding of Harvard College,* pp. 312–313.

What I received for the poor childrens transportation

In the first place, of Master George Walker one of the Re[c]eivers appointed by Parliament £ 339 8

Master Calamie our other Receiver £ 338 6

Of the other parishes which were behind that brought it not in to them with very much ade at last by the Lord Mayor's assistance I got £ 103 12 8

Sent us from a ladie £ 5

Procured from Dedham in Essex 17 17 6

Of childrens moneys the sum brought from that other side £ 804 4 2

From Yarmouth in Norfolk £ 12

From Sudbury in Suffolk £ 8 5

From Wrentham £ 2

The Lady Armine gave to transportation £ 30

. . . We got such of the poor childrens parents and friends as were able to lay down some thing toward their transportation which must be considered for them . . . in due time viz:

Mary Audleigh laid down by her father £ 1 10

John Littlefield by his master here £ 2 10

Judith Nichols by her father £ 2

John Stiles £ 2 £ 8

John Copland and his brother £ 2

Another whose name I know not £ 2

A child that came from Mary Stanning £ 1

John Emry £ 2 10

Edward Morgan £ 2 10 £ 10

£ 874 9 2

Use of Massachusetts as a reformatory, 1647

Colonial Laws of Massachusetts. Reprinted from the Edition of 1672, with the Supplement through 1686 (Boston, 1887), pp. 27–28.

The Bay Colony's reputation for piety prompted some English gentlemen to exile unruly sons there in hope of reform. That the device sometimes failed is indicated by this law.

Whereas sundry gentlemen of quality, and others, oft times send over their chidren into this country to some friends here, hoping (at least) thereby to prevent their extravagant and riotous courses, who notwithstanding (by means of some unadvised or ill affected persons, which give them credit, in expectation their friends either in favor to them or prevention of blemish to themselves, will discharge their debts) they are no less lavish and profuse here, to the great grief of their friends, dishonor of God, reproach of the country:

It is therefore ordered by this Court, that if any person after publication hereof, shall any way give credit to any such youth, or other person under one and twenty years of age, without order from their friends here or elsewhere under their hands in writing, they shall lose their debt whatever it be. And further, if such youth or person incur any penalty by such means and have not wherewith to pay, such person or persons as are occasions thereof, shall pay it as the delinquents in the like case should do.

Massachusetts offers a bounty for importing male servants, 1709

The Acts and Resolves, Public and Private,

of the Province of Massachusetts Bay . . . ,
I (Boston, 1869), 634.

From and after the first day of April . . .
any master, merchant, or others, that shall import or bring in and dispose in service within
this province any male servants of the kingdom
of Great Britain,[1] being between the age of
eight and twenty-five years, there shall be paid
unto such master, merchant, or other person,
the sum of forty shillings per head, gratis, for
every such male servant, *bona fide* disposed of
in service, out of the impost office, and the
commissioner is hereby ordered and impowered
to pay the same, any law, usage or custom to
the contrary notwithstanding.

Slave trading in New England and New York

---

1. Boston newspaper advertisements

Post Boy, June 22, 1752, in *Documents of the Slave Trade,* III, 66.

Kittery, Maine.

This day arrived the *Betsey,* Samuel Lan-
phier, Commander, from the Coast of Guinea,
with a Quantity of very likely Boys and Girls
of the blackest Sort: All Persons who incline
to be Purchasers may apply to me the Subscriber, where they shall be dealt with on reasonable terms. Alexander Rait.

News Letter, Oct. 18, 1759, in *Documents of the Slave Trade,* III, 67.

To be Sold, a Very likely Negro boy, has

---

1. As in the South Carolina Act of 1698 (see above,
sec. A, Colonial legislation to encourage immigration,
doc. 3), bounties were not paid for Irish servants.

been about twelve months from the Coast of
Guinea, speaks good English, straight limbed,
handsome featured, good natured, and has had
the smallpox. Enquire of the printer.

---

2. Letters about the trade

William Ellery, a Newport, R.I., merchant,
to Capt. Pollipus Hammond, Jan. 7, 1746, in
Documents of the Slave Trade,
III, 138–139.

You being Master of our Sloop *Anstis* and
ready to Sail, our orders are that you imbrace
the first opportunity and make the best of your
way for the Coast of Africa when please God
you arrive there dispose of our Cargoe to the
best advantage, make us returns in Negroes,
Gold Dust and whatever you think will answer.
If you have a good Trade for Negroes may
purchase forty or Fifty Negroes. Get most of
them mere Boys and Girl, some Men, let them
be Young, No very small Children. Make all
possable Dispatch, take care of your Vessells
Bottom. If you meet with disapointment in your
Trade and cannot get home some time in October next may go to Barbados and Dispose
of your Negroes, reserving Eight likely boyes
to bring home.

John Watts, a merchant of New York City,
tells Gedney Clarke of Barbados of the market
for slaves in New York, March 30, 1762,
in *Documents of the Slave Trade,* III, 457.

For this market they must be young, the
younger the better if not quite Children; those
advanced in years will never do. I should imagine a Cargo of them none exceeding thirty
might turn out at fifty pounds a head gross
sales. Males are best.

C. MIDDLE COLONIES

Children from Dutch almshouses bound out in New Netherland

---

1. The directors of the West India Company urge the importation of poor and orphaned children from the Netherlands, 1645

E. B. O'Callaghan and Berthold Fernow, eds., *Documents Relative to the Colonial History of the State of New York,* 15 vols. (Albany, 1856–1887), I, 364.

. . . We are of opinion that permission should be obtained from the Magistrates of some Provinces and Cities, to take from the almshouses or orphan asylums 300 to 400 boys and girls of ten, twelve to fifteen years of age, with their consent, however, and that their passage and board could be procured for 50 or 60 florins per head. With that recognition a large ship might be chartered, suitable for the conveyance of horses and salt from Curacao and afterwards return . . . with a cargo of logwood. It must be, further, declared that said children shall not remain bound to their masters for a longer term than six or seven years, unless being girls, they come meanwhile to marry, in which event they should have the option of hiring again with their masters or mistresses, or of remaining wholly at liberty and of settling there, on condition that they be allowed so much land as the Director shall consider it proper each should have for the support of her family . . .

---

2. The burgomasters of Amsterdam send a cargo of poor children to Peter Stuyvesant at Fort New Amsterdam, 1654

Documents Relative to the Colonial History of New York, I, 556.

Honorable, wise, prudent, right, discreet Sir!

Being informed by the governors of the almshouse of the vast number of poor people wherewith they are burdened and charged, we have concluded to relieve them and so do the Company a service, by sending some of them to New Netherland.

We have, therefore, sent over in the ship belonging to the bearer hereof, twenty-seven or twenty-eight boys and girls, requesting you, in a friendly manner, to extend to them your kind advice and assistance, and to advance them if possible; so that they, according to their fitness, may earn their board. If you consider that the population of that country could be advanced by sending over such persons, we shall, on being informed, lose no time to have some more forwarded. Meanwhile, we shall be much obliged by the aid and assistance you will extend in this instance.

---

3. An official of Fort New Amsterdam reports to commissioners at home on a cargo of poor children received in New Netherland and bound out to work, 1658

Documents Relative to the Colonial History of New York, II, 52.

The children sent over from the Almshouse have safely arrived and were in sufficient request, so that all are bound out with one and the other; the oldest for two years, the others, and the major portion, for three years, and the youngest for four years, earning forty, sixty, and eighty guilders during the above period, and at the end of the term will be fitted out in the same manner as they are at present; the conditions are no worse, but rather better than were prescribed in the form transmitted. Please to continue sending others from time to time; but, if possible, none ought to come less than fifteen years of age and somewhat strong, as little profit is to be expected here without labor; but from people with large families or many small children, little is to be expected. When the men die they do not leave a stiver behind. The public must provide the coffin, pay all the debts, and feed or maintain those who survive.

Tax exemption for colonists who bring or beget children in New Netherland, 1650

"Freedoms and Exemptions granted and allowed by the Incorporated Dutch West India Company to all those who shall be willing to repair to New Netherland. Exhibited May 24, 1650," in *Documents Relative to the Colonial History of New York,* I, 401.

On the arrival of the aforesaid persons in New Netherland, they shall be allowed and granted the privilege of choosing and taking up, under quit rent or as a fief, such parcels of land as they shall in any way be able to cultivate for the production of all sorts of fruits and crops of those parts, on condition that they shall be bound to commence the same within the year, on pain of being again deprived of said lands.

Said persons shall enjoy Exemption from Tenths of all aforesaid fruits and crops for the term of   years, and thenceforth one additional year's Exemption for every legitimate child they shall convey thither or get there.

The Palatine refugees and their children, 1710–1720

1. The governor of New York disposes of Palatine children

E. B. O'Callaghan, ed., *Documentary History of the State of New York,* III (Albany, 1850), 553.

The Palatine Germans were among the displaced persons of the War of the Spanish Succession. Approximately 3,000 of them, all poor and many sick, arrived in New York in 1709 and 1710; a large number, including the father of John Peter Zenger, one of the children bound out under the following order, died on shipboard. Young Zenger was apprenticed to the printer, William Bradford.

There having been several proposals made for the taking many of the Palatine children for a term of years, and there being many orphans who are unable to take care of themselves to work, and many who by sickness are rendered uncapable of doing any service for some time, and in that condition would be a great expense, and there being no prospect by settling them this summer by reason it's so much advanced, His Excellency [Governor Robert Hunter] does appoint Doctor Staats and Mr. Van Dam or either of them to take such proposals for placing out the orphans and other children whose parents have a numerous family, entering into an instrument in writing to clothe, victual and use them well and to deliver them to the government when called for.

It is ordered that an advertisement be printed signifying that His Excellency is willing to dispose of such orphans and other children as aforesaid, and directing all persons who are willing to take any to apply themselves to Doctor Staats or Mr. Van Dam or either of them.

2. Palatines protest loss of children

Documentary History of New York,
III, 707–708.

In 1720 the Palatines sent a petition to the
British government outlining "The Condition,
Grievances and Oppressions of the Germans
in his Majesty's Province of New York in
America." Some of the Palatines eventually
found a more cordial reception in
Pennsylvania.

In the year 1709 was the late Majesty Queen
Anne most graciously pleased to send a body
of between 3 and 4000 Germans to New York
under the inspection and care of Robert Hunter,
then Governor there, with particular orders and
instructions to settle them on lands belonging
to the Crown, and such as were most proper
for raising pitch, tar, and other naval stores.

Before they left England, they were promised five pounds in money per head, of which
they have received nothing at all.

It was likewise promised, that on their arrival there each of them should receive clothes,
utensils, tools, and other conveniencies belonging to husbandry, all which were sent with
them from England for their use, but of these
they received but very little.

They were moreover to have a grant of forty
acres of land to each person, but it was never
performed.

On their landing at New York, they were
quartered in tents on the common and divided
in six companies, over each of which was a
captain appointed to command them . . .
with an allowance of 15 £ per annum each,
but not one farthing has been hitherto paid
them.

About the same time took the said Governor, without and against their consent, many
children from them, and bound them to several of the inhabitants of that province till they
should arrive to the age of twenty one years,
particularly two sons from Captain Weiser, one
of twelve and another of thirteen years of age,
by which means they were deprived of the
comfort of their children's company and education, as well as the assistance and support
they might in a small time have reasonably expected from them.

A young thief exiled to Pennsylvania

"The speech of the Boy hang'd at Chester,"
American Weekly Mercury,
Aug. 16–23, 1722.

Many youthful offenders were transported
to the colonies as convict servants, but
William Battin, who was hanged for arson
and murder, had been sold as a servant
by his father.

I, William Battin, Son of William Battin of
White-Parish in Wiltshire in Great-Britain, do
think it necessary to leave a few Lines behind
me, that the World may in some Measure know
something of my past Life, and what ill Use I
have made of the time that God was pleased
to bestow upon me in this World.

I had my Education under my Parents, and
their Care was much over me; but I dishon-
oured and rebelled against them, and regarded
not their Care for me; and through the Insinuation of the Enemy I neglected their Business,
by wandering abroad. So without due Regard
to that which is good, I gave up my self to
serve the Devil, and to obey his Voice by yielding to his Temptations; which were Lying and
picking and Stealing other Men's Goods. I
shall briefly mention some of the gross Actions
which I have committed before and after the
Time of my running away from my Parents;
which was chiefly stealing of other Men's
Goods.

The first Thing that I stole was, to the best

of my Remembrance, a Whalebone Whip from
one Henry Whites, next a Cane from my Uncle
John Battin, next a Knife and Fork from one
Lawrence Tuch, a Great Coat from a Man in
White-Parish, and several other Things which
were found out by my Parents: For which I
was severely chastized by them.

.   .   .   .   .

The next Thing I stole was a Silver Watch,
of the Value of Five Pounds, from one that I
intended to serve an Apprentiship with, and
about an Hour after I had Stolen it, I sold it
to a Man for an English Half Crown; when my
intended Master came to understand that I had
stolen the Watch, he put me into Prison, and
after three Days he took me out again and
whipped me very severely: But I took no
Warning, and soon found an Opportunity to
make my Escape, taking with me a Beaver
Hat, a Suit of Clothes and a Shirt; since which
he never saw me.

This was the Course of Life which I followed whilst I was in England.

My Father seeing that there was not any
Good like to come of use, ordered me to be
brought over a Servant into this Province of
Pennsylvania. About 7 or 8 Days after the
Ship, which brought me over, was safely arrived here, I was sold to one John Hannam of
Concord in the Chester-County. I had scarcely
lived with him three Months before I fell again
into my old Practice of Stealing and running
away; for which Cause, after I had lived with
the said Hannam about one Year, he sold me
to Joseph Pyle of Bethel in the said County,
with whom I continued in the old Practice of
stealing, etc.

"An Oxford Scholar in the Situation of a
bought Servant," 1727

Leonard W. Labaree et al., eds., *The
Autobiography of Benjamin Franklin*
(New Haven, 1964), p. 109.

It was an odd Thing to find an Oxford
Scholar in the Situation of a bought Servant.
He was not more than 18 Years of Age, and
gave me this Account of himself; that he was
born in Gloucester, educated at a Grammar
School there, had been distinguish'd among the
Scholars for some apparent Superiority in performing his Part when they exhibited Plays;
belong'd to the Witty Club there, and had written some Pieces in Prose and Verse which were
printed in the Gloucester Newspapers. Thence
he was sent to Oxford; there he continu'd about
a Year, but not well-satisfy'd, wishing of all
things to see London and become a Player. At
length receiving his Quarterly Allowance of 15
Guineas, instead of discharging his Debts, he
walk'd out of Town, hid his Gown in a Furz
Bush, and footed it to London, where having
no Friend to advise him, he fell into bad Company, soon spent his Guineas, found no means
of being introduc'd among the Players, grew
necessitous, pawn'd his Cloaths and wanted
Bread. Walking the Street very hungry, and not
knowing what to do with himself, a Crimp's
Bill [1] was put into his Hand, offering immediate Entertainment and Encouragement to
such as would bind themselves to serve in
America. He went directly, sign'd the Indentures, was put into the Ship and came over;
never writing a Line to acquaint his Friends
what was become of him. He was lively, witty,
good-natur'd, and a pleasant Companion, but
idle, thoughtless and imprudent to the last
Degree.

1. Crimp: one whose business it was to lure or
entrap men into military or sea service, or to persuade
them to become indentured servants in return for
transportation to the colonies.

II Children in the Colonial Family

English writers of the late sixteenth and early seventeenth centuries, whether Puritan, orthodox Anglican, or secular in social outlook, agreed that the father's unquestioned rule was the only assurance of a proper discharge of the family's social obligations. In "the good man or master of the familie," wrote William Perkins (1558–1602), the leading Puritan divine of his time, "resteth the private and proper government of the whole household, and he comes not unto it by election, as it falleth out in other states, but by the ordinance of God, setled even in the order of nature. The husband indeed naturally beares rule over the wife, parents over their children, masters over their servants."[1] A champion of the divine right of monarchy, Sir Robert Filmer (ca. 1588–1653), reinforced his theory of royal authortiy with a parallel between family and kingdom. "I see not," he wrote, "how the children of Adam, or of any man else, can be free from subjection to their parents. And this subordination of children is the fountain of all regal authority."[2] The duties of fathers and kings, he continued, were the same. "We find them to be all one, without any difference at all but only in the latitude of extent of them. As the Father over one family, so the King as Father over many families, extends his care to preserve, feed, clothe, instruct and defend the whole Commonwealth."[3] Even Thomas Hobbes (1588–1679), the great theorist of sovereignty, and a far more modern thinker than either Perkins or

Filmer, assumed that families were the original and natural social unit existing prior to the creation of states. It followed, he wrote in *Leviathan,* "that a great Family if it be not part of some Common-wealth, is of it self, as to the Rights of Soveraignty, a little Monarchy . . . wherein the Father or Master is the Soveraign."[4] Although the creation of a national sovereign deprived fathers of their absolute rights over subordinates, they retained a substantial residue of authority since "the Father and Master being before the Institution of Common-Wealth, absolute Soveraigns in their own Families, they lose afterward no more of their Authority, than the Law of the Commonwealth taketh from them."[5] Father and monarch ruled their analogous realms unchallenged and unchallengeable by those arranged in hierarchy beneath them. So at least the theorists maintained.

Another common social idea was that the family or household served as the principal educator of children. Church and school, though valued for their contributions, were subservient to the family in turning unruly, immature children into dutiful subjects. The family introduced children to social customs and both cultivated and tested their ability to perform worthwhile services. "For the family," wrote William Gouge, a renowned Puritan preacher, "is a seminary of the Church and Common-wealth. It is a Bee-hive in which is the Stocke, and out of which are sent many swarms of Bees: for in families are all sorts of people bred and brought up and out of families are they sent into the Church and Com-

1. William Perkins, *Christian Oeconomie* (London, 1609), p. 164.
2. Peter Laslett, ed., *Patriarcha and Other Political Works of Sir Robert Filmer* (Oxford, 1949), p. 57. *Patriarcha* was written in the 1630's but not published until 1680.
3. *Ibid.,* p. 63.

4. Thomas Hobbes, *Leviathan* (London, 1924), p. 107; first published in 1651.
5. *Ibid.,* p. 124.

mon-wealth . . . Whence it followeth, that a conscionable performance of domesticall and household duties, tend to the good ordering of Church and Common-wealth." [6]

This neat social diagram drawn by preachers and philosophers did not encompass all of the realities of family life in either England or America. Aspiration and fact were combined in their portrait of the paterfamilias earnestly transmitting to his heirs and other dependents his own loyalties. Yet the ideals and needs of family life were sufficiently strong to inspire a determined effort in the colonies to duplicate the English model and even improve upon it. The requirements, as viewed by the colonists themselves, were different in New England and the southern colonies. The Puritans initially saw the New World as a means of liberating the family from Old World restraints. In leaving England, they escaped the evils of interference in their daily lives from improper ecclesiastical and governmental authorities. In America, they believed, the family would surmount the hardships of a wilderness to flourish and grow as nature and God intended, uniting with church and state to create a Christian commonwealth. In the South, however, where migration had been commercial in its character and implemented by individuals rather than families, deliberate policies were required merely to make possible the formation of families. With a population disproportionately composed of men, the permanence of the colonies and the transplantation of the rudiments of civilization required the provision of wives for the planters. Brides were among the essential provisions sent to the colonists of Virginia.

Even in New England, where it was expected the ideals of family life would have the best opportunity for fulfillment, ministerial exhortation, advice, and eventually legislation were found necessary to shore up the desired family style. The younger generation frequently seemed to be on the verge of a decline into impiety and insubordination. Their behavior

6. William Gouge, *Of Domesticall Duties* (London, 1622), pp. 17–18.

in home, church, and school was constantly examined and often found wanting. Some congregations set aside sections of the meetinghouse for them where they could be easily observed and praise, reproof, or correction administered as occasion demanded. Severe punishments for disobedience, including even the penalty of death, were decreed in Massachusetts and Connecticut, although there are no recorded instances of its imposition. More or less constant surveillance was the lot of the young in New England.

Repression was not the only device used by the leaders of the New England colonies to sustain authority. More important was a series of laws designed to encourage parents to meet the responsibilities that social theory and biblical injunction placed upon them. Beginning with the Massachusetts law of 1642 that required parents to see that their children and other dependents were taught reading and a trade, the New England colonies tried to make the family function as a broadly educational and socializing institution. Town officials were obligated to enforce the laws, but, after repeated failures, the General Court of Massachusetts created a new class of officers in 1675, the tithingmen, charged with the inspection of families. Although parents were brought before the authorities for neglecting the proper rearing of children, some repeatedly, in many towns it apparently was impossible to secure obedience to the law. A comparable manifestation of the family ideal was the attempt to bring single persons whatever their age under family government. Relying upon Psalms 68:6, "God setteth the solitary in families," the authorities required single persons to attach themselves to a household. But this measure too seems to have been only partially effective.

No colony's population of children consisted entirely of those in natural families. There were anomalies, such as bastards and orphans who, through no fault or failure of their own, could not provide for themselves and were without families for protection and nurture. In general, the American colonists attempted to continue the traditional English way of caring for unfortunate children. Bastards, for example, were to be supported by the father if he could be determined, if not, then by the parish or town. In case a father failed to acknowledge his child, the word of the mother given during the crisis of childbirth was to be accepted, although a court could relieve a man of a manifestly false charge. The large number of bound servants in the southern colonies created a special situation. At first Virginia penalized women servants who bore illegitimate children by adding two years to their term of service, laying upon the father the obligation to provide for the child. This law had to be changed to prevent unscrupulous masters from adding to the terms of their female servants by forcing them to bear children. The solution was to deprive the master of the additional time, transferring it to the parish.

Orphans were another familiar category of dependency. Their care in England had been provided by binding them out to foster parents and this method was readily employed in America. Novel uncertainties, however, sometimes threw upon the traditional system a weight it could scarcely bear. Such, for instance, was the case when Indian massacres, natural disasters, or epidemics created homeless orphans in large numbers. The only response then was to consider some form of institutional care.

Another anomaly in New World society was the child of mixed parentage. The establishment of a slave system resting upon racial identity added a third category of persons to the traditional two of the free and the servant. Slaves, servants, and free persons of both sexes and races and of all ages mingled together in the colonies. English experience obviously gave little guidance in establishing the legal status and the rights of the children who resulted. Although authority frowned upon unions between white servant women and Negro slave men as unnatural, unchristian, and socially disruptive, it is clear that they sometimes took place. Laws were passed to discourage informal matings, to outlaw marriage between those of different races, and to ensure that the children born out of wedlock to a slave mother would inherit her status.

In sum, America presented many new circumstances that required adjustments in traditional English institutions. The family that the colonists brought with them could not solve all of the problems it encountered. The belief that it could serve as the theater for the drama of child-rearing began to give way before the pressures of the New World environment. As children grew restive under the rule of parents less in touch than they with the requirements for success and happiness in a land of greater opportunity, they prompted the initiation of a search by the leaders of society for variations and innovation in institutions that would supplement the family.

A. THE FAMILY IN THE SOCIAL ORDER

Failure of English and Indians to marry

Robert Beverley, *The History and Present State of Virginia,* ed. Louis B. Wright (Chapel Hill, 1947), pp. 37–39; first published in 1705.

In contrast to the practice in the French and Spanish colonies, Englishmen and Indian women rarely married. After nearly a century of settlement, Robert Beverley of Virginia, an able historian, regretted this failure on the grounds that intermarriage might have averted much strife and bloodshed between Indians and English.

Anno 1612, Two Ships more arriv'd with Supplies: and Capt. *Argall,* who commanded one of them, being sent in her to *Patowmeck* to buy Corn, he there met with *Pocahontas*, the Excellent Daughter of *Powhatan*; and having prevail'd with her to come Aboard to a Treat, he detain'd her Prisoner, and carried her to *James-Town*, designing to make Peace with her Father by her Release: But on the Contrary, that Prince resented the Affront very highly; and although he loved his Daughter with all imaginable Tenderness, yet he would not be brought to Terms by that unhandsome Treachery; till about Two Years after a Marriage being proposed between Mr. *John Rolfe,* an *English* Gentleman, and this Lady; which *Powhatan* taking to be a sincere Token of Friendship, he vouchsafed to consent to it, and to conclude a Peace.

Intermarriage had been indeed the Method proposed very often by the *Indians* in the Beginning, urging it frequently as a certain Rule, that the *English* were not their Friends, if they refused it. And I can't but think it wou'd have been happy for that Country, had they embraced this Proposal: For, the Jealousie of the *Indians*, which I take to be the Cause of most of the Rapines and Murders they committed, wou'd by this Means have been altogether prevented, and consequently the Abundance of Blood that was shed on both sides wou'd have been saved; the great Extremities they were so often reduced to, by which so many died, wou'd not have happen'd; the Colony, instead of all these Losses of Men on both Sides, wou'd have been encreasing in Children to its Advantage; the Country wou'd have escaped the *Odium* which undeservedly fell upon it, by the Errors and Convulsions in the first Management; and, in all Likelihood, many, if not most, of the *Indians* would have been converted to Christianity by this kind Method; the Country would have been full of People, by the Preservation of the many *Christians* and *Indians* that fell in the Wars between them. Besides, there would have been a Continuance of all those Nations of *Indians* that are now dwindled away to nothing by their frequent Removals, or are fled to other Parts;

not to mention the Invitation that so much Success and Prosperity would have been for others to have gone over and settled there, instead of the Frights and Terrors that were produced by all those Misfortunes that happen'd.

Tobacco brides of Virginia, 1619–1623

To reduce discontent among the planters, and strengthen the settlement and enhance its prospects, officers of the Virginia Company encouraged the settlers to marry and have children by sending over young "tobacco brides." Later in the seventeenth century, the French government sent girls to New France and offered bounties for children "born in lawful wedlock." [1]

1. Sir Edwin Sandys, treasurer of the Virginia Company, proposes that brides be sent to the Virginia planters, November 1619

Va. Co. Records, I, 256–257.

He wished that a fit hundred might be sent of women, maids young and uncorrupt, to make wives to the inhabitants and by that means to make the men there more settled and less moveable who, by defect thereof (as is credibly reported), stay there but to get something and then to return for England, which will breed a disillusion and so an overthrow of the plantation. These women, if they marry to the public farmers, to be transported at the charges

1. *Edits, Ordonnances Royaux, Déclarations et Arrets du Conseil D'État du doi Concernant le Canada,* I (Quebec, 1854), 67–68; Charles Woolsey Cole, *Colbert and a Century of French Mercantilism* (New York, 1939), II, 70–73.

of the Company. If otherwise, then those that take them to wife to pay the said Company their charges of transportation, and it was never fitter time to send them than now, corn being here at home so cheap and plentiful, and great promises there for the harvest ensuing.

---

2. The Company informs the colonists of a shipment of brides and sets out the terms on which they may be purchased

Letter from the Virginia Company in London to the Governor and Council in Virginia, Aug. 12, 1621, in *Va. Co. Records*, III, 493–494.

We send you in this ship one widow and eleven maids for wives for the people in Virginia. There hath been especial care had in the choice of them; for there hath not any one of them been received but upon good commendations, as by a note herewith sent you may perceive. We pray you all therefore in general to take them into your care; and more especially we recommend them to you Master Pountis, that at their first landing they may be housed, lodged and provided for of diet till they be married, for such was the haste of sending them away, as that straitened with time we had no means to put provisions aboard, which defect shall be supplied by the magazine ship. And in case they cannot be presently married, we desire they may be put to several householders that have wives till they can be provided of husbands. There are near fifty more which are shortly to come, are sent by our most honorable Lord and Treasurer the Earl of Southampton and certain worthy gentlemen, who taking into their consideration that the Plantation can never flourish till families be planted and the respect of wives and children fix the people on the soil, therefore have given this fair beginning, for the reimbursing of whose charges it is ordered that every man that marries

them give 120 lbs. weight of the best leaf tobacco for each of them, and in case any of them die, that proportion must be advanced to make it up upon those that survive . . . And though we are desirous that marriage be free according to the law of nature, yet would we not have these maids deceived and married to servants, but only to freemen or tenants as have means to maintain them. We pray you therefore to be fathers to them in this business, not enforcing them to marry against their wills; neither send we them to be servants, save in case of extremity, for we would have their condition so much bettered as multitudes may be allured thereby to come unto you. And you may assure such men as marry those women that the first servants sent over by the Company shall be consigned to them, it being our intent to preserve families and to prefer married men before single persons. The tobacco that shall be due upon the marriage of these maids we desire Master Pountis to receive and to return by the first . . . To conclude, the Company, for some weighty reasons too long to relate, have ordered that no man marrying these women expect the proportion of land usually allotted for every head, which to avoid clamor or trouble hereafter, you shall do well to give them notice of.

---

3. A second shipment of brides in 1621 goes astray but still arrives safe in Virginia

Letter from the Virginia Council in London to the Governor and Council in Virginia, Sept. 11, 1621, in *Va. Co. Records,* III, 505.

By this ship and pinnace called the *Tiger,* we also send as many maids and young women as will make up the number of fifty, with those twelve formerly sent in the *Marmaduke,* which we hope shall be received with the same Christian piety and charity as they are sent from hence. The providing for them at their first landing, and disposing of them in marriage (which is our chief intent) we leave to your care and wisdom to take that order as may most conduce to their good, and satisfaction of the Adventurers . . .

"A Note of the Shipping, Men, and Provisions sent and Provided for Virginia . . . 1621," in *Va. Co. Records,* III, 640.

The voyage of the *Tiger* with its cargo of brides was anything but routine. Among the unusual occurrences of the year 1621 was noted:

The admirable deliverance of divers ships, and namely of the *Tiger,* which being driven strangely near 200 leagues out of her course, fell into the Turks' hands and yet came safe to Virginia.

---

4. A settler objects to the insufficient number of women in Virginia, 1623

Thomas Niccols to Sir John Worsenholme, *Va. Co. Records,* IV, 231–232.

Women are necessary members for the Colony, but the poor men are never the nearer for them, they are so well sold, for I myself have ever since my coming paid 3 £ sterling per annum for my washing . . . A hard case . . . having had for all the service I have done the Company not one pipe of tobacco consideration. I am sure for all these women your poor tenants that have nothing die miserably through nastiness and many depart the world . . . for want of help in their sickness. Wherefore for prevention I could wish women might be sent over to serve the Company for that purpose for certain years, whether they marry or no. For all that I can find that the multitude of women do is nothing but to devour the food of the land without doing any day's deed whereby any

benefit may arise either to the Company or Country.

Honor thy father and thy mother — and thy superiors

Children and parents, especially those in New England, were the targets of a steady stream of moral advice. The very young learned of their obligations to parents, church, and society by memorizing the correct responses to the questions in catechisms. Parents were told what to do to secure obedience and good manners and how to raise their children as faithful Christians and loyal subjects.

---

1. John Cotton, 1646

John Cotton, *Spiritual Milk for Boston Babes in either England. Drawn out of the Breasts of both Testaments for their Souls Nourishment* (Cambridge, Mass., 1656), p. 4; first published in 1646.

Cotton (1584–1652), leading clergyman and author, came to Massachusetts in 1633, where he figured prominently in affairs of church and state. His catechism was the standard work for rearing New England children.

Question. *What is the fifth commandment?*
Answer.   Honor thy father and thy mother, that thy days may be long in the land which the Lord thy God giveth thee.
Question. *Who are here meant by father and mother?*
Answer.   All our superiors, whether in family, school, church, and commonwealth.
Question. *What is the honor due to them?*
Answer.   Reverence, obedience, and (when I am able) recompence.

2. John Eliot, 1678

John Eliot, *The Harmony of the Gospels* (Boston, 1678), p. 29.

Eliot (1604–1690), famous apostle to the New England Indians and translator of the Bible, reached Boston in 1631. He took time from his missionary labors to prepare a work on Christian doctrine, containing some words of advice for parents.

It is a very false and pernicious principle that many people and parents are tainted with, viz., that youth must be suffered awhile to take their swing, and sow their wild oats, to travail into the world, to follow the fashions, company, and manners of the times, hoping they will be wiser hereafter. Oh false principle; God speaks fully to the contrary. Prov. 19:18. *Chasten thy son while there is hope, and let not thy soul spare for his crying.* Prov. 13:24. *He that spareth the rod, hateth his son, but he that loveth him, chasteneth him betimes.* The gentle rod of the mother is a very soft and gentle thing; it will break neither bone nor skin; yet by the blessing of God with it, and upon the wise application of it, it would break the bond that bindeth up corruption in the heart. Prov. 22:15. *Yea, yet greater is the power of this gentle thing.* Prov. 23:13–14. *Withhold not correction from the child, for if thou beatest him with the rod he shall not die; thou shalt beat him with the rod and shalt deliver his soul from Hell.*

3. Eleazar Moody, 1715

Eleazar Moody, *The School of Good Manners. Composed for the Help of Parents in Teaching their Children How to carry it in their Places during their Minority* (Boston, 1772), pp. 17–19.

This work, first reprinted in the American colonies in 1715, derived from a line of sixteenth- and seventeenth-century English guides to behavior of similar title.

When at Home

1. Make a bow always when you come home, and be immediately uncovered.
2. Be never covered at home, especially before thy parents or strangers.
3. Never sit in the presence of thy parents without bidding, tho' no stranger be present.
4. If thou passest by thy parents, and any place where thou seest them, when either by themselves or with company, bow towards them.
5. If thou art going to speak to thy parents, and see them engaged in discourse with company, draw back and leave thy business until afterwards; but if thou must speak, be sure to whisper.
6. Never speak to thy parents without some title of respect, viz., Sir, Madam, &c.
7. Approach near thy parents at no time without a bow.
8. Dispute not, nor delay to obey thy parents commands.
9. Go not out of doors without thy parents leave, and return within the time by them limited.
10. Come not into the room where thy parents are with strangers, unless thou art called, and then decently; and at bidding go out; or if strangers come in while thou art with them, it is manners, with a bow to withdraw.
11. Use respectful and courteous but not insulting or domineering carriage or language toward the servants.
12. Quarrel not nor contend with thy brethren or sisters, but live in love, peace, and unity.
13. Grumble not nor be discontented at anything thy parents appoint, speak, or do.
14. Bear with meekness and patience, and without murmuring or sullenness, thy parents reproofs or corrections: Nay, tho' it

should so happen that they be causeless or undeserved.

. . . . . .

In Their Discourse

1. Among superiors speak not till thou art spoken to, and bid to speak.
2. Hold not thine hand, nor any thing else, before thy mouth when thou speakest.
3. Come not over-near to the person thou speakest to.
4. If thy superior speak to thee while thou sittest, stand up before thou givest any answer.
5. Sit not down till thy superior bid thee.
6. Speak neither very loud, nor too low.
7. Speak clear, not stammering, stumbling nor drawling.
8. Answer not one that is speaking to thee until he hath done.
9. Loll not when thou art speaking to a superior or spoken to by him.
10. Speak not without, Sir, or some other title of respect.
11. Strive not with superiors in argument or discourse; but easily submit thine opinion to their assertions.
12. If thy superior speak any thing wherein thou knowest he is mistaken, correct not nor contradict him, nor grin at the hearing of it; but pass over the error without notice or interruption.
13. Mention not frivolous or little things among grave persons or superiors.
14. If thy superior drawl or hesitate in his words, pretend not to help him out, or to prompt him.
15. Come not too near two that are whispering or speaking in secret, much less may'st thou ask about what they confer.
16. When thy parent or master speak to any person, speak not thou, nor hearken to them.
17. If thy superior be relating a story, say not, "I have heard it before," but attend to it as though it were altogether new. Seem not

to question the truth of it. If he tell it not right, snigger not, nor endeavor to help him out, or add to his relation.
18. If any immodest or obscene thing be spoken in thy hearing, smile not, but settle thy countenance as though thou did'st not hear it.
19. Boast not in discourse of thine own wit or doings.
20. Beware thou utter not any thing hard to be believed.
21. Interrupt not any one that speaks, though thou be his familiar.
22. Coming into company, whilst any topic is discoursed on, ask not what was the preceding talk but hearken to the remainder.
23. Speaking of any distant person, it is rude and unmannerly to point at him.
24. Laugh not in, or at thy own story, wit or jest.
25. Use not any contemptuous or reproachful language to any person, though very mean or inferior.
26. Be not over earnest in talking to justify and avouch thy own sayings.
27. Let thy words be modest about those things which only concern thee.
28. Repeat not over again the words of a superior that asketh thee a question or talketh to thee.

---

4. Benjamin Wadsworth, 1719

Benjamin Wadsworth, *The Well-Ordered Family* . . . (Boston, 1719), pp. 44–58.

A Boston clergyman, Wadsworth compiled this work from a series of his sermons.

They should love their children and carefully provide for their outward supply and comfort while unable to provide for themselves . . . Parents should nourish in themselves a very tender love and affection to their children, and should manifest it by suitably providing for their outward comforts. Here I might say, as soon as the mother perceives herself with child, she should be careful not to do any thing injurious to herself or to the child God has formed in her. A conscientious regard to the Sixth Commandment (which is, *Thou shalt not kill*) should make her thus careful. If any purposely endeavor to destroy the fruit of their womb (whether they actually do it or not) they're guilty of murder in God's account. Further, before the child is born, provision should be made for its comfort when born. Some observe concerning our Saviour's Mother (the Virgin Mary) that though she was very poor and low and far from home when delivered of her Son, yet she had provided swaddling clothes to wrap her Son in. Mothers also, if able, should suckle their children. . . . Those mothers who have milk and are so healthy as to be able to suckle their children, and yet through sloth or niceness neglect to suckle them, seem very criminal and blameworthy. They seem to dislike and reject that method of nourishing their children which God's wise bountiful Providence has provided as most suitable. Having given these hints about mothers, I may say of parents (comprehending both father and mother) they should provide for the outward supply and comfort of their children. They should nourish and bring them up . . . They should endeavor that their children may have food suitable for quality and quantity, suitable *raiment* and *lodging*. In case of sickness, lameness, or other distress on children, parents should do all they can for their health or relief. *He that provides not for his own, especially those of his own house, hath denied the faith, and is worse than an infidel* I Tim. 8 . . . Therefore, if they can help it, they should not suffer their children to want any thing that's really good, comfortable, and suitable for them, even as to their outward man. Yet by way of caution I might say, let wisdom and prudence sway, more than fond indulgent fancy, in feeding and clothing your children. Too much niceness and delicateness in these things is not good; it tends not to make

them healthy in their bodies, nor serviceable and useful in their generation, but rather the contrary. Let not your children (especially while young and unable to provide for themselves) want any thing needful for their outward comfort.

.   .   .   .   .

Parents should govern their children well, restrain, reprove, correct them, as there is occasion. A Christian householder should rule well his own house . . . Children should not be left to themselves, to a loose end, to do as they please; but should be under tutors and governors, *not being fit to govern* themselves . . . Children being bid to obey their parents in all things . . . plainly implies that parents should give suitable precepts to, and maintain a wise government over their children; so carry it, as their children may both fear and love them. You should restrain your children from sin as much as possible . . . You should reprove them for their faults; yea, if need be, correct them too . . . Divine precepts plainly show that, as there is occasion, you should chasten and correct your children; you dishonor God and hurt them if you neglect it. Yet, on the other hand, a father should pity his children . . . You should by no means carry it ill to them; you should not frown, be harsh, morose, faulting and blaming them when they don't deserve it, but do behave themselves well. If you fault and blame your children, show yourself displeased and discontent when they do their best to please you, this is the way to provoke them to wrath and anger, and to discourage them; therefore you should carefully avoid such ill carriage to them. Nor should you ever correct them upon uncertainties, without sufficient evidence of their fault. Neither should you correct them in a rage or passion, but should deliberately endeavor to convince them of their fault, their sin; and that 'tis out of love to God's honor and their good (if they're capable of considering such things) that you correct them. Again, you should never be cruel nor barbarous in your corrections, and if milder ones will reform them, more severe ones should never be used. Under this head of government I might further say, you should refrain your children from bad company as far as possibly you can . . . If you would not have your sons and daughters destroyed, then keep them from ill company as much as may be . . . You should not suffer your children needlessly to frequent taverns, nor to be abroad unseasonably on nights, lest they're drawn into numberless hazards and mischiefs thereby. You can't be too careful in these matters.

godliness, but all in a hurry about the world; every one for himself, little care of public or common good.

It hath been God's way, not to send sweeping judgments, when the chief magistrates are godly and grow more so. I beseech all the Bay-ministers to call earnestly upon magistrates (that are often among them) tell them that their godliness will be our protection: if they fail, I shall fear some sweeping judgment shortly. The clouds seem to be gathering.

The trouble with the younger generation

1. "The young brood doth much afflict me," 1657

Ezekiel Rogers to a minister of Charlestown, Mass., 1657, in Cotton Mather, *Magnalia Christi Americana* (London, 1702), III, 103–104.

. . . I find greatest trouble and grief about the *rising generation.* Young people are little stirred here; but they strengthen one another in evil, by example, by counsel. Much ado I have with my own family; hard to get a servant that is glad of catechising, or family-duties: I had a rare blessing of servants in Yorkshire; and those that I brought over were a blessing: but the young brood doth much afflict me. Even the children of the godly here, and elsewhere, make a woful proof. So that, I tremble to think, what will become of this glorious work that we have begun, when the ancient shall be gathered unto their fathers. I fear grace and blessing will die with them, if the Lord do not also show more signs of displeasure, even in our days. We grow worldly every where; methinks I see little

2. Massachusetts General Court proclaims a day of humiliation, 1661

N. B. Shurtleff, ed., *Records of the Governor and Company of the Massachusetts Bay in New England (1628–1686),* 5 vols. (Boston, 1853–1854), IV, pt. 2 (1854), 34–35; hereafter cited as *Mass. Records.*

Most of Massachusetts Bay's problems in 1661 were political in nature; the General Court, however, characteristically linked the sins of the rising generation to the colony's other tribulations.

It being obvious to all pious and serious persons amongst us that we are called of God deeply to humble ourselves for the many and great sins and evils of the country, as our unprofitableness, neglect, and indisposedness to a full inquiry and practice of the order of the gospel; the great ignorance and inclination of the rising generation to vanity, profaneness, and disobedience; the sinful indulgence in family government; pride and excess in apparel; inordinate love of the world and the things thereof; insensibleness of evil occurences; and in special, God's suffering many enemies and underminers to multiply complaints against us to our sovereign lord the king. . . . This Court doth commend the serious consideration of the aforesaid things, with others of like nature, together with the afflicted condition of the people of God elsewhere, unto all the churches and inhabitants of this jurisdiction, and do[th] appoint the second day of January next to be kept a day of solemn humiliation and supplication to the Lord for a thorough redress and return from the said iniquities, and also for the diverting [of] such calamities as are coming upon us and the people of God the Christian world throughout.

---

3. Disorder and rudeness in youth, 1675

Mass. Records, V (1854), 59, 60–61.

Whereas there is manifest pride openly appearing amongst us in that long hair, like women's hair, is worn by some men, either their own or others hair made into periwigs, and by some women wearing borders of hair, and their cutting, curling, and immodest laying out their hair, which practise doth prevail and increase, especially among the younger sort:

This Court doth declare against this ill custom as offensive to them, and divers sober Christians among us, and therefore do hereby exhort and advise all persons to use moderation in this respect; and further, do empower all grand juries to present to the County Court such persons, whether male or female, whom they shall judge to exceed in the premises; and the County Courts are hereby authorized to proceed against such delinquents either by admonition, fine, or correction, according to their good discretion.

.   .   .   .   .

Whereas there is much disorder and rudeness in youth in many congregations in time of the worship of God, whereby sin and profaneness is greatly increased, for reformation whereof:

It is ordered by this Court, that the selectmen do appoint such place or places in the meeting house for children or youth to sit in where they may be most together and in public view, and that the officers of the churches, or selectmen, do appoint some grave and sober person or persons to take a particular care of and inspection over them, who are hereby required to present a list of the names of such who, by their own observance or the information of others, shall be found delinquent, to the next magistrate or Court, who are empowered for the first offense to admonish them, for the second offense to impose a fine of five shillings on their parents or governors, or order the children to be whipped, and if incorrigible, to be whipped with ten stripes or sent to the house of correction for three days.

Punishment of rebellious children

---

1. Connecticut, 1642

J. Hammond Trumbull, ed., *Public Records of the Colony of Connecticut,* I (Hartford, 1850), 78; hereafter cited as *Conn. Records.*

Forasmuch as incorrigeableness is also adjudged to be a sin of death, but no law yet amongst us [has been] established for the execution thereof: For the preventing [of] that great evil it is ordered, that whatsoever child or servant within these liberties shall be convicted of any stubborn or rebellious carriage against their parents or governors, which is a forerunner of the forementioned evil, the Governor or any two Magistrates have liberty and power from this Court to commit such person or persons to the house of correction, and there to remain under hard labor and severe punishment so long as the Court or the major part of the Magistrates shall judge meet.

2. Massachusetts, 1646

Mass. Records, III (1854), 101.

If any child[ren] above sixteen years old and of sufficient understanding shall curse or smite their natural father or mother, they shall be put to death, unless it can be sufficiently testified that the parents have been very un-christianly negligent in the education of such children, or so provoked them by extreme and cruel correction that they have been forced thereunto to preserve themselves from death or maiming. . . .

If a man have a stubborn or rebellious son of sufficient years of understanding, viz. sixteen, which will not obey the voice of his father or the voice of his mother, and that when they have chastened him will not harken unto them, then shall his father and mother, being his natural parents, lay hold on him and bring him to the magistrates assembled in Court, and testify to them by sufficient evidence that this their son is stubborn and rebellious and will not obey their voice and chastisement, but lives in sundry notorious crimes. Such a son shall be put to death.

3. Connecticut, 1651

Franklin B. Dexter, ed., *Ancient Town Records,* I (New Haven, 1917), 88–89.

In 1650 Connecticut followed the example of Massachusetts in adopting the Mosaic law which imposed the death penalty on rebellious children. In practice, as the following case suggests, less stringent punishments were employed.

———— How, the daughter of Captain How, was called before the Court (her mother being present), and told that she is complained of for a profane swearer, not only as she is a Christian, and by her soul, but by the Holy name of God; with other stubborn miscarriages to her mother, and in a profane wicked way speaking of the scriptures, saying it was not worth the reading, or to that purpose. She was asked what she said to the charge, and wished to own her sin and show her repentence for it. She boldly refused, and said she desired it might be proved. She was told by such ways she will but make her punishment more heavy.

Mistress How said that her daughter hath learned some of this ill carriage at Goodwife Wickams, where she went to school. She was told that the Court will inquire after that, for they will not suffer any to be instruments of corrupting children if they know it, specially such as keep school.

———— Seward, the wife of William Seward, testified upon oath that she is certain she heard ———— How swear by God, and as she was a Christian was common, and by the bottom of her soul, and that she saw her looking in a Bible, and turned over a leaf, and said it was not worth reading, and one time when her mother called her she said, a pox of the devil, what lacks this woman.

Rebecca Rose, the wife of Robert Rose, testified upon oath that she heard ———— How swear by God, and as she is a Christian, and by her faith, and by her soul, and that she saw her turn over a leaf of the Bible, and said it was not worth reading, and one time her mother called her and she said, a pox of the devil, what ails this mad woman.

The Court upon consideration of what is testified, ordered that for her swearing she pay ten shillings, and for her cursing speeches and rebellion to her mother, and profane speeches of the scriptures, tending to blasphemy, that she be corrected publicly by whipping, suitable to her years, and if this be not a warning but that she go on in these courses, it will come to a higher censure.

4. Massachusetts, 1654

Mass. Records, III, 355.

Forasmuch as it appears by too much experience that divers children and servants do behave themselves too disrespectively, disobediently, and disorderly towards their parents, masters, and governors, to the disturbance of families and discouragement of such parents and governors: For the ready prevention whereof it is ordered by this Court and the authority thereof that it shall henceforth be in the power of any one magistrate, by warrant directed to the constable of that town where such offender dwells, upon complaint, to call before him any such offender, and upon conviction of such misdemeanors to sentence him or them to endure such corporal punishment by whipping or otherwise as in his judgment the merit of the fact shall deserve, not exceeding ten stripes for one offence, or bind the offender to appear at the next Court of that county. And further, it is also ordered, that the commissioners for the town of Boston, and the three commissioners for towns where no magistrate dwells, shall have the like power, provided the person or persons so sentenced shall have liberty to make their legal appeal to the next County Court, if they desire it in any of these cases.

5. Laws of the Duke of York, 1676

George Staughton et al., eds., *Charter to William Penn and Laws of the Province of Pennsylvania Passed between 1682 and 1700, Preceded by the Duke of York's Book of Laws (1676–1682)* (Harrisburg, Pa., 1879), pp. 19–20.

. . . If any children of servants become rude, stubborn, or unruly, refusing to harken to the voice of their parents or masters, the constable and overseers (where no justice of peace shall happen to dwell within ten miles of the said town or parish), have power upon the complaint of their parents or masters [to] call before them such an offender, and to inflict such corporal punishment as the merit of the fact in their judgment shall deserve, not [exceeding] ten stripes, provided that such children and servants be of sixteen years of age.

Legislation strengthening family government, Massachusetts, 1642–1682

Among the Puritans there was a settled conviction that most of what was amiss in society stemmed from defects in family government. Beginning in 1642 Massachusetts Bay passed a series of acts intended to compel parents to "train up" their children properly and authorizing magistrates to take children from parents who neglected their duties.

1. Massachusetts Bay law for the training of children and servants in the home, 1642

Mass. Records, II (1853), 8–9.

This Court, taking into consideration the great neglect in many parents and masters in training up their children in learning, and labor, and other employments which may be profitable to the commonwealth, do hereupon order and decree that in every town the chosen men appointed for managing the prudential affairs of the same shall henceforth stand charged with the care of the redress of this evil, so as they shall be liable to be punished or fined for the neglect thereof, upon any presentment of the grand jurors or other information or complaint in any plantations in this jurisdiction . . . For this end they, or the greater part of them, shall have power to take account from time to time of [the] parents and masters and of their children, concerning their calling and employment of their children, especially of their ability to read and understand the principles of religion and the capital laws of the country, and to impose fines upon all those who refuse to render such account to them when required . . . They shall have power (with consent of any Court or magistrates) to put forth [as] apprentices the children of such as shall not be able and fit to employ and bring them up, nor shall take course to dispose of them . . . They are to take care that such as are set to keep cattle be set to some other employment withal, as spinning . . . knitting, weaving tape, etc.; and that boys and girls be not suffered to converse together so as may occasion any wanton, dishonest, or immodest behavior . . . For their better performance of this trust committed to them, they may divide the town amongst them, appoint to every of the said townsmen a certain number of families to have special oversight of. They are also to provide that a sufficient quantity of materials as hemp, flax, etc., may be raised in their several towns, and tools and implements provided for working out the same . . . For their assistance in this so needful and beneficial employment, if they meet with any difficulty or opposition which they cannot well master by their own power, they may have recourse to some of the magistrates, who shall take such course for their help and encouragement as the occasion shall require, according to justice . . . The said townsmen, at the next Court in those limits after the end of their year, shall give a brief account in writing of their proceedings herein. Provided, that they have been so required by some Court or magistrate a month at least before . . . This order to continue for two years and till the Court shall take further order.

2. Massachusetts selectmen ordered to enforce the law for training children and servants within the family, 1648

Max Farrand, ed., *Laws and Liberties of Massachusetts, Reprinted from the Copy of the 1648 edition* . . . (Cambridge, Mass., 1929), p. 11.

Forasmuch as the good education of children is of Singular behoof and benefit to any commonwealth, and whereas many parents and masters are too indulgent and negligent of their duty in that kind: It is therefore ordered that the selectmen of every town, in the several precincts and quarters where they dwell, shall have a vigilant eye over their brethren and neighbors to see, first, that none of them shall suffer so much barbarism in any of their families as not to endeavor to teach by themselves, or others, their children and apprentices so much learning as may enable them perfectly to read the English tongue and knowledge of the capital laws, upon penalty of twenty shillings for each neglect therein.

Also that all masters of families do once a week (at the least) catechize their children and servants in the grounds and principles of religion . . . If any be unable to do so much, that then at the least, they procure such children or apprentices to learn some short orthodox catechism without book, that they may be able to answer unto the questions that shall be propounded to them out of such catechism by their parents or masters or any of the selectmen when they shall call them to a trial of what they have learned in this kind.

And further that all parents and masters do breed and bring up their children and apprentices in some honest lawful calling, labor, or employment, either in husbandry, or some other trade profitable for themselves and the commonwealth, if they will not or cannot train them up in learning to fit them for higher employments. And if any of the selectmen, after admonition by them given to such masters of families, shall find them still negligent of their duty in the particulars aforementioned, whereby children and servants become rude, stubborn, and unruly, the said selectmen with the help of two Magistrates or the next County Court for that shire, shall take such children or apprentices from them and place them with some masters for years (boys till they come to twenty-one, and girls eighteen years of age complete) which will more strictly look unto, and force them to submit unto government according to the rules of this order, if by fair means and former instructions they will not be drawn unto it.

---

3. Enforcement of the literacy and catechism law, Watertown, Massachusetts, 1670–1676

Watertown Records . . . , I (Watertown, Mass., 1894), 102–103, 121–122, 128.

[1670]. Ordered that John Edy, Senior, shall go to John Fisk's house and to George Lawrence's and William Priest's houses to inquire about their children, whether they be learned to read the English tongue and in case they be defective to warn in the said John, George, and William to the next meeting of the Selectmen.

·   ·   ·   ·   ·

William Priest, John Fisk, and George Lawrence, being warned to a meeting of the Selectmen at John Bigulah's house, they making their appearance and being found defective, were admonished for not learning their children to read the English tongue: were convinced, did acknowledge their neglects, and did promise amendment.

·   ·   ·   ·   ·

[1674]. Agreed that Thomas Fleg, John Whitney, and Joseph Bemus should go about the

town to see that children were taught to read the English tongue and that they were taught some orthodox catechism and to see that each man has in his house a copy of the capital laws. For which end the Selectmen agreed there should be copies procured by Captain Mason at the printers and they to be paid for out of the town rate and the men above mentioned to carry them along with them to such of the inhabitants as have none.

·   ·   ·   ·   ·

Thomas Fleg, John Whitney, and Joseph Bemus gave in an account of what they had found concerning children's education and John Fisk being found wholly negligent of educating his children as to reading or catechizing, the Selectmen agreed that Joseph Bemus should warn him into answer for his neglect at the next meeting of the Selectmen.

·   ·   ·   ·   ·

[1676]. Ordered that Captain Mason and Simon Stone shall go to John Fisk to see if his children be taught to read English and their catechism.

---

4. Children removed from unsuitable homes, 1675, 1678

Samuel Eliot Morison, ed., "Records of the Suffolk County Court, 1671–1680," CSM *Publications,* XXX (1933), 599, 915.

[1675]. William Scant of Braintree being bound over to this court to answer for his not ordering and disposing of his children as may be for their good education, and for refusing to consent to the Selectmen of Braintree in the putting of them forth to service as the law directs; the court having duly weighed and considered what was alleged by him and the state of his family do[th] leave it to the prudence of the Selectmen of Braintree to dispose of his children to service so far forth as the necessity of his family will give leave.

[1678]. Robert Styles of Dorchester presented for not attending the public worship of God, negligence in his calling, and not submitting to authority, testified upon the oaths of Thomas Davenport and Isaac Jones, grandjurymen. Sentenced to be admonished, and order[ed] that he put forth his children, or otherwise the selectmen are hereby empowered to do it according to Law.

---

5. Responsibilities of tithingmen, 1679

Mass. Records, VI, 240–241.

The office of tithingman was established in the 1670's to assist selectmen and constables in supervising family government. Each tithingman was "diligently to inspect" ten or twelve families in his neighborhood. Edmund S. Morgan, *The Puritan Family* (New York, 1966), pp. 148–149.

It is ordered . . . that henceforth the selectmen of each town take care that tithingmen be annually chosen in their several precincts of the most prudent and discreet inhabitants, and sworn to the faithful discharge of their trust . . .

The tithingmen are required diligently to inspect the manner of all disorderly persons, and where by more private admonitions they will not be reclaimed, they are from time to time to present their names to the next Magistrate, or Commissioner invested with magistratical power, who shall proceed against them as the law directs. As also they are in like manner to present the names of all single persons that live from under family government, stubborn and disorderly children and servants, night-walkers,

tipplers, Sabbath breakers by night or by day, and such as absent themselves from the public worship of God on the Lord's days, or whatever else course or practice of any person or persons whatsoever tending to debauchery, irreligion, profaneness, and atheism amongst us, whether by omission of family government, nurture, and religious duties, [or] instruction of children and servants, or idle, profligate, uncivil or rude practices of any sort, the names of all which persons with the fact whereof they are accused, and witnesses thereof, they shall present to the next Magistrate or Commissioner, where any are in the said town invested with magistratical power, who shall proceed against and punish all such misdemeanours by fine, imprisonment, or binding over the county court as the law directs.[1]

Witchcraft and children in Massachusetts

The spectacular Salem witch trials of 1692 were preceded by seizures and trials in other New England towns. The prominence of young people in these proceedings suggests that accusations of witchcraft may have been an acceptable way of protesting against adult dominance of children's lives and of temporarily reversing the usual relationship.

---

1. The behavior of Elizabeth Knapp of Groton, Massachusetts, in 1671

Samuel Willard, minister at Groton, to Cotton Mather, 1672, in S. A. Green, *Groton in the*

1. In 1682 tithingmen were given additional responsibilities in investigating and reporting idle persons who failed to support their families. Morgan, *The Puritan Family*, p. 373.

Witchcraft Times (Groton, Mass., 1883),
pp. 17–20.

It was not many days ere she was hurried again into violent fits after a different manner, being taken again speechless, and using all endeavors to make away with herself, and do mischief unto others: striking those that held her, spitting in their faces, and if at any time she had done any harm or frightened them, she would laugh immediately, which fits held her sometimes longer, sometimes shorter. Few occasions she had of speech, but when she could speak, she complained of a hard heart, counselled some to beware of sin, for that had brought her to this, bewailed that so many prayers had been put up for her, and she still so hard hearted, and no more good wrought upon her. But being asked whether she were willing to repent, shaked her head and said nothing. Thus she continued till the next sabbath in the afternoon, on which day, in the morning, being somewhat better than at other times, she had but little company tarried with her in the afternoon, when the Devil began to make more full discovery of himself. It had been a question before whether she might properly be called a Demoniac, a person possessed of the Devil, but it was then put out of question. He began (as the persons with her testify) by drawing her tongue out of her mouth most frightfully to an extraordinary length and greatness, and many amazing postures of her body; and then by speaking vocally in her. Whereupon her father and another neighbor were called from the meeting, on whom (as soon as they came in), he railed, calling them rogues, charging them for folly in going to hear a black rogue who told them nothing but a parcel of lies, and deceived them, and many like expressions. After exercise I was called, but understood not the occasion till I came and heard the same voice, a grim, low, yet audible voice it was. The first salutation I had was, Oh! You are a great rogue. I was at the first something daunted and amazed, and many reluctances I had upon my spirits, which brought me to a silence and amazement in my spirits, till at last God heard my groans and gave me both refreshment in Christ and courage. I then called for a light to see whether it might not appear a counterfeit, and observed not any of her organs to move. The voice was hollow, as if it issued out of her throat. He then again called me great black rogue. I challenged him to make it appear. But all the answer was, You tell your people a company of lies. I reflected on myself, and could not but magnify the goodness of God not to suffer Satan to bespatter the names of his people with those sins which he himself hath pardoned in the blood of Christ. I answered, Satan, thou art a liar and deceiver, and God will vindicate his own truth one day. He answered nothing directly, but said, I am not Satan. I am a pretty black boy; this is my pretty girl. I have been here a great while. I sat still and answered nothing to these expressions. But when he directed himself to me again, Oh! You black rogue, I do not love you, I replied through God's grace, I hate thee . . . On Friday in the evening she was taken again violently, and then the former voice . . . was heard in her again, not speaking, but imitating the crowing of a cock, accompanied with many other gestures, some violent, some ridiculous, which occasioned my going to her, where by signs she signified that the Devil threatened to carry her away that night. God was again then sought for her. And when in prayer that expression was used, that God had proved Satan a liar, in preserving her once when he had threatened to carry her away that night, and was entreated so to do again, the same voice, which had ceased two days before, was again heard by the by-standers five times distinctly to cry out, Oh! You are a rogue, and then ceased. But the whole time of prayer, sometimes by violence of fits, sometimes by noises she made, she drowned her own hearing from receiving our petition, as she afterwards confessed. Since that time she hath continued for the most part speechless, her fits coming upon her sometimes often, sometimes with greater intermission, and with great varieties in the manner of them, sometimes by violence, sometimes by making her sick, but (through God's goodness) so abated in violence that now one person can as well rule her as formerly four or five. She is observed always to fall into her fits when any strangers go to visit her, and the more go the more violent are her fits.

---

2. The children of John Goodwin possessed by a witch, Boston, 1688

Cotton Mather, *Memorable Providences, Relating to Witchcrafts and Possessions* (Boston, 1689), in George L. Burr, ed., *Narratives of the Witchcraft Cases, 1648–1706* (New York, 1914), pp. 99–103.

There dwells at this time, in the south part of Boston, a sober and pious man, whose Name is John Goodwin, whose Trade is that of a Mason, and whose Wife . . . has made him the Father of six (now living) Children. Of these Children, all but the Eldest, who works with his Father at his Calling, and the Youngest, who lives yet upon the Breast of its mother, have laboured under the direful effects of a . . . stupendous *Witchcraft* . . .

The four Children [13, 11, 7, and 5 years old] had enjoyed a Religious Education. . . . They had an observable Affection unto Divine and Sacred things; and those of them that were capable of it, seem'd to have such a [feeling for] their eternal Concernments as is not altogether usual. Their Parents also kept them to a continual Employment, which did more than deliver them from the Temptations of Idleness, and as young as they were, they took a delight in it, it may be as much as they should have done. In a word, Such was the whole Temper and Carriage of the Children, that there cannot easily be any thing more unreasonable, than to imagine that a Design to Dissemble

could cause them to fall into any of their odd Fits . . .

About Midsummer, in the year 1688, the Eldest of these Children, who is a Daughter, saw cause to examine their Washerwoman, upon their missing of some Linnen, which twas fear'd she had stollen from them . . . This Laundress was the Daughter of an ignorant and a scandalous old Woman in the Neighbourhood; whose miserable Husband before he died, had sometimes complained of her, that she was undoubtedly a Witch . . . This Woman in her daughters Defence bestow'd very bad Language upon the Girl that put her to the Question; immediately upon which, the poor child became variously indisposed in her health, and visited with strange Fits, beyond those that attend an Epilepsy, or a Catalepsy . . .

It was not long before one of her Sisters, and two of her Brothers, were seized, in Order one after another . . . Within a few weeks, they were all four tortured every where in a manner so very grievous, that it would have broke an heart of stone to have seen their Agonies. Skilful Physicians were consulted for their Help, and particularly our worthy and prudent Friend Dr. Thomas Oakes, who found himself so [perplexed] by the Distempers of the children, that he concluded nothing but an hellish Witchcraft could be the Original of these Maladies. And that which yet more confirmed such Apprehension was, That for one good while, the children were tormented just in the same part of their bodies all at the same time together; and tho they saw and heard not one anothers complaints . . .

. . . Sometimes they would be Deaf, sometimes Dumb, and sometimes Blind, and often, all this at once. One while their Tongues would be drawn down their Throats; another-while they would be pull'd out upon their Chins, to a prodigious length . . . The same would happen to their Shoulder-Blades, and their Elbows, and Hand-wrists, and several of their joints. They would at times ly in a benumbed condition; and be drawn together . . . and presently be stretched out, yea, drawn Backwards, to such a degree that it was fear'd the very skin of their Bellies would have crack'd. They would make most pitteous out-cries, that they were cut with Knives, and struck with Blows that they could not bear. Their Necks would be broken, so that their Neck-bone would seem dissolved unto them that felt after it; and yet on the sudden, it would become again so stiff that there was no stirring of their Heads . . . Thus they lay some weeks most pittiful Spectacles; and this while as a further Demonstration of Witchcraft in these horrid Effects, when I went to Prayer by one of them, that was very desireous to hear what I said, the Child utterly lost her Hearing till our Prayer was over.

It was a Religious Family that these Afflictions happened unto; and none but a Religious Contrivance to obtain Releef, would have been welcome to them . . . Accordingly they requested the four Ministers of Boston, with the Minister of Charlstown, to keep a Day of Prayer at their thus haunted house; which they did in the Company of some devout people there. Immediately upon this Day, the youngest of the four children was delivered, and never felt any trouble as afore. But there was yet a greater Effect of these our Applications unto our God!

The Report of the Calamities of the Family for which we were thus concerned, arrived now unto the ears of the Magistrates, who presently and prudently apply'd themselves, with a just vigour, to enquire into the story. The Father of the Children complained of his Neighbour, the suspected ill woman, whose name was Glover; and she being sent for by the Justices, gave such a wretched Account of herself, that they saw cause to commit her unto the Gaolers Custody. Goodwin had no proof that could have done her any Hurt; but the Hag had not power to deny her interest in the Enchantment of the Children . . . An Experiment was made, Whether she could recite the Lords Prayer; and it was found, that tho clause after clause was most carefully repeated unto

her, yet when she said it after them that prompted her, she could not possibly avoid making Nonsense of it, with some ridiculous Depravations . . . Upon the Commitment of this extraordinary Woman, all the Children had some present ease; until one (related unto her) accidentally meeting one or two of them, entertain'd them with her Blessing, that is, Railing; upon which Three of them fell ill again, as they were before.

Death in the Colonial family

1. A father's sermon at the funeral of his three daughters, 1659

Mather, "The Life of Mr. Samuel Danforth" in *Magnalia Christi Americana*, IV, 156–157.

In December 1659 the (until then unknown) Malady of Bladders in the Windpipe,[1] invaded and removed many children; by opening of one of them the malady and Remedy (too late for very many) were discovered. Among those many that thereby expired, were the Three Children of the Reverend Mr. S. D. the Eldest of whom (being upward of five years and half; so gracious and intelligent were her expressions and behaviour both living and dying and so evident her faith in Christ) was a luculent commentary on that marvellous prophecy, that the Child should dye an Hundred years old. How the Sorrowful Father entertained this Solemn Providence may be partly gathered from what he expressed unto such as came to attend his Branches unto their graves . . .

"My Friends,

1. Probably scarlet fever or diphtheria. John Duffy, *Epidemics in Colonial America* (Baton Rouge, La., 1953), pp. 115–116.

If any that see my grief should say unto me as the Danites unto Micah, What aileth thee? I thank God, I cannot answer as he did, They have taken away my Gods. My heart was indeed somewhat set upon my children, especially the eldest; but they were none of my Gods, none of my Portion; my Portion is whole and untouched to this day.

. . . . .

Had our children replyed when we corrected them, we could not have born it: But poor hearts, they did us Reverence; how much rather should we be subject to the Father of Spirits and live. You know, that Nine years since, I was in a desolate condition without Father, without Mother, without wife, without children: But what a Father, and Mother, and wife have been bestowed upon me, and are still continued tho' my children are removed. And above all, although I cannot deny, but that it pierceth my very heart to call to rememberance the voice of my dear children, calling Father, Father! a Voice not now heard: Yet I bless God, it doth far more abundantly refresh and rejoice me, to hear the Lord calling unto me. My Son, My Son! My Son, despise not the chastening of the Lord, nor faint thou when thou are corrected of him. And blessed be God, that doth not despise the affliction of the afflicted, nor hides his face from him . . . and if the Lord will glorify himself by my family, by these awful strokes upon me, quickening parents unto their duty, and awakening their children to seek after the Lord, I shall desire to be content, though my name be cut off: And I beseech you be earnest with the Lord for us, that he would keep us from sinning against him; and that he would teach us to sanctify his name, and tho' our dear Branches have forsaken us, yet that He that hath promised to be with his children in six troubles and in seven, would not forsake us. My heart truly would be consumed, and would dye within me, but that the good will of Him that dwelt in the Burning Bush, and His good word of promise are my trust and stay."

2. Cotton Mather's crosses, 1713

Cotton Mather, *Diary, 1709–1724* in *Collections* of the Massachusetts Historical Society, 7th ser., VIII (1912), 248, 252–262; hereafter cited as MHS *Collections*.

Cotton Mather (1663–1728) was the father of fifteen children, only two of whom survived him. During the measles epidemic of 1713, in the space of less than two weeks, his wife and three of his children died.

October 18, 1713. The Measles coming into the Town, it is likely to be a Time of Sickness, and much Trouble in the Families of the Neighbourhood. I would by my public Sermons and Prayers, endeavour to prepare the Neighbours for the Trouble which their Families are likely to meet withal.[1]

The Apprehension of a very deep Share, that my Family may expect in the common Calamity of the spreading Measles, will oblige me to be much in pleading the Great Family-Sacrifice, that so the Wrath of Heaven may inflict no sad Thing on my Family; and to quicken and augment the Expressions of Piety, in the daily Sacrifices of my Family; and to lay hold on the Occasion to awaken Piety, and Preparation for Death, in the Souls of the children.

November 4, 1713. In my poor Family, now, first, my Wife has the *Measles* appearing on her; we know not yett how she will be handled.

My Daughter *Nancy* is also full of them; not in such uneasy Circumstances as her prædecessors.

My Daughter *Lizzy,* is likewise full of them; yett somewhat easily circumstanced.

1. Duffy, *Epidemics in Colonial America*, p. 254, calls Mather's pamphlet, *A Letter about a Good Management under the Distemper of the Measles* (Boston, 1739), "one of the colonial medical classics . . . a shining light amid the quackery of the period."

My Daughter *Jerusha,* droops and seems to have them appearing.

My Servant-maid, lies very full and ill of them.

Help Lord; and look mercifully on my poor, sad, sinful Family, for the Sake of the Great Sacrifice!

November 7, 1713. I sett apart this Day, as I had much Cause, and it was high Time, to do, for Prayer with Fasting before the Lord. Not only are my Children, with a Servant, lying sick, but also my Consort is in a dangerous Condition, and can gett no Rest; Either Death, or Distraction, is much feared for her. It is also an Hour of much Distress in my Neighbourhood. So, I humbled myself before the Lord, for my own Sins, and the Sins of my Family; and I presented before Him the great Sacrifice of my Saviour, that His wrath may be turned away from me, and from my Family; and that the Destroyer might not have a Commission to inflict any deadly Stroke upon us.

November 8, 9, 1713. This Day, I entertained my Neighbourhood, with a Discourse, on Joh. XVIII. II. *The Cup which my Father has given me shall not I drink it?* And, lo, this Day, my Father is giving me a grievous and bitter Cup, which I hop'd, had pass'd from me.

For these many Months, and ever since I heard of the venemous Measles invading the Countrey sixty Miles to the Southward of us, I have had a strong Distress on my Mind, that it will bring on my poor Family, a Calamity, which is now going to be inflicted. I have often, often express'd my Fear unto my Friends concerning it. And now, *the Thing that I greatly feared is coming upon me!*

When I saw my Consort safely delivered, and very easy, and the Measles appearing with favourable Symptomes upon her, and the Physician apprehending all to look very comfortably, I flattered myself, that my Fear was all over.

But this Day we are astonished, at the sur-prising Symptomes of Death upon her; after an extreme Want of Rest by Sleep, for diverse whole Dayes and Nights together.

To part with so desireable, so agreeable a Companion, a Dove from such a Nest of young ones too! Oh! the sad Cup, which my Father has appointed me! I now see the Meaning and the Reason of it, that I have never yett been able to make any Work of it, in Prayers and Cries to God, that such a Cup as this might pass from me. My Supplications have all along had, a most unaccountable Death and Damp upon them!

Tho' my dear Consort, had been so long without Sleep, yett she retain'd her Understanding.

I had and us'd my Opportunities as well as I could, continually to be assisting her, with Discourses that might support her in this Time, and prepare her for what was now before us.

It comforted her to see that her [step] children . . . were as fond of her, as her own could be!

God made her willing to Dy. God extinguished in her the Fear of Death. God enabled her to committ herself into the Hands of a great and good Saviour; yea, and to cast her Orphans there too, and to beleeve that He had merciful and wonderful Things to do for them.

I pray'd with her many Times, and left nothing undone, that I could find myself able to do for her Consolation.

On Munday [November 9, 1713] between three and four in the Afternoon, my dear, dear, dear Friend expired.

Whereupon, with another Prayer in the melancholy Chamber, I endeavoured the Resignation to which I am now called, and cried to Heaven for the Grace that might be suitable to the calamitous Occasion, and carried my poor Orphans unto the Lord.

It comforts me to see how extremely Beloved, and lamented a Gentlewoman, I now find her to be in the Neighbourhood.

Much weakness continues on some of my other Children. Especially the Eldest. And the poor Maid in the Family, is very like to dy.

2. G. D. Oh! the Prayers for my poor Children, oh! the Counsils to them, now called for!

The particular Scriptures, I shall direct them to read! And the Sentences thereof to be gotten by heart.

3. G. D. My Relatives, especially those of my deceased Consort, I will entertain with Books of Piety, that shall have in them a Memorial of her.

November 14, 1713. This Morning, the first Thing that entertains me, after my rising, is, the Death of my Maid-servant, whose Measles passed into a malignant Feaver, which has proved mortal to her.

Tis a Satisfaction to me, that tho' she had been a wild, vain, airy Girl, yett since her coming into my Family, she became disposed unto serious Religion; was awakened unto secret and fervent Supplications; gave herself to God in His Covenant: (upon which, a few Weeks ago, I baptised her:) and my poor Instructions, were the means that God blessed for such happy Purposes.

And now, as I am called still unto more Assiduities in my Præparations for my own Death, and unto more exquisite Projections and Contrivances, how a Family visited with so much Death, may become an Exemple of uncommon Piety: So, I must have my Repentance for my Miscarriages in my Behaviour towards my Servants, very much excited and promoted.

Oh! the Trial, which I am this Day called unto in the threatning, the dying Circumstances of my dear little *Jerusha!* The Resignation, with which I am to offer up that Sacrifice! *Father, Lett that Cup pass from me. Nevertheless —*

The Two Newborns, are languishing in the Arms of Death.

November 15, 1713. Tis a Time of much Calamity in my Neighbourhood, and a Time of much Mortality seems coming on. My Public Prayers and Sermons must be exceedingly adapted for such a Time.

I am this day called unto a great Sacrifice;

for so I feel my little *Jerusha.* The dear little Creature lies in dying Circumstances. Tho' I pray and cry to the Lord, for the Cup to pass from me, yett the glorious One carries me thro' the required Resignation. I freely give her up. Lord, she is thine! Thy will be done!

November 16, 1713. Little *Jerusha* begins a little to revive.

November 17–18, 1713. About Midnight, little *Eleazar* died.

November 20, 1713. Little *Martha* died, about ten a clock, A.M.

I am again called unto the Sacrifice of my dear, dear, *Jerusha.*

I begg'd, I begg'd, that such a bitter Cup, as the Death of that lovely child, might pass from me. *Nevertheless!* — My glorious Lord, brought me to glorify Him, with the most submissive Resignation.

November 21, 1713. This Day, I attended the Funeral, of my two: *Eleazar* and *Martha.*

Betwixt 9 h. and 10 h. at Night, my lovely *Jerusha* Expired. She was two years, and about seven Months, old. Just before she died, she asked me to pray with her; which I did, with a distressed, but resigning Soul; and I gave her up unto the Lord. The Minute that she died, she said, *That she would go to Jesus Christ.* She had lain speechless, many Hours. But in her last Moments, her speech returned a little to her.

Lord, I am oppressed; undertake for me!

November 22, 1713. It will be a great Service unto my Flock, for me to exemplify, a patient Submission to the Will of God, under many and heavy Trials, and a most fruitful Improvement of my Crosses . . .

My poor Family is now left without any Infant in it, or any under seven Years of Age. I must now apply myself with most exquisite Contrivance, and all the Assiduity imaginable, to cultivate my Children, with a most excellent

Education. I have now singular Opportunities for it. Wherefore I must in the first Place, earnestly look up to the glorious Lord, who gives Wisdome, for Direction.

B. SINGLE PERSONS, BASTARDS, AND ORPHANS

New England laws requiring single persons to live in families, 1636–1676

1. Massachusetts, 1636

Mass. Records, I (1853), 186.

It is ordered that all towns shall take care to order and dispose of all single persons and inmates within their town to service, or otherwise; and if any be grieved at the order of a town, the parties to have liberty to appeal to the Governor and Council, or the Court.

2. Connecticut, 1637

Conn. Records, I, 8.

It is ordered that no young man that is neither married nor hath any servant, and be no public officer, shall keep house by himself, without consent of the town where he lives . . . under pain of 20s. per week.

It is ordered that no master of a family shall give habitation or entertainment to any young man to sojourn in his family, but by the allowance of the inhabitants of the said town where he dwells under the like penalty of 20s. per week.

3. Plymouth, 1669

William Brigham, ed., *The Compact with the Charter and Laws of the Colony of New Plymouth* (Boston, 1836), p. 156.

Whereas great inconvenience hath arisen by single persons in the Colony being for themselves and not betaking themselves to live in well governed families, it is enacted by the Court that henceforth no single person be suffered to live of himself or in any family but such as the selectmen of the town shall approve of. And if any person or persons shall refuse or neglect to attend such order as shall be given them by the selectmen, that such person or persons shall be summoned to the Court to be proceeded with as the matter shall require.

4. Watertown, Massachusetts, 1672

Watertown Records, I, 113.

James Hollon appearing before the selectmen to answer for his living from under family government and misspending his time by idleness, the selectmen gave him a fortnight's time to provide himself a master, and in case he did it not in that time, that then they would provide one for him.

5. Suffolk County, Massachusetts, 1675

Morison, "Suffolk Co. Court Records," in CSM *Publications,* XXX, 647.

Captain James Johnson being complained of for disorderly carriages in his family, giving entertainment to persons at unseasonable hours of the night, and other misdemeanors, the court orders the said Captain Johnson to break up housekeeping and to dispose of himself into some good orderly family within one fortnight next following, or that then the Selectmen of Boston take care to dispose of him as abovesaid.

6. Connecticut, 1676

Conn. Records, II (1852), 281–282.

Whereas it is observed that young persons getting from under the government of parents or masters before they are able to govern themselves, which early liberty hath or may be an occasion of many evils and inconveniences, and hath moved this Court seriously and heartily to recommend it to the selectmen of the several plantations to be careful to prohibit and not to grant liberty to unmeet persons to entertain boarders or sojourners; and it is also ordered by this Court that all such boarders or sojourners as do live in families as such shall carefully attend the worship of God in those families where they so board or sojourn, and be subject to the domestic government of the said family, and shall be ready to give an account of their actions upon all demands, upon the penalty of forfeiting of five shillings for every breach of this order; and that no children shall be at liberty to dispose of themselves upon pretence of lawful age without the parents'

consent and approbation of the authority of the place.

Colonial laws on bastards

1. Massachusetts, 1660

Colonial Laws of Massachusetts, Reprinted from the Edition of 1660 (Boston, 1889), p. 257.

Whereas there is a law provided by this Court for punishing of fornicators, but nothing as yet for the easing of towns where bastards are born, in regard of the poverty of the parent or parents of such children sometimes appearing, nor any rule held forth touching the reputed father of a bastard for legal conviction:

It is therefore ordered and by this Court declared that where any man is legally convicted to be the father of a bastard child, he shall be at the care and charge to maintain and bring up the same, by such assistance of the mother as nature requireth and as the Court, from time to time (according to circumstances), shall see meet to order. And in case the father of a bastard, by confession or other manifest proof upon trial of the case, does not appear to the Court's satisfaction, then the man charged by the woman to be the father, she holding constant in it (especially being put upon the real discovery of the truth of it in the time of her travail), shall be the reputed father, and accordingly be liable to the charge of maintenance as aforesaid (though not to other punishment) notwithstanding his denial, unless the circumstances of the case and pleas be such, on the behalf of the man charged, as that the Court that have the cognizance thereon shall see reason to acquit him, and otherwise dispose of the child and education thereof . . .

2. Virginia, 1661–1662

W. W. Hening, ed., *Statutes at Large of Virginia,* II (New York, 1823), 115; hereafter cited as *Va. Statutes at Large.*

. . . And if it happen a bastard child to be gotten in such fornication, then the woman, if a servant, in regard of the loss and trouble her master doth sustain by her having a bastard, shall serve two years after her time by indenture is expired, or pay two thousand pounds of tobacco to her master, besides the fine or punishment for committing the offence; and the reputed father to put in security to keep the child and save the parish harmless.

Va. Statutes at Large, II, 167.

Whereas by act of Assembly every woman servant having a bastard is to serve two years, and late experience show[s] that some dissolute masters have gotten their maids with child and yet claim the benefit of their service, and on the contrary, if a woman got with child by her master should be freed from that service it might probably induce such loose persons to lay all their bastards to their masters. It is therefore thought fit and accordingly enacted, and be it enacted henceforward, that each woman servant got with child by her master shall, after her time by indenture or custom is expired, be by the churchwardens of the parish where she lived when she was brought to bed of such a bastard, sold for two years, and the tobacco to be employed by the vestry for the use of the parish.

Va. Statutes at Large, II, 168.

Whereas by the present law of this country the punishment of a reputed father of a bastard child is the keeping the child and saving the parish harmless, and if it should happen the reputed father to be a servant who can no way accomplish the penalty of that act; be it enacted by the authority aforesaid that where any bastard child is gotten by a servant, the parish shall take care to keep the child during the time of the reputed father's service by indenture or custom, and that after he is free, the said reputed father shall make satisfaction to the parish.

Support of illegitimate children

1. Maryland, ca. 1658

"Charles County Court Proceedings, 1658–1672," in G. Hall Pleasants, ed., *Md. Archives,* LIII (1936), 78.

Anne Williams, plaintiff, Richard Smith, defendant: The plaintiff desires maintenance for a child the defendant hath got by her and desires by her petition that he may be sworn to several interrogatories she hath in equity propounded. But he being unwilling to be deposed to them . . . present[ed] his declaration as followeth:

To the Honorable Governor and worshipful Commissioner of Charles County.

The humble declaration of Richard Smith most humbly showeth that whereas this impudent woman hath most scandalously cast aspersions upon me, and I having taken it into my consideration for the injury, I do think it most meet for me to let her run on in her own perdition as she hath begun. If so [it] be that you will be pleased to permit her to take her deposition concerning the allegation she hath alleged against me, I am contented thereupon to take the child and to maintain it, trusting in the severe judgment of God against perjured persons.

It is therefore ordered that the said Richard Smith maintain the child. And that the woman for her fact committed be whipped and have thirty lashes well laid on.

---

2. Massachusetts, ca. 1673

Morison, "Suffolk Co. Court Records," in CSM *Publications,* XXIX (1933), 254–255.

Mary Hunter bound over to this Court for committing of fornication and having an illegitimate child which she owned in Court and charged Joseph Cowell with being the father of her child and took her oath thereof as followeth. You do here swear by the great and dreadful name of the Everliving God that the child lately born of your body, being a son, was begotten by Joseph Cowell and that he and no man else is the father thereof, so help you God.

Sworn in Court, May 1, 1673 . . .

The Court having considered of [Mary Hunter's] offence, do sentence her to be severly whipped with thirty stripes and to pay fees of court, standing committed till the sentence be performed.

Joseph Cowell, being bound over to this Court to answer upon suspicion of his committing fornication with Mary Hunter, he being called to answer to it, did not appear, his sureties being called to bring him in made no answer. The Court ordered a default to be entered, but afterwards, appearing and being convict[ed] of too much familiarity with the said Hunter, and she swearing that he and only he was the father of her illegitimate child. The Court sentenceth the said Cowell to be whipped severely with thirty stripes and to pay four shillings a week, one third in money, one third in goods, and one thirds in provisions towards the maintenance of the child lately born of the body of the said Mary Hunter, until he either marry with her or this Court take further order; and to pay fees of Court standing committed. The said Cowell next day sent in a petition to the Court wherein he did confess that he was the father of the child lately born of said Mary Hunter.

Morison, "Suffolk Co. Court Records." in CSM *Publications,* XXIX, 433–434.

Joseph Cowell bound over to this Court to answer what should be alleged against him by Hanna Tower of Hingham for committing fornication with her, by whom she hath had a bastard child, of which she made oath in Court and he did not deny it. The Court declares the said Cowell to be the reputed father of the child according to law, and order[s] him to pay three shillings per week in money to the said Hanna Tower towards the maintenance of the said child until the Court take further order, and to give in bond with sureties of fifty pounds for his good behavior till the next Court of this county, and then to appear standing committed until he give in such bond.

Morison, "Suffolk Co. Court Records," in CSM *Publications,* XXIX, 1012.

Thomas Curtice, charged by Sarah Tower for committing fornication with her, by whom she saith she hath had a child, and made oath in Court that he and no man else is the father of the child late born of her body begotten by him in fornication. The Court sentenced said Curtice to give bond of twenty pounds with two sufficient sureties for the payment of two shillings six pence per week in money to be paid weekly to said Sarah Tower or her order towards the maintenance of her child, from the time of its birth until this Court take further order, and to pay fees of Court standing committed.

3. Rhode Island, 1688

John Russell Bartlett, ed., *Records of the Colony of Rhode Island,* III (Providence, 1858), 244.

At a General Quarter Sessions holden at Rochester, for Rhode Island . . . in September 1688

.   .   .   .   .

Mary Cory, of Portsmouth, single woman, being called in Court, to answer to an indictment by the Grand Jury found against her for having a child born of her body, in June last past, appeared, and being demanded who was the father of the said child, she answered John Wickham.

The Court sentence the said Mary Cory for her offence to pay a fine of twenty shillings in money; and also that she bear the town of Portsmouth, free from all charges concerning, maintaining and bringing up the said child.

Status of children with one slave or servile parent

1. Inheritance of status through the mother, Virginia, 1662

Va. Statutes at Large, II, 170.

Was a child with one slave and one free parent slave or free? English common law derived the status of children from the father. To follow that course in Virginia, however, would result in freedom for the children of white men and Negro slave women. The Virginia law, which established inheritance of slave status through the mother, was copied in the later southern colonies.

Negro women's children to serve according to the condition of the mother.

Whereas some doubts have arisen whether children got by any Englishman upon a Negro woman should be slave or free, Be it therefore enacted . . . that all children born in this country shall be held bond or free only according to the condition of the mother. And that if any Christian shall commit fornication with a Negro man or woman, he or she so offending shall pay double the fines imposed by the former act.

2. Inheritance through the father, Maryland, 1664

Md. Archives, I (1883), 533–534.

Maryland seems to have taken for granted that children born to slave women were unfree; a special problem, however, was presented by the marriage of white women servants to Negro slaves.

All Negroes or other slaves already within the Province and all Negroes and other slaves to be hereafter imported into the Province shall serve *durante vita*. And all children born of any Negro or other slave shall be slaves as their fathers were for the term of their lives. And forasmuch as divers freeborn English women, forgetful of their free condition and to the disgrace of our nation, do intermarry with Negro slaves, by which also divers suits may arise touching the issue of such women and a great damage doth befall the masters of such Negroes, for prevention whereof, for deterring such freeborn women from such shameful matches, Be it further enacted . . . that whatsoever freeborn woman shall intermarry with any slave from and after the last day of this present Assembly shall serve the master of such slave during the life of her husband. And that all the issue of such freeborn women so married shall be slaves as their fathers were. And Be it further enacted that all the issues of English or other freeborn women that have already married Negroes shall serve the masters of their parents till they be thirty years of age and no longer.[1]

3. Virginia law prescribes penalties for a white woman having a bastard child by a Negro and sets thirty-one years as a term of service for the child, 1705

Va. Statutes at Large, III
(Philadelphia, 1823), 453.

If any woman servant shall have a bastard child by a negro, or mulatto, over and above the years service due to her master or owner, she shall immediately, upon the expiration of her time to her then present master or owner, pay down to the church-wardens of the parish wherein such child shall be born, for the use of the said parish, fifteen pounds current money of Virginia, or be by them sold for five years, to the use aforesaid: And if a free Christian white woman shall have such bastard child, by a negro, or mulatto, for every such offence, she shall, within one month after her delivery of such bastard child, pay to the church-wardens for the time being, of the parish wherein such child shall be born, for the use of the said parish fifteen pounds current money of Virginia, or be by them sold for five years to the use aforesaid: And in both the said cases, the church-wardens shall bind the said child to be

1. In 1681 Maryland attempted to discourage marriages between slaves and white women servants by imposing a heavy fine on masters who permitted such unions and manumitting children born of the marriage. *Md. Archives,* VII (1889), 203–205.

a servant, until it shall be of thirty-one years of age.

4. Bastard child of a female mulatto servant compelled to serve until thirty-one regardless of father's color, 1723

Va. Statutes at Large, IV
(Richmond, 1820), 433.

Where any female mullatto, or indian, by law obliged to serve 'till the age of thirty or thirty-one years, shall during the time of her servitude, have any child born of her body, every such child shall serve the master or mistress of such mullatto or indian, until it shall attain the same age the mother of such child was obliged by law to serve unto.[1]

Inheritance, guardianship, and foster care

1. Inheritance when parents die intestate, Massachusetts, 1641

Colonial Laws of Massachusetts, Reprinted from the Edition of 1660, p. 51.

When parents die intestate, the elder son shall have a double portion of his whole es-

1. In 1770, in the case of Howell *v.* Netherland, the Virginia courts denied freedom to a mulatto boy who was two generations removed from the union between a white servant woman and a Negro man. The boy was required to serve until thirty-one years of age. See Helen C. Catterall, ed., *Judicial Cases Concerning American Slavery and the Negro,* I (Washington, D.C., 1926), 90–91.

tate, real and personal, unless the General Court, upon just cause alleged, shall judge otherwise.

When parents die intestate having no heirs males of their bodies, their daughters shall inherit as copartners, unless the General Court, upon just cause alleged, shall judge otherwise.

.   .   .   .   .

No orphan during their minority, which was not committed to tuition or service by the parents in their lifetime, shall afterwards be absolutely disposed of by any kindred, friend, executor, township, or church, nor by themselves without the consent of some Court, wherein two Assistants at least shall be present.

---

2. A resident of Plymouth Colony provides for the family government of his children and other dependents in his will, 1633

Mayflower Descendant, I (1899), 24–29.

I, Samuel Fuller the elder, being sick and weak but by the mercy of God in perfect memory ordain this my last will and testament. And first of all I bequeath my soul to God and my body to the earth until the resurrection. Item. I do bequeath the education of my children to my Brother Will Wright and his wife, only that my daughter Mercy be and remain with Goodwife Wallen so long as she will keep her at a reasonable charge. But if it shall please God to recover my wife out of her weak estate of sickness, then my children to be with her or disposed by her. Also, whereas there is a child committed to my charge called Sarah Converse, my wife dying as afore, I desire my Brother Wright may have the bringing up of her. And if he refuse then I commend her to my loving neighbor and brother in Christ, Thomas Prince,

desiring that whosoever of them receive her perform the duty of a step father unto her and bring her up in the fear of God as their own, which was a charge laid upon me by her sick father when he freely bestowed her upon me, and which I require of them. Item. Whereas Elizabeth Cowles was committed to my education by her father and mother still living at Charlestown, my will is that she be conveniently apparaled and return to her father or mother or either of them. And for George Foster, being placed with me upon the same terms by his parents still living at Saugus, my will is that he be restored to his mother likewise. Item. I give unto Samuel my son my house and lands at the Smeltriver to him and his heirs forever. Item. My will is that my house and garden at town be sold and all my moveables there and at the Smeltriver (except my cattle) together with the present crop of corn there standing by my overseers hereafter to be mentioned, except such as they shall think meet in the present education of my two children, Samuel and Mercy, my debts being first paid out of them, the overplus to be disposed of towards the increase of my stock of cattle for their good at the discretion of my overseers . . . Item. Whereas I have disposed of my children to my Brother Will. Wright and Priscilla his wife, my will is that in case my wife die he enter upon my house and land at the Smeltriver, and also my cattle not disposed [of], together with my two servants, Thomas Symens and Robert Cowles, for the remainder of their several terms, to be employed for the good of my children; he being allowed for their charge, viz. my children's, what my overseer shall think meet. But if in case my said brother Will Wright or Priscilla his wife die, then my said children Samuel and Mercy, together with the said joint charge committed to the said Will and Priscilla, be void except my overseers or the survivor of them shall think meet. To whose godly care in such case I leave them to be disposed of elsewhere as the law shall direct them . . . Item. My will is that when my children come to age of discretion, then my over-seers make a full valuation of that stock of cattle and the increase thereof, and that it be equally divided between my children. And if any die in the meantime, the whole to go to the survivor or survivors. Item. My will is that they be ruled by my overseers in marriage. Also, I would have them enjoy that small portion the Lord shall give them when my overseers think them to be of fit discretion, and not at any set time or appointment of years . . .

---

3. Widows, orphans, and guardians,
New Amsterdam, 1655

Berthold Fernow, ed. and trans., *The Minutes of the Orphanmasters of New Amsterdam, 1655 to 1683* (New York, 1902), pp. 3–9.

Whereas *Johan van Beeck* has perished in the last disaster[1] Therefore their Worships, the Burgomasters, as Orphan Masters, consider it necessary, that agreeably to the customs of the Fatherland guardians for the infant child be appointed and for this purpose there has been summoned *Maria Verleth,* the widow of said *J. van Beeck,* and the matter was laid before her; but as she could not so quickly resolve, whom to name and refused some, who were proposed, she was given time to think of it un-til the next meeting of the Orphan Masters, next Tuesday at 10 o. c. and the case deferred until then.

Whereas *Pieter Cecer,* alias *Mallemock,* and his wife have lately died, leaving six small chil-dren, Therefore their Worships, the Burgomas-ters, as Orphan Masters, have deemed it nec-essary, that tutors and guardians for said chil-dren be appointed and they have selected as such and herewith appoint *Pieter van Linde* as

1. Probably the Indian onslaught of September 15, 1655. [Editor's note in *Minutes of the Orphanmasters.*]

being the stepfather of the mother, and *Isaacq Kip* as witness . . . for the youngest child. They are hereby authorized to sell or employ the goods and property, left by deceased, for the benefit of the children, to hire out or bind out the children to honest and suitable people and to do everything, what time and circum-stances point out as proper. They shall be held, when called upon, to render account, produce vouchers etc to the Orphan Masters. Thus done etc. November 9, 1655.

Whereas *Cornelis Hendricksen of Dort* has perished in the late disaster and has left besides a widow a small child and whereas as yet no inventory has been taken of his estate, There-fore his widow *Madaleen Direx* has been sum-moned to appear before their Worships, the Burgomasters, as Orphan Masters, and she was asked, whether she knew of any relatives of her husband here in the country; she answered, she knew of none and as their Worships consider it necessary, to appoint, according to the cus-toms of the Fatherland, guardians for the small child, they have chosen and appointed, as they herewith do, *Jan Vinje,* as being related to the widow, and *Hendrick Kip,* an old Burgher and inhabitant here, who are hereby authorized to take within three days from date in the pres-ence of the Secretary an inventory of the estate of said *Cornelis Hendricksen* dec'd and to sub-mit the same next Tuesday to the Orphanmas-ters who will then decide upon the disposition of it. Done as above.

Whereas *Cornelis Clasen Swits* and *Tobias Teunissen* perished in the last disaster and their widows and children are still with the savage barbarians and whereas quite lately in gather-ing the cattle on the Island some heads were found and brought in, belonging to said *Cor-nelis Clasen* and *Tobias Teunissen* dec'd, There-fore their Worships, the Burgomasters, as Or-phanmasters, have deemed it necessary, that proper care be taken to have said cattle put to use for the benefit of the widows and orphans. For this purpose they have chosen and ap-pointed, as they herewith do, *Egbert Wouter-sen, Tomas Hall* and *Cornelis Aertsen,* who are hereby authorized to dispose of said cattle, as they according to time and circumstances shall consider best for the heirs. They shall be bound to report such disposals with proofs, vouchers etc. to the Orphan masters. Done November 10, 1655.

Jan Vinje appeared at the Secretary's office and declared, that he could not attend to the guardianship of the small child of *Cornelis Hendricksen of Dort* dec'd, as he had too much to do with his own business and had also been refused by the widow *Madaleene.*

Tuesday, the 16th of November [1655] . . . Whereas *Maria Verleth,* widow of *Joh. van Beeck,* was at the last meeting on the 9th inst given time until to-day, to consider, whom she should name as guardian of her infant child, therefore it has been decided to send the messenger for said widow to appear: which being done, the Messenger reports, that she had said, she were busy and could not come.

Then the Orphanmasters decreed as follows:

Whereas Sieur *Johannes van Beeck* has lately perished in the last disaster and has left behind in this country not only a widow, but also a small minor child. Therefore the Burgomasters of this City as Orphanmasters have deemed it necessary, that following the usages of our Fatherland guardians be appointed for said child, in order that neither the child nor the widow may be injured in their rights and inherited property and having called the widow *Maria Verleth* to appear they have after due deliberation appointed and commissioned as guardians, as they hereby do, Sieur *Joost van Beeck,* the brother of *Johannes van Beeck* deceased, and *Nicolas Verleth,* the brother of the widow, who are hereby authorized as such guardians, first to make in the presence of the Secretary an inventory of the estate, including furniture, real and personal property, debts and credits, here in the country due to and by deceased, which inventory they are to hand to the Orphanmasters as soon as possible, then to make with their advice a proper disposition. Done this 16th of November 1655.

It is further ordered, that a copy of the foregoing order shall be delivered by the Court Messenger to Sieur *Joost van Beeck.*

Whereas *Madaleen Dircksen,* widow of *Cornelis Hendricksen of Dort,* has refused to accept the guardians, appointed by the Orphanmasters and whereas up to date no inventory of the estate has been taken, therefore their Worships have decided, to call said widow before them, that she may give her reasons and state, whom she wishes. Appearing the widow says, she refuses the formerly appointed guardians, because *Jan Vinje* is her adversary and has never had any conversation with her or her late husband, while *Hendrick Kip* is in no wise a relative or friend. She requests, that the Orphanmasters, if they decide, that guardians are necessary, will please to commission *Abraham Verplanck* and *Andries de Haes.* Not knowing any reasons, why the named persons should not be made guardians, the Orphanmasters grant the widow's request and the men are sent for. Having accepted the charge they are commissioned in the manner as the preceding guardians and ordered to bring the inventory of the estate to the next meeting. . . .

Tuesday, November 23, [1655] . . . *Lourens Jansen* appearing before their Worships, the Burgomasters as Orphanmasters, reported that one *Barent Driesen* and *Aeltie N.,* his wife, had perished on Staten Island during this last disaster and that there remained a minor child, called *Jan Barensen,* about 7 years, who was at his house; also, that there were still running on Staten Island some cattle and other animals of the deceased. He requests therefore, that guardians might be appointed, to look after and administer said cattle and what else is left for the benefit of the child. Considering the request reasonable the Orphanmasters have chosen and commissioned *Jan Eversen Bout* and *Lourens Jansen,* who as guardians of said infant child are authorized to make an inventory of the animals and of whatever else the deceased have left and to administer upon the property for the best of said child, they being obliged to render and prove accounts to the Orphanmasters, when required.

4. Foster care in Maryland, 1661

Md. Archives, LIII, 136–137.

Know all men by these presents that I, Eleanor Empson, late wife to William Empson, deceased, have bargained and sold unto Richard Dod, to him, his heirs, executors, administrators, or assigns, two heifers of two years old apiece or thereabouts . . . which two heifers I, the said Eleanor Empson, am constrained to dispose of unto Richard Dod for the nursing, keeping, and relieving of Mary Empson, daughter of the aforesaid William Empson, deceased, from the day of the date hereof until two years be expired. And it is to be understood that I, the said Richard Dod, take the said child with this proviso that whether the said child live or die in the said term of time, I, the said Dod, am to enjoy the said two heifers, me and my heirs forever. Also I, the foresaid Richard Dod, doth take the said two heifers as delivered, they and their increase forever. Note that I, the said Eleanor Empson, am constrained to dispose of the said child above specified for the present relief, otherwise it might have perished in the condition I am left in . . . witness our hand this first of April, 1661.

Preservation of orphans' estates, Virginia and Maryland

1. Virginia, 1661/62

Va. Statutes at Large, II, 92–94.

Concerning orphan's estates, be it enacted that all wills and testaments be firm and inviolable, unless the executors or overseers do refuse to execute the trust reposed in them by the testator, in which case the court may appoint others to act according to the will; but if the said will be so made that no person will undertake the managing of the estate, or education of the orphans according to the tenor of it, then that the estate by appointment of the court shall be managed according to the rules set down for the ordering the estate of persons intestate, as followeth:

First, that no account be allowed for diet, clothes, physic, or else against any orphan's estate, but that to be educated and provided for by the interest of the estate and increase of their stock according to the proportion of their estates, if it will bear it. But if the estate be so mean and inconsiderable that it will not extend to a free education, then it is enacted that such orphans shall be bound apprentices to some handicraft trade until one and twenty years of age, except some kinsman or relation will maintain them for the interest of the small estate they have, without diminution of the principal, which, whether great or small, [is] always to be delivered to the orphans at the years appointed by the law.

That all cattle, horses and sheep be returned in kind by the guardian according to age and number, according as he received them . . .

That all plate and money be preserved and delivered in kind according to the weight and quantity; that other household stuff and lumber be apprised in money and the value thereof paid by the guardian to the orphan when he comes to age, in the country commodity [tobacco] at the price current as it shall be worth at the time, in the place where the orphan's estate is managed.

That the court take able and sufficient security for orphans' estates and inquire yearly of the security, and if the court see cause, to have it changed and called in and placed as the court shall think fit; the court also to inquire whether orphans be kept, maintained, and educated according to their estates, and if they find any notorious defects to remove the orphans to other guardians; also for those that are bound apprentices to change their masters if they use them rigorously or neglect to teach them his trade.

That such orphans as are not bound apprentices shall, after seventeen years of age, have the produce of their own labor and industry, and liberty to dispose thereof at their discretion, the guardians still allowing them their maintenance for the interest of their estate . . .

2. Maryland, 1671

Md. Archives, II (1884), 18, 325–329.

The Maryland statute of 1671 followed the Virginia law of 1661 but adopted new provisions regarding slave property, bound servants, education of orphans in the religion of parents, and legal age of girls.

Forasmuch as the former laws made in this province concerning orphans' estates are found by experience to be very defective and noways sufficient for the preservation of orphans' estates according to the ends and purposes thereby intended and desired, the delegates in this present Assembly now assembled pray that it may be enacted. And be it enacted by the Right Honorable the Lord Proprietary of this Province with the advice and consent of the upper and lower House of this present General Assembly and the authority of the same: That all last wills and testaments shall be firm and inviolable unless the executor or overseers thereby appointed do refuse to execute the trust in them reposed by the testator, in which case the Chief Judge for probate of wills and granting administration shall grant administration with the will annexed to some other person as in his discretion shall seem meet . . . always provided the children, if any, be committed to persons of the same religion of their deceased parents. And it is further enacted . . . that when any person whatsoever dieth intestate . . . the said Judge upon the account given by

the said administrators . . . shall make division of the overplus of the estate, after debts paid and funeral expenses defrayed, allowing to the wife of the intestate, if she be then living, one third part thereof, and the rest is to be divided amongst the children, if he have any then living; and in case he have no children, then to the next of the blood of the deceased intestate.

.   .   .   .   .

. . . that no Negroes or other slaves shall be sold or disposed of by any administrator for payment of debts or otherwise or reserved for the administrator's own use in satisfaction for any debt due to the said administrator, nor any execution served upon any Negroes or other slaves so long as there shall be other goods of the deceased sufficient to satisfy the just debts of the deceased . . .

.   .   .   .   .

. . . That every male orphan shall be accounted to be of full age at the years of one and twenty and at that age to receive his estate from the guardian, but in case any person by his last will and testament do appoint any person to be executor that is full seventeen years of age, that person so appointed shall be adjudged of sufficient age to administer as executor . . .

. . . That every female orphan shall be accounted of full age to receive her estate at the age of sixteen years or day of marriage which shall first happen, provided she be above sixteen years of age at the day she is married.

. . . That all Negroes and other slaves shall be, after the transmitting of the estate to the County Courts as aforesaid, appraised to the administrators and guardians and be preserved by them and employed to the said administrators and guardians use and benefit, and the like number of slaves and of like abilities returned to the said orphans out of their increase if any be at their several full ages by this law limited, and if any of the said slaves be grown aged or otherwise impotent or be lamed, and that the increase will not make the original stock good as to number and ability of body, that then they shall again be appraised by the said County Courts and the administrators and guardians shall pay to the said orphans so much money or tobacco as the County Courts shall judge the orphan's stock of Negroes then to be of less value than they were of at the time of the first apprais[al] and delivery of the said slaves to the said administrators and guardians . . .

That all that are servants for years be likewise returned in kind according to their number, several ages, and sexes, number of years they have to serve, and outward appearance of ability of body, to the orphans by the administrators and guardians as they received them when the orphan shall accomplish the age by this Act appointed.

Guardianship and maintenance cases,
North Carolina, 1694

No. Car. Records, I, 396, 398.

A petition exhibited to the Court by Eliza Arnold showing that her husband Lawrence Arnold left his estate to his son John Arnold to be enjoyed at thirteen years of age, but being incapable to manage it by reason of his tender years, prayeth to choose Jonathan Bateman for his guardian. Ordered that Jonathan Bateman be his guardian and that his mother do bring in an inventory of all the said estate to the next Court.

Upon a petition exhibited by Jabell Alford praying to have liberty to choose a guardian. Ordered that the said Jabell Alford be bound to Mistress Susanna Hartley, widow, until he be one and twenty years of age, and that the said Mistress Hartley be bound and enter into bond to learn him the trade of a carpenter or joiner within the said time.

Upon a petition exhibited by Thomas Has-

sold showing that a child named Thomas Snoden was left with him by his [step father] Edmund Pirkins upon condition to pay him 600 pounds of tobacco per year for his diet. Ordered that the said Thomas Snoden serve the said Hassold until his [step father] come for him or else till he arrive at the age of twenty-one years.

Care of orphans

1. Indenture of an orphan,
Delaware country, 1678/79 [1]
Records of the Court of New Castle on Delaware, 1676–1681
(Lancaster, Pa., 1904), p. 294.

Anna the daughter of Barent Egbertsen deceased was this day by Doctor Thomas Spry and Rebecca his wife, with the consent and approbation of the court, put out to William Grant and his heirs for the term of six years, now next ensuing the date hereof, during which time he, the said William Grant, did engage to find her, the said Anna, with sufficient meat, drink, washing, lodging and apparel, and at the expiration of the said time to give her as good clothes (if not better) as she now brings, as also two heifers with two calves and a sow with pig or with pigs by her side.
(February the 5th, 1678/9).

2. The first orphanage in the United States,
New Orleans, 1728

In 1727 seven Ursuline nuns arrived in

1. For other cases of the binding out of poor orphans see below, Chap. III.

New Orleans to operate a hospital and conduct a school for the Company of the Indies. As the following documents indicate, the nuns soon accepted additional responsibilities, including the care of orphans. The number of orphans under their care increased in 1730 when children of French victims of the Natchez massacre were brought to the convent. In 1731 the Sisters were caring for forty-nine girls ranging in age from three to twelve years. The Company of the Indies paid the Ursulines 150 livres per year for each orphan; in 1732 the French government contributed an annual subsidy of 4,500 livres to the orphanage.[1]

a. A school for Negro and Indian girls and women

Sister Mary Madeleine Hachard, New Orleans, to her father, in Henry Churchill Semple, *The Ursulines in New Orleans, A Record of Two Centuries* (New York, 1925), pp. 199, 230.

January 1, 1728.

We keep also a school to instruct the negro and Indian girls and women; they come every day from one o'clock in the afternoon to half-past two. You see, my dear father, that we are not useless in this country, I assure you that all our moments are counted and that we have not a single one to ourselves. We have lately taken charge of a little orphan girl who was serving in a house where she did not have a very good example. It is further the intention of Rev. Father de Beaubois that we should take charge, through charity, of some little orphan girls; and he tells us, in order to engage us to do it, that he and Mr. Perier charge themselves with all the orphan boys . . .

1. Jean Delangler, *French Jesuits in Lower Louisiana* (New Orleans, 1935), p. 283.

April 24, 1728.

Our little community is increasing from day to day. We have twenty boarders, of whom eight have to-day made their First Communion; three lady boarders, and three orphans whom we take through charity. We have also seven slave boarders to teach and prepare for Baptism and First Communion. Besides we have a large number of day-scholars and negresses and savages who come two hours a day to be instructed. . . .

b. The Ursulines have not arrived soon enough

Father le Petit, Missionary, New Orleans, to Father D'Avangour, Procurator of the Missions in North America, July 12, 1730, in Semple, *The Ursulines in New Orleans,* pp. 272–273.

One could not help being moved to pity, on seeing arrive in this city the French women whom the Natchez had made their slaves. The miseries which they suffered were painted on the countenance; however, it appears that they soon forgot them; at least, many among them were in a great hurry to marry again; and we have been assured that there were great demonstrations of joy at their weddings.

The little girls, whom none of the inhabitants wished to adopt, have greatly enlarged the interesting company of orphans who the religious are bringing up. The great number of these children serve but to augment their charity and attentions. They have formed into a separate class, of which two teachers have charge.

There is not one of this holy community who is not delighted to have crossed the ocean, were she to do no other good save that of preserving these children in their innocence, and of giving a polished and Christian education to young French girls who were in danger of being little better bred than slaves. The hope is held out to these holy religious that, ere the end of the year, they will occupy the new house which is destined for them, and for which they have so long been sighing.

When they shall be settled there, to the instruction of the borders, the orphans, the day-scholars and negresses, they will add also the care of the sick in the hospital, and a house of refuge for women of questionable character. Perhaps, later on, they will even be able to aid in affording regularly each year a retreat to a large number of ladies, in accordance with the task with which we have inspired them.

So many works of charity would, in France, suffice to occupy several communities and different institutions. But what cannot great zeal effect? These various labors do not at all startle seven Ursulines; and they rely upon being able, with the help of God's grace, to sustain them, without detriment to the religious observance of their rules. As for me, I fear that, if some assistance do not arrive, they will sink under the weight of so much fatigue. Those who before knowing them used to say they were coming too soon and in too great a number, have entirely changed their views and their language; witnesses of their edifying conduct and the great services they render to the Colony, they find that they have not arrived soon enough, and that there could not come too many of the same virtue and merit.

---

3. Disposition of orphans in Georgia, 1735

Edw. Jenkins and John Deane, Savannah, to James Oglethorpe, undated but 1735, PRO, CO 5/636, no. 120.

The letter was written about five years before the founding of Whitefield's Bethesda Orphanage. On the orphanage see below, Part Two, Chap. IV, sec. B, The Bethesda Orphan House, Georgia, 1739–1742.

In this packet we have enclosed an account of the orphans' effects, and must, I fear, be forced to take out executions against most that have not paid. We gain from many people a great deal of ill will by being pretty urgent to get the orphans' money. But as it was your Honor's desire we should undertake it, we will do to the utmost of our power in behalf of the orphans.

Mr. Causton tells us we must pay for the orphans' clothing out of their effects; we wait for your Honor's orders about it.

The children are placed as follows:

The daughter of Henery Clark with Mr. Hetherinton. I can't speak much in praise of the place.

Goddard's son with Mr. Gristwater it's [not] to be doubted will be ruined. We would be glad to have your order to remove him.

The daughter with Mr. Carwell . . . proves an unlucky child. I fear the ill conduct of the master and mistress is too much the cause. Mr. Causton refused paying them for the keeping the girl and order we to pay it which we desire to know where we must or no.

The two sons of Peter Tondees with Mr. Amatis. And by his ill conduct of taking a scandalous wench to himself instead of a wife, I very much fear how they will be taken care of.

John Millige ha[s] got him up a hut by the help of Mr. Young and some of his neighbors. He desired we would let his brother and sisters live with him as we have consented to. But I fear it's too young a family to do well. If they do not we will part them.

Mrs. Doyle being dead and left two sons, the eldest with Mr. Causton.

The youngest with James Turner who has learned to be a taylor and proved an honest man as any in the town and takes a great deal of care of the child.

Mr. Little's child with Mrs. Mercer. They are very kind to the child.

Mary Simons that you gave to Mr. Egcome, as soon as you went from hence he sold her to James Moore. Moore sold her to Wilson. Wilson sold her to Cheseright, which is a very bad debauched house, so that amongst them all, I fear the girl is undone; it's thought by the midwife she is with child. Mr. Causton thought, as she was a gift to Egcome, he could not qualify the selling of her, so took her away from Cheseright and thinks she comes under our care. So we have taken her and placed her to Mr. Tollafield, who is married to a careful woman. If any in the town can break her from her ill habit they will. I remain your Honored Most obedient and humble servant.

III The Care of Dependent Children

During the first century of colonization English settlers, in contrast to the French and Spanish, established almost no institutions for dependent children. A few "workhouses" at which poor children could be instructed in spinning and weaving were projected, but the customary method was to utilize family settings for the care and nurture of needy children. Some children, including infants and those who were sick, crippled, or idiotic — that is, those who could not work — received relief in their own homes or were boarded out at the expense of the town or the parish. The usual method of providing for orphaned, destitute, or neglected children, however, was to bind or indenture them at as early an age as possible and on the best terms that could be arranged. The indenture obliged the children to serve during minority as servants or apprentices to persons willing to maintain them and to train them in husbandry, a trade, or domestic service.

Binding out poor children derived from English practice and law, notably sixteenth-century legislation intended to suppress vagrancy and mendicancy and the Poor Law of 1601. The system was well suited to the needs and ethos of a pioneer society in which life was hard and precarious, labor was scarce, and where even small children were expected and required to make themselves useful. The acknowledged purpose of the system was to get the poor off the town or parish rolls. Binding out, whether of adults or children, was intended to relieve not only the needy but also the community of the cost of their support. Binding out was, in addition, a means of social control. It was a way of finding foster homes for orphans and illegitimate children; and it was used by magistrates to secure new family situations for children of parents who were deemed incompetent to provide suitable homes or who allowed their children to grow up in idleness and ignorance. Hence, in numerous instances, the sanctity of the family and the authority of the natural parent were subordinated to the welfare of the child and the good of the community. It is hard to read the documents without believing that these objectives were earnestly sought. It is also hard to read them without feeling that the desire or necessity for economy in providing for the poor sometimes overrode all other considerations.

Tudor legislation for binding out poor children

---

1. Apprenticing poor children under Henry VIII, 1535

27 Henry VIII, 1535 — ch. 25, Great Britain, *Statutes at Large,* II, 229.

. . . Children under fourteen years of age, and above five, that live in idleness, and be taken begging, may be put to service by the governors of cities, towns, etc., to husbandry, or other crafts or labours . . .

---

2. The Elizabethan Poor Law, 1601

43 Elizabeth, 1601 — ch. 2, Great Britain, *Statutes at Large,* II, 685–686.

. . . The church-wardens of every parish, and four, three, or two substantial householders there, as shall be thought meet, having respect to the proportion and greatness of the same parish and parishes, to be nominated yearly in Easter week, or within one month after Easter, under the hand and seal of two or more justices of the peace in the same county . . . shall be called overseers of the poor of the same parish: and they, or the greater part of them, shall take order from time to time, by and with the consent of two or more such justices of peace . . . for setting to work the children of all such whose parents shall not by the said church-wardens and overseers, or the greater part of them, be thought able to keep and maintain their children . . . and also for the putting out of such children to be apprentices, to be gathered out of the same parish, according to the ability of the same parish. . . .

And be it further enacted, That it shall be lawful for the said church-wardens and overseers, or the greater part of them, by the assent of any two justices of the peace . . . to bind any such children . . . to be apprentices, where they shall see convenient, till such manchild shall come to the age of four and twenty years, and such woman-child to the age of one and twenty years, or the time of her marriage; the same to be as effectual to all purposes, as if such child were of full age, and by indenture of covenant bound him or her self . . .

Putting poor children to work in Virginia

---

1. The workhouse at James City, 1646

Va. Statutes at Large, I (New York, 1823), 336–337.

Whereas sundry laws and statutes by Act of Parliament established have, with great wisdom ordained, for the better educating of youth in honest and profitable trades and manufactures, as also to avoid sloth and idleness wherewith such young children are easily corrupted, as also for relief of such parents whose poverty extends not to give them breeding; that the justices of the peace should, at their discretion, bind out children to tradesmen or husbandmen to be brought up in some good and lawful calling. And whereas God Almighty, among many his other blessings, hath vouchsafed increase of children to this colony, who now are multiplied to a considerable number, who if instructed in good and lawful trades may much improve the honor and reputation of the country and no less their own good and their parents' comfort, but, forasmuch as for the most part the parents, either through fond indulgence or perverse obstinacy, are most averse and unwilling to part with their children: *Be it therefore enacted by authority of this Grand Assembly,* according to the aforesaid laudable custom in the kingdom of England, that the commissioners of the several counties respectively do, at their discretion, make choice of two children in each county of the age of eight or seven years at the least, either male or female, which are to be sent up to James City between this and June next to be employed in the public flax houses under such master and mistress as shall be there appointed, in carding, knitting, and spinning, etc. And that the said children be furnished from the said county with six barrels of corn, two coverlets or one rug and one blanket, one bed, one wooden bowl or tray, two pewter spoons, a sow shoat of six months old, two laying hens, with convenient apparel both linen and woollen, with hose and shoes. And for the better provision of housing for the said children, *it is enacted,* that there be two houses built by the first of April next of forty foot long apiece, with good and substantial timber, the houses to be twenty foot broad apiece, eight foot high in the pitch, and a stack of brick chimneys standing in the midst of each house, and that they be lofted with sawn boards and made with convenient partitions. And it is further thought fit that the commissioners have caution not to take up any children but from such parents who by reason of their poverty are disabled to maintain and educate them. *Be it likewise agreed* that the Governor hath agreed with the Assembly for the sum of 10,000 lbs. of tobacco to be paid him the next crop, to build and finish the said houses in manner and form expressed.

2. "An act empowering county courts to build work houses," 1668

Va. Statutes at Large, II, 266–267.

Whereas the prudence of all states ought as much as in them lies endeavor the propagation and increase of all manufactures conducing to the necessities of their subsistence, and God having blessed this country with a soil capable of producing most things necessary for the use of man if industriously improved, *It is enacted by this Grand Assembly and the authority thereof* that for the better converting wool, flax, hemp, and other commodities into manufactures, and for the increase of artificers in the country, that the commissioners of each county court, with the assistance of the respective vestries of the parishes in their counties, shall be and hereby are empowered to build houses for the educating and instructing poor children in the knowledge of spinning, weaving, and other useful occupations and trades, and power granted to take poor children from indigent parents to place them to work in those houses.

3. "An act for suppressing of vagabonds and disposing of poor children to trades," 1672

Va. Statutes at Large, II, 298.

In the colonies the upper age limit for apprentices was twenty-one for boys and eighteen for girls, whereas the limits set by the Elizabethan Poor Law were twenty-four and twenty-one, respectively.

Whereas several wholesome laws and statutes have by the wisdom of several parliaments of England been made and are in force as well for the suppression of vagrants and idle persons as setting the poor on work, the neglect of which laws amongst us hath encouraged and much increased the number of vagabonds idle and disolute persons, Be it enacted, and it is hereby enacted and ordained by the governor, council and burgesses of this grand assembly, and the authority thereof, that the justices of peace in every county do put the laws of England against vagrant, idle and disolute persons in strict execution, and the respective county courts shall, and hereby are empowered and authorized to place out all children, whose parents are not able to bring them up apprentices to tradesmen, the males till one and twenty years of age, and the females to other necessary employments, till eighteen years of age, and no longer, and the churchwardens of every parish shall be strictly enjoined by the courts to give them an account annually at their orphans' court of all such children within their parish as they judge to be within the said capacity.

Virginia children bound out by church authorities, 1706–1716

1. Vestry orders church wardens to bind out parish children

C. G. Chamberlayne, *The Vestry Book of St. Paul's Parish* (Richmond, 1940), pp. 11, 22, 74, 103.

August 12, 1706.
Ordered that Elizabeth Williams, a parish child, which is at John Lawson's be forthwith bound out to Thomas Carr of King William County by the church wardens.

.   .   .   .   .

January 1, 1707/8.
Whereas John Burnley has appeared in vestry and relinquished his rights in Phoebe Anderson: Therefore, it is ordered that the said Phoebe shall be bound out to Anthony Winston, upon condition the said Anthony Winston shall pay unto the said Phoebe six hundred pounds of good, sound, sweet-scented tobacco in cask, when she shall become of age.

.   .   .   .   .

July 22, 1716.
Ordered that the clerk make indentures to bind Charles Goodall, a poor orphan child, unto Robert Tate, until he comes to 21 years of age; and for Lucy Foster, a poor orphan girl, to be bound to Jane Thomson widow, until she come to 18 years of age.

the age as the law directs,[1] to serve him, the said Ralph Bevis, his heirs, etc., in all manner of lawful services and employments that he shall set him about. And the said Ralph Bevis doth bind and oblige himself [and] his heirs, etc. to give the said mulatto boy three years schooling and to carefully instruct him afterwards that he may read well in any part of the Bible; also to instruct and learn him the said mulatto boy such lawful way or ways that he may be able after his indented time expired to get his own living, and to allow him sufficient meat, drink, washing, and apparel until the expiration of the said time. And after the finishing of the said time to pay the said George Petsworth all such allowances as the law directs in such cases; as also to keep the aforesaid parish during the aforesaid indented time from all manner of charges or being any way burdensome to the said parish.

New England laws for binding out poor and idle children

2. Parish clerk binds out mulatto boy, 1716

Edgar W. Knight, *A Documentary History of Education in the South Before 1860*, I (Chapel Hill, 1949), 60.

This indenture made the thirtieth day of October in the year of our Lord God 1716 . . . witnesseth that I, Thomas May, clerk of Petsworth Parish in Gloucester County [Virginia], do firmly in the name and behalf of the vestry of the parish abovesaid bind unto Ralph Bevis of the said parish and county a mulatto boy named George Petsworth of the age of two years old the sixth day of March next insuing, the date of these presents until he arrives at

1. Plymouth, 1641

David Pulsifer, ed., *Records of the Colony of New Plymouth: Laws 1623–1682* (Boston, 1861), p. 38.

7th December, 1641: It is enacted that those that have relief from the towns and have children and do not employ them, that then it shall be lawful for the town28 to take order that those children shall be put to work in fitting employment according to their strength and abilities or placed out by the towns . . .

1. See above, Chap. II, sec. B, Status of children with one slave or servile parent, doc. 3, for the law of 1705 setting thirty-one years as the term of service of illegitimate mulatto children.

2. Massachusetts, 1646

Mass. Records, II, 180.

Every township, or such as deputed or order the prudentials thereof, shall have power to present to the Quarter Court all idle and unprofitable persons, and all children who are not diligently employed by their parents, which Court shall have power to dispose of them for their own welfare and improvement of the common good . . .

3. Connecticut, ca. 1673

Acts and Laws of His Majesties Colony of Connecticut in New-England (New London, 1715), pp. 95–96.

. . . If any poor person or persons that have had or shall have relief or supplies from any town, shall suffer their children to live idly or misspend their time in loitering, and neglect to bring them up or employ them in some honest calling which may be profitable unto themselves and the public; or if there be any family that cannot, or do[es] not provide competently for their children, whereby they are exposed to want and extremity; it shall and may be lawful for the selectmen and overseers of the poor in each town, and they are hereby ordered and empowered, with the assent of the next magistrate or justice of the peace, to bind any poor children belonging to such town to be apprentices where they shall see convenient: a man child until he shall come to the age of twenty-one years, and a woman child to the age of eighteen years or time of marriage; which shall be as effectual to all intents and purposes as if any such child were of full age, and by indenture of covenant had bound him or herself.

New England towns remove children from poor families

1. Watertown, Massachusetts, 1671

Watertown Records, I, 103–104, 105, 107.

January 3, 1671. At a meeting of the Selectmen at the house of Isaac Sterns, John Bigulah and Thomas Fleg, Senior, were appointed to treat with Edward Sanderson and his wife about getting a service for the biggest of [the] two least of his children where it may be to their own content and the good education of the child in learning and labor. And the town will be helpful to them in it if they desire it. And to acquaint them that if themselves do not that, then the town will provide a service for it.

·   ·   ·   ·   ·

March 3, 1671. There coming a complaint to us the selectmen concerning the poverty of Edward Sandersons family: that they had not wherewith to maintain themselves and children either with supply of provision or employment to earn any, and considering that it would be the charge of the town to provide for the whole family which will be hard to do this year, and not knowing how to supply them with provision, we considering if we should supply them and could do it, yet it would not tend to the good of the children for their good education and bringing up so they may be useful in the commonwealth or themselves to live comfortably and usefully in time to come; we have, therefore, agreed to put out two of his children into some honest families where they may be educated and brought up in the knowledge of God and some honest calling or labor. And, therefore, we do order that Thomas Fleg and John Bigulah shall have power to bind them prentices with some honest people with the consent of their parents, if it may be had, and if the parents shall oppose them to use the help of the Magistrate, in the name and with the consent of the Selectmen, Thomas Hastings.

.   .   .   .   .

Thomas Fleg, Senior, and John Bigulah at a meeting of the Selectmen March 3, 1672 were appointed to put out the children of Edward Sanderson apprentice. The return of Thomas Fleg and John Bigulah was that they had put out the oldest of the two, of a matter of eight years of age, to John Fleg, an apprentice till she be eighteen years of age. The said John Fleg was to have her well apparelled at her coming to him and to have for his encouragement fifty shillings to be paid in his rates to the town. And the above said John Fleg does engage to bring her up in all respects as an apprentice according as the law require[s] and to allow her double apparel at the end of the term of her time fitting for an apprentice.

2. Boston, 1672

"Boston Records, 1600–1701," in *Seventh Report of the Boston Record Commissioners* (Boston, 1881), p. 67.

It was ordered that notice be given to the several persons under-written that they, within one month after the date hereof, dispose of their several Children (herein nominated or mentioned) abroad for servants, to serve by Indentures for some term of years, according to their ages and capacities, which if they refuse or neglect to do the Magistrates and Selectmen will take their said children from them, and place them with such masters as they shall provide according as the law directs. And that they that do according to this order dispose of their children do make return of the names of Masters and children so put out to service, with their Indentures to the Selectmen at their next monthly Meeting being the last Monday in April next.

John Glovers daughter about twelve years of age.

Bryan Morphews daughter-in-law Martha Dorman about twelve years.

John Bohamans daughter Mary about fourteen years.

Robert Peggs daughter Alice above twelve years.

John Griffens daughter about ten years.

William Spowells daughter about twenty years.

William Brownes daughter about fifteen years unless she can excuse the service of a Nurse attending upon her weak Mother.

Widow Crocums three daughters.

William Hambeltons daughter about twelve years.

Edward Golds son about twenty years.

John Dawes his son about seventeen years.

Thomas Williams his son Charles about eight years.

3. Hartford, Connecticut, 1693/94

Collections of the Connecticut Historical Society, III (1897), 235.

A town meeting held at Hartford,
March 13, 1693/94.

The town by their vote left it with the townsmen or the major part of them, with the advice of the magistrates in this town or any two of them, to bind out Ruth Grant's two boys to apprentice upon the best terms they can, and with as little charge to the town as may be, and for Ruth to procure a good service for her if she cannot support and provide for herself. And what the said townsmen shall do therein, the town will stand by them in it and make it good.

*North Carolina and New York
provide for dependent children*

Richard Morris, ed., *Select Cases of the
Mayor's Court of New York City, 1674–1784*
(Washington D.C., 1935), pp. 69–70,
184–185.

1. Provision for orphans, North Carolina,
1699, 1703

No. Car. Records, I, 522, 527.

Perquimans Precinct Court, January, 1699.

Jonathan Taylor and William Taylor, orphans being left distressed, ordered that they be bound to William Long and Sarah his wife till they come of age.

Thomas Tailer, orphan being left distressed, ordered that he be bound to John Lawrence and Hannah his wife till he comes of age.

Mary Tayler, orphan being left distressed, ordered that she be bound to Master Caleb Calleway and Elisabeth his wife till she comes of age.

Thomas Hallom, orphan being left distressed, ordered that he be bound to Francis Foster and Hannah his wife till he comes of age.

.   .   .   .   .

Perquimans Precinct Court, March, 1703.

Upon a petition of Gabriel Newby for two orphans left him by Mary Hancock the late wife of Thomas Hancock, and proving the same by the oaths of Elizabeth Steward and her daughter, the Court do[es] agree to bind them unto him, he engaging and promising before the Court to do his endeavor to learn the boy the trade of a wheelwright and likewise give him at the expiration of his time one year-old heifer, and to the girl at her freedom one cow and calf besides the custom of the country, and has promised at the next orphans' court to sign indentures for that effect.

2. Parish relief for the perishing, New York,
1714–1731

May 18, 1714.

Order'd that Richard Blanck Aged about ten years who was lately brought hither from Bristol to an Uncle who has left the Country and the said Richard Blanck being fatherless and Motherless and destitute of Other friends or Relations and being likely to be Chargeable to this City Order'd the Church Wardens to bind him Apprentice unto Joseph Phillips of this City Watchmaker for the term of Eleven years with Covenants that the said Master Shall teach him his Trade to Read and write and to find him with Meat drink Cloths washing and lodging.

June 4, 1728.

Whereas A female Child aged about two or three Months was lately left in this City on the Bed of one Patience Ashton by one Mary Huggins Supposed to be the Mother thereof who is Run away and left the same upon the Parish, which Child was Ordered by the Mayor to be Nursed by Elizabeth Allen wife of Samuell Allen Boatman to preserve the same from perishing. It is therefore Order'd the Church Wardens do provide for the maintenance of the Said Child till Such time as they Can put out the same for the Term of one and twenty years and that they take Care to put out the same as soon as possible.

December 16, 1729.

A Woman from Ireland lately Transported into this City in the Speedwell John Ray Master whose name is Nancy Killpatrick now being big with Child and near her delivery, and her Husband sold A servant somewhere in New Jersey to her unknown and she not being in a Condition to labour for her livelyhood and allmost ready to Perish it is Order'd by the Court that the Church Wardens do take Care for her Relief untill She Shall be delivered and able to

Labour for her livelyhood She Appearing to the Court to be an Object of Charity.

January 6, 1729/30.

Order'd the Church Wardens Visit the Petitioner Elizabeth Clarke and inquire into the Allegations of the Petitioner and if She and her two Children are in such deplorable and poor Circumstances as therein is sett forth to grant them such further and Additional Relief as they shall see needfull they Appearing to the Court to be great Objects of Charity.

August 18, 1730.

Whereas one Mary Gleson A prisoner in the Common Gaol of this City hath left two Small Children at the house of one Samuell Taylor a Soldier belonging to the Garrison who is not of ability to Maintain them and therefore either must become a Charge to the Parish or Perish it is therefore Ordered by the Court that the Church Wardens Satisfie the Said Samuel Taylor for the Maintainance of the said Children untill they Otherwise provide for their Maintainance, and that the said Church Wardens do as soon as they can bind the Said Children out Apprentices untill they attain each the Age of one and twenty years.

May 18, 1731.

Order'd the Church Wardens Visit Jane Mackintosh Widow whose husband was lately unfortunately drownded and who is left with four small Children and nothing to Support herself or them and if they find them Objects of Charity to Support them as they Shall see needfull untill such time as the Children Can be put out or till further Order.

IV Schooling

As soon as Europeans reached American shores they turned their attention to the needs of the natives' souls. Each nation defended its imperialism with the claim that it sought to carry the good news of the gospel to the far corners of the earth and to assist the Indians in acquiring the learning they would need to receive the message. Immense effort and self-sacrifice testified to the sincerity of the Europeans' evangelical zeal. Although a far more elaborate and effective organization was perfected by the Spanish colonists to the south, the English were by no means backward in launching missionary experiments. In both Virginia and Massachusetts large sums were donated for both secular and Christian instruction. Dedicated men such as John Eliot, the Puritan missionary and translator of the Bible, gave years to the task of converting the Indians to Christianity. These efforts, however, produced few tangible results. Harvard College, for example, collected funds and constructed a building for the education of likely Indian lads but graduated only one, Caleb Cheeshahteamauk, and he died shortly after leaving college. Much the same thing happened in Virginia: substantial effort, but little to show for it.

This failure owed something to the Indian's lack of interest in the white men's ways and to his justified suspicion of their intentions. The missionary purpose was often in conflict with the designs of other colonists on the Indians. Missionaries found, for example, that traders, soldiers, and even some colonial officials resented and undermined missionary endeavors. In 1712 Rev. Francis Le Jau, a missionary in South Carolina, reported that the Yamasees were eager to welcome a gospel messenger but

"the Indian traders have always discouraged me by raising a world of Difficultyes when I proposed anything to them relating to the Conversion of the Indians. It appears they do not care to have Clergymen so near them who doubtless would never approve those perpetual warrs they promote amongst the Indians for the onely reason of making slaves to pay for their trading goods." [1] Missionaries could rarely bridge the chasm of mistrust and hostility that resulted from wars, massacres, and broken promises. With so many colonists regarding the Indians as the chief threat to their security and the Indians looking upon the colonists as hypocrites, it is little wonder that attempts to win converts and to educate should fail.

Far more successful were the transplanted Englishmen's efforts to educate their own children. Their cultural inheritance included an educational structure in which parents, masters of trades, clergymen, grammar schoolmasters, and college fellows participated. Parents, masters, and clergymen were responsible for the earliest training of the young. Grammar schools, supported by endowments and fees, carried a few students on to mastery of ancient languages in preparation for the learned professions. The universities took in an even smaller number, perfected their classical education, and trained them for the clergy, medicine, law, teaching, or public service. With many important variations, this structure was brought to America.

Ordinarily education began in the home. Parents taught their children the alphabet and the rudiments of reading and writing; in similar

1. Fulham Palace MSS., South Carolina, no. 10, in Verner W. Crane, *The Southern Frontier, 1670–1732* (Ann Arbor, 1956), p. 152.

fashion masters were expected to instruct servants and apprentices. Lack of time, inclination, or ability in teaching prompted many parents to send their children to a neighbor, usually a poor widow, for this earliest instruction. Such was the origin of the "dame schools" attended by the very young, common throughout New England and present elsewhere. Although the earliest plans for grammar schools were formulated in Virginia, the first schools were actually established in the compact and homogeneous towns of Massachusetts. In the Puritan settlements the migration of families and the exhortation of the clergy led to the immediate founding of schools. Formal instruction was supplemented by participation in ordinary household activities — chores, care of the livestock, and assistance to parents engaged in their daily tasks.

The children of the poor mainly relied upon the apprenticeship system for whatever training they received outside the home. Colonial laws required masters to instruct apprentices in their trade and to teach them to read and write, sometimes with the addition of elementary arithmetic. Masters might give this instruction themselves but they often preferred to send their apprentices to a private teacher during a part of the day or in the evening.

Training in the home or in the master's household did not always work out according to the theory. From an early date, especially in Massachusetts, concern was expressed that parents and masters were neglecting their duty and that illiteracy, infidelity, and barbarism were overtaking the younger generation. In 1642, within a few years of the colony's foundation, Massachusetts resorted to legal coercion to enforce educational responsibilities with a law that affirmed parents' and masters' responsibilities and provided penalties should they fail to meet them.

The General Court of Massachusetts, going beyond reliance upon the household, took the first step in establishing a system of public education. In 1647 the Court required towns of fifty households to maintain a schoolmaster

for elementary skills and required larger towns of one hundred households to maintain a grammar schoolmaster capable of preparing boys in Latin and Greek for entrance to college. Fines were to be exacted from the selectmen for failure to comply. It was left to the town to choose the means of supporting the school: either by all of the inhabitants or only by the parents of the children who attended. In practice, both methods were used, sometimes in combination. Connecticut and New Hampshire followed Massachusetts' example. The laws, impressive on the statute book, were imperfectly applied. Numerous complaints and repeated prosecutions show that many towns, particularly in the interior, refused to obey the school law, managing either to evade the fines or finding it cheaper to pay them than to hire a schoolmaster. Nevertheless, the result was the closest approach to a system of free public education that had yet been made in Europe or America. The children of New England enjoyed a far greater opportunity for education, defective though it may have been, than the children of any other American colony. The role of government was strictly limited. Although the legislature required towns to maintain schools, it did not require attendance and it left the choice of means of support to the local community.

Outside of New England little was done by government to encourage education or impose educational standards. In the middle-Atlantic colonies the churches with other private assistance helped to maintain some elementary schools, but by and large they were confined to poor children. If parents could afford to pay, they were expected to do so. Secondary education in the middle colonies was entirely private.

The southern colonies fell behind those to the north in offering opportunities for formal education. For the most part the only elementary schools were charity schools for poor children supported by local authorities or a private endowment. Secondary education in the South was even more poorly provided, being almost entirely confined to a few expensive private schools in southern towns. Not until the very end of the century when the College of William and Mary was founded did it become possible for young southerners to obtain collegiate instruction on their native soil. Wealthy southerners hired tutors either from the northern colonies or England or they might secure an indentured servant who could act as a schoolmaster. A few of the very wealthy sent their sons abroad for schooling.

In all schools a single master taught the different subjects to children of all ages, with only now and then an exception in the larger towns where the grammar school master might have an assistant. The common method of instruction was memorization of the lessons by the pupil, followed by recitations in the presence of the master. Standard manuals, like the *New-England Primer* for beginning readers, were used throughout the colonies. In some secondary schools, more utilitarian subjects began to

be offered to young men who had no intention of going to college. As towns grew and commerce flourished, schoolmasters set up classes in surveying, navigation, accounting, and foreign languages for ambitious youth who hoped to succeed in business.

Deficient as colonial education may seem in retrospect, it nevertheless created and maintained a level of elementary skill and achievement unmatched in the seventeenth century. By 1700 in New England, nineteen of twenty men could sign their own names to legal documents. This may be a crude way of measuring literacy, but it is the only test available.[2] Although the proportion of the literate declined to the southward, it is still probably the case that more Americans could read and write than any other element of comparable size and social diversity within the realm of European culture.

2. Samuel E. Morison, *The Intellectual Life of Colonial New England* (New York, 1956), pp. 82–85.

A. EDUCATIONAL CONTACTS BETWEEN EUROPEANS AND INDIANS

Indian children receive the Word

---

1. King Ferdinand of Spain orders the education of the sons of Indian chiefs: the Laws of Burgos, 1512

Lesley Byrd Simpson, *Studies in the Administration of the Indians of New Spain* (Berkeley, 1934), p. 18.

Law XVII: Furthermore, we command that all the sons of the caciques[1] of the said island [Hispaniola] who are under thirteen years of age are to be handed over to the friars of the

1. Indian nobles appointed by the Spanish government as local officials.

Order of St. Francis so that the said friars teach them how to read and write and all things pertaining to Our Holy Catholic Faith; [the friars] are to keep these children for four years and then shall return them to their *encomenderos*[2] so that they will teach other Indians.

---

2. Virginia Company officials authorized to kidnap Indian children in order to bring them up Christians, 1609

2. Spanish colonists who were granted estates with Indian inhabitants to reward their services and to evangelize the Indians.

Virginia Council [London], "Instructions, orders, and constitutions to Sir Thomas Gates, Knight, Governor of Virginia," in *Va. Co. Records,* III, 14–15.

You shall, with all propenseness and diligence, endeavor the conversion of the natives to the knowledge and worship of the true God and their Redeemer, Christ Jesus, as the most pious and noble end of this plantation, which the better to effect you must procure from them some convenient number of their children to be brought up in your language and manners. And if you find it convenient, we think it reasonable you first remove . . . them from their . . . priests by a surprise of them all and detain them prisoners, for they are so wrapped up in the fog and misery of their iniquity, and so terrified with their continual tyranny, chained under the bond of Death unto the Devil, that while [the priests] live among them to poison and infect . . . their minds, you shall never make any great progress into this glorious work, nor have any civil peace or concur with them. And in case of necessity or conveniency, we pronounce it not cruelty nor breach of charity to deal more sharply with them and to proceed even to dash with these murderers of souls and sacrificers of gods' images to the devil . . .

---

3. Education of Indian children held as hostages, Virginia, 1656

Va. Statutes at Large, I, 396.

If the Indians shall bring in any children as gauges of their good and quiet intentions to us and amity with us, then the parents of such children shall choose the persons to whom the care of such children shall be entrusted; and the country by us their representatives do engage that we will not use them as slaves, but do their best to bring them up in Christianity, civility, and the knowledge of necessary trades. And on the report of the commissioners of each respective county that those under whose tuition they are do really intend the bettering of the children in these particulars, then a salary shall be allowed to such men as shall deserve and require it.

Gifts and bequests for the education of Indian youth and their disposition

The founders of Virginia were required by the charter of 1606 to commit themselves to "propagating the Christian religion to such people, as yet live in darkness and miserable ignorance." A sum in excess of £2,000 in money and goods was collected and plans drawn for "Henrico College," but a succession of mishaps and errors prevented the establishment of the school. The revocation of the charter in 1624, transforming Virginia into a royal colony, delayed any substantial effort until the end of the seventeenth century.

---

1. An anonymous London philanthropist gives £500 for the education of Indian children in Virginia, 1619

Va. Co. Records, I, 307–308.

A letter from an unknown person was read, directed to Master Treasurer [Sir Edwin Sandys], promising five hundred pounds for the educating and bringing up [of] infidel children in Christianity which Master Treasurer, not willing to meddle therewith alone, desired the Court to appoint a select committee for the managing and employing of it to the best . . .

The copy of which letter ensueth.

Sir, your charitable endeavors for Virginia

hath made you a father, we a favorer, of those good works which although heretofore hath come near to their birth, yet for want of strength could never be delivered (envy and division dashing these younglings even in the womb), until your helpful hand with other honorable personages gave them both birth and being. For the better cherishing of which good and pious work, seeing many casting gifts into the Treasury, I am encouraged to tender my poor mite. And although I cannot, with the Princes of Issaker, bring gold and silver covering, yet offer here what I can, some goat's hair, necessary stuff for the Lord's Tabernacle. . . . To the furtherance of which good work, the converting of infidels to the faith of Christ, I promised by my good friends 500 £ for the maintenance of a convenient number of young Indians taken at the age of seven years or younger and instructed in the reading and understanding the principles of Christian religion unto the age of twelve years, and then as occasion serveth to be trained and brought up in some lawful trade with all humanity and gentleness until the age of one and twenty years, and then to enjoy like liberties and privileges with our native English in that place.

the proceeds sent to the president and masters of the College of William and Mary, which had been chartered in 1693, to be expended for the education of Indian youths.

All sum and sums of money already or that should thereafter be received out of the said manor . . . should be thereafter remitted to the said President and masters for the time being.

. . . The said President and masters, and his and their successors, should thereout expend so much as should be necessary towards fitting and furnishing lodgings and rooms for such Indian children as should be thereafter brought into the said College.

. . . The said President and masters, and his or their successors, should keep at the said College so many Indian children in sickness and health, in meat, drink, washing, lodging, clothes, medicines, books and education, from the first beginning of letters till they should be ready to receive orders, and be thought sufficient to be sent abroad to preach and convert the Indians, at the rate of fourteen pounds per annum for every such child, as the yearly income of the premises, subject to the deduction aforesaid should amount to.

---

2. Education of Indian children at the College of William and Mary, ca. 1693

Herbert L. Ganter, "Some Notes on the Charity of the Honorable Robert Boyle . . . ," *William and Mary College Quarterly,* ser. 2, XV (1935), 6, 17–18.

Robert Boyle (1627–1691), the English chemist and natural philosopher, left the residue of his estate "for the advance or propagation of the Christian religion amongst infidels." The sum was invested in the manor of Brafferton in Yorkshire and the bulk of

3. Reforms proposed for the education of Indian youth at the College of William and Mary, 1724

Hugh Jones, *The Present State of Virginia,* ed. Richard L. Morton (Chapel Hill, 1956), pp. 114–116; first published in London in 1724.

Hugh Jones (ca. 1670–1760) was on the faculty of the College and was familiar with the situation there.

The Indians who are upon Mr. Boyle's foundation have now a handsom apartment for themselves and their master, built near the College, which useful contrivance ought to be carried on to the utmost advantage in the real education and conversion of the infidels; for hitherto but little good has been done therein, though abundance of money has been laid out, and a great many endeavours have been used, and much pains taken for that purpose.

The young Indians, procured from the tributary or foreign nations with much difficulty, were formerly boarded and lodged in the town; where abundance of them used to die, either through sickness, change of provision, and way of life; or as some will have it, often for want of proper necessaries and due care taken with them. Those of them that have escaped well, and been taught to read and write, have for the most part returned to their home, some with and some without baptism, where they follow their own savage customs and heathenish rites.

A few of them have lived as servants among the English, or loitered and idled away their time in laziness and mischief.

But 'tis great pity that more care is not taken about them, after they are dismissed from school.

They have admirable capacities when their humours and tempers are perfectly understood; and if well taught, they might advance themselves and do great good in the service of religion; whereas now they are rather taught to become worse than better by falling into the worst practices of vile nominal Christians, which they add to their own Indian manners and notions.

To prevent this therefore, let there be chosen continually four Indian servitors[1] out of the Indian school, as the other four out of the grammar school.

Let these be maintained in the Indian house, and wait upon the four lower tables: Let them be instructed as the other servitors, or as their genius most aptly may require, but particularly in religion; and when they are found qualified let them be sent to England, or placed out to captains of ships or trades . . . for a few years; then let them return and be allowed a small exhibition,[2] and encouraged in their separate callings and occupations; and let them settle among the English, and others return to their own nations.

Undoubtedly many of them would become excellent artists and proficients in trade; and thus when reason and experience has convinced them of the preference of our religion and manners, certainly they may not only save their own souls; but also be extreamly instrumental in the conversion of their barbarous friends and relations.

In proceeding thus, any that seem capable or inclinable to study divinity, should by all means be encouraged and forwarded in it, and sent over for a small time to one of our universities with an allowance of a fellow; after which, if such were admitted into orders, and then sent out missionaries among their own country-folks, what great good might we not expect from such, when thoroughly converted and instructed in Christianity, and made truly sensible of the advantages of religion, the deadly state of infidelity, and the miserable lives and customs of the Indians?

In a work of this kind undoubtedly several good Christians would contribute their charitable assistance; 'till which the present fund should be applied in this method, though the managers should be obliged to reduce the number of Indian scholars upon this account; since this was the main intent of the benefaction, and no other method can well answer this design; which may be evidenced by experience both from the colleges of Virginia and New England too, as I have been credibly informed from good authors, as well as my own experience.

By such methods in process of time might the Indian obstinacy be mollified, their seeming dulness might be cleared from rust; and the gates of heaven be opened for their admission upon their perfect conversion to the faith of

1. Students who acted as servants to the faculty of a college in return for their expenses.

2. A subsidy.

Christ. In such glorious designs as these neither should humour, interest, nor prejudice divert any from their charitable assistance therein, especially such as are concerned in affairs of this kind, and engaged by duty to lend their best aid in leading the infidels into the pale of Christ's Church, and making them by mild and most gentle measures to accompany his flock; since all the force in the world would rather drive them from, than guide them, to the congregation of the faithful and communion of saints.

By some such prudent and mild methods alone may they be made to live and die as true Christians, and not like the most savage brutes, as they generally do.

Massachusetts Puritans catechize Indian children, 1646

[John Wilson?], *The Day-Breaking if Not the Sun-Rising of the Gospell with the Indians in New-England* (New York, 1865), pp. 9–10; first published in London in 1647.

In New England early missionary activity centered around a few dedicated clergymen, particularly John Eliot, minister of First Church of Roxbury, Massachusetts, and translator of the Bible into the Algonkian language. In this tract, attributed to Eliot's friend and associate John Wilson, minister and teacher of First Church, Boston, the visit of four clergymen to a village of the Waban Indians is described. Eliot delivered a sermon and catechized the Indian children.

Upon November 11, 1646, we came the second time unto the same wigwam of Wabon. We found many more Indians met together than the first time we came to them; and having seats provided for us by themselves, and being sat down a while, we began again with prayer in the English tongue. Our beginning this time was with the younger sort of Indian children in catechizing of them, which being the first time of instructing them, we thought meet to ask them but only three questions in their own language, that we might not clog their minds or memories with too much at first. The questions (asked and answered in the Indian tongue) were these three:

1. Question: Who made you and all the world?
   Answer: God.
2. Question: Who do you look should save you and redeem you from sin and hell?
   Answer: Jesus Christ.
3. Question: How many commandments hath God given you to keep?
   Answer: Ten.

These questions being propounded to the children severally, and one by one, and the answers being short and easy, hence it came to pass that before we went through all, those who were last catechized had more readily learned to answer to them, by hearing the same question so often propounded and answered before their fellows. And the other Indians who were grown up to more years had perfectly learned them, whom we therefore desired to teach their children again when we were absent, that so when we came again we might see their profiting, the better to encourage them hereunto, we therefore gave something to every child.

B. NEW ENGLAND SCHOOLS AND SCHOOLTEACHERS

Public establishment and control of schools

---

1. A town grammar school,
Massachusetts, 1645

Regulations adopted by Dorchester, Mass.,
1645, in *Fourth Report of the Boston Record
Commissioners* (Boston, 1880), pp. 54–57.

The desire to maintain literacy and learning
was so strong in early Massachusetts that
schools, modeled on the traditional English
grammar school, were created soon after
the towns themselves were founded.
Arrangements and details varied from place to
place, but both the process and the institution
depicted here are broadly representative.

Upon a general and lawful warning of all the
inhabitants, the 14th of the 1st month 1645,
these rules and orders presented to the town
concerning the school of Dorchester are confirmed by the major part of the inhabitants then
present.

First . . . three able and sufficient men of
the plantation shall be chosen to be wardens or
overseers of the school abovementioned, who
shall have the charge, oversight, and ordering
thereof and of all things concerning the same
. . . and shall continue in their office and place
for term of their lives respectively, unless by
reason of any of them removing his habitation
out of the town, or for any other weighty
reason, the inhabitants shall see cause to elect
or choose others in their room.

. . . . . .

Secondly, the said wardens shall have full
power to dispose of the school stock, whether
the same be in land or otherwise, both such as
is already in being and such as may by any good
means hereafter be added, and shall collect
and receive the rents, issues, and profits arising
and growing of and from the said stock . . .

Thirdly, the said wardens shall take care,
and do their utmost, and best endeavor, that
the said school may from time to time be supplied with an able and sufficient schoolmaster,
who nevertheless is not to be admitted into the
place of schoolmaster without the general consent of the inhabitants or the major part of them.

Fourthly, so often as the said school shall
be supplied with a schoolmaster . . . the
wardens shall from time to time pay or cause
to be paid unto the said schoolmaster such
wages . . . as shall of right come due to be
paid.

Fifthly, the said wardens shall from time to
time see that the schoolhouse be kept in good
and sufficient repair . . .

Sixthly, the said wardens shall take care
that every year, at or before the end of [Decem-
ber], there be brought to the schoolhouse
twelve sufficient cart- or wainloads of wood for
fuel, to be for the use of the schoolmaster and
the scholars in winter . . .

Lastly, the said wardens shall take care that
the schoolmaster for the time being do faithfully perform his duty in his place, as school-
masters ought to do, as well as in other things
as in these which are hereafter expressed, viz.:

First, that the schoolmaster shall diligently
attend his school and do his utmost endeavor
for benefiting his scholars according to his best
discretion without unnecessarily absenting himself to the prejudice of his scholars and hindering their learning.

Secondly, that from the beginning of
[March], until the end of [September], he shall
every day begin to teach at seven of the clock
in the morning and dismiss his scholars at five

in the afternoon. And for the other five months, that is from the beginning of [October], until the end of [February], it shall every day begin at eight of the clock in the morning and end at four in the afternoon.

Thirdly, every day in the year the usual time of dismissing at noon shall be at eleven, and to begin again at one, except that

Fourthly, every second day in the week he shall call his scholars together between twelve and one of the clock to examine them what they have learned on the Sabbath day preceding, at which time also he shall take notice of any misdemeanor or disorder that any of his scholars shall have committed on the Sabbath, to the end that at some convenient time due admonition and correction may be administered by him according as the nature and quality of the offense shall require; at which said examination any of the elders of other inhabitants that please may be present to behold his religious care herein and to give their countenance and approbation of the same.

Fifthly, he shall equally and impartially receive and instruct such as shall be sent and committed to him for that end, whether their parents be poor or rich, not refusing any who have right and interest in the school.

Sixthly, such as shall be committed to him he shall diligently instruct as they shall be able to learn, both in humane learning and good literature, and likewise in point of good manners and dutiful behavior towards all, especially their superiors, as they shall have occasion to be in their presence whether by meeting them in the street or otherwise.

Seventhly, every sixth day of the week at two of the clock in the afternoon he shall catechize his scholars in the principles of Christian religion, either in some catechism which the wardens shall provide and present, or in defect thereof, in some other.

Eighthly, and because all man's endeavors without the blessing of God must needs be fruitless and unsuccessful, therefore, it is to be a chief part of the schoolmaster's religious care to commend his scholars and his labors amongst them unto God by prayer, morning and evening, taking care that his scholars do reverently attend during the same.

Ninthly, and because the rod of correction is an ordinance of God necessary sometimes to be dispensed unto children, but such as may easily be abused by overmuch severity and rigor on the one hand, or by overmuch indulgence and lenity on the other, it is therefore ordered and agreed that the schoolmaster, for the time being, shall have full power to minister correction to all or any of his scholars without respect of persons, according as the nature and quality of the offense shall require whereto. All his scholars must be duly subject and no parent or other of the inhabitants shall hinder or go about to hinder the master therein. Nevertheless, if any parent or others shall think there is just cause of complaint against the master for too much severity, such shall have liberty, friendlily and lovingly, to expostulate with the master about the same; and if they shall not attain to satisfaction, the matter is then to be referred to the wardens who shall impartially judge betwixt the master and such complainants . . .

And because it is difficult, if not impossible, to give particular rules that shall reach all cases which may fall out, therefore, for a conclusion, it is ordered and agreed in general, that where particular rules are wanting, there it shall be a part of the office and duty of the wardens to order and dispose of all things that concern the school, in such sort as in their wisdom and discretion they shall judge most conducible for the glory of God and the training up of the children of the town in religion, learning, and civility . . .

---

2. The first Massachusetts school law, 1647
Mass. Records, II, 203.

Fear that the law of 1642 (see above, Chap. II, sec. A, Legislation strengthening family government, Massachusetts, 1642–

1682, doc. 1) would fail to secure literacy prompted the General Court to require towns to maintain schoolmasters to teach youngsters to read and write and the larger towns to support in addition a schoolmaster to instruct boys in Latin and Greek.

It being one chief project of that old deluder Satan to keep men from the knowledge of the Scriptures, as in former times by keeping them in an unknown tongue, so in these latter times by persuading from the use of tongues, that so at least the true sense and meaning of the original might be clouded by false glosses of saint-seeming deceivers, that learning may not be buried in the grave of our fathers in the church and commonwealth, the Lord assisting our endeavors:

It is therefore ordered, that every township in this jurisdiction, after the Lord hath increased them to the number of fifty householders, shall then forthwith appoint one within their town to teach all such children as shall resort to him to write and read, whose wages shall be paid either by the parents or masters of such children, or by the inhabitants in general by way of supply, as the major part of those that order the prudentials of the town shall appoint. Provided, those that send their children be not oppressed by paying much more than they can have them taught for in other towns. And it is further ordered, that where any town shall increase to the number of 100 families or householders, they shall set up a grammar school, the master thereof being able to instruct youth so far as they may be fitted for the university. Provided, that if any town neglect the performance hereof above one year, that every such town shall pay five pounds to the next school till they shall perform this order.

The other New England colonies, except for Rhode Island, copied the Massachusetts school law with some variations. All shared the problem of securing town implementation of the laws' requirements. Even fines and other forms of financial pressure often failed to produce compliance.

Ordered and enacted by the Governor, Council and Representatives in General Court assembled . . . that there shall be four grammar schools constantly kept, at the four county towns of this colony, viz., at Hartford, New Haven, New London and Fairfield. And all other towns consisting of seventy families and upwards shall constantly keep up from year to year a public and sufficient school for the teaching children to write and read. And that all towns within this colony of any number of families under seventy shall keep up yearly a public school, for the teaching to read and write for one half of the year, these schools to be furnished with able and sufficient schoolmasters, according to law. And towards the maintenance of the schools respectively, it is ordered that from the colony rates . . . shall be yearly paid forty shillings upon every thousand pounds of the public list of persons and estates unto the several towns of this colony, and proportionally for lesser sums, for the use of their schools as aforesaid. And if any town shall be wanting of a sufficient and able schoolmaster as aforesaid, then for the fine they shall not have the allowance as aforesaid, but the sum of the forty shillings upon the thousand pounds shall be paid to the public treasury, provided that one month's want shall not be any bar to them . . .

---

3. Enforcement of school laws, Connecticut, 1700

C. J. Hoadly, ed., *Conn. Records*, IV (1868), 331.

4. A private school master of colonial Boston, 1727

A newspaper advertisement in Robert F.

Seybolt, *The Private Schools of Colonial Boston* (Cambridge, Mass., 1935), p. 17.

Instruction in the public and endowed schools of the towns was supplemented by the teaching of private school masters. Girls as well as boys were taught the elementary and some advanced subjects not included in the classical curriculum of the grammar schools. Any teacher who could attract a clientele qualified; any child whose parents could pay the fee might attend.

A person of this town who hath got some experience in the instruction of youth, and whose desire and office is to do good to others, is apt to think that he might be serviceable to the public in keeping a boarding school, wherein learning and godliness were cultivated together. In order to that, he doth propose to keep an usher and to teach writing, cyphering, Latin, French, geography, etc. so that young people in the same place may learn what they are feign to learn now in several places. He designs that Latin and French shall be spoken in his house by turns every month, which practical way of learning and teaching will save them three quarters of the time they spend now in learning, only in the common schools and books. It is also intended that in three languages they shall read such books in which they may learn sciences and useful things besides the language. It is likewise intended that their very recreations shall be made profitable to them, either to their health or understanding, or rather to both; that virtue and godliness shall be encouraged amongst them, and vice discountenanced by all means possible; and that their understanding, judgment, and parts shall be tried and improved every way. The keeping of such a school is intended if the aforesaid person is assured to have a competent number of boarders. Therefore he desires to know within two months time those that are inclined to put their children with him. They may inquire of the printer hereof and know further.

What children were taught

1. *The New England Primer*

Paul L. Ford, ed., *The New England Primer* (New York, 1897), pp. 65–72.

The New England Primer, first published around 1690, remained popular in various editions until the end of the eighteenth century. It was used throughout the colonies to teach children to read and spell. In addition to the A.B.C.'s, it contained a catechism, maxims, and lists of words.

Now the Child being entred in his Letters and Spelling, let him learn these and such like Sentences by Heart, whereby he will be both instructed in his Duty, and encouraged in his Learning.

The Dutiful Child's Promises,

I will fear GOD, and honour the KING.
I will honour my Father & Mother.
I will Obey my Superiours.
I will Submit to my Elders.
I will Love my Friends.
I will hate no Man.
I will forgive my Enemies, and pray to God for them.
I will as much as in me lies keep all God's Holy Commandments.
I will learn my Catechism.
I will keep the Lord's Day Holy.
I will Reverence God's Sanctuary,
For our GOD is a consuming Fire.

An Alphabet of Lessons for Youth.

A wise Son makes a glad Father, but a foolish Son is the heaviness of his Mother.
Better is a little with the fear of the Lord, than great treasure and trouble therewith.

Come unto CHRIST all ye that labour and are heavy laden, and He will give you rest.

Do not the abominable thing which I hate, saith the Lord.

Except a Man be born again, he cannot see the Kingdom of God.

Foolishness is bound up in the heart of a Child, but the rod of Correction shall drive it far from him.

Grieve not the Holy Spirit.

Holiness becomes God's House for ever.

It is good for me to draw near unto God.

Keep thy Heart with all Diligence, for out of it are the issues of Life.

Liars shall have their part in the lake which burns with fire and brimstone.

Many are the Afflictions of the Righteous, but the Lord delivers them out of them all.

Now is the accepted time, now is the day of salvation.

Out of the abundance of the heart the mouth speaketh.

Pray to thy Father which is in secret, and thy Father which sees in secret, shall reward thee openly.

Quit you like Men, be strong, stand fast in the Faith.

Remember thy Creator in the days of thy Youth.

Salvation belongeth to the Lord.

Trust in God at all times ye people pour out your hearts before him.

Upon the wicked God shall rain an horrible Tempest.

Wo to the wicked, it shall be ill with him, for the reward of his hands shall be given him.

eXhort one another daily while it is called to day, lest any of you be hardened through the deceitfulness of Sin.

Young Men ye have overcome the wicked one.

Zeal hath consumed me, because thy enemies have forgotten the words of God.

Choice Sentences.

1. Praying will make thee leave sinning, or sinning will make thee leave praying.

2. Our Weakness and Inabilities break not the bond of our Duties.

3. What we are afraid to speak before Men, we should be afraid to think before God.

---

2. A Boston boy at school, ca. 1690

"Autobiography of the Rev. John Barnard," in MHS *Collections,* 3d ser., V (1836), 178–180.

I was born at Boston, 6th Nov. 1681; descended from reputable parents, viz. John and Esther Barnard, remarkable for their piety and benevolence, who devoted me to the service of God, in the work of the ministry, from my very conception and birth; and accordingly took special care to instruct me themselves in the principles of the Christian religion, and kept me close at school to furnish my young mind with the knowledge of letters. By that time I had a little passed my sixth year, I had left my reading-school, in the latter part of which my mistress made me a sort of usher, appointing me to teach some children that were older than myself, as well as smaller ones; and in which time I had read my Bible through thrice. My parents thought me to be weakly, because of my thin habit and pale countenance, and therefore sent me into the country, where I spent my seventh summer, and by the change of air and diet and exercise I grew more fleshy and hardy; and that I might not lose my reading, was put to a school-mistress, and returned home in the fall.

In the spring of my eighth year I was sent to the grammar-school, under the tuition of the aged, venerable, and justly famous Mr. Ezekiel Cheever. But after a few weeks, an odd accident drove me from the school. There was an older lad entered the school the same week with me; we strove who should outdo; and he beat me by the help of a brother in the upper class, who stood behind master with the accidence[1] open for him to read out of . . . but I who had no such help, and was obliged to commit all to memory, could not keep pace with him; so that he would be always one lesson before me. My ambition could not bear to be outdone, and in such a fraudulent manner, and therefore I left the school. About this time arrived a dissenting minister from England, who opened a private school for reading, writing, and Latin. My good father put me under his tuition, with whom I spent a year and a half. The gentleman receiving but little encouragement, threw up his school, and returned me to my father, and again I was sent to my aged Mr. Cheever, who placed me in the lowest class . . .

In the time of my absence from Mr. Cheever, it pleased God to take to himself my dear mother, who was not only a very virtuous, but a very intelligent woman. She was exceeding fond of my learning, and taught me to pray. My good father also instructed me, and made a little closet for me to retire to for my morning and evening devotion. But, alas! how childish and hypocritical were all my pretensions to piety, there being little or no serious thoughts of God and religion in me.

.   .   .   .   .

Though my master advanced me . . . yet I was a very naughty boy, much given to play, insomuch that he at length openly declared. "You Barnard, I know you can do well enough if you will; but you are so full of play that you hinder your classmates from getting their lessons; and therefore, if any of them cannot perform their duty, I shall correct you for it." One unlucky day, one of my classmates did not look into his book, and therefore could not say his lesson, though I called upon him once and again to mind his book; upon which our master beat me. I told master the reason why he could not

say his lesson was, his declaring he would beat me if any of the class were wanting in their duty; since which this boy would not look into his book, though I called upon him to mind his book, as the class could witness. The boy was pleased with my being corrected, and persisted in his neglect, for which I was still corrected, and that for several days. I thought, in justice, I ought to correct the boy, and compel him to a better temper; and therefore, after school was done, I went up to him, and told him I had been beaten several times for his neglect; and since master would not correct him I would, and I should do so as often as I was corrected for him; and then drubbed him heartily. The boy never came to school any more, and so that unhappy affair ended.

Though I was often beaten for my play, and my little roguish tricks, yet I don't remember that I was ever beaten for my book more than once or twice. One of these was upon this occasion. Master put our class upon turning Aesop's Fables into Latin verse. Some dull fellows made a shift to perform this to acceptance; but I was so much duller at this exercise, that I could make nothing of it; for which master corrected me, and this he did two or three days going. I had honestly tried my possibles to perform the task; but having no poetical fancy, nor then a capacity opened of expressing the same idea by a variation of phrases, though I was perfectly acquainted with prosody, I found I could do nothing; and therefore told my master, that I had diligently labored all I could to perform what he required, and perceiving I had no genius for it, I thought it was in vain to strive against nature any longer; and he never more required it of me. Nor had I any thing of a poetical genius till after I had been at College some time, when upon reading some of Mr. Cowley's[2] works, I was highly pleased, and a new scene opened before me.

I remember once, in making a piece of Latin, my master found fault with the syntax of one word, which was not so used by me heedlessly,

---

1. An introductory Latin text and grammar. A full account of a grammar school curriculum is in Kenneth B. Murdock, "The teaching of Latin and Greek at the Boston Latin School in 1712," in CSM *Publications,* XXVII (1927), 23–25.

2. Abraham Cowley (1618–1667), English poet.

but designedly, and therefore I told him there was a plain grammar rule for it. He angrily replied, there was no such rule. I took the grammar and showed the rule to him. Then he smilingly said, "Thou art a brave boy; I had forgot it." And no wonder; for he was then above eighty years old.

Higher learning in New England

Massachusetts colonists were justly proud of having established a college within a few years of the first settlement. These documents elucidate the community's purpose in founding Harvard College and show what was expected of students. In 1701 Yale College was founded in Connecticut.

---

1. The founding, government, rules, and first course of study in Harvard College, 1636–1642

New England's First Fruits in Morison, *Founding of Harvard College,* pp. 423–436.

After God had carried us safe to New England, and we had builded our houses, provided necessaries for our livelihood, reared convenient places for God's worship, and settled the civil government, one of the next things we longed for, and looked after, was to advance learning and perpetuate it to posterity, dreading to leave an illiterate ministry to the churches when our present ministers shall lie in the dust. And as we were thinking and consulting how to effect this great work, it pleased God to stir up the heart of one Mr. Harvard (a godly gentleman and a lover of learning, there living amongst us) to give the one half of his estate (it being in all about 1700 £) towards the erecting of a College, and all his library. After him another gave 300 £, others after them cast in more, and the public hand of the state added the rest. The College was, by common consent, appointed to be at Cambridge (a place very pleasant and accommodate), and is called (according to the name of the first founder) Harvard College.

The edifice is very fair and comely within and without, having in it a spacious hall (where they daily meet at commons, lectures, [and] exercises), and a large library with some books to it, the gifts of divers of our friends, their chambers and studies also fitted for and possessed by the students, and all other rooms of office necessary and convenient, with all needful offices thereto belonging. And by the side of the College a fair grammar school, for the training up of young scholars, and fitting of them for academical learning, that still, as they are judged ripe, they may be received into the College of this school: Master Corlet is the master, who hath very well approved himself for his abilities, dexterity, and painfulness in teaching and education of the youth under him.

Over the College is Master Dunster placed, as President, a learned, conscionable, and industrious man, who hath so trained up his pupils in the tongues and arts, and so seasoned them with the principles of Divinity and Christianity, that we have to our great comfort, (and in truth) beyond our hopes, beheld their progress in learning and godliness also.[1] The former of these hath appeared in their public declamations in Latin and Greek, and disputations logical and philosophical which they have been wonted (besides their ordinary exercises in the college hall) in the audience of the magistrates, ministers, and other scholars, for the probation of their growth in learning, upon set days, constantly once every month to make and uphold. The latter hath been manifested in sundry of

---

1. Henry Dunster (1609–1658/59), the first president of Harvard, was forced to resign in 1654 because of his heretical beliefs regarding the efficacy of infant baptism although he was a satisfactory president in all other respects.

them by the savory breathings of their spirits in their godly conversation. Insomuch that we are confident, if these early blossoms may be cherished and warmed with the influence of the friends of learning and lovers of this pious work, they will by the help of God come to happy maturity in a short time.

Over the College are twelve Overseers chosen by the General Court. Six of them are of the magistrates, the other six of the ministers, who are to promote the best good of it and (having a power of influence into all persons in it) are to see that every one be diligent and proficient in his proper place.

Rules and Precepts that are observed in the College

1. When any scholar is able to understand Tully, or such like classical Latin author *extempore,* and make and speak true Latin in verse and prose . . . and decline perfectly the paradigms of nouns and verbs in the Greek tongue, let him then and not before be capable of admission into the College.

2. Let every student be plainly instructed and earnestly pressed to consider well [that] the main end of his life and studies is *to know God and Jesus Christ which is eternal life,* John 17:3, and therefore to lay Christ in the bottom, as the only foundation of all sound knowledge and learning. And seeing the Lord only giveth wisdom, let everyone seriously set himself by prayer in secret to seek it of him . . .

3. Everyone shall so exercise himself in reading the Scriptures twice a day that he shall be ready to give such an account of his proficiency therein, both in theoretical observations of the language and logic, and in practical and spiritual truths, as his tutor shall require, according to his ability . . .

4. That they, eschewing all profanation of God's name, attributes, word, ordinances, and times of worship, do study with good conscience carefully to retain God and the love of His

truth in their minds, else let them know that (notwithstanding their learning) God may give them up to strong delusions, and in the end to a reprobate mind . . .

5. That they studiously redeem the time: observe the general hours appointed for all the students, and the special hours for their own classes, and then diligently attend the lectures without any disturbance by word or gesture. And if in anything they doubt, they shall inquire, as of their fellows, so (in case of *non satisfaction*), modestly of their tutors.

6. None shall, under any pretence whatsoever, frequent the company and society of such men as lead an unfit and dissolute life. Nor shall any without his tutors leave, or (in his absence) the call of parents or guardians, go abroad to other towns.

7. Every scholar shall be present in his tutor's chamber at the seventh hour in the morning, immediately after the sound of the bell, at his opening the Scripture and prayer; so also at the fifth hour at night, and then give account of his own private reading, as aforesaid in particular the third, and constantly attend lectures in the hall at the hours appointed. But if any (without necessary impediment) shall absent himself from prayer or lectures, he shall be liable to admonition, if he offend above once a week.

8. If any scholar shall be found to transgress any of the laws of God, or the school, after twice admonition, he shall be liable, if not *adultus,* to correction; if *adultus,* his name shall be given up to the Overseers of the College, that he be admonished at the public monthly act.

The times and order of their studies, unless experience shall show cause to alter:

[1.] The second and third day of the week, read lectures as followeth:

To the first year at eight of the clock in the morning Logic the first three quarters, Physics the last quarter.

To the second year, at the ninth hour, Ethics and Politics at convenient distances of time.

To the third year at the tenth [hour] Arithmetic and Geometry the three first quarters, Astronomy the last.

Afternoon

The first year disputes at the second hour.

The second year at the third hour.

The third year at the fourth, everyone in his Art.

[2.] The fourth day read Greek.

To the first year the Etymology and Syntax at the eighth hour.

To the second at the ninth hour, Prosodia and Dialects.

Afternoon

The first year at second hour practice the precepts of Grammar in such authors as have a variety of words.

The second year at third hour practice in Poesy, Nonnus, Duport, or the like.

The third year perfect their Theory before noon, and exercise Style, Composition, Imitation, Epitome, both in Prose and Verse, afternoon.

[3.] The fifth day read Hebrew and the Eastern Tongues.

Grammar to the first year hour the eighth.

To the second, Chaldee at the ninth hour.

To the third, Syriac at the tenth hour.

Afternoon

The first year practice in the *Bible* at the second hour.

The second in Ezra and Daniel at the third hour.

The third at the fourth hour in Trostius' New Testament.

[4.] The sixth day read Rhetoric to all at the eighth hour.

Declamations at the ninth. So ordered that every scholar may declaim once a month. The rest of the day [free from studies].

[5.] The seventh day read Divinity Catechetical at the eighth hour.

Commonplaces at the ninth hour.

Afternoon

The first hour reads history in the winter, the nature of plants in the summer.

The sum of every lecture shall be examined before the new lecture be read.

Every scholar, that on proof is found able to read the originals of the Old and New Testament into the Latin tongue, and to resolve them logically, withal being of godly life and conversation, and at any public act hath the approbation of the Overseers and Master of the College, is fit to be dignified with his first degree.

Every scholar that giveth up in writing a system, or synopsis, or sum of Logic, Natural and Moral Philosophy, Arithmetic, Geometry and Astronomy, and is ready to defend his theses or positions, withal skilled in the originals as abovesaid, and of godly life and conversation, and so approved by the Overseers and Masters of the College, at any public act, is fit to be dignified with his second degree.

---

2. Higher learning defended against its detractors, 1663

Jonathan Mitchell, "A Model for the Maintaining of Students and Fellows of Choice Abilities at the College in Cambridge," in CSM *Publications,* XXXI (1935), 311, 321–322.

In this plan submitted to the General Court, Mitchell, senior fellow and teacher at Harvard College, urged endowment of fellowships for prospective ministers, schoolteachers, and magistrates. He systematically stated and refuted some of the leading objections to greater expenditures for higher learning then current in Massachusetts.

We in this country, being far removed from the more cultivated parts of the world, had need to use utmost care and diligence to keep up learning and all helps of education among us, lest degeneracy, barbarism, ignorance, and irreligion do by degrees break in upon us. We have great cause of thankfulness to God for what He hath done for us already in erecting not only other schools but a College among us by the pious gift of Master John Harvard, founder thereof.

.   .   .   .   .

An answer to some objections that may be raised against this work:

Objection 1: What need we so much [of] book-learning or a learned ministry? May we not do well enough without it?

Answer: He that despises book-learning forgets that God hath put our all into a book, or *Bible,* for the understanding and improving of which book all sorts of other useful books and all arts and sciences are no more than necessary. To despise any kind or degree of useful learning is to despise the prophetical office of Jesus Christ, the scope whereof is to restore knowledge to the sons of men, and inferior parts of knowledge [are] as needful and helpful to the superior. Neither can we do well without a learned ministry, yea such as are eminently learned in the arts and languages, as he will readily grant who considers that the Scriptures and the best helps to understand them are written in the learned languages; that there is the use and result of all arts in the Scriptures and all needful to a distinct understand[in]g thereof; that the opposition and disputes which Satan hath at all times and in these our days especially raised up against the truth, require much learning to resist and refute them . . .

Objection 2: But much hath been given to the College already. What becomes of that, and what needeth more?

Answer: 1. If we have any charity toward men, we may rest assured that what hath been given, being in the hands of men faithful and able, is carefully preserved, improved, and disposed in the best way that may be. The accounts of this have been presented to the General Court, viewed by their committees, and may be seen in the hands of the treasurer of the College by any that shall desire it. 2. What hath been given comes not to so much as many imagine. But if it were more than it is, it would fall far short of what is needful, as any one that considers the nature and compass of such a work will easily see. The whole annual revenues that any way come to the College (for support of the president, fellows, scholars and edifice) amount but to 250 £, and the greatest part of that in such ways as are difficult, troublesome, and inconvenient, though their necessity makes for a shift till better do occur. 3. The principal scope of this design is not so much to maintain the society of the College, as particular persons therein of choice abilities for the service of the country. And this will also make the society flourish, which now languisheth for want of students that continue.

Objection 3: The College, as it is, breedeth as many or more than can have employment in this small country in the work of the ministry.

Answer: 1. How is it then that some out-places are destitute and others not fully furnished? 2. The design of this model is not only to send forth ministers but choice and eminent ministers. The number will not, it may be, hereby be much augmented, but their abilities and advantages for greater attainments by being enabled to continue at the College and furnished with choice tutors there [will be]. 3. It sufficeth not to have supplies for the ministry, for time will show that unless we have the helps of learning and education to accomplish persons for the magistracy and other civil offices, things will languish and go to decay among us. 4. Advantages and preferments by learning here are not [as] attractive and considerable as they are in other places. Hence few will be of themselves at the charges to bring up their children to learning without help. We see by experience that most men, even the richer sort, do choose to put their children to more advantageous employments.

Objection 4: The College diet and accommodations [are] uncomfortable and prejudicial to the health of students there, also the manners of sundry are dissolute. These things are a discouragement both to parents from putting their children thither and to benefactors.

Answer: 1. There is and will be care taken that the accommodation at the College be in all respects as good as can be according to the present expenses and allowances. Yet it hath been the wisdom of all nations and ages to attend frugality and somewhat of severity in such societies. 2. If more and better be desired, the charge must needs be greater; and parents will find that heavy, unless some assistance be lent them, the obtaining whereof is our design of this proposal. 3. Were there more means to maintain good and able fellows in the College, both the manners of students and what else is amiss might by their help be rectified. 4. In all societies there will be bad as well as good; yet if we remember how many have been there bred of the better sort, we shall have no cause to insist too much on the former. But according to this model there will be such a careful election of scholars, and they kept under such obligations and inspection, as will through the blessing of God render them a rejoicing to all pious benefactors.

Objection 5: The country is poor and hath little to spare for such uses.

Answer: 1. Necessary things must be provided for, though we make the hardest shifts; and such a thing is the maintenance of learning for the work of present and after ages. 2. The proposal is tendered to such as God hath blessed with estates in some comfortable measure. 3. It is not great matters that we aim at, but a competent and necessary subsistence for learning according to our day of small things in a wilderness. 4. Though it is but little that each single person can do, yet many drops united may make a small stream. 5. It is hoped that in a little time God may raise up more Harvards whose dying bequeathments of their estates to this work (and haply to be improved according to this model) may give life to it. And thus the contributions of many particular persons may be spared. In the meantime let us creep as we can and be doing something that learning among us may not fall or languish, but may stand and flourish to the good of us and our posterity after us.

C. SCHOOLS AND LEARNING IN THE SOUTHERN COLONIES

Schools and learning in Virginia

Although the scattered farms and plantations of Virginia were a far less promising soil for the cultivation of learning than New England's compact towns, local schools appeared, tutors were employed by wealthy planters for their children, and some youths were sent to England for instruction. The earliest endowment for a free school in the colonies, consisting of two hundred acres of land and eight cows, was left in the will of Benjamin Syms of Virginia in 1634.[1] Nevertheless, when compared with New or old England, schooling in colonial Virginia was private, scanty, and haphazard.

1. The will is printed in Knight, *Education in the South*, I, 203–205.

1. The effects of Virginia's "scattered planting" on education, 1662

R. G., *Virginia's Cure, or An Advisive Narrative Concerning Virginia* (London, 1662), pp. 5–6, 9, 10–11.

Their almost general want of schools for the education of their children is another consequence of their scattered planting, of most sad consideration, most of all bewailed of parents there; and therefore the arguments drawn from thence most likely to prevail with them cheerfully to embrace the remedy. This want of schools, as it renders a very numerous generation of Christians' children born in Virginia (who naturally are of beautiful and comely persons and generally of more ingenious spirits than these in England) unserviceable for any great employments either in Church or State; so likewise it obstructs the hopefullest way they have for the conversion of the heathen, which is, by winning the heathen . . . to bring in their children to be taught and instructed in our schools together with the children of the Christians.

.   .   .   .   .

I shall humbly . . . endeavor to contribute towards the compassing this remedy by propounding:

1. That your Lordship would be pleased to acquaint the King with the necessity of promoting the building [of] towns in each county of Virginia, upon the consideration of the forementioned sad consequences of their present manner of living there.

2. That your Lordship . . . be pleased to move the pitiful and charitable heart of His Gracious Majesty (considering the poverty and needs of Virginia) for a collection to be made in all the churches of his three kingdoms . . . for the promoting a work of so great charity to the souls of many thousands of his loyal subjects, their children, and the generations after them, and of numberless poor heathen; and that the ministers of each congregation be enjoined with more than ordinary care and pains to stir up the people to a free and liberal contribution towards it . . .

2. The report of Sir William Berkeley, governor of Virginia, on the state of free schools, learning, and the ministry in the colony, 1671

"Enquiries to the Governor of Virginia," submitted by the Lords' Commissioners of Foreign Plantations, in *Va. Statutes at Large,* II, 517.

What course is taken about the instructing the people within your government in the christian religion; and what provision is there made for the paying of your ministry?

Answer. The same course that is taken in England out of towns; every man according to his ability instructing his children. We have forty-eight parishes, and our ministers are well paid, and by my consent should be better *if they would pray oftener and preach less.* But of all other commodities, so of this, *the worst are sent us,* and we had few that we could boast of, since the persecution in *Cromwell's* tyranny drove divers worthy men hither. But, I thank God, *there are no free schools* nor *printing,* and I hope we shall not have these hundred years; for *learning* has brought disobedience, and heresy, and sects into the world, and *printing* has divulged them, and libels against the best government.[1] God keep us from both!

1. Berkeley doubtless realized that a denunciation of heretical learning would be appreciated by officials of Charles II since they were fully prepared to attribute the recent English civil war to the spread of heresy.

3. The parish schools of Virginia in 1724

Jones, *Virginia,* p. 70.

In most parishes are schools (little houses being built on purpose) where are taught English and writing; but to prevent the sowing the seeds of dissention and faction, it is to be wished that the masters or mistresses should be such as are approved or licensed by the minister, and vestry of the parish, or justices of the county; the clerks of the parishes being generally most proper for this purpose; or (in case of their incapacity or refusal) such others as can best be procured.

4. Hugh Jones writes from England on the Virginian's attitude toward education, 1724

Jones, *Virginia,* pp. 45–47.

As for education, several are sent to England for it, though the Virginians being naturally of good parts (as I have already hinted), neither require nor admire as much learning as we do in Britain; yet more would be sent over were they not afraid of the smallpox, which most commonly proves fatal to them.

But indeed when they come to England they are generally put to learn to persons that know little of their temper, who keep them drudging on in what is of least use to them, in pedantic methods, too tedious for their volatile genius.

For grammar learning taught after the common roundabout way is not much beneficial nor delightful to them; so that they are noted to be more apt to spoil their school-fellows than improve themselves; because they are imprisoned and enslaved to what they hate and think useless, and have not peculiar management proper for their humor and occasion.

A civil treatment with some liberty, if permitted with discretion, is most proper for them, and they have most need of, and readily take polite and mathematical learning; and in English may be conveyed to them (without going directly to Rome and Athens) all the arts, sciences, and learned accomplishments of the ancients and moderns, without the fatigue and expense of another language, for which most of them have little use or necessity, since (without another) they may understand their own speech, and all other things requisite to be learned by them sooner and better.

Thus the youth might as well be instructed there as here by proper methods without the expense and danger of coming hither, especially if they make use of the great advantage of the College at Williamsburg, where they may (and many do) imbibe the principles of all human and divine literature, both in English and in the learned languages.

By the happy opportunity of this College may they be advanced to religious and learned education, according to the discipline and doctrine of the established Church of England; in which respect this College may prove of singular service and be an advantageous and laudable nursery and strong bulwark against the contagious dissensions in Virginia . . .

5. The early history of the College of William and Mary and proposals for its reform by a professor, 1724

Jones, *Virginia,* pp. 26–27, 83–87.

From the beginning of permanent settlement in Virginia considerable interest was expressed in the founding of a college, but none appeared until the chartering of William and Mary in 1693.

This royal foundation was granted and established by charter, by King William and

Queen Mary, and endowed by them, with some thousand acres of land, with duties upon furs and skins, and a penny a pound for all tobacco transported from Virginia and Maryland, to the other plantations; to which have been made several additional benefactions, as that handsome establishment of Mr. Boyle, for the education of Indians,[1] with the many contributions of the country, especially a late one of £1000 to buy Negroes for the College use and service.

The society is a corporation established for a president, six masters or professors, with a hundred scholars, more or less.

For some causes that I can't account for, the revenue is not improved as much as might be wished; neither is the College brought to that method of education and advantage, as it might be; though it is hoped, that in a few years it will, like the palm tree, grow to the greater perfection, under the weighty obstacles that load it.

The salary of the President, Mr. James Blair, has been lately ordered to be reduced from 150 to £100 per annum.

The salary of the fellows (one of which I have been several years) is £80 per annum each, with 20s. entrance, and 20s. a year for pupilage for each scholar: The payments are sometimes made in current Spanish money, and sometimes in sterling bills.

The nature of the country scarce yet admits of a possibility of reducing the collegians to the nice methods of life and study observed in Oxford and Cambridge; though by degrees they may copy from thence many useful customs and constitutions.

.   .   .   .   .

For it is now a college without a chapel, without a scholarship, and without a statute.

There is a library without books, comparatively speaking, and a president without a fixed salary till of late: A burgess without certainty of electors; and in fine, there have been disputes and differences about these and the like affairs of the college hitherto without end.

These things greatly impede the progress of sciences and learned arts, and discourage those that may be inclined to contribute their assistance or bounty towards the good of the College.

Nevertheless the difficulties of this kind might be removed by some such regulations as follow, viz.

Let none be permitted to teach school in any parish, but such as shall be nominated by the minister and vestry, and licensed by the president of the College.

Let such lads as have been taught to read and instructed in the grounds of the English language in those schools, be admitted into the grammar school at the College, if they pass examination before the president and masters; together with such youth as shall be sent from Maryland, who have a right to be educated at this College.

Provided always that the number of grammar scholars shall never exceed one hundred.

Let them be boarded and lodged in the dormitory, as they are at present; or upon such terms as may from time to time seem most proper to the president and masters, or to the governors, till a transfer be obtained.

These lads should be two years under the care of the usher,[2] and two more under the grammar master; and by them instructed in Latin and Greek, in such methods as the president and masters shall direct.

And during these four years, at certain appointed times they should be taught to write as they now are in the writing-school, or in such methods as the president and masters may judge better: There also should the writing master teach them the grounds and practice of arithmetick, in order to qualify such for business, as intend to make no farther progress in learning.

Out of the grammar school should be yearly elected by the president and masters (or professors) five scholars upon the foundation, who

1. See above, sec. A, Gifts and bequests for the education of Indian youth and their disposition, doc. 2.

2. An assistant to the schoolmaster.

should be allowed their board, education, and lodging in proper apartments gratis; and should also be provided with cloaths and gowns . . .

These scholars should continue three years upon the foundation; during which time, at appointed terms they should be instructed in languages, in religion, in mathematicks, in philosophy, and in history, by the five masters or professors appointed for that purpose; who with the grammar master make up the number appointed by the charter.

Besides the scholars, the professors should for a certain sum instruct such others as may be entered commoners in the College out of the grammar school, or from elsewhere, by the approbation of the president and masters, who should be obliged to wear gowns, and be subject to the same statutes and rules as the scholars; and as commoners[3] are in Oxford. These should maintain themselves, and have a particular table, and chambers for their accommodation.

For to wait at the four high tables hereafter mentioned, there should be elected by the president and masters four servitors, who should have their education, and such allowances, as the servitors in Oxford.

Such scholars, commoners, and servitors, as have behaved themselves well, and minded their studies for three years, and can pass proper examination, and have performed certain exercises, should have the degree of a batchellor of arts conferred upon them; should eat at a table together, and be distinguished by a peculiar habit; maintain themselves, be subject to certain rules, and pursue proper studies; being allowed the use of the Library as well as the masters, paying proper fees upon their admission for the good of the Library.

Out of these batchellors should be yearly elected by the presidents, and masters, one fellow to be allowed £20 for his passage to England, and £20 per annum for three years after his speedy entrance and continuance in some certain college in Oxford or Cambridge;

3. A student who pays for his own board.

after which he should commence master of arts; which degree, with all others in our universities, should be conferred in the same manner in this college by the president and masters.

Out of the graduates above batchellors should the masters or professors be chosen by the election of the said masters or professors, with the president; who also every seven years should chose a new chancellor, to whose determination all disputes and differences should be referred.

And when the president's place is vacant, it should be filled by such of the masters as has belonged first to the College.

.   .   .   .   .

Such an establishment would encourage the bright youth of Virginia to apply to their studies, and in some measure would compel them to improve themselves; whereas now being left to their own liberty, they proceed but superficially . . . Here too would be great inducements for their friends to advise and persuade them to go through with their learning; when they are certain, that they will thus be regularly improved, and have prospect of a cheap education, and hopes of the best preferment in their country in Church and State; and have equal (if not superior) chance with others for promotion abroad in the world; being bred compleat gentlemen and good Christians, and qualified for the study of the gospel, law, or physick; and prepared for undertaking trade, or any useful projects and inventions.

Educational work of the Society for the Propagation of the Gospel in Foreign Parts

This Society, chartered in England in 1701 and supported by philanthropy, sent many schoolmasters and missionaries to the southern and middle-Atlantic colonies in America. Its purpose was to gain converts to the Church of England, with elementary instruction one means to that end. Its schoolmasters cooperated with parish clergy. The Society was the leading agency of Anglican good works in America.

---

1. Instructions to schoolmasters, 1706

Charles F. Pascoe, comp., *Classified Digest of the Records of the Society for the Propagation of the Gospel in Foreign Parts, 1701–1892* (London, 1893), pp. 944–945.

I. That they well consider the end for which they are employed by the Society, *viz.,* the instructing and disposing children to believe and live as Christians.

II. In order to this end, that they teach them to read truly and distinctly, that they may be capable of reading the Holy Scriptures and other pious and useful books for informing their understandings and regulating their manners.

III. That they instruct them thoroughly in the Church-Catechism; teach them first to read it distinctly and exactly, then to learn it perfectly by heart, endeavoring to make them understand the sense and meaning of it by the help of such expositions as the Society shall send over.

IV. That they teach them to write a plain and legible hand, in order to the fitting them for useful employments, with as much arithmetic as shall be necessary to the same purpose.

V. That they be industrious, and give constant attendance at proper school hours.

VI. That they daily use, morning and evening, the prayers composed for their use in this collection with their scholars in the school, and teach them the prayers and graces composed for their use at home.

VII. That they oblige their scholars to be constant at church on the Lord's Day, morning and afternoon, and at all other times of public worship. That they cause them to carry their Bibles and Prayer Books with them, instructing them how to use them there and how to demean themselves in the several parts of worship. That they be there present with them, taking care of their reverent and decent behavior, and examine them afterwards as to what they have heard and learned.

VIII. That when any of their scholars are fit for it, they recommend them to the minister of the parish to be publicly catechized in the church.

IX. That they take especial care of their manners, both in their schools and out of them, warning them seriously of those vices to which children are most liable, teaching them to abhor lying and falsehood and to avoid all sorts of evil-speaking, to love truth and honesty, to be modest, gentle, well-behaved, just and affable, and courteous to all their companions, respectful to their superiors, particularly towards all that minister in holy things and especially to the minister of their parish, and all this from a sense and fear of Almighty God, endeavoring to bring them in their tender years to that sense of religion which may render it the constant principle of their lives and actions.

X. That they use all kind and gentle methods in the government of their scholars that they may be loved as well as feared by them; and that when correction is necessary, they make the children to understand that it is given them out of kindness for their good, bringing them to a sense of their fault as well as of their punishment.

XI. That they frequently consult with the minister of the parish in which they dwell about the methods of managing their schools, and be ready to be advised by him.

XII. That they do in their whole conversation show themselves examples of piety and virtue to their scholars and to all with whom they shall converse.

XIII. That they be ready, as they have opportunity, to teach and instruct the *Indians* and *Negroes* and their children.

XIV. That they send to the Secretary of

the Society, once in every six months, an account of the state of their respective schools, the number of their scholars, with the methods and success of their teaching.

---

2. A schoolmaster describes his curriculum and some of his problems, Charlestown, South Carolina, 1723–1726

Report of Thomas Morritt in Helen E. Livingston, "Thomas Morritt, Schoolmaster at the Charleston Free School, 1723–1728," *Historical Magazine of the Protestant Episcopal Church*, XIV (1945), 151–167.

The Latin tongue is the intent of my mission and for that method I shall observe no other than what is usually practiced in other grammar schools in England . . . And in order to give the boys a taste of class[ical] geography I shall cause to be read Dionysius Periegetis and Cluver *Geographia* and these I shall be somewhat particular upon to compare them with the modern geography . . . Justin and others I shall cause to be frequently read and perused to give the boys a taste of chronology . . . Kennet's *Goodwin* and Potter's *Antiquity* shall be also read in order to be acquainted with the rights, customs, and ceremonies of the ancients, these at spare times or at home I shall endeavor to oblige the boys to read over together with the history of the heathen gods, pantheon, etc. But as for those boys which I shall have constantly in the house with me and such as are boarders, I do intend besides these books already mentioned to make them read three times a week at least, if not every night, classic history, especially such historians as we have translated into our language. Those books I will cause to be read an hour at nights between eight and nine, and I shall not

omit at that time to instruct them in chronology and geography and teach them the use of the globes.

. . . . .

[Morrit complains about newcomers starting schools with easier curricula, 1723.]

I could heartily wish they were suppressed, for instead of being a furtherance to learning they're a great hindrance. It is customary here for a newcomer to set up for a schoolmaster and in a little time either grow weary or meet with some other employ. In the meantime, these intruders amuse the people and baulk the public school so much that I wish the humble Society would be pleased to interest themselves and represent this grievance to the Government.

. . . . .

I have ten boys sent me out of the country beside one that came from Philadelphia and another that came from the Bahaman Islands which are boarders, and ten charity boys recommended by the commissioners, two of which are mulattos; in all fifty-two, of which I daily expect an augmentation rather than a decrease.

. . . . .

Such are the difficulties I have met and struggled with, yet I thank God I have brought the school to something even beyond expectation, but yet would be much better was I in a convenient house, both convenient for boarders and more convenient for the town children. But this I live in is so crazy that some make a scruple of sending their children by day, lest it fall down. It is a brick house, two stories and a half high, and supported by sixteen shores, which is a hindrance to the increase of my boarders; and as for the new house, as it will not be ready against the hurricane season, so I must be obliged to have one at my own expense for the security of my goods and books, in which I suffered no small damage about two years ago, so much that I was obliged to write for new furniture which are now, I hope in God, safe at sea, with £35 sterling, school books, and part of my library I left behind me. I have drawn over a considerable interest into this country, so much that I cannot be able to remove out of it this two years, at least, without a considerable loss. And I have likewise 1000£ this currency owing me, which is not readily called in, as it is known I am fettered, so I am insulted and used the worse for it, which is very hard. I must thus be disturbed of my quiet and as it were ferreted out of my settlement . . .

The Society for the Propagation of the Gospel and the question of education for slaves

In its attempt to reach slaves the Society faced a difficult situation. Many masters feared that if slaves were baptized they would claim their freedom. If they were taught to read and write, the master's control would be jeopardized. The Society, on the other hand, felt bound to prepare slaves for baptism and, as far as its limited resources would allow, to supply elementary instruction. The first dilemma was resolved when the assemblies of the southern colonies and finally the British government itself declared that baptism gave no claim to freedom. No resolution of the conflict over the instruction of slaves was reached in this period. In practice the Society provided instruction only to a minute proportion of the slave population.

1. A missionary reports on the risks of teaching Negroes to read, 1710

Rev. Francis Le Jau to the London office of the Society for the Propagation of the

Gospel, Feb. 1, 1710, in Knight, *Education in the South,* I, 107.

I should say something of propagating the Christian knowledge. We want a schoolmaster in [the] parish for our white people's children, but as for the Negroes or Indians, with all submission, I would desire that such a thing should be taken into consideration as the importance of the matter and the consequences which may follow do deserve. The best scholar of all the Negroes in my parish, and a very sober and honest liver, through his learning was like to create some confusion among all the Negroes in this country. He had a book wherein he read some description of the several judgments that chastise men because of their sins in these latter days; that description made an impression upon his spirit and he told his masters abruptly there would be a dismal time and the moon woud be turned into blood and there would be dearth of darkness and went away. When I heard of that I sent for the Negro who ingeniously told me he had read so in a book. I advised him and charged him not to put his own constructions upon his reading after that manner, and to be cautious not to speak so, which he promised to me, but yet would never show me the book. But when he spoke those few words to his master some Negro overheard a part, and it was publicly blazed abroad that an angel came and spake to the man; he had seen a hand that gave him a book, he had heard voices, seen fires, etc. As I had opportunities, I took care to undeceive those who asked me about it. Now it is over. I fear that those men have not judgment enough to make a good use of their learning; and I have thought most convenient not to urge too far that Indians and Negroes should be indifferently admitted to learn to read, but I leave it to the discretion of their masters whom I exhort to examine well their inclinations. I have often observed and lately hear that it had been better if persons of melancholy constitution or those that run into the search after curious matter had never seen a book.

---

2. Conversion to Christianity does not affect the slave's status, South Carolina, 1711

J. Brevard, ed., *Digest of the Public Statute Law of South Carolina,* II (Charleston, 1814), 229.

Masters frequently refused their slaves any religious instruction for fear that conversion would entitle them to freedom. In South Carolina the issue was settled by legislation.

Since charity and the Christian religion which we profess obliges us to wish well to the souls of all men, and that religion may not be made a pretence to alter any man's property and right, and that no persons may neglect to baptize their Negroes or slaves, or suffer them to be baptized for fear that thereby they should be manumitted and set free: *Be it therefore enacted,* that it shall be, and is hereby declared, lawful for any Negro or Indian slave, or any other slave or slaves whatsoever, to receive and profess the Christian faith, and be thereunto baptized. But that notwithstanding such slave or slaves shall receive and profess the Christian religion, and be baptized, he or they shall not thereby be manumitted or set free, or his or their owner, master, or mistress lose his or their civil right, property, and authority over such slave or slaves, but that the slave or slaves, with respect to his or their servitude, shall remain and continue in the same state and condition that he or they was in before the making of this act.

---

3. A missionary of the Society discusses the baptism issue, North Carolina, 1719

A report from Mr. Taylor, April 23, 1719, to the Society, in *No. Car. Records,* II (1886), 331–333.

In this year I caused a pretty many of the children to learn our catechism, and catechized them in public. In this year I baptized one adult white young woman and thirty white children, and one adult Negro young woman, and one mustee[1] young woman and three mustee young children, in all thirty-six. I hope I took a method with the Negro young man, and with the mustee young woman whom I baptized which will please the Society, which was this. I made them get our Church Catechism perfectly without book, and then I took some pains with them to make them understand it, and especially the baptismal covenant, and to persuade them, faithfully and constantly to perform the great things they were to promise at their baptism and ever after to perform to God. And then I caused them to say the catechism one [on the] Lord's Day, and the other [on another] Lord's Day before a large congregation without book, which they did both distinctly, and so perfectly that all that heard them admired their saying it so well. And with great satisfaction to myself I baptized these two persons . . .

I had for some time great hopes of being the minister that should convert and baptize the rest of Esquire Duckenfield's slaves, which I was very desirous and ambitious to be, and I would have begrudged no pains but would, most freely and with the greatest pleasure, have done all I could to promote and accomplish this so great, and so good work. And in order thereunto, I was preparing four more of them for baptism, and had taught one of those four [his] catechism very perfectly and the other three a good part of it, and now as I was about this good work, the enemies to the conversion and baptism of slaves industriously and very busily buzzed into the peoples' ears that all slaves that were baptized were to be set free.

1. A person of mixed European and Indian ancestry.

And this silly bugbear so greatly scared Esquire Duckenfield that he told me plainly I should baptize no more of his slaves till the Society had got a law made in England that no baptized slave should be set free because he is baptized, and sen[t] it here. And many more are of the same mind, and so this good work was knocked in the head, which is a great trouble to me because so many slaves are so very desirous to become Christians without any expectation of being set free when they are baptized. I fear this good work will not be revived and prosper here till such a law is enacted by the Parliament of Great Britain and this people are acquainted with it, for I perceive nothing else will satisfy them.

---

4. A clergyman supports religious instruction of slaves, but opposes teaching them to read and write, Virginia, 1724

Jones, *Virginia,* pp. 70–71.

As for baptizing Indians and Negroes, several of the people disapprove of it; because they say it often makes them proud, and not so good servants: But these, and such objections, are easily refuted, if the persons be sensible, good, and understand English, and have been taught (or are willing to learn) the principles of Christianity, and if they be kept to the observance of it afterwards; for Christianity encourages and orders them to become more humble and better servants, and not worse, than when they were heathens.

But as for baptizing wild Indians and new Negroes, who have not the least knowledge nor inclination to know and mind our religion, language and customs, but will obstinately persist in their own barbarous ways; I question whether baptism of such (till they be a little weaned of their savage barbarity) be not a prostitution of a thing so sacred.

But as for the Children of Negroes and Indians, that are to live among Christians, undoubtedly they ought all to be baptized; since it is not out of the power of their masters to take care that they have a Christian education, learn their prayers and catechism, and go to church, and not accustom themselves to lie, swear and steal, though such (as the poorer sort in England) be not taught to read and write; which as yet has been found to be dangerous upon several political accounts, especially self-preservation.

D. SCHOOLS IN THE MIDDLE COLONIES

Schooling in New Netherland and New York

The Dutch settlers in New Netherland, familiar with private elementary schools in Holland, soon felt a need for public support of schools and of other institutions for children. However, education in that colony remained largely in the hands of private teachers with some regulation by the authorities. In the eighteenth century schoolmasters of the Society for the Propagation of the Gospel were active in New York.

---

1. A plea from officers of the colony for a public school, 1649

"The Remonstrance of New Netherland to the High and Mighty Lords States General of the United Netherlands by the People of New Netherland on the 28th of July, 1649," in O'Callaghan, *Documents Relative to the Colonial History of New York,* I, 317.

Although we are satisfied and fully aware, that, as respects public reforms, we are but as children, and that your High Mightinesses are fully competent in the case, yet we beseech you to pardon and excuse us, if we, according to our humble conception thereof, make a few suggestions in addition to what we have already considered, in our petition to your High Mightinesses, to be necessary.

.   .   .   .   .

There ought to be . . . a public school provided with at least two good teachers, so that the youth, in so wild a country, where there are so many dissolute people, may, first of all, be well instructed and indoctrinated not only in reading and writing, but also in the knowledge and fear of the Lord. Now, the school is kept very irregularly, by this one or that, according to his fancy, as long as he thinks proper. There ought to be, likewise, asylums for aged men, for orphans, and similar institutions . . .

---

2. Instructions from the burgomasters of New Amsterdam to a teacher, 1661

Thomas E. Finegan, *Free Schools: A Documentary History of the Free School Movement in New York State* (Albany, 1921), pp. 16–17.

---

1. He shall take good care, that the children, coming to his school, do so at the usual hour, namely at eight in the morning and one in the afternoon.

2. He must keep good discipline among his pupils.

3. He shall teach the children and pupils the Christian prayers, commandments, baptism, Lord's supper, and the questions with answers of the catechism, which are taught here on every Sunday afternoon in the church.

4. Before school closes he shall let the pupils sing some verses and a psalm.

5. Besides his yearly salary he shall be allowed to demand and receive from every pupil quarterly as follows: For each child, whom he teaches the a b c, spelling, and reading, 30 stivers; for teaching to read and write, 50 stivers; for teaching to read, write and cipher, 60 stivers; from those who come in the evening and between times pro rata a fair sum. The poor and needy, who ask to be taught for God's sake, he shall teach for nothing.

---

3. A schoolmaster licensed and given a monopoly of instruction in English at Albany, New York, by the governor of the colony, 1665

Daniel J. Pratt, *Annals of Public Education in the State of New York from 1626 to 1746* (Albany, 1872), p. 57.

In 1664 the English gained control of New York from the Dutch. Richard Nicolls, who issued this license, was the first English governor of the colony.

John Shutte is Licensed to Teach in Albany, New York, 1665.

Whereas, the teaching of the English tongue is necessary in this government; I have, therefore, thought fitt to give license to John Shutte to be the English Schoolmaster at Albany; And, upon condition that the said John Shutte shall not demand any more wages from each Schollar than is given by the Dutch to their Dutch Schoolmasters, I have further granted to the said John Shutte that hee shall bee the onely English Schoolmaster at Albany.

Education for life in Pennsylvania

Although higher learning held few attractions for the early Friends in America, they established private schools for elementary instruction. More than other colonists, they distrusted conventional, formal instruction, favoring a simpler mode of education that would directly prepare the young for the practical duties of life.

1. Parents, masters, and guardians must see that children learn reading, writing, and a trade, 1682

Staughton et al., *Charter to Willliam Penn,* p. 142.

This forward-looking law was disallowed by the Crown on the grounds that it was contrary to English educational traditions. Although it was re-enacted in a modified form in 1693, it was never enforced.

And to the end that poor as well as rich may be instructed in good and commendable learning, which is to be preferred before wealth, *Be it enacted,* That all persons in this Province and territories thereof having children, and all the guardians or trustees of orphans, shall cause such to be instructed in reading and writing, so that they may be able to read the Scriptures, and to write by that time they attain to twelve years of age. And that they be taught some useful trade or skill, that the poor may work to live, and the rich, if they become poor, may not want. Of which every County Court shall take care. And in case such parents, guardians, or overseers shall be found deficient in this respect, every such parent, guardian, or overseer, shall pay for every such child, five pounds, except there should appear an incapacity in body or understanding to hinder it.

2. Proposal for a system of public schools to teach academic subjects and trades, 1685

Thomas Budd, *Good Order Established in Pennsylvania and New Jersey,* ed. Frederick J. Shepard (Cleveland, 1902), pp. 43–49; first published in 1685.

Budd, a leader of the Quaker settlement during its early years, hoped that this plan would attract colonists to Pennsylvania and New Jersey. Although his scheme was not adopted, it serves as a statement of Friends' objectives in education.

1. Now It might be well if a Law were made by the Governours and general Assemblies of *Pennsilvania* and New-Jersey, that all Persons inhabiting in the said Provinces, do put their Children seven years to the publick School, or longer, if the Parents please.

2. That Schools be provided in all Towns and Cities, and persons of known honesty, skill and understanding be yearly chosen by the Governour and General Assembly, to teach and instruct Boys and Girls in all the most useful Arts and Sciences that they in their youthful capacities may be capable to understand, as the learning to *Read* and *Write true English, Latine,* and other useful Speeches and Languages, and *fair Writing, Arithmatick* and *Book-keeping;* and the Boys to be taught and instructed in some Mystery or Trade, as the making of *Mathematical Instruments, Joynery, Turnery,* the making of *Clocks* and *Watches, Weaving, Shoe-making,* or any other useful Trade or Mystery that the School is capable of teaching; and the Girls to be taught and in-

structed in *Spinning* of *Flax* and *Wool,* and *Knitting of Gloves* and *Stockings, Sewing,* and making of all sorts of useful *Needle-Work,* and the making of *Straw-Work,* as *Hats, Baskets, &c.* or any other useful Art or Mystery that the School is capable of teaching.

3. That the Scholars be kept in the Morning two hours at *Reading, Writing, Book-keeping, &c.* and other two hours at work in that Art, Mystery or Trade that he or she most delighteth in, and then let them have two hours to dine, and for Recreation; and in the afternoon two hours at *Reading, Writing, &c.* and the other two hours at work at their several Imployments.

4. The seventh day of the Week the Scholars may come to school only in the fore-noon, and at a certain hour in the afternoon let a Meeting be kept by the School-masters and their Scholars, where after good instruction and admonition is given by the Masters, to the Scholars and thanks returned to the Lord for his Mercies and Blessings that are daily received from him, then let a strict examination be made by the Masters, of the Conversation of the Scholars in the week past, and let reproof, admonition and correction be given to the Offendors, according to the quantity and quality of their faults.

5. Let the like Meetings be kept by the School-Mistresses, and the Girls apart from the Boys. By strictly observing this good order, our Children will be hindred of running into that Excess of Riot and Wickedness that youth is incident to, and they will be a comfort to their tender Parents.

6. Let one thousand Acres of Land be given and laid out in a good place, to every publick School that shall be set up, and the Rent or incom of it to go towards the defraying of the charge of the School.

7. And to the end that the Children of poor People, and the Children of *Indians* may have the like good Learning with the Children of Rich People, let them be maintained free of charge to their Parents, out of the Profits of the school, arising by the Work of the Scholars, by which the Poor and the *Indians,* as well as the

Rich, will have their Children taught, and the Remainder of the Profits, if any be, to be disposed of in the building of School-houses, and Improvements on the thousand Acres of Land, which belongs to the School.

.   .   .   .   .

3. A gentle protest against the book learning of schools when achieved at the cost of familiarity with nature, God and self, 1693

William Penn, "Reflections and Maxims," in *Select Works of William Penn* (London, 1782), pp. 119–122.

Ignorance

1. It is admirable to consider how many millions of people come into and go out of the world ignorant of themselves and of the world they have lived in.

2. If one went to see Windsor Castle or Hampton Court, it would be strange not to observe and remember the situation, the building, the gardens, fountains, etc. that make up the beauty and pleasure of such a seat. And yet few people know themselves; no, not their own bodies, the houses of their minds, the most curious structure of the world, a living, walking tabernacle; nor the world of which it was made, and out of which it is fed; which would be so much our benefit, as well as our pleasure, to know. We cannot doubt of this when we are told that the invisible things of God are brought to light by the things that are seen, and consequently we read our duty in them as often as we look upon them, to him that is the Great and Wise Author of them, if we look as we should do.

3. The world is certainly a great and stately volume of natural things, and may be not improperly styled the hieroglyphics of a better. But, alas! how very few leaves of it do we

seriously turn over! This ought to be the subject of the education of our youth who, at twenty, when they should be fit for business, know little or nothing of it.

Education

4. We are in pain to make them scholars, but not men! To talk, rather than to know; which is true canting.

5. The first thing obvious to children is what is sensible, and that we make no part of their rudiments.

6. We press their memory too soon, and puzzle, strain, and load them with words and rules; to know grammar and rhetoric, and a strange tongue or two, that it is ten to one may never be useful to them; leaving their natural genius to mechanical and physical, or natural knowledge uncultivated and neglected, which would be of exceeding use and pleasure to them through the whole course of their life.

7. To be sure, languages are not to be despised or neglected. But things are still to be preferred.

8. Children had rather be making the tools and instruments of play, shaping, drawing, framing, and building, etc. than getting some rules of propriety of speech by heart; and those, also, would follow with more judgment and less trouble and time.

9. It were happy if we studied nature more in natural things, and acted according to nature, whose rules are few, plain, and most reasonable.

10. Let us begin where she begins, go her pace, and close always where she ends, and we cannot miss of being good naturalists.

11. The creation would not be longer a riddle to us; the heavens, earth, and waters, with their respective various and numerous inhabitants; their production, natures, seasons, sympathies and antipathies; their use, benefit, and pleasure, would be better understood by us; and an eternal wisdom, power, majesty, and goodness very conspicuous to us through those sensible and passing forms; the world wearing the mark of its Maker, whose stamp is everywhere visible, and the characters very legible to the children of wisdom.

12. And it would go a great way to caution and direct people in their use of the world that they were better studied and knowing in the creation of it.

13. For how could men find the conscience to abuse it while they should see the Great Creator look them in the face in all and every part thereof?

14. Therefore ignorance makes them insensible, and to that insensibility may be ascribed their hard usage of several parts of this noble creation, that has the stamp and voice of Diety everywhere, and in everything, to the observing.

15. It is pity, therefore, that books have not been composed for youth by some curious and careful naturalists, and also mechanics, in the Latin tongue, to be used in schools that they might learn things with words, things obvious and familiar to them and which would make the tongue easier to be attained by them.

16. Many able gardeners and husbandmen are yet ignorant of the reason of their calling, as most artificers are of the reason of their own rules that govern their excellent workmanship. But a naturalist and mechanic of this sort is master of the reason of both and might be of the practice too if his industry kept pace with his speculation, which were very commendable, and without which he cannot be said to be a complete naturalist or mechanic.

17. Finally, if man be the index or epitome of the world, as philosophers tell us, we have only to read ourselves well to be learned in it. But because there is nothing we less regard than the characters of the Power that made us, which are so clearly written upon us, and the world he has given us, and can best tell us what we are and should be, we are even strangers to our own genius: the glass in which we should see that true, instructing, and agreeable variety which is to be observed in nature, to the admiration of that wisdom, and adoration of that power, which made us all.

V Apprenticeship and Child Labor

Children were an integral part of the colonial labor system because the work of children was inseparable from family relationships. In the English colonies, as in the mother country, the family was the basic unit of production and the framework within which labor was ordinarily performed. Children as young as six years of age or under assisted parents in farm and domestic tasks, as well as in stores and workshops. The labor of children was a social fact, not a social problem.[1]

Settlement of an undeveloped continent put a premium on the labor of both children and adults. If the new settlements were to survive, everybody had to work. Shortage of textiles seems to have been a crucial problem in all the colonies. As early as 1654, Edward Johnson praised the people of Rowley, Massachusetts, because they had "built a fulling mill, and caused their little ones to be very diligent in spinning cotten wool." [2] In 1641 the General Court of Massachusetts ordered: "all masters of families should see that their children and servants should bee industriously implied . . . that the honest and profitable custome of England may bee practised amongst us, so as all hands may bee implied for the working out of hemp and flaxe, and other needfull things for cloathing, without abridging any such servants of their due times for foode and rest, or other needfull refreshings." [3] A decade and a half later the General Court decreed: "all hands not necessaryly imployd on other occasions, as woemen, girles, and boyes, shall, and hereby are, enjoyned to spin according to their skill and abillitie; and that the select men in every towne doe consider the condition and capacitie of every familie, and accordingly to assess them, as one or more spinners." [4]

If necessity justified the labor of young children, religion sanctified it. From an early age children were warned that idleness destroyed souls and undermined the social system. In the Puritan ethic, work was essential to salvation and the mark of good citizenship. These exhortations were not confined to New England. Children in Pennsylvania entered daily in their copybooks: "By the sweat of thy brow thou shalt eat thy bread." [5] It was not uncommon in New England for well-to-do parents to bind their children to other households to serve as servants or apprentices so that they would experience and profit from the discipline of work.

Both family and government had a part in keeping everyone constructively employed. It was the child's duty to work, the father's legal obligation to prepare him for a useful occupation, and the responsibility of the magistrates

---

1. On the economic function of the child within the colonial family see Edmund Morgan, *The Puritan Family*; for England, see Peter Laslett, *The World We Have Lost* (London, 1965); and for the Continent, Philippe Ariès, *Centuries of Childhood* (New York, 1962). The best historical summary of child labor in colonial America is still Edith Abbott, "A Study of the Early History of Child Labor in America," *The American Journal of Sociology*, XIV (July 1908), 15–37.
2. "Wonder-Working Providence," MHS *Collections*, 2d ser., VII (1826), 12–13.

3. *Mass. Records,* I (1853), 322–323. The previous year, the Massachusetts General Court ordered the magistrates to inquire "what course may be taken for teaching the boyes and girles . . . the spinning of the yarne." Order of the General Court of Massachusetts, May 1640 (I, 294)
4. Order of the General Court of Massachusetts, May 1656, *Mass. Records,* III (1854), 396–397.
5. Monica Kiefer, "Early American Childhood in the Middle Atlantic Area," *Pennsylvania Magazine of History and Biography*, LXVIII (1944), 5.

to provide work for the poor and punish the idle. Neglect by parents and masters of the obligation of "training up their children in learning and labor," among other considerations, led to the passage of a Massachusetts statute in 1642 that required parents and masters to provide for the "calling and imployment of their children." [6] Penn's charter for Pennsylvania in 1682 prescribed that all children in the province, on reaching the age of twelve, should be taught some trade or skill "to the end that none may be idle, but the poor may work to live, and the rich, if they become poor, may not want." [7]

In addition to husband, wife, and children, the labor force of a household might include slaves, servants, and apprentices. The slave was a chattel, but servants and apprentices had the status of children and lived and functioned as part of the family.

Servants were bound by indenture to serve a certain number of years, without any specification of the type of labor. Child servants came to the colonies either as redemptioners, who entered into agreements voluntarily, promising to pay for their passage by labor in America, or as refugees from orphanages and workhouses in England. These sources of supply were supplemented by "spiriting," often a lucrative business. A survey of the seventeenth-century county court records of most colonies made by Richard B. Morris suggests the predominance of children among imported servants. Most servants were under nineteen years old, the average being between fourteen and sixteen years. Some were as young as six. [8]

6. Order of the General Court of Massachusetts, 1642, *Mass Records,* II (1853), 8–10.

7. "The Charter of the Province, The Several Frames of Government, The Laws Agreed Upon in England," George E. Reed, ed., *Pennsylvania Archives,* 4th ser., I (Harrisburg, 1900), 42.

8. Those servants here referred to were those who had come to America without indentures. Their age was determined by county judges when they were indentured. It is possible that the judges deliberately estimated a lower age, thus giving the masters a longer service term until the servant reached twenty-one. Richard B. Morris, *Government and Labor in Early America* (New York, 1946), p. 391.

Although the law defined servitude and apprenticeship as two separate institutions, apprenticeship in practice was often merely a specialized form of servitude. The main distinction between apprentice and servant was in the master's obligation to teach the former a specific trade. Even this difference disappeared, however, in the case of poor and dependent children, who were bound out as "apprentices," but actually worked as servants.

Apprenticeship was both an educational and economic institution. By training children in a trade, it added to the skilled labor force; at the same time it supplied masters' workshops and households with additional labor. Town and church officials, by binding out poor and orphan children used apprenticeship as a means of social control and public welfare. Thus, two types of apprenticeship developed side by side: voluntary, where the child and his parents or guardians entered into the agreement on their own initiative, and compulsory, where orphan or poor or neglected children were bound out by the authorities. [9] Masters were required to train voluntary apprentices for particular trades, and courts sometimes released the apprentice if his master failed to keep his part of the bargain. Compulsory apprenticeship more nearly resembled servitude, because the child or his parents, if present, had little voice in the choice of master or trade.

Voluntary apprentices normally served for seven years. Boys were apprenticed between ten and fourteen years of age and served until they were twenty-one. Girls served to age eighteen or until marriage. Compulsory apprentices on the other hand served until they were twenty-one, regardless of their age at the time of indenture. Since some were placed in infancy, their term of service often far exceeded seven years. The mutual obligations between master and apprentice were formalized in an indenture, signed by both parties before witnesses, and subsequently registered in court.

Apprenticeship was integrated with the func-

9. On the binding out of poor and orphan children see above, Chap. III, passim.

tions of the family. Apprenticeship has been defined as "the contractual exchange of vocational training in an atmosphere of family nurture for absolute personal service over a stated period of years." [10] The apprentice lived in the master's household and saw his own family rarely — and only with his master's permission — even if the family lived nearby. The master acted *in loco parentis,* assuming responsibility for the apprentice's material and spiritual welfare, and empowered to enforce his rules with the usual means of discipline. The apprentice, on his part, owed his master service, obedience, and loyalty.

Colonial apprenticeship stemmed from medieval practice, as institutionalized in the Elizabethan Statute of Artificers, but, because of American conditions, developed along different lines. In England the purpose of apprenticeship was to control competition among craft guilds. In the colonies, owing to the prevailing labor shortage, this objective was unrealistic. In consequence, colonial apprenticeship emphasized trade education instead of restrictions and controls. Benjamin Franklin was not required to prove that he had completed his apprenticeship when he sought his first job as a printer, but he did have to demonstrate his skill. In view of the labor shortage, the colonial master could hardly afford to impose property qualifications on the parents of prospective apprentices, or demand high training fees, as was customary in England. Nor was the seven year training term always observed in voluntary apprenticeship agreements. In New York, although the common council tried to uphold the seven year period in an order of 1711, four years was nearer the norm.[11] In Massachusetts the longer term was generally unenforced, although Boston in 1660 required seven years, since youths training for shorter periods had

shown themselves "incapable of being artists in their own trades." [12] In the tobacco colonies, where the bulk of the labor force consisted of compulsory apprentices, the term was normally longer than four years.

The most important difference between English and American apprenticeship systems was the American emphasis on general education. More often than not, articles of apprenticeship in England failed to require masters to teach reading and writing. American indentures, on the other hand, obligated masters to instruct apprentices in reading, writing, and simple arithmetic. The educational laws passed in various colonies from 1642 to 1731 reflect a continuous concern with the education of apprentices. The Massachusetts law of 1642 obligated not only parents but masters to supply instruction.[13] Connecticut passed a similar law in 1650, and New Haven in 1655. The Duke of York's Law (New York) of 1665, patterned after the Massachusetts law, required the instruction of all children and apprentices "in matters of Religion and the Laws of the county . . . and in some honest and Lawful Calling." A Massachusetts law of 1703 required that poor apprentices be taught to read and write. Amendments in 1710, 1720, and 1731, specified that males be taught reading, writing, and ciphering; females reading and writing. Although intended initially for poor, involuntary apprentices, these requirements applied to all children.[14] When masters were illiterate or unwilling to spend time on education, they were supposed to send apprentices to schools and pay tuition for their instruction. In Massachusetts the towns helped masters who were unable to pay. In New York masters sent apprentices to evening schools, usually kept for three months in the winter, which were apparently created specifically for the teaching of apprentices. In Massachusetts

10. Bernard Bailyn, *Education in the Forming of American Society* (Chapel Hill, 1960), p. 17.

11. The act of 1711 reversed a New York City Common Council Act of 1694 which permitted four year terms. Robert F. Seybolt, *Apprenticeship and Apprenticeship Education in Colonial New England and New York* (New York, 1917), p. 91.

12. *Boston Town Records,* II, 156–157. For an extensive discussion of the apprenticeship term see Morris, *Government and Labor,* pp. 372–376.

13. See above, Chap. II, sec. A, Legislation strengthening family government, Massachusetts, 1642–1682, Doc. 1.

14. Seybolt, *Apprenticeship,* pp. 105–106.

apprentices attended day schools.[15] The colo-

15. Seybolt found the first mention of formal schooling in a Harlem indenture, dated November 25, 1690, in which the master promised that his apprentice

nies tried to assure the apprentice the skills needed for usefulness and advancement.

"shall have the privilege of going to the evening school." *Apprenticeship,* p. 96.

A. APPRENTICESHIP

The Elizabethan Statute of Artificers legalizes and regulates apprenticeship, 1562

"An Act Containing Divers Orders for Artificers, Labourers, Servants of Husbandry, and Apprentices," 5 Elizabeth, 1562 — ch. 4, Great Britain, *Statutes at Large,* II, 527–535.

XXV. . . . Every person being an householder, and having and using half a ploughland at the least in tillage, may have and receive as an apprentice any person above the age of ten years, and under the age of eighteen years, to serve in husbandry, until his age of one and twenty at the least, or until the age of twenty-four years, as the parties can agree, and the said retainer and taking of an apprentice, to be made and done by indenture.

XXVI. . . . Every person being an householder, and twenty-four years old at the least, dwelling or inhabiting . . . in any city or town corporate, and using and exercising any art, mystery or manual occupation there, shall and may . . . have and retain the son of any freeman, not occupying husbandry, nor being a labourer, and inhabiting in the same . . . to serve and be bound as an apprentice after the custom and order of the city of London,[1] for

1. "The chief features of the London system were binding by indenture, the due recording of the agreement, a minimum term of seven years . . . and the close personal relation of master and apprentice, inseparable from which was the master's entire control of the boy." O. Jocelyn Dunlap and Richard D. Denman, *English Apprenticeship and Child Labour, a History* (London, 1912), p. 65.

seven years at the least, so as the term and years of such apprentice do not expire or determine afore such apprentice shall be of the age of twenty-four years at the least.

XXVII. Provided always . . . That it shall not be lawful to any person dwelling in any city or town corporate, using or exercising any of the mysteries or crafts of a merchant trafficking . . . trade into any of the parts beyond the sea, mercer, draper, goldsmith, ironmonger, imbroiderer or clothier, that doth or shall put cloth to making and sale, to take any apprentice or servant to be instructed or taught in any of the arts, occupations, crafts or mysteries which they or any of them do use or exercise; except such servant or apprentice be his son; or else that the father and mother of such apprentice or servant, shall have, at the time of taking such apprentice or servant, lands, tenements or other hereditaments, of the clear yearly value of forty shillings of one estate of inheritance or freehold at the least.

. . . . .

XXX. . . . It shall be lawful to any person using or exercising the art or occupation of a smith, wheel-wright, plough-wright, mill-wright, carpenter, rough mason, plaisterer, sawyer, lime-burner, brick-maker, brick-layer . . . wheresoever he or they shall dwell or inhabit, to have or receive the son of any person as apprentice in manner and form aforesaid, to be taught and instructed in these occupations only, and in none other, albeit the father or mother of any such apprentice have not any lands, tenements or hereditaments.

XXXI. . . . After the first day of May next coming, it shall not be lawful to any person or persons, other than such as now do lawfully use or exercise any art, mystery or manual occupation, to set up, occupy, use or exercise any craft, mystery or occupation, now used or occupied within the realm of England or Wales; except he shall have been brought up therein seven years at the least as an apprentice, in manner and form above-said; nor to set any person on work in such mystery, art or occupation, being not a workman at this day; except he shall have been apprentice as is aforesaid; or else having served as an apprentice as is aforesaid, shall or will become a journeyman, or be hired by the year; upon pain that every person willingly offending or doing the contrary, shall forfeit and lose for every default forty shillings for every month.

.   .   .   .   .   .

XXXV. . . . And if any such master shall misuse or evil intreat his apprentice, or that the said apprentice shall have any just cause to complain, or the apprentice do not his duty to his master, then the said master or apprentice being grieved, and having cause to complain, shall repair unto one justice of peace within the said county, or to the mayor . . . of the city . . . where the said master dwelleth, who shall by his wisdom and discretion take such order and direction between the said master and his apprentice, as the equity of the cause shall require; and if for want of good conformity in the said master, the said justice of peace, or the said mayor . . . cannot compound and agree the matter between him and his apprentice, then the said justice, or the said mayor . . . shall take bond of the said master to appear at the next [court] sessions then to be holden in the said county, or within the said city . . . and upon his appearance and hearing of the matter before the said justices . . . if it be thought meet unto them to discharge the said apprentice of his apprenticehood, that then the said justices . . . shall have power by authority hereof, in writing under their hands and

seals, to pronounce and declare, That they have discharged the said apprentice of his apprenticehood, and the cause thereof; and the said writing so being made and enrolled by the clerk of the peace or town-clerk, amongst the records that he keepeth, shall be a sufficient discharge for the said apprentice against his master, his executors and administrators; the indenture of the apprenticeshiphood, or any law or custom to the contrary notwithstanding. And if the default shall be found to be in the apprentice, then the said justices, or the said mayor or other head officer, with the assistance aforesaid, shall cause due correction and punishment to be ministered unto him, as by their wisdom and discretions shall be thought meet.

Standard form of indenture for an apprentice, Virginia, 1659

Philip A. Bruce, *Economic History of Virginia,* II (New York and London, 1896), 1–2n.

This indenture made the 6th day of June in the year of our Lord Christ 1659, witnesseth, that Bartholomew Clarke the son of John Clarke of the City of Canterbury, sadler, of his own liking and with the consent of Francis Plumer of the City of Canterbury, brewer, hath put himself apprentice unto Edward Rowzie of Virginia, planter, as an apprentice with him to dwell from the day of the date above mentioned unto the full term of four years from thence next ensuing fully to be complete and ended, all which said term the said Bartholomew Clarke well and faithfully the said Edward Rowzie as his master shall serve, his secrets keep, his commands most just and lawful he shall observe, and fornication he shall not commit, nor contract matrimony with any woman during the said term; he shall not do hurt unto his master, nor consent to the doing of any, but to his power shall hinder and prevent the doing of any;

at cards, dice or any unlawful games he shall not play; he shall not waste the goods of his said master nor lend them to anybody without his master's consent; he shall not absent himself from his said master's service day or night, but as a true and faithful servant, shall demean himself. [A]nd the said Edward Rowzie in the mystery, art, and occupation of a planter . . . the said Bartholomew shall teach or cause to be taught, and also during said term shall find and allow his apprentice competent meat, drink, apparel, washing, lodging with all other things fitting for his degree, and in the end thereof, fifty acres of land to be laid out for him, and all other things which according to the custom of the country is or ought to be done.

Punishment of unruly apprentices

1. Apprentice whipped and sentenced to house of correction, Salem, Massachusetts, 1669

Records and Files of the Quarterly Courts of Essex County, IV (Salem, 1914), 200.

Daniel Rumball's complaint: That whereas your said petitioner, having taken into his custody as an apprentice Charles Hill certain years last past, for and during the space of four or five years, the greatest part of which time is now expired, but finding by experience the said Charles to be grown to such an unruly frame of spirit and carriage that it is both troublesome and dangerous to bear with any longer, as in particular, by laying violent hands upon his said master and throwing him down twice and fetching blood of him, threatening to break his neck, running at his face with a chair, and vowing to be the death of some of them, as also by customary lying, swearing, and other like miscarriages, speaking slightingly and contemptuously of the honored mayor and of legal proceedings against him, too intolerable to be borne in a family, etc. Witnesses: Thomas Brocket, Alastair Gryme and Peter, the Frenchman [who] works with master Humber.

Order of Court: Charles Hill, for many disorderly and abusive carriages in the family, and swearing, was sentenced to be whipped and sent to the house of correction to remain during the court's pleasure.

2. Apprentice sold and term of service extended, 1682

Records of Essex County, VIII (1921), 302.

Thomas Bettes, servant to John Simmons, often running away and being incorrigible, said Simmons was discharged of his obligation of teaching the trade of a weaver.

Mr. William Cogswell having taken Thomas Bettes, who was sentenced to be whipped, and paying 40s., said Bettes had his corporal punishment remitted, and in consideration of his master Cogswell buying off his whipping, he agreed to serve him one year more than the time of his indenture and the six months ordered to serve his master Simmons by Ipswich court, Mar. 29, 1682 . . .

3. Charge for whipping equals one month's service, 1696

H. Clay Reed and G. C. Miller, eds., *The Burlington Court Book; A Record of Quaker Jurisprudence in West New Jersey, 1680–1709* (Washington, 1944), p. 186.

Upon complaint of Daniel Sutton against William Sanford, his apprentice, for running away and stealing and cheating; said Daniel being willing to part with his said apprentice and the apprentice also willing to leave him and to go to John Petty, the court ordered the said Daniel Sutton to pass over his apprentice to said John Petty or to any other person, and the said apprentice to serve such master seven years from this February 20, 1696. And ordered that said Sanford shall be severely whipped at a cart's tail (only the execution to be remitted until his first misbehavior) and the charge of whipping to be at his master's charge, and his master to be allowed a month's service more for it.

Whereas William Alcot being bound to Thomas Emley for nine years and three months to learn the trade of a carpenter, and the said William Alcot being assigned to William Budd Jr. who is no carpenter to serve the said term of years, therefore the court orders that he the said William Budd, when the said William Alcot has served seven years and three months of the term abovesaid, shall have his choice either for his apprenticeship to expire then or to serve the whole term and have the trade of a cooper or receive ten pounds now current money without a trade . . .

Apprentices complain of not being taught a trade

---

1. The jury finds for the defendant, 1672

"Records of the Suffolk County Court, 1671–1680," in CSM *Publications*, XXIX (1933), 155.

Smith contra Carrington: Mathias Smith, plaintiff, contra Edward Carrington, defendant, in an action of the case for not learning and instructing him fully in the trade of a turner according as by indenture he is bound, but employing him in other servile work, whereby the said Mathias is damnified for want of being perfected in the trade of a turner to the damage of twenty pounds or thereabout, and other due damages according to attachment dated 17th of October, 1672 . . . The jury . . . found for the defendant, costs of court being 19s. 2d.

---

2. An apprentice bound to learn trade of carpenter is assigned to a cooper, 1705

The Burlington Court Book, pp. 312–313.

Preparing one's child for a calling

Although a child started working at age six, it was usually at age fourteen that his father decided to choose a calling for him. In the Puritan ethic a calling meant more than a means of gaining a livelihood. God called an individual for a particular occupation, by giving him the talent and inclination for it. In choosing a calling for his son, a father had to carry out God's plan, as well as be sure that the occupation chosen would be of service to society.

---

1. The heavenly calling and the worldly calling

Cotton Mather, *A Christian at His Calling; Two Brief Discourses, one Directing a Christian in his General Calling; Another Directing him in his Personal* (Boston, 1701), pp. 36–45.

. . . There are *Two Callings* to be minded by *All Christians.* Every Christian hath a GENERAL CALLING; which is, to Serve the Lord

Jesus Christ, and Save his own Soul, in the Services of *Religion,* that are incumbent on all the Children of men. . . . But then, every Christian hath also a PERSONAL CALLING; or a certain *Particular Employment,* by which his *Usefulness,* in his Neighborhood, is distinguished. God hath made man a *Sociable* Creature. *We* expect Benefits from *Humane Society.*

.   .   .   .   .

But upon that Enquiry, *What is your Occupation?* a Christian should be able to give this further Account, *That he hath an Allowable Occupation, yea an Agreeable Occupation; and that he Entered into it with a suitable Disposition* . . . If our *Calling* be that whereby God will be *Offended,* it cannot be a *Calling* wherein we shall be our selves *Befriended.*

.   .   .   .   .

But this is not enough. A Christian should have it contrived, That his *Calling* be *Agreeable,* as well as *Allowable.* It is a wonderful Inconvenience for a man to have a *Calling* that won't *Agree* with him. See to it, O *Parents,* that when you choose *Callings* for your *Children,* you wisely consult their *Capacities,* & their *Inclinations;* lest you Ruine them. And, Oh! cry mightily to God, by *Prayer,* yea with *Fasting & Prayer,* for His Direction when you are to resolve upon a matter of such considerable consequence. But, O *Children,* you also should be *Thoughtful* and *Prayerful,* when you are going to fix upon your *Callings;* and above all, propose deliberately *Right Ends* unto your selves in what you do . . .

_____

2. The prerequisites for a proper calling

Wadsworth, *The Well-Ordered Family,*
pp. 41–51.

_____

Parents should bring up their children to be diligent in some lawful business. It's true, time

for lawful recreation now and then, is not altogether to be denied them. Even when Jerusalem is a City of Truth, a Holy Mountain, it shall be full of boys and girls playing in the streets . . . Yet for such to do little or nothing else but play in the streets, especially when almost able to earn their living, is a great sin and shame. They should by no means be brought up in idleness, or merely to learn fashions, ceremonious compliments, and to dress after the newest mode, etc. Such folly as this ruins many children. Boys and girls should be brought up diligently in such business as they are capable of, and as is proper for them. Adam (our First Parent) brought up his two sons . . . one to keep sheep, the other to till the ground . . . Nay when Adam himself was innocent, God allowed him not to be idle, but set him to dress and keep the Garden . . . Peter, Andrew, James and John, were called by Christ from following their particular occupation, to be apostles . . . These godly men, these eminent Saints, were not lazy, idle drones. They had their particular callings [or] trades [and] were employed in lawful business; and were so diligent therein, they would not leave the same to set a preaching or prophesying, till they had a plain clear call from God so to do. And from these instances we might learn by the way that for men to be diligent in their own proper calling, trade, or business, acting suitably in their own sphere, is the way to meet with God's blessing, and to be advanced by God, to be great blessings to others . . .

And when you put them out (if you do put them out) to some trade or calling; to be sure see that 'tis a lawful calling, and such as suits (as much as may be) the abilities and inclinations of your children. Put them into religious families, the heads whereof will say, with [Joshua] . . . *As for me and my house, we will serve the Lord.* Charge them also to be dutiful and faithful to those under whose care they must be. Some are more fit for a studious life, to serve the public with their heads, pens, tongues; and some for a more mechanic employment. If you're careful to bring them up diligently in proper business, you take a good method for their comfortable substance in this world (and for their being serviceable in their generation), you do better for them than if you should bring them up idly and yet leave them great estates.

---

3. Finding a calling for a son

Samuel Sewall, *Diary, 1674–1729* in MHS *Collections,* 5th ser., V (1878), 421–422, 423, 452.

Sewall's eldest son, unhappy in his apprenticeship with Captain Checkly, a general merchant, wished to find a proper calling and eventually secured employment with Mr. Wilkins, a bookseller.

Sixth-day, February 7th., [1695/6]. Last night Sam could not sleep because of my brother's speaking to him of removing to some other place, mentioning Mr. Usher's. I put him to get up a little wood, and he even fainted, at which brother was much startled, and advised to remove him forthwith and place him somewhere else, or send him to Salem and he would do the best he could for him. Since, I have expressed doubtfulness to Sam as to his staying there.

He mentioned to me Mr. Wadworth's Sermon against Idleness, which was an affliction to him. He said his was an idle calling, and that he did more at home than there, take one day with another. And he mentioned Mr. Stoddard's words to me, that [I] should place him with a good master, and where [he] had fulness of employment. It seems Sam overheard him, and now alleged these words against his being where he was because of his idleness. Mentioned also the difficulty of the employment by reason of the numerousness of goods and hard to distinguish them, many not being marked; whereas books, the price of them was set down, and so could sell them readily. I spoke to Captain

Checkly again, and again . . . he gave me no encouragement that his being there would be to Sam's profit; and Mrs. Checkly always discouraging.

Mr. Willard's Sermon from those words, "What doest thou hear Elijah?" was an occasion to hasten the removal.

February 10, Second-day. I went to Mr. Willard to ask whether had best keep him at home today. He said no, but tell Captain Checkly first. But when I came back, Sam was weeping and much discomposed, and loath to go because it was a little later than usual, so I thought 'twas hardly fit for him to go in that case, and went to Captain Checkly and told him how it was, and thanked him for his kindness to Sam, Captain Checkly desired Sam might come to their house and not be strange there, for which I thanked him very kindly. He presented his service to my wife, and I to his who was in her chamber. Captain Checkly gave me Sam's copybook that lay in a drawer.

Just before I got thither, I met Mr. Grafford who told me that Mumford said I was a knave. The good Lord give me Truth in the inward parts, and finally give rest unto my dear son and put him into some calling wherein He will accept of him to serve Him . . .

Sabbath, February 16, 1695/6. Captain Checkly's son Samuel is baptized with us. I was very sorrowful by reason of the unsettledness of my Samuel . . .

February 26, 1695/6. I prayed with Sam alone that God would direct our way as to a calling for him.

.   .   .   .   .

April 8, 1697. . . . In the morning agreed with Mr. Wilkins about Sam's living with him.

Second-day, April 12, 1697. Sam begins to go to Mr. Wilkins. Sold some of the Joy of Faith and some of Dr. Goodwin's third volume. At night we read Gal. 6:9 — in due season we shall reap, if we faint not. Lord furnish father and son with faith.

Benjamin Franklin's tribulations as apprentice

The Autobiography of Benjamin Franklin,
pp. 52–53, 57–59, 68–71, 77.

My elder Brothers were all put Apprentices to different Trades. I was put to the Grammar School at Eight Years of Age, my Father intending to devote me as the Tithe of his Sons to the Service of the Church. My early Readiness in learning to read (which must have been very early, as I do not remember when I could not read) and the Opinion of all his Friends that I should certainly make a good Scholar, encourag'd him in this Purpose of his. My uncle Benjamin too approv'd of it, and propos'd to give me all his Shorthand Volumes of Sermons I suppose as a Stock to set up with, if I would learn his Character. I continu'd however at the Grammar School not quite one Year, tho' in that time I had risen gradually from the Middle of the Class of that Year to be the Head of it, and farther was remov'd into the next Class above it, in order to go with that into the third at the End of the Year. But my Father in the mean time, from a View of the Expence of a College Education which, having so large a Family, he could not well afford, and the mean Living many so educated were afterwards able to obtain, Reasons that he gave to his Friends in my Hearing, altered his first Intention, took me from the Grammar School, and sent me to a School for Writing and Arithmetic kept by a then famous Man, Mr. Geo. Brownell, very successful in his Profession generally, and that by mild encouraging Methods. Under him I acquired fair Writing pretty soon, but I fail'd in the Arithmetic, and made no Progress in it.

At Ten Years old, I was taken home to assist my Father in his Business, which was that of a Tallow Chandler and Sope-Boiler. A Business he was not bred to, but had assumed on his Arrival in New England and on finding his Dying Trade would not maintain his Family, being in little Request. Accordingly I was em-

ployed in cutting Wick for the Candles, filling the Dipping Mold, and the Molds for cast Candles, attending the Shop, going of Errands, &c. I dislik'd the Trade and had a strong Inclination for the Sea; but my Father declar'd against it . . .

.   .   .   .   .

I continu'd thus employ'd in my Father's Business for two Years, that is till I was 12 Years old; and my Brother John, who was bred to that Business having left my Father, married and set up for himself at Rhodeisland, there was all Appearance that I was destin'd to supply his Place and be a Tallow Chandler. But my Dislike to the Trade continuing, my Father was under Apprehensions that if he did not find one for me more agreable, I should break away and get to Sea, as his Son Josiah had done to his great Vexation. He therefore sometimes took me to walk with him, and see Joiners, Bricklayers, Turners, Braziers, &c. at their Work, that he might observe my Inclination, and endeavour to fix it on some Trade or other on Land. It has ever since been a Pleasure to me to see good Workmen handle their Tools; and it has been useful to me, having learnt so much by it, as to be able to do little Jobs my self in my House, when a Workman could not readily be got; and to construct little Machines for my Experiments while the Intention of making the Experiment was fresh and warm in my Mind. My Father at last fix'd upon the Cutler's Trade, and my Uncle Benjamin's Son Samuel who was bred to that Business in London being about that time establish'd in Boston, I was sent to be with him some time on liking. But his Expectations of a Fee with me displeasing my Father, I was taken home again.

From a Child I was fond of Reading, and all the little Money that came into my Hands was ever laid out in Books . . .

This Bookish Inclination at length determined my Father to make me a Printer, tho' he had already one Son (James) of that Profession. In 1717 my Brother James return'd from England with a Press and Letters to set up his Business in Boston. I lik'd it much better than that of my Father, but still had a Hankering for the Sea. To prevent the apprehended Effect of such an Inclination, my Father was impatient to have me bound to my Brother. I stood out some time, but at last was persuaded and signed the Indentures, when I was yet but 12 Years old. I was to serve as an Apprentice till I was 21 Years of Age, only I was to be allow'd Journeyman's Wages during the last Year. In a little time I made great Proficiency in the Business, and became a useful Hand to my Brother . . .

.   .   .   .   .

Tho' a Brother, he considered himself as my Master, and me as his Apprentice; and accordingly expected the same Services from me as he would from another; while I thought he demean'd me too much in some he requir'd of me, who from a Brother expected more Indulgence. Our Disputes were often brought before our Father, and I fancy I was either generally in the right, or else a better Pleader, because the Judgment was generally in my favour: But my Brother was passionate and had often beaten me, which I took extreamly amiss; and thinking my Apprenticeship very tedious, I was continually wishing for some Opportunity of shortening it, which at length offered in a manner unexpected.[1]

One of the Pieces in our News-Paper, on some political Point which I have now forgotten, gave Offence to the Assembly. He was taken up, censur'd and imprison'd for a Month by the Speaker's Warrant, I suppose because he would not discover his Author. I too was taken up and examin'd before the Council; but tho' I did not give them any Satisfaction, they contented themselves with admonishing me, and dismiss'd me; considering me perhaps as an Apprentice who was bound to keep his Master's Secrets. During my Brother's Confinement,

which I resented a good deal, notwithstanding our private Differences, I had the Management of the Paper, and I made bold to give our Rulers some Rubs in it, which my Brother took very kindly, while others began to consider me in an unfavourable Light, as a young Genius that had a Turn for Libelling and Satyr. My Brother's Discharge was accompany'd with an Order of the House (a very odd one) *that James Franklin should no longer print the Paper called the New England Courant.* There was a Consultation held in our Printing House among his Friends what he should do in this Case. Some propos'd to evade the Order by changing the Name of the Paper; but my Brother seeing Inconveniences in that, it was finally concluded on as a better Way, to let it be printed for the future under the Name of *Benjamin Franklin.* And to avoid the Censure of the Assembly that might fall on him, as still printing it by his Apprentice, the Contrivance was, that my old Indenture should be return'd to me with a full Discharge on the Back of it, to be shown on Occasion; but to secure to him the Benefit of my Service I was to sign new Indentures for the Remainder of the Term, which were to be kept private. A very flimsy Scheme it was, but however it was immediately executed, and the Paper went on accordingly under my Name for several Months. At length a fresh Difference arising between my Brother and me, I took upon me to assert my Freedom, presuming that he would not venture to produce the new Indentures. It was not fair in me to take this Advantage, and this I therefore reckon one of the first Errata of my Life: But the Unfairness of it weigh'd little with me, when under the Impressions of Resentment, for the Blows his Passion too often urg'd him to bestow upon me. Tho' he was otherwise not an ill-natur'd Man: Perhaps I was too saucy and provoking.

When he found I would leave him, he took care to prevent my getting Employment in any other Printing-House of the Town, by going round and speaking to every Master, who accordingly refus'd to give me Work. I then thought of going to New York as the nearest

---

1. I fancy his harsh and tyrannical Treatment of me, might be a means of impressing me with that Aversion to arbitrary Power that has stuck to me thro' my whole Life. [Franklin's note.]

Place where there was a Printer: and I was the rather inclin'd to leave Boston, when I reflected that I had already made myself a little obnoxious to the governing Party; and from the arbitrary Proceedings of the Assembly in my Brother's Case it was likely I might if I stay'd soon bring myself into Scrapes; and farther that my indiscrete Disputations about Religion began to make me pointed at with Horror by good People, as an Infidel or Atheist. I determin'd on the Point: but my Father now siding with my Brother, I was sensible that if I attempted to go openly, Means would be used to prevent me. My Friend Collins therefore undertook to manage a little for me. He agreed with the Captain of a New York Sloop for my Passage, under the Notion of my being a young Acquaintance of his that had got a naughty Girl with Child, whose Friends would compel me to marry her, and therefore I could not appear or come away publickly. So I sold some of my Books to raise a little Money, Was taken on board privately, and as we had a fair Wind in three Days I found my self in New York near 300 Miles from home, a Boy of but 17, without the least Recommendation to or Knowledge of any Person in the Place, and with very little Money in my Pocket.

My Inclinations for the Sea, were by this time worne out, or I might now have gratify'd them. But having a Trade, and supposing my self a pretty good Workman, I offer'd my Service to the Printer of the Place, old Mr. Wm. Bradford (who had been the first Printer in Pensilvania, but remov'd from thence upon the Quarrel of Geo. Keith). He could give me no Employment, having little to do, and Help

enough already: But, says he, my Son at Philadelphia has lately lost his principal Hand, Aquila Rose, by Death. If you go thither I believe he may employ you. Philadelphia was 100 Miles farther. I set out, however, in a Boat for Amboy, leaving my Chest and Things to follow me round by Sea . . .

.   .   .   .   .

I made my self as tidy as I could, and went to Andrew Bradford the Printer's. I found in the Shop the old Man his Father, whom I had seen at New York, and who travelling on horse back had got to Philadelphia before me. He introduc'd me to his Son, who receiv'd me civilly, gave me a Breakfast, but told me he did not at present want a Hand, being lately supply'd with one. But there was another Printer in town lately set up, one Keimer, who perhaps might employ me; if not, I should be welcome to lodge at his House, and he would give me a little Work to do now and then till fuller Business should offer.

The old Gentleman said, he would go with me to the new Printer: And when we found him, Neighbour, says Bradford, I have brought to see you a young Man of your Business, perhaps you may want such a One. He ask'd me a few Questions, put a Composing Stick in my Hand to see how I work'd, and then said he would employ me soon, tho' he had just then nothing for me to do . . .[2]

2. Neither Bradford nor Keimer appears to have required Franklin to produce documentary evidence that he had completed an apprenticeship. Keimer was willing to employ Franklin after satisfying himself that Franklin knew his trade.

B. INDENTURED SERVANTS

*Colonial laws on
indentured servants*

1. Connecticut, 1644

Conn. Records, I, 105.

Whereas many stubborn, refractory, and discontented servants and apprentices withdraw themselves from their masters' services, to improve their time to their own advantage, for the preventing whereof: It is ordered that whatsoever servant or apprentice shall hereafter offend in that kind, before their covenants or term of service shall expire, shall serve their said masters, as they shall be apprehended or retained the treble term, or threefold time of their absence in such kind.

2. Massachusetts, 1648

Laws and Liberties of Massachusetts, p. 38.

Masters, Servants, Laborers: It is ordered by this Court and the authority thereof that no servant, either man or maid, shall either give, sell, or truck any commodity whatsoever without license from their masters during the time of their service under pain of fine or corporal punishment at the discretion of the Court as the offense shall deserve.

And that all workmen shall work the whole day, allowing convenient time for food and rest.

It is also ordered that when any servants shall run from their masters or any other inhabitants shall privily go away with suspicion of ill intentions, it shall be lawful for the next magistrate, or the constable and two of the chief inhabitants where no magistrate is, to press men and boats or pinnaces at the public charge to pursue such persons by sea or land and bring them back by force of arms.

3. Pennsylvania, 1700

James T. Mitchell and Henry Flanders, comps., *The Statutes at Large of Pennsylvania from 1682 to 1801,* II (Harrisburg, 1896), 54–55.

This statute is discussed in Respublica *v.* Keppele, 2 Dallas (Penna.) 197 (1783) (see below, Part Two, Chap. II, sec. A, Children not to be bound as servants).

. . . No servant, bound to serve his or her time in this province or counties annexed, shall be sold or disposed of to any person residing in any other province or government, without the consent of the said servant and two justices of the peace of the county wherein he lives or is sold, under the penalty of ten pounds, to be forfeited by the seller.

. . . No servant shall be assigned over to another person by any in this province or territories but in the presence of one justice of peace of the county, under the penalty of ten pounds; which penalty, with all others in this act expressed, shall be levied by distress and sale of goods of the party offending.

. . . Every servant that shall faithfully serve four years or more, shall, at the expiration of their servitude, have a discharge, and shall be duly clothed with two complete suits of apparel, whereof one shall be new; and shall also be furnished with one new ax, one grubbing hoe and one weeding hoe, at the charge of their master or mistress.

And for prevention of servants quitting their master's service.

Be it enacted . . . that if any servant shall absent him or herself from the service of their master or owner for the space of one day or more, without leave first obtained for the same, every such servant shall, for every such day's absence, be obliged to serve five days after the expiration of his or her time, and shall further make such satisfaction to his or her master or owner for the damages and charges sustained by such absence as the respective county court shall see meet, who shall order as well the time to be served as other recompense for damages sustained.

And whoever shall apprehend or take up any runaway servant, and shall bring him or her to the sheriff of the county, such person shall, for every such servant, if taken up within ten miles of the servant's abode, receive ten shillings; and if ten miles or upwards, twenty shillings reward, of the said sheriff, who is hereby required to pay the same and forthwith to send notice to the master or owner, of whom he shall receive five shillings prison fees, upon the delivery of the said servant, together with all other disbursements and reasonable charges for and upon the same.

---

4. North Carolina, 1715

Walter Clark, ed., *No. Car. Records,* XXIII (Goldsboro, N.C., 1904), 62–66.

. . . Every Christian servant whether so by importation or by contract made in this govern-

ment that shall, at any time or times absent him or herself from his or her master's or mistress' service without his or her license first had shall make satisfaction by serving after the time by custom or indenture or contract for serving is expired, double the time of service lost or neglected by such time or times of absence and also such longer time as the court shall see fit to adjudge in consideration of any further charge or damages accruing to the master or mistress by such time or times of absence as aforesaid.

. . . If any Christian servant shall lay violent hands on his or her master or mistress or overseer, upon proof thereof made, shall for every offence suffer such corporal punishment as the court shall think fit to adjudge. And as an encouragement for Christian servants to perform their service with fidelity and cheerfulness.

. . . Every master or mistress shall provide for their servants so imported or indented competent diet, clothing, and lodging. And shall not exceed the bounds of moderation in correcting them beyond their demerits. And that it shall and may be lawful for any servant having just cause of complaint to repair to the next magistrate who is hereby empowered, required and directed to bind over such master or mistress to appear and answer the complaint the next precinct court and there to stand to and abide by such orders and judgment as the court shall think fit to pass thereon. And if the magistrate shall see just cause he shall also take further security that he or she shall not in the meantime abuse such servant. And as a further encouragement for the faithful discharge of the such imported or indented servants' services. . . . Every Christian servant shall be allowed by their master or mistress at the expiration of his or her time of service three barrels of Indian corn and two new suits of apparel of the value of five pounds at least or, in lieu of one suit of apparel, a good well-fixed gun, if he be a man servant.

Colonial laws establish length of service owed by imported servants

1. Maryland, 1638/39

Md. Archives, I, 80.

. . . All persons being Christians (slaves excepted) of the age of eighteen years or above and brought into this province at the charge and adventure of some other person shall serve such person at whose charge and adventure they were so transported for the full term of four years only, to commence from his or their arrival in the province (except any other time were contracted for by covenant) . . .

And all persons under the age of eighteen years transported into this province at the charge and adventure of some other person shall serve such person at whose charge he or they were so transported until such person or persons so transported shall be of the full age of four and twenty years (except likewise any other time were contracted for by covenant).[1]

And every maid servant . . . of the age of twelve years old or under shall be bound to serve the party or parties transporting her or them for seven years and if she [be] above the age of twelve years she shall serve for four years only (except it were otherwise conditioned by covenant) and at the end of any the said terms of service expired, the master or mistress of such servant (at the time when the said term is expired) shall give unto such man or maid servant such conditions as were covenanted by the indentures or first covenants or (in default of such covenant) shall give unto them three barrels of corn, a hilling hoe and a weeding hoe and a felling axe, and to a man

servant one new cloth suit, one new shirt, one pair of new shoes, one pair of new stockings and a new monmouth cap, and to a maid servant one new petticoat and waistcoat, one new smock, one pair of new shoes, one pair of new stockings and the clothes formerly belonging to the servant . . .

2. Virginia, 1642/43

Va. Statutes at Large, I, 257.

Whereas divers controversies have risen between masters and servants being brought into the colony without indentures or covenants to testify their agreements, whereby both masters and servants have been often prejudiced, *Be it therefore enacted and confirmed* for prevention of future controversies of the like nature, that such servants as shall be imported having no indentures or covenants, either men or women, if they be above twenty year old to serve four year, if they shall be above twelve and under twenty to serve five years, and if under twelve to serve seven years.

3. Virginia, 1657/58

Va. Statutes at Large, I, 441–442.

. . . Such persons as shall be imported, having no indenture or covenant, either men or women, if they be above sixteen years old shall serve four years, if under fifteen to serve till he or she shall be one and twenty years of age, and the courts to be judges of their ages.

---

1. As amended in 1654 and again in 1661, the law required children under fifteen to serve their masters only until twenty-one years of age. *Md. Archives,* I, 352–353, 409.

4. Virginia, 1662

Va. Statutes at Large, II, 169.

. . . Every master buying or bringing in a servant without indenture shall be enjoined to carry him to the court within four months after he hath brought him, when they may have judgment of his age, or else that the servant shall serve no longer than those of sixteen years of age by custom of the country.[1]

5. North Carolina, 1715

No. Car. Records, XXIII, 62–66.

. . . All Christian servants imported or to be imported into this government above sixteen years of age without indentures shall serve five years. And all under the age of sixteen years at the time of their importation shall serve till they be two and twenty years of age. And the age of such servant or servants to be adjudged by the precinct court where the master or mistress of such servant resides. Provided the master or mistress of such servant to carry him or her to the said court within six months after their importation. Otherwise such servant or servants shall serve no longer than those of sixteen years are above appointed to serve by virtue of this act.

Courts adjudge age and determine term of service of child servants

1. Pennsylvania, ca. 1700

Chester County Court Records, in John S.

1. That is, no longer than four years.

Futhey and Gilbert Cope, *History of Chester County, Pennsylvania* (Philadelphia, 1881), pp. 430–431.

Francis Chadsey brought a boy whose name was Alexander Steward, who was adjudged to serve eight years from the 14th of September last past, to be taught to read and write, or else to serve but seven years; also, he had a servant maid whose name is Ann Bearn, who was adjudged to serve five years from this Court, to said Francis Chadsey or his assigns.

William Cope brought a boy whose name is Thomas Harper, who was adjudged to serve five years and three quarters, if he be taught to read and write, or else to serve but five years, to him or his assigns.

Elizabeth Withers brought a servant girl whose name is Margaret Mongey, who was adjudged to be eleven years of age, and to serve ten years to Thomas Withers or his assigns.

Henry Nayl brought a servant boy to the Court whose name is Alexander Stewart, whose time the said Nayl had bought of Francis Chadsey, and the said boy consents and agrees to serve the said Henry Nayl one year and a quarter above his time by record, if the said Henry Nayl teach him the trade of shoemaker; if not, the said Nayl to allow the said boy satisfaction for the overplus time as the Court shall allow.

Elinor Clayton, an orphan of the age of fourteen years, was ordered by the Court to serve Daniel Hoopes for the term of seven years, on condition that he should teach her to read, knit and sew, and pay £12 according to the order of the Court.

2. A Scotch boy, brought to New Jersey and sold there without indenture, has his term of service established in court, 1697

The Burlington Court Book, p. 197.

. . . John Scott of Wellingborough in the county of Burlington exhibited to the court a Scotch boy named George Douglass which he, the said Scott, bought of James Trent as by a certain bill of sale given by the said Trent to him the said Scott dated the twenty first day of July last past [1697] may more fully appear. And the said Scott, having no indenture with his said boy, he requests of the court to assertain and fix a certain term of years for the said George Douglass serving him, the said Scott, according as the law in that case directs; which said boy is ordered by the bench to serve nine years from this ninth day of August 1697 to him the said John Scott his heirs, executors, administrators, or assigns.

Children bound out by parents or guardians

---

1. Children bound out without consent of father, New Haven, 1651

Ancient Town Records, I, 89–90.

William Bunill declareth that while he was gone for England, his wife and her father put forth his son to Nicholas Elsy and his daughter to Samuel Whithead, to apprentice without his consent, which when he came he disallowed of [and] only was willing they should keep them a while, but now desires that he may have them again for his help.

Nicholas Elsy said that the grandfather of the boy came to him and desired him to take him, and he did. Goodman Willmot, the grandfather of the boy, was asked the ground thereof. He said his son Bunill was in the Bay and was a charge to the country there; after [he] went to England, [he] left his wife and children but no means to maintain them. After he was gone, she and her children came up hither to him, but he was not able to keep them; therefore they did advise together and agreed to put forth the children, and did put the boy to Nicholas Elsy.

Samuel Whithead said for the girl he sought her not; but Goodwife Bunill came to his house, declared her condition which was to be pitied, having divers small children and no means to maintain them, and desired him to take her daughter, which they did upon the terms they agreed. Goodwife Bunill was asked what direction her husband left for providing for the children; she said he left little or nothing to maintain them and she asked him what she should do with them. He said they were hers as well as his and he left them with her. And the boy saith he remembers his father did say so to his mother.

William Pecke said that his wife heard Goodman Bunill say after he came here from England that he was well satisfied with the children where they were; and Luke Atkinson said he heard Goodman Bunill say he was well satisfied in the placing of the children. Goodman Bunill said he meant for the present, a year or two or so. Goodman Bunill was told he must not think that they will take children small and keep them till now and let him have them again, but he must allow what is just for keeping them, which he is not able to do; and the case was such it seems that if they had not placed them, the magistrate must have taken care to dispose of them. Wherefore, all things considered, the court cannot but confirm the placing of them; but if they find the time too long, they will consider that some of it be abated, or something allowed to them.

---

2. Brother and sister bound to different masters, Maryland, 1661

Md. Archives, LIII, 183–184.

Anne Guest, the relict of Walter Guest deceased, doth here in open court bind over unto Mr. Thomas Baker, his heirs, executors, administrators but not assigns, Mary Guest her [step]daughter to serve the said Baker as aforesaid, from the day of the date hereof until the 28th day of January, 1667, in all such services and employments as he, the said Baker, his heirs, executors, administrators shall employ her in, and the said Mary being demanded in open court whether she was thereunto condescending, who very freely replied that she was therewith very well contented.

Whereupon it was ordered that the said Mary Guest should serve the said Baker, his heirs, executor, administrators but not assigns, the full and just term of six years from the day of the date hereof in all such services and employments as he or they shall employ her in, he and they, during the term of the said time, finding and allowing her sufficient meat, drink and good lodging fitting for a servant in that kind. Anne, the relict of Walter Guest, doth hereby in open court bind over unto Mr. Henry Adams, his heirs, executors, administrators, but not assigns one Lewis Guest her son, being about three years old, from the day of the date hereof the full and just term of eighteen years, to serve him or them in all such services and employments as he or they shall employ him in during the said term of time.

And for the confirmation of the said assignment, it is ordered that the said Lewis Guest shall serve the said Mr. Adams, his heirs, executors, administrators but not assigns, from the day of the date hereof the full and just term of time of eighteen years in all such services and employments that he or they shall employ him in, he and they during the said term finding and allowing the said Lewis Guest sufficient meat, drink, washing and lodging fitting for a servant.

3. Beginning and end of an indenture, 1671–1685

Charles Thornton Libby, ed., *Province and Court Records of Maine,* II (Portland, 1931), 431–432.

15 May, 1671.

It is mutually agreed between Joanna Crawley, wife unto Thomas Crawley on the one party, and Alexander Maxwell of York on the other party, that the said Joanna, with her free consent upon good considerations doth dispose of her daughter's . . . child named Samuel, a boy of about three years old, into the custody of Alexander Maxwell for the full term of eighteen years from the date hereof, who is to provide for him meat, drink, apparel, washing and lodging during the said time of his service fit and convenient for a servant; and the said Alexander Maxwell is to use his best endeavors to teach the said child to write and read before his time be expired and to give him a cow seven years hence to be disposed of to some of his friends for the boy's best advantage, and twenty acres of land at the end of his time. And in case that Alexander Maxwell should die before the boy's time of eighteen years be run out, that then he shall serve the remainder of his time with his Dame Annas Maxwell.

20 November, 1685.

Whereas Samuel Crawley, who by consent of his grandmother Joanna Crawley was bound, as by records appears, to his master and Dame Alexander Maxwell . . . for the term of eighteen years from the 15th of May 1671; and having served in May next fifteen years of his time, wherein, until the 20th of this instant November he did remain unchargeable of any notorious transgression, at what time he . . . [was] convicted for felony, sentenced, and branded according to law, and afterwards returned into the constable's hands by order of the court to tender said Crawley to his master to serve out his full time with him, which the constable doth assert he did, but master refused to accept of him and gave his man Crawley freely his time, in confirmation whereof he returned him unto the custody of William Worm-wood the constable with his indenture.

---

4. Spinster binds out four year old son as "apprentice and servant," 1723

"Indentures of Apprentices, 1718–1727," in *Collections* of the New York Historical Society for the Year 1909, XLII (1910), 155–156.

Indenture of Margaret Perry, spinster and mother of John Hames her natural son by one John Hames, late of the same city of New York, mariner, deceased . . . by these presents doth put her said son John Hames, aged four years, an apprentice and servant unto John Vanloo, Gent., with him to live and after the manner of an apprentice and servant to serve him the said John Vanloo in any place or places whatsoever he the said John Vanloo shall think fit to reside or inhabit from the twelfth day of July, 1721, till the said child shall arrive at the age of eighteen years . . . During all which term the said mother doth promise, covenant, and agree to and with the said John Vanloo and his assigns that he the said John Hames shall dwell with and faithfully serve the said John Vanloo or his assigns.

.   .   .   .   .

That he shall at the age of ten years, if he so long live, by an indenture under his own hand and seal bind himself to his said master for and during all the residue of the said time which shall be then unexpired, if his said master or his assigns shall so require. And the said master during the said term shall by the best means or methods that he can teach or cause the said servant to be taught the art which he now useth, and shall find and provide unto the said apprentice or servant sufficient meat, drink, apparel, lodging and washing fitting for such an apprentice and servant, and shall also teach or

cause the said servant to be taught to read and to write. For the true performance of all and every these covenants and agreements the said Margaret Perry and the said John Vanloo do bind themselves either of them to the other of them firmly by these presents in the penal sum of one hundred pounds current money of the province of New York.

Indenture by other means

---

1. Indenture of Hans Peter Kaul, age 16, to Thomas Lawrence, September 26, 1752

Box 9C, Collections, Historical Society of Pennsylvania, Philadelphia, Pa.

THIS INDENTURE witnesseth that Hans Peter Kaul [?], in consideration of £14 Paid for him to Alex Ray by Thos. Lawrence, Esq. as also for other good causes; he, the said Hans Peter Kaul hath bound and put himself and by these Presents doth bind and put himself Servant to the said Thos. Lawrence Esq.; to serve him or his Executors and Assigns, from the Day of the Date hereof, for and during the full Term of Five Years thence next ensuing. During all which Term, the said Servant his said Master or his Executors or Assigns, faithfully shall serve, and that honestly and obediently in all Things as a good and dutiful Servant ought to do. AND the said Master or his Executors and Assigns, during the said Term, shall find and provide for the said Servant sufficient Meat, Drink, Apparell, Washing and Lodging.

And at Expiration shall give him the usual freedom dues AND for the true performance hereof, both the said Parties bind themselves firmly unto each other by these Presents. *In Witness* whereof, they have hereunto interchangeably set their Hands and Seals. Dated this Eighteenth Day of September, in the 26th Year of His Majesty's Reign, Annoque Domini 1752.

2. Order form for one Negro lad and one hundred bushels of salt, May 11, 1769

Mary Harvey to Thomas Clifford, May 11, 1769, Clifford-Pemberton Papers, V, 113, Pennsylvania Historical Society.

Wilmington, May 11th, 1769

Friend Clifford

I have Recd. thy Letter This Day Which Informs me thy Vessel is arrived With Salt & Servants. Would Request the favour of thee to Send me down the Boy Thou Mentioned if he is Not Disposed of already and Likewise one hundred Bushels of Salt By one of our Boats as they are Both Up   From thy   Friend Mary Harvey.

3. Indenture of the manumitted Negress Kitty, May 18, 1804

Gratz-Crogham Etting Papers, II, 93, Pennsylvania Historical Society.

THIS INDENTURE WITNESSETH, That Negress Kitty, aged about four years, whom Reuben Etting, on the eighteenth day of May, Eighteen hundred and four, in the City of Baltimore, in the State of Maryland manumitted from slavery, In compliance with the terms and conditions of the said manumission hath put herself, and by these Presents, with the advise and consent of her friend Thos. Harmion, a member of the Abolition Society, doth voluntarily, and of her own free will and accord, put herself Apprentice to the said Reuben Etting of the City of Philadelphia to learn the Art, Trade, and Mystery of a Cook and house-waiter and after the manner of an Apprentice to serve the said Reuben Etting, his Executors and assigned administrators from the day of the date hereof, for and during, and to the full end and term of twenty-three years . . .

C. PROTECTION OF CHILDREN AGAINST ABUSE BY MASTERS

Masters tried for manslaughter or murder of apprentices or servants

1. A doubtful case, Salem, 1639

John Winthrop, *The History of New England from 1630 to 1649,* ed. J. Savage (Boston, 1853), I, 318–319.

At the court of assistants, one Marmaduke Perry, of Salem, was arraigned for the death of one [*blank*] his apprentice. The great inquest found the bill for murder; the jury of life and death could not agree; so they were adjourned to the next court, and Perry was let to bail by the governor and some other of the magistrates after the court. At the court in December, the prisoner appeared, and the jury, being called, had further evidence given them, which tended to the clearing of Perry; yet two of the jury dissented from the rest, who were all agreed to acquit him. In the end it had this issue, that these two were silent, and so the verdict was received. The cause was this: The boy was ill disposed, and his master gave him unreasonable correction, and used him ill in his diet. After, the boy got a bruise on his head, so as there appeared a fracture in his skull, being dissected after his death. Now, two things were in the evidence, which made the case doubtful; one, the boy was charging his master, before his death, to have given him that wound with his meatyard and with a broomstaff (for he spoke of both at several times;) the other was, that he had told another, that his hurt came with the fall of a bough from a tree; and other evidence there was none.

2. Master reportedly executed for murder of servant, Boston, 1643

"Rev. John Eliot's Records of the First Church in Roxbury, Massachusetts," in *Sixth Report* of Boston Record Commissioners (Boston, 1881), p. 187.

There happened (by God's providence) a dreadful example of God's judgement this year upon one William Frankling who belonged to Boston town . . . But he spent his sabbath at our town, being nearer, and after a season desired to join to our church and had approbation so to do, and was received.

But Satan presently did enter into him and having a boy whom he had bought for some years time, and proving sick and naughty, after he was joined to the church he grew more passionate, cruel, and fierce against him, though he had been sharp before, yet unknown or undisposed to us. But now he grew outrageous, so that by sundry cruel stripes and other kinds of ill usage, the boy died under his rigorous hand, and that (by a strange providence of God and his own folly) at Boston, as if God meant to bring him on the stage for an example to all others. For which sin that day [and] month that he was admitted, he was excommunicated,

and though much pains were taken to have brought him to repentance and reconciliation to the church, yet all in vain; he protesting partly to deny and partly to mince his cruel actions towards the boy. So that in that estate he was executed at Boston as public records will show.

3. A battered child, Plymouth, 1655

Nathaniel B. Shurtleff, ed., *Records of Plymouth Colony, Court Orders,* III (Boston, 1855), 71–72.

John Walker was about twelve years of age; Latham, the master, was subsequently found guilty of manslaughter and ordered "burned in the hand" and "all his goods confiscate."

We, whose names are underwritten, being appointed a jury by Master John Alden to view the dead body of John Walker, servant to Robert Latham, of this town, and to find the cause how he came to his untimely end:

We, upon due search and examination, do find that the body of John Walker was blackish and blue, and the skin broken in divers places from the middle to the hair of his head, viz., all his back with stripes given him by his master, Robert Latham, as Robert himself did testify; and also we found a bruise of his left arm, and one of his left hip, and one great bruise of his breast; and there was the knuckles of one hand and one of his fingers frozen, and also both his heels frozen, and one of the heels the flesh was much broken, and also one of his little toes frozen and very much perished, and one of his great toes frozen, and also the side of his foot frozen; and also, upon the reviewing the body, we found three gaules like holes in the hams, which we formerly, the body being frozen, thought they had been holes; and also we find that the said John was forced to carry a log which was beyond his strength, which he endeavoring to do, the log fell upon him, and he, being down, had a stripe or two, as Joseph Beedle doth testify; and we find that it was some few days before his death; and we find, by the testimony of John Howland and John Adams, that heard Robert Latham say that he gave John Walker some stripes that morning before his death; and also we find the flesh much broken of the knees of John Walker, and that he did want sufficient food and clothing and lodging, and that the said John did constantly wet his bed and his clothes, lying in them, and so suffered by it, his clothes being frozen about him; and that the said John was put forth in the extremity of cold, though thus unabled by lameness and soreness to perform what was required; and therefore in respect of cruelty and hard usage he died; and also, upon the second review, the dead corpse did bleed at the nose.

[*Signatures of twelve men*]

Masters admonished for immoderate punishment of apprentices and servants

1. Salem, Massachusetts, ca. 1680–1685

Records of Essex County, VIII (1921), 302–303.

Phillip Fowler was presented for abusing his servant, Richard Parker, and although court justified any person in giving meet correction to his servant, which the boy deserved, yet they did not approve of the manner of punishment given in hanging him up by the heels as butchers do beasts for the slaughter, and cautioned said

Fowler against such kind of punishment. He was ordered to pay costs.

2. New York City, 1683

R. B. Morris, ed., *Select Cases of the Mayor's Court of New York City, 1674–1784* (Washington, 1935), p. 182.

The plaintiff declared against the defendant for detaining his apprentice and servant from him to his damage nineteen pounds, nineteen shillings. The defendant pleaded that the apprentice was his son and that by reason of the plaintiff's ill usage towards him by unreasonable correction he was forced to leave his service and come to his father where he now is. After full hearing of both parties the Court ordered that the said apprentice do return to his master and serve his time according to indenture, and if the plaintiff for the future shall misuse him by undue or unreasonable correction on proof made thereof, he shall be freed from his service. The plaintiff to pay the costs.

Apprentices and servants freed or transferred because of abuse by masters

1. Massachusetts, 1640

Mass. Records, I, 311.

Samuel Hefford, having been much misused by his master Jonathan Wade, he is freed from the said master Wade and is put to John Johnson for three years, and to have 6£

wages paid, and for the other 1½ years, it is referred to the Court.

---

2. Maryland, 1660

Md. Archives, LIII, 410–411.

Master Arthur Turner, being summoned to give a reason why the orphan John Ward hath been so ill treated in his house, insomuch that the voice of the people crieth shame thereat, and also to bring the said Ward and his indenture to the court with him, all which accordingly here were produced . . .

The said Ward, with a most rotten filthy, stinking, ulcerated leg that even loathed all the beholders thereof, his apparel being all ragged and torn and his hair seemed to be rotted off with ashes, whose indenture is as followeth:

This indenture, made the twentieth day of April in the year of our Lord God 1652 between Arthur Turner of the one party and John Ward on the other party, witnesseth that the said John Ward doth hereby covenant and grant to and with the said Arthur Turner, his executors and assigns, from the day of the date hereof for and during the term of time until I, the said John, be at the age of twenty years, to serve in such service and employment as the said Arthur Turner shall [me] employ; in consideration whereof the said Arthur Turner doth covenant and grant to and with the said Ward to find and allow his meat, drink, and apparel, and lodging, with other necessaries during the said term, and at the end of the said term to pay unto him double apparel, three barrels of corn, a cow, and a sow, with fifty acres of land, and if in case the said Arthur cannot bring the said John to reading in the time of his service, then the said Arthur doth covenant and bind himself to teach the said John the trade of a cooper or a carpenter . . .

John Nevill sworn and examined in open court sayeth that he knew John Ward ever since he came into the country, which is seventeen years ago, and that he was then to his judgment about four or five years old, and further sayeth not.

Mr. William Marshall declares upon oath, that to the best of his judgment, John Ward was about nine or ten years old when he came to master Turner.

It is therefore ordered that the said Ward should be free from the said Turner.

---

3. Salem, Massachusetts, 1674

Records of Essex County, V (1916), 417–419.

In this case the father of an abused apprentice sought reimbursement from the master for the cost of caring for and treating the boy. Verdict was rendered for the plaintiff.

Writ: Hugh March, Sr., of Newbury *v.* Benjamin Lowle of Newbury for not keeping his servant Hugh March, Jr., and for not providing for him sufficiently in time of his sickness, also for not teaching him his art or trade according to indenture . . .

Indenture, dated September 29, 1674, Hugh March, son of Hugh March of Newbury, of his own will and with the consent of his parents was apprenticed to Benjamin Lowle of Newbury, blacksmith, for six years, to learn the trade of a blacksmith, and said Lowle was to perfect him in writing and casting accounts, in reading English and in the trade of making or mending locks . . .

Daniel Ela deposed that he saw the young lad Hugh March at said March's house in Newbury when Mr. John Dole was called to treat him and they did not expect him to live through the night. He was lame in his knee for fifteen months and his thigh was very painful night and day, the flesh and bones being very sore. Deponent saw him often and was called to dress the leg, and Hugh had gotten so much cold and numbness, together with his melancholy, that all the means they used did no good for a long time . . .

Jonathan March deposed that when his brother was sick at Lowle's house, "I was riding along in the street, and about the midway between my father's house and the house of Benjamin Lowle I met with Benjamin Lowle. He asked me whither I was going with a pillion beside me. I said, to his house for to fetch my brother, if you will let me have him. He made me this answer, 'that's very well,' and no more that I do remember. Then I went to the house and asked his dame whether she would let me have my brother to carry him home and she said yes. She went to him and fitted on his clothes and helped him down the stairs, and she and her mother helped him upon the horse and wrapped the clothes about him and I brought him home . . . I did lay with him two nights at his master Lowle's house when he was sick, and . . . the thing he lay on was a cotton wool bag, or such like thing, filled with chaff and straw and upon it was a piece of old curtain, and his covering was an old cotton rug and a sheet which was all the bedclothes he had, in the coldest winter night that came . . ."

Judith March deposed that she went to Lowle's to see her son Hugh, and told said Lowle that she was busy and could not attend to him and that he must have a doctor for him. When the doctor came he said the place was not fit for a sick person to be in on account of the coldness of the room. "His dame urged me to take him home. I was not willing and gave her reason for it, as that we were building of our house and had many workmen to lodge, besides the occasions of the ordinary. And her answer was to me: she could not attend him to go up and down the stairs; therefore, urged me very hard to take him, and said he would be better contented with me for he did nothing but lie and cry yesterday almost all day long.

So he was fetched from thence and remains with us to this day . . ."

Elizabeth Broune, formerly a servant to Hugh March and of Jonathan March his son, testified that the continual hearing of his doleful crying out night and day for a long time was a great distraction to the family, and his attendance was extraordinary. And for a long time . . . his parents, the Doctor, and we did think that he would not have lived until the morning. And helping sometimes to carry him from the bed to the fire and sometimes lifting him to and fro and leading him, it was for a long time most of the whole family's work to attend him . . . Hugh March, Junior, came in to his father's house one bitter cold night in the winter foregoing and was asked from whence he came. He said from Rowley, and coming to the fire, in a little time, cried out and was not able to stand still. His mother seeing what kind of breeches he had on (which was two stiff leather things like boards about him) she put her hand to see whether he had any drawers on and there was nothing but a rag . . .

And the inside of the thigh . . . so rough, not like flesh, but like some rough board.

---

4. New York City, 1726

Cases of The Mayor's Court of New York City, p. 185.

Upon hearing the Complaint of William Lewis an Apprentice to John Schutz of this City, Barber and Wigmaker, against his Master for Immoderately Correcting him without any Just Cause, and upon hearing the said John Schutz in his Defence, and it Visibly Appearing to this Court that the Said John Schutz hath Immoderately Corrected the said Apprentice: It is the Opinion of the Court that the Said William Lewis be discharged from his Said Apprenticeship.

Protection of servants against mistreatment,
Virginia, ca. 1700

Beverley, *Virginia,* pp. 271–274.

Because I have heard how strangely cruel
and severe the service of this country is represented in some parts of England, I can't fore-
bear affirming that the work of their servants
and slaves is no other than what every common
freeman does. Neither is any servant required
to do more in a day than his overseer. And I
can assure you with a great deal of truth that
generally their slaves are not worked near[ly]
so hard, nor so many hours in a day, as the
husbandmen and day laborers in England. An
overseer is a man, that having served his time,
has acquired the skill and character of an experienced planter, and is therefore entrusted
with the direction of the servants and slaves.

But to complete this account of servants, I
shall give you a short relation of the care their
laws take that they be used as tenderly as possible.

By the laws of their country.

1. All servants whatsoever have their complaints heard without fee or reward, but if the
master be found faulty, the charge of the complaint is cast upon him, otherwise the business
is done *ex officio.*

2. Any justice of peace may receive the
complaint of a servant, and order everything
relating thereto till the next county court, where
it will be finally determined.

3. All masters are under the correction and
censure of the county courts to provide for
their servants good and wholesome diet, clothing, and lodging.

4. They are always to appear, upon the first
notice given of the complaint of their servants,
otherwise to forfeit the service of them until
they do appear.

5. All servants' complaints are to be received at any time in court without process,
and shall not be delayed for want of form, but

the merits of the complaint must be immediately inquired into by the justices; and if the
master cause any delay therein, the court may
remove such servants, if they see cause, until
the master will come to trial.

6. If a master shall at any time disobey an
order of court, made upon any complaint of a
servant, the court is empowered to remove such
servant forthwith to another master who will be
kinder, giving to the former master the produce
only (after fees deducted), of what such servants shall be sold for by public outcry.

7. If a master should be so cruel as to use
his servant ill that is fallen sick or lame in his
service, and thereby rendered unfit for labor,
he must be removed by the church wardens out
of the way of such cruelty, and boarded in
some good planter's house till the time of his
freedom, the charge of which must be laid be-
for the next county court, which has power
to levy the same from time to time, upon the
goods and chattels of the master. After which,
the charge of such boarding is to come upon
the parish in general.

8. All hired servants are entitled to these
privileges.

9. No master of a servant can make a new
bargain for service or other matter with his
servant, without the privity and consent of a
justice of peace, to prevent the master's over-
reaching or scaring such servant into an unreasonable compliance.

10. The property of all money and goods
sent over thither to servants, or carried in with
them, is reserved to themselves and remain[s]
entirely at their disposal.

11. Each servant at his freedom receives of
his master fifteen bushels of corn (which is
sufficient for a whole year), and two new suits
of clothes, both linen and woolen; and then
becomes as free in all respects and as much
entitled to the liberties and privileges of the
country, as any other of the inhabitants or natives are.

12. Each servant has then also a right to
take up fifty acres of land, where he can find
any unpatented. But that is no great privilege,

for anyone may have as good a right for piece of eight.

This is what the laws prescribe in favor of servants, by which you may find that the cruelties and severities imputed to that country are an unjust reflection. For no people more abhor the thoughts of such usage than the Virginians, nor take more precaution to prevent it.

Part Two   Children and Youth in the Age of Voluntarism and Self-Help, 1735–1820

I Children in the Enlightenment and the Revolution

During the first half of the eighteenth century the people of the American colonies steadily increased in numbers and prosperity. On the seaboard, peaceful towns and secure farms replaced wilderness outposts. At the same time a secular outlook advanced at the expense of traditional religion. Although the religious establishment in the colonies remained outwardly intact, religious emotions and loyalties were eroded by a more materialistic view of life. John Locke (1632–1704), the English philosopher, exemplified this new common-sense rationalism. Natural rights, the social contract, and environmentalism — his political, social, and psychological doctrines — seemed to be confirmed by the leading characteristics of American experience. Little wonder that his writings were welcomed by Americans who derived private rights from nature, could recall the moment when their society was created, and recognized among themselves the emergence of a distinct character in this new environment. Locke's American counterpart was Benjamin Franklin (1706–1790), who shared with the Englishman this secular and utilitarian point of view. Observation and practical reason were the means of formulating rules of behavior which then had to pass the test of actual life. Providentially, morality by and large coincided with the rules for the pursuit of worldly success and esteem. In the universe of Locke and Franklin, governed by a benevolent if remote deity, the harmony between the moral law for individuals and the means of social progress inspired a fervent belief in the future. In pursuing his own good every man joined in the great procession of American advance. Franklin's many plans for uniting private and public improvement were characteristic expressions of the age.

Belief in progress and individualism was reinforced by the Great Awakening, the first sustained religious revival in America. Seemingly an attempt to return to a simpler world of biblical certainties, the Great Awakening did not in fact look to the past. Its revivalists preached an evangelistic Calvinism in which the individual initiated a search for salvation. Jonathan Edwards (1703–1758) and George Whitefield (1714–1770) fixed the attention of their listeners upon the future. Men, women, and even children would earn an eternal habitation in hell or heaven through their own decisions and actions.

Revivalistic Calvinism created new forms of participation by children in religious life. As much as adults, they were capable of the faith and feeling which composed religious experience as revivalists understood and preached it. The intricate structure of abstruse theological doctrines erected by the Puritan divines was subordinate or even irrelevant to the teachings of the heart. Although a powerful thinker like Jonathan Edwards subjected religious ideas to a rigorous exposition, the beliefs he explicated were compatible with experiential religion. Furthermore, while the denominational divisions that resulted from the Great Awakening assisted in the establishment of several new colleges in the middle years of the eighteenth century, and thereby enlarged opportunities for higher education, these colleges were in the main untroubled by any sense of incompatibility between their intellectual objectives and the religion of feeling.

Puritan parents had expected their children passively to accept the religious truth that was supplied to them, but in the Great Awakening children became active seekers of redemption. Awareness of sin and the need for salvation — the most important of life's lessons — came characteristically during youth, often with a devastating suddenness. A few gifted souls might apprehend the truth during childhood. Their example was used to show others, including their elders, how to proceed in the pursuit of righteousness. Since this movement challenged the supremacy of adult males in the crucially important matter of perceiving fundamental truth, it provoked a spirited counterattack from the guardians of tradition. Revivals, asserted the orthodox, were divisive, prone to excess and disorder. Evangelicalism set child against parent, wife against husband, and the lower orders against their betters, and threatened the established institutions of church, state, and society. These fears were not unfounded: the Great Awakening prefigured both a recurring pattern of religious and social unrest and the prominent part henceforth to be taken by young people in the discovery and dramatization of moral and social truths.

The American Revolution and the attainment of independence, like the Great Awakening, tended to enhance the status of the young. Debates over public policy and the tactics of protest raged in colonial schools and colleges; when the fighting commenced they contributed many of their students to service in the army. Some of the leading figures in the struggle for independence were remarkable for their relative youthfulness. Thomas Jefferson was only thirty-three when he wrote the Declaration of Independence in 1776, his fellow Virginian James Madison was twenty-five, and Alexander Hamilton, soon to be a member of Washington's staff, was a youngster of twenty-one. The American Revolution enlisted youth's sympathy and loyalty and in turn offered them new opportunities in an independent nation.

Most important, perhaps, was the impetus the secular version of the idea of progress received from the movement for independence. The successful defiance of the most powerful imperial nation of Europe, followed by the creation of a large and independent national republic, confirmed the view that a remarkable experiment in human improvement was occurring in the New World. The doctrine of material and moral progress directed attention to the young. Future generations were bound to be better than those of the past and present. If the new generation fell short of expectations, as often seemed to be the case, then the fault most likely lay with parents. The formulation of a national creed around the belief in progress accentuated generational distinctiveness and tended to give the young the benefit of the doubt in a conflict of moral values with their elders. Children and youth, further along the road to perfection, enjoyed a natural superiority over those who had already reached maturity.

Family authority and self-discipline

1. John Locke's advice on family government, 1690

John Locke, "Some Thoughts Concerning Education," in *The Works of John Locke,* IX (London, 1823), sections 40–46.

Locke, colonial America's favorite philosopher, although unmarried and childless himself, offered characteristic advice on authority in the family. "Some Thoughts Concerning Education" was written in 1690, but the ideas contained in it express the eighteenth-century faith in reason and common sense as guides to the good life.

Those . . . that intend ever to govern their children, should begin it whilst they are very little; and look that they perfectly comply with the will of their parents. Would you have your son obedient to you, when past a child? Be sure then to establish the authority of a father, as soon as he is capable of submission, and can understand in whose power he is. If you would have him stand in awe of you, imprint it in his infancy; and, as he approaches more to a man, admit him nearer to your familiarity: so shall you have him your obedient subject (as is fit) whilst he is a child, and your affectionate friend when he is a man. For methinks they mightily misplace the treatment due to their children, who are indulgent and familiar when they are little, but severe to them, and keep them at a distance, when they are grown up. For liberty and indulgence can do no good to children: their want of judgment makes them stand in need of restraint and discipline. And, on the contrary, imperiousness and severity is but an ill way of treating men, who have reason of their own to guide them, unless you have a mind to make your children, when grown up, weary of you; and secretly to say within themselves, "When will you die, father?"

I imagine every one will judge it reasonable, that their children, when little, should look upon their parents as their lords, their absolute governors; and, as such, stand in awe of them: and that, when they come to riper years, they should look on them as their best, as their only sure friends: and, as such, love and reverence them. The way I have mentioned, if I mistake not, is the only one to obtain this. We must look upon our children, when grown up, to be like ourselves; with the same passions, the same desires. We would be thought rational creatures, and have our freedom; we love not to be uneasy under constant rebukes and brow-beatings; nor can we bear severe humours, and great distance, in those we converse with. Whoever has such treatment when he is a man, will look out other company, other friends, other conversation, with whom he can be at ease. If therefore

a strict hand be kept over children from the beginning, they will in that age be tractable, and quietly submit to it, as never having known any other: and if, as they grow up to the use of reason, the rigour of government be, as they deserve it, gently relaxed, the father's brow more smoothed to them, and the distance by degrees abated: his former restraints will increase their love, when they find it was only a kindness for them, and a care to make them capable to deserve the favour of their parents, and the esteem of every body else.

Thus much for the settling your authority over children in general. Fear and awe ought to give you the first power over their minds, and love and friendship in riper years to hold it: for the time must come, when they will be past the rod and correction; and then, if the love of you make them not obedient and dutiful; if the love of virtue and reputation keep them not in laudable courses; I ask, what hold will you have upon them, to turn them to it? Indeed, fear of having a scanty portion, if they displease you, may make them slaves to your estate; but they will be nevertheless ill and wicked in private, and that restraint will not last always. Every man must some time or other be trusted to himself, and his own conduct; and he that is a good, a virtuous, and able man, must be made so within. And therefore, what he is to receive from education, what is to sway and influence his life, must be something put into him betimes: habits woven into the very principles of his nature; and not a counterfeit carriage, and dissembled outside, put on by fear, only to avoid the present anger of a father, who perhaps may disinherit him.

This being laid down in general, as the course ought to be taken, it is fit we come now to consider the parts of the discipline to be used, a little more particularly. I have spoken so much of carrying a strict hand over children, that perhaps I shall be suspected of not considering enough what is due to their tender age and constitutions. But that opinion will vanish, when you have heard me a little farther. For

I am very apt to think, that great severity of punishment does but very little good; nay, great harm in education: and I believe it will be found, that, those children who have been most chastised, seldom make the best men. All that I have hitherto contended for, is, that whatsoever rigour is necessary, it is more to be used, the younger children are; and, having by a due application wrought its effect, it is to be relaxed, and changed into a milder sort of government.

A compliance, and suppleness of their wills, being by a steady hand introduced by parents, before children have memories to retain the beginnings of it, will seem natural to them, and work afterwards in them, as if it were so; preventing all occasions of struggling, or repining. The only care is, that it be begun early, and inflexibly kept to, till awe and respect be grown familiar, and there appears not the least reluctancy in the submission and ready obedience of their minds. When this reverence is once thus established (which it must be early, or else it will cost pains and blows to recover it, and the more, the longer it is deferred) it is by it, mixed still with as much indulgence as they made not an ill use of, and not by beating, chiding, or other servile punishments, they are for the future to be governed, as they grow up to more understanding.

That this is so, will be easily allowed, when it is best considered what is to be aimed at, in an ingenuous education; and upon what it turns.

1. He that has not a mastery over his inclinations, he that knows not how to resist the importunity of present pleasure or pain, for the sake of what reason tells him is fit to be done, wants the true principle of virtue and industry; and is in danger of never being good for any thing. This temper, therefore, so contrary to unguided nature, is to be got betimes; and this habit, as the true foundation of future ability and happiness, is to be wrought into the mind, as early as may be, even from the first dawnings of any knowledge or apprehension in children; and so to be confirmed in them, by all the care and ways imaginable, by those who have the oversight of their education.

2. On the other side, if the mind be curbed, and humbled too much in children; if their spirits be abased and broken much, by too strict an hand over them; they lose all their vigour and industry, and are in a worse state than the former. For extravagant young fellows, that have liveliness and spirit, come sometimes to be set right, and so make able and great men: but dejected minds, timorous and tame, and low spirits, are hardly ever to be raised, and very seldom attain to any thing. To avoid the danger that is on either hand is the great art: and he that has found a way how to keep up a child's spirit, easy, active, and free; and yet, at the same time, to restrain him from many things he has a mind to, and to draw him to things that are uneasy to him; he, I say, that knows how to reconcile these seeming contradictions, has, in my opinion, got the true secret of education.

---

2. Benjamin Franklin's first project for public improvement

Leonard W. Labaree et al., eds., *The Autobiography of Benjamin Franklin* (New Haven, 1964), pp. 53–54.

. . . Living near the Water, I was much in and about it, learnt early to swim well, and to manage Boats, and when in a Boat or Canoe with other Boys I was commonly allow'd to govern, especially in any case of Difficulty; and upon other Occasions I was generally a Leader among the Boys, and sometimes led them into Scrapes, of which I will mention one Instance, as it shows an early projecting public Spirit tho' not then justly conducted. There was a Salt Marsh that bounded part of the Mill Pond, on the Edge of which at Highwater, we us'd to stand to fish for Minews. By much Trampling, we had made it a mere Quagmire. My Proposal was to build a Wharf there fit for us to stand upon, and I show'd my Comrades a large Heap of Stones which were intended for a new House near the Marsh, and which would very well suit our Purpose. Accordingly in the Evening when the Workmen were gone, I assembled a Number of my Playfellows, and working with them diligently like so many [ants] sometimes two or three to a Stone, we brought them all away and built our little Wharff. The next Morning the Workmen were surpriz'd at Missing the Stones; which were found in our Wharff; Enquiry was made after the Removers; we were discovered and complain'd of; several of us were corrected by our Fathers; and tho' I pleaded the Usefulness of the Work, mine convinc'd me that nothing was useful which was not honest.

---

3. A young man's plan for moral perfection

The Autobiography of Benjamin Franklin, pp. 148–150.

It was about this time [ca. 1721] that I conceiv'd the bold and arduous Project of arriving at moral Perfection. I wish'd to live without committing any Fault at any time; I would conquer all that either Natural Inclination, Custom, or Company might lead me into. As I knew, or thought I knew, what was right and wrong, I did not see why I might not *always* do the one and avoid the other. But I soon found I had undertaken a Task of more difficulty than I had imagined. While my *Attention was taken up* in guarding against one Fault, I was often surpriz'd by another. Habit took the Advantage of Inattention. Inclination was sometimes too strong for Reason. I concluded at length, that the mere speculative Conviction that it was our Interest to be compleatly virtuous, was not sufficient to prevent our Slipping, and that the contrary Habits must be broken and good ones acquired and established, be-

fore we can have any Dependance on a steady uniform Rectitude of Conduct. For this purpose I therefore contriv'd the following Method.

In the various Enumerations of the moral Virtues I had met with in my Reading, I found the Catalogue more or less numerous, as different Writers included more or fewer Ideas under the same Name. Temperance, for Example, was by some confin'd to Eating and Drinking, while by others it was extended to mean the moderating every other Pleasure, Appetite, Inclination or Passion, bodily or mental, even to our Avarice and Ambition. I propos'd to myself, for the sake of Clearness, to use rather more Names with fewer Ideas annex'd to each, than a few Names with more Ideas; and I included under Thirteen Names of Virtues all that at that time occurr'd to me as necessary or desirable, and annex'd to each a short Precept, which fully express'd the Extent I gave to its Meaning.

These Names of Virtues with their Precepts were

1. TEMPERANCE.

Eat not to Dulness.
Drink not to Elevation.

2. SILENCE.

Speak not but what may benefit others or yourself. Avoid trifling Conversation.

3. ORDER.

Let all your Things have their Places. Let each Part of your Business have its Time.

4. RESOLUTION.

Resolve to perform what you ought. Perform without fail what you resolve.

5. FRUGALITY.

Make no Expence but to do good to others or yourself: i.e. Waste nothing.

6. INDUSTRY.

Lose no Time. Be always employ'd in something useful. Cut off all unnecessary Actions.

7. SINCERITY.

Use no hurtful Deceit.

Think innocently and justly; and, if you speak, speak accordingly.

8. JUSTICE.

Wrong none, by doing Injuries or omitting the Benefits that are your Duty.

9. MODERATION.

Avoid Extreams. Forbear resenting Injuries so much as you think they deserve.

10. CLEANLINESS.

Tolerate no Uncleanness in Body, Cloaths or Habitation.

11. TRANQUILITY.

Be not disturbed at Trifles, or at Accidents common or unavoidable.

12. CHASTITY.

Rarely use Venery but for Health or Offspring; Never to Dulness, Weakness, or the Injury of your own or another's Peace or Reputation.

13. HUMILITY.

Imitate Jesus and Socrates.

My Intention being to acquire the *Habitude* of all these Virtues, I judg'd it would be well not to distract my Attention by attempting the whole at once, but to fix it on one of them at a time, and when I should be Master of that, then to proceed to another, and so on till I should have gone thro' the thirteen . . .

Children in the Great Awakening

1. A religious prodigy, 1735

Jonathan Edwards, *A Narrative of Many Surprising Conversions in Northampton and Vincinity (1736) Together with some Thouhts on the Revival in New England (1740)* (Worcester, Mass., 1832), pp. 66–69.

I now proceed to the other instance that I would give an account of, which is of the little child forementioned. Her name is Phebe Bartlet, daughter of William Bartlet. I shall give the account as I took it from the mouths of her parents, whose veracity, none that know them doubt.

She was born in March, in the year 1731. About the latter end of April, or beginning of May, 1735, she was greatly affected by the talk of her brother, who had been hopefully converted a little before, at about eleven years of age, and then seriously talked to her about the great things of religion. Her parents did not know of it at that time, and were not wont, in the counsels they gave to their children, particularly to direct themselves to her, by reason of her being so young, and, as they supposed not capable of understanding; but after her brother had talked to her, they observed her very earnestly to listen to the advice they gave to the other children, and she was observed very constantly to retire, several times in a day, as was concluded, for secret prayer, and grew more and more engaged in religion, and was more frequent in her closet, till at last she was wont to visit it five or six times in a day, and was so engaged in it, that nothing would at any time divert her from her stated closet exercises. Her mother often observed and watched her, when such things occurred, as she thought most likely to divert her, either by putting it out of her thoughts, or otherwise engaging her inclinations, but never could observe her to fail. She mentioned some very remarkable instances.

She once, of her own accord, spake of her unsuccessfulness, in that she could not find God, or to that purpose. But on Thursday, the last day of July, about the middle of the day, the child being in the closet, where it used to retire, its mother heard it speaking aloud, which was unusual, and never had been observed before; and her voice seemed to be as of one exceeding importunate and engaged, but her mother could distinctly hear only these words (spoken in her childish manner, but seemed to be spoken with extraordinary earnestness, and out of distress of soul), Pray BLESSED LORD give me salvation! I PRAY, BEG pardon all my sins! When the child had done prayer, she came out of the closet, and came and sat down by her mother, and cried out aloud. Her mother very earnestly asked her several times, what the matter was, before she would make any answer, but she continued exceedingly crying, and wreathing her body to and fro, like one in anguish of spirit. Her mother then asked her whether she was afraid that God would not give her salvation. She then answered yes, I am afraid I shall go to hell! Her mother then endeavored to quiet her at all — but she continued thus earnestly crying and taking on for some time, till at length she suddenly ceased crying and began to smile, and presently said with a smiling countenance, Mother, the kingdom of heaven is come to me! Her mother was surprised at the sudden alteration, and at the speech, and knew not what to make of it, but at first said nothing to her. The child presently spake again, and said, there is another come to me, and there is another, there is three; and being asked what she meant, she answered, One is thy will be done; and there is another, enjoy him forever; by which it seems that when the child said there is three come to me, she meant three passages of its catechism that came to her mind.

After the child had said this, she retired again into her closet; and her mother went over to her brother's, who was next neighbor; and when she came back, the child being come out of the closet, meets her mother with this cheering speech; I can find God now! Referring to what she had before complained of, that she could not find God. Then the child spoke again, and said, I love God! Her mother asked her how well she loved God, whether she loved God better than her father and mother; she said, yes. Then she asked her whether she loved God

better than her little sister Rachel, she answered yes, better than any thing!

. . . . . .

The same day the elder children, when they came home from school, seemed such affected with the extraordinary change that seemed to be made in Phebe; and her sister Abigail standing by, her mother took occasion to counsel her, now to improve her time, to prepare for another world; on which Phebe burst out in tears, and cried out, poor Nabby! Her mother told her, she would not have her cry, she hoped that God would give Nabby salvation; but that did not quiet her, but she continued earnestly crying for some time; and when she had in a measure ceased, her sister Eunice being by her, she burst out again, and cried, poor Eunice! and cried exceedingly; and when she had almost done, she went into another room, and there looked upon her sister Naomi, and burst out again, crying poor Amy! Her mother was greatly affected at such behaviour in the child, and knew not what to say to her. One of the neighbors coming in a little after, asked her what she had cried for. She seemed, at first, backward to tell the reason. Her mother told her she might tell that person, for he had given her an apple; upon which she said, she cried because she was afraid they would go to hell.

---

2. Self-righteous children criticize their elders, 1743
Charles Chauncy, *Seasonable Thoughts on the State of Religion in New England* (Boston, 1743), pp. 168–170.

Reverend Charles Chauncy (1705–1787), minister of the First Church in Boston, complained of the divisive effects of the Great Awakening, particularly in spreading disrespect and insubordination among youth.

The Subjects . . . of these Terrors . . . are Children, Women, and youngerly Persons. Not that others han't been wrought upon. Instances there have been of Men; and these, both middle-aged, and advanced in Years, who have both cried out, and fallen down: But 'tis among Children, young People and Women, whose Passions are soft and tender, and more easily thrown into a Commotion, that these Things chiefly prevail. I know, 'tis thus in those Places, where I have had Opportunity to make Inquiry. And from the Accounts transmitted to me from Friends, in other Places, it appears to have been so among them also.

.   .   .   .   .

They often begin with a single Person, a Child, or Woman, or Lad, whose Shrieks set others a Shrieking; and so the Shrieks catch from one to another, 'till the whole Congregation is alarmed, and such an awful Scene, many Times, open'd, as no Imagination can paint to the Life. To this Purpose is that in the Boston-*Post-Boy,* when after an Account of the terrible Language made Use of by the Itinerants, 'tis added, "This frequently frights the little Children, and sets them a Screaming; and that frights their tender Mothers, and sets them to Screaming, and by Degrees spreads over a great Part of the Congregation: And 40, 50, or an 100, of them screaming all together, makes such an awful and hideous Noise as will make a Man's Hair stand on End. Some will faint away, fall down upon the Floor, wallow and foam. Some Women will rend off their Caps, Handkerchiefs, and other Clothes, tear their Hair down about their Ears, and seem perfectly bereft of their Reason."

.   .   .   .   .

I shall not exceed the literal Truth, when I say, that there never was a Time, since the Settlement of New England, wherein there was so much bitter and rash Judging; Parents con-demning their Children, and Children their Parents; Husbands their Wives, and Wives their Husbands; Masters their Servants, and Servants their Masters; Ministers their People, and People their Ministers. Censoriousness, to a high Degree, is indeed the constant Appendage of this religious Commotion.

Wherever it takes Place, the Subjects of it, too generally, are uncharitable to Neighbours, to Brethren of the same Community, to Relatives, to Ministers in an especial Manner; yea, to all the World that are not in their Way of thinking and speaking.

.   .   .   .   .

I shall, as an Illustration of this Censoriousness, insert here some Part of a Letter, wrote to me by a Friend, upon his own Knowledge. Says he, " 'Tis remarkable, those, who were said to be struck with Conviction, immediately seem'd to be fill'd with a censuring and judging Spirit against almost all others . . . declaring them to be in an unconverted State. — One Instance among many others, I shall mention. There was a young Woman about 15 Years of Age, who fell under this Conviction, and for about four Hours together she, in this Manner, exhorted. At first, she began with her Father, and told him, she could see the Image of the Devil then in his Face, and that he was going Post-haste down to Hell; and that all the Prayers he had ever made in his Family were nothing but Abomination in the Ears of the Almighty, and that all the Counsels he had ever given her, had no better a Tendency than to instruct her, how she should please the Devil; and that both he, and his Wife, were no better than the Devil. Many such Instances there were of Children condemning their Parents. And many old Persons also, though, as well as the Parents above, Persons of unblemish'd Characters, a good Profession, sober, and Lovers of Religion, were called, and by Children too, old Hypocrites, Heirs of eternal Damnation, going the Road that would lead them to Hell, &c."

3. Jonathan Edwards advocates "dealing plainly and thoroughly with children, in the concerns of their souls," 1740

Edwards, *Conversions and Revival in New England,* pp. 202–203.

What has more especially given offence to many, and raised a loud cry against some preachers, as though their conduct were intolerable, is their frightening poor innocent children, with talk of hell fire, and eternal damnation. But if those that complain so loudly of this, really believe, what is the general profession of the country, viz. That all are by nature the children of wrath, and heirs of hell; and that every one that has not been born again, whether he be young or old, is exposed, every moment, to eternal destruction, under the wrath of Almighty God; I say, if they really believe this, then such a complaint and cry as this, betrays a great deal of weakness and inconsideration. As innocent as children seem to be to us, yet, if they are out of Christ, they are not so in God's sight, but are young vipers, and are infinitely more hateful than vipers, and are in a most miserable condition, as well as grown persons; and they are naturally very senseless and stupid, being *born as the wild asses colt,* and need much to awaken them. Why should we conceal the truth from them? Will those children that have been dealt tenderly with, in this respect, and lived and died insensible of their misery, until they come to feel it in hell, ever thank parents, and others, for their tenderness, in not letting them know what they were in danger of. If parents' love towards their children was not blind, it would affect them much more to see their children every day exposed to eternal burnings, and yet senseless, than to see them suffer the distress of that awakening, that is necessary in order to their escape from them, and that tends to their being eternally happy, as the children of God. A child

that has a dangerous wound, may need the painful lance, as well as grown persons; and that would be a foolish pity, in such a case, that should hold back the lance, and throw away the life. I have seen the happy effects of dealing plainly, and thoroughly with children, in the concerns of their souls, without sparing them at all, in many instances; and never knew any ill consequences of it in any one instance.

Children in the Revolution

1. Harvard College students support the cause of American liberty, 1769

Andrew Eliot to Thomas Hollis, December 25, 1769, Hollis Papers, Massachusetts Historical Society.

Andrew Eliot (1718–1778) of Boston was secretary of the Harvard Corporation and a close observer of the college and its students.

I shall be sorry if the Court should be at Cambridge.[1] It hinders the Scholars in their studies. The young Gentlemen are already enough taken up with politics. They have imbibed the Spirit of the times. Their declamations and forensic disputes breathe the Spirit of Liberty. This has always been encouraged, but they have sometimes wrought themselves up to such a pitch of Enthusiasm that it has been difficult to keep them within due bounds. But their tutors are fearful of giving too great a check to a disposition which may hereafter fill the Country with Patriots and choose to

1. It had been suggested that the meeting of the General Court be moved to Cambridge owing to the presence of British troops in Boston.

leave it to age and experience to correct their ardor.

2. Disorder at Harvard College over the drinking of tea, March 1, 1775

"Records of the College Faculty, Harvard College, March 1, 1775," IV (1775–1781), 4–5, Harvard University Archives.

March 1. At a Meeting of the President, Professors and Tutors

A disorder having arisen this morning in the Hall at breakfast, between some of the students, respecting the drinking of India Tea; and some of the utensils for breakfasting having been broke; and the parties having been heard — *Resolved* — 1. We disapprove of the conduct on both sides as imprudent.

Resolved — 2. That the regulation of the Hall belongs exclusively to the Government of the College, and consequently that no students have a right to interpose with regard thereunto, and that those students who have thus interposed have conducted disorderly in this respect, and ought to make restitution for the property of their fellow students by such interposition destroyed.

Resolved — 3. Since the carrying India Teas into the Hall is found to be a source of uneasiness and grief to many of the students, and as the use of it is disagreeable to the people of this Country in general; and as those who have carried Tea into the hall declare that the drinking of it in the Hall is a matter of trifling consequence with them; that they be advised not to carry it in for the future, and in this way that they, as well as the other students in all ways, discover a disposition to promote harmony, mutual affection, and confidence, so well becoming members of the same society: that so peace and happiness may be preserved within the walls of the college whatever convulsions may unhappily distract the State abroad.

3. Thomas Paine, the pamphleteer of the Revolution, compares the colonies' need for independence to that of grown up children, 1776

Thomas Paine, "The Crisis," *The Political Writings of Thomas Paine,* I (Middletown, N.J., 1837), 181; first published in 1776.

The title which [Great Britain] assumed, of parent country, led to, and pointed out the propriety, wisdom and advantage of a separation; for, as in private life, children grow into men, and by setting up for themselves, extend and secure the interest of the whole family, so in the settlement of colonies large enough to admit of maturity, the same policy should be pursued, and the same consequences would follow. Nothing hurts the affections both of parents and children so much, as living too closely connected, and keeping up the distinction too long. Domineering will not do over those, who, by a progress in life, have become equal in rank to their parents, that is, when they have families of their own; and though they may conceive themselves the subjects of their advice, will not suppose them the objects of their government. I do not, by drawing this parallel, mean to admit the title of *parent country,* because, if it is due any where, it is due to Europe collectively, and the first settlers from England were driven here by persecution. I mean only to introduce the term for the sake of policy and to show from your title the line of your interest.

4. A New Hampshire youth leaves home to serve on an American warship, 1779

Andrew Sherburne, *Memoirs,* 2d ed. (Providence, 1831), pp. 18–21.

Ships were building, prizes taken from the enemy unloading, privateers fitting out, standards waved on the forts and batteries, the exercising of soldiers, the roar of cannon, the sound of martial music and the call for volunteers so infatuated me, that I was filled with anxiety to become an actor in the scene of war. My eldest brother, Thomas, had recently returned from a cruise on board the "General Mifflin," of Boston, Capt. Mc'Neal. This ship had captured thirteen prizes, some of which, however, being of little value, were burnt, some were sold in France, others reached Boston, and their cargoes were divided among the crew of that ship. On my brother's return, I became more eager to try my fortune at sea. My father, though a high Whig, disapproved the practice of privateering. Merchant vessels, at this period, which ran safe, made great gains, seamen's wages were consequently very high. Through my father's influence Thomas was induced to enter the merchants' service. Though not yet fourteen years of age, like other boys, I imagined myself almost a man. I had intimated to my sister, that if my father would not consent that I should go to sea, I would run away, and go on board a privateer. My mind became so infatuated with the subject, that I talked of it in my sleep, and was overheard by my mother. She communicated what she had heard to my father. — My parents were apprehensive that I might wander off and go on board some vessel without their consent. At this period it was not an uncommon thing for lads to come out of the country, step on board a privateer, make a cruise and return home, their friends remaining in entire ignorance of their fate, until they heard it from themselves. Others would pack up their clothes, take a cheese and a loaf of bread, and steer off for the army. There was a disposition in commanders of privateers and recruiting officers to encourage this spirit of enterprise in young men and boys. Though these rash young adventurers did not count the cost, or think of looking at the dark side of the picture, yet this spirit, amidst the despondency of many, enabled our country to maintain a successful struggle and finally achieve her independence.

The continental ship of war Ranger, of eighteen guns, commanded by Thomas Simpson, Esq. was at this time shipping a crew in Portsmouth. This ship had been ordered to join the Boston and Providence frigates and the Queen of France of twenty guns, upon an expedition directed by Congress. My father having consented that I should go to sea, preferred the service of Congress to privateering. He was acquainted with Capt. Simpson. — On board this ship were my two half uncles, Timothy and James Weymouth. Accompanied by my father, I visited the rendezvous of the Ranger and shipped as one of her crew. There were probably thirty boys on board this ship. As most of our principal officers belonged to the town, parents preferred this ship as a station for their sons who were about to enter the naval service. Hence most of these boys were from Portsmouth. As privateering was the order of the day, vessels of every description were employed in the business. Men were not wanting who would hazard themselves in vessels of twenty tons or less, manned by ten or fifteen hands. Placing much dependence on the protection of my uncles, I was much elated with my supposed good fortune, which had at last made me a sailor.

I was not yet fourteen years of age. I had received some little moral and religious instruction, and was far from being accustomed to the habits of town boys, or the maxims or dialect of sailors. The town boys thought themselves vastly superior to country lads; and indeed in those days the distinction was much greater than at present. My diffidence and aversion to swearing, rendered me an object of ridicule to those little profane chaps. I was insulted, and frequently obliged to fight. In this I was sometimes victorious. My uncles, and others, prompted me to defend my rights. I soon began to improve in boxing, and to indulge in swearing. At first this practice occasioned some remorse of conscience. — I however endeavored to persuade myself that there was a necessity for it. I at length became a proficient in this abominable practice. To counterbalance my guilt in this, I at the same time became more constant in praying; heretofore I had only prayed occasionally; now I prayed continually when I turned in at night, and vainly imagined that I prayed enough by night to atone for the sins of the day. Believing that no other person on board prayed, I was filled with pride, concluding I had as much or more religion than the whole crew besides. The boys were employed in waiting on the officers, but in time of action a boy was quartered to each gun to carry cartridges. I was waiter to Mr. Charles Roberts, the boatswain, and was quartered at the third gun from the bow. Being ready for sea, we sailed to Boston, joined the Providence frigate, commanded by Commodore Whipple, the Boston frigate and the Queen of France. I believe that this small squadron composed nearly the entire navy of the United States. We proceeded to sea some time in June, 1779. A considerable part of the crew of the Ranger being raw hands and the sea rough, especially in the gulf stream, many were exceedingly sick, and myself among the rest. We afforded a subject of constant ridicule to the old sailors.

---

5. The happy farmer and his household, 1782

Michel-Guillaume Jean de Crèvecoeur, *Letters from an American Farmer* (New York, 1963), pp. 47–49, 58–59, 305–307; first published in 1782.

Crèvecoeur (1735–1813), born in Normandy, served under Montcalm in the French and Indian War. He came to New York in 1759, married in 1765, and settled on a farm, "Pine Hill," in Orange County, New York. He was in France in 1782 when *Letters from an American Farmer* was first published. On his return to America in 1783 Crèvecoeur found his wife dead, farmhouse burned, and children scattered.

When I contemplate my wife, by my fire-side, while she either spins, knits, darns, or suckles our child, I cannot describe the various emotions of love, of gratitude, of conscious pride which thrill in my heart, and often overflow in involuntary tears. I feel the necessity, the sweet pleasure of acting my part, the part of an husband and father, with an attention and propriety which may entitle me to my good fortune. It is true these pleasing images vanish with the smoke of my pipe, but though they disappear from my mind, the impression they have made on my heart is indelible. When I play with the infant, my warm imagination runs forward, and eagerly anticipates his future temper and constitution. I would willingly open the book of fate, and know in which page his destiny is delineated; alas! where is the father who in those moments of paternal extacy can delineate one half of the thoughts which dilate his heart? I am sure I cannot; then again I fear for the health of those who are become so dear to me, and in their sicknesses I severely pay for the joys I experienced while they were well. Whenever I go abroad it is always involuntary. I never return home without feeling some pleasing emotion, which I often suppress as useless and foolish. The instant I enter on my own land, the bright idea of property, of exclusive right, of independence exalt my mind. Precious soil, I say to myself, by what singular custom of law is it that thou wast made to constitute the riches of the freeholder?

.   .   .   .   .

Often when I plough my low ground, I place my little boy on a chair which screws to the beam of the plough — its motion and that of the horses please him, he is perfectly happy and begins to chat. As I lean over the handle, various are the thoughts which croud into my mind. I am now doing for him, I say, what my father formerly did for me, may God enable him to live that he may perform the same operations for the same purposes when I am worn out and old! I relieve his mother of some trouble while I have him with me, the odoriferous furrow exhilarates his spirits, and seems to do the child a great deal of good, for he looks more blooming since I have adopted that practice; can more pleasure, more dignity be added to that primary occupation? The father thus ploughing with his child, and to feed his family, is inferior only to the emperor of China ploughing as an example to his kingdom.

.   .   .   .   .

At home my happiness springs from very different objects; the gradual unfolding of my children's reason, the study of their dawning tempers attract all my paternal attention. I have to contrive little punishments for their little faults, small encouragements for their good actions, and a variety of other expedients dictated by various occasions. But these are themes unworthy your perusal, and which ought not to be carried beyond the walls of my house, being domestic mysteries adapted only to the locality of the small sanctuary wherein my family resides. Sometimes I delight in inventing and executing machines, which simplify my wife's labour. I have been tolerably successful that way; and these, Sir, are the narrow circles within which I constantly revolve, and what can I wish for beyond them? I bless God for all the good he has given me; I envy no man's prosperity, and with no other portion of happiness than that I may live to teach the same philosophy to my children; and give each of them a farm, shew them how to cultivate it, and be like their father, good substantial independent American farmers — an appellation which will be the most fortunate one, a man of my class can possess, so long as our civil government continues to shed blessings on our husbandry.

.   .   .   .   .

6. What is an American? 1782

Crèvecoeur, *Letters from an American Farmer,* pp. 63–64.

What attachment can a poor European emigrant have for a country where he had nothing? The knowledge of the language, the love of a few kindred as poor as himself, were the only cords that tied him: his country is now that which gives him land, bread, protection, and consequence: *Ubi panis ibi patria,* is the motto of all emigrants. What then is the American, this new man? He is either an European, or the descendant of an European, hence that strange mixture of blood, which you will find in no other country. I could point out to you a family whose grandfather was an Englishman, whose wife was Dutch, whose son married a French woman, and whose present four sons have now four wives of different nations. He is an American, who leaving behind him all his ancient prejudices and manners, receives new ones from the new mode of life he has embraced, the new government he obeys, and the new rank he holds. He becomes an American by being received in the broad lap of our great *Alma Mater.* Here individuals of all nations are melted into a new race of men, whose labours and posterity will one day cause great changes in the world. Americans are the western pilgrims, who are carrying along with them that great mass of arts, sciences, vigour, and industry which began long since in the east; they will finish the great circle. The Americans were once scattered all over Europe; here they are incorporated into one of the finest systems of population which has ever appeared, and which will hereafter become distinct by the power of the different climates they inhabit. The American ought therefore to love this country much better than that wherein either he or his forefathers were born. Here the rewards of his industry follow with equal steps the progress of his labour; his labour is founded on the basis of nature, self-interest; can it want a stronger allurement? Wives and children, who before in vain demanded of him a morsel of bread, now, fat and frolicsome, gladly help their father to clear those fields whence exuberant crops are to arise to feed and to clothe them all; without any part being claimed, either by a despotic prince, a rich abbot, or a mighty lord. Here religion demands but little of him; a small voluntary salary to the minister, and gratitude to God; can he refuse these? The American is a new man, who acts upon new principles; he must therefore entertain new ideas, and form new opinions. From involuntary idleness, servile dependence, penury, and useless labour, he has passed to toils of a very different nature, rewarded by ample subsistence. — This is an American.

II Child Labor

Industrial child labor began in America at the end of the eighteenth century. The novelty of this development should not obscure the fact that during the eighteenth and nineteenth centuries most children continued to work in their homes, on the farm, and in their parents' workshops.[1]

With the increase of patriotic enthusiasm for national industries in the last third of the eighteenth century, there was an increasing premium on the work of women and children in the household, especially in the production of wool and cotton. In 1767, Sir Henry Moore, governor of New York reported with great satisfaction that "every house swarms with chidren, who are set to work as soon as they are able to spin and card."[2] Alexander Hamilton declared in 1790: "It is computed in a number of districts that two thirds, three fourths, and even four fifths, of all the clothing of the inhabitants, are made by themselves. The importance of so great a progress as appears to have been made in family manufactures, within a few years, in both a moral and political view, renders the fact highly interesting."[3]

1. For an extensive discussion of this question see Rolla M. Tryon, *Household Manufactures in the United States* (Chicago, 1917). On the development of the cotton industry in America and on the employment of women and children see Edith Abbott, *Women in Industry* (New York, 1913) and Caroline F. Ware, *The Early New England Cotton Manufacture: A Study in Industrial Beginnings* (Boston and New York, 1931)

2. "Governor Moore to the Lords of Trade, 12 January, 1767," E. B. O'Callaghan, ed., *Documents Relative to the Colonial History of the State of New York*, VII (Albany, 1856), 888.

3. "Manufactures December 5, 1791," *American State Papers, Finance*, I (Washington, 1832), 132.

In the 1760's small shops took over several stages in the production of wool and cotton. Although housewives continued to spin at home, they found it more efficient to have the wool and cotton carded and fulled in the workshop. Sometimes, too, they brought the spun wool to be dyed. Thus, these shops became the nuclei of later factories, serving as a transitional stage between household industry and the large factory. Since carding, fulling, and spinning had been children's occupations in the home, it was only natural to transfer children to such workshops. This form of employment, however, could not yet be considered industrial child labor; it was merely a variation on traditional household work. The labor force in such shops consisted of the master's household — his children, his servants, and his apprentices.

The cotton industry in New England brought the industrial revolution to America, and with it the introduction of children as an industrial labor force. In 1789 William Almy and Moses Brown invited Samuel Slater, "the father of American manufactures," to join them as a partner in their Providence, Rhode Island, factory. An apprentice and later employee of Jedidiah Strutt, the leading English manufacturer of cotton and a partner of Richard Arkwright, Slater had smuggled himself and the plans for Arkwright's machinery to New York. He joined Almy and Brown and produced satisfactory yarn in 1791. For the first time in America all stages of manufacture from raw cotton to yarn were worked in the factory by machinery (except the cleaning, which children too young to work in the factory still performed at home).[4]

The Slater factory demonstrated in practice the arguments of the advocates of the new industrial system: diversification of labor and the introduction of power machinery were ideally suited for the employment of children. The first employees at Almy, Brown, and Slater were nine boys from poor families in the vicinity. In contrast to earlier practice these children were factory laborers, rather than apprentices. Slater had intended to keep apprentices as well but in the words of his son, "it did not suit the American temperament, and was abandoned."[5] By 1801, the number of children increased to one hundred, ranging in age from four to ten. They worked in one room where all the machinery was concentrated under the supervision of a foreman, spreading the cleaned cotton on the carding machine to be combed and passing it through the roving machine, which turned the cotton into loose rolls ready to be spun. Most of the children tended the spindles, removing and attaching bobbins. Small, quick fingers were admirably suited for picking up and knotting broken threads. To the delight of Tench Coxe, a champion of American industry, the children became "the little fingers . . . of the gigantic automatons of laborsaving machinery."[6]

In the twenty years after its establishment the Slater system spread rapidly through New England. In 1810 Albert Gallatin reported twenty-seven mills in operation in Rhode Island, southern Massachusetts, and eastern Connecticut.[7]

All these mills were fashioned after the Slater model. For 1809 Gallatin estimated the number of employees in the cotton mills as 4,000. Those consisted of 500 men and 3,500 women and children.[8] The later growth of the industry was so rapid that the Committee on Manufactures reported in 1816 that the mills then employed 100,000 hands, of whom 24,000 were "boys under seventeen" and 66,000 "women and girls." Thus, children and women comprised 90 per cent of the labor force.[9] The computation in the *Digest of Manufactures* separates women from children. Children formed 47 per cent of the labor force in Massachusetts cotton mills, 55 per cent in Rhode Island, and 55 per cent in Connecticut. In the wool industry, which used traditional methods of production, children comprised only 22 to 27 per cent.

Two systems developed for the recruitment of children to the factory. Samuel Slater followed the English plan of employing entire families. This family system dominated the smaller factories in Rhode Island, Connecticut, and southern Massachusetts. The alternative, established first in the textile mill in Waltham, was the boardinghouse system, where some children and mostly young girls worked in the factory, while their parents continued to live on the farm. This practice would be more common after the 1820's in large factories employing older girls: in Lowell and Lawrence, Massachusetts, in Dover, Manchester, Exeter, and Portsmouth, New Hampshire, and in Maine.

Under the family system, rural families moved to the mill and lived in a compact community built and owned by the company. They payed an average rent of 25 cents per week for the tenement and obtained provisions through a company store, often as a partial or whole substitute for money wages. Every member of the family above age seven worked in the factory from sunrise to sunset, six days a week. Their only holidays were Christmas, Easter, and

4. Ware, *Early New England Cotton Manufacture,* passim.

5. "H. N. Slater's Reminiscences of Samuel Slater, his Father, April 26, 1884," in William B. Weeden, *Economic and Social History of New England, 1670–1789,* II (Boston and New York, 1891), 913.

6. Tench Coxe, quoted in United States Bureau of Labor, *Report on Condition of Woman and Child Wage-Earners in the United States,* 19 volumes (Washington, D.C., 1910–1913), VI, 48.

7. "Manufactures, April 17, 1810," *American State Papers, Finance,* II (Washington, 1832), 433. These factories produced yarn, not finished cloth. Only with the introduction of the power loom to Waltham, Massachusetts, in 1814 was the process from raw cotton to cloth completed.

8. *American State Papers, Finance,* II, 427.

9. "Protection to the Manufactures of Cotton Fabrics, February 13, 1816," *American State Papers, Finance,* III (Washington, 1834), 82.

half a day on the Fourth of July. The father was often a mechanic or skilled spinner; his wife and children provided the unskilled labor force. In other instances, however, the father continued to farm.

Children's wages were calculated and graded according to age. A child under ten normally received 50 cents a week. Some companies paid as little as 37 cents. While 50 cents a week was the standard pay in the Slater factory, children of the Rier family in Lancaster received higher weekly wages (the youngest eight years old, 75 cents, and the oldest, sixteen years old, $2.00). In contrast, the Troy mill at Fall River paid the youngest children only 25 or 10 cents a week. Henry Bradshaw Fearon, a British traveler, must have exaggerated when he reported that at the Slater mill in Pawtucket children from 6 to 10 years were earning $1.12 1/2 a week, children from 11 to 16 years $1.67 a week, women $2 a week, and men from $4.50 to $5.25 a week.[10]

The significance of these wages is clearer in view of the fact that in 1814 the company store of the Slater mill charged $1.34 for a bushel of corn, 9 cents for a pound of flour, 16 cents for a bushel of potatoes, 23 cents for a pound of sugar, 20 cents for a pound of candles, and 16 cents for a pound of soap. A pair of shoes cost $2. Families rarely purchased other items, except occasionally beef, coffee, and tobacco.[11] The account books of the Slater and Tiffany cotton mill suggest that families, even with the continued earnings of all children, carried a debt from one period to the next and rarely broke even. Accounts went unsettled for long periods, usually a full year. William Howland, for example, ordinarily discovered at Christmas time that his labor and the work of his seven children had failed to cancel his debt to the company. Howland earned $6 a week, and his children earned respectively $4, $2.50, 85 cents, 66 cents, and 50 cents a week each. For the period from May 27, 1814, to December 20, 1814, he owed the company $587.98 for "sundries" and rent. The family's combined earnings came to $582.46. He was still $2.08 short, after the company credited him with $3.44. From the next settlement period, in December 1815, he carried a debt of $37.07. April 3, 1816, marked the beginning of a period of solvency, since he was credited with $10.49. On December 20, 1816, he was credited again with $50.51. But, by January 20, 1818, he found himself short again, this time by the amount of $45.86. On May 2, 1818, Mr. Howland finally managed to settle the account with $4.22 to his credit.[12]

Sally Maine, on the other hand, who had three children working in the factory fared worse. On November 9, 1815, she discovered that she was $98.24 short. (She had spent $445.50 and earned only $347.26.) To cope with the emergency Mrs. Maine took in four woman boarders and sent her two boys to work full time. But by November 4, 1817, she owed again $70.92. The purchase record of Mrs. Maine suggests that she rarely bought anything in the store but essential staples, although she did have a high sugar and coffee consumption. During the entire period she purchased two pairs of shoes and six yards of gingham. All eighteen families listed in the mill's account books from 1817 to 1819 continuously struggled with debt. The record books do not show even one case of savings.

In principle, the employment of children in factories was not drastically different from the colonial precedent of child labor. Moreover, Virginia had established the pattern for commercial employment of children early in the colonial period. Advocates of infant industries used the existing views of the sanctity of work and fear of idleness as persuasive arguments in favor of the new manufactures. They declared that new industries would not displace

10. Quoted in United States Bureau of Labor, *Report on Condition of Woman and Child Wage-Earners,* VI, 62.

11. Slater and Tiffany, Cotton, "Ledger, 1814–1823," Slater Papers, Baker Library, Harvard University Graduate School of Business Administration, Boston, Mass.

12. Slater and Tiffany, Cotton, "Accounts Settled, 1817–1819" and "Ledger 1814–1823," Slater Papers.

farmers from their labor and would not strain the labor market, since they would draw on women and children. By harnessing children to machinery, factories would not only increase industrial production at minimum expense but would also put the poor, idle, and potentially vicious elements of society to useful employment.

In reality, the labor of children in factories introduced novel conditions and required special adjustment. In the earlier practice of household production children were not distinguished from adults. They shared in the burden of domestic chores and industries. They worked whenever and wherever it was necessary. In the factory system, on the other hand, the household ceased to be a self-governing economic unit. Paternal authority became separate from labor instruction and supervision. A child now answered to two masters: a foreman in the factory and a father at home. The father still had to decide whether his child should be employed, to sign contracts for him, and to collect his wages. But even in the family employment system, where whole families were hired as a unit, the contract spelled out the wages of each child independently. In the factory room, the members of the family became part of a crowd, each repeating a specific function and being disciplined by a foreman.

The disruption of the family as an independent economic unit in this period was evident not only in the factory system. Even in household industry the master-apprentice relationship lost its paternal-filial character as the personal, non-vocational obligations binding master and servant declined. In the eighteenth century many apprentices were acquiring not only their general education, but also their trade education in schools.[13]

The factory system redefined child labor. It classified children as a distinct labor force. Advertisers of new machinery estimated and measured the efficiency of their product in terms of the necessary boy or girl power to produce a certain amount of yarn. John Baxter assured prospective customers that his new machines with six and twelve spindles respectively could be easily turned by "children of from five to ten years of age," while the twelve-spindle machine would require "girls from ten to twenty." [14] Not unlike slave families, the number of employable children determined the economic assets and desirability of raising a family. Children received payment as laborers, rather than maintenance and instruction as apprentices.[15]

One can only speculate on the impact of factory labor on the independence of child workers. The meager wages earned went into the family pocket. Long hours of work from sunrise to sunset left little time for schooling or recreation. On the other hand, the factory experience occasionally produced experts at an early age. In one instance a thirteen-year-old boy was employed by the Globe Company in Tiverton, Rhode Island, to repair and set into operation idle machinery, and in another a fifteen-year-old was sent by his father to Burrillville, Rhode Island, to superintend and equip a mill and put it into operation. The boys had had six to seven years experience. If the factory confined the horizons of the children of mill families, it still loomed high in the dreams of young boys and girls in impoverished rural areas. Lured by visions of an independent income, life with their peers in boardinghouses, and a change of environment, they viewed the mill as an escape from drudgery on the farm. Thus, the factory began to compete with the sea as an outlet for restless youngsters.

The new child labor force in the factory was not governed by the traditional laws of appren-

13. Bailyn, *Education in the Forming of American Society,* p. 32.

14. *Niles' Weekly Register,* March 5, 1814, p. 16.
15. The distinction between apprenticeship and factory labor was not clear in all early factories. For instance, at Dickson's factory in Hell Gates, New York, the child workers were all bound by indenture and treated and maintained as apprentices. In an advertisement in 1793 this same factory called for apprentices who "will be found in everything during their apprenticeship and taught the different branches of the cotton business." Quoted in Abbott, *Women in Industry,* p. 45.

ticeship or servitude, although some customs lingered. Thus, the paternalism of Samuel Slater and General Humphreys derived as much from the traditional conceptions of master-apprentice relationships as from personal benevolence. Ideally all members of the company village were envisioned as one large family. In reality, unlike the apprentice's master, the factory owner was under no obligation to teach the child a trade, unless he was explicitly taken on as an apprentice. Nor was he required to provide him with a general education. Unlike apprentices, factory children had no legal recourse in the case of abuse in this early period. The nation's leaders, delighting in the contribution of little children to economic independence, struggled to secure national protection for infant industries but did not find it necessary to protect the "little fingers" that worked them.

A. APPRENTICES AND SERVANTS

Laws regulating apprenticeship, 1731–1788

1. New York City, 1731

"A Law for Regulating Indentures of Apprenticeship," November 18, 1731, *Minutes of the Common Council of the City of New York, 1675–1776,* IV (New York, 1905), 97; hereafter cited as *N.Y.C. Council Minutes.*

. . . No merchant, shopkeeper or handy craft tradesman shall take any apprentice to teach or instruct them in their trade or calling within this City, without being bound by indenture before the Mayor, Recorder or one of the Aldermen of the said City, and enroling the same in the Town Clerk's Office. And that at the expiration of the said indentures the said apprentice shall be made free of this City by the master, if he hath well and truly served him. And the Clerk shall have for enroling each indenture of apprenticeship the sum of three shillings to be paid by the master of such apprentice bound as aforesaid.

.   .   .   .   .

And whereas the emigration of poor persons from Europe hath conduced greatly to the settlement of this State, while a colony; and whereas doubts have arisen tending to the discouragement of further importation of such poor persons; therefore be it further enacted by the authority aforesaid, That every contract already made or hereafter to be made by any infant or other person, coming from beyond sea . . . the party entering into the same, for such term and for such services as shall be therein specified . . . But that no contract shall bind any infant longer than until his or her arrival to the full age of twenty one years; excepting such as are or shall be bound in order to raise money for the payment of their passages, who may be bound until the age of twenty four years, provided the term of such service shall not exceed four years in the whole.

.   .   .   .   .

And whereas, many persons are taken as apprentices or servants, when they are very young, and for several years of their apprenticeships or service, are rather a burthen, than otherwise, to their masters or mistresses: And whereas it frequently happens that such apprentices or servants, when they might be expected to be useful to their masters or mistresses, absent themselves from their service: And whereas the laws in being are not sufficient to prevent these inconveniences: For remedy whereof: Be it further enacted by the authority aforesaid, That from and after the passing of this act, if any apprentice or servant shall absent him or herself, from his or her master's or mistress's service, before the term of his or her apprenticeship or service shall be expired, every such apprentice or servant shall, at any time or times thereafter, whenever he or she shall be found, be compelled to serve his or her said master or mistress, for double the time he or she shall have so absented him or herself from such service, unless he or she shall make satisfaction to his or her master or mistress for the loss he or she shall have sustained by such absence from his or her service; and so from time to time, as often as any such apprentice or servant, shall, without leave of his or her master or mistress, absent himself or herself from his or her service, before the term of his or her contract shall be fulfilled.

Provided always . . . That nothing in this clause of this act shall extend to any apprentice, whose master or mistress shall have received with such apprentice any sum or sums of money to learn such art, craft, mystery, profession, trade or employment. And also that no apprentice or servant shall be compelled to serve for any time or term or to make any satisfaction to any master or mistress, after the expiration of three years, next after the end of the term for which such apprentice or servant, shall have contracted to serve; any thing herein contained to the contrary notwithstanding.

2. South Carolina, 1740

"An act concerning masters and apprentices" in Thomas Cooper, ed., *Statutes at Large of South Carolina,* III (Columbia, S.C., 1838), pp. 544–546; hereafter cited as *So. Car. Statutes at Large.*

. . . All and every person and persons whatsoever, that now are or at any time or

times after the passing of this Act shall be bound by indentures to serve as an apprentice within this Province, in any lawful employment, calling, art, mystery or trade, although such apprentice or any of them have been or shall be within the age of twenty-one years at the time of making their several indentures, shall be bound to serve for the years in their several indentures contained, as fully and effectually, to every intent, as if the said apprentice had been of full age at the time of making such indentures, and shall be bound, accepted and taken as an apprentice, accordingly . . . and provided also, that nothing in this Act contained shall extend to oblige any male apprentice to serve after he shall have attained the age of one-and-twenty years, or a female after she shall have attained the age of eighteen years.

. . . Every person or persons under the age of one-and-twenty years, and hereafter intending to be bound by indenture as an apprentice, in this Province, shall execute such indenture in the presence and with the approbation of his or her father, mother or guardian; and if such intended apprentice hath neither father, mother or guardian, in the presence and with the approbation of the church-wardens of the parish where such person is indented . . . which indenture or indentures, so executed . . . shall be good and effectual, to all intents and purposes, as if such apprentice had been of full age and by indenture of covenant had bound him or herself, or otherwise shall be void and of none effect.

.   .   .   .   .

. . . It shall and may be lawful to and for the master or mistress of any apprentice, indented to serve within this Province as aforesaid, upon sufficient cause, to be approved of by the parent or guardian, or where there is no parent or guardian, by the church-wardens of the parish where such master or mistress resides, to assign and transfer the indenture of such apprentice to any other master or mistress, exercising within this Province the same employment, calling, trade, art or mystery; which said indenture, so assigned, shall be valid and effectual to the assignee as to the time remaining unexpired, as if the said apprentice had been originally indented to such assignee; and the said assignee, on accepting such assignment, shall be equally bound to the said apprentice, according to the tenor or the said indenture, as the original master or mistress was.

.   .   .   .   .

And it be further enacted by the authority aforesaid, That if any master or mistress within this Province shall misuse or evilly intreat his or her apprentice, or if the said apprentice shall have any just cause to complain, or do not his or her duty to the said master or mistress, then and in such case the said master, mistress or apprentice being grieved, and having just cause to complain, shall repair and make such complaint to any two justices of the peace within the county where such master or mistress resides, who shall and are hereby authorized and required by their wisdom and discretion to make such order and give such direction between the said master, mistress and apprentice, as the equity and justice of the case shall require . . .

3. New York, 1788

"An act concerning apprentices and servants," 1788 — ch. 15, *Laws of the State of New York . . . 1785–1788,* II (Albany, 1866), 621–625.

. . . If any person, who shall bind him or herself, by and with the consent of his or her parent or other guardian . . . or who shall be bound by the overseers of the poor and justices or mayor or recorder and aldermen . . . to serve, as an apprentice or servant in the manner in this act above directed and prescribed, shall refuse so to do . . . the said justice or the said mayor or recorder or alderman respectively, shall have power and authority . . . to commit him or her unto ward in the bridewell or house of correction if any there be, or if there be no bridewell or house of correction, in the gaol of the city or county wherein such refusal shall take place, there to remain until he or she be contented and will serve as an apprentice or servant should serve, according to the true intent and meaning of this act.

And to the end that the time of the continuance of the service of such apprentice or servant may the more plainly and certainly appear, the age of every such infant so to be bound apprentice or servant, shall be mentioned and inserted in his or her indentures; and where the binding is by the overseers of the poor . . . the same . . . shall, as fully as they can, inform themselves of such infant's age, and from such information shall insert the same in the said indentures; and the age of such infant so inserted and mentioned in the said indentures (in relation to the continuance of his or her service) shall be taken to be his or her true age, without any further proof thereof.

And whereas the emigration of poor persons from Europe hath conduced greatly to the settlement of this State, while a colony; and whereas doubts have arisen tending to the discouragement of further importation of such poor persons; therefore be it further enacted by the authority aforesaid, That every contract already made or hereafter to be made by any infant or other person, coming from beyond sea . . . the party entering into the same, for such term and for such services as shall be therein specified . . . But that no contract shall bind any infant longer than until his or her arrival to the full age of twenty one years; excepting such as are or shall be bound in order to raise money for the payment of their passages, who may be bound until the age of twenty four years, provided the term of such service shall not exceed four years in the whole.

.   .   .   .   .

And whereas, many persons are taken as apprentices or servants, when they are very young, and for several years of their apprenticeships or service, are rather a burthen, than otherwise, to their masters or mistresses: And whereas it frequently happens that such apprentices or servants, when they might be expected to be useful to their masters or mistresses, absent themselves from their service: And whereas the laws in being are not sufficient to prevent these inconveniences: For remedy whereof: Be it further enacted by the authority aforesaid, That from and after the passing of this act, if any apprentice or servant shall absent him or herself, from his or her master's or mistress's service, before the term of his or her apprenticeship or service shall be expired, every such apprentice or servant shall, at any time or times thereafter, whenever he or she shall be found, be compelled to serve his or her said master or mistress, for double the time he or she shall have so absented him or herself from such service, unless he or she shall make satisfaction to his or her master or mistress for the loss he or she shall have sustained by such absence from his or her service; and so from time to time, as often as any such apprentice or servant, shall, without leave of his or her master or mistress, absent himself or herself from his or her service, before the term of his or her contract shall be fulfilled.

Provided always . . . That nothing in this clause of this act shall extend to any apprentice, whose master or mistress shall have received with such apprentice any sum or sums of money to learn such art, craft, mystery, profession, trade or employment. And also that no apprentice or servant shall be compelled to serve for any time or term or to make any satisfaction to any master or mistress, after the expiration of three years, next after the end of the term for which such apprentice or servant, shall have contracted to serve; any thing herein contained to the contrary notwithstanding.

. . . . .

Advertisements for runaway servants and apprentices

Boston Evening Post, Oct. 20, 1735.

Ran away from Mr. Thomas Keighley of Boston, Twine and Line spinner, on the 30th of October last an English Servant Boy named John Long, about 17 Years old, well set, of a black complexion, with a large Head, a wide Mouth, and large Ears. He had on an old black coloured Jacket, a pair of trousers, a Cotton and Linnen Shirt, yarn Stockings, and old Shoes. All Masters of Vessels and others, are hereby forbid to harbour, conceal, or carry off the said Servant, as they will avoid the Penalty of the Law in that Case made and provided.

Whoever brings the said Servant to his above said Master shall have Forty Shillings Reward, and all necessary Charges paid.

Boston Evening Post, Oct. 7, 1751.

Ran away from his Master Benjamin Renken of Boston, Taylor, on Tuesday morning last, an Irish Lad named James Hatherton, but has sometimes called himself James Smith. He is well set, and of a midling Stature, has large Legs, and speaks pretty good English. Carried away with him a Gun, under Pret[ence] of goi[ng] to train. Had on when he went away, a Beaver Hat newly drest, and a worsted Cap, a blue Coat lined with Red, trim'd with Yellow Metal Buttons, the Jacket was double breasted, blue yarn Rib'd Stockings, peeked toed turned pumps, with white Metal Buckles.

Whoever shall apprehend said Servant, and bring or convey him to his said Master in Boston, near the Draw-Bridge, shall have Four Dollars Reward, and all necessary Charges paid by me. Benjamin Renken.

All Masters of Vessels and others, are hereby cautioned not to conceal, entertain, or carry off the Said Servant, as they would avoid the

Penalty of the Law in that Case made and Provided.

Pennsylvania Gazette, July 4, 1751.

Ran away on the 1st instant, from Daniel Bates of Gloucester county, an English servant man, named George M'Cartney, about 19 years of age, a short fellow, pretty well set, of a yellow complexion, a little pitted with smallpox; Had on when he went away, an old felt hat, with a piece sewed on part of the brim of it, a ragged linnen cap, a blue jacket, without lining, with soal-leather buttons on it, coarse, dirty ozenbrigs trowsers, a check shirt, and an old pair of women's shoes, with the heels out, and pieces of leather put in the room of them. Whoever takes up and secures said servant, so that his master may have him again, shall have Forty Shillings reward, and reasonable charges, paid by

Daniel Bates

.   .   .   .   .

Pennsylvania Gazette, July 18, 1751.

Run away on the 12th inst., from William Oakford, at the head of Alloway's Creek, Salem county, a servant man, named Joseph Steel, of a middle stature, short black curl'd hair, about 28 years of age . . . He took with him a Negroe boy named Caesar: Had on when he went away, a new lead colour'd thick cloth coat and vest, leather breeches, short trowsers, thread stockings and half-worn shoes; he had also two felt hats, and two shirts, one white the other brown. The said servants took with them a bay horse, has got the pole-evil, and paces well; a rifle barrel gun, and a large yellow dog, with a white ring round his neck. Whoever takes up and secures said servants, so that their master may have them again, shall have Forty Shillings reward for each, and reasonable charges, paid by

William Oakford.

N.B. The said Steel has serv'd a time in Bucks county, about 17 miles from Philadelphia, on Bristol road; and the Negroe boy was bought out of Philadelphia, about two years since.

Pennsylvania Gazette, April 3, 1760.

Run away last Night from William Scott, of this City, an Apprentice Boy, named Job Goodman, by Trade a Taylor, about 16 or 17 years old, a well looking Boy, tall and slim, has a very innocent Look and Speech, wears brown Hair, tied behind with a black Ribbon (but it is likely he will cut it off, for he has got a blue and white Cotton Cap). Had on when he went away, a light coloured Cloth Coat and Breeches, with yellow carved Metal Buttons, black Jacket, check Shirt, and a pair of Silver Buckles on his Shoes. Whoever takes up the said Apprentice, and brings him home to his said Master shall be rewarded with Forty Shillings, and all reasonable Charges, paid by William Scott.

NB It is likely he may change his Clothes, as he has got, in a greenish coloured Bag, a new blue German Serge Coat, with Buttons and Lining of the Colour, and sundry other clothes, etc. All Masters of Vessels are forbid to carry him off at their peril. If the above Apprentice is inlisted in any of his Majesty's Troops, the Subscriber would be much obliged to any Person that would let him know.

Pennsylvania Gazette, March 6, 1776.

This present instant on the fourteenth day,
My apprentice boy did run away;
Thomas Stillenger he is called by name,
His indenture further testifies the same;
He has always been a vexatious lad,
One reason why he is so meanly clad;

.   .   .   .   .

To describe the rest I am not inclined,
Cloth for a jacket he left behind;
Of apple pies he took with him but five,

For to preserve himself alive;
Three quarter dollars are missed of late,
Which perhaps he took to pay his freight;
Believe him not if you be wise,
He is very artful in telling lies;

.   .   .   .   .

For which I whipt him, I thought severe,
But did not make him shed one tear.
Whoever doth him safely secure
Of a reward they may be sure,
Six-pence at least I do propose
To give for him with all his clothes;
Or clear me of him forever and mine.
And his indentures away I will sign;
Now to inform you further still,
I keep a saw and fulling mill;
In East-Fallowfield township
and Chester County is the place of my abode,
I subscribe my name unto the same, and that is
   William Moode.

Bargains, black and white

Boston Evening Post, Oct. 21, 1751.

To be given away, a fine Negro Male Child.
Enquire of the Printer.

Boston Evening Post, Dec. 9, 1751.

To be sold, a Negro Girl of twelve Years old,
that can be well recommended. Enquire of the
Printer.

Pennsylvania Gazette, Jan. 28, 1755.

To be sold, A likely Negro woman and child.
Enquire at the New Printing Office.

A likely brisk Servant lad, about 16 years of
Age, and is to serve till he's 21 years old, he's
this country born, and brought up to plantation

work, can read, write, and cypher. Any person
that he will suit, may agree with Mr. James
Whitehead, Keeper of the Workhouse, in Philadelphia, who has the selling of him.

Pennsylvania Gazette, April 3, 1760.

To be sold by Thomas Overrend, at the
Drawbridge, Two white Boys and a Negro Lad;
all about fourteen Years of Age. Also very
good Lime juice, by the Hogshead or Gallon.

Servant complains of harsh treatment,
Maryland, 1756

Elizabeth Sprigs, Maryland, to John Sprigs,
London, England, Sept. 22, 1756, in
Isabel M. Calder, *Colonial Captivities,
Marches and Journeys* (New York, 1935),
pp. 151–152.

Betty may have been a convict servant.
According to a census taken in 1755, out of
Maryland's total white population of 107,000,
indentured servants numbered 6,870 and
approximately 2,000 were convict servants.
Abbot E. Smith, *Colonists in Bondage:
White Servitude and Convict Labor in
America, 1607–1776* (Chapel Hill,
1947), p. 324.

Honred Father
   My being for ever banished from your sight,
will I hope pardon the Boldness I now take of
troubling you with these. My long silence has
been purely owing to my undutifullness to you,
and well knowing I had offended in the highest
Degree, put a tie to my tongue and pen, for
fear I should be extinct from your good Graces
and add a further Trouble to you. But too well
knowing your care and tenderness for me so
long as I retain my Duty to you, induced me
once again to endeavour if possible, to kindle
up that flame again. O Dear Father, believe

what I am going to relate the words of truth and sincerity, and Ballance my former bad Conduct [to] my sufferings here, and then I am sure you'll pitty your Destress[ed] Daughter. What we unfortunat English People suffer here is beyond the probility of you in England to Conceive, let it suffice that I one of the unhappy Number, am toiling almost Day and Night, and very often in the Horses druggery, with only this comfort . . . ["]You Bitch you do not halfe enough,["] and then tied up and whipp'd. To that Degree that you'd not serve an Animal, scarce any thing but Indian Corn and Salt to eat and that even begrudged nay many Neagroes are better used. Almost naked no shoes nor stockings to wear, and the comfort after slaving dureing Masters pleasure, what rest we can get is to rap ourselves up in a Blanket and ly upon the Ground. This is the deplorable Condition you poor Betty endures, and now I beg if you have any Bowels of Compassion left show it by sending me some Relief, Cothing is the principal thing wanting, which if you should condiscend to, may easely send them to me by any of the ships bound to Baltimore Town Patapsco River Maryland, and give me leave to conclude in Duty to you and Uncles and Aunts, and Respect to all Friends

    Honred Father
    Your undutifull and Disobedient Child
    Elizabeth Sprigs

Redemptioners and their children, ca. 1750–1818

---

1. Commerce in human beings, 1750

Gottlieb Mittelberger, *Journey to Pennsylvania,* ed. and trans. Oscar Handlin and John Clive (Cambridge, Mass., 1960), pp. 17–19; first published in 1756.

    Mittelberger's journey extended from 1750 to 1754.

Before I begin to describe how this commerce in human beings takes place I must report what the voyage to Philadelphia or Pennsylvania costs. Any one older than ten years has to pay £10, or 60 florins, for the passage from Rotterdam to Philadelphia. Children between five and ten pay half fare, that is to say £5, or 30 florins. All children under the age of five get free passage. In return the passengers are transported across the ocean; and as long as they are at sea, they get their board, however bad it is (as I reported above).

All this covers only the sea voyage; the cost of land transportation from home to Rotterdam, including the Rhine passage, comes to at least 40 florins no matter how economically one tries to live on the way. This does not include the expenses of any extraordinary contingencies. I can assure readers of this much — that many travelers on the journey from their homes to Philadelphia spent 200 florins, even with all possible thrift.

This is how the commerce in human beings on board ship takes place. Every day Englishmen, Dutchmen, and High Germans come from Philadelphia and other places, some of them very far away, sometime twenty or thirty or forty hours' journey, and go on board the newly arrived vessel that has brought people from Europe and offers them for sale. From among the healthy they pick out those suitable for the purposes for which they require them. Then they negotiate with them as to the length of the period for which they will go into service in order to pay off their passage, the whole amount of which they generally still owe. When an agreement has been reached, adult persons by written contract bind themselves to serve for three, four, five, or six years, according to their health and age. The very young, between the ages of ten and fifteen, have to serve until they are twenty-one, however.

Many parents in order to pay their fares in this way and get off the ship must barter and sell their children as if they were cattle. Since the fathers and mothers often do not know where or to what masters their children are to be sent, it frequently happens that after leaving the vessel, parents and children do not see each other for years on end, or even for the rest of their lives.

People who arrive without the funds to pay their way and who have children under the age of five, cannot settle their debts by selling them. They must give away these children for nothing to be brought up by strangers; and in return these children must stay in service until they are twenty-one years old. Children between five and ten who owe half-fare, that is, thirty florins, must also go into service in return until they are twenty-one years old, and can neither set free their parents nor take their debts upon themselves. On the other hand, the sale of children older than ten can help to settle a part of their parents' passage charges.

A wife must be responsible for her sick husband and a husband for his sick wife, and pay his or her fare respectively, and must thus serve five to six years not only for herself or himself, but also for the spouse, as the case may be. If both should be ill on arrival, then such persons are brought directly from the ship into a hospital, but not until it is clear that no purchaser for them is to be found. As soon as they have recovered, they must serve to pay off their fare, unless they have the means immediately to discharge the debt.

It often happens that whole families — husband, wife, and children — being sold to different purchasers, become separated, especially when they cannot pay any part of the passage money. When either the husband or the wife has died at sea, having come more than halfway, then the surviving spouse must pay not only his or her fare, but must also pay for or serve out the fare of the deceased.

When both parents have died at sea, having come more than halfway, then their children, especially when they are still young and have nothing to pawn or cannot pay, must be responsible for their own fares as well as those of their parents, and must serve until they are twenty-one years old. Once free of service, they receive a suit of clothing as a parting gift, and if it has been so stipulated the men get a horse and the women a cow.

---

2. Parents freed by indenture of children, 1818

Jacob Böller, Philadelphia, to Friedrich Rapp, Harmony, Indiana, Nov. 4 and Dec. 7, 1818, in Karl J. R. Arndt, *George Rapp's Harmony Society, 1785–1847* (Philadelphia, 1965), pp. 191–193.

German immigrants, mistakenly believing that George Rapp's Harmony Society would pay their passage to America, were stranded when the Society failed to do so. As in Mittelberger's day, parents with children of working age sold them as servants on the best terms they could arrange. Böller was the Philadelphia agent of the Rapp colony.

Meanwhile the parents are beginning to indenture (*verbinden*) their children and are laying as much of their own passage on them as they can bear! Yesterday, one, Hoffman, allowed a girl of ten years to be indentured for ten years for $80.

· · · · · ·

Schiller and wife, who placed their passage on their children, are free, except a small one. She has just borne a child. Hoffman and wife are free through their children. Schnabel and wife are free by your order, are working industriously, and are saving. It is expected that she will soon bear a child, Schwerdt, wife, and one child are not yet free. Vogt, who with his wife has already indentured several of his beautiful children, but upon whom $200 still rests, is therefore still on the ship. She lies in the hospital giving birth to a child. The Vogt family while they were still all together was an interesting family. Widow Kuenzler is free through her four grown children; the oldest daughter Christiana Frederica lives with us and is an honor to her countrymen. Widow Hass, who lost her husband at sea, and her two children are still on the ship in a deserted condition. Gutbrod and family, not yet free. Witmayer and family not yet free. The people are no longer on board ship but in a storehouse nearby where one can have heat . . . seemingly they are willing to resign themselves to their fate and the direction of the Lord. The Vogt woman, however, does not want to give up *Harmonie* and her friends there. Likewise widow Kuenzler who has a brother there.

Special practices of apprenticeship among the Moravians in North Carolina reconciling the Law of the Land with the Rules of the Brethren

1. Moravians dispose of unruly apprentices by apprenticing them outside the community: indenture of a shoemaker, 1769

Adelaide L. Fries, ed., *Records of the Moravians in North Carolina,* II (Raleigh, 1925), 608–609.

AND during the whole Time of his Apprenticeship lodgeth and boards him the said Andrew Kremser, in the Single Brethren's house, according to the Custom of the United Brethren. AND if the said Apprentice should turn out to be of such Life and Manners, that according to the Rules of the Brethren he could not be tolerated amongst them, and in that Case at the Request of the said Frederic Marshall or his Heirs the said Jacob Frederic Pfeil shall bind out his said Apprentice to an other Master not residing at the Settlement aforesaid.

2. Strict supervision of the conduct of apprentices by the governing council of elders (Aeltester Conferenz)

Extracts from the minutes of the Aeltester Conferenz, Aufseher Collegium, and Grosse Helfer Conferenz, 1773, in *Records of the Moravians,* II, 765–766.[1]

March 2. (Aelt. Conf.) Br. Bonn, as Executor, acting for Sr. Merk, wishes to bind Br. Merk's two apprentices, Jacob Wohlfart and Strub, to other Masters, and asks the opinion of Conference.

Brn. Broesing and Triebel were suggested, and after consulting with the Masters, with Br. Bonn, with the widow, and with both boys, and finding all willing, the boys moved from Bethabara to Salem Brothers House on March 6th, and were taken by the Masters for eight days on trial.

March 9. (Aelt. Conf.) Little G*** K***, who ran away last Sunday from his foster-father and Master, Br. Aust, will be taken back today, by Br. Petersen, and will be told that he must learn obedience before any one can think of letting him learn a profession.

.   .   .   .   .

Before boys are bound to Masters the Aufseher Collegium shall speak with both parties, and then the boy shall be bound by a Justice, with Brethren from the Collegium present as witnesses.

When an Apprentice becomes of age he becomes free, according to the Constitution of the land; and his Indenture shall be canceled by the Aufseher Collegium, with the approval of the Hand-work Committee. And if either Master or Apprentice has anything to complain of it shall be discussed at that time, and settled, so that there may be no after-talk, or groundless accusation.

1. The governing councils of the community, which regulated all economic affairs.

Minutes of the Aeltesten Conferenz of
Wachovia, N.C., Jan. 14, 1774, in
Records of the Moravians, II, 714.

Jan. 14. L*** M*** has written a note to
the Conferenz—his Master, A***, has dismissed him from the workshop. There is fault
on both sides, but a Master has not the right
to dismiss a journeyman or apprentice, but
should try to train the boys so as to make orderly and useful men of them. As there seems
to be hope of doing something with M*** we
will try to bring the two together again, and
persuade them to bury the past, Br. Tiersch will
speak with A***, and Br. Muschbach with
M***.

Extracts from the minutes of the Aufseher
Collegium of Salem, N.C., 1772, Tuesday,
Dec. 1, in *Records of the Moravians,*
II, 709.

. . . It is not well that during work hours
journeymen should be idle, should go pleasure-
walking into the woods or elsewhere, or should
go to the mill, to Bethabara or Bethania, without object, and without permission from their
Masters or the House officials. The apprentices
should also be kept in better order, and there
should be an understanding between the Choir
officials, the Brethren in charge of the Boys,
and the Masters, to hold them to their duties,
that they go to the work-shops at the proper
time, that they work diligently and well, that
they do not linger too long at meals, and that
they continue to work until stopping time, or
until the Master gives permission to lay the
work aside. Much of this can be adjusted in a
conference of Master-workmen.

Children not to be bound as servants,
Pennsylvania, 1793

Respublica *v.* Keppele, 2 Dallas (Penna.)
197 (1793).

According to this decision, parents or
guardians could not bind out children except
as apprentices to learn a trade. In practice,
trade was given a liberal interpretation.
"The art and trade of housewifery," for
example, was a euphemism for servitude.
The same was true of apprenticeship in many
agricultural and industrial employments. See
Herrick A. Cheeseman, *White Servitude in
Pennsylvania, Indentured and Redemption
Labor in Colony and Commonwealth*
(Philadelphia, 1926), p. 108.

A *habeus corpus* was issued to bring up the
body of Benjamin, a minor about fourteen
years old, who had been bound by his guardian's consent to the defendant, to serve her till
he should arrive to the age of fifteen. Having
absconded from her service, he was commtted
to gaol for that cause, and a general question
was made whether an infant could be bound
as a servant in Pennsylvania.

The Court was unanimously of opinion that
the indenture, in this case, was void and gave
their opinions *seriatim.*

The opinion of Justice Bradford (which is
all I have in my notes), entered fully into the
principles of the decision as follows.

Bradford, Justice: The imprisonment of this
infant, if justified at all, must be supported under the Act of 1700 respecting servants, so that
the only question for our determination is
whether he be a servant within the meaning
of that act of Assembly.

It is clear that this indenture, by which the
infant is bound to serve, and not to learn any
trade, occupation, or labor, cannot be supported upon the principles of common law nor
by the express words of any statute. But, it is
said, that it depends upon the custom of the
country, and it is evident that such a custom is
referred to in our laws. I have taken some pains
to ascertain its origin and extent.

This custom seems to have originated with
the first adventurers to Virginia and to have
arisen from the circumstances of the country.
Persons desirous of coming to America, and

unable to pay for their passage in any other way, shipped themselves and their children as servants. If they were imported under indenture, those indentures were held good, and they were to serve according to their stipulation; but if there was no indenture, they were to serve according to the custom, to wit, five years if of full age or above seventeen, and if under seventeen, till they arrived at the age of twenty-two, or in some places till twenty-four. The early laws of Virginia and Maryland (some of them so early as 1638) speak of these servants thus imported. They are called "servants according to the custom," "servants bound to serve the accustomary five years," and sometimes are described as "servants sold for the custom."

These servants were in a very degraded situation. They were a species of property, holding a middle rank between slaves and freemen; they might be sold from hand to hand and they were under the correction of laws exceedingly severe.

It appears by all the early laws on this subject that the custom extended to imported servants only, and it extended to all such as were imported, whether minors or adults. The custom was founded on necessity, and it was thought to be mutually beneficial to the colony and to the emigrant. But no such necessity existed as to the children who were already in the province. The custom, therefore, never extended to them, and there was in all the colonies, and particularly in Pennsylvania, a marked distinction between these two classes of minors. This is to be found in the articles of the laws agreed on in England, and more fully in the laws of 1682. These speak only of imported servants, and direct how long such servants, brought into the province without indentures, shall serve; but in Chapter 112, all parents and guardians in the province are enjoined to teach the children under their care to read and write till they are twelve years old, and that they be instructed in some useful trade or skill. This policy of putting children out as apprentices is carried into our poor laws and those which relate to orphans. Overseers of the poor and the Orphans Courts have no authority to bind out minors as servants, even such as are the objects of public charity. They must be bound apprentices to some "art, trade, occupation, or labor."

There have been instances of children here being bound out as servants, but this has not been general and the courts of justice have always frowned on the attempts.

I agree that it is not necessary to determine how far a father may transfer to another the right which he has to the service of his children, in consideration of that other's instructing him in reading, writing, and the like; nor whether the Court would interfere to take the child out of such person's custody. But, I think it right to say that no parent, under any circumstances, can make his child a servant, in the sense in which this boy is held as such. Though he is entitled to the service of his child, he cannot enforce it, as a master can that of his servants. He cannot commit him to gaol if he runs away; he cannot demand the penalty of five days service for every day of absence, and therefore it is impossible that he can transfer such right to another.

I am, therefore, of opinion with the rest of the Court that this boy is not a servant within the meaning of the Act of 1700, and consequently he must be discharged.

Apprentice prefers to stay with master rather than return to join natural mother

Commonwealth *v.* Hamilton, 6 Mass. Reports 273 (1810).

Catharine Cuddy was apprenticed by her mother to a master in Canada. Later the master moved to Massachusetts, and the girl accompanied him willingly. Catharine's mother remarried and brought a suit to secure her return.

The chief justice enquired of the child if she was restrained against her wishes; to which she answered that she was not, but that she was very desirous of continuing in the family, and under the protection of *Mr. Hamilton.*

By the court. By the return of this writ, it appears that *Catharine Cuddy* was bound as an apprentice to the defendant, agreeably to the laws of *Upper Canada* where the parties then resided. Although it may be true, that on removing into this state, the defendant could not have compelled her to accompany him, yet as she came voluntarily, and as the defendant is under obligation to provide for her; which obligation it is by no means certain that the laws of this commonwealth would not enforce in a case situated like the present; as there is no evidence of any neglect of that duty on his part, but on the contrary, the child appears to have been well treated, and to be attached to the family of the defendant; it would be unreasonable to take her from his care and deliver her to her mother, who by her marriage to her present husband ceased to have any power of controuling her own actions, or of providing for the support and education of her child. Whatever rights she might have had as guardian by nurture, they have certainly ceased at the age [fourteen] of this child; and the husband is under no legal obligations to be at any expense for that object. Let the child be discharged with liberty to remain in the defendant's family, as she has requested: and we further order that neither the said *Margaret,* nor any other person or persons, molest, interrupt or disturb her in respect to her residence in the family of the said *Hamilton.*

The making of a printer, 1809–1826

1. Thurlow Weed's experience, 1809

Thurlow Weed, *The Autobiography of*

Thurlow Weed (Boston, 1883), pp. 2–3, 10, 21–26.

When Thurlow Weed (1797–1882) was apprenticed to a printer at the age of twelve, he had already acquired a variety of work experiences. As in Franklin's case almost a century earlier, failure to complete the apprenticeship did not bar Weed's employment as a printer.

My first employment, when about eight years old, was in blowing a blacksmith's bellows for a Mr. Reeves, who gave me six cents per day, which contributed so much towards the support of the family. I stood upon a box to enable me to reach the handle of the bellows. My next service was in the capacity of boy of all work, at a tavern in the village of Jefferson, two miles from Catskill, kept by a Captain Baker, who had, I remember, made a great mistake in exchanging the command of a ship for a tavern. After the sheriff took possession of Captain Baker's wrecked hotel, I got a situation as cabin boy on board the sloop Ranger, Captain Grant. This gratified a desire I had to see the city of New York. I was then (1806) in my ninth year. I remember, as if it were but yesterday, after carrying the small hair trunk of a passenger from Coenties Slip to Broad Street, finding myself in possession of the first shilling that I could call my own. I remember, too, how joyfully I purchased with that shilling three twopenny cakes and three oranges for my brother and sister, how carefully I watched them on the passage back, and how much happiness they conferred . . . After the Ranger was either condemned or laid up (I don't know which), I went as cabin boy on board the sloop Jefferson, Captain Jacobus Bogardus. I believe I went one trip with Captain Bogardus in the old sloop Washington before the Jefferson was finished.

.   .   .   .   .

1806.—I greatly enjoyed life as a sloop's cabin boy. The trip between Catskill and New York

Tombstone of the Cutler children, Charlestown, Massachusetts, 1680.

Tombstone of the Langley children, Newport, Rhode Island, 1778.

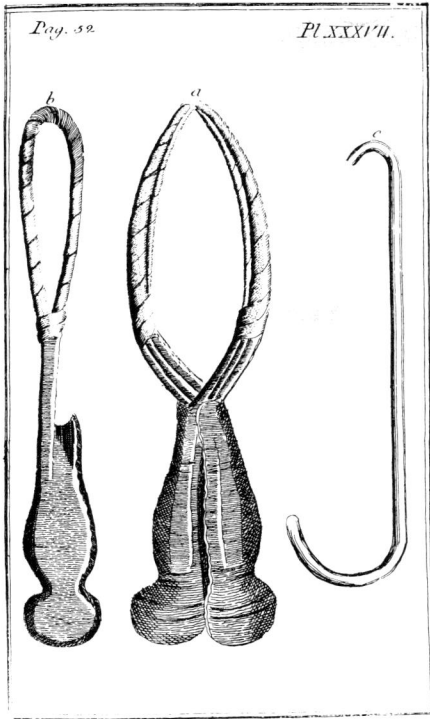

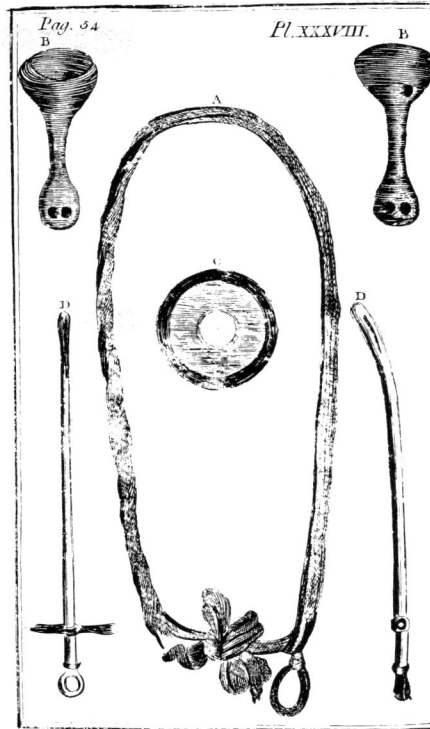

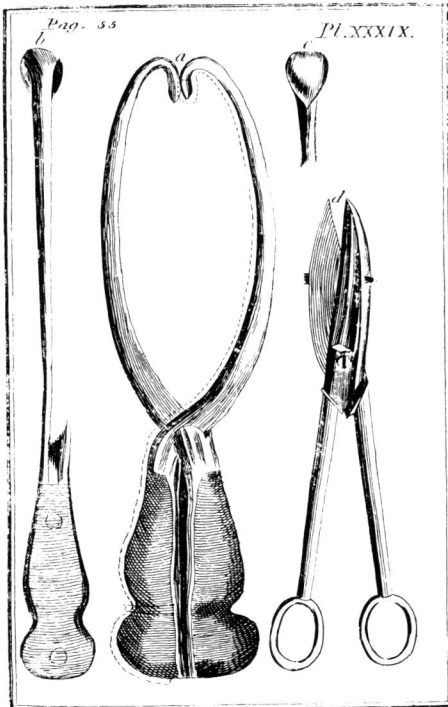

Obstetrical Instruments, 1786.

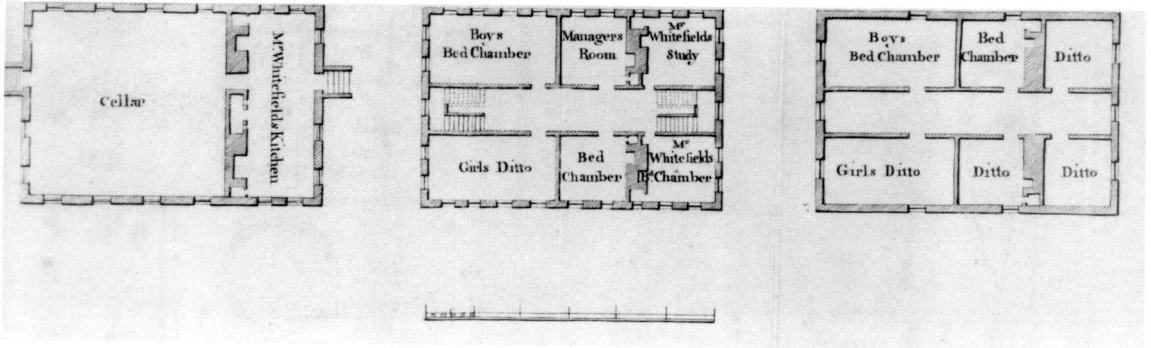

Plan of the Orphan House, Georgia, 1741.

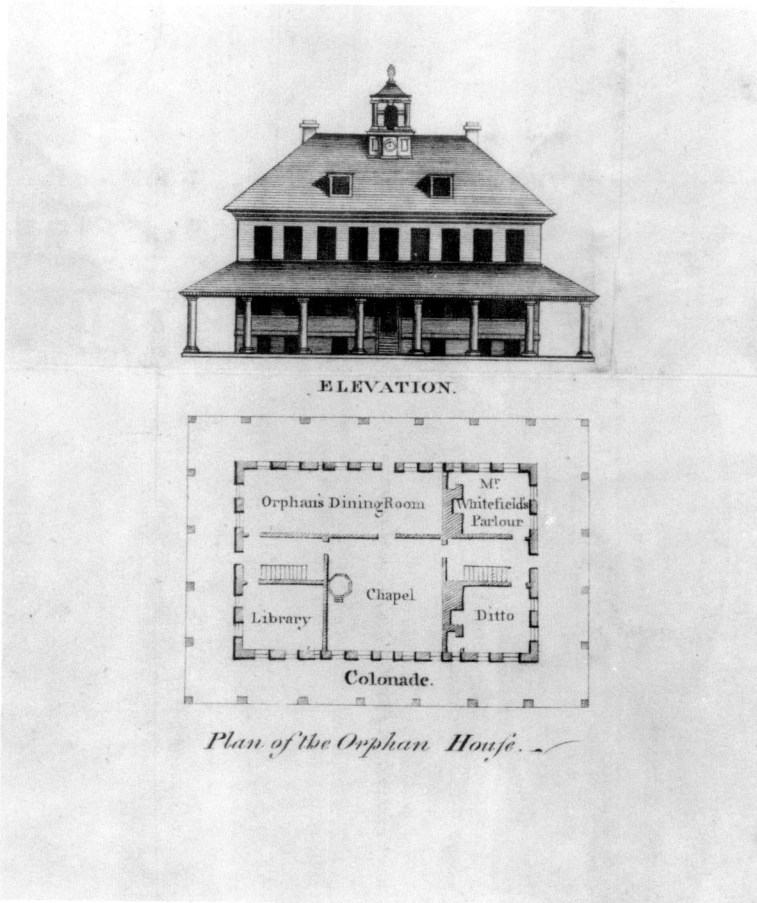

ELEVATION.

Plan of the Orphan House.

averaged from four to ten days. When be-calmed we would go ashore in a small boat to obtain vegetables, fruit, etc. I was soon familiar with all the villages and all the points of historical interest along the river. I became during that time much attached to a sailor named James Van Dervoort, a tall, handsome man, who sang "Cease, rude Boreas," and other nautical songs, with great effect. Van Dervoort, when navigation closed, shipped for a winter voyage to China, or the East Indies. In the "yarns" he used to "spin" about the wonders of the East I was greatly interested, and but for the circumstance that I could not go aloft without becoming dizzy-headed, I should have gone to sea with my friend Van Dervoort.

Thus, but for an infirmity which incapaci-tated me for the most essential part of a sailor's duty, my occupation would have been that of a seaman instead of a printer.

.   .   .   .   .

In the fall and winter of 1808, I was equivo-cally attached to the office of the "Catskill Recorder." I say equivocally, because I was not regularly apprenticed, and yet I carried the paper to the village subscribers, and did "chores" about the office, with a strong desire and hope that I should be received as an ap-prentice. But the hope was disappointed by the removal of my father, with his family, to the town of Cincinnatus, Cortland County, in March, 1808 . . . I bitterly lamented this change, because it cut off my cherished design of becoming either a sailor or a printer.

.   .   .   .   .

Late that autumn [1809] I was rejoiced with the information that printing materials had ar-rived at Onondaga Hollow, where a newspaper was to be published. My father, anxious to see me in the way of learning a trade, gratified my own wishes by making an application in my behalf as an apprentice. But my spirit was crushed on his return, with an answer that no apprentice was wanted, one having been al-ready engaged. I applied to Mr. Hopper, who

was a leading patron of the embryo paper, for his interposition with its proprietor, who finally consented to take me on trial, remarking in no encouraging tone and manner that I was too big and clumsy for a printer, but that I could cut wood and make fires. This ungracious re-ception, however, did not discourage me. The ambition to be a printer was irrepressible.

My first employment as an apprentice, beside cutting wood and making fires in the printing-office, was in "treading pelts," a duty of which the present generation of printers is growing up in ignorance.

The balls, which have been succeeded by rol-lers, were made of green sheepskins, which had to undergo a sort of tanning process between your feet and the floor. It was a long and tedi-ous operation, as every printer whose appren-ticeship commenced previous to 1812 will at-test.

In 1814 dressed deerskin began to be used instead of pelts, but it required time to induce old printers to become reconciled to this in-novation.

.   .   .   .   .

I was now a half-made printer out of place. A few weeks previous one Royal T. Chamber-lin had established a paper called the "Tocsin" at Union Springs, Cayuga County. In that paper I saw that "A boy who has worked some at the business is wanted as an apprentice at this office." I therefore started on foot for Union Springs, and was received by Mr. Royal T. Chamberlin as the boy who had worked some at the business. His office was in the old town of Scipio, some nine miles above the Cayuga bridge. We boarded with the editor and pub-lisher's father, who lived on a farm about two miles from the office. We took an early break-fast, brought our dinner with us, and returned to supper in the evening. I enjoyed this very much, especially as it was in peach season and Mr. Chamberin's father had the fruit in great abundance and perfection.

.   .   .   .   .

I went to work again in the furnace until December, when, having earned some clothes and finding myself with three dollars in cash, I started on foot for Utica, where I had the good fortune to get employment in the printing-office of Messrs. Seward & Williams.

To my application for a situation Mr. Williams, after looking me over somewhat deliberately, replied that he had no work for me; but as I was leaving the office, evidently depressed and as evidently in need of employment, he called me back, and inquired where I came from, how old I was, and why I had not served out my apprenticeship. My answers proving satisfactory, he put a composing stick in my hand, placed some copy before me, and in an encouraging way remarked that he would see what I could do. When he returned two or three hours afterwards, he read over the matter that I had been "settingup," and remarked kindly that I could go with the other boys to supper. I was therefore at work in the office and domiciled in the house of a gentleman (William Williams) who became and ever remained my warm friend, and for whose memory I cherish a grateful remembrance.

2. New York City journeymen printers complain of competition of "half-way journeymen," 1811

Circular of the New York Typographical Society, July 13, 1811, in New York State Department of Labor, *Annual Report of Bureau of Labor Statistics, 1911* (Albany, 1912), pp. 67–69.

In this circular the New York Typographical Society is attempting to regulate apprenticeships.

To the Master Printers
of the City of New York:
Gentlemen: — Viewing with deep concern the improper practices in many of the printing offices in this city the journeymen composing the New York Typographical Society have appointed the undersigned a committee to address you on the subject and represent the many evil effects they have on the art of printing in general and the demoralizing effects on the professors.

The practice of employing what is usually styled "half-way journeymen" in preference to those who have served their time, while it holds encouragement to boys to elope from their master as soon as they acquire sufficient knowledge of the art to be enabled to earn their bread, is a great grievance to the journeymen and almost certain ruin to the boys themselves. Becoming masters of their own conduct at a period of life when they are incapable of governing their passions and propensities they plunge headlong into every species of dissipation and are often debilitated by debauchery before they arrive at the age of manhood; and it also tends to an unnecessary multiplication of apprentices, inasmuch as the place of every boy who elopes from his master is usually supplied by another, while at the same time the runaway supplies after a manner the place of . . . a regular journeyman and one who probably has a family dependent on his labor for support.

· · · · ·

To render an art respectable it is indispensably necessary that professors should be perfect masters of their calling, which can only be acquired by serving a proper apprenticeship. And in our art it is not always true that time will perfect the printer. Regard should always be paid to the capacity and requirements of a boy before he should be suffered to learn the art of printing; for it is too often the case that boys of little or no education are taken as apprentices, which the first services as devil frequently preclude the knowledge of, until they are bound, when the discovery is too late to be remedied. Owing to this deficiency they make the sorry printers; whereas, had they learned some trade which does not particularly require a good education they might have been perfect masters of it and better able to gain a livelihood.

These are the evils, gentlemen, which we sorely feel, and which it is in your power to remedy, and we sincerely hope that this appeal to your justice and your humanity may meet with that consideration which its importance demands.

---

3. Horace Greeley's experience, 1826

James Parton, *The Life of Horace Greeley* (Boston, 1872), pp. 49–55.

. . . "Are you the man that carries on the printing office?"

Mr. Bliss then turned, and resting upon his hoe, surveyed the person who had thus addressed him. He saw standing before him a boy apparently about fifteen years of age, of a light, tall, and slender form, dressed in the plain, farmer's cloth of the time, his garments cut with an utter disregard of elegance and fit. His trowsers were exceedingly short and voluminous; he wore no stockings; his shoes were of the kind denominated "high-lows," and much worn down; his hat was of felt, "one of the old stamp, with so small a brim, that it looked more like a two-quart measure inverted than anything else"; and it was worn far back on his head; his hair was white, with a tinge of orange at its extremities, and it lay thinly upon a broad forehead and over a head "rocking on shoulders which seemed too slender to support the weight of a member so disproportioned to the general outline." The general effect of the figure and its costume was so *outré,* they presented such a combination of the rustic and ludicrous, and the apparition had come upon him so suddenly, that the amiable gardener could scarcely keep from laughing.

He restrained himself, however, and replied, "Yes, I'm the man."

Whereupon the stranger asked, "Don't you want a boy to learn the trade?"

"Well," said Mr. Bliss, "we have been thinking of it. Do *you* want to learn to print?"

"I've had some notion of it," said the boy in true Yankee fashion, as though he had not been dreaming about it, and longing for it for years.

Mr. Bliss was both astonished and puzzled — astonished that such a fellow as the boy *looked* to be, should have ever thought of learning to print, and puzzled how to convey to him an idea of the absurdity of the notion. So, with an expression in his countenance, such as that of a tender-hearted dry-goods merchant might be supposed to assume if a hod-carrier should apply for a place in the lace department, he said, "Well, my boy — but, you know, it takes considerable learning to be a printer. Have you been to school much?"

"No," said the boy, "I haven't had much chance at school. I've read some."

"What have you read?" asked Mr. Bliss.

"Well, I've read some history, and some travels, and a little of most everything."

"Where do you live?"

"At Westhaven."

"How did you come over?"

"I came on foot."

"What's your name?"

"Horace Greeley."

Now it happened that Mr. Amos Bliss had been for the last three years an Inspector of Common Schools, and in fulfilling the duties of his office — examining and licensing teachers — he had acquired an uncommon facility in asking questions, and a fondness for that exercise which men generally entertain for any employment in which they suppose themselves to excel. The youth before him was — in the language of medical students — a "fresh subject," and the Inspector proceeded to try all his skill upon him, advancing from easy questions to hard ones, up to those knotty problems with which he had been wont to "stump" candidates for the office of teacher. The boy was a match for him . . . In Mr. Bliss's own account of the interview, he says, "On entering into conversation, and a partial examination of the qualifications of my new applicant, it required but little time to discover that he possessed a mind of no common order, and an acquired intelligence far beyond his years. He had had but little opportunity at the common school, but he said "he had read some," and what he had read he well understood and remembered. In addition to the ripe intelligence manifested in one so young, and whose instruction had been so limited, there was a single-mindedness, a truthfulness and common sense in what he said, that at once commanded my regard."

After half an hour's conversation with the boy, Mr. Bliss intimated that he thought he would do, and told him to go into the printing-office and talk to the foreman. Horace went to the printing-office, and there his appearance produced an effect on the tender minds of the three apprentices who were at work therein, which can be much better imagined than described, and which is most vividly remembered by the two who survive. To the foreman Horace addressed himself, regardless certainly, oblivious probably, of the stare and the remarks of the boys. The foreman, at first, was inclined to wonder that Mr. Bliss should, for one moment, think it possible that a boy got up in that style could perform the most ordinary duties of a printer's apprentice. Ten minutes' talk with him, however, effected a partial revolution in his mind in the boy's favor, and as he was greatly in want of another apprentice, he was not inclined to be over particular. He tore off a slip of proof-paper, wrote a few words upon it hastily with a pencil, and told the boy to take it to Mr. Bliss. That piece of paper was his fate. The words were: "Guess we'd better try him." Away went Horace to the garden, and presented his paper. Mr. Bliss, whose curiosity had been excited to a high pitch by the extraordinary contrast between the appearance of the boy and his real quality, now entered into a long conversation with him,

questioned him respecting his history, his past employments, his parents, their circumstances, his own intentions and wishes; and the longer he talked, the more his admiration grew. The result was, that he agreed to accept Horace as an apprentice, provided his father would agree to the usual terms; and then, with eager steps, and a light heart, the happy boy took the dusty road that led to his home in Westhaven.

A day or two after, Horace packed up his wardrobe in a small cotton handkerchief. Small as it was, it would have held more; for its proprietor never had more than two shirts, and one change of outer-clothing, at the same time, till he was of age. Father and son walked, side by side, to Poultney, the boy carrying his possessions upon a stick over his shoulder.

At Poultney, an unexpected difficulty arose, which for a time made Horace tremble in his high-low shoes. The terms proposed by Mr. Bliss were, that the boy should be bound for five years, and receive his board and twenty dollars a year. Now, Mr. Greeley had ideas of his own on the subject of apprenticeship, and he objected to this proposal, and to every particular of it. In the first place, he had determined that no child of his should ever be bound at all. In the second place, he thought five years an unreasonable time; thirdly, he considered that twenty dollars a year and board was a compensation ridiculously disproportionate to the services which Horace would be required to render; and finally, on each and all of these points, he clung to his opinion with the tenacity of a Greeley. Mr. Bliss appealed to the established custom of the country; five years was the usual period; the compensation offered was the regular thing; the binding was a point essential to the employer's interest. And at every pause in the conversation, the appealing voice of Horace was heard: "Father, I *guess* you'd better make a bargain with Mr. Bliss"; or, "Father, I guess it won't make much difference"; or, "Don't you think you'd better do it, father?" At one moment the boy was reduced to despair. Mr. Bliss had given it as his *ultimatum* that the proposed binding was absolutely indispensable; he "could do business in no other way." "Well, then, Horace," said the father, "let us go home." The father turned to go; but Horace lingered; he could not give it up; and so the father turned again; the negotiation was re-opened, and after a prolonged discussion, a compromise was effected. What the terms were, that were finally agreed to, I cannot positively state, for the three memories which I have consulted upon the subject give three different replies. Probably, however, they were — no binding, and no money for six months; then the boy could, if he chose, bind himself for the remainder of the five years, at forty dollars a year, the apprentice to be boarded from the beginning. And so the father went home, and the son went straight to the printing office and took his first lesson in the art of setting type.

.   .   .   .   .

The new apprentice took his place at the font, and received from the foreman his "copy," composing stick, and a few words of instruction, and then he addressed himself to his task. He needed no further assistance. The mysteries of the craft he seemed to comprehend intuitively. He had thought of his chosen vocation for many years; he had formed a notion how the types must be arranged in order to produce the desired impression, and, therefore, all he had to acquire was manual dexterity. In perfect silence, without looking to the right hand or to the left, heedless of the sayings and doings of the other apprentices, though they were bent on mischief, and tried to attract and distract his attention, Horace worked on, hour after hour, all that day; and when he left the office at night could set type better and faster than many an apprentice who had had a month's practice. The next day, he worked with the same silence and intensity. The boys were puzzled. They thought it absolutely incumbent on them to perform an initiating rite of some kind; but the new boy gave them no handle, no ex-

cuse, no opening. He committed no greenness, he spoke to no one, looked at no one, seemed utterly oblivious of everything save only his copy and his type. They threw type at him, but he never looked around. They talked saucily *at* him, but he threw back no retort. This would never do. Towards the close of the third day, the oldest apprentices took one of the large black balls with which printers used to *dab* the ink upon the type, and remarking that in his opinion Horace's hair was of too light a hue for so black an art as that which he had undertaken to learn, applied the ball, well inked, to Horace's head, making four distinct dabs. The boys, the journeyman, the pressman and the editor, all paused in their work to observe the result of this experiment. Horace neither spoke nor moved. He went on with his work as though nothing had happened, and soon after went to the tavern where he boarded, and spent an hour in purifying his dishonored locks. And that was all the "fun" the boys "got out" of their new companion on *that* occasion. They were conquered. In a few days the victor and the vanquished were excellent friends.

Horace was now fortunately situated. Ampler means of acquiring knowledge were within his reach than he had ever before enjoyed; nor were there wanting opportunities for the display of his acquisitions and the exercise of his powers.

A boy ships
before the mast, 1817 [1]

Robert Bennett Forbes, *Personal Reminiscences* (Boston, 1878), pp. 30–52.

Robert Forbes (1804–1889) went to sea in 1817 when thirteen years old. By the age of twenty he was master of one of the ships owned by his uncles, James and Thomas H.

1. For additional documents on boys at sea, see below, Part Three, Chap. IV, sec. C.

Perkins. Forbes subsequently became a China trader and shipowner.

I must now go back, and allude to the reasons for my going to sea before the mast. I confess to having often left my legitimate business on Foster's Wharf, where my uncles fitted out their ships; I was very fond of going aloft, sky-larking, and of pulling an oar, and sailing. My cousin, James Perkins, residing at Pine Bank on Jamaica Pond, had often instructed me in his sailboat in the mysteries of luffing, bearing away, beating to windward, &c.; and my experiences at sea in the "Midas," the "Orders in Council," the "Caroline," and the "Leda," had naturally invested me with a maritime prestige; and sometimes my uncle T. H. Perkins would remark at table, when supplying me with pudding, that I should not get any so good off the Cape of Good Hope. I thus became familiar with the idea that I was *born to eat bad puddings off the Cape.* I had no real proclivities for the sea; I was not particularly robust or courageous, and but for the casual remarks of my uncle, to whom I looked up as to the highest known authority, I should have been content to stick to the counting-room of my cousins, in the line of promotion. My brother Thomas was in the office of my uncles, and I fully realized that his superiority in age and acquirements gave him the start of me.

In the early part of October, 1817, I was one day on my usual visit to the ships, when my uncle came on board; and, seeing me actively employed, said, "Well, Ben, which of these ships do you intend to go in?" What more could be said to a boy of thirteen, who had already had so many hints as to the Cape and bad puddings! I answered, "I am ready to go on this one" (the "Canton Packet."). My uncle gave his assent, and told me to go home and see my mother. I did so, and found her much overcome at the idea; but when she saw that I had made up my mind to conform to the destiny imposed upon me by fate and my revered uncle, she gave her consent. I cut short

my connection with oats and shorts, collecting wharfage bills, catching rats, and copying letters in a very bad hand, and took orders from my uncle to go to Gedney King, and get a quadrant, a Bowditch's navigator, a log book, &c.; and he detailed one of the older clerks named Archibald, who had been to sea, to go to some slop-shop, and procure for me a chest and a full outfit of sailor's clothes. I think they consisted of new, unwashed checked shirts, duck trousers much too large, socks, shoes, a pea-jacket, a tin pot, an iron spoon, and several knives, a bed filled with pig's hair, and a blanket or two. The smaller luxuries were to be drawn from home.

. . . . .

Preparations for my departure were made at home, — a supply of thread, needles, buttons, &c., was put into what sailors call a "ditty bag." Some well-darned socks, some well-patched clothes, a Testament from my aunt, Mrs. Abbot of Exeter, a bottle of red lavender, one of essence of peppermint, a small box of broken sugar, and a barrel of apples from that good friend and neighbor, Dr. Holbrook, completed my equipment. My mother wanted to give me a pillow and some sheets and pillow-cases, but I scorned the idea, having been told that sailors never used them, but usually slept with a stick of wood with the bark on for a pillow! My good mother, who had been at sea herself, and fully realized the dangers and temptations to which I should be exposed, felt that there could be but one more severe trial for her, and that was to put me into my grave. My uncle contributed a letter full of excellent advice, recommending me to fit myself to be a good captain, and promising to keep me in mind. Mr. William Sturgis, who had always been a warm friend of my mother, and who had much experience of the sea, took an interest in me, and gave me this advice: "Always go straight forward, and if you meet the devil cut him in two, and go between the pieces; if any one imposes on you, tell him to whistle against a north-wester, and to bottle up moonshine." The moral of the first part of these injunctions I have endeavored to keep constantly before me.

The day for our departure came, Oct. 19, 1817. I took leave of home amidst the tears of the children, and, with my mother's blessing, embarked in the "Canton Packet," Captain John King; chief mate, George W. Stetson; second mate, William Rowson; and got under way in company with the ship "Levant," Captain Charles S. Cary. I had the satisfaction of seeing the captain and mate casting up their accounts while I remained well; but this was not of long duration. We had a good run off the coast, which, however, is a mere matter of tradition, as I was soon taken deadly sea-sick; and, could I have gone back then, my nautical career would have terminated. I had no kind mother to hold my dizzy head, and no sister's kind words to cheer me; and when I went to the weather-side to transfer to Neptune what I could not retain, I was roughly told that nothing must be thrown to windward save ashes and hot water! I cared little if they cast me overboard. When I was carried down to the dark steerage, and put upon my own resources, I found my trunk or chest knocking about, my bed unpacked, my tin pot flattened into a small compass. I threw myself down on the bare deck, and slept from mere exhaustion. When I awoke, the ship was tumbling about awfully. I lay smothered in onions, owing to the strings chafing off as they hung over my head. I then called upon my ill stars for sending me to sea, and sighed to be back among the oats and shorts. After a day or two of tears and lamentations, during which the captain was too much engaged to think of me, I crawled on deck, and sat me down to leeward of the main-mast in the coil of the fore-brace. Soon an order was given to square the fore-yard; and the party who let fly the lee-brace no doubt anticipated the result, for I was pitched into the lee-scuppers. I now remembered the injunctions of my mother; namely, whenever I felt sea-sick or faint to take a few drops of peppermint or red lavender on a piece of sugar: the natural result was that I plied the bottles to such an extent that I was

nearly killed thereby. I went to the captain for relief, and he gave me some powerful pills. During the night a gale had come on, and I was obliged, by imperative calls, to go on deck; I crawled along the lee-side of the long-boat bound to the fore-channels. I returned stealthily to the steerage-hatch as naked as I was born, cold, and thoroughly exhausted. In stealing down the ladder, I met the carpenter, Johnny Heatman, coming up; he put his hand against my cold body, and fell back with an emphatic ejaculation of fear: as I found out later, he supposed I was the ghost of the steward who blew up the "Canton Packet" on election day.

During my illness, I was green enough to inform the older boys, one of whom, named Brush, had been in a man-of-war, and knew a thing or two, that I had a barrel of apples in the hold, to which they were welcome; the inevitable result was that when I came to my stomach the barrel was empty. My mother had also provided for me a small bag of hard-baked ginger-nuts, which, for safe-keeping, I had put into a bag containing my boots and shoes; I hung this at the foot of my bunk, an upper one, the lower being occupied by Brush. He very soon realized that my bag contained something besides leather, and he shifted his head forward, made a small hole in my bag, and gradually appropriated the ginger-nuts. These early lessons caused me to be less trustful of human nature, and especially of big boys who had seen service in vessels of war!

When I went into my dark quarters, unincumbered by clothes, I opened my chest, and arrayed myself in a new check shirt, a pair of long duck trousers, and went to my bunk. For several days, I lay there ill and uncared for, and when at last I came to my stomach, and went on deck, I found myself completely tatooed like an Indian by the check shirt.

.   .   .   .   .

With a return of health, after two or three weeks of intense mental and bodily suffering, came an exorbitant appetite; salt beef, pork and beans, hard duff, and harder bread disappeared with wonderful fleetness. My rusty knife, my iron spoon, and battered tin pot came into constant use.

We had by this time got into the north-east trade winds, and were bowling along at the rate of seven or eight knots; a bright moon shone over us, and I remembered that I was born to *higher* purposes than merely keeping the bread from moulding. I asked leave to *go aloft* and furl a royal, and did not have to solicit the favor a second time. I had often gone above the tops, at the wharf, through the "lubbers' hole"; but now that I had become a sailor, my dignity forbade any such course. I made a desperate effort, and went up the futtock shrouds, and was glad, when fairly over the top-rim, to pause and take breath. I furled the sail, as I thought, very well; but I noticed that a man went up after me to mend the job. Night came. I had not been ordered as yet to stand my watch, but, remembering the injunctions of my uncle, I asked leave to do so, and was put into the second mate's watch, and ordered to keep a good lookout for land in the lee gang-way, from eight to ten. Having some knowledge of geography, I knew there was no land near. By and by, I followed the example of my comrades by settling myself for a nap under the lee of the long-boat. At twelve o'clock I went to my sweet sleep, feeling proudly conscious that I had actually begun my career as a sailor. Four A.M. came very quickly. I heard the watch called; the moon had gone down, and a rain squall had come on. The appalling sound of three thumps on the booby-hatch, and the cry of "starboard watch, ahoy!" caused very unpleasant sensations; it appeared to me that I had not been asleep more than ten minutes. I did not like the pattering of the rain on deck, and, thinking I should not be missed, I kept still, and prepared to finish my short nap, so rudely broken. I soon heard Mr. Rowson crying down the hatchway, "You boy, Bob! where are you? If not on deck in five minutes, I shall be after you with a rope's end." At first, I made no answer, thinking that my insignificant services would not pay for a second call. I argued thus: I am very comfortable where I am, and very sleepy; the scene on deck has changed much, the moon has gone down, and the rain is pouring merrily. And I did not relish the thought of going from one extreme to the other.

But the mate reiterated something about the royal clewline and my back. Not relishing this aspect of royalty, I grunted an unwilling "Ay, ay, sir!" and went on deck, when the following dialogue occurred: —

"Well, sir, why not on deck when the watch was called?"

Answer. — "I tried keeping watch at my own request, but, not liking it, I concluded not to go up."

"You began to keep watch to please yourself, my boy, and now you must continue in order to please me."

Although I was not quite convinced of the justice of this style of reasoning, I soon became accustomed to turn out quickly, and *stand* my watch by sleeping on deck much of the time, or in spinning yarns with my shipmates.

．　　．　　．　　．　　．

Of the boys, my companions in the mess, we had John Brush, who had swept up most of my apples and ginger-nuts. He had been taken in the "President" frigate, had been in Dartmoor prison, and was strongly infected by contact with hard characters. Harry Farnham was the son of a respectable silver-ware merchant of Boston. He was very smart, and disliked his position as aid to the cook, Harris; and as I was a great favorite with the sable king of the pantry, and got many tid-bits from him, there grew up a rivalry between us, of which more by and by. John Heatman must have been lost at sea; he was too careful and too tough ever to die a natural death . . .

On our way to China, off the Cape, we lost overboard, one dark night, a sailor named Harry Neal; he was knocked over in furling the spanker. The night was dark, and, when the alarm was given, the ship was rounded to, a boat lowered, and search made for poor Harry. Stetson and four men went to look for him at great risk, but failed to find him, and had great difficulty in regaining the ship. This accident made a great impression on me. The Sunday following, his effects were sold by auction to his shipmates, and the memory of poor Harry soon became a blank.

.   .   .   .   .

We arrived at Canton, March 13, 1818, by the eastern passage, and I soon became domesticated with my cousin, John P. Cushing, then at the head of the house of Perkins & Co., Canton. Here began an epoch in my life which was of great importance: a connection which led directly to fortune, and which never ended but with the life of my cousin, in April, 1861.

The way to wealth

Benjamin Franklin, *Advice to a Young Tradesman* (Boston, 1762), unpaged.

Remember that TIME is Money. He that can earn ten Shillings a Day by his Labour, and goes abroad or sits idle one Half of that Day, though he spends but Six-Pence during his Diversion or Idleness, ought not to reckon *that* the only Expence, he has really spent, or rather thrown away, five Shillings besides.

.   .   .   .   .

Remember this Saying — The good Paymaster is Lord of another Man's Purse. He that is known to pay punctually and exactly to the Time he promises, may at any Time, and on any Occasion, raise all the Money his Friends can spare. This is sometimes of great Use. After Industry and Frugality, Nothing contributes more to the Raising a young Man in the World than *Punctuality* and Justice in all his Dealings: Therefore never keep borrowed Money an Hour beyond the Time you promised, lest a Disappointment shuts up your Friend's Purse forever.

.   .   .   .   .

Be encouraged to Diligence in your Calling, and trust in Providence. Establish a Character as an *honest* and *faithful,* as well as *skilful* Workman, and you need not fear the Want of Employment. Industry pays Debts, while Despair increases them. Something doing, something coming. Industry is sure of Profit.

.   .   .   .   .

In short, the Way to Wealth, if you desire it, is as plain as the Way to Market. It depends chiefly on two Words, INDUSTRY and FRUGALITY; that is, *Waste neither Time nor Money, but make the best Use of both.* Without Industry and Frugality nothing will do, and with them every Thing. He that gets all he can honestly, and saves all he gets (necessary Expences excepted) will certainly become RICH — If that Being who governs the World, to whom all should look for a Blessing on their honest Endeavours, doth not, in his wise Providence, otherwise determine.

B. INFANT INDUSTRIES

The economic value of children in America

---

1. Adam Smith on child power as the nation's wealth, 1776

Adam Smith, *An Inquiry into the Nature and Causes of the Wealth of Nations,* I (London, 1819), 94–95; first published in 1776.

Those who live to old age, it is said, frequently see there [North America] from fifty to a hundred, and sometimes many more descendants from their own body. Labor is there so well rewarded that a numerous family of children, instead of being a burden, is a source of opulence and prosperity to the parents. The labor of each child before it can leave their house, is computed to be worth a hundred pounds clear gain to them. A young widow with four or five young children, who, among the middling or inferior ranks of people in Europe would have so little chance for a second husband, is there frequently counted as a sort of fortune. The value of children is the greatest of all encouragement to marriage. We cannot, therefore, wonder that the people in North America should generally marry very young. Notwithstanding the great increase occasioned by such early marriages, there is a continual complaint of the scarcity of hands in North America.

conducted by the Germans in extending human happiness, is manifested by the joy they express upon the birth of a child. No dread of poverty, nor distrust of Providence from an encreasing family, depress the spirits of these industrious and frugal people. Upon the birth of a son, they exult in the gift of a ploughman or a waggoner; and upon the birth of a daughter, they rejoice in the addition of another spinster, or milkmaid to their family. Happy state of human society! what blessings can civilization confer, that can atone for the extinction of the ancient and patriarchal pleasure of raising up a numerous and healthy family of children, to labour for their parents, for themselves, and for their country; and finally to partake of the knowledge and happiness which are annexed to existence! The joy of parents upon the birth of a child is the grateful echo of creating goodness. May the mountains of Pennsylvania be for ever vocal, with songs of joy upon these occasions! They will be the infallible signs of innocence, industry, wealth and happiness in the state.

2. Value of children among Pennsylvania Germans, 1789

Benjamin Rush, "An Account of the Manners of the German Inhabitants of Pennsylvania," in *Essays, Literary, Moral, and Philosophical,* 2d ed. (Philadelphia, 1806), pp. 232–233.

The Germans seldom *hire* men to work upon their farms. The feebleness of that authority which masters possess over hired servants, is such that their wages are seldom procured from their labour, except in harvest, when they work in the presence of their masters. The wives and daughters of the German farmers frequently forsake, for a while, their dairy and spinning wheel, and join their husbands and brothers in the labour of cutting down, collecting and bringing home the fruits of their fields and orchards. The work of the gardens is generally done by the women of the family.

.   .   .   .   .   .

The favourable influence of agriculture, as

Arguments in support of manufacturing, 1775–1791

To overcome the prejudice against manufacturing — as inimical to and less desirable than agriculture — advocates regularly cited the usefulness of manufacturing as a means of providing employment for young children and women. Daniel Roberdeau (1727–1795), a Philadelphia merchant, was president of the Pennsylvania Society for the Encouragement of Manufactures; Tench Coxe, also a Philadelphian and president of the Society for the Encouragement of Manufactures, was assistant secretary of the treasury at the time Hamilton, as secretary, presented his "Report on Manufactures."

1. Child labor will make cloth cheap, 1775

Daniel Roberdeau, "A Speech Delivered in Carpenter's Hall . . . before the Subscribers towards a fund for establishing Manufacturing . . . in the City of Philadelphia, 1775," in Peter Force, ed., *American Archives . . . ,* 4th ser., II (Washington, D.C., 1839), 143.

. . . There is an endless variety in the geniuses of men; and it would be to preclude the exertion of the faculties of the mind to confine them entirely to the simple arts of agriculture. Besides, if these Manufactories were conducted as they ought to be, two-thirds of the labour of them will be carried on by those members of society who cannot be employed in agriculture, namely, by women and chidren.

A second objection is, that we cannot manufacture cloths so cheap here, as they can be imported from *Britain* . . . The expense of manufacturing cloth will be lessened from the great share women and children will have in them; and I have the pleasure of informing you that the machine lately brought into this City for lessening the expense of time and hands in spinning, is likely to meet with encouragement from the Legislature of our Province. In a word, the experiments which have been already made among us, convince us that woollens and linens of all kinds may be made and bought as cheap as those imported from *Britain;* and I believe every one who has tried the former, will acknowledge that they wear twice as well as the latter.

2. "We shall deliver them from the curse of idleness"

A plain, but real Friend to America, "On American Manufactures," *American Museum,* I (Feb. 1787), 118–119.

. . . What period shall we appoint for ourselves when to begin? How long will it take us until we arrive at sufficient age, and are fit to go to work? — Surely, the time of youth is a very proper period to serve our apprenticeship. This I have found in common life. We seldom see a person fond of labour in old age, who has lived an idle life when young. But if we neglect arts and manufactures much longer, we shall find it still more difficult to begin.

.   .   .   .   .

By manufacturing ourselves, and employing our own people, we shall deliver them from the curse of idleness. We shall hold out to them a new stimulus and encouragement to industry and every useful art. We shall open an extensive field to many laudable pursuits. The speculative, the ingenious, as well as the laborious, may all employ their time and talents to valuable purposes. Idleness may be justly termed the bane of the mind, and the grand inlet to numerous vices. Nations that are remarkable for idleness and sloth, are for the most part prone to luxury, effeminacy, and extravagance. What hasty strides have we not taken since the peace to gain the summit of those refinements! O may the good genius of America now step forth, and inspire her infatuated sons, to make a solemn pause, to consider, and to amend!

3. The employment of persons who would otherwise be idle, 1791

Alexander Hamilton, "Report on Manufactures, December 5, 1791," *Works,* III (New York, 1850), 207–208.

As to the additional employment of classes of the community, not originally engaged in the particular business.

This is not among the least valuable of the means, by which manufacturing institutions contribute to augment the general stock of industry and production. In places where those institutions prevail, besides the persons regularly engaged in them, they afford occasional and extra employment to industrious individuals and families, who are willing to devote the leisure resulting from the intermissions of their ordinary pursuits to collateral labours, as a resource for multiplying their acquisitions or their enjoyments. The husbandman himself experiences a new source of profit and support, from the increased industry of his wife and daughters; invited and stimulated by the demands of the neighbouring manufactories.

Beside this advantage of occasional employment to classes having different occupations, there is another of a nature allied to it, and of a similar tendency. This is, the employment of persons who would otherwise be idle (and in many cases a burden on the community), either from the bias of temper, habit, infirmity of body, or some other cause, indisposing or disqualifying them for the toils of the country. It is worthy of particular remark, that, in general, women and children are rendered more useful, and the latter more early useful, by manufacturing establishments, than they would otherwise be. Of the number of persons employed in the cotton manufactories of Great-Britain, it is computed that four-sevenths nearly are women and children; of whom the greatest proportion are children, and many of them of a tender age.

And thus it appears to be one of the attributes of manufactures, and one of no small consequence, to give occasion to the exertion of a greater quantity of industry, even by the *same number* of persons, where they happen to prevail, than would exist, if there were no such establishments.

Tench Coxe, *A View of the United States of America* (Philadelphia, 1794), pp. 54–55.

Opinions had prevailed in America, that manufacturing employments were injurious to the best interests of the country; that the pursuit of agriculture should occupy all our citizens; and that labour was so dear, as to preclude all chances of success. Yet it was observed, that many emigrators, and others in the manufacturing branches, had actually succeeded; and it was manifest, that the civil and religious freedom of the country, and the low price of food, of fuel, and of raw materials, would continue to attract persons of that description. Further investigation and reflection threw new and pleasing lights upon the subject. It was perceived, that children, too young for labour, could be kept from idleness and rambling, and of course from early temptations to vice, by placing them for a time in manufactories, and that the means of their parents to clothe, feed, and educate them, could be thereby increased; that women, valetudinarians, and old men, could be employed; that the portions of time of housewives and young women, which were not occupied in family affairs, could be profitably filled up; that machinery, horses, fire, water, and various processes requiring only some incipient labour, were the principal means of manufacturing in Britain; that manufactures, instead of impeding agriculture in that country, are actually its greatest and most certain support, and that, in truth, *they are indispensably necessary to the prosperity of its landed interest.*

Employment of children in the early manufactures

---

4. Manufactories keep children from idleness and rambling, 1794

1. George Washington favorably impressed by the work of young girls in a duck factory, Boston, 1789

John C. Fitzpatrick, ed., *The Diaries of George Washington, 1748–1799,* IV (Boston, 1925), 37–38.

October 28, 1789. Went after an early breakfast, to visit the duck manufacture, which appeared to be carrying on with spirit, and is in a prosperous way. They have manufactured 32 pieces of duck of 30 or 40 yds. each in a week; and expect in a short time to increase it to [   ]. They have 28 looms at work, and 14 girls spinning with both hands (the flax being fastened to their waste). Children (girls) turn the wheels for them, and with this assistance each spinner can turn out 14 lbs. of thread per day when they stick to it, but as they are paid by the piece, or work they do, there is no other restraint upon them but to come at 8 o'clock in the morning, and return at 6 in the evening. They are the daughters of decayed families, and are girls of character — none others are admitted. The number of hands now employed in the different parts of the work is [   ] but the managers expect to increase them to [   ]. This is a work of public utility and private advantage.

2. Boy-power in James Davenport's industry, 1794

Advertisement in *Massachusetts Mercury,* Aug. 24, 1798, in William R. Bagnall, *Textile Industries of the United States,* I (Cambridge, Mass., 1893), 225.

James Davenport received the first patent issued in the United States for his spinning machinery in Philadelphia (1794). He set up his machinery for spinning and weaving by water power at the Globe Mills, Philadelphia. The labor was chiefly performed by boys, one of whom was able to spin 292,000 feet of flax or hempen thread in a day of ten hours.

Spinning by Machinery
Into Thread and Twine

James Davenport proposes to sell or erect his Machine for spinning Hemp, Flax and Tow; he will complete it, and let it to work, and instruct any person inclined to purchase. These who have seen the machine at work will allow that the subjoined statement is strictly correct.

Thread. Two boys and one man can spin from 20 to 60 lb. per day; according to the fineness, regular and even.

Twine, Seine, or *Sewing.* This Machine will double twist, and finish from 50 to 60 lbs. per day, with 3 boys from 10 to 12 years old, which for regularity and excellence cannot be surpassed by the twisting by hand of the best workmen.

. . . . .

Any person willing to treat for the purchase of this invaluable invention, may hear the terms by applying to J. Davenport, at John Baker's Hotel, Water-street.

Wanted, A Partner, who will find it advantageous.

3. Impressions of Henry Wansey, the Wiltshire clothier, of his visit to the Dickson, Livingston & Co. factory, Hellgates, New York, on May 31, 1794

Henry Wansey, *Journal of an Excursion to the United States* (London, 1798), p. 60.

Went with a party to see Dickson's Cotton Factory at Hell-Gates, about five miles from New York. It is worked by a breast water-wheel, twenty feet in diameter. There are two large buildings, four stories high, and eighty feet long. In one shop, I saw twenty-six looms at work, weaving fustians, calicoes, nankeens, nankinets, dimities, &c., and there are ten other looms in the neighbourhood. They have the new-invented spring-shuttle. They also spin by water, using all the new improvements of Arkwright and others. Twelve or fourteen workmen are from Manchester. All the machinery in wood, steel, and brass were made on the spot from models, brought from England and Scotland. They are training up women and children to the business, of whom I saw twenty or thirty at work. They give the women two dollars a week, and find them in board and lodging. The children are bound apprentices till twenty-one years of age, with an engagement to board, clothe, and educate them. They have the machine called the mule, at which they have spun cotton so fine as twenty-one hundred scains to the pound, and they propose making muslins.

4. "Pity those little creatures . . . ," 1801

"Journey of Josiah Quincy through Southern Parts of New England, 1801," MHS *Proceedings,* 2d ser., IV (1887–1889), 124.

Josiah Quincy, later Mayor of Boston, and subsequently president of Harvard, expressed compassion for toiling children. His position was exceptional at a time when child labor was generally viewed as beneficial to the child and society.

These consist chiefly of Iron, paper, and cotton works, in the last of which a very complicated and ingenious machinery performs all the requisite labor . . . All the processes of turning cotton from its rough into every variety of marketable thread state, such as cleaning, carding, spinning, winding, etc., are here performed by machinery operating by water wheels only by children from four to ten years old, and one superintendent. Above one hundred of the former are employed at the rate of from 12 to 25 cents for a day's labor. Our attendant was very eloquent on the usefulness of this manufacture, and the employment is supplied to so many poor children. But an eloquence

was exerted on the other side of the question more commanding than this, which calls us to pity those little creatures, plying in a contracted room, among flyers and coggs, at an age when nature requires for them air, space and sports. There was a dull dejection in the countenance of all of them.

5. Advertisement for child workers, eight to twelve years old, 1808

Federal Gazette (Baltimore), Jan. 4, 1808.

Baltimore Cotton Manufactory.

This manufactory will go into operation in all this month, where a number of boys and girls, from eight to twelve years of age, are wanted, to whom constant employment and encouraging wages will be given; also, work will be given out to women at their homes, and widows will have the preference in all cases where work is given out, and satisfactory recommendations will be expected. This being the first essay of the kind in this city, it is hoped that those citizens, having a knowledge of families, having children destitute of employment, will do an act of public benefit, by directing them to this institution. Applications will be received by Thomas White, at the Manufactory, near the Friends' Meetinghouse, Old Town, or by the subscriber.

Isaac Burneston, No. 196 Market Street.

6. Women and children in the early textile labor force, 1811

Albert Gallatin, "Manufactures, April 19, 1810," *American State Papers, Finance,* II (1832), 427.

Returns have been received of eighty-seven mills, which were erected at the end of the year 1809; sixty-two of which (forty-eight, water, and fourteen, horse, mills) were in operation, and worked, at that time, thirty-one thousand spindles. The other twenty-five will all be in operation in the course of this year, and, together with the former ones, (almost all of which are increasing their machinery) will, by the estimate received, work more than eighty thousand spindles at the commencement of the year 1811.

The capital required to carry on the manufacture, on the best terms, is estimated at the rate of one hundred dollars for each spindle; including both the fixed capital applied to the purchase of the mill-seats, and to the construction of the mills and machinery, and that employed in wages, repairs, raw materials, goods on hand, and contingencies. But it is believed that no more than at the rate of sixty dollars for each spindle is generally actually employed. Forty-five pounds of cotton, worth about 20 cents a pound, are, on an average, annually used for each spindle; and these produce about thirty-six pounds of yarn, of different qualities, worth, on an average, one dollar and twelve and a half cents a pound. Eight hundred spindles employ forty persons, viz: five men and thirty-five women and children. On those data, the general results for the year 1811, are estimated in the following table:

		Persons employed		
			Women and	
Mills	Spindles	Men	children	Total
87	80,000	500	3,500	4,000

The increase of carding and spinning of cotton by machinery, in establishments for that purpose, and exclusively of that done in private families, has, therefore, been fourfold, during the two last years, and will have been tenfold in three years.

Child workers and families in the early textile factories

1. The first workers in the Slater textile mill were all children, Providence, 1790

Letter of Smith Wilkinson to George White, May 30, 1835, in George S. White, *Memoir of Samuel Slater,* 2d ed. (Philadelphia, 1836), p. 76.

Mr. Slater came to Pawtucket early in January, 1790, in company with Moses Brown, William Almy, Obadiah Brown, and Smith Brown, who did a small business in Providence, at manufacturing on billies and pennies, driven by men, as also were the carding machines. They wove and finished jeans, fustians, thicksetts, velveretts, etc., the work being mostly performed by Irish emigrants. There was a spinning-frame in the building, which used to stand on the southwest abutment of Pawtucket Bridge, owned by Ezekiel Carpenter, which was started for trial after it was built for Andrew Dexter and Lewis Peck, by Joseph and Richard Anthony, who are now living at or near Providence. But the machine was very imperfect and made very uneven yarn. The cotton for this experiment was carded by hand, and roped on a woolen wheel by a female. Mr. Slater entered into contract with William Almy and Smith Brown, and commenced building a water-frame of 24 spindles, two carding machines, and the drawing and roping frames, necessary to prepare for the spinning, and soon after added a frame of 48 spindles. He commenced sometime in the fall of 1790, or winter of 1791. I was then in my tenth year, and went to work for him, and began tending the breaker. Four children of David Arnold — Turpin, Charles, Eunice and Ann — also Smith Wilkinson, Jabez Jenks, John and Sylvanus Jenks, and Otis Barrows, were the operatives in 1790 and 1791. These children were from seven to twelve years of age.

2. Family labor force in the Slater
factory, 1813

List extracted from Time Books for 1813 in
Cotton Mills, 1813–1816, Slater Papers,
Harvard Business School.

1 family with 8 members working
1 family with 7 members working
2 families each with 5 members working
4 families each with 4 members working
5 families each with 3 members working
8 single men
4 single women

3. The Gifford family at the Troy mill,
Fall River, Massachusetts, 1815

Quoted in Otey, "Children in the Cotton
Industry," p. 63.

Daniel Gifford and family to have the following price for one year from the time of his
moving into our house — which was on the
5th of 5th mo., 1815 — to have one half of the
1st. one-story house at $30.

Himself per day $1.00
Oldest boy to tend picker 67
2nd boy 50
3rd girl 42
4th do 44
5th do 25
6th boy 25
7th girl 10
8th and 9th boy and girl . . . .

4. The Rier family, Lancaster,
Massachusetts, 1815

Plant and Poignaud Papers in the
Lancaster Town Library, in Otey, "Children
in the Cotton Industry," p. 64.

Dennis Rier had the authority to sign a
contract not only for his own family, but
for his sister and her children as well. It is
quite possible that the sister was a widow
and therefore dependent on Rier.

Dennis Rier of Newbury Port has this day
engaged to come with his family to work in our
factory on the following conditions. He is to
be here about the 20th of next month [January
1815] and is to have the following wages per
week:

Himself	$5.00
His son Robert Rier, 10 years of age	.83
Daughter Mary, 12 years of age	1.25
Son William, 13 years of age	1.50
Son Michael, 16 years of age	2.00
	10.58
His sister, Abigail Smith	2.33
Her daughter Sally, 8 years of age	.75
Son Samuel, 13 years of age	1.50
	4.58

House rent to be from $20. to $30.[1] Wood cut
up $2. per cord.

6. Wanted, children and families for the mills

Massachusetts Spy (Worcester),
May 13, 1818, p. 3.

WANTED,

A steady, active BOY, from
twelve to fifteen years of age, as an Apprentice
to the *Carding Wool and Clothiers Business.*
One that can produce good recommendations,

1. This amount would be for one year.

will meet with good encouragement. — inquire at the *Spy* office.

Massachusetts Spy, May 27, 1818, p. 3.

Family wanted

Wanted, at Samuel Slayter's Factory, in Oxford, a FAMILY with 5 or 6 Children, to work to the Mills. One that has worked in a Mill would be preferred.
Good recommendations will be required.—
Apply at the Factory
    Oxford, May 20, 1818.

Massachusetts Spy, March 8, 1820, p. 3.

WANTED,

At the Factory of Leland
Morse & Co. two or three FAMILIES,
of four or five children each. Those who are in the habit of profanity or Sabbath breaking, and intend to continue these practices, are invited not to make application.

Paternalism in the textile factories

1. The first Sunday school in America was for factory children

White, *Samuel Slater,* pp. 107–108.

Mr. Samuel Slater, on the establishment of the old mill, introduced among the labourers therein such regulations, as his previous observations of cotton mills in Derbyshire had shown to be useful and applicable to the circumstances of an American population. Amongst these, that which every philanthropist will deem the most important, was the system of Sunday-school instruction — which had been for some time in full operation, at all the mills of Messrs. Strutt and Arkwright, when Mr. Slater left England.

These schools, the first of the kind in America, are still continued at the present day. They have been copied, and extended with the extension of the cotton manufacture through this country; and they have prompted the establishment of similar schools in our seaport towns and in foreign countries. It was from Pawtucket that they were introduced into Providence in 1815, by the young men of the latter place, one of whom, William Jenkins, had been a clerk with Mr. Slater. These institutions were at first considered as charity schools only; and the teachers paid by the young men. They were subsequently taken under the care and patronage of the different religious societies, by whom they have been made to serve the purpose of biblical instruction. In addition to these schools for Sunday instruction, the establishment and support of common day schools was promoted at all the manufactories in which Mr. Slater was interested; and in some cases, the teachers were wholly paid by himself. Regular and stated public worship, also, was liberally supported at those points where the people could be most conveniently assembled. A strict, though mild and paternal scrutiny of the conduct of the workpeople was maintained; and prudent and effectual regulations against disorderly and immoral behaviour secured the peace, harmony, and quiet, of the mill companies. The introduction of manufacturing was thus, in every place, a harbinger of moral and intellectual improvement, to the inhabitants of the vicinage, and the numerous operatives from remote and secluded parts of the country, attracted to the manufacturing villages by the employment, comforts, and conveniences which they afforded. Hundreds of families of the latter description, originally from places where the general poverty had precluded schools and public worship, brought up illiterate and without religious instruction, and disorderly and vicious in consequence of their lack of regular employment, have been transplanted to these new creations of skill and enterprise; and by the ameliorating effects of study, industry, and instruction, have been reclaimed, civilised, Christianised. Not a few of them have accumulated and saved, by close application and moderate economy, very handsome estates. Indeed, such have been the blessed results of concentrating and giving employment to a population formerly considered almost useless to the community, that there is among our manufacturing population at this moment, a greater number of males, of from twenty to thirty years old, who are worth from $300 to $1000 each, and of marriageable females worth from $100 to $800 each, than can be found in any population, out of the manufacturing villages.

---

2. Purchase of equipment for the Sunday school in the Slater-Howard mill, 1824

Woolen file, Slater & Howard Memoranda, 1827–1829, XXVI, Slater Papers.

Prior to compulsory education laws the Sunday school system was the only form of education for factory children.

Dudley, Feb. 25th 1824

Left with Slater & Howard to sell and account for or return on demand the following Books.

18	W. Spelling Books	2.25
4	English Readers	1.67
2	School Bibles	1.34
1	Murray's Grammer	.50
4	" " abridged	.42
1	Walker's Dictionary	.67
2	Watts Psalms & Hymns (course)	.67
		7.52
1	[?]	.37

For Holbrook & Fessenden
Timothy Knight

---

3. Conditions in the Humphreysville Manufacturing Company, Connecticut, 1810

Timothy Dwight, *Travels; in New-England and New York,* III (New Haven, 1822), 392–394.

General David Humphreys (1752–1818), a Revolutionary war hero and Federalist statesman, became acquainted with the value of Merino sheep in 1802, while serving as United States minister to Spain. He imported Merinos to Derby, Connecticut, and subsequently established a wool manufacture. In 1810 he smuggled John Winterbotham, an expert in the manufacture of wool, out of England. Winterbotham eventually became Humphreys' partner.

The houses can accommodate, with a comfortable residence, about one hundred and fifty persons. Ten others in the neighborhood will furnish comfortable residences for upwards of one hundred and fifty more. Gardens, on a beautiful plat in the rear of the manufactories, furnish all the vegetables necessary for the establishment. The institution contains four broad and eight narrow looms and eighteen stocking-frames. The principal part of the labour in attending the machinery in the cotton and woolen manufactories is done by women and children; the former hired at from fifty cents to one dollar per week, the latter, apprentices, who are regularly instructed in reading, writing, and arithmetic. The wages of the men are from five dollars to twenty-one dollars per month.

In Europe great complaints have been made of manufacturing establishiments as having been, very commonly seats of vice and disease. General Humphreys began this with a determination either to prevent these evils, or, if this could not be done, to give up the design. With regard to the health of the people it is sufficient to observe that, from the year 1804 to the year 1810, not an individual belonging to the institution died; and it is believed that, among the other equal number of persons, there has been less disease. With respect to vice it may be remarked that every person who is discovered to be openly immoral is discharged. At the commencement of the institution, discreet parents were reluctant to place their children in it, from unfavorable apprehensions concerning the tendency of such establishments. Since that time they have been offered in more than sufficient numbers.

In 1813 the Legislature, at the instance of General Humphreys, passed a law, constituting the selectmen and magistracy of the several towns, in which manufactories had been or should be established, visitors of those institutions. This law required the proprietors to control, in a manner specified, the morals of all their workmen and to educate the children as other children, in plain families throughout the State, are educated.[1] The visitors were directed to inquire annually into the manner in which the proprietors conformed to this law. The reports of the visitors in Derby concerning the establishment at Humphreysville have been, in a high degree, honorable both to the proprietor and his people.

The manufactures at Humphreysville are esteemed excellent. The best broadcloth, made here, is considered as inferior to none which is imported. None but Americans are employed in this institution. Americans make all the machinery, and have invented several kinds of machines which are considered as superior to such as have been devised in Europe for the same purposes.

In this manufactory he has, I think, fairly established three points of great importance. One is that these manufactures can be carried on with success; another, that the workmen can be preserved in as good health as that enjoyed by any other class of men in the country; and the third, that the deterioration of morals in such institutions, which is so often complained of, is not necessary, but incidental; not inherent in the institution itself, but the fault of the proprietor.

1. See the following document.

First law in the United States requiring schooling of children in manufactures, Connecticut, 1813

"An act in addition to an act, entitled 'An act relating to masters and servants, and apprentices,'" 1813 — ch. 2, *Public Statutes of Connecticut, Oct. 1808–May 1819,* May Session, 1813 (Hartford, 1813) pp. 117–118.

The law was passed at the instigation of General David Humphreys. As with later child labor legislation, it was laxly enforced.

The president and directors of all factories which now are, or hereafter shall be legally incorporated, and the proprietor or proprietors of all other manufacturing establishments in this state, shall cause that the children employed in such factory or establishment, whether bound by indenture, by parol agreement, or in any other manner, be taught to read and write, and also that they be instructed in the four first rules of arithmetic (provided the term of their service shall be of so long duration that such instruction can be given,) and that due attention be paid to the preservation of their morals; and that they be required by their masters or employers regularly to attend public worship, as is by law provided with regard to the other citizens of this state.

The civil authority and select-men for and within such towns in which such factories or manufacturing establishments, do or may exist, or a committee by them appointed, shall be and they are hereby constituted a board of visitors; and it shall be the duty of such board of visitors, in the month of January annually, or at such other time or times as they shall appoint, carefully to examine, and to ascertain whether the requisitions of this act, which relate to the instruction and the preservation of the morals of the children employed as aforesaid, be duly observed: and if on such examination, such board of visitors shall discover that the president and directors of any incorporated factory, or the proprietor or proprietors of any manufacturing establishment have neglected to perform the duties enjoined on them by this act, such board of visitors shall report such neglect to the next county court within the county within which the same shall have occurred, and thereupon such county court shall cause the president and directors of such incorporated factory, or the proprietor or proprietors of such manufacturing establishment, to appear before such court to answer in the premises; and if on due enquiry, it shall be found that such president and directors, or the proprietor or proprietors of such establishment, do not duly attend to the education of the children by them respectively employed, as is by this act required; or that due attention is not paid to preserve the morals of such children, it shall be the duty of such court, and they are hereby authorized, at their discretion, either to discharge the indentures or contracts, relating to such minors, and by which they may be bound to render services in such establishments, or they may impose such fine or forfeiture on the proprietor or proprietors of such establishment as they may consider just and reasonable: Provided the same shall not exceed the sum of one hundred dollars.

us of our dependence of foreigners and quieting their intrigues — and raising up an American interest to supercede the servility and devotion of those who deal in foreign goods to foreign interests. These establishments have made wonderful progress towards perfection; but they have not yet arrived at a degree of strength competent to meet, on equal grounds, the more wealthy and older institutions of Europe. They must be protected and assisted for a while by the government — which owes to the exertion of its people what a good mother owes to her child. There certainly is not much *profit* in raising children — a woman might assuredly earn more *money* if, instead of nursing her infant and nourishing it as she ought, she were to cast it on the ground and apply herself to labor. But what would we think of a *calculation* like this? For, altho' the mother may have no affection for her child, she owes a duty to the society in which she lives to rear it with care. It belongs to the state, and is to be added to the national strength. I consider that the manufacturers of the United States stand to the government in the precise relation of an infant to its mother — if they are cherished, they will repay, in the future peace and prosperity of the country, all that is done for them.

Economic and moral justification of manufacturing and child labor, 1816–1823

1. The "Infant Industries" argument, 1816

"The Manufacturing Interest," *Niles' Weekly Register,* Jan. 27, 1816, p. 1.

Manufactories grew up as if by magic — and they promised fair, in due season, to supply the chief part of our wants — thus releasing

2. "Two hundred children create a value of 13,500 dollars a year. 317,000 children would . . . make us independent of all nations," 1816

Niles' Weekly Register, Oct. 5, 1816, pp. 86–87.

Note that the writer calculates age seven as the standard for commencement of labor.

By calculations made upon the data furnished by the census of 1810, it appears that the children, under 10 years, averaged, for the middle states, are 35 per cent. of the whole population; and that those of 10 and under 16, in like manner, are about 15 per cent. making together 50 per cent. Or, in other words, that the children under 16 years of age are one half of all the inhabitants of this section of the United States.

A certain town, in one of these states, well situated and healthy, had by that census 4416 inhabitants; and, consequently, the children under 16 years old may be estimated at 2208.

But we have no datum to determine what proportion of these children were under 7 years — we may suppose them at a half, or 1104; which we may also suppose incapable of any employment other than the little services they can render in domestic affairs; — and we have 1104 between the ages of 7 and 16 capable of some sorts of business not immediately connected with the concerns of the families of which they are members. By an actual enumeration of the children at school, in the town alluded to, in 1814, they amounted to 650 — but of these 60 were from other places, and the number of *town* children was only 590, leaving of 1104 a balance of 514. Of which 514 we may suppose 100 were apprenticed — 50 at school in other places, and 100 in the employ of their parents, who prefer keeping them at home to sending them to earn a living in the manufactories adjacent — deducting, then, 250 from the 514, we have 264 in the town unemployed, unless they be engaged in the cotton, woolen or card-making establishments, within it or in its neighborhood. Say 200 — and let us attempt to calculate the difference to the community in employing them and suffering them to remain unemployed.

A cotton manufactory of 5 or 6000 spindles will employ those 200 children, and their wages may be reckoned as follows:

100 at 125 cents per week,	$125	00
50 at 150	do.	75	00
50 at 200	do.	100	00
	300	00
Say for 45 weeks in the year,	$13,500	00

Calculations pretty accurately made show that it will require $25 a year to clothe a child of 7 years old, in an economical way — the clothing of these children would cost 5000 dollars, leaving 8,500 dollars towards their board and education. If we suppose, that, before the establishment of these manufactories, there were 200 children, between 7 and 16 years of age, that contributed nothing towards their maintenance and that they are now employed, it makes an *immediate* difference of 13,500 dollars a year to the value produced in the town, and may also make a considerable saving by reducing the cost of clothing. Let us see the effects of this employment on agriculture and commerce.

Daily experience teaches us, that as the means of subsistence are facilitated, the people are disposed to enjoy what is called the comforts of life — to eat better or richer food, and wear better or more costly clothing; and as these 200 children create a value of 13,500 dollars a year, we may fairly suppose that nearly so much more will be expended for these things . . .

If such be the effects of the introduction of manufactures into a small district (I do not wish to be understood as meaning only those of cotton and wool, but of all that give employment to children from 7 to 16 years of age) let us see how the calculation will apply to all the United States.

It is pretty clear that a gross population of 4,416 persons *may* have 200 children wanting employment — the United States contains 7 millions of white inhabitants, and, by the same ratio, may have 317,000 such children, whose annual wage, as above, would amount to $21,397,500. This is more than the average annual revenue of the general and state governments, united, and equal to about half the value of our exports of domestic produce and manufacture.

But it cannot be thought possible to employ all the children in the United States as calculated above: 1st, because they are too widely scattered to be brought into such employment; and 2ndly, because it supposes a progress in manufactures that we may not attain to for a generation to come, if so soon as that — for to employ 317,000 children would require the establishment of nearly 8 millions of cotton spindles, or of something else equivalent thereto — an increase not to be expected or desired: but there are a great variety of businesses yet to be introduced amongst us, necessary to secure to us what we consider the comforts, if not the necessaries of life, and make us independent of all nations . . .

3. Factories as seats of health, cheerfulness, and learning, 1817

Address of The American Society for the Encouragement of Domestic Manufactures, To the People of The United States (New York, 1817), p. 14.

. . . Our fabrics will not require to be situated near mines of coal, to be worked by fire or steam, but rather on chosen sites, by the fall of waters and the running stream, the seats of health and cheerfulness, where good instruction will secure the morals of the young, and good regulations will promote, in all, order, cleanliness, and the exercise of the civil duties. This, with the beneficial clauses usual in our indentures of apprenticeship, and the vigilant eye of the magistrate to enforce them, will obviate every apprehension. And we hazard nothing by the assertion, that some of the best educated of the poorer class, in this country, are those brought up in factories, and such as would otherwise have been destitute of education altogether; and those whose tenderness inclines them to make this objection are requested to reflect, that the paternal regard of the legislature is awake to this subject; and that, to every institution of this kind a school will be appendant.

4. Work people, six to twelve years old, 1817

Niles' Weekly Register, June 7, 1817, pp. 226–227.

The great objection to manufactures was, that they abstracted labor from the more profitable and more healthy pursuits of agriculture. And this might have been a reasonable objection when able-bodied men were doing the work that is now better done by little girls from six to twelve years old . . . Messrs. *Robert* and *Alexander M'Kim* have a cotton mill in Baltimore, driven by steam, capable of making a certain quantity of yarn per annum. The cost of the raw material used, at its present high price, is estimated at $35,200, and the value of the yarn produced, at its present low rate, at $58,500. The difference between these sums ($23,300) variously disbursed, and some part retained for profit or interest on capital employed, is nearly as much as value *created* and thrown into the general wealth, as if the Messrs. M'Kims were capable of transmitting some useless substance into pure gold of that value; for in the whole establishment they employ but two or three men; — all the rest, in number about 100, are girls from 6 to 12 or 13 years of age, and a few women; *who, without this employ, would earn nothing at all.* Mr. A. M'Kim (the late member of congress from this city) informs me, that many of his little work-people read and write handsomely. They live with their parents, who are generally poor, but not the most indigent; and their wages assist in sending them to school or furnish them with clothes to appear decently there. The little girls often seek employment for the avowed purpose of earning money to buy clothes to go to school in, and no difficulty is found in obtaining as many hands as are wanted. We feel warranted in saying that this factory is a blessing and a comfort to many families in its neighborhood. The yarn spun at this mill, if wove into cloth, would give us about 315,000 yards 7–8 wide, at 25 cents per yard, or

$78,750, and leave a gross value *created* of $43,550, *per annum* — but the weaving is chiefly done by men.

---

5. Edifying impact of manufactures on poor children, 1819

Letter to editor, *Niles' Weekly Register,* Jan. 30, 1819, pp. 418–419.

I am unfortunately concerned in three cotton factories — one of them has for a long time been standing still — the other two were in operation about 18 months, when we stopped one of them; the last is yet going, but it is doubtful whether we shall keep it working much longer. The latter originally cost 150,000 dollars — we bought it at sheriff's sale for 50,000 — and since May 1817 have had upwards of 4000 spindles running in it — but I do not believe that the profit made is equal to one cent per spindle, per annum — we therefore think of stopping them. This factory is well situated, and known to have made the very best goods. The children employed were chiefly taken from the poor-masters of the country towns, and from the alms-house in this city, where there are now upwards of 700 of them, many of whom might be usefully employed in such establishments — the remainder were orphans, or children of infirm parents or widows, some of the latter also, were in our employ. It is a pleasing fact, that the young man who is the clerk of our factory and keeps our books, being a cripple, was taken from the overseers of the poor of a country town about six years ago, and is indebted for his learning to the *school of the factory, where all the children enjoy the same advantages he did.* The value that these children, assisted by machinery, have produced, is to the country as so much specie gained without any labor at all — *a clear profit to its whole amount.* To estimate this properly, we must understand that one girl, at Manchester, fully assisted by machinery, produces as much value as eight laborers in our field . . .

---

6. Idle man's life altered by labor of his children, 1823

Niles' Weekly Register, Nov. 29, 1823, p. 195.

Many persons apprehend that large manufacturing establishments are the great seats of vice and immorality. Whatever may be the case in Europe, they are not so in the United States, nor will they be, until our population is much more dense than it is, and our immense tracts of vacant lands are occupied; *then,* if the people shall also have lost the rights and privileges which they at present enjoy, perhaps the manufacturers may become as corrupt as the population of some of our cities is now.

An able correspondent of the New York "Statesman" gives the following account of a visit to the Matteawan Factory, near the Fishkill mountains, when the proprietor, Mr. Schenck, gave him the following narrative:

"Before I commenced the erection of these works, said Mr. S., and established in this place the branch of cotton manufacture, the process of which you have been just examining, the man who built, and now owns that neat little tenement, had no place to shelter himself and his numerous family, but the wretched hovel which you may observe at a few rods distance from his present abode. At that time, continued my informant, his only occupation was that of fishing: or rambling in the mountains in pursuit of such game as chance might throw in his way. Of the little he obtained by this occasional and precarious mode of subsistence, a large proportion was expended in the purchase of rum; in the use of which he indulged to such an extent as to brutalize his faculties, and render him a pest to society, as well as a curse to his family; which he kept in a state of the most deplorable and squalid poverty. Of his children three or four were daughters, of various ages, from seven or eight to fourteen years; these, said Mr. S. on commencing my establishment, I took into the factory; where, from that period to the present time, they have always had constant and regular employment. The proceeds of their first week's labor, amounting to six or seven dollars, when paid and taken home to their parents, was an amount which, it is probable, they never before at any one time possessed. The almost immediate effect on the mind of the father appears to have been a conviction that his children, instead of being a burthen which he despaired of supporting, and, therefore, never before made an effort to accomplish, would, on the contrary, by the steady employment now provided for them, be able, by their industry, not only to sustain themselves, but also contribute to the maintenance and support of the other members of the family. From that moment, it would appear, as if he had determined to reform his vicious habit, and to emerge from that state of degradation and wretchedness into which he had plunged himself and his family. He has done so, said Mr. S. and, instead of being a pest, he has become a useful member of society; instead of being a curse to his family, and occupying with them that wretched hovel yonder, fit only for swine to wallow in, he has by his own exertions, aided by the industry and good conduct of his children, lately purchased the soil, and erected the comfortable cottage, which, said Mr. S. smiling, appears so powerfully to attract your notice."

III Education

After 1730 the tasks of education were carried out in a new social and cultural setting. The arrival of Scots, Irish, Germans, and Negro slaves, all entering in large numbers for the first time, added human variety and social diversity to the older English and Dutch populations. Accumulations of wealth in commerce and agriculture gave rise to towns and produced more clearly defined social classes. Although the great majority of Americans still lived on farms, influential numbers resided in Boston, New York, Philadelphia, and other bustling ports along the coast. The towns drew ambitious and able youths away from the farms and villages with a promise of greater rewards in wealth and status. Young John Adams, who made his way from the family farm in Quincy to Harvard College and then on to a career as a Boston lawyer, and Thomas Hancock, son of a country clergyman who acquired sufficient wealth as a merchant to leave a fortune of £100,000 to his nephew John, followed a course that was becoming both a pattern and an ideal. A wealthy colonial aristocracy emerged, exercising political and social leadership. A diverse middle class of professional men, merchants, and independent farmers lived in comfort and esteem and managed local politics. A lower class of servants, artisans, farm laborers, and Negro slaves supplied the muscle and hard work that enabled the colonies to participate in the expanding trade and increasing wealth of the Western world.

In these circumstances naturally there were opportunities and pressures for new departures in education. The academy, a modification of the old grammar school, was the most important attempt to supply a kind of training suitable for a mixed economy and society with commercial as well as professional and agricultural components. It was fitting that the academy movement should have been initiated by Benjamin Franklin, the prophet of the new America. Although private schoolmasters in colonial towns and villages had given instruction in practical and useful subjects, the decision of Franklin and some friends to launch an academy in Philadelphia was the first attempt to create an institution for secondary education designed to complement and implement the more materialistic outlook of the eighteenth-century American. Franklin recognized that any school dependent upon public patronage would have to supply instruction in the ancient languages, but he proposed to include new subjects such as modern languages, and to add substantial amounts of science, mathematics, and history. To his mind the most novel and important proposal was the English school, a separate branch of the academy which would prepare students for careers in trades and professions. Although the academy at Philadelphia did not exactly follow Franklin's model, it roughly conformed to it and, more important, it was imitated throughout America. By a century later several thousand academies had been formed. To describe them as either exclusively private or public schools is misleading. Most, but by no means all, obtained charters from colonial assemblies or, after 1776, from state legislatures. They often received financial assistance in some form from government and their doors were open to all who could pay the fees. They were governed however by private self-perpetuating boards of trustees, and they were free to teach subjects and fix requirements and regulations as they wished. Usually drawing financial support and students from a particular region or vicinity, they are most accurately described as secondary schools of a mixed private and public character.

Colleges remained closely tied to religion although they were by no means immune to secular currents in thought and styles of life. The foundation of new colleges between 1740 and the War for Independence was mainly the result of the impact of the Great Awakening on religious feeling, denominational growth, and rivalry. With the proliferation of schisms in denominations, the weakening of church establishments, and the spread of tolerance, denominations sought to enhance their chances of popular acceptance and support by founding colleges. In these new institutions the children of the faithful would be instructed and a supply of trained ministers assured. New Light Presbyterianism was sufficiently established to open Princeton in 1746. New England Baptists founded Brown in 1764, the Dutch Calvinists established Rutgers in 1766, and frontier Congregationalists secured a charter for Dartmouth in 1769. Only Columbia, the object of an inconclusive denominational struggle, and the University of Pennsylvania, which developed out of the movement for Franklin's academy in Philadelphia, came into existence without benefit of a denominational connection. Since New York and Philadelphia were religiously and socially more diverse than any other colonial cities, it is not surprising that nonsectarianism should have commenced there. Although the denominational colleges maintained a religious connection to the extent of asking for funds from churches and drawing their presidents, board members, and teachers from denominational ranks, none could cavalierly take the position that students should be admitted only from that same source. Both students and funds were too scarce and their supply too precarious for a college to exclude anyone who wanted to come. No tests besides adequate preparation and financial ability were therefore imposed.

Through the second half of the eighteenth century the curriculum of the colleges reflected the progress of rationalism and natural religion. Although all colleges, nonsectarian as well as denominational, continued to foster a way of life and instruction for undergraduates built around Christian piety, they introduced new works and concepts from Newton's science and Locke's philosophy. God was not, of course, dismissed from the colonial college, but He was required to share the stage. The champions of traditional religious and educational views, disturbed by the growth of rival denominations and religious voluntarism as well as by rationalism, vigorously counterattacked the encroachments of a more worldly outlook. Despite the insistence of college officials like Thomas Clap (1703–1767), rector and later president of Yale, that colleges should mainly serve to train prospective ministers, the colleges steadily broadened their intellectual and social perspectives.

The winning of national independence marked an epoch in the history of ideas about public control of education. Before 1776 education was almost entirely a local responsibility. New England colonial governments had obligated towns to supply certain kinds of instruction, but the actual conduct of education was in local hands and the requirements of colonial assemblies were frequently ignored. The mother country provided a model for colonial education and furnished philanthropic assistance for schools and colleges; the British government, however, had not regulated or encouraged education in any way.

Even before the end of the war, thoughtful Americans began to contemplate the kind of education needed for the free citizens of independent republics. Recognizing that self-governing republics resting upon consent were the revolutionary element in the struggle for independence, statesmen looked ahead to the educational system that would secure popular loyalty and release the energy needed to maintain such untried, experimental forms of government. The promises of rights and opportunities had to be given institutional form if the sacrifices of war and the disruption of old loyalties were to be justified. The most imaginative proposal came from Thomas Jefferson in 1779. Jefferson's plan for public education comprised a part of his work as a member of a committee of the Virginia Assembly assigned to revise the laws of the state in accordance with republican principles. He had two objectives: to supply all the children of the commonwealth with the elementary instruction necessary to make them useful, responsible citizens, and to prepare a select group to assume positions of political and social leadership. Jefferson's proposal was only the first of a succession of schemes for educational reform that appeared between the War for Independence and the War of 1812. Both prominent and obscure champions of a republican and national way of life — Noah Webster, Benjamin Rush, George Washington, and William Manning — offered their ideas on the mode of education needed to secure liberty and order among free men.

The effect of these plans on the actual conduct of education is difficult to measure. Jefferson's Virginia proposal was not adopted, nor were the more elaborate plans of some of his successors such as Samuel Harrison Smith and Samuel Knox who, in proposals submitted to the American Philosophical Society in 1797, daringly advocated uniform national school systems.[1] The more feasible plan of Washington for a national university, endorsed by all of his successors in the presidency before Jackson, likewise failed to be acted on. In each case a commitment of resources was required that was beyond the capability of the young nation. Nevertheless, the projects reveal a serious attempt to come to grips with the social and political needs of a republic: to supply the trained and loyal citizens necessary to make self-government work, and to secure to every citizen the means of self-improvement which would make a republican government worth the

effort. They publicized the need for education and furnished a standard for judging current practices. From the Revolution onward, the connection between popular education and a healthy self-governing body politic was acknowledged.

The expansion of national boundaries to include new, largely unsettled areas had important implications for education. The treaty of 1783 recognized the American claim to lands as far as the Mississippi River. Americans were familiar with the various procedures for building new communities in the wilderness, but there was a range of opinion concerning the proper methods for such an undertaking. In the South it had been customary for individuals to venture on the frontier by themselves or in their families with the institutions of civilization left more or less to look after themselves. In practice, this meant that schools and churches were not established until the populace was sufficiently large and dense to support them out of payments by the settlers who made use of their services. In New England, a more orderly method of community building had often been followed. There bands of like-minded citizens had moved to a frontier location, securing grants of land and governing privileges from the authorities before they went. Almost always the grant included lands for the support of the church and its minister and for support of a school. When the United States government fell heir to the western lands some of the states had claimed under their colonial charters, a choice between the two methods of frontier settlement was necessary. Each had its champions but a group of New England men, accustomed to the land system of that section and committed to the notion that pioneers should not venture into the woods without the accoutrements of civilized life, was influential in obtaining a decision in favor of the New England method of community planting. The Land Ordinance of 1785, the Northwest Ordinance of 1787, and the land contracts subsequently negotiated with the Ohio Company, all followed this method. The reservation of lands

---

1. For the essays of Smith and Knox, with others of a similar character, see Frederick Rudolph, ed., *Essays on Education in the Early Republic* (Cambridge, Mass., 1965).

for educational purposes set precedents which were followed in virtually all subsequent government grants of land to territories and states. Ultimately the precedents were broadened to include a great variety of federal government financial aids to education.

Another discernible change following the American Revolution was the establishment and strengthening of state administrative agencies. The states, much more powerful than their colonial counterparts, began to assume a part of the responsibility for the promotion, support, and regulation of education within their boundaries. State constitutions uniformly required legislatures to support education, although they rarely stipulated the means to be followed. State legislatures commonly designated certain revenues like excise taxes for support of education or granted private promoters or towns the right to hold lotteries to raise funds; ordinarily state support was confined to aiding the instruction of the children of pauper parents. A few states, with New York in the lead, contemplated the creation of state offices of education to collect statistics about the schools and administer the distribution of the limited state funds that were available. A framework for more efficient and uniform school administration began to be constructed. Southern states such as Georgia and North Carolina, bereft of colleges in comparison with northern states, chartered the first state universities.

Although the American Revolution encouraged the states to stake out claims to greater power and responsibility in education, no substantial shift in the actual balance between private and public enterprise in education occurred. The educational "system" remained a mixed collection of public schools of a limited and specific character in New England and New York, with private schools, often receiving some kind of public recognition and assistance, supplementing public schools in some areas and substituting for them elsewhere. Legal protection for chartered private schools and colleges was secured in the famous Dartmouth College Case of 1819 when the United States Supreme Court blocked the attempt of the State of New Hampshire to establish control over a private college. The decision protected the intentions and donations of the founders of private institutions and, once a charter had been granted, guarded these schools and colleges against almost any state interference with their activities. It helped to assure the future of private education just on the eve of pressures for the expansion and reform of public schooling in the common school revival.

A. EDUCATION IN THE LATE COLONIAL PERIOD

The Academy Movement

In the latter half of the eighteenth century private academies appeared in some of the more densely settled parts of the colonies. Although they by no means rejected the preparation of boys for college, they usually enlarged the curriculum to include useful subjects that would prepare students for commerce and other business pursuits.

1. Benjamin Franklin proposes an academy

Benjamin Franklin, *Proposals Relating to the Education of Youth in Pensilvania* (Philadelphia, 1749), in Leonard W. Labaree et al., eds., *The Papers of Benjamin Franklin,* III (New Haven, 1961), 399–419.

Among his many projects to advance the public welfare, Franklin was instrumental in

the establishment of an academy in Philadelphia. This essay became the most influential
statement in behalf of these new schools.
Most of Franklin's notes, containing lengthy
quotations from authorities, have been omitted.

The good Education of Youth has been es-
teemed by wise Men in all Ages, as the surest
Foundation of the Happiness both of private
Families and of Common-wealths. Almost all
Governments have therefore made it a principal
Object of their Attention, to establish and en-
dow with proper Revenues, such Seminaries of
Learning, as might supply the succeeding Age
with Men qualified to serve the Publick with
Honour to themselves, and to their Country.

Many of the first Settlers of these Provinces,
were Men who had received a good Education
in Europe, and to their Wisdom and good Management we owe much of our present Prosperity. But their Hands were full, and they
could not do all Things. The present Race are
not thought to be generally of equal Ability:
For though the American Youth are allow'd not
to want Capacity; yet the best Capacities require Cultivation, it being truly with them, as
with the best Ground, which unless well tilled
and sowed with profitable Seed, produces only
ranker Weeds.

That we may obtain the Advantages arising
from an Increase of Knowledge, and prevent as
much as may be the mischievous Consequences
that would attend a general Ignorance among
us, the following *Hints* are offered towards
forming a Plan for the Education of the Youth
of Pennsylvania, viz.

It is propos'd,

THAT some Persons of Leisure and publick
Spirit, apply for a CHARTER, by which they may
be incorporated, with Power to erect an ACAD-
EMY for the Education of Youth, to govern the
same, provide Masters, make Rules, receive
Donations, purchase Lands, &c. and to add to
their Number, from Time to Time such other
Persons as they shall judge suitable.

That the Members of the Corporation make
it their Pleasure, and in some Degree their

Business, to visit the Academy often, encourage
and countenance the Youth, countenance and
assist the Masters, and by all Means in their
Power advance the Usefulness and Reputation
of the Design; that they look on the Students
as in some Sort their Children, treat them with
Familiarity and Affection, and when they have
behav'd well, and gone through their Studies,
and are to enter the World, zealously unite, and
make all the Interest that can be made to establish them,[1] whether in Business, Offices, Marriages, or any other Thing for their Advantage,
preferably to all other Persons whatsoever even
of equal Merit.

·   ·   ·   ·   ·

That a House be provided for the ACADEMY,
if not in the Town, not many Miles from it; the
Situation high and dry, and if it may be, not far
from a River, having a Garden, Orchard,
Meadow, and a Field or two.

That the House be furnished with a Library
(if in the Country, if in the Town, the Town
Libraries may serve) with Maps of all Countries, Globes, some mathematical Instruments,
an Apparatus for Experiments in Natural Philosophy, and for Mechanics; Prints, of all Kinds,
Prospects, Buildings, Machines, &c.

That the RECTOR be a Man of good Understanding, good Morals, diligent and patient,
learn'd in the Languages and Sciences, and a
correct pure Speaker and Writer of the English
Tongue; to have such Tutors under him as shall
be necessary.

That the boarding Scholars diet together,
plainly, temperately, and frugally.

---

1. Something seems wanting in America to incite
and stimulate Youth to Study. In Europe the Encouragements to Learning are of themselves much greater
than can be given here. Whoever distinguishes himself there, in either of the three learned Professions,
gains Fame, and often Wealth and Power: A poor
Man's Son has a Chance, if he studies hard, to rise,
either in the Law or the Church, to gainful Offices
or Benefices; to an extraordinary Pitch of Grandeur;
to have a Voice in Parliament, a Seat among the
Peers; as a Statesman or first Minister to govern Nations, and even to mix his Blood with Princes. [Frank-
lin's note.]

That to keep them in Health, and to strengthen and render active their Bodies, they be frequently exercis'd in Running, Leaping, Wrestling, and Swimming, &c.

That they have peculiar Habits to distinguish them from other Youth, if the Academy be in or near the Town; for this, among other Reasons, that their Behaviour may be the better observed.

As to their STUDIES, it would be well if they could be taught *every Thing* that is useful, and *every Thing* that is ornamental: But Art is long, and their Time is short. It is therefore propos'd that they learn those Things that are likely to be *most useful* and *most ornamental,* Regard being had to the several Professions for which they are intended.

All should be taught to write a *fair Hand,* and swift, as that is useful to All. And with it may be learnt something of *Drawing,* by Imitation of Prints, and some of the first Principles of Perspective.

Arithmetick, Accounts, and some of the first Principles of *Geometry* and *Astronomy.*

The English Language might be taught by Grammar; in which some of our best Writers, as Tillotson, Addison, Pope, Algernon Sidney, Cato's Letters, &c. should be Classicks: The *Stiles* principally to be cultivated, being the *clear* and the *concise.* Reading should also be taught, and pronouncing, properly, distinctly, emphatically; not with an even Tone, which *under-does,* nor a theatrical, which *over-does* Nature.

To form their Stile, they should be put on Writing Letters to each other, making Abstracts of what they read; or writing the same Things in their own Words; telling or writing Stories lately read, in their own Expressions. All to be revis'd and corrected by the Tutor, who should give his Reasons, explain the Force and Import of Words, &c.

To form their Pronunciation, they may be put on making Declamations, repeating Speeches, delivering Orations, &c. The Tutor assisting at the Rehearsals, teaching, advising, correcting their Accent, &c.

But if HISTORY be made a constant Part of their Reading, such as the Translations of the Greek and Roman Historians, and the modern Histories of antient Greece and Rome, &c. may not almost all Kinds of useful Knowledge be that Way introduc'd to Advantage, and with Pleasure to the Student? As

GEOGRAPHY, by reading with Maps, and being required to point out the Places *where* the greatest Actions were done, to give their old and new Names, with the Bounds, Situation, Extent of the Countries concern'd, &c.

CHRONOLOGY, by the Help of Helvicus[2] or some other Writer of the Kind, who will enable them to tell *when* those Events happened; what Princes were Contemporaries, what States or famous Men flourish'd about that Time, &c. The several principal Epochas to be first well fix'd in their Memories.

ANTIENT CUSTOMS, religious and civil, being frequently mentioned in History, will give Occasion for explaining them; in which the Prints of Medals, Basso Relievo's, and antient Monuments will greatly assist.

MORALITY, by descanting and making continual Observations on the Causes of the Rise or Fall of any Man's Character, Fortune, Power, &c. mention'd in History; the Advantages of Temperance, Order, Frugality, Industry, Perseverance, &c. &c. Indeed the general natural Tendency of Reading good History, must be, to fix in the Minds of Youth deep Impressions of the Beauty and Usefulness of Virtue of all Kinds, Publick Spirit, Fortitude, &c.

History will show the wonderful Effects of ORATORY, in governing, turning and leading great Bodies of Mankind, Armies, Cities, Nations. When the Minds of Youth are struck with Admiration at this, then is the Time to give them the Principles of that Art, which they will study with Taste and Application. Then they may be made acquainted with the best Models among the Antients, their Beauties being particularly pointed out to them. Modern Political

2. Christophorus Helvicus, *The Historical and Chronological Theatre* (London, 1687). [Editor's note in *Papers of Benjamin Franklin.*]

Oratory being chiefly performed by the Pen and Press, its Advantages over the Antient in some Respects are to be shown; as that its Effects are more extensive, more lasting, &c.

History will also afford frequent Opportunities of showing the Necessity of a *Publick Religion,* from its Usefulness to the Publick; the Advantage of a Religious Character among private Persons; the Mischiefs of Superstition, &c. and the Excellency of the CHRISTIAN RELIGION above all others antient or modern.

History will also give Occasion to expatiate on the Advantage of Civil Orders and Constitutions, how Men and their Properties are protected by joining in Societies and establishing Government; their Industry encouraged and rewarded, Arts invented, and Life made more comfortable: The Advantages of *Liberty,* Mischiefs of *Licentiousness,* Benefits arising from good Laws and a due Execution of Justice, &c. Thus may the first Principles of sound *Politicks* be fix'd in the Minds of Youth.

On *Historical* Occasions, Questions of Right and Wrong, Justice and Injustice, will naturally arise, and may be put to Youth, which they may debate in Conversation and in Writing. When they ardently desire Victory, for the Sake of the Praise attending it, they will begin to feel the Want, and be sensible of the Use of *Logic,* or the Art of Reasoning to *discover* Truth, and of Arguing to *defend* it, and *convince* Adversaries. This would be the Time to acquaint them with the Principles of that Art. Grotius, Puffendorff, and some other Writers of the same Kind, may be used on these Occasions to decide their Disputes. Publick Disputes warm the Imagination, whet the Industry, and strengthen the natural Abilities.

.   .   .   .   .

With the History of Men, Times and Nations, should be read at proper Hours or Days, some of the best *Histories of Nature,* which would not only be delightful to Youth, and furnish them with Matter for their Letters, &c. as well as other History; but afterwards of great Use to them, whether they are Merchants,

Handicrafts, or Divines; enabling the first the better to understand many Commodities, Drugs, &c. the second to improve his Trade or Handicraft by new Mixtures, Materials, &c. and the last to adorn his Discourses by beautiful Comparisons, and strengthen them by new Proofs of Divine Providence. The Conversation of all will be improved by it, as Occasions frequently occur of making Natural Observations, which are instructive, agreeable, and entertaining in almost all Companies. *Natural History* will also afford Opportunities of introducing many Observations, relating to the Preservation of Health, which may be afterwards of great Use. Arbuthnot on Air and Ailment, Sanctorius on Perspiration, Lemery on Foods,[3] and some others, may now be read, and a very little Explanation will make them sufficiently intelligible to Youth.

While they are reading Natural History, might not a little *Gardening, Planting, Grafting, Inoculating,* &c. be taught and practised; and now and then Excursions made to the neighbouring Plantations of the best Farmers, their Methods observ'd and reason'd upon for the Information of Youth. The Improvement of Agriculture being useful to all, and Skill in it no Disparagement to any.

The History of *Commerce,* of the Invention of Arts, Rise of Manufactures, Progress of Trade, Change of its Seats, with the Reasons, Causes, &c. may also be made entertaining to Youth, and will be useful to all. And this, with the Accounts in other History of the prodigious Force and Effect of Engines and Machines used in War, will naturally introduce a Desire to be instructed in *Mechanicks,*[4] and to be inform'd of the Principles of that Art by which weak

3. John Arbuthnot, *An Essay concerning the Effects of Air on Human Bodies* (London, 1733), and *An Essay concerning the Nature of Aliments* (2 vols., London, 1731–32); *Medicina Statica: being the Aphorisms of Sanctorius* (London, 1712); and Louis Lémery, *Traité des Aliments* (Paris, 1702). [Editor's note in *Papers of Benjamin Franklin*.]
4. How many Mills are built and Machines constructed, at great and fruitless Expence, which a little Knowledge in the Principles of Mechanics would have prevented? [Franklin's note.]

Men perform such Wonders, Labour is sav'd, Manufactures expedited, &c. &c. This will be the Time to show them Prints of antient and modern Machines, to explain them, to let them be copied,[5] and to give Lectures in Mechanical Philosophy.

With the whole should be constantly inculcated and cultivated, that *Benignity of Mind,* which shows itself in *searching for* and *seizing* every Opportunity *to serve* and *to oblige;* and is the Foundation of what is called GOOD BREEDING; highly useful to the Possessor, and most agreeable to all.

The Idea of what is *true Merit,* should also be often presented to Youth, explain'd and impress'd on their Minds, as consisting in an *Inclination* join'd with an *Ability* to serve Mankind, one's Country, Friends and Family; which *Ability* is (with the Blessing of God) to be acquir'd or greatly encreas'd by *true Learning;* and should indeed be the great *Aim* and *End* of all Learning.

---

2. Franklin's appeal to the Philadelphia Common Council for support of the Academy, July 31, 1750

The Papers of Benjamin Franklin, IV (1961), 34–37.

The academy, having secured some public

5. We are often told in the Journals of Travellers, that such and such Things are done in foreign Countries, by which Labour is sav'd, and Manufactures expedited, &c. but their Description of the Machines or Instruments used, are quite unintelligible for want of good Drafts. Copying Prints of Machines is of Use to fix the Attention on the several Parts, their Proportions, Reasons, Effects, &c. A Man that has been us'd to this Practice, is not only better able to make a Draft when the Machine is before him, but takes so much better Notice of its Appearance, that he can carry it off by Memory when he has not the Opportunity of Drawing it on the Spot. Thus may a Traveller bring home Things of great Use to his Country. [Franklin's note.]

support, opened in 1751. The University of Pennsylvania developed from this foundation.

The Trustees of the Academy have already laid out near £800, in the Purchase of the Building, and will probably expend near as much more in fitting up Rooms for the Schools, and furnishing them with proper Books and Instruments for the Instruction of Youth.

The greatest Part of the Money paid and to be paid, is subscribed by the Trustees themselves, and advanced by them; many of whom have no Children of their own to educate, but act from a View to the Public Good, without Regard to Sect or Party. And they have engaged to open a Charity School within two Years for the Instruction of Poor Children gratis, in Reading, Writing and Arithmetick, and the first Principles of Virtue and Piety.

The Benefits expected from this Institution, are,

1. That the Youth of Pensilvania may have an Opportunity of receiving a good Education at home, and be under no Necessity of going abroad for it; whereby not only a considerable Expence may be saved to the Country, but a stricter Eye may be had over their Morals by their Friends and Relations.

2. That a Number of our Natives will hereby be qualified to bear Magistracies, and execute other public Offices of Trust, with Reputation to themselves and Country; there being at present great Want of Persons so qualified in the several Counties of this Province. And this is the more necessary now to be provided for by the English here, as vast Numbers of Foreigners are yearly imported among us, totally ignorant of our Laws, Customs, and Language.

3. That a Number of the poorer Sort will hereby be qualified to act as Schoolmasters in the Country, to teach Children Reading, Writing, Arithmetick, and the Grammar of their Mother Tongue; and being of good Morals and known Characters, may be recommended from the Academy to Country Schools for that Purpose; The Country suffering at present very

much for want of good Schoolmasters, and oblig'd frequently to employ in their Schools, vicious imported Servants, or concealed Papists, who by their bad Examples and Instructions often deprave the Morals or corrupt the Principles of the Children under their Care.

4. It is thought that a good Academy erected in Philadelphia, a healthy Place, where Provisions are plenty, situated in the Center of the Colonies, may draw Numbers of Students from the Neighbouring Provinces, who must spend considerable Sums yearly among us, in Payment for their Lodging, Diet, Apparel &c. which will be an Advantage to our Traders, Artisans, and Owners of Houses and Lands. This Advantage is so considerable, that it has been frequently observed in Europe, that the fixing a good School or College in a little inland Village, has been the Means of making it a great Town in a few Years; And therefore the Magistrates of many Places, have offer'd and given great yearly Salaries, to draw learned Instructors from other Countries to their respective Towns, merely with a View to the Interest of the Inhabitants.

Numbers of People have already generously subscribed considerable Sums to carry on this Undertaking; but others, well disposed, are somewhat discouraged from contributing, by an Apprehension lest when the first Subscriptions are expended, the Design should drop. The great Expence of such a Work is in the Beginning: If the Academy be once well-open'd, good Masters provided, and good Orders established, there is Reason to believe (from many former Examples in other Countries) that it will be able after a few Years, to support it self. Some Assistance from the Corporation is immediately wanted and hoped for; and it is thought that if this Board, which is a perpetual Body, take the Academy under their Patronage, and afford it some Encouragement, it will greatly strengthen the Hands of all concern'd, and be a Means of Establishing this good Work, and continuing the good Effects of it down to our late Posterity.

3. Sample advertisements for private schools in Boston newspapers in 1751 and 1754

Robert F. Seybolt, *The Private Schools of Colonial Boston* (Cambridge, Mass., 1935), pp. 34–35, 37–38.

Private instruction in practical subjects, readily available in the cities, supplemented both the grammar schools and the new academies.

ALL MANNER OF INSTRUMENTS in Writing, and Conveyances in the Law, now in Use and Practice, are carefully drawn and ingross'd. Also young Gentlemen and Ladies may be boarded and educated, and taught English, Writing and Arithmetick, both Vulgar and Decimal; with several other Branches of the Mathematicks, after a very easy and concise Method.

By George Suckling.

Also young Ladies may be taught plain Work, Dresden, Point (or Lace) Work for Child Bed Linnen, Crossstitch, Tentstitch, and all other Sorts of Needle Work.

By Bridget Suckling.

.   .   .   .   .

IN NEW-BOSTON near the Meeting-House are Taught these Mathematical Sciences, viz. Arithmetic, Geometry, Trigonometry, Navigation, Astronomy, Projections of the Sphere, useful Problems in Geography, the use of the plain Scale, Gunter and sliding Gunter and Sector in measuring Superficies and Solids, &c. &c. by Capt. George Mackay. N.B. Young Gentlemen boarded.

AT THE WIDOW ROBINS's at the North-End, near Mr Gledden's Ship-Yard, is kept a School by JOHN LEACH, from LONDON, who teaches the following Branches, viz. Arithmetick, common, vulgar and decimal; Geometry, Trigonometry; Navigation and Journal keeping in a practical Method; either with all kinds of Books and Instruments in use, or without any; from several Years Experience in His Majesty's Service and three Voyages in the Hon. East-India Company's: — Mensuration of Superficies, Solids, Heights and Distances both accessible and inaccessible; — Gauging, either with or without the Callipars; — Surveying, with or without the Theodolite: Also, Drawing, as far as it is useful for a compleat Sea-Artist, as it respects taking Prospects of Land and surveying Harbours, &c. &c. With the Use and Construction of each Instrument us'd in the above Science. N.B. He keeps an Evening School from 6 to 9 P.M. during the Winter Season. — Also, surveys Land, draws Plans, &c.

---

4. A formal statement of the objectives of private academies as set out by Samuel and John Phillips, founders of Phillips Academy in Andover, Massachusetts, 1778

The Constitution of Phillips Academy in Andover (Andover, 1828), pp. 3–4, 8–12.

A SHORT reflection upon the grand design of the great PARENT OF THE UNIVERSE in the creation of mankind, and the improvements, of which the mind is capable, both in knowledge and virtue as well, as upon the prevalence of ignorance and vice, disorder and wickedness, and upon the direct tendency and certain issue of such a course of things, must occasion, in a thoughtful mind, an earnest solicitude to find the source of these evils and their remedy; and a small acquaintance with the qualities of young minds — how susceptible and tenacious they are of impressions, evidences that YOUTH is the important period, on the improvement or neglect of which depend the most important consequences to individuals themselves and the community.

A serious consideration of the premises, and an observation of the growing neglect of YOUTH, have excited in us a painful anxiety for the event, and determined us to make, in the following Conveyance, a humble dedication to our HEAVENLY BENEFACTOR of the ability, wherewith he hath blessed us, to lay the foundation of a public free SCHOOL or ACADEMY for the purpose of instructing Youth, not only in English and Latin Grammar, Writing, Arithmetic, and those Sciences, wherein they are commonly taught; but more especially to learn them the GREAT END AND REAL BUSINESS OF LIVING.

Earnestly wishing that this Institution may grow and flourish; that the advantages of it may be extensive and lasting; that its usefulness may be so manifest, as to lead the way to other establishments on the same principles; and that it may finally prove an eminent means of advancing the Interest of the great REDEEMER, to His patronage and blessing we humbly commit it.

·　·　·　·　·

No person shall be chosen, as a principal Instructor, unless a professor of the CHRISTIAN RELIGION, of exemplary manners, of good natural abilities and literary acquirements, of a good acquaintance with human nature, of a natural aptitude for instruction and government; and, in the appointment of any Instructor, regard shall be had to qualifications only, without preference of kindred or friend, place of birth, education, or residence.

·　·　·　·　·

It shall be ever considered, as the first and principal duty of the Master, to regulate the tempers, to enlarge the minds, and form the Morals of the Youth, committed to his care.

There shall be taught in this Seminary the English, Latin, and Greek Languages, Writing, Arithmetic, Music, and the Art of Speaking; also practical Geometry, Logic, and any other of the liberal Arts and Sciences, or Languages, as opportunity and ability may hereafter admit, and as the TRUSTEES shall direct.

The Master is to give special attention to the

health of the Scholars, and ever to urge the importance of a habit of Industry. For these purposes it is to be a part of his duty, to encourage the Scholars to perform some manual labor, such as gardening, or the like; so far as it is consistent with cleanliness and the inclination of their parents; and the fruit of their labor shall be applied, at the discretion of the TRUSTEES, for procuring a Library, or in some other way increasing the usefulness of this Seminary.

But, above all, it is expected, that the Master's attention to the disposition of the *Minds* and *Morals* of the Youth, under his charge, will exceed every other care; well considering that, though goodness without knowledge (as it respects others) is weak and feeble; yet knowledge without goodness is dangerous; and that both united form the noblest character, and lay the surest foundation of usefulness to mankind.

It is therefore required, that he most attentively and vigorously guard against the earliest irregularities; that he frequently delineate, in their natural colours, the deformity and odiousness of vice, and the beauty and amiableness of virtue; that he spare no pains, to convince them of their numberless and indispensable obligations to abhor and avoid the former, and to love and practise the latter; of the several great duties, they owe to GOD, their country, their parents, their neighbour, and themselves; that he critically and constantly observe the variety of their natural tempers, and solicitously endeavour to bring them under such discipline, as may tend most effectually to promote their own satisfaction and the happiness of others; that he early inure them to contemplate the several connexions and various scenes, incident to human life; furnishing such general maxims of conduct, as may best enable them to pass through all with ease, reputation, and comfort.

And, whereas many of the Students in this Seminary may be devoted to the sacred work of the gospel ministry; that the true and fundamental principles of the Christian Religion may be cultivated, established, and perpetuated in the Christian Church, so far, as this Institution may have influence; it shall be the duty of the Master, as the age and capacities of the Scholars will admit, not only to instruct and establish them in the truth of Christianity; but also early and diligently to inculcate upon them the great and important scripture doctrines of the existence of One true GOD, the FATHER, SON, and HOLY GHOST; of the fall of man, the depravity of human nature; the necessity of an atonement, and of our being renewed in the spirit of our minds; the doctrines of repentance toward God and of faith toward our Lord Jesus Christ; of sanctification by the Holy Spirit, and of justification by the free grace of God, through the redemption, that is in Jesus Christ (in opposition to the erroneous and dangerous doctrine of justification by our own merit, or a dependence on self righteousness) together with the other important doctrines and duties of our HOLY CHRISTIAN RELIGION.

And, whereas the most wholesome precepts, without frequent repetition, may prove ineffectual; it is farther required of the Master, that he not only urge and reurge; but continue from day to day, to impress these instructions.

And let him ever remember that the design of this Institution can never be answered, without his persevering, incessant attention to this duty.

Protestants only shall ever be concerned in the TRUST or Instruction of this Seminary.

.   .   .   .   .

This Seminary shall be ever equally open to Youth, of requisite qualifications, from every quarter; provided, that none be admitted, till in common parlence they can read English well, excepting such particular numbers, as the TRUSTEES may hereafter license.

And, in order to prevent the smallest perversion of the true intent of this Foundation, it is again declared, that the *first* and *principal* object of this Institution is the promotion of true PIETY and VIRTUE; the *second,* instruction in the English, Latin, and Greek Languages, together with Writing, Arithmetic, Music, and the Art of Speaking; the *third,* practical Geometry, Logic, and Geography; and the *fourth,* such other of the liberal Arts and Sciences or Languages, as opportunity and ability may hereafter admit, and as the TRUSTEES shall direct. And these Regulations shall be read by the President, at the annual meetings of the TRUSTEES.

The Outlook of Friends

Anthony Benezet, *Some Serious and Awful Considerations, recommended to All, particularly the Youth . . .* (Philadelphia, [1769]), pp. 2–3.

Trying to maintain a distinctive religious perspective, Quaker schoolmasters warned against the encroachment of worldly motives on the ultimate spiritual purpose of education. The Friends maintained schools for their own children to which they admitted children of the poor and, in some instances, Negroes.

Benezet (1713–1784), born in France, came to Philadelphia in 1731, where he taught at the Friends' English Public School and, in 1755, opened a girls' school. A prolific writer, he was influential in movements promoting education and the amelioration of the condition of Negro slaves.

All that has been said by the greatest saints and dying men, when the fullest of light and divine knowledge, of the necessity of piety, of the excellency of virtue, of our duty to God, of the vanity of worldly enjoyments; and all the maxims of the wisest philosophers, when in their highest state of wisdom, are proper objects of meditation for the serious minded, and ought, particularly, to constitute the daily lessons of youthful minds. Such was the education of the youth who attended Plato and Socrates; their every day's instruction were so many lectures upon the nature of man, his true end, and the right use of his faculties. Now as Christianity has set every thing that is reasonable, wise, holy and desirable, in its true point of light, so it might well be expected, that the education of the youth should be as much bettered and amended by Christianity, as the faith and doctrines of religion are. But, alas, our modern education is not of this kind, whatever way of life we intend the youth for, we apply to the fire of their minds, and exhort them to improvement from corrupt motives. We generally stir them to action from principles of covetousness, or a desire of distinction, that they may accumulate wealth, excel others, and shine in the eyes of the world. We repeat and inculcate these motives upon them, till they think it a part of their duty to make gain and worldly distinction the chief object of their desire. That this is generally the nature of the education of our sons, is too plain to need any proof. And it is much to be lamented that our daughters, whose right education is of the utmost importance to human life, should not only be brought up in pride, but in the lowest and most contemptible part of it; such as a fondness for their persons, a desire of beauty, and a love of dress; and indeed almost every thing they meet with seems to conspire to make them think of little else. And after all this we complain of the pernicious effects that pride and covetousness have in the world; we wonder to see grown persons actuated and govern'd by these pernicious principles, not considering that they were all the time of their youth called upon to form their actions and industry upon the same principles. An education under Plato and Socrates had no other end, but to teach youth to think, judge, act and follow such rules of life as Plato and Socrates used, and is it not our indispensable duty to use our best endeavour that the end of a Christian education, may be to teach our youth how to think and judge, and act, and live agreeable to the precepts and practice of our blessed Lord and Saviour Jesus Christ.

Teaching in colonial Virginia

1. A teacher advertises for students in the *Virginia Gazette,* November 17, 1752

Edgar W. Knight, ed., *A Documentary History of Education in the South,* I (Chapel Hill, 1949), 655–656.

JOHN WALKER,

Lately arriv'd in *Williamsburg* from *London,* and who for ten Years past has been engag'd in the Education of Youth, undertakes to instruct young Gentlemen in Reading, Writing, Arithmetick, the most material Branches of Classical Learning, and ancient and modern Geography and History; but, as the noblest End of Erudition and Human Attainments, he will exert his principal Endeavours to improve their Morals, in Proportion to their Progress in Learning, that no Parent may repent his Choice in trusting him with the Education of his Children.

Mrs. *Walker,* likewise, teaches young Ladies all Kinds of Needle Work; makes Capuchins, Shades, Hats, and Bonnets; and will endeavour to give Satisfaction to those who shall honour her with their Custom.

The above-mentioned *John Walker,* and his Wife, live at Mr. *Cobb's* new House, next to Mr. *Coke's,* near the Road going down to the Capitol Landing; where there is also to be sold, Mens Shoes and Pumps, *Turkey* Coffee, Edging and Lace for Ladies Caps, and some Gold Rings.

2. Children should be educated in accordance with their social rank and expectations, 1762

Helen D. Bullock, ed., "A Dissertation on Education in the Form of a Letter from James Maury to Robert Jackson, July 17, 1762," *Papers of the Albemarle County Historical Society,* II (Charlottesville, Va., 1942), 40–46, 57–58.

Rev. James Maury was one of Thomas Jefferson's teachers.

An Acquaintance with the Languages, antiently spoken in Greece & Italy, is necessary, absolutely necessary, for those, who wish to make any reputable Figure in Divinity, Medicine or Law.

It is also delightful, ornamental & useful, nay even necessary to such, as, in some other Parts of the World, turn in the more exalted Spheres of Life.

For Instance, it is so to the English Gentleman of the upper Class, whose Opulence places him far above the perplexing Pursuits & sordid Cares, in which Persons of inferior Fortunes are usually engaged.

It is likewise most eminently to the British Nobleman, whose vast annual Revenues rank him with, nay set him above, many, who, in other Countries, claim the royal Stile & Title; & warrant his indulging himself in the Enjoyment of that calm Retreat from the Bustle of the World, of that studious Leisure and Philosophic Repose, which furnish him with the happiest Opportunities, not barely of making transient Visits to, but even fixing his Residence within, those sacred Recesses, sequestered Seats & classic Grounds, which are the Muses' favourite Haunts; a Repose, a Leisure, a Retreat, which nought, but his Countries pressing Calls, on some great Emergencies, has a Right to break in upon or interrupt.

.   .   .   .   .

It long has been, & still is, Matter of Doubt with me whether the Study of the Grecian & Roman Tongues be (I do not say necessary, for it seems quite obvious it is not, but even) proper for all our Youth, who are sent to a Grammar-school, who have Genius equal to the Task, & the circumstances of whose Parents bid fair for placing them above manual Labor & servile Employments, after their Attainment to Manhood. In the Instances above-mentioned, indeed, the Propriety, & even Necessity, of these Studies, are undeniable: but in this Case, which involves almost all our Youth above the lower Ranks in this Quarter of the World, I am far from convinced, that they are necessary or proper.

In Education it can be no irrational Maxim, that the Part, which, either the Circumstances, the natural Turn, the inclination, or the Talents of The Learner may either require or incline or capacitate him to act in the World, be ever in his Teacher's View; & that even his puerile Studies & earlier Exercises always converge & centre in that one Point.

What his future Circumstances may be in Reference to Fortune, may with Probability be conjectured from those of his Parents; which, if they be but a Remove or two from the Vulgar, are generally nearly guessed at in this Country.

Whether he may have a natural Turn or Genius for either of the learned Professions,[1] is what cannot usually be discovered very early in Life. However, as I cannot at present recollect that the Son of any one Parent of a larger Fortune has, of late Years, been brought up to either of the three; since the Profits of neither are adequate to the Expence of a proper Education for, or to the Fatigue of a diligent Discharge of, the Duties of either of them; a Tutor, methinks, may hence conclude, that such Parents will not judge it eligible to train up their Sons for either of them.

.   .   .   .   .

It is then to be considered, what Kind of Education may be most suited for such, who, when they shall settle in the World, are to be masters of competent Fortunes, which they are to improve, either by the Culture of our Staple, by Merchandise, or by some other Method, than either of the Learned Professions. And such are most of those among us, who class with the Gentry.

Now, Sir, the Business, which these are usually obliged to pursue; — the Variety of Cares, insep[ar]able from their Situation & Way of Life; render it quite obvious, they can have but little Opportunity or Leisure, after they launch out into the busy World, to apply to the Study of the Languages. — Moreover, few, very few of them prosecute their Studies, either in private or public Schools, so long as their twentieth Year. Besides, they commonly marry very Young, & are thence in the early Stages of Life encumbered with Families. And, tho' you suppose them born to the greatest Fortunes, yet the prudent Management of a large Virginia Estate requires so frequent & close an Inspection, in Order, not only to improve, but preserve it, that the Possessor, when once he comes to be charged with the Care of it, can expect but little of that Leisure & Repose, which are requisite for a pleasurable or successful Engagement in such Parts of Literature, as the Languages, Criticism, & curious & deep Researches into Antiquity.

And yet, Sir, Parts of Literature there evidently are, with which even a Virginia Gentleman ought to have some Acquaintance; destitute of which, he must inevitably make but a ridiculous & awkward Figure in Life. And the Rudiments of these must be acquired in Childhood & Youth, or not at all.

For, if he have not some general Acquaintance with History, he can give or receive but very little Satisfaction or Benefit in private Conversation; nor can acquit himself with any tolerable Measure of Honor & Dexterity in any of those public Stations, which are generally filled by Persons of his Rank. Some of his Time then must be spent this Way.

.   .   .   .   .

But, Sir, let us change the Prospect. From viewing a Virginia Gentleman, born to an affluent Fortune, of which we have but very few

---

1. Law, divinity, and medicine.

. . . let us contemplate another, who will be obliged to call in the Assistance of some lucrative Business to help out his little Patrimony to support himself & his Family, when he shall have one, in such Manner, as to prevent his mingling with & being lost among the vulgar Herd. And here, I trust, the Reasonableness of what has been said, will be still more evident & conspicuous.

Here then is a Person, to be educated, who, when come to a state of Manhood, besides the necessary Cares of Oconomy & good Husbandry, must recur to some profitable Vocation to preserve & improve his patrimonial Estate.

It will not, I believe, be denied, that about his 14 or 15th Year he should be put under some Person, eminent in the Business he chooses, in Order to gain an Insight into all it's Modes, Forms & Mysteries, without which it is not to be carried on with Reputation or Success. The earlier then he lays a Foundation for the general Knowledge, mentioned above, as necessary for every Gentleman, the sooner he will be at Liberty to engage in Exercises, peculiarly adapted to qualify him for the Part he is to act. And the sooner this can be done, so much the better.

Gentlemen of this Sort are frequently called to the highest Posts of Honor & Trust in this Country. It is therefore reasonable to crowd as much of this most useful Knowlege as possible into that short Parenthesis of Time (if the Expression may be allowed) which stands between these two Periods, his beginning to learn the first Elements, & his quitting his scholastic Studies, to apply himself principally to acquire a Skill in the destined Business, whatever it be. But, if that short Space be filled with Latin & Greek; I doubt, his Pains & Time cannot justly be said to have been laid out to Advantage. For it is not possible for him to acquire a tolerable Stock of classical Knowledge, at the same Time have Leisure for such useful & necessary Studies, as English Grammar, reading, writing, arithmetic, History, Geography, Chronology, the more practical Parts of the Mathematics, Rhetoric, Eloquence & other Species of polite & useful Learning; nor for gaining an Acquaintance with, & taste for, some of the most instructive, entertaining & finished Productions of Genius in his own Language.

.   .   .   .   .

The Truth of it is, where there is a Strong Presumption, that a Youth, when he shall have attained unto Manhood, will become a Man of Business; it is but reasonable he should, while under his Tutor, be chiefly employed in Studies, that will be useful to him in the approaching active Scenes of Life. Others, however valuable, curious, or entertaining in themselves, yet, if they lend not this Way, are not to him worth the Time & Paines, that must be bestowed on them.

---

3. The duties of a tutor in an aristocratic Virginia family

Hunter D. Farish, ed., *Journal and Letters of Philip Vickers Fithian, 1773–1774: A Plantation Tutor of the Old Dominion* (Williamsburg, Va., 1945), pp. 34–35, 66–67, 72, 208–222.

Fithian, a young graduate of the College of New Jersey (Princeton), was tutor of the children of Robert Carter of Nomini Hall.

LETTER TO THE REVEREND
ENOCH GREEN

Decemr 1st 1773.

REVD SIR.

As you desired I may not omit to inform you, so far as I can by a letter, of the business in which I am now engaged, it would indeed be vastly agreeable to me if it was in my power to give you particular intelligence concerning the state and plan of my employment here.

I set out from home the 20th of Octr and arrived at the Hon: Robert Carters, of Nominy, in Westmorland County, the 28th I began to teach his chidren the first of November. He has two sons, and one Nephew; the oldest Son is turned of seventeen, and is reading Salust and the greek grammer; the others are about fourteen, and in english grammer, and Arithmetic. He has besides five daughters which I am to teach english, the eldest is turned of fifteen, and is reading the spectator; she is employed two days in every week in learning to play the Forte-Piana, and Harpsicord — The others are smaller, and learning to read and spell. Mr Carter is one of the Councellors in the general court at Williamsburg, and possest of as great, perhaps the clearest fortune according to the estimation of people here, of any man in Virginia: He seems to be a good scholar, even in classical learning, and is remarkable one in english grammar; and notwithstanding his rank, which in general seems to countenance indulgence to children, both himself and Mrs Carter have a manner of instructing and dealing with children far superior, I may say it with confidence, to any I have ever seen, in any place, or in any family. They keep them in perfect subjection to themselves, and never pass over an occasion of reproof; and I blush for many of my acquaintances when I say that the children are more kind and complaisant to the servants who constantly attend them than we are to our superiors in age and condition. Mr Carter has an overgrown library of Books of which he allows me the free use. It consists of a general collection of law books, all the Latin and Greek Classicks, vast number of Books on Divinity chiefly by writers who are of the established Religion; he has the works of almost all the late famous writers, as Locke, Addison, Young, Pope, Swift, Dryden, &c. in Short, Sir, to speak moderately, he has more than eight times your number — His eldest Son, who seems to be a Boy of genius and application is to be sent to Cambridge University, but I believe will go through a course either in Philadelphia or Princeton College first. As to what

is commonly said concerning Virginia that it is difficult to avoid being corrupted with the manners of the people, I believe it is founded wholly in a mistaken notion that persons must, when here frequent all promiscuous assemblies; but this is so far from truth that any one who does practise it, tho' he is accused of no crime, loses at once his character; so that either the manners have been lately changed, or the report is false, for he seems now to be best esteemed and most applauded who attends to his business, whatever it be, with the greatest diligence. I believe the virginians have of late altered their manner very much, for they begin to find that their estates by even small extravagance, decline, and grow involved with debt, this seems to be the spring which induces the People of fortune who are the pattern of all behaviour here, to be frugal, and moderate.

.　　　.　　　.　　　.　　　.

[*Wednesday,* January 5, 1774]

Rose at Seven. The morning very stormy. *Bob & Nancy* before Breakfast had a quarrel — Bob called Nancy a Lyar; Nancy upbraided Bob, on the other Hand, with being often flog'd by their Pappa; often by the Masters in College; that he had stol'n Rum, & had got drunk; & that he used to run away &c — These Reproaches when they were set off with Miss Nancys truely feminine address, so violently exasperated *Bob* that he struck her in his Rage — I was at the time in my Chamber; when I enter'd the Room each began with loud and heavy complaints, I put them off however with sharp admonitions for better Behaviour.

. . . Immediately after Breakfast Ben came over with a Message from Mr *Carter,* that he desired me to correct *Bob* severely immediately — Bob when I went into School sat quiet in the corner, & looked sullen, and penitent; I gave some orders to the Children, and went to my Room. — I sent for Bob — He came crying — I told him his Fathers Message; he confess'd himself guilty — I sent him to call up *Harry* —

He came — I talked with them both a long Time recommended Diligence, & good Behaviour, but concluded by observing that I was obliged to comply with Mr Carter's request; I sent *Harry* therefore for some Whips. — *Bob* and poor I remained trembling in the chamber (for Bob was not more uneasy than I it being the first attempt of the kind I have ever made — The Whips came! — I ordered Bob to strip! — He desired me to whip Him in his hand in Tears — I told him no — He then patiently, & with great deliberation took of his Coat and laid it by — I took him by the hand and gave him four or five smart twigs; he cring'd, & bawld & promis'd — I repeated then about eight more, & demanded and got immediately his solemn promise for peace among the children, & Good Behaviour in general — I then sent him down — He conducts himself through this day with great Humility, & unusual diligence, it will be fine if it continues.

. . . . .

Tuesday [January 11, 1774]

The morning very cold — . . . I put Ben to construe some Greek, he has yet no Testament, I gave him therefore Esops Fables in Greek, and Latin. I also took out of the Library, and gave him to read Gordon, upon Geography. Ben seem'd scared with his Greek Lesson, he swore, & wished for Homer that he might kick Him, as he had been told Homer invented Greek.

. . . . .

Letter to John Peck, "On going to Virginia in Character of a Tutor." Nomini Hall August 12th 1774.

. . . . .

You will act wisely, if, from the begining, you convince all your Scholars which you may easily do, of your abilities in the several branches, which you shall profess to teach; you are not to tell them, totidem Verbis, "that you

understand, perhaps as well as any man on the Continent both the Latin & Greek Classicks"; "& have gone through the usual Course in the noted College of New-Jersey, under Dr Witherspoon, so universally known & admired, where you have studied Criticism, Oratory, History, not to mention Mathematical & philosophical Studies, & dipt a good way into the French-Language, & that you have learn'd a smattering of Dancing, Cards &c. &c. &c." For Dun-p or Hack — n or the most profound dunce in your College or School would have too much sense to pass such impudence by, & not despise and reproach it; but you may speedily & certainly make them think you a "Clever Fellow" (which is a phrase in use here for a good Scholar) if you never mention any thing before them, only what you seem to be wholly master of — This will teach them never to dispute your determination, & always to rely upon your Judgment; two things which are most essential for your peace, & their advantage. That you may avoid yourself of this with certainty I shall recommend for your practice the following method, as useful at least, if not intirely necessary. Read over carefully, the lessons in Latin & Greek, in your leisure hours, that the story & Language be fresh in your memory, when you are hearing the respective lessons; for your memory is treacherous, & I am pretty certain it would confound you if you should be accosted by a pert School-Boy, in the midst of a blunder, with "Physician heal thyself"! — You ought likewise to do this with those who are working Figures; probably you may think that because the highest Cypherer is only in decimal arithmetic, it is not there fore worth your critical attention to be looking previously into the several Sums. But you are to consider that a sum in the Square-Root, or even in the Single Rule of three direct, is to your Pupils of as great importance, as the most abstruse problem in the Mathematicks to an able artist; & you may lay this down for a Maxim, that they will reckon upon your abilities, according as they find you acquainted & expert in what they themselves are studying. If therefore you have resolution (as I do not question your ability) to carry this plan which I have laid down into execution; you will thereby convince them of the propriety of their Subordination to you, & obedience to your instructions, so that you may lead them, without any resistance, and fix them to the Study of whatever Science you think proper, in which they will rise according to their respective Capacities.

.   .   .   .   .

Another current difficulty will be petitions for holidays. You must have good deal of steadiness if you are able to evade cleverly this practice which has grown so habitual to your little charge from a false method in their early education that they absolutely claim it as a necessary right. You must also as much as you can, avoid visible partiality. At least you must never suffer your fondness for one Scholar to grow so manifest, as that all your School shall see you look over a fault in him or her which same fault, if committed by another, you severely chastise. This will certainly produce in the others hatred & contempt. A fourth difficulty, and the last I shall mention, consists in knowing when, & in what measure to give the Boys Liberty to go from Home. The two younger Boys are wholly under your inspection; so that not only the progress they make in learning, but their moral Conduct (for both of these are critically observed & examined) either justifies or condemns your management to the World. If you keep them much at home, & close to business, they themselves will call you unfeeling and cruel; & refuse to be industrious; if you suffer them to go much abroad they are certainly out of the way of improvement by Study, probably, by discovering their gross Ignorance, they will expose to ridicule both themselves & all their former instructors, & possibly they may commit actual Crimes so as very much to injure themselves; & scandalize their family; but in each of these you will have a large share of blame, perhaps more than the parents, or even the Boys themselves — It will be said that the parents gave them no licence

relying wholly on your Judgment & prudence, this will in good measure Justify them to the world. And as to the Boys they are full of youthful impetuosity & vigour, & these compel them, when they are free of restraint, to commit actions which with proper management they had surely avoided. I say, when you lay these things together, & view them on every side you will find so many perplexities arising in your mind, from a sense of ignorance of your duty, that you will proceed with caution & moderation, & will be carefull to examine with some precision into the circumstances of *time, company, & Business* when you license them to go out entirely at the risk of your Reputation.

Sectarianism in the colleges

One result of the growth of the colonies was the founding of six colleges between 1745 and 1770. Denominational rivalries resulting in part from the Great Awakening made sectarian control an important issue.

---

1. Jonathan Edwards proposes that colleges should continue to be *"the schools of the prophets,"* 1740

Edwards, *Conversions and Revival in New England,* pp. 339–340.

Edwards was chosen president of the College of New Jersey in 1757 but died only a few months after taking office.

And though it may be thought, that I go out of my proper sphere, to intermeddle in the affairs of the colleges, yet I will take the liberty of an Englishman (that speaks his mind freely concerning public affairs) and the liberty of a minister of Christ (who doubtless may speak his mind as freely about things that concern the kingdom of his Lord and master) to give my opinion, in some things, with respect to those societies; the original and main design of which is to train up persons, and fit them for the work of the ministry. And I would say in general, that it appears to me that care should be taken, some way or other, that those societies should be so regulated, that they should, in fact, be nurseries of piety. Otherwise, they are fundamentally ruined and undone, as to their main design, and most essential end. They ought to be so constituted, that vice and idleness should have no living there. They are intolerable in societies, whose main design is, to train up youth in Christian knowledge and eminent piety, to fit them to be pastors of the flock of the blessed Jesus. I have heretofore had some acquaintance with the affairs of a college, and experience of what belonged to its tuition and government; and I cannot but think that it is practicable enough, so to constitute such societies, that there should be no being there, without being virtuous, serious and diligent. It seems to me to be a reproach to the land, that ever it should be so with our colleges that instead of being places of the greatest advantages for true piety, one cannot send a child thither, without great danger of his being infected, as to his morals; as it has certainly sometimes been with these Societies. It is perfectly intolerable; and any thing should be done, rather than it should be so. If we pretend to have any colleges at all, under any notion of training up youth for the ministry, there should be some way found out, that should certainly prevent its being thus. To have societies for bringing persons up to be ambassadors of Jesus Christ, and to lead souls to heaven, and to have them places of so much infection, is the greatest nonsense and absurdity imaginable.

And, as thorough and effectual care should be taken that vice and idleness are not tolerated in these societies, so certainly, the design of them requires, that extraordinary means should be used in them, for training up the students

in vital religion, and experimental and practical godliness; so that they shoud be holy societies, the very place should be as it were sacred. They should be, in the midst of the land, fountains of piety and holiness. There is a great deal of pains taken, to teach the scholars human learning; there ought to be as much, and more care, thoroughly to educate them in religion, and lead them to true and eminent holiness. If the main design of these nurseries, is to bring up persons to teach Christ, then it is of the greatest importance that there should be care and pains taken, to bring those that are there educated, to the knowledge of Christ. It has been common in our public prayers, to call these societies, *the schools of the prophets;* and if they are schools, to train up young men to be prophets, certainly there ought to be extraordinary care there taken, to train them up to be Christians.

---

2. An attack upon sectarianism during the debate in New York at the founding of King's College (Columbia University), 1753: a series of essays entitled "Remarks on Our Intended College"

William Livingston et al., *The Independent Reflector, or weekly Essays on Sundry Important Subjects more particularly adapted to the Province of New-York,* ed. Milton Klein (Cambridge, Mass., 1963), pp. 171, 174–176, 178–181, 188–189, 199–203.

Livingston (1723–1790) was an ambitious young politician who later represented New York at the First and Second Continental Congresses.

March 29, 1753

It is in the first Place observable, that unless [the] Constitution and Government [of the college] be such as will admit Persons of all protestant Denominations, upon a perfect Parity as to Privileges, it will itself be greatly prejudiced, and prove a Nursery of Animosity, Dissention and Disorder. The sincere Men of all Sects, imagine their own Profession, on the whole, more eligible and scriptural than any other. It is therefore very natural to suppose, they will exert themselves to weaken and diminish all other Divisions, the better to strengthen and enlarge their own. To this Cause must in a great Measure be ascribed, that Heat and Opposition, which animate the Breasts of many Men of religious Distinctions, whose intemperate and misapplied Zeal, is the only Blemish that can be thrown upon their Characters. Should our College, therefore, unhappily thro' our own bad Policy, fall into the Hands of any one religious Sect in the Province: Should that Sect, which is more than probable, establish its religion in the College, shew favour to its votaries, and cast Contempt upon others; 'tis easy to foresee, that Christians of all other Denominations amongst us, instead of encouraging its Prosperity, will, from the same Principles, rather conspire to oppose and oppress it. Besides *English* and *Dutch* Presbyterians, which perhaps exceed all our other religious Professions put together, we have Episcopalians, Anabaptists, Lutherans, Quakers, and a growing Church of Moravians, all equally zealous for their discriminating Tenets: Which-soever of these has the sole Government of the College, will kindle the Jealousy of the Rest, not only against the Persuasion so preferred, but the College itself. Nor can any Thing less be expected, than a general Discontent and Tumult; which, affecting all Ranks of People, will naturally tend to disturb the Tranquility and Peace of the Province.

In such a State of Things, we must not expect the Children of any, but of that Sect which prevails in the Academy will ever be sent to it: For should they, the established Tenets must either be implicitly received, or a perpetual religious War necessarily maintained. Instead of the liberal Arts and Sciences, and such At-tainments as would best qualify the Students to be useful and ornamental to their Country, Party Cavils and Disputes about Trifles, will afford Topics of Argumentation to their incredible Disadvantage, by a fruitless Consumption of Time. Such Gentlemen, therefore, who can afford it, will give their Sons an Education abroad, or at some of the neighbouring Academies, where equally imbibing a Zeal for their own Principles, and furnished with the Arts of defending them, an incessant Opposition to all others, on their Return, will be the unavoidable Consequence . . .

Others, and many such there may be, who not able to support the Expence of an Education abroad, but could easily afford it at Home, thro' a Spirit of Opposition to the predominant Party, will rather determine to give their Children no Education at all. From all which it follows, that a College under the sole Influence of a Party, for want of suitable Encouragement, being but indifferently stocked with Pupils, will scarce arrive to the Usefulness of a *Schola illustris,* which being inferior to a College is, I hope, much short of what is intended by Ours.

Another Argument against so pernicious a Scheme is, that it will be dangerous to Society . . . And have we not reason to fear the worst Effects of it, where none but the Principles of one Persuasion are taught, and all others depressed and discountenanced? Where, instead of Reason and Argument, of which the Minds of the Youth are not capable, they are early imbued with the Doctrines of a Party, enforced by the Authority of a Professor's Chair, and the combining Aids of the President, and all the other Officers of the College? That religious Worship should be constantly maintained there, I am so far from opposing, that I strongly recommend it, and do not believe any such Kind of Society, can be kept under a regular and due Discipline without it. But instructing the Youth in any particular Systems of Divinity, or recommending and establishing any single Method of Worship or Church Government, I am convinced would be both useless and hurtful.

.   .   .   .   .

A Third Argument against suffering the College to fall into the Hands of a Party, may be deduced from the Design of its Erection, and Support by the Public.

The Legislature to whom it owes its Origin, and under whose Care the Affair has hitherto been conducted, could never have intended it as an Engine to be exercised for the Purposes of a Party. Such an Insinuation, would be false and scandalous. It would therefore be the Height of Insolence in any to pervert it to such mean, partial and little Designs. No, it was set on Foot, and I hope will be constituted for general Use, for the public Benefit, for the Education of all who can afford such Education: And to suppose it intended for any other less public-spirited Uses, is ungratefully to reflect upon all who have hitherto, had any Agency in an Undertaking so glorious to the Province, so necessary, so important and beneficial.

.   .   .   .   .

April 19, 1753

First: That all the Trustees be nominated, appointed, and incorporated by the Act, and that whenever an Avoidance among them shall happen, the same be reported by the Corporation to the next Sessions of Assembly, and such Vacancy supplied by Legislative Act. They hold their Offices only at the good Pleasure of the Governor, Council and General Assembly: and that no Person of any Protestant Denomination be, on Account of his religious Persuasion, disqualified for sustaining any Office in the College.

.   .   .   .   .

The Fifth Article I propose is, that no religious Profession in particular be established in the College; but that both Officers and Scholars be at perfect Liberty to attend any Protestant Church at their Pleasure respectively: And that the Corporation be absolutely inhibited the making of any By-Laws relating to Religion, except such as compel them to attend Divine Service at some Church or other, every Sabbath, as they shall be able, lest so invaluable a Liberty be abused and *made a Cloak for Licenciousness.*

To this most important Head, I should think proper to subjoin,

Sixthly: That the whole College be every Morning and Evening convened to attend public Prayers, to be performed by the President, or in his Absence, by either of the Fellows; and that such Forms be perscribed and adhered to as all Protestants can freely join in.

Besides the Fitness and indisputable Duty of supporting the Worship of God in the College; obliging the Students to attend it twice every Day, will have a strong Tendency to preserve a due Decorum, Good Manners and Virtue amongst them, without which the College will sink into Profaness and Disrepute. They will be thereby forced from the Bed of Sloth, and being brought before their Superiors, may be kept from Scenes of Wickedness and Debauchery, which they might otherwise run into, as hereby their Absence from the College will be better detected.

.   .   .   .   .

Seventhly: That Divinity be no Part of the public Exercises of the College. I mean, that it be not taught as a Science: That the Corporation be inhibited from electing a Divinity Professor; and that the Degrees to be conferred, be only in the Arts, Physic, and the Civil Law.

---

3. Rev. Thomas Clap, president of Yale College, argues for the sectarian character of colleges, 1754

Thomas Clap, *The Religious Constitution of Colleges* (New London, Conn., 1754), pp. 4–10, 12–13.

Colleges, are *Religious Societies,* of a Superior Nature to all others. For whereas Parishes, are Societies, for training up the *common People;* Colleges, are *Societies of Ministers,* for training up Persons for the Work of the *Ministry.* And therefore *all their Religious Instructions, Worship, and Ordinances, are carried on, within their own Jurisdiction, by their own Officers, and under their own Regulation.*

.   .   .   .   .

Religious, Worship, Preaching, and Instruction on the Sabbath, being one of the most important Parts, of the Education of Ministers; it is more necessary, that it should be under the Conduct, of the Authority, of the College, than any other Part of Education. The Preaching, ought to be adapted, to the superior Capacity, of those, who are to be qualified, to be *Instructors of others;* and upon all Accounts *Superior,* to that, which is ordinarily to be expected, or indeed requisite, in a common Parish.

.   .   .   .   .

YALE-COLLEGE in *New-Haven;* does not come up, to the Perfection, of the Ancient Established Universities, in *Great Britain;* yet, would endeavour, to Imitate them, in most things, as far, as its present State, will admit of.

It was FOUNDED, A.D. 1701. By *Ten Principal Ministers,* in the Colony of CONNECTICUT; upon the Desire, of many other Ministers, and People in it; with the *Licence, and Approbation, of the General Assembly.* Their main Design, in that *Foundation,* was to *Educate Persons, for the Ministry of these* Churches, commonly called *Presbyterian,* or *Congregational,* according to their own *Doctrine, Discipline,* and *Mode of Worship.*

.   .   .   .   .

The *Founders,* at their first Meeting, in 1701; make, a *Formal Foundation,* of the College, by an *Express Declaration;* and *giving, a Number of Books,* for a Library . . . Particularly Prescribing, what Books of Divinity, they should Recite; and *no other, but such, as the Trustees should order;* and, that special Care, should be taken, in the Education, of the Students, not to suffer them, to be Instructed, in any different Principles, or Doctrines; and that, all proper Measures, should be taken, to promote, the *Power, and Purity, of Religion;* and *the Peace, and best Edification, of those Churches.* And particularly Order, *that the Students, should attend, Morning, and Evening Prayers,* and *other religious Exercises; and* especially, the *Worship of God, on the Lord's Day;* on Penalty, not exceeding, *Six-pence* Sterling.

The present Governors, of the College; esteem themselves, bound by *Law,* and the more *sacred Ties of Conscience, and Fidelity to their Trust, committed to them, by their Predecessors;* to pursue, and carry on, the pious Intention, and Design, of the *Founders;* and to improve, all the *College Estate,* descended to them, for that purpose.

.   .   .   .   .

Some indeed, have supposed, that, the only Design of Colleges, was to teach the Arts, and Sciences; and that Religion, is no part, of a College Education: And therefore, there ought to be, no religious Worship upheld, or enjoined, by the Laws of the College; but every Student, may Worship, where, and how, he pleaseth; or, as his Parents, or Guardian, shall direct.

But, it is probable, that there is not a College, to be found upon Earth, upon such a Constitution; without any Regard, to Religion. And we know, that Religion, and the Religion of these Churches, in particular; both, as to *Doctrine,* and *Discipline,* was the main Design, of the *Founders,* of this College (agreeable, to the minds, of the *Body, of the People*); and, this Design, their Successors, are bound in Duty, to pursue. And indeed, Religion, is a matter, of so great Consequence, and Importance; that the Knowledge, of the Arts, and Sciences, how excellent soever, in themselves, are comparatively, worth but little, without it.

---

4. An ethical system for college students

Samuel Johnson, *Elementa Philosophica . . .* (Philadelphia, 1752), pp. 2–4, 6–10, 18–22.

Eighteenth-century colleges taught a Christianity harmonized with natural principles. This text by the first president of King's College represents the philosophical outlook students were expected to adopt.

---

3. ETHICS is the Art of living happily, by the right Knowledge of ourselves, and the Practice of Virtue: Our *Happiness* being the End, and *Knowledge* and *Virtue,* the Means to that End.

4. We are said to live happily when we enjoy ourselves, and all that is really good for us, in the whole of our Nature and Duration; *i.e.* considered, not only as sensitive, but as reasonable, free, active, social and immortal Creatures. For *Happiness* means that Pleasure which ariseth in us from our Enjoyment of ourselves, and all that is really good for us, or suitable to our Natures, and conducive to our Happiness in the whole.

5. The Enjoyment of ourselves, and all that is truly good, depends on a good Habit, or State of the Soul, united with, and delighting in its proper Objects, which are *Truth* and *Good;* the first being the Object of the Understanding; and the other of the Will and Affections: And this good Habit is the same Thing with *Virtue.*

.   .   .   .   .

And as Ease, Pleasure or Happiness, is what we call natural Good; so Uneasiness, Pain or Misery, we call natural Evil.

10. In order to make a right Judgment of *natural Good* and *Evil,* as being the Test of *moral,* we must (as I said) take into the Ac-

count, the *whole of our Nature and Duration,* as being *sensitive* and *rational, social* and *immortal* Creatures. It must therefore be the Good and Happiness of the *whole human Nature,* and the *whole moral System,* in *Time,* and to all *Eternity.* Hence the Good of the *animal Body,* or the *Pleasure of Sense,* is but imaginary, and ceaseth to be *Good,* and hath even the Nature of *Evil,* so far forth as it is inconsistent with the Good and Happiness of the *Soul:* Which is also the Case of *private Good,* so far forth as it is inconsistent with the *Good* of the *Publick;* and *temporal Good,* so far forth as it is inconsistent with that which is *eternal.*

.   .   .   .   .

15. (1.) The Law of *Reason* and *Conscience* is, I think, the same Thing which some have called the *moral Sense,* being a kind of quick and almost intuitive Sense of Right and Wrong, deriving, as I conceive, from the perpetual Presence and Irradiation of the Deity in our Minds, and dictating with a strong and commanding Force what is reasonable, fair and decent, and so fit and right to be done, and giving us Applause and Satisfaction when we conform to it, and blaming and reproaching us, and filling us with Uneasiness and Remorse, when we act contrary to its Dictates: It being the Law of our Nature, that we should always affect and act conformable to the inward Sense of our own Minds and Consciences. And those consequent pleasing or uneasy Sentiments, considering it as a Law, are its Sanctions.

16. (2.) The Law of *Self-love* and *Self-preservation,* which makes us solicitous for the Continuance of our Existence, and the Enjoyment of ourselves, and ariseth from the Consciousness of our Existence, and of Pleasure or Pain, naturally attending certain Conditions in which we are, or may be . . . For it is manifest that we are, by the Author of our Nature, laid under a Necessity of valuing ourselves and our own *Interest,* and of seeking and pursuing our own *Preservation* and *Well-being* or Happiness, and whatever we find tends to it, or is

connected with it; and consequently that of the Society to which we belong, with which we find our own is, in the Nature of Things, necessarily connected.

17. From whence ariseth (thirdly) the Law of *Benevolence,* or that Disposition we find also implanted in us towards the Good of others, arising from Reflection, whereby we are led to put ourselves in each other's Stead, and to have a secret Pleasure or Uneasiness in the good or ill Condition of others, from a Consciousness of our own, in the like Situation; which Sentiments therefore are its Sanctions. This Principle makes us desirous of each other's Esteem and Goodwill, and puts us upon doing what we know may be pleasing and advantageous to each other, and to the whole; so that *self* and *social Good* cannot be considered in themselves, as at all interfering, but as being intirely coincident and subservient to each other.

. . . . .

19. (2.) The *external* and *moral Obligation* we are under . . . ariseth from *moral Government,* or the Consideration that they are the Will and Law of a Superior who aims at our Happiness in enjoying them, to whom we are therefore accountable for our Behaviour, and by whom we shall be rewarded or punished; *i.e.* made to feel Pleasure or Pain, according as we behave well or ill . . .

20. (1.) The *political Obligation* to the Practice of these moral Actions and Forebearances, is the Consideration that they are the publick Will, or the Will and *Law of the Society* or Government we live under, and to which we are accountable (whether indeed it be a *Family* or a *State*) enforced by the Sanctions of temporal Rewards and Punishments. In this View *moral Laws* become *political Laws,* and *moral Good, political Good,* to which many others might be added, for promoting of the publick Weal.

21. But here again, tho' GOD is the Founder of Government, both economical and political, yet while we rest on this Foot, and act meerly under these political Views, and with a Regard only to our Interest in this World, tho' we may be said to be meer *moral Men* (as that Expression is commonly used) or *good Citizens,* and *good Common-wealthmen,* we cannot be said to be *religious,* no, not even in those Actions that relate to GOD *himself.* But,

22. (2.) The *religious Obligation* we are under to those Actions and Forebearances that are necessary to our Happiness in the whole, is the Consideration that they are the Will and *Law of* GOD, our Creator, Preserver, and supreme moral Governor, the great Author, Head and Lord of the whole social System, enforced by the Sanctions of *eternal Rewards* and *Punishments,* to whom we are justly accountable for all our Behaviour, and by whom we must expect to be treated well or ill, according as that shall be found to be good or bad.

. . . . .

25. So that upon the whole it appears, That *Morality,* in the just Extent of it, is the same Thing with the *Religion of Nature,* or that *Religion* which is founded in the *Nature* of Things; and that it may be defined, *the Pursuit of our true Happiness by Thinking, Affecting and Acting, according to the Laws of Truth and right Reason, under a Sense of the Duty that we owe to Almighty GOD, and the Account we must expect to give of ourselves to Him.*

. . . . .

§10. I also find, upon looking about me, an endless Variety of sensible Objects; a glorious Heaven above me, and a spacious Earth beneath me, furnished with a surprizing Variety of Inhabitants, all connected (together with my own Body, one of the most curious Machines of them all) in a most wonderful Manner one with another. So that it is manifest from their Dependence and Subserviency, that they are contrived and designed to constitute, as in Fact they do, one harmonious, beautiful and useful System; one complete and intire Whole; in which I find every Thing fitted, in the best Manner, to my own Conveniences and Pleasures, both for the comfortable Subsistence of my Body, and the Entertainment and Delight of my Soul; but so, that it was, at the same time, the manifest Design of them to excite, engage, direct and employ my Activity, without which I find I cannot comfortably enjoy either myself or them.

§11. I can moreover carry my Thoughts and Imaginations throughout the vast Spaces of Heaven and Earth, and have a mighty Curiosity to pry and search out the Secrets and Laws of Nature, and discover and conceive, as much as I can, of the great Author of it, and what Sort of Behaviour and Conduct is suitable to my Nature, and the Relation I stand in to Him and my Fellow Creatures . . .

§13. As to those of my own Species (from which by Analogy I may form some Notion of them) I find we were evidently made for Society, being furnished with the Power of *Speech* as well as *Reason,* whereby we are capable of entering into the Understanding of each other's Minds and Sentiments, and of holding mutual Intercourse and Conversation one with another, and jointly conspiring to promote our common Well-being; to which we are naturally led by a Principle of *Benevolence,* and *social Dispositions* and *Affections,* founded in the Frame and Condition of our Nature, which not only placeth us in the various Relations of *Husbands* and *Wives, Parents* and *Children,* and other *Relatives;* but also lays us under a Necessity of mutual Dependence one upon another, which obligeth us to enter into Compacts for our Defence and Safety, and for maintaining both private Right and publick Order, and promoting the common Good of our Species, in the several Communities to which we belong. And as I have a quick Sense of what is right in others towards me as being what I am, and of my own Ease and Comfort, so I cannot divest myself of a Sense of what must, for the same Reason, be right in me towards others, and a Sense of Tenderness and Compassion for those that are in Misery, whereby I am strongly prompted to relieve them: And these Tendencies and Affections of *the social Kind,* are evidently planted in us for promoting our

social Happiness. And finally; as I cannot long enjoy myself in a State of Solitude, and have a strong Passion for Society; so I find, in Fact, that my true Interest and Enjoyment of myself, depends on the general Interest and good Order of the Community, and this, in Addition to those social Dispositions, strongly prompts me to the Love of my Country, and to be forward and active in whatever may promote the publick Weal. Such are my Abilities and Advantages, and such my Condition, Circumstances and Tendencies, and those of the Kind to which I stand related.

.　　　.　　　.　　　.　　　.

§16. At the same time we find, by sad Experience, that we are daily liable to many Infirmities and Diseases, Pains and Miseries, Losses and Disappointments, and perpetual Uncertainty, with respect to Life and Health, and every Thing about us, and must expect, in a little Time to quit our present State of Being, and resign to the common Fate of a Dissolution, which is called *Death,* that King of Terrors, who is incessantly making his Approaches towards us in one Shape or another. Such a strange Mixture is human Nature! Such a various Creature is Man! Such his noble Abilities and Excellencies on the one Hand, and such his Imperfections and Wretchedness on the other.

---

5. Philip Fithian, a recent graduate of the College of New Jersey, fondly recalls the diversions of student life, 1774

Journal and Letters of Philip Fithian, pp. 253–254.

Every time I reflect on that Place of retirement & Study, where I spent two years which I call the most pleasant as well as the most important Period in my past life — Always when I think upon the *Studies,* the *Discipline,* the *Companions,* the *Neighbourhood,* the *exercises, & Diversions,* it gives me a secret & real Pleasure, even the Foibles which often prevail there are pleasant on recollection; such as giving each other *names & characters;* Meeting & Shoving in the dark entries; knocking at Doors & going off without entering; Strewing the entries in the night with greasy Feathers; freezing the Bell; Ringing it at late Hours of the Night; — I may add that it does not seem disagreeable to think over the Mischiefs often practised by wanton Boy's — Such are writing witty pointed anonymous Papers, in *Songs, Confessions, Wills, Soliliques, Proclamations, Advertisements &c —* Picking from the neighbourhood now & then a plump fat Hen or Turkey for the private entertainment of the Club "instituted for inventing & practising several new kinds of mischief in a secret polite Manner" — Parading bad Women — Burning Curse-John — Darting Sun-Beams upon the Town-People Reconoitering Houses in the Town, & ogling Women with the Telescope — Making Squibs, & other frightful compositions with Gun-Powder, & lighting them in the Rooms of timorous Boys, & new *comers* — The various methods used in naturalizing Strangers, of incivility in the Dining-Room to make them bold; writing them sharp & threatning Letters to make them smart; leading them at first with long Lessons to make them industrious — And trying them by Jeers & Repartee in order to make them choose their Companions &c &c —

B. EDUCATION IN THE EARLY REPUBLIC

The impact of independence

Although the American Revolution temporarily interrupted the work of many schools and colleges, its most important effect in the long run was to encourage innovations to end cultural as well as political and economic dependency. Education was affected by this spirit. While it was difficult, as always, to translate ideas into practice, men throughout the country tried to create new patterns in education appropriate for the people of an independent and republican nation.

---

1. Pennsylvania schoolmasters and officers of academies and colleges required to swear allegiance to the United States and the Commonwealth of Pennsylvania during the War for Independence, 1777

James T. Mitchell and Henry Flanders, comps., *The Statutes at Large of Pennsylvania from 1682 to 1801,* IX (n.p., 1903), 111–112, 239–240; hereafter cited as *Penna. Statutes at Large*

I, ..., do swear (or affirm) that I renounce and refuse all allegiance to George the Third, King of Great Britain, his heirs and successors, and that I will be faithful and bear true allegiance to the commonwealth of Pennsylvania as a free and independent state, and that I will not at any time do or cause to be done any matter or thing that will be prejudicial or injurious to the freedom and independence thereof, as declared by Congress; and also that I will discover and make known to some one justice of the peace of the said state all treasons or traitorous conspiracies which I now know or hereafter shall know to be formed against this or any of the United States of America.

.   .   .   .   .

And be it enacted, That all trustees, provosts, rectors, professors, masters and tutors of any college or academy, and all schoolmasters and ushers . . . who shall at any time after the first day of June next, be admitted into or enter upon any of the before mentioned preferments, offices or places, or shall come into any such capacity, or shall take upon him or them any such practice, employment or business as aforesaid without having first taken and subscribed the before mentioned oath or affirmation, he or they shall be ipso facto adjudged incapable and disabled in law, to all intents and purposes whatsoever, to have, occupy or enjoy the said preferment or preferments office or offices, employment or employments or any part of them, or any matter or thing aforesaid, or any profit or advantage appertaining to them, or any of them, and every such office or place of trust shall be void and is hereby adjudged void; and any person that shall be lawfully convicted of the premises, or any of them in or upon any presentment, or indictment in any court of record in this state, shall also forfeit any sum, not exceeding five hundred pounds, which the court shall adjudge, together with costs, one-half of which said fine shall go to the use of the State, and the other half to him, her or them who shall commence and carry on such prosecution with effect.

---

2. The Georgia legislature penalizes young men who are educated abroad, 1785

Allen D. Candler, comp., *The Colonial Records of the State of Georgia,* XIX, pt. 2 (Atlanta, 1911), 378; hereafter cited as *Ga. Colonial Records.*

If any Person or persons under the age of sixteen Years shall after the passing of this Act be sent abroad without the limits of the United States and reside there three Years for the purpose of receiving an education under a foreign power. such person or persons after their return to this State shall for three Years be considered and treated as Aliens in so far as not to be eligable to a Seat in the Legislature or Executive authority or to hold any office civil or Military in the State for that term and so in proportion for any greater number of Years as he or they shall be absent as aforesaid, but shall not be injured or disqualified in any other respect.

---

3. Noah Webster (1758–1843), a leading spokesman for nationalism argues that American youth should be educated at home, 1788

The American Magazine, I (May 1788), 370–374.

Before I quit this subject, I beg leave to make some remarks on a practice which appears to be attended with important consequences; I mean that of sending boys to Europe for an education, or sending to Europe for teachers. That this was right before the revolution will not be disputed; at least so far as national attachments were concerned; but the propriety of it ceased with our political relation to Great Britain.

In the first place, our honor as an independent nation is concerned in the establishment of literary institutions, adequate to all our own purposes; without sending our youth abroad, or depending on other nations for books and instructors. It is very little to the reputation of America to have it said abroad, that after the heroic achievements of the late war, this independent people are obliged to send to Europe for men and books to teach their children A B C.

But in another point of view, a foreign education is directly opposite to our political interests, and ought to be discountenanced, if not prohibited.

Every person of common observation will grant, that most men prefer the manners and the government of that country where they are educated. Let ten American youths be sent, each to a different European kingdom, and live there from the age of twelve to twenty, & each will give the preference to the country where he has resided.

The period from twelve to twenty is the most important in life. The impressions made before that period are commonly effaced; those that are made during that period *always* remain for many years, and *generally* thro' life.

Ninety-nine persons of a hundred, who pass that period in England or France, will prefer the people, their manners, their laws, and their government to those of their native country. Such attachments are injurious, both to the happiness of the men, and to the political interests of their own country. As to private happiness, it is universally known how much pain a man suffers by a change of habits in living. The customs of Europe are and ought to be different from ours; but when a man has been bred in one country, his attachments to its manners make them in a great measure, necessary to his happiness; on changing his residence, he must therefore break his former habits, which is always a painful sacrifice; or the discordance between the manners of his own country and his habits, must give him incessant uneasiness; or he must introduce, into a circle of his friends, the manners in which he was educated. All these consequences may follow at the same time, and the last, which is inevitable, is a public injury. The refinement of manners in every country should keep pace exactly with the increase of its wealth — and perhaps the greatest evil America now feels is, an improvement of taste and manners which its wealth cannot support.

A foreign education is the very source of this evil — it gives young gentlemen of fortune a relish for manners and amusements which are not suited to this country; which, however, when introduced by this class of people, will always become fashionable.

But a corruption of manners is not the sole objection to a foreign education: An attachment to a *foreign* government, or rather a want of attachment to our *own,* is the natural effect of a residence abroad, during the period of youth . . .

It may be said that foreign universities furnish much better opportunities of improvement in the sciences than the American. This may be true, and yet will not justify the practice of sending young lads from their own country. There are some branches of science which may be studied to much greater advantage in Europe than in America, particularly chemistry. When these are to be acquired, young gentlemen ought to spare no pains to attend the best professors. It may, therefore, be useful, in some cases, for students to cross the atlantic to *complete* a course of studies; but it is not necessary for them to go early in life, nor to continue a long time. Such instances need not be frequent even now; and the necessity for them will diminish in proportion to the future advancement of literature in America.

It is, however, much questioned whether, in the ordinary course of study, a young man can enjoy greater advantages in Europe than in America. Experience inclines me to raise a doubt, whether the danger to which a youth must be exposed among the sons of dissipation abroad, will not turn the scale in favor of our American colleges. Certain it is, that four fifths of the great literary characters in America never crossed the Atlantic.

---

4. Thomas Jefferson's plan for a Virginia school system, 1779

Julian P. Boyd, ed., *Papers of Thomas Jefferson,* II (Princeton, 1950), 526–533.

Jefferson proposed this comprehensive system of public schools to prepare the ablest youths for the professions and public service. He was a member of the Virginia House of Delegates and chairman of its committee to revise the laws, but the legislature refused to pass the bill.

A Bill for the More General Diffusion of Knowledge

Whereas it appeareth that however certain forms of government are better calculated than others to protect individuals in the free exercise of their natural rights, and are at the same time themselves better guarded against degeneracy, yet experience hath shewn, that even under the best forms, those entrusted with power have, in time, and by slow operations, perverted it into tyranny; and it is believed that the most effectual means of preventing this would be, to illuminate, as far as practicable, the minds of the people at large, and more especially to give them knowledge of those facts, which history exhibiteth, that, possessed thereby of the experience of other ages and countries, they may be enabled to know ambition under all its shapes, and prompt to exert their natural powers to defeat its purposes; And whereas it is generally true that that people will be happiest whose laws are best, and are best administered, and that laws will be wisely formed, and honestly administered, in proportion as those who form and administer them are wise and honest; whence it becomes expedient for promoting the publick happiness that those persons, whom nature hath endowed with genius and virtue, should be rendered by liberal education worthy to receive, and able to guard the sacred deposit of the rights and liberties of their fellow citizens, and that they should be called to that charge without regard to wealth, birth or other accidental condition or circumstance; but the indigence of the greater number disabling them from so educating, at their own expence, those of their children whom nature hath fitly formed and disposed to become useful instruments for the public, it is better that such should be sought for and educated at the common expence of all, than that the happiness of all should be confided to the weak or wicked:

Be it therefore enacted by the General Assembly, that in every county within this commonwealth, there shall be chosen annually, by the electors qualified to vote for Delegates, three of the most honest and able men of their county, to be called the Aldermen of the county.

.   .   .   .   .

The said Aldermen on the first Monday in October, if it be fair, and if not, then on the next fair day, excluding Sunday, shall meet at the court-house of their county, and proceed to divide their said county into hundreds, bounding the same by water courses, mountains, or limits, to be run and marked, if they think necessary, by the county surveyor, and at the county expence, regulating the size of the said hundreds, according to the best of their discretion, so as that they may contain a convenient number of children to make up a school, and be of such convenient size that all the children within each hundred may daily attend the school to be established therein, distinguishing each hundred by a particular name; which division, with the names of the several hundreds, shall be returned to the court of the county and be entered of record, and shall remain unaltered until the increase or decrease of inhabitants shall render an alteration necessary . . .

The electors aforesaid residing within every hundred shall meet on the third Monday in October after the first election of Aldermen, at such place, within their hundred, as the said Aldermen shall direct . . . The electors being so assembled shall choose the most convenient place within their hundred for building a school-house . . . The said Aldermen shall forthwith proceed to have a school-house built at the said place, and shall see that the same be kept in repair, and, when necessary, that it be rebuilt; but whenever they shall think necessary that it be rebuilt, they shall give notice as before directed, to the electors of the hundred to meet at the said school-house, on such day as they shall appoint, to determine by vote, in the manner before directed, whether it shall be rebuilt at the same, or what other place in the hundred.

At every of these schools shall be taught reading, writing, and common arithmetick, and the books which shall be used therein for instructing the children to read shall be such as will at the same time make them acquainted with Grecian, Roman, English, and American history. At these schools all the free children, male and female, resident within the respective hundred, shall be intitled to receive tuition gratis, for the term of three years, and as much longer, at their private expence, as their parents, guardians or friends, shall think proper.

Over every ten of these schools (or such other number nearest thereto, as the number of hundreds in the county will admit, without fractional divisions) an overseer shall be appointed annually by the Aldermen at their first meeting, eminent for his learning, integrity, and fidelity to the commonwealth, whose business and duty it shall be, from time to time, to appoint a teacher to each school, who shall give assurance of fidelity to the commonwealth, and to remove him as he shall see cause; to visit every school once in every half year at the least; to examine the schollars; see that any general plan of reading and instruction recommended by the visiters of William and Mary College shall be observed; and to superintend the conduct of the teacher in every thing relative to his school.

Every teacher shall receive a salary of by the year, which, with the expences of building and repairing the school-houses, shall be provided in such manner as other county expences are by law directed to be provided and shall also

have his diet, lodging, and washing found him, to be levied in like manner . . .

And in order that grammar schools may be rendered convenient to the youth in every part of the commonwealth, Be it farther enacted, that on the first Monday in November, after the first appointment of overseers for the hundred schools . . . the said overseers . . . shall meet . . . and shall fix on such place in some one of the counties in their district as shall be most proper for situating a grammar school-house, endeavouring that the situation be as central as may be to the inhabitants of the said counties, that it be furnished with good water, convenient to plentiful supplies of provision and fuel, and more than all things that it be healthy.

.   .   .   .   .

The said overseers shall forthwith proceed to have a house of brick or stone, for the said grammar school, with necessary offices, built on the said lands, which grammar school-house shall contain a room for the school, a hall to dine in, four rooms for a master and usher, and ten or twelve lodging rooms for the scholars.

To each of the said grammar schools shall be allowed out of the public treasury, the sum of pounds, out of which shall be paid by the Treasurer, on warrant from the Auditors, to the proprietors or tenants of the lands located, the value of their several interests . . . and the balance thereof shall be delivered to the said overseers to defray the expence of the said buildings.

In these grammar schools shall be taught the Latin and Greek languages, English grammar, geography, and the higher part of numerical arithmetick, to wit, vulgar and decimal fractions, and the extraction of the square and cube roots.

A visiter from each county constituting the district shall be appointed, by the overseers, for the county, in the month of October annually, either from their own body or from their county at large, which visiters or the greater part of them, meeting together at the said grammar school on the first Monday in November . . . shall have power to choose their own Rector, who shall call and preside at future meetings, to employ from time to time a master, and if necessary, an usher, for the said school, to remove them at their will, and to settle the price of tuition to be paid by the scholars. They shall also visit the school twice in every year at the least, either together or separately at their discretion, examine the scholars, and see that any general plan of instruction recommended by the visiters of William and Mary College shall be observed. The said masters and ushers, before they enter on the execution of their office, shall give assurance of fidelity to the commonwealth.

A steward shall be employed, and removed at will by the master, on such wages as the visiters shall direct; which steward shall see to the procuring provisions, fuel, servants for cooking, waiting, house cleaning, washing, mending, and gardening on the most reasonable terms; the expence of which, together with the steward's wages, shall be divided equally among all the scholars boarding either on the public or private expence. And the part of those who are on private expence, and also the price of their tuitions due to the master or usher, shall be paid quarterly by the respective scholars, their parents, or guardians, and shall be recoverable, if withheld, together with costs, on motion in any Court of Record . . . The said steward shall also, under the direction of the visiters, see that the houses be kept in repair, and necessary enclosures be made and repaired . . .

Every overseer of the hundred schools shall, in the month of September annually, after the most diligent and impartial examination and enquiry, appoint from among the boys who shall have been two years at the least at some one of the schools under his superintendance, and whose parents are too poor to give them farther education, some one of the best and most promising genius and disposition, to proceed to the grammar school of his district;

which appointment shall be made in the court-house of the county, on the court day for that month . . . in the presence of the Aldermen, or two of them at the least, assembled on the bench for that purpose, the said overseer being previously sworn by them to make such appointment, without favor or affection, according to the best of his skill and judgment, and being interrogated by the said Aldermen, either on their own motion, or on suggestions from the parents, guardians, friends, or teachers of the children, competitors for such appointment; which teachers shall attend for the information of the Aldermen. On which interrogatories the said Aldermen, if they be not satisfied with the appointment proposed, shall have right to negative it; whereupon the said visitor may proceed to make a new appointment, and the said Aldermen again to interrogate and negative, and so toties quoties until an appointment be approved.

Every boy so appointed shall be authorised to proceed to the grammar school of his district, there to be educated and boarded during such time as is hereafter limited; and his quota of the expences of the house together with a compensation to the master or usher for his tuition, at the rate of twenty dollars by the year, shall be paid by the Treasurer quarterly on warrant from the Auditors.

A visitation shall be held, for the purpose of probation, annually at the said grammar school on the last Monday in September . . . at which one third of the boys sent thither by appointment of the said overseers, and who shall have been there one year only, shall be discontinued as public foundationers, being those who, on the most diligent examination and enquiry, shall be thought to be of the least promising genius and disposition; and of those who shall have been there two years, all shall be discontinued, save one only the best in genius and disposition, who shall be at liberty to continue there four years longer on the public foundation, and shall thence forward be deemed a senior,

The visiters for the districts which, or any part of which, be southward and westward of James river . . . in every other year, to wit, at the probation meetings held in the years, distinguished in the Christian computation by odd numbers, and the visiters for all the other districts at their said meetings to be held in those years, distinguished by even numbers, after diligent examination and enquiry as before directed, shall chuse one among the said seniors, of the best learning and most hopeful genius and disposition, who shall be authorised by them to proceed to William and Mary College, there to be educated, boarded, and clothed, three years; the expence of which annually shall be paid by the Treasurer on warrant from the Auditors.

---

5. Jefferson's explanation and defense of his plan for public education, 1783

Thomas Jefferson, *Notes on Virginia* (Paris, 1783), pp. 268–275.

Another object . . . is, to diffuse knowledge more generally through the mass of the people. This bill proposes to lay off every county into small districts of five or six miles square, called hundreds, and in each of them to establish a school for teaching reading, writing, and arithmetic. The tutor to be supported by the hundred, and every person in it entitled to send their children three years gratis, and as much longer as they please, paying for it. These schools to be under a visitor, who is annually to chuse the boy, of best genius in the school, of those whose parents are too poor to give them further education, and to send him forward to one of the grammar schools, of which twenty are proposed to be erected in different parts of the country, for teaching Greek, Latin, geography, and the higher branches of numerical arithmetic. Of the boys thus sent in any

one year, trial is to be made at the grammar schools one or two years, and the best genius of the whole selected and continued six years, and the residue dismissed. By this means twenty of the best geniusses will be raked from the rubbish annually, and be instructed, at the public expence, so far as the grammar schools go. At the end of six years instruction, one half are to be discontinued (from among whom the grammar schools will probably be supplied with future masters); and the other half, who are to be chosen for the superiority of their parts and disposition, are to be sent and continued three years in the study of such sciences as they shall chuse, at William and Mary college, the plan of which is proposed to be enlarged, as will be hereafter explained, and extended to all the useful sciences. The ultimate result of the whole scheme of education would be the teaching all the children of the state reading, writing, and common arithmetic: turning out ten annually of superior genius, well taught in Greek, Latin, geography and the higher branches of arithmetic: turning out ten others annually of still superior parts, who, to those branches of learning, shall have added such of the sciences as their genius shall have led them to: the furnishing to the wealthier part of the people convenient schools, at which their children may be educated, at their own expence. The general objects of this law are to provide an education adapted to the years, to the capacity, and the condition of every one, and directed to their freedom and happiness . . . The first stage of this education being the schools of the hundreds, wherein the great mass of the people will receive their instruction, the principal foundations of future order will be laid here. Instead therefore of putting the Bible and Testament into the hands of the children, at an age when their judgments are not sufficiently matured for religious enquiries, their memories may here be stored with the most useful facts from Grecian, Roman, European and American history. The first elements of morality too may be instilled into their minds; such as, when further developed as their judgments advance in strength, may teach them how to work out their own greatest happiness, by shewing them that it does not depend on the condition of life in which chance has placed them, but is always the result of a good conscience, good health, occupation, and freedom in all just pursuits. Those whom either the wealth of their parents or the adoption of the state shall destine to higher degrees of learning, will go on to the grammar schools, which constitute the next stage, there to be instructed in the languages. The learning Greek and Latin, I am told, is going into disuse in Europe. I know not what their manners and occupations may call for: but it would be very ill-judged in us to follow their example in this instance. There is a certain period of life, say from eight to fifteen or sixteen years of age, when the mind, like the body, is not yet firm enough for laborious and close operations. If applied to such, it falls an early victim to premature exertion; exhibiting indeed at first, in these young and tender subjects, the flattering appearance of their being men while they are yet children, but ending in reducing them to be children when they should be men. The memory is then most susceptible and tenacious of impressions; and the learning of languages being chiefly a work of memory, it seems precisely fitted to the powers of this period, which is long enough too for acquiring the most useful languages antient and modern. I do not pretend that language is science. It is only an instrument for the attainment of science. But that time is not lost which is employed in providing tools for future operation: more especially as in this case the books put into the hands of the youth for this purpose may be such as will at the same time impress their minds with useful facts and good principles. If this period be suffered to pass in idleness, the mind becomes lethargic and impotent, as would the body it inhabits if unexercised during the same time. The sympathy between body and mind during their rise, progress and decline, is too strict and obvious to endanger our being misled while we reason from the one to the other. As soon as they are of sufficient age, it is supposed they will be sent on from the grammar schools to the university, which constitutes our third and last stage, there to study those sciences which may be adapted to their views. By that part of our plan which prescribes the selection of the youths of genius from among the classes of the poor, we hope to avail the state of those talents which nature has sown as liberally among the poor as the rich, but which perish without use if not sought for and cultivated. But of all the views of this law, none is more important, none more legitimate, than that of rendering the people the safe, as they are the ultimate, guardians of their own liberty. For this purpose the reading in the first stage, where *they* will receive their whole education, is proposed, as has been said, to be chiefly historical. History by apprising them of the past will enable them to judge of the future; it will avail them of the experience of other times and other nations; it will qualify them as judges of the actions and designs of men; it will enable them to know ambition under every disguise it may assume; and knowing it, to defeat its views. In every government on earth is some trace of human weakness, some germ of corruption and degeneracy, which cunning will discover, and wickedness insensibly open, cultivate, and improve. Every government degenerates when trusted to the rulers of the people alone. The people themselves therefore are its only safe depositories. And to render even them safe their minds must be improved to a certain degree. This indeed is not all that is necessary, though it be essentially necessary. An amendment of our constitution must here come in aid of the public education. The influence over government must be shared among all the people. If every individual which composes their mass participates of the ultimate authority, the government will be safe; because the corrupting the whole mass will exceed any private resources of wealth: and public ones cannot be provided but by levies on the people. In this case every man would have to pay his own price . . . It has been thought that corruption is restrained by confining the right of suffrage to a few of the wealthier people: but it would be more effectually restrained by an extension of that right to such numbers as would bid defiance to the means of corruption.

---

6. The plan of Dr. Benjamin Rush for a public system of education in Pennsylvania, 1786

Benjamin Rush, *A Plan for the Establishment of Public Schools and Diffusion of Knowledge in Pennsylvania . . .* (Philadelphia, 1786), pp. 4–10.

Rush (1745–1813), a famous physician of Philadelphia, proposed reforms in many fields of public life.

For the purpose of diffusing knowledge through every part of the state, I beg leave to propose the following simple plan.

I. Let there be one university in the state, and let this be established in the capital. Let law, physic, divinity, the law of nature and nations, economy, &c. be taught in it by public lectures in the winter season, after the manner of the European universities, and let the professors receive such salaries from the state as will enable them to deliver their lectures at a moderate price.

II. Let there be four colleges. One in Philadelphia — one at Carlisle — a third, for the benefit of our German fellow citizens, at Manheim — and a fourth, some years hence, at Pittsburgh. In these colleges, let young men be instructed in mathematics and in the higher branches of science, in the same manner that they are now taught in our American colleges. After they have taken a degree in one of these colleges, let them, if they can afford it, complete their studies by spending a season or two in attending the lectures in the university. I prefer four colleges in the state to one or two,

for there is a certain size of colleges as there is of towns and armies, that is most favourable to morals and good government. Oxford and Cambridge in England are the seats of dissipation, while the more numerous, and less crouded universities and colleges in Scotland, are remarkable for the order, diligence, and decent behaviour of their students.

III. Let there be an academy established in each county, for the purpose of instructing youth in the learnd languages, and thereby preparing them to enter college.

IV. Let there be free schools established in every township, or in districts consisting of one hundred families. In these schools, let children be taught to read and write the English and German languages, and the use of figures. Such of them as have parents that can afford to send them from home, and are disposed to extend their education, may remove their children from the free school to the county academy.

By this plan, the whole state will be tied together by one system of education. The university will in time furnish masters for the colleges, and the colleges will furnish masters for the academies and free schools, while the free Schools, in their turn, will supply the academies — the colleges, and the university, with scholars — students, and pupils. The same systems of grammar, oratory and philosophy will be taught in every part of the state, and the literary features of Pennsylvania will thus designate one great, and equally enlightned family.

A question now rises, and that is, How shall this plan be carried into execution? — I answer —

The funds of the university of Pennsylvania (if the English and other schools were separated from it) are nearly equal to the purpose of supporting able professors in all the arts and sciences that are taught in the European universities.

A small addition to the funds of Dickinson college, will enable it to exist without any further aid from government.

Twenty thousand acres of good land in the late Indian purchase, will probably afford a revenue large enough to support a college at Manheim, and another on the banks of the Ohio, in the course of twenty years.

Five thousand acres of land, appropriated to each county academy, will probably afford a revenue sufficient to support them in twenty years. In the mean while let a tax from £200 to £400 a year be laid on each county for that purpose, according to the number and wealth of its inhabitants.

Let sixty thousand acres of land be set apart, to be divided, twenty years hence, among the free schools. In the mean while let a tax from £30 to £60 a year be levied upon each district of one hundred families, for the support of the schoolmaster, and to prompt him to industry in encreasing his school, let each scholar pay him from 1/6 to 2/6 every quarter.

But, how shall we bear the expence of these literary institutions under the present weight of our taxes? — I answer — These institutions are designed to lessen our taxes. They will enlighten us in the great business of finance — they will teach us to encrease the ability of the state to support government, by encreasing the profits of agriculture, and by promoting manufactures. They will teach us all the modern improvements and advantages of inland navigation. They will defend us from hasty and expensive experiments in government, by unfolding to us the experience and folly of past ages, and thus, instead of adding to our taxes and debts, they will furnish us with the true secret of lessening and discharging both of them.

But, shall the estates of orphans, batchelors and persons who have no children be taxed to pay for the support of schools from which they can derive no benefit? I answer in the affirmative, to the first part of the objection, and I deny the truth of the latter part of it. Every member of the community is interested in the propagation of virtue and knowledge in the state. But I will go further, and add, it will be true economy in individuals to support public schools. The batchelor will in time save his tax for this purpose, by being able to sleep with fewer bolts and locks to his doors, the estates

of orphans will in time be benefited, by being protected from the ravages of unprincipled and idle boys, and the children of wealthy parents will be less tempted, by bad company, to extravagance. Fewer pillories and whipping posts, and smaller jails, with their usual expences and taxes, will be necessary when our youth are properly educated, than at present. I believe it could be proved, that the expences of confining, trying and executing criminals amount every year, in most of the counties, to more money than would be sufficient to maintain all the schools that would be necessary in each county. The confessions of these criminals generally show us, that their vices and punishments are the fatal consequences of the want of a proper education in early life.

---

7. Rush's suggestions for methods of recreation and discipline suitable for future citizens of a republic, 1790

"Thoughts upon the Amusements and Punishments which are proper for Schools. Addressed to George Clymer, Esq. by Benjamin Rush, M.D.," *The Universal Asylum and Columbian Magazine,* V (1790), 67–73.

Montesquieu informs us that the exercises of the last day of the life of Epaminondas, were the same as his amusements in his youth. Herein we have an epitome of the perfection of education. The amusements of Epaminondas were of a military nature; but as the profession of arms is the business of only a small part of mankind, and happily much less necessary in the United States than in ancient Greece, I would propose that the amusements of our youth, at school, should consist of such exercises as will be most subservient to their future employments in life. These are: 1. agriculture; 2. mechanical occupations; and 3. the business of the learned professions.

1. There is a variety in the employments of agriculture which may readily be suited to the genius, taste, and strength of young people. An experiment has been made of the efficacy of these employments, as amusements, in the Methodist College at Abington, in Maryland; and, I have been informed, with the happiest effects. A large lot is divided between the scholars, and premiums are adjudged to those of them who produce the most vegetables from their grounds, or who keep them in the best order.

2. As the employments of agriculture cannot afford amusement at all seasons of the year, or in cities, I would propose, that children should be allured to seek amusements in such of the mechanical arts as are suited to their strength and capacities. Where is the boy who does not delight in the use of a hammer — a chissel — or a saw? and who has not enjoyed a high degree of pleasure in his youth, in constructing a miniature house? How amusing are the machines which are employed in the manufactory of cloathing of all kinds! and how full of various entertainment are the mixtures which take place in the chemical arts! each of these might be contrived upon such a scale, as not only to amuse young people, but to afford a profit to their parents or masters . . .

If, in these amusements, an appeal should be made to that spirit of competition which is so common among young people, it would be the means of producing more pleasure to the children, and more profit to all who are connected with them. The wealth of those manufacturing towns in England, which employ the children of poor people, is a proof of what might be expected from connecting amusement and labour together, in all our schools. The product from the labour obtained in this way, from all the schools in the United States, would amount to a sum which would almost exceed calculation.

3. To train the youth who are intended for the learned professions, or for merchandize, to the duties of their future employments, by means of useful amusements, which are *related* to those employments, will be impracticable; but their amusements may be derived from cultivating a spot of ground; for where is the lawyer, the physician, the divine, or the merchant, who has not indulged or felt a passion, in some part of his life, for rural improvements? Indeed I conceive the seeds of knowledge in agriculture will be most productive, when they are planted in the minds of this class of scholars.

I have only to add under this head, that the common amusements of children have no connection with their future occupations. Many of them injure their clothes, some of them waste their strength, and impair their health, and all of them prove, more or less, the means of producing noise, or of exciting angry passions, both of which are calculated to beget vulgar manners . . .

Do not think me too strict if I here exclude *gunning* from among the amusements of young men. My objections to it are as follow:

1. It hardens the heart, by inflicting unnecessary pain and death upon animals.

2. It is unnecessary in civilized society, where animal food may be obtained from domestic animals, with greater facility.

3. It consumes a great deal of time, and thus creates habits of idleness.

4. It frequently leads young men into low, and bad company.

5. By imposing long abstinence from food, it leads to intemperance in eating, which naturally leads to intemperance in drinking.

6. It exposes to fevers, and accidents. The news-papers are occasionally filled with melancholy accounts of the latter, and every physician must have met with frequent and dangerous instances of the former, in the course of his practice.

I know the early use of a gun is recommended in our country, to teach our young men the use of fire-arms, and thereby to prepare them for war and battle. But why should we inspire our youth, by such exercises, with hostile ideas towards their fellow creatures? Let us rather instill into their minds sentiments of universal benevolence to men of all nations and colours. Wars originate in error and vice. Let us eradicate these, by proper modes of education, and wars will cease to be necessary in our country . . .

I have hinted at the injury which is done to the health of young people by some of their amusements; but there is a practice common in all our schools, which does more harm to their bodies than all the amusements that can be named, and that is, obliging them to sit too long in *one place,* or crowding too many of them together *in one room.* By means of the former, the growth and shape of the body have been impaired; and by means of the latter, the seeds of fevers have often been engendered in schools. In the course of my business, I have been called to many hundred children who have been seized with indispositions in school, which evidently arose from the action of morbid effluvia, produced by the confined breath and perspiration of too great a number of children in one room. To obviate these evils, children should be permitted, after they have said their lessons, to amuse themselves in the open air, in some of the useful and agreeable exercises which have been mentioned. Their minds will be strengthened, as well as their bodies relieved by them. To oblige a sprightly boy to sit *seven* hours in a day, with his little arms pinioned to his sides, and his neck unnaturally bent towards his book; and for *no crime!* — what cruelty and folly are manifested, by such an absurd mode of instructing or governing young people!

I come next to say a few words upon the subject of Punishments which are proper in schools.

In barbarous ages every thing partook of the complexion of the times. Civil, ecclesiastical, military, and domestic punishments were all of a cruel nature. With the progress of reason and christianity, punishments of all kinds have become less severe. Solitude and labour are now substituted in many countries, with success, in the room of the whipping-post and the gallows. The innocent infirmities of human nature are

no longer proscribed, and punished by the church. Discipline, consisting in the vigilance of officers, has lessened the supposed necessity of military executions; and husbands —fathers —and masters now blush at the history of the times, when wives, children, and servants, were governed only by force. But unfortunately this spirit of humanity and civilization has not reached our schools. The rod is yet the principal instrument of governing them, and a school-master remains the only despot now known in free countries. Perhaps it is because the little subjects of their arbitrary and capricious power have not been in a condition to complain. I shall endeavour therefore to plead their cause, and to prove that corporal punishments (except to children under four or five years of age) are never necessary, and always hurtful, in schools. The following arguments I hope will be sufficient to establish this proposition.

1. Children are seldom sent to school before they are capable of feeling the force of rational or moral obligation. They may therefore be deterred from committing offences, by motives less disgraceful than the fear of corporal punishments.

2. By correcting children for ignorance and negligence in school, their ideas of *improper* and *immoral* actions are confounded, and hence the moral faculty becomes weakened in after life. It would not be more cruel or absurd to inflict the punishment of the whipping-post upon a man, for not dressing fashionably or neatly, than it is to ferule a boy for blotting his copy-book, or misspelling a word.

3. If the natural affection of a parent is sometimes insufficient, to restrain the violent effects of a sudden gust of anger upon a child, how dangerous must the power of correcting children be, when lodged in the hands of a school-master, in whose anger there is no mixture of parental affection! Perhaps those parents act most wisely, who never trust themselves to inflict corporal punishments upon their children, after they are four or five years old, but endeavour to punish, and reclaim them, by con-

finement, or by abridging them of some of their usual gratifications, in dress, food or amusements.

4. Injuries are sometimes done to the bodies, and sometimes to the intellects of children, by corporal punishments. I recollect, when a boy, to have lost a school-mate, who was said to have died in consequence of a severe whipping he received in school. At that time I did not believe it possible, but from what I now know of the disproportion between the violent emotions of the mind, and the strength of the body in children, I am disposed to believe, that not only sickness, but that even *death* may be induced, by the convulsions of a youthful mind, worked up to a high sense of shame and resentment.

The effects of thumping the head, boxing the ears, and pulling the hair, in impairing the intellects, by means of injuries done to the brain, are too obvious to be mentioned.

5. Where there is *shame,* says Dr. Johnson, there may be *virtue.* But corporal punishments, inflicted at school, have a tendency to destroy the sense of shame, and thereby to destroy all moral sensibility. The boy that has been often publicly whipped at school, is under great obligations to his maker, and his parents, if he afterwards escape the whipping-post or the gallows.

6. Corporal punishments, inflicted at school, tend to beget a spirit of violence in boys toward each other, which often follows them through life; but they more certainly beget a spirit of hatred, or revenge, towards their masters, which too often becomes a ferment of the same baneful passions towards other people . . . I think I have known several instances of this vindictive, or indignant spirit, to continue towards a cruel and tyrannical school-master, in persons who were advanced in life, and who were otherwise of gentle and forgiving dispositions.

7. Corporal punishments, inflicted at schools, beget a hatred to instruction in young people. I have sometimes suspected that the devil, who knows how great an enemy knowl-

edge is to his kingdom, has had the address to make the world believe that *feruling, pulling* and *boxing ears, cudgelling, horsing,* &c. and, in boarding-schools, a *little starving,* are all absolutely necessary for the government of young people, on purpose that he might make both schools, and school-masters odious, and thereby keep our world in ignorance; for ignorance is the best means the devil ever contrived, to keep up the number of his subjects in our world.

8. Corporal punishments are not only hurtful, but altogether unnecessary, in schools. Some of the most celebrated and successful school-masters, that I have ever known, never made use of them.

9. The fear of corporal punishments, by debilitating the body, produces a corresponding debility in the mind, which contracts its capacity of acquiring knowledge. This capacity is enlarged by the tone which the mind acquires from the action of hope, love, and confidence upon it; and all these passions might easily be cherished, by a prudent and enlightened school-master.

10. As there should always be a certain ratio between the strength of a remedy, and the excitability of the body in diseases, so there should be a similar ratio between the force employed in the government of a school, and the capacities and tempers of children. A kind rebuke, like fresh air in a fainting fit, is calculated to act upon a young mind with more effect, than stimulants of the greatest power; but corporal punishments level all capacities and tempers, as quack-medicines do all constitutions and diseases. They dishonour and degrade our species; for they suppose a total absence of all moral and intellectual feeling from the mind. Have we not often seen children suddenly improve by changing their schools? The reason is obvious. The successful teacher only accomodated his manner and discipline to the capacities of his scholars.

11. I conceive corporal punishments, inflicted in an arbitrary manner, to be contrary to the spirit of liberty, and that they should not

be tolerated in a free government. Why should not children be protected from violence and injuries, as well as white and black servants? Had I influence enough in our legislature to obtain only a single law, it should be to make the punishment for striking a school-boy, the same as for assaulting and beating an adult member of society.

.   .   .   .   .

If . . . prudent . . . measures should fail of preventing offences at school, then let the following modes of punishment be adopted.

1. *Private* admonition. By this mode of rebuking, we imitate the conduct of the divine Being towards his offending creatures, for His first punishment is always inflicted privately, by means of the still voice of conscience.

2. Confinement after school-hours are ended; but with the knowledge of the parents of children.

3. Holding a small sign of disgrace, of any kind, in the middle of the floor, in the presence of a whole school.

If these punishments fail of reclaiming a bad boy, he should be dismissed from school, to prevent his corrupting his school-mates. It is the business of parents, and not of schoolmasters, to use the last means for eradicating idleness and vice from their children.

The world was created in love. It is sustained by love. Nations and families that are happy, are made so only by love. Let us extend this divine principle, to those little communities which we call schools. Children are capable of loving in a high degree. They may therefore be governed by love.

The occupation of a school-master is truly dignified. He is (next to mothers) the most important member of civil society. Why then is there so little rank connected with that occupation? Why do we treat it with so much neglect, or contempt? It is because the voice of reason, in the human heart, associates with it the idea of despotism and violence. Let schoolmasters cease to be tyrants, and they will soon enjoy the respect and rank, which are naturally connected with their profession.

We are grosly mistaken in looking up wholly to our governments, and even to ministers of the gospel, to promote public and private order in society. Mothers and school-masters plant the seeds of nearly all the good and evil which exist in our world. Its reformation must therefore be begun in nurseries and in schools. If the habits we acquire there, were to have no influence upon our future happiness, yet the influence they have upon our governments, is a sufficient reason why we ought to introduce new modes, as well as new objects of education into our country.

----

8. Noah Webster's appeal for a republican mode of education, 1790

Noah Webster, *A Collection of Essays and Fugitiv[1] Writing, on Moral, Historical, Political and Literary Subjects* (Boston, 1790), pp. 3–4, 14–19, 22–26.

Education is a subject which has been exhausted by the ablest writers, both among the ancients and moderns. I am not vain enough to suppose I can suggest any new ideas upon so trite a theme as Education in general; but perhaps the manner of conducting the youth in America may be capable of some improvement. Our constitutions of civil government are not yet firmly established; our national character is not yet formed; and it is an object of vast magnitude that systems of Education should be adopted and pursued, which may not only diffuse a knowlege of the sciences, but may implant, in the minds of the American youth, the principles of virtue and of liberty; and inspire them with just and liberal ideas of government, and with an inviolable attachment to their own

1. Among other innovations, Webster advocated spelling reform.

country. It now becomes every American to examin the modes of Education in Europe, to see how far they are applicable in this country, and whether it is not possible to make some valuable alterations, adapted to our local and political circumstances.

.   .   .   .   .

The first error that I would mention, is, a too general attention to the dead languages, with a neglect of our own . . .

The high estimation in which the learned languages have been held, has discouraged a due attention to our own. People find themselves able without much study to write and speak the English intelligibly, and thus have been led to think rules of no utility. This opinion has produced various and arbitrary practices, in the use of the language, even among men of the most information and accuracy; and this diversity has produced another opinion, both false and injurious to the language, that there are no rules or principles on which the pronunciation and construction can be settled.

This neglect is so general, that there is scarcely an institution to be found in the country, where the English tongue is taught regularly, from its elements to its true and elegant construction, in prose and verse. Perhaps in most schools, boys are taught the definition of the parts of speech, and a few hard names which they do not understand, and which the teacher seldom attempts to explain; this is called *learning grammar*. This practice of learning questions and answers without acquiring any ideas, has given rise to a common remark, *that grammar is a dry study;* and so is every other study which is prosecuted without improving the head or the heart . . . In general, when a study of any kind is tiresome to a person, it is a presumptive evidence that he does not make any proficiency in knowledge, and this is almost always the fault of the instructor.

.   .   .   .   .

Young gentlemen, designed for the mercantile line, after having learned to write and speak English correctly, might attend to French, Italian, or such other living language, as they will probably want in the course of business. These languages should be learned early in youth, while the organs are yet pliable; otherwise the pronunciation will probably be imperfect. These studies might be succeeded by some attention to chronology, and a regular application of geography, mathematics, history, the general regulations of commercial nations, principles of advance in trade, of insurance, and to the general principles of government.

It appears to me that such a course of Education, which might be completed by the age of fifteen or sixteen, would have a tendency to make better merchants than the usual practice which confines boys to Lucian, Ovid and Tully, till they are fourteen, and then turns them into a store, without an idea of their business, or one article of Education necessary for them, except perhaps a knowlege of writing and figures.

Such a system of English Education is also much preferable to a university Education, even with the usual honors; for it might be finished so early as to leave young persons time to serve a regular apprenticeship, without which no person should enter upon business. But by the time a university Education is completed, young men commonly commence *gentlemen;* their age and their pride will not suffer them to go thro the drudgery of a compting house, and they enter upon business without the requisite accomplishments. Indeed it appears to me that what is now called a *liberal Education,* disqualifies a man for business. Habits are formed in youth and by practice; and as business is, in some measure, mechanical, every person should be exercised in his employment, in an early period of life, that his habits may be formed by the time his apprenticeship expires. An Education in a university interferes with the forming of these habits; and perhaps forms opposite habits; the mind may contract a fondness for ease, for pleasure or for books, which no efforts can overcome. An academic Education, which should furnish the youth with some ideas of men and things, and leave time for an apprenticeship, before the age of twenty one years, would in my opinion, be the most eligible for young men who are designed for activ employments.

The method pursued in our colleges is better calculated to fit youth for the learned professions than for business. But perhaps the period of study, required as the condition of receiving the usual degrees, is too short. Four years, with the most assiduous application, are a short time to furnish the mind with the necessary knowlege of the languages and of the several sciences. It might perhaps have been a period sufficiently long for an infant settlement, as America was, at the time when most of our colleges were founded. But as the country becomes populous, wealthy and respectable, it may be worthy of consideration, whether the period of academic life should not be extended to six or seven years.

But the principal defect in our plan of Education in America, is, the want of good teachers in the academies and common schools. By good teachers I mean, men of unblemished reputation, and possessed of abilities, competent to their stations. That a man should be master of what he undertakes to teach, is a point that will not be disputed; and yet it is certain that abilities are often dispensed with, either thro inattention or fear of expense.

To those who employ ignorant men to instruct their children, permit me to suggest one important idea: That it is better for youth to have *no* Education, than to have a bad one; for it is more difficult to eradicate habits, than to impress new ideas. The tender shrub is easily bent to any figure; but the tree, which has acquired its full growth, resists all impressions.

Yet abilities are not the sole requisites. The instructors of youth ought, of all men, to be the most prudent, accomplished, agreeable and respectable. What avail a man's parts, if, while he is the "wisest and brightest," he is the "meanest of mankind?" The pernicious effects of bad example on the *minds* of youth will probably be acknowledged; but with a view to *improvement,* it is indispensably necessary that the

teachers should possess good breeding and agreeable manners. In order to give full effect to instructions, it is requisite that they should proceed from a man who is loved and respected. But a low bred clown, or morose tyrant, can command neither love nor respect; and that pupil who has no motive for application to books, but the fear of a rod, will not make a scholar.

The rod is often necessary in school; especially after the children have been accustomed to disobedience and a licentious behavior at home. All government originates in families, and if neglected there, it will hardly exist in society; but the want of it must be supplied by the rod in school, the penal laws of the state, and the terrors of divine wrath from the pulpit. The government both of families and schools should be absolute. There should, in families, be no appeal from one parent to another, with the prospect of pardon for offences. The one should always vindicate, at least apparently, the conduct of the other. In schools the master should be absolute in command; for it is utterly impossible for any man to support order and discipline among children, who are indulged with an appeal to their parents. A proper subordination in families would generally supersede the necessity of severity in schools; and a strict discipline in both is the best foundation of good order in political society.

If parents should say, "we cannot give the instructors of our children unlimited authority over them, for it may be abused and our children injured"; I would answer, they must not place them under the direction of any man, in whose temper, judgement and abilities, they do not repose perfect confidence. The teacher should be, if such can be found, as judicious and reasonable a man as the parent.

There can be little improvement in schools, without strict subordination; there can be no subordination, without principles of esteem and respect in the pupils; and the pupils cannot esteem and respect a man who is not in himself respectable, and who is not treated with respect by their parents. It may be laid down as an invariable maxim, that a person is not fit to superintend the Education of children, who has not the qualifications which will command the esteem and respect of his pupils. This maxim is founded on a truth which every person may have observed; that children always *love* an *amiable* man, and always *esteem* a *respectable* one. Men and women have their passions, which often rule their judgement and their conduct. They have their caprices, their interests and their prejudices, which at times incline them to treat the most meritorious characters with disrespect. But children, artless and unsuspecting, resign their hearts to any person whose manners are agreeable, and whose conduct is respectable. Whenever, therefore, pupils cease to respect their teacher, he should be instantly dismissed.

.   .   .   .   .

From a strange inversion of the order of nature, the cause of which it is not necessary to unfold, the most important business in civil society, is, in many parts of America, committed to the most worthless characters. The Education of youth, an employment of more consequence than making laws and preaching the gospel, because it lays the foundation on which both law and gospel rest for success; this Education is sunk to a level with the most menial services. In most instances we find the higher seminaries of learning intrusted to men of good characters, and possessed of the moral virtues and social affections. But many of our inferior schools, which, so far as the heart is concerned, are as important as colleges, are kept by men of no breeding, and many of them, by men infamous for the most detestable vices. Will this be denied? will it be denied, that before the war, it was a frequent practice for gentlemen to purchase convicts, who had been transported for their crimes, and employ them as private tutors in their families?

Gracious Heavens! Must the wretches, who have forfeited their lives, and been pronounced unworthy to be inhabitants of a *foreign* country, be entrusted with the Education, the morals, the character of *American* youth?

Will it be denied that many of the instructors of youth, whose examples and precepts should form their minds for good men and useful citizens, are often found to sleep away, in school, the fumes of a debauch, and to stun the ears of their pupils with frequent blasphemy? It is idle to suppress such truths; nay more, it is wicked. The practice of employing low and vicious characters to direct the studies of youth, is, in a high degree, criminal; it is destructive of the order and peace of society; it is treason against morals, and of course, against government; it ought to be arraigned before the tribunal of reason, and condemned by all intelligent beings. The practice is so exceedingly absurd, that it is surprising it could ever have prevailed among rational people. Parents wish their children to be *well bred,* yet place them under the care of *clowns.* They wish to secure their hearts from *vicious principles* and *habits,* yet commit them to the care of men of the most *profligate lives.* They wish to have their children taught *obedience* and *respect* for superiors, yet give them a master that both parents and children *despise.* A practice so glaringly absurd and irrational has no name in any language! Parents themselves will not associate with the men, whose company they *oblige* their children to keep, even in that most important period, when habits are forming for life.

.   .   .   .   .

Another defect in our schools, which, since the revolution, is become inexcusable, is the want of proper books. The collections which are now used consist of essays that respect foreign and ancient nations. The minds of youth are perpetually led to the history of Greece and Rome or to Great Britain; boys are constantly repeating the declamations of Demosthenes and Cicero, or debates upon some political question in the British Parliment. These are excellent specimens of good sense, polished stile and perfect oratory; but they are not interesting to children. They cannot be very useful, except to young gentlemen who want them as models of reasoning and eloquence, in the pulpit or at the bar.

But every child in America should be acquainted with his own country. He should read books that furnish him with ideas that will be useful to him in life and practice. As soon as he opens his lips, he should rehearse the history of his own country; he should lisp the praise of liberty, and of those illustrious heroes and statesmen, who have wrought a revolution in her favor.

.　　.　　.　　.　　.

Two regulations are essential to the continuance of republican governments: 1. Such a distribution of lands and such principles of descent and alienation, as shall give every citizen a power of acquiring what his industry merits. 2. Such a system of education as gives every citizen an opportunity of acquiring knowlege and fitting himself for places of trust. These are fundamental articles; the *sine qua non* of the existence of the American republics.

Hence the absurdity of our copying the manners and adopting the institutions of Monarchies.

In several States, we find laws passed, establishing provision for colleges and academies, where people of property may educate their sons; but no provision is made for instructing the poorer rank of people, even in reading and writing. Yet in these same States, every citizen who is worth a few shillings annually, is entitled to vote for legislators. This appears to me a most glaring solecism in government. The constitutions are *republican,* and the laws of education are *monarchical.* The *former* extend civil rights to every honest industrious man; the *latter* deprive a large proportion of the citizens of a most valuable privilege.

In our American republics, where governments is in the hands of the people, knowlege should be universally diffused by means of public schools. Of such consequence is it to society, that the people who make laws, should be well informed, that I conceive no Legislature can be justified in neglecting proper establishments for this purpose.

When I speak of a diffusion of knowlege, I do not mean merely a knowlege of spelling books, and the New Testament. An acquaintance with ethics, and with the general principles of law, commerce, money and government, is necessary for the yeomanry of a republican state. This acquaintance they might obtain by means of books calculated for schools, and read by the children, during the winter months, and by the circulation of public papers.

.　　.　　.　　.　　.

It is said, indeed by many, that our common people are already too well informed. Strange paradox! The truth is, they have too much knowlege and spirit to resign their share in government, and are not sufficiently informed to govern themselves in all cases of difficulty.

There are some acts of the American legislatures which astonish men of information; and blunders in legislation are frequently ascribed to bad intentions. But if we examin the men who compose these legislatures, we shall find that wrong measures generally proceed from ignorance either in the men themselves, or in their constituents. They often mistake their own interest, because they do not foresee the remote consequences of a measure.

It may be true that all men cannot be legislators; but the more generally knowlege is diffused among the substantial yeomanry, the more perfect will be the laws of a republican state.

Every small district should be furnished with a school, at least four months in a year; when boys are not otherwise employed. This school should be kept by the most reputable and well informed man in the district. Here children should be taught the usual branches of learning; submission to superiors and to laws; the moral or social duties; the history and transactions of their own country; the principles of liberty and government. Here the rough manners of the wilderness should be softened, and the principles of virtue and good behaviour inculcated. The *virtues* of men are of more consequences to society than their *abilities;* and for this reason, the *heart* should be cultivated with more assiduity than the *head.*

Such a general system of education is neither impracticable nor difficult; and excepting the formation of a federal government that shall be efficient and permanent, it demands the first attention of American patriots. Until such a system shall be adopted and pursued; until the Statesman and Divine shall unite their efforts in *forming* the human mind, rather than in loping its excrescences, after it has been neglected; until Legislators discover that the only way to make good citizens and subjects, is to nourish them from infancy; and until parents shall be convinced that the *worst* of men are not the proper teachers to make the *best;* mankind cannot know to what a degree of perfection society and government may be carried. America affords the fairest opportunities for making the experiment, and opens the most encouraging prospect of success.

The assembly to which I address myself, is too enlightened not to be fully sensible how much a flourishing state of the arts and sciences contributes to national prosperity and reputation. True it is, that our country, much to its honor, contains many seminaries of learning highly respectable and useful; but the funds upon which they rest are too narrow to command the ablest professors, in the different departments of liberal knowledge, for the institution contemplated, though they would be excellent auxiliaries.

Amongst the motives to such an institution, the assimilation of the principles, opinions, and manners of our countrymen, by the common education of a portion of our youth from every quarter, well deserves attention. The more homogeneous our citizens can be made in these particulars, the greater will be our prospect of permanent union; and a primary object of such a national institution should be, the education of our youth in the science of government. In a republic, what species of knowledge can be equally important, and what duty more pressing on its legislature, than to patronize a plan for communicating it to those, who are to be the future guardians of the liberties of the country?

---

9. President George Washington recommends the establishment of a national university to foster unity and train young men for public positions, 1796

Jared Sparks, ed., *The Writings of George Washington* . . . , XII (Boston, 1837), 70–71.

I have heretofore proposed to the consideration of Congress, the expediency of establishing a national university, and also a military academy. The desirableness of both these institutions has so constantly increased with every new view I have taken of the subject, that I cannot omit the opportunity of once for all recalling your attention to them.

---

10. A Massachusetts farmer, William Manning, on the kind of education needed in a free republic, 1798

William Manning, *The Key to Libberty, Shewing the Causes Why a Free Government Has Always Failed, and a Remidy Against it* (Billerica, Mass., 1922), pp. 19–21, 35–36.

Manning (1747–1814), a Jeffersonian Republican in politics, was born, worked, and died on a farm in North Billerica, Massachusetts. His thoughts on the causes of despotism and the importance of popular education in maintaining a republic give a clue to the outlook of ordinary men. The manuscript was not published until 1922.

---

1. On the Ignorance of the Many

Solomon said, Train up a Child in the way he should go, & when he is old he will not depart from it. And it is as true that if a child is trained up in the way he should not go, when he is old he will keep to it. It is the universal custom & practis of monorcal & dispotick government to train up their subjects as much in ignorance as they can in matters of government, & to teach them to reverance & worship grate men in office, & to take for truth what ever they say without examining for themselves. Consiquently when ever Revolutions are brought about & free governments established it is by the influence of a few leeding men, who after they have obtained their object (like other men) can neaver receiv compensation & honours anough from the people for their services, & the people being brought up from their uths to reverance & respect such men they go on old ways & neglect to search & see for themselves & take care of their own interists. Also being naturally very fond of being flattered, they redily hear to measures proposed by grate men who they are convinced have done them good services. This is the prinsaple ground on which the few work to Destroy a free government.

.   .   .   .   .

3. On Larning

Larning is of the gratest importance to the seport of a free government, & to prevent this the few are always crying up the advantages of costly collages, national acadimyes & grammer schooles, in ordir to make places for men to live without work, & so strengthen their party. But are always opposed to cheep schools & woman schools, the ondly or prinsaple means by which larning is spred amongue the Many.

4. On Knowledge

The gratest & best meens of obtaining the knowledge nesecary for a free man to have, is by the Liberty of the Press, or publick Newspapers. To counter act and destroy this priviledge the few spare no pains to make them as costly as posable & to contradict everything in them that favours the interests of the Many, puting Darkness for Light, & Light for Darkness, falsehood for truth, & truth for falsehood, &cc.

.   .   .   .   .

On Larning

No person who is a frind to Libberty will be against a large expence in Larning, but it aught to be promoted in the cheepest & best manner possable, which in my oppinnion would be: — For every State to maintain as many Coledges in conveniant parts thereof as would be attended upon to give the highest Degrees of Larning, & for every County to keep as many Grammer Schools or Acadimies in conveniant parts thereof as would be attended too by both sects summer & winter, & no student or scholer to pay anything for tuition, and for the County Schooles to pay a particuler attention to teaching the Inglish langueg & qualifying its scholors to teach & govern Common Schools for little children.

And for Every Town to be obliged to keep as Much as six weeks of wrighting school in the winter & twelve weeks of a woman school in the summer in every parte of the town. So that none should be thronged with two many schollers, nor none have too far to travel, & every person be obliged to send his children to school, for the publick are as much interested in the Larning of one child as an other.

If this method of Larning was established we should soone have a plenty of school masters & mistrises as cheep as we could hire other labour, & Labour & Larning would be conected together & lesen the number of those that live without work. Also we should have a plenty of men to fill the highest offices of State for less than halfe we now give. But insted of this mode of Larning the few are always striving to oblige us to maintain grait men with grate salleryes & to maintain Grammer Schools in every town to teach our Children a b c all which is ondly to give imploy to gentlemens sons & make places for men to live without worke. For their is no more need of a mans haveing a knowledge of all the languages to teach a Child to read write & cifer than their is for a farmer to have the marinors art to hold plow.

Encouragement of education in state constitutions

Nearly all state constitutions committed the state to the support of education. Most of the early education laws, however, were permissive rather than mandatory, authorizing rather than requiring local officials to maintain schools.

1. Clause on education in the North Carolina Constitution of 1776

F. N. Thorpe, ed., *The Federal and State Constitutions* . . . (Washington, 1909), V, 2794.

XLI. That a school or schools shall be established by the Legislature, for the convenient instruction of youth, with such salaries to the masters, paid by the public, as may enable them to instruct at low prices; and all useful learning shall be duly encouraged, and promoted, in one or more universities.

2. Constitution of Vermont provides for the establishment of schools, 1777

The Federal and State Constitutions, IV, 3748.

Section XL. A school or schools shall be established in each town, by the legislature, for the convenient instruction of youth, with such salaries to the masters, paid by each town; making proper use of school lands in each town, thereby to enable them to instruct youth at low prices. One grammar school in each county, and one university in this State, ought to be established by direction of the General Assembly.

3. The commitment to support education in the Massachusetts Constitution of 1780

The Federal and State Constitutions, III, 1907–1908.

CHAPTER V
Section II. — The Encouragement
of Literature, etc.

Wisdom and knowledge, as well as virtue, diffused generally among the body of the people, being necessary for the preservation of their rights and liberties; and as these depend on spreading the opportunities and advantages of education in the various parts of the country, and among the different orders of the people, it shall be the duty of legislatures and magistrates, in all future periods of this commonwealth, to cherish the interests of literature and the sciences, and all seminaries of them; especially the university at Cambridge, public schools and grammar schools in the towns; to encourage private societies and public institutions, rewards and immunities, for the promotion of agriculture, arts, sciences, commerce, trades, manufactures, and a natural history of the country; to countenance and inculcate the principles of humanity and general benevolence, public and private charity, industry and frugality, honesty and punctuality in their dealings; sincerity, good humor, and all social affections, and generous sentiments, among the people.

4. The Northwest Ordinance requires the government of the Northwest Territory to encourage education, 1787

The Federal and State Constitutions, II, 961.

Article III

Religion, morality, and knowledge being necessary to good government and the happiness of mankind, schools and the means of education shall forever be encouraged . . .

5. Education in the Indiana Constitution of 1816

The Federal and State Constitutions, II, 1068–1069.

ARTICLE IX

SECTION 1. Knowledge and learning, generally diffused through a community, being essential to the preservation of a free government, and spreading the opportunities and advantages of education through the various parts of the country being highly conducive to this end, it shall be the duty of the General Assembly to provide, by law, for the improvement of such lands as are or hereafter may be granted by the United States to this State for the use of schools, and to apply any funds which may be raised from such lands or from any other quarter to the accomplishment of the grand object for which they are or may be intended. But no lands granted for the use of schools or seminaries of learning shall be sold by authority of this State prior to the year 1820; and the moneys which may be raised out of the sale of any such lands, or otherwise obtained for the purposes aforesaid, shall be and remain a fund for the exclusive purpose of promoting the interest of literature and the sciences, and for the support of seminaries and public schools. The General Assembly shall, from time to time, pass such laws as shall be calculated to encourage intellectual, scientific and agricultural improvements, by allowing rewards and immunities for the promotion and improvement of arts, sciences, commerce, manufacture and natural history; and to countenance and encourage the principles of humanity, honesty, industry and morality.

SEC. 2. It shall be the duty of the General Assembly, as soon as circumstances will permit, to provide, by law, for a general system of education, ascending in a regular gradation from township schools to a State University, wherein tuition shall be gratis, and equally open to all.

SEC. 3. And for the promotion of such salutary end, the money which shall be paid, as an equivalent, by persons exempt from military duty, except in times of war, shall be exclusively, and in equal proportion, applied to the support of County Seminaries; also, all fines assessed for any breach of the penal laws, shall be applied to said seminaries in the County wherein they shall be assessed.

6. Education in the Alabama Constitution of 1819

The Federal and State Constitutions, I, 110–111.

EDUCATION

Schools, and the means of education, shall forever be encouraged in this State; and the general assembly shall take measures to preserve, from unnecessary waste or damage, such lands as are or hereafter may be granted by the United States for the use of schools within each township in this State, and apply the funds, which may be raised from such lands, in strict conformity to the object of such grant. The general assembly shall take like measures for the improvement of such lands as have been or may be hereafter granted by the United States to this State, for the support of a seminary of learning, and the moneys which may be raised from such lands, by rent, lease, or sale, or from any other quarter, for the purpose aforesaid, shall be and remain a fund for the exclusive support of a State university, for the promotion of the arts, literature and the sciences; and it shall be the duty of the general assembly, as early as may be, to provide effectual means for the improvement and permanent security of the funds and endowments of such institution.

State support and regulation of public education

Although most school expenses were met out of local taxes and fees, other devices were also used to obtain financial support for the schools. These included grants of public lands by the national government, lotteries, fines, and excise taxes. In addition to supplying limited amounts of funds, governments in the northern states tried, not always successfully, to set minimum standards and exercise a general supervision over local school practices.

precedent for a similar provision in the Land Ordinance of 1785.

A petition of Joshua Lamb, Joseph Ruggles, Timothy Ruggles, and Ebenezer Pierpoint, praying that this court would please to make a grant to the petitioners and their associates for a tract of land lying on Ware River for a township, upon such conditions as the court shall judge proper.

Read and in answer to this petition:

Ordered that there be and hereby is granted unto the petitioners and their associates a tract of land of the contents of six miles square for a township at the place petitioned for to be laid out in a regular form by a surveyor and chainmen under oath, a plan thereof to be presented to this court at the next session for confirmation, the said land by them to be settled on the conditions following, viz., that they within the space of five years settle and have on ye spot sixty families (the settlers are to be none but such as are natives of New England), each settler to build a good and convenient dwelling house of one story high, and eighteen feet square at the least, and clear and bring to four acres fit for improvement and three acres more well stocked with English grass, and also lay out three shares throughout the town, each share to be one sixty third part of the said town, one share for the first settled minister, one for the ministry, and the other for the school, and also build a convenient meeting house and settle a learned orthodox minister within the term aforesaid.

1. The General Court of Massachusetts grants land for the support of a school in a new town on the frontier, 1732

The Acts and Resolves, Public and Private, of the Province of Massachusetts Bay . . . , XI (Boston, 1903), 656–657.

The New England custom of granting lands for the support of town schools provided a

2. Lands set aside by the national government for the support of public schools in the Land Ordinance of 1785

John C. Fitzpatrick, ed., *Journals of the Continental Congress, 1774–1789,* XXVIII (Washington, 1933), 378.

There shall be reserved for the United States out of every township, the four lots, being numbered 8, 11, 26, 29, and out of every fractional part of a township, so many lots of the same numbers as shall be found thereon, for future sale. There shall be reserved the lot N 16, of every township, for the maintenance of public schools, within the said township; also one third part of all gold, silver, lead and copper mines, to be sold, or otherwise disposed of as Congress shall hereafter direct.

---

3. Massachusetts school law, 1789

The Laws of the Commonwealth of Massachusetts, 1780–1800 (Boston, 1801), I, 469–473.

This law codified practices which had developed over the previous century pertaining to town support of lower and grammar schools, the division of towns into school districts, instruction in morals, and certification of teachers.

Every town or district within this Commonwealth, containing *fifty* families, or householders, shall be provided with a School-Master or School-Masters, of good morals, to teach children to read and write, and to instruct them in the English language, as well as in arithmetic, orthography, and decent behaviour, for such term of time as shall be equivalent to *six months* for one school in each year. And every town or district containing *one hundred* families, or householders, shall be provided with such School-Master or School-Masters, for such term of time as shall be equivalent to *twelve* months for one school in each year. And every town or district containing *one hundred and fifty* families, or householders, shall be provided with such School-Master or School-Masters, for such term of time as shall be equivalent to *six months* in each year; and shall, in addition thereto, be provided with a School-Master or School-Masters, as above described, to instruct children in the English language, for such term of time as shall be equivalent to *twelve months* for one school in each year. And every town or district containing *two hundred* families, or householders, shall be provided with a grammar School-Master, of good morals, well instructed in the Latin, Greek and English languages; and shall, in addition thereto, be provided with a School-Master or School-Masters, as above described, to instruct children in the English language, for such term of time as shall be equivalent to *twelve months* for each of said schools in each year.

And whereas by means of the dispersed situation of the inhabitants of several towns and districts in this Commonwealth, the children and youth cannot be collected in any one place for their instruction, and it has thence become expedient that the towns and districts, in the circumstances aforesaid, should be divided into separate districts for the purpose aforesaid:

. . . the several towns and districts in this Commonwealth, be and they are hereby authorized and empowered, in town-meetings, to be called for that purpose, to determine and define the limits of school districts within their towns and districts respectively.

And to the end that grammar School-Masters may not be prevented in their endeavours to discharge their trust in the most useful manner:

. . . no youth shall be sent to such grammar schools unless they shall have learned, in some other school or in some other way, to read the English language, by spelling the same; or the Selectmen of the town where such grammar school is, shall direct the grammar School-Master to receive and instruct such youth.

. . . It shall be and it is hereby made the duty of the President, Professors and Tutors of the University at Cambridge, Preceptors and

Teachers of Academies, and all other instructors of youth, to take diligent care, and to exert their best endeavours, to impress on the minds of children and youth committed to their care and instruction, the principles of piety, justice, and a sacred regard to truth, love to their country, humanity, and universal benevolence, sobriety, industry and frugality, chastity, moderation and temperance, and those other virtues which are the ornament of human society, and the basis upon which the Republican Constitution is structured. And it shall be the duty of such instructors, to endeavour to lead those under their care (as their ages and capacities will admit) into a particular understanding of the tendency of the before mentioned virtues, to preserve and perfect a Republican Constitution, and to secure the blessings of liberty, as well as to promote their future happiness; and the tendency of the opposite vices to slavery and ruin.

And to the end that improper persons may not be employed in the important offices before mentioned:

. . . no person shall be employed as a School-Master as aforesaid, unless he shall have received an education at some College or University, and, before entering on the said business, shall produce satisfactory evidence thereof, or unless the person to be employed as aforesaid, shall produce a certificate from a learned minister, well skilled in the Greek and Latin languages, settled in the town or place where the school is proposed to be kept, or two other such ministers in the vicinity thereof, that they have reason to believe that he is well qualified to discharge the duties devolved upon such School-Master by this Act; and, in addition thereto, if for a grammar school, "that he is of competent skill in the Greek and Latin languages, for the said purpose." And the candidate of either of the description aforesaid, shall moreover produce a certificate from a settled minister of the town, district, parish or place, to which such candidate belongs, or from the Selectmen of such town or district, or committee of such parish

or place, "That to the best of his or their knowledge, he sustains a good moral character."

Provided nevertheless, This last certificate, respecting morals, shall not be deemed necessary where the candidate for such school belongs to the place where the same is proposed to be actually kept; it shall however be the duty of such Selectmen or Committee who may be authorized to hire such School-Master, specially to attend to his morals; and no settled minister shall be deemed, held, or accepted to be a School-Master, within the intent of this Act.

. . . If any town or district having the number of *fifty* families, or householders, and less than *one hundred,* shall neglect the procuring and supporting a School-Master or School-Masters, to teach the English language as aforesaid, by the space of *six* months in one year, such deficient town or district shall incur the penalty of *Ten Pounds,* and a penalty proportionable for a less time than *six* months in a year, upon conviction thereof; and, upon having the number of *one hundred* families, or householders, and upwards, shall neglect the procuring and supporting such School-Master or School-Masters, as is herein required to be kept by such town, for the space of one year, every such deficient town or district shall incur the penalty of *Twenty Pounds,* and a proportionable sum for a less time than a year, upon conviction of such neglect. And every town or district having *one hundred and fifty* families, or householders, which shall neglect the procuring and supporting such School-Masters, and for such term of time as the schools aforesaid are herein required to be kept by such town or district, in any one year, shall incur the penalty of *Thirty Pounds,* and a proportionable sum for a less time, upon conviction of such neglect. And every town or district having *two hundred* families, or householders, and upwards, that shall neglect the procuring and supporting such grammar School-Master, as aforesaid, for the space of one year, shall incur the penalty of *Thirty Pounds,* and a proportionable sum for a less time than a year, upon conviction of such neglect.

. . . It shall be the duty of the Minister or Ministers of the Gospel and the Selectmen (or such other persons as shall be specially chosen by each town or district for that purpose) of the several towns or districts, to use their influence and best endeavours, that the youth of their respective towns and districts do regularly attend the schools appointed and supported as aforesaid, for their instruction; and once in every six months at least, and as much oftener as they shall determine it necessary, to visit and inspect the several schools in their respective towns and districts, and shall inquire into the regulation and discipline thereof, and the proficiency of the scholars therein, giving reasonable notice of the time of their visitation.

. . . All plantations which shall be taxed to the support of Government, and all parishes and precincts, are hereby authorized and empowered, at their annual meeting in *March* or *April,* to vote and raise such sums of money upon the polls and rateable estates of their respective inhabitants for the support and maintenance of a School-Master to teach their children and youth to read, write and cypher, as they shall judge expedient, to be assessed by their Assessors in due proportion, and to be collected in like manner with the public taxes.

And whereas schools for the education of children in the most early stages of life, may be kept in towns, districts or plantations, which schools are not before particularly described in this Act; and that the greatest attention may be given to the early establishing just principles in the tender minds of such children, and carefully instructing them in the first principles of reading:

. . . no person shall be allowed to be a Master or Mistress of such school, or to keep the same, unless he or she shall obtain a certificate from the Selectmen of such town or district where the same may be kept, or the Committee appointed by such town, district or plantation, to visit their schools, as well as

from a learned Minister settled therein, if such there be, that he or she is a person of sober life and conversation, and well qualified to keep such school. And it shall be the duty of such Master or Mistress, carefully to instruct the children, attending his or her school, in reading (and writing, if contracted for) and to instil into their minds a sense of piety and virtue, and to teach them decent behaviour. And if any person shall presume to keep such school without a certificate as aforesaid, he or she shall forfeit and pay the sum of *Twenty Shillings,* one moiety thereof to the informer, and the other moiety to the use of the poor of the town, district or plantation where such school may be kept.

. . . No person shall be permitted to keep, within this Commonwealth, any school described in this Act, unless, in consequence of an Act of naturalization, or otherwise, he shall be a citizen of this or some other of the United States. And if any person who is not a citizen of this or some one of the United States, shall presume to keep any such school within this State for the space of one month, he shall be subjected to pay a fine of *Twenty Pounds,* and a proportionable sum for a longer or shorter time; the one half of which fine shall be to the use of the person who shall sue for the same, and the other half thereof to the use of this Commonwealth.

---

4. Financial support of schools in Connecticut, 1796

"An Act for appointing, encouraging, and supporting Schools," *Acts and Laws of the State of Connecticut in America* (Hartford, 1796), pp. 372–373.

School monies were drawn from local taxes, a fund derived from the sale of public lands, and levies upon town residents and the parents of the children who attended school.

---

5. *And for the Encouragement and Maintenance of . . . Schools and School-Masters:*

. . . the Treasurer of this State shall annually deliver the Sum of *Two Dollars* upon every *Thousand Dollars* in the Lists of the respective Towns in this State, and proportionably for lesser Sums, out of the Rate of each Town, as the same shall be brought into the public Treasury by the several Constables, in such Money, or Bills of Public Credit, as the Rate shall be paid in; out of which the same is to be taken, unto the School-Committees . . .

Provided. The said School-Committees or Select-men shall deliver their Certificates, that there hath been a School kept in each of the Towns and Societies they desire to take the Money out for, in the preceding Year, according to this Act.

6. *And whereas the several Towns and Societies in this State, which made and computed Lists of their Polls and rateable Estate . . . received by their Committees respectively, for that Purpose appointed, considerable Monies, or Bills of public Credit, raised by the Sale of certain Townships laid out in the western Lands, then so called, . . . to be let out, and the Interest thereof used for the support of the respective Schools aforesaid, for ever, and to no other Use.*[1]

And whereas certain Sums of Money have likewise been received by the several Towns and Societies in this State, by Virtue of an Act of this Court . . . directing the Treasurer to pay out of the public Treasury to the several Towns the principal Sums paid in by them as Excise Money, together with the Interest due at the Time of Payment . . . appropriating the same, solely to the Use of the respective Schools.

Be it therefore enacted, That if at any Time after the Receipt of said Monies aforesaid, or if at any Time hereafter, the said Monies, or Interest thereof, hath been or shall be, by order

of such Town or Society, or the Communities chosen by them, put to, or employed for any other Use than for the support of a School, as aforesaid, such sum of Money received as aforesaid, shall be returned into the State Treasury; and the Treasurer of this State, upon Refusal thereof, shall recover the same Sum or Sums of such Town or Society, for the Use of the State.

7. And such Town or Society that misapplies such Money, shall forever lose the Benefit thereof.

8. That where, in any Town or Society, there is not a sufficiency of Money or Interest provided, in the Manner aforesaid, or by charitable Donations, or Sequestrations, or any other Ways procured for the maintenance of a School as aforesaid, therein, and a suitable School-Master to keep the same, a sufficient Maintenance shall be made up, the one Half by the Inhabitants of such Town or Society, and the other Half thereof by the Parents or Masters of the Youth or Children that go to such School; unless any Town or Society shall agree otherwise; which they are hereby empowered to do.

9. And every such Town and Society by their Vote, shall have full Power to grant Rates for the support of such School, and choose a Collector to gather and collect such Rates. And what such Town or Society shall agree upon and enact respecting the Encouragement and Support of the School aforesaid, among themselves, shall be obligatory upon the whole Town or Society, and every Member therein.

---

5. The Delaware school fund, 1796

"An Act to create a fund sufficient to establish schools in this state," 1796–ch. 105, *Laws of the State of Delaware* (Newcastle, 1797), II, 1296–1298.

In this act the state established a fund drawn from stipulated revenues. The money

---

1. The fund from the sale of lands was established by the General Court in 1733. C. J. Hoadly, ed., *Public Records of the Colony of Connecticut,* VII (Hartford, 1873), 459.

that accumulated was to be used for starting new schools. No funds were actually paid out until 1817 when the money was spent for the education of poor children.

The money paid into the state treasury on account of marriage and tavern licences . . . between the passing of this act and the first day of January, in the year of our Lord One Thousand Eight Hundred and Six, shall be, and is hereby appropriated, as part of a fund hereafter to be applied, under the direction of the Legislature, for establishing schools in this state.

. . . The money so as aforesaid appropriated, and all other money and estate hereafter given or appropriated for the said purpose, shall be distinguished and known by the name of *The fund for establishing schools in the state of Delaware.*

. . . *The Trustee of the fund* . . . shall be and is hereby impowered, authorised and required, to take care of the said fund, to receive, apply for, and recover, by suit or action, in his name as Trustee of the said fund, any gift, donation, or bequest, which any person or persons, disposed to promote the establishment of seminaries of learning, may think proper to make; and for the application of every such gift, donation, or bequest, to the purpose of establishing schools as aforesaid, the public faith of this state is hereby most solemnly pledged . . .

Whenever the money in the treasury, arising from marriage and tavern licences, gifts, and bequests, shall amount to a sum equal to the purchase of a share in either the Bank of Delaware, the United States, of Pennsylvania, or of North America, the said Trustee shall be, and is hereby authorised, impowered, and required, to purchase, on the best terms to be procured, in the name of the Trustee of the fund for establishing schools in the state of Delaware, a share in one of the said banks, to demand and receive the dividend on every such share, as often as it becomes due, and to apply the same, with the other money in the treasury belonging to this fund, to the purchasing another share in one of the said banks, as often as the same may be adequate thereto.

.   .   .   .   .

The said fund shall be applied to the establishment of schools in the several hundreds, or districts, of the respective counties of this state, for the purpose of instructing the children of the inhabitants thereof in the English language, arithmetic, and such other branches of knowledge as are most useful and necessary, in completing a good English education; and that the same shall not be applied to the erecting or supporting any academy, college, or university in this state.

---

6. Rhode Island legislature grants the right to conduct a lottery for support of an academy, 1801

"Lottery granted to James Helme," *Acts and Resolves of Rhode Island, 1800–1801* (n.p., n.d.), p. 10.

Upon the petition of James Helme and others, praying leave to raise the sum of two thousand five hundred dollars, by lottery, for the purpose of building an academy in the town of South-Kingstown, *It is Voted and Resolved,* That the prayer of said petition be granted, and that Messrs. Elisha R. Potter, James Helme and Samuel E. Gardnier, be appointed managers of said lottery, they giving bonds to the General-Treasurer in the sum of ten thousand dollars for the faithful execution of said trust; and that the said managers have power to raise said sum in one or more classes, and by such scheme or schemes as they may think proper, and that no expense of said lottery be charged to this State.

7. Hiring a schoolmaster in a country district

Caleb Bingham, *The Columbian Orator* . . . (Hartford, 1807), pp. 158–165.

This satire exposed some of the evils of excessive local authority in school matters.

Dialogue Between a School-Master, and School-Committee.

(N.B. *The Author is happy in believing, that the following Dialogue is applicable to but few towns and few teachers in this country; but, so long as there are any remaining to whom it may apply, he thinks a sufficient apology exists for its publication.*)

SCENE, *a Public House in the Town of* ———.

Enter School-Master, *with a pack on his back.*

Schoolmaster. How fare you, landlord? what have you got that's good to drink?

Landlord. I have gin, West-India, genuine New-England, whiskey, and cider brandy.

Schoolm. Make us a stiff mug of sling. Put in a gill and a half of your New-England; and sweeten it well with lasses.

Land. It shall be done, sir, to your liking.

Schoolm. Do you know of any vacancy in a school in your part of the country, landlord?

Land. There is a vacancy in our district; and I expect the parson, with our three school-committee men will be at my house directly, to consult upon matters relative to the school.

Schoolm. Well, here's the lad that will serve them as *cheap* as any man in America; and I believe I may venture to say as *well* too; for I profess no small share of skill in that business. I have kept school eleven winters, and have often had matter of fifty scholars at a time. I have teach'd a child its letters in a day, and to read in the Psalter in a fortnight: and I always feel very much ashamed, if I use more than one quire of paper in larnin a boy to write as

well as his master. As for government, I'll turn my back to no man. I never flog my scholars; for that monstrous doctrine of whippin children, which has been so long preached and practiced by our rigid and superstitious fore-fathers, I have long since exploded. I have a rare knack of *flattering* them into their duty. And this according to a celebrated Doctor at Philadelphia,[1] whose works I have heard of, though I never read them, is the grand criterion of school government. It is landlord, it is the very philosopher's stone. I am told, likewise, that this same great Doctor does not believe that Solomon and others really meant *licken,* in the proper sense of the word, when they talked so much about using the rod, &c. He supposes that they meant confining them in dungeons; starving them for three or four days at a time; and then giving them a portion of tatromattucks, and such kinds of mild punishment. And, zounds, landlord, I believe he's above half right.

Land. (Giving the cup to the master.) Master ——— What may I call your name, Sir, if I may be so bold?

Schoolm. Ignoramus, at your service, Sir.

Land. Master Ignoramus, I am glad to see you. You are the very man we wish for. Our committee won't hesitate a moment to employ you, when they become acquainted with your talents. Your sentiments on government I know will suit our people to a nicety. Our last master was a tyrant of a fellow, and very extravagant in his price. He grew so important, the latter part of his time, that he had the frontery to demand *ten dollars* a month and his board. And he might truly be said to rule with a rod of iron; for he kept an *ironwood* cudgel in his school, four feet long; and it was enough to chill one's blood to hear the shrieks of the little innocents, which were caused by his barbarity. I have heard my wife say, that Sue Gossip told her, that she has seen the marks of

1. A reference to Dr. Benjamin Rush whose ideas on discipline the schoolmaster has appropriated and distorted. See above, The impact of independence, doc. 7.

his lashes on the back of her neighbour Rymple's son Darling, for twelve hours after the drubbing. At least, the boy told her with his own mouth, that they *might* be seen, if they would only take the trouble to strip his shirt off. And, besides, Master Ignoramus, he was the most niggardly of all the human race. I don't suppose that my bar-room was one dollar the richer for him, in the course of the whole time which he tarried with us. While the young people of the town were recreating themselves, and taking a social glass, of an evening, at my house, the stupid blockhead was eternally in his chamber, poring over his musty books. But finally he did the job for himself, and I am rejoiced. The wretch had the dacity to box little Sammy Puney's ears at such an intolerable rate, that his parents fear the poor child will be an idiot all the days of his life. And all this, for nothing more, than partly by design, and partly through mere accident, he happened to spit in his master's face. The child being nephew to the 'squire, you may well suppose, that the whole neighbourhood was soon in an uproar. The indignation of the mother, father, aunts, uncles, cousins, and indeed the whole circle of acquaintance, was roused; and the poor fellow was hooted out of town in less than twenty-four hours.

Schoolm. (*Drinking off his liquor.*) This is a rare dose. Believe me, landlord, I have not tasted a drop before, since six o'clock this morning. (*Enter Parson and Committee Men.*) Your humble sarvant, gentlemen. I understand you are in want of a school-master.

Parson. Yes Sir; that is the occasion of our present meeting. We have been so unfortunate as to lose one good man; and we should be very glad to find another.

1st Committee Man. Pray don't say *unfortunate,* Parson. I think we may consider ourselves as very *fortunate,* in having rid the town of an extravagant coxcomb, who was draining us of all the money we could earn, to fill his purse, and rig himself out with fine clothes.

2d Com. Ten dollars a month, and board,

for a man whose task is so easy, is no small sum.

3d Com. I am bold to affirm, that we can procure a better man for half the money.

Schoolm. That I believe, friend; for, though I esteem myself as good as the best; that is to say, in the common way; yet I never ax'd but five dollars a month in all my life.

Par. *For* my own part, whatever these gentlemen's opinion may be, I must tell you, that I am much less concerned about the wages we are to give, than I am about the character and abilities of the man with whom we intrust the education of our children. I had much rather you had said you had received forty dollars a month, than five.

1st. Com. Dear Sir, you are beside yourself. You will encourage the man to *rise* in his price; whereas I was in hopes he would have *fallen,* at least one dollar.

Par. Before we talk any further about the price, it is necessary that we examine the gentleman according to law, in order to satisfy ourselves of his capability to serve us. Friend, will you be so obliging as to inform us where you received your education, and what your pretensions are, with respect to your profession?

Schoolm. Law, Sir! I never went to college in my life.

Par. I did not ask you whether you had been to college or not. We wish to know what education you have had; and whether your abilities are such, as that you can do yourself honor in taking the charge of a common English school.

Schoolm. Gentlemen, I will give you a short history of my life. From seven, to fifteen years of age, I went to school perhaps as much as one year. In which time, I went through Dilworth's Spelling-Book, the Psalter, the New-Testament: and could read the newspaper without spelling more than half the words. By this time, feeling a little above the common level, I enlisted a soldier in the army, where I continued six years; and made such proficiency in the military art, that I was frequently talked of for a corporal. I had likewise learn'd to write considerably, and to cypher as fur as Division. The multiplication table I had at my tongue's end, and have not forgot it to this day. At length, receiving a severe flogging for nothing at all, I am not ashamed to own that I deserted, and went into one of the back settlements, and offered myself as a teacher. I was immediately employed in that service; and, though I am obliged to say it myself, I do assure you I soon became very famous. Since that time, which is eleven years, I have followed the business constantly; at least, every winter; for in the summer, it is not customary in the towns in general, to continue a man's school. One thing I would not forget to mention; and that is, I have travelled about the country so much, and been in the army so long (which is allowed to be the best school in the world) that I consider myself as being thoroughly acquainted with mankind. You will not be insensible, gentlemen, of what great importance this last acquisition is, to one who has the care of youth.

3d Com. I admire his conversation. I imagine, by this time, you have cyphered *clear through;* have you not, Sir?

Schoolm. Why, as to that, I have gone so fur that I thought I could *see through*. I can tell how many minutes old my great grandfather was when his first son was born; how many barley corns it would take to measure round the world; and how old the world will be at the end of six thousand years from the creation.

1st Com. It is very strange! You must have studied hard, to learn all these things, and that without a master too.

Schoolm. Indeed I have, Sir; and if I had time, I could tell you things stranger still.

Par. Can you tell in what part of the world you were born; whether in the torrid, frigid, or temperate zone?

Schoolm. I was not born in the *zoon,* Sir, nor in any other of the West-India Islands; but I was born in New-England, in the state of New-Jersey, and Commonwealth of the United States of America.

Par. Do you know how many parts of speech there are in the English language?

Schoolm. How many speeches! Why as many as there are "stars in the sky, leaves on the trees, or sands on the sea shore."

1st Com. Please to let me ask him a question, Parson, How many commandaments are there?

Schoolm. Ten, Sir; and I knew them all before I went into the army.

2d Com. Can you tell when the moon changes, by the almanac?

Schoolm. No! but I'll warrant you, I could soon tell by cyphering.

3d Com. How many varses are there in the 119th Psalm?

Schoolm. Ah! excuse me there, if you please, Sir; I never meddle with psalmody, or metaphysics.

Par. Will you tell me, my friend, what is the difference between the circumference and the diameter of the globe?

Schoolm. There you are to hard for me again. I never larn'd the rule of circumstance nor geometry. I'll tell you what, gentlemen, I make no pretensions to minister larnin, lawyer larnin, or doctor larnin; but put me upon your clear schoolmaster larnin, and there I am even with you.

1st Com. I am satisfied with the gentleman. He has missed but one question, and that was such a metatisical one, that it would have puzzled a Jesuit himself to have answered it. Gentlemen, shall the master withdraw a few minutes, for our further consultation?

(*Exit Master.*)

2d Com. I am much pleased with the stranger. He appears to be a man of wonderful parts; and I shall cheerfully agree to employ him.

3d Com. For my part, I don't think we shall find a *cheaper* master; and I move for engaging him at once.

Par. Gentlemen, how long will you be blind to your own interest? I can say with you, that I am perfectly satisfied — that the man is, in his profession, emphatically what he calls himself by name, an *ignoramus;* and totally incapable of instructing our children. You know not who he is, or what he is; whether he be a thief, a liar, or a drunkard. The very terms, on which he offers himself, ought to operate as a sufficient objection against him. I am sensible that my vote will now be of no avail, since you are all agreed. I have been for years striving to procure a man of abilities and morals, suitable for the employment; and such a one I had obtained; but, alas! we were unworthy of him. We aspersed his character; invented a multitude of falsehoods; magnified every trifling error in his conduct; and even converted his virtues into vices. We refused to give him that pecuniary reward which his services demanded; and he knowing his own worth, and our unworthiness, has left us forever.

1st Com. Come, come, Parson, it is easy for salary men to talk of *liberality,* and to vote away money which they never earned; but it won't do. The new master I dare engage, will do as well or better than the old one. Landlord, call him in for his answer.

Par. I protest against your proceedings, and withdraw myself forever from the committee. But I must tell you, your children will reap the bitter consequences of such injudicious measures. It has always been surprising to me, that people in general are more willing to pay their money for any thing else, than for "the one thing needful," that is, for the education of their children. Their tailor must be a workman, their carpenter, a workman, their hairdresser, a workman, their hostler, a workman; but the instructor of their children must — work *cheap!*

(*Exit Parson.*)

Re-enter School-Master.

1st Com. We have agreed to employ you, Sir; and have only to recommend to you, not to follow the steps of your predecessor. This is an "age of reason"; and we do not imagine our children so stupid, as to need the rod to quicken their ideas, or so vicious, as to require a moral lesson from the ferule. Be gentle and accommodating, and you have nothing to fear.

Land. I'll answer for him. He's as generous and merry a lad as I've had in my house this many a day.

---

8. State supervision and support of schools in New York, 1812

"An Act for the Establishment of Common Schools," 1812 — ch. 242, *Laws of the State of New York . . . 1812* (Albany, 1812), pp. 600–606.

This law established the office of superintendent of common schools and provided for the distribution of the school fund among the schools of towns and districts. The school fund monies were to be used to pay the wages of teachers, and the expense of constructing and maintaining school buildings was to be met from local taxes. To qualify for state funds, a district had to guarantee that school was kept during at least three months of the year.

. . . There shall be constituted an officer within this state, known and distinguished as the superintendent of common schools, which superintendent shall be appointed by the council of appointment, and shall keep his office at the seat of government, and shall be allowed an annual salary of three hundred dollars, but not to be under pay until he shall give notice of the first distribution of the school money . . .

It shall be the duty of the superintendent . . . to digest and prepare plans for the improvement and management of the common school fund, and for the better organization of common schools; to prepare and report estimates and expenditures of the school monies, to superintend the collection thereof, to execute such services relative to the sale of the lands, which now are or hereafter may be appropriated, as a permanent fund for the support of common schools, as may be by law required of him; to give information to the legislature respecting all matters referred to him by either branch thereof, or which shall appertain to his office; and generally to perform all such services relative to the welfare of schools, as he shall be directed to perform . . .

No distribution of the interest of the school funds shall take place amongst the common schools in this state, until it shall arise to fifty thousand dollars a year, and it shall not be lawful for the superintendent . . . to distribute any more than fifty thousand dollars a year until he shall find he will be able to distribute sixty thousand, and the sum of sixty thousand until the interest shall arise to seventy thousand, and so on as often as the interest shall increase ten thousand dollars, it shall be lawful for the superintendent to add to the sum last distributed ten thousand dollars more.

.   .   .   .   .

The superintendent of common schools shall, in the month of January . . . send a notice in writing to each of the county clerks in this state, informing them that there will be a distribution of the interest of the school fund in the month of February . . . stating the amount that will be assigned to each county. And it shall be the duty of the said county clerks, to send a like notice to the clerk of the board of supervisors, and to each town clerk in his county, stating the amount of money to be distributed, and the time when, which notice the town clerk shall read at the opening of the next town meeting, to the intent that the town meeting may direct by their vote the supervisor, to levy on said town, at the next meeting of the board aforesaid, the sum for the support of common schools, required by this act to entitle said town to its proportion of the interest of said fund to be distributed . . .

The inhabitants living within the limits of the several towns within this state, and within the cities of Hudson and Schenectady, who by law have, or may have, a right to vote in town meetings, shall on the days of their annual town meetings, choose, by ballot, three of the inhabitants of their respective towns, commissioners, to superintend and manage the concerns of the schools within said towns respectively, and to perform all such services relative to schools as they shall be directed to perform . . .

And the inhabitants of said towns respectively shall choose, a suitable number of persons within their respective towns, not exceeding six, who, together with the commissioners aforesaid, shall be inspectors of the schools of said towns respectively; which inspectors shall examine the teachers, and approve or disapprove of the same, and also shall visit the several schools within their respective towns, quarterly, or oftener, if they deem it necessary; three or more of the said inspectors shall be competent both to examine the teachers, and the respective schools, and no person shall be employed as a teacher in any of the schools, in any of the districts of this state, who shall not have been previously examined by the inspectors aforesaid, and have received a certificate, signed by at least two of said inspectors, importing that he is duly qualified to teach a common school, and is of good moral character . . .

The commissioners . . . are hereby authorized and empowered to divide their respective towns into a suitable and convenient number of districts, for keeping their schools, and to alter and regulate the same from time to time, as there may be occasion . . .

.   .   .   .   .

Freeholders and inhabitants, or a majority of them . . . are hereby authorised and empowered to appoint a moderator for the time being, to designate a site for their school house, to vote a tax on the resident inhabitants of such district as a majority present shall deem sufficient to purchase a suitable site for their school house, and build, keep in repair, and furnish it with necessary fuel and appendages; also to choose three trustees to manage the concerns of such district, whose duty it shall be to build and keep in repair the school house, and from time to time, as occasion may require, to agree with and employ instructors, and to pay them . . . and it shall be the further duty of the trustees of each district as soon as may be after the district meeting have voted a tax, to make a rate bill or tax list, which shall raise the sum voted, with five cents on a dollar for collector's fees, on all the taxable inhabitants of said district, agreeable to the levy on which the town tax was levied the preceding year, and annex to said tax list or rate bill a warrant . . .

.   .   .   .   .

The several towns in this state which shall conform to the provisions of this act, shall be entitled to such monies, to be distributed to them severally, according to the number of inhabitants in each town, to be ascertained by the respective census under the constitution of the United States, subject nevertheless to a distribution thereof, by said town, to the several school districts therein . . .

The several school districts within the several towns in this state which shall conform to the provisions of this act, shall be entitled to the monies deposited with the commissioners as aforesaid, to be distributed to said districts severally, according to the number of children within each district, between the ages of five and fifteen inclusive . . . Monies shall be applied and expended by said trustees in paying the wages of the teachers to be employed, and for no other purpose . . . After the first year, no order shall be accepted, nor shall the commissioners aforesaid deliver the monies, directed to be delivered as aforesaid, until two of the trustees of such district shall have certified in writing . . . that the school in said district hath been kept for three months at least, during the year ending on the first day of May last, by an instructor duly appointed and approved in all respects, according to law, and that all monies by us drawn from the commissioners for said year, appropriated for

schools, have been faithfully applied and expended in paying the wages of said instructor.

_____

9. Clarification of the boundary between public and private education by Chief Justice John Marshall in the Dartmouth College Case, 1819

The Trustees of Dartmouth College v. Woodward, 17 U.S.518 (1819).

This famous case originated with the attempted revocation of the 1769 charter of Dartmouth College by the New Hampshire legislature in 1816. The Supreme Court, holding that the charter was a contract within the meaning of the federal Constitution and therefore irrevocable, gave private schools and colleges a secure legal position. The decision signaled a turn toward strict separation between private and public institutions.

_____

This is an action of trover, brought by the Trustees of Dartmouth College against William H. Woodward, in the state court of New Hampshire, for the book of records, corporate seal, and other corporate property, to which the plaintiffs allege themselves to be entitled . . . The superior court of judicature of New Hampshire rendered a judgment upon this verdict for the defendant, which judgment has been brought before this court by writ of error. The single question now to be considered is, do the acts to which the verdict refers violate the constitution of the United States?

This court can be insensible neither to the magnitude nor delicacy of this question. The validity of a legislative act is to be examined; and the opinion of the highest law tribunal of a state is to be revised — an opinion which carries with it intrinsic evidence of the diligence, of the ability, and the integrity, with which it was formed.

.   .   .   .   .

It can require no argument to prove, that the circumstances of this case constitute a contract. An application is made to the crown for a charter to incorporate a religious and literary institution. In the application, it is stated, that large contributions have been made for the object, which will be conferred on the corporation, as soon as it shall be created. The charter is granted, and on its faith the property is conveyed. Surely, in this transaction every ingredient of a complete and legitimate contract is to be found. The points for consideration are, 1. Is this contract protected by the constitution of the United States? 2. Is it impaired by the acts under which the defendant holds?

1. On the first point, it has been argued, that the word "contract," in its broadest sense, would comprehend the political relations between the government and its citizens, would extend to offices held within a state, for state purposes, and to many of those laws concerning civil institutions, which must change with circumstances, and be modified by ordinary legislation; which deeply concern the public, and which, to preserve good government, the public judgment must control. That even marriage is a contract, and its obligations are affected by the laws respecting divorces. That the clause in the constitution, if construed in its greatest latitude, would prohibit these laws. Taken in its broad, unlimited sense, the clause would be an unprofitable and vexatious interference with the internal concerns of a state, would unnecessarily and unwisely embarrass its legislation, and render immutable those civil institutions, which are established for purposes of internal government, and which, to subserve those purposes, ought to vary with varying circumstances. That as the framers of the constitution could never have intended to insert in that instrument, a provision so unnecessary, so mischievous, and so repugnant to its general spirit, the term "contract" must be understood in a more limited sense. That it must be understood as intended to guard against a power, of at least doubtful utility, the abuse of which had been extensively felt; and to restrain the legislature in future from violating the right to property. That, anterior to the formation of the constitution, a course of legislation had prevailed in many, if not in all, of the states, which weakened the confidence of man in man, and embarrassed all transactions between individuals, by dispensing with a faithful performance of engagements. To correct this mischief, by restraining the power which produced it, the state legislatures were forbidden "to pass any law impairing the obligation of contracts," that is, of contracts respecting property, under which some individuals could claim a right to something beneficial to himself; and that, since the clause in the constitution must in construction receive some limitation, it may be confined, and ought to be confined, to cases of this description; to cases within the mischief it was intended to remedy.

The general correctness of these observations cannot be controverted. That the framers of the constitution did not intend to restrain the states in the regulation of their civil institutions, adopted for internal government, and that the instrument they have given us, is not to be so construed, may be admitted. The provision of the constitution never has been understood to embrace other contracts, than those which respect property, or some object of value, and confer rights which may be asserted in a court of justice. It never has been understood to restrict the general right of the legislature to legislate on the subject of divorces . . .

The parties in this case differ less on general principles, less on the true construction of the constitution in the abstract, than on the application of those principles to this case, and on the true construction of the charter of 1769. This is the point on which the cause essentially depends. If the act of incorporation be a grant of political power, if it create a civil institution, to be employed in the administration of the government, or if the funds of the college be public property, or if the State of New Hampshire, as a government, be alone interested in its transactions, the subject is one in which the legislature of the state may act according to its own judgment, unrestrained by any limitation of its power imposed by the constitution of the United States.

But if this be a private eleemosynary institution, endowed with a capacity to take property, for objects unconnected with government, whose funds are bestowed by individuals, on the faith of the charter; if the donors have stipulated for the future disposition and management of those funds, in the manner prescribed by themselves; there may be more difficulty in the case, although neither the persons who have made these stipulations, nor those for whose benefit they were made, should be parties to the cause. Those who are no longer interested in the property, may yet retain such an interest in the preservation of their own arrangements, as to have a right to insist, that those arrangements shall be held sacred. Or, if they have themselves disappeared, it becomes a subject of serious and anxious inquiry, whether those whom they have legally empowered to represent them for ever, may not assert all the rights which they possessed, while in being; whether, if they be without personal representatives, who may feel injured by a violation of the compact, the trustees be not so completely their representatives, in the eye of the law, as to stand in their place, not only as respects the government of the college, but also as respects the maintenance of the college charter. It becomes then the duty of the court, most seriously to examine this charter, and to ascertain its true character.

.   .   .   .   .

Are the trustees and professors public officers, invested with any portion of political power, partaking in any degree in the administration of civil government, and performing duties which flow from the sovereign authority? That education is an object of national con-

cern, and a proper subject of legislation, all admit. That there may be an institution, founded by government, and placed entirely under its immediate control, the officers of which would be public officers, amenable exclusively to government, none will deny. But is Dartmouth College such an institution? Is education altogether in the hands of government? Does every teacher of youth become a public officer, and do donations for the purpose of education necessarily become public property, so far that the will of the legislature, not the will of the donor, becomes the law of the donation? These questions are of serious moment to society, and deserve to be well considered.

.   .   .   .   .

Whence, then, can be derived the idea, that Dartmouth College has become a public institution, and its trustees public officers, exercising powers conferred by the public for public objects? Not from the source whence its funds were drawn; for its foundation is purely private and eleemosynary — not from the application of those funds; for money may be given for education, and the persons receiving it do not, by being employed in the education of youth, become members of the civil government. Is it from the act of incorporation? Let this subject be considered.

A corporation is an artificial being, invisible, intangible, and existing only in contemplation of law. Being the mere creature of law, it possesses only those properties which the charter of its creation confers upon it, either expressly, or as incidental to its very existence. These are such as are supposed best calculated to effect the object for which it was created. Among the most important are immortality, and, if the expression may be allowed, individuality; properties, by which a perpetual succession of many persons are considered as the same, and may act as a single individual. They enable a corporation to manage its own affairs, and to hold property, without the perplexing intricacies, the hazardous and endless necessity, of perpetual conveyances for the purpose of transmitting it from hand to hand. It is chiefly for the purpose of clothing bodies of men, in succession, with these qualities and capacities, that corporations were invented, and are in use. By these means, a perpetual succession of individuals are capable of acting for the promotion of the particular object, like one immortal being.

.   .   .   .   .   .

From this review of the charter, it appears, that Dartmouth College is an eleemosynary institution, incorporated for the purpose of perpetuating the application of the bounty of the donors, to the specified objects of that bounty; that its trustees or governors were originally named by the founder, and invested with the power of perpetuating themselves; that they are not public officers, nor is it a civil institution, participating in the administration of government; but a charity school, or a seminary of education, incorporated for the preservation of its property, and the perpetual application of that property to the objects of its creation.

.   .   .   .   .   .

This is plainly a contract to which the donors, the trustees and the crown (to whose rights and obligations New Hampshire succeeds) were the original parties. It is a contract made on a valuable consideration. It is a contract for the security and disposition of property. It is a contract, on the faith of which, real and personal estate has been conveyed to the corporation. It is, then, a contract within the letter of the constitution, and within its spirit also, unless the fact, that the property is invested by the donors in trustees, for the promotion of religion and education, for the benefit of persons who are perpetually changing, though the objects remain the same, shall create a particular exception, taking this case out of the prohibition contained in the constitution.

It is more than possible, that the preservation of rights of this description was not particularly in the view of the framers of the constitution, when the clause under consideration was introduced into that instrument. It is probable, that interferences of more frequent occurrence, to which the temptation was stronger, and of which the mischief was more extensive, constituted the great motive for imposing this restriction on the state legislatures. But although a particular and a rare case may not, in itself, be of sufficient magnitude to induce a rule, yet it must be governed by the rule, when established, unless some plain and strong reason for excluding it can be given. It is not enough to say, that this particular case was not in the mind of the convention, when the article was framed, nor of the American people, when it was adopted. It is necessary to go further, and to say that, had this particular case been suggested, the language would have been so varied, as to exclude it, or it would have been made a special exception. The case being within the words of the rule, must be within its operation likewise, unless there be something in the literal construction, so obviously absurd or mischievous, or repugnant to the general spirit of the instrument, as to justify those who expound the constitution in making it an exception.

On what safe and intelligible ground, can this exception stand? There is no expression in the constitution, no sentiment delivered by its contemporaneous expounders, which would justify us in making it . . .

Almost all eleemosynary corporations, those which are created for the promotion of religion, or charity or of education, are of the same character. The law of this case is the law of all. In every literary or charitable institution, unless the objects of the bounty be themselves incorporated, the whole legal interest is in trustees, and can be asserted only by them. The donors, or claimants of the bounty, if they can appear in court at all, can appear only to complain of the trustees. In all other situations, they are identified with, and personated by, the trustees; and their rights are to be defended and maintained by them. Religion, charity and education are, in the law of England, legatees or donees, capable of receiving bequests or donations in this form. They appear in court, and claim or defend by the corporation. Are they of so little estimation in the United States, that contracts for their benefit must be excluded from the protection of words, which in their natural import include them? Or do such contracts so necessarily require new modelling by the authority of the legislature, that the ordinary rules of construction must be disregarded, in order to leave them exposed to legislative alteration?

.   .   .   .   .

If the insignificance of the object does not require that we should exclude contracts respecting it from the protection of the constitution; neither, as we conceive, is the policy of leaving them subject to legislative alteration so apparent, as to require a forced construction of that instrument, in order to effect it. These eleemosynary institutions do not fill the place, which would otherwise be occupied by government, but that which would otherwise remain vacant. They are complete acquisitions to literature. They are donations to education; donations, which any government must be disposed rather to encourage than to discountenance. It requires no very critical examination of the human mind, to enable us to determine, that one great inducement to these gifts is the conviction felt by the giver, that the disposition he makes of them is immutable. It is probable, that no man ever was, and that no man ever will be, the founder of a college, believing at the time, that an act of incorporation constitutes no security for the institution; believing, that it is immediately to be deemed a public institution, whose funds are to be governed and applied, not by the will of the donor, but by the will of the legislature. All such gifts are made in the pleasing, perhaps, delusive hope, that the charity will flow for ever in the channel which the givers have marked out for it. If every man finds in his own bosom strong evidence of the universality of this sentiment, there can be but little reason to imagine, that

the framers of our constitution were strangers to it, and that, feeling the necessity and policy of giving permanence and security to contracts, of withdrawing them from the influence of legislative bodies, whose fluctuating policy, and repeated interferences, produced the most perplexing and injurious embarrassments, they still deemed it necessary to leave these contracts subject to those interferences.

.   .   .   .   .

The opinion of the court, after mature deliberation, is, that this is a contract, the obligation of which cannot be impaired, without violating the constitution of the United States. This opinion appears to us to be equally supported by reason, and by the former decisions of this court.

2. We next proceed to the inquiry, whether its obligation has been impaired by those acts of the legislature of New Hampshire, to which the special verdict refers?

From the review of this charter, which has been taken, it appears that the whole power of governing the college, of appointing and removing tutors, of fixing their salaries, of directing the course of study to be pursued by the students, and of filling up vacancies created in their own body, was vested in the trustees. On the part of the crown, it was expressly stipulated, that this corporation, thus constituted, should continue for ever; and that the number of trustees should for ever consist of twelve, and no more. By this contract, the crown was bound, and could have made no violent alteration in its essential terms, without impairing its obligation.

By the revolution, the duties, as well as the powers, of government devolved on the people of New Hampshire. It is admitted, that among the latter was comprehended the transcendent power of parliament, as well as that of the executive department. It is too clear, to require the support of argument, that all contracts and rights respecting property, remained unchanged by the revolution. The obligations, then, which were created by the charter to Dartmouth

College, were the same in the new, that they had been in the old government. The power of the government was also the same. A repeal of this charter, at any time prior to the adoption of the present constitution of the United States, would have been an extraordinary and unprecedented act of power, but one which could have been contested only by the restrictions upon the legislature, to be found in the constitution of the state. But the constitution of the United States has imposed this additional limitation, that the legislature of a state shall pass no act "impairing the obligation of contracts."

It has been already stated, that the act "to amend the charter, and enlarge and improve the corporation of Dartmouth College," increases the number of trustees to twenty-one, gives the appointment of the additional members to the executive of the state, and creates a board of overseers, to consist of twenty-five persons, of whom twenty-one are also appointed by the executive of New Hampshire, who have power to inspect and control the most important acts of the trustees.

On the effect of this law, two opinions cannot be entertained. Between acting directly, and acting through the agency of trustees and overseers, no essential difference is perceived. The whole power of governing the college is transferred from trustees, appointed according to the will of the founder, expressed in the charter, to the executive of New Hampshire. The management and application of the funds of this eleemosynary institution, which are placed by the donors in the hands of trustees named in the charter, and empowered to perpetuate themselves, are placed by this act under the control of the government of the state. The will of the state is substituted for the will of the donors, in every essential operation of the college. This is not an immaterial change . . . This system is totally changed. The charter of 1769 exists no longer. It is re-organized; and re-organized in such a manner, as to convert a literary institution, moulded according to the will of its founders, and placed under the control of

private literary men, into a machine entirely subservient to the will of government. This may be for the advantage of this college in particular, and may be for the advantage of literature in general; but it is not according to the will of the donors, and is subversive of that contract, on the faith of which their property was given.

.   .   .   .   .

It results from this opinion, that the acts of the legislature of New Hampshire, which are stated in the special verdict found in this cause, are repugnant to the constitution of the United States; and that the judgment on this special verdict ought to have been for the plaintiffs. The judgment of the state court must, therefore, be reversed.

---

10. Rhode Island grants the proceeds from lotteries for the support of public schools, 1828

"An Act to Establish Public Schools,"
*Acts and Resolves of Rhode Island
1827–1828* (Providence, 1828), pp. 9–10.

Be it enacted . . . That from and after the passing of this act, all money that shall be paid into the General Treasury, by managers of lotteries or their agents, also all money that shall be paid into said Treasury by auctioneers, for duties accruing to the State, shall be set apart and paid over to the several towns in this State in manner hereinafter mentioned, in proportion to their respective population under the age of sixteen years, as exhibited in the census provided by law to be taken from time to time, under the authority of the United States; always adopting for said ratio the census next preceding the time of paying out each annual appropriation of said money as herein provided, to be by said towns appropriated to and for the exclusive purpose of keeping public schools, and paying the expenses thereof; the sum, however, hereby appropriated, to be paid over in any one year, not to exceed ten thousand dollars.

Public support for schools for poor children

Although few Americans were ready to support free schools for all children out of taxation, the education of poor children had a special appeal. Government had long been held to a general responsibility for the education of children otherwise unprovided for. A fear of social chaos unless the virtues of order and discipline were inculcated in the disparate American population moved philanthropists to contribute their own funds for poor children's education and to seek government support for the cause.

1. The plan of Benjamin Rush for free schools for the poor children of Philadelphia, 1787

A letter "To the Citizens of Philadelphia, and of the District of Southwark and the Northern Liberties," in *The Independent Gazetteer,* March 28, 1787, in Lyman H. Butterfield, ed., *Letters of Benjamin Rush* (Princeton, 1951), I, 412–415.

Rush, conceding that his projected state system of public education was premature, believed that Philadelphia and its environs could sustain schools for poor children out of taxation.

The blessings of knowledge can be extended to the poor and laboring part of the community only by the means of FREE SCHOOLS.

The remote and unconnected state of the settlements in the new counties will forbid the establishment of those schools for some years to come by a general law; but there is nothing to prevent this being set on foot immediately in the city of Philadelphia and in the old and thick-settled counties of the state.

To a people enlightened in the principles of liberty and Christianity, arguments, it is to be hoped, will be unnecessary to persuade them to adopt these necessary and useful institutions. The children of poor people form a great proportion of all communities. Their ignorance and vices when neglected are not confined to themselves; they associate with and contaminate the children of persons in the higher ranks of society. Thus they assist after they arrive at manhood in choosing the rulers who govern the whole community. They give a complexion to the morals and manners of the people. In short, where the common people are ignorant and vicious, a nation, and above all a republican nation, can never be long free and happy. It becomes us, therefore, as we love our offspring and value the freedom and prosperity of our country, immediately to provide for the education of the poor children who are so numerous in the thick-settled parts of the state.

The following plan for beginning this important business in the capital of the state is submitted to the consideration of the citizens of Philadelphia and of the districts of Southwark and the Northern Liberties.

FIRST, Let an application be made to the legislature for a law to assess 100*l.* upon all estates in the city and liberties of Philadelphia, to be appropriated for the maintenance of schoolmasters, for the rent of schoolhouses, and other expenses connected with this undertaking. This mode of establishing free schools has many advantages over that of trusting them to the precarious support of charitable contributions. In Scotland and New-England the free schools are maintained by *law;* hence education and knowledge are universal in those countries. In England the free schools are supported chiefly by charity sermons; hence education and knowledge are so partially diffused through that country, and hence too the origin of the numerous executions and inventions to punish and extirpate criminals of which we daily read such melancholy accounts in the English newspapers. Charitable contributions fall unequally upon the different members of society — a tax will be more equally borne and will be so light as scarcely to be felt by anybody. The price of a bottle of wine or of a single fashionable feather will pay the tax of an ordinary freeholder for a whole year to those schools. Besides, there will be real economy in the payment of this tax; by sowing the seeds of good morals in the schools and inspiring the youth with habits of industry, the number of the poor and of course the sum of the tax paid for their maintenance will be diminished. By lessening the quantity of vice, we shall moreover lessen the expenses of jails and of the usual forms of law which conduct people to them. Above all, we shall render an acceptable service to the Divine Being in taking care of that part of our fellow creatures who appear to be the more immediate objects of his compassion and benevolence.

SECONDLY, Let the children who are sent to those schools be taught to read and write the English and (when required by their parents) the German language. Let the girls be instructed in needlework, knitting, and spinning, as well as in the branches of literature that have been mentioned. Above all, let both sexes be carefully instructed in the principles and obligations of the Christian religion. This is the most essential part of education — this will make them dutiful children, teachable scholars, and, afterwards, good apprentices, good husbands, good wives, honest mechanics, industrious farmers, peaceable sailors, and, in everything that relates to this country, good citizens. To effect this important purpose it will be necessary,

THIRDLY, That the children of parents of the same religious denominations should be educated together in order that they may be instructed with the more ease in the principles and forms of their respective churches. By these means the schools will come more immediately under the inspection of the ministers of the city, and thereby religion and learning be more intimately connected.

After the experience we have had of the advantages derived by the Friends from connecting their schools and their church together in forming the morals of their youth, nothing further need be added in favor of this part of the plan.

FOURTHLY, Let the money to be raised for the support of the schools be lodged in the hands of the city treasurer, to be appropriated in the following manner: Let a certain number of persons of each religious society be appointed trustees of the free schools of their respective churches, and let a draft signed by the president of a quorum of these trustees be a voucher to the treasurer to issue three or four pounds a year for every scholar who is educated by them. As soon as the number of scholars belonging to any religious society exceeds fifteen, let 30l. a year be allowed to them for the rent of the school room and for paper, ink, pens, books, and firewood, and 60l. a year when the number of scholars becomes so great as to require two schoolrooms. If any religious society should decline accepting of the bounty of the city, from having provided for the education of their poor by private contribution, let their proportion of it be thrown into the poor tax of the city if it should not be required for the poor children of the less wealthy societies. And,

LASTLY, Let the accounts and expenditures of the schools be open at all times to inspectors, to be appointed by the law, and published every year.

Citizens of Philadelphia, awaken at last to check the vice which taints the atmosphere of our city. The profane and indecent language which assaults our ears in every street can only be restrained by extending education to the children of poor people. The present is an era of public spirit — the Dispensary and the Humane Society will be lasting monuments of the humanity of the *present* citizens of Philadelphia. But let not the health and lives of the poor exhaust the whole stock of our benevolence. Their morals are of more consequence to society than their health or lives; and their minds must exist forever. "Blessed is he that considereth the poor, the Lord will deliver him in time of trouble. The Lord will preserve him, and keep him alive upon the earth — he will not deliver him into the will of his enemies."

---

2. The Pennsylvania legislature authorizes the overseers of the poor to provide for the education of poor children at public expense, 1802

"An Act to provide for the education of poor children gratis," 1802 — ch. 2247, *Pa. Statutes at Large from 1802 to 1805,* XVII (1915), 81–82.

The Pennsylvania Constitution of 1790, which Benjamin Rush helped to secure, authorized the legislature to provide for the establishment of free schools for the poor. No law was passed, however, until 1802.

. . . From and after the passing of this act, the guardians and overseers of the poor of the city of Philadelphia, the district of Southwark and township of the Northern Liberties, and every township and borough within this commonwealth, shall ascertain the names of all those children whose parents or guardians they shall judge to be unable to give them necessary education, and shall give notice in writing to such parents or guardians, that provision is made by law for the education of their children or the children under their care, and that they have a full and free right to subscribe, at the usual rates, and send them to any school in their neighborhood, giving notice thereof, as

soon as may be, to the guardians or overseers, of the term for which they have subscribed, the number of scholars, and the rate of tuition; and in those townships where there are no guardians or overseers of the poor, the supervisors of the highways shall perform the duties herein required to be done by the guardians or overseers of the poor.

. . . Every guardian, overseer of the poor, or supervisor of the highway, as the case may be, in any township or place where any such child or children shall be sent to school as aforesaid, shall enter in a book, the name or names, age and length of time such child or children shall have been so sent to school, together with the amount of schooling, school books and stationery, and shall levy and collect, in the same way and manner, and under the same regulations as poor taxes or road taxes are levied and collected, a sufficient sum of money from their respective townships, boroughs, wards, or districts, to discharge such expenses, together with the sum of five per centum for their trouble.

---

3. Schools for the poor children of Washington, D.C., 1804

"An act to establish and endow a permanent institution for the education of youth in the city of Washington," in U.S. Department of Education, *Special Report of the Commissioner of Education on the Condition and Improvement of Public Schools in the District of Columbia . . . 1870* (Washington, 1871), pp. 50–51.

Thomas Jefferson was chosen first president of the school board established in the act.

Impressed with the inseparable connection between the education of youth and the prevalence of pure morals, with the duties of all communities to place within the reach of the poor as well as the rich the inestimable blessing of knowledge, and with the high necessity of establishing at the seat of general government proper seminaries of learning, the city council of Washington do pass the following act:

. . . The superintendence of public schools within the city of Washington shall be placed under the direction of a board of thirteen trustees; whereof seven shall be annually chosen by the joint ballots of the council from among the residents of the city; and six shall be annually chosen by individuals contributing to the promotion of schools hereinafter provided . . . They shall have power to pass all necessary bylaws not inconsistent with this act; to receive donations, and to vest and apply the funds placed under their care in such manner as they may see fit. They shall make an adequate provision, and pay at such rates as they deem reasonable and proper for the education of children residing in the city, whose parents or guardians are unable to defray the expenses of their education; they shall keep a journal of their proceedings, and shall on the second Monday in June, in each year, make a full report of them to the councils, excepting the names of those children who shall receive education without any charge being made therefor.

And be it enacted . . . That so much of the net proceeds of taxes laid, or to be laid on slaves, on dogs, on licenses for carriages and hacks, for ordinaries and taverns, for retailing of wines and spirituous liquors, for billiard tables, for theatrical and other public amusements, for hawkers and pedlars, be appropriated as the trustees may decide to be necessary for the education of the poor of the city . . . *Provided,* That if the said net proceeds exceed annually the sum of $1,500, the surplus shall be retained by the treasurer of the city, subject to the disposition of the council.

---

4. Public funds for poor children's education in Virginia, 1810–1811

"An Act to appropriate certain Escheats, Penalties, Confiscations and Forfeitures to the Encouragement of Learning," 1810 — ch. 14, *Acts Passed at a General Assembly of the Commonwealth of Virginia* (Richmond, 1810), p. 15. "An Act to Provide for the Education of the Poor," 1811 — ch. 8, *Acts . . . of Virginia* (1811), pp. 8–10.

In 1810 the legislature of Virginia established a literary fund with stipulated sources of revenue and in 1811 it directed that the proceeds of the fund should be used to support schools for the poor.

All escheats, confiscations, fines, penalties and forfeitures, and all rights in personal property accruing to the commonwealth, as derelict, and having no rightful proprietor, be, and the same are hereby appropriated to the encouragement of learning; and . . . the auditor of public accounts be, and he is hereby required to open an account to be designated The Literary Fund. To which he shall carry every payment hereafter made into the treasury on account of any escheat or confiscation, which has happened or may happen, or any fine, penalty or forfeiture which has been or may be imposed, or which may accrue: *Provided always,* That this act shall not apply to militia fines.

.   .   .   .   .

The fund aforesaid shall be divided and appropriated as to the next legislature shall seem best adapted to the promotion of literature: *Provided always,* That the aforesaid fund shall be appropriated to the sole benefit of a school or schools, to be kept in each and every county within this commonwealth, subject to such orders and regulations as the general assembly shall hereafter direct.

.   .   .   .   .

[The Act of 1811] All sums of money which have accrued, or may hereafter accrue to the literary fund . . . are hereby vested in the following persons, to wit: The governor, lieutenant governor, treasurer, attorney general and president of the court of appeals of this commonwealth for the time being, and they and their successors are hereby constituted a body politic and corporate under the denomination of the president and directors of the literary fund . . .

In further aid of the said fund, the said president and directors are hereby empowered to raise annually for a term of years not exceeding seven, by lottery, any sum not exceeding thirty thousand dollars . . . It shall be lawful for the said president and directors to conduct all the operations of such lottery in person or by commissioners or agents by them appointed for that purpose, or, if it be deemed more advisable, to contract for the drawing of the said lottery, with any undertaker or undertakers for such share of the profit thereof as to them may appear reasonable, reserving to the fund which it is designed to aid, or not, at their discretion, a greater or less interest in such lottery.

.   .   .   .   .

As soon as a sufficient fund shall be provided for the purpose, it shall be the duty of the directors thereof to provide a school or schools for the education of the poor in each and every county of the commonwealth.

5. College training for one orphan boy annually in South Carolina, 1811

D. J. McCord, ed., *So. Car. Statutes at Large*, VII (1840), 132–133.

Whereas, from the number of orphan children from every part of this State, educated and supported by the munificence of the citizens of Charleston, in the Orphan House of that city, an ample opportunity is offered of making a judicious selection of talents and genius; in order, therefore, to further the patriotic and liberal views of the patrons of that institution,

. . . from and immediately after the passing of this Act, the commissioners of the Orphan House in the city of Charleston shall be, and they are hereby, authorized and empowered to select, annually, one youth from the number educated and maintained on the bounty of that institution, for the purpose of completing his education at the South Carolina College, graduate and receive the degrees conferred at the said College.

. . . The Trustees, the President and Professors, shall be, and they are hereby, directed to receive and cause to be educated and allowed to graduate at the South Carolina College, the boys to be selected as aforesaid; subject, nevertheless, to all the rules, orders and regulations of the said South Carolina College.

. . . All expense incident to the education and maintenance of the said boys so to be selected (clothing excepted) shall be defrayed from the amount annually appropriated by the Legislature to the South Carolina College.

. . . As the youths so chosen shall graduate, or in case of the death, expulsion or removal of them, or any of them, the commissioners aforesaid are hereby authorized and impowered to fill up any vacancy occasioned thereby.

. . . The sum of one hundred and forty dollars be, and is hereby, annually appropriated for the cloathing of each of the said boys while they remain at the said College; *Provided nevertheless,* that they shall not continue beyond the term usually allowed to candidates for the first degree.

6. Appropriations from the Delaware school fund for the education of poor children, 1817

"An Act appropriating part of the school fund for the education of poor children," 1817 — ch. 146, *Laws of the State of Delaware Passed at a Session of the General Assembly* (Dover, 1818), pp. 251–255.

The trustee of the fund for establishing schools . . . is hereby required . . . to place in the hands of each of the county treasurers of the several counties within this State, in four equal quarter yearly payments, the sum of one thousand dollars, from any money in his hands, belonging to the fund for establishing schools, not otherwise appropriated . . .

The county treasurers of the respective counties aforesaid, are authorised and required to pay, to the order or orders of the trustees herein before appointed, or a majority of them, in their several hundreds respectively, any moneys which may come into their hands in pursuance of this act . . .

. . . . . .

The trustees, herein appointed, to superintend the education of the poor children of their several hundreds respectively, are authorised and required, to draw for, and receive, the several sums, allotted to their hundreds respectively, and the same, or any part thereof that may be found necessary, or as fast as the same may be required, to expend, in the payment of such school masters, or teachers of reading, writing and arithmetic, as may, by the trustees aforesaid, or a majority of them, within their several hundreds respectively, be intrusted with the tuition and education of poor children: *Provided however,* that nothing, herein contained, shall be deemed or taken, to authorise any of the trustees, herein appointed, to expend any of the money, by this act, made subject to their order, except only for the benefit of instructing, in reading, writing and arithmetic, such children as may be obviously unable to receive the rudiments of an English education from any private or other source, except as is herein before provided.

. . . The trustees hereby appointed, in the several counties, and in their respective hundreds, keep a regular and distinct account, of all moneys by them received and expended, under and by virtue of this act, as well in relation to the manner of its expenditure, the names, ages, condition, and progress in learning made by the child or children, for whose benefit the same has been expended; as to the number, character and situation of the different schools and school houses, in their respective neighbourhoods, also the exact number, name and ages of all the poor white children within their respective hundreds, and their opinions as to the amount of money required to pay for their tuition, together with such other particulars as they may deem necessary, to enable the general assembly, at their next session, to determine the competency, of the nett proceeds of the fund for establishing schools, to defray the expense, which might be incurred by the tuition of all the poor children within the state . . .

The Public School Society of New York City

This society was founded to provide schools for those poor children of the city who did not attend the charity schools maintained by religious denominations. Backed by a group of prominent and wealthy residents, the Society secured funds from government and contributions from individuals.

---

1. A petition to the New York legislature for a charter for the Public School Society of New York City, 1805

William O. Bourne, *History of the Public School Society of New York* (New York, 1870), pp. 3–4.

Your memorialists have viewed with painful anxiety the multiplied evils which have accrued, and are daily accruing, to this city, from the neglected education of the children of the poor. They allude more particularly to that description of children who do not belong to, or are not provided for, by any religious society; and who, therefore, do not partake of the advantages arising from the different Charity Schools established by the various religious societies in this city. The condition of this class is deplorable indeed; reared up by parents who, from a variety of concurring circumstances are become either indifferent to the best interests of their offspring, or, through intemperate lives, are rendered unable to defray the expense of their instruction, these miserable and almost friendless objects are ushered upon the stage of life, inheriting those vices which idleness and the bad example of their parents naturally produce. The consequences of this neglect of education are ignorance and vice, and all those manifold evils resulting from every species of immorality, by which public hospitals and almshouses are filled with objects of disease and poverty, and society burthened with taxes for their support. In addition to these melancholy facts, it is to be feared that the laboring class in the community is becoming less industrious, less moral, and less careful to lay up the fruit of their earnings. What can this alarming declension have arisen from, but the existence of an error which has ever been found to produce a similar effect — a want of a *virtuous education,* especially at that early period of life when the impressions that are made generally stamp the future character?

The rich having ample means of educating their offspring, it must be apparent that the laboring poor — a class of citizens so evidently useful — have a superior claim to public support.

The enlightened and excellent Government under which we live is favorable to the general diffusion of knowledge; but the blessings of such a Government can be expected to be enjoyed no longer than while its citizens continue *virtuous,* and while the majority of the people, through the advantage of a proper early education, possess sufficient knowledge to enable them to understand and pursue their best interests . . .

Trusting that the necessity of providing suitable means for the prevention of the evils they have enumerated will be apparent to your honorable Body, your memorialists respectfuly request the patronage and assistance of the Legislature in establishing a free school, or schools, in this city, for the benevolent purpose of affording education to those unfortunate children who have no other mode of obtaining it.

The personal attention to be bestowed on these children for the improvement of their morals, and to assist their parents in procuring situations for them, where industry will be inculcated and good habits formed, as well as to give them the learning requisite for the proper discharge of the duties of life, it is confidently hoped will produce the most beneficial and lasting effects.

The more effectually to accomplish so desirable an object, your memorialists have agreed to form an association under the name of "The Society for Establishing a Free School in the City of New York." They therefore respectfully solicit the Legislature to sanction their undertaking by an Act of Incorporation, and to grant them such pecuniary aid or endowment as, in your wisdom, may be deemed proper for the promotion of the benevolent object of your memorialists.

---

2. The act incorporating the Public School Society, April 9, 1805

"An Act to incorporate the society instituted in the city of New York, for the establishment of a free school for the education of poor children . . . ," 1805 — ch. 108, *Laws of the State of New York . . . 28 Sess.* (1805), pp. 515–522.

Whereas De Witt Clinton and others, have associated themselves for the laudable purpose of establishing a free school in the city of New York, for the education of the children of persons in indigent circumstances . . . *And whereas* the said persons have presented a petition to the legislature, setting forth the benefits which would result to society from the education of such children, by implanting in their minds the principles of religion and morality, and by assisting their parents in providing suitable situations for them, where habits of industry and virtue may be acquired, and that it would enable them more effectually to accomplish the benevolent objects of their institution, if their association were incorporated: Therefore,

Be it enacted [that] . . . all such . . . persons as now are and shall hereafter become members of the said society, shall be and are hereby ordained, constituted and declared to be a body corporate and politic, in fact and in name . . . and they . . . shall be forever hereafter capable in law to purchase, take, receive, hold and enjoy any estate real or personal whatsoever, of whatever nature or quality soever, to the use of them and their successors: *Provided always,* That the yearly income of the real and personal estate and hereditaments held by the said corporation, doth not nor shall at any time exceed the sum of ten thousand dollars . . .

There shall be forever hereafter thirteen trustees of the said corporation, who shall conduct and manage all the affairs of the said corporation, and . . . the said trustees shall be members of the said corporation, and actually residing in the city of New York; and the first trustees of the said corporation shall be De Witt Clinton, Samuel Osgood, Brockholst Livingston, John Murray, junior, Samuel Miller, Joseph Constant, Thomas Eddy, Thomas Pearsall, Thomas Franklin, Matthew Clarkson, Leonard Bleecker, Samuel Russell and William Edgar, who shall hold their offices until the first day of May next; and the trustees . . . for the time being, shall have power to establish two or more free schools in the city of New-York.

.   .   .   .   .   .

The mayor, recorder, aldermen and assistants of the city of New York, shall and may be, *ex officio,* members of the said corporation, and . . . any person who shall subscribe and contribute to the benefit of the said society the sum of eight dollars, shall, by virtue of such contribution, be a member of the said corporation . . .

---

3. Address of De Witt Clinton, first president of the Public School Society, 1805

Bourne, *The Public School Society of New York,* pp. 6–8.

Clinton issued this appeal for support to the people of New York, providing further explanation of the Society's purpose.

While the various religious and benevolent societies in this city, with a spirit of charity and zeal which the precepts and example of the Divine Author of our religion could alone inspire, amply provide for the education of such poor children as belong to their respective associations, there still remains a large number living in total neglect of religious and moral instruction, and unacquainted with the common rudiments of learning, essentially requisite for the due management of the ordinary business of life. This neglect may be imputed either to the extreme indigence of the parents of such children, their intemperance and vice; or to a blind indifference to the best interests of their offspring. The consequences must be obvious to the most careless observer. Children thus brought up in ignorance, and amidst the contagion of bad example, are in imminent danger of ruin; and too many of them, it is to be feared, instead of being useful members of the community, will become the burden and pests of society. Early instruction and fixed habits of industry, decency, and order, are the surest safeguards of virtuous conduct; and when parents are either unable or unwilling to bestow the necessary attention on the education of their children, it becomes the duty of the public, and of individuals, who have the power, to assist them in the discharge of this important obligation. It is in vain that laws are made for the punishment of crimes, or that good men attempt to stem the torrent of irreligion and vice, if the evil is not checked at its source; and the means of prevention, by the salutary discipline of early education, seasonably applied. It is certainly in the power of the opulent and charitable, by a timely and judicious interposition of their influence and aid, if not wholly to prevent, at least to diminish, the pernicious effects resulting from the neglected education of the children of the poor.

.   .   .   .   .

The particular plan of the school, and the rules for its discipline and management, will be made known previous to its commencement. Care will be exercised in the selection of teachers, and, besides the elements of learning usually taught in schools, strict attention will be bestowed on the morals of the children, and all suitable means be used to counteract the disadvantages resulting from the situation of their parents. It is proposed, also, to establish, on the first day of the week, a school, called a Sunday School, more particularly for such children as, from peculiar circumstances, are unable to attend on the other days of the week. In this, as in the Common School, it will be a primary object, without observing the peculiar forms of any religious Society, to inculcate the sublime truths of religion and morality contained in the Holy Scriptures.

This Society . . . interferes with no existing institution, since children already provided with the means of education, or attached to any other Society, will not come under its care. Humble gleaners in the wide field of benevolence, the members of this Association seek such objects only as are left by those who have gone before, or are fellow-laborers with them in the great work of charity. They, therefore,

look with confidence for the encouragement and support of the affluent and charitable of every denomination of Christians; and when they consider that in no community is to be found a greater spirit of liberal and active benevolence than among the citizens of New York, they feel assured that adequate means for the prosecution of their plan will be easily obtained.

---

4. The Lancastrian system of instruction in the schools of the Public School Society, 1809

Address of DeWitt Clinton to benefactors and friends of the Society, in William Campbell, *DeWitt Clinton* (New York, 1849), pp. 317–319.

This method, propagated by Joseph Lancaster (1778–1838), an English author and teacher, made use of the more advanced pupils under the supervision of a teacher to instruct the beginners. Its chief recommendation was its cheapness.

It comprehends reading, writing, arithmetic, and the knowledge of the Holy Scriptures. It arrives at its object with the least possible trouble and at the least possible expense. Its distinguishing characters are economy, facility, and expedition, and its peculiar improvements are cheapness, activity, order, and emulation . . . Reading in all its processes, from the alphabet upwards, is taught at the same time with writing, commencing with sand, proceeding to the slate, and from thence to the copybook . . . Solitary study does not exist in the establishment. The children are taught in companies. Constant habits of attention and vigilance are formed, and an ardent spirit of emulation kept continually alive. Instruction is performed through the instrumentality of the scholars. The school is divided into classes of ten, and a chief, denominated a Monitor, is appointed over each class, who exercises a didactic and supervisional authority. The discipline of the school is enforced by shame, rather than by the infliction of pain. The punishments are varied with circumstances; and a judicious distribution of rewards, calculated to engage the infant mind in the discharge of its duty, forms the keystone which binds together the whole edifice.

. . . . .

When I perceive that many boys in our school have been taught to read and write in two months, who did not before know the Alphabet, and that even one has accomplished it in three weeks — when I view all the bearings and tendencies of this system — when I contemplate the habits of order which it forms, the spirit of emulation which it excites — the rapid improvement which it produces — the purity of morals which it inculcates — when I behold the extraordinary union of celerity in instruction, and economy of expense — and when I perceive one great assembly of a thousand children, under the eye of a single teacher, marching with unexampled rapidity, and with perfect discipline, to the goal of knowledge, I confess that I recognize in Lancaster, the benefactor of the human race.

5. The Public School Society requires children at its schools to attend worship, 1819

From the ninth annual report of the Society, in Bourne, *The Public School Society of New York,* p. 638.

In furtherance of the . . . object, the children have been required to assemble at their respective schools on the morning of every Sabbath, and proceed, under the care of a monitor, to such place of public worship as was designated by their parents or guardians.

This requisition has been regularly attended to by many, but the want of suitable clothing has prevented others from complying with it. In cases where an attendance at school previous to going to church is particularly inconvenient, liberty has been given for the children to attend public worship in company with their parents or guardians.

6. The Public School Society's attitude toward the parents of poor children, 1819

An Address to the Parents and Guardians of the Children Belonging to the Schools under the care of the New-York Free-School Society, by the Trustees of the Institution (New York, 1819), pp. 4–8.

This Institution holds out much encouragement, and you are bound by every moral obligation, to avail yourselves of the advantages which your children may derive from a steady attendance at school, where they may acquire, not only school learning to qualify them for business, but be improved in their morals, and manners.

Many of you have not been favoured with the privileges your children now enjoy, that of a gratuitous education. Every parent who is solicitous for the welfare of his offspring, but whose circumstances may be such, as not to be able to pay the expense, is invited to come forward, and place them where they may be instructed in literature, in the paths of virtue, and in the road to happiness.

The Trustees may venture to say, that this Institution may be productive of great good to you, and to your children, especially, if on your part there is a disposition to promote it. We wish your children may be furnished with a good education, and early acquire good habits. As they grow in years, they should be impressed with the importance of INDUSTRY, and FRUGALITY; these are virtues necessary to form useful characters.

You know that many evils grow out of *Idleness,* and many more out of the improper use of *Spirituous Liquors;* that they are ruinous and destructive to morals, and debase the human character below the lowest of all created beings: we therefore, earnestly desire, you may be watchful, and careful in this respect, otherwise in vain may we labour to promote the welfare of your children.

In domestic life, there are many virtues which are requisite, in order to promote the comfort, and welfare of families. TEMPERANCE and ECONOMY, are indispensable, but without CLEANLINESS, your enjoyments as well as your reputation, will be impaired; it is promotive of HEALTH, and ought not to be neglected. Parents can perhaps scarcely give a greater proof of their care for their children, than by keeping them *clean,* and *decent,* especially when they are sent to school, where it is expected they will appear with their hands, faces, and heads perfectly clean, and their clothing clean and in good order: the appearance of children exhibits to every observing mind, the character of the mother.

Among other moral, and religious duties, that of a due observance of the First Day of the week, commonly called SUNDAY, we consider of importance to yourselves, and to your children. PUBLIC WORSHIP, is a duty we owe to our CREATOR, it is of universal obligation; and you ought to be good examples therein, encouraging your families to the due observance thereof, and believing, as we do, that the establishment of what is called SUNDAY SCHOOLS, has been a blessing to many, and may prove so to many more, we are desirous you may unite in the support of a plan, so well calculated to promote the religious duties of that day, which ought to be appropriated to public worship, retirement, and other duties connected with the improvement of the mind.

Seeing, next to your own souls, your children, and those placed under your care, are, or ought to be, the immediate objects of your constant attention, and diligent concern, you ought to omit no opportunity to instruct them early in the principles of the *Christian Religion,* in order to bring them in their youth to a sense of the unspeakable love, and infinite wisdom and power of their *Almighty Creator.*

---

7. Religious exercises in the schools of the Public School Society, 1830

From a teacher's "Manual" prepared for use in the primary grades and published by the trustees of the Society, in Bourne, *The Public School Society of New York,* pp. 643–644.

Although the Society was nondenominational, it included religious instruction and exercises of a Protestant character in its course of study. This caused Catholic parents to refuse to allow their children to attend the Society's schools.

Teacher. My dear children, the intention of this school is to teach you to be good and useful in this world, that you may be happy in the world to come. What is the intention of this school?

T. We therefore first teach you to "remember your Creator in the days of your youth." What do we first teach you?

T. It is our duty to teach you this, because we find it written in the Holy Bible. Why is it our duty to teach you this?

T. The Holy Bible directs us to "train you up in the way you should go." What good book directs us to train you up in the way you should go?

T. Therefore, my children, you must obey your parents.

Scholar. I must obey my parents.

T. You must obey your teachers.

S. I must obey my teachers.

T. You must never tell a lie.

S. I must never tell a lie.

T. You must never steal the smallest thing.

S. I must never steal the smallest thing.

T. You must never swear.

S. I must never swear.

T. God will not hold him guiltless that taketh His name in vain.

S. God will not hold him guiltless that taketh His name in vain.

T. God always sees you. (*Slowly, and in a soft tone.*)

S. God always sees me.

T. God hears all you say.

S. God hears all I say.

T. God knows all you do.

S. God knows all I do.

T. You should fear to offend Him, for He is most holy.

S. I should fear to offend Him, for He is most holy.

T. You should depart from evil, and learn to do well.

S. I should depart from evil, and learn to do well.

T. May all you, dear children, learn, while attending this school, to be good and useful in this world.

S. May we all, while attending this school, learn to be good and useful in this world.

T. And, with God's blessing, may you be happy in the world to come.

S. And, with God's blessing, may we be happy in the world to come.

---

8. Compulsory attendance of poor children in New York City schools, 1832

Twenty-Seventh Annual Report of the Trustees of the Public School Society of New York (New York, 1832), pp. 14–16.

Alarmed by the amount of truancy, the Public School Society asked for authority to compel children's attendance regardless of the wishes of parents.

Truantship in [Boston] is deemed a criminal offence in children, and those who cannot be reclaimed, are taken from their parents by the Police, and placed in an Institution called the "School of Reformation," corresponding in many respects with our House of Refuge — from which they are bound out by the competent authority, without again returning to their parents. As a necessary consequence, the percentage of absentees, or the difference between the number of children on register and the actual attendance, is less in the Boston Public Schools than those of New-York. This subject has during the past, as in former years, received the attention of the Trustees, and will probably be brought before the next Board, in connection with the general subject of non-attendance at any school, which exists to such an alarming extent in this city. Efforts have been made by the present Board to obtain in some way, the active co-operation of the city government in applying a remedy to this extensive evil. Every political compact supposes a surrender of some individual rights for the general good. In a government like ours, "founded on the principle that the only true sovereignty is the will of the people," universal education is acknowledged by all, to be, not only of the first importance, but necessary to the permanency of our free institutions. If then persons are found so reckless of the best interests of their children, and so indifferent to the public good, as to withhold from them that instruction, without which they cannot beneficially discharge those civil and political duties which devolve on them in after life, it becomes a serious and important question, whether so much of the natural right of controlling their children may not be alienated, as is necessary to qualify them for usefulness, and render them safe and consistent members of the political body. The expediency of such a measure would be confined pretty much, perhaps entirely, to large seaport towns, and in its practical operation would be found to affect but few native citizens. The number of families arriving in this city almost daily from Europe, is so great as to require some measure of the kind — for the means heretofore used to induce the attendance of their children at the Public Schools have proved insufficient. The objectionable manner in which these children are employed on their arrival here, needs no description — it cannot have escaped the notice of any observing citizen.

9. The New York City Board of Aldermen threatens to withhold public charity from parents who fail to send their children to school, 1832

Proceedings of the Board of Aldermen [of New York City] from December 16, 1831 to May 8, 1832 (New York, 1835), II, 380–382.

Your Committee have had an interview with the said Trustees of Public Schools, and are fully sensible of the lamentable truth, that owing to the indifference of careless, intemperate and unworthy parents, thousands of children in this city, where instruction is, literally speaking, brought to their doors, are bred up by their parents wholly destitute of even the necessary information to enable the young and tender mind to discriminate between right and wrong; instead of being educated and fitted for useful members of society, such children are permitted to waste the morning of their youth in the streets and places of resort for idle and dissolute persons, subjected to the influence of vice and temptation.

Your Committee are . . . of opinion that a large proportion of the improvident parents, here referred to, are of the class of persons who are in the habit of resorting to the Commissioners of the Alms House for support.

Your Committee would therefore recommend, as far as the influence of our public charities can consistently be brought to bear, in the behalf of such unfortunate children, that the Common Council grant the prayer of the laudable petition made by the Trustees of the Public School Society; in the hope that it may induce parents, who are now indifferent about the education of their offspring, from a regard at least of their own welfare, to be sensible of one of the most important duties which they owe to their young and tender offspring.

It must, however, be obvious, that any regulation of this nature in order to be efficacious, must receive the cordial cooperation and support of the Commissioners of the Alms House. Your Committee have, therefore, consulted those gentlemen, and are authorized to state, that in addition to their now arduous duties, the Commissioners will also lend their aid and exertions to carry the proposed experiment into effect. Your Committee respectfully submit the following resolutions:

Resolved. That the Trustees of the Public School Society and the Commissioners of the Alms House, be requested to make it known to parents, and all persons, whether emigrants or otherwise, having children in charge capable to receive instruction, and being between the ages of five and twelve years, that unless such parents and persons do or shall send such children to some public or other daily school, for such time in the year as the Trustees of the Public School Society may from time to time designate, that all such persons must consider themselves without the pale of public charities, and not entitled, in case of misfortune, to receive public favor.

IV Care of Dependent Children

In the late eighteenth and early nineteenth centuries binding out or apprenticeship remained the preferred way of caring for children who were dependent on the public for support. For various reasons the age at which the children were bound out tended to rise and consequently the period during which the community continued to be responsible for their care lengthened. Whereas in the seventeenth and early eighteenth century it had been customary to bind the children to masters when they were barely out of infancy, the newer tendency was to maintain them as public charges until they reached the age of eight, ten, or twelve. When it was possible to bind out children at earlier ages it may be assumed that poor law officials took advantage of the opportunity. The growth of humanitarian sentiment led to greater appreciation for the special needs of very young children and on the seaboard, at least, the conquest of the wilderness had proceeded far enough by the 1740's to make it seem less necessary to set tiny boys and girls to work. Moreover, with the spread of slavery and the greater availability of indentured servants and redemptioners, it became more difficult to find masters and mistresses willing to accept children whose extreme youthfulness made them more trouble to keep than their labor was worth.

Public acceptance of responsibility for dependent children during a longer period of childhood did not necessarily mean that the responsibility was well or cheerfully discharged. The majority of dependent children, like the majority of dependent adults, were maintained in their own homes or boarded out at public expense — if they could meet the often stringent requirements for settlement and other tests of eligibility for relief. The "New England" or vendue method of pauper relief was an ingenious and thrifty variant of boarding out: the town poor, young and old, were auctioned off, either singly or in lots, to the lowest bidders. It sometimes happened that a likely looking youth, old enough to be useful on a farm or in a shop, might be "bid down" to nothing, then "bid up," and finally "struck off" to someone who was willing to pay the town for the boy's labor.[1]

During the latter half of the eighteenth century the larger cities, where the problem of poor relief was most serious, maintained almshouses which, by the 1800's, housed hundreds of paupers.[2] Many of these were children, who, despite some efforts to segregate the inmates, mingled with older paupers, the insane, and persons suffering from venereal disease. Prior to 1800 orphan homes or asylums for unfortunate children were rare. A few such institutions had been founded under the pressure of emergencies[3] or, as in the case of George Whitefield's Bethesda, in response to the effort and determination of a dominant personality. The increasingly active part women took in benevolent activities after the Revolution led to an increase in the number of orphan homes, many of which were intended to shelter girls who might otherwise have had to go to the alms-

1. For an example see Grace Abbott, *The Child and the State* (Chicago, 1938), II, 4.
2. For developments in urban poor relief in the mid-eighteenth century see Carl Bridenbaugh, *Cities in Revolt: Urban Life in America, 1743–1776* (New York, 1964), pp. 124–126.
3. On the founding of the first orphanage in the United States in New Orleans in 1728 see Part One, Chap. II, sec. B, Care of orphans, doc. 2.

house. When the great age of orphanage founding set in after 1830, precedents had already been established for granting public subsidies to private institutions. Since the orphanages, although managed and operated by private associations, performed services that were beneficial to society, they were deemed entitled to assistance from public funds.

Whether maintained at home, in almshouses, or orphan homes, poor children, upon reaching "suitable age," were bound out to serve farmers, tradesmen, sea captains, or housewives during the rest of their minority. There are instances of overseers of the poor binding children to work in factories, but this practice was less prevalent in the United States than in England.

The practice of consigning free born boys and girls to involuntary servitude simply because they were poor hardly squared with the political philosophy of the Revolution and the young republic. The practice continued, but under the legal fiction that the children were being apprenticed.[4] By the end of the eighteenth century laws governing the apprenticing of poor children sometimes contained provisions offering slightly more protection than formerly to bound children and requiring overseers of the poor to ascertain that the terms of the indenture were observed by the master. The extent to which these provisions were carried out varied greatly, not only from state to state, but also from town to town, city to city, and county to county. Weak as the protection afforded children indentured under the poor law was, the public standard for working age (the age at which children were bound out) generally was higher than that observed by those parents who allowed or compelled their own children to go to work at a tender age.

4. See above, Chap. II, sec. A, Children not to be bound as servants, for the case of Respublica *v.* Keppele, 2 Dallas (Penna.) 197 (1793).

A. BINDING OUT AND OUTDOOR RELIEF

Care of dependent children in Virginia, 1748–1785

1. Church wardens to bind out poor and neglected children, 1748

W. W. Hening, ed., *Statutes at Large of Virginia,* VI (Richmond, 1819), 32; hereafter cited as *Va. Statutes at Large.*

. . . To prevent the evil consequences attending the neglect or inability of poor people to bring up their children in an honest and orderly course of life . . . where any persons or persons shall be, by their county court, judged incapable of supporting and bringing up their child or children in honest courses, or where it shall appear to the court that he, she, or they neglect to take due care of the education of his, her, or their child or children, and their instruction in the principles of Christianity, in any such case it shall be lawful for the churchwardens of the parish where such child or children inhabit, by order of their county court, to bind every such child or children apprentices, in the same manner, and under such covenants and conditions as the law directs for poor orphan children.

2. Outdoor relief, 1748–1753

C. G. Chamberlayne, *The Vestry Book of St. Paul's Parish* (Richmond, 1940), pp. 202–205, 324–327, 332–333.

Despite the law of 1748 parishes continued to rely on families for the care of poor children and assisted parents of handicapped or defective children. The figures represent pounds of tobacco.[1]

At a vestry held for St. Paul's Parish, November 18, 1748.

Present: The Reverend Patrick Henry, John Henry, Thomas Anderson, John Bickerton, Robert Jennings, Barttelot Anderson, John Darracott, William Taylor Gent.

The following charge was brought in against the said parish and levied on the inhabitants thereof:

To Matthew Wellman for keeping a bastard child and clothing it.	800
To Richard Anderson to maintain his daughter	500
To Richard Humphreys for nursing Robert Nairn	250
To Edward Lankford for keeping a bastard child a year.	800
To Samuel White for keeping James Axley's two children 5½ months.	700
To Henry Wood for keeping his son a year	800
To Sarah Blalack for keeping six poor people one year.	4200

.   .   .   .   .

At a vestry held for St. Paul's Parish, November 20, 1749 . . .

To Matthew Wellman for keeping a bastard child a year.	800
To Richard Anderson towards maintaining his daughter.	500
To Henry Wood for keeping his son a year	800

To Sarah Blalack for keeping six poor people a year.	4200

.   .   .   .   .

At a vestry held for St. Paul's Parish, November 6, 1750 . . .

To Matthew Wellman for keeping a bastard child a year.	650
To Richard Anderson for keeping his daughter a year.	500
To Henry Wood for keeping his son a year	700
To Mary Garratt for keeping a bastard child a year.	700

.   .   .   .   .

At a vestry held for St. Paul's Parish, October 15, 1751 . . .

To Joseph Allen for keeping and burying Esther Wood's child.	300
To Matthew Wellman for keeping a bastard child a year.	500
To [Matthew Wellman] for keeping two mulatto children a year.	700

.   .   .   .   .

At a vestry of St. Paul's Parish held . . . on Saturday the 20th day of October, 1753.

To Esther Watson for keeping Mary Hogg, a bastard child one year.	700
To Henry Wood for keeping David Burnet's son	500
To John Barker for keeping Sinclair children	500
To Matthew Wellman[1] for keeping a bastard child one year.	400

---

1. In Virginia, because specie was scarce, tobacco receipts circulated as money. The estimated price of tobacco in 1748 was 4 cents per pound. Howard Mackey, "The Operation of the English Old Poor Law in Colonial Virginia," *The Virginia Magazine of History and Biography*, LXXIII (April 1965), 33–34; Arthur W. James, "Foster Care in Virginia—1679–1796," *Public Welfare*, VIII (March 1950), 60.

3. Overseers of the poor supersede churchwardens, 1785

1. At a vestry held December 29, 1780, it was announced that Matthew Wellman had bequeathed "five hundred pounds for the education of the poor children in St. Paul's Parish" (p. 565).

"An act to provide for the poor of the several counties within the commonwealth," 1785 — ch. 4, *Va. Statutes at Large,* XII (1823), 28.

After the disestablishment of the Church of England the poor-relief duties formerly performed by churchwardens were assigned to the overseers of the poor.

And be it enacted, The overseers of the poor in each district, shall monthly make returns to the court of their county of the poor orphans in their district, and the said court is hereby authorized to direct the said overseers, or either of them, to bind out such poor orphans, apprentices to such person or persons as the court on due enquiry shall approve of, and the indentures of such apprentices shall be filed in the office of the clerk of the county, and not transferrable to any person whatsoever, without the approbation of the court. The said overseers shall, on or before the tenth day of August annually, make up in a book to be kept for that purpose, an exact account of the persons to and for whom such monies are to be paid, the purposes for which, and the particular sums, a transcript of which, they shall once in every year return to the court to be there entered of record; a copy of which they shall also, on or before the same day, deliver to the collector of the public taxes, who is hereby authorized and required to collect the same, together with the list of persons chargeable with the poor rates, and of the sum each person is liable to pay; which collector shall give bond with good security to the court for the faithful discharge of his duty herein, and shall have the same powers to collect the said poor rates, and have the same commission, and be subject to the same fines, forfeitures, and prosecutions, as in the case of county levies. The said collector shall pay the money or tobacco, as the case may be, to the several persons, or to their order, for whom it was levied, on or before the first day of October in every year; and in default

thereof, it shall be lawful for the court of the county to render judgment for the same, with costs on complaint of the party, or on motion by the overseers: provided that the collector has ten days previous notice of such motion.

Binding out poor children in Massachusetts

1. "An act for the support of the poor," 1781

Acts and Laws of the Commonwealth of Massachusetts, 1788–1789 (Boston, 1894), p. 99.

. . . the Overseers of the Poor in any Town or District where such Officers are chosen, otherwise the Selectmen or the Major part of them, are hereby fully Authorized & Impowered by and with the Assent of two Justices of the Peace, to set to work, or bind out Apprentice, all such Children, whose Parents shall in their Opinion be unable to maintain them (whether they receive Alms, or are chargeable to the Town or District or not) . . . Male Children until they arrive to the age of twenty one years, and Females to the age of Eighteen, unless such females are sooner married, which binding shall be as good and effectual in Law to every intent & purpose, as if such Child being of full Age, had by Deed of Indenture or Covenant bound himself: Provision to be made in the Indenture for instructing the Males to read, write & cypher, and Females to read & write, as they respectively may be capable; And it shall be the duty of the Overseers or Selectmen, to make enquiry into the treatment of Children, bound out by themselves, or their Predecessors in Office, And if they find them at any time injured, to seek a redress thereof . . .

2. Protection of indentured children in Boston, 1792

Letter of Stephen Miller, Jr., to his uncle, Col. Edward Winslow, New Brunswick, Canada, in MHS *Proceedings,* n.s., II (1866), 242.

Boston, Nov. 15, 1792

Dear Sir, — I have waited on the principal Overseer of the Poor in this place for the purpose of knowing the conditions on which I could procure a lad or two for you, but find them as follow, viz.: that they must not go out of the State, must either be taught some mechanical profession, or have twenty pound's when free, and the person who takes them must have a *recommendation from the selectmen of the town.* These circumstances preclude the possibility of procuring any from the almshouse. But you may depend on my best endeavors, sir, to procure some from another quarter, in which, if I succeed, shall inform you. With my best respects to Aunt Winslow, and love to your little family, I am, with much respect,

Your affectionate nephew,

Stephen Miller, Jr.

Instructions for apprenticing poor children, Maryland, 1793

"An act for the better regulation of Apprentices," 1793 — ch. 45, *Laws of Maryland* . . . (Baltimore, 1811), II, 202–203.

Most states and even territories had laws authorizing overseers of the poor to bind out poor orphans or children whose parents were unable to support them. The Maryland law paid more attention to the interest of the children and the wishes of parents than was customary.

Whereas, it has been found by experience, that poor children, orphans and illegitimate children, for want of some efficient system, have been left destitute of support, and have become useless or depraved members of society: and whereas it would greatly conduce to the good of the public in general, and of such children in particular, that necessary instructions in trades and useful arts should be afforded them; therefore,

Sec. 2. *Be it enacted by the General Assembly of Maryland,* That the justices of the several and respective orphan courts, shall and may bind out as an apprentice every orphan child (the increase or profits of whose estate, whether real or personal, is or are not sufficient for maintenance, support or education, of the said child) to some manufacturer, mechanic, mariner, handicraftsman, or other person, at the discretion of the said justices, until such orphan child, if a male, shall arrive to the age of twenty-one years, or if a female, to the age of sixteen years; and the said justices are hereby directed, in all cases where they can, to make it a part of the contract on the part of the master or mistress of such apprentice, that he or she shall give such orphan child reasonable education in reading and writing, or in reading, writing and arithmetic, to be particularized therein, and also teach such orphan, especially if a male, some useful art or trade, and in all cases supply suitable clothing and maintenance; and the said justices shall and may also bind out as apprentices, such children as are suffering through the extreme indigence or poverty of their parents, also the children of beggars, and also illegitimate children, and the children of persons out of this state, where a sufficient sustenance is not afforded, in like manner, and on like terms; provided always, that when any child is about to be bound out, the parent or parents of said child, if living in the county, shall be summoned to appear before the said justices, and the inclination of the said parent or parents so far as is reasonable, shall be consulted in the choice of the person to whom the said child shall be bound out; and provided always, that when any child shall be before the court for the purpose of being bound out as an apprentice, if any relation or other person will, with good and sufficient security, enter into bond in the penalty of one hundred pounds, for the due and comfortable maintenance, and for the providing sufficient and proper clothing for such child till of age as aforesaid, and also for the reasonable schooling and education of such child, then the court shall not proceed to bind out such child as aforesaid.[1]

The short and simple annals of the poor, North Carolina, 1796–1797

Person County [North Carolina], Wardens of the Poor Records, 1792–1831, Southern Historical Collection, University of North Carolina, Chapel Hill.

17 September 1793: Ordered that James Jones be allowed the Sum of Ten Pounds for the support of a base begotten child of Mary Dixon from Easter 1793 to Easter 1794.

25 April 1795: Ordered that Robert Jones be allowed the sum of Ten Pounds for the support of a base begotten child of Mary Dixon providing that no person will do it for less from Easter 1795 to Easter 1796.

June 1, 1795: Ordered that Elizabeth Long be allowed the sum of eight pounds ten shillings for the support of a base begotten child of Mary Dixon . . . from Easter 1795 to Easter 1796.

December 7, 1795: no order shall be issued to Elizabeth Long for supporting a base begotten Child which is now dead until she shall bring in her charge before the Board of Wardens.

March 28, 1796: Ordered that Elizabeth Long be allowed the sum of seven pounds for the support of a Bastard child of Mary Dixon, now deceased, for seven months from Easter 1795 —.

· · · · ·

March 6, 1797: Ordered that Robert Jones be allowed the sum of thirteen shillings for the support of a base begotton child of Mary Dixon a small time in the year 1796.

New York City seeks permission from state legislature to bind out poor children outside the city, 1812

N.Y.C. Council Minutes 1784–1831, VII (1917), 83–84.

Your Memorialists [mayor and aldermen] further represent to your Honorable Body [state legislature] that the number of Poor children under the care of the Commissioners of the Alms House & Bridewell of the City of New York is and hath heretofore been so great that the said Commissioners have not been and are not able to bind the whole of them as Apprentices or Servants in the City and County of New York, and that they have therefore occasionally bound out some of them in other parts of this State and in the States of New Jersey & Connecticut. Your Memorialists therefore pray that your Honorable Body will be pleased to confirm the same, and to permit the Commissioners hereafter to bind the said poor children to persons residing in any part of this State or in the States of New Jersey or Connecticut.

The vendue system of poor relief

1. In 1819 Maryland provided for the binding out of free Negro children on the same terms as white *except* that the period of service of Negro girls was extended to eighteen years of age and judges were authorized to substitute payment of $30.00 in extra freedom dues for the requirement of instruction in reading and writing.

1. Massachusetts, ca. 1817

Rev. A. P. Marvin, *History of Winchendon, Massachusetts* (Winchendon, 1868), pp. 267–268.

The next step in the way of supporting the poor, was the singular, and now almost forgotten practice of having them put up at auction, and bid off to the lowest bidder. This was sometimes called "selling the poor." Careless readers of the Records might hastily infer that this was a relic of white slavery, when it was simply a mode of providing homes for the weak and indigent. Suppose a family consisting of an infirm man, who yet might do some slight work; of an old woman, who could render a little aid in the household; and a boy old enough to drive the cows and drop corn. How shall they be provided for? Instead of going from house to house, to find a home for them, this course was pursued. On an appointed day, a vendue was held, and men were called upon to say what they would charge for the support of the family, for one year. The bidders would take into consideration their own conveniences for having such a family in their houses; what their board and clothing would cost; how much they could reasonably expect to get in return by way of labor; and putting all things together, they made their bids. He who would take the family for the least sum of money, had them put into his charge, by the Selectmen, or the Overseers of the Poor. But they exercised their discretion. If the man who made the lowest bid was not of good character; if he were hard and cruel; if he was one who would scrimp and abuse the poor, the officers could decline to deliver these wards of the town to his keeping. Besides, it was often stipulated that children thus "bid off," should have so many weeks or months of schooling, annually. In addition to these safeguards, an enlightened and humane public sentiment went far to guard the poor from illtreatment. It was competent for the Selectmen, at any time, to take the custody of the poor into their own hands, if they were subject to abuse or unkindness. Perhaps this was the best policy that could be pursued before the towns entered upon the more modern plan of providing houses and farms for the support of the poor.

2. New York, 1820

Samuel Hopkins Adams, "Grandfather Attends a Vendu," in *Grandfather Stories* (New York, 1955), pp. 282–287. © 1955 Random House, Inc.

Rome, New York, in 1820, was a very active and affording town, Grandfather said. On an October morning he rode Spiderfoot into the village without a care in his twenty-one year old head but to turn an honest dollar into two. At the town hall, he reined in to look over the hoardings, for one never could tell what matter of interest might turn up: offers of reward for fugitive slaves; sales of furs, fish, cattle and rope; postings of errant wives whose husbands would no longer be responsible for their debts; the parmateering appeals of political candidates; sheriffs' warnings of jail-broken criminals; notices of runagate apprentices; and bids for "mechanics" to work on the swiftly progressing canal. One printed broadside caught Grandfather's eye. The Rome selectmen, having voted the sum of five hundred dollars for the relief of the poor, had resolved that "said poor be set up at Public Vendu by the Overseers, and go to the lowest bidders." The vendu was set for that very afternoon, and Grandfather resolved to go.

John said, "Lowest bidders? Didn't it mean the *highest* bidders, Grandpa?"

"Not at a poor vendu," the old gentleman replied. "At a poor vendu, the person on the block went to the bidder who offered board, lodging and care at the lowest rate per month, a sum the selectmen were obligated to pay from the fund they had voted."

"Just like slavery!" Jenny said indignantly.

"Not very different," Grandfather agreed. "The occupants of the poor-bench, when I arrived, looked quite as wretched as slaves."

"Couldn't the poor people do anything about it, sir?" John asked.

"Oh, yes," the old gentleman said. "If they

did not choose to be bid off, they could lie out and starve or freeze. Humane persons did not approve of these pauper auctions. Nevertheless, they went on for many years. The 'New England system,' it was called. I suppose the custom derived from there. It was so well established in this region that a farmer of my acquaintance used to bid for the entire pauper list of Amsterdam, New York. Three hundred and fifty dollars per annum was his stated offer. Nobody ever underbid him, so he got the lot, year after year."

"Why did you go to the auction, Grandpa?" Charlie asked. "Did you want to buy a poor?"

"I had no such conceit at the time, Charles," said Grandfather. "I went there out of idle curiosity."

The Rome town square, the old gentleman continued, was shrouded in dreary, October fog. Sixty or seventy townsfolk stood about paying little heed to the auctioneer, a facetious fellow named Schley. It was an unpromising vendu, Grandfather thought. A scant dozen figures were huddled on the poor-bench. An obliging bystander identified several of them for the stranger's benefit. There were two recent widows, the local half-wit, a pock-marked redemptioner who had been turned out of the farmstead where she worked as not worth her keep, a county pauper who was not properly a town charge, a rheumatism-doubled cripple, and a befreckled urchin of ten or eleven, unknown to the informant. Among the whole sorry lot, this boy was the only one who kept a straight back.

As Grandfather dismounted, Auctioneer Schley was exercising his wit upon a bleary and tremulous crone who could hardly stand upright, she was so weak from hunger.

"Exhibit B for Beauty," the auctioneer said merrily. "Any traveling poppet show would hire her on sight. How old are you, Mrs. Nosegay?"

The answer was an unhappy mumble. Taking her chin between thumb and forefinger, Schley pulled down her jaw. "Look!" he cried. "No teeth! Can't eat! Cheap to feed! What's the offer?"

After a few scattered bids, the woman was knocked down to the lockkeeper's wife for twelve shillings, and her place on the block was taken by the frightened young redemptioner. On her quavering admission that she could cook and wash, she went to a quick-bidding canal-labor contractor and was led away weeping. The rheumatic cripple followed, and was offered by Schley with the cunning suggestion that whoever got him would not have to keep him long. Bored and depressed, Grandfather was about to re-mount and go his way, when the auctioneer's raised voice checked him.

"Here's a fine bit of goods!" Schley called. "Up with you, spratling!"

The urchin rose and walked, straight, steady, and scowling, to the block. He was skeleton thin. Shapeless pantaloons of well-worn fustian flapped around his legs. His coat was fashioned from a large jute bag. Oversized wooden shoes were held on his meager feet with strings. His wretched and defiant look moved Grandfather to a kind of admiration.

"How old are you, brat?" Schley began.

"Dunno."

"Come on! Make a guess, young Web. That's your name, ain't it?" he added, consulting his auction list.

"Yup."

"What's the rest of it? Web what?"

"Web Loakes."

"Loakes, hey? Where's your folks-y, young Web Loakes-y?"

Amidst the paroxysms of merriment provoked by this sally, Grandfather heard the boy mutter, "Ain't got any."

"Well, well! Foundling, huh? Nobody around to stir up trouble about you. That's good. And you don't know how old you are. Call it ten. How you been living?"

"Traveling circuit with a show," said the boy. "Poppet and animal. I tended the bestial."

"What happened? You run away?"

"No. Monkey died. Bear bit the boss. Show busted."

"So you get you on the poor rates. Can you read?"

The boy stared at him. "No," he grunted.

"Well, I wouldn't expect it of you. Write nor figger, neither, I reckon."

The boy shook his head.

"See?" the auctioneer said to the onlookers. "No book learning to set him above his vittles. A stout fellow, too; stout and willing, ain't you, boy?"

"No," the boy said.

"Yes!" Mr. Schley corrected, cuffing him beside the head. "Now, what's the bid on this brisk spratling?"

A scissors-grinder opened with thirteen shillings, which pleased the auctioneer, though he feigned disappointment.

"You could keep him a year on that!" he cried.

The local whitesmith, who was looking for an apprentice, bid twelve. A taproom keeper cut a shilling under. A motherly-looking boarding-house mistress sent to ten.

"Nine shilling!" came a bellow from a hulking citizen in a painted castor hat, who had been lolling against an oak.

Grandfather, who recognized him as Dunk Snedeker, captain of the line boat, "Try and Catch Me," felt sorry for any human chattel who might fall into the Captain's brutal hands. It was none of Grandfather's business, however.

A Peter Funk — a spurious bidder, the accomplice of the auctioneer — now offered eight-and-six. Captain Snedeker underbid him, and was, himself, capped by the scissors-grinder. Again the Captain shouted a bid, and the Peter Funk kept the bidding going once more.

It was now down to five-and-six.

"Five, blast ye all!" Dunk Snedeker bawled, glaring about him. "Any man unders that, he'll have me to deal with."

"That's no manner of talk," protested the official, discountenanced. "Don't let him scare you off, folks. Next bid?"

Nobody responded. The Captain was an ugly customer.

"Do I hear the four?" the auctioneer cried. "Well, four and the penny? Four and tuppence? Going, once. Going — Hey, grab him!"

The merchandise had plunged from the platform and was scrambling through the crowd. He was tripped, collared and dragged back. Grandfather caught sight of his face. It was filled with hate and terror.

"One shilling!" Grandfather called, startled to hear his own voice.

"Who spoke?" the auctioneer asked, peering around.

"One shilling," Grandfather repeated firmly.

"Done!" cried the auctioneer. "Get down, boy. The next article is — "

Grandfather heard no more. He was making for his mare, with one eye out for the Captain and one hand on the collar of the boy. He swung into the saddle, and the boy swarmed up behind him. Captain Snedeker was pushing through the crowd toward them. There was no chance of evading him. Grandfather pulled the mare around, set her straight at the Captain, and bowled him over like a ninepin.

"And that," the old gentleman told us, "is how I got my first apprentice."

"I think it was noble of you, Grandfather," Jenny said.

"Why, I was rather of that opinion myself," said Grandfather.

B. INSTITUTIONAL CARE OF POOR CHILDREN

The Bethesda Orphan House, Georgia, 1739–1742

1. George Whitefield raises funds for an orphan house in Georgia, 1739–1740
The Autobiography of Benjamin Franklin,
pp. 176–178.

George Whitefield (1714–1770) combined evangelistic fervor for saving souls with prowess in fund raising. The principal object of his philanthropic labors was the orphan house in Georgia which he projected in 1738 on his first visit to America.[1] Late in 1739, after the Georgia trustees awarded him 500 acres of land for the orphanage, Whitefield returned to America. The incident Franklin describes occurred in the course of this second visit, when Whitefield was about twenty-five years of age.

Mr. Whitfield, in leaving us, went preaching all the Way thro' the Colonies to Georgia. The Settlement of that Province had lately been begun; but instead of being made with hardy industrious Husbandmen accustomed to Labour, the only People fit for such an Enterprise, it was with Families of broken Shopkeepers and other insolvent Debtors, many of indolent and idle habits, taken out of the Goals, who being set down in the Woods, unqualified for clearing Land, and unable to endure the Hardships of a new Settlement, perished in Numbers, leaving many helpless Children unprovided for. The Sight of their miserable Situation inspired the benevolent Heart of Mr. Whitefield with the Idea of building an Orphan House there, in which they might be supported and educated. Returning northward he preach'd up this Charity, and made large Collections; for his Eloquence had a wonderful Power over the Hearts and Purses of his Hearers, of which I myself was an Instance. I did not disapprove of the Design, but as Georgia was then destitute of Materials and Workmen, and it was propos'd to send them from Philadelphia at a great Expence, I thought it would have been better to have built the House here and brought the Children to it. This I advis'd, but he was resolute in his first Project, and rejected my Counsel, and I thereupon refus'd to contribute. I happened soon after to attend one of his Sermons, in the Course of which I perceived he intended to finish with a Collection, and I silently resolved he should get nothing from me. I had in my Pocket a Handful of Copper Money, three or four silver Dollars, and five Pistoles in Gold. As he proceeded I began to soften, and concluded to give the Coppers. Another Stroke of his Oratory made me asham'd of that, and determin'd me to give the Silver; and he finish'd so admirably, that I empty'd my Pocket wholly into the Collector's Dish, Gold and all. At this Sermon there was also one of our Club, who being of my Sentiments respecting the Building in Georgia, and suspecting a Collection might be intended, had by Precaution emptied his Pockets before he came from home; towards the Conclusion of the Discourse however, he felt a strong Desire to give, and apply'd to a Neighbour who stood near him to borrow some Money for the Purpose. The Application was unfortunately to perhaps the only Man in the Company who had the firmness not to be affected by the Preacher. His Answer was, *At any other time, Friend Hopkinson, I would lend to thee freely; but not now; for thee seems to be out of thy right Senses.*

1. For disposition of orphans in Georgia shortly before Whitefield's visit see Part One, Chap. II, sec. B, Care of orphans, doc. 3.

2. Whitefield's description of Bethesda, 1740

George Whitefield's Journals (London, 1960),
pp. 395–397; first published 1738–1741.

Bethesda was the second orphanage in
Georgia, German settlers having established
one at Ebenezer in 1738. Both Bethesda and
Ebenezer were modeled after the orphanage
at Halle, Germany, founded
by August Francke.[1]

Savannah

Friday, January 11, 1740. Went this morning, with some friends, to view a tract of land,
consisting of five hundred acres, which Mr.
Habersham, whom I left schoolmaster of Savannah, was directed, I hope by Providence, to
make choice of for the Orphan House. It is
situated on the northern part of the colony,
about ten miles from Savannah, and has various
kinds of soil in it; a part of it very good. Some
acres, through the diligence of my friend, are
cleared. He has also stocked it with cattle and
poultry. He has begun the fence, and built a
hut, which will greatly forward the work. I
choose to have it so far off the town, because
the children will be more free from bad examples, and can more conveniently go up on
the land to work. For it is my design to have
each of the children taught to labour, so as to
be qualified to get their own living. Lord, do
Thou teach and excite them to labour also for
that meat which endureth to everlasting life!

Thursday, Jan. 24. Went this morning and
took possession of my lot. I called it Bethesda,
that is, the House of Mercy; for I hope many
acts of mercy will be shewn there, and that
many will thereby be stirred up to praise the
Lord, as a God Whose mercy endureth for
ever.

Tuesday, Jan. 29. Took in three German
orphans, the most pitiful objects, I think, I
ever saw. No new negroes could look more
despicable, or require more pains to instruct
them. They have been used to exceedingly
hard labour, and though supplied with provisions from the trustees, were treated in a
manner unbecoming even heathens. Were all
the money I have collected, to be spent in
freeing these three children from slavery, it
would be well laid out. I have also in my house
near twenty more, who, in all probability, if
not taken in, would be as ignorant of God and
Christ as the Indians. Blessed be God, they
begin to live in order. Continue this and all
other blessings to them, for Thy mercies' sake,
O Lord.

This day I began the cotton manufacture,
and agreed with a woman to teach the little
ones to spin and card. I find annual cotton
grows fairly well in Georgia; and to encourage
the people, I bought to-day, three hundred
pounds weight, and have agreed to take all the
cotton, hemp, and flax that shall be produced
the following year through the whole province.
Though there are fewer inhabitants in Savannah, yet I think they are in a better situation
than when I was here last. They now live independent on a public store. Provisions (flour
especially) are much cheaper, cattle more
plentiful; and if any manufacturer can be raised
among themselves, to prevent them exporting
so much money, they may yet do well. My
congregations are as large as usual. The Court
House is generally full; and I keep as near as
possible to my old way of proceeding. We
have the Sacrament every Sunday, and public
prayer and exposition twice every day in the
week.

Wednesday, Jan. 30. Went with the carpenter
and surveyor, and laid out the ground whereon
the Orphan House is to be built. It is to be
sixty feet long and forty wide. The foundation
it to be brick, and is to be sunk four feet
within, and raised three feet above the ground.
The house is to be two stories high, with a hip
roof: the first ten, the second nine feet high. In

1. Clyde E. Buckingham, "Early American Orphanages: Ebenezer and Bethesda," *Social Forces,* XXVI
(1947), 311–321.

all, there will be nearly twenty commodious rooms. Behind are to be two small houses, the one for an infirmary, the other for a workhouse. There is also to be a still-house for the apothecary; and, I trust, before my return to England, I shall see the children and family quite settled. I find it will be an expensive work; but it is for the Lord Christ. He will take care to defray all charges. The money that will be spent, on this occasion, will keep many families from leaving the colony, and in all probability, bring many others over. There are nearly thirty working at the plantation already, and I would employ as many more, if they were to be had. Whatsoever is done for God, ought to be done speedily, as well as with all our might.

Monday, Feb. 4. Met, according to appointment, all the magistrates, who heard the Recorder read the grant given me by the Trustees, and took a minute of their approbation of the same. Lord, grant I may carefully watch over every soul that is or shall be committed to my charge.

Monday, Feb. 11. Took in four fresh orphans, and set out with two friends, to Frederica, in order to pay my respects to General Oglethorpe, and to fetch the orphans in the southern parts of the colony.

---

3. Mistreatment of orphan at Bethesda, 1741

"Journal of Colonel William Stephens,"
Ga. Colonial Records, IV Supplement
(1908), 166–168.

Whitefield returned to England in December 1740 leaving Jonathan Barber in charge of spiritual matters at Bethesda and James Habersham in charge of business affairs. William Stephens was secretary of the colony of Georgia.

June 16, 1741. Complaint being made to Bailiff Parker, that one of the Orphan Boys, under the Care of Mr. Whitefield, had been treated with unwarrantable Correction, by Mr. Barber the Presbyterian Minister there, he was summoned to appear at Savannah, by Warrant to the Constable, under the Hands of Mess. Parker, Fallowfield, and Pye the Recorder: To which he appeared; and the Matter was examined into by them,

.   .   .   .   .

The Boy who had suffered (it seems) had run away to Mr. Parker for Protection, at his Plantation in the Isle of Hope; where Parker being not well at that Time, had delay'd coming to Town for near a fortnight, to have it enquir'd into; by which Means the Stripes he had seen fresh upon the Boy, did not now appear so terrible as at first: However, the Boy being now present, and stripp'd, it is yet too visible from Scars and Wounds not yet healed, that great Cruelty had been used: It was not denied, that the Boy was made naked to the Waist, after the Manner of common Malefactors, and lashed with five strong Twigs tied together, as long as they would hold, whereby his whole Back, Shoulders, Loins, Flank and Belly, were in a dreadful Condition. The Cause of this Severity, as alledged by the Boy, was, that he had wrote a Letter some Time before, to Mr. Parker, therein then complaining of severe Usage; which Mr. Parker now owned he received, but did not take great Notice of it, thinking it the common Case of many School-Boys under the Chastisement of a Rod; but now it was made appear, that the Boy's writing that Letter, was come to their Knowledge, and was the Occasion of his being thus dealt with and threatened to have his Punishment renewed, unless he would write to Mr. Parker again, and contradict all he had said before; which the Anguish he was under forced him to promise; but he made his Escape as aforesaid. During this Proceeding, it is said Mr. Barber found courteous Treatment; but upon offering nothing in his own Vindication, only that he thought himself the proper Judge, without Controul, in what Manner to govern the Boys that he had the Care of, and questioning the Powers by which they acted; they told him, they should convince him farther of that very soon, when they intended, by Virtue of that Power, to visit the Orphan-House, and make farther Enquiry into whatever they found amiss, and appeared to them contrary to the Design of the Trustees, by their Grant: And thereupon taking the Boy away, with Intent to dispose of him by Apprenticeship, as they saw proper, they parted.

---

4. "Let the orphan house alone," 1742

Letter from George Whitefield presumably to the Trustees of the Colony of Georgia, Aug. 17, 1742, in *Ga. Colonial Records,* XXIII (1914), 392–395.

As early as 1740 disputes arose between Whitefield and the Georgia magistrates and trustees over the extent of Whitefield's authority over orphans and the autonomy of the orphan house. Whitefield was accused of taking orphans from the homes of relatives who were able and willing to support them.

. . . I am sorry also to inform Your Honrd. Gentlemen that five very small Swiss or Dutch Children, whose Parents lately died in their passage from England, have had their goods sold at Vandue, & been bound out to the Age of twenty one Years. This I think directly contrary to the Grant given me by You Honrd. Gentlemen — For thereby I was impower'd to take in as many Orphans into the Orphan-house as my fund would admit of — The Magistrates I understand also have been at the Orphan-house & claim a power to take away the Children when they please, whether the Children chuse it or complain of ill treatment or not — This grieves some of the Children, & makes others of them Insolent who are hereby taught that they have a power to go away when they will — This Honrd. Gentlemen must be very

discouraging to those who are entrusted with their Education, & who I am persuaded aim at nothing but the Glory of God, the welfare of the Colony & the Salvation of the Children's souls — I suppose the Magistrates (I mean Mr. Parker & Fallowfield) have taken such liberty from some of the Instructions which were sent Honrd. Gentlemen from You some time agoe But Mr. Jones has told them they have misunderstood You — And His Excellency General Oglethorp I find has wrote to you Honrd. Gentlemen about it — By the Accounts I have, our Plantation thrives well, & Mr. Habersham writes me word He hopes we shall do with white Servants — I do assure you Honrd. Gentlemen I will do all I can, with the most disinterested view to promote the good of Georgia — Only I beg the Management of the Orphanhouse & Orphans may be secured to to me & my Successors for Ever, & the Magistrates not be suffered to disturb us when there is no ground of complaint — They acknowledged when att the Orphan-house last that the Children were taken good care of both as to Body & soul — And will it not then Honrd. Gentlemen tend much to the Welfare of the Colony that the Orphan-house should meet with all possible encouragement? . . . Indeed Honrd. Gentlemen, I do not desire to find fault — I doubt not but You have been prejudiced against me & my Friends — The Event will shew what Friends we are to Georgia — The Orphanhouse will certainly be an Addition to the Colony, & the Children educated therein I trust will be the Glory of the Society to which they belong — They are bred up to Industry as well as other things, & taught to fear God & honour the King — If You please Honrd. Gentlemen I will wait upon You when I return to London, & with all humility lay these matters before You — I am glad to hear You have lately sent over a Gentleman who (as is supposed) will do justice — I think I desire nothing else & heartily pray God to bless him & You Honrd. Gentlemen & all that are concerned in the management of the Georgia affairs — I hope to be in Town in about two months — In the mean while I would beg the favour of [a] line, by Your Secretary, & also entreat You Honrd. Gentlemen to write to the Magistrates of Savannah to let the Orphan-house alone till I have laid matters before You & arrive at Georgia which God willing at the furthest will be the beginning of next Year — If I or my friends should happen to say or do any thing amiss, I assure You Honrd. Gentlemen, You shall have all possible satisfaction given You by them, as also by, Honrd. Gentlemen

Your very humble Servt.

George Whitefield

Public institutions

1. The first public orphanage, Charleston, South Carolina, 1790

"An Ordinance for the establishment of an orphan house in the City of Charleston," ratified Oct. 18, 1790, in George B. Eckhard, *A Digest of the Ordinance of the City Council of Charleston, From the Year 1783 to October 1844* (Charleston, 1844), pp. 188–189.

WHEREAS, the present mode of supporting and educating poor children at different schools, has been found by experience to be attended with heavy expense and many inconveniences, and the establishment of an Orphan House properly organized and conducted, will be attended with less expense, more convenience and benefit, and may tend to give general satisfaction to the citizens, and induce the benevolent to assist in the support of so charitable and laudable an institution:

Be it ordained, That a lot of land, not less than two hundred feet square, shall be immediately laid out by the Committee of the City Lands, on the most healthy and convenient spot, and reserved for the building and erecting an Orphan House, as soon as the funds of the corporation will admit, or any practical plan to defray the expense thereof can be devised. And that all such poor orphan children and children of poor distressed or disabled parents as shall be deemed proper objects of admission by the Commissioners, who shall be vested with powers for managing the said Orphan House, shall be admitted into the same, and shall be supported, educated and maintained at the expense of the corporation, during such term and under such regulations as the City Council shall from time to time prescribe or sanction.

·   ·   ·   ·   ·

Until the said Orphan House shall be erected, a proper house and lot of land conveniently situated, shall be rented as an Orphan House, by the Commissioners [elected by City Council] who shall have the direction and management of the same, and who shall admit, and take charge of the clothing, maintenance and education of the children of the Orphan House; and it shall be the duty of the Commissioners to choose and appoint proper assistants, nurses and domestics, and to superintend and manage the Orphan House, the officers and servants thereof, and the children therein, to the best of their judgment and skill, subject to the control of the City Council.

It shall be the duty of the Steward of the Orphan House to see that good and wholesome provisions are sent for the use of the children and other persons residing in the Orphan House, by the butchers, bakers, and other persons employed to furnish such articles as may be necessary; to take care of the articles delivered him for the use of the Orphan House; to keep a book of fair and regular accounts of all receipts and expenditures, which shall be subject at all times, to the examination of the Commissioners, to perform all the duties of a good Steward, to obey the directions and regulations of the Commissioners; and to enable the said Steward to discharge faithfully the duties required of him, he shall reside in the Orphan

House, and shall receive necessary provisions for himself.

A Matron of good capacity and character shall be elected by the City Council on the last Monday in October, annually, but if no Council shall meet on that day, then on the first day of the Council thereafter, as School Mistress and Matron of the Orphan House, whose duty it shall be to teach the children to read and sew, to take care that their clothes are properly made, washed and preserved, to keep the children and their rooms cleanly, and to watch over their morals and conduct; to direct the assistants and nurses, and to see that they discharge their duties faithfully, and to distribute them properly among the children, in the different rooms; to take care that the victuals provided for the children are wholesome, cleanly and well prepared; to preserve order and decorum at table and elsewhere, and to conduct the children regularly to some place of worship on the Sabbath, and to obey all the directions of the Commissioners. And to enable the said Mistress and Matron to perform her duties she shall reside in the Orphan House, and shall receive necessary provisions for herself.

The Commissioners who shall be appointed by the City Council, shall have power and authority to make and frame such rules and regulations as they may think necessary, for the good government and conducting the business of the Orphan House, and all persons therein. *Provided,* all such rules and regulations are presented to, and approved of by the City Council, within ten days after the same are framed, and that the City Council shall and may confirm, alter and amend or annul the same.

2. Care of children in New York City Almshouse, 1800

"Rules for the Government of the Alms-House," Oct. 6, 1800, in *N.Y.C. Council Minutes, 1784–1831,* II, 671.

1. Care shall be taken to provide healthy and proper nurses for such of the children as may require them; and where this can be done out of the house, it shall be preferred.

2. Such children as have arrived at a suitable age, shall regularly attend the school, provided for them, and shall be instructed in reading, writing, and arithmetic.

3. The girls shall be taught plain work and knitting, by a proper person to be provided for that purpose, and shall be employed therein, at least three afternoons in every week.

4. Care shall be taken that the children are kept clean and neat; that they receive their food regularly, and that they behave themselves in a decent and orderly manner. They shall be allowed such sports and pastime, as may contribute to their health, but always in the presence of some discreet and sober person; and shall be kept, as much as possible, from any intermixture with the other paupers.

5. If any of the children distinguish themselves by their good behaviour and capacity, the board will direct their being instructed in the higher kinds of learning, and will take measures that they may profit thereby in their future situations in life.

6. The children shall be kept in separate apartments, according to their different sexes.

7. The schoolmaster, or some proper person, shall twice on each Sunday, read to the children, and such of the adult paupers as may chuse to attend, proper prayers and sermons, with some passages or parts of the bible, or some other religious book.

8. When any of the children arrive at proper ages, they shall be bound out to suitable trades or occupations, and provision shall be made in their indentures for their due maintenance and instruction.

9. If any of those who shall have been so bound out, shall be injured or ill-treated, the superintendent shall consider it as his duty to procure them redress. They are to be considered, in every respect, as the children of the public, under his care.

Female Associations for the benefit of children

1. Origins of the Boston Female Asylum, 1800

Abby L. Wales, *Reminiscences of the Boston Female Asylum* (Boston, 1844), pp. 7–12.

In these times of excitement and movement, when societies for every imaginable purpose have become so common as for the very name to provoke a smile or a sarcasm, and yet when every new project finds friends and supporters, it is difficult to appreciate the deep yet timid feeling, which prompted a few high minded and kind hearted women, to step beyond what was then considered the limit of female duty, and associate to found, in the year 1800, an asylum for female orphan children.

.   .   .   .   .

Our city now numbering its hundred thousand inhabitants, then contained but twenty thousand, nor had the great tide of foreign immigration poured in its thousands of the poor; yet even then the want of an Orphan Asylum was felt; and this want was brought to express itself under apparently accidental circumstances. A case of individual wrong and suffering, in which she became much interested, was made known to Mrs. Hannah Stillman, wife of the Rev. Dr. Stillman, one of the most popular and beloved clergymen of that day. An orphan girl told her story of early destitution, and betrayal; and it was known that there were many exposed to like wants and trials. Mrs. Stillman spoke of this, and of her wish to provide an Asylum for such, to her friends. One of them, Mrs. Ozias Goodwin, had accounts of such establishments brought by her husband from Europe. A plan was talked of, and a correspondence opened on the subject in the Boston Gazette, edited by Mr. John Russell, in which that gentleman took a part, and was from the beginning a friend and helper in the project. Although several other ladies joined

Mrs. Stillman, it was difficult to get a sufficient number who were willing to give their names as subscribers. It was the first time here that women had combined for any public purpose. Many looked suspiciously, and many opposed the design. Yet its friends were of that character and station in society that sympathy and confidence could not be long withheld.

The first meeting for the purpose of organizing the society, was held at the house of Mrs. Jonathan Mason Sen'r, September 26, 1800 . . . At this first meeting a plan was proposed and accepted, and several ladies were chosen to fill the offices necessary for carrying it into effect. Some of these, though expressing great interest in the object, declined for various reasons to serve in this way.

At the second meeting, the Treasurer reported that she had received donations amounting to three hundred and eighteen dollars, and annual subscriptions to two hundred and ninety-one dollars. She was directed to invest the donations in bank stock, and keep the subscriptions until called for. It was with this slender capital, the managers advertised that they were ready to receive the most needy of the orphans who might be presented, according as their means would permit. It had been agreed, that a suitable person should be provided who would take the children to board and instruct them under the supervision of the managers. Mrs. Susanna Draper was chosen for this purpose, and one dollar and fifty cents per week was to be paid for the board of each child.

At this meeting too, the first child, Betsey D., was admitted. Of this child, Dr. Stillman in his anniversary sermon says: — "The first child was admitted into this Asylum under circumstances extremely affecting. Having lost her parents when about five years of age, she was received by an aunt, affectionate but poor, who adopted her as her own. Soon after disease attacked this aunt and she expected to die. Her principal anxiety now was what would become of this destitute child. In the moment of her distress, she was visited by a friend, who told her that a place was just established under the management of the ladies of Boston for female orphan children, and that they would certainly receive the child on application being made to them. Overjoyed at this unexpected information, she exclaimed 'Thank Got! that place is provided for my little girl!' "

At the next meeting two others were admitted.

At the December meeting, it was recorded that a child having a mother in a very distressed situation was offered for admission. The original design of some of the managers seems to have been to confine the privilege of admission to those who had "neither father nor mother." And the record says there was much discussion on the subject. Some advocating strict adherence to the rule, while others pleaded for a larger construction of the term orphan. The votes being taken, eight were found to be in favor of receiving the child and five against it. She was accordingly admitted. It may be permitted to add the following words from the record: "Madam Perkins then rose and laid on the table a ten dollar bill, as a mark of her approbation of the decision . . .

From this time it was never made an objection to the admission of a suffering child that one of its parents was living.

2. Female Charitable Society, Salem, Massachusetts, 1802–1807

William Bentley, D.D., *Diary*, II (Salem, 1905), 408–409; III (1911), 299.

January 19, 1802. Female associations for the benefit of the female children are adopted through the United States. There has been one lately established at Savanna. There has been one at Baltimore & one in this Town, besides there are in several other places, Boston, Philadelphia, N.Y. The widow of Gen. Fiske is Directress of that at Salem & they have upon the printed List above 140 members. I am happy to find the concurrence of many of my own parish. In the List I find of my own Females, 6 out of the 8 & one third of the members.

June 9, 1807. Application in turn to preach the Annual Sermon before the Female Charitable Society in Salem. Some late difficulties have become serious to this Institution. The Nine Female Children subject to its care have been entrusted lately to a woman who is represented for the purpose of her avarice to have withholden necessary food from them. Enquiries have been made but not with full satisfaction in the result as there never can be when both parties are not without friends & when the public jealousies are awakened. The strict economy required by the managers, when directed by ignorance & avarice, may have a terrible appearance before those who see the poor daily supplied abundantly with food, when they really are in want of everything besides.

3. Contract between Sisters of Charity and the managers of St. Joseph's Orphan Asylum, Philadelphia, 1820

"Mother Seton's Daughters in Philadelphia in 1820," *Records* of the American Catholic Historical Society, XVIII (1917), 277–279.

The Sisters of Charity of St. Joseph, founded in 1809 by Elizabeth Ann Seton (1774–1821), staffed many of the early Roman Catholic schools, hospitals, and orphanages in the United States. Although this contract was made in 1820, the sisters had taken charge of the orphanage in 1814. A similar contract was entered into in 1817 between the Sisters of Charity and the managers of the New York Catholic Asylum.

AN agreement entered into between the Superior-general of the Sisters of Charity of St. Joseph's near Emmittsburg, Maryland, in their name and in their behalf, and the managers of the Roman Catholic Society of St. Joseph, for educating and maintaining poor Orphan Children in Philadelphia:

1. The Rev. John Dubois, Superior General of the Sisters of Charity of St. Joseph's engages to supply four sisters, who shall undertake the management of the Orphan House in Philadelphia, to attend to the economy of the house, the care of the children, their schooling and religious instruction.

2. All donations received by the sisters to be accounted for by them to the managers of St. Joseph's Society, who have the exclusive direction of the funds belonging to that institution.

3. No children to be admitted into the Asylum other than by the managers, whose duty it shall be from time to time to consult the head sister thereon.

4. The managers hereby engage to support the house, supplying from time to time, any monies that may be wanted, should donations prove insufficient for that purpose.

5. Flour and wood will be provided by the managers, all articles of clothing by the Ladies' Society, established for that purpose. Groceries generally to be purchased by the sisters, at the same time leaving it optional with the head sister to purchase those articles themselves or to have them bought by the managers.

6. No other duties or charges shall be imposed on the sisters without the consent of the central government, the managers being desirous that they shall attend to the Orphans exclusively.

7. The regulation and management of the house to be left to the discretion of the sisters, in whom the managers repose entire confidence and with whose rules and customs they will not interfere.

8. The managers by their appointment feel themselves in duty bound to attend to the wants of the children, and of course reserve to themselves the right to visit the house at proper hours and seasons, it being understood that they are not to interfere or interrupt the sisters

in their religious exercises, these visits to be confined to the school and lower parts of the house.

9. The Ladies who undertake to provide for and furnish the Asylum with clothing and other necessaries are to have the privilege of visiting every part of the house. It being nevertheless understood that they shall appoint monthly or quarterly committees for that purpose, consisting of at least two members — the visits to be at such times as not to interfere with the sisters in their religious duties. The Ladies at their quarterly meetings to examine the children, when small premiums shall be distributed by them to the most deserving.

10. Strangers visiting the Asylum, may be introduced to all parts of the house for the first time, either by one or more of the managers, or by the sisters, if these visits are repeated they can only be received in the parlors; the same privilege is allowed also the person or persons who may introduce said strangers for the first time, although themselves may have repeated the visits frequently.

11. The sisters to board at the Asylum conformable to the simplicity of their rules.

12. The Ladies will pay to the head sister, thirty-one dollars per annum for each sister employed in the Asylum for their clothing, and furnish them with shoes, but in case of their not so doing, the managers hereby engage to do the same.

13. The travelling expenses of the sisters, coming to or going from Philadelphia shall be paid by the managers, when the health of any one of the sisters, or any reasonable cause may be such as to require her removal to Emmittsburg, and of course, another will have to supply her place, whose expenses will also be borne. In case of the decease of any one of the sisters at the Asylum, the managers to pay the funeral expenses, all removals of the sisters other than the foregoing to be paid by the central government.

In confirmation whereof the said parties have set their hands and seals the twenty-eighth day of July 1820.

JOHN DUBOIS, Superintendent of the Sisters of Charity of St. Joseph's.

JOSEPH SNYDER, Secretary of the Board of Managers of St. Joseph's Society.

The New York Orphan Asylum, 1806–1819

The Orphan Asylum Society was organized on March 15, 1806, at a meeting presided over by Mrs. Isabella Marshall Graham.

Mrs. Graham was the first directress of the Society for the Relief of Poor Widows with Small Children, founded in 1797. The Orphan Asylum Society was an outgrowth of the earlier society. It was incorporated in 1807 and granted authority to indenture its orphan wards in 1809.

---

1. Collection proposed for the benefit of the Orphan Asylum Society, 1807

New York Evening Post, June 5, 1807.

Orphan Asylum Society — The attention of the public is most respectfully solicited to the merits, the importance, and the wants of a recent but valuable institution, "The Orphan Asylum Society of New-York," which commenced in March, 1806. There are already about twenty orphans cloathed, fed, and educated under the care of this Society. In the space of fourteen months, many of the children who knew not the alphabet when they entered, can now read the Bible fluently, and their progress in writing is also considerable. As yet a hired building has sufficed, but the surprising number of Orphans and the propriety of a permanent and extensive Asylum have induced the venerable Clergy of New-York almost unanimously to propose a general collection in their several churches. Christian Friends and Fellow-

Citizens — you will rejoice in this opportunity of affording your bountiful and efficient aid to this more than common charity. Each Minister will appoint in his own congregation the day deemed proper for taking up the desired contributions and many a good Samaritan will be able to pour oil and wine into the wounds of deprived infancy —

. . . . .

Four lots of ground are already purchased; and there is reason to hope, the patronage of a people . . . will produce a fund fully adequate to the erection of a handsome and commodious building. It will be an external ornament to our city, and an eternal consolation to all its inhabitants.

---

2. "The institution is considerably in debt . . . ," 1810

New York Evening Post, July 31, 1810.

The contributions to this institution have been liberal, and do honor to the patrons and conductors of so noble an establishment. But we are sorry to observe that the institution is considerably in debt. The benevolent zeal of the disinterested conductors, has outrun their means. However, this cannot long be the case — the wealthy and liberal citizens of this prosperous city, will never suffer an institution of such heavenly origin, to droop and die for want of the necessary pecuniary support . . .

---

3. Grant of a state subsidy

a. New York recognizes the Orphan Asylum Society, 1811

"An act for the benefit of the Orphan Asylum Society," 1811 — ch. 86, *Laws of the State of New York . . . 1811* (1811), p. 159.

Be it enacted by the People of the State of New York, represented in Senate and Assembly: That the Treasurer shall pay, until the further order of the legislature, to the trustees of the orphan asylum society in the city of New York, the annual sum of five hundred dollars out of the fund arising from auction duties, and appropriated to the support of foreign poor in the city of New York, and that the first payment under this Act shall be made on the first day of May next.[1]

b. The Society gratefully acknowledges the annual subsidy, 1820

1. In similar fashion the state of Louisiana began the practice of subsidizing private charitable agencies by making annual grants, first (1819) to the Female Orphan Society and subsequently to an ever increasing number of "homes" and asylums. Elizabeth Wisner, *Public Welfare Administration in Louisiana* (Chicago, 1930), pp. 187–188.

Orphan Asylum Society in the City of New York, *Thirteenth Annual Report* (New York, 1819), p. 94.

. . . We have not been accustomed to consider this as a public institution, being, we may say, wholly supported by private beneficence.[2] The only exception to this is an annual sum of $500 from the State Legislature, procured for us through the kind offices of a gentleman long known as the patron of every good institution and who always cheered us in our course.

Our respect, our gratitude, and best wishes are associated with the name of DeWitt Clinton, in whom, during the long period he was chief magistrate of this city, we always found a steady friend and dignified protector . . .

2. In 1809 the state legislature awarded the Society $5,000 from the proceeds of a lottery to be held for the benefit of the Board of Health. This sum finally became available in 1816 enabling the society to pay off the mortgage on the asylum property and make an addition to the building. *Third Annual Report* (1809), p. 32; *Tenth Annual Report* (1816), p. 75.

V Child Health

In the early eighteenth century, medically speaking the concept of child health hardly existed. Children, though they suffered particularly from the absence of medical knowledge and from various epidemics, were treated like their elders. Young and old alike fought sickness by drinking exotic concoctions of herbs and other vegetable and animal matter and by alternately dieting and bleeding, purging and sweating. Two eminent physicians and practical philosophers, John Locke and William Cadogan, advised parents to preserve their children's health by hardening them to the environment. Cadogan wrote encouragingly, "There are many instances, both ancient and modern, of infants exposed and deserted, that have lived several days." [1]

Whether from this advice or for other reasons, the mortality rate for infants and children was high. "Tis a frequent thing for parents to bury their *children*," said Cotton Mather in 1711. "Else we could not see, as they say we do, at least half the children of men dying short of twenty." [2] Smallpox, diphtheria, and yellow fever appeared in epidemic forms and, of these, diphtheria particularly affected children. Those children who survived epidemics were sometimes left without one or both parents. The prevailing belief that original sin was the ultimate cause of illness often discouraged remedial action such as inoculation of children against smallpox. On the other hand, Mather,

a firm believer in original sin, surmounted dogma to support inoculation. Still, in 1735 a diphtheria epidemic, particularly severe among younger people in Kingston, New Hampshire, was attributed to "the holy displeasure of almighty God."

The dismal state of obstetrical care also contributed to the high rate of infant and maternal mortality. Pregnant women were left to the care of often ignorant and superstitious midwives and, as a result, they frequently perished along with their infants. After 1750, this tragedy was partially mitigated with the introduction of English obstetrical methods based upon better knowledge of gestation and delivery. William Smellie, the leading English authority on midwifery, trained or influenced many of the first American obstetricians, including James Lloyd of Boston, William Shippen, Jr., of Philadelphia, and William Moultrie of Charlestown.

Children who escaped unskilled midwives often suffered at the hands of ignorant doctors. "Our practitioners deal much in quackery and quackish medicines," wrote the Boston physician William Douglass in 1751. [3] To fight quackery, New York City (ca. 1760) and the province of New Jersey (1772) adopted examination and licensing programs for physicians. Here too developments in English medicine improved American practice. Many skilled Scottish physicians like William Moultrie emigrated to the colonies seeking better opportunities than were available to them in Britain.

During the latter half of the eighteenth cen-

1. William Cadogan, "An Essay upon Nursing and the Management of Children, from their Birth to Three Years of Age," in Logan Clendening, comp., *Sourcebook of Medical History* (New York, 1942), p. 270.

2. Cotton Mather, *Orphanotrophium. Or, Orphans Well-provided for* (Boston, 1711), p. 11.

3. William Douglass, *A Summary, Historical and Political, of the First Planting, Progressive Improvements, and Present State of the British Settlements in North America . . . ,* II (Boston, 1751), 351–352.

tury, some children also benefited from the availability and improved quality of hospital care in a few urban centers. Hospital departments existed in the larger public almshouses prior to this time, but the first charter for a hospital was issued in 1751 to Dr. Thomas Bond and the other founders of the Pennsylvania Hospital. Modeled after English hospitals, this institution admittted charity cases while depending upon philanthropic donors and fee paying patients. New York Hospital, a similar institution built "upon the plan of the Royal Infirmiry at Edinburgh," was destroyed by fire shortly before its scheduled opening in 1775 but was rebuilt in 1791 with the aid of state and city funds. In 1765 children began to benefit specifically from the Pennsylvania Hospital when Dr. William Shippen, Jr., opened a private school of midwifery; however, a lying-in department was not officially added to the hospital until 1803.

Similarly, children profited from the improved professional standards which resulted from the founding of medical schools at the College of Philadelphia (1765), King's College (1767), and Harvard University (1782). Here, practitioners began to develop obstetrics and child care into fields of specialized and precise inquiry. Dr. Samuel Bard of Columbia, formerly King's College, gave an original account of diphtheria; Benjamin Rush, the leading clinician of his time and a member of the staff of both the College of Philadelphia and its successor, the University of Pennsylvania, described cholera infantum and influenza. In 1796 Rush's pupil, Charles Caldwell, wrote the first monograph on pediatrics to be submitted as a dissertation for the medical degree.

The most important medical advance of the early nineteenth century was the prevention and control of smallpox by vaccination, introduced into this country by Benjamin Waterhouse of Harvard Medical School. In contrast to the response to inoculation, vaccination was gratefully accepted, not only by the medical profession but also by the public and by the national and state governments. Waterhouse was less interested in the moral condition of the sufferer and more concerned with "the unspeakable advantages that might accrue to this country" with the development of the technique. Vaccination, therefore, represented both a medical breakthrough and a change in attitudes toward disease.

Advice on child health

1. John Locke's rules for preserving and improving health in children, 1690

Locke, "Some Thoughts Concerning Education," *Works,* IX, section 4–7, 23, 27.

Locke was a physician as well as philosopher. He wrote this essay in 1690 with the needs of a young English gentleman in mind, but his advice on raising healthy, reasonable children was pertinent to the simpler social and cultural setting of the American colonies in the eighteenth century.

The consideration I shall here have, of health, shall be, not what a physician ought to do, with a sick or crazy child; but what the parents, without the help of physic, should do for the preservation and improvement of an healthy, or, at least, not sickly constitution, in their children: and this perhaps might be all despatched in this one short rule, viz. that gentlemen should use their children as the honest farmers and substantial yeomen do theirs. But because the mothers, possibly, may think this a little too hard, and the fathers, too short, I shall explain myself more particularly; only laying down this, as a general and certain observation for the women to consider, viz. that most children's constitutions are either spoiled, or at least harmed, by cockering and tenderness.

The first thing to be taken care of is, that children be not too warmly clad or covered, winter or summer. The face, when we are born, is no less tender than any other part of the body: it is use alone hardens it, and makes it more able to endure the cold . . . Our bodies will endure any thing, that from the beginning they are accustomed to.

.   .   .   .   .

Give me leave, therefore, to advise you not to fence too carefully against the cold of this our climate: there are those in England, who wear the same clothes winter and summer, and that without any inconvenience, or more sense of cold than others find. But if the mother will needs have an allowance for frost and snow, for fear of harm, and the father, for fear of censure, be sure let not his winter-clothing be too warm; and amongst other things remember, that when nature has so well covered his head with hair, and strengthened it with a year or two's age, that he can run about by day without a cap, it is best that by night a child should also lie without one; there being nothing that more exposes to head-ach, colds, catarrhs, coughs, and several other diseases, than keeping the head warm.

I have said [he] here, because the principal aim of my discourse is, how a young gentleman should be brought up from his infancy, which in all things will not so perfectly suit the education of daughters; though, where the difference of sex requires different treatment, it will be no hard matter to distinguish.

I would also advise his feet to be washed every day in cold water; and to have his shoes so thin, that they might leak and let in water, whenever he comes near it. Here, I fear, I shall have the mistress, and maids too, against me. One will think it too filthy; and the other, perhaps, too much pains to make clean his stockings. But yet truth will have it, that his health is much more worth than all such considerations, and ten times as much more. And he that considers how mischievous and mortal a thing taking wet in the feet is, to those who

have been bred nicely, will wish he had, with the poor people's children, gone barefoot; who, by that means, come to be so reconciled by custom, to wet their feet, that they take no more cold or harm by it than if they were wet in their hands. And what is it, I pray, that makes this great difference between the hands and the feet in others, but only custom? I doubt not, but if a man from his cradle had been always used to go barefoot, whilst his hands were constantly wrapped up in warm mittins, and covered with handshoes, as the Dutch call gloves; I doubt not, I say, but such a custom would make taking wet in his hands as dangerous to him, as now taking wet in their feet is to a great many others. The way to prevent this, is to have his shoes made so as to leak water, and his feet washed constantly every day in cold water. It is recommendable for its cleanliness: but that, which I aim at in it, is health. And therefore I limit it not precisely to any time of the day. I have known it used every night with very good success, and that all the winter, without the omitting it so much as one night, in extreme cold weather: when thick ice covered the water, the child bathed his legs and feet in it; though he was of an age not big enough to rub and wipe them himself; and when he began this custom, was puling and very tender. But the great end being to harden those parts, by a frequent and familiar use of cold water, and thereby to prevent the mischiefs that usually attend accidental taking wet in the feet, in those who are bred otherwise; I think it may be left to the prudence and convenience of the parents, to choose either night or morning. The time I deem indifferent, so the thing be effectually done. The health and hardiness procured by it would be a good purchase at a much dearer rate. To which if I add the preventing of corns, that to some men would be a very valuable consideration. But begin first in the spring with lukewarm, and so colder and colder every time, till in a few days you come to perfectly cold water, and then continue it so, winter and summer. For it is to be observed in this, as in all other alterations from our ordinary way of living, the changes must be made by gentle and insensible degrees; and so we may bring our bodies to any thing, without pain, and without danger.

.   .   .   .   .

One thing more there is, which hath a great influence upon the health, and that is going to stool regularly; people that are very loose have seldom strong thoughts, or strong bodies. But the cure of this, both by diet and medicine, being much more easy than the contrary evil, there needs not much to be said about it; for if it come to threaten, either by its violence or duration, it will soon enough, and sometimes too soon, make a physician be sent for: and if it be moderate or short, it is commonly best to leave it to nature. On the other side, costiveness has too its ill effects, and is much harder to be dealt with by physic; purging medicines, which seem to give relief, rather increasing than removing the evil.

.   .   .   .   .

I would therefore advise, that this course should be taken with a child every day, presently after he has eaten his breakfast. Let him be set upon the stool, as if disburdening were as much in his power as filling his belly; and let not him or his maid know any thing to the contrary, but that it is so: and if he be forced to endeavour, by being hindered from his play, or eating again till he has been effectually at stool, or at least done his utmost, I doubt not but in a little while it will become natural to him. For there is reason to suspect that children being usually intent on their play, and very heedless of any thing else, often let pass those motions of nature, when she calls them but gently; and so they, neglecting the seasonable offers, do by degrees bring themselves into an habitual costiveness. That by this method costiveness may be prevented, I do more than guess: having known, by the constant practice of it for some time, a child brought to have a stool regularly after his breakfast, every morning.

2. "Children in general are over-cloathed and over-fed"

William Cadogan, "An Essay upon Nursing and the Management of Children, from their Birth to Three Years of Age," in Clendening, *Sourcebook of Medical History,* pp. 269–273.

Cadogan (1711–1797), a London physician who specialized in cures for gout, wrote this treatise in 1748. It was well received in both England and the colonies.

You perceive, Sir, by the hints I have already dropped, what I am going to complain of is, that Children in general are over-cloathed and over-fed; and fed and cloathed improperly. To these causes I impute almost all their diseases. But to be a little more explicit. The first great mistake is, that they think a new-born infant cannot be kept too warm: from this prejudice they load and bind it with flannels, wrappers, swathes, stays, &c. which altogether are almost equal to it's own weight; by which means a healthy child in a month's time is made so tender and chilly, it cannot bear the external air; and if, by any accident of a door or window left carelessly open too long, a refreshing breeze be admitted into the suffocating atmosphere of the lying-in bed-chamber, the child and Mother sometimes catches irrecoverable colds. But, what is worse than this, at the end of the month, if things go on apparently well, this hotbed plant is sent out into the country to be reared in a leaky house, that lets in wind and rain from every quarter. Is it any wonder the child never thrives afterwards? The truth is, a new-born Child cannot well be too cool and loose in its dress; it wants less cloathing than a grown person in proportion, because it is naturally warmer, as appears by the thermometer, and would therefore bear the cold of a winter's night much better than any adult person whatever. There are many instances, both antient and modern, of infants exposed and deserted, that have lived several days. As it was the practice of antient times, in many parts of the world, to expose all those whom the parents did not care to be incumbered with; that were deformed, or born under evil stars; not to mention the many Foundlings picked up in LONDON streets. These instances may serve to shew, that Nature has made Children able to bear even great hardships, before they are made weak and sickly by their mistaken Nurses. But, besides the mischief arising from the weight and heat of these swaddling-cloaths, they are put on so tight, and the Child is so cramped by them, that its bowels have not room, nor the limbs any liberty, to act and exert themselves in the free easy manner they ought. This is a very hurtful circumstance; for limbs that are not used will never be strong, and such tender bodies cannot bear much pressure: the circulation restrained by the compression of any one part, must produce unnatural swellings in some other, especially as the fibres of infants are so easily distended. To which doubtless are owing the many distortions and deformities we meet with everywhere; chiefly among Women, who suffer more in this particular than the Men.

I would recommend the following dress: A little flannel waistcoat, without sleeves, made to fit the body, and tie loosely behind; to which there should be a petticoat sewed, and over this a kind of gown of the same material, or any other that is light, thin, and flimsey. The petticoat should not be quite so long as the Child, the gown a few inches longer; with one cap only on the head, which may be made double if it be thought not warm enough. What I mean is, that the whole coiffure should be so contrived, that it might be put on at once, and neither bind nor press the head at all: the linen as usual. This I think would be abundantly sufficient for the day; laying aside all those swathes, bandages, stays, and contrivances that are most ridiculously used to close and keep the head in it's place, and support the body. As if Nature, exact Nature, had produced her chief work, a human creature, so carelessly unfinished as to want those idle aids to make it perfect. Shoes and stockings are very needless incumbrances, besides that they keep the legs wet and nasty, if they are not changed every hour, and often cramp and hurt the feet: a child would stand firmer, and learn to walk much sooner without them. I think they cannot be necessary till it runs out in the dirt. There should be a thin flannel shirt for the night, which ought to be every way quite loose. Children in this simple, pleasant dress, which may be readily put on and off without teazing them, would find themselves perfectly easy and happy, enjoying the free use of their limbs and faculties, which they would very soon begin to employ when they are thus left at liberty. I would have them put into it as soon as they are born, and continued in it till they are three years old; when it may be changed for any other more genteel and fashionable: tho' I could wish it was not the custom to wear stays at all; not because I see no beauty in the sugar-loaf shape, but that I am apprehensive it is often procured at the expence of the health and strength of the body. There is an odd notion enough entertained about change, and the keeping of children clean. Some imagine that clean linen and fresh cloaths draw, and rob them of their nourishing juices. I cannot see that they do any thing more than imbibe a little of that moisture which their bodies exhale. Were it, as is supposed, it would be of service to them; since are are always too abundantly supplied, and therefore I think they cannot be changed too often, and would have them clean every day; as it would free them from stinks and sournesses, which are not only offensive, but very prejudicial to the tender state of infancy.

The feeding of Children properly is of much greater importance to them than their cloathing. We ought to take great care to be right in this material article, and that nothing be given them but what is wholesome and good for them, and in such quantity as the body calls for towards it's support and growth; not a grain more. Let us consider what Nature directs in the case: if we follow Nature, instead of leading or driving it, we cannot err. In the business of Nursing, as well as Physick, Art is ever destructive, if it does not exactly copy this original. When a Child is first born, there seems to be no provisions at all made for it; for the Mother's milk, as it is now managed, seldom comes till the third day; so that according to this appearance of Nature a Child would be left a day and a half, or two days, without any food. Were this really the case, it would be a sufficient proof that it wanted none; as indeed it does not immediately; for it is born full of blood, full of excrement, it's appetites not awake, nor it's senses opened; and requires some intermediate time of abstinence and rest to compose and recover the struggle of the birth and the change of circulation (the blood running into new channels), which always put it into a little fever. However extraordinary this might appear, I am sure it would be better that the Child was not fed even all that time, than as it generally is fed; for it would sleep the greatest part of the time, and, when the milk was ready for it, would be very hungry, and suck with more eagerness; which is often necessary, for it seldom comes freely at first. But let me endeavour to reconcile this difficulty, that a Child should be born thus apparently unprovided for. I say apparently, for in reality it is not so. Nature neither intended that a Child should be kept so long fasting, nor that we should feed it for her. Her design is broke in upon, and a difficulty raised that is wholly owing to mistaken management. The Child, as soon as it is born, is taken from the Mother, and not suffered to suck till the Milk comes of itself; but is either fed with strange and improper things, or put to suck some other Woman, whose Milk flowing in a full stream, overpowers the newborn infant, that has not yet learnt to swallow, and sets it a coughing, or gives it a hiccup; the Mother is left to struggle with the load of her Milk, unassisted by the sucking of the Child. Thus two great evils are produced, the one a prejudice to the Child's health, the other, the danger of the Mother's life, at least the retarding her recovery, by

causing what is called a milk-fever; which has been thought to be natural, but so far from it, that it is entirely owing to this misconduct. I am confident, from experience, that there would be no fever at all, were things managed rightly; were the Child kept without food of any kind, till it was hungry, which it is impossible it should be just after the birth, and then applied to the Mother's breasts; it would suck with strength enough, after a few repeated trials, to make the milk flow gradually, in due proportion to the Child's unexercised faculty of swallowing, and the call of it's stomach. Thus the Child would not only provide for itself the best of nourishment, but, by opening a free passage for it, would take off the Mother's load, as it increased, before it could oppress or hurt her; and therefore effectually prevent the fever; which is caused only by the painful distension of the lacteal vessels of the breasts, when the milk is injudiciously suffered to accumulate. . . .

There is usually milk enough with the first Child; sometimes more than it can take: it is poured forth from an exuberant, overflowing urn, by a bountiful hand, that never provides sparingly. The call of Nature should be waited for to feed it with any thing more substantial, and the appetite ever precede the food; not only with regard to the daily meals, but those changes of diet, which opening, increasing life requires. But this is never done in either case, which is one of the greatest mistakes of all Nurses. Thus far Nature, if she be not interrupted, will do the whole business perfectly well; and there seems to be nothing left for a Nurse to do, but to keep the Child clean and sweet, and to tumble and toss it about a good deal, play with it, and keep it in good humour.

When the Child requires more solid sustenance, we are to enquire what, and how much, is most proper to give it. We may be well assured, there is a great mistake either in the quantity or quality of Children's food, or both, as it is usually given them; because they are made sick by it; for to this mistake I cannot help imputing nine in ten of all their diseases. . . .

It is not common for people to complain of ails they think hereditary, 'till they are grown up; that is, 'till they have contributed to them by their own irregularities and excesses, and then are glad to throw their own faults back upon their Parents, and lament a bad constitution, when they have spoiled a very good one.

The inoculation controversy, Boston, 1721

Cotton Mather, although patiently submitting to the will of God, was quick to adopt and advocate measures to avert unnecessary death. During the severe smallpox epidemic of 1721, Mather, concerned about the safety of his children, induced Dr. Zabdiel Boylston to try the experiment of inoculation as a means of preventing fatal cases of the disease. Boylston inoculated both his own and Mather's children. For many years after 1721 the practice of inoculation remained a controversial issue, defended and attacked on both theological and medical grounds.[1]

1. The introduction of smallpox inoculation, 1721

Zabdiel Boylston, *An Historical Account of the Smallpox Inoculated in New England, Upon All Sorts of Persons, Whites, Blacks, and of All Ages and Constitutions* . . . (London, 1726; Boston, 1730), pp. ii–vi.

I began the practice indeed from a short consideration thereof; for my children, whose

1. On the inoculation controversy see John Duffy, *Epidemics in Colonial America* (Baton Rouge, 1953), pp. 23–40.

lives were very dear to me, were daily in danger of taking the infection, by my visiting the sick in the natural way; and although there arose such a cloud of opposers at the beginning, yet finding my account in the success, and easy circumstances of my patients (with the encouragement of the good ministers), I resolved to carry it on for the saving of lives, not regarding any, or all the menaces, and opposition that were made against it.

I have not, in this practice, left room for anyone to cavil, and say, that my experiments have not been fair, and full proofs, that inoculating the smallpox is a certain means of moderating that distemper, to the greatest demonstration. This, the warmest opposers of that practice, who have seen any fair trials made, are convinced of; and the only difficulty of convincing all mankind, is how to make them eye-witnesses to a number sick of the smallpox in both ways of infection; and this would do it at once, and very much to their satisfaction in, and approbation of this method. And here it should be considered how rashly our patients, even whole families together, rushed into this practice . . .

I have not used this practice only to the healthful and strong, but to the weak and diseased, the aged and the young. Not only to the rich, but have carried it into the houses of the poor, and laid down whole families; and though through my own hurry in business, and their living out of town, I have been forced to leave them to the management of unexperienced nurses, yet they all did well.

.   .   .   .   .

We met with no . . . terrible effects (save that death is terrible in all its shapes) from the smallpox inoculated, as was common amongst us in the natural way, viz. purple spots, convulsion fits, bloody urine, violent inflammations in the eyes, throat, and other parts, scarred faces, some who had lost both eyes, and, as it has been thought, near an hundred one eye, with many more melancholy symptoms too tedious here to enumerate; not to mention parents being left childless, children without parents, and sometimes parents and children's being both carried off, and many families broken up by the destruction the smallpox made in the natural way. Indeed, we had some resemblance of those effects; but in none where it was not evident, that they were infected in the natural way before; and though we met with but five or six cases that bordered on, or resembled more or less those symptoms, yet it would not have been strange had there been six times that number; for in Boston, and in the middle of Roxbury, no one knew who were, or who were not infected, before inoculated; and I verily believe that twenty five, if not thirty of my patients were infected before inoculated. And this reason I can give for every one's believing so, that in all and everyone whom I inoculated, and that had not been exposed to an infected air, and which were above one hundred, not any of them had the least shadow of such symptoms upon them, through the whole course of their distemper. However, I do not recommend this practice to be carried on and managed by old women and nurses; no, I would have it carried on and managed by good physicians and surgeons, where they are to be had; but rather than the people should be left a prey to the smallpox in the natural way, let it be managed by nurses, for I cannot help thinking that even in their hands, many less would die of the smallpox by inoculation, than there does in the natural way, though in the best of hands, and under the best of care.

.   .   .   .   .

I do not call upon or exhort the physicians and surgeons who are already in the practice, and have used their endeavors to promote it, nor do I pretend to inform or instruct them. My design is only to stir up those who have not yet come into and used this method, and to lay before the people a fair state of the distemper in both ways of infection, that they may be apprized of the danger in the one, and the reasonable expectation they have of doing well in the other. My reasonings and opinions I submit to those of better judgment, but as we are rational creatures, we do, or should delight in acting upon principles of reason; and those who consider this method, and make use of it, I think may be said so to act.

I hope the reader will excuse me for troubling him with some of the difficulties that I met with. I have been basely used and treated by some who were enemies to this method, and have suffered much in my reputation and in my business too, from the odiums and reflections cast upon me for beginning and carrying on this practice in New England; which ill usage I think justly entitles me to make the necessary reflections, and relate matters of fact in my own justification, and to recommend and do justice to the method, which was so exposed and condemned by their misrepresentations, which have been spread abroad in the world; and to set things in a good light, that the world may impartially judge between the parties (if I may be allowed the term) which of the two have acted most like men and Christians, viz. whether those who have opposed and exclaimed against this method without due consideration of, or knowing scarce anything about it; or those who have considered well, been in the practice of, and have proved by their own experience, or that have seen the good effects and benefit of it, and from such reasons have recommended it to others?

Indeed I can easily forgive and pity those who through tenderness, or in point of conscience, have refused the offered mercy, and that have gently appeared against it. Such, with the assistance of a divine, together with the exercise of their own reason upon it, may easily get through their difficulties. But for those who out of private piques, or views, have exclaimed and railed against it, and who have trumpt up the groundless ill consequences that would attend or follow it. Such I leave to sweat it out with just reflection and due repentance. As for my own part, I know of no better way of judging between moral and immoral methods of medical practice, than from the good or ill success that does, or may attend them.

2. Inoculation is a "lawful practice and
. . . has been blessed by GOD," 1721

Increase Mather, *Several Reasons Proving
that Inoculating or Transplanting the
Small Pox, is a Lawful Practice, and that
it has been Blessed by God for the Saving
of Many a Life* (Boston, 1721).

It has been questioned, whether inoculating
the small pox be a lawful practice. I incline to
the affirmative, for these reasons.

I.　Because I have read, that in Smyrna, Con-
stantinople, and other places, thousands of
lives have been saved by inoculation, and not
one of thousands has miscarried by it. This is
related by wise and learned men who would
not have imposed on the world a false narrative. Which also has been published by the
Royal Society; therefore a great regard is due
to it.

II.　We hear that several physicians, have recommended the practice hereof to His Majesty,
as a means to preserve the lives of his subjects,
and that His wise and excellent Majesty King
George, as also His Royal Highness the Prince
have approved hereof, and that it is now coming into practice in the nation. In one of the
public prints are these words, "Inoculating the
small pox is a safe and universally useful experiment." Several worthy persons lately arrived from England inform us, that it is a
successful practice there: If wise and learned
men in England, declare their approbation of
this practice, for us to declare our disapprobation will not be for our honor.

III.　GOD has graciously owned the practice
of inoculation, among us in Boston, where
some scores, yes above an hundred have been
inoculated, and not one miscarried; but they
bless GOD, for His discovering this experiment
to them. It has been objected, that one that was
inoculated, died, viz. Mrs. D———; but she
had the small pox, in the common way before,

and her friends and nearest relations declare
that she received no hurt by inoculation, but
was by a fright put into fits that caused her
Death. It is then a wonderful providence of
GOD, that all that were inoculated should have
their lives preserved; so that the safety and usefulness of this experiment is confirmed to us
by ocular demonstration: I confess I am afraid,
that the discouraging of this practice, may
cause many a life to be lost, which for my own
part, I should be loth to have any hand in, because of the Sixth Commandment.

IV.　It cannot be denied but that some wise
and judicious persons among us, approve of inoculation, both magistrates and ministers;
among ministers I am one, who have been a
poor preacher of the gospel in Boston above
threescore years, and am the most aged, weak
and unworthy minister now in New England.
My sentiments, and my son's also, about this
matter are well known. Also we hear that the
reverend and learned Mr. Solomon Stoddard
of Northampton concurs with us; so doth the
Reverend Mr. Wise of Ipswich, and many other
younger divines, not only in Boston, but in
the country, join with their fathers. Furthermore, I have made some inquiry, whether there
are many persons of a profane life and conversation, that do approve and defend inoculation,
and I have been answered, that they know but
of very few such. This is to me a weighty consideration. But on the other hand, though there
are some worthy persons, that are not clear
about it; nevertheless, it cannot be denied, but
that the known children of the wicked one, are
generally fierce enemies to inoculation . . .
For my part I should be ashamed to join with
such persons; O my soul come not thou into
their secret, unto their assembly be not thou
united. I am far from reflecting upon all that
are against inoculation. I know there are very
worthy persons (with whom I desire to live and
die) that are not clear in their judgments for it,
and they are greatly to be commended and
honored in that they will not act against a
doubting conscience; yet it may be some of

them might change their minds, if they would advise with those who are best able to afford them scripture light in this as well as in other cases of conscience.

.   .   .   .   .

A most successful, and allowable method of preventing Death, and many other grievous miseries, by the small pox, is not only lawful but a Duty, to be used by those who apprehend their lives immediately endangered by the terrible distemper.

---

3. A physician's criticism of "inoculation, practised at random," 1722

Jared Sparks, ed., "Letters from Dr. William Douglass to Dr. Cadwallader Colden of New York," in *Collections* of the Massachusetts Historical Society, 4th ser., II (1854), 168–171; hereafter cited as MHS *Collections.*

William Douglass (ca. 1691–1752), born in Scotland and trained in medicine in Edinburgh, Leyden, and Paris, settled in Boston in 1718. For a fuller statement of his views see *A Dissertation Concerning Inoculation of the Small-Pox* (Boston, 1730). By 1751 he had become convinced of the beneficial results of the practice of inoculation. Cadwallader Colden (1688–1776), a noted botanist and physicist, was a leading advocate of public health measures in New York City. He served as lieutenant-governor of the colony from 1760 to 1774.

May 1, 1722.

After nineteen years intermission we received via Saltertudas from Barbadoes the small-pox, middle of April 1721, and by the January following it was nearly over, having affected only Boston and two or three adjacent Towns . . .

Our small-pox burials were as follows, May 1; June 8; July 20; August 26; September 101; October 402; November 249; December 31; January 6; in all 844 persons in Boston. Last February an exact scrutiny was made, it was found that Boston consisted of 10,565 souls whereof 6,000 have now had the small-pox and of those 899 dyd; about 700 who never had it escaped and a few who remained in the country are free of it.

Having, sometime before the small-pox arrived, lent to a credulous vain preacher Mather, Jr., the philosophical Transactions No. 339 and 377 which contain Timonius' and Pylermus' accounts of Inoculation from the Levant; that he might have something to send home to the Royal Society who had long neglected his communications as he complained; he sets inoculation to work in month of June; by 18th of November one hundred were inoculated, and by January in all some few more than 250 in Town and Country. Whereof some have been inoculated oftener than once before it took effect; with some it never wrought; they all complained much of head disorders, even with those who had but very few and these imperfect pustules their incisions grew up in a few days as in common superficial wounds of the skin; but about the seventh or eighth day generally they begin to complain (some few sooner or later), are feverish, their incisions inflame, open, and discharge profusely with a peculiar noisome fetor, and continue running some weeks after their small-pox pimples are dried up and they abroad about their affairs infect wherever they go (this spreading the infection and consequently rendering it more intense is a great objection against inoculation practised at random in a place whose greatest part of the people are liable to the distemper). We all knew of nine or ten inoculation deaths besides abortions that could not be concealed, we suspect more who died in the height of the small-pox, it being only known to their nearest relations whether they died of inoculation or in the natural way . . .

I oppose this novel and dubious practice not being sufficiently assured of its safety and consequences; in short I reckon it a sin against society to propagate infection by this means and bring on my neighbor a distemper which might prove fatal and which perhaps he might escape (as many have done) in the ordinary way, and which he might certainly secure himself against by removal in this Country where it prevails seldom. However many of our clergy had got into it and they scorn to retract; I had them to appease, which occasioned great heats (you may perhaps admire how they reconcile this with their doctrine of predestination) . . . Our People at present are generally averse to it.

July 25, 1722.

We are now clear of the small-pox, and inoculation here made a poor exit; for the last six inoculated persons were in danger of violence from the people. They were by warrant of the Justices removed out of the town and sent two leagues down the Bay to an island, and were afterwards, though well, confined there by a resolve of the Assembly till the beginning of July; the three grown persons were very full of the small-pox, one of them was in danger of his life, the three children had the distemper favorable. The number of all that have been inoculated in New-England is circiter 240 persons.

Epidemics in the eighteenth century

---

1. Measles in New York City, 1729

James Alexander to Cadwallader Colden, March 14 and March 26, 1729, Cadwallader Colden Papers, I, *Collections* of the New-York Historical Society (1917), 276–277.

Alexander (1691–1756) was a New York lawyer and member of the Council of New York.

[March 14, 1729]

There was never So great a mortality here Since I came to this place as now, theres no day but what theres numbers of buryings, Some of the measles but most of the pain of the Side there's hardly a house in town but what had severals Sick of the one or other of these Distempers Some have half a Score at a time four of our children have had the Measles two almost quite recovered two Sick as yet, our negro Jupiter had them Struck out yesterday which is comeing more deliberatly than in most other familys we have three children more & three more negroes which we Expect Every day to have them, So you may Easyly think the town is in not a little Distress

.   .   .   .   .

[March 26, 1729]

My wife is brought Low with the Measles & dare not come out of her room yet, Johnie is ill of a Relapse after them, Mattie's measles were at the height yesterday but I think is in no danger, Jammee was dangerously ill, but now Sets up & plays, Billie was taken yesternight wt a fever I Suppose its the Measles, my children at Nurse have had them & are not quite recovered yet, four of our Negroes have the Measles, & one we are afraid is getting them this day, So that there is but davie & my Self of whites & one black wench that I can call well in our family, but if Something alleviats the Distress that we are not Singular few families in toun being much better off, In all my days I never saw So generall a Sickness in a place nor a greater mortality

---

2. A public fast for "the younger people [that] have been removed by death," in the "throat distemper" epidemic, 1735

Massachusetts Bay (Province), Governor, *By His Excellency Jonathan Belcher, Esq.*

Captain-General and Governour in Chief, In and Over His Majesty's Province of the Massachusetts-Bay in New England. A Proclamation for a Publick Fast (Boston, 1735).

The fast was proclaimed on the occasion of the first major epidemic of "throat distemper" (diphtheria and scarlet fever), which broke out in Kingston, New Hampshire, in May 1735 and gradually spread through New England. The chief victims were young children. In the parish of Hampton Falls, New Hampshire, twenty families buried all their children. Within one year the community lost 210 persons out of a population of about 1,200; 95 per cent of the victims were below the age of twenty.[1]

Whereas among other tokens of the holy displeasure of almighty GOD towards this sinful people, He hath been pleased to visit several of the towns within this province with a very unusual, malignant and mortal distemper, by which great numbers, especially of the *younger people,* have been removed by death; and there is great danger that the said sickness will become more epidemical so as to spread throughout the land.

I have therefore thought fit, with the advice of Majesty's Council, and at the desire of the representatives, in the present session, to appoint Thursday the eighth day of January next, to be observed as a day of solemn prayer and humiliation with fasting, throughout this province; hereby, exhorting both ministers and people devoutly to attend the same, by humble and penitent confession of their sins, and sincere and fervent supplications to the GOD of all grace, that in his infinite mercy, he would spare this unworthy people, and put a stop to the progress of this mortal distemper, or restrain the malignity thereof, and command the destroying angel to stay his hand;

1. Duffy, *Epidemics in Colonial America*, pp. 117–118.

and above all, that he would sanctify this visitation to the spiritual good and advantage of this people; and that the fruit of all may be to purge away our sin and make us the partakers of his holiness; that he would pour out his holy spirit upon all orders of men among us, and especially on the rising generation, that they may seek the Lord GOD of their fathers, and serve Him with a perfect heart and willing mind; and likewise that he would be pleased to give light and direction to the government of this province in all their administrations, and graciously protect all our religious and civil interests: And that he would hasten the coming and kingdom of our lord and saviour JESUS CHRIST, and fill the whole earth with his glory.

3. Worm fever in South Carolina, 1770

D. Milligan, "A Short Description of the Province of South Carolina," in B. R. Carroll, comp., *Historical Collections of South Carolina,* II (1836), 511.

Worm-fevers are very frequent, and common to all ages, though children under 5 years of age suffer most, particularly in the spring and beginning of summer. The sweet potato, Indian corn or maize, and pompion, all much used in diet, seem to have a larger share of the eggs of these mischievous insects, than the rest of the farinaceous or leguminous kind.

When a fever, in young people particularly, is attended with irregular symptoms, and is of a longer duration than usual, not easily otherwise accounted for, we may be assured that worms are the cause of them: In such cases I know of no medicine more likely to be of service than the decoction of pink-root . . . to be continued till the disease terminates; blisters, and other medicines proper for particular symptoms that may occur, are not to be neglected.

---

4. Yellow fever in Philadelphia, 1793

Benjamin Rush, *An Account of the Bilious Remitting Yellow Fever, as it Appeared in the City of Philadelphia, in the Year 1793* . . . (Philadelphia, 1794), pp. 122–128.

Between 1760 and 1793 the United States was free of yellow fever. In the latter year a fearful epidemic of the disease broke out in Philadelphia. One-tenth of the city's population died in the epidemic. Benjamin Rush (1745–1813) was the city's leading physician, a prolific writer, and promoter of humanitarian reforms. The practice of "depletion" (heavy bleeding) which Rush advocated and employed probably helped increase mortality rates in the epidemic.

Thus far have I delivered the history of the yellow fever as it affected the human body with sickness and death. I shall now mention a few of those circumstances of public and private distress which attended it. I have before remarked, that the first reports of the existence of this fever were treated with neglect or contempt. A strange apathy pervaded all classes of people. While I bore my share of reproach for "terrifying our citizens with imaginary danger," I answered it by lamenting "that they were not terrified enough." The publication from the college of physicians soon dissipated this indifference and incredulity. Fear or terror now sat upon every countenance. The disease appeared in many parts of the town, remote from the spot where it originated; although in every instance it was easily traced to it. This set the city in motion. The streets and roads leading from the city were crowded with families flying in every direction for safety to the country. Business began to languish. Water

Street between Market and Race Streets became a desert. The poor were the first victims of the fever. From the sudden interruption of business, they suffered for awhile from poverty, as well as disease. A large and airy house at Bush-hill about a mile from the city, was opened for their reception. This house, after it became the charge of a committee appointed by the citizens on the 14th of September, was regulated and governed with the order and cleanliness of an old and established hospital. An American and French physician had the exclusive medical care of it after the 22d of September.

The contagion after the second week in September, spared no rank of citizens. Whole families were confined by it. There was a deficiency of nurses for the sick, and many of those who were employed were unqualified for their business. There was likewise a great deficiency of physicians from the desertion of some, and the sickness and death of others. At one time, there were only three physicians who were able to do business out of their houses, and at this time, there were probably not less than 6,000 persons ill with the fever.

During the first three or four weeks of the prevalence of the disorder, I seldom went into a house the first time, without meeting the parents or children of the sick in tears. Many wept aloud in my entry, or parlor, who came to ask for advice for their relations. Grief, after awhile descended below weeping, and I was much struck in observing that many persons submitted to the loss of relations and friends, without shedding a tear, or manifesting any other of the common signs of grief.

A cheerful countenance was scarcely to be seen in the city for six weeks. I recollect once in entering the house of a poor man, to have met a child of two years old that smiled in my face. I was strangely affected with this sight (so discordant to my feelings and the state of the city) before I recollected the age and ignorance of the child. I was confined the next day by an attack of the fever, and was sorry to hear upon my recovery, that the father and mother of this little creature died, a few days after my last visit to them.

The streets everywhere discovered marks of the distress that pervaded the city. More than one half the houses were shut up, although not more than one third of the inhabitants had fled into the country. In walking for many hundred yards, few persons were met, except such as were in quest of a physician, a nurse, a bleeder, or the men who buried the dead. The hearse alone kept up the remembrance of the noise of carriages or carts in the streets. Funeral processions were laid aside. A black man, leading, or driving a horse, with a corpse on a pair of chair wheels, with now and then half a dozen relations or friends following at a distance from it, met the eye in most of the streets of the city at every hour of the day, while the noise of the same wheels passing slowly over the pavements, kept alive anguish and fear in the sick and well, every hour of the night.

But a more serious source of the distress of the city arose from the dissentions of the physicians, about the nature and treatment of the fever. It was considered by some, as a modification of the influenza, and by others as the jail fever. Its various grades, and symptoms were considered as so many different diseases, all originating from different causes. There was the same contrariety in the practice of the physicians that there was in their principles. The newspapers conveyed accounts of both to the public every day. The minds of the citizens were distracted by them, and hundreds suffered and died from the delays which were produced by an erroneous opinion of a plurality of diseases in the city, or by indecision in the choice, or a want of confidence in the remedies of their physician.

The science of medicine is related to everything, and the philosopher as well as the Christian will be gratified by knowing the effects of a great and mortal epidemic upon the morals of a people. It was some alleviation of the distress produced by it, to observe its influence upon the obligations of morality and religion. It was remarked during this time, by many people that the name of the Supreme Being was seldom profaned either in the streets, or in the intercourse of the citizens with each other. Two robberies only, and those of a trifling nature, occurred in nearly two months, although many hundred houses were exposed to plunder, every hour of the day and night. Many of the religious societies met two or three times a week, and some of them every evening, to implore the interposition of heaven to save the city from desolation. Humanity and charity kept pace with devotion. The public have already seen accounts of their benevolent exercises in other publications. It was my lot to witness the uncommon activity of those virtues upon a smaller scale. I saw little to blame, but much to admire and praise in persons of different professions, both sexes, and of all colors. It would be foreign to the design of this work, to draw from the obscurity which they sought, the many acts of humanity and charity, of fortitude, patience, and perseverance which came under my notice. They will be made public, and applauded elsewhere.

But the virtues which were excited by our calamity, were not confined to the city of Philadelphia. The United States wept for the distresses of their capital. In several of the states, and in many cities, and villages, days of humiliation and prayer were set apart to supplicate the father of mercies in behalf of our afflicted city. Nor was this all. From nearly every state in the union, the most liberal contributions of money, provisions, and fuel, were poured in for the relief and support of such as had been reduced to want, by the suspension of business, as well as by sickness, and the death of friends.

Midwifery and childbearing

---

1. Dr. William Shippen, Jr., of Philadelphia proposes a course in midwifery

Pennsylvania Gazette, Jan. 31, 1765.

Shippen (1736–1808) received his M.D. at Edinburgh in 1761. His first class, held at the Pennsylvania Hospital, stimulated the establishment of the Medical School of the College of Philadelphia (1765), later the University of Pennsylvania. In 1791 Shippen was appointed professor of anatomy, surgery and midwifery at the University.

Dr. Shippen Jr., having been lately called to the assistance of a number of women in the country, in difficult labors, most of which was made so by the unskillful old women about them, the poor women having suffered extremely, and their innocent little ones being entirely destroyed, whose lives might have been easily saved by proper management, and being informed of several desperate cases in the different neighborhoods which had proved fatal to the mothers as to their infants, and were attended with the most painful circumstances too dismal to be related, he thought it his duty immediately to begin his intended courses in Midwifery, and has prepared a proper apparatus for that purpose, in order to instruct those women who have virtue enough to own their ignorance and apply for instructions, as well as those young gentlemen now engaged in the study of that useful and necessary branch of surgery, who are taking pains to qualify themselves to practice in different parts of the country with safety and advantage to their fellow citizens.

The Doctor proposes to begin his first course as soon as a number of pupils sufficient to defray necessary expence shall apply . . .

In order to make the course more perfect, a convenient lodging is provided for the accommodation of a few poor women, who otherwise might suffer for want of the common necessaries on those occasions, to be under the care of a sober honest matron, well acquainted with lying-in women, employed by the Doctor for that purpose.[1]

2. Pennsylvania authorizes "a lying-in and foundling hospital," 1793

"An act for extending the benefits experienced from the institution of the Pennsylvania Hospital," 1791–1793 — ch. 1693, *Statutes at Large of Pennsylvania,* XIV (Harrisburg, 1909), 440.

The managers of the Hospital, reluctant to assume the financial burden of caring for pregnant women without means, did not establish a lying-in department until 1803. The new department accommodated forty patients without charge.

Be it further enacted . . . That as the relief of unfortunate women laboring in child birth and not able to provide for the expenses necessarily incident thereto, and also the misfortunes of suffering and forsaken infancy, are objects very deserving of some humane provision, it shall and may be lawful for the managers of the Pennsylvania Hospital to provide commodious apartments, for the purpose of answering the ends intended by a lying-in and foundling hospital, whenever moneys shall be placed in their hands for such a purpose, and that they are hereby authorized to call for any such sums as may now be detained for such an use, whenever they shall be in a situation to carry the benevolent design, for which such moneys were granted, into full effect, anything in the constitution or charter of the said hospital to the contrary thereof notwithstanding.

1. On July 17, 1765, "a female child of Martha Robinson a poor patient" became the first child born within the hospital. See Thomas G. Morton, *The History of the Pennsylvania Hospital, 1751–1895* (Philadelphia, 1895), p. 234.

3. Childbearing, 1795

Journal of Elizabeth Sandwith Drinker,
April 6–7, 1795, in Cecil K. Drinker, *Not
So Long Ago: A Chronicle of Medicine
and Doctors in Colonial Philadelphia*
(New York, 1937), pp. 51–52.

Elizabeth Drinker (1735–1807), wife of a
Quaker merchant, was interested in health
and disease and filled her journal with
accounts of various medical incidents. Here
she describes the labor of her eldest
daughter, Sally Downing. Dr. William
Shippen, Jr., in the custom of the day,
attended Mrs. Downing at home.

[April 6, 1795] There was a time, that if
either of my beloved children were in the situation that my dear Sally is at present, I could
not have found in my heart to have made
a memorandum; is it that as we grow in years
our feelings become blunted and callous? or
does pain and experience cause resignation?
'tis now past eleven at night my dear afflicted
child has just taken anodoyne from Dr. Shippen,
she has been all this evening in afflictive pain
'tho unprofitable, I came here yesterday afternoon, went to bed at eleven o'clock. Jacob
[Downing] call'd me up after two this morning
when I had just fallen a sleep, Sally being
rather worse, before four o'clock Jacob went for
Hannah Yerkes. After breakfast we sent for
Dr. Shippen, he felt her pulse, said he hoped
she was in a good way — he din'd with us, and
as Sally did not wish his stay, he left us, saying he would return in the evening. She continu'd in pain at times, all day, was worse
towards evening, Neighbor Waln, H. Yerkes
and sister with us — sent for the Doctor who
soon came, towards night we perceived that
all things were not right, I did not venture to
question the Doctor, but poor Sally was not
sparing in that particular — she suffer'd much
to little purpose, — when the anodoyne was

given, two opium pills, the Doctor went to lay
down, when all was quiet for a short time, but
poor Sally who instead of being compos'd grew
worse. The Doctor was call'd, when he came I
quited the room, knowing that matters must
'eer long come to a crisis, I was down stairs
in back parlor by myself an hour and half as
near as I can judge, when observing that my
dear child ceas'd her lamentation and a bustle
ensu'd — with a fluttering heart I went up
stairs, in a state of suspense, not knowing if the
child was born, or Sally in a fit, as I heard no
crying of a child. — It was mercy fully born,
the Doctor blowing in its mouth and slapping
it, it came to and cry'd. — The Doctor then
told us, that a wrong presentation had taken
place; which with poor Sally's usual difficulties
call'd for his skill more particularly; by good
management he brought on a footling labour,
which 'tho severe, has terminated by divine
favour, I trust, safely, —

[April 7, 1795] Heavy rain in the night with
some thunder and lightning — wind N.E. —
Henry Downing, the second of the name, was
born in the seventh of the fourth month, between one and two in the morning on the third
day of the week — Sally is this morning as
well as can be all things consider'd — the
effects of the anodoyne not gone off.

Problems of immigrants, 1750–1805

1. Sickness and accidents among children on immigrant ships, ca. 1750

Mittelberger, *Journey to Pennsylvania,*
pp. 14–15.

One can scarcely conceive what happens at
sea to women in childbirth and to their in-

nocent offspring. Very few escape with their lives; and mother and child, as soon as they have died, are thrown into the water. On board our ship, on a day on which we had a great storm, a woman about to give birth and unable to deliver under the circumstances, was pushed through one of the portholes into the sea because her corpse was far back in the stern and could not be brought forward to the deck.

Children between the ages of one and seven seldom survive the sea voyage; and parents must often watch their offspring suffer miserably, die, and be thrown into the ocean, from want, hunger, thirst, and the like. I myself, alas, saw such a pitiful fate overtake thirty-two children on board our vessel, all of whom were finally thrown into the sea. Their parents grieve all the more, since their children do not find repose in the earth, but are devoured by the predatory fish of the ocean. It is also worth noting that children who have not had either measles or smallpox usually get them on board the ship and for the most part perish as a result.

On one of these voyages a father often becomes infected by his wife and children, or a mother by her small children, or even both parents by their children, or sometimes whole families one by the other, so that many times numerous corpses lie on the cots next to those who are still alive, especially when contagious diseases rage on board.

Many other accidents also occur on these ships, especially falls in which people become totally crippled and can never be completely made whole again. Many also tumble into the sea.

It is not surprising that many passengers fall ill, because in addition to all the other troubles and miseries, warm food is served only three times a week, and at that is very bad, very small in quantity, and so dirty as to be hardly palatable at all. And the water distributed in these ships is often very black, thick with dirt, and full of worms. Even when very thirsty, one is almost unable to drink it without loathing. It is certainly true that at sea one would often spend a great deal of money just for one good piece of bread, or one good drink of water — not even to speak of a good glass of wine — if one could only obtain them.

---

2. Acadian children exposed to "contagious distempers" in America

George S. Brookes, *Friend Anthony Benezet* (Philadelphia, 1937), pp. 477–478.

The Acadians or French residents of Nova Scotia were forcibly displaced by the Crown at the outbreak of the Seven Years War (1755) and scattered throughout the American colonies. As foreign-speaking Catholics, their arrival was often resented. In Philadelphia, however, Benezet (1713–1784), the famous educator and anti-slavery leader, aided their settlement and prepared this memorial for them.

EXTRACT OF THE MEMORIAL TO THE KING OF GREAT BRITAIN IN BEHALF OF THE ACADIANS, DRAFTED AT THEIR REQUEST, IN THE YEAR 1760

. . . We were transported into the English colonies; and this was done in so much haste, and with so little regard to our necessities, and the tenderest ties of nature, that from the most social enjoyments and affluent circumstances, many found themselves destitute of the necessaries of life, and separated parents from children and husbands from wives, some of whom have not to this day met again. We were so crowded in the transport vessels, that we had not room even for all our bodies to lay down at once; and consequently were prevented from carrying with us proper necessaries, especially for the comfort, and support of the aged and weak; many of whom quickly ended their misery with their lives. And even those amongst us who had suffered deeply for your Majesty, on account of their attachment to your Majesty, were equally involved in the common calamity, of which Rene Lablanc, the notary public . . . is a remarkable instance.

He was seized, confined, and brought away among the rest of the people; and his family, consisting of twenty children, and about one hundred and fifty grandchildren, were scattered in different colonies, so that he was put on shore at New York with only his wife and two youngest children, in an infirm state of health, from whence he joined three more of his children at Philadelphia; where he died without any more notice being taken of him than any of us, notwithstanding his many years labour, and deep suffering for your Majesty's service.

The miseries we have since endured, are scarce sufficiently to be expressed; being reduced for a livelihood to toil and hard labour, in a southern climate, so disagreeable to our constitutions, that most of us have been prevented by sickness from procuring the necessary subsistence for our families; and therefore are threatened with that which we esteem the greatest aggravation of all our sufferings; even of having our children forced from us and bound out to strangers, and exposed to contagious distempers unknown in our native country. This compared with the affluence and ease we enjoyed, shows our condition to be extremely wretched. We have already seen in this province two hundred and fifty of our people, half the number that were landed here, perish through misery and various diseases.

---

3. Poor father seeks release of daughter from Pennsylvania Hospital, 1765

Morton, *History of Pennsylvania Hospital,* pp. 134–135.

To the Managers of the Pennsylvania Hospital

The Petition of Conrad I. Döer the Father of Mary Elizabeth Döer, a Child about 13 years of Age, a Convalescent in your Hospital.

Give me leave Gentlemen to lay before you a true State of my Case. To represent to you my deep Concern for my said Daughter and that I may endeavour to move your goodness to gratify the natural desire of a Father by restoring to him his darling Child which is now in a better Condition than when she was committed to your Charitable Care.

I embarked on board the Ship Hero with my late dear Wife and four Children. My said Wife and one Child died when we were in the Mouth of the River Maase and my unhappy Daughter was at the moment of her parting with her dear Mother seized with so violent a Grief as would not yield to any Comfort, her Mind was disturbed and she cried Day and Night etc.

In this Condition we arrived in the Port of Philadelphia, when Ralph Foster the Commander of the Ship told me she must be brought to the Hospital and that her Cure and Maintenance should not cost me a Penny, In which particular I never mistrusted the Captain As the General notion we entertain of Hospitals in Germany is that they are founded by public or private Benevolence for the relief of the poor unhappy sick and that never anything is charged to their Account, Except in the Case of Rich Pensioners whose relations sometimes agree with the Governors of such Hospitals for a better accommodation than common.

I then settled with the Owners of the Ship, all the Freight money for my poor Family was paid to them So that the Contract between the Owners of the Ship and me is entirely ended. I was bound a Servant for the Term of 3 years to . . . Patten Esq. but I agreed with my Master that I would Serve him one Year longer in Case he would suffer a little Child of mine 3 years Old to live with his Family during the Term of my Servitude.

When I lately had an Account from Philadelphia that my Daughter in the Hospital was pretty well again, I addressed my kind Master to give me leave to fetch my Child up to his House and he gave me leave that she might stay six Months at his House and I agreed with a Neighbour of my Master to maintain her till I was free. So having provided every thing for the reception of my Daughter and flattering myself how soon I would have her near me and see her daily, I came to the Philadelphia Hospital and was told that the Managers would deliver up the Girl to the Owners of the Ship who had assumed to pay for her cure and Accommodation and that these Merchants would sell her for the Charges of the Hospital. As I expect that the Captain will have forgot his Word he gave me when I gave up my Daughter to the Hospital, or put me off with an Equivocation that it will not cost me Money but that it must cost me my Daughter who is as dear to me as my own Life, As I expect no Mercy from the Merchants, who look upon poor Germans as upon other Merchandize and as the obtaining of Justice against them if they should attempt to sell my Child against my will is too expensive for a poor Stranger, All My hopes is in you Gentlemen who preside over the Contributions of a Wealthy and charitable people in this and the neighbouring Provinces.

And your petitioner humbly prayeth that you will be pleased to forgive the Cost of Curing and Maintaining my poor Child and not to commit me to an Argument with Merchants in which they might get the better of me when I being a poor Servent myself may be unable to support my natural Right to my Daughter.

And your Petitioner shall every pray.

Conrad I. Döer

---

4. Mistreatment of German redemptioners on the American ship *General Wayne*, 1805

Report of Andreas Geyer, Jr., to the Hon. H. Muhlenberg, president of the German Society of Philadelphia, April 27, 1805, "On the Conditions of German Redemptioners on Board of the American ship *General Wayne*," in Friedrich Kapp, *Immigration and the Commissioners of Emigration of the State of New York* (New York, 1870), pp. 183–186.

I went to visit those unfortunate people, and in truth they may be called unfortunate. And I must confess I have seen a number of vessels at Philadelphia with redemptioners, but never did I see such a set of miserable beings in my life. Death, to make use of the expression, appeared to be staring them in the face.

· · · · ·

They . . . set sail [from Hamburg in November 1804] and after fourteen days had elapsed the captain informed them that they would get nothing to eat except two biscuits, one pint of water, and the eighth part of a pound of meat per day. This regulation continued for two or three weeks, when they one and all declared they could not any longer exist on the small allowance they received; that they must, without doubt, perish. The hunger and thirst being at this time so great, and the children continually crying out for bread and drink, some of the men resolved, at all events, to procure bread, broke open the apartment wherein it was kept, and took some. This was discovered by the captain, as were also those who did the same, when each of them was ordered to, and actually did, receive, after being first tied, a number of lashes on their bare backs well laid on. The whole of the passengers were also punished for this offence. The men received no bread, the women but one biscuit. This continued for nine days, when the men were again allowed one biscuit per day; however, the captain would at least make or proclaim a fast day. In this situation their condition became dreadful, so much so that five and twenty men, women, and children actually perished for the want of bread . . . The hunger was so great on board that all the bones about the ship were hunted up by them, pounded with a hammer and eaten; and what is more lamentable, some of the deceased persons, not many hours before their death, crawled on their hands and feet to the captain, and begged him, for God's sake, to give them a mouthful of bread or a drop of water to keep them from perishing, but their supplications were in vain; he most obstinately refused, and thus did they perish. The cry of the children for bread was, as I am informed, so great that it would be impossible for man to describe it, nor can the passengers believe that any other person excepting Captain Conklin would be found whose heart would not have melted with compassion to hear those little inoffensive ones cry for bread. The number of passengers, when the ship arrived at Amboy, amounted to one hundred and thirty-two. Fifty-one remained there still; the others have been disposed of.

The passengers further state that they did not receive the tobacco, the fish, nor the potatoes, as they ought to have received, and which they were entitled to as by their contract with the captain, neither did they receive their dram but four or five times during their passage, and no butter after they left the British port until within three or four days ago.

Observations on insanity in
children, 1812

Benjamin Rush, *Medical Inquiries and Observations, Upon the Diseases of the Mind* (Philadelphia, 1812), pp. 51–57.

For twenty years after 1783, Rush was a member of the staff of the Pennsylvania Hospital. His book on diseases of the mind was based on his work with the insane at the Hospital.

There are severeal peculiarities which attend this disease [madness], where the predisposition to it is hereditary, which deserve our notice.

1. It is excited by more feeble causes than in persons in whom this predisposition has been acquired.

2. It generally attacks in those stages of life in which it has appeared in the patient's ancestors . . .

3. Children born previously to the attack of madness in their parents are less liable to inherit it than those who are born after it.

4. Dr. Burton, in his *Anatomy of Melancholy*, remarks, that children born of parents who are in the decline of life, are more predisposed to one of the forms of partial insanity than children born under contrary circumstances.

5. A predisposition to certain diseases seated in parts contiguous to the seat of madness, often descends from parents to their children. Thus we sometimes see madness in a son whose father or mother had been afflicted only with hysteria, or habitual head-ache. The reverse of this remark likewise sometimes takes place . . .

6. There are instances of families in which madness has existed, where the disease has passed by the understanding in their posterity, and appeared in great strength and eccentricity of the memory, and of the passions, or in great perversion of their moral faculties. Sometimes it passes by all the faculties of the mind, and appears only in the nervous system, in persons descended from deranged parents, and again we see madness in children whose parents were remarkable only for eccentricity of mind.

There are several diseases which attack the children of the same family, which did not exist in their ancestors. I have called them *filial* diseases. They are chiefly consumption and epilepsy . . .

.   .   .   .   .

Madness, it has been said, seldom occurs under puberty. To the small number of instances of it that are upon record, I shall add four more. Two boys, the one of eleven, and the other of seven years of age, were admitted into our Hospital with this disease (the latter during the time of my attendance in 1799) and both discharged cured. I have since seen an instance of it in the year 1803, in a child of two years old, that had been affected with cholera infantum; and another in a child of the same age, in the year 1808, that was affected with internal dropsy of the brain. They both discovered the countenance of madness, and they both attempted to bite, first their mothers, and afterwards their own flesh. The reason why children and persons under puberty are so rarely affected with madness must be ascribed to mental impressions, which are its most frequent cause, being too transient in their effects, from the instability of their minds, to excite their brains into permanently diseased actions . . .

Vaccination against smallpox, 1800–1813

During the first decade of the nineteenth century, vaccination, developed by Edward Jenner in the 1790's, replaced inoculation as the preventive of smallpox. Dr. Benjamin Waterhouse (1754–1846), professor of the theory and practice of medicine at Harvard, played a large part in publicizing the new method.

1. Vaccination tested on children, 1800

Benjamin Waterhouse, *A Prospect of Exterminating the Small-Pox; The History of the Kine-Pox, commonly called the Cow-Pox* (Cambridge, Mass., 1800), pp. 3–4, 18–21, 23–25.

In the beginning of the year 1799, I received from my friend Dr. Lettsom of London, a copy of Dr. Edward Jenner's "inquiry into the causes and effects of the Variolae Vaccinae, or Cow-Pox," a disease totally unknown in this quarter of the world. On perusing this work, I was struck with the unspeakable advantages that might accrue to this country, and indeed to the human race at large, from the discovery of a mild distemper that would ever after secure the constitution from that terrible scourge, the small-pox.

.   .   .   .   .

Under a serious impression of effecting a public benefit, and conceiving it, moreover, a duty in my official situation in this University, I sent to England for some of the *vaccine* or *cow-pox-matter* for trial. After several fruitless attempts, I obtained some by a short passage from Bristol, and with it I inoculated all the younger part of my family.

The first of my children that I inoculated, was a boy of five years old, named Daniel Oliver Waterhouse. I made a slight incision in the usual place for inoculation in the arm, inserted a small portion of the infected thread, and covered it with a sticking-plaster. It exhibited no other appearances than what would have arisen from any other extraneous substance, until the 6th day, when an encreased redness called forth my attention. On the 8th, he complained of pain under the inoculated arm, and on the 9th, the inoculated part exhibited evident signs of virulency. By the 10th, any one, much experienced in the inoculated small-pox, would have pronounced the arm infected. The pain and swelling under his arm went on, gradually encreasing, and by the 11th day from inoculation, his febrile symptoms were pretty strongly marked. The sore in the arm proceeded exactly as Drs. Jenner and Woodville describe, and appeared to the eye very like the second plate in Dr. Jenner's elegant publication. In short, the appearance and symptoms of this disease, in the *old* world, and in the *new,* were more completely alike than I expected . . .

The inoculated part in this boy, was surrounded by an efflorescence which extended from his shoulder to his elbow, which made it necessary to apply some remedies to lessen it; but the "symptoms," as they are called, scarcely drew him from his play more than an hour or two; and he went through the disease in so light a manner, as hardly ever to express any marks of peevishness . . .

Satisfied with the appearances and symptoms in this boy, I inoculated another of three years of age, with matter taken from his brother's arm, for he had no pustles on his body. He likewise went through the disease in a perfect and very satisfactory manner. This child pursued his amusements with as little interruption as his brother. Then I inoculated a servant boy of about 12 years of age, with some of the infected thread from England. His arm was pretty sore, and his "symptoms" pretty severe. He treated himself rather harshly by exercising unnecessarily in the garden, when the weather was extremely hot (Farht. Thermr. 96, in the shade!) and then washing his head and upper parts of his body under the pump, and setting, in short, all rules at defiance, in my absence. Nevertheless, this boy went through the disorder without any other accident than a sore throat and a stiffness of the muscles of the neck, all which soon vanished by the help of a few remedies.

.   .   .   .   .   .

From a full maturated pustle in my little boy of three years old, I inoculated his infant sister, already weaned, of one year. At the same time, and from the same pustle, I inoculated its nursery maid. They both went through the disease with equal regularity. As this woman was the first adult person on whom I had performed the operation, I was more constant in my enquiries, and more careful to note symptoms as they arose. They were very similar to those of the lighter kind from inoculation for the small-pox, viz. a slight dizziness and nausea, watery eyes, chilliness, soreness of the flesh, usually called by the common

people in this country, "bones'-ache," a general lassitude, transient pains in the region of the stomach, loins and head, with a disinclination to animal food and exercise; yet none of these symptoms were so oppressive as to diminish for a moment her attention to her little charge, whose symptoms, we conjectured, kept pace with those of its nurse.

.   .   .   .   .

Having thus traced the most important facts respecting the causes and effects of the *kine-pox* up to their source in England, and having confirmed most of them by actual experiment in America, one experiment only remained behind to complete the business. To effect this, I wrote the following letter to Dr. Aspinwall, physician to the *small-pox hospital* in the neighbourhood of Boston.

Cambridge, Aug. 2d, 1800.

Dear Doctor,

You have doubtless heard of the newly discribed disorder, known in England by the name of the *cow-pox,* which so nearly resembles the small-pox, that it is now agreed in Great-Britain, that the former will pass for the latter.

I have collected every thing that has been printed, and all the information I could procure from my correspondents, respecting this distemper, and have been so thoroughly convinced of its importance to humanity, that I have procured some of the vaccine matter, and therewith inoculated seven of my family. The inoculation has proceeded in six of them exactly as described by Woodville and Jenner; but my desire is to confirm the doctrine by having some of them inoculated by you.

I can obtain variolous matter, and inoculate them privately, but I wish to do it in the most open and public way possible. As I have imported a new distemper, I conceive that the public have a right to know exactly every step I take in it. I write this, therefore, to enquire whether you will, on philanthropic principles, try the experiment of inoculating some of my children who have already undergone the cow-pox. If you accede to my proposal, I shall consider it as an experiment in which we have co-operated for the good of our fellow-citizens, and relate it as such in the pamphlet I mean to publish on the subject.

I am &c. &c.

B.W.

Hon. William Aspinwall, Esq.
  Brookline.

To this letter the Dr. returned a polite answer, assuring me of his readiness to give any assistance in his power, to ascertain *whether the cow-pox would prevent the small-pox;* observing, that he had at that time fresh matter that he could depend on, and desiring me to send the children to the hospital for that purpose. Of the three which I offered, the Dr. chose to try the experiment on the boy of 12 years of age, mentioned in page 20, whom he inoculated in my presence by two punctures, and with matter taken that moment from a patient who had it pretty full upon him. He at the same time, inserted an infected thread, and then put him into the hospital, where was one patient with it the natural way. On the 4th day, the Dr. pronounced the *arm* to be infected. It became every hour sorer, but in a day or two it dried off, and grew well, without producing the slightest trace of a disease; so that the boy was dismissed from the hospital and returned home the 12th day after the experiment. One fact, in such cases, is worth a thousand arguments.[1]

---

2. Massachusetts vaccination law, 1810

Massachusetts, *The Cow Pox Act, with the Order of the Legislature; and a Com-*

munication, Relative to the Subject, from the Selectmen of the Town of Milton (Boston, 1810).

. . . It shall be the duty of every Town, District, or Plantation, within this Commonwealth, wherein no Board of Health shall be established by law, at their annual meeting in the months of March or April, annually, to choose in the manner in which other officers are by law chosen, three or more suitable persons, whose duty it shall be, to superintend the inoculation of the inhabitants of such Town, District, or Plantation with the Cow Pox.

.   .   .   .   .

Amongst the multiplied instances of the love of a kind Providence, none seems to be more evident, than the admirable dispensation, which has bestowed on Man, the means of a perfect security against the small pox. The nature of the benefit is so great and so simple, that no one can mistake the source . . .

To diffuse the blessing among every class of our fellow citizens appears to be an object highly desirable, and it will be found that a public inoculation of the Cow Pox, if pursued with zeal, is easy and rapid in its progress, but method will facilitate the process and render it more safe in its operation; to that effect we would wish to offer to the consideration of our fellow citizens, the propriety of the following arrangements.

.   .   .   .   .

It is therefore proposed, that in every County the inoculation should begin in the Shire, or other conveniently situated Towns, as early in June as possible, and that as soon as the people there are under the operation of the disease, the other Towns should send, for a supply of Vaccine matter, to begin their inoculation with. The month of June, appears to be peculiarly favourable for the inoculation; the state of the weather being in general steady and moderate, the inoculated would be less exposed to casual disorders, which by interfer-

---

1. Five more of my family, including three of my children, are now in Dr. Aspinwall's hospital. [Waterhouse's note.]

ing with the inoculation, might possibly impair the credit due to the Vaccine affection; it is perfectly safe, mild, and inoffensive in its operation; but the friends of Vaccination, should use every caution to secure that credit by judicious arrangements.

The inoculation from arm to arm, is more likely to take, and to produce the real disease, than when performed with dry matter; it is recommended therefore, that individuals under the operation of the disease, should volunteer to go, and transmit to their friends in the neighbouring Towns, the benefit which they have secured for themselves.

.   .   .   .   .

The Superintendants are invited to call upon every family, and use their best exertions, to persuade all that are exposed to the small pox, to attend . . . and it is presumed, that in every Town, the arrangements would be such, as to secure the Benefit at the expense of the Town, to such of the inhabitants as may be destitute.

On the day appointed for the inoculation, it is proposed, that the superintendants should make a note of the names and age of every person inoculated, with a number to it, and should give to every such person, a ticket with the corresponding number, as per form No. 2.

That they should appoint a second meeting eight days after, for the physicians to determine the result of the inoculation. That, at this second meeting, they should add to the notes first taken, the result of the inoculation of every person, and that said result should be written on the back of the respective tickets, and signed by the physician.

.   .   .   .   .

If the attainment of so great an end, as a security against the small pox, is desirable for every Town, it is equally so, that much caution should be used, to avoid being deceived into a false security. The security will depend upon using genuine Cow Pox matter, and employing physicians, who have had an opportunity to acquire a practical knowledge of the characters of the disease.

.   .   .   .   .

In the ordinary course of life, every Parent who has procured the security of his children against the small pox, by successive inoculations, cannot do otherwise than feel grateful and happy, he cannot be otherwise than an honourable object of praise and imitation; exalting is the thought of the numerous family of a Commonwealth, where not one life would be suffered to go to waste, by that dreaded Pestilence; annual inoculations in every Town would procure that happy result.

Amongst the officers which we are in the habit of electing annually in our Towns, is there any, whose trust is of equal interest to that, of those Superintendants, who would warn the Mother of the danger of her Child, who would annually contribute to the safety and welfare of the State, by preserving its inhabitants? Can any Town feel safe, without the annual appointment of such officers?

---

3. Federal law to encourage vaccination, 1813

"An act to encourage vaccination," *Annals of the Congress of the United States,* 12 Cong., 2 Sess. (1813), pp. 1336–1337.

The President of the United States . . . is hereby authorized to appoint an agent to preserve the genuine vaccine matter, and to furnish the same to any citizen of the United States, whenever it may be applied for, through the medium of the post office; and such agent shall, previous to his entering upon the execution of the duties assigned to him by this act, and before he shall be entitled to the privilege of franking any letter or package as herein allowed, take and subscribe the following oath or affirmation, before some magistrate, and cause a certificate thereof to be filed in the General Post Office: "I, A.B., do swear (or affirm, as the case may be) that I will faithfully use my best exertions to preserve the genuine vaccine matter, and to furnish the same to the citizens of the United States; and also, that I will abstain from everything prohibited in relation to the establishment of the post office of the United States." And it shall be the duty of the said agent to transmit to the several postmasters in the United States a copy of this act; and he shall also forward to them a public notice, directing how and where all application shall be made to him for vaccine matter.

. . . All letters or packages, not exceeding half an ounce in weight, containing vaccine matter, or relating to the subject of vaccination, and that alone, shall be carried by the United States' mail free of any postage, either to or from the agent who may be appointed to carry the provisions of this act into effect: *Provided always,* That the said agent, before he delivers any letter for transmission by the mail, shall, in his own proper handwriting, on the outside thereof, endorse the word "vaccination," and thereto subscribe his name, and shall previously furnish the postmaster of the office where he shall deposite the same with a specimen of his signature . . .

VI Children in Trouble

Although eighteenth-century American society continued to rely upon family government to teach the public laws as well as domestic manners, increasing numbers of young people, mostly apprentices and indentured servants, escaped this authority by fleeing to the rapidly growing seaboard towns. There they mixed anonymously with their fellows and with newly-arrived immigrants. The Puritans had warned, "Early liberty hath or may be an occasion for many evils and inconveniences," and town officials, plagued by the misdeeds of these youthful vagrants, had no reason to doubt the truth of this maxim.

Many of the children in trouble had histories of personal unhappiness prior to their emigration, often forced, from England, Ireland, and Scotland. Young felons had been transported to the plantations of Virginia and Maryland as convict servants. Lesser offenders, youthful "rogues and vagabonds" who crowded Bridewell and local jails, had been persuaded or intimidated into signing indentures for service in the colonies. Other children, innocent of any crime save that of being poor, had been gathered from city and country parishes and transported to the colonies either separately or in groups. The harsh discipline and miserable working conditions which these unwilling immigrants sometimes encountered in America disposed them to unruly behavior.

In the eighteenth century no special facilities existed for the correction or reformation of young offenders. Indeed, the concept of juvenile delinquency hardly existed. Colonial authorities recognized the inadvisability of incarcerating youths with adult criminals but they could not even afford to maintain the children, much less to establish separate institutions for them. Instead of holding delinquents in jail, town officials bound them out — in effect, sold them for their keep. Jailers attempted to collect from masters the cost of supporting their servants or apprentices. Philadelphia levied a maintenance tax to discourage masters from abandoning their incarcerated servants.

In both England and America, common law and statutory law provided young children with the greatest protection from imprisonment. Sir William Blackstone was explicit on common law safeguards: "Under seven years of age indeed an infant cannot be guilty of felony; for then a felonious discretion is almost an impossibility in nature: but at eight years old he may be guilty of felony. Also, under fourteen, though an infant shall be *prima facie* adjudged to be *doli incapax* [incapable of mischief]; yet if it appear to the court and jury, that he was *doli capax,* and could discern between good and evil, he may be convicted and suffer death." [1] Although the dictum *maleta supplet aetatem* [malice supplies the want of age] occasionally resulted in the conviction of young children, courts and juries more often exercised their discretionary power by refusing to prosecute children or by acquitting them after a nominal trial. Moreover, individual colonies statutorily exempted young children from certain punishments. In Pennsylvania, for example, only youths over sixteen could be sentenced to a public whipping for disobeying parents or masters. On the other hand, statutes and ordinances often dealt specifically with

1. Sir William Blackstone, *Commentaries on the Laws of England,* IV (London, 1795), 23.

307

childish offenses such as sledding on the Sabbath or playing ball on public thoroughfares.

Common law and statutory safeguards and sympathetic judges and juries were only partially successful in preventing the imprisonment of juvenile offenders. Even after 1800 there were instances of children under fourteen years of age convicted of felonies and sentenced to penitentiaries. The Society for the Prevention of Pauperism in the City of New York, established in 1817, called attention to "those unfortunate children from 10 to 18 years of age, who from neglect of parents, from idleness and misfortune, have . . . contravened some penal statute without reflecting on the consequences, and for a hasty violation, been doomed to the penitentiary by the condemnation of the law." [2] As in the colonial period, the continuous and chaotic growth of urban areas exacerbated this problem. By 1820, however, state or municipal plans for reforming delinquent children had yet to be formulated.

Runaway servants and apprentices in — or escaped from — jails

1. Convict servant lad, Philadelphia, 1752

Pennsylvania Gazette, Sept. 14, 1752.

Made his escape from Patrick Hamilton, on Sunday night last Florence M'Carty, a convict servant lad, who was taken out of Trenton gaol, and belongs to John Flannigan, in Cecil county, Maryland, and was going home; he is of a middle size, pale complexion, wears a cap, and a lock of hair behind, has light grey eyes; has two green jackets on, one of good cloth, white trousers, thread stockings and pumps,

with large carved pewter buckles. Any body that will secure him in any gaol, and give notice to James Whitehead, keeper of the work-house, in Philadelphia, so as he may be had again, shall have Three Pounds reward, and if brought to him, all charges, paid by

James Whitehead.

2. An iron collar about his neck

Pennsylvania Journal, Dec. 26, 1752, in William Nelson, ed., *Documents Relating to the Colonial History of the State of New Jersey,* XIX (Paterson, 1897), 229.

Chester, December 18, 1752.

Run aways in Chester county gaol, Viz. Andrew Dun, born in Ireland, as he says; he was bought by one Joshua Roberts, in West New Jersey, and sold by the said Roberts to one William Walker, in Northampton township, Burlington province aforesaid. Thomas Wood, an English man, 19 years of age, a short set fellow, about 5 feet 5 inches high, swarthy complexion, pretends to be a sailor. Had on when committed, an iron collar, about his neck; brought with him a brown gelding, and says his master's name is John Smith, and lives in Maryland, within four miles of Patapsco. John Simmonds, born in England, in the city of Norwich, 20 years of age, of a sandy complexion, and says he runaway from John Boham, in Lancaster county, Brickmaker by trade. David Greenwood, about 60 years of age, born in England, and speaks broad English, a weaver by trade, a lusty, big-boned man, and says he has been in the country 11 years, but will not give any account where he lived, or from whence he came.

These are to desire the owners to come and pay the charges, otherwise they will be sold out for their keeping.

William Hay, Gaol Keeper.

2. Society for the Prevention of Pauperism in the City of New York, *Second Annual Report, 1819* (New York, 1820), p. 32.

3. Run-a-way or disorderly apprentices maintained in jail at master's expense

"Rules, Orders and Regulations, for the Gaol, of the City and County of Philadelphia," in Caleb Lownes, *An Account of the Alteration and Present State of the Penal Laws of Pennsylvania* . . . (Boston, 1799), p. 32.

Runaway or disorderly apprentices and servants shall be separately fed, lodged, and employed, and the keeper shall give notice to their masters or mistresses, at the time of their commitment, of the charge that will accrue for their daily maintenance, who may at their option agree to pay the same, or provide the necessary food themselves.

A thirteen-year-old girl tried for murder, 1806

State *v.* Mary Doherty, 2 Overton's Tenn. Reports 80 (1806).

The grand jury having found a true bill for the murder of her father, lately resident in Hawkins county, —

On Saturday she was brought to the bar, and appeared to be between twelve and thirteen years of age. Upon being arraigned, she stood mute. The Court assigned attorneys Grey and Powel as her counsel, being poor, and without friends or relations to assist her.

After this assignment of counsel, she was remanded.

The Monday following she was again brought to the bar, and again stood mute. The Court directed a jury to be impanelled and sworn in the following manner: —

"You swear that you will well and truly inquire whether the person at the bar, Mary Doherty, stands mute through malice or the visitation of God."

Mr. Beaty, a witness, was called, who de-posed that he had lived about a mile from the deceased Michael Doherty. Had known the girl about three years, and she always appeared to have common sense. Had heard her talk frequently as other people, was in the jail to see her last week, and spoke to her, and particularly respecting her brothers and sisters.

Several other persons then spoke to her, but she made no answer, and appeared to be senseless.

Her eyes appeared to be nearly closed, and, whilst speaking to her, saw no difference in her manner. M. Shiply lived close to where the deceased resided. The last time he saw the prisoner was when she was arrested and taken from home; she talked more that day than he ever heard her, for she usually did not talk much.

He always believed she could talk as well as others until lately. He was in the jail this day week, talked to her, but saw no sign of understanding nor alteration in her countenance. Mr. Patten, the jailer, heard her speak three or four times, soon after she came, but they were the monosyllables *yes* or *no;* had not heard her speak for eight weeks; she had been in jail about four months, three months of the time he had acted as jailer. When he first had the care of her, he endeavored to get her to eat for several days, but without effect; he left the victuals with her, after being afraid that she would perish.

The victuals left were gone, though he cannot say that she ate them, but supposes she did. She seems to have been insane ever since her being in jail, about four months.

He told her to change her clothes and to sweep the jail, and found it done afterwards, though he has once or twice known the jail swept without telling.

She lay on a bed of straw, and he always found her on her right side, covered with a blanket, in the hottest weather.

She did not discover any uneasiness from confinement. He always had to raise her up; she has not swept the jail for two or three weeks.

He often made efforts to get her to speak himself, and many others in his presence, but all without effect.

When he heard her speak, it was to a black girl of Mr. M'Allister. Had lately seen the negro girl try to get her to speak, but she did not. At another time he heard her speak; it was when Mr. Fane was in the jail. Mr. Fane told her he was to stay in jail with her, and asked her if she would give him her blanket; she answered no.

This morning her brother went into jail, and spoke to her, but saw no alteration in her countenance. Her eyes are, as you usually see them, nearly closed, and I do not recollect to have seen her wink them.

Mr. Fane heard her speak six or eight weeks before, once or twice; had been in the jail several times, but she did not speak.

Mr. Long, the former jailer, kept the jail about thirty days; during that time never heard her speak but once, and that was to the negro girl of Mr. M'Allister. He was in the jail once or twice every day, and at first she did not eat any thing without force. He thought she would perish with hunger. During his care of her, he never saw the least alteration in her looks; her eyes were always closed. When he went into jail he always found her lying. He tried frequently to get her to speak by persuasion and threats, but never could. Once he saw her smile when the black girl was dressing her.

.   .   .   .   .

After a short retirement, the jury returned, and found that the defendant was mute by the visitation of God; upon which the Court ordered the pleas of not guilty to be entered for her.

Being late in the evening, and it appearing to the Court that the defendant would neither eat nor drink when any person was near, they ordered her to be remanded, and brought out next day for trial.

On Tuesday she was brought to the bar, and put on trial on the plea of not guilty.

.   .   .   .   .

Mr. Beaty was sworn in chief. He did not know the age of the prisoner, but supposed she was about thirteen years of age, or perhaps more. Was told by a person that the deceased was missing four nights and four days; believed he was dead; with another man he went to his house, and all over the plantation, supposing that he was dead somewhere about it, as he was subject to intoxication. Inquired of the children, of whom the oldest was the defendant. He proposed to stay with the children all night, as they might be afraid. The defendant answered that she had stayed before, and was not afraid. The house the old man lived in was built of logs, and raised a small distance from the ground; when standing on the outside of the house with several others, he by chance descried something under the house. Upon raising a puncheon of the floor on the inside, the deceased was found under the floor dead. He then made the following observation to the prisoner, Mary Doherty. "Now you knew this." She answered, "Beaty, you lie." He went for the coroner, and was upon the inquest. He saw blood upon an axe that was found upon the bed and wall of the house, near the head of the bed, and on a wheelbarrow.

The axe appeared to have been washed, but there was some in the eye of it. The deceased had blood on his shirt and about his head. The bed appeared to have been washed, but the blood was still to be seen. The house floor had been washed, but there was the stain of blood plainly to be seen on it, between the bed and where the deceased was found, which was five or six feet.

The prisoner said the last time she saw her father was four days before that, and about 150 yards from the house; this was before he was found.

Knowing that the deceased usually wore a greatcoat, he asked the prisoner where it was; she answered, "You need not care." He told her that he wanted to see it; she then went to the bed where the deceased was supposed to have been murdered, and got it from thence, gave it to him, saying, "There, I suppose you are satisfied." The prisoner did not discover any concern when her father was found, nor when she was examined before the coroner, and looked and talked with a great deal of assurance.

The family of the deceased consisted of the prisoner, the little boy who had been offered as a witness in court, and two other younger children. He had lost his wife. Never saw the prisoner except once off the plantation, and never saw any of the family at a place of worship.

The deceased was found a few days before the 13th or 14th of April, when the coroner's inquest was held. He never saw the prisoner employed except once or twice, and then she was providing some victuals, nor did she ever go to school.

The house of the deceased was not much resorted to; they lived to themselves principally; did not know whether the prisoner was accustomed to converse with other children in the neighborhood or not. As to any difference in the understanding of the boy and the prisoner he had not observed. The other children were present when the body was found, and none of them appeared to be alarmed in the smallest degree. When found, the deceased looked as if he had been dead several days; the side of his head looked black, as if it had been bruised, but did not know whether his skull was broken or not. He had seen the deceased a few days before his death, going, by his house, home.

There was not any thing remarkable in the character of the deceased, nor did he know any thing of the conduct of the deceased to his family. He never saw him intoxicated at his own house; and always thought the prisoner possessed as much understanding as common. Of this he judged from her answers to questions he had asked her; but when he was there, which was frequently the case, she did not appear to be employed as girls of her age usually are. At the inquest, she did not say any thing from which he could collect an idea that

she was sensible of the atrocity of the crime committed.

John Miller was sworn. He was one of the inquest. Beside the several things stated by Mr. Beaty, he observed that when the deceased was taken from under the floor the right side of his head was cut, and on the other side his skull was broken, from which blood flowed; saw the blood on the chairs, on the floor, on his clothes, and against the wall at the head of the bed, where he supposed it to have sprinkled.

At the inquest, the prisoner was tied with some tow strings, and appeared to be hurt.

There was a parcel of old women pushing her about, and sometimes reviling her; he loosed her, took her to a branch, and told her to wash herself, as she was extremely dirty. He then talked to her familiarly, upon which she began to shed tears.

As she had been beaten and hauled about by several who were there, he pitied her, and told her she must not run away, to stay with him, and no person should injure her, nor should she be served in the manner she had been any more.

Having thus used persuasion with her, he told her she must tell him. The counsel for the prisoner objected, that no confession obtained from the prisoner by hope or fear should be given in evidence against her, and it was manifest that whatever she did tell this witness must have been extorted from her by an irresistible impulse, arising from the hope of better treatment.

The witness being asked if he did not believe this to be the case, he acknowledged he did.

.   .   .   .   .

John Sheflet, a witness for the State, deposed to many of the facts stated by Mr. Miller. He believed the deceased to have been murdered, heard a number of persons examine the defendant, but she constantly denied knowing any thing about the death of her father.

There appeared to be a difference in her countenance when her father was found. She appeared to be scared; had been acquainted with the family about three years, and lived a near neighbor. He never saw her at work nor ever abroad.

She appeared to be of an obstinate disposition.

He stayed all night at the house after the body was found. She did not discover any disposition to make her escape, though she might have done so.

The deceased was at his house, and was telling him that this girl and two of his children had run away, and then stated the ages of his children; but did not recollect them.

The prisoner was tied early in the morning, and remained so until the inquest.

White, J., stated to the jury the circumstances that were necessary to constitute murder. Their inquiry was, whether the prisoner was the person who took the life of the deceased, and, if they were of that opinion, to inquire whether it were done with malice aforethought.

From the circumstances appearing, there seemed to be no doubt as to malice, except what had been attempted on the ground of the tender years of the prisoner. Neither argument nor authority had been introduced on this point. He stated what he conceived to be the law on this point, and, if incorrect, should be glad to be corrected from any quarter.

If a person of fourteen years of age does an act, such as stated in this indictment, the presumption of the law is that the person is *doli capax*. If under fourteen and not less than seven, the presumption of law is that the person cannot discern between right and wrong. But this presumption is removed, if from the circumstances it appears that the person discovered a consciousness of wrong. The jury retired, and, after being absent a few hours, returned a verdict *not guilty*.[1]

1. Overton reported (pp. 88–89) that one day after the trial Mary Doherty was observed sitting on the courthouse steps. "Her eyes were open, clear, animated, and emitted striking sensations of complacency."

Children in jail and on trial, New York City, 1812–1820

1. The case of Little Tom, 1812

State Prison Record Book, John Stanford Papers, New York Historical Society, New York City.

John Stanford (1754–1834) was the first chaplain to visit regularly the public charitable and penal institutions of New York City.

The Case of T———s C———d: This unfortunate youth sad to relate is said to have been nursed upon the lap of vice, by his own parent and eventually committed that offence which brought him to the State Prison, when he was only twelve years of age. He was entirely unacquainted with the first rudiments of learning; but through the benevolence of the head keeper the unfortunate youth being favoured with an evening school, little Tom, for so they called him, was indulged with this privilege, and made a very rapid progress. His application to the trade assigned him was such that he was able to turn out more work than his companions. His conduct was so discreet that he gained the attention of the head keeper as that of his fellow prisoners.

In the month of June 1812 Tom was seized with a sore throat, and an affection of the lungs. In this state I found him, in the prison hospital; with tenderness & faithfulness I conversed with him, on the great necessity of pardon and peace with God. He could scarce speak, but said, "Yes, Sir, I know it." When I visited him again, though I gave him my best advice, he was unable to speak; but the tears which flowed from his eyes spoke the impression of his heart. Every effort was used; all were interested to recover little Tom. Mr. K. being convinced that the boy could not long survive, in a tender manner intimated his approaching end. Tom said he was willing to die; he then asked him if he wished to see his mother. At first he declined, but afterwards consented. The next day, his mother, if such may be called, with his little sister came. The mother indifferently asked him how he did, and immediately turned aside to some of the men prisoners indulging [in] improper language. Returning again to Tom's bed, to bid him good bye, the little girl got upon his bed to kiss her brother. The hypocritical mother condescended to embrace him also. Tom said to her, "Mother can you not get me away from here, perhaps I may then get well." The monster of a woman half intoxicated immediately replied, "No Tom, you will not get out till you are carried out in the cold meat box." This it was supposed by the bye standers to mean his coffin. This was told me by those who heard her.

The next day, Sunday morning when I entered the Chapel to perform service, the prisoner who took the lead in singing stopped me at the foot of the pulpit stairs, and said, "Sir, little Tom is dead. Please to remember the occurence in your prayer; it may produce some impression upon the people." I did so. In the interval of worship Mr. R. expressed his regret on the loss of the boy, as there was a great prospect of his becoming a useful member of society. I said had I known this event I would have provided a suitable discourse for the afternoon. Mr. R. suggested that I might yet accomplish it. I therefore went aside; and formed a Sermon on Eccls. 12.4, which with much emotion of heart I delivered; [I] gave a short narrative of poor Tom, and made suitable addresses, particularly of the young prisoners.

---

2. Suspended sentence for a young girl, 1816

Daniel Rogers, comp., *The New York City-Hall Recorder for the Year 1816* (New York, 1817), p. 6.

The prisoner, a young female, was indicted for Grand Larceny, in stealing a pocket-book containing 140 dollars, the property of Nathaniel Hopping. It appeared, that a few days before the trial, Hopping, who is a married man, came from New-Jersey about 8 o'clock in the evening, and with another countryman, went to the house of Mrs. Daniel, at the corner of Cherry and Walnut-streets. The prisoner, with others, was dancing; and on the appearance of Hopping, she manifested much fondness towards him, and (as he expressed it) hung round him. He joined in the dance, and in the course of the evening, called for some gin and treated the prisoner. She absented herself; and Hopping went out of the door and saw her, when she fled from him. In a short time after, he missed his pocket-book, which he carried in the side-pocket of his coat. He could not find her that night. The next day he called on her, with a friend, when she begged of them not to carry her to Bridewell, and she would restore the money. She paid back twenty-eight dollars, and said she had lost the pocket-book.

It appeared that she paid several debts the same evening that she was with Hopping; the principal one of which was a debt of thirty-one dollars due Mrs. Daniel.

Price contended, that there was not sufficient evidence of an actual felonious taking in this case to constitute the offence. No doubt she found the pocket-book on the floor: the prosecuter, perhaps, in *hopping* about right merrily at the sound of the viol, with these Cyprian damsels, dropped it inadvertently. The circumstance of paying her debts rather operated in her favour. She did no more than what every *honest* girl ought to do.

Hamilton contra.

The Jurors immediately pronounced her *Guilty,* but recommended her to mercy, by reason of her youth.

Her sentence was suspended until the next Term.

3. Seven-year-old boy acquitted, 1820

Daniel Rogers, comp., *The New York City-Hall Recorder for the Year 1820* (New York, 1821), pp. 137–138.

The prisoner, a boy, was indicted with another named Byrnes, for petit larceny, in stealing ten pounds of copper bolts, the property of Robert M'Queen and Alexander M. Muir, on the 8th of October.

It appeared, that the prisoner carried the goods to the grocery of George M'Pherson, to whom he sold it.

The mother of the boy, being sworn in his favour, testified, that he was but a few weeks more than seven years of age; and that, in consequence of falling on his head, his senses were impaired.

No evidence was offered on the part of the prosecutor to show the boy's capacity.

Wilson submitted to the Court, that as a child of seven was held incapable of crime, and between that age and fourteen it was necessary to show his capacity; and that, in proportion as he approached to seven, the inference in his favour was the greater, and as he approached to fourteen the less, that there was not sufficient evidence in this case to support the prosecution, especially as strong evidence of incapacity had been produced on his part.

Upon this principle, the Mayor charged the Jury, who immediately acquitted the prisoner.

4. Children between seven and fourteen convicted and sentenced to state prison, 1820

Rogers, comp., *New York City-Hall Recorder for 1820*, pp. 177–178.

The prisoners were all infants, between seven and fourteen years of age. The one first named was indicted for a grand larceny, in stealing a lady's dressing box, containing several pair of pearl ear-rings, a necklace, a breast-pin, and other valuable articles of jewelry, of the value of $150, the property of George Hearsey, on the 25th of November last; and the other prisoners were indicted for petit larceny, in stealing a bearskin, the property of Charles Dickinson, on the 31st of December last.

On the traverse of the first mentioned indictment, it appeared from the testimony of Eliza Hearsey, the lady of George Hearsey, that on the day laid in the indictment, she saw the prisoner going out of the entry of the house with the box, which was taken from her bedchamber, under his arm, endeavouring to escape out of the back door; and, when she seized him, for the purpose of getting away the box, he tried to bite her, and retain it by force. He cried, and alleged that another boy had told him to take it away. He told the lady that he was eight years old.

There was no other evidence of capacity offered; and, after the remarks of the respective counsel, the Mayor charged the Jury, that with regard to an infant, between the age of seven and fourteen, the Jury should be satisfied that he had a capacity of knowing good from evil. And proof of this may be given either by extrinsic testimony, or it may arise from the circumstances of the case. In this case, the fact of concealment, and of an attempt to escape, appear; and it will rest with the Jury to determine, whether this boy did not know, at the time he stole this property, that he was doing wrong.

He was convicted, and sentenced to the state prison three years.

On the traverse of the other indictment, it appeared by the testimony of Charles Dickinson, that the bearskin was stolen out of his stable, and concealed in an oven in an adjoining yard. He did not see the property in possession of the prisoners; but, in a short time after it was stolen, the prisoners were brought to his house, and, on his threatening that if they did not confess the fact, he would send them to Bridewell, they acknowledged that they stole it, and concealed it in the oven where it was found. One of the boys accused the others of inducing him to commit the theft, and they were all detained in the prosecutor's yard, until Azel Conklin was sent for, to whom they made a similar confession; and, on being carried into the police-office the next morning, made an ample confession before one of the magistrates.

David Graham addressed the Jury on behalf of the prisoners, and insisted, that the confession made to Mr. Dickinson, being made under the influence of threats, influenced those made subsequently; and, therefore, the whole ought to be rejected.

Van Wyck, contra.

The Mayor charged the Jury, that if they believed that the confession made in the police was influenced by that previously made to the prosecutor, it ought to be rejected; but the Mayor thought that this confession ought to be considered as standing on a different ground from the confessions made to the prosecutor, and afterwards to the officer. The confession made in the police was on the next day, and no threats are ever used there to extort a confession. But, in this case, there is fact independent of any confession.

The property was found concealed in an oven, where the prisoners acknowledged it to be. This is good evidence.

Kellet, on being arraigned, pleaded guilty; and the others were convicted by the Jury, and the whole sentenced to the penitentiary three years.

VII Negro and Indian Children

The encounter between white society and nonwhite children — Negro and Indian — became more acute during the eighteenth century. Slave or free, the child of nonwhite parents was reared in a different way from the free white child, and the way in which the state and the organized community impinged upon his young life was dissimilar. Shifts in the magnitude and distribution of the population help to explain some of the changes in law and custom. The numbers of both black slaves and freemen increased dramatically throughout the eighteenth century. In 1700 there were approximately twenty-five thousand Negro slaves, or about one in every ten inhabitants. When the War for Independence broke out seventy-five years later, there were about five hundred thousand slaves, or one Negro in every five inhabitants, a proportion that has not since been equaled. In South Carolina at the time of the Revolution over two-thirds of the population was black. Whereas southern farmers had previously relied on their own families and servants for cheap, unskilled labor, the wealthier among them increasingly turned to black workers from Africa.

Owing to several causes, there was a small number of free Negroes in the American colonies. Released from slavery as a reward for services, or allowed to purchase their freedom, they might be found scattered throughout colonial towns engaged in trades and common labor. A large addition to their ranks resulted from the War for Independence. Some blacks earned freedom through service in the armies; others obtained it on the basis of the principles of natural right and human equality that justified the war. In Massachusetts, suits for freedom were brought by slaves, the best known being the case of Quok Walker in 1783, on the grounds that slavery was incompatible with the protection of individual rights in the new state constitution.[1] By 1790 the federal census in Massachusetts failed to report any slaves still in the state. The movement of the northern economy toward trade and even manufacturing made emancipation seem economically advantageous. One after another, northern states made provision for the freedom of slaves. In most instances a scheme for the gradual abolition of slavery was adopted, granting freedom as the children of slaves reached a stipulated age; in some states the mechanism was so slow in its operation that a few slaves were to be found in northern states on the eve of the Civil War itself.

Gradual emancipation plans, such as Pennsylvania's, the first to be enacted by one of the original thirteen colonies, freed the next generation rather than the present one. In fixing a legal status for black children, northern legislators followed the model of bond servitude, making some alterations. For example, the period in which a Negro child could be held in servitude before becoming entirely free was longer than was customary for whites who were bound out as servants in infancy or childhood. Rarely did legislators provide any special protection or assume new obligations in behalf of Negro children; it was even more rare for them to keep promises. In Rhode Island, for example, where the emancipation statute obligated towns to supply an elementary

1. See Arthur Zilversmit, *The First Emancipations: The Abolition of Slavery in the North* (Chicago, 1967), pp. 112–116.

education to free black children, many grew up without schooling. Private schools were the principal recourse for black children since the states and other governing agencies assumed no consistent policy of support. Religious societies with an interest in their education continued to maintain schools. Anthony Benezet, the Philadelphia Quaker, taught Negro students until his death in 1784. The Philadelphia Society for Free Instruction of Colored People, founded five years later, encouraged and coordinated Quaker instruction of black children in Baltimore, Providence, Newport, and Burlington, New Jersey.[2] The manumission societies of northern towns and states characteristically turned to education once emancipation statutes had been enacted. These philanthropic organizations, ordinarily led by influential and capable white citizens, sometimes succeeded in obtaining intermittent public support for their schools. In addition, black parents, despite limits on their resources, participated in the founding of schools for their children. In Washington, D.C., as in Philadelphia and even some southern cities and towns, such as New Orleans and Charleston, they contributed money and time to the instruction of black children. Even with these efforts probably most free black children grew up without formal instruction. The magnitude of the task far exceeded the resources that were devoted to it.

Following emancipation in the North most Negro children were still slaves. The federal census of 1820, the first to record the nation's black population by age, listed 763,747 blacks under fourteen years; of this number only 93,551 were free while 670,196 were in slavery. The conditions of life for these children as well as adult slaves varied enormously by place, kind of work, and master. No simple generalization covers all cases. Masters had virtually complete legal authority. Willful murder could be punished, provided there were white witnesses willing to testify, but short of

murder a master could do almost anything to his slave. On the other hand, masters were subject to internal ethical, religious, and economic restraints on their behavior, and they had to face the fact that slaves might respond to mistreatment with slow-downs, sabotage, or flight. Between these two poles lay a vast arena of conflict in which masters contended with the dilemmas of interest versus conscience and slaves sought the means of preserving life and a measure of comfort and dignity as best they could. The situation of slave families amply illustrates the insecurity of personal relationships. In a legal sense the slave family did not exist. Although marriage was sometimes sanctified by a religious ceremony and respected by slaves themselves, it was not protected by the bonds of the law. In the eighteenth century masters could sunder husband and wife, parents and children, as they wished. Some whites acknowledged the humanity of slaves and their capacity for feeling by assisting them in maintaining the forms of family life. A kindly judge might prevent separate sale of a slave mother and her children to satisfy the debts of a deceased master or to facilitate the division of property among heirs. Such instances were exceptional although not altogether rare. In general, slaves of the same family were kept together or divided as the interests of the master dictated.

Before the eighteenth century the slave population was so small that its education presented few sustained issues for decision. Missionaries here and there had tried to supply that small amount of training required for conversion to Christianity. This might consist of no more than memorization of a simple catechism although some missionaries tried to instruct slave children in the rudiments of reading and writing. Despite the fact that it touched relatively few, the education of slaves raised serious questions for masters. If educated slaves accepted Christianity, did they then acquire a claim to freedom? If slaves assembled to learn to read and write, would not rebellion be encouraged? If they gained even a small amount

2. Winthrop D. Jordan, *White Over Black: American Attitudes Toward the Negro, 1550–1812* (Chapel Hill, 1968), pp. 356–359.

of learning, would not enhanced self-esteem lead them to scorn field and domestic labor? The answers given to these questions tended to curtail opportunities for the education of slaves. Although the ancient idea that acceptance of Christianity was incompatible with the status of a slave was struck down by both colonial and imperial authority, the education of slaves found little encouragement in other ways. As the number of slaves in the southern colonies increased, their lives were hedged with restrictions designed to maintain white power. Missionaries still kept schools for slaves but the trend in southern colonies was directed against any kind of education. The first assembly action came in 1740 in South Carolina. A wave of fear swept that colony following the Stono rebellion in which a band of perhaps one hundred slaves had risen, killed some whites, and set out for Spanish Florida for refuge before they were headed off and rounded up by the militia. Severe measures were adopted by the assembly to prevent a recurrence, including a law making it a crime to teach a slave to write. The same law, with a lesser penalty, was enacted in Georgia in 1770, and in South Carolina, following another rebellion scare in 1800, meetings of slaves "for the purpose of mental instruction in a confined or secret place" were outlawed.[3] For the time being, these laws were not imitated in other slave states and even in South Carolina and Georgia they were not ordinarily enforced. Conscientious masters, missionaries, free Ne-

3. Joseph Brevard, ed., *An Alphabetical Digest of the Public Statute Law of South Carolina* (Charleston, 1814), II, 254.

groes, and other patrons of slaves taught many to read and write, and in other colonies the provision of elementary education for slaves was not uncommon. Nevertheless, the laws of 1740 and 1800 suggested a willingness to keep slave children in utter ignorance if that was deemed necessary for the security of whites.

Education occasioned few contacts between Indian children and whites in the eighteenth century. Some missionary organizations, like the Society for the Propagation of the Gospel, continued their efforts. John Eliot had his successors in David Brainerd and Eleazar Wheelock, and in the Southwest Spanish Catholic padres built churches at mission stations where Indians worshipped and worked. The main thrust in relations between whites and Indians, however, ran counter to the peaceful pursuits of the church and the school. A long and devastating series of colonial and national wars, at first between the English colonists and the French, later between the Americans and the British in Canada, drew Indian tribes into diplomatic and military alliances that worked against the presence of missionaries and schoolmasters among them. Not until the conclusion of frontier wars with the American victory over the northwest tribes in the War of 1812 was a peaceful status established sufficient to encourage sustained missionary and educational endeavors. In the eighteenth century, with a few exceptions such as Eleazar Wheelock's Indian school in Connecticut and later New Hampshire, the principal modes of contact and influence between whites and Indians, including children, were trade and warfare.

A. INDIAN CHILDREN IN SCHOOLS AND MISSIONS

Schools

1. A plan for training Indian youth as teachers and missionaries to their people, 1763

Eleazar Wheelock, *A Plain and Faithful Narrative of the Original Design, Rise, Progress and present State of the Indian Charity–School at Lebanon, in Connecticut* (Boston, 1763), pp. 9–29.

Wheelock (1711–1779), a Congregationalist minister, opened a school for Indians in 1754. Disappointed with the results of his work in Connecticut, he obtained a charter from Governor John Wentworth of New Hampshire in 1769 and transferred the school to that colony where it became Dartmouth College.

Understanding there are numbers of religious and charitably disposed persons, who only wait to know where their charities may be bestowed in the best manner for the advancement of the kingdom of the great Redeemer; and supposing there may also be in some, evil surmisings about, and a disposition to discredit a cause which they don't love, and have no disposition to promote; I have, to gratify the one, and prevent the mischiefs of the other, thought it my duty to give the publick a short, plain, and faithful narrative of the original design, rise, progress, and present state of the Charity-School here, called *Moor's Indian-Charity School, etc.*

.   .   .   .   .   .

And as there were few or none who seemed so much to lay the necessity and importance of the case to heart, as to exert themselves in earnest, and lead the way therein, I was naturally put upon consideration and enquiry what methods might have the greatest probability of success; and upon the whole was fully perswaded that this, which I have been pursuing, had by far the greatest probability of any that had been proposed, viz. by the mission of their own sons in conjunction with the *English;* and that a number of girls should also be instructed in whatever should be necessary to render them fit to perform the female part, as house-wives, school-mistresses, tayloresses, etc. and to go and be with these youth, when they shall be hundreds of miles distant from the *English* on the business of their mission: And prevent a necessity of their turning savage in their manner of living, for want of those who may do those offices for them, and by this means support the reputation of their mission, and also recommend to the savages a more rational and decent manner of living, than that which they are in — and thereby, in time, remedy and remove that great, and hitherto insuperable difficulty, so constantly complained of by all our missionaries among them, as the great impediment in the way to the success of their mission, viz. their continual rambling about; which they can't avoid so long as they depend so much upon fishing, fowling, and hunting for their support. And I am more and more perswaded, that I have sufficient and unanswerable reasons to justify this plan.

As,

1. The deep rooted prejudices they have so generally imbibed against the *English,* that they are selfish, and have secret designs to incroch upon their lands, or otherwise wrong them in their interests. This jealousy seems to have been occasioned, nourished, and confirmed by some of their neighbours, who have got large tracts of their lands for a very inconsiderable

part of their true value, and, it is commonly said, by taking the advantage of them when they were intoxicated with liquor. And also, by unrighteous dealers, who have taken such advantage to buy their skins and furrs at less than half price, etc. And perhaps these jealousies may be, not a little, increased by a conciousness of their own perfidy and inhumanity towards the *English*. And it seems there is no way to avoid the bad influence and effects of these prejudices, at present, unless it be by the mission of their own sons . . .

2. An *Indian* missionary may be supported with less than half the expence, that will be necessary to support an *Englishman,* who can't conform to their manner of living, and who will have no dependence upon them for any part of it. And an *Indian* who speaks their language, it may reasonably be supposed, will be at least four times as serviceable among them, supposing he be otherwise equally qualified as one who can communicate to or receive nothing from them, but by an interpreter: He may improve all opportunities not only in public, but, "when he sits in the house, walks by the way, when he lies down, and when he rises up:" And speak with as much life and spirit as the nature and importance of the matter require, which is very much lost when communicated by an interpreter.

3. Indian missionaries may be supposed better to understand the tempers and customs of *Indians,* and more readily to conform to them in a thousand things than the *English* can; and in things wherein the nonconformity of the *English* may cause disgust, and be construed as the fruit of pride, and an evidence and expression of their scorn and disrespect.

4. The influence of their own sons among them will likely be much greater than of any *Englishman* whatsoever. They will look upon such an one as one of them, his interest the same with theirs; and will naturally esteem him as an honour to their nation, and be more likely to submit patiently to his instructions and reproofs than to any English missionary . . .

5. The acquaintance and friendship which

Indian boys from different and distant tribes and places, will contract and cultivate, while together at school, may, and if they are zealously affected will, be improved much for the advantage and furtherance of the design of their mission; while they send to, hear from, or visit one another, confirming the things which have been spoken . . .

6. Indian missionaries will not disdain to own English ones, who shall be associated with them (where the *English* can be introduced) as elder brethren; nor scorn to be advised or reproved, counselled or conducted by them; especially so long as they shall be so much dependent upon the *English* for their support; which will likely be till God has made them his people; and then, likely, they will not stand in such need of *English* guides and counsellors . . .

7. In this school, children of different nations may, and easily will learn one another's language, and English youth may learn of them; and so save the best expence and trouble of interpreters; and their ministry be much more acceptable and edifying to the *Indians.*

8. There is no such thing as sending *English* missionaries, or setting up and maintaining *English* schools to any good purpose, in most places among them, as their temper, state and condition have been and still are . . . There is no such thing at present as introducing either *English* schoolmasters or missionaries to continue with them; such are their prejudices in general, and such the malevolent, and ungovernable temper of some, that none but an Indian would dare venture his life among them.

And besides all this, they are so extremely poor, and depend so much upon hunting for a livelihood, that they are in no capacity to support their children at school, if their disposition for it were ever so good.

· · · · ·

9. There are very few or no interpreters, who are suitable and well-accomplished for the business, to be had . . . How many na-

tions are there for whom there is no interpreter at all, except, it may be, some ignorant and perhaps vicious person, who has been their captive, and whom it is utterly unsafe to trust in matters of such eternal consequence. And how shall this difficulty be remedied? . . .

When, and as soon as the method proposed by the Rev'd. Mess. *Sergeant* and *Brainerd,* can be put into execution, viz. to have land appropriated to the use of *Indian* schools, and prudent skilful farmers, or tradesmen, to lead and instruct the boys, and mistresses to instruct the girls in such manufactures as are proper for them, at certain hours, as a diversion from their school exercises, and the children taken quite away from their parents, and the pernicious influence of *Indian* examples, there may be some good prospect of great advantage by schools among them.

And must it be esteemed a wild imagination, if it be supposed that well-instructed, sober, religious *Indians,* may with special advantage be employed as masters and mistresses in such schools; and that the design will be much recommended to the Indians thereby; and that there may be special advantage by such, serving as occasional interpreters for visitors from different nations from time to time; and they hereby receive the fullest conviction of the sincerity of our intentions and be confirmed and established in friendly sentiments of us; and encouraged to send their children, etc.?

I am fully perswaded from the acquaintance I have had with them, it will be found, whenever the trial shall be made, to be very difficult if not impossible, unless the arm of the Lord should be revealed in an eminent manner, to cure them of such savage and sordid practices, as they have been inured to from their mother's womb, and form their minds and manners to proper rules of virtue, decency and humanity, while they are daily under the pernicious influence of their parents example, and their many vices made familiar thereby.

10. I have found by experience, there may be a thorough and effectual exercise of government in such a school, and as severe as shall be necessary, without opposition from, or offence taken by, any . . .

11. We have the greatest security we can have, that when they are educated and fitted for it, they will be employed in that business. There is no likelihood at all that they will, though ever so well qualified, get into business, either as school-masters or mistresses, among the *English;* at least till the credit of their nations be raised many degrees above what it is now, and consequently they can't be employed as will be honorable for them, or in any business they will be fit for, but among their own nation . . .

And there may also be admitted into this school, promising *English* youth of pregnant parts, and who from the best principles, and by the best motives, are inclined to devote themselves to that service; and who will naturally care for their state.

.   .   .   .   .

In such a school their studies may be directed with a special view to the design of their mission. Several parts of learning which have no great subserviency to it, and which will consume much time, may be less pursued, and others most necessary made their chief study. And they may not only learn the pagan languages, but will naturally get an understanding of their tempers, and many of their customs, which must needs be useful to missionaries. And instead of a delicate manner of living, they may by degrees, as their health will bear, enure themselves to such a way of living as will be most convenient for them to come into when on their mission.

And if the one half of the *Indian* boys thus educated shall prove good and useful men, there will be no reason to regret our toil and expence for the whole. And if God shall deny this blessing on our endeavours, as to the general design, it may be these particular youth may reap eternal advantage by what we do for them; and if but one in ten does so, we shall have no cause to think much of the expence.

And if a blessing be denied to all, "we shall notwithstanding be unto God a sweet savour of Christ in them that perish."

---

2. A description of the Indian school in a letter of a Boston merchant, John Smith, May 18, 1764

James D. McCallum, ed., *The Letters of Eleazar Wheelock's Indians* (Hanover, N.H., 1932), pp. 73–75.

In rideing last week to new London I turned some miles out of my way to see Mr Wheelocks Indian School; nor do I repent my Trouble I had heard in general that it consisted of Twenty or more Indian Boys & Girls of the Mohawks & other Tribes of Indians And that a number of the Ministers of that Province had spoken well of Mr Wheelock & of this undertaking of his, But this I thought was seeing with the Eyes of others & therefore Chose to use my own.

.   .   .   .   .   .

I reached his House a little before the Evening Sacrifice & was movingly Touched on giving out the Psalm to hear an Indian Youth set the Time & the others following him, & singing the Tenor, & Base, with remarkable Gravity & Seirousness, & tho' Mr Wheelock, The Schoolmaster & a minister from our Province (called as I was by Curiosity) joined in Praise; yet they unmoved seemed to have nothing to do but to sing to the Glory of God.

I omit Mr Wheelocks Prayer & pass to the Indians in the morning when on Ringing the School house Bell they Assemble at Mr Wheelocks House about 5 oClock with their Master; who named the Chapter in Course for the Day & called upon the near Indian who read 3 or 4 Versus till the Master said *Proximus,* & then the next Indian read some Verses & so on till all the Indians had read the whole chapter.

After this Mr Wheelock Prayes And then they each Indian perse a Verse or two of the Chapter they had read. After this they entered Successively on Prosodia & then on Disputations on some Questions propounded by themselves in some of the Arts & Sciences. And it is really charming to see Indian Youths of Different Tribes & Languages in pure English reading the Word of God & speaking with Exactness & accuracy on points (either chosen by themselves or given out to them) in the Severall arts & Sciences, And especially to see this done with at Least a seeming Mixture of Obedience to God; a fillial Love & Reverence to Mr Wheelock, & yet with great Ambittion to Excell each other And indeed in this Morning Exercies I saw a Youth Degraded one lower in the Class who before the Exercises were finished not only recovered his own place but was advanced two Higher.

I learnt hear that my surprize was common to ministers & other persons of Litterature who before me had been to visit this School or rather Colledge for I doubt whither in Colledges in General a better Education is to be expected & in mentioning this to a Gentleman in this Town who had visited this Seminary, He acquainted me that he intended at his own Charge to send his Son to obtain his Education in Mixture with these Indians. There were 4 or 5 of these Indians from 21 to 24 years of age who did not mix with the youth in these Exercies — These I learnt were Perfected in their Literature & stand ready to be sent among the Indians to keep Schools & occasionally to preach as doors open.

Missions

---

1. Indian children at worship in a New Mexico mission, 1773

Fray Joaquin de Jesús Ruiz, "The form of government used at the missions of San Diego de los Jímez and San Agustín de la Isleta," in Adolph F. A. Bandelier, ed., *Historical Documents relating to New Mexico, Nueva Vizcaya, and Approaches Thereto, to 1773*, III (Washington, D.C., 1937), 502–503.

The bell is rung at sunrise in summer, and in winter a little later; when the catechumens gather in the churchyard each has his own place assigned to him, the *fiscal* endeavoring to see that they do not change their places, so that the father teacher may easily see if any are missing, and not delay the roll-call. The method for prayer is to put all the little ones, boys as well as girls, in front, separated from one another by a distance of half a vara, so that they cannot talk or amuse themselves with gestures that distract their attention. In the same way the larger girls are placed behind the children, with their faces uncovered, not being permitted to cover them with their shawls, for then they occupy themselves in chewing *exquite,* or in some other nasty habit that they practice. After them come the young men, in the same order as those first named. Two young cantors stand up with the catechism in their hands and begin the recitation in a loud voice, and all respond. They recite first from the "Todo Fidel Christiano" as far as the "Credo," then from the "Salve" as far as the "Sacramentos," and then the explanation of the principal mysteries, closing each recitation with the angelical salutation and the "Alabado" of the Holy Trinity. At the last the responsory is sung, accompanied by the tolling of the bell.

The cantor for the week repeats the prayer together with the sacristans, and the little serving girls with the *fiscal* for the week, in the same order as the catechism. When it is finished the father goes to eat his supper and send away the women cooks, not permitting them under any pretext to sleep in the convent, nor are they permitted to hold any intercourse with the sacristans and young men servants in the kitchen, but must treat them harshly, though without striking them, and when they offend they must be punished through the fiscal. At the ringing of the Ave Marías these last repair to their cells and recite the angelical salutation. When there is work to be done in the way of sweeping, white-washing, or any other task in the convent, they [the men and women] are not permitted to work together, for they do not behave as they ought, and from this come intrigues.

---

2. The birth and work of Indian children at the Mission of San Carlos, Monterey, 1801

Fermin Francisco de Lasuén, "Refutation of Charges, 1801," in *Writings,* II (Washington, D.C., 1965), 210–211.

Fray Fermin Francisco de Lasuén, the head of this Franciscan mission, replied in this document to charges of cruelty to the Indians and mismanagement brought against him by another priest. Lasuén was exonerated as the result of the ensuing investigation.

Knowing full well the inhuman crimes these Indian women so often commit, especially those who live between San Luis Obispo Mission and San Buenaventura, how they commit abortion, and are guilty of suffocating their infants, we employ for their correction all the care and vigilance, all the expedients, and all the diligence which a matter of such importance demands. I once heard a missionary say, in connection with this question, that in his mission the only service the expectant mother accomplishes in the course of five years is to add to the problems of the missionary. And, to tell the truth, if all the missions were taken into account, this would not be much of an exaggeration, for, during the entire period of pregnancy, during the year that follows the birth, and the two years more after that, whether or not the mother nurses the infant, when she settles down to work it is never far from her side, the same as if she were actually nursing it. Then, either the child cries, or is made to cry, or it points with its finger to its head, or to its breast, or to some other part of the body to show that that's where it hurts; and so the mother quits working.

. . . . . .

As regards the young boys and young girls: these are kept busy in a manner befitting their age and sex. It is our aim that, as far as possible, as they grow older they may acquire an inclination towards work and not have such an aversion or repugnance for it as their parents.

Everyone knows that idleness is the most fruitful source of lawlessness and crime; that a child can be taught easily and without compulsion to grow accustomed to work; and that he can grow to like what he has grown accustomed to; and that this liking can increase with the years. We have long known, and experience has strengthened our knowledge, that if anyone spends his childhood, and consequently his youth, in idleness and indolence he will find it morally impossible to feel inclined to work.

B. FREE BLACK CHILDREN IN THE NORTH

Abolition statutes

1. The abolition of slavery in Pennsylvania, with provision for children, 1780

"An Act for the Gradual Abolition of Slavery," 1780 — ch. 881, *Penna. Statutes at Large,* X (Harrisburg, 1904), 68–69.

And whereas the condition of those persons who have heretofore been denominated negro and mulatto slaves, has been attended with circumstances which not only deprived them of the common blessings that they were by nature entitled to, but has cast them into the deepest afflictions by an unnatural separation and sale of husband and wife from each other, and from their children, an injury the greatness of which can only be conceived by supposing that we were in the same unhappy case. In justice, therefore, to persons so unhappily circumstanced, and who, having no prospect before them whereon they may rest their sorrows and their hopes, have no reasonable inducement to render that service to society which they otherwise might, and also in grateful commemoration of our own happy deliverance from that state of unconditional submission to which we were doomed by the tyranny of Britain . . .

Be it enacted . . . That all persons, as well negroes and mulattoes as others who shall be born within this state, from and after the passing of this act, shall not be deemed and considered as servants for life or slaves; and that all servitude for life or slavery of children in consequence of the slavery of their mothers, in the case of all children born within this state from and after the passing of this act as aforesaid, shall be and hereby is utterly taken away, extinguished and forever abolished . . .

Provided always . . . That every negro and mulatto child born within this state after the passing of this act as aforesaid who would in case this act had not been made, have been born a servant for years or life or a slave, shall be deemed to be and shall be, by virtue of this act the servant of such person or his or her assigns who would in such case have been entitled to the service of such child until such child shall attain unto the age of twenty-eight years, in the manner and on the conditions whereon servants bound by indenture for four years are or may be retained and holden, and shall be liable to like correction and punishment, and entitled to like relief in case he or she be evilly treated by his or her master or mistress, and to like freedom dues and other privileges as servants bound by indenture for four years are or may be entitled unless the person to whom the service of any such child shall belong shall abandon his or her claim to the same, in which case the overseers of the poor of the city, township or district, respectively where such child shall be so abandoned, shall [by indenture] bind out every child so abandoned as an apprentice for a time not exceeding the age hereinbefore limited for the service of such children.

2. The Pennsylvania legislature remedies defects in the abolition statute, 1788

"An Act to Explain and Amend an Act Entitled 'An Act for the Gradual Abolition of slavery,' " 1788 — ch. 1345, *Penna. Statutes at Large 1787–1790,* VIII (1908), 52–56.

This act was passed to close loopholes that had appeared in the earlier law.

And be it further enacted . . . That no negro or mulatto slave or servant for term of years . . . shall be removed out of this state with the design and intention that the place of abode or residence of such slave or servant shall be thereby altered or changed or with the design and intention that such slave or servant if a female and pregnant shall be detained and kept out of this state till her delivery of

the child of which she is or shall he pregnant or with the design and intention that such slave or servant shall be brought again into this state, after the expiration of six months from the time of such slave or servant having been first brought into this state without his or her consent . . .

And be it further enacted . . . That all persons who now are or hereafter shall be possessed of any child or children born after the first day of March, one thousand seven hundred and eighty, who would by the said act be liable to serve till the age of twenty-eight years, shall on or before the first day of April one thousand seven hundred and eighty-nine, or within six months next after the birth of any such child, deliver or cause to be delivered in writing to the clerk of the peace of the county, or the clerk of the court of record of the city of Philadelphia in which they shall respectively inhabit the name, surname and occupation or profession of such possessor and of the county, township, district or ward in which they reside and also the age (to the best of his or her knowledge) name and sex of every such child or children, under the pain and penalty of forfeiting and losing all right and title to every such child and children, and of him, her or them immediately becoming free, which said return or account in writing shall be verified by the oath or affirmation of the party which the said clerks are hereby respectively authorized and required to administer, and the said clerks shall make and preserve records thereof, copies and extracts of which shall be good evidence in all courts of justice when certified under their hands and seals of office.

.   .   .   .   .

And whereas the practice of separating which is too often exercised by the masters and mistresses of negro and mulatto slaves or servants for terms of years, in separating husbands and wives and parents and children, requires to be checked so far as the same may be done without prejudice to such masters or mistresses.

. . . Be it enacted . . . That if any owner

or possessor of any negro or mulatto slave or slaves or servant or servants for term of years shall from and after the first day of June next separate or remove or cause to be separated or removed a husband from his wife, a wife from her husband, a child from his or her parent or a parent from child, of any or either of the descriptions aforesaid, to a greater distance than ten miles with the design and intention of changing the habitation or place of abode of such husband, or wife, parent or child, unless such child shall be above the age of four years or unless the consent of such slave or servant for life or years shall have been obtained and testified in the manner hereinbefore described, such person or persons shall severally forfeit and pay the sum of fifty pounds with costs of suit for every such offense to be recovered by action of debt, bill, plaint or information, in the supreme court or in any court of common pleas, at [the] suit of any person who will sue for the same, one moiety thereof when recovered, for the use of the plaintiff the other moiety for the use of the poor of the city, township or place from which such husband or wife, parent or child shall have been taken and removed.

3. Rhode Island's abolition statute, 1784

"An Act authorizing the Manumission of Negroes, Mulattoes and others, and for the gradual Abolition of Slavery," *Laws of Rhode Island* (Providence, 1784), p. 7.

February, 1784.

No Person or Persons, whether Negroes, Mulattoes, or others, who shall be born within the Limits of this State, on or after the First Day of March, A.D. 1784, shall be deemed or considered as Servants for Life, or Slaves; and . . . all Servitude for Life, or Slavery of Children, to be born as aforesaid, in Consequence of the Condition of their Mothers, be, and the same is hereby taken away, extinguished and for ever abolished.

And whereas Humanity requires, that Children declared free as aforesaid remain with their Mothers a convenient Time from and after their Birth; to enable therefore those who claim the Services of such Mothers to maintain and support such Children in a becoming Manner, *It is further Enacted* . . . That such Support and Maintenance be at the Expence of the respective Towns where those reside and are settled: *Provided however,* That the respective Town-Councils may bind out such Children as Apprentices, or otherwise provide for their Support and Maintenance, at any Time after they arrive to the Age of One Year, and before they arrive to their respective Ages of Twenty-one, if Males, and Eighteen, if Females.

And whereas it is the earnest Desire of this Assembly, that such Children be educated in the Principles of Morality and Religion, and instructed in Reading, Writing and Arithmetic: *Be it further Enacted* . . . That due and adequate Satisfaction be made as aforesaid for such Education and Instruction. And for ascertaining the Allowance for such Support, Maintenance, Education and Instruction, the respective Town-Councils are hereby required to adjust and settle the Accounts in this Behalf from Time to Time, as the same shall be exhibited to them: Which Settlement so made shall be final; and the respective Towns by Virtue thereof shall become liable to pay the Sums therein specified and allowed.

Schools conducted by abolition societies and free Negroes

1. Reports of abolition societies in New York and Philadelphia on the schools for

black children maintained in those cities, 1797

Minutes of the Proceedings of the Fourth Convention of Delegates from the Abolition Societies Established in Different Parts of the United States, Assembled at Philadelphia, May 3, 1797 (Philadelphia, 1797), pp. 29–34.

After the abolition of slavery in the northern states during the last quarter of the eighteenth century, the abolition societies directed their attention to the education of young Negroes.

New-York Society.

The New York society many years since, instituted a school for the instruction of African descendants, in various species of knowledge; this institution, which considerable experience has proved to be of the highest importance to the progress of emancipation and the welfare of the subjects of our care, has since the last Convention received a new share of our attention, undergone a renovation, and is now on a more flourishing and respectable footing than at any former period. By an appropriation of the principal part of the funds of the society, to this object, together with the annual dividend of the bounty of the state, and the contributions of individuals, we have, at an expense of more than fourteen hundred pounds, purchased a building and lot suitable for our purpose, and the school is now maintained at the rate of about one thousand dollars a year. This institution, as the Convention will observe from the constitution of the society, is under the immediate inspection of a board of Trustees. It is provided with a master, usher and mistress, by whom the pupils are taught reading, penmanship, arithmetic, English grammar and geography, and the female scholars, in addition, needlework. The number of scholars on the first of January 1797, was

one hundred and twenty-two; of whom sixty-three were males, and fifty-nine females, and this is about the usual number; many of them being of sufficient age to be occasionally serviceable to their parents and masters, some irregularity unavoidably happens in their attendance, but this is not so considerable but that more than two-thirds are generally present. The appearance, conduct and progress of this school, in the opinion of the Trustees, would do credit to any institution of the kind, and is exceeded by none in the city.

On the whole they exhibit an example of successful industry, highly honorable to themselves, gratifying to their parents, encouraging to their patrons and consoling to humanity. Mean while the spirit of improvement has diffused itself among many of their color, who have attained to years of maturity, without the benefits of instruction. An evening school under the patronage of the Board of Trustees, but not at the expense of the society, has been instituted the last winter; this school which is conducted by the master and usher of the society school, for their own emolument, is supported by the pupils, who amount to forty-four, of both sexes, and themselves defray the charges of their education. Hitherto a degree of decorum and industry has prevailed among them much to their honor and advantage; and it will no doubt be gratifying to the Convention to learn that the usher in either school, is himself of African descent, and discharges the duties of his office with a zeal, fidelity and success, worthy of his character as a man, and his profession as a Christian.

Pennsylvania Society.

Early in the year 1793, the committee of the Abolition Society, for improving the condition of the free blacks, purchased on a ground rent of fifteen pounds per annum, a lot of ground situated on the north side of Cherry street, between Sixth and Seventh streets, on which they soon after placed a frame building and opened a free school for the instruction of children of color of both sexes; in this school are taught, spelling, reading, and needle work. Eleanor Harris, a black woman, being judged well qualified, has been employed as their teacher since the opening of the school. Her salary is one hundred dollars per annum; she is also provided with a dwelling in the house, and with fire wood. The children are furnished with the necessary school-books. The expenses of this school are defrayed out of the particular funds of this committee, raised by donations, legacies and annual subscriptions. The school is regularly visited every month by the committee of education. The number of scholars who generally attend is thirty.

With a view further to extend the benefits of education to the Africans and their descendants, the above named committee for improving the condition of the free blacks, have lately procured additional contributions, supposed sufficient to enable them to establish two more schools, which it is expected will shortly be opened, one in the northern, and the other in the southern part of the city.

The committee for improving the condition of the free blacks have also afforded pecuniary assistance to a society of young men, chiefly members of the Abolition Society, who have kept an evening school since the year 1788, for the instruction of black men, in reading, writing and arithmetic, during the fall and winter months. A school room was furnished them by the overseers of the school held in Willings-alley, hereafter to be mentioned; they have generally employed a master, and have themselves served alternately as his assistants. The blacks are provided with books, &c. and taught gratis. The expense is now defrayed by voluntary contributions of the society of young men. About sixty scholars are at present taught in this school. A First-day or Sunday school is kept at this house in the summer season, for the instruction of black men in reading and writing by the same society of young men.

Besides the schools more particularly under the care and direction of the society, there are several others in this city, established for the improvement of the people of color in various branches of useful learning.

In the year 1771, two schools for the instruction of black children, male and female, were instituted by the society of Friends, on a lot of ground belonging to them in Willings-alley — An house was built, and the school supported by voluntary contributions from the members of that society, until the year 1786, when by a legacy of Anthony Benezet, amounting to a ground rent of ninety pounds per annum, a donation of five hundred pounds sterling from England, and some legacies in this country, all of which were vested in ground rents, the yearly income of the school was near two hundred pounds — the salaries of the master and mistress, expense of fire wood, books and stationary, amount to about two hundred and thirty-two pounds per annum. The balance is made up by the society of Friends. The teachers live in the house, rent free, and are provided with fire-wood — no children of color whether slaves or others are refused admittance to this school. The average number in each school is about forty scholars. These schools are under the care of a committee of twelve persons appointed by the society of Friends, who visit them regularly once a month.

In the year 1795, a number of young women of this city, formed a society for the purpose of teaching black women and girls reading and writing. They have procured a school room, give their personal attendance as teachers alternately, provide fire wood, and for those who are not able to procure them, books and stationary. The expense is defrayed by voluntary contributions — the school is held in the evening during the fall and winter months — the average number of scholars who attend is thirty.

In the winter of 1796, a First-day or Sunday school for the education of the black people in reading and writing was opened by a member of the Abolition Society at the

Methodist African meeting house on Sixth street, and held between the hours of public worship. From sixty to ninety persons, chiefly adults of both sexes, usually attended. The original institutor of this school was soon afterwards assisted by several young men, mostly members of the Abolition Society. The generality of the scholars were furnished with books gratis; the fund for defraying the necessary expenses was raised by contributions solicited by the founder, who proposes in lieu of the day school to keep one in the evening on a similar plan, during the winter season.

All the accounts procured of the different schools concur in declaring, that the improvement and behaviour of the people of color is encouraging and satisfactory.

---

2. An advertisement for a school for black children in Washington, D.C., 1818

National Intelligencer, Aug. 29, 1818.

Negro parents founded schools for their children in the absence of adequate public schools.

A SCHOOL

Founded by an association of free people of color of the city of Washington, called the "Resolute Beneficial Society," situate near the Eastern public school, and the dwelling of Mrs. Fenwick, is now open for the reception of children of free people of color, and others that ladies or gentlemen may think proper to send, to be instructed in reading, writing, arithmetic, English grammar, or other branches of education, applicable to their capacities, by a steady, active and experienced teacher, whose attention is wholly devoted to the purposes described. It is presumed, that free colored families will embrace the advantages thus presented to them, either by subscribing to the funds of the society, or by sending their children to the school; the terms in either case being remarkably moderate. An improvement of the intellect and morals of colored youth being the leading object of this institution, the patronage of benevolent ladies and gentlemen, by donation or subscription, is humbly solicited in aid of the fund, — the demands thereon being heavy, and the means at present much too limited. For the satisfaction of the public, the constitution and articles of association are printed and published. And, to avoid disagreeable occurrences, no writings are to be done by the teacher for a slave, neither directly nor indirectly to serve the purposes of a slave, on any account whatsoever. Further particulars may be known, by applying to any of the undersigned officers.

WILLAM COSTIN, President.
GEORGE HICKS, Vice President.
JAMES HARRIS, Secretary.
GEORGE BELL, Treasurer.
ARCHIBALD JOHNSON, Marshal.
FRED. LEWIS, Chairman of the Com.
ISAAC JOHNSON } Committee.
SCIPIO BEENS,

N.B. An evening school will commence on the premises, on the first Monday in October, and continue throughout the season.

The managers of Sunday schools in the Eastern District, are thus most dutifully and respectfully informed, that on Sabbath days the school-house belonging to this society, if required, for the tuition of colored youth, will be uniformly at their service.

C. SITUATION OF SLAVE CHILDREN

Slave children in families

1. John Woolman's description of the treatment of slave families in 1757

John Woolman, *A Journal of the Life, Gospel Labors and Christian Experience of that Faithful Minister of Jesus Christ, John Woolman* . . . (Philadelphia, 1860), pp. 79–80.

Woolman (1720–1772), a devout Quaker of the Province of West Jersey, journeyed through Virginia, Maryland, and North Carolina in the interests of the Society of Friends.

The prospect of a road lying open to . . . degeneracy, in some parts of this newly settled land of America, in respect to our conduct toward the negroes, hath deeply bowed my mind in this journey; and though to relate briefly how these people are treated is no agreeable work, yet, after often reading over the notes I made as I travelled, I find my mind engaged to preserve them. Many of the white people in those provinces take little or no care of negro marriages; and when negroes marry after their own way, some make so little account of those marriages, that, with views of outward interest, they often part men from their wives by selling them far asunder; which is common when estates are sold by executors at vendue. Many whose labor is heavy being followed at their business in the field by a man with a whip, hired for that purpose, having in common little else allowed but one peck of Indian corn and some salt for one week, with a few potatoes; the potatoes they commonly raise by their labor on the first day of the week.

The correction ensuing on their disobedience to overseers, or slothfulness in business, is often very severe, and sometimes desperate. Men and women have many times scarely clothes enough to hide their nakedness, and boys and girls, ten and twelve years old, are often quite naked amongst their master's children. Some of our Society, and some of the society called New Lights, use some endeavors to instruct those they have in reading; but in common this is not only neglected, but disapproved. These are the people by whose labor the other inhabitants are in a great measure supported, and many of them in the luxuries of life; these are the people who have made no agreement to serve us, and who have not forfeited their liberty, that we know of; these are the souls for whom Christ died: and for our conduct toward them, we must answer before Him who is no respecter of persons.

2. The children of slaves legally equated with the offspring of animals, South Carolina, 1809

M'Vaughters, Administrator of M'Lain *v.* Elder, 2 Brevard 307 (1809).

It appeared . . . that M'Lain, the intestate, left at his death a female slave, named Bet, and a mare named Pol Jones, which property, after his death, came into the possession of Margaret M'Grew, who claimed the same, as his next of kin and legal heir. After having the slave in possession, from 1795 or 1796 till 1800, she sold her to the defendant, from whom she was demanded by the plaintiff. At the time of the demand, the wench had two children, who were born while she was in the possession of Mrs. M'Grew. The mare died while in Mrs. M'Grew's possession, having had three colts during the time of her being in the possession of Mrs. M'Grew, which were grown at the time of the demand. Margaret M'Grew died in the year 1805, intestate, and without ever having administered on the estate of M'Lain. Immediately after her death, the plaintiff obtained letters of administration, as administrator of M'Lain; and having demanded the negroes and horses abovementioned, from the defendant, who had them in possession, and refused to deliver them up, commenced this action.

.   .   .   .   .

[The Court held] . . . it follows that Margaret M'Grew had no right to intermeddle with, or dispose of the property in question; and that the defendant could not derive any valid title from her, or right to retain the goods from the administrator of M'Lain.

But it has been contended, the plaintiff is not entitled to recover damages for the conversion of the offspring of the female slave, and of the mare in question, because they were not in the possession of the intestate at the time of his death, either in deed, or in law.

The answer to this objection is, that by our law, the brood, or offspring, of tame and domestic animals, is similar to the civil law, which declares that the issue shall follow the condition of the mother, or dam . . . This law applies to the young of slaves, because as objects of property, they stand on the same footing as other animals, which are assets to be administered by the personal representative of the deceased owner. If the defendant had, indeed, been the lawful temporary owner of the mother of the young negroes, and of the mare in question, there might be a doubt who should be entitled to young brought forth during the period of the lawful possession of the defendant. But as the defendant . . . never had any lawful right of property, or possession, in the mothers of the young slaves and horses, he can have no more right, than any mere stranger, to claim the offspring and increase in question.

Separation of mother and child

---

1. The Court of Appeals of Virginia facilitates keeping slave mothers and infants together, 1801

Fitzhugh v. Foote, 3 Call 13 (1801).

Litigation occurred over the proper division among the heirs, a widow, Margaret Foote Fitzhugh, and two sons, Richard and William H. Foote, of an estate consisting of land and slaves.

The Court is of opinion, that the appellant, Margaret, is entitled to dower in all the slaves whereof her former husband, Richard Foote, was possessed at the time of his death, as the sale of any of them was not necessary for the payment of his debts; and, therefore, that the commissioners, appointed by the Court of Chancery to enquire whether more slaves were retained by the said Margaret than she was entitled to for dower, ought, in the valuation of all the slaves of the said Richard Foote, which was made by them, to have ascertained the value of the widow's third part of the said slaves, to have included the value of the slave Lucy, said to have been appointed for, and delivered to Mrs. Alexander, the daughter of the said Richard, which they omitted to do: That an equal division of slaves, in number or value, is not always possible, and sometimes improper, when it cannot be exactly done without separating infant children from their mothers, which humanity forbids, and will not be countenanced in a Court of Equity: so, that a compensation for excess must, in such cases, be made and received in money: And, that under all the circumstances of the present case, as stated in the proceedings in this cause, between children and parents, a new division of the slaves of the said Richard Foote, ought not, after such a length of time, for a small excess, to have been ordered; especially as the whole of the dower slaves, with their increase, will belong to the appellees on the death of the said Margaret, their mother . . .

2. The separation of a slave mother from her children, 1807

Garland *v.* Bugg, Hening and Mumford 374 (1807).

A Virginia master attempted to prevent the separation of a slave mother and her two children after he had sold them. The Virginia Supreme Court of Appeals blocked the attempt on technical grounds.

The appellee brought an action of detinue[1] against the appellant, for a negro woman: — the defendant pleaded *non detinet;* — and moreover a special plea in bar, "That he had sold the said negro woman with her two children to the plaintiff, who, by his deed in writing, bearing date, &c., did agree that the sale of the slave in the declaration mentioned should be void and defeasible, and the title of the plaintiff in her forfeited and vested in the defendant, if the said plaintiff should sell, hire, convey away, or otherwise divide the said slave from her two children, until they should respectively attain the age of ten years, unless such sale, &c. should be of the mother and children collectively and all together, upon the defendant's paying to the plaintiff the sum of 500 dollars; that the plaintiff had broken the condition of the said agreement, and forfeited his title in the said negro woman, by making a distinct sale of her in exclusion of her children

1. An action for the recovery of a personal chattel wrongfully detained.

before they respectively attained their age of ten years, whereby, &c.; and that the defendant tendered to the plaintiff the 500 dollars, which he refused to accept."

3. A Kentucky court upholds the sale of a slave mother and child together, 1811

Lawrence *v.* Speed, 2 Bibb 401 (1811).

This execution was directed to the sheriff of Mercer county, and put into the hands of his deputy, who by virtue thereof seized four negroes, to wit, Joseph, Milly, Ruth and David, of the estate of David Lawrence, deceased, and sold the same at public auction in the town of Danville.

Joseph and Milly were first severally sold, the former at the price of $115 50 cents, and the latter for $293. There still remaining between 250 and $300 of the execution unsatisfied, the sheriff sold Ruth, and David her son, between two and three years old, in one lot at the price of $400. The sale was advertised at the courthouse door; but it does not appear that an advertisement was set up any where else in the county. The defendants in the execution however had seen the advertisement, and the sales seem to have been effected at a fair price. No fraud is imputed either to the sheriff or the purchasers. At the next term of the court after the sale, the defendants in the execution moved the court to quash the sale, having previously given notice for that purpose, but the court overruled the motion and gave judgment against the defendants; to which they have prosecuted this writ of error.

It is contended in the first place, that the sale is wholly void and ought to have been quashed, because the sheriff failed to advertise agreeably to law; and in the second place, if the sale be not wholly void, that it is so at least so far as respects Ruth and David, because they were sold together, whereas they ought to have been sold separately, and because the sale of both was not necessary to make the money then due on the execution.

. . . . . .

As to the second point, it cannot be denied to be in general true that it is the duty of the sheriff to sell separately property which is divisible in its nature, and that he would be responsible for any injury done by a violation of his duty in this respect; and cases may be imagined where the transaction would manifest such gross fraud that the purchaser could not but be cognizant of it. In such cases the sale itself would be void and might be set aside. But the present case does not appear to be of that description. The mother and child were indeed physically divisible, but morally they were not so; and the sheriff in selling them together certainly acted in conformity to the dictates of humanity, and probably in pursuance of the interest of the owner. If the child had been sold separately from its mother, it is pretty certain its value would have been greatly diminished, and most unquestionably would not have satisfied the execution. It would in that case have still been the indispensable duty of the sheriff to have sold the mother: if the mother had been first sold, it is not improbable that her value might have been lessened in the estimation of purchasers, and we cannot tell with certainty that she would have commanded a price that would have been sufficient to satisfy the execution. Consequently we cannot say that the sheriff has exceeded his authority in selling both, and where it is not clear that the sheriff has exceeded his authority or grossly abused it, we ought not to set aside the sale upon motion, but leave the party to his remedy by action.

Slave children cannot inherit a beneficial interest in property, North Carolina, 1801

Thomas Cunningham's Heirs *v.* Thomas

Cunningham's Executors, Cameron and Norwood, 353 (1801).

A slave owner tried to make provision for the children of one of his slaves, but failed owing to the legal incapacity of slaves.

Thomas Cunningham, in September, 1792, duly made his last will and testament, by which, amongst other things, he devised as follows: "It is my will and desire, that . . . the house where Mr. Potts is now resident, be at the expiration of the lease rented out for the maintenance of a negro woman of mine, named Rachel, and the maintenance and education of her three mulatto children named Mary, Ritty and Chrissy, and the child of which she is now pregnant." After devising part of a lot to Edmund Robeson, the will proceeds thus, "and the rest and residue of the said lot to be rented yearly for the maintenance of Rachel and her three children, already named, with the child of which she is now pregnant; with all the rest of the land lying between Lee's creek and Deep Inlet creek, between Rachel and her three children, share and share alike, to them and their heirs.

"Item. I will and desire that my negro men, Virgil and Quash, together with my negro woman Tamer, should live on the plantation where I now reside, on Lee's creek, to work for the maintenance of Rachel's children, during the natural life of the said negroes. Item. I will and desire that Rachel and her children should be set free immediately after my decease." [1]

The defendant, as executor of Thomas Cunningham, the testator, took possession of that part of the real estate, the rents of which are directed by the will to be applied towards the maintenance and education of the negro woman Rachel and her children. For this part of the estate the action was brought.

Rachel and all her children, before and at

---

1. Cunningham failed to comply with all of the requirements for manumission; hence his wish was not carried out.

the time of making the will, and ever since, have been slaves.

For the defendant, it was insisted, that by the words of the will, he is entitled to the possession of the real estate, in order to receive the rents and profits, and to pay the same to the negro woman Rachel.

The plaintiff's claim was rested on the following grounds: I. That supposing the words of the will are sufficient to pass the estate to the negro woman Rachel and her children, yet, by law, negro slaves are incapable of taking or holding real estate: II. And admitting they are capable, yet there is no express devise of the lands in question to the executors; consequently, the lands descend to the plaintiffs, as heirs at law of the testator.

Hall, J. I think that the devise in question is void, and cannot take effect. The maintenance and education of some of the devisees, is what the testator appears to have been anxious for. How can it be effected? They are slaves, and their owners have a right to them and their services; if they are educated, it must be by his permission, and if it is attempted without, it is a violation of his right . . .

Taylor, J. The intention of the testator seems plainly to have been, to transfer the beneficial interest in the lands to Rachel and her children; and were there no legal impediments to the effecting of such an object, I should think the words made use of equivalent to an express devise of the land. But it is indispensible to the validity of every devise, that there be a devisee appointed who is competent to take: Slaves have not that competence; for a civil incapacity results from the nature and condition of slavery. And it would be a solecism, that the law should sanction or permit the acquisition of property by those, from whom it afterwards withholds that protection without which property is useless.

Punishments for crimes committed by three slave boys, Maryland, 1748

W. H. Browne, ed., *Archives of Maryland,* XXVIII (Baltimore, 1908), 431–432.

The Governor's Council voided a death sentence from a lower court for commission of a felony.

His Excellency [Governor Samuel Ogle] having communicated to this Board the report made to him by the Judges of Assize of the Western Shore of the proceedings in their Circuit held in September last, whereby it appears that they had passed sentence of death upon Negro Tom a boy belonging to Col Thomas Lee, and on Negro Cheshire a boy belonging to John Lee, and on Mullato James a slave belonging to a certain Bayne Smallwood, for house breaking and felony by them committed in Charles County . . . and it also appearing to this Board by the return of the said Justices that the Negro boys Tom and Cheshire were not above twelve or fourteen years old and were objects of mercy, but that Mullato James bore a very ill character and had been a notorious rogue for some years . . . It is therefore the humble advice of this Board to his Excellency that he be pleased to grant his Lordships pardon to the aforesaid Negro Tom and Negro Cheshire . . . And that he would be pleased to order warrant for the execution of the said Mulatto James; which pardons and warrant issued accordingly.

A slave boy hired out by his master, Maryland, 1781

Memorandum of an agreement between John Smith and Joseph Pemberton, Jan. 3, 1781, Pemberton Papers, XXXV, 75, The Historical Society of Pennsylvania, Philadelphia.

Hiring out slaves whose labor the master could not effectively use was a common practice in many parts of the South, particularly in cities. In this instance a slave boy's services were sold.

The said John Smith hath bound unto the said Joseph Pemberton a Negro lad called Isaac to serve the said Joseph Pemberton or his assigns for the term of four years from the date of these presents. During which time the said Pemberton doth covenant and agree to provide the said Negro with sufficient cloath-ing, to pay any assessment or other expenses he may be subject to, and at the expiration of each and every year to pay unto the said John Smith or his assigns the sum of twenty Spanish silver dollars in case the said Negro should live so long, or in proportion for the term he does live. For the true performance of the above contract the said parties bind themselves each to the other in the sum of one hundred silver dollars money aforesaid as witness those hands the day and year above written.

D. EDUCATION OF NEGRO CHILDREN

Education under the auspices of religious organizations

---

1. A plan for the education of slaves in South Carolina, 1740

Alexander Garden to Philip Bearcroft, May 6, 1740, in Frank J. Klingberg, *An Appraisal of the Negro in Colonial South Carolina* (Washington, D.C., 1941), pp. 104–105.

The Reverend Alexander Garden (1685–1756), leading Episcopalian official in the colony, established a school for slaves and other blacks in Charleston in 1743; it continued until 1764. In this letter to an officer of the Society for the Propagation of the Gospel, Garden described his plan and its novel features. Although it seems likely that many of the students were free blacks, the presence of slaves in the school illustrates the lax enforcement of the South Carolina law of 1740 on teaching slaves (see below, Prohibitions on education, doc. 2).

Touching the most effectual Method, for Instructing the Negro and Indian Slaves, in the principles of our holy Religion, as it has been a Matter of my long and Serious Attention, I shall now humbly offer my final sentiments upon it, to the Honorable Society, in these few following Conclusions.

1st This good Work must not be attempted in the Gross, or inclusive of the whole Body of Slaves, of so many various Ages, Nations, Languages etc. For in this View it always has, and ever will appear insuperable. But

2dly It must commence, and be carried on among such of them only, as are Home-Born, and under the Age of Ten years.

3dly Neither will the work thus limited ever turn out to any tolerable Effect, in the Hands of the Masters and Mistresses of Slaves; much less in the hands of any White Schoolmasters or Mistresses that may be sent from England, or any otherwise employed in it, And therefore

4. My 4th Conclusion is, that the above effectual Method of Proceeding in the Work as above limited, must be by *Negro* School-masters, Home-born, and equally Property as other Slaves, but educated for this Service, and employed in it during their Lives, as the others are in any other Services whatsoever.

Pursuant to this last Conclusion I long since Proposed, that every owner of Eighty or a Hundred Slaves ('mong whom there are seldom fewer than Ten or Twelve Children from Ten years old and under) should be at the charge of sending to School One or other of the Males, as should appear most capable and best disposed, 'till he be Taught to read the *Bible,* to say the *Church Catechism* by heart, and to use the *Common Prayer;* and who from thenceforth should be employ'd by the Said Owner, as a Schoolmaster, and in that Service only during his life, to instruct in the same manner all the Slave children not only of that Plantation, but of the smaller Plantations, that may be in the Neighbourhood. But alas! this Proposal how practicable soever allowed to be, yet it contains in it the loss of the Annual Profit from the labour of One Slave, no Body would be prevailed with to put it in Practice. I then consulted the Members of our Assembly here whether the Proposal might not be En-forced by a Law, or Act of Assem[bly] passed for the purpose; but was answer'd, that as it would touch on . . . Properties, they could pass no such Law (or rather would not do it, being most of them Parties concerned) I farther also had some thoughts . . . whether the Honorable Society might not obtain his Majesty's Recommendation for the Passing such a Law in the respective Colonies; But ob-serving how frequently such Recommendations, or even Instructions are either postponed or otherwise evaded, when there is no Mind to comply, I have likewise laid aside all such thoughts, and finally concluded —

5. In the last Place, to rest the Matter wholly on the Bottom of Charity; and in no hands so proper or promising of Success, as those of the Honorable Society . . .

2. The Church of England clergymen of New York City secure a teacher for Negro children, 1760

The New-York Mercury, Aug. 4, Sept. 15, 1760, in Morgan Dix, *A History of the Parish of Trinity Church in the City of New York* (New York, 1898), pp. 294–295.

Wanted immediately, a sober Woman, of a fair Character and Qualifications, necessary to keep a School, for the instruction of Thirty Negro Children, in reading, sewing, &c. Such a persons by applying to any one of the Clergy of the Church of England, in this City, may be informed of the Terms, which are advan-tageous.

N.B. The intended School will be chiefly Supported by a Charitable Society of worthy and well disposed Christians in England: It is therefore hop'd that such Persons as have a Regard for the Souls of their poor Young Slaves, especially those born in their house, will be ready to assist in forwarding and pro-moting this laudable Undertaking.

. . . . .

This is to inform the Public, that a Free School is opened near the New-Dutch-Church, for the instruction of 30 Negro Children, from 5 years old and upwards, in Reading, and in the Principles of Christianity, and likewise sewing and knitting; which School is entirely under the Inspection and Care of the Clergy of the Church of England in this City: Those Persons therefore that have the present Useful-ness, and future Welfare of their young Slaves at Heart (especially those born in their Houses), are desired to apply to any one of the Clergy, who will immediately send them to the aforesaid School, and see that they be faithfully instructed.

N.B. All that is required of their Masters and Mistresses, is that they find them in Wood for the Winter. Proper Books will be pro-vided for them gratis.

State authorized education

1. Slave children in New Jersey to be taught to read, 1788

"A Supplement to an Act entitled, 'An Act to prevent the Importation of Slaves into the State of New Jersey, and to authorize the Manumission of them under certain restrictions, and to prevent the Abuse of Slaves,' " *Acts of the Thirteenth General Assembly of the State of New Jersey* (Trenton,1788), p. 488.

New Jersey abolished slavery in 1804 by a gradual emancipation scheme.

And be it further enacted . . . that every person or persons within this State, who shall be the owner or owners of any Negro or Mulatto slave or slaves, servant or servants, for life, or years, born after the Publication of this Act, shall cause every such slave or slaves, servant or servants, while under the age of twenty-one years, to be taught and instructed to read; and every owner or owners of any such Negro or Mulatto slave or slaves, servant or servants, who shall neglect or refuse to cause his, her or their slave or slaves, servant or servants, to be taught and instructed as afore-said, shall forfeit and pay the sum of five pounds, to be recovered by Action of Debt, before any Justice of the Peace within this State, by any person or persons who shall or may prosecute for the same.

2. A Massachusetts politician suggests public education for all Negro children, 1795

James Sullivan to Jeremy Belknap, July 30, 1795, in MHS *Collections,* 5th ser., III (1877), 414–415.

Sullivan (1744–1808), a Republican, served as a delegate to the Massachusetts Constitutional Convention, justice of the Supreme Judicial Court, attorney-general, and governor.

From the difficulties suggested . . . it would seem as if the case was without remedy, and that a state of slavery is entailed for ever on some part of the inhabitants of free America. But there is, in my mind, this resource; and I am obliged to think that it is the only one in the case, and that a very slow one. As there is no way to eradicate the prejudice which education has fixed in the minds of the white against the black people, otherwise than by raising the blacks, by means of mental improvements, nearly to the same grade with the whites, the emancipation of the slaves in United America must be slow in its progress, and ages must be employed in the business. The time necessary to effect this purpose must be as extensive, at least, as that in which slavery has been endured here. The children of the slaves must, at the public expence, be educated in the same manner as the children of their masters; being at the same schools, &c., with the rising generation, that prejudice, which has been so long and inveterate against them on account of their situation and colour, will be lessened within thirty or forty years. There is an objection to this, which embraces all my feelings; that is, that it will tend to a mixture of blood, which I now abhor; but yet, as I feel, I fear that I am not a pure Republican, delighting in the equal rights of all the human race. This mode of education will fit the rising progeny of the black people either to participate with the whites in a free government, or to colonize, and have one of their own. The negroes born after a certain future day may be considered as free at 40 years, those after another at 30, and those after another at 21 years of age. This will, in the course of time, emancipate all the slaves. To induce them to be industrious members of community, a certain portion of property ought to be considered as necessary to their holding civil offices, or enjoying civil privileges, in common with other citizens. This process, I know, is too slow for the warm and philanthropic feelings of your elegant correspondent; and carries with it the idea of a curse being entailed in the Southern States from the fathers to the children, to the third and fourth generation. Be that as it may, I think the best way is to make haste slowly, and to bear for a time an evil with patience, rather than to aggravate its miseries, and render future attempts discouraging. There have been few instances indeed, in history, where a man educated as a slave has been capable of enjoying freedom. In the most despotic governments, there have appeared champions for liberty; but the event has generally evinced to the world that the greater part of these had acted only from a spirit of ambitious heroism, because they have generally been tyrants as soon as they had established their own power to rule.

There is no doubt a great disparity in the natural abilities of mankind, and we have great reason to believe that the organization of the Africans is such as prevents their receiving the more fine and sublime impressions equally with the white people; and yet we do not know but that, giving them the same prospects, placing them under the force of the same motives, and conferring upon them the same advantages for the space of time in which 3 or 4 generations shall rise and fall, will so mend the race, and so increase their powers of perception, and so strengthen their faculty for comparing ideas, and understanding the nature and connexion of the external things with which man is surrounded on this globe, as that they may exceed the white people.

Prohibitions on education

1. South Carolina prohibits teaching slaves to write, 1740

So. Car. Statutes at Large, VII, 413.

Although this law, the earliest statutory prohibition of education for slaves, was not usually enforced, it discouraged efforts to educate slaves.

And *whereas,* the having of slaves taught to write, or suffering them to be employed in writing, may be attended with great inconveniences; *Be it therefore enacted . . .* That all and every person and persons whatsoever, who shall hereafter teach, or cause any slave or slaves to be taught, to write, or shall use or employ any slave as a scribe in any manner of writing whatsoever, hereafter taught to write, every such person and persons, shall, for every such offence, forfeit the sum of one hundred pounds current money.

---

2. South Carolina punishes "unlawful assemblages of persons of colour" including meetings for purposes of instruction, 1800

So. Car. Statutes at Large, VII, 440–441, 448–449.

The second clause of this act, prohibiting mixed meetings of Negroes and whites for religious worship, was altered in 1802 to prevent disruption without a warrant of religious services when a majority of the participants were white.

Whereas, the laws heretofore enacted for the government of slaves, free negroes, mulattoes and mestizoes, have been found insufficient for keeping them in due subordination.

Be it therefore enacted . . . That from and after the passing this law, all assemblies and congregations of slaves, free negroes, mulattoes and mestizoes, whether composed of all or any of the above description of persons, or of all or any of the above described persons and of a proportion of white persons, assembled or met together for the purpose of mental instruction, in a confined or secret place of meeting, or with the gates or doors of such place of meeting barred, bolted or locked, so as to prevent the free ingress and egress to and from the same, shall be, and the same is hereby declared to be, an unlawful meeting; and the magistrates, sheriffs, militia officers, and officers of the police, being commissioned, are hereby directed, required and empowered, to enter into such confined places where such unlawful assemblies are convened, and for that purpose to break doors, gates or windows, if resisted, and disperse such slaves, free negroes, mulattoes or mestizoes . . .

And be it further enacted . . . That from [and] after the passing of this Act, it shall not be lawful for any number of slaves, free negroes, mulattoes or mestizoes, even in company with white persons, to meet together and assemble for the purpose of mental instruction or religious worship, either before the rising of the sun or after the going down of the same; and all magistrates, sheriffs, militia officers, and officers of the patrol, being commissioned, city or town guard, or watchmen, are hereby vested with all the powers and authority for dispersing such assemblies, before day or after sun set, as is herein and hereby given to them in the first clause of this Act . . .

Part Three   The American Child, 1820–1865

I Children in a Democracy

No brief formula adequately explains or summarizes the varieties of family and child life that existed in the United States by the early nineteenth century. Variety was bound to be the lot of a people drawn together through different means and for different purposes from the ends of the earth. Except for the inevitable disruption of their lives and a common sea voyage, the first migrants shared virtually nothing. Vast groups inherited contrasting cultural beliefs. Religious, class, and ethnic divisions abounded. Some even denied the humanity of others. What did slave children, immigrant children in city slums, children of pioneer farmers, children of a doctor or minister in a comfortable home, and the children of a proud aristocrat on a plantation or those of a wealthy New England merchant really have in common? Little more, one suspects, than the land itself; a mere geographical location, and even in that simple respect there was greater diversity in the American environment than in any of the many nations and provinces from which the ancestors of the American young had come. Little wonder then that experiences of childhood and youth are so elusive. At that early point in life when social institutions have had little opportunity to produce some semblance of uniformity, the spectrum of potential experience stretched wider than at any other time.

The difficulties of doing justice to the varieties of childhood are compounded by the paucity of records for all classes of children. Children themselves are incapable of producing records until they reach a certain age. Even then the inherent obstacles to expression are rarely overcome. Children of the middle class, however, figure in the literary contributions of adults. Reminiscences, school and other official records, imaginative literature, and traveler's descriptions contain numerous portraits of the favored child of white, native born parents who grew up in comfortable circumstances. The children of the poor, the immigrant, Negroes, and Indians rarely receive more than incidental mention, are only fugitive shades in the records of the past, and when they do appear are seen through the distorting prism of another's perception. Rarely do they speak for themselves. Consequently, the images formed of childhood are drawn from the middle class despite the fact that most children for most of American history grew up under different conditions and according to different rules.

By 1820 the middle-class American family did not merely duplicate Western European patterns of family life and childhood. The processes and principles of an individualistic, laissez-faire, white democracy were penetrating government, the economy, churches, and even so traditionally aristocratic an institution as the family. The Western world had not seen the like of the American family before. Many Europeans, with more fear than hope, sensed in American novelties the signs of their own future. A steady flow of travelers from abroad testified with nearly one voice to differences in tone and organization of family life and to the enhanced role of children in this new setting. They fully agreed that the American child was a new creature, although they disagreed over whether American parents should be praised or blamed for what they had done. Members of American families, some travelers averred, regarded themselves as equals, united, though often only temporarily, in a common endeavor for the pursuit of ends of mutual advantage. The hierarchical family, reaching its apex in the father, was undermined and finally leveled by the force of democratic social principles. The new model family encouraged its children to form new habits and attitudes of mind and temperament. American children were more independent, individualistic, and socially precocious than their European counterparts; they were less polite and deferential to adults. Many European travelers were appalled by the children's ready challenges to their parents' statements and their ceaseless assertion of their own views and personalities. Captain Frederick Marryat, a British naval officer and acidulous critic of democracy, believed that the power balance between American parents and their children was accurately depicted in this conversational encounter he overheard in the United States in 1837:

" 'Johnny, my dear, come here,' says his mamma.

'I won't,' cries Johnny.

'You must, my love, you are all wet, and you'll catch cold.'

'I won't,' replies Johnny.

'Come, my sweet, and I've something for you.'

'I won't.'

'Oh! Mr. ———, do, pray make Johnny come in.'

'Come in, Johnny,' says the father.

'I won't.'

'I tell you, come in directly, sir — do you hear?'

'I won't,' replies the urchin, taking to his heels.

'A sturdy republican, sir,' says his father to me, smiling at the boy's resolute disobedience." [1]

Happily, some observers were able to report that equality did not always lead to willful disobedience. Another Englishman watched a father and his fourteen-year-old son chatting and singing together during a train trip on terms of equality, respect, and affection. "There was no attempt," he wrote, "at keeping up the dignity of a parent, as might have been considered necessary and proper with us. There was no reserve. They were . . . already on an equal footing of persons of the same age." [2] Middle-class children had become then the most republican and democratic of all Americans in their feelings and manners. Individualism, progress, and an opportunity for those like themselves to move ahead according to their merits and diligence were the guides to their beliefs and the key to their behavior.

Owing in large part to the new status of children many American parents were puzzled about how to raise them. Parents had never, of course, been without advice in this important matter. Ministers had preached sermons and legislators had passed laws on the subject. In the first half of the nineteenth century, however, the initiative for such advice came from parents themselves. They were not simply responding to the wishes of others who wanted to pattern the lives of their children in ways that would maintain an orderly society. Instead, they searched for the proper ways of rearing children, implicitly confessing that changing times required a new approach. Many manuals on the proper methods of child-rearing appeared after the 1820's. Some looked toward a restoration of family relations on a traditional, hierarchical model, maintained by repeated applications of piety and discipline. Most, however, looked for a middle way between authority and permissiveness, in which family relations were governed by affection and maintained by mutual respect with severe discipline resorted to on only rare occasions. The ideal child was one who would be independent but in agreement on essentials with parents as a result of free choice. The welfare of children had become the preeminent goal of family life.

1. Frederick Marryat, *A Diary in America* (London, 1839), III, 284–285.

2. Foster Barham Zincke, *Last Winter in the United States* (London, 1868), p. 71.

The legal status of American children was subject to conflicting pressures and interests. On the one hand, the welfare of the child — his prospects for personal growth and even happiness — was encroaching upon the rights of parents and the convenience of society as guiding principles in the law of family relations. Family law had been primarily established by judges in the course of deciding actual conflicts over the rights of parents and children, custody, and illegitimacy, with occasionally a statute to codify a trend or resolve inconsistencies. During the first half of the nineteenth century the judges' determination of the welfare of the child involved in a particular case began to override the formal rights of parents, particularly fathers. This trend was most apparent in custody cases. Courts began to favor mothers in disputes over custody on the grounds that the child's future welfare depended upon a mother's care. A willingness to restrict the authority of a parent was one important result of the enhanced social status of children to which so many testified. On the other hand, racial biases deprived some children of this concern for their future well-being. When the children of free and slave Negroes encountered the law, their interests were regularly subordinated to those of someone else. The child with one free and one slave parent was regarded as illegitimate because marriage of slaves had no legal foundation. Children of slaves were still denied legal protection for family life, although, as before, some masters tried to keep families together. As in many other ways, the black child paid for the ease, convenience, and profit of the white.

Negro and Indian children of the early nineteenth century are more visible to historians than were their predecessors. Few personal documents exist from earlier times; some sources, however, for the study of the lives of nineteenth-century children of black and red minorities have been preserved. Plantation account books and letters between masters and their overseers contain information about relations between owners and slaves, one-sided

as the point of view always is. Many documents of value derive from the abolition movement. Many fugitive slaves and freedmen left accounts of their travails and escapes. These sources serve to counterbalance a one-sided view and to give depth of understanding to black experience and history. Their existence testifies to the weakening hold of the slave system. As there were more fugitives, and as they came into contact with sympathetic, educated persons or learned to read and write, they drew up accounts of their lives in slavery and escape that served as an inspiration to the abolition cause and an impetus to the education of Negroes. These accounts reinforced points known or suspected for a long time. They made clear, often in the most graphic language, the sufferings of slave families, the disregard of masters for ordinary human decencies in their regulation of slaves, the sacrifices that slaves and free Negroes were willing to make in each others behalf, and the risks they were willing to run in order to be free. Perhaps no single event was more persuasive in convincing white Americans that blacks were indeed human beings and deserving of humane treatment than the appearance of slave narratives. They taught that heroism, self-sacrifice, and idealism could all exist in a black man. The most famous of these documents was Frederick Douglass' *Narrative*. A man of energy and intelligence, Douglass devoted himself after his escape from slavery to the advancement of the abolitionist cause, lecturing widely throughout the North, publishing several newspapers, and participating in the affairs of abolitionist organizations. His life was a refutation of the racist assumptions so prevalent through the South and widely accepted in the North. His account of it, written in a clear and affecting style, probably did more than any other work by a black author to convince whites of the great injustice and degradation of a slave system which tried to bind such a man to a life of labor for others.

The slave system itself was outwardly thriving and expansive. Carried westward as southerners advanced from the seacoast states to the interior, it was fastened firmly into the economic and social life of the Southwest. The planting of the fertile soil of the Gulf states created a steady and sometimes spectacular demand for slave labor. Slaves in gangs with their masters or in the coffles of professional traders moved westward. Although masters of the Old Dominion and other eastern and border state areas with a surplus of slaves often prided themselves on their refusal to break up slave families, they were under such relentless pressure to sell that only the most scrupulous could resist. Perhaps at no other period were there more frequent and more frequently valid charges of slavemongering and the deliberate breeding of slaves for a distant market. The expanding economy of the nineteenth century added to the prosperity and self-confidence of the country, but for black children and their parents progress all too often meant only more work and the pain of separation.

Indian children found themselves in an unenviable situation. The traditional tribal ways were being subverted by American culture. Deprived of effective allies by American domination of the continent, the Indian tribes were thrown back upon their own inadequate resources to stem the tide of frontier advance. With fewer and fewer exceptions they recognized the hopelessness of their cause. Indian parents tried to continue to raise their children in time-honored ways appropriate to the nomadic, rugged life so many of the tribes pursued. In fact, before American power rendered ineffectual the Indian's defenses and destroyed their trust in themselves and the ways of their ancestors, their life together exhibited qualities envied by those whites who traveled among them and observed their customs without distortions of bias and fear. In particular, they pointed out the affection Indian parents, especially fathers, had for their children and the efficient way they reared the children to assume an acknowledged place and role in tribal life. Their lives, often enough, were hard and brief, but they had the security and self-respect that resulted from knowing that traditional ways worked. The future held no such satisfactions for them. Caught between the dying world of tribal culture and the inattainable world of white society, Indian children were destined for a limbo of misunderstanding and neglect.

A. THE AMERICAN FAMILY

The impact of democracy on the American family

Mathew Carey (1760–1839), publisher, economist, and civic leader in Philadelphia, emigrated from Ireland to the United States in 1824. He was the father of nine children, three of whom died young.

---

1. "The endearing relation between parents and children," 1826

Mathew Carey, *Reflections on the Subject of Emigration from Europe* . . . (Philadelphia, 1826), p. 14.

The endearing relation between parents and children partakes largely of the same mild character. The austerity, the harshness, and the severity which characterise this relation in some parts of Europe, are here unknown, except among a few foreigners, who have brought hither the manners of their own countries. Children are scarcely ever banished into nurseries, or entrusted wholly to the care of hired servants, as is too frequently the case there. From an early period they are made companions by their parents, which affords an opportunity of expanding their ideas long before they would reach maturity, in the seclusion to which children in Europe are often subjected. They are likewise much earlier introduced into company than in that quarter. This inspires a confidence in themselves, extremely advantageous in their progress through life. In many cases, however, indulgence is here carried to a censurable extreme, and parental authority not sufficiently exercised. But in general the happy medium is preserved between over indulgence and degrading severity. I have known some foreigners, who used a whip or other instrument of correction to their children at 18, 19, 20, and even beyond the period when minority had expired. No such case is to be found among natives of this country. A man who struck his child at that age, would be regarded with disgust.

The pernicious and unnatural system of primogeniture, whereby the rights, the happiness, and the fortunes of the junior branches of a family are sacrificed for the aggrandizement of the oldest son, is execrated in this country, and unknown to its laws and constitutions.

---

2. Tocqueville on the American family

Alexis de Tocqueville, *Democracy in America,* trans. Henry Reeve, ed. Phillips Bradley, II (New York: Alfred A. Knopf, 1945), 192–197; first published in 1835.

Tocqueville (1805–1859), traveled in the United States in 1831–1832, then returned to France to write his classic analysis of the working of the democratic principle in American society.

It has been universally remarked that in our time the several members of a family stand upon an entirely new footing towards each other; that the distance which formerly separated a father from his sons has been lessened; and that paternal authority, if not destroyed, is at least impaired.

Something analogous to this, but even more striking, may be observed in the United States. In America the family, in the Roman and aristocratic signification of the word, does not exist. All that remains of it are a few vestiges in the first years of childhood, when the father exercises, without opposition, that absolute domestic authority which the feebleness of his children renders necessary and which their interest, as well as his own incontestable superiority, warrants. But as soon as the young American approaches manhood, the ties of filial obedience are relaxed day by day; master of his thoughts, he is soon master of his conduct. In America there is, strictly speaking, no adolescence: at the close of boyhood the man appears and begins to trace out his own path.

It would be an error to suppose that this is preceded by a domestic struggle in which the son has obtained by a sort of moral violence the liberty that his father refused him. The same habits, the same principles, which impel the one to assert his independence predispose the other to consider the use of that independence as an incontestable right. The former does not exhibit any of those rancorous or irregular passions which disturb men long after they have shaken off an established authority; the latter feels none of that bitter and angry regret which is apt to survive a bygone power. The father foresees the limits of his authority long beforehand, and when the time arrives, he surrenders it without a struggle; the son looks forward to the exact period at which he will be his own master, and he enters upon his freedom without precipitation and without effort, as a possession which is his own and which no one seeks to wrest from him.

It may perhaps be useful to show how these changes which take place in family relations are closely connected with the social and political revolution that is approaching its consummation under our own eyes.

There are certain great social principles that a people either introduces everywhere or tolerates nowhere. In countries which are aristocratically constituted with all the gradations of rank, the government never makes a direct appeal to the mass of the governed; as men are united together, it is enough to lead the foremost; the rest will follow. This is applicable to the family as well as to all aristocracies that have a head. Among aristocratic nations social institutions recognize, in truth, no one in the family but the father; children are received by society at his hands; society governs him, he governs them. Thus the parent not only has a natural right but acquires a political right to command them; he is the author and the support of his family, but he is also its constituted ruler.

In democracies, where the government picks out every individual singly from the mass to make him subservient to the general laws of the community, no such intermediate person is required; a father is there, in the eye of the law, only a member of the community, older and richer than his sons.

When most of the conditions of life are extremely unequal and the inequality of these conditions is permanent, the notion of a superior grows upon the imaginations of men; if the law invested him with no privileges, custom and public opinion would concede them. When, on the contrary, men differ but little from each other and do not always remain in dissimilar conditions of life, the general notion of a superior becomes weaker and less distinct; it is vain for legislation to strive to place him who obeys very much beneath him who commands; the manners of the time bring the two men nearer to one another and draw them daily towards the same level.

Although the legislation of an aristocratic people grants no peculiar privileges to the heads of families, I shall not be the less convinced that their power is more respected and more extensive than in a democracy; for I know that, whatever the laws may be, superiors always appear higher and inferiors lower in aristocracies than among democratic nations.

When men live more for the remembrance of what has been than for the care of what is, and when they are more given to attend to what their ancestors thought than to think themselves, the father is the natural and necessary tie between the past and the present, the link by which the ends of these two chains are connected. In aristocracies, then, the father is not only the civil head of the family, but the organ of its traditions, the expounder of its customs, the arbiter of its manners. He is listened to with deference, he is addressed with respect, and the love that is felt for him is always tempered with fear.

When the condition of society becomes democratic and men adopt as their general principle that it is good and lawful to judge of all things for oneself, using former points of belief not as a rule of faith, but simply as a means of information, the power which the opinions of a father exercise over those of his sons diminishes as well as his legal power.

Perhaps the subdivision of estates that democracy brings about contributes more than anything else to change the relations existing between a father and his children. When the property of the father of a family is scanty, his son and himself constantly live in the same place and share the same occupations; habit and necessity bring them together and force them to hold constant communication. The inevitable consequence is a sort of familiar intimacy, which renders authority less absolute and which can ill be reconciled with the external forms of respect.

Now, in democratic countries the class of those who are possessed of small fortunes is precisely that which gives strength to the notions and a particular direction to the manners of the community. That class makes its opinions preponderate as universally as its will, and even those who are most inclined to resist its commands are carried away in the end by its example. I have known eager opponents of democracy who allowed their children to address them with perfect colloquial equality.

Thus at the same time that the power of aristocracy is declining, the austere, the conventional, and the legal part of parental authority vanishes and a species of equality prevails around the domestic hearth. I do not know, on the whole, whether society loses by the change, but I am inclined to believe that man individually is a gainer by it. I think that in proportion as manners and laws become more democratic, the relation of father and son becomes more intimate and more affectionate; rules and authority are less talked of, confidence and tenderness are often increased, and it would seem that the natural bond is drawn closer in proportion as the social bond is loosened.

In a democratic family the father exercises no other power than that which is granted to the affection and the experience of age; his orders would perhaps be disobeyed, but his advice is for the most part authoritative. Though he is not hedged in with ceremonial respect, his sons at least accost him with confidence; they have no settled form of addressing him, but they speak to him constantly and are ready to consult him every day. The master and the constituted ruler have vanished; the father remains.

Nothing more is needed in order to judge of the difference between the two states of society in this respect than to peruse the family correspondence of aristocratic ages. The style is always correct, ceremonious, stiff, and so cold that the natural warmth of the heart can hardly be felt in the language. In democratic countries, on the contrary, the language addressed by a son to his father is always marked by mingled freedom, familiarity, and affection, which at once show that new relations have sprung up in the bosom of the family.

A similar revolution takes place in the mutual relations of children. In aristocratic families, as well as in aristocratic society, every place is marked out beforehand. Not only does the father occupy a separate rank, in which he enjoys extensive privileges, but even the children are not equal among themselves. The age and sex of each irrevocably determine his rank and secure to him certain privileges. Most of these distinctions are abolished or diminished by democracy.

In aristocratic families the eldest son, inheriting the greater part of the property and almost all the rights of the family, becomes the chief and to a certain extent the master of his brothers. Greatness and power are for him; for them, mediocrity and dependence. But it would be wrong to suppose that among aristocratic nations the privileges of the eldest son are advantageous to himself alone, or that they excite nothing but envy and hatred around him. The eldest son commonly endeavors to procure wealth and power for his brothers, because the general splendor of the house is reflected back on him who represents it; the younger sons seek to back the elder brother in all his undertakings, because the greatness and power of the head of the family better enable him to provide for all its branches. The different members of an aristocratic family are therefore very closely bound together; their interests are connected, their minds agree, but their hearts are seldom in harmony.

Democracy also binds brothers to each other, but by very different means. Under democratic laws all the children are perfectly equal and consequently independent; nothing brings them forcibly together, but nothing keeps them apart; and as they have the same origin, as they are trained under the same roof, as they are treated with the same care, and as no peculiar privilege distinguishes or divides them, the affectionate and frank intimacy of early years easily springs up between them. Scarcely anything can occur to break the tie thus formed at the outset of life, for brotherhood brings them daily together without embarrassing them. It is not, then, by interest, but by common associations and by the free sympathy of opinion and of taste that democracy unites brothers to each other. It divides their inheritance, but allows their hearts and minds to unite.

Such is the charm of these democratic manners that even the partisans of aristocracy are attracted by it; and after having experienced it for some time, they are by no means tempted to revert to the respectful and frigid observances of aristocratic families. They would be glad to retain the domestic habits of democracy if they might throw off its social conditions and its laws; but these elements are indissolubly united, and it is impossible to enjoy the former without enduring the latter.

. . . . . .

. . . Democracy loosens social ties, but tightens natural ones; it brings kindred more closely together, while it throws citizens more apart.

---

3. Thomas Jefferson's opinion of the effects of slaveowning on the formation of character

Thomas Jefferson, *Notes on the State of Virginia,* ed. William Peden (Chapel Hill: University of North Carolina Press, 1955), p. 162; first published in 1787.

There must doubtless be an unhappy influence on the manners of our people produced by the existence of slavery among us. The whole commerce between master and slave is a perpetual exercise of the most boisterous passions, the most unremitting despotism on the one part, and degrading submissions on the other. Our children see this, and learn to imitate it; for man is an imitative animal. This quality is the germ of all education in him. From his cradle to his grave he is learning to do what

he sees others do. If a parent could find no motive either in his philanthropy or his self-love, for restraining the intemperance of passion towards his slave, it should always be a sufficient one that his child is present. But generally it is not sufficient. The parent storms, the child looks on, catches the lineaments of wrath, puts on the same airs in the circle of smaller slaves, gives a loose to his worst of passions, and thus nursed, educated, and daily exercised in tyranny, cannot but be stamped by it with odious peculiarities. The man must be a prodigy who can retain his manners and morals undepraved by such circumstances.

---

4. The republican manners of American children

Harriet Martineau, *Society in America* (New York, 1837), III, 166–167.

Miss Martineau (1802–1876), English author and reformer, traveled in the United States between 1834 and 1836.

The early republican consciousness of which I have spoken, and the fact of the more important place which the children occupy in a society whose numbers are small in proportion to its resources, are the two circumstances which occasion that freedom of manners in children of which so much complaint has been made by observers, and on which so much remonstrance has been wasted; — I say "wasted," because remonstrance is of no avail against a necessary fact. Till the United States cease to be republican, and their vast area is fully peopled, the children there will continue as free and easy and as important as they are. For my own part, I delight in the American children; in those who are not overlaid with religious instruction. There are instances, as there are everywhere, of spoiled, pert, and selfish children. Parents' hearts are pierced there, as elsewhere. But the independence and fearlessness of children were a perpetual charm in my eyes. To go no deeper, it is a constant amusement to see how the speculations of young minds issue, when they take their own way of thinking, and naturally say all they think. Some admirable specimens of active little minds were laid open to me at a juvenile ball at Baltimore. I could not have got at so much in a year in England. If I had at home gone in among eighty or a hundred little people, between the ages of eight and sixteen, I should have extracted little more than "Yes, ma'am," and "No, ma'am." At Baltimore, a dozen boys and girls at a time crowded round me, questioning, discussing, speculating, revealing in a way which enchanted me. In private houses, the comments slipped in at table by the children were often the most memorable, and generally the most amusing part of the conversation. Their aspirations all come out. Some of these are very striking as indicating the relative value of things in the children's minds. One affectionate little sister, of less than four years old, stimulated her brother William (five) by telling him that if he would be very very good, he might in time be called William Webster; and then he might get on to be as good as Jesus Christ.

Guides for parents and children

1. An authoritarian outlook on rearing children

Heman Humphrey, *Domestic Education* (Amherst, Mass., 1840), pp. 16–19, 27–29, 36–37.

A graduate of Yale and president of Amherst College from 1823 to 1845, Humphrey represented the views of conservative New England congregationalism.

Every family is a little state, or empire within itself, bound together by the most endearing attractions, and governed by its patriarchal head, with whose prerogative no power on earth has a right to interfere. Nations may change their forms of government at pleasure, and may enjoy a high degree of prosperity under different constitutions; and perhaps the time will never come, when any *one* form will be adapted to the circumstances of all mankind. But in the family organization there is but one model, for all times and all places. It is just the same now, as it was in the beginning, and it is impossible to alter it, without marring its beauty, and directly contravening the wisdom and benevolence of the Creator. It is at once the simplest, the safest and the most efficient organization that can be conceived of. Like everything else, it may be perverted to bad purposes; but it is a divine model, and must not be altered.

Every father is the constituted head and ruler of his household. God has made him the supreme earthly legislator over his children, accountable, of course, to Himself, for the manner in which he executes his trust; but amenable to no other power, except in the most extreme cases of neglect, or abuse. The will of the parent is the law to which the child is bound in all cases to submit, unless it plainly contravenes the law of God. Children are brought into existence and placed in families, not to follow their own wayward inclinations, but to look up to their parents for guidance; not to teach, but to be taught; not to govern but to be governed. You may think that your neighbor's family is badly managed. You may see and know, that the education of his children is greatly neglected, and that he has not a single patriarchal qualification. Under these circumstances you may *advise* him as earnestly as you please — you may point out his duties — you may expostulate with him — you may adjure him by all that is tender and sacred, to consider where he stands, and to think of the account which he must render; but if he turns a deaf ear, you have no remedy. God has placed him and not you at the head of his family. You have no right, if you had the inclination, to enter his house, and order him to stand aside, and assume the reins of government yourself, and absolve his children from their natural allegiance. It may be true that they would be infinitely better off under your control and instruction than his; but you may not thus interfere with one of God's ordinances. Such a general allowance would subvert the whole domestic system.

Nor has *civil government* any right to interfere with the head of a family, unless it be where he is guilty of extreme neglect, or abuse. If he becomes a sot, or a reprobate in any other form of abandonment; or if he plays the tyrant in his own house, so as to put the lives of his children in jeopardy, it is no doubt the right and the duty of the magistrate to come to their rescue. It is an extreme case, and none but extreme remedies will reach it. But in all ordinary cases, even of great delinquency, the guilty parent must be left to answer for his abuse of power, or neglect of duty, to him who "ruleth over all." It would be impossible for any government in the world, to take upon itself parental authority and discharge parental duties; and if it were possible, such an innovation would soon derange and destroy the whole social system.

And as no power on earth may forcibly take the reins out of a parent's hands, neither may he abandon his post, or refuse to act as the vicegerent of God in his own house. When a father finds himself surrounded by a rising family, it is too late for him to decide whether or not he will assume the responsibility of supporting and educating his children. That question is already settled. "Necessity is laid upon him." . . . However unfit he may find himself to discharge the duties of a parent, or however anxious he may be to shift them off upon somebody else, he must stand in his lot and meet them the best way he can. He is not indeed precluded from availing himself of the assistance of others, by sending his children abroad for a part of their education, when he thinks it will be for their advantage; but let him not forget that he is accountable to God for the judicious exercise of this discretion. The authority which he cannot exercise over his children when they are away from home, he must delegate to those who receive them under their care; and in no case may he place them where they will be left to themselves, and exposed without counsel or restraint, to bad influences.

.   .   .   .   .

The rights and duties of parents . . . extend through the whole period of the child's minority. It is not enough for parents to bring their children early under proper subjection, and then leave their authority to take care of itself. There is no such executive energy in any domestic code, however wise or reasonable. The work is only commenced, when you have subdued the refractory spirit of your child. It is indeed an auspicious beginning; and if you keep the advantage which you have gained, the task will ever after be comparatively easy. But you must never let go the reins. If you relax, if you leave the child after it has once yielded, to follow its own depraved inclinations, it will soon becomes as head-strong as ever; and if it does not get entirely beyond your reach, it may cost you infinite trouble to regain the ground which you have lost. All the natural tendencies in the minds of our children are downward; and there is no overcoming this gravitating power, but by constant effort. "Line must be upon line, precept upon precept, here a little and there a little."

A judicious parent will not use exactly the same means to govern a boy of eight years old, as he does to govern a child of two; nor will he deal with a grown up son of fifteen, just as he does with a lad of ten. But though the *means* will be different, the *end* is the same. The young man of twenty, in his father's house, has no more right to say that he will use his own discretion, in regard to observing the rules and regulations of the family, than a child of ten; and that parent sins against God, against the community in which he lives, and against his own family, who throws up his authority, before his children can safely be left to govern and take care of themselves.

---

2. Rearing the innocent child on
the principle of affection

Lydia Maria Child, *The Mother's Book*
(Boston, 1831), pp. 22–29.

Holding a more charitable view of human
nature than that of Heman Humphrey,
Lydia Child (1802–1880), a prolific authoress
and humanitarian reformer, advised parents
to consider their children's feelings
as they guided their behavior.

The good old fashioned maxim that "example is better than precept," is the best thing to begin with. The great difficulty in education is that we give *rules* instead of inspiring *sentiments*. The simple fact that your child never saw you angry, that your voice is always gentle, and the expression of your face always kind, is worth a thousand times more than all the rules you can give him about not beating his dog, pinching his brother, &c. It is in vain to load the understanding with rules, if the affections are not pure. In the first place, it is not possible to make rules enough to apply to all manner of cases; and if it were possible, a child would soon forget them. But if you inspire him with right *feelings,* they will govern his *actions.* All our thoughts and actions come from our affections; if we love what is good, we shall think and do what is good. Children are not so much influenced by what we say and do in particular reference to them, as by the general effect of our characters and conversation. They are in a great degree creatures of imitation. If they see a mother fond of finery, they become fond of finery; if they see her selfish, it makes them selfish; if they see her extremely anxious

for the attention of wealthy people, they learn to think wealth is the only good.

Those whose early influence is what it should be, will find their children easy to manage, as they grow older.

An infant's wants should be attended to without waiting for him to cry. At first, a babe cries merely from a sensation of suffering — because food, warmth, or other comforts necessary to his young existence, are withheld; but when he finds crying is the only means of attracting attention, he soon gets in the habit of crying for everything. To avoid this, his wants should be attended to, whether he demand it or not. Food, sleep, and necessary comforts should be supplied to him at such times as the experience of his mother may dictate. If he has been sitting on the floor, playing quietly by himself a good while, take him up and amuse him, if you can spare time, without waiting for weariness to render him fretful. Who can blame a child for fretting and screaming, if experience has taught him that he cannot get his wants attended to in any other manner?

Young children should never be made to cry by plaguing them, for the sake of fun; it makes them seriously unhappy for the time, and has an injurious effect upon their dispositions. When in any little trouble, they should be helped as quick as possible. When their feet are caught in the rounds of a chair, or their playthings entangled, or when any other of the thousand and one afflictions of baby-hood occur, it is an easy thing to teach them to wait by saying, "Stop a minute, and I will come to you." But do not say this, to put them off; attend to them as quick as your employments will permit; they will then wait patiently should another disaster occur. Children, who have entire confidence that the simple truth is always spoken to them, are rarely troublesome.

A silent influence, which they do not perceive, is better for young children than direct rules and prohibitions. For instance, should a child be in ill humor, without any apparent cause (as will sometimes happen) — should he push down his playthings, and then cry because he has injured them — chase the kitten, and then cry because she has run out of his reach — it is injurious to take any direct notice of it, by saying, "How cross you are today, James. What a naughty boy you are. I don't love you today." This, in all probability, will make matters worse. The better way is to draw off his attention to pleasant thoughts by saying, "I am going in the garden" — or, "I am going out to see the calf. Does James want to go with me?" If, in the capriciousness of his humor, he says he does not want to go, do not urge him: make preparations to go, and he will soon be inclined to follow. A few flowers, or a little pleasant talk about the calf, will, in all probability produce entire forgetfulness of his troubles. If the employment suggested to him combine usefulness with pleasure, — such as feeding the chickens, shelling peas for dinner, &c, so much the better. The habit of assisting others, excites the benevolent affections, and lays the foundation of industry.

When a little child has been playing, and perhaps quarrelling, out of doors, and comes in with his face all of a blaze, sobbing and crying, it is an excellent plan to take him by the hand and say, "What is the matter, my dear boy? Tell me what is the matter. But, how dirty your face is! Let me wash your face nicely, and wipe it dry, and then you shall sit in my lap and tell me all about it." If he is washed gently, the sensation will be pleasant and refreshing, and by the time the operation is finished, his attention will be drawn off from his vexations; his temper will be cooled, as well as his face. Then seat him in your lap, encourage him to tell you all about his troubles, comb his hair gently in the meantime, and in a few minutes the vexation of his little spirit will be entirely soothed. This secret of calling off the attention by little kind offices is very valuable to those who have the care of invalids, or young children. Bathing the hands and feet, or combing the hair gently, will sometimes put a sick person to sleep when they can obtain rest in no other way.

.   .   .   .   .   .

By such expedients as I have mentioned, ill-humor and discontent are driven away by the influence of kindness and cheerfulness; "evil is overcome with good." Whipping and scolding could not have produced quiet so soon; and if they could, the child's temper would have been injured in the process.

I have said that example and silent influence were better than direct rules and commands. Nevertheless, there are cases where rules must be made; and children must be taught to obey implicitly. For instance, a child must be expressly forbidden to play with fire, to climb upon the tables, &c. But whenever it is possible, restraint should be invisible.

The first and most important step in management is, that whatever a mother says, always *must* be done. For this reason, do not require too much; and on no account allow your child to do at one time, what you have forbidden him at another. Sometimes when a woman feels easy and good-natured, and does not expect any company, she will allow her children to go to the table and take lumps of sugar; but should visiters be in the room, or she out of humor with the occurrences of the day, she will perhaps scold, or strike them for the self same trick. How can a mother expect obedience to commands so selfish and capricious? What inferences will a child draw from such conduct? You may smile at the idea that very young children draw inferences; but it is a fact, that they do draw inferences — and very just ones too. We mistake, when we trust too much to children's not thinking, or observing. They are shrewd reasoners in all cases where their little interests are concerned. They know a mother's ruling passion; they soon discover her weak side, and learn how to attack it most successfully . . .

The necessity of obedience early instilled is the foundation of all good management. If children see you governed by a real wish for their good, rather than by your own selfishness, or capricious freaks, they will easily acquire this excellent habit. Wilful disobedience should never go unpunished. If a little child disobeys you from mere forgetfulness and frolic, it is best to take no notice of it; for his intention is not bad, and authority has greater effect when used sparingly, and on few occasions. Should he forget the same injunction again, look at him very seriously, and tell him that if he forgets it again, you shall be obliged to punish him. Should he commit the offence the third time, take from him the means of committing it; for instance, if you tell him not to tear his picturebook, and he does tear it, take it away from him. Perhaps he will pout and show ill humor; — will push off with his little chair, and say "I don't love you, mother." — If so, take no notice. Do not laugh, for that would irritate him, without performing the least use; do not seem offended with him, for that will awaken a love of power in his little mind. It excites very bad feelings in a child, to see that he can vex a parent, and make her lose her self-command. In spite of his displeasure, therefore, continue your employment tranquilly, as if nothing had happened. If his ill humor continue, however, and show itself in annoyances to you, and others around him, you should take him by the hand, look very seriously in his face, and say, "James, you are such a naughty boy, that I must punish you. I am very sorry to punish you; but I must, that you may remember to be good next time." This should be done with perfect calmness, and a look of regret. When a child is punished in anger, he learns to consider it a species of revenge; when he is punished in sorrow, he believes that it is done for his good.

The punishment for such peevishness as I have mentioned should be being tied in an armchair, or something of that simple nature. I do not approve of shutting the little offender in the closet. The sudden transition from light to darkness affects him with an undefined species of horror, even if he has been kept perfectly free from frightful stories. A very young child will become quite cold in a few minutes, at midsummer, if shut in a dark closet. If the culprit is obstinate, and tries to seem as if he did not care for his punishment, let him remain in confinement till he gets very tired; but in the meanwhile be perfectly calm yourself, and follow your usual occupations. You can judge by his actions, and the expression of his countenance, whether his feelings begin to soften. Seize a favorable moment, and ask him if he is sorry he has been so naughty; if he says "yes," let him throw himself into your arms, kiss him, and tell him you hope he will never be naughty again; for if he is, you must punish him, and it makes you very sorry to punish him. Here is the key to all good management: always punish a child for wilfully disobeying you in the most trifling particular; but never punish him in anger.

---

3. The way to success and respectability

Anonymous, *Bosses and Their Boys* (Philadelphia, ca. 1853), pp. 138–142.

This book was one of hundreds of edifying publications for children and youth of the American Sunday School Union, an interdenominational organization of evangelical churches founded in 1825 to assist in the establishment of Sunday schools for children, especially those of poor parents.

John Munson was out of his term of apprenticeship some three years before James, but he continued to work as a journeyman, and the wages that he made he was careful to lay up in the SAVINGS BANK . . . By the time that James Stevens had completed his term, he too had something ahead, and they began to think about going into business for themselves.

Mr. Stone had been more and more interested in the progress of his apprentices. It was by his direction that James's wages had been increased from time to time, more rapidly than they would have been but for the favour of his employer, who had been an attentive observer of the habits of his men ever since he had been roused to a sense of his high responsibility as an employer. He had been compelled to dismiss several from his service, on the ground of unfaithfulness growing out of their bad habits; and when he saw the mischief which these were working, he could not fail to notice with approbation the deportment and abilities of such a youth as James Stevens.

Mr. Stone found in James what he had long been looking for — *"one who would make his employer's interest his own"* — a young man who would labour and watch with the same zeal and fidelity for the interest of his employer that he would if the establishment belonged to him. This is the secret of securing the favourable regard of one who "owns the concern." Most business men keep a bright look out for their own interest. It is not an easy matter to find help that suits. Very few young men are disposed to work for others as they would work for themselves. They do not think that they are working for themselves when they are serving an employer for wages. It is very short-sighted in them to take such a view of the case; for it will be found in the long run, that he who is faithful in a few things will by-and-by have the charge of many things; and though merit is sometimes suffered to lie unobserved in this world, it is generally appreciated; and success that is not built on merit is not worth having.

Mr. Stone was a fair sample of manufacturers and merchants and capitalists generally. He was willing to do well by those who were disposed to do well by him. When he saw that a young man would do no more than just enough to keep his place and get his wages, working as if he grudged every minute and every blow, Mr. Stone set him down as a lazy and indifferent fellow, not worthy of his regard. But he saw Stevens and Munson always ready for any thing that would promote the efficiency of the business. Early and late, in season and out of season, they were always ready; and if they had owned the shop, and were making fortunes out of the business, they could not have more faithfully laboured in it.

He was now getting well on in life. Most of his children were grown up. He had taken a fancy to these young men, and he advised them to go into business on their own account. They urged the want of capital as a fatal objection; but he removed that difficulty by telling them that he would put them in the way of beginning a small concern, and they might come to him for help whenever they were in need.

They could not refuse so favourable an opening, and, taking a building of moderate dimensions, they set up business for themselves under the firm of

Stevens and Munson,
Coach and Carriage Manufacturers.

In a manufacturing community such as this, the social position of the people is of course not regulated by birth and education. There are fewer distinctions in society than elsewhere. These young men found themselves at once entitled to the respect, as they had long enjoyed the entire confidence of the community, so far as they were known. James Stevens was often at Mr. Stone's house; and it came to pass that, in the lapse of time, James Stevens became the son-in-law of Mr. Stone; and not very long after that important event, Mr. Stone proposed to James to take his business and carry it on in his name, as he, Mr. Stone, was now advanced in age, and was anxious to retire. To this James said he had but one objection; and that was, he was in partnership with John Munson, and he was not willing to leave him, however his prospects might be improved by so tempting an offer as Mr. Stone had made him. The old gentleman told him it would be very easy to get along with that matter, as Munson could come into the new arrangement, putting in whatever sum of money he might be able to command. Mr. Stone himself consented to remain, if the young men would take the entire charge of the business and let him act only as a silent partner. So they formed a new firm under the name of

Stevens, Munson and Co.,
Coach, Carriage and Car Manufacturers;
and under this firm they are doing business at

this very time. Mr. Stone has ceased to give any attention to the concern, but is enjoying the evening of life with his children and grand-children around him.

James Stevens, who sent his first dollar to his parents, was glad to spend the first thou-sand dollars that he was worth in improving the house they occupied in Shellton; and from time to time he added to it all the comforts which the old people could desire. The same good spirit led him to provide for the education of the younger children; and as they come on in life, he will see that they are put into the way of earning an honest livelihood as he has done before them.

---

4. Growing up as a Shaker in Enfield, New Hampshire

Hervey Elkins, *Fifteen Years in the Senior Order of Shakers* (Hanover, N.H., 1853), pp. 37–38, 40–43.

The Senior Order of Shakers at Enfield consisted of those who had proved them-selves worthy and fit for full membership in the Shaker community.

My mother and only brother are now mem-bers of the Society, at Enfield, being caught with my father in the meshes of Shakerism at the time that I, a tender and sensitive plant, was transplanted from my native soil, into one of a more stiff and tenacious texture. Be-reft at once of the gentle accents and caresses of maternal care, by the rigidity of that regime which mildly severs man and wife, parent and child, from each other's embraces and directs them all to seek a less local, and that more general bond of union, which folds to its bosom the whole household of faith, and reduces to practice the ideal of other christians . . . yet by the novelty and systematic order which I witnessed, and by the excellent caretakers and

cheerful countenances which I saw around me, I soon took root in the soil of deep and un-harassed contentment. I lived with my parents in the Novitiate Order[1] for about four months. I saw them often and conversed freely upon the harmony and exoteric beauty of our new habitation.

My father, a man of mediocre fortune, of inflexible honesty, and eccentric views, re-mained for a time; but at last refused implicit submission to *men* anointed as leaders of Christ's church and aspired, as he said, "to a more immediate communication of God's will direct from the impulse given to conscience," and returned to his old domain; leaving be-hind him my mother, my brother, and myself.

.   .   .   .   .

In the Senior Order I was placed as ap-prentice, with the tailor who, as I said before, is now a bishop . . . For nearly three years I was submitted to his temporal and spiritual guidance; and week after week and month after month we plied together the needles which fabricated the beautiful drab garments worn by other brethren; occasionally, however, to promote a healthy condition and development of the bodily function, I climbed the mountains in company with those of my age, or sauntered along the shores, or rowed the skiffs over the burnished surface of the lake. In spring, I sometimes helped the other boys to gather, boil and eat the delicacies of the sugar maple, and roll away from the mill the blocks of wood for fuel, cut the desired length by a large saw carried by water power horizontally across the log. In the summer I would accompany them in gathering strawberries, raspberries and blackberries: and in the hay-field, my master and all who were able, would lend a helping hand. The Senior Order was generally four or five weeks engaged in the hay harvest, in which time three hundred acres of land would be stripped of their products, by about twenty-five men and as many boys . . .

1. The Novitiate Order was made up of applicants for admission.

My tutor had also the supervision of the school, and the spiritual guidance of all the male children. He taught us to be honest, pure and clean; and might have been a consummate master of youth had he better understood the art of inspiring them with the ideas of beauty, nobility, and love of piety, in lieu of monotonously drilling them by admonitions for every trifling offence. He wished to urge us by a "hot-bed" process, to understand and ponder upon the abstract essences of divinity. He desired fickle and puerile minds, who could not be made sensible of a lofty conception, or a sublime sentiment, to see those spiritual beauties that he had seen, to hear those soft whispers that he had heard, and to feel the gentle impressions which he had felt. Frequent rebukes, however gentle, serve to harden the heart and fortify it for opposition. The capricious child of nature delights to break down moral, as well as physical, restraints, which are raised before him in consequence of distrust . . . His scientific knowledge was good, but from the day he joined the Shakers, he added, to his previously acquired stock, not a groat, unless we except a knowledge of music, which was all acquired after he became a member of the Shaker society. For reading or writing music, few men in this, or any other country, can excel him.

The delirium of pleasure, which I had so rapturously anticipated from the enchanting scenes of my new home, was only interrupted by my separation from my parents, and the recollection of the sweet company of my maternal parent, who knew that I was happy and well. In my new abode, I saw no very repulsive look or frowns, unless elicited by a few of my sarcastic and wayward companions, of which in spite of religious discipline, some were found. Some few aged ones, having made through life many crooks and turns and digressions from the straight road — some false movements in the great battle field with their spiritual enemy, displayed occasionally to their subsequent chagrin, a pique incompatible with their pacific rule of faith. Yet, on the whole,

great harmony appeared to exist. Our juvenile meetings, where the boys, about twenty in number, and the caretakers, the one our spiritual, the other our temporal supervisor, met for worship, were conducted by my tutor with all the religious sincerity and fervor of devotion. The songs, the dances, the ministrations, the lapses into a visionary or abducted state, heightened immeasurably in interest and excitement by the announcement of angels and departed spirits, causing the instruments to join simultaneously in the evolutions and caroles of complicated dances and songs of immediate creation — scenes common in the family meetings which Sundays we attended, and not uncommon even among the children, exercised upon my mind a curiosity and inclination to investigate the cause, or else reason away, by the pretext of impossibility of such power being exercised over mortals. More than a score of new dances were performed with an attitude of grace and with the precision of a machine, by about twenty female clairvoyants. They *said* they learned them of seraphs before the throne of God.

I was doubtful of their assertions; for such things were to me novel. I however determined not to overstep the bounds of prudence, and declare the work an illusion, for fear that I might blaspheme a higher power. I communicated my doubts to a few of my companions, and one, less cautious than myself, immediately broke forth in imprecations against it. I never was secretly opposed, but a turbulent disposition or a love for dramatic scenes, prompted by the hope of detecting either the validity or deception of such phenomana, impelled me to wink opposition to my reckless companion. In the devotional exercises, which served as a preliminary to the entrance of the mind into a superior condition, such as whirling, twisting and reeling, we all took part. Henry, for that was the name of the youth who was so zealous in his aspersions, united awkwardly and derisively in these exercises. Amidst so many arms, legs and bodies, revolving, oscillating, staggering and tripping, it is not remarkable that a few should be thrown prostrate, (not violently however,) upon the floor. One evening, in a boy's meeting at a time of great excitement, when the spirits of some of our companions were reported to be in spiritual spheres, and other departed spirits were careering their mortal ladies in the graceful undulations of a celestial dance, Henry and many others, among whom I was seen, were whirling, staggering, and rolling, striving, in vain, by all the humility we could assume, to be also admitted into the regions of spiritual recognition, Henry suddenly tripped and fell. One of his visionary companions instantly sprang, passed his hands with great rapidity over him as though binding him with invisible cords, and then returned to his graceful employment. The clairvoyant's eyes were closed, as indeed were the eyes of all while in that condition. In vain Henry struggled to rise, to turn or hardly to move. He was fettered, bound fast by invisible manacles. The brethren were summoned to witness the sight. In the space of perhaps half an hour the clairvoyant returned, loosened his fetters and he arose mortified and confounded. Singularly disposed, he ever after treated these gifts with virulent ridicule and never was heard to utter any serious remarks concerning this transaction. The clairvoyant after this event was the butt of his satire and jests and received them without revenge, so long as Henry remained, which was about five years: — a reckless, abandoned, evil-minded person, eventually severed by that same power which he strove incessantly to ridicule. All these strange operations and gifts are attributed by the Shakers to the influence of superhuman power like that manifested in the Primitive Church.

---

5. "Christian Nurture" in the home, 1861

Horace Bushnell, *Christian Nurture* (New Haven: Yale University Press 1960), pp. 12–13, 40, 44–51; first published in 1861.

Bushnell (1802–1876), a Congregationalist minister of Hartford, Connecticut, appalled by the excesses and ineffectiveness of revivalistic methods in winning converts to Christ, advised parents to suffuse their children's upbringing with piety in order to lead them naturally and gradually into the Christian way. This enhanced the importance of the family in rearing children.

Christian piety should begin in other and milder forms of exercise than those which commonly distinguish the conversion of adults . . . Christ himself, by that renewing Spirit who can sanctify from the womb, should be practically infused into the childish mind; in other words, . . . the house, having a domestic Spirit of grace dwelling in it, should become the church of childhood, the table and hearth a holy rite, and life an element of saving power. Something is wanted that is better than teaching, something that transcends mere effort and will-work — the loveliness of a good life, the repose of faith, the confidence of righteous expectation, the sacred and cheerful liberty of the Spirit — all glowing about the young soul, as a warm and genial nurture, and forming in it, by methods that are silent and imperceptible, a spirit of duty and religious obedience to God. This only is Christian nurture, the nurture of the Lord.

.   .   .   .   .

We conclude, not that every child can certainly be made to grow up in Christian piety — nothing is gained by asserting so much, and perhaps I could not prove it to be true, neither can any one prove the contrary — I merely show that this is the true idea and aim of Christian nurture as a nurture of the Lord. It is presumptively true that such a result can be realized, just as it is presumptively true that a school will forward the pupils in knowledge, though possibly sometimes it may fail to do it. And, without such a presumption, no parent can do his duty and fill his office well, any more than it is possible to make a good school, in the expectation that the scholars will learn something five or ten years hence, and not before.

.   .   .   .   .

What motives are laid upon all Christian parents, by the doctrine I have established, to make the first article of family discipline a constant and careful discipline of themselves. I would not undervalue a strong and decided government in families. No family can be rightly trained without it. But there is a kind of virtue, my brethren, which is not in the rod — the virtue, I mean, of a truly good and sanctified life. And a reign of brute force is much more easily maintained than a reign whose power is righteousness and love. There are, too, I must warn you, many who talk much of the rod as the orthodox symbol of parental duty, but who might really as well be heathens as Christians; who only storm about their house with heathenish ferocity, who lecture, and threaten, and castigate, and bruise, and call this family government. They even dare to speak of this as the nurture of the Lord. So much easier is it to be violent than to be holy, that they substitute force for goodness and grace, and are wholly unconscious of the imposture. It is frightful to think how they batter and bruise the delicate, tender souls of their children, extinguishing in them what they ought to cultivate, crushing that sensibility which is the hope of their being, and all in the sacred name of Christ Jesus. By no such summary process can you dispatch your duties to your children. You are not to be a savage to them, but a father and a Christian. Your real aim and study must be to infuse into them a new life, and, to this end, the Life of God must perpetually reign in you. Gathered round you as a family, they are all to be so many motives, strong as the love you bear them, to make you Christ-like in your spirit. It must be seen and felt with them that religion is a first thing with you. And it must be first, not in words and talk, but visibly first in your love — that which fixes your aims, feeds your

enjoyments, sanctifies your pleasures, supports your trials, satisfies your wants, contents your ambition, beautifies and blesses your character. No mock piety, no sanctimony of phrase, or longitude of face on Sundays will suffice. You must live in the light of God, and hold such a spirit in exercise as you wish to see translated into your children. You must take them into your feeling, as a loving and joyous element, and beget, if by the grace of God you may, the spirit of your own heart in theirs.

This is Christian education, the nurture of the Lord. Ah, how dismal is the contrast of a half-worldly, carnal piety; proposing money as the good thing of life; stimulating ambition for place and show; provoking ill-nature by petulance and falsehood; praying, to save the rule of family worship; having now and then a religious fit, and, when it is on, weeping and exhorting the family to undo all that the life has taught them to do; and then, when the passions have burnt out their fire, dropping down again to sleep in the embers, only hoping still that the family will sometime be converted! When shall we discover that families ought to be ruined by such training as this? When shall we return ourselves wholly to God, and looking on our children as one with us and drawing their character from us, make them arguments to duty and constancy — duty and constancy not as a burden, but, since they are enforced by motives so dear, our pleasure and delight? For these ties and duties exist not for the religious good of our children only, but quite as much for our own. And God, who understands us well, has appointed them to keep us in a perpetual frame of love; for so ready is our bad nature to kindle with our good, and burn with it, that what we call our piety, is, otherwise, in constant danger of degenerating into a fiery, censorious, unmerciful, and intolerant spirit.

. . . Therefore God hath set Israel in families, that the argument to duty may come upon the gentle side of your nature, and fall, as a baptism, on the head of your natural affections. Your character is to be a parent character, infolding lovingly the spirits of your children, as birds are gathered in the nest, there to be sheltered and fed, and got ready for the flight. Every hour is to be an hour of duty, every look and smile, every reproof and care an effusion of Christian love. For it is the very beauty of the work you have to do that you are to cherish and encourage good, and live a better life into the spirits of your children.

It is to be deeply considered, in connection with this view of family nurture, whether it does not meet many of the deficiencies we deplore in the Christian character of our times, and the present state of our churches. We have been expecting to thrive too much by conquest, and too little by growth. I desire to speak with all caution of what are very unfortunately called revivals of religion; for, apart from the name, which is modern, and from certain crudities and excesses that go with it — which name, crudities, and excesses are wholly adventitious as regards the substantial merits of such scenes — apart from these, I say, there is abundant reason to believe that God's spiritual economy includes varieties of exercise, answering, in all important respects, to these visitations of mercy, so much coveted in our churches. They are needed. A perfectly uniform demonstration in religion is not possible or desirable. Nothing is thus uniform but death. Our exercise varies every year and day from childhood onward. Society is going through new modes of exercise in the same manner, excited by new subjects, running into new types of feeling, and struggling with new combinations of thought. Quite as necessary is it that all holy principle should have a varied exercise — now in one duty, now in another; now in public aims and efforts, now in bosom struggles; now in social methods, now in those which are solitary and private; now in high emotion, now in deliberative thought and study. Accordingly the Christian church began with a scene of extraordinary social demonstration, and the like, in one form or another, may be traced in every period of its history since that day.

But the difficulty is with us that we idolize such scenes, and make them the whole of our religion. We assume that nothing good is doing, or can be done at any other time. And what is even worse, we often look upon these scenes, and desire them, rather as scenes of victory than of piety. They are the harvest-times of conversion, and conversion is too nearly every thing with us. In particular we see no way to gather in disciples save by means of certain marked experiences, developed in such scenes, in adult years. Our very children can possibly come to no good save in this way. Instrumentalities are invented to compass our object that are only mechanical, and the hope of mere present effect is supposed to justify them . . .

. . . Let us try if we may not train up our children in the way that they should go. Simply this, if we can do it, will make the church multiply her numbers many fold more rapidly than now, with the advantage that many more will be gained from without than now. For she will cease to hold a mere piety whose chief use is to get up occasions; she will follow a gentler and more constant method, as her duty is more constant and blends with the very life of her natural affections. Her piety will be of a more even and genial quality, and will be more respected. She will not strive and cry, but she will live. The school of John the Baptist will be succeeded by the school of Christ, as a dew comes after a fire. Families will not be a temptation to you, half the time hurrying you on to get money and prepare a show, and the other half a motive to repentance and shame, and profitless exhortation; but all the time an argument for Christian love and holy living.

Then, also, the piety of the coming age will be deeper, and more akin to habit than ours, because it began earlier. It will have more of an air of naturalness, and will be less a work of will. A generation will come forward, who will have been educated to all good undertakings and enterprises — ardent without fanaticism, powerful without machinery. Not born, so generally, in a storm, and brought to Christ by an abrupt transition, the latter portion of life will not have an unequal war to maintain with the beginning, but life will be more nearly one and in harmony with itself. Is not this a result to be desired? Could we tell our American churches, at this moment, what they want, should we not tell them this? Neither, if God, as many fear, is about to bring upon his church a day of wrath and stormy conflict, let any one suspect that such a kind of piety will want vigor and nerve to withstand the fiery assaults anticipated. See what turn the mind of our apostle took when he was arming his disciples for the great conflict of their age. Children, obey your parents — Fathers, provoke not your children — Servants, be obedient to your masters — Masters, forbear threatening — Finally, to include all, put on the whole armor of God. As if the first thought, in arming the church for great trials and stout victories, was to fill common life and the relations of the house with a Christian spirit. There is no truer truth, or more sublime. Religion never thoroughly penetrates life, till it becomes domestic. Like that patriotic fire which makes a nation invincible, it never burns with inextinguishable devotion till it burns at the hearth.

Parents who are not religious in their character, have reason, in our subject, seriously to consider what effect they are producing, and likely to produce, in their children. Probably you do not wish them to be irreligious; few parents have the hardihood or indiscretion to desire that the fear of God, the salutary restraints of religion, should be removed from their children. Possibly you exert yourselves, in a degree, to give them religious counsel and instruction. But, alas! how difficult is it for you to convince them, by words, of the value of what you practically reject yourselves. Have I not shown you that they are set in organic connection with you, to draw their spirit, and principles, and characters from yours? What, then, are they daily deriving from you, but that which you yourselves reveal in your prayerless house and at your thankless table? Is it a spirit of duty and Christian love, a faith that has its home and rest in other worlds, or is it the carnal spirit of gain, indifference to God, deadness to Christ, love of the world, pride, ambition, all that is earthly, nothing that is heavenly?

Do not imagine that you have done corrupting them when they are born. Their character is yet to be born, and, in you, is to have its parentage. Your spirit is to pass into them, by a law of transition that is natural, and well nigh irresistible. And then you are to meet them in a future life, and see how much of blessing or of sorrow they will impute to you — to share their unknown future, and look upon yourselves as father and mother to their destiny. Such thoughts, I know, are difficult for you to meet; difficult because they open real scenes, which you are, one day, to look upon. Loving these your children, as most assuredly you do, can you think that you are fulfilling the office that your love requires? Go home to your Christless house, look upon them all as they gather round you, and ask it of your love faithfully to say, whether it is well between you? And if no other argument can draw you to God, let these dear living arguments come into your soul and prevail there.

B. THE LEGAL STATUS OF THE CHILD IN THE FAMILY

Parents and children

1. Rights and duties of parents under the common law in the United States, 1827

James Kent, *Commentaries on American Law,* 11th ed. (Boston, 1867), II, 189–205.

James Kent (1763–1847), chief justice of New York Supreme Court and chancellor of New York state, was professor of law at Columbia University. His lectures or *Commentaries* were published in four volumes, 1826–1830.

1. Of the duties of parents. — The duties of parents to their children, as being their natural guardians, consist in maintaining and educating them during the season of infancy and youth, and in making reasonable provision for their future usefulness and happiness in life, by a situation suited to their habits, and a competent provision for the exigencies of that situation.

(1) *Of maintaining children.* — The wants and weaknesses of children render it necessary that some person maintain them, and the voice of nature has pointed out the parent as the most fit and proper person. The laws and customs of all nations have enforced this plain precept of universal law. The Athenian and the Roman laws were so strict in enforcing the performance of this natural obligation of the parent, that they would not allow the father to disinherit the child from passion or prejudice, but only for substantial reasons, to be approved of in a court of justice.

The obligation on the part of the parent to maintain the child continues until the latter is in a condition to provide for its own maintenance, and it extends no further than to a necessary support. The obligation of parental duty is so well secured by the strength of natural affection, that it seldom requires to be enforced by human laws. According to the language of Lord Coke, it is "nature's profession to assist, maintain, and console the child." A father's house is always open to his children. The best feelings of our nature establish and consecrate this asylum . . .

All the provision that the statute law of New York has made on this subject applies to the case of necessary maintenance; and as the provision was borrowed from the English statutes of 43 Eliz. and 5 Geo. I., and is dictated by feelings inherent in the human breast, it has probably been followed, to the extent at least of the English statutes, throughout this country. The father and mother, being of sufficient ability, of any poor, blind, lame, old, or decrepit person whomsoever, not being able to maintain himself, and becoming chargeable to any city or town, are bound, at their own charge and expense, to relieve and maintain every such person, in such manner as the overseers of the poor of the town shall approve of, and the court of general sessions shall order and direct. If the father, or if the mother, being a widow, shall abscond and leave their children a public charge, their estate is liable to be sequestered, and the proceeds applied to the maintenance of the children. The statute imposes a similar obligation upon the children, under like circumstances. This feeble and scanty statute provision was intended for the indemnity of the public against the maintenance of paupers, and it is all the injunction that the statute law pronounces in support of the duty of parents to maintain their adult children. During the minority of the child, the case is different, and the parent is absolutely bound to provide reasonably for his maintenance and education; and he may be sued for necessaries furnished, and schooling given to a child, under just and reasonable circumstances. The father is bound to support his minor children, if he be of ability, even though they have property of their own; but this obligation in such a case does not extend to the mother, and the rule, as to the father, has become relaxed. The courts now look with great liberality to the circumstances of each particular case, and to the respective estates of the father and children; and in one case, where the father had a large income, he was allowed for the maintenance of his infant children, who had still a larger income. The legal obligation of the father to maintain his child ceases as soon as the child is of age, however wealthy the father may be, unless the child becomes chargeable to the public as a pauper . . .

And in consequence of the obligation of the father to provide for the maintenance, and, in some qualified degree, for the education of his infant children, he is entitled to the custody of their persons, and to the value of their labor and services. There can be no doubt that this right in the father is perfect, while the child is under the age of fourteen years. But as the father's guardianship, by nature, continues until the child has arrived to full age, and as he is entitled by statute to constitute a testamentary guardian of the person and estate of his children until the age of twenty-one, the inference would seem to be, that he was, in contemplation of the law, entitled to the custody of the persons, and to the value of the services and labor, of his children, during their minority . . .

The father may obtain the custody of his children by the writ of *habeas corpus,* when they are improperly detained from him; but the courts, both of law and equity, will investigate the circumstances, and act according to sound discretion, and will not always, and of course, interfere upon *habeas corpus,* and take a child, though under fourteen years of age, from the possession of a third person, and deliver it over to the father against the will of the child. They will consult the inclination of an infant, if it be of a sufficiently mature age to judge for itself, and even control the right of the father to the possession and education of his child when the nature of the case appears to warrant it . . .

2. *Of the rights of parents.* — The rights of parents result from their duties. As they are bound to maintain and educate their children, the law has given them a right to such authority; and in the support of that authority, a right to the exercise of such discipline as may be requisite for the discharge of their sacred trust. This is the true foundation of parental power; and yet the ancients generally carried the power of the parent to a most atrocious extent over the person and liberty of the child. The Persians, Egyptians, Greeks, Gauls, and Romans tolerated infanticide, and allowed to fathers a very absolute dominion over their offspring; but the Romans, according to Justinian, exceeded all other people, and the liberty and lives of the children were placed within the power of the father . . .

. . . In everything that related to the domestic connections, the English common law has an undoubted superiority over the Roman. Under the latter, the paternal power continued during the son's life, and did not cease even on his arriving at the greatest honors. The son could not sue without his father's consent, or marry without his consent; and whatever he acquired, he acquired for the father's advantage; and in respect to the father, the son was considered rather in the light of property than a rational being.

The father (and on his death, the mother) is generally entitled to the custody of the infant children, inasmuch as they are their natural protectors, for maintenance and education. But the courts of justice may, in their sound discretion, and when the morals, or safety, or interests of the children strongly require it, withdraw the infants from the custody of the father or mother, and place the care and custody of them elsewhere . . .

2. "The principle of parental authority and filial obedience," 1842

Commonwealth *v.* Armstrong, 1 Penna. Law Journal, 392 (1842).

Ellis Lewis (1798–1871) was chief justice of the Pennsylvania Supreme Court from 1854 to 1857. His opinion in the Armstrong case was widely distributed and praised by authorities such as Chancellor Kent.

Lewis, J. — This is an application on behalf of the Rev. William S. Hall, a minister of the gospel of the Baptist persuasion, for an order of this Court requiring the defendant to give surety for keeping the peace. The circumstances of the case are these: On the last Sunday in February last, the defendant prohibited the complainant from administering the ordinance of baptism, by immersion, to his minor daughter, aged about seventeen, she having already been baptized in the Presbyterian church, to which her mother belonged. This prohibition was accompanied with threats of personal injury to the complainant if he baptized her, the defendant declaring that he would shoot him if he did so. On the second Sabbath in April following, the complainant having an opportunity, baptized the daughter, by immersion, in the absence, and without the knowledge of the father, and contrary to his known and positive commands. This proceeding came to the knowledge of the parent afterwards, and on the Monday after the occurrence, he followed the complainant through the street, threatening him with personal injury to such an extent as to induce the present application for surety of the peace.

Whatever may be the rights of the parent, in defence of his child, and in the exercise of his lawful authority over it, in order to prevent any act of disobedience on its part, or any interference with his authority on the part of others, it is clear that no man has a right to take the law into his own hands, to be the judge and executioner in his own case, and inflict punishment upon those who have already injured him. This is vengeance, and not defence. Vengeance does not belong to man. The court therefore order the defendant to give surety in the sum of $500 to keep the peace for six months towards the Rev. William S. Hall, and all other citizens of this Commonwealth.

Thus far we have acted without hesitation or doubt. But under the Act of Assembly of the 28th of March, 1814, it is the duty of the Court, in cases of surety of the peace, to direct the defendant, the prosecutor, or the county to pay the costs. In the exercise of this discretion, it becomes necessary to inquire into the conduct of the parties, and to ascertain whose wrongful act produced the necessity for this application for the preservation of the public peace. If the prosecutor was acting within the line of his duty, he ought not to pay them. If, on the contrary, he has interfered with the lawful authority of the father over his own offspring, in its minority, and therefore provoked him in his excited feelings, to meditate the personal injury, and to make the threats complained of, it would be just that the prosecutor should pay the costs which his own first wrongful act had occasioned.

The authority of the father results from his duties. He is charged with the duties of maintenance and education. These cannot be performed without the authority to command and to enforce obedience. The term education is not limited to the ordinary instruction of the child in the pursuits of literature. It comprehends a proper attention to the moral and religious sentiments of the child. In the discharge of this duty, it is the undoubted right of the father to designate such teachers, either in morals, religion or literature, as he shall deem best calculated to give correct instruction to the child. No teacher, either in religion or in any other branch of education, has any authority over the child, except what he derives from its parent or guardian; and that authority may be withdrawn whenever the parent, in the exercise of his discretionary power, may think proper. If he should come to the conclusion that the attendance of his child upon the ministration of any particular religious instructor is not conducive to its welfare, he may prohibit such attendance, and confine it to such religious teachers as he believes will be most likely to give correct instruction and to secure its welfare here, and its eternal happiness in the world to come. He cannot force it to adopt opinions contrary to the dictates of its own conscience, but he has a right to its time and its attention during its minority, for the purpose of enabling him to make the effort incumbent on him as a father, of "training it up in the way it should go." He may not compel it, against its own convictions of right, to become a member of any religious denomination; but after it has been initiated, with its own free will, into the religious communion in which its parent belongs, he may lawfully restrain it, during its legal infancy, from violating the religious obligations incurred in its behalf, by placing itself under the control of a minister whose opinions do not meet its parent's approbation.

The patriarchal government was established by the Most High, and, with the necessary modifications, it exists at the present day. The authority of the parent, over the youth and inexperience of his offspring, rests on foundations far more sacred than the institutions of man. "Honour thy father and thy mother," was the great law proclaimed by the King of kings. It was the first commandment accompanied with a promise of blessing upon those who obeyed it: while the dread penalty of death was inflicted upon all who were guilty of its infraction. "The eye that mocketh at his father, and despiseth to obey his mother, the ravens of the valley shall pick it out, and the young eagles shall eat it." *Proverbs xxx. 17.* "The stubborn and rebellious son who will not obey the voice of his father shall be stoned with stones that he may die, and all Israel shall hear and fear." *Deuteronomy xxi. 21.* Abraham commanded his children, and his household after him, to keep the way of the Lord. Joshua resolved both for himself and his house to serve the Lord. And the house of Eli was destroyed because his sons made themselves vile and he restrained them not. "My son keep the instruction of thy father and forsake not the law of thy mother." *Proverbs i. 8, 9;* and *Proverbs vi. 20.* "A fool despiseth his father's instruction." *Proverbs xviii. 1.* "Cursed be he that setteth light by his father or his mother, and all the people shall say, Amen." *Deuteronomy xxvii. 16.*

.   .   .   .   .

Dr. [Francis] Wayland, President of Brown University, and a distinguished minister of the Gospel, of the same denomination with the prosecutor, declares in his work on moral science, "the right of the parent is to command — the duty of the child is to obey. Authority belongs to the one, submission to the other. The relation," he continues, "is established by our Creator. The failure of one party does not annihilate the obligations of the other. If the parent be unreasonable, this does not release the child. He is still bound to honour and obey and reverence his parent. The duty of parents is to educate their children in such a manner as they (the parents) believe will be most for their future happiness, both temporal and eternal. The parent is under obligations to cause his child to be instructed in those religious sentiments which he the parent believes to be according to the will of God. With his duty in this respect no one has a right to interfere. If the parent be in error, the fault is not in teaching the child what he believes, but in believing what is false without having used the means which God has given him to arrive at the truth. In such matters he is the ultimate and the only responsible authority. While he exercised his parental duties, within their prescribed limits, he is, by the law of God, exempt from interference both from individuals and from society. In infancy (under 21) the control of the parent over the child is absolute — that is, it is exercised without any respect whatever to the wishes of the child."

These are the sentiments of a man of great learning, piety, purity of heart — of one whose fame has extended into every part of the widespread Union, and the learned and good of other nations have been taught to know and to appreciate his exalted worth. His works will remain, after the present generation shall have passed away, an imperishable monument of his memory.

The doctrines of the common law are in accordance with these principles. It is the duty of the parent to maintain and educate the child, and he possesses the resulting authority to control it in all things necessary to the accomplishment of these objects. The law has assigned no limits to the authority of the parent over the child, except that it must not be exercised in such manner as to endanger its safety or morals. If the parent should transcend his authority in this respect, an appeal does not lie to the minister of the Gospel of any denomination whatever. Application for relief can only be made to the authorities entrusted by the supremacy of the law, with the high power of controlling parental authority where the morals or safety of the child require such interference.

. . . The Orphans' Court have by law the right to appoint guardians for orphan children — but so careful have the legislature been of the right of the parent to have his offspring brought up in the religious persuasion to which he belongs, that the Court are bound to have respect to this consideration in the selection of guardians, and persons of the same religious faith as the parents must be preferred over all others.

.   .   .   .   .

The principle of parental authority and filial obedience has its home in the human heart — is in accordance with the law of nature, and will ever be near and dear to every good man

of every religion under the sun. It has already been remarked, that there is no limit to that authority save that which is necessary for the preservation of the health and morals of the child.

Without the slightest disrespect for the Baptists, for whom we have every respect for their virtues and piety, it may safely be affirmed that the morals of the child were not endangered by remaining within the folds of the Presbyterian church, in which it had been baptized, and to which its mother belonged. There was therefore no just ground for interfering with the parent's authority, or for participating in the act of filial disobedience committed by the child. This proceeding cannot be justified under any claim founded upon the rights of conscience. The child whose conscience stimulates it into open rebellion against the lawful authority of its father, stands more in need of proper instruction and discipline under that authority than any other. If every child, under a claim founded upon the supposed rights of conscience, were allowed to carry into effect every decision of its immature judgment, where is that to end? Who shall prescribe limits to the crude conceptions of its youth and inexperience? — Shall it be allowed, under this pretence, to violate the law of God? to repudiate the Christian religion? to become a Jew or a Mohammedan? Or, retaining the Christian name, shall it be allowed to mingle with the battle-axe community, who make it a matter of conscience to disregard the holy institution of marriage? Or, upon this pretence, shall the beloved daughter of a Christian parent, in a moment of delusion, and in the tender years of her minority, be allowed to become one of the secret wives of the Mormon prophet?

It is dangerous to depart from established principles. Parental authority is not to be subverted so long as it is exercised within the limits which the law has prescribed. It is the duty of the parent to regulate the conscience of the child, by proper attention to its education; and there is no security for the offspring during the tender years of its minority but in obedience to the authority of its parents, in all things not injurious to its health or morals.

We wish it to be distinctly understood, that no imputations are cast upon the motives of the Rev. Mr. Hall. We believe that he acted conscientiously as he conceived to be right. But, in our opinion, he has transcended the divine and human law, in disregarding the authority of the father over his own offspring while in its minority. This is the opinion of the constitutional authority — the result of our conscientious convictions of the law, and it is hoped that he will feel himself bound to respect it accordingly, in any after proceedings. In refusing to render unto Caesar, the things that are Caesar's, he has fallen under the condemnation of the law.

It is therefore ordered that he pay the costs of this application.

Illegitimate children

1. Status of illegitimate children in the United States, 1827

James Kent, *Commentaries on American Law,* 14th ed. (Boston, 1896), II, 210–216.

A bastard being in the eye of the law *nullius filius,* or, as the civil law, from the difficulty of ascertaining the father, equally concluded, *patrem habere non intelliguntur,* he has no inheritable blood, and is incapable of inheriting as heir, either to his putative father, or his mother, or to any one else, nor can he have heirs but of his own body. This rule of the common law, so far at least as it excludes him from inheriting as heir to his mother, is supposed to be founded partly in policy, to discourage illicit commerce between the sexes . . . Bastards are incapable of taking in New York, under the law of descents, and under the statute of distribution of intestates' effects; and they are equally incapable in several of the

other United States, which follow, in this respect, the rule of the English law. But in Vermont, Connecticut, Virginia, Kentucky, Ohio, Indiana, Missouri, Illinois, Tennessee, North Carolina, Alabama, and Georgia, bastards can inherit from, and transmit to, their mothers, real and personal estate, under some modifications, which prevail particularly in the states of Connecticut, Illinois, North Carolina, and Tennessee; and in New York, the estate of an illegitimate intestate descends to the mother, and the relatives on the part of the mother . . .

This relaxation in the laws of so many of the states, of the severity of the common law, rests upon the principle that the relation of parent and child, which exists in this unhappy case, in all its native and binding force, ought to produce the ordinary legal consequences of that consanguinity . . .

The mother, or reputed father, is generally in this country chargeable by law with the maintenance of the bastard child; and in New York it is in such way as any two justices of the peace of the county shall think meet; and the goods, chattels, and real estate of the parents are seizable for the support of such children, if the parents have absconded. The reputed father is liable to arrest and imprisonment until he gives security to indemnify the town chargeable with the maintenance of the child. These provisions are intended for the public indemnity, and were borrowed from several English statutes on the subject; and similar regulations to coerce the putative father to maintain the child, and indemnify the town or parish, have been adopted in the several states . . .

2. Legitimatizing and adopting children, Alabama, 1852

John J. Ormand, Arthur P. Bagby, George Goldthwaite, eds., *Code of Alabama, 1852* (Montgomery, 1852), pp. 384–385.

The marriage of the mother and reputed father of a bastard child, renders it legitimate, if recognized by the father as his child.

The father of a bastard child may legitimate it, and render it capable of inheriting his estate, by making a declaration in writing, attested by two witnesses, setting forth the name of the child proposed to be legitimated, its sex, supposed age, and the name of the mother, and that he thereby recognises it as his child, and capable of inheriting his estate, real and personal, as if born in wedlock; the declaration being acknowledged by the maker before the probate judge of the county of his residence, or its execution proved by the attesting witnesses, filed in the office of the probate judge, and recorded on the minutes of his court, has the effect to legitimate such child.

The father may at the same time change the name of such child, stating in his declaration the name it is then known by, and the name he wishes it afterwards to have.

Any person desirous to adopt a child, so as to make it capable of inheriting his estate, real and personal, or to change the name of one previously adopted, may make a declaration in writing, attested by two witnesses, setting forth the name, sex, and age of the child he wishes to adopt, and the name he wishes it thereafter to be known by; which, being acknowledged by the declarant before the probate judge of the county of his residence, filed and recorded as in the two preceding sections, has the effect to make such child capable of inheriting such estate of the declarant, and of changing its name to the one stated in the declaration; and for services under this chapter, the judge of probate is entitled to a fee of one dollar.

The adoption of children

1. Adoption by deed, Texas, 1850

Laws of the State of Texas, 1850 (Austin, 1898), ch. 39.

In the 1850's American states began to make legal provision for adoption, a procedure which did not exist under the common law. The Texas law, which remained in effect until 1931, made adoption analogous to the transfer of real property.

Be it enacted by the Legislature of the State of Texas, That any person wishing to adopt another as his or her legal heir, may do so by filing in the office of the Clerk of the County Court in which county he or she may reside, a statement in writing, by him or her signed and duly authenticated or acknowledged, as deeds are required to be, which statement shall recite in substance, that he or she adopts the person named therein as his or her legal heir, and the same shall be admitted to record in said office.

Be it further enacted, That such statement in writing, signed and authenticated, or acknowledged and recorded as aforesaid, shall entitle the party so adopted to all the rights and privileges, both in law and equity, of a legal heir of the party so adopting him or her. Provided, however, that if the party adopting such person have, at the time of such adopting, or shall thereafter have a child or children, begotten in lawful wedlock, such adopted child or children shall in no case inherit more than the one-fourth of the estate of the party adopting him or her, which can be disposed of by will.

2. Massachusetts adoption law, 1851

"An Act to provide for the adoption of children," 1851 — ch. 324, *Massachusetts Acts and Resolves, 1851* (Boston, 1851), pp. 815–816.

The Massachusetts law establishing judicial procedures for adoption became the model for other states.

Any inhabitant of this Commonwealth may petition the judge of probate, in the county wherein he or she may reside, for leave to adopt a child not his or her own by birth.

If both or either of the parents of such child shall be living, they or the survivor of them, as the case may be, shall consent in writing to such adoption; if neither parent be living, such consent may be given by the legal guardian of such child; if there be no legal guardian, no father nor mother, the next of kin of such child within the State may give such consent; and if there be no such next of kin, the judge of probate may appoint some discreet and suitable person to act in the proceedings as the next friend of such child, and give or withhold such consent.

If the child be of the age of fourteen years or upwards, the adoption shall not be made without his or her consent.

No petition by a person having a lawful wife shall be allowed unless such wife shall join therein, and no woman having a lawful husband shall be competent to present and prosecute such petition.

If, upon such petition, so presented and consented to as aforesaid, the judge of probate shall be satisfied of the identity and relations of the persons, and that the petitioner, or, in case of husband and wife, the petitioners, are of sufficient ability to bring up the child, and furnish suitable nurture and education, having reference to the degree and condition of its parents, and that it is fit and proper that such adoption should take effect, he shall make a decree setting forth the said facts, and ordering that, from and after the date of the decree, such child should be deemed and taken, to all legal intents and purposes, the child of the petitioner or petitioners.

A child so adopted, as aforesaid, shall be deemed, for the purposes of inheritance and succession by such child, custody of the person and right of obedience by such parent or parents by adoption, and all other legal consequences and incidents of the natural relation of parents and children, the same to all intents and purposes as if such child had been born in lawful wedlock of such parents or parent by adoption, saving only that such child shall not be deemed capable of taking property expressly limited to the heirs of the body or bodies of such petitioner or petitioners.

The natural parent or parents of such child shall be deprived, by such decree of adoption, of all legal rights whatsoever as respects such child; and such child shall be freed from all legal obligations of maintenance and obedience, as respects such natural parent or parents.

Any petitioner, or any child which is the subject of such a petition, by any next friend, may claim and prosecute an appeal to the supreme judicial court from such decree of the judge of probate, in like manner and with the like effect as such appeals may now be claimed and prosecuted in cases of wills, saving only that in no case shall any bond be required of, nor any costs awarded against, such child or its next friend so appealing.

The custody of children

1. The child's welfare requires the mother's custody, 1813

Commonwealth *v.* Addicks and wife, 5 Binney, 520 (1813).

This custody case, one of the earliest in which the interests of the children were the paramount consideration, was decided in the Supreme Court of Pennsylvania. It was frequently cited in later cases elsewhere.

The Court, upon the application of Joseph Lee, granted a *habeas corpus* to the defendants, to bring up two female children, his daughters, in their custody; and they were accordingly brought into Court, under the care of their mother, Barbara Addicks, with whom, as was stated in the return, they had lived ever since their birth.

One of the children was ten, the other about seven years old.

J. R. Ingersoll for the father, read to the Court the proceedings in the Common Pleas, upon a libel for divorce by Lee against Barbara, at present the wife of Addicks, by which it appeared, that about the beginning of the present year, she had had a child by Addicks, and for some time before, and constantly since, had lived with him. Lee was divorced from her *a vinculo,* for this cause, on the 12th of June 1813; and since that time, the wife and Addicks were married . . . He contended that the father, as the natural guardian of the children, had a right to their custody, and that the nature of the intercourse between their mother and Addicks, rendered it highly improper to permit them to remain under her care.

Hopkinson contra, replied, that it was entirely in the Court's discretion to interfere or not, as there was no illegal restraint of the children; and for the purpose of enabling the Court to exercise a sound discretion upon the subject, he gave to them an outline of the mother's history, her marriage with Lee, his conduct to her and his family, and the circumstances under which her acquaintance with Addicks and her subsequent indiscretion had originated. From the whole it appeared, that she was at least as unfortunate, as she was culpable; that for four years prior to the divorce, from the embarrassments of Lee, and other causes, he had made no provision for either his wife or these children, although he had been applied to for this purpose. That during this period, the mother had kept a boarding house, and had educated the children herself, having applied in this manner the accomplishments she had acquired in the course of an excellent education in Canada. That the marriage with Addicks had taken place without a knowledge of

the legal impediment, and that in no respect had her intercourse with him, interfered with the attention that was due to the children, whose sex as well as age, particularly required the care of a mother.

J. R. Ingersoll on the other hand, made a statement to exculpate the husband, and to shew that his pecuniary circumstances, which at one time prevented him from giving aid to his family, now enabled him to educate and maintain the daughters, as he did a son of the same marriage, who had always been under his care.

One fact was not disputed, that the children were well treated and educated by the mother, and had hitherto in no respect suffered under her care.

After holding the case under advisement for a day, the Chief Justice now delivered the Court's opinion.

Tilghman C.J. We have considered the law, and are of opinion, that although we are bound to free the person from all illegal restraints, we are not bound to decide who is entitled to the guardianship, or to deliver infants to the custody of any particular person. But we may in our discretion do so, if we think that, under the circumstances of the case, it ought to be done . . . The present case is attended with peculiar and unfortunate circumstances. We cannot avoid expressing our disapprobation of the mother's conduct, although so far as regards her treatment of the children, she is in no fault. They appear to have been well taken care of in all respects. It is to them, that our anxiety is principally directed; and it appears to us, that considering their tender age, they stand in need of that kind of assistance, which can be afforded by none so well as a mother. It is on their account, therefore, that exercising the discretion with which the law has invested us, we think it best, at present, not to take them from her. At the same time, we desire it to be distinctly understood, that the father is not to be prevented from seeing them. If he does not choose to go to the house of their mother, she ought to send them to him, when he desires it, taking it for granted that he will not wish to carry them abroad, so much as to interfere with their education.

---

2. Denial of father's absolute right to custody, 1824

U.S. *v.* Green, 26 Fed. Cas. 30 (1824).

Joseph Story (1779–1845), a leading jurist and legal writer, was appointed to the United States Supreme Court in 1811. Simultaneously, he sat on the United States circuit bench for the northeastern states.

Habeas corpus upon the petition of Aaron Putnam, a citizen of New York, against Timothy Green, a citizen of Rhode Island, to bring up the body of Eliza A. Putnam, an infant daughter of Putnam, about ten years old, alleged to be wrongfully detained in the custody of the defendant, who was her grandfather. Upon the execution of the writ, a special return was made by the defendant, alleging, that the infant was the child of his daughter Mary, who married Putnam, and had since deceased; that in 1817, Putnam became embarrassed, and brought his wife and the said infant to reside at his house in North Providence, where they lived for two years; that they were subsequently removed to Connecticut, and again came back to his house with the consent of Putnam; that the wife died in his family in 1820, and upon her death-bed requested her parents to keep and bring up the said infant as their own; that they promised accordingly so to do: that the infant had ever since, until within a few months, resided in his family, and she was then placed by them in the Friends' Seminary at Providence for education;

STORY, Circuit Justice. As to the question of the right of the father to have the custody of his infant child, in a general sense it is true. But this is not on account of any absolute right of the father, but for the benefit of the infant, the law presuming it to be for his interest to be under the nurture and care of his natural protector, both for maintenance and education. When, therefore, the court is asked to lend its aid to put the infant into the custody of the father, and to withdraw him from other persons, it will look into all the circumstances, and ascertain whether it will be for the real, permanent interests of the infant; and if the infant be of sufficient discretion, it will also consult its personal wishes. It will free it from all undue restraint, and endeavour, as far as possible, to administer a conscientious, parental duty with reference to its welfare. It is an entire mistake to suppose the court is at all events bound to deliver over the infant to his father, or that the latter has an absolute vested right in the custody.

---

3. The father's "paramount" right to custody, New Hampshire, 1860

State *v.* Richardson, 40 N.H. 272 (1860).

The development of child custody law in the United States in the nineteenth century is surveyed in U.S. Bureau of Education, Circular of Information No. 3, 1880, *Legal Rights of Children* (Washington, 1880), pp. 23–28.

. . . In this case the father, and natural guardian of the child, is seeking . . . to have it restored to his custody, and we are required to determine whether, in the exercise of a sound discretion, the custody of the child ought, or ought not to be awarded to the father.

In determining this question the court will

take into consideration the right of the father, his ability and inclination to perform faithfully the trust imposed upon him, the present condition of the child, and, if of years of discretion, its wishes upon the subject. *Primâ facie,* however, the right of custody is in the father; and when the application is resisted upon the ground that he is unfit for the trust, by reason of grossly immoral conduct, harsh usage of his child, or other cause, a proper regard to the sanctity of the parental relation will require that the objection be sustained by clear and satisfactory proofs . . .

The discretion to be exercised is not an arbitrary one, but, in the absence of any positive disqualification of the father for the proper discharge of his parental duties, he has, as it seems to us, a paramount right to the custody of his infant child, which no court is at liberty to disregard. And while we are bound also to regard the permanent interests and welfare of the child, it is to be presumed that its interests and welfare will be best promoted by continuing that guardianship which the law has provided, until it is made plainly to appear that the father is no longer worthy of the trust . . . The breaking of the ties which bind the father and the child can never be justified without the most solid and substantial reasons. Upon the father the child must mainly depend for support, education and advancement in life, and as security for this he has the obligation of law as well as the promptings of that parental affection which rarely fail to bring into the service of the child, the best energies and the most thoughtful care of the father. In any form of proceeding the sundering of these ties will always be approached by the courts with great caution, and with a deep sense of responsibility.

In the case before us, the child, a female, was ten years old in February last, and is quite intelligent and well educated, for her years; and it appears that for nearly the whole of her life she has resided in the family of the respondent, and that it is her wish to remain there. It also appears that the respondent, the maternal uncle of the child, and his family, consisting of his mother and an unmarried sister, are in every way suitable persons to have the charge of such a child, and that it has been treated by them uniformly with great kindness, and that between the child and the family there exists a strong mutual affection. On the other hand, there is no evidence of the unfitness of the father for the proper discharge of his parental duties toward the child, or of the want of proper parental affection, but the evidence shows both the father and uncle to be highly respectable clergymen of the same religious sect, both suitable persons to have the charge of such a child, and, so far as the evidence goes, having equal means.

Under these circumstances, and upon the principles we have stated, we are satisfied that the father is entitled to the custody of the child, and that, in the exercise of a sound judicial discretion, we are not at liberty to allow his right to be controlled by the wishes of a child of such tender years.

.   .   .   .   .

In this case, there being no evidence that the father is unfit for the trust imposed upon him, there is no solid or substantial ground for refusing to award to him the custody of his child, unless we give to its wishes an influence which is not based upon either authority or reason, and might seriously and extensively interfere with that parental control which is wisely committed to the natural guardian of children.

C. CHILDREN IN SLAVERY

Family relations and legal status

---

1. A classic account of a childhood and youth spent in slavery

Benjamin Quarles, ed., *Narrative of the Life of Frederick Douglass, Written by Himself* (Cambridge, Mass.: Harvard University Press, 1960), pp. 23–27, 51–53; first published in 1845.

Douglass (1817?–1895), following his escape from slavery in Maryland in 1838, carved a notable career as a champion of the rights of Negro citizens.

I was born in Tuckahoe, near Hillsborough, and about twelve miles from Easton, in Talbot county, Maryland. I have no accurate knowledge of my age, never having seen any authentic record containing it. By far the larger part of the slaves know as little of their age as horses know of theirs, and it is the wish of most masters within my knowledge to keep their slaves thus ignorant. I do not remember to have ever met a slave who could tell of his birthday. They seldom come nearer to it than planting-time, harvest-time, cherry-time, spring-time, or fall-time. A want of information concerning my own was a source of unhappiness to me even during childhood. The white children could tell their ages. I could not tell why I ought to be deprived of the same privilege. I was not allowed to make any inquiries of my master concerning it. He deemed all such inquiries on the part of a slave improper and impertinent, and evidence of a restless spirit. The nearest estimate I can give makes me now between twenty-seven and twenty-eight years of age. I come to this, from hearing my master

say, some time during 1835, I was about seventeen years old.

My mother was named Harriet Bailey. She was the daughter of Isaac and Betsey Bailey, both colored, and quite dark. My mother was of a darker complexion than either my grandmother or grandfather.

My father was a white man. He was admitted to be such by all I ever heard speak of my parentage. The opinion was also whispered that my master was my father; but of the correctness of this opinion, I know nothing; the means of knowing was withheld from me. My mother and I were separated when I was but an infant — before I knew her as my mother. It is a common custom, in the part of Maryland from which I ran away, to part children from their mothers at a very early age. Frequently, before the child has reached its twelfth month, its mother is taken from it, and hired out on some farm a considerable distance off, and the child is placed under the care of an old woman, too old for field labor. For what this separation is done, I do not know, unless it be to hinder the development of the child's affection toward its mother, and to blunt and destroy the natural affection of the mother for the child. This is the inevitable result.

I never saw my mother, to know her as such, more than four or five times in my life; and each of these times was very short in duration, and at night. She was hired by a Mr. Stewart, who lived about twelve miles from my home. She made her journeys to see me in the night, travelling the whole distance on foot, after the performance of her day's work. She was a field hand, and a whipping is the penalty of not being in the field at sunrise, unless a slave has special permission from his or her master to the contrary — a permission which they seldom get, and one that gives to him that gives it the proud name of being a kind master. I do not recollect of ever seeing my mother by the light of day. She was with me in the night. She would lie down with me, and get me to sleep, but long before I waked she was gone. Very little communication ever took place between us. Death soon ended what little we could have while she lived, and with it her hardships and suffering. She died when I was about seven years old, on one of my master's farms, near Lee's Mill. I was not allowed to be present during her illness, at her death, or burial. She was gone long before I knew any thing about it. Never having enjoyed, to any considerable extent, her soothing presence, her tender and watchful care, I received the tidings of her death with much the same emotions I should have probably felt at the death of a stranger.

Called thus suddenly away, she left me without the slightest intimation of who my father was. The whisper that my master was my father, may or may not be true; and, true or false, it is of but little consequence to my purpose whilst the fact remains, in all its glaring odiousness, that slaveholders have ordained, and by law established, that the children of slave women shall in all cases follow the condition of their mothers; and this is done too obviously to administer to their own lusts, and make a gratification of their wicked desires profitable as well as pleasurable; for by this cunning arrangement, the slaveholder, in cases not a few, sustains to his slaves the double relation of master and father.

I know of such cases; and it is worthy of remark that such slaves invariably suffer greater hardships, and have more to contend with, than others. They are, in the first place, a constant offence to their mistress. She is ever disposed to find fault with them; they can seldom do any thing to please her; she is never better pleased than when she sees them under the lash, especially when she suspects her husband of showing to his mulatto children favors which he withholds from his black slaves. The master is frequently compelled to sell this class of his slaves, out of deference to the feelings of his

white wife; and, cruel as the deed may strike any one to be, for a man to sell his own children to human flesh-mongers, it is often the dictate of humanity for him to do so; for, unless he does this, he must not only whip them himself, but must stand by and see one white son tie up his brother, of but few shades darker complexion than himself, and ply the gory lash to his naked back; and if he lisp one word of disapproval, it is set down to his parental partiality, and only makes a bad matter worse, both for himself and the slave whom he would protect and defend.

· · · · ·

As to my own treatment while I lived on Colonel Lloyd's plantation, it was very similar to that of the other slave children. I was not old enough to work in the field, and there being little else than field work to do, I had a great deal of leisure time. The most I had to do was to drive up the cows at evening, keep the fowls out of the garden, keep the front yard clean, and run of errands for my old master's daughter, Mrs. Lucretia Auld. The most of my leisure time I spent in helping Master Daniel Lloyd in finding his birds, after he had shot them. My connection with Master Daniel was of some advantage to me. He became quite attached to me, and was a sort of protector of me. He would not allow the older boys to impose upon me, and would divide his cakes with me.

I was seldom whipped by my old master, and suffered little from any thing else than hunger and cold. I suffered much from hunger, but much more from cold. In hottest summer and coldest winter, I was kept almost naked — no shoes, no stockings, no jacket, no trousers, nothing on but a coarse tow linen shirt, reaching only to my knees. I had no bed. I must have perished with cold, but that, the coldest nights, I used to steal a bag which was used for carrying corn to the mill. I would crawl into this bag, and there sleep on the cold, damp, clay floor, with my head in and feet out. My feet have been so cracked with the frost, that the pen with which I am writing might be laid in the gashes.

We were not regularly allowanced. Our food was coarse corn meal boiled. This was called *mush*. It was put into a large wooden tray or trough, and set down upon the ground. The children were then called, like so many pigs, and like so many pigs they would come and devour the mush; some with oyster-shells, others with pieces of shingle, some with naked hands, and none with spoons. He that ate fastest got most; he that was strongest secured the best place; and few left the trough satisfied.

I was probably between seven and eight years old when I left Colonel Lloyd's plantation. I left it with joy. I shall never forget the ecstasy with which I received the intelligence that my old master (Anthony) had determined to let me go to Baltimore, to live with Mr. Hugh Auld, brother to my old master's son-in-law, Captain Thomas Auld. I received this information about three days before my departure. They were three of the happiest days I ever enjoyed. I spent the most part of all these three days in the creek, washing off the plantation scurf, and preparing myself for my departure.

The pride of appearance which this would indicate was not my own. I spent the time in washing, not so much because I wished to, but because Mrs. Lucretia had told me I must get all the dead skin off my feet and knees before I could go to Baltimore; for the people in Baltimore were very cleanly, and would laugh at me if I looked dirty. Besides, she was going to give me a pair of trousers, which I should not put on unless I got all the dirt off me. The thought of owning a pair of trousers was great indeed! It was almost a sufficient motive, not only to make me take off what would be called by pig-drovers the mange, but the skin itself. I went at it in good earnest, working for the first time with the hope of reward.

The ties that ordinarily bind children to their homes were all suspended in my case. I found no severe trial in my departure. My home

was charmless; it was not home to me; on parting from it, I could not feel that I was leaving any thing which I could have enjoyed by staying. My mother was dead, my grandmother lived far off, so that I seldom saw her. I had two sisters and one brother, that lived in the same house with me; but the early separation of us from our mother had well nigh blotted the fact of our relationship from our memories. I looked for home elsewhere, and was confident of finding none which I should relish less than the one which I was leaving. If, however, I found in my new home hardship, hunger, whipping, and nakedness, I had the consolation that I should not have escaped any one of them by staying. Having already had more than a taste of them in the house of my old master, and having endured them there, I very naturally inferred my ability to endure them elsewhere, and especially at Baltimore . . .

2. A slave family broken up and partially reunited

Life of Josiah Henson, as Narrated by Himself (Boston, 1849), pp. 1–5.

Henson (1789–1883), reputedly the original of Harriet Beecher Stowe's Uncle Tom, escaped from slavery in 1830 and spent the remainder of his life in Canada.

I was born, June 15, 1789, in Charles County, Maryland, on a farm belonging to Mr. Francis N., about a mile from Port Tobacco. My mother was the property of Dr. Josiah McP., but was hired by Mr. N., to whom my father belonged. The only incident I can remember, which occurred while my mother continued on N.'s farm, was the appearance of my father one day, with his head bloody and his back lacerated. He was in a state of great excitement, and though it was all a mystery to me at the age of three or four years, it was explained at a later period, and I understood that he had been suffering the cruel penalty of the Maryland law for beating a white man. His right ear had been cut off close to his head, and he had received a hundred lashes on his back. He had beaten the overseer for a brutal assault on my mother, and this was his punishment. Furious at such treatment, my father became a different man, and was so morose, disobedient, and intractable, that Mr. N. determined to sell him. He accordingly parted with him, not long after, to his son, who lived in Alabama; and neither my mother nor I, ever heard of him again. He was naturally, as I understood afterwards from my mother and other persons, a man of amiable temper, and of considerable energy of character; but it is not strange that he should be essentially changed by such cruelty and injustice under the sanction of law.

.   .   .   .   .

In consequence of [the decease of my master], it became necessary to sell the estate and the slaves, in order to divide the property among the heirs; and we were all put up at auction and sold to the highest bidder, and scattered over various parts of the country. My brothers and sisters were bid off one by one, while my mother, holding my hand, looked on in an agony of grief, the cause of which I but ill understood at first, but which dawned on my mind, with dreadful clearness, as the sale proceeded. My mother was then separated from me, and put up in her turn. She was bought by a man named Isaac R., residing in Montgomery county, and then I was offered to the assembled purchasers. My mother, half distracted with the parting forever from all her children, pushed through the crowd, while the bidding for me was going on, to the spot where R. was standing. She fell at his feet, and clung to his knees, entreating him in tones that a mother only could command, to buy her *baby* as well as herself, and spare to her one of her little ones at least. Will it, can

it be believed that this man, thus appealed to, was capable not merely of turning a deaf ear to her supplication, but of disengaging himself from her with such violent blows and kicks, as to reduce her to the necessity of creeping out of his reach, and mingling the groan of bodily suffering with the sob of a breaking heart? Yet this was one of my earliest observations of men; an experience which has been common to me with thousands of my race, the bitterness of which its frequency cannot diminish to any individual who suffers it, while it is dark enough to overshadow the whole after-life with something blacker than a funeral pall. — I was bought by a stranger. — Almost immediately, however, whether my childish strength, at five or six years of age, was overmastered by such scenes and experiences, or from some accidental cause, I fell sick, and seemed to my new master so little likely to recover, that he proposed to R., the purchaser of my mother, to take me too at such a trifling rate that it could not be refused. I was thus providentially restored to my mother; and under her care, destitute as she was of the proper means of nursing me, I recovered my health, and grew up to be an uncommonly vigorous and healthy boy and man.

---

3. A purchase of slave children in order to prevent separation from their mother. Virginia, 1834

Tabb's Curator *v*. Cabell, 17 Grattan 160 (1834).

The will of Landon Cabell deceased was admitted to probate in the County court of Amherst in January, 1834. By his will, after giving to his wife Judith S. Cabell a number of slaves in absolute property, he gave her for her life three men and three women [Burgess, Jordan, Cyrus, Margaret, Lucinda, and

Charity] and he directed that after the death of Mrs. Cabell, the slaves given her for life and their increase should be sold, and the proceeds equally divided among his three children, Robert H. and Landon R. Cabell and Elizabeth Preston . . . And he directed all his property, not specifically disposed of by his will, to be sold by his executor, and the proceeds to be divided among his wife and children.

In March, 1834, the executor sold the property.

.   .   .   .   .

At the sale . . . the girl Lucinda was sold, and in her stead this defendant purchased two small negroes, Edward and Matilda, the children of the above named woman Margaret. This was done by consent of parties, to prevent a separation of families.

---

4. A runaway slave woman suspected of rejoining her children, 1836

Richmond Enquirer, Aug. 5, 1836.

$50 REWARD — I will give the above reward to anyone who will apprehend my Negro woman, FANNY, if she is taken out of the State of Virginia, and secured in jail, so that I get her again; or $15, if taken in the said State, and delivered to me, near Tappahannock in Essex county. Fanny left me about the 1st of July; is of a brown color, a little above the middle size, very intelligent, and when in the act of speaking, contracts her forehead into wrinkles, and shews the whites of her eyes more than at other times. I know of no scars or other peculiarities by which she can be distinguished. I purchased her of Dr. A. Brockenbrough, of Tappahannock, and think it is probable she may be at or near the farm of his son, John, in the county of King William, where several of her children are living, but

have some reasons to think she has left this state.

RICHARD T. HUNDLEY

---

5. The effects of slavery on the domestic affections of slaves

Martineau, *Society in America,* II, 154–155.

It is true that slaves will often leave their infants to perish, rather than take any trouble about them; that they will utterly neglect a sick parent or husband; while they will nurse a white mistress with much ostentation. The reason is obvious. Such beings are degraded so far below humanity that they will take trouble, for the sake of praise or more solid reward, after they have become dead to all but grossly selfish inducements. Circumstances will fully account for a great number of cases of this sort: but to set against these, there are perhaps yet more instances of domestic devotion, not to be surpassed in the annals of humanity. Of these I know more than I can here set down; partly from their number, and partly from the fear of exposing to injury the individuals alluded to.

A friend of mine was well acquainted at Washington with a woman who had been a slave; and who, after gaining her liberty, worked incessantly for many years, denying herself all but absolute necessaries, in order to redeem her husband and children. She was a sick-nurse, when my friend knew her; and, by her merits, obtained good pay. She had first bought herself; having earned, by extra toil, three or four hundred dollars. She then earned the same sum, and redeemed her husband; and had bought three, out of her five, children when my friend last saw her. She made no boast of her industry and self-denial. Her story was extracted from her by questions; and she obviously felt that she was doing what was merely unavoidable. It is impossible to help instituting a comparison between this woman and the gentlemen who, by their own licentiousness, increase the number of slave children whom they sell in the market. My friend formerly carried an annual present from a distant part of the country to this poor woman: but it is not known what has become of her, and whether she died before she had completed her object, of freeing all her family.

---

6. Fanny Kemble on the increase of slave population, 1838

Frances A. Kemble, *Journal of a Residence on a Georgian Plantation in 1838–1839,* ed. John A. Scott (New York: Alfred A. Knopf, 1961), pp. 94–96; first published in 1863.

Miss Kemble (1809–1893) married Pierce Butler, heir to a large Georgia plantation, in 1834 after a sparkling stage career in England and America. Already opposed to slavery, she was appalled by conditions on his plantation where they lived in 1838–1839. She left her husband in 1846 but refused to publish the journal of her stay on the plantation until the Civil War broke out, when she hoped it would influence British opinion in behalf of the Union.

[I]t has occurred to me that whereas the increase of this ill-fated race is frequently adduced as a proof of their good treatment and well-being, it really and truly is no such thing, and springs from quite other causes than the peace and plenty which a rapidly increasing population are supposed to indicate. If you will reflect for a moment upon the overgrown families of the half-starved Irish peasantry and English manufacturers, you will agree with me that these prolific shoots by no means necessarily spring from a rich or healthy soil. Peace and plenty are certainly causes of human increase, and so is recklessness; and this, I take it, is the impulse in the instance of the English manufacturer, the Irish peasant, and the Negro slave. Indeed here it is more than recklessness, for there are certain indirect premiums held out to obey the early commandment of replenishing the earth which do not fail to have their full effect. In the first place, none of the cares, those noble cares, that holy thoughtfulness which lifts the human above the brute parent, are ever incurred here by either father or mother. The relation indeed resembles, as far as circumstances can possibly make it do so, the short-lived connection between the animal and its young. The father, having neither authority, power, responsibility, or charge in his children, is of course, as among brutes, the least attached to his offspring; the mother, by the natural law which renders the infant dependent on her for its first year's nourishment, is more so; but as neither of them is bound to educate or to support their children, all the unspeakable tenderness and solemnity, all the rational, and all the spiritual grace and glory of the connection, is lost, and it becomes mere breeding, bearing, suckling, and there an end. But it is not only the absence of the conditions which God has affixed to the relation which tends to encourage the reckless increase of the race; they enjoy, by means of numerous children, certain positive advantages. In the first place, every woman who is pregnant, as soon as she chooses to make the fact known to the overseer, is relieved of a certain portion of her work in the field, which lightening of labor continues, of course, as long as she is so burdened. On the birth of a child certain additions of clothing and an additional weekly ration are bestowed on the family; and these matters, small as they may seem, act as powerful inducements to creatures who have none of the restraining influences actuating them which belong to the parental relation among all other people, whether civilized or savage. Moreover, they have all of them a most distinct and perfect knowledge of their value to their owners as property; and a woman thinks, and not much amiss, that the more frequently she adds to the number of her master's livestock by bringing new slaves into the world, the more claims she will have upon his consideration and good will. This was perfectly evident to me from the meritorious air with which the women always made haste to inform me of the number of children they had borne, and the frequent occasions on which the older slaves would direct my attention to their children, exclaiming: "Look, missis! little niggers for you and massa; plenty little niggers for you and little missis!"

---

7. William Wells Brown, a slave assistant to a slavetrader, recounts the separation of a mother from her baby by the trader

William W. Brown, *Narrative of the Life of William W. Brown* (Boston, 1847), pp. 48–51.

Brown (ca. 1816–1884), hired out to several employers by his master, was a fugitive from slavery in 1834. Later he became a prominent abolitionist and pioneer historian of black people in America.

He soon commenced purchasing to make up the third gang. We took steamboat, and went to Jefferson City, a town on the Missouri river. Here we landed, and took stage for the interior of the State. He bought a number of slaves as he passed the different farms and villages. After getting twenty-two or twenty-three men and women, we arrived at St. Charles, a village on the banks of the Missouri. Here he purchased a woman who had a child in her arms, appearing to be four or five weeks old.

We had been travelling by land for some days, and were in hopes to have found a boat at this place for St. Louis, but were disappointed. As no boat was expected for some days, we started for St. Louis by land. Mr. Walker had purchased two horses. He rode one, and I the other. The slaves were chained together, and we took up our line of march, Mr. Walker taking the lead, and I bringing up the rear. Though the distance was not more than twenty miles, we did not reach it the first day. The road was worse than any that I have ever travelled.

Soon after we left St. Charles, the young child grew very cross, and kept up a noise during the greater part of the day. Mr. Walker complained of its crying several times, and told the mother to stop the child's d——d noise, or he would. The woman tried to keep the child from crying, but could not. We put up at night with an acquaintance of Mr. Walker, and in the morning, just as we were about to start, the child again commenced crying. Walker stepped up to her, and told her to give the child to him. The mother tremblingly obeyed. He took the child by one arm, as you would a cat by the leg, walked into the house, and said to the lady,

"Madam, I will make you a present of this little nigger; it keeps such a noise that I can't bear it."

"Thank you, sir," said the lady.

The mother, as soon as she saw that her child was to be left, ran up to Mr. Walker, and falling upon her knees begged him to let her have her child; she clung around his legs, and cried, "Oh, my child! my child! master, do let me have my child! oh, do, do, do. I will stop its crying, if you will only let me have it again." When I saw this woman crying for her child so piteously, a shudder, — a feeling akin to horror, shot through my frame.

.   .   .   .   .

Mr. Walker commanded her to return into the ranks with the other slaves. Women who had children were not chained, but those that had none were. As soon as her child was disposed of, she was chained in the gang.

8. A slave father fails in an attempt to purchase two of his children, South Carolina, 1846

Gist *v.* Toohey, 2 Richardson 424 (1846).

The plaintiff, Elizabeth P. Gist, sued to recover $100 which her slave, William, who hired out his time, had paid to the defendant toward the purchase of his children.

It appeared that in April, 1841, William, a slave of the plaintiff, who had earned one hundred dollars over and above his wages, placed that sum in the hands of the defendant, under an agreement that the defendant should purchase, for William, two of his children, for three hundred and fifty dollars; and that when William should repay to the defendant the balance of the purchase money, with an additional sum of fifty dollars for each year that the balance should remain unpaid, he, the defendant, would execute a bill of sale to William, of the children. In pursuance of this agreement, the defendant bought the negroes for three hundred and fifty dollars.

The Recorder charged the jury, that if the defendant acted in good faith, the plaintiff was not entitled to recover the one hundred dollars advanced by William, unless the balance of the money paid by the defendant to accomplish the purchase, had been tendered to him, and a conveyance of the children required to be made, either to William or the plaintiff. The jury found for the plaintiff one hundred dollars, with interest from April, 1841.

The defendant appealed, and now moved for a new trial.

.   .   .   .   .

Curia, per Wardlaw, J. This verdict may have been found upon the conclusion of the jury, formed from the evidence, that the defendant had not acted in good faith; but even upon a contrary supposition, this court thinks it must stand. The promises of a master to a slave, are binding only in conscience and honor; at law, notwithstanding any such promise, that the slave shall have certain acquisitions, all the acquisitions of the slave in possession, are the property of the master. A dealing or trafficking with the slave concerning such acquisitions, without the license of the master, is as much contrary to our statutory regulations, as other unlicensed dealings with a slave. Sometimes an executed contract with a slave might transfer a title to a third person, upon the ground of the master's implied consent; but an executory agreement with a slave (not the agent of the master therein) can give no right of action, either to the slave or master . . . Then the $100 in William's possession, belonged to the plaintiff; the defendant violated the law in receiving it from him under a bargain; or, to say the least, acted with great imprudence in resting his justification for dealing with the slave to such an amount, when the owner was near, upon the implied permission of the owner, and not obtaining express license. Such assent of the plaintiff as would make William her agent, cannot be presumed against the verdict; and the defendant must refund the $100, as money received in an unlawful transaction, wherein the plaintiff did not participate — or as money received upon consideration of an agreement which the law regards as worthless.

---

9. The causes of loose family ties among slaves

Nehemiah Adams, *A South Side View of Slavery* (Boston, 1854), pp. 82–85.

Adams (1806–1878), a New England Congregationalist minister, traveled through the South in 1854. Although he concluded that southern slaveowners had been unfairly criticized by their abolitionist detractors, he was not unaware of the devastating effects of slavery on family relations.

Husbands and wives, in a large proportion of cases, belong to different masters, and reside on separate plantations, the husband sometimes walking several miles, night and morning, to and from his family, and many of them returning home only on Saturday afternoon. In cities, also, husbands and wives most commonly belong to different families. Laboring apart, and having their meals apart, *the bonds of domestic life are few and weak.* A slave, his wife, and their children, around that charmed centre, a family table, with its influences of love, instruction, discipline, humble as they necessarily would be, yet such as God had given them, are too seldom seen. To encourage and protect their homes generally would be in effect to put an end to slavery as it is.

It was remarked to me by an eminent and venerable physician at the south, that maternal attachments in slave mothers are singularly shortlived. Their pain and grief at the sale of their children, their jealousy, their self-sacrificing efforts for them, are peculiar; but they are easily supplanted. The hen, and even the timid partridge, is roused when her young are in danger, and her demonstrations of affection then are unsurpassed. Yet in a few weeks she will treat her offspring as strangers. Maternal instincts in slave mothers (my friend observed) were more like this than the ordinary parental feelings of white people.

I told him that this disclosed to me one of the most affecting illustrations of slavery, and that I needed not to ask him for his explanation of it. Every one can see, not only the probability, but the cause, of this limited parental affection. From the first moment of maternal solicitude, the idea of property on the part of the owner in the offspring is connected with the maternal instinct. It grows side by side with it, becomes a neutralizing element, prevents the inviolable links of natural affection from reaching deep into the heart. We need no slave auctions or separations of families to make us feel the inherent, awful nature of the present system of slavery, in view of this illustration.

Some use it in mitigation of the alleged wrongfulness of separating mothers and young children. Human nature refuses to hear one who is capable of using such an argument.

The same day that my friend made his remark to me, I had an accidental confirmation of it in the conversation of an intelligent landlord, who was telling me of the recent lamentable death of an old slave mother who had nursed him and all his brothers and sisters. His mother said to the dying woman, "How do you feel about leaving your children?" for she had several, who were still young. "O missis," she said, "you will take care of them; I don't mind them. I don't want to leave you, missis, and your Charley and Ann. What will they do without me, little dears?" The gentleman mentioned it as affecting illustration, as it certainly is, of the disinterested affection in these colored servants; but I felt that there was something back of all this. Slavery had loosened the natural attachments of this woman to her offspring, and those attachments had sought and found objects to grow upon in the children of another. There must be something essentially wrong in a system which thus interferes with the nature which God has made.

The drapery of words is hardly sufficient, perhaps, to clothe an idea which a slave mother in one of the best of Christian families expressed; but she was deprecating the possibility of being a mother again. She said, "You feel when your child is born that you can't have the bringing of it up."

One evening, in a prayer meeting of slaves, the white brother who presided read the chapter in Matthew containing the Lord's Prayer, and asked me to make some remarks. I alluded to the Lord's Prayer, which had just been read, and was proceeding to remark upon portions of it. I found myself embarrassed, however, at once, in speaking about that overwhelming name of love — Our Father, who art in heaven; for it flashed upon me, these slaves, although they have the spirit of sons, although they cry, "Abba, Father," as I seldom ever heard other Christians use the name, can not appreciate any illustrations of it which I may draw from earthly parentage; they know the thing; the illustration they cannot fully appreciate, for in effect the slave has no father. He more frequently remembers his mother; but who was his father? His knowledge of him is far less frequent. The annihilation by slavery, to a great extent, of the father in the domestic relations of the slaves, is inseparable from it, as it exists at present.

Take a further illustration. I was in a large colored Sabbath school. The superintendent at the close gave the scholars a kind word of exhortation to this effect: "Now, children, I want to repeat what I have said to you so often; you must all try to be good children, wherever you are, remembering that you are never out of God's sight. If you love and obey him, if you are good children at home, what a comfort you will be to your" (I expected the words *fathers* and *mothers*) "masters and mistresses." I felt as when I have heard the earth fall upon a stranger's coffin; it was all correct, all kind; but the inability to use those names, the perfect naturalness with which other names came in to fill the place of *father* and *mother,* brought to my heart the truth, the slaves generally have no homes.

---

10. A slave woman and her children in the Richmond slave market

Charles R. Weld, *A Vacation Tour in the United States and Canada* (London, 1855), pp. 302–304.

Charles Weld (1813–1869), author of many travel books, was an English historian and scientist.

As all the slaves present were now sold, I thought business was over in this establishment; but just as the last woman was led away, a mulatto entered the room with another woman followed by two little children about three and four years old, and carrying a third still younger in her arms. These were the children announced for sale. The circumstance of this woman, or lot, as she and the children were called, being brought in alone, led me to suppose there was some distinction between her and the preceding slaves. In slavery none, — she and her children were slaves like those just sold; but in appearance the difference was great. She was a remarkably handsome mulatto, and her children were nearly, if not fully, as white as the fairest Americans. If any doubt existed in my mind respecting the revolting nature of this human traffic, the case of this woman would have determined my judgment. Her story was brief: she was not married, and the man whose passions had made her his mistress as well as slave, willed that she should be sold with *his* children. More she would not divulge; nor would she answer questions relative to her occupation. All attempts at extracting further information were met by a scornful refusal to divulge aught of her past life, and when her small soft hands and bosom were examined, on which her infant was reposing, her eyes flashed fire, and I sincerely believe, had a knife been within her grasp she would have plunged it in the hearts of her tormentors. Followed by her two little children, who clung to her dress like scared lambs, shrinking from the gaze of the rough men who pressed round them, she ascended the platform, and the auctioneer recommenced his business. Whether he dreaded a scene, or that he deemed it unnecessary, I am unable to say; but he limited his prefatorial harangue to the simple announcement that he had a fine young woman to offer, with her children, who would not be sold separate, adding that in a few years the boys would be fit for work. What could he say of her, whose heart's finest affections were perhaps at the moment lacerated to satisfy the greed of a man? He set a high price on the woman and her children, declaring he expected at least 2500 dollars for the lot. The first bid was 800; languid biddings succeeded, until the amount reached 900 dollars. The woman was then ordered down, and followed by her little children, was made to walk up and down the room. On resuming her place on the platform, the biddings became a little brisker; but as no eloquency on the part of the auctioneer could raise them above 1100 dollars, the lot was withdrawn. I was informed the woman alone would have realised more than this amount, but there is a strong aversion against purchasing white children.

Care of infants and children on plantations

1. The slave "settlement" and the infirmary, Georgia, 1838–1839

Kemble, *Journal,* pp. 67–70, 72–73, 98–99, 169–170, 229–230.

[January 1839] I walked down the settlement toward the infirmary or hospital, calling in at one or two of the houses along the row. These cabins consist of one room, about twelve feet by fifteen, with a couple of closets smaller and closer than the staterooms of a ship, divided off from the main room and each other by rough wooden partitions, in which the inhabitants sleep. They have almost all of them a rude bedstead, with the gray moss of the forests for mattress, and filthy, pestilential-looking blankets for covering. Two families (sometimes eight and ten in number) reside in one of these huts, which are mere wooden frames pinned, as it were, to the earth by a brick chimney outside, whose enormous aperture within pours down a flood of air, but little counteracted by the miserable spark of fire, which hardly sends an attenuated thread of lingering smoke up its huge throat. A wide ditch runs immediately at the back of these dwellings, which is filled and emptied daily by the tide. Attached to each hovel is a small scrap of ground for a garden, which, however, is for the most part untended and uncultivated.

Such of these dwellings as I visited today were filthy and wretched in the extreme, and exhibited that most deplorable consequence of ignorance and an abject condition, the inability of the inhabitants to secure and improve even such pitiful comfort as might yet be achieved by them. Instead of the order, neatness, and ingenuity which might convert even these miserable hovels into tolerable residences, there was the careless, reckless, filthy indolence which even the brutes do not exhibit in their lairs and nests, and which seemed incapable of applying to the uses of existence the few miserable means of comfort yet within their reach. Firewood and shavings lay littered about the floors, while the half-naked children were cowering round two or three smouldering cinders. The moss with which the chinks and crannies of their ill-protecting dwellings might have been stuffed was trailing in dirt and dust about the ground, while the back door of the huts, opening upon a most unsightly ditch, was left wide open for the fowls and ducks, which they are allowed to raise, to travel in and out, increasing the filth of the cabin by what they brought and left in every direction.

In the midst of the floor, or squatting round the cold hearth, would be four or five little children from four to ten years old, the latter all with babies in their arms, the care of the infants being taken from the mothers (who are driven afield as soon as they recover from child labor), and devolved upon these poor little nurses, as they are called, whose business it is to watch the infant, and carry it to its mother whenever it may require nourishment. To these hardly human little beings I addressed my remonstrances about the filth, cold, and unnecessary wretchedness of their room, bidding the older boys and girls kindle up the fire, sweep the floor, and expel the poultry. For a long time my very words seemed unintelligible to them, till, when I began to sweep and make up the fire, etc., they first fell to laughing, and then imitating me. The incrustations of dirt on their hands, feet, and faces were my next object of attack, and the stupid Negro practice (by-the-by, but a short time since nearly universal in enlightened Europe) of keeping the babies with their feet bare, and their heads, already well capped by nature with their woolly hair, wrapped in half a dozen hot, filthy coverings.

.   .   .   .   .

The infirmary is a large two-story building, terminating the broad orange-planted space between the two rows of houses which form the first settlement; it is built of whitewashed wood, and contains four large-sized rooms. But how shall I describe to you the spectacle which was presented to me on entering the first of these? But half the casements, of which there were six, were glazed, and these were obscured with dirt, almost as much as the other window-less ones were darkened by the dingy shutters, which the shivering inmates had fastened to in order to protect themselves from the cold. In the enormous chimney glimmered the power-less embers of a few sticks of wood, round which, however, as many of the sick women as could approach were cowering, some on wooden settles, most of them on the ground, excluding those who were too ill to rise; and these last poor wretches lay prostrate on the floor, without bed, mattress, or pillow, buried in tattered and filthy blankets, which, huddled round them as they lay strewed about, left hardly space to move upon the floor . . . Here lay women expecting every hour the terrors and agonies of childbirth, others who had just brought their doomed offspring into the world, others who were groaning over the anguish and bitter disappointment of miscarriages — here lay some burning with fever, others chilled with cold and aching with rheumatism, upon the hard cold ground, the draughts and dampness of the atmosphere increasing their sufferings, and dirt, noise, and stench, and every aggravation of which sickness is capable, combined in their condition — here they lay like brute beasts, absorbed in physical suffer-ing; unvisited by any of those Divine influences which may ennoble the dispensations of pain and illness, forsaken, as it seemed to me, of all good; and yet, O God, Thou surely hadst not forsaken them! Now pray take notice that this is the hospital of an estate where the owners are supposed to be humane, the over-seer efficient and kind, and the Negroes re-markably well cared for and comfortable.

.   .   .   .   .

In the hospital were several sick babies, whose mothers were permitted to suspend their field labor in order to nurse them. Upon ad-dressing some remonstrances to one of these, who, besides having a sick child, was ill her-self, about the horribly dirty condition of her baby, she assured me that it was impossible for them to keep their children clean; that they went out to work at daybreak, and did not get their tasks done till evening, and that then they were too tired and worn out to do any-thing but throw themselves down and sleep. This statement of hers I mentioned on my re-turn from the hospital, and the overseer ap-peared extremely annoyed by it, and assured me repeatedly that it was not true.

.   .   .   .   .

My next agreeable office in the infirmary this morning was superintending the washing of two little babies, whose mothers were nurs-ing them with quite as much ignorance as zeal. Having ordered a large tub of water, I desired Rose to undress the little creatures and give them a warm bath; the mothers looked on in unutterable dismay; and one of them, just as her child was going to be put into the tub, threw into it all the clothes she had just taken off it, as she said, to break the unusual shock of the warm water. I immediately rescued them; not but what they were quite as much in want of washing as the baby, but it appeared, upon inquiry, that the woman had none others to dress the child in when it should have taken its bath; they were immediately wrung and hung by the fire to dry; and the poor little patients, having undergone this novel operation, were taken out and given to their mothers. Anything, however, much more helpless and inefficient than these poor ignorant creatures you cannot conceive; they actually seemed incapable of drying or dressing their own babies, and I had to finish their toilet myself. As it is only a very few years since the most absurd and disgusting customs have become exploded among ourselves, you will not, of course, wonder that these poor people pin up the lower part of their infants, bodies, legs, and all, in red flannel as soon as they are born, and keep them in the selfsame envelope till it literally falls off.

.   .   .   .   .

[February 1839] I was assailed by a small gang of children, clamoring for the indulgence of some meat, which they besought me to give them. Animal food is only allowed to certain of the harder working men, hedgers and ditchers, and to them only occasionally, and in very moderate rations. My small cannibals clamored round me for flesh, as if I had had a butcher's cart in my pocket, till I began to laugh, and then to run, and away they came, like a pack of little black wolves, at my heels, shrieking: "Missis, you gib me piece meat — missis, you gib me meat," till I got home. At the door I found another petitioner, a young woman named Maria, who brought a fine child in her arms, and demanded a present of a piece of flannel. Upon my asking her who her husband was, she replied, without much hesitation, that she did not possess any such appendage. I gave another look at her bonny baby, and went into the house to get the flannel for her. I afterward heard from Mr. [Butler] that she and two other girls of her age, about seventeen, were the only instances on the island of women with illegitimate children.

After I had been in the house a little while, I was summoned out again to receive the petition of certain poor women in the family way to have their work lightened. I was, of course, obliged to tell them that I could not interfere in the matter; that their master was away, and that, when he came back, they must present their request to him: they said they had already begged "massa," and he had refused, and they thought, perhaps, if "missis" begged "massa" for them, he would lighten their task. Poor "missis," poor "massa," poor woman, that I am to have such prayers addressed to me! I had to tell them that, if they had already spoken to their master, I was afraid my doing so would be of no use, but that when he came back I would try; so, choking with crying, I turned away from them, and re-entered the house, to the chorus of "Oh, thank you, missis! God bless you, missis!"

.   .   .   .   .

[February 28–March 2, 1839] You will see how miserable the physical condition of many of these poor creatures is; and their physical condition, it is insisted by those who uphold this evil system, is the only part of it which is prosperous, happy, and compares well with that of Northern laborers. Judge from the details I now send you; and never forget, while reading them, that the people on this plantation are well off, and consider themselves well off, in comparison with the slaves on some of the neighboring estates.

Fanny has had six children; all dead but one. She came to beg to have her work in the field lightened.

Nanny has had three children; two of them are dead. She came to implore that the rule of sending them into the field three weeks after their confinement might be altered.

Leah, Caesar's wife, has had six children; three are dead.

Sophy, Lewis's wife, came to beg for some old linen. She is suffering fearfully; has had ten children; five of them are dead. The principal favor she asked was a piece of meat, which I gave her.

Sally, Scipio's wife, has had two miscarriages and three children born, one of whom is dead.

She came complaining of incessant pain and weakness in her back. This woman was a mulatto daughter of a slave called Sophy, by a white man of the name of Walker, who visited the plantation.

Charlotte, Renty's wife, had had two miscarriages, and was with child again. She was almost crippled with rheumatism, and showed me a pair of poor swollen knees that made my heart ache. I have promised her a pair of flannel trousers, which I must forthwith set about making.

Sarah, Stephen's wife; this woman's case and history were alike deplorable. She had had four miscarriages, had brought seven children into the world, five of whom were dead, and was again with child. She complained of dreadful pains in the back, and an internal tumor which swells with the exertion of working in the fields; probably, I think, she is ruptured. She told me she had once been mad and had run into the woods, where she contrived to elude discovery for some time, but was at last tracked and brought back, when she was tied up by the arms, and heavy logs fastened to her feet, and was severely flogged. After this she contrived to escape again, and lived for some time skulking in the woods, and she supposes mad, for when she was taken again she was entirely naked. She subsequently recovered from this derangement, and seems now just like all the other poor creatures who come to me for help and pity. I suppose her constant childbearing and hard labor in the fields at the same time may have produced the temporary insanity.

Sukey, Bush's wife, only came to pay her respects. She had had four miscarriages; had brought eleven children into the world, five of whom are dead.

Molly, Quambo's wife, also only came to see me. Hers was the best account I have yet received; she had had nine children, and six of them were still alive.

This is only the entry for today, in my diary, of the people's complaints and visits. Can you conceive a more wretched picture than that which it exhibits of the conditions under which these women live?

---

2. A plantation nursery on the "Rice Coast" of South Carolina, ca. 1853

Frederick Law Olmsted, *A Journey in the Seaboard Slave States, with Remarks on Their Economy (New York,* 1856), pp. 423–425.

The cabin nearest the overseer's house was used as a nursery. Having driven up to this, Mr. X inquired first how the children were; whether there had been any births since his last visit; spoke to two convalescent young mothers, that were lounging on the floor of the portico, with the children, and then asked if there were any sick people.

"Nobody, oney dat boy, Sam, sar."

"What Sam is that?"

"Dat little Sam, sar; Tom's Sue's Sam, sar."

"What's the matter with him?"

"Don' 'spec dere's noting much de matter wid him now, sar. He came in Sa'dy, complainin' he had de stomach-ache, an' I gin him some ile, sar; 'spec he mus' be well, dis time, but he din go out dis mornin'."

"Well, I'll see to him."

Mr. X went to Tom's Sue's cabin, looked at the boy, and, concluding that he was well, though he lay abed, and pretended to cry with pain, ordered him to go out to work. Then, meeting the overseer, who was just riding away, on some business off the plantation, he remained some time in conversation with him, while I occupied myself in making a sketch of the nursery and the street of the settlement in my note-book. On the verandah and the steps of the nursery, there were twenty-seven children, most of them infants, that had been left there by their mothers, while they were working their tasks in the fields. They probably make a visit to them once or twice during the day, to nurse them, and receive them to take to their cabins, or where they like, when they have finished their tasks — generally in the middle of the afternoon. The older children were fed with porridge, by the general nurse. A number of girls, eight or ten years old, were occupied in holding and tending the youngest infants. Those a little older — the crawlers — were in the pen, and those big enough to toddle were playing on the steps, or before the house. Some of these, with two or three bigger ones, were singing and dancing about a fire that they had made on the ground. They were not at all disturbed or interrupted in their amusement by the presence of their owner and myself. At twelve years of age, the children are first put to regular field-work; until then no labor is required of them, except, perhaps, occasionally, they are charged with some light kind of duty, such as frightening birds from corn. When first sent to the field, one quarter of an able-bodied hand's day's work is ordinarily allotted to them, as their task.

But very few of the babies were in arms; such as were not, generally lay on the floor, rolling about, or sat still, sucking their thumbs. The nurse was a kind-looking old negro woman, with, no doubt, philoprogenitiveness well developed; but she paid very little attention to them, only sometimes chiding the older ones for laughing or singing too loud. I watched for half an hour, and in all that time not a baby of them began to cry; nor have I ever heard one, at two or three other plantation-nurseries which I have visited . . . I make a note of it, as indicating how young the little twig is bent, how early the formation of habits commences, and that, even in babyhood, the "product of happiness is to be found, not so much in in-

creasing your numerator, as in lessening your denominator."

Slave children as hirelings and apprentices

1. Slave boys hired out, 1825

Richmond Enquirer, Jan. 13, 1825.

HIRELINGS — BOYS WANTED

The subscriber wishes to hire fifty boys from 12 to 18 years of age, to be employed in a tobacco factory, under a contract that he may retain them in his service for six years, paying hire for them annually.

The labour of boys so engaged is considerably more productive to their owners than if employed in any other business, and the yearly increase in their value enhanced in a much higher degree, while the service performed is easy and wholesome.

COLLIN MCRAE

2. Slave boys hired out as blacksmith's apprentices, 1832

Richmond Enquirer, Dec. 28, 1832.

TO OWNERS OF SLAVES — The subscribers are in want of four or five boys as apprentices, to learn the blacksmith's business. Application may be made to James Bosher, or to

JACOB F. BARNES & CO.

D. THE LEGAL STATUS OF FREE NEGRO CHILDREN IN THE SOUTH

Children of a free mother and a slave father may be bound out by overseers of the poor because legally they are bastards. Virginia, 1848

Brewer *v.* Harris, 5 Grattan 285 (1848).

In October 1848 Retha Harris, a free woman of colour, and whose husband was a slave, on behalf of herself and her three children, Sally, Joannah and Milly Harris, applied to the Judge of the Circuit Court of Henry county for a writ of *habeas corpus,* to require John S. Brewer to bring the said Sally, Joannah and Milly into Court; and charging that they were illegally detained in custody by Brewer. The writ was awarded; and Brewer, in obedience thereto, brought the parties into Court, and certified their cause of detention to be, that they had been bound to him as apprentices by one of the overseers of the poor of the county of Henry, by virtue of an order of the County Court; and he made the indentures of apprenticeship and the order of the Court a part of his return to the writ.

The order of the Court was made on the 13th of May, A.D. 1844, and ordered that the overseers of the poor bind out Sally Harris, Joannah Harris and Milly Harris, bastard children of Retha Harris, a free woman of colour, to John S. Brewer; and that they require the said Brewer to pay an annual hire to the said Retha, the mother, for said apprentices, of one dollar each, from the age of fourteen to seventeen; and that he pay to each of them 12 dollars for the last year of their servitude.

The indentures bore date the 12th day of November 1844, and were made "between Richard G. Lamkin, one of the overseers of the county of Henry, of the first part, and John S. Brewer, of the same county, of the second part;" and witnessed that Lamkin, in his character of overseer of the poor aforesaid, and pursuant to the order of the County Court, which was set out in the indentures, bound the said Sally, Joannah and Milly to Brewer, as apprentices, until they attained the age of 17 years. And he covenanted with Brewer, that the apprentices should serve him faithfully, and honestly demean themselves. The covenants by Brewer, which were the same in all of the indentures, were as follows: "And the said John S. Brewer, on his part, doth covenant and agree to and with the overseers of the poor for the county of Henry, and their successors, to pay unto the said Retha Harris, the mother of the said Milly, the annual sum of one dollar, for the services of her daughter, from the age of fourteen to seventeen years; and that he will instruct and cause the said Milly to learn and be taught all the art, trade and mystery of washing and spinning; and that he will at all times treat the said apprentice Milly with humanity, and furnish her with good and wholesome food and raiment during the time of her apprenticeship; and moreover will pay unto the said Milly the full sum of 12 dollars at the expiration of her said apprenticeship." The indentures were executed by Lamkin and Brewer; and they were endorsed by the clerk of the County Court as filed in his office on the 12th of November 1844.

The case came on to be tried at the October term of the Court for 1848, when the Court held that the said Sally, Joannah and Milly Harris were illegally detained in the custody of John S. Brewer, and ordered them to be discharged, with their costs. Brewer, thereupon, applied to this Court for a *supersedeas* to the judgment, which was awarded.

.   .   .   .   .

In this case, the apprentices in question are bastards, their father being a slave, and therefore incapable of contracting matrimony in the mode prescribed by our law. And the County Court exercised its legitimate jurisdiction, by ordering them to be bound out by the overseers of the poor of the county, upon prescribed terms, to a person designated in the order. It cannot be supposed that the Court meant the overseers in a corporate character, or all of them individually, instead of such and so many of them as the law directs; and the law is obeyed, and the substantial purpose of the Court accomplished, when the act is performed by one or more of the overseers.

The indentures in question, therefore, were executed by due authority, and between the proper parties, and moreover express the relative legal obligations of the master and apprentice. This is enough in these statutory indentures to give adequate remedies to the apprentice, and others entitled, in their own names, for any failure of duty on the part of the master, whatever may be the form of the covenants.

.   .   .   .   .

The judgment of the Circuit Court ought to be reversed, and the apprentices remanded into the custody and service of their master . . .

Children of free Negro women may not be bound as apprentices to masters objectionable to their mothers, Kentucky, 1855

Baker (of Color) *v.* Winfrey, 15 B. Mon 499 (1855).

The Kentucky Court of Appeals reversed the decision of a lower court.

These . . . cases are brought by appeals from the proceedings of the County Court in binding out the appellants, free persons of color, of whom some are the children of Eliza Baker and others the children of Mary Baker, free women of color. It appears that a summons issued against each of the mothers to appear at the October term of the County Court, and show cause why her children should not be bound out, etc. That on their appearance, the county attorney moved the court to bind out the children, ten in number, to five persons whom he named; to which the mothers, by their counsel, objected, claiming the right to choose the masters to whom their children should be bound, and naming four persons whom they selected under that right. But the court . . . denied the right claimed; and without any evidence of the condition or character of the mothers, or of their ability or inability to support the children, or their disposition to bring them up in moral courses, proceeded to bind out to the persons named by the county attorney each of the ten children, the males to learn farming, and the females to learn house-keeping. It appears from the orders and the indentures that several of the children were between ten and fourteen years of age, one three years old, another five, and the others between five and ten. It is somewhat singular that in two or three months after these proceedings most of the persons to whom the children were bound came again into court, and on their several motions, and as the order says, for good cause shown, they were severally released from the indentures, and the children were immediately bound again to other persons. In most of these instances the mothers, by their attorney, again objected. The indentures contain all of the stipulations required, except education, which is prohibited to free negroes.

[The county court] erred in overruling the objection of the mother[s] to the persons proposed by the county attorney as the masters to whom the children were to be bound, and in disallowing their right to choose the masters, and in proceeding to bind out the children severally to the different persons objected to by the mothers . . . The mere fact that these are colored persons does not put them out of the protection of the law, nor subject them to be dealt with or disposed of with a view merely to the interest of individuals. There must be some ground of necessity, in view of the requirements of the law, to authorize the binding out of these children . . . No such necessity is shown to have existed . . . We only say further, that although the statutes do not in terms require it, the indentures ought, in all propriety, to contain a covenant on the part of the master to teach his apprentice the art or business for the purpose of learning which he is bound to him.

A dispute among the children and heirs of a free Negro man reveals the complications of legal status that result from a mixed slave and free social system, North Carolina, 1858

Frances Howard *v.* Sarah Howard, 6 Jones N.C. 235 (1858).

Miles Howard, a free man of color, died intestate in 1857 . . .

About the year 1818, he being then the slave of the late Thomas Burgess, Esquire, without other ceremony, took for his wife, by consent of his master, and a Mr. Burt, *Matilda,* a slave of the latter, and was immediately thereafter duly emancipated. *Miles* then bought his wife, *Matilda,* and by her had issue, the lessor Frances, when the said *Matilda* was duly emancipated. After this event, they had other issue, to wit: the lessors, Robert, Eliza, Miles, Charles, Lucy, Ann, Thomas, when the said Matilda died.

In a few years afterwards, the said Miles took another wife, a free woman of color, and had issue, the defendants, Sarah, John, Nancy, and Andrew. The latter marriage was performed with due ceremony, the former was celebrated in the manner usual among slaves, and the

parties lived together ever afterwards as man and wife, and kept house together as such.

In 1836, the lessor, Frances, with other children, who died before the intestate, Miles, was emancipated as the children and slaves of the said Miles Howard, by an act of the Legislature.

The plaintiff's lessors claimed to be tenants in common with the defendants — which the defendants denied, and claim to be the only legitimate children, and sole heirs of their father. The Court, upon consideration of the case submitted, gave judgment in favor of the defendants; from which the lessors of the plaintiffs appealed.

.   .   .   .   .

Marriage is based upon contract; consequently the relation of "man and wife" cannot exist among slaves. It is excluded, both on account of their incapacity to contract, and of the paramount right of ownership in them, as property.

.   .   .   .   .

Both parents were slaves when the relation was entered into. Afterwards, the father was emancipated, and bought the mother, and *held her as his slave,* at the birth of the lessor, Frances. This presents a question, in many respects, different from that of the *status* of a child born while both parents were slaves, and lived together as man and wife; for the relation of master and slave is wholly incompatible with even the qualified relation of husband and wife, as it is supposed to exist among slaves, and the idea that a husband may own his wife as property and sell her, if he chooses, or that a parent may own his children and sell or give them away as chattels, and that the wife or the children, are, nevertheless, entitled to any of the civil rights incident to those relations, involves, a legal absurdity. The relations are repugnant; and as that of master and slave is fixed and recognised by law, the other cannot exist; and it follows that the lessor, Frances, does not take as one of the heirs of her father.

The other lessors are in a condition still more unfortunate; for, while relieved from the incongruity, which is involved in the case of their sisters, by the fact, that their mother, at the time of their birth, was free, yet, that circumstance caused them to be unlawfully begotten. Their parents, having become free persons, were guilty of a misdemeanor in living together as man and wife, without being married, as the law required; so that, there is nothing to save them from the imputation of being "bastards."

．　　　．　　　．　　　．　　　．

The relation between slaves is essentially different from that of man and wife joined in lawful wedlock. The latter is indissoluble during the lives of the parties, and its violation is a high crime; but with slaves it may be dissolved at the pleasure of either party, or by a sale of one or both, dependant on the caprice or necessity of the owners. So the union is formed, and the consent given in reference to this state of things, and no ground can be conceived of, upon which the fact of emancipation can, not only draw after it the qualified relation, but by a sort of magic, convert it into a relation of so different a nature. In our case, the emancipation of the father could not draw after it the prior relation, because the mother was not then free, and, in fact, afterwards became his slave. So the relation was not connected with the *status* of the parties in a way to follow as an incident. Suppose, after being free, the father had married another woman, could he have been convicted of bigamy, on the ground that a woman, who was his slave, was his wife? Or, after both were freed, would the penalty of the law have attached, if either had married a third person, l[ea]ving the other? Certainly not; because the averment of a prior, lawful marriage could not be supported, and yet, if the marriage followed the emancipation as an incident, it would present an instance of a marriage relation, which either is at liberty to dissolve at pleasure.

The parties after being freed, ought to have married according to law; it is the misfortune of their children that they neglected or refused to do so, for no court can avert the consequences.

E. INDIAN CHILDREN

Childbirth and child-rearing among the plains Indians, 1819–1820

Edwin James, "Account of an Expedition from Pittsburgh to the Rocky Mountains Performed in the Years 1819, 1820," in Reuben Gold Thwaites, *Early Western Travels,* XV (Cleveland, 1905), 18–23.

James, a botanist and geologist, accompanied Major Stephen Long on his famous expedition across the plains to the Rockies.

If, on a march, a pregnant woman feels the pains of parturition, she retires to the bushes, throws the burden from her back, and, without any aid, brings her infant into the world. After washing in water, if at hand, or in melted snow, both herself and the infant, she immediately replaces the burden upon her back, weighing, perhaps, between sixty and an hundred pounds, secures her child upon the top of it, protected from the cold by an envelop of bison robe, and then hurries on to overtake her companions.

It is only at the delivery of the first child

that any difficulty is ever anticipated; and, on this occasion, as there are no professed midwives, the young wife calls in some friendly matron to assist in case of need. The aid which these temporary midwives afford, seems to be limited to the practice of tying a belt firmly about the waist of the patient, and shaking her, generally in a vertical direction, with considerable violence. In order to facilitate the birth, a vegetable decoction is sometimes administered; and the rattle of the rattle-snake is also given with, it is said, considerable effect. The singular appendages of this animal are bruised by pounding, or comminuted by friction between the hands, mixed with warm water; and about the quantity of two segments constitutes a dose.

The art of *turning* does not appear to be known, neither is blood-letting practised in their obstetrics. We heard of no case of retention of the placenta after parturition, nor of the affection of longing, or of nausea of the stomach during pregnancy.

On the delivery of her first child, the young mother, who appears to be but little enfeebled by the process, arises almost immediately, and attends to the ordinary housework; but she does not, in general, undergo any laborious occupation, such as cutting and carrying wood, until the lapse of two or three days. The second child is brought forth without difficulty, and the parent, after bathing, ties it to a board, after their usual manner, then proceeds with her daily work, as if nothing extraordinary had occurred.

Mammary abscess is very rare; a squaw of the Sioux nation died with this complaint.

Sterility, although it does occur, is not frequent, and seems to be mostly attributable to the husband, as is evinced by subsequent marriages of the squaws.

The usual number of children may be stated at from four to six in a family, but in some families are ten or twelve. Of these the mother has often two at the breast simultaneously, of which one may be three years of age. At this age, however, and sometimes rather earlier, the child is weaned by the aid of ridicule, in which the parents are assisted by visitors.

The catalogue of the diseases, of both children and adults, probably bears a similar proportion to that of the white people, and is far less extensive and appalling. The summer complaint, so destructive to children in our region, appears to be uncommon with the Omawhaw infants; but, during their first year, they suffer more from constipation of the bowels than from any other complaint, but which is occasionally remedied by passing a small piece of soap (which is obtained from the traders,) cut into the proper shape, into the rectum.

Dentition seems to be productive of no great distress; the gums are never cut, but the teeth are permitted to force their way through. The shedding of the teeth is also accomplished without much difficulty; the milk-teeth, being forced out by the permanent ones, either fall from the mouth, or are gently extracted by the fingers of the parent.

Monstrous births sometimes occur, though rarely; and it is not known that infants are ever destroyed by their parents in consequence of deformity, unless the degree of malformation is excessive. The Indians mention two monsters which were born in their village; one of these they represent as resembling a white bear, and the other a cray-fish; they were both destroyed. The husband of the squaw, who gave birth to the former, said that she must have had connection with a white bear; but she asserted that the production of the monster was occasioned by a fright, which she received at seeing her husband suddenly, whilst he was personating that animal both in dress and gesture.

The magi affect to converse with the fœtus in utero, when the mother perceives it to be uneasy; they also sometimes venture to predict its sex.

Abortion is effected, agreeably to the assertions of the squaws, by blows with the clenched hand, applied upon the abdomen, or by repeated and violent pressure upon that part, or by rolling on the stump of a tree, or other hard body. The pregnant squaw is induced thus to procure abortion, in consequence of the jealousy of her husband, or in order to conceal her illicit amours, to which all the married squaws, with but few exceptions, are addicted.

The infant, when recently born, is of a reddish-brown colour; but in a short time it becomes whitish, though never so pure a white as that of the children of white people. The change to the national complexion is then gradual, and independent of exposure; inasmuch as those parts of their bodies, which are perpetually concealed from the light, change simultaneously with the face.

The abdomen of the children protrudes very considerably; and the sole article of dress, which the younger boys wear during the warm season, is a small belt of cloth around the middle of the abdomen, leaving every other part of the body perfectly naked. In wintry weather they have the addition of leggings, mockasins, and a small robe.

The female children are furnished with a short piece of cloth, in imitation of a petticoat, but destitute of a seam, belted round the loins, and depending as low as the knees. Their hair, when dressed, is parted longitudinally on the top of the head, and collected on each side behind the ear, into a vertical cylindric form, of the length of five or six inches, decorated with silver and brass rings and ribands; the line of separation of the hair is coloured with vermilion.

This disposition of the hair into two rolls is generally observed in the girls, and is often continued one or two years after their residence with a husband.

The girl is kept in a state of considerable subjection; she habitually conforms to all the commands of the mother, and is obliged to assist her in her ordinary occupations; if she is refractory, she receives a blow upon the head or back from the hand of the mother, but hardly ever from the father. At the age of four or five years, she is taught the use of the *hoppas,* and is gradually familiarised to carry burdens. They are trained up to industry, and are taught to cut wood, to cultivate maize, to

perform the scalp dance, and are early informed of the sexual relations of men and women, and warned against the arts which will be aimed at the subjugation of their virtue.

The experienced parent, however, in addition to these salutary counsels, keeps a vigilant eye to the deportment of her unmarried daughter, and so sedulously guards her steps, that the arts of seduction, notwithstanding the free use of the licentiousness of language, appear to be more rarely triumphant over the Omawhaw maid, than over the civilized fair.

Hence a prostitute, who has never been married, is of exceedingly rare occurrence. Yet, notwithstanding the vigilance of the parent, the daughter sometimes elopes with a favoured lover, but not until she has ascertained that his intentions are perfectly honourable.

The girl displays the most affectionate regard for her parents, and grand parents.

Whilst the deportment of the sister is thus trenched and guarded, the brother roams at large, almost uncontrolled. Should his conduct be at any time flagrantly outrageous, he will, perhaps, in the anger of his parents, receive a harsh reproof; but an ill-judged affection soon prompts them to assuage his grief, and dry his tears, by presents and soothing expressions. At a very early age he is furnished with a bow and arrows, with the use of which he delights to employ himself, that he may be qualified for a hunter and warrior.

From the age of about five years to that of ten or twelve, custom obliges the boy to ascend to a hill-top, or other elevated position, fasting, that he may cry aloud to the Wahconda. At the proper season, his mother reminds him that "the ice is breaking up in the river, the ducks and geese are migrating, and it is time for you to prepare to go in clay." He then rubs his person over with a whitish clay, and is sent off to the hill-top at sunrise, previously instructed by his mother what to say, and how to demean himself in the presence of the Master of life. From this elevation he cries out to the great Wahconda, humming a melancholy tune, and calling on him to have pity on him, and make him a great hunter, horse-stealer, and warrior. This is repeated once or twice a week, during the months of March and April.

It is only when his pride is concerned, that the boy is obedient to the injunctions of his parents; on other occasions he disregards them, or replies only with ridicule. A boy in anger discharged an arrow at his mother, which penetrated her thigh; when, instead of chastising him for the act, she applauded his spirit, declaring him to be a gallant fellow, the early promise of a great warrior. But though he does not scruple thus to insult his parents, he would unhesitatingly revenge an indignity offered them by another.

He soon becomes ambitious of martial distinction, in consequence of frequently hearing the old warriors narrate their feats of arms, and eagerly anticipates the age which will justify his enrolling himself in the ranks of a war-party.

At the age of twelve or thirteen, having received every instruction respecting their mode of warfare, his wishes are gratified, and he is accepted as a volunteer in the path of honour.

The reminiscences of Poor Wolf, chief of the Gros Ventre, ca. 1825

Poor Wolf, "Autobiography," *Collections* of the State Historical Society of North Dakota, I (1906), 439–441.

Poor Wolf dictated his memoirs in 1906 when he was eighty-six years old.

I was born on the Knife river in the middle of the three Gros-ventre villages near the mouth of that stream . . .

When I was a child of five winters, perhaps only four, I prayed to the spirits of animals, to the stars, the sun and the moon. My words were not many, but I prayed. I was afraid of the enemy in the dark. My father had heard of the white man's God through a trader but nothing clearly. We sometimes prayed to the white man's God who made us and could make us grow.

We had female divinities above, and we prayed to the four winds, and to the earth that makes the corn grow. There are many songs concerning these things, some of the songs speak of the different colored flowers. These things were taught for a great price, by the priests of the tribe.

When I was about five winters old a white chief visited our village on the Knife river. He said that the Gros Ventres should obey the Great Father, and consider their hunting grounds as extending from Devil's lake to the Yellowstone river. I remember saying to my father: Will I be a white man now? And my father said, Yes. That was 77 years ago, and I have been a friend to the whites ever since.

These men had eight boats. They were drawn by ropes that the men pulled. They were soldiers with stripes on their breasts and arms . . .

When I was 17 year of age I had the small pox. I was left alone in a lodge, helpless, weak, and my eyes nearly closed. A bear came in and walked up to where I was lying. He sat down with his back pressed against me, and began to scratch his breast with his fore paws. By and by he got up and walked out of the lodge. Was I dreaming or had it really happened? While I was thinking it over the bear returned, and while I trembled for fear, went through the same motions again, and then went off, leaving me unharmed. I thought surely the bear has had mercy on me. When my father came again we talked it over and agreed that the bear had pitied me. After that I worshiped the bear, and in the dance I wore anklets of bear's teeth.

When I was 19 or 20 years of age, I went fasting for 20 days. I would not eat anything nor smoke for four days. On the fifth day I would eat a little, and then fast again. My mother and friends would try to have me give up, but I persisted. I cried during this time, and then, for a year after, though I did not fast I kept on crying. After this I was tattooed on my arms and neck and other places on my body. This was done with great ceremony. Song was used in the performance. They would sing: Let his body be pictured, his face, his spirit also, and O! White Father in heaven, and ye four winds, make him blue. Let him not be bitten by rattle snakes. It was thought that the tattooing would give courage and afford protection; one would not be struck by bullets. One could suck out snake poison without harm. This last I did not like to try, but my father assured me it could be done. The tattooing left me sore, swollen, and itching. After a while I moved about slowly and painfully, and ate a little. I was rubbed with grease and then the sores healed and the blue patterns came out. In tattooing five little sharp instruments were fastened side by side. They were like needles, and pricked painfully into the flesh.

At the Knife river a party of Sioux once attacked us in the winter. The Gros Ventres were running away. I walked right up to the Sioux who were on horseback. They ran. Then two of them came against me on foot. They shot at me, but the bullets struck my beaded shirt and did no harm. I was then 21 years of age.

Indian boys and girls, 1851

Hiram M. Chittenden and Alfred T. Richardson, eds., *Life, Letters and Travels of Father Pierre-Jean De Smet* (New York, 1905), III, 1006–1007.

Father De Smet was a Belgian Jesuit missionary. This account of Plains Indians was included in a letter to his niece.

You expect, no doubt, that I will tell you something about the savages of America. Here is how they stand in regard to education, which I know is a matter that interests you. The only school in which the Indian youth learn to form

their head and heart, is the example of their elders. They give them no preceptors. In the family, the father has charge of the boys, the mother of the girls, and the old proverb, "like father like son," applies more strictly among the Indians than anywhere else. In general, great attention is paid to the physical development of the children and they are prepared from their tenderest infancy for the hardest kind of life. As soon as the child is born, in whatever season, regardless of the severest cold or the greatest heat, they at once plunge it several times into water. Then, suitably wrapped up, it is placed and entrusted in the hands of some other nurse than its mother. After the first week the parents take it back, and it is put into the cradle, or *berceau* — a machine that deserves to be patented, and which the little individual does not leave until he is able to walk. This is the simple construction of it — a small hide-covered board, about a foot longer than its little occupant. The child is placed upon it and tied tightly with bandages, beginning with the legs and covering it to the shoulders; they are made tightest about the loins and the pit of the stomach, in order to force out the chest as much as possible. Neatly arranged in this style, the little party occupies a place in the lodge, out of harm's way. When the weather is fine, he is set in the doorway of the lodge. If the nurse goes away, she hangs the cradle to the branch of a tree, where the baby warms himself tranquilly in the sun, or on hot days is in the shade, and is in no danger from dogs, wolves or snakes, which are often plentiful in the neighborhood. When they travel, the cradle is hung from the saddle-bow, where it is out of the rider's way and offers no danger to the little prisoner.

After he has learned to walk, and up to the time when he can provide for his own subsistence, he remains attached to his parents' lodge, doing no hard work. At about the age of twelve, he begins to take care of his father's band of horses, and to handle the bow or fire-arms in the chase. At sixteen or eighteen he is invested with the honors and responsibilities of the warrior; he shares the labors and takes part in all the amusements of the village elders. The girls enjoy no such liberty as do the boys. They are early made to help their mother in all her labors; they cut and bring in firewood, help prepare the food, which is no small matter among the Indians, who often dine six or eight times a day; mend and make shoes and garments, with a very great number of etceteras, and when a girl is of age, her father sells her for a horse or two and she becomes the slave of a man to whom very likely she may never have spoken.

II Immigrant Children

Unlike working children or juvenile delinquents, immigrant children of the first half of the nineteenth century cannot be studied separately from adults. Immigrant children experienced with their parents the pain of uprooting, the vicissitudes of crossing, and the tribulations of adjustment. Public laws and regulations did not distinguish between children and adults, except in the calculation of fares and space allotted aboard ships. Immigration laws extended no special protection to children and made no allowances for their needs.

An unprecedented wave of migrations in the middle of the nineteenth century confronted Americans with new social problems. From 1790 to 1820 only about 250,000 immigrants entered the United States, while from 1815 to 1860 5,000,000 immigrants poured into a population which in 1820 numbered about 10,000,000 and in 1860, 31,000,000. This movement began with 151,000 in the 1820's and reached 2,314,000 in the 1850's. It consisted largely of displaced Scandinavian tenant farmers and of Irish and German peasants fleeing potato famines. The first Scandinavians arrived in 1825, but their immigration did not gain momentum until the 1840's. The Irish wave peaked between 1845 and 1849 after the great famine, the German between 1846 and 1855. From the 1840's on, most immigrants arrived virtually penniless. Unable to continue their journey inland, many remained in the coastal cities to swell the rolls of unskilled labor and the dependent poor. This was especially true of the Irish.[1]

The immigrants of the 1830's and 1840's shared the aspirations and expectations of the many generations of newcomers who ventured to improve their lives and to secure a better future for their children. "When children are born they are called blessings here," wrote a man from New York to his brother in England.[2] The theme of a new world for children was expressed in all waves of migration as well as in the westward movement within the American continent.

America became the common man's utopia in the first half of the nineteenth century. Across the Atlantic prospective immigrants eagerly read printed reports and long-awaited "America letters" from friends and relatives.[3] John West, a shoemaker who had come to Pennsylvania from Corsley, England, advised his relatives: "A man can do better here with a family than with none. For children at six years old can work and get some money."[4] Stephen and Elizabeth Watson, paupers in England who had emigrated at parish expense, reported from Dearborn, Indiana: "We can get our children educated better than one could at your place. The free school here is the Lancastrian system; it has four hundred scholars, both rich and poor, who pay one dollar a quarter, and some not more than a shilling sterling; the scholars are taught reading, writing, arithmetic, geography."[5] Such glowing re-

1. On the Irish situation see Oscar Handlin, *Boston's Immigrants: A Study in Acculturation* (rev. and enl. ed., Cambridge, Mass., 1959).

2. Luke Bentley to his brother, March 27, 1818, in Edith Abbott, *Historical Aspects of the Immigration Problem* (Chicago, 1926), p. 42.

3. On this point see Marcus Lee Hansen, *The Atlantic Migration, 1607–1800* (New York, 1961), pp. 146–172.

4. Letter of John West, May 20, 1831, in Abbott, *Immigration Problem*, p. 78.

5. Letter of March 29, 1824, to their parents, in Abbott, *Immigration Problem*, p. 247.

ports from the promised land infected relatives and neighbors with the fever of migration. En route to utopia immigrants crossed overland routes and spent several months in cramped steerage quarters of freight vessels. If they survived "floating pestilence," starvation, and abuse, they became prey to "sharpers" and thieves on their arrival.

The initiative for the protection of the immigrant came from the federal government. In 1819 Congress set a limit on the number of passengers a vessel could carry. A law passed in May 1848 required adequate ventilation of the ship, set minimum quantities of food, water, and fuel for each passenger, called for the installation of cooking ranges, and made the captain responsible for maintaining "good discipline, and such habits of cleanliness . . . as will tend to the preservation and promotion of the health." The act of 1855, which superseded all previous legislation, protected families by insisting that double-berths be occupied only by combinations of two women; a husband and wife; two men of the same family; a woman and two children under age eight; or a man and two of his own children under age eight.[6] The laws went generally unobserved. Thus, while the laws did not improve the circumstances of the individual immigrant, they indicate the government's conception of responsibility for the protection of immigrants in transit.

The states, on the other hand, were more concerned with the protection of their own populations from immigrant paupers than with the welfare of newcomers. The first permanent state agency for the protection and relief of immigrants — and indeed the first state welfare agency in America — was the New York State Board of Commissioners of Emigration. Its goals, in the words of Friedrich Kapp, a leading member of the Board, were "to protect

the newcomer, to prevent him from being robbed, to facilitate his passage through the city to the interior, to aid him with good advice, and, in cases of the most urgent necessity, to furnish him with a small amount of money; in short, not to treat him as a pauper with the ultimate view of making him an inmate of the Almshouse, but as an independent citizen, whose future career would become interwoven with the best interests of the country." [7]

The commissioners of emigration collected head taxes and indemnity bonds imposed on immigrants and crew and vessels arriving at the various New York ports. Using these funds to aid immigrants and to reimburse local communities for relief granted to immigrants, the commissioners acted on the principle that the immigrant was *entitled* to relief, since he had paid for it. In 1855, to protect immigrants from boardinghouse runners and unscrupulous transportation agents, the commissioners established a central compulsory landing depot in Castle Garden at the foot of Manhattan. There they provided information on lost luggage, transportation, guidance, and job placement. Initially the commissioners restricted their health activities to immigrants suffering from contagious diseases. In 1848 they leased Ward's Island in the East River where they established a general hospital, a lying-in hospital for mothers, and a refuge for unemployable immigrants. Recognizing the need of children for special treatment, the commissioners took charge of illegitimate children, administered the property of orphans, and maintained a nursery and a school on Ward's Island.

The new waves of the great migration had a direct impact on the urbanization and industrialization of the Northeast. The expanding textile, iron, and construction industries absorbed the immigrant labor force. Irish canal builders worked their way from Boston to Lowell, while their women and children entered the textile factories. Yankees in New England factory towns complained of recent immigrants

6. "An Act Regulating Passenger Ships and Vessels," 1819 — ch. 46, *The Public Statutes of the United States of America 1789–1845*, III (Boston, 1850), 488–489. "An Act to provide for the Ventilation of Passenger Vessels, and for other Purposes," 1848 — ch. 41, *The Statutes at Large and Treaties of the United States of America, 1845–1851* (Boston, 1851), pp. 220–223

7. Friedrich Kapp, *Immigration and the Commissioners of Emigration of the State of New York* (New York, 1870), p. 85.

who, in their readiness to work for any wage, were displacing young women of native stock in the mills.[8] In a report issued in 1858, a Massachusetts legislative committee, using familiar rhetoric, held immigrants and corporations responsible for the social problems of towns with a high percentage of foreigners: "Monster corporations import by the shipload the employees who fill their mills, [and] do the base drudgery of their workshops and their degrading, ill paid, menial services in every branch of business. They allow them to erect in their cities and towns the most miserable shanties for dwellings, or else, the capitalists, who profit by their labor, do it in their stead. In these are made the paupers of the state." [9]

Not even the unskilled labor market could absorb the immigrant flood that poured in during the 1840's and early 1850's. Boston, New York, Baltimore, and New Orleans complained of the burden of charity and poor relief. Young immigrant rag-and-bone and coal pickers, petty thieves, beggars, and street arabs became part of the scene in the Five Points district of New York, in Boston's North End, and in the newly christened "Irish Channel" section of New Orleans. Theodore Lyman, mayor of Boston from 1831 to 1835 and, in 1847, a principal figure in the establishment of the first state institution for delinquents, warned in 1835 "we shall have among us a race that will never be infused into our own . . . Their children will be brought up in ignorance and idleness; disregarding themselves every comfort and neglecting every decency of life." [10]

The immigrant child did not import delinquency and dependency to America. Yet, the staggering influx of immigrant poor aggravated existing conditions of destitution. By mid-century immigrant children and children of foreign-born parents composed about 50 per cent of the inmates in reformatories and houses of refuge.[11] Hence, benevolent societies, holding the immigrant responsible for the impersonal forces which seemed to threaten the existing order, were startled by what they considered a "vast influx of foreign pauperism, ready-made and hatched abroad, ignorant, squalid and degraded, alien to our institutions, usages, habits and laws." [12]

In their concern for the protection of society from the potential criminal in a neglected immigrant child, philanthropic organizations found the obvious answer in Americanization. Protestant missionary organizations which undertook the rescue of immigrant children in the mid-nineteenth century conceived of Americanization as a method of social control and a proselytizing effort, rather than a cultural movement. Many made the welfare of the immigrant secondary to their desire to rescue souls from Catholicism. "Boston is a dreadful place for making Protestants of people, and you must be careful, especially of the children, or they will get them from you," an Irish priest in Hali-

8. On the increase of Irish factory labor in Lowell see Caroline Ware, *Early New England Cotton Manufacture* (New York, 1966), pp. 228–232. Ware argues that the Irish did not displace the native girls, but rather filled the spaces which they had left. The readiness of the Irish to work for low wages, however, precipitated the departure of large numbers of women from the factories.

9. Massachusetts, Senate, "Report on Public Charitable Institutions," *Sen. Doc. No. 2* (Boston, 1859), pp. 81–82.

10. Theodore Lyman, Jr., *Addresses Made to the City Council of Boston* (Boston, 1835), pp. 17–24.

11. In 1850 Catholic boys comprised 41 per cent of the inmates of the State Reform School at Westborough, Massachusetts. Most of these were Irish. The foreign-born population of Massachusetts was 18.93 per cent. Michael B. Katz, *The Irony of Early School Reform: Educational Innovation in Mid-Nineteenth Century Massachusetts* (Cambridge, Mass., 1968), pp. 176–177. Similarly, the annual reports of the New York Children's Aid Society suggest that about half the children under the Society's care were immigrants themselves or children of immigrants. The statistical evidence is inconclusive, however, because the reports do not distinguish between immigrant children and children of foreign parentage. Moreover, the reports usually list about 25 per cent of "unknown" origin.

12. Annual Report of the Boston Industrial Aid Society for 1858, in Francis E. Lane, *American Charities and the Child of the Immigrant* (Washington, D.C., 1932), p. 64.

fax warned a mother about to move to Boston.[13]

In their uplifting work Americanizers discovered that education and labor — the traditional weapons in the war on pauperism — were insufficient in dealing with the immigrant. An entire transformation of character was necessary. The Massachusetts State Board of Charities insisted that if immigrant children were trained in proper homes and mingled freely with native children, their "habits and character must be radically changed; they will be no more foreigners but Americans — the alien will become naturalized." [14]

Because of the enormity of the task of coping with entire families and because of the lack of cooperation from parents, missionaries had to concentrate on the children alone. Boston's Benevolent Fraternity of Churches, despairing of its ability to hand relief to the increasing "swarms of immigrants" which descended on the city's quays, found a new challenge in the rescue of the souls of immigrant children. "These persons are ignorant of even the alpha-

bet of useful or domestic economy," wrote one of the Fraternity's women workers about the immigrant poor. She warned that their children could never be instructed "unless they are driven faster by stern necessity from their wretched homes, and compelled to learn some useful occupation." [15] The New York Children's Aid Society, founded in 1853, went even further by placing children from New York slums with farmer's families in the West, thus rescuing them from the "dangerous classes" and a corrupting environment. Usually half the children shipped west by the Society were immigrants, or of foreign parentage.

Societies such as the New York Association for the Improvement of the Condition of the Poor, the Boston Provident Association, the Howard Mission and the Five Points House of Industry in New York, and the Children's Mission to the Children of the Destitute in Boston all tried to rescue immigrant children by sending them elsewhere. Even if the old generation was lost, the children could be redeemed as Americans.

13. Lane, *American Charities*, p. 47.

14. Massachusetts, Board of State Charities, *First Annual Report; January 1865* (Boston, 1865), pp. xxv–xxvi.

15. Rev. J. B. Torricelli, *21st Annual Report of the Executive Committee of the Benevolent Fraternity of Churches* (Boston, 1855), pp. 14–15.

A. REPORTS FROM THE PROMISED LAND

Lack of educational opportunities for immigrant children in rural America, 1805

Friedrich Herman, "Die Deutschen in Nord Amerika," *Minerva,* II (April–June 1805), 53–55; translated by the editors.

It is easy to understand that elementary instruction under these circumstances must be in a very sad state. In the countryside there are usually no qualified teachers. Those who can

bring themselves to undertake the hard and poorly paid work of a school teacher in these remote and still very desolate areas are only too often men who could not make a go of it elsewhere — pedagogical quacks, ignorant, without principles, and often of bad character. Even if a locality is lucky enough to have a good teacher in its preacher or some other person, it can scarcely be very happy about that. In the first place the individual houses are often too far from the school, and so separated from it by water holes, thick woods, and the like, that a person can scarcely hazard sending his children (especially if they are of tender age) to school all year round. Secondly a person lacking hired help needs the children too much at home for field work or housekeeping to part with them willingly. Thus the benefit of the children is secondary to their parents' needs. In this way nothing is done for the up-bringing and education of the child except what the parents are able to do at home. How little this is, however, a person can easily gather from the fact that they themselves can be compared almost to children in their lack of knowledge. They don't have the slightest idea how to treat these tender hearts, and even worse they are hindered by their endless tasks in the fields from giving them the necessary supervision. There are two fundamental principles which a father seeks to inculcate in his child and which indeed should be omitted from no education, though they by no means constitute its entirety. The first is: Fear God! This embraces all religion, in which, however, the parents themselves are guided more by obscure emotions than by clear thinking. Therefore they are in a position to instruct the young spirits only very imperfectly. The second is: Be industrious! This [commandment] covers the entire range of their duties as citizens, which consist largely in manual labor to be sure and, according to their fathers, should not encompass anything further. One can see that this practice hardly suffices to protect the heart from vice, not to speak of filling it with a real love for virtue. If the simple habits of the parents, the ignorance of luxury, and the distance they live from big cities and their depravity were not more effective than this upbringing, youth would be in real danger.

"Nothing has made me more happy . . . than the fact that we . . . journeyed to this country"

Letter of Gjert Gregoriussen Hovland, April 22, 1835, in George M. Stephenson, "A Typical 'American Letter,'" *Mississippi Valley Historical Review,* IX (1922–1923), 69–72.

Hovland came to America in 1831 and settled in western New York, in a colony founded in 1825 by the first group of Norwegian immigrants to America. Hundreds of copies of Hovland's letters circulated in southern Norway. They aroused interest among peasants, and apparently influenced the Norwegian migration to America in 1836 and 1837.

I must take this opportunity to let you know that we are in the best of health, and that we — both my wife and I — find ourselves exceedingly well satisfied. Our son attends the English school, and talks English as well as the native-born. Nothing has made me more happy and contented than the fact that we left Norway and journeyed to this country. We have gained more since our arrival here than I did during all the time that I lived in Norway, and I have every prospect of earning a livelihood here for myself and my family — even if my family were larger, so long as God gives me good health.

Such excellent plans have been developed here that, even though one be infirm, no one need suffer want. Competent men are elected whose duty it is to see that no needy persons, either in the cities or in the country, shall have to beg for their living. If a man dies and is survived by a widow and children who are unable to support themselves — as is often the case — they have the privilege of petitioning these officials. To each one will then be given every year as much as is needed of clothes and food, and no discrimination will be shown between the native-born and those from foreign countries. These things I have learned through daily observation, and I do not believe there can be better laws and arrangements for the benefit and happiness of the common man in the whole world.

.   .   .   .   .

No, everyone must work for his living here, and it makes no difference whether he is of low or of high estate. It would heartily please me if I could learn that everyone of you who are in need and have little chance of gaining support for yourselves and your families would make up your mind to leave Norway and to come to America, for, even if many more were to come, there would still be room here for all. For all those who are willing to work there is no lack of employment and business here. It is possible for all to live in comfort and without suffering want.

"Your interest in your children must be the deciding factor"

Letter of Herman Steines to his parents, brothers, and friends, St. Louis, Mo., Nov. 8, 1833, in William G. Bek, "The Followers of Duden," *Missouri Historical Review,* XIV (1919–1920), 64–70.

In May 1833, Herman and Frederick Steines, natives of Rhenish Prussia, sailed from Bremen leading a group of pioneers to settle in Missouri.

. . . Those whose line of work is in demand will prosper . . . Fortunately [Cousin Adolph] found work at once, and now earns from $1.25 to $3.00 per day, since he is working by the piece. But it must be remembered that one cannot buy as much for $2.00 in St. Louis as one can buy for $1.00 in Solingen or any other German city. Almost all necessities are twice as high here as abroad. Meat and vegetables are in some instances cheaper here, or at least as cheap as at home. But even at that they are able to save something. Adolph's daughter Ida works at the house where I am staying and earns five dollars a month, while his son William is an apprentice to a furniture maker. He is obliged to work four years for this man, and receives an annual wage of $30.00 and has an allowance of $1.50 per week for board and lodging which he has with his own parents. During half the year his master sends the boy to school, part of the time to the day school and part time to the night school. In case of sickness he receives free medical attention and at the end of his apprenticeship he will get a number of tools . . . A young single man is not so much to be pitied, because he can fight his way thru for some time, but if the disappointed person happens to be the father of a family, then it is hard indeed. I repeat that $666.00 is the absolute minimum with which one should attempt to make a start here . . .

.   .   .   .   .

Now a few words to you, my mother and my sisters, in order that you not become intimidated by my letter, for I did not intend to do that. If you feel strong enough in body to endure the hardships of the journey, and buoyant enough in spirit to participate in the attempt of realizing the fond dream of your men folks, then we shall all be happy and greatly benefitted. The older members of our family will not be materially benefitted by coming here, but your interest in your children must be the deciding factor if you take this step. You women must have a clear understanding with your men.

Farewell, Norway, 1847

Anonymous poem in *Nordlyset,* Aug. 19, 1847, in Martin B. Ruud, ed. and trans., "Norwegian Emigrant Songs," *Norwegian-American Studies and Records,* II (Northfield, Minn. 1927), 5–6.

Farewell, Norway, and God bless thee. Stern and severe wert thou always, but as a mother I honor thee, even though thou skimped my bread. All things vanish. Grief and care sink down upon the heart; still the memory of thee refereshes the soul like the deep sleep of a child.

Other lands offer me independence, and for my labor well-being to my children. These, oh Norway, thou didst not give me, for thou art a land of lords and slaves, where the great ones ruled and we obeyed.

Once more, God bless thee; to the day of my death I will pray God to keep thee; for thou wert the keeper of my childhood and the joys of childhood thou gavest me. I will remember thee always, whatever life may bring, and I will pray, "Throw off the chains that embittered my youth for me."

"To spare my children the slavish drudgery"

Letter from Stephan Stephanson, May 17, 1854, in George H. Stephenson, "When America was the Land of Canaan," *Minnesota History,* X (September 1929), 254.

I am glad that I migrated to this land of liberty, in order to spare my children the slavish drudgery that was my lot; in this country if a laborer cannot get along with his employer, he can leave his job at any time, and the latter is obliged to pay him for the time he has put in at the same wage that was agreed upon for the month or year. We are free to move at any time and to any place without a certificate from the employer or from the pastor, because neither passports nor certificates are in use here.

Life and death in the promised land

Letter from Andrew Pauley to his uncle and family in Philadelphia, Aug. 21, 1854,

courtesy of Professor Arnold Schrier, University of Cincinnati.

There has been a long silence between you and me and it seems my fate to be the first to break that silence. I have to relate to you some things that has been rather unpleasant to me, within the last year.

On the 7th of July last our youngest child "Mary Ann" died being about 6 months old. She was only about 2 days sick. A few days afterwards I started to Ohio to see Father & Mother & Bro. remained there about a week sister Mary came back here again with me . . . but when I got home I met with more trouble, for a few days after I returned, our son William took sick, and lived 2 or 3 days. He was 2¼ years old when he died. This was full trying enough on both Margaret and me to loose the two in such a short time. Of course Margaret feels bad about them. It has left us now all alone only Sister Mary is staying with us at present, this has been a very sickly summer here and a great many deaths. Some weeks as high as 4 or 6 hundred deaths. There is a report that the cholera is bad here but I do not know whether it is or not.

I have got along very well since I came here and has saved some money. I never regretted coming out here, and any young person that cannot got along well there would do well to come here if they intended to conduct themselves decently. Yet I would not say to any one to come for most people dislike it for a while and have difficulties at first too but they can get over that and make money if they only help themselves right. But if they don't intend to do that they had better stay at home for they be only in disgrace to themselves and then friends here. But old people have no great chance here except their families are with them, and go to the country and can give themselves a little to farming for they can do nothing living in a city, but are a burden to themselves and their family. And then they cannot enjoy themselves aged in the city as they could in the country as they have been used all their life.

But young people can more easily suit themselves to any locality.

———————

An immigrant family on the Minnesota frontier, 1862–1866

Letter from Guri Olsdatter to relatives, Dec. 2, 1866, in Theodore C. Blegen, "Immigrant Women and the American Frontier," *Norwegian-American Studies and Records,* V (Northfield, Minn., 1930), pp. 26–29.

Guri Olsdatter was the wife of Lars Endreson; her husband and son were among the several hundred white settlers killed during the Sioux massacre of 1862.

———————

DEAR DAUGHTER AND YOUR HUSBAND AND CHILDREN, AND MY BELOVED MOTHER:

I have received your letter of April fourteenth, this year, and I send you herewith my heartiest thanks for it, for it gives me great happiness to hear from you and to know that you are alive, well, and in general thriving. I must also report briefly to you how things have been going with me recently, though I must ask you to forgive me for not having told you earlier about my fate. I do not seem to have been able to do so much as to write to you, because during the time when the savages raged so fearfuly here I was not able to think about anything except being murdered, with my whole family, by these terrible heathen. But God be praised, I escaped with my life, unharmed by them, and my four daughters also came through the danger unscathed. Guri and Britha were carried off by the wild Indians, but they got a chance the next day to make their escape; when the savages gave them permission to go home to get some food, these young girls made use of the opportunity to flee and thus they got away alive, and on the third day after they had been taken, some Americans came along who found them on a large plain or prairie and brought them to people. I myself wandered aimlessly around on my land with my youngest daughter and I had to look on while they shot my precious husband dead, and in my sight my dear son Ole was shot through the shoulder. But he got well again from this wound and lived a little more than a year and then was taken sick and died. We also found my oldest son Endre shot dead, but I did not see the firing of this death shot. For two days and nights I hovered about here with my little daughter, between fear and hope and almost crazy, before I found my wounded son and a couple of other persons, unhurt, who helped us to get away to a place of greater security. To be an eyewitness to these things and to see many others wounded and killed was almost too much for a poor woman; but, God be thanked, I kept my life and my sanity, though all my movable property was torn away and stolen. But this would have been nothing if only I could have had my loved husband and children — but what shall I say? God permitted it to happen thus, and I had to accept my heavy fate and thank Him for having spared my life and those of some of my dear children.

I must also let you know that my daughter Gjærtru has land, which they received from the government under a law that has been passed, called in our language "the Homestead law," and for a quarter section of land they have to pay sixteen dollars, and after they have lived there five years they receive a deed and complete possession of the property and can sell it if they want to or keep it if they want to. She lives about twenty-four American miles from here and is doing well. My daughter Guri is away in house service for an American about a hundred miles from here; she has been there working for the same man for four years; she is in good health and is doing well; I visited her recently, but for a long time I knew nothing about her, whether she was alive or not.

My other two daughter, Britha and Anna, are at home with me, are in health, and are thriving here. I must also remark that it was four years on the twenty-first of last August since I had to flee from my dear home, and since that time I have not been on my land, as it is only a sad sight because at the spot where I had a happy home, there are now only ruins and remains left as reminders of the terrible Indians. Still I moved up here to the neighborhood again this summer. A number of families have moved back here again so that we hope after a while to make conditions pleasant once more. Yet the atrocities of the Indians are and will be fresh in memory; they have now been driven beyond the boundaries of the state and we hope that they never will be allowed to come here again. I am now staying at the home of Sjur Anderson, two and a half miles from my home. I must also tell you how much I had before I was ruined in this way. I had seventeen head of cattle, eight sheep, eight pigs, and a number of chickens; now I have six head of cattle, four sheep, one pig; five of my cattle stayed on my land until February, 1863, and lived on some hay and stacks of wheat on the land; and I received compensation from the government for my cattle and other movable property that I lost. Of the six cattle that I now have three are milk cows and of these I have sold butter, the summer's product, a little over two hundred and thirty pounds; I sold

this last month and got sixty-six dollars for it. In general I may say that one or another has advised me to sell my land, but I would rather keep it for a time yet, in the hope that some of my people might come and use it; it is difficult to get such good land again, and if you, my dear daughter, would come here, you could buy it and use it and then it would not be necessary to let it fall into the hands of strangers. And now in closing I must send my very warm greetings to my unforgetable dear mother, my dearest daughter and her husband and children, and in general to all my relatives, acquaintances, and friends. And may the Lord by his grace bend, direct, and govern our hearts so that we sometime with gladness may assemble with God in the eternal mansions where there will be no more partings, no sorrows, no more trials, but everlasting joy and gladness, and contentment in beholding God's face. If this be the goal for all our endeavors through the sorrows and cares of this life, then through his grace we may hope for a blessed life hereafter, for Jesus sake.

Always your devoted
GURI OLSDATTER

Write to me soon.

B. THE CROSSING

A ship agent's contract with shipowners to carry emigrants, Bremen, 1833

Bek, "The Followers of Duden," pp. 42–46.

Bremen was the chief direct port of departure from Germany. The Bremen city government, unlike Liverpool, the Irish ports, and Hamburg, passed regulations for the protection of emigrants as early as 1832. Generally, however, these laws remained unobserved and, therefore, the services offered differed dramatically from those promised in the contract. The usual height of the steerage deck ranged from four to six feet. Steerage quarters five feet high often contained two tiers of berths. Below was the "orlop deck" — a hole to which no law applied.[1]

1. Kapp, *Immigration and the Commissioners of Emigration of the State of New York*, pp. 19–25.

Conditions under which J. D. Luedering in Bremen, the authorized ship's agent, who has been appointed by the government to receive emigrants and to assist them to their ships, agrees to make contracts for the passage from Bremen to the United States of North America.

1) For the transportation of passengers only such ships are accepted as are provided with roomy steerage quarters and whose efficiency has been duly tested and investigated and is vouched for by the insurance company prior to the beginning of the journey.

2) During the journey the passengers receive their board free, board such as it is customary to serve on board of ship, consisting of salt beef, salt and smoked bacon, shelled beans, green and yellow peas, groats, rice, farinaceous foods, potatoes, etc., everything in sufficient quantity and well prepared; in addition to this — in the morning coffee or tea, toast, fresh water, etc. For the men a drink of brandy is provided in the morning. In case of sickness the patients receive appropriate food and necessary medicine, of which a sufficient supply is on board. In order that no want may arise during the journey, the above named supplies are taken in a superfluous quantity, calculated sufficient for a journey of ninety days.

3) The ordinary traveling baggage of passengers is conveyed free of charge. Under the term "ordinary traveling baggage" is meant a trunk or chest of about twenty cubic feet content per passenger. In this matter only the size and not the weight of the chest is taken into consideration.

4) Passengers will find suitable bedsteads, but they must supply their own bedding or straw mattresses, as well as their own dishes, spoons, knives and forks.

5) The rate of steerage passage to Baltimore, New York, or Philadelphia is the following per individual:

Persons over twelve years of age 40 Thaler in gold.[2]

Children from eight to twelve years 30 Thaler in gold.

Children from four to eight years 20 Thaler in gold.

Children from one to four years 10 Thaler in gold.

Children under one year of age 5 Thaler in gold.

Since however, according to an American law, only a certain number of passengers may be transported on each steamer (for every five tons of the ship's displacement only two passengers), and since children are estimated equal to adults in this matter, therefore it is assumed that under the above quoted rates for children their number will be such proportion to the number of adults that a sufficiently large average sum per head will be realized.[3] The now customary sum, required of families or parties, amounts to thirty-five Thaler in gold per head, according to which only one child is allowed with three adults. If there are more children than can be apportioned according to the above scale, additional payment must be made. Families will therefore do well to combine with other adult persons whose fare is uniformly forty Thaler. I myself shall endeavor to make the passage of families as cheap as possible by securing combinations with other adults.

6) The age of children must be certified to by birth certificates, and every passenger must be provided with a passport to the foreign country.

7) In a few places in North America, especially in New York and Philadelphia, the government demands a poor-tax (Armen-Taxe) of immigrants upon their arrival. This amounts to a sum ranging from one to four Spanish Thaler or one and a half to five Thaler in gold. This fee passes under the term of Commutation money. All passengers sailing to any of these points must deposit this amount at the time they pay their fare.

.   .   .   .   .

2. Forty thaler was approximately $16.00.

3. The American law referred to here is the Act of March 2, 1819.

The purpose of the undersigned is by no means to encourage emigration, but to assist those who have made up their minds to emigrate and to provide for them the best and at the same time the cheapest possible passage. This I am enabled to do since I am always sending suitable passenger ships to Baltimore, and also dispatch the regularly going packet ships to New York. I shall be glad to give further detailed information upon receipt of postage prepaid inquiries. Passengers are under no obligation to pay me any commission.

May 9, 1833.

J. D. Luedering, Ship's Agent,
Langenstrasse, No. 39, Bremen.

"If crosses and tombstones could be erected on the water . . . the whole route of the emigrant vessel from Europe to America would long since have assumed the appearance of crowded cemeteries"

Kapp, *Immigration,* pp. 19–25, 39–44.

Friedrich Kapp (1824–1884), journalist, historian, and New York state commissioner of emigration, 1867–1870, was born in Ham, Westphalia. Disappointed by the failure of the Revolution of 1848, he emigrated to New York in 1850. While practicing law in New York City, he wrote for newspapers and periodicals including the *Nation,* edited the New York *Abendzeitung,* and became an influential leader of the German community. After three years on the Board of Commissioners of Emigration he returned to Berlin in 1870, relinquished his American citizenship, and served as a member of the Reichstag from 1871 until 1884.

Thus the owner of the vessel had not the least concern or interest in the welfare or good treatment of the passengers; all he looked for was the payment of the stipulated price for that part of the ship which he had let. The steerage passengers were simply additional and unwelcome freight; they had to follow the directions of the owner, and were subordinate to what he considered his more important interests. They had to wait for their departure as long as it pleased him, and had no right than to occupy the ten or twelve square feet which were allotted to them. To the owner, they were less than a box of goods, and handled with less care, as they did not break, nor, if injured, require to be paid for. The agents, in order to make the business lucrative, sent on board as many passengers as they could get hold of, without the smallest reference to the conveniences of the steerage, the number of berths, the separation of sexes, or anything, except their own immediate profit. Besides assigning a space, however small, to the emigrants, they had no responsibility and ran no risk whatever. There was no check to the overloading of the vessel. Even if it had more than double the number of passengers that it could accommodate, there was no authority to which the emigrants could apply for protection. The agents did just as they pleased. A vessel which was not good and safe enough to be used as a transport for goods and merchandise was, nevertheless, employed for the conveyance of passengers. Thus, for instance, the destruction of life by shipwrecks has been most appalling among the emigrants who have been enticed on board the worn-out vessels engaged in the Canadian timber trade; seventeen being shipwrecked in a single season in the Gulf of St. Lawrence, and more than seven hundred lives lost.

.   .   .   .   .

To give an adequate idea of recent losses of human life on board of ill-provided, ill-ventilated vessels, it may be stated here that out of 98,105 poor Irish emigrants shipped to Canada by their landlords after the great famine of 1846, during the summer of 1847 there died 5,293 at sea, 8,072 at Gross Isle (Quarantine) and Quebec, and 7,000 in and above Montreal, making 20,365, besides those who afterwards perished whose number will never be ascertained. Thus the *Lark* reported at Quebec on August 12, 1847, from Sligo, sailed with 440 passengers, of whom 108 died on the passage and 150 were sick, almost all of whom died a short time after landing. The *Virginius* sailed with 496; 158 died on the passage, 186 were sick, and the remainder landed feeble and tottering; the captain, mates, and crew were all down. At that period, the ratio of the sick per one thousand was 30 on board British, $9\frac{2}{5}$ on American, and $8\frac{3}{5}$ on German vessels. Ship-fever and want of food were almost unheard of on board vessels from Northern Europe, and particularly those from Hamburg and Bremen.

.   .   .   .   .

The first law which prescribed the space to be allotted to each steerage passenger was that passed by Congress on March 2, 1819, according to which a ship was forbidden to carry more than two passengers for every five tons, Custom House measure. This law, however benevolent its purpose, proved insufficient; for it did not prohibit the orlop-deck, nor provide for proper ventilation or side-lights, nor deduct the freight-room and accommodations for the officers and first-class passengers from the computation of the total amount of tonnage. Thus a ship which measured 1,000 tons and had a steerage of only 500 tons, could nevertheless take steerage passengers for the whole tonnage, that is, 400 instead of 200. Nothing was said about the height of the steerage. It must always be borne in mind that the construction of ships for the express purpose of carrying passengers only began about the year 1830; that up to that time all space which could not be used for shipping merchandise was temporarily arranged for steerage passengers; that often at the last moment, a few days before going to sea, the superfluous room was sold to an agent, and that in those days a steerage five feet high was considered fully sufficient for making two tiers of beds along their sides. And

the hole beneath this hole was called orlop-deck, and likewise used for the transport of passengers.

.   .   .   .   .

Although the most lucrative article of import, emigrants were treated with the least possible care, with the utmost disregard of decency and humanity. With rare exceptions, they were robbed and plundered, from the day of their departure to the moment of their arrival in their new homes, by almost every one with whom they came in contact. They received less consideration on the voyage than even trees in course of transplantation. They were treated worse than beasts, and less cared for than slaves, who, whatever their condition may be in other respects, represent more or less capital, and as valuable chattels, are sure to receive protection and assistance in case of danger or sickness. There seemed to be a secret league, a tacit conspiracy, on the part of all concerned in dealing with emigrants, to fleece and pluck them without mercy, and pass them from hand to hand as long as anything could be made out of them. The poor foreigners were virtually helpless against any sort of imposition and fraud. The thousands who died, or were killed, on the voyage, were thrown into the ocean with as little ceremony as old sacks or broken tools. If crosses and tombstones could be erected on the water as on the Western deserts, where they indicate the resting-places of white men killed by savages or by the elements, the whole route of the emigrant vessel from Europe to America would long since have assumed the appearance of crowded cemeteries. And, what is still worse, the sufferings of the emigrants seem destined to last for ever. The experience of one does not help the other, for the emigrants, after their arrival in America, disperse into all parts of the great continent. They seldom bring charges or make complaints, being satisfied that they will not be heard, or being eager to reach their new homes. Only here and there some victims tell of their ill-treatment, and it is almost exclusively upon their recitals, and upon the meagre official data, that we have to rely for a history of later emigration.

Emigrant ships from Ireland declared worse than those in African slave trade

Extract from the *Montreal Advertiser,* in *Niles' Weekly Register,* Sept. 27, 1834, pp. 55–56.

We have frequently heard the character of emigrant ships from Ireland declared to be worse than that of those concerned in the slave trade of Africa; the account given by the passengers of the "Thomas Gelston," from Londonderry, substantiates the opinion.

The passengers by this vessel state the number, including children, to have been somewhere from 450 to 517. They were nine weeks on the passage, and suffered much from want of water and provisions. Besides two tiers of berths on the sides, the vessel was filled with a row of berths down the center, between which and the side berths there was only a passage of about three feet. The passengers were thus obliged to eat in their berths, each of which contained a great many persons, say five and upwards. In one were a man, his wife, his sister and five children; in another were six full-grown young women, while that above them contained five men, and the next one eight men.

.   .   .   .   .   .

Although these people landed safely at Grosse Isle, a great deal of sickness has broke out among them since. A part of them came up by the "Canadian Eagle" on Wednesday, from which about a dozen persons were taken to the cholera hospital soon after their arrival.

The death ship *Leibnitz,* 1868
Report of Commissioners Kapp and Bissinger

to the Board of Commissioners of Emigration of New York, Jan. 21, 1868, in Kapp, *Immigration,* pp. 189–195.

The case of the ship *Leibnitz* demonstrated the ineffectiveness of the United States Emigrant Passengers Act of 1855. In January 1868, the commissioners rushed to inspect the ship after 105 of its 544 passengers had died on the voyage. In concluding their report the commissioners recommended a petition to Congress for legislation requiring: 1. The appointment of a physician or surgeon on all emigrant vessels with more than fifty passengers; 2. The elimination of the orlop-deck; 3. A more stringent rule for enforcing payment of the penalty for dead passengers; 4. The power of obtaining redress to be lodged in the hands of the parties injured — the emigrants themselves; 5. Summary proceedings for the recovery of damages.

Last summer, she went to Quebec with about seven hundred passengers, of whom she lost only a few on her passage; this time she left Hamburg, Nov. 2, 1867, Capt. H. F. Bornhold, lay at Cuxhaven, on account of head-winds, until the 11th, whereupon she took the southern course to New York. She went by the way of Madeira, down to the Tropics, 20th degree, and arrived in the Lower Bay on Jan. 11, 1868, after a passage of 61 days, or rather 70 days — at least, as far as the passengers are concerned, who were confined to the densely crowded steerage for that length of time.

The heat, for the period that they were in the lower latitudes, very often reached . . . 94 degrees of Fahrenheit. Her passengers 544 in all — of whom 395 were adults, 103 children, and 46 infants — came principally from Mecklenburg, and proposed to settle as farmers and laborers in Illinois and Wisconsin; besides them, there were about 40 Prussians from Pomerania and Posen, and a few Saxons and Thuringians.

It is not proven by any fact, that the cholera

(as has been alleged) raged or had raged in or near their homes when or before they left them. This statement appears to have been made by or in behalf of those who have an interest in throwing the origin of the sickness on its poor victims. Of these 544 German passengers, 105 died on the voyage, and three in port, making in all 108 deaths — leaving 436 surviving.

The first death occurred on Nov. 25th . . . The sickness did not abate until toward the end of December, and no new cases happened when the ship had again reached the northern latitudes; five children were born; during the voyage some families had died out entirely; of others, the fathers or mothers are gone; here, a husband had left a poor widow, with small children; and there, a husband had lost his wife. We spoke to some little boys and girls, who, when asked where were their parents, pointed to the ocean with sobs and tears, and cried, *"Down there!"*

Prior to our arrival on board, the ship had been cleansed and fumigated several times, but not sufficiently so to remove the dirt, which, in some places, covered the walls. Mr. Frederick Kassner, our able and experienced Boarding Officer, reports that he found the ship and the passengers in a most filthy condition, and that when boarding the *Leibnitz* he hardly discovered a clean spot on the ladder, or on the ropes, where he could put his hands and feet. He does not remember to have seen anything like it within the last five years.

.   .   .   .   .

As to the interior of the vessel, the upper steerage is high and wide. All the spars, beams, and planks which were used for the construction of temporary berths had been removed. Except through two hatchways and two very small ventilators, it had no ventilation, and not a single window or bull's-eye was open during the voyage. In general, however, it was not worse than the average of the steerages of other emigrant ships; but the lower steerage, the so-called orlop-deck, is a perfect pest-hole, cal-

culated to kill the healthiest man. It had been made a temporary room for the voyage by laying a tier of planks over the lower beams of the vessel, and they were so little supported that they shook when walking on them. The little light this orlop-deck received came through one of the hatchways of the upper-deck. Although the latter was open when we were on board, and although the ship was lying in the open sea, free from all sides, it was impossible to see anything at a distance of two or three feet. On our enquiring how this hole had been lighted during the voyage, we were told that some lanterns had been up there, but that on account of the foulness of the air, they could scarcely burn. It had, of course, much less than the upper-deck draft or ventilation, and was immediately over the keel, where the bilge-water collects, and adjoining part of the cargo, which consisted of wool and hides. And in this place about 120 passengers were crowded for 70 days, and for a greater part of the voyage in a tropical heat, with scanty rations and a very inadequate supply of water, and worse than all, suffering from the miasma below, above, and beside them, which of itself must create fever and pestilence!

The captain himself stated to us that the passengers refused to carry the excrements on deck, and that "the urine and ordure of the upper-steerage flowed down to the lower." As the main-deck was very difficult of access from the orlop-deck, the inmates of the latter often failed to go on deck even to attend to the calls of nature. There were only six water-closets for the accommodation of all the passengers.

.   .   .   .   .

All the passengers concur in the complaint that their provisions were short, partly rotten, and that, especially, the supply of water was insufficient, until they were approaching port.

.   .   .   .   .

The treatment of the passengers was heartless in the extreme. The sick passengers received the same food with the healthy, and high prices were exacted for all extras and comforts. A regular traffic in wine and beer, and liquors was carried on between the passengers on the one side and the steward and crew on the other. A man by the name of Frederick Hildebrand, from Wirsitz, in Posen, who lost two children, paid 35 Prussian thalers extra for beer and wine to sustain himself and his sick wife. A bottle of rum cost him one dollar; a bottle of bad wine even more.

.   .   .   .   .

When the first deaths occurred, the corpses were often suffered to remain in the steerage for full twenty-four hours. In some cases the bodies were covered with vermin before they were removed.

There was no physician on board. Although we found a large medicine-chest, it was not large enough for the many cases of sickness, and was, in fact, emptied after the first two weeks of the voyage.

.   .   .   .   .

The physicians above mentioned, to whose report we refer for particulars, most positively declare that it was not the Asiatic cholera, but intestinal and stomach catarrh (*catarrh ventriculi et intestinorum*), more or less severe, and contagious typhus, which killed the passengers. From what we saw and learned from the passengers, we likewise arrive at the conclusion that the shocking mortality on board the *Leibnitz* arose from want of good ventilation, cleanliness, suitable medical care, sufficient water, and wholesome food.

The present case is another instance of the mortality on board the Hamburg sailing-vessels, and increases their bad reputation. Of 917 passengers on board of two ships of the Sloman line, not less than 183 died within one month! As often as complaint has been made here, it has not induced them to make any improvement. It appears that the Hamburg authorities either did not care to examine the merits of the charges brought against their ships or that they were imposed upon by their officials. On the other hand, local interests, friendly feelings, family connections, and other personal considerations, usually prevailing in small political communities, seem to stand in the way of energetic administration of the police of emigrant ships, and of the removal of the several grievances.

.   .   .   .   .

In our opinion, it is of great importance for the interest of humanity, in which both Europe and this country are concerned, and as a matter of political economy, that the transportation of emigrants across the Atlantic to this port should be confined to steam-vessels, as they not only convey the passengers more comfortably and land them in better health, but, in consequence of the regularity and rapidity of the passage, save an immense amount of labor for their own benefit and that of this country.

We are sorry to say that our laws afford very inadequate relief for the punishment of these crimes against humanity, and that, in the majority of cases, the institution of legal proceedings for redress, and the prosecution of the guilty parties, is almost an impossibility.

Much of the suffering, disease, and death on board of emigrant ships could have been prevented, and a recurrence of such abhorrent scenes hereafter be avoided, by proper enactments of Congress, enforced by suitable penalties.

Abuse of immigrants under the bonding system

1. "The emigrant was utterly without protection of the law"

Testimony of Alderman George H. Purser in New York Assembly, "Report of the Select Committee to examine into the condition, business accounts, and management of the trusts under the charge of the Commissioner of Emigration," *Assembly Doc. 34* (Albany, 1852), pp. 170–172.

The state of New York required masters of vessels to post a bond of $300 for each alien passenger who was a potential public charge. Shipmasters usually transferred the responsibility for indemnifying passengers to brokers, who abused the system. To avoid forfeiting bond money they placed sick or destitute immigrants in private hospitals and poorhouses maintained especially for this purpose.

. . . With the gradual but vast increase of emigration from 1843 to 1846, the competition in this [bond-brokerage] business increased, while it was conducted naturally with less humanity. In 1845, 78,788 emigrant passengers arrived at the port of New York, of which 71,068 were bonded, and in 1846 about 110,000 arrived, of which 100,000 were bonded, the aggregate bonds taken amounting to $56,636,400. In 1846, within seven months, one passenger agent gave bonds to the extent of $3,360,600, who afterwards failed and absconded, and was very recently a prisoner in England. The proprietors of these establishments were always interested in giving insufficient and indifferent food and accommodation. In all cases their profits were measured by this economy, and in some instances when they had made a bad speculation in relation to a ship's entire passengers, cruelty, evasion, and neglect were resorted to as the only means by which they could escape bankruptcy. Under this system, the emigrant was utterly without protection of the law, the hopeless victim of private rapacity.

If a woman and helpless children in a starving condition applied to the alms house, and they appeared to be bonded passengers, all aid was refused. If they turned their weary steps to the counting house of the merchant who had actually bonded them, they were unceremo-

niously referred to some passenger agent, or the office of the proprietor of some emigrant hospital or poor house, where they almost universally received abuse, and too frequently denial as well as insult.

. . . The provision made for the sick in these miscalled hospitals was wholly inadequate. The buildings employed were usually selected in the suburbs of the city, rather for economy than for adaptation, and almost necessarily deficient in ventilation. In a two-story dwelling house at Bloomingdale, 46 by 40 feet, the proprietors admitted that 120 patients had been crowded, though several of the rooms were exclusively occupied by the officers and servants. The food, clothing and attendance, insufficient; the sick and convalescent, the old and young huddled together, and police arrangements, so essential in such establishments to maintain health and morals, utterly disregarded . . .

One peculiar and deplorable result was the neglect of the children in these establishments; they were permitted to wander where they pleased; they were placed under no special government; never in any instance received the elements of education, but were exposed to influences and language calculated to corrupt and degrade them. Frequently so scantily provided with food that they were constrained to go out begging with their parents, and the neighbors informed me that they often furnished them with meals; on many occasions they were separated from their parents and handed over to employers from distant locations with the probability of never seeing their friends again.

Another evil was the want of reliability in the information given in relation to labor, the object was to get rid of them and they were often induced to accept cheap conveyances to distant States with the expectation of employment where none could be obtained. In one instance 500 Germans, chiefly aged paupers and young children, were shipped by subscription from their homes and arrived in a fearful condition of suffering and destitution; the passenger agents engaged lighters to take them to Albany, but being alderman of the ward in which the ship landed them, I interfered, and they were removed in wagons to the alms house where many died. The city eventually received 4 or 5 dollars per head from the shipping merchants as a commutation fee . . .

2. Abuse and death of children in the Topscott Poor-House and Hospital

New York City, Board of Assistant Aldermen, "Visit of the Committee of the Board of Assistant Aldermen to the Topscott Poor-House and Hospital, 1846," Doc. no. 20, *Proceedings and Documents 1845–1846,* XXVII.

The Topscott Poor-House and Hospital was established by the firm of W. & S. T. Topscott, passenger-brokers in New York. It was used as a dumping place for sick and indigent immigrants.

Margaret Bertram, an inmate for nearly twelve months in the institution, "recollects that two children died there. The mother of one died at sea; no particular nurse took charge of it; several of us had milk, perhaps four or five, and each took it by turns; it died of summer complaint. The other infant died five weeks since; it was brought here by a woman not its mother; it was a weakly child; we suckled it turn and turn about; no particular person attended to it; several now in the New York Almshouse nursed it."

Fannie Mitchell: "That the child referred to by Margaret Bertram was sent over from Topscott's office, and lived about a fortnight afterwards; that it came on Saturday, and Mr. Topscott called on the Sunday following, and, an objection being made to nurse the infant,

declared that any one who refused should be turned right out of doors. Under such circumstances the women consented, and took it turn and turn about."

Ann Doyle: "While I was there, some of the women induced a man who was cutting up some meat to give them a few slices, one of the women alleging that she wanted it for a sick child. They obtained about a pound, and Miller (the superintendent) discovered it in the evening, and went and informed Topscott, who came the next morning and turned the women out; one had the sick child before mentioned."

3. Exploitation of the immigrant

"Walks among the New-York poor: Emigrants and emigrants' children," *New-York Daily Times,* June 28, 1853.

If you would see, for a moment, one of the streams in the great current which is always pouring through New-York, go down a Summer afternoon to the North River wharves. A German emigrant ship has just made fast. The long wharf is crowded full of trucks and carts, and drays, waiting for the passengers. As you approach the end you come upon a noisy crowd of strange faces and stranger costumes. Moustached peasants in Tyrolese hats are arguing in unintelligible English with truck-drivers; runners from the German hotels are pulling the confused women hither and thither; peasant girls with bare heads, and the rich-flushed, nut brown faces you never see here, are carrying huge bundles to the heaps of baggage; children in doublets and hose, and queer little caps, are mounted on the trunks, or swung off amid the laughter of the crowd with ropes from the ship's sides. Some are just welcoming an old face, so dear in the strange land, some are letting down the huge trunks, some swearing in very genuine low Dutch, at the endless noise and distractions. They bear the plain marks of the Old World. Healthy, stout frames, and low, degraded faces with many stamps of inferiority; dependence, servitude on them; little graces of costume too — a colored headdress or a fringed coat — which never could have originated here; and now and then a sweet face, with the rich bloom and the dancing blue eye, that seem to reflect the very glow and beauty of the vine hills of the Rhine.

It is a new world to them — oppression, bitter poverty behind — here, hope, freedom, and a chance for work, and food to the laboring man. They may have the vaguest ideas of it all — still, to the dullest some thoughts come of the New Free World.

Every one in the great City, who can make a living from the freshly arrived immigrant, is here. Runners, sharpers, peddlers, agents of boarding-houses, of forwarding-offices, and worst of all, of the houses where many a simple emigrant girl, far from friends and home, comes to a sad end. Very many of these, who are now arriving, will start to-morrow at once for the far West. Some will hang about the German boarding-houses in Greenwich-street, each day losing their money, their children getting out of their control, until they at last seek a refuge in Ward's Island, or settle down in the Eleventh Ward, to add to the great mass of foreign poverty and misery there gathered. From there, you shall see their children sallying out these summer mornings, as soon as light, to do the *petty work* of the City, rag-picking, bone-gathering, selling chips, peddling, by the thousands, radishes, strawberries and fruit through every street.

Federal legislation for the protection of immigrants aboard ships, 1860

U.S. Congress, "An Act to Amend an Act entitled, 'An Act to regulate the Carriage of Passengers in Steamships and Other Vessels,' approved March third, eighteen hundred and fifty-five, for the better Protection of Female Passengers, and Other Purposes," U.S. *Statutes at Large,* VIII, 36th Cong., 1st Sess. (1860), 3–4.

Every master or other officer, seaman or other person employed on board of any ship or vessel of the United States, who shall, during the voyage of such ship or vessel, under promise of marriage, or by threats, or by the exercise of his authority, or by solicitation, or the making of gifts or presents, seduce and have illicit connexion with any female passenger, shall be guilty of a misdemeanor, and upon conviction, shall be punished by imprisonment for a term not exceeding twelve months, or by a fine not exceeding one thousand dollars: *Provided,* That the subsequent intermarriage of the parties seducing and seduced may be pleaded in bar of a conviction.

. . . Neither the officers, seamen, or other persons employed on board of any ship or vessel bringing emigrant passengers to the United States, or any of them, shall visit or frequent any part of such ship or vessel assigned to emigrant passengers, except by the direction or permission of the master or commander of such ship or vessel first made or given for such purpose; and every officer, seaman, or other person employed on board of such ship or vessel, who shall violate the provisions of this section shall be deemed guilty of a misdemeanor, and, on conviction thereof, shall forfeit to the said ship or vessel his wages for the voyage of the said ship or vessel during which the said offence has been committed. Any master or commander who shall direct or permit any officer or seaman or other employed on board of such ship or vessel, to visit or frequent any part of said ship or vessel assigned to emigrant passengers, except for the purpose of doing or performing some necessary act or duty as an officer, seaman, or person employed on board of said ship or vessel, shall be deemed guilty of a misdemeanor, and shall, on conviction thereof, be punished by a fine of fifty dollars for each occasion on which he shall so direct or permit the provisions of this section to be violated by any officer, seaman, or other person employed on board of such ship or vessel.

. . . It shall be the duty of the master or commander of every ship or vessel bringing emigrant passengers to the United States to post a written or printed notice in the English, French, and German languages containing the provisions of the second section of this act in a conspicuous place on the forecastle, and in the several parts of the said ship or vessel assigned to emigrant passengers, to do, he shall be deemed guilty of a misdemeanor, and, on conviction thereof, shall be punished by a fine not exceeding five hundred dollars.

. . . In case of the conviction of any person under the provisions of the first section of this act, and the imposition of a fine, the court sentencing the person so convicted may, in its discretion, by an order to be entered on its minutes, direct the amount of the fine when collected, to be paid for the use or benefit of the female seduced, or her child or children, if any.

. . . No conviction shall be had under the provisions of this act on the testimony of the female seduced uncorroborated by other evidences, nor unless the indictment shall be found within one year after the arrival of the ship or vessel at the port for which she was destined when the offence was committed.

APPROVED, March 24, 1860.

C. THE IMMIGRANT CHILD AS A SOCIAL PROBLEM

Failure in adjustment

1. "Why should I have children? . . . They say the childer here all is ruined"

"Walks among the New-York poor," *New-York Daily Times,* June 28, 1853.

This account is by a member of the New York Children's Aid Society who visited immigrant families in their tenements.

It is a fact worth noticing, that of all the many children who come under our operations, very seldom, indeed, is ever one an American or a Protestant. The Irish emigrants are generally more degraded, even, than the German. They rise more slowly, and are cursed with that scourge of their race — Intemperance.

I visited lately one of their lodging houses for the newly-arrived — a den such as I had no idea existed in New-York. It was in the neighborhood of Water-street — a high, respectable-looking brick house on the outside. A number of ragged children were playing at the door; within, the hall was dark and reeking with the worst filth. I climbed the dirty stairway, knocked at the door, and entered a little room where some women were cooking; in the room adjoining, a little closet of a place, half-a-dozen Irish girls were sitting, making coarse straw bags, "for a cent a-piece," as I was afterwards informed. I told my object to a sharp-looking man in charge. He said there were no children there, and directed me up stairs. The girls looked overdone, and were probably freshly arrived, and not in the best hands. I wanted to have a few words with them, but it seemed hardly advisable, and I went up stairs. A knock again, and this time, a little room, five feet by fifteen; two women sitting and another, younger, on a bed. "Have you any children here you would like to get work for in the country?" "No, Sir, we haven't — yes,

The Lowell Offering (December 1845), cover.

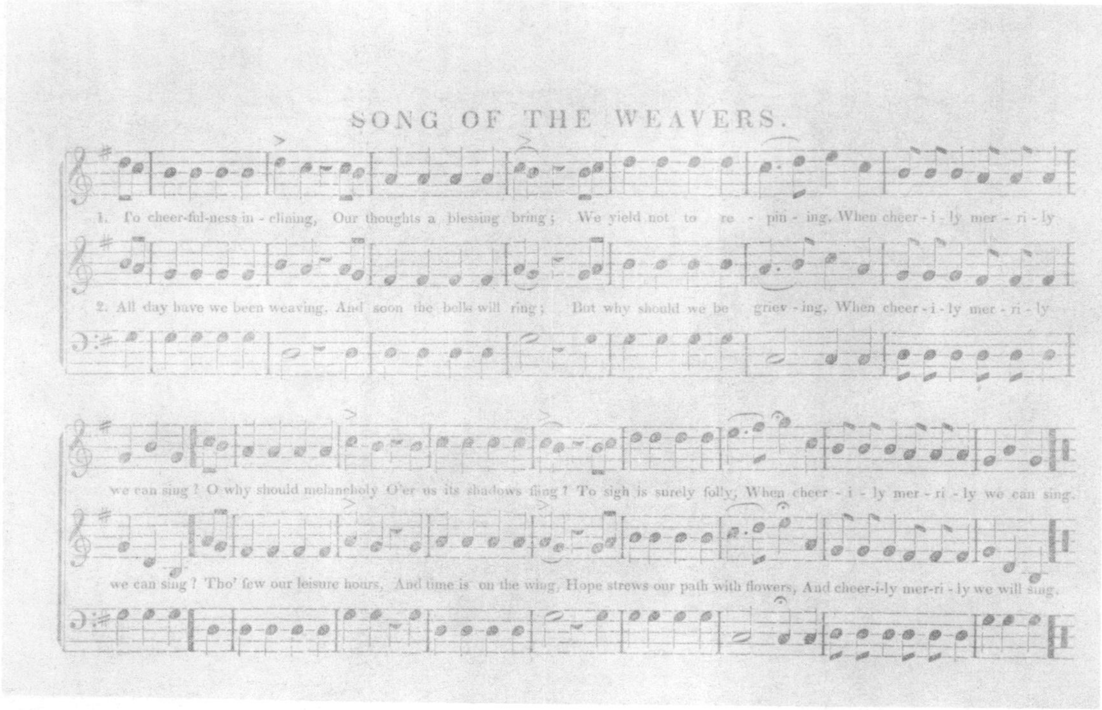

"Song of the Weavers." *The Lowell Offering* (December 1845).

Carryl children, ca. 1840.

Advertisement for The Children's Hospital, *Public Ledger* (Philadelphia), Nov. 22, 1855.

though — there's NELLY!" said one; "and what is the work, plase?" I told them, and said a little of the dangers for a poor man's children in a great city. They allowed it: "Oh, NELLY, Sir — she's not my child; but then I love her as mine; and, plase God, I never meant to lave her. But, then, you see, Sir, we can't take care of her. She's only fourteen, and she's away and in the streets so much, and I'd rather have her dead than in some places."

"It's ruin here! — I've lived it all! I know it," said the young woman on the bed. I turned, and saw for the first time, how care-worn and wretched her face was.

"But could you get a respectable situation, Sir, for NELLY?" I told her what we could do, and NELLY is to come up to the office.

The upper part of the house was filled with little narrow rooms, each one having five or six occupants; all very filthy. The people seemed very poor, honest Irish, not long here, and without work, usually. Women and men, evidently not of the same family, were herded in the same rooms, as one sees them in peasants' cabins in Ireland. They all looked depressed, worn, degraded. "Oh, yes, Sir," said an old woman, as I asked her, "I do want my boy out of the City. I can't do nothin' with him. He sleeps out nights, now, and he gets in with the bad boys. It's all thrue what ye say, Sir, and I fear ivry day to have had news of him amang the Police."

In an attic room, a young woman with a black eye and bloody face was making a fire of shavings, and a child was beside her. "Children!: she said, wildly, hardly looking at me — "No, thank God! I have none but her. Why should I have children? It was *he* bate me — he strikes me. They say the childer here all is ruined — I know it," and, turning abruptly to me, "Yes, Sir, there be paple down below that set their ain children to stale cotton. I've seen it — I know it, Sir. They *makes* 'em thieves. But what does *he* care, wid his liquor?" She spoke of her husband, who was lying on the floor in the corner — "It is he who is a murthering us!"

I was glad to leave as soon as possible. There were other rooms in the same way, filled with these poor, half-brutalized men and women. The girls and the boys left to themselves in the street — not a family sent children to school.

The whole was very depressing. It seemed like the worst part of old Europe transplanted. There was not even intelligence about their sensuality. You felt hopeless of ever reforming such natures — and, under all common probabilities, the children must be beggars, and prostitutes, and thieves.

You appreciated the dangers if many such colonies were scattered about in our cities.

. . . . .

Our work with this immense class of poor children is often very discouraging.

The suspicions and prejudices of their parents, brought with them from another society — the aspect it gives of the crushing temptations to evil over all the poor and friendless in our great cities — the difficulty of arousing even good men from their old accustomed ways, to help in new channels — and the sad contrast of the unresting activity of society, when those whom they once neglected are to be hunted and punished. Almost every week there is the gloomy knell of some new execution through the land — generally of young men, once the street boys, the poor or neglected children of our great cities.

The papers are full of the conviction of young offenders. One cannot but think how easy, a few years ago, a cure might have been. We could have made a useful man of the vagrant lad then — now, we can only hang him.

2. Illegitimate births among immigrant mothers

Massachusetts, House, "Report of the Commissioners of Alien Passengers and Foreign

Paupers, 1853," Doc. 18, *Documents, 1853* (Boston, 1853), pp. 14–19.

Whole number of children examined 2,896; number of children of American birth, but of foreign parentage, under 12 years, is 1,573.

```
Number from 1 day to 4 years old,   1,211
   "      "  4 years to 8  "    "      903
   "      "  8  "  " 12  "    "      782
                                  ——— 2,896
Of the foregoing number there are girls, 1,263
   "        "       "       "    " boys,  1,633
                                  ——— 2,896
```

Of those under one year of age, a very large number are illegitimate children, whose mothers have been assisted to this country by the fathers of such children, or have been seduced soon after landing here. By many women our almshouses are made lying-in hospitals; these women go there and remain until they recover after their delivery, while their husbands are able to maintain them at home. No less than 94 births of the above classes have taken place at the House of Industry, South Boston, during the last year, and 96 in the year 1851. Some of those, and many of a larger class, are now orphan children, and must be maintained at the expense of the State until they grow up or are qualified to provide for themselves. There is another class of paupers, who are more expensive to the community, and less likely to *ever* become good mothers, than those who are inmates of our public institutions.

---

3. Deportation of an Irish mother and her illegitimate child, 1855

Boston Daily Advertiser, May 16, 1855.

Yesterday morning there sailed from this port a splendid packet-ship bearing the noble name of "Daniel Webster," which fitly belongs to so fine a vessel. Yet so many fine ships sail out of our harbor that the reader may inquire why we make this departure the occasion for such conspicuous notice.

Among the crowd of human beings on board that proud vessel was one poor woman, with an infant daughter. Her passage and that of her child were paid by the rich and powerful commonwealth of Massachusetts. She left our free and happy shores unwilling and reluctant. She went away against her own free will, constrained by force of the civil authorities of the State. Her cries as she begged not to be thus so cruelly banished, were, we are told, most piteous, and such as to cause the accidental witness of the scene to burn with indignation.

The offence of this poor woman, for which she was thus violently and ignominiously expelled from Massachusetts, was the fact that she was born in Ireland and is called a pauper. Her infant daughter, who unconsciously shares her mother's sad fate, is a native of the commonwealth of Massachusetts; but she too partakes of that hard lot of poverty which it has been reserved for Massachusetts to make a crime, and a crime which Massachusetts punishes as no other crime is punished in America, by banishment — banishment from one's native land.

The name of this victim to Know-Nothing intolerance was Mary Williams; and her infant, Bridget, is but a few weeks old. About thirty-five paupers, perhaps more, were sent away at the same time, in the same vessel, at the expense of the State. These facts we learn from eye-witnesses of the scene, and from other certain and authentic sources of information.

Our readers are aware that there exists upon our statute book a law which authorizes any Justice of the Peace upon complaint, by a warrant directed to and to be executed by any constable, or any other person there designed, to cause any pauper to be removed out of the State, to any place beyond the sea where he belongs, if the Justice thinks proper, and he may be conveniently removed, and also that, independently of this provision of law, a practice has arisen by which the Commissioner of Alien Passengers undertakes, even without the warrant of a Justice of the Peace, to send back paupers in cases in which he sees fit, and pays the expenses from money in his hands belonging to the State Treasury.

On account of the temporary absence of the Commissioner of Alien Passengers, and none of the gentlemen in his office being possessed of the facts, we are unable to state which of these two methods was employed as the pretext of authority for effecting the rendition of the unfortunate creatures who sailed yesterday in the "Daniel Webster"; nor can we state by what Justice of the Peace, if any, the warrant was issued. But the facts that they were sent away and that the State paid their passage, and that the piteous cries of this poor woman with her child were such as to attract the attention of the bystanders as she was led on board the vessel — these facts we have certainly ascertained.

The Citizen (New York), May 26, 1855.

Subsequent investigation also has put the case of Mary Williams in a worse form than it was at first represented. The Boston *Atlas* has sifted the matter to the bottom, and declares:

She was not a pauper abroad, and she never had been a pauper . . . She came here with an aunt who is now living in the State, and is not a pauper. This girl — for she is quite young — had been deceived abroad, and she came here to conceal her shame. When near the time of her confinement, she was sent to the alms-house; and when next we hear of her, she is torn from the only being who loves her, and is sent over the sea. Before she could make her wants known, before she could appeal to benevolent men or women for aid, before she could effect any arrangement for supporting herself by her own labor, she is driven by force out of this hospitable Commonwealth — to want, to loneliness, to irreclaimable infamy. And all of this cost the State of Massachusetts just $12 passage money! . . .

4. Female street beggars and pilferers in Boston

Massachusetts, House, "Report of the Commissioners of Alien Passengers and Foreign Paupers, 1853," pp. 15–19.

The Commissioners refer to young female street beggars, and pilferers, who are to be found in all the cities, and many of the large towns in this Commonwealth. These cases are so numerous that it appears to the Commissioners highly necessary to give them some consideration; they have had many interviews with various officers of different humane societies, and gentlemen having charge of the municipal affairs in some of our cities, and all admit that something should be done to check the crime, and prevent the miseries of the many young girls, who are continually growing up in idleness, or what is worse, are hangers on or errand girls for the vilest haunts of iniquity that our cities are infested with.

It is a subject in which the Commissioners themselves feel a deep interest, claiming as they do some little knowledge of the misfortunes of young females in the city of Boston, and the causes, which finally end in degradation misery and ruin; and although they feel their inability to point out all the particulars necessary for a thorough reform of this class of persons, yet they are fully convinced that an effort should be made towards such a reform. They therefore ask leave to introduce a few statistics, and suggest a plan, which if carried out, will do much towards accomplishing a very desirable end, and will greatly improve the condition of many young females. One week's report by the police of Boston, in January, 1851, says:

25 girls, between the ages of 7 and 15 years have been seen picking up chips in various parts of the city, ... 25

7 have been seen with baskets apparently going begging, ... 7

37 have been seen peddling apples, ... 37
 2 stealing cotton, ...   2
10 picking over ashes for coal, ... 10
 2 picking up junk, ...   2
37 begging in the street, ... 37
 4 idle and strolling about streets, ...   4
                                              124

. . . 1,263 girls under 12 years of age, were inmates of the various almshouses during the past year; many of them are orphans, and will be compelled to remain inmates a long time, unless some other mode be adopted for their support. True, many of our cities and large towns have connected with their pauper institutions, schools, that are well conducted; but it is very certain that children of any number cannot receive the instruction both mental and physical, that is necessary for their future welfare, in institutions where the halt, the lame and the imbecile of all kinds, assemble together, and where much improper language is spoken, and many influences of an unfavorable character operate on these young females, and their continuance so precarious, as they would in an institution peculiarly adapted to their wants; one that would possess all the elements necessary to train the young mind for all the virtuous walks of life.

---

5. Facing the danger of immigrant paupers

New York Children's Aid Society, *First Annual Report* (New York, 1854), pp. 3–6.

The Children's Aid Society, founded in 1853, addressed itself specifically to problems of neglected and delinquent youth.[1]

This Association — the Children's Aid Society — has sprung from the increasing sense among our citizens of the evils of the city.

1. See below, Chap. VI, sec. C, The Children's Aid Society, New York, 1853–1860.

Thirty years ago, the proposal of an important organization, which should devote itself entirely to the class of vagrant, homeless and criminal children in New York, would have seemed absurd. There were vile streets, and destitute and abandoned people; but the city was young and thriving . . .

In these considerations, one element was forgotten. During the last twenty years, a tide of population has been setting towards these shores, to which there is no movement parallel in history. During the year 1852 alone, 300,992 alien passengers have landed in New York, or nearly at the rate of *one thousand* a day, for every week day. Of these 118,131 were from Ireland, and 118,611 were from Germany. A portion of this immigration has been good — sober, hard-working people, who have spread over the country and become mingled with our population. Another part has been bad, almost the worst — the off-scouring of the poorest districts and the most degraded cities of the Old World. The pauperism and poverty of England and Ireland has been drained into New York. If this could have spread over our land, to be influenced by the new circumstances, the effect would not have been so bad. But in the main, it has settled and stagnated in the city. The poor immigrants could not afford to go to the West, or with the natural caution of ignorance, they dreaded to go. Our poorest streets began to be filled up with a thriftless, beggared, dissolute population. As is always the case in such circumstances, vice and laziness stimulated each other. The poor and idle of a street grew worse for having poor and idle neighbors. The respectable and industrious moved out of certain quarters; and such places as the Five Points began to be known. Streets once inhabited by the best of people, as Lower Pearl, and Cherry, and Dover streets, were abandoned, and have since been held mostly by lodging-houses of the poorest immigrants.

   .   .   .   .   .

Crime among boys and girls has become organized, as it never was, previously. The Police state that picking pockets is now a profession among a certain class of boys. They have their haunts, their "flash" language, their "decoys," and "coverers," as they are called, or persons who will entice others where they can be plundered, and protect the thieves if they are caught.

There is a class of young lads now in the city, known as "feelers," who are employed by older rogues, to ascertain where their depredations can be most easily committed.

Cotton-picking on the wharves, iron stealing in the drydocks, "smashing" of baggage, in other words, pilfering under pretence of carrying it, and "book-bluffing," which is a species of mock book-selling, are all means of livelihood for the dishonest poor boys of New York.

Of the young girls in the city, driven to dishonest means of living, it is most sad to speak. Privation, crime, and old debasement in the pure an sunny years of childhood.

It must not be thought that all our street children are engaged in dishonest business. In the district east of the Bowery, near the foot of Houston and Rivington streets, will be found thousands of children, whose sole occupation is picking rags and bones in the street to sell. They are Germans, and mostly Bavarians. The work is filthy, laborious, and dangerous to the morals, but it is honest. The little street-sweepers come often from the same class. There are besides match selling and candy selling — in themselves honest trades; hundreds and thousands of children make their living from them. Among the little traders of the city rank the news boys, the shrewdest and sharpest of them all — a class numbering several hundreds, living solely on their own earnings, and the mass of them sleeping in boxes or printing-house alleys, constantly exposed to the worst influences.

All these little trades are honest, and are infinitely better than begging; but the danger is that the roving, vagabond life will lead to the worst habits. The children are liable to the most bitter want, and are exposed to every temptation. They are growing up to be citizens, or women, under the vilest influences.

---

6. What is done for the poor female servants

Five Points Monthly Record (New York, 1854), pp. 113–116.

Our Female Domestic Servants form a class whose moral wants exact, from our sympathies and self-interest alike, a peculiar regard. No class of persons exists in this country, to whom the name of stranger, with all its painfullest associations, so truly belongs. Aliens to our race, our soil, our institutions, and our faith, they are also thrown into a position of antagonism in interest and feeling, which every year that passes over them, embitters more and more. They enter into no truly humane and social relation with our families, of which they are never members, but only uncomfortable appendages, tolerated because we cannot do without them. There are no ties of long attachment between us and them, connecting each to each from generation to generation, by the endearing links of infancy and old age, of birth and death; the utmost average duration of this heartless and mercenary connection, being probably not longer than six months. Among us but not of us, serving us but not loving us or loved by us, they are in a most pitiable sense outcasts; and if the element of contempt be essential to that condition, they suffer it in fuller measure than any other lawful and recognized class in society. No American girl is so poor or degraded as not to think herself superior to the condition or the person of a domestic servant. A consequence of this contempt, indeed, is to produce such a scarcity of domestics, as gives the class a fictitious importance and an unnatural advantage over their employers; aggravating the evils inseparable from the existence of an unwilling servitude, by the addition of presumption, jealousy and contention.

The consequence of all this is plainly to be seen, and exactly what might be expected. We have the worst servants in the world; the most dishonest, unserviceable, unruly and changeable, and as a class they are daily growing worse. Our dependence on Roman Catholic immigration for domestics, is commonly considered the main cause of this great evil; but the cause of this dependence, and the barrier to any natural corrective of its inconveniences, are the same, and will be found in the perverted relation of employer as it exists among us. A vulgar purse-pride, and a mercenary habit of mind, have thrust apart the poor servant from the circle of our domestic sympathies and consideration, denying her a home among us, thus driving the native laboring class to other and more endurable situations, and degrading and alienating those whose necessities compel them to take service in our houses. If servants were as plenty as blackberries, their miserable character and entire recklessness of our interests, could never be remedied, while the relation of employer continued to be filled in such a spirit as at present.

The vagrant character of our female domestics, produces employment in the city of New York for some twenty-six intelligence offices, which are supported in nearly equal proportions by the employers and employed. The most of these are mere mercenary establishments, and it is difficult to decide whether the servant or the employer is on the whole the worse abused by their intervention. They serve to lighten the inconvenience of changing servants frequently, and as plainly aggravate the same evil a hundred-fold, besides training the girls to proficiency in the worst faults of their class.

A Christian Home for Female Servants, is a noble enterprise, at once expedient and philanthropic, in a high degree. New and better ideas of the qualifications of a domestic servant, must be communicated to that friendless class of beings, by the interposition of Christian kindness and instruction with respect to their temporal and spiritual interests. The Christian philanthropist who makes himself their friend and patron, receiving no fee from their hard earnings, will shortly gain an influence over them which may compete even with that of the priesthood. On the other hand, employers will

be insensibly conducted by the mediation of Christian love into a new relation and sense of responsibility to those who live in their households as servants, and who ought to be members with them of that holy and divine institution, the family. Finally, as a convenience to those who desire good servants, there can be no other sort of intelligence office comparable to this: insomuch that it cannot be doubtful that such an institution, well conducted, would be liberally supported by the fees which employers will gladly pay, with a considerable margin for charitable and religious purposes relating to the class to which it is devoted.

An institution of this nature was opened on the 29th of May last, at No. 614 Sixth Avenue, corner of Thirty-Sixth-street, under the direction of a voluntary committee of most respectable ladies. The energy and enthusiasm of its projector and superintendent, Mrs. JOSEPH L. LINFORD, who has devoted herself personally to the management, have already realized the most encouraging results. We are informed that not less than a thousand females have already received from this institution good situations, with affectionate, maternal advice, and religious instruction, appropriate to their circumstances. Of these, perhaps a third have applied in circumstances of destitution and distress, and many a heart-rending and well authenticated tale of wrong, neglect and suffering, has been brought to light and to a happy conclusion, by means of this yet infant enterprise.

No fee is received from the applicant registered at this institution for a situation. On the contrary, if destitute of a place or home, and of money, she is gratuitously provided with board, lodging, opportunities for washing, and all the advantages of the establishment. About one-third, as was just observed, of the applicants have been in these distressed circumstances, and have been thus gratuitously relieved until good situations could be found for them. In a word, this establishment is intended to be, according to its title, a Christian Home for the Female Servant, where not only situations may be obtained, but where every blessing of a Christian family which can be imparted, is freely offered to all females in want of friends or employment, without money and without price; those able to pay, and those only, being charged with the actual expenses of their board while they remain inmates of the house; while those who simply register name and address for situations, are subjected to no expense whatever. One exception only is made to this extended offer, and that only until a suitable separate building can be appropriated to the class excluded; until then, none can be admitted as inmates or registered for situations, unless provided with satisfactory testimonials of good character. It is obviously improper and unjust, both to the girl of good character and to the employer, that the virtuous and the vicious should be mingled in the same establishment, or brought into familiar contact with each other.

Among the special advantages of the Home, may be instanced, first, family devotion, morning and evening, at which (as it should be in every Christian family, whatever the Roman priesthood may say) each inmate is expected to be present, whatever her religious persuasion; but at which only the pure and universal principles of Christianity and morals, are recognized or adverted to, and no real offence or violence is done to the feelings of any devout member of any sect.

Next, a daily evening school is open to all who choose to enter, in which useful branches of education are pursued. The neat and convenient sitting room is also furnished with desks, miscellaneous books and bibles, and is always accessible.

On Sunday evenings a religious service is held with females exclusively, of the class for whom the institution is designed, and also ladies who are heads of families and desire to witness the instructions and exhortations afforded to the inmates.

A small store is kept on the ground floor, for the sale of articles made by those out of employment, who are furnished with plain sewing for their support while unemployed, and for the purpose of supplying them with such articles as they need, at the lowest prices, without danger of imposition.

Employers are received, and their particular wishes noted, with their address, in a distinct part of the establishment. If a girl supposed to be suitable is at hand, she is sent for and introduced to the employer. If not, the superintendent undertakes, if possible, the task of finding a person suitable to the wishes of the applicant, who is promptly sent to her address. Employers pay according to a certain schedule of prices; or, frequently make liberal contributions to the benevolent purposes of the Home, without regard to the prescribed amount.

Such are some of the features of the institution in its present infant condition. We understand its ultimate plan to be more extensive and reformatory. At present its moral efforts are, from circumstances, confined to the improvement of those who already bear a good outward character. A large building or suite of buildings is projected, and partly arranged for, in which different departments and classes may be instituted with reference to character and wants. These schemes we will not now anticipate. As it stands, the establishment is eminently worthy of encouragement and sympathy, and affords, without doubt, the best office for obtaining domestic servants in the city or elsewhere. Its liberality towards the poor servant necessarily attracts a very large number of candidates for the employer's choice; its parental interest in her character, history, and spiritual wants, tends to sift out the hardened and depraved, by mutual repulsion, and to attract the well-disposed and manageable; its influence will naturally be strong, and the dread of incurring the disapprobation of the Superintendent, influential over the servant to a degree quite unknown with respect to the mercenary intelligence offices of the day; and the confidence reasonably to be indulged in the judgment and disposition of the Superintendent, by the Christian lady who is anxious for servants whom she can trust, and to whom she can hope to do good, is a privilege not elsewhere accessible. It is impossible to set bounds to the influence of such an institution, well carried forward in the pure spirit of Christianity, upon the minds and characters of the class to which it is devoted, upon the interest which the community has in blending the foreign immigration harmoniously and freely in living social relations with ourselves, and upon the welfare and comfort of our families, to which that immigration is now an incalculable detriment.

---

7. The ruin of female honor

Thurlow Weed, in John F. Maguire, *The Irish in America* (London, 1868), p. 340.

Thurlow Weed, member of the New York Commissioners of Emigration, addressed himself to the plight of immigrant girls in his speech at the laying of the foundation stone of the Emigrant Hospital on Ward's Island, 1864.

Referring to the helpless condition of the emigrant before the present admirable system was organised in New York, he says: "Families were frequently plundered of all the money they possessed, and left to the charity of the city. Young and friendless females coming from abroad, to find their friends, or seeking employment, *were not unfrequently outraged . . . Innocent and unprotected girls came consigned to houses of prostitution.*" Mr. Weed was referring to what frequently occurred some years before; but it is notorious that similar evils have existed at a later period, and are not yet effectually suppressed. The panderers to the lust of great cities are constantly on the watch to drag into their dens of infamy the young,

the innocent, and the unsuspecting. There is scarcely a House of Protection under the care of a Religious Order in America, which cannot record cases of young girls snatched from the jaws of danger. Many, it is true, are saved; but what can the helpless do against the snares and traps and frauds of those who live by the vilest crime? The contest is unequal: the lamb is helpless in the talons of the vulture, or the fangs of the wolf. As a single instance of the peril awaiting the unsuspecting, may be mentioned that of a young and handsome Irish girl who was lately trapped into hiring, in a Western city, with a person of infamous character. She was fortunately observed by a poor old Irish woman, who, knowing the peril in which the young creature stood, boldly rushed to her rescue, and, at personal risk to herself, literally tore the prey from the grasp of the enemy. The rescued girl was taken to the Refuge in the Convent of Mercy, where she was at once in safety; and though she lost all her clothes, save those in which she then stood, she congratulated herself that she had never crossed the threshold of a house of ill-fame.

Perils by sea, and perils by land, is it wonderful that fraud and violence so often triumph over innocence and helplessness? — that human wrecks occasionally strew the highways of the centres of wealth, of luxury, and of vice?

I have in another place referred to the evils of overcrowding, in lowering the tone of the community, and exposing the humbler classes to dangers of various kinds, moral as well as sanitary. Besides the temptations of poverty and passion, of youth and thoughtlessness, there is the terrible mischief of daily and hourly association in the densely-populated lodging-house, in which it too often happens that, even with the best intentions, the most ordinary decency cannot be maintained. There is not a physician or a clergyman in New York who will not say that this system is fraught with danger to the health of soul and body. It is in the last degree unfavourable to the development of virtue . . . .

8. San Francisco, the ideal home for the Irish girl

Maguire, *The Irish in America,* pp. 276–277.

Of the Irish girls in America I have spoken elsewhere; but any notice of the race in San Francisco, in which special mention of the Irish girls of that city was not made, would be most incomplete. They form a considerable and valuable portion of its population, and are deservedly esteemed by all classes of its citizens. They are industrious, intelligent, faithful, generous, high-spirited, and intensely devoted to their religion, of which they are the proudest ornaments and best examples. So justly esteemed are these Irish girls for purity and honour, that some 2,000 of them have been well married — fully half of that number to men of substance and good position. It may be remarked that a considerable number of them had been tenderly reared at home, where they received a fair education; but, driven by circumstances to emigrate, they were of necessity obliged to accept even the humblest situations in a foreign land. They soon, however, rose above the lowly condition which they dignified by their intelligence and worth, and found in an honourable marriage ample compensation for all their former trials. It is estimated that seventy-five per cent. of the Irish girls in domestic employment in San Francisco can read fairly, while more than fifty per cent. can both write and read well. The rate of wages for domestic employment ranges from 20 to 40 dollars a month. The average would come to 60*l.* a year. Out of this income they save a certain portion, indulge their Celtic love of finery, gratify their charitable and religious instincts by generous contributions to church, to convent, to orphanage, and to asylum; and the balance is devoted to the twofold purpose, with them almost equally sacred — to assist their parents or aged relatives in the old country, or bring out a brother or a sister to their adopted home. It

is calculated by those who have every means of ascertaining the fact, that the Irish girls employed in San Francisco annually remit to Ireland, for the purposes stated, the sum of 270,000 dollars! What eulogium can equal the mere mention of this fact?

Uplifting and Americanizing the immigrant child

1. The poor Germans insist upon using their children to earn money

New York Children's Aid Society, *Third Annual Report* (New York, 1856), pp. 14–15.

To meet the needs of immigrant children, the Society established a series of industrial schools for respective foreign groups. Among these were the German School at 14 Avenue C, the German Industrial School of Calvary Church, composed of sixty German Protestant children, and an Italian school at the Five Points House of Industry.

THE GERMAN SCHOOL — AT NO. 14 AVENUE C.

There has been a difficulty in regard to the School for the German children, which has not been felt to such a degree in any other school. The poor Germans insist upon using their children to earn money, whether they have had any education or not. They prefer the present shillings to any future spiritual or moral benefit for the child, which may be offered. For this reason, the older scholars have been constantly withdrawn from the School, sometimes merely for street trades; and much of the hard labor for them, has *seemed* to have been wasted. And yet, in the assault of temptations from every side, which must meet the poor foreign girl in New York, who can say what the refined example and the Christian instructions of such schools may not effect! . . . About forty volunteer teachers have come to the School every week through this most inclement winter — some a distance of two miles. If the plan, now under consideration, of forming a work-room where a regular trade can be taught, shall be successfully carried out, there can be no doubt of the School regaining its influence over the older girls, who have temporarily left it.

Whole number in attendance through the year, 235; average daily attendance, 97; number sent to public schools, 50; number sent to the country and into families, 42. Cost of provisions for one year, $250; number of dinners given, 10,352; number of garments and shoes distributed, 227. Salaried teachers and matron, 3. Expenses, $1,687.47.

2. "Not one family in a hundred ever send their children to school"

"Walks among the New-York poor,"
New-York Daily Times, June 28, 1853.

We have now a German gentleman, the Rev. Mr. BOGEN, employed in visiting in that quarter, and he reports that not one family in a hundred ever send their children to school.[1] They were forced to school them in Germany; here they want the pleasure of having their own way. The boys, some of them, do well — though very many fall in with the multitude of young thieves and vagrants of that Ward. The girls, in the great proportion of cases, as soon as they ma-

1. Reverend Bogen was a visitor for the Children's Aid Society. He collected children from the streets and took them to the industrial school at the Calvary Church in New York City. The school, affiliated with the Children's Aid Society, had an average of fifty pupils, all German.

ture, are more or less dissolute in morals. The filthy habits of their parents, and the open street-life which they must pursue, seem of necessity to degrade their morals.

Yet, the children themselves long to do better. In visiting for the Girls Industrial School, in Avenue D., the difficulty to all has always been with the parents, not the girls. They jump at the chance of learning something beyond what their parents have known; and, as that school shows, only want the opportunity to make great progress . . .

3. Making the Italians understand that they are not like brutes

Rev. J. B. Torricelli, *27th Annual Report of the Executive Committee of the Benevolent Fraternity of Churches* (Boston, 1861), pp. 27–29.

The Benevolent Fraternity of Churches, a missionary Protestant society, was founded in Boston ca. 1835. Among its members were Unitarian and Congregational churches and other private religious and voluntary associations. It was dedicated to educational work in the poverty districts of Boston. Although originally interested in the native poor, the association adjusted grudgingly to meet the needs of poor immigrants as the "swarms of [Irish] immigrants descended upon" the quays of Boston. By 1860 the Association had German and Italian agents for those respective groups.

It is now a little over ten months since I began my mission among the Italians of this city and vicinity . . .

The obstacles I have met on my way have been many, and not easily removed; especially the utter indifference, the deadly apathy, with which every thing spiritual is regarded by the class of people committed to my care. The slanders and intrigues of the malevolent, the prejudices and superstitions of the ignorant, the corruption and degradation of a large majority, — all these things together are not so difficult to be conquered as that only one. Even when aroused by the apprehension of their own danger, they fall back into their lethargy, as soon as the voice that shook them is silent.

.   .   .   .   .

As the result of the influence acquired over many of them, I will mention a few facts. Several parents, who were strongly prejudiced against our common and evening schools, were prevailed upon to send their children; and thus from thirty to forty boys and girls were taken from the streets, and are now under a better influence. In some instances, I took them to school myself, and helped their friends to clothe them, or make up for the little they used to bring home by peddling and begging . . .

A few copies of the Scriptures were given to such as desired them, and several volumes on different matters are circulated among those who know how to read; but, owing to the fact that very few can read our language well enough to enjoy and profit by English reading, this means of instruction cannot be extended, and rendered more useful. Italian works which they would read with advantage are not many at my disposal. The few I own are accessible to any one that can use them: when my means will permit, their number will be increased.

. . . several families received substantial aid that enabled them to go back to their country, after it had been found the only possible way of benefiting them. Twenty-seven individuals — men, women, and children — left for Italy during last summer and fall.

On the whole, the good done to the Italians through this mission has been more material and temporal than moral and spiritual; not because the moral and spiritual is not wanted and possible, but because they are not prepared. With most of them, the work must begin by making them understand that they are not like brutes. Once awakened to a sense of their dignity as human beings, I have no doubt that our efforts to make them better and happier would prove successful.

---

4. Drawing German children into the sabbath school

A. Ubelacker, *26th Annual Report of the Executive Committee of the Benevolent Fraternity of Churches* (Boston, 1860), pp. 22–23.

A portion of the Germans have a strong prejudice toward both church and minister, arising from the deplorable union of Church and State in Germany; in consequence of which, the Church is an institution of the State, and the minister, in some degree, a civil officer.

.   .   .   .   .

. . . I have endeavored to draw the children of German parentage into the sabbath school, and have found but little difficulty in persuading them to attend; and generally the parents are also willing. Such expressions as, "If we do not attend services ourselves, we will not deprive our children of gospel privileges," &c., are of common occurrence . . .

.   .   .   .   .

The Young Men's Association, which I organized some time ago, has done much good in keeping young men from bad company, and leading them to devote their leisure hours to profitable instruction.

I have visited two hundred and sixty families, and made over three hundred calls.

---

5. American Germans neglect the education of their children

Francis Lieber, ed., *Letters to a Gentleman in Germany* (Philadelphia, 1834), pp. 213, 216–217.

Lieber (1800–1872), German-born educator and political scientist, was himself the writer of the letters. The work was later issued under the title *The Stranger in America*.

I believe I have descanted already, in a former letter, on the great advantage which accrues to all parties, if the Germans, who come to this country, assimilate with the predominating race. I repeat it — they are a valuable addition to our population, if they mix. But let truth prevail every where: twisting of facts, and stating or being silent according to convenience, is an unmanly thing — unworthy of a lover of his species, and a man who thinks he has expanded his views by travelling into other countries, and by studying history back into other ages. It is painful, indeed, for a German, that the descendants of his nation in this country, where they live closely together, have not only done less for the common education of their offspring, than their neighbors, but have actually often frustrated the endeavors of government to establish a system of general education.[1] How a scion of a people, who have done more for education than any other on earth, comes thus to neglect one of the most sacred duties, would be inexplicable, were it not for the fact, on which I think I have touched on a former occasion, that it is difficult for a community, severed from the mother country, and separated from a surrounding population by the barrier of a different language, to prevent mental stagnation . . .

1. We say with the author, let truth prevail; thus only can evils be corrected. It has been stated, that the act lately passed by the legislature of Pennsylvania, providing for the education of the poor and of the children of people not favorably circumstanced, is far from meeting with ready and cheerful support from the German population of that state. Even obstacles are thrown in the way of this salutary law. [Lieber's note.]

The care of immigrant children under the New York State Board of Commissioners of Emigration

1. Care of pregnant women and newborn babies

Commissioners of Emigration of the State of New York, "Fifth Annual Report for the Year 1851," *Annual Reports of the Commissioners of Emigration of the State of New York, 1847–60* (New York, 1861), pp. 98–99.

Women, during all periods of gestation, are received at the Emigrants' Refuge, in large and well ventilated wards, and enjoy those indulgences and privileges to which their parturient state entitles them. Here they remain until the premonitory symptoms of labor appear, when they are transferred to the Lying-in ward, and receive immediate attendance of one of the resident physicians of this department; upon one of whom it is obligatory to attend in all such cases, or in event of any serious difficulty occurring, to request the aid of Dr. Williams.

After delivery, the patient remains in the hospital until convalescence is completely established, when, their infants having been vaccinated, they are transferred to other wards appropriated to infants of this tender age, where they still continue to be under the control of the physicians of the mid-wifery department.

The diet of lying-in women, during the first week after delivery, consists of farina, milk, weak tea, broths, and other light articles of this nature, unless circumstances call for a more stimulating course. During the second week more substantial food is allowed, as beef, or chicken tea, bread, tea or coffee, and small quantities of solid animal food. Thus they are permitted gradually to return to their regular mode of living.

Women who have been but lately delivered, either privately or otherwise, and who have not recovered from its debilitating effects, or such as are suffering from puerperal or other diseases peculiar to the female, are, on application, received into this division of the hospital.

Connected with the Lying-in department, and under the same medical control, are the Nursery and Infants' wards, both of which receive daily attendance from the visiting and resident physicians. The latter consists of two large well-ventilated wards, each capable of accommodating sixty mothers with infants. In the former are the Orphans' ward, and one appropriated to the reception of all diseases of the scalp and skin occurring in children.

2. Sickness, deaths, and births among passengers (see table below)

Commissioners of Emigration, "Table A: Statement of Vessels with Emigrants that have arrived at the Port of New York, in the year 1849," *Annual Reports, 1847–60,* p. 289.

3. The mortality rates are high

Commissioners of Emigration, "Medical and Surgical Report of the State Immigrant Hospitals (Jan. 7, 1854)," *Annual Reports, 1847–60,* p. 324.

Pregnant women are also confined on shipboard, and come to us immediately after having landed; some directly after confinement in the city are received, both mother and child often in a desperate condition; others, but a few days in the country, reach the hospital, and are prematurely delivered of feeble infants, many of which merely breathe and then cease to exist; others linger a few hours or days at most; and in this way they swell our bills of mortality, without being in any way amenable to the physician's skill, or the surgeon's art; they end their sufferings almost as soon as begun, but they are as prominent in the necrology of the hospital as if they had reached adult life.

4. Admissions and dispositions of emigrants (see table on next page)

Commissioners of Emigration, *Annual Reports, 1847–60,* p. 302.

Nation of vessel	Number of vessels	Passengers	Sick	Deaths	Births	Ratio of sick	Ratio of deaths	Ratio of births
American	594	134,657	921	1,556	113	.61·100	1.16·100	0.9·100
British	371	62,463	475	658	76	.76·100	1.5·100	.12·100
German	85	10,966	66	87	11	.60·100	.79·100	.10·100
French	12	1,779	1	1	1	.60·100	.60·100	.60·100
Belgian	8	810	—	4	—	—	.49·100	—
Swedish, Norwegian, &c.	581	13,718	18	41	10	—	—	—
Total	1,651	224,393	1,481	2,357	211			

| | NUMBER ADMITTED AND CLASSIFIED | | | | | | | Total number of admissions and births, showing the whole number of persons cared for and treated | NUMBER OF DEATHS CLASSIFIED | | | | |
| | | | | DISTRIBUTION | | | | | IN HOSPITALS | | | | |
Year	Adults	Children 1–12 years	Infants under 1 year	To hospital	To refuge	Total admissions	Number of births		Adults	Children 1–12 years	Infants under 1 year	In refuge	Total deaths
1847	—	—	—	—	—	1,629	29	1,658	164	10	40	—	214
1848	—	—	—	—	—	3,491	177	3,668	194	44	67	—	305
1849	—	—	—	—	—	6,827	346	7,173	740	100	390	—	1,230
1850	—	—	—	7,084	1,014	8,098	384	8,482	429	129	204	132	894
1851	—	—	—	10,928	1,586	12,514	493	13,007	877	197	250	330	1,654
1852	—	—	—	9,336	3,217	12,553	523	13,076	831	220	150	342	1,543
1853	—	—	—	10,794	723	11,517	644	12,161	504	167	151	286	1,108
1854	—	—	—	9,803	2,684	12,487	701	13,188	729	322	387	269	1,707
1855	7,801	949	342	6,349	2,743	9,092	641	9,733	543	202	298	235	1,278
1856	4,402	643	294	3,625	1,714	5,339	406	5,745	229	65	94	138	526
1857	5,499	911	291	4,405	2,296	6,701	468	7,169	224	59	111	125	519
1858	3,967	415	243	3,282	1,343	4,625	366	4,991	205	44	123	115	487
1859	2,660	226	162	2,319	729	3,048	261	3,309	113	18	47	84	262
1860	3,144	382	175	2,662	1,039	3,701	264	3,965	128	19	43	36	226
Total	—	—	—	—	—	101,622	5,703	107,325	5,910	1,596	2,355	2,092	11,953

Note: The records do not show the ages of the persons admitted previous to 1855, nor the distribution of those admitted during the years 1847, 1848, and 1849.

The table above shows the number of admissions to, and births and deaths in the State Emigrant Refuge and Hospitals, Ward's Island, under the charge of the Commissioners of Emigration, from the organization of the Commission, May 5, 1847, to Dec. 31, 1860.

5. Authority of the New York State commissioners of emigration over poor, orphan, and illegitimate immigrant children

"An act to amend an act entitled 'An act concerning passengers in vessels coming to the city of New-York,' passed May 5, 1847," 1847 — ch. 483, *New York Laws of 1847* (Albany, 1847), II, 716–717.

The commissioners of emigration, or any one or more of them, shall have and exercise the same powers and authority, in relation to poor children actually chargeable upon, or receiving support from said commissioners, as are now conferred by law upon the "commissioner of the alms house department," of the city of New-York, respecting the "act concerning apprentices and servants."

.   .   .   .   .

In all cases in which the minor children of alien passengers shall become orphans, by their parents or last surviving parent, dying on the passage to the port of New-York, or in the marine hospital on Staten Island, the personal property which said parents or parent may have had with them, shall be taken in charge by the commissioners of emigration to be by them appropriated for the sole benefit of said orphan children; and said commissioners shall give in their annual report to the legislature, a minute statement of all cases in which property shall come into their possession by virtue of this section, and the disposition made of the same. And the commissioners of emigration are hereby authorized to prescribe rules requiring the health officer to make such reports to them respecting the persons and property at said hospital as they may consider necessary.[1]

1. This act was amended in 1849 to cover "any other establishment under the charge of the commissioners" in addition to the Marine Hospital.

Parent	Vessel	Where from	Date of death of parents	Children	Age	Amount	Disposition of property
John Hall	India	Liverpool	19 Feb. 1848	Sarah	17	$190.00	$95.00 paid for clothing and
				Elizabeth	13	and a watch.	nursing infant. Balance on
				Jane	11	—	deposit in savings bank.
				Mary	—	—	
				Hannah	3½	—	
Catharine Moore	Digby	Liverpool	23 Mar. 1848	Matthew	15	140.07	In savings bank.
Andrew Hannon	Virginia	"	1 May, 1848	Anderoga	8	1.25	" "
				Michael	7	—	
				Edward	4	—	
John Perry	Wm. Carson	Dublin	16 Aug. 1848	Peter	12	4.83	" "
				Mary	11	—	
Elizabeth Whaley	Memnon	Liverpool	9 Oct. 1848	Lavinia	12	14.76	" "
				James	10	—	
Robert O'Reilly	New World	"	3 Mar. 1849	William	14	5.00	$2.50 paid to William; balance
				Eliza	—	—	in savings bank.
Jacob Burkle	—	—	7 June, 1849	Anton	8	316.17	
				Adam	10	—	$117.87 paid for clothing, board,
				Mary	5	—	&c. Balance in savings bank.
				Henry	2	—	
Auguste Pfau	E. Harbeck	Bremen	1 Aug. 1849	Carl	19	502.70	$66.05 paid for clothing. Balance
				Edward	9	—	in bank.
				Robert	8 mos.	—	
Matilda Pohlig	Belvidere	Antwerp	Oct. 1849	Albert	—	1,176.00	$10.75 paid for clothing, &c.
				Matilda	—	—	Balance in bank.
Ferdinand Seidler	Avalanche	Bremen	—	Ferdinand	9	120.90	$24.70 paid for clothing.
H. Jan Oonk	E. Denison	do.	—	—	—	25.25	$1.00 " cartage.

6. Administration of property belonging to orphan children (see table above)

"Table No. V: Statement of Moneys received by the Commissioners of Emigration on account of Minor Children becoming orphans; made in accordance with Section 10, Act of April 11, 1849," in Commissioners of Emigration, *Annual Reports, 1847–60,* p. 362.

7. Status of American-born children of immigrant parents while under the authority of the commissioners of emigration, 1854

Commissioners of Emigration, "Report of the subjects in dispute between the Commissioners of Emigration and the Alms-house Department of the City of New York," *Annual Reports, 1847–60,* pp. 399–404.

The Commissioners are authorized to take care of emigrants alone. During the seven years of their existence, many emigrant females have been delivered of children in the hospitals of the Commissioners. These children are not emigrants, but native-born, and their care and maintenance belong to the Governors of the Alms-house; and the expense of taking care of them, your Committee is advised, is an equitable set-off, to some extent at least, to the claims of the Governors for lunatics and small-pox patients. This is denied by the latter, and the Commissioners are told to send such children to the alms-house. They are willing, and have offered, to do so provided the Governors will also take charge of the mothers, for whose expenses they will be indemnified. This is refused, on the ground that the mothers, being emigrants, are properly inmates of the Institutions on Ward's Island, and will not be received into the poor-house. And thus the Commissioners are obliged to be either guilty of the inhumanity of separating tender babes from their mothers, or must bear the expenses of thousands of infants chargeable of right to another fund and another body. The Commissioners have adopted the latter alternative, and will, for humanity's sake, continue so to do . . .

.   .   .   .   .   .

The above has been the case for over eight years, and the amount expended for such children is computed to exceed $50,000. The Governors, however, refuse to allow it; and it is therefore to be the subject of arbitration or litigation. It is well worth while, however, to observe in the above statement, the ground upon which its disallowance is placed by the honorable the Governors, and to consider whether it may not be that the "quibble" — the mote in the eye of the Commission — is not seen by the Governors from behind a beam in their own optics.

Even, however, allowing that the Commissioners are in error in claiming an equitable allowance on this account, equal at least to the balance claimed by the Governors, still assuredly, when it is considered that this unadjusted balance of $20,700 is on a long account, upon which payments of seven times that amount have been actually made, and that over a hundred times that amount have been expended for the use of the city by this Commission, a little delay in settlement can hardly justify the broad charges of the Governors, and still less can it afford any ground for the assertion, that it will "compel this department to call for a sum of not less than $100,000 for the special purpose of providing for the impositions of the Commissioners of Emigration not otherwise provided for."

If a deficiency in the large grants to the Governors has occurred, requiring such an additional call from the department, it must arise from "impositions" from some other quarter than the Commissioners of Emigration.

———————————————

8. Post-mortems performed on immigrant children without consent of parents, 1850

Commissioners of Emigration, "Report of the Committee to inquire and report in relation to certain abuses, alleged to have taken place . . . in the Hospitals and Refuge at Ward's Island, November 27, 1850," *Annual Reports, 1847–60,* pp. 386–394.

In November 1850, the New York City papers accused the hospital on Ward's Island of the illegal dissection of two deceased children. The committee appointed by the commissioners of emigration to investigate the scandal was divided in its conclusions. Gulian C. Verplank, president of the commission, and Adolf Rodewald, president of the German Society, argued that the proceedings had been legal, since the doctors performed a post-mortem, rather than dissection. They censured, however, the conduct of one of the younger doctors, who had stolen the body of one of the two children from Potter's Field, after interment. On the other hand, Gregory Dillon, president of the Irish Society, saw this case as a violation of the rights of the poor.

———————————————

In the two cases of children which had been stated in certain city papers to have been dissected, were both of them cases of . . . post-mortem examinations. One of them died of a disease of the throat . . . The parts affected were opened, and the examinations made by Dr. Cox, and afterwards sewed up, the whole being done, as the committee was assured, precisely as it would have been done in the chambers of the wealthy in private practice, and without defacing the body. It was stated by Dr. Carnochan, that this post-mortem inspection was not only valuable as to general medical skill, but had resulted in immediate advantages in the treatment of similar cases in the practice of the hospital.

The other . . . body was also opened by direction of Dr. Macneven, who had attended the case, and the examination made in the manner usual in private practice.

.   .   .   .   .

If the dissections had been confined to those patients who were here without friends or relatives, it would have involved simply a violation of the rights of the dead; but two cases were proved to us, in which children were dissected without permission of their parents, and in wanton violation of their rights and feelings, although the parents had been to the island to make preparations for the decent burial of their offspring. In one of these cases, even after the child had been buried, one of the young physicians so far forgot the rights of the father and his own duty, that in the dead of night he, in company with two other house physicians, went to the grave-yard at Potter's Field, and with his own hands dug up the remains of the child and carried them to the dead-house for dissection, thus superadding to the other enormities of this transaction a violation of a law of the State. It also appeared before the committee, that in some cases, after dissection, the bodies were not buried entire, but parts were taken away by the physicians as it pleased them; and that portions of different bodies were thrown into the same coffin and buried together.

.   .   .   .   .

The late scandalous proceedings at Ward's Island may be traced to another cause, which penetrates through all our establishments, and works quietly but with the most baleful effect. I refer to the opinion entertained by many that the emigrants are paupers, and are, therefore, entitled only to pauper consideration. This is a radical error . . . They are not paupers in any just sense of the term; they were called paupers when they were a charge upon the city, and before this commission was established; but the returns show that they never have been paupers, and are not paupers now. Every emigrant that comes to our shores pays a dollar and fifty cents to this Commission. Those who have health spread over the country, to increase our wealth and prosperity; those who are sick are relieved by the fund to which all, both well and sick, have contributed,

and the fund is sufficient, and in my opinion more than sufficient under proper management. The whole class, therefore, are, as it were, underwriters for each of their members, and by their own aggregate contributions alone relieve the misfortunes of one another.

---

9. Wanted — immigrant children

New York Daily Tribune, Sept. 26, 1850, p. 5.

Wanted — Situations for a number of excellent girls and children, recently arrived, free from city habits and associations, and willing to work for moderate wages. Application to be made at the office of Commissioners of Emigration, in the Park. No charges.

---

10. Request for state support of the school sponsored by the New York commissioners of emigration on Ward's Island

Commissioners of Emigration, "Fifth Annual Report for the Year 1851," pp. 91–93.

[The school] consists of boys and girls of suitable age, who are in care of a male and female teacher, of excellent qualifications and experience, aided by competent assistants. The average attendance in the former part of the year, was *one hundred and forty-three;* but during the last six months, the number had increased to *two hundred and four.* The same course of instruction is pursued as in the City Public Schools; and the discipline and order maintained, as also the improvement of the pupils in their respective studies, it is believed, will favorably compare with any of them. The Board, regarding the young, impressible children as a peculiarly interesting and hopeful portion of their charge, have spared no exertions to render these means of instruction as beneficial as the circumstances admit.

They would observe, moreover, in this connection, that a primary class has also been formed, and is in charge of a carefully selected instructress, for the benefit of young children, five years of age, and under. Being without maternal care, their tender age required such a guardianship as this provision is designed to supply. Having an apartment to themselves, nothing needful to their comfort is withheld; while by appropriate exercises of body and mind, the health and vigor of both are promoted. Recitations, interspersed with singing, marching, and other agreeable recreations suited to their years, will doubtless, in their case, as experience has shown in others, tend to their present enjoyment and lasting advantage.

From the rapid succession of children in these schools, and the comparatively short period they remain there, the system of instruction cannot be carried so far, ordinarily, as in the larger Public Schools of the State. But for the same reason, this instruction, so far as it goes, reaches a greater number in proportion to the number there at any one time, and is found of much value in habituating children to order and attention, and preparing them to derive immediate benefit from other schools, whenever they leave the island.

The cost of maintaining these schools has been hitherto defrayed from the income of the Emigration Fund.

As all these children are part of the population of the State, and destined to become its citizens, there seems no reason why they should not partake of the general benefits of the liberal provision made by the State for public education. On the contrary, it seems right that the Emigration Fund, limited in amount in comparison with the large demands upon it, should be relieved from every charge which does not of necessity fall within its objects. The Commissioners have had it under consideration to have their schools, on Ward's Island, organized under the authority of the Board of Education, on the footing of a ward school. But on further consideration and consultation with the officers of the Board of Education, various difficulties presented themselves as to such an organization, the requirements of the law transferring the property and control of such schools to other hands, whilst the efficiency and good order of the establishment required that the teachers resident and employed in the Emigrant Refuge, should be subject to the appointment and authority of the Commissioners, and their officers.

The Commissioners, therefore, respectfully submit to the Legislature the propriety and justice of placing the schools in the Emigrant Refuge, on the same footing with those of the New York Public School Society, the Orphan Asylum, and the Half Orphan Asylum, the Institution for the Blind, and the School of the Mechanics' Society, all of which, with some others, are, by law, authorized to receive a proportional share of the school moneys, on compliance with the general system of instruction, and being subject to the visitation and inspection of the Board of Education. The immediate control and government would then remain with the Commissioners, as they do with the Trustees of the several above-named institutions in relation to their own schools.

III Education

The story of education between 1820 and 1865 is dominated by the common school movement. No age in the history of American schools matches it in the list of impressive laws placed upon the statute books or in the quality of argument that this movement inspired. A long roster of names evokes the caliber of its leadership: Horace Mann preeminently, striving ever, as he once movingly advised the young, to win at least one battle for humanity. Henry Barnard, James Carter, Calvin Wiley, Samuel Lewis, and many others scattered throughout the Union publicized, lobbied for, and administered the new and improved school systems. Imaginative and dedicated as these men were, the American common school did not spring fully fashioned from their minds. Popular schools had been ably advocated before. Thomas Jefferson among other thinkers of the first years of independence, grasping the connection between popular education and popular government, had supported education for all. Their recommendations, unhappily, had resulted in few new schools. With the exception of the New England states, free instruction was still confined to those pauper children whose parents were willing to testify to their inability to provide schooling for them.

New social and economic conditions prompted a re-examination of public and private institutions and processes in the middle of the nineteenth century and brought a new urgency to the cause of public education. Generally speaking, the public school movement was an attempt to secure a common core of belief and loyalty in order to maintain a balance between social stability and liberty. Challenges to the uniformity of American character appeared on every side. Immigrants came from abroad in unprecedented numbers. Old communities were uprooted and destroyed as new lands in the West drew off the farmers and youth of established agricultural areas which could not compete with the fertile expanse of the Mississippi valley, while the growing factory towns and cities of the eastern states similarly drained upland farms and villages of their youth and talent. Manchester, Lowell, Buffalo, and, by the 1850's, Chicago, were the emblems of an industrial-urban way of life that was fast encroaching upon the simple agrarian and commercial society of earlier decades. A new America emerged of factories as well as fields, of Irishmen as well as Yankees, Catholics as well as Protestants.

Probably there was more sustained analysis and speculation about the character of institutions in the four decades before the Civil War than in any other comparable period of American history. The social role of the schools was at the center of this reconsideration. On the one hand, schools were expected to mold the young into loyal and useful American citizens, an uncertain procedure at best but clearly one of greater difficulty as the population became more varied. On the other hand, they were supposed to assist the young in developing and fulfilling their capabilities, helping them to unlock the potentials of mind and character that would free them from error and narrowness. The two aims were theoretically brought together in the process of social mobility: by developing his mind and skill each individual would find the place he merited in the social order. If mobility worked efficiently, all would be both happy and useful. Unfortunately, it did not always work that way. The demanding task of the common school reformer was to find and sustain a balance between serving order by shaping young Americans and serving young Americans by helping them find themselves.

It was no accident that the common school movement took hold in precisely those areas where the pluralistic character of society was most evident. Although the New England states and those of the middle-Atlantic area had progressed farther than any others in building schools, they were also the states where the new society and economy made the deepest and most rapid inroads. The population of Massachusetts increased from 523,287 in 1820 to 1,231,066 forty years later. Inevitably this threw a burden upon the schools. They had to accommodate the new immigrants and the shifting school population that resulted from internal population movements. In addition, faith in the very idea of public schools had to be revived. Under the Massachusetts law of 1789 authorizing the "district school," financial support had fallen off, buildings were in disrepair, teachers' salaries had dwindled, and the school year had been shortened. The reputation of free schools declined, while private schools attended by the children of the wealthy flourished and spread. Horace Mann's task, following his appointment as secretary of the Massachusetts Board of Education in 1837, was no less than to restore the support of the public for free schools, which he did with astounding energy and ingenuity.

Even where it took hold, the common school movement fell short of its aims. It was difficult to strike an entirely satisfactory balance between the school as a means of inculcating the value of social stability and the school as a means of personal growth and liberation. Ironically the mobile character of the American population accentuated the need for uniformity of instruction. The separation of students into grades, the standardization of textbooks, and uniform training for teachers were in part attempts to accommodate learning to the desire of so many Americans to be on the move from an old place to a new where they hoped better

fortune awaited them. If instruction could be classified, children could move freely with their parents from place to place taking up schoolwork where it had been dropped at their old place of residence.[1] But such classification inevitably meant that different pupils (and teachers) were steered into niches fashioned for them by someone else.

In other parts of the nation the educational problems of industrial and urban growth were not so acute. Where frontier conditions lingered, sparseness of settlement and a moving rural population worked against effective schools. A legal framework for uniform public education was created in the Midwest, closely following the models of the New England and middle-Atlantic states. Building schools and hiring good teachers, however, lagged behind. As states like Ohio and Michigan attained a settled population accompanied by some industrial growth toward the middle of the century, their school systems became indistinguishable from those in the older states in the East.

In southern states the difficulties in founding free schools were of a different character. A people predominantly rural, living in isolation from each other, and lacking liquid wealth, had to overcome both aristocratic educational and social traditions and the blighting effects of slavery. Despite the obstacles public education had its champions, particularly Calvin Wiley who laid the foundations for a state school system in North Carolina during the decade preceding the Civil War. Actual free schooling in the South, however, remained confined to pauper education at public expense, some city school systems that provided education for all, and a very few districts that chose to avail themselves of the permissive school legislation passed by southern legislatures.

Higher education, although further removed than the common schools from the immediate

1. For the evils of a failure to standardize instruction see William Burton, *The District School as It Was* (New York, 1938), pp. 35–40; graded schools are advocated in George B. Emerson, "Address on Education," *Common School Journal*, X (1848), 321–326.

stress and strain of demographic, social, and economic changes, felt the pressure of similar forces. The colleges, among the most aristocratic institutions of the country, had to face charges that their course of study was irrelevant and their methods of governing the lives of undergraduates undemocratic. Student restlessness and criticism were commonplace in the early part of the nineteenth century, stemming from dissatisfaction with the course of study and the student's unhappiness with the restraints the faculty imposed upon their lives. Although denominational interests and competition continued to be crucial in the founding of private colleges, the harmful effects of sectarian rivalry were frequently recognized and deplored. State universities suffered from the indifference of a public that was preoccupied with numerous denominational colleges. Consequently, with exceptions like the Universities of Virginia and Michigan, they remained subordinate to private colleges. Some experiments were undertaken with the college curriculum, although most institutions preferred to stand by the prescribed classical studies. At Harvard a limited trial of elective study began through the prompting of George Ticknor, a young professor who had studied at a German university and had there glimpsed what a university might be. Ticknor became so discouraged over the lack of faculty interest in expanding the curriculum and giving students a choice of subjects that he resigned. Yale, with its hearty commitment to prescription, the ancient languages, and the theory of mental discipline, pointed to a familiar and appealing way. Only toward the middle of the century when college enrollments began to decline and the volume of criticism increased did serious discussion of sweeping changes in studies and the formation of true universities as centers of research and scholarship as well as of teaching begin to take place. In many ways the most important outcome of this desire for new institutions was the passage of the Morrill Act in 1862 which launched the land-grant colleges. Initiating a democratization of higher education by supply-ing training in more practical subjects at less cost than the traditional college, the land-grant colleges anticipated an enlargement of the college-attending group and a commitment of federal government support for learning.

The education of blacks came under closer restriction after the Nat Turner revolt of 1831. One southern legislature after another, fearing assemblies of slaves and their communication with each other and with free Negroes, outlawed elementary instruction. Most of these laws remained in force until the Civil War, although some of the harshness was removed from them by allowing instruction for free Negroes when carried out under the auspices of trusted whites acceptable to the legislature or local authorities. Because of the weak administration and enforcement of law, occasional slaveowners acquiesced in the instruction of their slaves and even participated in it themselves. The literate slave was not, then, unknown in the old South, but he was a rarity. Eighty per cent of nonwhites in 1870 were illiterate according to the federal census of that year, the first to attempt such estimates. Two considerations should be remembered in interpreting this figure. First, the 20 per cent who were literate by the census definition were mainly the free blacks of the ante-bellum era and their descendants. Second, by 1870 there had been five years of freedom in which private and public agencies had made an impressive attempt to supply ex-slaves with an education sufficient to assure literacy.

The situation of free Negro children was substantially the same in North and South. In neither section was there equality before the law. Discriminatory legislation in civil rights, access to courts, occupations, property, and schools could be found in every southern state and in nearly all those of the North. Segregated schools were the rule. Only in remote areas and small towns with few Negro inhabitants was it common for black and white children to attend school together. In some towns and states separate schools for Negro children were maintained by law. Financing of schools was often carried out in a discriminatory fashion. Negro property owners were liable for the payment of local taxes for the support of schools which their children could not attend. In some states legislation provided for the division of local school funds in accordance with the payment of taxes by blacks and whites. In no instance were funds divided according to the number of black and white children attending school, nor were other efforts made to assure that the separate schools children went to should be equal in length of the school term, pay of teachers, or expenditures on equipment. Black children in separate public schools in the North almost uniformly received less attention and care than their white counterparts.

Only in Massachusetts was legal action successful in changing this situation. In Boston segregated primary schools for blacks were maintained by the School Committee. A Negro father sued in behalf of his daughter for admittance into a nearby all-white school. Although the state Supreme Court upheld the School Committee's racial discrimination among pupils, the legislature, responsive to opinion outside Boston in the rural and small town portions of the state, reversed the court's decision in 1855. This was the only legislative victory that black parents and children in the North could claim before the war in their struggle for equal rights.

The federal government first assisted in the education of Indian children after the War of 1812. The Treaty of Ghent ended the series of conflicts stretching back to the late seventeenth century in which Indian tribes, in alliance with foreign powers, tried to stem the advance of white Americans. Warfare did not, of course, cease in 1815, but the subjugation of the Indians was a foregone conclusion once the possibility of outside assistance had been eliminated. The American government, therefore, reached a turning point in its relations with the tribes. With less need for a military approach, the government turned to what it called a civilization policy. Having been brought under control, the Indians would now be trans-formed into white Americans, or at least made into a manageable and partial facsimile.

The task of civilizing the Indian did not lie with government alone. Cooperation with private agencies was an accepted means of carrying on a multitude of tasks of a public character. So it is not surprising that the government should have adopted subsidization of private, missionary religious agencies as the primary means of educating the Indian child. Many religious groups were eager to take the field. They had a long history, without great success, of seeking contact with Indians and trying to bring Indian youth into schools and convert them to Christianity. In 1819 the federal government committed a small portion of its resources through the establishment of an Indian "civilization fund," at first only ten thousand dollars each year, to pay the expenses of missionaries and teachers chosen by denominational associations or ecumenical bodies in schools scattered among the Indian tribes.

The kind of schooling and community that would be effective for Indian children was difficult to determine. Most of the teachers tried to impart the ordinary kinds of elementary instruction combined with lessons in piety. This seldom produced more than a veneer of education which was stripped away as soon as the Indian child returned to the tribe. An exception existed among the Cherokees of the Southeast who established villages, cleared fields, raised domestic animals, learned trades, and went to school and church in large numbers until during Jackson's administration they were forced to surrender their lands and move westward. Thus the only really successful experiment in acculturation before the Civil War failed because of the desire of white men for the lands the Indians occupied.

Once the failure of conventional education was recognized, those concerned began to cast about for alternatives. They hit upon combining a measure of conventional education with instruction in manual trades. Mastery of a trade, it was hoped, would supply the Indian child with a way of making a living while contributing to the progress of all and the assimilation of his fellow Indians. Another possibility was the boarding school in which children were removed from the influence of parents and tribal ways in the hope that they would adopt the outlook of whites. This movement, in its infancy before the Civil War, was to be implemented in the late nineteenth century.

How successful was education for minority children? In general, government only indirectly affected most aspects of their lives. They were mainly influenced by unofficial, less formal institutions of society. In education, government largely maintained legal and social-cultural distinctions between the treatment of the children of these minority groups and the children of the white middle class. Where it was possible for Negro children to go to school at all, laws were passed to keep them in segregated schools. Very few Indian children were given any kind of instruction. The broad impact of institutions under government control or influence on children of minority groups was to enforce an alien way of life and a degrading conception of themselves incompatible with growth and fulfillment.

A. THE COMMON SCHOOL MOVEMENT

Common school education before the reform movement

1. Tocqueville's observations on the character and efficiency of instruction in the United States

Tocqueville, *Democracy in America,* I (1945), 315–318.

The observer who is desirous of forming an opinion on the state of instruction among the Anglo-Americans must consider the same object from two different points of view. If he singles out only the learned, he will be astonished to find how few they are; but if he counts the ignorant, the American people will appear to be the most enlightened in the world. The whole population, as I observed in another place, is situated between these two extremes.

In New England every citizen receives the elementary notions of human knowledge; he is taught, moreover, the doctrines and the evidences of his religion, the history of his country, and the leading features of its Constitution. In the states of Connecticut and Massachusetts, it is extremely rare to find a man imperfectly acquainted with all these things, and a person wholly ignorant of them is a sort of phenomenon.

When I compare the Greek and Roman republics with these American states; the manuscript libraries of the former, and their rude population, with the innumerable journals and the enlightened people of the latter; when I remember all the attempts that are made to judge the modern republics by the aid of those of antiquity, and to infer what will happen in our time from what took place two thousand years ago, I am tempted to burn my books in order to apply none but novel ideas to so novel a condition of society.

What I have said of New England must not, however, be applied to the whole Union without distinction; as we advance towards the West or the South, the instruction of the people diminishes. In the states that border on the Gulf of Mexico a certain number of individuals may be found, as in France, who are devoid even of the rudiments of instruction. But there is not a single district in the United States sunk in complete ignorance, and for a very simple reason. The nations of Europe started from the darkness of a barbarous condition, to advance towards the light of civilization; their progress has been unequal; some of them have improved rapidly, while others have loitered in their course, and some have stopped and are still sleeping upon the way.

Such has not been the case in the United States. The Anglo-Americans, already civilized, settled upon that territory which their descendants occupy; they did not have to begin to learn, and it was sufficient for them not to forget. Now the children of these same Americans are the persons who, year by year, transport their dwellings into the wilds, and, with their dwellings, their acquired information and their esteem for knowledge. Education has taught them the utility of instruction and has enabled them to transmit that instruction to their posterity. In the United States society has no infancy, but it is born in man's estate.

The Americans never use the word *peasant,* because they have no idea of the class which that term denotes; the ignorance of more remote ages, the simplicity of rural life, and the rusticity of the villager have not been preserved among them; and they are alike unacquainted with the virtues, the vices, the coarse habits, and the simple graces of an early stage of civilization. At the extreme borders of the confederated states, upon the confines of society and the wilderness, a population of bold adventurers have taken up their abode, who pierce the solitudes of the American woods and seek a country there in order to escape the poverty that awaited them in their native home. As soon as the pioneer reaches the place which is to serve him for a retreat, he fells a few trees and builds a log house. Nothing can offer a more miserable aspect than these isolated dwellings. The traveler who approaches one of them towards nightfall sees the flicker of the hearth flame through the chinks in the walls; and at night, if the wind rises, he hears the roof of boughs shake to and fro in the midst of the great forest trees. Who would not suppose that this poor hut is the asylum of rudeness and ignorance? Yet no sort of comparison can be drawn between the pioneer and the dwelling that shelters him. Everything about him is primitive and wild, but he is himself the result of the labor and experience of eighteen centuries. He wears the dress and speaks the language of cities; he is acquainted with the past, curious about the future, and ready for argument about the present; he is, in short, a highly civilized being, who consents for a time to inhabit the backwoods, and who penetrates into the wilds of the New World with the Bible, an axe, and some newspapers. It is difficult to imagine the incredible rapidity with which thought circulates in the midst of these deserts. I do not think that so much intellectual activity exists in the most enlightened and populous districts of France.

It cannot be doubted that in the United States the instruction of the people powerfully contributes to the support of the democratic republic; and such must always be the case, I believe, where the instruction which enlightens the understanding is not separated from the moral education which amends the heart. But I would not exaggerate this advantage, and I am still further from thinking, as so many people do think in Europe, that men can be instantaneously made citizens by teaching them to read and write. True information is mainly derived from experience; and if the Americans had not been gradually accustomed to govern themselves, their book-learning would not help them much at the present day.

I have lived much with the people in the United States, and I cannot express how much I admire their experience and their good sense. An American should never be led to speak of Europe, for he will then probably display much presumption and very foolish pride. He will take up with those crude and vague notions which are so useful to the ignorant all over the world. But if you question him respecting his own country, the cloud that dimmed his intelligence will immediately disperse; his language will become as clear and precise as his thoughts.

He will inform you what his rights are and by what means he exercises them; he will be able to point out the customs which obtain in the political world. You will find that he is well acquainted with the rules of the administration, and that he is familiar with the mechanism of the laws. The citizen of the United States does not acquire his practical science and his positive notions from books; the instruction he has acquired may have prepared him for receiving those ideas, but it did not furnish them. The American learns to know the laws by participating in the act of legislation; and he takes a lesson in the forms of government from governing. The great work of society is ever going on before his eyes and, as it were, under his hands.

2. A teacher's description of conditions in a rural New England school on the eve of the common school revival

"History of a Common School, from 1801–1831," *American Annals of Education and Instruction for the Year 1831,* I (1831), 468–472.

SCHOOL HOUSE AND GENERAL ARRANGEMENTS

The school house stood near the centre of the district, at the junction of four roads, so near the usual track of carriages, that a large stone was set up at the end of the building to defend it from injury. Except in the dry season the ground is wet, permitting small collections of water on the surface, and the soil by no means firm. The spot is peculiarly exposed to the bleak winds of winter; nor are there at present any shade trees near, to shelter the children from the scorching rays of the summer's sun during their recreations. There were a few formerly; but they were cut down many

years ago. Neither is there any such thing as an outhouse of *any kind,* not even a wood shed.

The size of the building was twenty two feet long, by twenty broad. From the floor to the ceiling, it was seven feet. The chimney and entry took up about four feet at one end, leaving the school room itself, twenty feet by eighteen. Around three sides of the room, were connected desks, arranged so that when the pupils were sitting at them, their faces were towards the instructor and their backs towards the wall. Attached to the sides of the desks nearest to the instructor, were benches for small pupils. The instructor's desk and chair occupied the centre. On this desk were stationed a rod or ferule; sometimes both. These, with books, writings, inkstands, rules, and plummets, with a fire shovel, and a pair of tongs (often broken), were the principal furniture.

The windows were five in number, of twelve panes each. They were situated so low in the walls, as to give full opportunity to the pupils, to see every traveller as he passed, and to be easily broken. The places of the broken panes, were usually supplied with hats, during the school hours. The entry was four feet square. A depression in the chimney on one side of the entry, furnished a place of deposit for about half of the hats, and spare clothes of the boys; and the rest were left on the floor, often to be trampled upon. The girls generally carried their bonnets, &c. into the school room. The floor and ceiling were level, and the walls were plastered.

The room was warmed by a large and deep fire place. So large was it, and so little efficacious in warming the room otherwise, that I have seen about *one eighth of a cord of good wood,* burning in it at a time. In severe weather, it was estimated that the amount usually consumed, was not far from a cord, or one hundred and twenty eight feet, a week.

The new building erected about five years since, has many improvements upon the former. It is of brick; the room is larger and higher; it is better lighted, and has an improved fire place. The writing desks for the pupils are attached to the walls, and the seats for the smaller pupils have backs. Besides, the local situation of the house is changed. It stands two or three rods from the road side, on a firm soil; but there are no shade trees near, nor any out houses. Like the former house, it has a cold bleak situation in winter. With regard to an entry, however, there now is none. The whole building forms but one room.

The school was not unfrequently broken up for a day or two for want of wood in former years; but since they have used a smaller fire place, this occurrence has been more rare. The instructor or pupils were, however, sometimes compelled to cut or saw it, to prevent the closing of the school. The wood was left in the road near the house, so that it was often buried in the snow or wet with the rain. At the best, it was usually burnt green. The fires were to be kindled, about half an hour before the time of beginning the school. Often, the scholar, whose lot it was, neglected to build it. In consequence of this, the house was frequently cold and uncomfortable about half the forenoon, when the fire being very large, the excess of heat became equally distressing. Frequently too, we were annoyed by smoke. The greatest amount of suffering, however, arose from excessive heat, particularly at the close of the day. The pupils being in a free perspiration when they retired, were very liable to take cold.

The ventilation of the school room, was as much neglected as its temperature; and its cleanliness, more perhaps than either. Situated as the house was, the latter might seem to be in a measure unavoidable. There were, however, no arrangements made for cleaning feet at the door, or for washing floors, windows, &c. In the summer the floor was washed, perhaps once in two or three weeks.

The winter school has usually been opened about the first of December, and continued from twelve to sixteen weeks. The summer school is commenced about the first of May. Formerly this was also continued about three or four months; but within ten years the term has been lengthened usually to twenty weeks. Males have been uniformly employed in winter, and females in summer.

The instructors have usually been changed every season, but sometimes they have been continued two successive summers or winters. A strong prejudice has always existed against employing the same instructor more than once or twice in the same district. This prejudice has yielded in one instance, so far that an instructor who had taught two successive winters, twenty five years before, was employed another season. I have not been able to ascertain the exact number of different instructors who have been engaged in the school during the last thirty years; but I can distinctly recollect *thirty-seven*. Many of them, both males and females, were from sixteen to eighteen years of age, and a few, over twentyone.

Good moral character, and a thorough knowledge of the common branches, were formerly considered as indispensable qualifications in an instructor. The instructors were chiefly selected from the most respectable families in town. But for fifteen or twenty years, these things have not been so much regarded. They have indeed been deemed desirable; but the most common method now seems to be, to ascertain as near as possible the dividend for that season from the public treasury, and then, fix upon a teacher who will take charge of the school three to four months, for this money. He must indeed be able to obtain a license from the Board of Visitors; but this has become nearly a matter of course, provided he can spell, read, and write. In general, the candidate is some favorite or relative of the District Committee. It gives me great pleasure, however, to say that the *moral* character of almost every instructor, so far as I know, has been unexceptionable.

Instructors have usually boarded in the families of the pupils. Their compensation has varied from seven to eleven dollars a month for males; and from sixtytwo and a half cents to one dollar a week for females. Within the last ten years, however, the price of instruction has rarely been less than nine dollars in the former case, and seventyfive cents in the latter. In the few instances in which the instructors have furnished their own board, the compensation has been about the same; it being supposed that they could work at some employment of their own, enough to pay their board, especially females. The only exceptions which I can recollect are two; both within five years. In one of these instances the instructor received twelve dollars, and in the other, eleven dollars and fifty cents a month.

It often happens that no family of the district is prepared to receive the Instructor. In such cases it is expected he will repair to the house of the District Committee. Some, however, from delicacy, or other causes, choose to go to their own homes, when near, until a place is provided.

Two of the Board of Visitors usually visit the winter schools twice during the term. In the summer, their visits are often omitted. These visits usually occupy from one hour to an hour and a half. They are spent in merely hearing a few hurried lessons, and in making some remarks, general in their character. Formerly, it was customary to examine the pupils in some approved catechism; but this practice has been omitted for twenty years.

The parents seldom visit the school, except by special invitation. The greater number pay very little attention to it at all. There are, however, a few who are gradually awaking to the importance of good instruction; but there are also a few, who oppose every thing which is suggested, as at the least, useless; and are scarcely willing their children should be governed in the school.

The school books have been about the same for thirty years. Webster's Spelling Book, the American Preceptor, and the New Testament, have been the principal books used. Before the appearance of the American Preceptor, Dwight's Geography was used as a reading book. A few of the Introduction to the American Orator were introduced about twelve years since, and more recently, Jack Halyard.[1]

Until within a few years, no studies have been permitted in the day school, but spelling, reading and writing. Arithmetic was taught by a few instructors, one or two evenings in a week. But in spite of a most determined opposition, arithmetic is now permitted in the day school, and a few pupils study geography.

---

3. Report of the superintendent in Schoharie County, New York, 1843

New York State, *Annual Report of the Superintendent of Common Schools with the Reports of the Deputy Superintendent, 1843* (Albany, 1843), pp. 332–335.

The greatest portion of the schools in the county were found by me in a most deplorable condition; as the following statistical information, relating to them, will, without any other proof, clearly show.

The number of school districts in the county (as will be found in the abstract of the copies of the reports of the commissioners) is 180
Number of district schools visited by me during the year, once, ... 175
Number of district schools visited by me during the year, twice 116
Number visited in company with one or more of the town inspectors 65

Last winter, the terms in many of the districts were so short, that several of them had closed before I could get around, and conse-

1. William S. Cardell, *The Story of Jack Halyard, The Sailor Boy; or The Virtuous Family,* 4th ed. (New York, 1825); as noted on title page, "Designed for American Children in Families and Schools."

quently I have not been able to visit them but once, although I have visited nearly all the *districts* in the county twice. During the year there has been a school in every district in the county except two. In these, the number of children is small; besides, there is an indifference among the people about a school, and a want of union.

. . . . . .

It appears from the reports of the commissioners, that the number of children in the county, over 5 and under 16 years of age, is 9593

The number of children in attendance in all the district schools taught this year in the county, except three, was, when visited by me, ... 4026

According to this, the number of children absent that should have been in school, was 5567

The number reported as being in attendance in the 175 schools, when first visited by me, is probably a fair statement of the average attendance. A part of these schools were visited in the summer, and a part in the winter. There are but few private schools in the county. The whole number of children in the county that have attended the private schools and academies during the present year, will not exceed 350. Making allowance for these, and for the number of children that usually attend the schools in the three districts in which I found no schools at the time of my visits, and for those in the other two districts in which there have been no schools the present year, and we shall then find that more than half of the children in the county, over 5 and under 16 years of age, have, the present year, been daily absent from school.

Condition of the School Houses.

Number built of stone, ... 3
  do do wood framed, ... 164
  do do logs, ... 13
do having but one room, ... 77
do having one room and an entry, . . 103
do in good repair, ... 53
do in a bad or decaying condition, . . 127
do having no prives, ... 160
do having two privies, ... 3
do having one privy, ... 17

Fifty-three of the school houses I have reported in good repair; but these though in such a condition as to protect the children from the storms and cold of winter; and though furnished with whole benches and firm desks, yet they are nearly all in every respect badly planned, and ill adapted to the purposes for which they are designed. And I regret most deeply to be compelled to say, that all the school houses in the county, with few exceptions, are not in such a condition as either to secure the health, comfort or convenience of the children. Nineteen-twentieths of them are badly located; and a great many of them are, in fact, apparently situated, so far as regards the physical well being of the children, in the very worst places in the districts. A very large number of them are built at the forks of the highways, or on the corners made by their intersection, and often standing, at the same time, on bleak hills, without any kind of out buildings, or even a tree to break off the chilling blasts of winter, or shade them from the scorching rays of the summer's sun. They almost all stand nearly on the line of the highway, and in most cases, they are very far from having any thing like appropriate play grounds, or the requisite or even out buildings of any kind whatever connected with them. In selecting the site for their school house, the all-absorbing object of the people would, indeed, seem to have been, either to find the central point in the district, or some corner at the intersection of the public roads, at the sacrifice of every nobler and more important consideration.

In size they are generally too small. This, though even now an inconvenience, yet it is not commonly so, in consequence of so many children in several of the districts being daily out of school. In regard to their interior accommodations, the construction and arrangement of the desks and benches, they are more defective than in their location. In my visits through the county, I found one-half of the children in seven-eighths of the school houses, seated on narrow benches without any backs, and so high too, that their feet could not reach the floor; and many of them while thus seated, were employed in trying to learn to write at writing desks, to the edges of which they could scarcely reach their chins. In constructing the desks and benches, no attention has, in fact, been paid to the comfort, health or convenience of the children.

I have, at every opportunity, endeavored to apprise the patrons of the schools, of the great danger to which their offspring are exposed by being confined in such painful positions, and in such miserable buildings; of undermining their constitutions, and sowing the seeds of disease; and it gives me great pleasure to be able to state, that the desks and benches in many parts of the county are undergoing a reformation.

I found the school houses generally destitute of all kinds of apparatus; only a few being furnished even with a black-board. But I am happy to say, that several black-boards have lately been introduced.

I would state that the wretched condition of the school houses generally in the county, is not often owing to the want of means to re-build better, but to the leaden apathy upon the subject of education, and to the belief among many farmers, that their money can be more profitably invested in building better barns and stables for their cattle and horses, than in constructing more comfortable and commodious school houses for the children of their bosom.

But to the credit of the people and the county, it gives me pleasure to mention, that three school houses are now building, and one of them of stone, and though not so large, yet they are on the most approved plans, with ample play grounds; and provisions are making for all the requisite out buildings. And I trust that an example so commendable, will next summer be followed in a large number of districts.

---

4. A dame school for very young children

Lucy Larcom, *A New England Girlhood* (Boston, 1889), pp. 42–44.

Lucy Larcom (1824–1893), author and teacher, attended this school in Beverly, Massachusetts.

Aunt Hannah used her kitchen or her sitting-room for a schoolroom, as best suited her convenience. We were delighted observers of her culinary operations and other employments. If a baby's head nodded, a little bed was made for it on a soft "comforter" in the corner, where it had its nap out undisturbed. But this did not often happen; there were so many interesting things going on that we seldom became sleepy.

Aunt Hannah was very kind and motherly, but she kept us in fear of her ferule, which indicated to us a possibility of smarting palms. This ferule was shaped much like the stick with which she stirred her hasty pudding for dinner, — I thought it was the same, — and I found myself caught in a whirlwind of family laughter by reporting at home that "Aunt Hannah punished the scholars with the pudding-stick."

There was one colored boy in school, who did not sit on a bench, like the rest, but on a block of wood that looked like a backlog turned endwise. Aunt Hannah often called him a "blockhead," and I supposed it was because he sat on that block. Sometimes, in his absence, a boy was made to sit in his place for punishment, for being a "blockhead" too, as I imagined. I hoped I should never be put there. Stupid little girls received a different treatment, — an occasional rap on the head with the teacher's thimble; accompanied with a half-whispered, impatient ejaculation, which sounded very much like "Numskull!" I think this was a rare occurrence, however, for she was a good-natured, much-enduring woman.

One of our greatest school pleasures was to watch Aunt Hannah spinning on her flax-wheel, wetting her thumb and forefinger at her lips to twist the thread, keeping time, meanwhile, to some quaint old tune with her foot upon the treadle.

.   .   .   .   .

I began to go to school when I was about two years old, as other children about us did. The mothers of those large families had to resort to some means of keeping their little ones out of mischief, while they attended to their domestic duties. Not much more than that sort of temporary guardianship was expected of the good dame who had us in charge.

But I learned my letters in a few days, standing at Aunt Hannah's knee while she pointed them out in the spelling-book with a pin, skipping over the "a b abs" into words of one and two syllables, thence taking a flying leap into the New Testament, in which there is concurrent family testimony that I was reading at the age of two years and a half. Certain it is that a few passages in the Bible, whenever I read them now, do not fail to bring before me a vision of Aunt Hannah's somewhat sternly smiling lips, with her spectacles just above them, far down on her nose, encouraging me to pronounce the hard words.

---

5. Example of inadequate schoolkeeping in Ohio, 1838

Ohio, *First Annual Report of the Superintendent of Common Schools made to the Thirty-Sixth General Assembly of the State of Ohio, January, 1838, by Samuel Lewis* (Columbus, 1838), pp. 8–10.

Samuel Lewis (1799–1854) was the first superintendent of common schools in Ohio and a leading western advocate of free schools for all.

As it will be impossible to give a full history of my observations, an example of the several classes must suffice. In one town a free school is taught three months in the year, by one teacher, in a district where more than one hundred children desire to attend; they rush in and crowd the school so as to destroy all hope of usefulness, the wealthy, and those in comfortable circumstances, seeing this, withdraw their children or never send them; the school thus receives the name of a school for the poor, and its usefulness is destroyed. This example is one that represents nearly all the free schools in the State, as well in the country, as in the cities and towns.

Another and much larger number of the districts, adopt a practice of which the following is an example.

The district has funds which would pay a teacher one quarter or less; but in order to keep up a school as long as possible, it is divided between two or more quarters; the teacher makes his estimate of the amount, besides public money, that must be paid by each scholar, and gets his subscription accordingly. Here none send but those who can pay the balance; of course, the children of the poor, the very intemperate and careless, with sometimes the inordinate lovers of money, are left at home. This mode, though it defeats the primary object of the law, really secures a greater aggregate amount of instruction than the other. Another class proceeds on the same plan, with the exception that the teacher is bound to take the very poor free, if they prove their total inability to pay. This is but little, if any, better than the last, since the poor woman must humble herself, and in effect take the benefit of the poor law, before she can get her children into school; and then, both she and her children must suffer, constantly, deep mortification, which frequently drives from the school some of the most promising children, who (right or wrong) are too proud to brook such humiliating conditions. It effectually banishes the children of those who love money better than learning, as well as those of the intemperate, whose sensibilities are too much vitiated to care for this subject at all. Besides, if the poor go on these terms, it invariably crowds the school to a ruinous extent; and if the teacher cannot instruct all, he will, of course, take care of his patrons first; let him be as honest as he may, he will endeavor to satisfy those that support him; and the poor, whose conscientiousness of poverty always make them jealous and watchful, detect the smallest partiality, and leave the school in disgust, or stay to scatter the seeds of discontent and insubordination. Another part of this class is, where the directors agree with the teacher at so much per month, and, after expending the school money, levy, under the statute, a tax on the scholars for the residue, sometimes admitting the poor, and sometimes rejecting all that are unable to pay the difference.

In some towns, all the teachers receive a portion of the public money at the rate of so much per scholar, which they deduct from the subscription price. In these cases, the schools are all strictly private, and no provision whatever is made for the poor. The officers in one place where this practice prevails, said that "if the schools were free, they would be so crowded as to be useless, unless they had more funds; but, by the mode they adopted, every man who sent to school, got a part of the public money;" if he was not able to pay the balance, he was punished by losing the whole; which is certainly a bad feature in the practice, and a gross violation of law. Another custom is not to draw the school money for several years, and then say once in two or three years, they can keep a crowded free school from three to six months. In some places public schools have not been taught this two years. These examples give the practice of all the school districts in the State; the second and third named prevail the most generally; but it is not uncommon to find all the examples adopted in different districts in the same township.

No correct idea can be given of the particular system of instruction adopted in the schools; it embraces almost every system; and in our public, as well as in our private schools, is found every variety from the very best, to those esteemed the most defective. But a small proportion of schools in the State have sufficient permanence to have adopted any specific plan, nor is it possible to produce or preserve any thing like system, until the schools have more permanence, and the art of teaching is recognized as something valuable.

In towns and large villages, the *common* schools are poorer than in the country. In the latter, neighborhoods depend more on them, and of course take a deeper interest in their control; while in the former, there is too frequently but little attention paid to these schools, by persons able to provide other means of instruction. Private schools are considered the best, and being patronized by the wealthy, create a distinction that is ruinous. I am unwilling to repeat the remarks in reference to this point, that I have often heard made; it may be sufficient to say, that in many instances, the whole tendency is to bring the schools into disrepute, if not positive disgrace.

---

6. Horace Mann's advocacy of common schools, 1838

Massachusetts, Board of Education, *First Annual Report* (Boston, 1838), pp. 46–51, 53–57.

Mann's work from 1837 to 1848 as secretary of the Massachusetts Board of Education established him as the leading champion of common schools. In his reports he took up the major educational issues of the time.

Another topic . . . is the apathy of the people themselves towards our common schools.

The wide usefulness of which this institution is capable is shorn away on both sides, by two causes diametrically opposite. On one side there is a portion of the community who do not attach sufficient value to the system to do the things necessary to its healthful and energetic working. They may say excellent things about it, they may have a conviction of its general utility; but they do not understand, that the wisest conversation not embodied in action, that convictions too gentle and quiet to coerce performance, are little better than worthless. The prosperity of the system always requires some labor. It requires a conciliatory disposition, and oftentimes a little sacrifice of personal preferences. A disagreement about the location of a school-house, for instance, may occasion the division of a district, and thus inflict permanent impotency upon each of its parts. In such cases, a spirit of forbearance and compromise averting the evil, would double the common fund of knowledge for every child in the territory. Except in those cases, where it is made necessary by the number of the scholars, the dismemberment of a district, though it may leave the body, drains out its life-blood. So through remissness or ignorance on the part of parent and teacher, the minds of children may never be awakened to a consciousness of having, within themselves, blessed treasures of innate and noble faculties, far richer than any outward possessions can be; they may never be supplied with any foretaste of the enduring satisfactions of knowledge; and hence, they may attend school for the allotted period, merely as so many male and female automata, between four and sixteen years of age . . . It is generally believed, that there is an increasing class of people amongst us, who are losing sight of the necessity of securing ample opportunities for the education of their children. And thus, on one side, the institution of common schools is losing its natural support, if it be not incurring actual opposition.

Opposite to this class, who tolerate, from apathy, a depression in the common schools, there is another class who affix so high a value upon the culture of their children, and understand so well the necessity of a skilful preparation of means for its bestowment, that they turn away from the common schools, in their depressed state, and seek, elsewhere, the helps of a more enlarged and thorough education. Thus the standard, in descending to a point corresponding with the views and wants of one portion of society, falls below the demands and the regards of another. Out of different feelings grow different plans; and while one remains fully content with the common school, the other builds up the private school or the academy. The education fund is thus divided into two parts. Neither of the halves does a quarter of the good which might be accomplished by a union of the whole. One party pays an adequate price, but has a poor school; the other has a good school, but at more than four-fold cost. Were their funds and their interest combined, the poorer school might be as good as the best; and the dearest almost as low as the cheapest. This last mentioned class embraces a considerable portion, perhaps a majority of the wealthy persons in the state; but it also includes another portion, numerically much greater, who, whether rich or poor, have a true perception of the sources of their children's individual and domestic well-being, and who consider the common necessaries of their life, their food and fuel and clothes, and all their bodily comforts as superfluities, compared with the paramount necessity of a proper mental and moral culture of their offspring.

The maintenance of free schools rests wholly upon the social principle. It is emphatically a case where men, individually powerless, are collectively strong. The population of Massachusetts, being more than eighty to the square mile, gives it the power of maintaining common schools. Take the whole range of the western and south-western states, and their population, probably, does not exceed a dozen or fifteen to the square mile. Hence, except in favorable localities, common schools are impossible; as the population upon a territory of convenient size for a district, is too small to sustain a school. Here, nothing is easier. But by dividing our funds, we cast away our natural advantages. We voluntarily reduce ourselves to the feebleness of a state, having but half our density of population.

It is generally supposed, that this severance of interests, and consequent diminution of power, have increased much of late, and are now increasing in an accelerated ratio. This is probable, for it is a self-aggravating evil. Its origin and progress are simple and uniform. Some few persons in a village or town, finding the advantages of the common school inadequate to their wants, unite to establish a private one. They transfer their children from the former to the latter. The heart goes with the treasure. The common school ceases to be visited by those whose children are in the private. Such parents decline serving as committee men. They have now no personal motive to vote for or advocate any increase of the town's annual appropriation for schools; to say nothing of the temptation to discourage such increase in indirect ways, or even to vote directly against it. If, by this means, some of the best scholars happen to be taken from the common school, the standard of that school is lowered. The lower classes in a school have no abstract standard of excellence, and seldom aim at higher attainments than such as they daily witness. All children, like all men, rise easily to the common level. There, the mass stop; strong minds only ascend higher. But raise the standard, and, by a spontaneous movement, the mass will rise again and reach it. Hence the removal of the most forward scholars from a school is not a small misfortune. Again; the teacher of the common school rarely visits or associates except where the scholars of his own school are the origin of the acquaintance, and the bond of attachment. All this inevitably depresses and degrades the common school. In this depressed and degraded state, another portion of the parents find it, in fitness and adequacy, inferior to their wants; and, as there is now a private school in the neighborhood, the strength of the inducement,

and the facility of the transfer, overbalance the objection of increased expense, and the doors of the common school close, at once, upon their children, and upon their interest in its welfare. Thus another blow is dealt; then others escape; action and reaction alternate, until the common school is left to the management of those, who have not the desire or the power either to improve it or to command a better. Under this silent, but rapid corrosion, it recently happened, in one of the most flourishing towns of the state, having a population of more than three thousand persons, that the principal district school actually run down and was not kept for two years. I have been repeatedly assured, where every bias of my informants would lead them to extenuate and not to magnify the facts, that, in populous villages and central districts, where there is naturally a concentration of wealth and intelligence, and a juster appreciation of the blessings of a good education, and where, therefore, the common school ought to be the best in the town, it was the poorest.

.   .   .   .   .

Some objections are urged, on both sides, to a restitution of our system to its original design; but, as they are anti-social in their nature, they must be dissipated by a more enlarged view of the subject. Citizens, living remote from the place, where the town school would probably be kept, allege the difference in the distances of residence, and the consequent inequality of advantages, derivable from it, as arguments against its maintenance. They, therefore, resist its establishment, and thus extinguish all chances of a better education for a vast majority of the children in the town, whatever may be their talents or genius. They debar some, perhaps their own offspring, from the means of reaching a higher sphere of usefulness and honor. They forbid their taking the first steps, which are as necessary as the last, in the ascension to excellence. They surrender every vantage ground to those who can and will, in any event, command the means of a higher education for their children. Because the balance of advantages cannot be mathematically adjusted, as in the nature of things it cannot be, they cast their own shares into the adverse scale; as though it were some compensation, when there is not an absolute equality, to make the inequality absolute. The cost of education is nothing to the rich, while the means of it are every thing to the poor.

.   .   .   .   .

On the other hand, the patrons of the private school plead the moral necessity of sustaining it, because, they say, some of the children in the public school are so addicted to profanity or obscenity, so prone to trickishness or to vulgar and mischievous habits, as to render a removal of their own children from such contaminating influences an obligatory precaution. But would such objectors bestow that guardian care, that parental watchfulness upon the common schools, which an institution, so wide and deep-reaching in its influences, demands of all intelligent men, might not these repellent causes be mainly abolished? Reforms ought to be originated and carried forward by the intelligent portion of society; by those who can see most links in the chain of causes and effects; and that intelligence is false to its high trusts, which stands aloof from the labor of enlightening the ignorant and ameliorating the condition of the unfortunate. And what a vision must rise before the minds of all men, endued with the least glimmer of foresight, in the reflection, that, after a few swift years, those children, whose welfare they now discard, and whose associations they deprecate, will constitute more than *five-sixths* of the whole body of that community, of which their own children will be only a feeble minority, vulnerable at every point, and utterly incapable of finding a hiding-place for any earthly treasure, where the witness, the juror and the voter cannot reach and annihilate it!

The theory of our laws and institutions undoubtedly is, *first,* that in every district of every town in the Commonwealth, there should be a free district school, sufficiently safe, and sufficiently good, for all the children within its territory, where they may be well instructed in the rudiments of knowledge, formed to propriety of demeanor, and imbued with the principles of duty: and, *secondly,* in regard to every town, having such an increased population as implies the possession of sufficient wealth, that there should be a school of an advanced character, offering an equal welcome to each one of the same children, whom a peculiar destination, or an impelling spirit of genius, shall send to its open doors, — especially to the children of the poor, who cannot incur the expenses of a residence from home in order to attend such a school. It is on this common platform, that a general acquaintanceship should be formed between the children of the same neighborhood. It is here, that the affinities of a common nature should unite them together so as to give the advantages of pre-occupancy and a stable possession to fraternal feelings, against the alienating competitions of subsequent life.

After the state shall have secured to all its children, that basis of knowledge and morality, which is indispensable to its own security; after it shall have supplied them with the instruments of that individual prosperity, whose aggregate will constitute its own social prosperity; then they may be emancipated from its tutelage, each one to go withersoever his well-instructed mind shall determine. At this point, seminaries for higher learning, academies and universities, should stand ready to receive, at private cost, all whose path to any ultimate destination may lie through their halls. Subject, of course, to many exceptions; — all, however, inconsiderable, compared with the generality of the rule, — this is the paternal and comprehensive theory of our institutions; and, is it possible, that a practical contradiction of this theory can be wise, until another shall be devised, offering some chances at least of equally valuable results?

Amongst any people, sufficiently advanced in intelligence, to perceive, that hereditary opinions on religious subjects are not always coincident with truth, it cannot be overlooked, that the tendency of the private school system is to assimilate our modes of education to those of England, where churchmen and dissenters, — each sect according to its own creed, — maintain separate schools, in which children are taught, from their tenderest years to wield the sword of polemics with fatal dexterity; and where the gospel, instead of being a temple of peace, is converted into an armory of deadly weapons, for social, interminable warfare. Of such disastrous consequences, there is but one remedy and one preventive. It is the elevation of the common schools. Until that is accomplished (for which, however, they ought to cooperate), those who are able, not only will, but they are bound by the highest obligations, to provide surer and better means for the education of their children.

It ought not to be omitted, that it is urged, in defence of the private school system, that it is preparing a class of better teachers for the common schools than they could otherwise obtain. Suppose, however, that the common schools were what they should be, could not they prepare the teachers as well?

I trust I shall not be deemed to have given an undue importance to the different interests involved in this topic, when it is considered that more than *five-sixths* of the children in the state are dependant upon the common schools for instruction, and would have no substitute if they became valueless; while less than *one-sixth* are educated in the private schools and academies, and these would be educated, even if the common schools were abolished. To hold *one-sixth* of the children to be equal to five-sixths, I should deem to be as great an error in morals as it would be in arithmetic.

The debate over the common school

1. A conservative politician's estimation of the social utility of popular education, 1820

Daniel Webster, "First Settlement of New England," in Edward Everett, ed., *The Works of Daniel Webster* (Boston, 1851), I, 41–42.

Webster (1782–1852) was practicing law in Boston when he delivered this address at Plymouth on December 22, 1820.

I must yet advert to another most interesting topic, — the Free Schools. In this particular, New England may be allowed to claim, I think, a merit of a peculiar character. She early adopted, and has constantly maintained the principle, that it is the undoubted right and the bounden duty of government to provide for the instruction of all youth. That which is elsewhere left to chance or to charity, we secure by law. For the purpose of public instruction, we hold every man subject to taxation in proportion to his property, and we look not to the question, whether he himself have, or have not, children to be benefited by the education for which he pays. We regard it as a wise and liberal system of police, by which property, and life, and the peace of society are secured. We seek to prevent in some measure the extension of the penal code, by inspiring a salutary and conservative principle of virtue and of knowledge in an early age. We strive to excite a feeling of respectability, and a sense of character, by enlarging the capacity and increasing the sphere of intellectual enjoyment. By general instruction, we seek, as far as possible, to purify the whole moral atmosphere; to keep good sentiments uppermost, and to turn the strong current of feeling and opinion, as well as the censure of the law and the denunciations of religion, against immorality and crime. We hope for a security beyond the law, and above the law, in the prevalence of an enlightened and well-principled moral sentiment. We hope to continue and prolong the time, when, in the villages and farm-houses of New England, there may be undisturbed sleep within unbarred doors. And knowing that our government rests directly on the public will, in order that we may preserve it we endeavor to give a safe and proper direction to that public will. We do not, indeed, expect all men to be philosophers or statesmen; but we confidently trust, and our expectation of the duration of our system of government rests on that trust, that, by the diffusion of general knowledge and good and virtuous sentiments, the political fabric may be secure, as well against open violence and overthrow, as against the slow, but sure, undermining of licentiousness.

---

2. Public education as a way of securing social unity, 1824

James G. Carter, *Letters to the Honorable William Prescott . . . on the Free Schools of New England* (Boston, 1824), pp. 44–46.

Carter (1795–1849), teacher, author of textbooks, publicist, and politician, was the pioneer of educational reform in Massachusetts.

In publick and large seminaries of learning, which bring together young men from different towns, states, and sections of the country, the change in habits, manners, and feelings towards each other, is astonishingly rapid. They come together with feelings and prejudices, and oftentimes with a dialect peculiar to the different places, from which they come, and each staring and wondering at the excessive *strangeness* of the other. But a very short time loosens their local prejudices, and teaches them, that all excellence is not peculiar to any one place. The whole exterior and deportment of the young man is often almost entirely transformed, in the short space of a few weeks. The change and improvement in this respect are more rapid at first, and quite as important and valuable to him, as his acquisitions in knowledge. What has a more direct tendency to improve "the

manners" and deportment of the children, who attend our schools, than to observe some refinement in their instructer? Such is the personal influence of an instructer in a common school, that whether he is refined or vulgar, or whether he attends to the manners of his pupils or not, his manners will infallibly be imitated and copied by all, for the time, as a model of perfection. The different sections of our country are more free from dialects of the same language than any other in the world. What has produced this uniformity of language, so desirable on every consideration, but our public and common seminaries of learning, — the frequent and intimate commercial and literary intercourse between different parts of the country, — and the numerous points of contact between the educated and uneducated parts of the community? For the interest and happiness of the whole, and especially, the lower and uneducated classes of the community, it is certainly desirable these points of contact and intercourse should be multiplied, rather than diminished. For these reasons, the employment of instructers in our schools, who have had the advantages of some publick school or college, is an object of great consideration. Besides being the most direct and effectual means, of inculcating "decent behaviour," — of reconciling the prejudices of different parts of the country, and different classes of the community; there is still another point of view, in which the measure is not less important. It tends more than any thing else, to lessen the distance and weaken the jealousies, which very generally subsist between the educated and uneducated. The talents and acquirements of a young man of publick education are often lost to the unlettered community for some years, while they have a delicious season of mutually hating and despising each other. These evils are in some degree obviated, when, by the kind of intercourse usually subsisting between a *publick* instructer and the *publick,* they are taught by experience their mutual worth and dependence as members of the same body politick.

3. The failure to educate the children
of the poor, 1838

Ohio, *First Annual Report of the
Superintendent of Common Schools,* pp.
16–18.

Though a great majority of our citizens are
enlightened and intelligent, it must be admitted,
that quite a number do not regard the education of their children with sufficient interest to
induce proper individual action; and unless
provision for these, other than parental, be
made, they will be even worse situated, in
many cases, than the orphan. It is common to
say of these, "They could educate their children, if they would": but visits to the houses
of many people, in different counties, of whom
this was said, would satisfy any man, as it has
satisfied me, that if they paid for schooling, it
must be taken from the already too scanty fare
of an unfortunate wife and poorly provided
family. In many cases, you may as well charge
fifteen dollars per quarter, as fifty cents. They
cannot, if they would, and too many would
not, if they could, pay, as individuals, any thing.

If such fathers were the only sufferers, we
might be excused from labors to avert the
evil; but such parents will have left the world,
long before society will feel its full extent.

The children are not to blame; nor are the
children of those in other circumstances, guilty
of any offence that will justify their fathers in
fixing upon them a great moral contagion, destroying their best interests.

The children of those several classes (and
there are not a few) are practically shut out of
our common schools, in nine cases out of ten,
in the State. For it makes but little difference,
whether we positively prohibit their attendance,
or prescribe such conditions as preclude them.
Nor is it a question that can influence us,
whether they are correct in their views. So long
as those views operate the hindrance, it is the
same thing to the public. It is not by any means

certain, that we should discourage a feeling of
independence, in parents or children. A mag-
nanimous friend, in doing the greatest favor,
seeks how he may do it so delicately, that the
favored party may not feel himself oppressed
with a sense of obligation.

Though common school is a civil, rather than
charitable institution, it must be admitted that
a primary object is, to bring under a wholesome influence, the classes of children I have
named.

Whether we regard this subject in reference
to *their* interest, or that of the whole people
forming the State, it is of too much importance
to be passed over lightly, or justify, for a moment, the conclusion that any portion of the
rising generation, on whom must devolve the
government of the country, can be abandoned
to accident or certain ruin. Men may discourse
eloquently about family instruction, and fire-
side education: it is all good; better than orators have spoken, or poets sung. But we must
not be misled by eloquence or poetry. The fact
is, a large part of our fellow citizens, who depend on their labor for a support (and they
are the majority) have no time for much of
this, if they had ability. If *we* should rise in the
morning, and before our little ones were even
dressed, hurry to our work, and devote the
entire day to it, returning when our fatigued
bodies, without other aid, admonished us of
approaching night, we should be exceptions to
all general rules, if we could undertake the
instruction of our sons by candle light. And
the cases of three-fifths of our mothers, is still
harder. Their labor begins on the first move
in the house, nor ends until the last candle is
out. They have, emphatically, no time to
educate their daughters. Exceptions, we know,
there are; persons who have risen above all
these obstacles, and educated both themselves
and their families. But we must stop until at
least one generation shall be educated, before
we can expect to make the exceptions, the
general rule. We should, in providing for the
people, look to their present condition as a

body, and not to what they should be according to the perfection of a few characters, perhaps over-drawn, if they ever existed, except in the inventive genius of vivid imaginations. I do not place a low estimate on the capacity of my countrymen; but it is out of their power to do the labor that custom requires of them, and do much toward educating their children at home. A very great number declare they cannot, if they had time.

4. Horace Mann analyzes the American moral crisis and calls for its solution by a new education, 1846

Massachusetts, Board of Education, *Ninth Annual Report* (1846), pp. 75–76.

Now it is too obvious to need remark, that the main tendency of institutions and of a state of society, like those here depicted, is to cultivate the intellect and to inflame the passions, rather than to teach humility and lowliness to the heart. Our civil and social condition holds out splendid rewards for the competitions of talent, rather than motives for the practice of virtue. It sharpens the perceptive faculties, in comparing different objects of desire; it exercises the judgment in arranging means for the production of ends; it gives a grasp of thought and a power of combination, which nothing else could so effectively impart; but, on the other hand, it tends not merely to the neglect of the moral nature, but to an invasion of its rights, to a disregard of its laws, and, in cases of conflict, to the silencing of its remonstrances and the denial of its sovereignty.

And has not experience proved what reason might have predicted? Within the last half century, has not speculation, to a fearful extent, taken the place of honest industry? Has not the glare of wealth so dazzled the public eye, as often to blind it to the fraudulent means by which the wealth itself had been procured? Have not men been honored for the offices of dignity and patronage they have held, rather than for the ever-during qualities of probity, fidelity, and intelligence, which alone are meritorious considerations for places of honor and power? In the Moral Price Current of the nation, has not Intellect been rising, while Virtue has been sinking in value? Though the nation, as a nation, and a very great majority of the States composing it, have performed all their pecuniary obligations, and preserved their reputation unsullied; yet have there not been great communities, acting through legislators, whom they themselves had chosen, that have been guilty of such enormous breaches of plighted faith, as would cause the expulsion of a robber from his brotherhood of bandits?

And who will say, even of the most favored portions of our country, that their advancement in moral excellence, in probity, in purity, and in the practical exemplification of the virtues of a Christian life, has kept pace with their progress in outward conveniences and embellishments? Can Virtue recount as many triumphs in the moral world, as Intellect has won in the material? Can our advances towards perfection, in the cultivation of private and domestic virtues, and in the feeling of brotherhood and kindness towards all the members of our households, bear comparison with the improvements in our dwellings, our furniture, or our equipage? Have our charities for the poor, the debased, the ignorant, been multiplied in proportion to our revenues? Have we subdued low vices, low indulgences and selfish feelings, and have we fertilized the waste places in the human heart, as extensively as we have converted the wilderness into plenteous harvest fields, or enlisted the running waters in our service? In fine, have the mightier and swifter agencies which we have created, or applied, in the material world, any parallel, in new spiritual instrumentalities by which truth can be more rapidly diffused, by which the high places of iniquity can be brought low, or its crooked ways made straight?

Must it not be acknowledged, that, morally

speaking, we stand in arrears to the age in which we live; and must not some new measures be adopted, by which, as philanthropists and Christians, we can redeem our forfeited obligations?

While then, the legislator continues to denounce his penalties against such wicked desires as break out into actual transgression; and while the judge continues to punish the small portion of offences that can be proved in court; the friends of Education must do whatever can be done, to diminish the terrible necessity of the penal law, and the judicial condemnation.

---

5. Mann asserts a natural right to education and points out the limitations it places on the rights of property, 1847

Massachusetts, Board of Education, *Tenth Annual Report* (1847), pp. 111–113, 119–120, 124–125.

I believe that this amazing dereliction from duty, especially in our own country, originates more in the false notions which men entertain *respecting the nature of their right to property,* than in any thing else. In the district school meeting, in the town meeting, in legislative halls, every where, the advocates for a more generous education could carry their respective audiences with them in behalf of increased privileges for our children, were it not instinctively foreseen that increased privileges must be followed by increased taxation. Against this obstacle argument falls dead. The rich man, who has no children, declares it to be an invasion of his rights of property to exact a contribution from him to educate the children of his neighbor. The man who has reared and educated a family of children denounces it as a double tax, when he is called upon to assist in educating the children of others also; or, if he has reared his own children, without educat-

ing them, he thinks it peculiarly oppressive to be obliged to do for others, what he refrained from doing even for himself. Another, having children, but disdaining to educate them with the common mass, withdraws them from the Public School, puts them under what he calls "selecter influences," and then thinks it a grievance to be obliged to support a school which he contemns. Or if these different parties so far yield to the force of traditionary sentiment and usage, and to the public opinion around them, as to consent to do something for the cause, they soon reach the limit of expense where their admitted obligation, or their alleged charity, terminates.

It seems not irrelevant, therefore, in this connection, to inquire into the nature of a man's right to the property he possesses, and to satisfy ourselves respecting the question, whether any man has such an indefeasible title to his estates, or such an absolute ownership of them, as renders it unjust in the government to assess upon him his share of the expenses of educating the children of the community, up to such a point as the nature of the institutions under which he lives, and the well-being of society require.

I believe in the existence of a great, immutable principle of natural law, or natural ethics, — a principle antecedent to all human institutions and incapable of being abrogated by any ordinances of man, — a principle of divine origin, clearly legible in the ways of Providence as those ways are manifested in the order of nature and in the history of the race, — which proves the *absolute right* of every human being that comes into the world to an education; and which, of course, proves the correlative duty of every government to see that the means of that education are provided for all.

In regard to the application of this principle of natural law, — that is, in regard to the extent of the education to be provided for all, at the public expense, — some differences of opinion may fairly exist, under different political organizations; but under a republican government, it seems clear that the minimum of this education can never be less than such as is sufficient to qualify each citizen for the civil and social duties he will be called to discharge; — such an education as teaches the individual the great laws of bodily health; as qualifies for the fulfilment of parental duties; as is indispensable for the civil functions of a witness or a juror; as is necessary for the voter in municipal affairs; and finally, for the faithful and conscientious discharge of all those duties which devolve upon the inheritor of a portion of the sovereignty of this great republic.

The will of God, as conspicuously manifested in the order of nature, and in the relations which he has established among men, places the *right* of every child that is born into the world to such a degree of education as will enable him, and, as far as possible, will predispose him, to perform all domestic, social, civil and moral duties, upon the same clear ground of natural law and equity, as it places a child's *right,* upon his first coming into the world, to distend his lungs with a portion of the common air, or to open his eyes to the common light, or to receive that shelter, protection and nourishment which are necessary to the continuance of his bodily existence. And so far is it from being a wrong or a hardship, to demand of the possessors of property their respective shares for the prosecution of this divinely-ordained work, that they themselves are guilty of the most far-reaching injustice, who seek to resist or to evade the contribution. The complainers are the wrongdoers. The cry, "Stop thief," comes from the thief himself.

.   .   .   .   .

But sometimes, the rich farmer, the opulent manufacturer, or the capitalist, when sorely pressed with his legal and moral obligation, to contribute a portion of his means for the education of the young, replies, — either in form or in spirit; — "My lands, my machinery, my gold and my silver, are mine; may not I do what I will with my own?" There is one supposable case, and only one, where this argument

would have plausibility. If it were made by an isolated, solitary being, — a being having no relations to a community around him, having no ancestors to whom he had been indebted for ninety-nine parts in every hundred of all he possesses, and expecting to leave no posterity after him, — it might not be easy to answer it. If there were but one family in this western hemisphere, and one only in the eastern hemisphere, and these two families bore no civil and social relations to each other, and were to be the first and last of the whole race, it might be difficult, except on very high and almost transcendental grounds, for either one of them to show good cause why the other should contribute to help to educate children not his own . . . In self-defence, or in selfishness, one might say to the other, "What are your fortunes to me? You can neither benefit nor molest me . . . But is this the relation which any man amongst us sustains to his fellows? In the midst of a populous community to which he is bound by innumerable ties, having had his own fortune and condition almost predetermined and foreordained by his predecessors, and being about to exert upon his successors as commanding an influence as has been exerted upon himself, the objector can no longer shrink into his individuality, and disclaim connection and relationship with the world. He cannot deny that there are thousands around him on whom he acts, and who are continually reäcting upon him. The earth is much too small, or the race is far too numerous, to allow us to be hermits, and therefore we cannot adopt either the philosophy or the morals of hermits. All have derived benefits from their ancestors, and all are bound, as by an oath, to transmit those benefits, even in an improved condition, to posterity. We may as well attempt to escape from our own personal identity, as to shake off the three-fold relation which we bear to others, — the relation of an associate with our contemporaries; of a beneficiary of our ancestors; of a guardian to those who, in the sublime order of Providence, are to follow us. Out of these relations, manifest duties are evolved. The society of which we necessarily constitute a part, must be preserved; and, in order to preserve it, we must not look merely to what one individual or family needs, but to what the whole community needs; not merely to what one generation needs, but to the wants of a succession of generations. To draw conclusions without considering these facts, is to leave out the most important part of the premises.

.   .   .   .   .

All moralists agree, nay, all moralists maintain, that a man is as responsible for his omissions as for his commissions; — that he is as guilty of the wrong which he could have prevented, but did not, as for that which his own hand has perpetrated. They then, who knowingly withhold sustenance from a newborn child, and he dies, are guilty of infanticide. And, by the same reasoning, they who refuse to enlighten the intellect of the rising generation, are guilty of degrading the human race! They who refuse to train up children in the way they should go, are training up incendiaries and madmen to destroy property and life, and to invade and pollute the sanctuaries of society! In a word, if the mind is as real and substantive a part of human existence as the body, then mental attributes during the periods of childhood, demand provision at least as imperatively as bodily appetites. The time when these respective obligations attach, corresponds with the periods when the nurture, whether physical or mental, is needed. As the right of sustenance is of equal date with birth, so the right to intellectual and moral training begins, at least as early as when children are ordinarily sent to school. At that time, then, by the irrepealable law of nature, every child succeeds to so much more of the property of the community as is necessary for his education. He is to receive this, not in the form of lands, or of gold and silver, but in the form of knowledge and a training to good habits. This is one of the steps in the transfer of the property of the present to a succeeding generation. Human

sagacity may be at fault in fixing the amount of property to be transferred, or the time when the transfer should be made, to a dollar or to an hour; but certainly, in a republican government, the obligation of the predecessors, and the right of the successors, extend to and embrace the means of such an amount of education as will prepare each individual to perform all the duties which devolve upon him as a man and a citizen. It may go further than this point; certainly, it cannot fall short of it.

---

6. The Americanizing mission of the schools, 1850

Benjamin Labaree, "The Education Demanded by the Peculiar Character of Our Civil Institutions," in *The Lectures Delivered Before the American Institute of Instruction, 1849* (Boston, 1850), pp. 33–35.

Most common school reformers believed the influx of non-English immigrants in the two decades before the Civil War posed a threat to the national unity they sought. Labaree (1801–1883) was president of Middlebury College and a writer on educational subjects.

The foreign element, which is becoming so prominent in our social and civil state, demands . . . forbearance and expansiveness of view, on the part of our public men and of the rising generation. The multitude of emigrants from the old world, interfused among our population, is rapidly changing the identity of American character. These strangers come among us, ignorant of our institutions, and unacquainted with the modes of thought and habits of life peculiar to a free people. Accustomed to be restrained by the strong arm of power, and to look upon themselves as belonging to an inferior class of the human race, they suddenly emerge from the darkness of oppression into the light and liberty of freemen. The transition is instantaneous, and admits of no preparation for the new life. Will not this sudden change in their political relations produce a corresponding change in their views respecting personal rights and duties? Would it be strange if in such circumstances, many should mistake lawless freedom from restraint, for true and rational liberty? Shall these adopted citizens become a part of the body politic, and firm supporters of liberal institutions, or will they prove to our republic what the Goths and Huns were to the Roman Empire? The answer to this question depends in a great degree upon the wisdom and fidelity of our teachers and associated influences. They have a two-fold duty to perform in regard to this class of our population. On the one hand they must act the part of master-builders, and by degrees mould these unprepared and uncongenial elements into the form and character which the peculiar nature of the edifice demands, and in due time the youth especially may become intelligent, enterprising and liberal-minded supporters of free institutions. On the other hand, our instructors must prepare our native population for the suitable reception and treatment of these strangers, must teach them to lay aside prejudices and animosities, to meet the newcomers in the spirit of kindness and benevolence, and to enlist their sympathies and good-will on the side of liberty, humanity and truth. If our country is to remain, as it has been, the asylum of the oppressed, and the home of the free, a wise and liberal policy must be pursued towards foreigners; resolute and persevering exertions must be made to engraft them upon the republican stock, and to qualify them for the duties of free and enlightened citizens.

---

7. Arguments in opposition to common schools, 1830

Editorials in the *Philadelphia National Gazette,* July 10, 12, Aug. 19, 1830, in John R. Commons et al., eds., *A Documentary History of American Industrial Society,* V (Cleveland, 1910), 107–112.

We remark the following toast in one of the lists which nearly fill the papers at this season.

"Education and general information — these must indeed constitute our only true National Bulwark. May the day soon come when in point of literary acquirements the poorest peasant shall stand on a level with his more wealthy neighbours."

It is our strong inclination and our obvious interest that literary acquirements should be universal; but we should be guilty of imposture, if we professed to believe in the possibility of that consummation. Literature cannot be acquired without leisure, and wealth gives leisure. Universal opulence, or even competency, is a chimera, as man and society are constituted. There will ever be distinctions of condition, of capacity, of knowledge and ignorance, in spite of all the fond conceits which may be indulged, or the wild projects which may be tried, to the contrary. The "peasant" must labor during those hours of the day, which his wealthy neighbor can give to the abstract culture of his mind; otherwise, the earth would not yield enough for the subsistence of all: the mechanic cannot abandon the operations of his trade, for general studies; if he should, most of the conveniences of life and objects of exchange would be wanting; langour, decay, poverty, discontent would soon be visible among all classes. No government, no statesman, no philanthropist, can furnish what is incompatible with the very organization and being of civil society. Education, the most comprehensive, should be, and is, open to the whole community; but it must cost to every one, time and money; and those are means which every one cannot possess simultaneously. Doubtless, more of education and of information is attainable for all in this republic, than can be had any where else by the poor or the operatives, so called.

It is an old and sound remark, that government cannot provide for the necessities of the People; that it is they who maintain the government, and not the latter the People. Education may be among their necessities; but it is one of that description which the state or national councils cannot supply, except partially and in a limited degree. They may endow public schools for the indigent, and colleges for the most comprehensive and costly scheme of instruction. To create or sustain seminaries for the tuition of all classes — to digest and regulate systems; to adjust and manage details, to render a multitude of schools effective, is beyond their province and power. Education in general must be the work of the intelligence, need, and enterprise of individuals and associations. At present, in nearly all the most populous parts of the United States, it is attainable for nearly all the inhabitants; it is comparatively cheap, and if not the best possible, it is susceptible of improvement and likely to be advanced. Its progress and wider diffusion will depend, not upon government, but on the public spirit, information, liberality and training of the citizens themselves, who may appreciate duly the value of the object as a national good, and as a personal benefit for their children. Some of the writers about universal public instruction and discipline, seem to forget the constitution of modern society, and declaim as if our communities could receive institutions or habits like those of Sparta. The dream embraces grand Republican female academies, to make Roman matrons!

We can readily pardon the editor of the United States *Gazette* for not perceiving that the scheme of Universal Equal Education at the expense of the State, is virtually "Agrarianism." It would be a compulsory application of the means of the richer, for the direct use of the poorer classes; and so far an arbitrary division of property among them. The declared object is, to procure the opportunity of instruction for the child or children of every citizen; to elevate the standard of the education of the working classes, or equalize the standard for all classes; which would, doubtless, be to lower or narrow that which the rich may now compass. But the most sensible and reflecting possessors of property sufficient to enable them to educate their children in the most liberal and efficacious way, and upon the broadest scale, would prefer to share their means for any other purpose, or in any other mode, than such as would injuriously affect or circumscribe the proficiency of their offspring. A public meeting of "the Mechanics and other Working Men of the City and County of New York," was held in the city, on the 17th inst., and among the principles for which they have "resolved" to contend, we find the following:

"In Education — The adoption of a general system of instruction, at the expense of the State, which shall afford to children, however rich or poor, equal means to obtain useful learning. To effect this, it is believed that a system of direct taxation will not be necessary, as the surplus revenue of the State and United States Governments will, in a very few years, afford ample means — but even if it were necessary to resort to direct taxation to accomplish this all-important object, and the amount paid by the wealthy should be far greater than that paid by our less eligibly situated fellow-citizens, an equivalent to them would be found in the increased ability and usefulness of the educated citizen to serve and to promote the best interests of the State; in the increased permanency of our institutions — and in the superior protection of liberty, person and property."

Thus, a direct tax for "the equal means of obtaining useful learning" is not deemed improbable, and it is admitted that the amount which would be paid by the wealthy would be "far greater" than that paid by their "less eligibly situated fellow citizens." Here, we contend, would be the action, if not the name, of the Agrarian system. Authority — that is, the State — is to force the more eligibly situated citizens to contribute a part (which might be very considerable) of their means, for the accommodation of the rest; and this is equivalent to the idea of an actual, compulsory partition of their substance. The more thriving members of the "mechanical and other working classes" would themselves feel the evil of the direct taxation; they would find that they had toiled for the benefit of other families than their own. One of the chief excitements to industry, among those classes, is the hope of earning the means of educating their children respectably or liberally: that incentive would be removed, and the scheme of State and equal education be thus a premium for comparative idleness, to be taken out of the pockets of the laborious and conscientious . . .

We have no confidence in any compulsory equalizations; it has been well observed that they pull down what is above, but never much raise what is below, and often "depress high and low together beneath the level of what was originally the lowest." By no possibility could a perfect equality be procured. A scheme of universal equal education, attempted in reality, would be an unexampled bed of Procrustes, for the understandings of our youth, and in fact, could not be used with any degree of equality of profit, unless the dispositions and circumstances of parents and children were nearly the same; to accomplish which phenomenon, in a nation of many millions, engaged in a great variety of pursuits, would be beyond human power . . .

Political aspects and laws of the common school movement in Pennsylvania

1. Pennsylvania legislators propose a system of common schools, 1834

"Report of the Joint Committee of the two Houses of the Pennsylvania Legislature, on the subject of a System of General

Education . . ." in *Hazard's Register of Pennsylvania,* XIII (1834), 97.

In Pennsylvania, as in many other states, common school reform consisted of replacing pauper schooling at public expense with schools free and open to all.

The number of voters in Pennsylvania, unable to read, have been computed . . . at many thousand; and two thousand five hundred, grow up to be voters annually, who are equally ignorant. In a republican government, no voter should be without the rudiments of learning; for aside from political considerations, education purifies the morals, and lessens crime. Our philanthropists, who visit our jails, have ascertained that more than half the convicts are unable to read. It is better to avert crime, by giving instruction to our youth, than punish them when men, as ignorant convicts.

A radical defect in our laws upon the subject of education, is that the public aid now given, and imperfectly given, is confined *to the poor.* Aware of this, your committee have taken care to exclude the word *poor,* from the bill which will accompany this report, meaning to make the system *general;* that is to say, to form an educational association between the rich, the comparatively rich, and the destitute. Let them all fare alike in the primary schools; receive the same elementary instruction; imbibe the same republican spirit, and be animated by a feeling of perfect equality. In after life, he who is diligent at school, will take his station accordingly, whether born to wealth or not. Common schools, universally established, will multiply the chances of success, perhaps of brilliant success, among those who may forever continue ignorant. It is the duty of the State to promote and foster such establishments. That done, the career of each youth will depend upon himself. The State will have given the first impulse; good conduct and suitable application must do the rest. Among the indigent, "some flashing of a mounting genius" may be found; and among both rich and poor, in the course of nature, many no doubt will sink into mediocrity, or beneath it. Yet let them start with equal advantages, leaving no discrimination then or thereafter, but such as nature and study shall produce.

---

2. Pennsylvania common school law, 1834

"An Act to Establish a General System of Education by Common Schools," 1834 — ch. 102, *Laws of Pennsylvania of the Session of 1833–1834* (Harrisburg, 1834), pp. 171–174.

The recommendations of the Joint Committee were written into this law providing free schooling for all. The financing scheme was designed to encourage school districts to vote taxes for schools without coercing them. Attendance was not compulsory.

Be it enacted . . . That each . . . district shall contain a competent number of common schools, for the education of every child within the limits thereof, who shall apply, either in person or by his or her parents, guardian or next friend, for admission and instruction.

.   .   .   .   .

There shall be held, at the county court-house in each division, a joint meeting of the county commissioners and one delegate from each board of school directors within said county or school division, in which it shall be decided whether or not a tax for the expenditure of each district be levied; and if a tax be authorized by a majority of the joint meeting, it shall be apportioned among the several districts as county rates and levies are now by law apportioned . . .

The appropriations made for the common schools, by the joint meeting, shall be considered part of the authorized estimates of county expenditures, and shall be levied and collected in the usual manner: *Provided,* That no tax shall be less in amount than double the funds which may be furnished to said county or school division, as hereinafter directed, out of the treasury of this Commonwealth, in aid of common schools organized according to the provisions of this act . . .

When such delegate meeting is organized, the vote on the question of making appropriations for common schools shall be taken by yeas and nays, a record whereof shall be kept by the county commissioners, and if it shall be determined, by a majority of said meeting, that no such appropriation shall be made for any division or county, then all the districts, whose delegates voted in the negative, shall for that year be entitled to no part of the money appropriated by this act, but the whole amount which such division would have been entitled to, had it determined to make such appropriation for common schools by tax, shall go and be appropriated to such district or districts in said division or county, whose delegates voted in the affirmative, in the ratio of the taxable inhabitants of said district . . .

Within twenty days after such joint meeting of the delegates as aforesaid, or at such time as such joint meeting shall fix and determine, if said delegate meeting shall have determined to make an appropriation as aforesaid, the people of the several school districts shall assemble in their respective wards or districts, at the usual place of holding ward or township elections . . . And it shall be in the power of said meeting to decide, by a majority of votes, whether they will raise for the current year a sum in addition to that determined on by the delegate meeting aforesaid, to be applied to the common schools of the said district . . .

---

3. Thaddeus Stevens' speech in the Pennsylvania House of Representatives opposing repeal of the school law, 1835

Hazard's Register of Pennsylvania,
XV (1835), 284–285.

Stevens is often given credit for
saving the bill of 1834.

The amendment which is now proposed as a substitute for the school law of last session, is, in my opinion, of a most hateful and degrading character. It is a re-enactment of the pauper law of 1809. It proposes that the assessors shall take a census, and make a record of the *poor;* This shall be revised, and a new record made by the county commissioners, so that the names of those who have the misfortune to be poor men's children shall be forever preserved, as a distinct class, in the archives of the county! The teacher, too, is to keep in his school a *pauper* book, and register the names and attendance of poor scholars. Thus pointing out and recording their poverty in the midst of their companions. Sir, hereditary distinctions of rank are sufficiently odious; but that which is founded on poverty is infinitely more so. Such a law should be entitled "an act for branding and marking the poor, so that they may be known from the rich and proud." — Many complain of this tax, not so much on account of its amount, as because it is for the benefit of others and not themselves. This is a mistake. It is for *their own* benefit, inasmuch as it perpetuates the government, and ensures the due administration of the laws under which they live, and by which their lives and property are protected. Why do they not urge the same objection against all other taxes? The industrious, thrifty, rich farmer pays a heavy county tax to support criminal courts, build jails, and pay sheriffs and jail keepers, and yet probably he never has and never will have any direct personal use of either. He never gets the worth of his money by being tried for a crime before the court, allowed the privilege of the jail on conviction: or receiving an equivalent from the sheriff or his hangman officers! He cheerfully pays the tax which is necessary to support and punish convicts; but loudly complains of that which goes to prevent his fellow being from becoming criminal, and to obviate the necessity of those humiliating institutions.

This law is often objected to, because its benefits are shared by the children of the profligate spendthrift equally with those of the most industrious and economical habits. It ought to be remembered, that the benefit is bestowed, not upon the erring parents, but the innocent children. Carry out this objection and you punish children for the crimes or misfortunes of their parents. You virtually establish castes and grades founded on no merit of the particular generation, but on the demerits of their ancestors; an aristocracy of the most odious and insolent kind — the aristocracy of wealth and pride.

It is said that its advantages will be unjustly and unequally enjoyed, because the industrious, money-making man keeps his whole family *constantly* employed, and has but little time for them to spend at school; while the idle man has but little employment for his family and they will constantly attend school. I know sir, that there are some men, whose whole souls are so completely absorbed in the accumulation of wealth; and whose avarice so increases with success that they look upon their very children in no other light than as instruments of gain — that they, as well as the ox and the ass within their gates, are valuable only in proportion to their annual earnings. And according to the present system, the children of such men are reduced almost to an intellectual level with their co-laborers of the brute creation. This law will be of vast advantage to the offspring of such misers. If they are compelled to pay their taxes to support schools, their very meanness will induce them to send their children to them to get the worth of their money. Thus it will extract good out of the very penuriousness of the miser . . .

Why, sir, are the colleges and literary institutions of Pennsylvania now, and ever have been, in a languishing, sickly condition? Why, with a fertile soil and genial climate, has she, in proportion to her population, scarcely one-third as many collegiate students, as cold, barren, New England? The answer is obvious — She has no free schools. Until she shall have, you may in vain endow college after college, they will never be filled; or filled only by students from other states. In New England free schools plant the seeds and the desire of knowledge in *every* mind, without regard to the wealth of the parent or the texture of the pupil's garments. When the seed thus universally sewn, happens to fall on fertile soil, it springs up and is fostered by a generous public, until it produces its glorious fruit. — Those who have but scanty means and are pursuing a collegiate education, find it necessary to spend a portion of the year in teaching common schools; thus imparting the knowledge which they acquire, they raise the dignity of the employment to a rank which it should always hold, honorable in proportion to the high qualifications necessary for its discharge. Thus devoting a portion of their time to acquiring the means of subsistence, industrious habits are forced upon them, and their minds and bodies become disciplined to a regularity and energy which is seldom the lot of the rich. It is no uncommon occurrence to see the poor man's son, thus encouraged by wise legislation, far outstrip and bear off the laurels from the less industrious heirs of wealth. Some of the ablest men of the present and past days never could have been educated except for that benevolent system.

New York City organizes its public schools

1. The controversy over the religious character of the public schools in New York City, 1842

Governor William H. Seward's message to the New York state legislature, 1842, in

Charles Lincoln, ed., *State of New York, Messages from the Governors,* III (Albany, 1909), 946–951.

The Public School Society, a private organization with public revenues, had managed the city's schools since 1809 (see above, Part Two, Chap. III, sec. B, The Public School Society of New York). Although nondenominational, it required religious instruction sufficiently Protestant in character to force faithful Roman Catholics to keep their children out of its schools. The legislature removed control of the schools from the Society and vested it in a public board of education.

It was among my earliest duties to bring to the notice of the Legislature the neglected condition of many thousand children, including a very large proportion of those of immigrant parentage in our great commercial city; a misfortune then supposed to result from groundless prejudices and omissions of parental duty. Especially desirous at the same time not to disturb in any manner the public schools which seemed to be efficiently conducted, although so many for whom they were established were unwilling to receive their instructions, I suggested, as I thought, in a spirit not inharmonious with our civil and religious institutions, that if necessary, it might be expedient to bring those so excluded from such privileges into schools rendered especially attractive by the sympathies of those to whom the task of instruction should be confided.[1] It has since been discovered that the magnitude of the evil was not fully known, and that its causes were very imperfectly understood. It will be shown . . . that twenty thousand children in the city of New York, of suitable age, are not at all instructed in any of the public schools, while the whole number in all the residue of the State, not taught in common schools, does not

1. Seward had earlier recommended that children should be taught by teachers of their faith and in the languages that they spoke.

exceed nine thousand. What had been regarded as individual, occasional and accidental prejudices, have proved to be opinions pervading a large mass, including at least one religious communion equally with all others entitled to civil tolerance — opinions cherished through a period of sixteen years, and ripened into a permanent conscientious distrust of the impartiality of the education given in the public schools. This distrust has been rendered still deeper, and more alienating, by a subversion of precious civil rights of those whose consciences are thus offended.

Happily in this, as in other instances, the evil is discovered to have had its origin no deeper than in a departure from the equality of general laws. In our general system of common schools, trustees chosen by taxpaying citizens, levy taxes, build school houses, employ and pay teachers, and govern schools which are subject to visitation by similarly elected inspectors, who certify the qualifications of teachers; and all schools thus constituted participate in just proportion in the public moneys, which are conveyed to them by commissioners also elected by the people. Such schools are found distributed in average spaces of two and a half square miles throughout the inhabited portions of the State, and yet neither popular discontent, nor political strife, nor sectarian discord, has ever disturbed their peaceful instructions or impaired their eminent usefulness. In the public school system of the city, one hundred persons are trustees and inspectors, and by continued consent of the common council, are the dispensers of an annual average sum of $35,000, received from the Common School Fund of the State, and a sum equal to $95,000, derived from an undiscriminating tax upon the real and personal estates of the city. They built school houses chiefly with public funds, they appoint and remove teachers, fix their compensation, and prescribe the moral, intellectual and religious instruction which one-eighth of the rising generation of the State shall be required to receive. Their powers, more effective and far reaching

than are exercised by the municipality of the city, are not derived from the community whose children are educated and whose property is taxed, nor even from the State, which is so great an almoner, and whose welfare is so deeply concerned, but from an incorporated and perpetual association which grants upon pecuniary subscription the privileges even of life membership and yet holds in fee simple the public school edifices, valued at eight hundred thousand dollars. Lest there might be too much responsibility, even to the association, that body can elect only one half of the trustees, and those thus selected appoint their fifty associates.

The philanthropy and patriotism of the present managers of the public schools, and their efficiency in imparting instruction, are cheerfully and gratefully admitted. Nor is it necessary to maintain that agents thus selected will become unfaithful, or that a system that so jealously excludes popular interference, must necessarily be unequal in its operation. It is only insisted that the institution, after a fair and sufficient trial, has failed to gain that broad confidence reposed in the general system of the State, and indispensable to every scheme of universal education. No plan for that purpose can be defended, except on the ground that public instruction is one of the responsibilities of the government. It is, therefore, a manifest legislative duty to correct errors and defects in whatever system is established. In the present case, the failure amounts virtually to an exclusion of all the children thus withheld. I cannot overcome my regret, that every suggestion of amendment encounters so much opposition from those who defend the Public School system of the metropolis, as to show that in their judgment it can admit of no modification, either from tenderness to the consciences or regard to the civil rights of those aggrieved, or even for the reclamation of those for whose culture the State has so munificently provided; as if society must conform itself to the public schools, instead of the public schools adapting themselves to the exigencies of society . . .

I submit, therefore, with entire willingness to approve whatever adequate remedy you may propose, the expediency of restoring to the people of the city of New York — what I am sure the people of no other part of the State would, upon any consideration, relinquish — the education of their children. For this purpose it is only necessary to vest the control of the common schools in a board to be composed of commissioners elected by the people; which board shall apportion the school moneys among all the schools, including those now existing, which shall be organized and conducted in conformity to its general regulations and the laws of the State, in the proportion of the number of pupils instructed. It is not left doubtful that the restoration to the common schools of the city, of this simple and equal feature of the common schools of the State, would remove every complaint, and bring into the seminaries the offspring of want and misfortune, presented by a grand jury, on a recent occasion, as neglected children of both sexes, who are found in hordes upon the wharves and in corners of the streets, surrounded by evil associations, disturbing the public peace, committing petty depredations and going from bad to worse, until their course terminates in high crimes and infamy.

This proposition, to gather the young from the streets and wharves into the nurseries which the State, solicitous for her security against ignorance, has prepared for them, has sometimes been treated as a device to appropriate the school fund to the endowment of seminaries for teaching languages and faiths, thus to perpetuate the prejudices it seeks to remove; sometimes as a scheme for dividing that precious fund among an hundred jarring sects, and thus increasing the religious animosities it strives to heal; sometimes as a plan to subvert the prevailing religion and introduce one repugnant to the consciences of our fellow citizens; while in truth, it simply proposes, by enlightening equally the minds of all, to enable them to detect error wherever it may exist, and to reduce uncongenial masses into one intelligent,

virtuous, harmonious and happy people. Being now relieved from all such misconceptions, it presents the questions whether it is wiser and more humane to educate the offspring of the poor, than to leave them to grow up in ignorance and vice; whether juvenile vice is more easily eradicated by the court of sessions than by common schools; whether parents have a right to be heard concerning the instruction and instructors of their children, and taxpayers in relation to the expenditure of public funds; whether in a republican government, it is necessary to interpose an independent corporation between the people and the schoolmaster, and whether it is wise and just to disfranchise an entire community of all control over public education, rather than suffer a part to be represented in proportion to its numbers and contributions. Since such considerations are now involved, what has hitherto been discussed as a question of benevolence and of universal education, has become one of equal civil rights, religious tolerance, and liberty of conscience. We could bear with us, in our retirement from public service, no recollection more worthy of being cherished through life, than that of having met such a question in the generous and confiding spirit of our institutions, and decided it upon the immutable principles on which they are based.

---

2. The legislature responds by requiring that public schools in New York City be nonsectarian, 1842

"An Act to extend to the city and county of New York the provisions of the general act in relation to common schools," 1842 — ch. 150, *Laws of the State of New York . . .* (Albany, 1842), pp. 187–188.

All children between the ages of four and sixteen, residing in said city and county, shall be entitled to attend any of the common schools therein; and the parents, guardians, or other persons having the custody or care of such children, shall not be liable to any tax, assessment, or imposition for the tuition of any such children, other than is herein before provided.

The schools of the Public School Society, the New-York Orphan Asylum school, the Roman Catholic Orphan Asylum school, the schools of the two Half Orphan Asylums, the school of the Mechanics' School Society, the Harlem school, the Yorkville Public school, the Manhattanville Free school, the Hamilton Free school, the Institution for the Blind, the school connected with the alms house of the said city, and the school of the Association for the Benefit of Colored Orphans, shall be subject to the general jurisdiction of the said commissioners of the respective wards in which any of the said schools now are or hereafter may be located, subject to the direction of the board of education . . .

No school above mentioned, or which shall be organized under this act, in which any religious sectarian doctrine or tenet shall be taught, inculcated, or practised, shall receive any portion of the school moneys to be distributed by this act, as hereinafter provided; and it shall be the duty of the trustees, inspectors, and commissioners of schools in each ward, and of the deputy superintendent of schools, from time to time, and as frequently as need be, to examine and ascertain, and report to the said board of education, whether any religious sectarian doctrine or tenet shall have been taught, inculcated, or practised in any of the schools in their respective wards . . .

With public schools come attendance laws

1. New York truancy law, 1853

"An act to provide for the care and instruction of idle and truant children," 1853 — ch. 185, *Laws of the State of New York . . .* (Albany, 1853), pp. 358–360.

Until the passage of general public school attendance laws, truancy laws requiring a citizen's complaint for enforcement were used. This legislation was an instrument for placing abandoned and neglected children in institutions.

1. If any child, between the ages of five and fourteen years, having sufficient bodily health and mental capacity to attend the public schools, shall be found wandering in the streets or lanes of any city or incorporated village, idle and truant, without any lawful occupation, any justice of the peace, police magistrates, or justices of the district courts, in the City of New-York, on complaint thereof by any citizen on oath, shall cause such child to be brought before him for examination, and shall also cause the parent, guardian, or master of such child, if he or she have any, to be notified to attend such examination. And if, on such examination, the complaint shall be satisfactorily established, such justice shall require the parent, guardian, or master to enter into an engagement in writing, to the corporate authorities of the city or village, that he will restrain such child from so wandering about, will keep him or her on his own premises, or in some lawful occupation, and will cause such child to be sent to some school at least four months in each year, until he or she becomes fourteen years old. And such justice may, in his discretion, require security for the faithful performance of such engagement. If such child has no parent, guardian, or master, or none can be found, or if such parent, guardian, or master refuse or neglect, within a reasonable time, to enter into such engagement, and to give such security, if required, such justice shall, by warrant under his hand, commit such child to such place as shall be provided for his or her reception, as hereinafter directed.

2. If such engagement be habitually or in-

tentionally violated, an action may be brought thereon, by the overseers of the poor, or either of them, of such city or village, in the name of the corporate authorities thereof, and on proof of such habitual or intentional violation, the plaintiff shall recover therein a penalty of not more than fifty dollars with costs. And thereupon, the magistrate or court, before whom such recovery shall be had, shall by warrant commit such child to the place so provided for his or her reception, as aforesaid.

3. The corporate authorities of every city and incorporated village shall provide some suitable place for the reception of every child that may be so committed, and for the employment of such child in some useful occupation, and his or her instruction in the elementary branches of an English education, and for his or her proper support and clothing. Every child so received shall be kept in such place until discharged by the overseers of the poor, or the commissioners of the alms-house of such city or village, and may be bound out as an apprentice by them or either of them, with the consent of any justice of the peace, or any of the aldermen of the city, or any trustee of the incorporated village where he may be, in the same manner, for the same periods, and subject to the same provisions, in all respects, as are . . . children whose parents have become chargeable on any city or town.

endangers life and property among us, and tenants our prisons and penitentiaries? It is because mere moral influence, opposed by parental authority, has been incompetent to effect their recovery; and because previous legislation had shrunk from its high duty in respect to them. The law, which is so omnipotent concerning adults, whose stringent provisions reach our modes of living, — which regulates the steamer, the rail-car, the stage-coach, — the markets which supply our food, — polices our streets, and ordains in what kind of houses we shall not live; which, with almost unlimited power, binds and unbinds the marriage tie, interferes between man and man, husband and wife, brother and sister, — has, until now, failed to extend its protecting care over unprotected and neglected children.

But this anomaly in legislation no longer exists. Our State has the merit of being foremost in this great work of reform, and of thus establishing for itself a lasting memorial of its wisdom and beneficence. By assuming the place of a parent to its helpless children, and undertaking their training, it raises them from the degradation of their previous condition to one of equality with the other pupils of our public schools, while it saves such pupils from the dread of debasement by intercourse with them.

2. Robert M. Hartley, founder and general secretary of the New York Association for Improving the Condition of the Poor, discusses the New York truancy law of 1853

New York Association for Improving the Condition of the Poor, *Annual Report, 1853* (New York, 1853), p. 71.

Why is it that the neglected children of our city have so long furnished the class which

3. The Massachusetts compulsory attendance law of 1852

"An Act concerning the Attendance of Children at School," 1852 — ch. 240, *Acts and Resolves Passed by the General Court of Massachusetts . . . 1852* (Boston, 1852), pp. 170–171.

This mandatory legislation replaced an ineffective law of 1850 which had permitted towns to require attendance. Other states did not adopt compulsory attendance legislation until after the Civil War.

Every person who shall have any child under his control, between the ages of eight and fourteen years, shall send such child to some public school within the town or city in which he resides, during at least twelve weeks, if the public schools within such town or city shall be so long kept, in each and every year during which such child shall be under his control, six weeks of which shall be consecutive.

Every person who shall violate the provisions of the first section of this act shall forfeit, to the use of such town or city, a sum not exceeding twenty dollars, to be recovered by complaint or indictment.

It shall be the duty of the school committee in the several towns or cities to inquire into all cases of violation of the first section of this act, and to ascertain of the persons violating the same, the reasons, if any, for such violation, and they shall report such cases, together with such reasons, if any, to the town or city in their annual report; but they shall not report any cases such as are provided for by the fourth section of this act.

If, upon inquiry by the school committee, it shall appear, or if upon the trial of any complaint or indictment under this act it shall appear, that such child has attended some school, not in the town or city in which he resides, for the time required by this act, or has been otherwise furnished with the means of education for a like period of time, or has already acquired those branches of learning which are taught in common schools, or if it shall appear that his bodily or mental condition has been such as to prevent his attendance at school, or his acquisition of learning for such a period of time, or that the person having the control of such child, is not able, by reason of poverty, to send such child to school, or to furnish him with the means of education, then such person shall be held not to have violated the provisions of this act.

---

4. School truancy in Lawrence, Massachusetts, 1853

Annual Report of the School Committee of the City of Lawrence for the School Year 1853 (Lawrence, 1854), pp. 20–21.

Despite the Massachusetts law of 1852, habitual truancy remained a problem in some industrial towns.

TRUANCY. — This is an alarming evil among us, and demands the serious consideration, not of the Committee alone, but of the whole community. It is not an occasional stolen half day's absence from school that is meant, for the tables given show that to be a very moderate evil, but it is the constant non-attendance at school of a large number of children. From the best available information, I judge that there are now in the city upwards of *two hundred* boys and girls between five and fifteen years old, who keep aloof from school and have no regular reputable employment. They spend their time in prowling about shops, alleys and backyards, pilfering swill, fuel, old-iron, and such more valuable articles as happen to be unprotected. Still, it can not be said that these children receive no education. Every child is in school learning daily lessons and forming habits which the energy and will of after life will find it difficult if not impossible to break. These two hundred little marauders rarely if ever enter a school of literature and science, of wisdom and virtue; but through each live-long day they are taught by example, and their knowledge fixed by practice, in the school of the street, where the violation of every moral precept and duty form the morning and the evening lesson. This is a subject of much importance when viewed in its minor bearings — the losses from theft, the malicious mischief done to public and private property, the occasional disturbance of schools and religious meetings, and the frequent and increasing insults to women and children; but how much graver does it become when we consider the influence of this "dangerous class" on such virtuous children as are unavoidably brought in contact with its members, and are thus introduced to the Primary School of vice, and when we remember that these uncared for youth will soon be parents and citizens, training up a new generation after their own ideas and exerting an equal power with the most exemplary in determining the character of our institutions . . . It would surely seem that our community in which $85,000 is now expending on a prison for adult criminals, might be led from mere considerations of economy to join in obtaining and enforcing some sufficient enactment for the suppression of this great promoter of crime and disorder.

The cause of popular education in the South

1. An open letter addressed to the North Carolina legislature in opposition to public schools, 1829

Raleigh Register, Nov. 9, 1829, in Charles L. Coon, ed., *The Beginnings of Public Education in North Carolina* (Raleigh, 1908), I, 432–433.

You will probably be asked, Gentlemen, to render some little assistance to the University of our State. But I hope you will strenuously refuse to do this . . . It is respectfully submitted . . . whether our good old-field schools are not abundantly sufficient for all our necessities. Our fathers and mothers jogged along uncomplainingly without colleges; and long experience proves them to be very expensive things. The University has already cost the people not a little; and the good it has accomplished thus far is extremely doubtful; if I might not rather allege it to have been productive of mischief. College learned persons

give themselves great airs, are proud, and the fewer of them we have amongst us the better. I have long been of the opinion . . . that establishments of this kind are aristocratical in their nature, and evidently opposed to the plain, simple, honest matter-of-fact republicanism, which ought to flourish among us. The branches of learning cultivated in them are, for the most part, of a lofty arrogant and useless sort. Who wants Latin and Greek and abstruse mathematics in these times and in a country like this? Might we not as well patronize alchymy, astrology, heraldry and the black art? . . . It is possible, but not very likely I confess, that you may be solicited to take some steps with regard to the establishment among us of common schools. Should so ridiculous a measure be propounded to you, you will unquestionably, for your own interest, as well as that of your constituents, treat it with the same contemptuous neglect which it has ever met with heretofore. Common schools indeed! Money is very scarce, and the times are unusually hard. Why was such a matter never broached in better and more prosperous days? Gentlemen, it appears to me that schools are sufficiently plenty, and that the people have no desire they should be increased. Those now in operation are not all filled, and it is very doubtful if they are productive of much real benefit. Would it not redound as much to the advantage of young persons, and to the honour of the State, if they should pass their days in the cotton patch, or at the plow, or in the cornfield, instead of being mewed up in a school house, where they are earning nothing? Such an ado as is made in these times about education, surely was never heard of before. Gentlemen, I hope you do not conceive it at all necessary, that *everybody* should be able to read, write and cipher. If one is to keep a store or a school, or to be a lawyer or physician, such branches may, *perhaps,* be taught him; though I do not look upon them as by any means indispensable: but if he is to be a plain farmer, or a mechanic, they are of no manner of use, but rather a detriment. There need no arguments to make clear so self-evident a proposition. Should schools be established by law, in all parts of the State, as at the North, our taxes must be considerably increased, possibly to the amount of one per cent. and six pence on a poll; and I will ask any prudent, sane, saving man if he desires his taxes to be higher?

You will doubtless be told that our State is far behind her sisters in things of this sort, — and what does this prove? Merely, that other states are before us; which is their affair, and not ours. We are able to govern ourselves without reference to other members of the confederation; and thus are we perfectly independent. We shall always have reason enough to crow over them, while we have power to say, as I hope we may ever have, that our taxes are lighter than theirs.

2. Virginia permissive school district law, 1829

"An Act to amend the several acts concerning the Literary Fund," 1829 — ch. 14, *Acts Passed at a General Assembly of . . . Virginia* (Richmond, 1829), pp. 13–14.

Be it enacted . . . That whenever the school Commissioners of any county shall believe that the funds appropriated to the education of the poor children of their county, can be employed to advantage in the manner hereinafter designated, it shall be lawful for them to cause their county to be divided into convenient districts . . .

Whenever the inhabitants of any one of the said districts shall, by voluntary contribution, have raised three-fifths of the amount necessary to build, either in the centre, or such other part of their district as may be agreed on with the School Commissioners of their county, a good and sufficient school-house of wood, stone or brick, it shall and may be lawful for

the said School Commissioners to appropriate, out of the annual quota of their county, the remaining two-fifths of the amount requisite for said buildings . . .

It shall moreover be lawful for the School Commissioners of any county to appropriate out of the annual quota of their county, a sum not exceeding one hundred dollars, for the employment of a good and sufficient teacher for any school-house vested in the President and Directors of the Literary Fund, in the manner prescribed in the foregoing section, or for any similar school-house erected by the inhabitants of any district in the centre, or such other part of their district as may be agreed on with the said School Commissioners: provided the inhabitants of said district shall raise by voluntary contribution, an equal or greater sum for the same purpose, and shall select no teacher that shall not have been examined and accepted by such person or persons as the School Commissioners may have appointed for that purpose. *And provided also,* That the said school shall be constituted into a free school for the instruction, without fee or reward, of every free white child within said district . . .

3. A southerner's criticism of permissive legislation on schools and pauper education, 1835

Lucian Minor, "An Address on Education, as Connected With the Permanence of our Republican Institution," *Southern Literary Messenger,* II (1835), 19–20.

Minor (1802–1858) was a Virginia lawyer, man of letters, temperance reformer, and later professor of law at the College of William and Mary.

A great and obvious difference between our primary school system, and the *common*-school systems of the northern states, is, that *they* take in ALL children: while we aim to instruct only the children of the *poor; literary paupers.* We thus at once create two causes of failure: first, *the slight value which men set upon what costs them nothing . . .* second, *the mortification to pride* (an honest though mistaken pride) in being singled out as an object of charity. As if these fatal errors had not sufficiently ensured the impotence of the scheme, the schools themselves are the least efficient that could be devised. Instead of teachers retained expressly for the purpose, — selected, after strict examination into their capacities, and vigilantly superintended afterwards, by competent judges — the poor children are *entered* by the neighboring commissioner (often himself entirely unqualified either to teach or to direct teaching) in the private school which chance, or the teacher's unfitness for any other employment, combined always with cheapness of price, may have already established nearest at hand. There, the little *protégé* of the commonwealth is thrown amongst pupils, whose parents pay for them and give some heed to their progress; and having no friend to see that he is properly instructed — mortified by the humiliating name of *poor scholar* — neglected by the teacher — and not rigorously urged to school by anyone — he learns nothing, slackens his attendance, and soon quits the temple of science in rooted disgust.

Observe now, I pray you, how precisely the results agree with what might have been foretold, of such a system. In 1833, nearly 33,000 *poor children* (literary paupers) were found in 100 counties of Virginia; of whom but 17,081 *attended school at all: and these* 17,081 *attended on an average, but* SIXTY-FIVE DAYS OF THE YEAR, EACH! The average of learning acquired by each, during those 65 days, would be a curious subject of contemplation: but I know of no arithmetical rule, by which it could be ascertained. That it bears a much less proportion to the *reasonable* attainments of a full scholastic year, than 65 bears to the number of days in that year, there can be no doubt.

· · · · ·

Judging by the number met with in *business* transactions, who cannot write their names or read, and considering how many there are whose poverty or sex debars them from such transactions, and lessens their chances of scholarship; we should scarcely exceed the truth, in estimating the *white adults of Virginia who cannot read or write, at twenty or thirty thousand.*

· · · · ·

Sagacious men have not been wanting among us, to see the radical defects of our primary school system: and in 1829, the late Mr. Fitzhugh of Fairfax, stimulated the Legislature to a feeble effort towards correcting them, by *empowering* the school commissioners of any county to lay it off into districts of not less than three nor more than seven miles square; and to pay, out of the public fund, *two-fifths* of the sum requisite for building a school house, and half a teacher's salary, for any one of those districts, whenever its inhabitants, by *voluntary subscription,* should raise the residue necessary for these purposes: and the schools thus established were to be open, gratuitously, alike to rich and poor. But the *permissive* phraseology of this statute completely neutralized its effect. It might have been foreseen, and it *was* foreseen, that *empowering* the commissioners to act, and leaving the rest to voluntary contributions, would be unavailing, where the workings of the school system had so long been regarded with apathy. The statute has been acted upon, so far as I have learned, in but *three* counties of the State; remaining, as to the other 107, a dead letter. I have the strongest warrant — that of *actual experiment,* in New York and in Massachusetts — for saying, that had the law *commanded* the commissioners to lay off districts in all counties where the census shewed a sufficiently dense white population; and had it then organized in the districts some local authorities, whose *duty* it should be to levy the needful amount upon their people; — I should have been saved the ungracious task of reproaching my county with her want of parental care; and Virginia would now be striding onward, speedily to recover the ground she has lost in the career of true greatness.

---

4. A South Carolinian argues against public schools and for education in accordance with social position, 1852

James Simmons, "Address delivered at the opening of the Free Schools in Charleston, June 26, 1852," *Southern Quarterly Review,* VI (1852), 461, 466–470.

Whenever a child is to be educated, it should be ascertained what is to be his probable destiny. We do not mean that his career is to be definitely marked out for him, that his profession is to be selected in advance; such a procedure would be unwise, if it were not impracticable. But his social position being ascertained, and the means provided for his maintenance being known, he should be educated in accordance with the condition in which he is expected to commence his career.

Every child should be taught to read, to write, and to cipher. These elements form the key to all knowledge, and should be placed within reach of all. They are as necessary to the moral and intellectual man, as food and raiment are to his body. But as the quality of the food and raiment of each man depends upon his means and his condition, so the same circumstances should determine whether the intellectual food and raiment should exceed that necessary modicum which the spirit of the age seems to require.

. . . . .

The only practicable means of improving our schools, so as to place a higher grade of education within reach of the very poor, must be found, either in a compulsory provision on the part of the State, which by directly taxing all for the support of common schools, should compel all persons of moderate fortunes to educate their children at them; or by a voluntary union of the primary schools supported by the State, with those which may be established by private enterprize. This latter plan is, we are informed, generally adopted in our upper districts. Whenever such a voluntary association of private with public means is made, we are content to rely implicitly on the wisdom which plans the arrangement. But the case is widely different when it is presented as a compulsory measure. The State has no more authority to levy a tax for a given school, than for a given church. And when men of moderate fortunes are compelled, by the operation of law, to send their children to the State school, or to none, it becomes absolute tyranny.

Many persons have well grounded objections to sending their children to schools which are open to all indiscriminately. And though it is true that wealth alone can not insure good morals, yet it has an undoubted right to seek such advantages, without being exposed to the risk of incurring insidious imputations.

. . . . .

There is as much cant on the subject of education as on that of religion. The politician and the preacher alike call for the education of the people. Education is not only the palladium of our liberties, but the guide which is to lead us to eternal truth. We believe in neither of these dogmas. They are both repugnant to fact and to common sense. If we lived in Utopia, and our numbers were limited, — if we were not required to struggle, not only for the means of living, but for life itself, — if the circumstances of every man were such that his necessary labours were only so great as to brace his nerves and his muscles for enjoyment during his hours of relaxation, — then would universal education be, not a sweetener of life only, but a necessity. It would be essential to the perfect development of Utopian life. But our world is one of fact. Life is a sober reality. In spite of the falsehoods which constitutions proclaim to the contrary, the privileged few must govern. To the mass of mankind the character of the government is a matter of practical indifference.

. . . . .

Men whose lives are spent in humble toil, have little time for reflection. They are as susceptible to evil impressions as to good. Education exposes them to the danger of attacks from the demagogue, as well as to the wholesome admonitions of the patriotic. As we go northward in our country, we find every phase of political doctrine. The spirit of agrarianism is rife. In New-York the landlord has had to resort to military force to collect his rents. Throughout the whole country, from the Hudson to the Bay of Fundy, a settled determination exists to abolish slavery at the South, though it is demonstrated that Northern prosperity is dependent upon Southern slavery. Is this fanaticism? There is no doubt that the people entertain an honest conviction of the sinfulness of slavery, inspired first by the preachings of enthusiasts, and afterwards fostered by aspirants after political power, who have taken advantage of this honesty of purpose in the masses to promote their own views. The diffusion of education in New-England is likely to effect a dissolution of the Union; and no one can venture to predict, under such a result, the endless horrors which threaten the future of that imperfectly educated, but self-sufficient and misguided people.

Education effects no change in the nature of man. It is but an instrument — to the good, of good, to the bad it is only a new element of evil. There is no necessary connection between learning and freedom. In ancient times, slaves were educated for the purpose of increasing their value, and we have never heard that their value has, in modern times, been in the slightest degree diminished by the amount of their instruction. Liberty is an instinct, not a principle. There is no more freedom enjoyed in Europe now, than in the time of Alfred. The races that were free then, continue so.

5. The necessity of educating the white people of the South, 1854

George Fitzhugh, *Sociology for the South, or the Failure of Free Society* (Richmond, 1854), pp. 144–148.

A champion of the slave system, George Fitzhugh (1806–1881) won renown in the South by attacking the free institutions of the North. So far as education was concerned, however, he argued that the southern states should emulate their northern counterparts.

The abolitionists taunt us with the ignorance of our poor white citizens. This is a stigma on the South that should be wiped out. Half of the people of the South, or nearly so, are blacks. We have only to educate the other half. At the North, they educate all. Our Southern free-trade philosophy, our favorite maxim, "every man for himself," has been the cause of the neglect of popular education. The civilized world differ from us and censure us. They say it is the first duty of government to provide for the education of all its citizens. Despotic Prussia compels parents to send their children to schools supported at public expense. All are educated and well educated. As our's is a government of the people, no where is education so necessary. The poor, too, ask no charity, when they demand universal education. They constitute our militia and our police. They protect men in possession of property, as in other countries; and do much more, they secure men in possession of a kind of property which they could not hold a day but for the supervision and protection of the poor. This very property has rendered the South merely agricultural, made population too sparse for neighborhood schools, prevented variety of pursuits, and thus cut the poor off as well from the means of living, as from the means of education.

Universal suffrage will soon attempt to remedy these evils. But rashness and precipitancy may occasion failure and bring about despondency. We are not yet prepared to educate all. Free schools should at once be established in all neighborhoods where a sufficient number of scholars can be collected in one school. Parents should be compelled to send their children to school. The obligation on the part of government, to educate the people, carries with it the indubitable right to employ all the means necessary to attain that end. But the duty of government does not end with educating the people. As far as is practicable, it should open to them avenues of employment in which they may use what they have learned. The system of internal improvements now carried on in the South, will directly and indirectly, quite suffice to attain this end, so far as government can aid properly in such an object. Government may do too much for the people, or it may do too little. We have committed the latter error.

The mail and the newspaper-press might be employed, as cheap and efficient agents, in teaching the masses. No family in the Union is so dull, stupid and indifferent, as not to be curious about the news of the day. Contemporaneous history is the most interesting and important part of history. That is to be had alone from newspapers. But newspapers contain on all subjects the most recent discoveries, and the most valuable information.

A large weekly newspaper might be furnished to every poor family in the State, at less than a dollar a family. If there were not a teacher within fifty miles, some member of each family would learn to read, first to get at the neighborhood news and scandals, the deaths, and marriages, and murders. Gradually they would understand and become interested in the proceedings of our government, and the news from foreign countries. The meanest newspaper in the country is worth all the libraries in Christendom. It is desirable to know what the ancients did, but it is necessary to know what our neighbors and fellow country-men are doing.

Our system of improvements, manufactures, the mechanic arts, the building up of our cities, commerce, and education should go hand in hand. We ought not to attempt too much at once. 'Tis time we were attempting something. We ought, like the Athenians, to be the best educated people in the world. When we employ all our whites in the mechanic arts, in commerce, in professions, &c., and confine the negroes to farm-work, and coarse mechanical operations, we shall be in a fair way to attain this result. The abolition movement is a harmless humbug, confined to a handful of fanatics, but the feeling of antipathy to negroes, the hatred of race, and the disposition to expel them from the country is daily increasing, North and South. Two causes are in active operation to fan and increase this hostility to the negro race. The one, the neglect to educate and provide means of employment for the poor whites in the South, who are thereby led to believe that the existence of negroes amongst us is ruin to them. The other, the theory of the Types of Mankind, which cuts off the negro from human brotherhood, and justifies the brutal and the miserly in treating him as a vicious brute. Educate all Southern whites, employ them, not as cooks, lacqueys, ploughmen, and menials, but as independent freemen should be employed, and let negroes be strictly tied down to such callings as are unbecoming white men, and peace would be established between blacks and whites. The whites would find themselves elevated by the existence of negroes amongst us. Like the Roman citizens, the Southern white man would become a noble and a privileged character, and he would then like negroes and slavery, because his high position would be due to them. Poor people can see things as well as rich people. We can't hide the facts from them. It is always better openly, honestly, and fearlessly to meet danger, than to fly from or avoid it. The last words we will utter on this subject are, — The path of safety is the path of duty! Educate the people, no matter what it may cost!

6. The education of young southerners at home, 1856

Resolutions of a southern commercial convention at Richmond, *De Bow's Review,* XXI (1856), 552–553.

A succession of regional conventions in the South attempted to promote southern influence and self-sufficiency as the feeling over sectional issues in politics intensified.

VI. EDUCATION. — With institutions of learning like those that have been long established and now flourish in the States of Maryland, Virginia, North and South Carolina, Georgia, Alabama, and Mississippi, must the youth of the South be longer doomed to exile in uncongenial climes, where the most sacred associations of their homes are denounced as those of the savage and the barbarian, the heritage of guilt and crime, and where grave and Reverend professors and Clergymen leave the pulpit and the desk to sign and circulate incendiary political addresses, substituting rifles for Euclid or the Bible, and finding in Kansas, fields more classic and consecrated than were ever before furnished to them by Attica or Palestine. Shall not our State legislatures, acting in concert, provide for an increased number of home institutions, extending at the same time the sphere of those already existing? With a larger proportion of thoroughly educated men than is to be found beyond our limits will we build up and encourage home literature and foster and encourage home publication houses? The time for action is *now.* It will be well, at least, to look to our school-books. Can the making of these be entrusted so exclusively to those, who by instilling an occasional heresy, dangerous to our repose, imagine that they serve at the same time God and mammon — their consciences and their pockets? The State Legislatures at the South alone are competent to heal this mischief. Property will submit to any amount of taxation for such a purpose. A system can and ought to be matured at the South by which the most ample encouragement shall be given to its educational system and to its press. Withdraw at once the contributions which

are returned too often to us now in contumely and insult.

Fellow-citizens of the South, we may not realize at once all of these hopes, but let us fondly cherish them, believing them to be attainable at no distant day, if we shall act in concert, moving in the same direction, under the dictates of a common interest — necessity and patriotism.

The effects of slavery on literacy, culture, and education in the South

Hinton R. Helper, *The Impending Crisis of the South* (New York, 1857), pp. 404–408.

Although a native of North Carolina, Hinton R. Helper (1829–1909) was violently opposed to slavery. The "peculiar institution" of the South, he believed, had reared up an aristocracy that oppressed common white men and retarded the region's progress. Nowhere was the gap between North and South so great as in the educational accomplishments of the two sections. His denunciation of slavery had an important effect on the politics of the sectional crisis; in 1859 a fund was raised by Republicans to print and distribute one hundred thousand copies of this publication.

WHAT HAS PRODUCED THIS LITERARY PAUPERISM OF THE SOUTH? One single word, most pregnant in its terrible meanings, answers the question. That word is — SLAVERY! But we have been so long accustomed to the ugly thing itself, and have become so familiar with its no less ugly fruits, that the common mind fails to apprehend the connection between the one, as cause, and the other as effect; and it therefore becomes necessary to give a more detailed answer to our interrogatory.

. . . The conditions requisite to a flourish-

ing literature are wanting at the South. These
are —

I. Readers. The people of the South are not
a reading people. Many of the adult population
never learned to read; still more, do not care
to read. We have been impressed, during a
temporary sojourn in the North, with the difference between the middle and laboring classes
in the Free States, and the same classes in the
Slave States, in this respect. Passing along the
great routes of travel in the former, or taking
our seat in the comfortable cars that pass up
and down the avenues of our great commercial
metropolis, we have not failed to contrast the
employment of our fellow-passengers with that
which occupies the attention of the corresponding classes on our various Southern routes of
travel. In the one case, a large proportion of
the passengers seem intent upon mastering the
contents of the newspaper, or some recently
published book. The merchant, the mechanic,
the artizan, the professional man, and even the
common laborer, going to or returning from
their daily avocations, are busy with their morning or evening paper, or engaged in an intelligent discussion of some topic of public interest.
This is their leisure hour, and it is given to the
acquisition of such information as may be of
immediate or ultimate use, or to the cultivation
of a taste for elegant literature. In the other
case, newspapers and books seem generally
ignored, and noisy discussions of village and
State politics, the tobacco and cotton crops,
filibusterism in Cuba, Nicaragua, or Sonora,
the price of negroes generally, and especially
of "fine-looking wenches," the beauties of
lynch-law, the delights of horse-racing, the excitement of street fights with bowie-knives and
revolvers, the "manifest destiny" theory that
justifies the stealing of all territory contiguous
to our own, and kindred topics, constitute the
warp and woof of conversation. All this is on
a level with the general intelligence of the Slave
States. It is true, these States have their educated men, — the majority of whom owe their
literary culture to the colleges of the North. Not
that there are no Southern colleges — for there

are institutions, so called, in a majority of the
Slave States. — Some of them, too, are not
deficient in the appointments requisite to our
higher educational institutions; but as a general
thing, Southern colleges are colleges only in
name, and will scarcely take rank with a third-
rate Northern academy, while our academies,
with a few exceptions, are immeasurably inferior to the public schools of New-York, Philadelphia, and Boston. The truth is, there is a
vast inert mass of stupidity and ignorance, too
dense for individual effort to enlighten or remove, in all communities cursed with the institution of slavery. Disguise the unwelcome
truth as we may, slavery is the parent of ignorance, and ignorance begets a whole brood
of follies and of vices, and every one of these
is inevitably hostile to literary culture. The
masses, if they think of literature at all, think
of it only as a costly luxury, to be monopolized
by the few.

The proportion of white adults over twenty
years of age, in each State, who cannot read
and write, to the *whole* white population, is as
follows:

Connecticut,	1 to every 568
Vermont,	1 to every 473
N. Hampshire,	1 to every 310
Massachusetts,	1 to every 166
Maine,	1 to every 108
Michigan,	1 to every 97
Rhode Island,	1 to every 67
New Jersey,	1 to every 58
New York,	1 to every 56
Pennsylvania,	1 to every 50
Ohio,	1 to every 43
Indiana,	1 to every 18
Illinois,	1 to every 17
Louisiana,	1 to every 38½
Maryland,	1 to every 27
Mississippi,	1 to every 20
Delaware,	1 to every 18
South Carolina,	1 to every 17
Missouri,	1 to every 16
Alabama,	1 to every 15
Kentucky,	1 to every 13½

Georgia,	1 to every 13
Virginia,	1 to every 12½
Arkansas,	1 to every 11½
Tennessee,	1 to every 11
North Carolina,	1 to every 7

In this table, Illinois and Indiana are the only Free States which, in point of education, are surpassed by any of the Slave States; and this disgraceful fact is owing, principally, to the influx of foreigners, and to immigrants from the Slave States. New-York, Rhode Island, and Pennsylvania have also a large foreign element in their population, that swells very considerably this percentage of ignorance. For instance, New-York shows, by the last census, a population of 98,722 who cannot read and write, and of this number, 68,052 are foreigners; Rhode Island, 3,607, of whom 2,359 are foreigners; Pennsylvania, 76,272, of whom 24,989 are foreigners. On the other hand, the ignorance of the Slave States is principally *native* ignorance, but comparatively few emigrants from Europe seeking a home upon a soil cursed with "the peculiar institution." North Carolina has a foreign population of only 340, South Carolina only 104, Arkansas only 27, Tennessee only 505, and Virginia only 1,137, who cannot read and write; while the aggregate of *native*

ignorance in these five States (exclusive of the *slaves,* who are debarred all education by *law*) is 278,948! No longer ago than 1837, Governor Clarke, of Kentucky, in his message to the Legislature of that State, declared that "by the computation of those most familiar with the subject, *one-third of the adult population of the State are unable to write their names*"; and Governor Campbell, of Virginia, reported to the Legislature, that "from the returns of ninety-eight clerks, it appeared that of 4,614 applications for marriage licenses in 1837, no less than 1,047 were made by men unable to write."

In the Slave States the proportion of free white children between the ages of five and twenty, who are found at any school or college, is not quite *one-fifth* of the whole; in the Free States, the proportion is more than *three-fifths*.

We could fill our pages with facts like these to an almost indefinite extent, but it cannot be necessary. No truth is more demonstrable, nay, no truth has been more abundantly demonstrated than this: that Slavery is hostile to general education; its strength, its very life, is in the ignorance and stolidity of the masses; it naturally and necessarily represses general literary culture.

B. EDUCATIONAL ISSUES IN SCHOOL AND COLLEGE

The status and recruitment of teachers

1. The ideal teacher

William A. Alcott, *A Word to Teachers; or, Two Days in a Primary School* (Boston, 1833), pp. 30–32.

Alcott (1798–1859), cousin of Bronson Alcott, was a teacher, reformer of popular education, and prolific author of works on education and health. The school he visited and here described was the First Public School in Hartford, Connecticut.

When the school bell commenced ringing for noon, the teacher had just begun to gratify a request from some of her pupils that she would read stories to them from the Juvenile Rambler. She was reading the adventures of Thomas Traveller; I think his journey from New York to Gibraltar. There was such a profound silence in the room, that you might have heard a pin fall. When the bell begun to ring she asked the pupils if she should not stop. "No; No;" they all said; "we wish you would go on with the story." "But do you not wish to go home to dinner?" said the teacher. "Yes, ma'am;" they replied: "But we want to hear the story first."

This reminds me of what I have been assured by a lady in the vicinity; that her little daughter, who attends here, seems to be happy nowhere else but with her teacher, and of a report which I have heard of another of the pupils, who is said in some instances to have solicited her parents to let her go to school without her breakfast. Indeed, I have actually known one school where the teacher made every thing so agreeable that the pupils used to run away from home without their meals; so much more fond were they of the school room than of any other place. Indeed I have no more confidence in the notion that some children naturally hate books and school, than I should have in the opinion that some, by nature, hate food. It is a disgust which is acquired; and no wonder.

Although the pupils were anxious to hear the whole of what the "traveller" had to say, the teacher did not think it proper to gratify them, but left off about the middle of the story, and prepared to dismiss them.

As the intermission is usually two hours in length, and as a large proportion of the scholars have but a little way to walk, they usually go to their homes as soon as they are dismissed, especially if the weather is not uncommonly severe or stormy . . . To those who go home great attention is paid by both the teacher to see that their clothing is properly put on, and to be sure that they leave nothing which they intended to take along with them. In short, the teachers take, so far as possible, the place

of parents; and not merely *instruct,* but *educate,* — and *make happy.*

2. A deputy superintendent of schools in a rural area of New York observes and ranks the teachers of his county, 1843

Report of A. Burgess, deputy superintendent for Allegheny county, in New York State, Department of Public Instruction, *Annual Report of the Superintendent of Common Schools . . . 1843* (Albany, 1843), pp. 77–80.

I have found them from first rate down to the lowest grade, whose services do more hurt than good, who communicate more error than truth, and who would establish more bad habits in the practice of scholars in a single term of four months than a thorough and competent instructor would break up in eight. I have found ladies and gentlemen engaged in the responsible business of directing the youthful mind in our common schools, whose only ambition seemed to be to shine in their profession, and benefit their juvenile charge all in their power; who would scorn alike the sneers of those engaged in private schools, and the contempt of those who consider the district school fit only for the instruction of the very lowest grade of community, whose *breath* is *contagion,* and whose *touch* is immediate *moral death.* The class of teachers to which I now refer, have established themselves in the estimation of the friends of popular education, by a course of well doing, and a strict attention to all the means within their reach intended to elevate the condition and character of district schools. They are systematic and thorough in every department of their labors . . . I believe that about one-sixth of all the teachers whose schools I have visited will rank in the first class, and their labors and persevering efforts do honor to the profession.

The next class I shall mention is more numerous than the former, and who appear to enter upon the business of teaching with high expectations and flattering prospects. For a time they go on with all that ardor and ambition peculiar to the character of the young, infusing all the energy of soul they possess into the feelings of their scholars, and drawing into requisition every power within their reach for the attainment of their high object. After pursuing this course for a time, they grow tired of the labor it imposes, and begin to relax in their exertions to do all in their power to elevate the standard of district schools; they begin to descend from the elevation they have gained, lose their influence over their pupils, their respect and subordination; their systematic course is in some measure abandoned; they have not that decision of purpose with which they set out; they become peevish and fretful, easily thrown out of a train of good humor, and are exposed to the mercy of their scholars, who, when they perceive they can make them appear ridiculous, will seek every pretext to harrass and irritate their feelings. This class, I am sorry to say, are much more numerous than the one before mentioned, and can be denominated no higher than second rate teachers.

A third class are those who enter upon the business of teaching for the purpose of raising a sum of money in a given time, which they could not do in any other business in which they could find employment. They enter not upon the discharge of these vast responsibilities because they love to teach, or because they have any desire to see the rising generation growing up with that knowledge so necessary to fit them for the transaction of business, and for usefulness in the community in which they may be placed, but for the pecuniary benefit derived from the employment. They have no desire so to manage their schools as to gain employment in that district again, for they wish to form new acquaintances, and therefore prefer to stay but one term in a place. It matters not with them whether they communicate ideas to those placed under their charge or not; whether their pupils have an understanding of what they are required to commit to memory, or whether they repeat their lessons parrot-like, without knowing what they mean . . .

Another, and the last class of teachers I will mention, are those who, to gain a notoriety, which is beyond their reach by any other means, thrust themselves upon the notice of the public to be employed in giving a proper turn to the youthful mind. They are such as have no definite ideas of the business they are about to engage in, or of those things they are required to teach. They enter their schools without seeing any thing clearly. Their minds are confused, and they know not what to do, how to act, or what to expect. They know not where to begin, or how to proceed after having begun. If called upon to explain the principle upon which any rule in arithmetic is founded, they are utterly at a loss to know what is meant by the question. It has never once entered their heads that the rules of arithmetic are founded upon any principles whatever. In the examination of a teacher, whose school I visited last winter, I asked him why he carried one for every ten in addition of whole numbers. "Because figures *decrease* from the right hand to the left in a tenfold proportion." "But, sir, you *cannot* mean '*decrease*' can you?" *Sartin,* I mean decrease, and that is what the *rule says;* for I have larnt it by heart." He could recite as he had learned them the tables of weights and measures in arithmetic; but could not answer one question in ten when asked promiscuously. I desired him to tell me what part of speech is "*wise*" in the following example: "Into the will and arbitration *wise* of the Supreme." After looking at it for some time with a vacant stare, he replied, "I don't git hold of the meanin of the author in that place, and don't know what part of speech *wise* is. I never studied grammar only about tu weeks, and I don't pretend to understand it perfectly; but I reckoned how I understood it well enough to keep the school in this dee-strick." I asked him to spell *potato,* and tell me which syllable had the full or primary accent? He spelled the word, and said "the full accent is on the last syllable." I then pronounced the word with the accent agreeably to his notion, and asked him if it was right? He thought not. He then said "it is the first;" but after making a practical application of accent to the first syllable, he perceived he was mistaken, and said "it is the second." I asked him which is the most northeastern State? He did "not know sartin, but he bleaved it was Ohio or Indiana." He was a most wretched reader and worse speller . . . This is an extreme case of the class of teachers I am now describing. How do many of them manage the affairs of their schools? After spending, perhaps, fifteen or twenty minutes in trying to produce silence in the school, a class is called upon to read. "Toe that crack," says the teacher to the children who are called upon to read. But instead of "toeing the crack," some face to the north, some to the south, some to the east, and some to the west. "Now stand up straight and speak up loud and distinct." The teacher, or rather the apology for one, takes a book to see if any mistakes are made by any in the class. Whilst the one at the head is reading, a boy presents his writing book for a copy. He at once lays aside the reading book and begins to write the copy. Whilst doing this, another bawls out, "will you mend my pen." Willing to accommodate all, he leaves the copy and takes the pen; and before he finishes that, another "wants a sum done;" another, "can't find a name on the map." All these calls are attended to forthwith by the teacher, and all of them left unfinished, to attend to something else. Thus, perhaps, from twenty to forty minutes have been spent, the class has become tired of reading, and some one calls out, "haint we read fur enough;" "I don't know," says the teacher, "how fur have you read?" "Six chapters;" "Wal, you have read fur enough, you needent read no furder, go long to your seats and *set* still, and tend to your studies."

3. The Massachusetts Board of Education recommends the establishment of state normal schools, 1838

"First Annual Report of the Board of Education, 1838," in Mary P. Mann, *Life and Works of Horace Mann* (Boston, 1891), II, 376–378.

Improvement and specialization in teacher training were major concerns of common school reformers. A gift of $10,000 from Edmund Dwight in 1838, matched by the legislature with public funds, enabled the Commonwealth to found three normal schools. The first opened at Lexington the following year.

The subject of the education of teachers has been more than once brought before the Legislature, and is of the very highest importance in connection with the improvement of our schools. That there are all degrees of skill and success on the part of teachers, is matter of too familiar observation to need repetition; and that these must depend, in no small degree, on the experience of the teacher, and in his formation under a good discipline and method of instruction in early life, may be admitted without derogating, in any measure, from the importance of natural gifts and aptitude, in fitting men for this as for the other duties of society. Nor can it be deemed unsafe to insist that, while occupations requiring a very humble degree of intellectual effort and attainment demand a long-continued training, it cannot be that the arduous and manifold duties of the instructor of youth should be as well performed without as with a specific preparation for them. In fact, it must be admitted, as the voice of reason and experience, that institutions for the formation of teachers must be established among us, before the all-important work of forming the minds of our children can be performed in the best possible manner, and with the greatest attainable success.

No one who has been the witness of the ease and effect with which instruction is imparted by one teacher, and the tedious pains-taking and unsatisfactory progress which mark the labors of another of equal ability and knowledge, and operating on materials equally good, can entertain a doubt that there is a mastery in teaching as in every other art. Nor is it less obvious that, within reasonable limits, this skill and this mastery may themselves be made the subjects of instruction, and be communicated to others.

We are not left to the deductions of reason on this subject. In those foreign countries, where the greatest attention has been paid to the work of education, schools for teachers have formed an important feature in their systems, and with the happiest result. The art of imparting instruction has been found, like every other art, to improve by cultivation in institutions established for that specific object. New importance has been attached to the calling of the instructor by public opinion, from the circumstance that his vocation has been deemed one requiring systematic preparation and culture. Whatever tends to degrade the profession of the teacher, in his own mind or that of the public, of course impairs his usefulness; and this result must follow from regarding instruction as a business which in itself requires no previous training.

The duties which devolve upon the teachers even of our Common Schools, particularly when attended by large numbers of both sexes, and of advanced years for learners (as is often the case), are various, and difficult of performance. For their faithful execution, no degree of talent and qualification is too great; and when we reflect that in the nature of things only a moderate portion of both can, in ordinary cases, be expected, for the slender compensation afforded the teacher, we gain a new view of the necessity of bringing to his duties the advantage of previous training in the best mode of discharging them.

A very considerable part of the benefit, which those who attend our schools might derive from them, is unquestionably lost for want of mere skill in the business of instruction, on the part of the teacher. This falls with especial hardship on that part of our youthful population, who are able to enjoy, but for a small portion of the year, the advantage of the schools. For them it is of peculiar importance, that, from the moment of entering the school, every hour should be employed to the greatest advantage, and every facility in imparting knowledge, and every means of awakening and guiding the mind, be put into instant operation: and where this is done, two months of schooling would be as valuable as a year passed under a teacher destitute of experience and skill. The Board cannot but express the sanguine hope, that the time is not far distant, when the resources of public or private liberality will be applied in Massachusetts for the foundation of an institution for the formation of teachers, in which the present existing defect will be amply supplied.

---

4. The damaging effects of frequent replacement of teachers in Connecticut, 1839

Connecticut, *First Annual Report of the Board of Commissioners of Common Schools in Connecticut, together with the First Annual Report of the Secretary of the Board, May 1839* (Hartford, 1839), pp. 37–38.

Henry Barnard (1811–1900), the author of this report, was a leader in common school reform who held many offices and published numerous volumes during a long career. His critical remarks on Connecticut's schools are especially significant owing to the state's deserved reputation for a superior system.

Most of the teachers employed the past winter, have not taught the same schools two successive seasons. Out of 1292 teachers returned, but 341 have taught the same school before. Omitting those who are engaged for the whole year, as permanent teachers, the number is less than 240. And these were not engaged in the summer, but only for the winter. In this single fact is found an explanation of many of the acknowledged defects in our schools.

In the first place, nearly one month of the school is practically lost in the time consumed by the teacher in getting acquainted with the temper, wants, dispositions, and previous progress of his various pupils, with a view to their proper classification, and to the adaptation of his own peculiar modes of government and instruction. By the time the school is in good progress, the scholars begin to drop away, the school money is exhausted, and the school dismissed. After a vacation of unnecessary length, as far as the recreation and relief of the children are concerned, the summer school commences with reduced numbers, under a less vigilant supervision, with a poorly compensated teacher, to go through the same course as before; and so on from year to year. The loss of time consequent on the change of teachers, and the long intermission between the two seasons of schooling, not only retards the progress of the school, but leads to the breaking up of regular habits of study, which will be felt in the whole future life.

In the second place, it leads to the perpetual and expensive change of school books, so much complained of, and so justly complained of, by parents. Every teacher has his favorite text books, and is naturally desirous of introducing them wherever he goes. And as there is no system adopted in relation to this subject in any society, he usually succeeds in introducing more or less of them into every school. The money now expended in the purchase of new books, caused by the change of teachers, would go far to continue the same teacher another month in the same school. Thus the district might practically gain, without any additional expense, two months schooling each year by employing the same teacher year after year.

In the third place, this practice excludes from our common schools nearly all those who have decided to make teaching a profession and drives them, almost as a matter of course, into private schools or academies. Out of the 1292 teachers employed, only 100 have been engaged in teaching for more than 10 years; and of this number a large proportion have only taught in the winter.

---

5. The superiority of women as teachers

Catherine E. Beecher, *The Evils Suffered by American Women and American Children: The Causes and the Remedy* (New York, 1846), pp. 9–10.

The replacement of men by women in the classroom was advocated by most of the common school reformers. Catherine E. Beecher (1800–1878), daughter of the famed preacher Reverend Lyman Beecher, was a leading spokesman for women's rights and interests, especially in education.

Now, without expressing any opinion as to the influence, on health and morals, of taking women away from domestic habits and pursuits, to labor with men in shops and mills, I simply ask if it would not be *better* to put the thousands of men who are keeping school for young children into the mills, and employ the women to train the children?

Wherever education is most prosperous, there woman is employed more than man. In Massachusetts, where education is highest, five out of seven of the teachers are women; while in Kentucky, where education is so much lower, five out of six of the teachers are men.

Another cause of depression to our sex is found in the fact that there is no profession for women of education and high position, which, like law, medicine, and theology, opens the way to competence, influence, and honor, and presents motives for exertion. Woman ought never to be led to married life except under the promptings of pure affection. To marry for an establishment, for a position, or for something to do, is a deplorable wrong. But how many women, for want of a high and honorable profession to engage their time, are led to this melancholy course. This is not so because Providence has not provided an ample place for such a profession for woman, but because custom or prejudice, or a low estimate of its honorable character, prevents her from entering it. *The education of children, that* is the true and noble profession of a woman — *that* is what is worthy the noblest powers and affections of the noblest minds.

Another cause which deeply affects the best interests of our sex is the contempt, or utter neglect and indifference, which has befallen this only noble profession open to woman. There is no employment, however disagreeable or however wicked, which custom and fashion cannot render elegant, interesting, and enthusiastically sought. A striking proof of this is seen in the military profession. This is the profession of *killing our fellow-creatures,* and is attended with everything low, brutal, unchristian, and disgusting; and yet what halos of glory have been hung around it, and how the young, and generous, and enthusiastic have been drawn into it! If one-half the poetry, fiction, oratory, and taste thus misemployed had been used to embellish and elevate the employment of training the mind of childhood, in what an altered position should we find this noblest of all professions!

As it is, the employment of teaching children is regarded as the most wearying drudgery, and few resort to it except from necessity; and one very reasonable cause of this aversion is the utter neglect of any arrangements for *preparing* teachers for this arduous and difficult profession. The mind of a young child is like a curious instrument, capable of exquisite harmony when touched by a skillful hand, but sending forth only annoying harshness when unskillfully addressed. To a teacher is committed a collection of these delicate contrivances; and, without experience, without instruction, it is required not only that each one should be tuned aright, but that all be combined in excellent harmony: as if a young girl were sent into a splendid orchestra, all ignorant and unskillful, and required to draw melody from each instrument, and then to combine the whole in faultless harmony. And in each case there are, here and there, individual minds, who, without instruction, are gifted by nature with aptness and skill in managing the music either of matter or of mind; but that does not lessen the folly, in either case, of expecting the whole profession, either of music or of teaching, to be pursued without preparatory training.

---

6. Teachers should become professionals

David P. Page, *Theory and Practice of Teaching* (Syracuse, 1847), pp. 270–287.

Page, a leading writer on educational subjects, was principal of the State Normal School at Albany, New York.

It has long been the opinion of the best minds . . . that teaching should be a profession. It has been alleged, and with much justice, that this calling, which demands for its successful exercise the best of talents, the most persevering energy, and the largest share of self-denial, has never attained an appreciation in the public mind at all commensurate with its importance. It has by no means received the emolument, either of money or honor, which strict justice would award in any other department to the talents and exertions required for this. This having been so long the conditions of things, much of the best talent has been attracted at once to the other professions; or if exercised awhile in this, the temptation of more lucrative reward, or of more speedy, if not more lasting honor, has soon diverted it from teaching, where so little of either can be realized, to engage in some other department of higher promise. So true is this, that scarcely a man can be found, having attained to any considerable eminence as a teacher, who was not several times solicited — and perhaps strongly *tempted* — to engage in some more lucrative employment; and while there have always been some strong men, who have preferred teaching to any other calling, — men who would do honor to any profession, and who, while exercising this, have found that highest of all rewards, the consciousness of being useful to others, — still it must be confessed that teachers have too often been of just that class which a knowledge of the circumstances might lead us to predict would engage in teaching; men of capacity too limited for the other professions, of a temperament too sluggish to engage in the labors of active employment, of manners too rude to be tolerated except in the society of children (!), and sometimes of a morality so pernicious as to make them the unfailing contaminators of the young whenever permitted — not to teach — but to "keep school." Thus two great evils have been mutually strengthening each other. The indifference of the employers to the importance of good teachers, and their parsimony in meting out the rewards of teaching, have called into the field large numbers, in the strictest sense, unworthy of all reward; while this very unworthiness of the teachers has been made the excuse for further indifference, and if possible for greater meanness on the part of employers. Such has been the state of the case for many years past, and such is, to a great extent, the fact at present.

It has been the ardent wish of many philanthropists that this deplorable state of affairs should be exchanged for a better. Hence they have urged that teaching should be constituted a profession; that none should enter this profession but those who are thoroughly qualified to discharge the high trust; and, as a consequence, that the people should more liberally reward and honor those who are thus qualified and employed. This would indeed be a very desirable change; it would be the educational millennium of the world. For such a period we all may well devoutly pray.

·   ·   ·   ·   ·

Section I. — Self-Culture.

The teacher should labor diligently to improve himself. This is a duty incumbent on all persons, but particularly upon the teacher. The very nature of his employment demands that his mind should be frequently replenished from the storehouses of knowledge.

·   ·   ·   ·   ·

1. *He should have a course of professional reading.* It will do much for his improvement to read the works of those who have written on the subject of education and the art of teaching. If possible he should collect and possess a small educational library . . .

2. *By pursuing systematically a course of general study.* Many teachers who have a desire to improve themselves, still fritter away their time upon little miscellaneous matters, without making real progress. It is well in this to have a plan. Let some one study, — it may be geology, or astronomy, or chemistry, or botany, or the pure mathematics, — let some one study receive constant attention till no mean attainments have been made in it . . .

3. *Keep a journal or common-place book.* The habit of composing daily is very valuable to the teacher. In this book he may record whatever plans he has devised with their results in practice. He may enter remarkable cases of discipline, — in short, any thing which in the course of his practice he finds interesting. Those valuable suggestions which he receives from others, or hints that he may derive from books, may be epitomized here, and thus be treasured up for future reference.

·   ·   ·   ·   ·

But there are other and direct duties which he owes to his profession, which I proceed to consider under the head of

Section II. — Mutual Aid.

Every teacher should be willing to impart as well as to receive good. No one, whatever may be his personal exertions, can monopolize all the wisdom of the world.

.   .   .   .   .

How can teachers encourage each other?

1. *By mutual visitation.* Very much may be done by social intercourse. Two teachers can scarcely converse together an hour without benefiting each other . . .

But not only should teachers visit one another, — it is profitable also for them to visit each other's schools. I have never spent an hour in the school of another without gaining some instruction. Sometimes a new way of illustrating a difficult point, sometimes an exhibition of tact in managing a difficult case in discipline, sometimes an improved method of keeping up the interest in a class, would suggest the means of making my own labors the more successful. And even should one's neighbor be a bad teacher, one may sometimes learn as much from witnessing glaring defects as great excellencies. Some of the most profitable lessons I have ever received, have been drawn from the deficiencies of a fellow teacher.

.   .   .   .   .

2. *By the use of the pen.* Every teacher should be a ready writer. Nearly every teacher could gain access to the columns of some paper, through which he could impart the results of his experience, or of his reflection. Such a course would benefit him specially, and at the same time it would awaken other minds to thought and action. In this way the attention, not only of teachers but parents, would be called to the great work of education . . .

3. *By Teachers' Associations or Institutes.* These are peculiarly adapted to the diffusion of the best plans of instruction. Rightly conducted, they can never fail of being useful . . .

As far as possible, such meetings should be made strictly practical. The older teachers, who usually have the most to do with the management of them, should bear in mind that they are mainly designed to diffuse practical ideas of teaching, particularly among the younger members. Too often, these meetings are made the arena of debate upon questions of very little practical importance to the teacher . . .

Another, and no inconsiderable advantage of such associations, is, that the teacher gains encouragement and strength, by being thus brought in contact with others engaged in the same pursuit. Toiling on alone, in his isolated district, surrounded by obstacles and discouragements, weighed down by care, and finding none to sympathize with him, he is almost ready to faint in his course, and perhaps to abandon his calling. At this crisis, he reads the notice for the teachers' meeting, and he resolves to go up once more to the gathering of his friends. From the various parts of the county, from the populous and crowded city, and from the byways of the country-towns, a goodly number collect together and greet each other. Smile answers to smile, the blood courses more freely through the veins, the spirits, long depressed perhaps, partake of the general glow, and each feels that he is not toiling alone. He feels that a noble brotherhood of kindred spirits are laboring in the same field, under trials and discouragements similar to those which have oppressed him. He derives new strength from the sympathy of friends.

A professional feeling is engendered, which will accompany him to his schoolroom; and when he goes home, it is with renewed vigor and fresh aspirings to be a better man, and a better teacher. He labors with more confidence in himself; and, enlightened by what he has seen and heard, he is far more successful than before. His pupils, too, respond to the new life they see enkindling in him, and go to their work more cheerfully. One difficulty after another vanishes, and he begins to think teaching, after all, is not the *worst* employment in the world . . .

---

7. A challenge to the authority of a teacher in a frontier school

Edward Eggleston, *The Hoosier Schoolmaster* (New York, 1871), pp. 109–114.

Eggleston (1837–1902), historian and man of letters, drew upon recollections of schooldays in his native Indiana for this classic fictional account of a frontier schoolmaster.

The school closed on Monday evening as usual. The boys had been talking in knots all day. Nothing but the bull-dog in the slender, resolute young master had kept down the rising storm. Let a teacher lose moral support at home, and he can not long govern a school. Ralph had effectually lost his popularity in the district, and the worst of it was that he could not divine from just what quarter the ill wind came, except that he felt sure of Small's agency in it somewhere. Even Hannah had slighted him, when he called at Mean's on Monday morning to draw the pittance of pay that was due him.

He had expected a petition for a holiday on Christmas day. Such holidays are deducted from the teacher's time, and it is customary for the boys to "turn out" the teacher who refuses to grant them, by barring him out of the school-house on Christmas and New Year's morning. Ralph had intended to grant a holiday if it should be asked, but it was not asked. Hank Banta was the ringleader in the disaffection, and he had managed to draw the surly Bud, who was present this morning, into it.

It is but fair to say that Bud was in favor of making a request before resorting to extreme measures, but he was overruled. He gave it as his solemn opinion that the master was mighty peart, and they would be beat any how some way, but he would lick the master fer two cents ef he warn't so slim that he'd feel like he was fighting a baby.

And all that day things looked black. Ralph's countenance was cold and hard as stone, and Shocky trembled where he sat in front of him. Betsey Short tittered rather more than usual. A riot or a murder would have seemed amusing to her.

School was dismissed, and Ralph, instead of returning to the Squire's, set out for the village of Clifty a few miles away. No one knew what he went for, and some suggested that he had "sloped." But Bud said "he warn't that air kind. He was one of them air sort as died in ther tracks, was Mr. Hartsook. They'd find him on the ground nex' morning, and he 'lowed the master war made of that air sort of stuff as would burn the dog-on'd ole school-house to ashes, or blow it into splinters, but what he'd beat. Howsumdever he'd said he was a-goin' to help, and help he would; but all the sinnoo in Golier wouldn' be no account again the cute they was in the head of the master."

But Bud, discouraged as he was with the fear of Ralph's "cute," went like a martyr to the stake and took his place with the rest in the school-house at nine o'clock at night. It may have been Ralph's intention to have preoccupied the school-house, for at ten o'clock Hank Banta was set shaking from head to foot at seeing a face that looked like the master's at the window. He waked up Bud and told him about it.

"Well, what are you a-tremblin' about, you coward?" growled Bud. "He won't shoot you; but he'll beat you at this game, I'll bet a hoss, and me, too, and make us both as 'shamed of ourselves as dogs with tin-kittles to their tails. You don't know the master, though he did duck you. But he'll larn you a good lesson this time, and me too, like as not." And Bud soon snored again, but Hank shook with fear every time he looked at the blackness outside the windows. He was sure he heard foot-falls. He would have given anything to have been at home.

When morning came, the pupils began to gather early. A few boys who were likely to prove of service in the coming siege were admitted through the window, and then everything was made fast, and a "snack" was eaten.

"How do you 'low he'll git in?" said Hank, trying to hide his fear.

"How do I 'low?" said Bud. "I don't 'low nothin' about it. You might as well ax me where I 'low nex' shootin' star is a-goin' to drap. Mr. Hartsook's mighty onsartin. But he'll git in, though, and tan your hide fer you, you see ef he don't. Ef he don't blow up the school-house with gunpowder!" This last was thrown in by way of alleviating the fears of the cowardly Hank, for whom Bud had a great contempt.

The time for school had almost come. The boys inside were demoralized by waiting. They began to hope that the master had "sloped." They dreaded to see him coming.

"I don't believe he'll come," said Hank, with a cold shiver. "It's past school-time."

"Yes, he will come, too," said Bud. "And he 'lows to come in here mighty quick. I don't know how. But he'll be a-standin' at that air desk when it's nine o'clock. I'll bet a thousand dollars on that. Ef he don't take it into his head to blow us up!" Hank was now white.

Some of the parents came along, accidentally of course, and stopped to see the fun, sure that Bud would thrash the master if he tried to break in. Small, on the way to see a patient perhaps, reined up in front of the door. Still no Ralph. It was just five minutes before nine. A rumor now gained currency that he had been seen going to Clifty the evening before, and that he had not come back, though in fact Ralph had come back, and had slept at Squire Hawkin's.

"There's the master," cried Betsey Short, who stood out in the road, shivering and giggling alternately. For Ralph at that moment emerged from the sugar-camp by the school-house, carrying a board.

"Ho! ho!" laughed Hank, "he thinks he'll smoke us out. I guess he'll find us ready." The boys had let the fire burn down, and there was now nothing but hot hickory coals on the hearth.

"I tell you he'll come in. He didn't go to Clifty fer nothin'," said Bud, who sat still on one of the benches which leaned against the door. "I don't know how, but they's lots of ways of killing a cat besides chokin' her with butter. He'll come in — ef he don't blow us all sky-high!"

Ralph's voice was now heard, demanding that the door be opened.

"Let's open her," said Hank, turning livid with fear at the firm, confident tone of the master.

Bud straightened himself up. "Hank, you're a coward. I've got a mind to kick you. You got me into this blamed mess, and now you want to flunk. You jest tech one of these ere fastenings, and I'll lay you out flat of your back afore you can say Jack Robinson."

The teacher was climbing to the roof with the board in hand.

"That air won't win," laughed Pete Jones outside. He saw that there was no smoke. Even Bud began to hope that Ralph would fail for once. The master was now on the ridge-pole of the school-house. He took a paper from his pocket, and deliberately poured the contents down the chimney.

Mr. Pete Jones shouted "Gunpowder!" and started down the road to be out of the way of the explosion. Dr. Small remembered, probably, that his patient might die while he sat there, and started on.

But Ralph emptied the paper, and laid the board over the chimney. What a row there was inside! The benches that were braced against the door were thrown down, and Hank Banta rushed out, rubbing his eyes, coughing frantically, and sure that he had been blown up. All the rest followed, Bud bringing up the rear sulkily, but coughing and sneezing for dear life.

Such a smell of sulphur as came from that school-house!

Betsey had to lean against the fence to giggle.

As soon as all were out, Ralph threw the board off the chimney, leaped to the ground, entered the school-house, and opened the windows. The school soon followed him, and all was still.

"Would he thrash?" This was the important question in Hank Banta's mind. And the rest looked for a battle with Bud.

"It is just nine o'clock," said Ralph, consulting his watch, "and I'm glad to see you all here promptly. I should have given you a holiday if you had asked me like gentlemen yesterday. On the whole, I think I shall give you a holiday any how. The school is dismissed."

And Hank felt foolish.

And Bud secretly resolved to thrash Hank or the master, he didn't care which.

And Mirandy looked the love she could not utter.

And Betsey giggled.

*The moral and social values
taught in the schools*

---

1. Lessons about goodness, honesty, and obedience as related in stories for young readers

William H. McGuffey, *McGuffey's Eclectic First Reader* (Cincinnati, 1853), pp. 30–31, 80–81, 94–96, 100–104.

McGuffey (1800–1873), a college professor in Ohio and Virginia, was the most famous American author of textbooks. Sales of his numerous spellers and readers exceeded 122,000,000 copies.

The Poor Old Man.

Jane, there is a poor old man at the door.

He asks for some-thing to eat. We will give him some bread and cheese.

He is cold. Will you give him some clothes too?

I will give him a suit of old clothes, which will be new to him.

Poor man! I wish he had a warm house to live in, and kind friends to live with him; then he would not have to beg from door to door.

We should be kind to the poor. We may be as poor as this old man, and need as much as he.

Shall I give him some cents to buy a pair of shoes?

No; you may give him a pair of shoes.

It is hard for the poor to have to beg from house to house.

Poor boys and girls some-times have to sleep out of doors all night. When it snows, they are ver-y cold, and when it rains, they get quite wet.

Who is it that gives us food to eat, and clothes to make us warm?

It is God, my child; he makes the sun to shine, and sends the rain up-on the earth, that we may have food.

God makes the wool grow up-on the lit-tle lambs, that we may have clothes to keep us warm.

.   .   .   .   .

Pe-ter Holt.

Pe-ter Holt was left at home one day by his par-ents, when they went out to take a ride.

His moth-er told him to stay in the house un-til she came back. "Be ver-y sure that you do not go out a-mong the hors-es," said she, "they may hurt you."

Pe-ter said he would do as he was bid. So his moth-er kiss-ed him and start-ed. He was soon ver-y tir-ed of stay-ing in the house; so he went to the door, and soon aft-er ran down in-to the lot, to look at a lit-tle colt, which his fa-ther had giv-en him.

It was ver-y tame, so he put his hand on its neck, and then on its head. At last he thought it was so tame and gen-tle that he would ride it. He led it to the fence and jump-ed on its back.

The colt had nev-er be-fore felt a-ny thing on his back, and was ver-y much a-larm-ed. It put down its head and ran off at a great rate, and, at last, kick-ed up its hind feet, and threw Pe-ter over its head.

Pe-ter was ver-y much hurt, but he crept home as well as he could. If he had been so bad-ly hurt as not to be a-ble to get home, he might have died in the field be-fore his moth-er came home.

Lit-tle chil-dren may learn from this, that they should al-ways o-bey their par-ents. How ma-ny lit-tle girls and boys have been hurt, because they did not do as they were bid!

I once knew of a lit-tle girl who was told not to cross the street be-fore a car-riage. But she would not stop; and when the car-riage came up, it ran di-rect-ly o-ver her.

.   .   .   .   .

The Lit-tle Chim-ney Sweep.

Some time a-go, there was a lit-tle chim-ney sweep, who had to sweep a chim-ney in the house of a ver-y rich la-dy. The lit-tle sweep went up at the kitch-en fire place, and came down in the cham-ber.

When he got in-to the cham-ber, he found him-self all a-lone. He stop-ped a mo-ment to look round up-on the rich things he saw there. As he look-ed on the top of the ta-ble, he saw a fine gold watch, with gold seals to it.

He had nev-er seen a-ny thing so beau-ti-ful be-fore, and he took it up in his hands. As he list-en-ed to hear it tick, it be-gan to play sweet mu-sic. He then thought, that if it was on-ly his own, how rich he would be; and then he thought he might hide it in his blank-et.

"Now," said he, "if I take it, I shall be a thief — and yet no bod-y sees me. No bod-y? Does not God see me? Could I ev-er a-gain be good? Could I then ev-er say my pray-ers a-gain to God? And what should I do when I come to die?"

.   .   .   .   .

More A-bout the Chim-ney Sweep.

While the lit-tle sweep was think-ing a-bout tak-ing the la-dy's watch, he felt cold all o-ver, and trem-bled with fear.

"No," said he, "I can not take this watch. I would rath-er be a sweep and al-ways be poor, than steal." And down he laid the watch, and crept up the chim-ney.

Now the la-dy who own-ed the watch was just in the next room, and she could look through, and see and hear all that pass-ed. She did not say a-ny thing to the boy then, but let him go a-way.

The next day she sent for him, and when he came, she said to him, "Well, my lit-tle friend, why did you not take my watch yes-ter-day?" The lit-tle sweep then fell up-on his knees and told the la-dy all a-bout it.

Now, as the lit-tle sweep did not steal the gold watch, nor tell a-ny sto-ries a-bout it, the la-dy let him stay and live in her house. For ma-ny years she sent him to school, and when he grew up, he be-came a good man, and nev-er for-got the com-mand-ment which says, "Thou shalt not steal."

Had he ta-ken the la-dy's watch, he would have sto-len. Then he would have been sent to jail.

Let no lit-tle boy or girl ev-er take things with-out leave, for it is steal-ing; and they who steal are thieves.

You can not steal the small-est pin, with-out its be-ing a sin, nor with-out be-ing seen by that eye which never sleeps.

.   .   .   .   .

The Bro-ken Win-dow.

George El-let had a fine New Year's gift. What do you think it was? A bright sil-ver dol-lar! A mer-ry boy was George, when he thought of all the fine things he might buy with it. And as soon as the sun be-gan to make the air feel a lit-tle warm, he put on his cap and gloves, and ran in-to the street.

The ground was cov-er-ed with snow, but the sun shone out, and ev-er-y thing look-ed bright. As George went skip-ping a-long, he met some boys who were throw-ing snow-balls. This is fine sport, and George pull-ed off his gloves, and was soon as bu-sy as the rest. See, how he gath-ers up the snow, and press-es it be-tween his hands.

Now he has hit James Ma-son. But the ball was soft, and James is not hurt. Now he has made an-oth-er ball, and if James does not dodge, George will hit him a-gain. A-way goes the ball! But it miss-ed James, and broke a win-dow on the oth-er side of the street. George was a-fraid that some one would come out of the house and whip him; so he ran off, as fast as he could.

As soon as he got round the next cor-ner, he stop-ped, be-cause he was ver-y sor-ry for what he had done. Just then he saw a man car-ry-ing a box with glass doors, full of pret-ty toys; and as George was on-ly eight years old, he for-got the bro-ken win-dow, and ran aft-er the man.

. . . . . .

More A-bout the Bro-ken Win-dow.

As George was a-bout to buy a lit-tle house with doors and chim-neys, and put his hand in his pock-et for the mon-ey, he thought of the bro-ken win-dow. Then he said to him-self, "I have no right to spend this dollar for a toy-house. I ought to go back, and pay for the glass I broke with my snow-ball."

So he gave back the house to the toy-man, and turn-ed round. But he was a-fraid of be-ing scold-ed or beat-en, and did not know what to do. He went up and down the street, and felt ver-y bad-ly. He wish-ed to buy some-thing nice with his mon-ey; and he al-so wish-ed to pay for the glass he had bro-ken.

At last he said to him-self, "It was wrong to break the win-dow, al-though I did not mean to do it. I will go and pay the man for it at once. If it takes all my mon-ey, I will try not to be sor-ry; and I do not think the man will hurt me, if I of-fer to pay for the mis-chief I have done." He then start-ed off, and felt much hap-pi-er for hav-ing made up his mind to do what was right.

He rang the door bell; and when the man came out, George said, "Sir, I threw a snow-ball through your win-dow. But I did not in-tend to do it, and am ver-y sor-ry, and I wish to pay you. Here is the dol-lar my fa-ther gave me as a New Year's gift, this morn-ing."

The man took the dol-lar, and ask-ed George if he had a-ny more mon-ey. George said he had not. "Well," said the man, "this will be e-nough." So aft-er ask-ing George where he liv-ed, and what was his name, he call-ed him an hon-est lad, and shut the door.

. . . . . .

More A-bout the Bro-ken Win-dow.

When George had paid the man, he ran a-way, and felt ver-y hap-py, be-cause he had done what he knew to be right. He play-ed ver-y mer-ri-ly all the fore-noon, al-though he had no mon-ey to spend; and went home at din-ner time, with a face as ro-sy, and eyes as bright, as if noth-ing had gone wrong.

At din-ner, Mr. El-let ask-ed George what he had bought with his mon-ey. George ver-y hon-est-ly told him all a-bout the bro-ken win-dow, and said he felt ver-y well, with-out a-ny mon-ey to spend. When din-ner was o-ver, Mr. El-let told George to go and look in his hat.

He did so, and found two sil-ver dol-lars. The man, whose win-dow had been bro-ken, had been there, and told George's fa-ther a-bout it. He al-so gave back the dol-lar which George had paid him, and an-oth-er one with it.

A few months aft-er that, the man came and told Mr. El-let that he want-ed a good boy to stay in his store, and would like to have George, as soon as he left school, for he was sure that George was an hon-est boy. George went to live with this man, who was a rich mer-chant. In a few years he be-came the mer-chant's part-ner, and is now rich. George oft-en thinks of the bro-ken win-dow.

---

2. The nature of philanthropy

William H. McGuffey, *McGuffey's Newly Revised Eclectic Reader* (Cincinnati, 1844), pp. 50–53.

True and False Philanthropy — *Anonymous*

Mr. Fantom. I despise a narrow field. O for the reign of universal benevolence! I want to make all *mankind* good and happy.

Mr. Goodman. Dear me! Sure that must be a wholesale sort of a job: had you not better try your hand at a *town* or *neighborhood* first?

Mr. F. Sir, I have a plan in my head for re-lieving the miseries of the *whole world*. Every-thing is bad as it now stands. I would alter all the laws, and put an end to all the wars in the world. I would put an end to all punishments; I would not leave a single prisoner on the face of the globe. *This* is what I call doing things on a grand scale.

Mr. G. A scale with a vengeance! As to releas-ing the prisoners, however, I do not much like that, as it would be liberating a few rogues at the expense of all honest men; but as to the rest of your plan, if all countries would be so

good as to turn *Christians,* it might be helped on a good deal. There would be still misery enough left indeed; because God intended this world should be earth and not heaven. But, sir, among all your changes, you must destroy human corruption, before you can make the world quite as perfect as you pretend.

Mr. F. Your project would *rivet* the chains which *mine* is designed to *break.*

Mr. G. Sir, I have no projects. Projects are, in general, the offspring of restlessness, vanity, and idleness. I am too busy for projects, too contented for theories, and I hope, have too much honesty and humility for a philosopher. The utmost extent of my ambition at present is, to redress the wrongs of a poor apprentice, who has been cruelly used by his master: in-deed, I have another little scheme, which is to prosecute a fellow, who has suffered a poor wretch in the poorhouse, of which he had the care, to perish through neglect, and you must assist me.

Mr. F. Let the town do that. You must not apply to me for the redress of such petty griev-ances. I own that the wrongs of the Poles and South Americans so fill my mind, as to leave me no time to attend to the petty sorrows of poorhouses, and apprentices. It is provinces, empires, continents, that the benevolence of the philosopher embraces; every one can do a little paltry good to his next neighbor.

Mr. G. Every one *can,* but I do not see that every one *does.* If they would, indeed, your business would be ready done to your hands, and your grand ocean of benevolence would be filled with the drops, which private charity would throw into it. I am glad, however, you are such a friend to the prisoners, because I am just now getting a little subscription, to set free your poor old friend Tom Saunders, a very honest brother mechanic, who first got into debt, and then into jail, through no fault of his own, but merely through the pressure of the times. A number of us have given a trifle every week towards maintaining his young family since he has been in prison; but we think we shall do much more service to Saunders, and indeed in the end, lighten our own expense, by paying down, at once, a little sum, to release him, and put him in the way of maintaining his family again. We have made up all the money except five dollars. I am already promised four, and you have nothing to do but to give me the fifth. And so, for a single dollar, without any of the trouble we have had in arranging the matter, you will, at once, have the pleasure of helping to save a worthy family from starving, of redeeming an old friend from jail, and of putting a little of your boasted benevolence into action. Realize! Mr. Fantom: there is nothing like realizing.

Mr. F. Why, hark ye, Mr. Goodman, do not think I value a dollar; no sir, I despise money; it is trash, it is dirt, and beneath the regard of a wise man. It is one of the unfeeling inventions of artificial society. Sir, I could talk to you half a day on the abuse of riches, and my own contempt of money.

Mr. G. O pray do not give yourself that trouble. It will be a much easier way of proving your sincerity, just to put your hand in your pocket, and give me a dollar without saying a word about it: and then to you, who value *time* so *much,* and *money* so *little,* it will cut the matter short. But come now, (for I see you will give nothing), I should be mighty glad to know what is the sort of good you do yourselves, since you always object to what is done by others.

Mr. F. Sir, the object of a true philosopher is, to diffuse light and knowledge. I wish to see the whole world enlightened.

Mr. G. Well, Mr. Fantom, you are a wonderful man, to keep up such a stock of benevolence, at so small an expense; to *love* mankind so dearly, and yet *avoid* all opportunities of doing them *good;* to have such a noble zeal for the *millions,* and to feel so little compassion for the *units;* — to long to free *empires* and enlighten *kingdoms,* and deny instruction to your

own *village* and comfort to your own *family.* Surely, none but a *philosopher* could indulge so much *philanthropy* and so much *frugality* at the same time. But come, do assist me in a partition I am making in our poorhouse, between the *old,* whom I want to have better *fed,* and the *young,* whom I want to have more *worked.*

Mr. F. Sir, my mind is so engrossed with the partition of Poland, that I cannot bring it down to an object of such insignificance. I despise the man, whose benevolence is swallowed up in the narrow concerns of his own family, or village, or country.

Mr. G. Well, now I have a notion, that it is as well to do one's *own* duty, as the duty of *another* man; and that to do good at *home,* is as well as to do good *abroad.* For *my* part, I had as lief help *Tom Saunders* to freedom, as a *Pole* or a *South American,* though I should be very glad to help *them too.* But one must begin to love somewhere; and I think it is as natural to love one's own family, and to do good in one's own neighborhood, as to any body else. And if every man in every family, village, and county did the same, why then all the schemes would meet, and the end of one village or town where I was doing good, would be the beginning of another village where somebody else was doing good; so my schemes would jut into my neighbor's; his projects would unite with those of some other local reformer; and all would fit with a sort of dovetail exactness.

Mr. F. Sir, a man of large views will be on the watch for great occasions to prove his benevolence.

Mr. G. Yes, sir; but if they are so distant that he cannot reach them, or so vast that he cannot grasp them, he may let a thousand little, snug, kind, good actions slip through his fingers in the meanwhile: and so, between the great things that he *cannot* do, and the little ones that he *will not* do, life passes, and *nothing* will be done.

3. The lessons of American history

John Bonner, *A Child's History of the United States* (New York, 1859), II, 319–320.

I have tried to recount how a few straggling bands of poor wanderers, seeking a scanty living on the wild sea-coast of America, have grown to be one of the greatest nations of the earth. It is a beautiful and a wonderful subject to write about, and I wish, for your sake, that I had written the story with more skill.

No other people, since the world began, ever grew out of so small a beginning to so towering a height of power and prosperity in so short a time. If you seek to know why your countrymen have outstripped all the nations of the earth in this respect, the reason is easily found. The founders of this nation were honest, true men. They were sincere in all they said, upright in all their acts. They feared God and obeyed the laws. They wrought constantly and vigorously at the work they had to do, and strove to live at peace with their neighbors. When they were attacked they fought like men, and, defeated or victorious, would not have peace till their point was gained. Above all, they insisted, from the very first, on being free themselves, and securing freedom for you, their children.

If you follow the example they set, and love truth, honor, religion, and freedom as deeply, and, if need be, defend them as stoutly as they did, the time is not far distant when this country will as far excel other countries in power, wealth, numbers, intelligence, and every good thing, as other countries excelled it before Columbus sailed away from Spain to discover the New World.

4. The history of the United States as presented to the children of the Confederacy, 1863

M. B. Moore, *Geographical Reader for the Dixie Children* (Raleigh, 1863), pp. 13–14.

Southerners tried to supply all of the elements of civilization during the Civil War including textbooks for schools. This is one example of that genre.

The United States.

1. This was once the most prosperous country in the world. Nearly a hundred years ago it belonged to England, but the English made such hard laws that the people said they would not obey them. After a long, bloody war of seven years, they gained their independence; and for many years were prosperous and happy.

2. In the mean time both English and American ships went to Africa and brought away many of those poor heathen negroes, and sold them for slaves. Some people said it was wrong and asked the King of England to stop it. He replied that "he knew it was wrong; but that slave trade brought much money into his treasury, and it should continue." But both countries afterwards did pass laws to stop this trade. In a few years, the Northern States finding their climate too cold for the negro to be profitable, sold them to the people living farther South. Then the Northern States passed laws to forbid any person owning slaves in their borders.

3. Then the northern people began to preach, to lecture, and to write about the sin of slavery. The money for which they sold their slaves, was now partly spent in trying to persuade the Southern States to send their slaves back to Africa. And when the territories were settled they were not willing for any of them to become slaveholding. This would soon have made the North much stronger than the South; and many of the men said they would vote for a law to free all the negroes in the country. The Southern men tried to show them

how unfair this would be, but still they kept on.

4. In the year 1860 the Abolitionists became strong enough to elect one of their men for President. Abraham Lincoln was a weak man, and the South believed he would allow laws to be made, which would deprive them of their rights. So the Southern States seceded, and elected Jefferson Davis for their President. This so enraged President Lincoln that he declared war, and has exhausted nearly all the strength of the nation, in a vain attempt to whip the South back into the Union. Thousands of lives have been lost, and the earth has been drenched with blood; but still Abraham is unable to conquer the "Rebels" as he calls the South. The South only asked to be let alone, and to divide the public property equally. It would have been wise in the North to have said to her Southern sisters, "If you are not content to dwell with us longer, depart in peace. We will divide the inheritance with you, and may you be a great nation."

5. This country possesses many ships, has fine cities and towns, many railroads, steamboats, canals, manufactures, etc. The people are ingenious, and enterprising, and are noted for their tact in "driving a bargain." They are refined, and intelligent on all subjects but that of negro slavery, on this they are mad.

6. The large lakes, the long rivers, the tall mountains, with the beautiful farms and pretty towns and villages, make this a very interesting country to travelers.

Continuity and change in the colleges

1. The Yale Report, 1828

"Original Papers in Relation to a Course of Liberal Education," *American Journal of Science and Arts,* XV (1829),

299–304, 306–310, 312–313, 323–325, 328–331.

The authors of this influential statement were President Jeremiah Day (1773–1867) and Professor James L. Kingsley (1778–1852). They defended the prescribed curriculum built around the classical languages against the charge that it was useless and antiquated. The report provided arguments for generations of academic conservatives and was used as a blueprint for the course of study in many of the nation's new colleges.

Perhaps the time has come, when we ought to pause, and inquire, whether it will be sufficient to make *gradual* changes, as heretofore; and whether the whole system is not rather to be broken up, and a better one substituted in its stead. From different quarters, we have heard the suggestion, that our colleges must be *new-modelled;* that they are not adapted to the spirit and wants of the age; that they will soon be deserted, unless they are better accommodated to the business character of the nation. As this point may have an important bearing upon the question immediately before the committee, we would ask their indulgence, while we attempt to explain, at some length, the nature and object of the present plan of education at the college.

.   .   .   .   .   .

What then is the appropriate object of a college? It is not necessary here to determine what it is which, in every case, entitles an institution to the *name* of a college. But if we have not greatly misapprehended the design of the patrons and guardians of this college, its object is to LAY THE FOUNDATION of a SUPERIOR EDUCATION: and this is to be done, at a period of life when a substitute must be provided for *parental superintendence.* The ground work of a thorough education, must be broad, and deep, and solid. For a partial or superficial education, the support may be of looser materials, and more hastily laid.

The two great points to be gained in intellectual culture, are the *discipline* and the *furniture* of the mind; expanding its powers, and storing it with knowledge. The former of these is, perhaps, the more important of the two. A commanding object, therefore, in a collegiate course, should be, to call into daily and vigorous exercise the faculties of the student. Those branches of study should be prescribed, and those modes of instruction adopted, which are best calculated to teach the art of fixing the attention, directing the train of thought, analyzing a subject proposed for investigation; following, with accurate discrimination, the course of argument; balancing nicely the evidence presented to the judgment; awakening, elevating, and controlling the imagination; arranging, with skill, the treasures which memory gathers; rousing and guiding the powers of genius. All this is not to be effected by a light and hasty course of study; by reading a few books, hearing a few lectures, and spending some months at a literary institution. The habits of thinking are to be formed, by long continued and close application. The mines of science must be penetrated far below the surface, before they will disclose their treasures. If a dexterous performance of the manual operations, in many of the mechanical arts, requires an apprenticeship, with diligent attention for years; much more does the training of the powers of the mind demand vigorous, and steady, and systematic effort.

In laying the foundation of a thorough education, it is necessary that *all* the important mental faculties be brought into exercise. It is not sufficient that one or two be cultivated, while others are neglected . . . When certain mental endowments receive a much higher culture than others, there is a distortion in the intellectual character. The mind never attains its full perfection, unless its various powers are so trained as to give them the fair proportions which nature designed. If the student exercises his reasoning powers only, he will be deficient in imagination and taste, in fervid and impressive eloquence. If he confines his attention to demonstrative evidence, he will be unfitted to decide correctly, in cases of probability. If he relies principally on his memory, his powers of invention will be impaired by disuse. In the course of instruction in this college, it has been an object to maintain such a proportion between the different branches of literature and science, as to form in the student a proper *balance* of character. From the pure mathematics, he learns the art of demonstrative reasoning. In attending to the physical sciences, he becomes familiar with facts, with the process of induction, and the varieties of probable evidence. In ancient literature, he finds some of the most finished models of taste. By English reading, he learns the powers of the language in which he is to speak and write. By logic and mental philosophy, he is taught the art of thinking; by rhetoric and oratory, the art of speaking. By frequent exercise on written composition, he acquires copiousness and accuracy of expression. By extemporaneous discussion, he becomes prompt, and fluent, and animated. It is a point of high importance, that eloquence and solid learning should go together; that he who has accumulated the richest treasures of thought, should possess the highest powers of oratory. To what purpose has a man become deeply learned, if he has no faculty of communicating his knowledge? And of what use is a display of rhetorical elegance, from one who knows little or nothing which is worth communicating? . . . Our course, therefore, aims at a union of science with literature; of solid attainment with skill in the art of persuasion.

No one feature in a system of intellectual education, is of greater moment than such an arrangement of duties and motives, as will most effectually throw the student upon the *resources of his own mind*. Without this, the whole apparatus of libraries, and instruments, and specimens, and lectures, and teachers, will be insufficient to secure distinguished excellence. The scholar must form himself, by his own exertions. The advantages furnished by a residence at a college, can do little more than stimulate and aid his personal efforts. The *inventive* powers are especially to be called into vigorous exercise. However abundant may be the acquisitions of the student, if he has no talent at forming new combinations of thought, he will be dull and inefficient. The sublimest efforts of genius consist in the creations of the imagination, the discoveries of the intellect, the conquests by which the dominions of science are extended. But the culture of the inventive faculties is not the *only* object of a liberal education. The most gifted understanding cannot greatly enlarge the amount of science to which the wisdom of ages has contributed. If it were possible for a youth to have his faculties in the highest state of cultivation, without any of the knowledge which is derived from others, he would be but poorly fitted for the business of life. To the discipline of the mind, therefore, is to be added instruction. The analytic method must be combined with the synthetic. Analysis is most efficacious in directing the powers of invention; but is far too slow in its progress to teach, within a moderate space of time, the circle of the sciences.

In our arrangements for the communication of knowledge, as well as in intellectual discipline, such branches are to be taught as will produce a proper symmetry and balance of character. We doubt whether the powers of the mind can be developed, in their fairest proportions, by studying languages alone, or mathematics alone, or natural or political science alone. As the bodily frame is brought to its highest perfection, not by one simple and uniform motion, but by a variety of exercises; so the mental faculties are expanded, and invigorated, and adapted to each other, by familiarity with different departments of science.

A most important feature in the colleges of this country is, that the students are generally of an age which requires, that a substitute be provided for *parental superintendence.* When removed from under the roof of their parents, and exposed to the untried scenes of temptation, it is necessary that some faithful and affectionate guardian take them by the hand, and guide their steps. This consideration determines the *kind* of government which ought to be maintained in our colleges. As it is a substitute for the regulations of a family, it should approach as near to the character of parental control as the circumstances of the case will admit. It should be founded on mutual affection and confidence. It should aim to effect its purpose, principally by kind and persuasive influence; not wholly or chiefly by restraint and terror. Still, punishment may sometimes be necessary. There may be perverse members of a college, as well as of a family. There may be those whom nothing but the arm of law can reach.

. . . . .

In giving the course of instruction, it is intended that a due proportion be observed between *lectures,* and the exercises which are familiarly termed *recitations;* that is, examinations in a text book. The great advantage of lectures is, that while they call forth the highest efforts of the lecturer, and accelerate his advance to professional eminence; they give that light and spirit to the subject, which awaken the interest and ardor of the student. They may place before him the principles of science, in the attractive dress of living eloquence. Where instruments are to be explained, experiments performed, or specimens exhibited; they are the appropriate mode of communication. But we are far from believing, that *all* the purposes of instruction can be best answered by lectures alone. They do not always bring upon the student a pressing and definite responsibility. He may repose upon his seat, and yield a passive hearing to the lecturer, without ever calling into exercise the active powers of his own mind. This defect we endeavor to remedy, in part, by frequent examinations on the subjects of the lectures. Still it is important, that the student should have opportunities of retiring by himself, and giving a more commanding direction to his thoughts, than when listening to oral instruction. To secure his steady and earnest efforts, is the great object of the daily examinations or recitations. In these exercises, a text-book is commonly the guide. A particular portion of this is assigned for each meeting. In this way only, can the responsibility be made sufficiently definite.

.　　.　　.　　.　　.

We deem it to be indispensable to a proper adjustment of our collegiate system, that there should be in it both Professors and Tutors. There is wanted, on the one hand, the experience of those who have been long resident at the institution, and on the other, the fresh and minute information of those who, having more recently mingled with the students, have a distinct recollection of their peculiar feelings, prejudices, and habits of thinking. At the head of each great division of science, it is necessary that there should be a Professor, to superintend the department, to arrange the plan of instruction, to regulate the mode of conducting it, and to teach the more important and difficult parts of the subject. But students in a college, who have just entered on the first elements of science, are not principally occupied with the more abstruse and disputable points. Their attention ought not to be solely or mainly directed to the latest discoveries. They have first to learn the principles which have been in a course of investigation, through successive ages; and have now become simplified and settled. Before arriving at regions hitherto unexplored, they must pass over the intervening cultivated ground. The Professor at the head of a department may, therefore, be greatly aided, in some parts of the course of instruction, by those who are not as deeply versed as himself in all the intricacies of the science. Indeed we doubt, whether elementary principles are always taught to the best advantage, by those whose researches have carried them so far beyond these simpler truths, that they come back to them with reluctance and distaste . . . Young men have often the most ardor, in communicating familiar principles, and in removing those lighter difficulties of the pupil, which, not long since, were found lying across their own path.

In the internal police of the institution, as the students are gathered into one family, it is deemed an essential provision, that some of the officers should constitute a portion of this family; being always present with them, not only at their meals, and during the business of the day; but in the hours allotted to rest. The arrangement is such, that in our college buildings, there is no room occupied by students, which is not near to the chamber of one of the officers.

But the feature in our system which renders a considerable number of tutors indispensable, is the subdivision of our classes, and the assignment of each portion to the particular charge of one man. Each of the three junior classes is formed into two or three divisions; and each division is committed to the superintendence of a tutor. Although he is not confined to the instruction of his own division; but makes such exchanges with the other tutors as will give to each the opportunity of teaching his favorite branch; yet by meeting them in the recitation rooms two or three times every day, and by minutely inspecting their conduct on other occasions, he renders a service to the police of the institution, which could be secured in no other way. It is intended that the government should be, as much as possible, of a parental character; a government of mild and grateful influence. But the basis of this must be mutual attachment; such as can spring only from daily and peculiar intimacy. If the same teacher instructs eight or ten different divisions, in rapid succession, it will be difficult for him to feel, that he stands in a very near relation to them all. If the same student attends on a dozen different instructers, in rotation, he may respect them all; but can hardly be expected to view them with any peculiar affection.

.　　.　　.　　.　　.

The collegiate course of study, of which we have now given a summary view, we hope may be carefully distinguished from several *other* objects and plans, with which it has been too often confounded. It is far from embracing *every thing* which the student will ever have occasion to learn. The object is not to *finish* his education; but to lay the foundation, and to advance as far in rearing the superstructure, as the short period of his residence here will admit. If he acquires here a thorough knowledge of the principles of science, he may then, in a great measure, educate himself. He has, at least, been taught *how* to learn. With the aid of books, and means of observation, he may be constantly advancing in knowledge. Wherever he goes, into whatever company he falls, he has those general views, on every topic of interest, which will enable him to understand, to digest, and to form a correct opinion, on the statements and discussions which he hears. There are many things important to be known, which are not taught in colleges, because they may be learned any where. The knowledge, though indispensable, comes to us as freely, in the way of our business, as our necessary supplies of light, and air, and water.

The course of instruction which is given to the undergraduates in the college, is not designed to include *professional* studies. Our object is not to teach that which is peculiar to any one of the professions; but to lay the foundation which is common to them all. There are separate schools for medicine, law, and theology, connected with the college, as well as in various parts of the country; which are open for the reception of all who are prepared to enter upon the appropriate studies of their several professions. With these, the academical course is not intended to interfere.

But why, it may be asked, should a student waste his time upon studies which have no immediate connection with his future profession? Will chemistry enable him to plead at the bar, or conic sections qualify him for preaching, or astronomy aid him in the practice of physic? Why should not his attention be confined to the subject which is to occupy the labors of his life? In answer to this, it may be observed, that there is no science which does not contribute its aid to professional skill. "Every thing throws light upon every thing." The great object of a

collegiate education, preparatory to the study of a profession, is to give that expansion and balance of the mental powers, those liberal and comprehensive views, and those fine proportions of character, which are not to be found in him whose ideas are always continued to one particular channel. When a man has entered upon the practice of his profession, the energies of his mind must be given, principally, to its appropriate duties. But if his thoughts never range on other subjects, if he never looks abroad on the ample domains of literature and science, there will be a narrowness in his habits of thinking, a peculiarity of character, which will be sure to mark him as a man of limited views and attainments. Should he be distinguished in his profession, his ignorance on other subjects, and the defects of his education, will be the more exposed to public observation. On the other hand, he who is not only eminent in professional life, but has also a mind richly stored with general knowledge, has an elevation and dignity of character, which gives him a commanding influence in society, and a widely extended sphere of usefulness. His situation enables him to diffuse the light of science among all classes of the community. Is a man to have no other object, than to obtain a *living* by professional pursuits? Has he not duties to perform to his family, to his fellow citizens, to his country; duties which require various and extensive intellectual furniture?

Professional studies are designedly excluded from the course of instruction at college, to leave room for those literary and scientific acquisitions which, if not commenced there, will, in most cases, never be made. They will not grow up spontaneously, amid the bustle of business . . .

As our course of instruction is not intended to complete an education, in theological, medical, or legal science; neither does it include all the minute details of *mercantile, mechanical, or agricultural* concerns. These can never be effectually learned except in the very circumstances in which they are to be practised. The young merchant must be trained in the counting room, the mechanic, in the workshop, the farmer, in the field. But we have, on our premises, no experimental farm or retail shop; no cotton or iron manufactory; no hatter's, or silver-smith's, or coach-maker's establishment. For what purpose, then, it will be asked, are young men who are destined to these occupations, ever sent to a college? They should not be sent, as we think, with an expectation of *finishing* their education at the college; but with a view of laying a thorough foundation in the principles of science, preparatory to the study of the practical arts. As every thing cannot be learned in four years, either theory or practice must be, in a measure at least, postponed to a future opportunity. But if the scientific theory of the arts is *ever* to be acquired, it is unquestionably first in order of time. The corner stone must be laid, before the superstructure is erected . . .

The question may be asked, What is a young man fitted for, when he takes his degree? Does he come forth from the college qualified for business? We answer, no, — if he stops here. His education is begun, but not completed. Is the college to be reproached for not accomplishing that which it has never undertaken to perform?

.　　.　　.　　.　　.

But why, it is asked, should *all* the students in a college be required to tread in the *same steps?* Why should not each one be allowed to select those branches of study which are most to his taste, which are best adapted to his peculiar talents, and which are most nearly connected with his intended profession? To this we answer, that our prescribed course contains those subjects only which ought to be understood, as we think, by every one who aims at a thorough education. They are not the peculiarities of any profession or art. These are to be learned in the professional and practical schools. But the principles of science, are the common foundation of all high intellectual attainments. As in our primary schools, reading, writing, and arithmetic are taught to all,

however different their prospects; so in a college, all should be instructed in those branches of knowledge, of which no one destined to the higher walks of life ought to be ignorant. What subject which is now studied here, could be set aside, without evidently marring the system. Not to speak particularly, in this place, of the ancient languages; who that aims at a well proportioned and superior education will remain ignorant of the elements of the various branches of the mathematics, or of history and antiquities, or of rhetoric and oratory, or natural philosophy, or astronomy, or chemistry, or mineralogy, or geology, or political economy, or mental and moral philosophy?

It is sometimes thought that a student ought not to be urged to the study of that for which he has *no taste or capacity.* But how is he to know, whether he has a taste or capacity for a science, before he has even entered upon its elementary truths? If he is really destitute of talent sufficient for these common departments of education, he is destined for some narrow sphere of action. But we are well persuaded, that our students are not so deficient in intellectual powers, as they sometimes profess to be; though they are easily made to believe, that they have no capacity for the study of that which they are told is almost wholly useless.

When a class have become familiar with the common elements of the several sciences, then is the proper time for them to *divide off* to their favorite studies. They can then make their choice from actual trial. This is now done here, to some extent, in our Junior year. The division might be commenced at an earlier period, and extended farther, provided the qualifications for admission into the college, were brought to a higher standard.

.　　.　　.　　.　　.

Our republican form of government renders it highly important, that great numbers should enjoy the advantage of a thorough education. On the Eastern continent, the *few* who are destined to particular departments in political life, may be educated for the purpose; while the mass of the people are left in comparative ignorance. But in this country, where offices are accessible to all who are qualified for them, superior intellectual attainments ought not to be confined to any description of persons. *Merchants, manufacturers,* and *farmers,* as well as professional gentlemen, take their places in our public councils. A thorough education ought therefore to be extended to all these classes. It is not sufficient that they be men of sound judgment, who can decide correctly, and give a silent vote, on great national questions. Their influence upon the minds of others is needed; an influence to be produced by extent of knowledge, and the force of eloquence. Ought the speaking in our deliberative assemblies to be confined to a single profession? If it is knowledge, which gives us the command of physical agents and instruments, much more is it that which enables us to control the combinations of moral and political machinery.

Young men intended for active employments ought not to be excluded from the colleges, merely on the ground that the course of study is not specially adapted to their pursuits. This principle would exclude those also who are intended for the professions. In either case, the object of the undergraduate course, is not to finish a preparation for business; but to impart that various and general knowledge, which will improve, and elevate, and adorn any occupation. Can merchants, manufacturers, and agriculturists, derive no benefit from high intellectual culture? They are the very classes which, from their situation and business, have the best opportunities for reducing the principles of science to their practical applications. The large estates which the tide of prosperity in our country is so rapidly accumulating, will fall mostly into their hands. Is it not desirable that they should be men of superior education, of large and liberal views, of those solid and elegant attainments, which will raise them to a higher distinction, than the mere possession of property; which will not allow them to hoard their treasures, or waste them in senseless extravagance; which will enable them to adorn

society by their learning, to move in the more intelligent circles with dignity, and to make such an application of their wealth, as will be most honorable to themselves, and most beneficial to their country?

The active, enterprising character of our population, renders it highly important, that this bustle and energy should be directed by sound intelligence, the result of deep thought and early discipline. The greater the impulse to action, the greater is the need of wise and skillful guidance. When nearly all the ship's crew are aloft, setting the topsails, and catching the breezes, it is necessary there should be a steady hand at helm. Light and moderate learning is but poorly fitted to direct the energies of a nation, so widely extended, so intelligent, so powerful in resources, so rapidly advancing in population, strength, and opulence. Where a free government gives full liberty to the human intellect to expand and operate, education should be proportionably liberal and ample. When even our mountains, and rivers, and lakes, are upon a scale which seems to denote, that we are destined to be a great and mighty nation, shall our literature be feeble, and scanty, and superficial?

.   .   .   .   .

The subject of inquiry now presented, is, whether the plan of instruction pursued in Yale College, is sufficiently accommodated to the present state of literature and science; and, especially, whether such a change is demanded as would leave out of this plan the study of the Greek and Roman classics, and make an acquaintance with ancient literature no longer necessary for a degree in the liberal arts.

.   .   .   .   .

In the British Islands, in France, Germany, Italy, and, indeed, in every country of Europe in which literature has acquired distinction and importance, the Greek and Roman classics constitute an essential part of a liberal education. In some countries, classical studies are reviving from a temporary depression; in others, where no such depression has been experienced, they are pursued with increased ardor; and in none, are they known to be declining in public estimation. There may be more variety of opinion than formerly, as to the use of classical learning in certain departments of life; but the conviction of its necessity in the highest education, that which has any claim or pretence to be denominated liberal, is not known to have sustained any considerable change. The literature of every country of Europe is founded more or less on classical literature, and derives from this source its most important illustrations. This is evident not only from such works as have long since appeared, and which form the standard literature of modern times, but from those most recently published, and even from the periodical works of the day. Classical learning is interwoven with every literary discussion. The *fact* only is here insisted on, and this is undeniable. Whoever, then, without a preparation in classical literature, engages in any literary investigation, or undertakes to discuss any literary topic, or associates with those who in any country of Europe, or in this country, are acknowledged to be men of liberal acquirements, immediately feels a deficiency in his education, and is convinced that he is destitute of an important part of practical learning. If scholars, then, are to be prepared to act in the literary world as it in fact exists, classical literature, from considerations purely practical, should form an important part of their early discipline.

But the claims of classical learning are not limited to this single view. It may be defended not only as a necessary branch of education, in the present state of the world, but on the ground of its distinct and independent merits. Familiarity with the Greek and Roman writers is especially adapted to form the taste, and to discipline the mind, both in thought and diction, to the relish of what is elevated, chaste, and simple. The compositions which these writers have left us, both in prose and verse, whether considered in reference to structure, style, modes of illustration, or general execution, approach nearer than any others to what

the human mind, when thoroughly informed and disciplined, of course approves; and constitute, what it is most desirable to possess, a standard for determining literary merit.

.   .   .   .   .

But the study of the classics is useful, not only as it lays the foundations of a correct taste, and furnishes the student with those elementary ideas which are found in the literature of modern times, and which he no where so well acquires as in their original sources; — but also as the study itself forms the most effectual discipline of the mental faculties. This is a topic so often insisted on, that little need be said of it here. It must be obvious to the most cursory observer, that the classics afford materials to exercise talent of every degree, from the first opening of the youthful intellect to the period of its highest maturity. The range of classical study extends from the elements of language, to the most difficult questions arising from literary research and criticism. Every faculty of the mind is employed; not only the memory, judgment, and reasoning powers, but the taste and fancy are occupied and improved.

Classical discipline, likewise, forms the best preparation for professional study. The interpretation of language, and its correct use, are no where more important, than in the professions of divinity and law. But in a course of classical education, every step familiarizes the mind with the structure of language, and the meaning of words and phrases. In researches of a historical nature, and many such occur in the professions, a knowledge, especially of the Latin language, is often indispensable. The use of a thorough knowledge of Greek to a theologian, no one will deny. It is admitted that instances may be found of distinguished success in these professions, where the advantages of a classical education were not enjoyed; — but success of this kind proves only that talents may sometimes force their way to eminence through powerful obstacles. In settling a plan of education, the inquiry should be, not what some men of uncommon endowments have done, but what most men find necessary. Even in cases of extraordinary success, such as have been now alluded to, the want of classical knowledge has been often felt and lamented.

In the profession of medicine, the knowledge of the Greek and Latin languages is less necessary now than formerly; but even at the present time it may be doubted, whether the facilities which classical learning affords for understanding and rendering familiar the terms of science, do not more than counterbalance the time and labor requisite for obtaining this learning. Besides, a physician, who would thoroughly investigate the history of his profession, will find a knowledge of the ancient languages, essential to his object. In all the professions, likewise, a knowledge of general literature is of high importance as a qualification for extensive intercourse with mankind. The formality of the professional character, where the course of reading and thinking is confined to one channel, has often been remarked. The mere divine, the mere lawyer, or the mere physician, however well informed he may be in his particular profession, has less chance of success, than if his early education had been of a more liberal character.

---

2. A critique of the sectarian influence
on American colleges, 1829

L. J. Halsey, ed., *The Works of Philip Lindsley*
(Philadelphia, 1859), I, 202–206.

Lindsley (1786–1855) was a graduate of Princeton and president of the University of Nashville where he delivered this baccalaureate address.

A principal cause of the excessive multiplication and dwarfish dimensions of Western colleges is, no doubt, the diversity of religious denominations among us. Almost every sect will have its college, and generally one at least in each State. Of the score of colleges in Ohio, Kentucky and Tennessee, all are sectarian except two or three; and of course few of them are what they might and should be; and the greater part of them are mere impositions on the public. This is a grievous and growing evil. Why colleges should be sectarian, any more than penitentiaries or than bank, road or canal corporations, is not very obvious. Colleges are designed for the instruction of youth in the learned languages — in polite literature — in the liberal arts and sciences — and not in the dogmatical theology of any sect or party. Why then should they be baptized with sectarian names? Are they to inculcate sectarian Greek, sectarian mathematics, sectarian logic, history, rhetoric, philosophy? Must every State be divided and subdivided into as many college associations as there are religious sects within its limits? And thus, by their mutual jealousy and distrust, effectually prevent the usefulness and prosperity of any one institution? Why does any sect covet the exclusive control of a college, if it be not to promote party and sectarian purposes?

I am aware that as soon as any sect succeeds in obtaining a charter for a *something* called a college, they become, all of a sudden, wondrously liberal and catholic. They forthwith proclaim to the public that their college is the best in the world — and withal, perfectly free from the odious taint of sectarianism. That youth of all religions may come to it without the slightest risk of being proselyted to the faith of the governing sect. This is very modest and very specious, and very hollow, and very hypocritical. They hold out false colours to allure and to deceive the incautious. Their college *is* sectarian, and they know it. It is established by a party — governed by a party — taught by a party — and designed to promote the ends of a party. Else why is it under the absolute and perpetual management and control of a party? They very eagerly and very naturally desire the patronage of other sects, for the double purpose of receiving pecuniary aid, and of adding to their numbers and strength from the ranks of other denominations.

Let any religious sect whatever obtain the absolute direction of a college — located in a small village or retired part of the country — where their religious influence is paramount, perhaps exclusive — where the youth must necessarily attend upon such religious instructions and exercises and ceremonies as they shall prescribe — where, in fact, they can witness no other — where every sermon and prayer and form, where all private conversation and ministerial services proceed from, or are directed by, the one sect — and, is it possible that youth, at the most susceptible period of their lives, should not be operated on by such daily influences, during a period of two, four or six years? How long will the people be gulled by such barefaced impudence — by such unreasonable and monstrous pretensions?

I do not object to any sect's being allowed the privilege of erecting and maintaining, at their own expense, as many schools, colleges and theological seminaries as they please. But, then, their sectarian views should be openly and distinctly avowed. Their purpose should be specified in their charters: and the legislature should protect the people from imposition by the very act which invests them with corporate powers. Hitherto, almost every legislature has pursued an opposite policy, and has aided the work of deception, by enacting that, in the said sectarian institution, youths of all sects should be entitled to equal privileges. Thus the sectarian manufactory goes into operation under the smiles, patronage and recommendation of the people's representatives. Its friends puff it off, and laud it as the people's school, and plead their liberal charter as the talisman that is to guard the people against every insidious attempt at proselytism; and urge the people to contribute their money to build up their promising and most catholic seminary. The bait is seized — the people are cheated — and the sect has its college. Students of all denominations frequent it. And no man of sense and reflection can doubt the consequences . . .

A *public* college — that is, a literary and scientific college designed for the public generally — ought to be independent of all religious sectarian bias, or tendency, or influence. And it ought, when practicable, to be situated in a town or city where the several sects, composing the body of the people, have their own places of public worship, to which their sons may have free access; and where the public eye may be constantly fixed on the conduct of the Trustees and Faculty. And where every artful attempt at proselytism would be instantly detected and exposed. Some men are so constituted that they cannot help being partisans and bigots. Such men are not fit to be the instructors of youth, except where it is intended that the dogmas of a sect shall be inculcated.

Science and philosophy ought to know no party in Church or State. They are degraded by every such connexion. Christianity, indeed, if rightly interpreted, breathes a pure angelic charity, and is as much a stranger to the strife, and intrigue, and rancour, and intolerance, and pharisaism of party, as science and philosophy can be. But so long as men are not content to be honest Christians, but will be zealous Presbyterians, Episcopalians, Methodist, Baptist, Quakers or Romanist, we must so organize our *public* seminaries of learning, as that all may intrust their sons to them without fear of danger to their religious faith.

---

3. A plan for a modern university, 1851

Henry P. Tappan, *University Education* (New York, 1851), pp. 68–70, 88–95.

Tappan (1805–1881), a professor of philosophy and author of many works on that subject, became president of the University of Michigan in 1852. There he attempted to implement the ideas set out in this work but encountered so much opposition that he resigned in 1863.

It were well to commence about this time some experiment of a different kind — a new experiment, and yet one of no doubtful issue, if we can carry it out to its issue. If we can give it a beginning and a middle, we know what its end must be. The establishment of Universities in our country will reform, and alone can reform our educational system. By the Universities we mean such as we have before described — *Cyclopædias* of education: where, in libraries, cabinets, apparatus, and professors, provision is made for studying every branch of knowledge in full, for carrying forward all scientific investigation; where study may be extended without limit, where the mind may be cultivated according to its wants, and where, in the lofty enthusiasm of growing knowledge and ripening scholarship, the bauble of an academical diploma is forgotten. When we have such institutions, those who would be scholars will have some place to resort to; and those who have already the gifts of scholarship will have some place where to exercise them. With such institutions in full operation, the public will begin to comprehend what scholarship means, and discern the difference between sciolists and men of learning. Then we shall hear no more inane discussions about the expediency of discarding Latin and Greek; for, classical scholars there will then be, who will have an opportunity of showing the value of the immortal languages, and the immortal writings of the most cultivated nations of antiquity. Then we shall have mathematicians prepared for astronomers and engineers. Then we shall have philosophers who can discourse without text-books. Then, too, we shall have no more acute distinctions drawn between scholastic and practical education; for, it will be seen that all true education is practical, and that practice without education is little worth; and then there will be dignity, grace, and a resistless charm about scholarship and the scholar.

The philosophic idea of education being thus developed in the highest form of an educational institution — where alone it can be adequately developed — it will begin to exert its power over all subordinate institutions. There will now be demanded a preparation suitable for undertaking the higher degrees of scholarship, and schools and colleges will receive a new impulse and will be determined to their proper form. We shall not now attempt to learn a little of everything in the lower institutions; but we shall learn that which is requisite to prepare for the higher, and we shall learn that well. The influence of the higher will be to give limitation, order, consistency, and thoroughness to the lower. And there will be diffused through all schools of every grade, and for both sexes, new ideas of intellectual discipline, and the sense of an elevated life and duty. Education now will have an authority to define it, examples to illustrate it, and the voice of a Divine spirit to call it forth.

We might have had Universities ere this, had we not wasted our means and energies in unfruitful schemes and misappropriations. We have wasted large sums in erecting expensive buildings in many different places for small collections of students, which, had they been concentrated, would have given for several uncertain colleges a stable University, with ample provision of books and the whole material of learning, and with endowed professorships.

.　　.　　.　　.　　.

We have delayed this great work of founding Universities too long. We cannot well afford to wait for any new sign from heaven before we begin this work. Is there any impertinence in calling upon all scholars and true friends of learning to consider whether we may not now create at least one great institution of learning that may vie with the best of the old world? And if we designed to show the spirit of this undertaking in a few words, we would say, that it is required for the successful development of such an institution, that it should neither cheapen its education at the expense of its intellectual life and aliment, nor be tempted to do so; that it should be adequate to educate the many, and yet not be destroyed if compelled, for a time, to educate the few; that it should be removed alike from the conflicts and jealousies of sects in the Church, and of parties in the State; and that it should be faithfully consecrated to science, literature, and art.

No part of our country presents equal facilities with the city of New York, for carrying out this great undertaking. New York is really the metropolitan city of our country. The centre of commercial activity, the vast reservoir of wealth, it takes the lead in the elegancies and splendor of life, in the arts of luxury and amusement. It is also the great emporium of books and the fine arts. Here resort the professors of music and of the arts of design. Here literary men are taking up their abode. Here literary institutions of various kinds and grades have already come into being. Here are libraries established by associations or by individual munificence, which are enlarging themselves from year to year. Commerce, wealth, and elegance invite, nay, demand the invigorating life, the counterbalancing power and activity of intellectual cultivation. Whatever is requisite for a great Institution of Learning can here be most readily collected; and here are the means in profusion of creating whatever the well-being and glory of our city and of our country may require. By adding to the natural attractions of a metropolitan city the attractions of literature, science, and art, as embodied in a great University, students from every part of the Union would be naturally drawn together. We should thus have a fully appointed national Institution where the bonds of our nationality would be strengthened by the loftiest form of education, the sympathy of scholars, and the noblest productions of literature.

A great Institution would collect together all that is now scattered and isolated among us, be the home of scholars, the nurse of scholar-like endeavors, the regulating and harmonizing centre of thought and investigation. Our whole population would feel the plastic power of intellectual development and progress; society would receive new forms and habitudes from a learned class, and knowledges be widely diffused by public lectures under the direction of an elite corporation.

But what shall be the form of this Institution?

We would take as models, in general, the University of Paris, the Universities of England before they were submerged in the Colleges, and the Universities of Germany.

In the creation of such a University we would at the very beginning collect a choice, varied, and ample library, second to none in the world in books to aid students in attaining ripe scholarship, and in promoting investigation in every department of knowledge — a library distinguished more for valuable and directly available resources of scholarship than for curious and antiquarian collections, estimated rather by the character than the number of its volumes. At the same time we would collect all the necessary apparatus for Physics and Chemistry; we would furnish a noble Observatory; we would found a rich Cabinet of Natural History; and we would open a gallery of the Fine Arts.

Thus with a full store of the material of science, literature, and the arts, would we lay the foundation of a University. We should thus meet aspirations and wants which, in our country, have hitherto been only disappointed, and call into the walks of learning, by commanding attractions, ingenuous minds that in despair have hitherto given themselves to other pursuits.

We would constitute four Faculties, a Faculty of Philosophy and Science, a Faculty of Letters and Arts, a Faculty of Law, and a Faculty of Medicine. Under these should be comprised a sufficient number of professorships to make a proper distribution of the various subjects comprehended under the general titles. These professorships should be endowed to an extent to afford the incumbents a competency independently of tuition fees. The necessity of such endowments must be obvious when we reflect that studious men require undisturbed minds, and that there are branches of knowledge which the interests of the world demand to have taught

— such as Philology, Philosophy, the higher Astronomy, Mathematics, and Physics, while at the same time the number of students will be comparatively few.

It may be a question whether fees of tuition should be required of students, or whether the lectures, together with the libraries and cabinets, should be thrown open gratuitously to the public, as is done in the University of Paris. In this case the professorships, of course, would require to be more amply endowed.

The Professors of the different Faculties should be required to give courses of lectures, on the subjects assigned to them, to the Academical Members of the University. They should also be required to give popular courses to the public in general, on subjects selected by themselves.

By the *Academical* Members, we mean those who shall be admitted upon examination, or upon a Bachelor's degree from any College, and who shall enrol themselves as candidates for the University degrees.

These degrees may be of two grades. The lower grade may comprise Master of Arts, Doctor of Philosophy, Doctor of Medicine, and Bachelor of Laws; the higher grade may comprise Doctor of Laws, Doctor of Theology, and other degrees to mark a high and honorable advance in Medicine, and in Philosophy, Science, Letters and Art.

Those of the first grade to be awarded after three or four years' study, and upon examination. Those of the second grade to be awarded as honorary degrees to men distinguished in the walks of life for their attainments and professional eminence, and to individuals who remain for a still longer term of years connected with the University in learned pursuits. It is, of course, understood that the provisions of the University are to be such as to enable students to pursue favorite branches of science, or learning in general, for an indefinite term of years.

One concurrent effect of this organization would be to elevate the character of Academical degrees, by making them the expression of real attainments, and honorable badges of real merit.

In connection with the popular courses of lectures, there should, also, be established courses particularly designed for the benefit of those engaged in commerce and the useful arts. This would give rise to another class of students besides the Academical, who might avail themselves of every advantage of the University possible to them under the degree of preparation they may have made, and under the pressure of daily business avocations. So also, others besides Academical students might attend the lectures in Law and Medicine, or indeed any courses which they might please to select, but without being considered as candidates for University degrees.

The result would be that the libraries, cabinets, laboratories, and lecture rooms of the University would become the resort of students of every grade; it would thus become the great centre of intellectual activity, and a fountain of learning open to the whole populace.

The different public libraries of the city might, also, be connected with it under their distinctive names; and new libraries might be founded by new donors, under new names, in the same connection, like the different libraries of the English Universities.

It will be remarked that we have omitted a Faculty of Theology in the constitution of this University. As each denomination of Christians has its peculiar Theological views and interests, it would be impossible to unite them harmoniously in one Faculty. It is most expedient, therefore, to leave this branch to the Theological Institutions already established by the several denominations. But still a connection of an unobjectionable character might be formed between Theological Institutions, especially those existing in this city, and the University, productive of very rich benefits. The students of the former might be admitted not only to the libraries of the latter, but also to the lectures on history, philosophy, philology, and general literature, when distinguished lecturers on these subjects gave promise of advantages additional to those enjoyed in the Theological Institutions. Indeed an arrangement might be made by which students undergoing prescribed examinations in philosophy, natural theology, philology, and history, and presenting certificates from their Professors of having completed satisfactorily their Theological courses, might be admitted to the degree of Bachelor in Theology. Students of the Free Academy, also, after having completed their courses in that Institution, might be admitted into the University as Academical Students, or otherwise according to the preparation they may have made.

Thus all our Institutions of learning would grow into a harmonious whole.

With respect to its religious and moral character it should embody in its constitution: First, an entire separation from ecclesiastical control and a renunciation of all sectarian partialities. Secondly, but as every thing that relates to human welfare, needs to be taken under the protecting and nurturing wings of Christianity, it should acknowledge Christianity to be the only true religion, the Bible to be of Divine inspiration, and the supreme rule of Faith and Duty, given freely to all men to be read and received with entire freedom of conscience and opinion.

To carry out these principles it should provide for an equal control of all denominations of Christians acknowledging these principles; it should institute a course of lectures on the evidences of Christianity and on Christian morality; and the reading of the Scriptures together with prayer should constitute a daily public service to be conducted by the Professors in the presence of the students.

No religious profession, however, should be required for admission to the University, but it should be open to students of all creeds as well as of all nations.

For the full development of such an institution, ample funds are required; but that private munificence can accomplish it we fully believe. If the attention of our community can be aroused to the necessity, the interest, the glory of such a work, the accomplishment of it cannot be long delayed.

---

4. The demands of democracy on higher education

Francis Wayland, *The Education Demanded by the People of the U. States* (Boston, 1855), pp. 24–27.

President Wayland (1796–1865) of Brown University drew attention in this essay to those circumstances of American life that were encouraging the colleges to redefine their purpose and reconstruct the curriculum. His reforms of 1850 in Brown's academic program placed the school among the innovative leaders in higher education.[1]

We have a population increasing in wealth with a rapidity wholly unprecedented. The intellect of this people is aroused to action by the means universally provided for common school education. This awakened intellect is stimulated to uncommon activity by the legitimate effects of the democratic principle. Now, can a philanthropist, a patriot, or a statesman, hesitate for a moment, when he is called upon to determine the principles by which the higher education of such a people should be governed?

Shall we, having educated the whole people up to a certain point, giving to all equal advantages for self-development, then reverse our whole system, and bestow the advantages of higher education only upon a few? Shall we say that the lawyer, and physician, and clergyman, need a knowledge of principles in order to pursue their callings with success, while the

1. [Francis Wayland], *Report to the Corporation of Brown University, on Changes in the System of Collegiate Education, Read March 28, 1850* (Providence, 1850).

farmer, the mechanic, the manufacturer, and the merchant require no knowledge of the laws upon which the success of every operation which they perform depends? Shall we say that we need a literary class of men, and for the education of these we will make ample provision, while for all the rest it makes no manner of difference whether they be thoughtful, independent and self-reliant, or nothing but mere hewers of wood and drawers of water? Shall we say that intellect is to be cultivated and talent developed in one direction alone, or developed in every possible direction? I cannot conceive it possible for American citizens to hold any divided opinion on this subject. He would certainly be a rare man who would openly contend for such a distinction as these questions suppose. We are all equal. We are all left each one for himself to work out his own destiny, and to make provision for those that shall come after him. Every one needs knowledge, knowledge of the laws which shall command success in his own avocation. Every one needs that knowledge which shall enable him to form correct judgments, and all men need it equally. Wherever a provision is made for education by private munificence, all men may reasonably expect to share it without distinction; where provision is made by the public, they may rightfully demand it. Nothing can be conceived of, more diametrically opposed to the first principles of our government, than to impose a tax upon the whole, and then appropriate it to the benefit of a part.

But it will, I presume, be answered, that I am contending where there is no adversary; that all our institutions of learning are equally open for all, and that all men may avail themselves of their advantages if they be so disposed. All this I grant. But I ask, for whom were our present systems of collegiate education devised? — for the few or for the many? They were originally designed exclusively for the clergy, and in the fatherland they have been perpetuated for the clergy and the aristocracy. They are, in this country, devised mainly for the professions, and their success is measured by their results upon the professions. The learning which they cultivate is in kind and amount measured by the demands of the professions. But I ask, as I have done before, have not the mechanic and the merchant, the farmer and the manufacturer, as much need of knowledge, each in his own profession, as the lawyer, the minister, and the physician? Have they not as just a claim on the money taken from their own earnings, as those classes which have been so exclusively favored? May they not then justly demand that not only education in higher knowledge shall be provided for them, but that it shall be education of which they may profitably avail themselves; so that they may enter upon their career in life, under as favorable auspices as those who prefer what are sometimes called literary professions?

It would seem then that, in devising a system of higher education for our country, we should commence with the self-evident maxim, that we are to labor not for the benefit of one but of all; not for a caste, or a clique, but for the whole community. Proceeding upon this ground, we should provide the instruction needed by every class of our fellow-citizens. Wherever an institution is established in any part of our country, our first inquiry should be, what is the kind of knowledge (in addition to that demanded for all) which this portion of our people needs, in order to perfect them in their professions, give them power over principles, enable them to develop their intellectual resources and employ their talents to the greatest advantage for themselves and for the country? This knowledge, whatever it may be, should be provided as liberally for one class as for another. Whatever is thus taught, however, should be taught, not only with the design of increasing knowledge, but also of giving strength, enlargement and skill to the original faculties of the soul. When a system of education formed on these principles shall pervade this country, we may be able to present to the world the legitimate results of free institutions; by pursuing any other career we may render them a shame and a by-word.

5. The Morrill Act, 1862, donating federal lands to the loyal states for the foundation and support of colleges

U.S. *Statutes at Large,* XII, 503–505.

Through this act, introduced by Representative Justin Morrill of Vermont, the federal government became a major sponsor of higher education. Although the act specifically required land-grant institutions to supply instruction in "agriculture and the mechanic arts," they were to offer traditional college subjects as well. Many important decisions regarding the organization and operation of the new colleges were left to the states.

Be it enacted by the Senate and House of Representatives of the United States of America in Congress assembled, That there be granted to the several States, for the purposes hereinafter mentioned, an amount of public land, to be apportioned to each State a quantity equal to thirty thousand acres for each senator and representative in Congress to which the States are respectively entitled by the apportionment under the census of eighteen hundred and sixty: *Provided,* That no mineral lands shall be selected or purchased under the provisions of this act.

.   .   .   .   .

Section 4. *And be it further enacted,* That all moneys derived from the sale of the lands aforesaid by the States to which the lands are apportioned, and from the sales of land scrip hereinbefore provided for, shall be invested in stocks of the United States, or of the States, or some other safe stocks, yielding not less than five per centum upon the par value of said stocks; and that the moneys so invested shall constitute a perpetual fund, the capital of which shall remain forever undiminished (except so far as may be provided in section fifth of this act) and the interest of which shall be invio-

lably appropriated, by each State which may take and claim the benefit of this act, to the endowment, support, and maintenance of at least one college where the leading object shall be, without excluding other scientific and classical studies, and including military tactics, to teach such branches of learning as are related to agriculture and the mechanic arts, in such manner as the legislatures of the State may respectively prescribe, in order to promote the liberal and practical education of the industrial classes in the several pursuits and professions in life.

.   .   .   .   .

No portion of said fund, nor the interest thereon, shall be applied, directly or indirectly, under any pretence whatever, to the purchase, erection, preservation, or repair of any building or buildings.

Any State which may take and claim the benefit of the provisions of this act shall provide, within five years, at least not less than one college, as described in the fourth section of this act, or the grant to such State shall cease; and said State shall be bound to pay the United States the amount received of any lands previously sold, and that the title to purchasers under the State shall be valid.

.   .   .   .   .

No State while in a condition of rebellion or insurrection against the government of the United States shall be entitled to the benefit of this act.

The higher education of women

1. Emma Willard proposes advanced instruction for women in "female seminaries," 1819

Emma Willard, *A Plan for Improving Female*

Education, reprint of the 2d ed., 1819 (Middlebury, Vt.: Middlebury College, 1918), pp. 5–6, 13–16.

Miss Willard (1787–1870) proposed to improve women's education but not to make it an exact copy of collegiate instruction for men. She felt education for women should be adjusted to women's needs and responsibilities by including "domestic instruction" and "the ornamental branches." Her hope of securing support from the New York legislature was disappointed but in 1821 she established the Troy (New York) Female Seminary with the assistance of citizens of that city.

The idea of a college for males will naturally be associated with that of a seminary, instituted and endowed by the public; and the absurdity of sending ladies to college, may, at first thought, strike every one to whom this subject shall be proposed. I therefore hasten to observe, that the seminary here recommended, will be as different from those appropriated to the other sex, as the female character and duties are from the male. The business of the husbandman is not to waste his endeavours, in seeking to make his orchard attain the strength and majesty of his forest, but to rear each, to the perfection of its nature.

That the improvement of female education will be considered by our enlightened citizens as a subject of importance, the liberality with which they part with their property to educate their daughters, is a sufficient evidence; and why should they not, when assembled in the legislature, act in concert to effect a noble object, which, though dear to them individually, cannot be accomplished by their unconnected exertions.

If the improvement of the American female character, and that alone, could be effected by public liberality, employed in giving better means of instruction; such improvement of one half of society, and that half, which barbarous and despotic nations have ever degraded, would of itself be an object, worthy of the most liberal government on earth; but if the female character be raised, it must inevitably raise that of the other sex: and thus does the plan proposed, offer, as the object of legislative bounty, to elevate the whole character of the community.

As evidence that this statement does not exaggerate the female influence in society, our sex need but be considered, in the single relation of mothers. In this character, we have the charge of the whole mass of individuals, who are to compose the succeeding generation; during that period of youth, when the pliant mind takes any direction, to which it is steadily guided by a forming hand. How important a power is given by this charge! yet, little do too many of my sex know how, either to appreciate or improve it. Unprovided with the means of acquiring that knowledge, which flows liberally to the other sex — having our time of education devoted to frivolous acquirements, how should we understand the nature of the mind, so as to be aware of the importance of those early impressions, which we make upon the minds of our children? — or how should we be able to form enlarged and correct views, either of the character, to which we ought to mould them, or of the means most proper to form them aright?

Studies and employments should . . . be selected, from one or both of the following considerations; either, because they are peculiarly fitted to improve the faculties; or, because they are such, as the pupil will most probably have occasion to practise in future life.

These are the principles, on which systems of male education are founded; but female education has not yet been systematized. Chance and confusion reign here. Not even is youth considered in our sex, as in the other, a season, which should be wholly devoted to improvement. Among families, so rich as to be entirely above labour, the daughters are hurried through the routine of boarding school instruction, and at an early period introduced into the gay world; and, thenceforth, their only object is amusement. — Mark the different treatment, which the sons of these families receive. While their sisters are gliding through the mazes of the midnight dance, they employ the lamp, to treasure up for future use the riches of ancient wisdom; or to gather strength and expansion of mind, in exploring the wonderful paths of philosophy. When the youth of two sexes has been spent so differently, is it strange, or is nature in fault, if more mature age has brought such a difference of character, that our sex have been considered by the other, as the pampered, wayward babies of society, who must have some rattle put into our hands, to keep us from doing mischief to ourselves or others?

Another difference in the treatment of the sexes is made in our country, which, though not equally pernicious to society, is more pathetically unjust to our sex. How often have we seen a student, who, returning from his literary pursuits, finds a sister, who was his equal in acquirements, while their advantages were equal, of whom he is now ashamed. While his youth was devoted to study, and he was furnished with the means, she, without any object of improvement, drudged at home, to assist in the support of the father's family, and perhaps to contribute to her brother's subsistence abroad; and now, a being of a lower order, the rustic innocent wonders and weeps at his neglect.

Not only has there been a want of system concerning female education, but much of what has been done, has proceeded upon mistaken principles.

One of these is, that, without a regard to the different periods of life, proportionate to their importance, the education of females has been too exclusively directed, to fit them for displaying to advantage the charms of youth and beauty. Though it may be proper to adorn this period of life, yet, it is incomparably more important, to prepare for the serious duties of maturer years. Though well to decorate the blossom, it is far better to prepare for the harvest. In the vegetable creation, nature seems but to sport, when she embellishes the flower;

while all her serious cares are directed to perfect the fruit.

Another errour is, that it has been made the first object in educating our sex, to prepare them to please the other. But reason and religion teach, that we too are primary existencies; that it is for us to move, in the orbit of our duty, around the Holy Centre of perfection, the companions, not the satellites of men; else, instead of shedding around us an influence, that may help to keep them in their proper course, we must accompany them in their wildest deviations.

I would not be understood to insinuate, that we are not, in particular situations, to yield obedience to the other sex. Submission and obedience belong to every being in the universe, except the great Master of the whole. Nor is it a degrading peculiarity to our sex, to be under human authority. Whenever one class of human beings, derive from another the benefits of support and protection, they must pay its equivalent, obedience. Thus, while we receive these benefits from our parents, we are all, without distinction of sex, under their authority; when we receive them from the government of our country, we must obey our rulers; and when our sex take the obligations of marriage, and receive protection and support from the other, it is reasonable, that we too should yield obedience. Yet is neither the child, nor the subject, nor the wife, under human authority, but in subservience to the divine. Our highest responsibility is to God, and our highest interest is to please him; therefore, to secure this interest, should our education be directed.

Neither would I be understood to mean, that our sex should not seek to make themselves agreeable to the other. The errour complained of, is that the taste of men, whatever it might happen to be, has been made a standard for the formation of the female character. In whatever we do, it is of the utmost importance, that the rule, by which we work, be perfect. For if otherwise, what is it, but to err upon principle? A system of education, which leads one class of human beings to consider the approbation of another, as their highest object, teaches, that the rule of their conduct should be the will of beings, imperfect and erring like themselves, rather than the will of God, which is the only standard of perfection.

---

2. A satire on a mother's ambitions for her daughter

Matte Hall, "I have brought my daughter to you to be taught everything," *Godey's Lady's Book,* XLVI (1853), 457.

Dear Madam, I've called for the purpose
    Of placing my daughter at school;
She's only thirteen, I assure you,
    And remarkably easy to rule.
I'd have her learn painting and music,
    Gymnastics and dancing, pray do,
Philosophy, grammar, and logic
    You'll teach her to read, of course, too.

I wish her to learn every study,
    Mathematics are down in my plan,
But of figures she scarce has an inkling,
    Pray instruct her in those, if you can.
I'd have her taught Spanish and Latin,
    Including the language of France;
Never mind her very bad English,
    Teach her *that* when you find a good chance.

On the harp she must be a proficient,
    And play the guitar pretty soon,
And sing the last opera music,
    Even though she can't turn a right tune,
You must see that her manners are finished,
    That she moves with a Hebe-like grace;
For, though she *is* lame and one-sided,
    That's nothing to do with the case.

Now, to you I resign this young jewel,
    And my words I would have you obey;
In six months you return her, dear madam,
    Shining bright as an unclouded day.
She's not aptness, I grant you, for learning
    And her memory oft seems to halt,
But, remember, if she's not *accomplished,*
    It will certainly all be your fault.

---

3. A sympathetic description of the first experiment in collegiate coeducation, 1854

Oberlin Evangelist, June 7, 1854, in Robert S. Fletcher, *A History of Oberlin College* (Oberlin, Ohio: Oberlin College, 1943), I, 379.

We take it the golden mean lies in so shaping the association of young gentlemen with young ladies as to make its general tone elevated and pure; the topics of conversation solid, not vapid; more sensible than sentimental; and drawn from the realms of literature, science and morals, rather than from the limbo of Vanity. Similar studies, common recitations, the daily measuring of mental strength, conduce greatly to the practical impression on each sex that the other are to be held and deemed as intellectual and social beings. The relation of beau and belle is in good measure displaced by the more healthful one of fellow-student. The idea that the young lady is a toy or a plaything is very thoroughly exploded by the practical working of intellectual competition on the college race ground, — to say nothing of the influence of that higher nobler Christian life, in which united efforts for the salvation of souls deeply engross the heart.

C. EDUCATION OF BLACKS AND INDIANS

Denial of education to slaves and free Negroes

1. Mississippi outlaws meetings of five or more slaves or free Negroes for instruction, 1823

"An Act to alter and amend an act entitled 'An Act to reduce into one the several acts concerning slaves, free negroes and mulattoes,'" *Laws of the State of Mississippi, Passed at the Sixth Session of the General Assembly* (Jackson, 1823), p. 60.

All meetings or assemblies of slaves, or free negroes, or mulattoes, mixing and associating with such slaves above the number of five, at any place of public resort, or at any meeting-house or houses, in the night, or at any school or schools, for teaching them reading or writing, either in the day or night, under whatsoever pretext, shall be deemed and considered an unlawful assembly, and any justice of the peace of the county or corporation wherein such assemblage shall be, either from his own knowledge, or the information of others, of such unlawful assemblage or meeting, may issue his warrant, directed to any sworn officer or officers, authorising him or them to enter the house or houses where such unlawful assemblages or meetings may be, for the purpose of apprehending or dispersing such slaves, free negroes or mulattoes, and to inflict corporal punishment on the offender or offenders, at the discretion of any such justice of the peace, not exceeding thirty-nine lashes . . .

2. Virginia prohibits instruction of free Negroes and slaves, 1831

"An Act to amend the act concerning slaves, free negroes and mulattoes," 1831 — ch. 39, *Acts Passed at a General Assembly of the Commonwealth of Virginia* (Richmond, 1831), pp. 107–108.

All meetings of free negroes or mulattoes, at any school-house, church, meeting-house or other place for teaching them reading or writing, either in the day or night, under whatsoever pretext, shall be deemed and considered as an unlawful assembly; and any justice of the county or corporation, wherein such assemblage shall be, either from his own knowledge, or on the information of others, of such unlawful assemblage or meeting, shall issue his warrant, directed to any sworn officer or officers, authorising him or them, to enter the house or houses where such unlawful assemblage or meeting may be, for the purpose of apprehending or dispersing such free negroes or mulattoes, and to inflict corporal punishment on the offender or offenders, at the discretion of any justice of the peace, not exceeding twenty lashes.

. . . If any white person or persons assemble with free negroes or mulattoes, at any school-house, church, meeting-house, or other place for the purpose of instructing such free negroes or mulattoes to read or write, such person or persons shall, on conviction thereof, be fined in a sum not exceeding fifty dollars, and moreover may be imprisoned at the discretion of a jury, not exceeding two months.

. . . If any white person, for pay or compensation, shall assemble with any slaves for the purpose of teaching, and shall teach any slave to read or write, such person, or any white person or persons contracting with such teacher so to act, who shall offend as aforesaid, shall, for each offence, be fined at the discretion of a jury, in a sum not less than ten, nor exceeding one hundred dollars, to be recovered on an information or indictment.

---

3. The Alabama legislature penalizes those who teach free Negroes or slaves to read, then makes an exception, 1832–1833

a. "An Act to Prevent the Introduction of Slaves into Alabama, and for other Purposes," *Acts Passed at the Thirteenth Annual Session of the General Assembly of the State of Alabama* (Tuscaloosa, 1832), p. 16.

Any person or persons who shall endeavor or attempt to teach any free person of color, or slave, to spell, read, or write, shall, upon conviction thereof by indictment, be fined in a sum not less than two hundred and fifty dollars nor more than five hundred dollars.

b. "An Act to authorize the instruction of certain free persons of color . . . ," *Acts Passed at the Annual Session of the General Assembly of the State of Alabama* (Tuscaloosa, 1834), p. 68.

Whereas, there are now residing in the city and county of Mobile and Baldwin, many free colored creoles of said city and counties, whose ancestors were residing there in the time of the change of the flag, and to whom, by the treaty entered into between the French republic and the United States of America, in 1803, were secured the enjoyments of all the rights, advantages and immunities of citizens of the United States: and whereas the said colored creoles have heretofore conducted themselves with uniform propriety and good order, and are anxious to have their offspring educated: therefore,

Be it enacted . . . That the mayor and aldermen of the city of Mobile shall have power to authorize and license such person or persons, as they may deem suitable to teach and instruct, for limited periods, the free colored creole children, residents within the limits of the city and counties of Mobile and Baldwin, who are descendants of those persons who were residents of the said city or counties, at the time the treaty made between the French republic and the United States of America, in April, 1803, was ratified: *Provided always,* that none of the colored children shall be so taught and instructed, until they shall first have the permission of the said mayor and aldermen of the city of Mobile, and they shall have recorded the names of such children in a book to be kept by them for that purpose.

---

4. South Carolina act on teaching slaves, 1834

"An Act to amend the Laws in relation to Slaves and Free Persons of Color," D. J. McCord, ed., *Statutes at Large of South Carolina,* VII (Columbia, 1840), 468.

If any person shall hereafter teach any slave to read or write, or shall aid or assist in teaching any slave to read or write, or cause or procure any slave to be taught to read or write, such person, if a free white person, upon conviction thereof, shall, for each and every offence against this Act, be fined not exceeding one hundred dollars, and imprisoned not more than six months; or if a free person of color, shall be whipped, not exceeding fifty lashes, and fined not exceeding fifty dollars, at the discretion of the court of magistrates and freeholders before which such free person of color is tried; and if a slave, to be whipped at the discretion of the court, not exceeding fifty lashes; the informer to be entitled to one half of the fine, and to be a competent witness. And if any free person of color or slave shall keep any school, or other place of instruction, for teaching any slave or free person of color to read or write, such free person of color or slave shall be liable to the same fine, imprisonment and corporal punishment, as are by this Act imposed and inflicted on free persons of color and slaves for teaching slaves to read or write.

---

5. A Petition to the North Carolina legislature from the Society of Friends asking for repeal of the recently enacted laws restricting the instruction of slaves, 1834

Charles L. Coon, *The Beginnings of Public Education in North Carolina, 1790–1840: A Documentary History* (Raleigh, 1908), II, 675–677.

The legislature failed to respond to this appeal.

Memorial and Petition of the Religious Society of Friends, Convened at New Garden, Guilford County, North Carolina, in the Eleventh Month, 1834. To the General Assembly of the State of North Carolina, Respectfully sheweth — That your Memorialists, entertaining a hope that you will be disposed seriously to consider any subject connected with the great principles of Civil and Religious Liberty, affecting every class of citizens, respectfully present this Memorial.

In this enlightened age and country, and before the Assembly to which your Memorialists now appeal, we deem it unnecessary to urge the incontrovertible arguments that might be advanced from reason and Religion, to prove that it is the indispensable duty of the Legislature of a Christian people to enact laws and establish regulations for the literary instruction of every class, within its limits; and that such provisions should be consistent with sound policy, tend to strengthen the hands of Government and promote the peace and harmony of the community at large.

Your Petitioners consider it a high privilege, that they are subjects of a Government, mild in its form and professedly Republican; that the people have annually the choice of their Legislatures — a circumstance that lessens the difficulty and delicacy of petitioning for the repeal of laws enacted by preceding Legislatures and encourages their hope of success.

Your Memorialists are therefore emboldened under a weighty concern of Religious duty, to petition the present General Assembly of North Carolina to repeal all those laws, enacted by preceding Legislatures of this State, against the literary instruction of Slaves, making it a finable offence for any to be found to be teaching them to read. And they respectfully request your consideration of the repeal of the law recently enacted, prohibiting all coloured persons in this State, bond or free, upon the penalty of corporeal punishment, from public preaching, exhorting, &c. in their respective Religious Congregations or Societies. We consider these laws unrighteous, offensive to God and contrary to the spirit and principles of the Christian Religion; and your Memorialists believe, if not repealed, will increase the difficulties and danger they were intended to prevent.

Your Petitioners, so far from using any measures, either publicly or privately, that would tend to increase their discontent with their situation, feel it their indispensable duty, upon all suitable occasions, to encourage slaves to obedience and faithfulness to their masters, as the most probable means of mitigating their sufferings, and ameliorating their present condition. We would exhort them in the language of the Apostle —

"Servants be obedient to your Masters" — and we do exhort Masters to be kind to their Slaves, as, we have no doubt, such Christian usage would induce a reciprocity of kindlier feelings between them, and ultimately tend to increase the happiness of both, and also promote the harmony and prosperity of the Civil and Religious community. And may we not believe that the more we live in the spirit and in the practice of the precepts of the Gospel of Jesus Christ, the more kind and gentle will be our treatment of every grade of our fellow creatures — for was not the harmonizing and evangelizing of the whole human family, one of the grand purposes for which this Religion was introduced into the world?

And lastly, your Petitioners would respectfully submit to your consideration, not only the repeal of those laws before mentioned, but the enacting of other laws and regulations for the general instruction of Slaves, in the doctrines and precepts of the Christian Religion, and in so much of literary education at least, as will enable them to read the Holy Scriptures, which would undoubtedly tend to the improvement of their general character, and condition, and greatly lessen if not wholly remove, the apprehensions of danger from them.

And may you be influenced by that wisdom which is from above, which is profitable to direct, and which the Apostle says, "is first pure, then peaceable, gentle and easy to be entreated, full of mercy and good fruits." That you may be enabled to enact righteous laws, the operation and execution of which may be a terror to evil-doers, an encouragement to those that do well, and to the praise of God; that violence may no more be heard in our land, but that Righteousness, which exalteth a nation, may so prevail, that the threatening judgments of Heaven on account of sin (which is a reproach to any people) may be averted . . .

been promulgated. The Americans of this portion of the Union have not, indeed, augmented the hardships of slavery; on the contrary, they have bettered the physical condition of the slaves. The only means by which the ancients maintained slavery were fetters and death; the Americans of the South of the Union have discovered more intellectual securities for the duration of their power. They have employed their despotism and their violence against the human mind. In antiquity precautions were taken to prevent the slave from breaking his chains; at the present day measures are adopted to deprive him even of the desire for freedom. The ancients kept the bodies of their slaves in bondage, but placed no restraint upon the mind and no check upon education; and they acted consistently with their established principle, since a natural termination of slavery then existed, and one day or other the slave might be set free and become the equal of his master. But the Americans of the South, who do not admit that the Negroes can ever be commingled with themselves, have forbidden them, under severe penalties, to be taught to read or write; and as they will not raise them to their own level, they sink them as nearly as possible to that of the brutes.

6. The imprisonment of the minds of slaves

Tocqueville, *Democracy in America,* I, 379–380.

The legislation of the Southern states with regard to slaves presents at the present day such unparalleled atrocities as suffice to show that the laws of humanity have been totally perverted, and to betray the desperate position of the community in which that legislation has

7. Chancellor William Harper of South Carolina defends the southern decision to keep slaves in ignorance

The Pro-Slavery Argument; as Maintained by the Most Distinguished Writers of the Southern States, Containing the Several Essays, on the Subject, of Chancellor Harper, Governor Hammond, Dr. Simms, and Professor Dew (Charleston, 1852), pp. 36–38.

Harper (1790–1847), South Carolina's leading lawyer and judge, had been active in the nullification movement of 1832. His essay on slavery was first published in 1837.

Odium has been cast upon our legislation, on account of its forbidding the elements of education to be communicated to slaves. But, in truth, what injury is done to them by this? He who works during the day with his hands, does not read in intervals of leisure for his amusement, or the improvement of his mind — or the exceptions are so very rare, as scarcely to need the being provided for. Of the many slaves whom I have known capable of reading, I have never known one to read any thing but the Bible, and this task they impose on themselves as matter of duty. Of all methods of religious instruction, however, this, of reading for themselves, would be the most inefficient — their comprehension is defective, and the employment is to them an unusual and laborious one. There are but very few who do not enjoy other means more effectual for religious instruction. There is no place of worship opened for the white population, from which they are excluded. I believe it a mistake, to say that the instructions there given are not adapted to their comprehension, or calculated to improve them. If they are given as they ought to be — practically, and without pretension, and are such as are generally intelligible to the free part of the audience, comprehending all grades of intellectual capacity, — they will not be unintelligible to slaves. I doubt whether this be not better than instruction, addressed specially to themselves — which they might look upon as a device of the master's, to make them more obedient and profitable to himself. Their minds, generally, show a strong religious tendency, and they are fond of assuming the office of religious instructors to each other; and perhaps their religious notions are not much more extravagant than those of a large portion of the free population of our country. I am not sure that there is a much smaller proportion of them, than of the free population, who make some sort of religious profession. It is certainly the master's *interest* that they should have proper religious sentiments, and if he fails in his duty towards them, we may be sure that the consequences will be visited not upon them, but upon him.

If there were any chance of their elevating their rank and condition in society, it might be matter of hardship, that they should be debarred those rudiments of knowledge which open the way to further attainments. But this they know cannot be, and that further attainments would be useless to them. Of the evil of this, I shall speak hereafter. A knowledge of reading, writing, and the elements of arithmetic, is convenient and important to the free laborer, who is the transactor of his own affairs, and the guardian of his own interests — but of what use would they be to the slave? These alone do not elevate the mind or character, if such elevation were desirable.

How slaves learned to read and write

1. Frederick Douglass in Baltimore, ca. 1825–1830

Narrative of the Life of Frederick Douglass, Written by Himself, pp. 58, 64–65, 70–71.

Very soon after I went to live with Mr. and Mrs. Auld, she very kindly commenced to teach me the A, B, C. After I had learned this, she assisted me in learning to spell words of three or four letters. Just at this point of my progress, Mr. Auld found out what was going on, and at once forbade Mrs. Auld to instruct me further, telling her, among other things, that it was unlawful, as well as unsafe, to teach a slave to read. To use his own words, further, he said, "If you give a nigger an inch, he will take an ell. A nigger should know nothing but to obey his master — to do as he is told to do. Learning would *spoil* the best nigger in the world.

Now," said he, "if you teach that nigger (speaking of myself) how to read, there would be no keeping him. It would forever unfit him to be a slave. He would at once become unmanageable, and of no value to his master. As to himself, it could do him no good, but a great deal of harm. It would make him discontented and unhappy." These words sank deep into my heart, stirred up sentiments within that lay slumbering, and called into existence an entirely new train of thought. It was a new and special revelation, explaining dark and mysterious things, with which my youthful understanding had struggled, but struggled in vain.

. . . . .

From this time I was most narrowly watched. If I was in a separate room any considerable length of time, I was sure to be suspected of having a book, and was at once called to give an account of myself. All this, however, was too late. The first step had been taken. Mistress, in teaching me the alphabet, had given me the *inch,* and no precaution could prevent me from taking the *ell.*

The plan which I adopted, and the one by which I was most successful, was that of making friends of all the little white boys whom I met in the street. As many of these as I could, I converted into teachers. With their kindly aid, obtained at different times and in different places, I finally succeeded in learning to read. When I was sent of errands, I always took my book with me, and by going one part of my errand quickly, I found time to get a lesson before my return. I used also to carry bread with me, enough of which was always in the house, and to which I was always welcome; for I was much better off in this regard than many of the poor white children in our neighborhood. This bread I used to bestow upon the hungry little urchins, who, in return, would give me that more valuable bread of knowledge. I am strongly tempted to give the names of two or three of those little boys, as a testimonial of the gratitude and affection I bear them; but prudence forbids; — not that it would injure me, but it might embarrass them; for it is almost an unpardonable offence to teach slaves to read in this Christian country.

. . . . .

The idea as to how I might learn to write was suggested to me by being in Durgin and Bailey's ship-yard, and frequently seeing the ship carpenters, after hewing, and getting a piece of timber ready for use, write on the timber the name of that part of the ship for which it was intended. When a piece of timber was intended for the larboard side, it would be marked thus — "L." When a piece was for the starboard side, it would be marked thus — "S." A piece for the larboard side forward, would be marked thus — "L.F." When a piece was for starboard side forward, it would be marked thus — "S.F." For larboard aft, it would be marked thus — "L.A." For starboard aft, it would be marked thus — "S.A." I soon learned the names of these letters, and for what they were intended when placed upon a piece of timber in the ship-yard. I immediately commenced copying them, and in a short time was able to make the four letters named. After that, when I met with any boy who I knew could write, I would tell him I could write as well as he. The next word would be, "I don't believe you. Let me see you try it." I would then make the letters which I had been so fortunate as to learn, and ask him to beat that. In this way I got a good many lessons in writing, which it is quite possible I should never have gotten in any other way. During this time, my copy-book was the board fence, brick wall, and pavement; my pen and ink was a lump of chalk. With these, I learned mainly how to write. I then commenced and continued copying the Italics in Webster's Spelling Book, until I could make them all without looking on the book. By this time, my little Master Thomas had gone to school, and learned how to write, and had written over a number of copy-books. These had been brought home, and shown to some of our near neighbors, and then laid aside. My mistress used to go to class meeting at the Wilk Street meeting-house every Monday afternoon, and leave me to take care of the house. When left thus, I used to spend the time in writing in the spaces left in Master Thomas's copy-book, copying what he had written. I continued to do this until I could write a hand very similar to that of Master Thomas. Thus, after a long, tedious effort for years, I finally succeeded in learning how to write.

2. Fanny Kemble gives a reading lesson on a Georgia plantation, 1839

Kemble, *Journal,* p. 300.

I must give you an account of Aleck's first reading lesson, which took place at the same time that I gave S[ally] hers this morning. It was the first time he had had leisure to come, and it went off most successfully. He seems to me by no means stupid, I am very sorry he did not ask me to do this before; however, if he can master his alphabet before I go, he may, if chance favor him with the occasional sight of a book, help himself on by degrees. Perhaps he will have the good inspiration to apply to cooper London for assistance; I am much mistaken if that worthy does not contrive that Heaven shall help Aleck, as it formerly did him, in the matter of reading.

3. Slaves on a Mississippi plantation who had learned to read

Frederick Law Olmsted, *A Journey in the Back Country* (New York, 1860), pp. 142–144.

The next morning when I turned out I found Yazoo looking with the eye of a connoisseur at the seven prime field-hands, who at half past

seven were just starting off with hoes and axes for their day's work. As I approached him, he exclaimed with enthusiasm:

"Are n't them a right keen lookin' lot of niggers?"

And our host soon after coming out, he immediately walked up to him, saying:

"Why, friend, them yer niggers o' yourn would be good for seventy bales of cotton, if you'd move down into our country."

Their owner was perfectly aware of their value, and said every thing good of them.

"There's something ruther singlar, too, about my niggers; I do n't know as I ever see any thing like it anywhere else."

"How so, sir?"

"Well, I reckon it 's my way o'treatin' 'em, much as any thing. I never hev no difficulty with 'em. Hen't licked a nigger in five year, 'cept maybe sprouting some of the young ones sometimes. Fact, my niggers never want no lookin' arter; they jus tek ker o' themselves. Fact, they do tek a greater interest in the crops than I do myself. There's another thing — I 'spose 't will surprise you — there ent one of my niggers but what can read; read good, too — better'n I can, at any rate."

"How did they learn?"

"Taught themselves. I b'lieve ther was one on 'em that I bought, that could read, and he taught all the rest. But niggers is mighty apt at larnin', a heap more'n white folks is."

I said that this was contrary to the generally received opinion.

"Well, now, let me tell you," he continued; "I had a boy to work, when I was buildin', and my boys jus teachin' him night times and such, he warn't here more'n three months, and he larned to read as well as any man I ever heerd, and I know he did n't know his letters when he come here. It did n't seem to me any white man could have done that; does it to you, now?"

"How old was he?"

"Warn't more'n seventeen, I reckon."

"How do they get books — do you get them for them?"

"Oh, no; get 'em for themselves."

"How?"
"Buy 'em."
"How do they get the money?"
"Earn it."
"How?"
"By their own work. I tell you my niggers have got more money 'n I hev."
"What kind of books do they get?"
"Religious kind a books ginerally — these stories; and some of them will buy novels, I believe. They won't let on to that, but I expect they do it."
They bought them of peddlers. I inquired about the law to prevent negroes reading, and asked if it allowed books to be sold to negroes. He had never heard of any such law — did n't believe there was any. The Yazoo man said there was such a law in his country. Negroes never had any thing to read there.

Education of free Negro children

1. John Chavis, a free Negro, teaches white and black children in North Carolina

Chavis (ca. 1763–1838), according to tradition, studied privately with President John Witherspoon of Princeton and then became a Presbyterian missionary and teacher in Virginia and North Carolina. His school for whites, attended by several who later became prominent North Carolinians, was famous. As the documents below indicate, he also taught free Negroes.

a. Chavis advertises his school, 1808

The Raleigh Register, Aug. 26, 1808, in Edgar W. Knight, "Notes on John Chavis," *North Carolina Historical Review,* VII (1930), 339, 343.

John Chavis takes this method of informing his employers, and the citizens of Raleigh in general, that the present quarter of his school will end the 15th of September, and the next will commence on the 19th. He will, at the same time, open an evening school for the purpose of instructing children of colour, as he intends, for the accommodation of some of his employers, to exclude all children of colour from his day school.

The evening school will commence at an hour by sun. When the white children leave the house, those of colour will take their places, and continue until ten o'clock.

The terms of teaching white children will be as usual, two and a half dollars per quarter; those of color, one dollar and three quarters. In both cases, the whole of the money is to be paid in advance to Mr. Benjamin S. King. Those who produce certificates from him of their having paid the money, will be admitted.

Those who think proper to put their children under his care, may rely upon the strictest attention being paid, not only to their education but to their morals, which he deems an *important* part of education.

He hopes to have a better school house by the commencement of the next quarter.

b. Chavis draws the praise of a newspaper editor

John Gale [editor], *The Raleigh Register,* April 22, 1830, in Knight, "Notes on John Chavis," p. 343.

On Friday last, we attended an examination of the free children of color, attached to the school conducted by John Chavis, also colored, but a regularly educated Presbyterian minister, and we have seldom received more gratification from any exhibition of a similar character. To witness a well regulated school, composed of this class of persons — to see them setting an example both in behavior and scholarship, which their white superiors might take pride in imitating, was a cheering spectacle to a philanthropist. The exercises throughout, evinced a degree of attention and assiduous care on the part of the instructor, highly creditable, and of attainment on the part of his scholars almost incredible. We were also much pleased with the sensible address which closed the examination. The object of the respectable teacher, was to impress on the scholars, the fact, that they occupied an inferior and subordinate station in society, and were possessed but of limited privileges; but that even *they* might become useful in their particular sphere by making a proper improvement of the advantages afforded them.

---

2. Connecticut forbids the attendance of Negro children from other states in private, unincorporated schools without the permission of the selectmen, 1833

The Public Statute Laws of the State of Connecticut (Hartford, 1835), pp. 321–322.

Connecticut, by this law, struck at the school of Prudence Crandall (1803–1889) in the town of Canterbury. Miss Crandall, admitting Negroes to her school for girls, aroused the ire and provoked abuse from her fellow townspeople. Arrested and imprisoned under this law in 1834, she discontinued her school and left the state.

Whereas, attempts have been made to establish literary institutions in this state for the instruction of colored persons belonging to other states and countries, which would tend to the great increase of the colored population of the state, and thereby to the injury of the people: Therefore,

Be it enacted . . . That no person shall set up or establish in this state any school, academy, or literary institution, for the instruction or education of colored persons who are not inhabitants of this state, nor instruct or teach in any school, academy, or other literary institution whatsoever in this state, or harbor or board, for the purpose of attending or being taught or instructed in any such school, academy, or literary institution, any colored person who is not an inhabitant of any town in this state, without the consent, in writing, first obtained of a majority of the civil authority, and also of the select-men of the town in which such school, academy, or literary institution is situated; and each and every person who shall knowingly do any act forbidden as aforesaid, or shall be aiding or assisting therein, shall, for the first offence, forfeit and pay to the treasurer of this state, a fine of one hundred dollars, and for the second offence shall forfeit and pay a fine of two hundred dollars, and so double for every offence of which he or she shall be convicted . . .

---

3. Ohio laws on public schools for Negro children, 1825–1859

Although the Ohio legislature passed a common school law in 1825, Negro children were excluded from public schools. In 1829 the exclusion was made explicit; at the same time, tax funds paid by Negroes were set aside for use by their children.

---

a. Negro taxes for Negro schools

"An Act to provide for the support and better regulation of Common Schools,"

Acts of a General Nature Passed at the First Session of the Twenty-Seventh Assembly of the State of Ohio (Columbus, 1829), pp. 72–73.

Be it enacted by the General Assembly of the State of Ohio, That a fund shall hereafter be raised in the several counties in this state, in the manner pointed out by this act, for the use of common Schools, for the instruction of youth of every class and grade without distinction, in reading, writing, arithmetic and other necessary branches of a common education: *Provided,* That nothing in this act contained, shall be so construed as to permit black or mulatto persons to attend the schools hereby established, or compel them to pay any tax for the support of such schools; but all taxes assessed on their property, for school purposes, in the several counties in this state, shall be appropriated as the Trustees of the several townships may direct, for the education of said black and mulatto persons therein, and for no other purpose, whatever.

b. School districts for Negroes authorized, 1849

"An Act to authorize the establishment of separate schools for the education of colored children, and for other purposes," *Acts of a General Nature Passed by the Forty-Seventh General Assembly of the State of Ohio* (Columbus, 1849), pp. 17–18.

The trustees of each incorporated township in this State, and the trustees, visitors, and directors of schools, or other officers having authority in the premises, of each city and incorporated town or village, shall be and they are hereby authorized and required respectively . . . to create one or more school districts for colored persons, in every such township, city, town or village . . .

Whenever any district shall be established as aforesaid, the trustees or other authorities establishing the same, shall give notice, by public advertisement, to the adult male colored tax payers residing in such district, to meet at a time and place specified in the notice, and choose their school directors . . .

The trustees or other authorities establishing separate districts, as aforesaid, shall cause an accurate list to be made as speedily as possible, of all colored tax payers, and of all colored youth over four and under twenty-one years of age, resident therein, and shall certify it to the county Auditor, who shall preserve the same in his office; and no property of any colored tax payer within said districts shall be charged with any special tax for district purposes, for the benefit of the schools in any regular district, composed wholly or in part of the same territory; and no property of any white person in any regular district, shall be charged with any such tax for the benefit of the schools in any separate district composed wholly, or in part, of the same territory.[1]

Every separate district, established as aforesaid, shall be held to include for school purposes, only the colored persons resident within its territorial limits, and from and after the establishment of the same, the colored youth resident therein, shall attend the schools organized under the directors of such district.

c. A court test of the Ohio school laws, 1859

Enos Van Camp *v.* The Board of Education of the Incorporated Village of Logan, n.s. 9, Ohio Reports, 408, 409–412, 414.

1. An amendment of March 14, 1853, entitled Negro children in separate schools to a proportionate share of the common school fund maintained by the state. Until then, their schools were supported solely by local taxes upon the property of Negroes,

A Negro parent, resident in a district which had provided no school for Negro children, brought suit to force the local board to admit his children to the schools, arguing that the children were in part of white ancestry. In a 3–2 decision, the justices of the Ohio Supreme Court maintained that the children were properly excluded by the laws of the state. The majority opinion was written by Justice Peck.

The plaintiff in error insists that his children, though in part of African descent, being more than one-half of white blood, are, under the law and the uniform decisions of this court, to be regarded as *white,* and were therefore wrongfully excluded by the defendants in error from the common schools of the incorporated village of Logan.

. . . . .

This act of 1853 . . . looks to and makes provision for the education of *all* the children within the state; — children of all races and shades of color. But in so doing, divides them into two classes, "white" and "colored," and imposes the duty of providing schools for both classes, though under different teachers, upon the same board of education. The law then is one of *classification* and not of *exclusion.* All the youth, within the prescribed ages, must fall within the one class or the other. All are to be instructed and to participate equally in the public fund, and the share of one class can never be diverted to the instruction of the other. It is true, that where the number of colored youth is too small to justify the organization or the continuance of a school for colored youth, such school must be temporarily delayed or suspended; but this is no more than might occur with the other class under similar circumstances. In determining what is to be understood by the terms "white" and "colored," as used in this act, we may look to the state of things existing at the time, the evils complained of, and the remedies sought to be applied. For nearly two generations, blacks and mulattoes

had been a proscribed and degraded race in Ohio. They were debarred from the elective franchise and prohibited from immigration and settlement within our borders, except under severe restrictions. They were also excluded from our common schools and all means of public instruction — incapacitated from serving upon juries, and denied the privilege of testifying in cases where a white person was a party. It would be strange, indeed, if such a state of things had not increased, in the present generation, the natural repugnance of the white race to communion and fellowship with them. Whether consistent with true philanthropy or not, it is nevertheless true, that in many portions, if not throughout the state, there was and still is an almost invincible repugnance to such communion and fellowship. It is also to be borne in mind, that a class had grown up among us, which, though partly black, had still a preponderance of white blood in their veins, and that the courts, influenced in some degree by the severe and somewhat penal character of the restrictions as to blacks and mulattoes, had held that such persons were not only entitled to vote at elections, and testify in our courts of justice, but were also admissible into the schools for white children. It is notorious that these decisions, especially the last, did not receive the hearty approval of the state at large. The prejudice of ages could not be dissipated by one or more judicial decisions, and the frequent suits brought to enforce such admission, evidence such feeling on the part of young and old.

Under this state of things the act of 1853 was enacted. Three objects seem to have been especially in view. To divide all the youth of the state, for educational purposes, into two classes, to provide more effectually for the education of both classes, and to require both classes to be separately instructed. To which of these classes do the children of the plaintiff in error belong — "white" or "colored?" They are not in the *ordinary,* if they are in a *legal sense,* white. The demurrer admits that they are, in fact, if not in law, *colored* children . . .

A person who has any perceptible admixture of African blood, is generally called a colored person. In affixing the epithet "colored," we do not ordinarily stop to estimate the precise shade, whether light or dark, though where precision is desired, they are sometimes called "light colored," or "dark colored," as the case may be. If we look at the evils the law was intended to remedy, we shall arrive at the same result. One of the evils undoubtedly was the repugnance felt by many of the white youths and their parents to mingling, socially and on equal terms, with those who had any perceptible admixture of African blood. This feeling or prejudice, if it be one, had been fostered by long years of hostile legislation and social exclusion. The general assembly, legislating for the people as they were, rather than as, perhaps, they ought to have been, while providing for the education and consequent ultimate elevation of a long degraded class, yielded for the time to a deep-seated prejudice, which could not be eradicated suddenly, if at all. Such an arrangement, in the present state of public feeling, is far better for both parties — for the colored youth as well as those entirely white. If those a shade more white than black were to be forced upon the white youth against their consent, the whole policy of the law would be defeated. The prejudice and antagonism of the whites would be aroused; bickerings and contentions become the order of the day, and the moral and mental improvement of both classes retarded. It would seem then, from this examination of the law of 1853, and the circumstances under which it was passed, that the words "white" and "colored," as used in that act, were both used in their ordinary and common acceptation, and that any other construction would do violence to the legislative intent, and perpetuate the very evils that act was intended to remedy. Such was also the construction, which the act upon its passage received in many portions, if not throughout the state. The colored population, whether more or less than mulatto, affiliated with the blacks. Schools were organized,

and a wholesome rivalry inaugurated between the two classes.

.   .   .   .   .

That the legislature have the power thus to classify the scholars, even when all are undeniably white, no one will question. It might, perhaps, have been better if some further and more definite provision had been made for the education of colored youth, in districts in which the number is so very limited, as it appears to be in the village of Logan. That, however, is a matter for the consideration of the legislature and not for the judiciary.

Division of school fund in New York

1. New York state grants permission to districts to establish separate schools for Negro children and provides for a division of school funds, 1841

"An Act to amend . . . the Revised Statutes, relating to Common Schools," 1841 — ch. 260, *Laws of the State of New York, Passed at the Sixty-fourth Session of the Legislature* (Albany, 1841), pp. 238–239.

A school for colored children may be established in any city or town of this state, with the approbation of the commissioners of common schools of such city or town, which shall be under the charge of the trustees of the district in which such school shall be kept; and in places where no school districts exist, or where from any cause it may be expedient, such school may be placed in charge of trustees to be appointed by the commissioners of common schools of the town or city, and if there be none, to be appointed by the superintendent.

Returns shall be made by the trustees of such schools to the commissioners of common schools, at the same time and in the same manner as now provided by law in relation to districts; and they shall particularly specify the number of colored children over five and under sixteen years of age, attending such school from different districts, naming such districts respectively, and the number from each. The commissioners shall apportion and pay over to the trustees of such schools, a portion of the money received by them annually, in the same manner as now provided by law in respect to school districts, allowing to such schools the proper proportion for each child over five and under sixteen years, who shall have been instructed in such school at least four months by a teacher duly licensed, and shall deduct such proportion from the amount that would have been apportioned to the district to which such child belongs; and in their reports to the superintendent the commissioners shall specially designate the schools for colored children in their town or city.

---

2. A criticism of inequitable distribution of school funds in New York City, 1859

Editorial in the *New York Tribune,* March 8, 1859.

We systematically deprive the black man of the opportunity of equal culture with the white; we deliberately withhold from him the humanizing and softening influences of education; we practically deny him the right which we theoretically maintain belongs to all men, and then we reproach him that he is not thrifty, not enlightened, not virtuous, but idle, indigent, and imbecile. Doing our best to make him a bad citizen, we complain of him, and reproach him for not being a good one. If the complaint and

reproach are not justified by the fact, it is from no merit of ours, but because the black man is so used to oppression that the virtue of moral resistance is strengthened by use, and he does not altogether succumb to the hard fate with which he is visited.

There are in this city about nine thousand colored adults, one thousand of whom are taxed on real estate to the value of nearly a million and a half of dollars, and to this amount may be added nearly two millions of personal estate and money in bank. Probably not less than three thousand more of these people, who are not owners of real estate, are heavily taxed as householders and rent payers, so that the proportion of the whole number who pay taxes for the support of our public schools is quite as large, if not larger, in proportion to the whole number, than that of the white population. Since the organization of the Board of Education the expenditure for school-houses has amounted to $1,600,000. The expenditure for colored schools, during the same period, has amounted to $1,000, the Old Public School Society having assigned to the Board two of the school-houses now used for colored children. The actual expenditure then has been as 1,600 to 1 in favor of the whites, while the proportion of colored children to white attending the schools is as 1 to 40. Nor does the injustice end here. The estimated number of colored children (from the census of 1850) is 3,000, and the average attendance on public schools and corporate schools, supported by school funds, is 1,153, giving an average of attendance to the whole number of 1 to 2.60. The estimated number of white children is 150,000, and the average attendance upon the public and corporate schools is 46,684, or to the whole number as 1 to 3.40. From this it appears that in proportion to the whole number there are nearly 25 per cent more of colored children than of white, who avail themselves of the advantages of education provided by the State. But a large proportion of the white children attend private and Catholic parochial schools;

and with this addition, even, it appears that the proportionate attendance of the two classes in schools of all kinds, is about equal. With an equal desire then for education, and with, at least, equal, if not greater proportionate taxation, the expenditure of the Board, as we have shown above, is as 1 to 1,600. This remarkable difference is easily accounted for. The schoolhouses for the whites are in situations where the price of lots is high, and on the buildings themselves no expenditure is spared to make them commodious and elegant, such as the halls of learning should be, where the State, with a paternal care, provides for the education of the rising generation. The schools for the blacks, on the contrary, are nearly all, if not all, old buildings, generally in filthy and degraded neighborhoods, dark, damp, small and cheerless, safe neither for the morals nor the health of those who are compelled to go to them, if they go anywhere, and calculated rather to repel than to attract them. For such a state of things there is of course no excuse other than the very poor one of an unreasonable prejudice, and an enlightened and prosperous people should be ashamed of being so governed by it as to make the least possible return in educational privileges to those who are most heavily taxed for them. It is breaking the promise to the ear as well as to the hope to assert the legal supposition of equality while the logical consistency only is maintained of granting a poorer quality of instruction to those who are held, by their very isolation, to be of a poorer quality of humanity. We are glad to see that the Special Commission in relation to the common schools of this city call particular attention to this state of things in their annual report to the Governor. Either the colored children should be as well educated as the white, or, if any distinction is made, it should extend to the taxes as well as the educational advantage. But no well-governed State can afford to do otherwise than to secure to those who are to become hereafter its men and women, every possible inducement and facility to intelligence and virtue.

Separate schools for Negroes in Boston

1. An account of the separate public grammar school for Negro children in Boston, 1845

Reports of the Annual Visiting Committees of the Public Schools of the City of Boston, 1845 (Boston, 1845), pp. 22–23.

The Committee on Grammar Schools consisted of Theophilus Parsons, Samuel Gridley Howe, and Rollin H. Neale. Its report, severely critical of the methods employed by teachers, stimulated a controversy which before running its course touched upon all aspects of the schools. Defenders of the schools characterized the visiting committee's report as "visionary and . . . pert." The Smith School, described below, was the only public grammar school for Negroes in Boston. The committee judged it the poorest of the eighteen schools visited in each of the four required grammar school studies — grammar, definitions, history, and geography. *Reports of the Annual Visiting Committees,* p. 149.

In regard to the Smith school, we have come to the conclusion that it is not only in an unsatisfactory, but in a deplorable condition. The attainments of the scholars are of the lowest grade; a few can read aloud from the first class reader, but cannot understand any other than the simplest passages. Their chattering about grammar shows only the power of their memories to retain the names of things which they do not understand; and their knowledge of geography is nothing but the faculty of repeating imperfectly names of states, towns, rivers, &c. There are certain parts of physical and political geography which we supposed might be made most interesting to colored

children, those relating to the West India Islands, the condition of the colored race in
Cuba, Jamaica, Hayti, &c.; the colonies in
Africa, the condition of the natives, &c.; but
the scholars of the Smith school seemed to know
nothing about them. They supposed Cuba to
be smaller than Massachusetts, knew little or
nothing of the other islands, and though one
or two had heard of the emancipation act, the
class knew nothing about it. They had only the
most crude and vague notions of history; and,
as for mathematical geography, astronomy, or
natural philosophy, the master declined any
examination.

But the intellectual deficiency which prevails in this school is not its worst feature; there
is a want of discipline; an indifference to verbal
requests for order, which indicates the frequency of appeal to more stirring motives; a
want of respectful attention, and many inde-
finable but clear indications of a low moral
tone.

Your Committee are aware, that there are
many circumstances to be considered before
blame should be laid on any individual, for the
present low state of the school; they are aware
of the difficulties in obtaining a good average
attendance, and they will not say that another
individual could at once inspire the colored
population with more interest in the school,
could secure a more punctual attendance, or
could awaken the faculties and interest the
attention of the scholars. But they do believe
that there is good sense enough among the
parents, and intellect enough among the children, if fairly enlisted in the subject, and directed by a zealous and discreet friend, to create
a school which shall reach at least to the rank
now attained by one half of the city schools.

It is to be regretted that the present incumbent has not more faith in the desire of
the colored population for the education of
their children, and in the capacities of the children themselves; for we fear that, without much
faith, and even some enthusiasm, no great
harvest can follow the teacher's labors. We
think this school calls loudly for improvement.

[William Brigham, J. I. T. Coolidge,
and Hiram A. Graves], "Report of the
Committee on Writing Schools," *Reports of the
Annual Visiting Committees,* pp. 158–159.

At the time of the examination, 163 belonged to [Smith School]. The average attendance since the first of April last has been 109.
This school is under the instruction of a master
and two female assistants. It is divided into
four classes. Twenty-seven are in the first class.
Four half days each week are devoted to writing and arithmetic. Of the first division of the
first class only five were present, whose average
age was twelve years and four months. There
seemed to be but few pupils present more than
ten or eleven years of age. The present master
has been connected with the school eleven
years.

The Committee do not hesitate to say that
they were disappointed in this school. With but
two or three exceptions the pupils had not gone
beyond the simplest questions in oral Arithmetic, and on examination they seemed to be
unable to answer any thing but the plainest
propositions. The school is in a low condition,
and does not appear to be answering the objects
for which it was instituted. There are, no
doubt, great difficulties in the management and
instruction of this school, arising from causes
which do not affect any other school in the
city. The children leave early and as soon as
they are able to obtain employment. Those
best educated and most capable usually go first.

They often, too, join the school at an advanced age, and without much previous education or discipline. They are inconstant in their
attendance, oftentimes tardy, and in many
cases exceedingly inattentive to their studies. It
is evident that in a school of this character,
other and greater efforts are required in its
management than in the other city schools. It
may not be made to compete with the other
schools, yet it is believed that it can be much
elevated, that its usefulness may be increased,
and that it may be placed on such a footing as
to answer the just expectations of its benevolent

founder, as well as the rightful claims of the colored population.

---

2. Negro citizens of Boston petition the School Committee for integrated primary schools, 1846

Report to the Primary School Committee, June 15, 1846, on the Petition of Sundry Colored Persons for the Abolition of the Schools for Colored Children (Boston, 1846), p. 2.

To the Primary School Committee of the City of Boston:

The undersigned colored citizens of Boston, parents and guardians of children *now* attending the exclusive Primary Schools for colored children in this City, respectfully represent; — that the establishment of exclusive schools for our children is a great injury to us, and deprives us of those equal privileges and advantages in the public schools to which we are entitled as citizens. These separate schools cost more and do less for the children than other schools, since all experience teaches that where a small and despised class are shut out from the common benefit of any public institutions of learning and confined to separate schools, few or none interest themselves about the schools, — neglect ensues, abuses creep in, the standard of scholarship degenerates, and the teachers and the scholars are soon considered and of course become an inferior class.

But to say nothing of any other reasons for this change, it is sufficient to say that the establishment of separate schools for our children is believed to be unlawful, and it is felt to be if not in intention, in fact, insulting. If, as seems to be admitted, you are violating our rights, we simply ask you to cease doing so.

We therefore earnestly request that such exclusive schools be abolished, and that our children be allowed to attend the Primary Schools established in the respective Districts in which we live.

(Signed)   George Putnam,
                    And Eighty-five Others.

---

3. Rejection of the petition by the Primary School Committee

Report of the Primary School Committee, pp. 28–30.

This report was adopted by the Committee by a vote of 59 to 16. A dissenting minority report, advocating integrated schools, was also presented.

What we claim, is,

That, under the law giving to the School Committee "the general charge and superintendence of all the public schools," and the power to "determine the number and qualification of the scholars to be admitted into the school," the Committee have the right to distribute, assign, and classify, all children, belonging to the schools in the City, according to their best judgement:

.   .   .   .   .

In applying these principles to the case of colored children, we maintain,

1. That their peculiar physical, mental, and moral structure, requires an educational treatment, different, in some respects, from that of white children. Teachers of schools in which they are intermingled, remark, that, in those parts of study and instruction in which progress depends on memory, or on the imitative faculties, chiefly, the colored children will often keep pace with the white children, but, when progress comes to depend chiefly on the faculties of invention, comparison, and reasoning, they quickly fall behind.

2. That the number of colored children, in Boston, is so great, that they can be advantageously placed in separate schools, where all needful stimulus, arising from numbers and competition, may be felt, without their being degraded or discouraged.

3. That they live so compactly, that in very few (if in any) cases, is it at all inconvenient to attend the special Schools provided for them.

4. That the facts, connected with the origin and history of these Schools, show, that, without them, the colored people would have remained ignorant and degraded, and very few would have been found in the Schools.

5. That if these special Schools were now abolished, the number of colored children in the Public Schools would be greatly diminished, while serious injury would also be done to the other Schools, and no benefit would result.

6. That the majority of the colored, and most of the white people, prefer the present system.

As, then, there is no statute, nor decision of the civil Courts, against classifying children in schools according to a distinction in races, color, or mental and physical peculiarities, the Committee believe that we have the right to classify on these principles; nor do they believe, that, by so doing, we defeat the intent, or violate the spirit, of the law, the Constitution, or the invaluable common-school system established by our fathers; nor in any way infringe the rights of the colored child, or degrade the colored people. These Schools were established for their special benefit: for the same reason we would have them vigorously sustained. No man, colored or white, who understands their real value to the colored people, would seek their destruction.

---

4. The Roberts case: an attack upon legal discrimination in access to the public schools, Boston, 1849

Sarah C. Roberts *v.* The City of Boston, 5 Mass. Reports, 200–201 (1849).

[The facts of the case:]

The plaintiff is a colored child, of five years of age, a resident of Boston, and living with her father, since the month of March, 1847, in Andover street, in the sixth primary school district. In the month of April, 1847, she being of suitable age and qualifications (unless her color was a disqualification) applied to a member of the district primary school committee, having under his charge the primary school nearest to her place of residence, for a ticket of admission to that school, the number of scholars therein warranting her admission, and no special provision having been made for her, unless the establishment of the two schools for colored children exclusively, is to be so considered.

The member of the school committee, to whom the plaintiff applied, refused her application, on the ground of her being a colored person, and of the special provision made as aforesaid. The plaintiff thereupon applied to the primary school committee of the district, for admission to one of their schools, and was in like manner refused admission, on the ground of her color and the provision aforesaid. She thereupon petitioned the general primary school committee, for leave to enter one of the schools nearest her residence. That committee referred the subject to the committee of the district, with full powers, and the committee of the district thereupon again refused the plaintiff's application, on the sole ground of color and the special provision aforesaid, and the plaintiff has not since attended any school in Boston. Afterwards, on the 15th of February, 1848, the plaintiff went into the primary school nearest her residence, but without any ticket of admission or other leave granted, and was on that day ejected from the school by the teacher.

The school established in Belknap street [a school for Negro children] is twenty-one hundred feet distant from the residence of the plaintiff, measuring through the streets; and in passing from the plaintiff's residence to the Belknap street school, the direct route passes the ends of two streets in which there are five primary schools . . . The distance from the plaintiff's residence to the nearest primary school is nine hundred feet. The plaintiff might have attended the school in Belknap street, at any time, and her father was so informed, but he refused to have her attend there.

---

5. Argument of Charles Sumner, attorney for the plaintiff, in the Roberts case, 1849

Argument of Charles Sumner Esq. Against the Constitutionality of Separate Colored Schools in the Case of Sarah C. Roberts vs. The City of Boston (Boston, 1849), pp. 4–5, 10–16, 19–20, 23–25, 29–30.

Sumner (1811–1874), on the threshold of a long and influential political career, claimed that the School Committee had unconstitutionally exceeded its powers in barring Negro children from certain schools under its control.

I. I begin with the principle, that, according to the spirit of American institutions, and especially of the Constitution of Massachusetts, *all men, without distinction of color or race, are equal before the law.*

I might, perhaps, leave this proposition without one word of comment. The equality of men will not be directly denied on this occasion, and yet it has been so often assailed of late, that I trust I shall not seem to occupy your time superfluously in endeavoring to show what is understood by this term, when used in laws, or constitutions, or other political instruments.

.   .   .   .   .   .

The equality which was declared by our fathers in 1776, and which was made the funda-mental law of Massachusetts in 1780, was *equality before the law*. Its object was to efface all political or civil distinctions, and to abolish all institutions founded upon *birth*. "All men are *created* equal," says the Declaration of Independence. "All men are *born* free and equal," says the Massachusetts Bill of Rights. These are not vain words. Within the sphere of their influence no person can be *created*, no person can be *born*, with civil or political privileges, not enjoyed equally by all his fellow-citizens, nor can any institution be established recognizing any distinctions of birth. This is the Great Charter of every person who draws his vital breath upon this soil, whatever may be his condition, and whoever may be his parents. He may be poor, weak, humble, black — he may be of Caucasian, of Jewish, of Indian, or of Ethiopian race — he may be of French, of German, of English, of Irish extraction — but before the Constitution of Massachusetts all these distinctions disappear. He is not poor, or weak, or humble, or black — nor Caucasian, nor Jewish, nor Indian, nor Ethiopian — nor French, nor German, nor English, nor Irish; he is a MAN, — the equal of all his fellow-men. He is one of the children of the State, which, like an impartial parent, regards all its offspring with an equal care. To some it may justly allot higher duties, according to their higher capacities, but it welcomes all to its equal, hospitable board. The State, imitating the divine justice, is no respecter of persons.

.   .   .   .   .

II. I now pass to the second stage of this argument, and ask attention to this proposition. The legislature of Massachusetts, in entire harmony with the Constitution, has made no discrimination of color or race, in the establishment of Public Schools.

If such discrimination were made by the laws, they would be unconstitutional and void. But the legislature of Massachusetts has been too just and generous, too mindful of the Bill of Rights, to establish any such privilege of *birth*. The language of the statutes is general, and applies equally to all children, of whatever color or race.

The provisions of the law regulating this subject are entitled, *Of the Public Schools.* (Revised Statutes, chap. 23.) It is to these that we must look in order to ascertain what constitutes a Public School. None can be legally such which are not established in conformity with the law. They may, in point of fact, be more or less public: yet, if they do not come within the terms of the law, they do not form a part of the beautiful system of our public schools — they are not public schools.

·   ·   ·   ·   ·

I conclude . . . that there is but one kind of public school established by the laws of Massachusetts. This is the general Public School, free to all the inhabitants. There is nothing in these laws establishing any exclusive or separate school for any particular class, whether rich or poor, whether Catholic or Protestant, whether white or black. In the eye of the law there is but *one class,* in which all interests, opinions, conditions and colors commingle in harmony — excluding none, comprehending all.

·   ·   ·   ·   ·

III. The Courts of Massachusetts have never recognized any discrimination, founded on color or race, in the administration of the Public Schools, but have recognized the equal rights of all the inhabitants.

There are a few decisions only of our Court bearing on this subject, but they all breathe one spirit. The sentiment of equality animates them. In the case of *Commonwealth* vs. *Davis,* 6 Mass. R. 146, while declaring the equal rights of all the inhabitants, both in the grammar and district schools, the Court said: "The schools required by the statute are to be maintained for the benefit of the whole town, *as it is the wise policy of the law to give all the inhabitants equal privileges for the education of their children in the public schools.* Nor is it in the power of the majority to deprive the minority of

this *privilege* . . . Every inhabitant of the town has a right to participate in the benefits of both descriptions of schools, and it is not competent for a town to establish a grammar school for the benefit of one part of the town to the exclusion of the other, although the money raised for the support of schools may be in other respects fairly apportioned."

·   ·   ·   ·   ·

IV. The exclusion of colored children from the Public Schools, open to white children, is a source of practical inconvenience to them and their parents, to which white persons are not exposed, and is, therefore, a violation of Equality. The black and the white are not equal before the law.

It appears from the statement of facts, that among the rules of the Primary School Committee, is one to this effect: "*Scholars to go to the school nearest their residence.* Applicants for admission to our schools (with the exception and provision referred to in the preceding rule) are especially entitled to enter the schools nearest to their places of residence." The exception here is "of those for whom special provision has been made" in separate schools; that is, colored children.

·   ·   ·   ·   ·

I may go, however, beyond the facts of this case, and show that the inconvenience arising from the exclusion of colored children, is of such a character as seriously to affect the comfort and condition of the African race in Boston. The two primary schools open to these children are in Belknap street and in Sun court. I need not add that the whole city is dotted with schools open to white children. The colored parents, anxious that their children should have the benefit of education, are compelled to live in the neighborhood of the schools, to gather about them, as in the East people come from a distance to rest near a fountain or a well. They have not, practically, the same liberty of choosing their homes, which belongs to the white man. Inclination, or business, or economy, may call them to another part of the city; but they are restrained on account of their children. There is no such restraint upon the white man, for he knows that wherever in the city inclination, or business, or economy, may call him, he will find a school open to his children near his door. Surely this is not equality before the law.

Or if a colored person, yielding to the necessities of his position, removes to a distant part of the city, his children may be compelled, at an inconvenience which will not be called trivial, to walk a long distance in order to enjoy the advantages of the school. In our severe winters, this cannot be disregarded by children so tender in years as those of the primary schools. There is a respectable colored person, I am told, who became some time since a resident at East Boston, separated by the water from the main land. There are, of course, proper public schools at East Boston, but none that were then open to colored children. This person, therefore, was obliged to send his children, three in number, daily, across the ferry to the distant African school. The tolls for these children amounted to a sum which formed a severe tax upon a poor man.

. . . . .

V. The separation of children in the Public Schools of Boston, on account of color or race, is in the nature of Caste, and is a violation of Equality.

The facts in this case show expressly that the child was excluded from the school nearest to her dwelling, the number in the school at the time warranting her admission, "on the sole ground of color." The first Majority Report presented to the School Committee, to which reference is made in the statement of facts, gives, with more fulness, the grounds of this discrimination, saying, "It is one of races, not of color, merely. The distinction is one which the Almighty has seen fit to establish, and it is founded deep in the physical, mental, and moral natures of the two races. No legislation, no social customs, can efface this distinction."

Words more apt than these to describe the heathenish relation of Caste, could not be chosen.

. . . . .

It will be vain to say that this distinction, though seeming to be founded on color, is in reality founded on natural and physical peculiarities, which are independent of color. These peculiarities, whatever they may be, are peculiarities of race, and any discrimination on account of them constitutes the relation of Caste. Disguise it as you will, it is this hateful institution. But the words Caste and Equality are contradictory. They mutually exclude each other. Where Caste is, there cannot be Equality. Where Equality is, there cannot be Caste.

It is unquestionably true that there is a distinction between the Ethiopian and Caucasian race. Each has received from the hand of God certain characteristics of color and form. The two may not readily intermingle, although we are told by Homer that Jupiter

— "did not disdain to grace
The feast of Ethiopia's blameless race."

One may be uninteresting or offensive to the other, precisely as different individuals of the same race and color may be uninteresting or offensive to each other. *But this distinction can furnish no ground for any discrimination before the law.*

We abjure nobility of all kinds; but here is a nobility of the skin. We abjure all hereditary distinctions; but here is an hereditary distinction, founded not on the merit of the ancestor, but on his color. We abjure all privileges derived from birth; but here is a privilege which depends solely on the accident, whether an ancestor is black or white. We abjure all inequality before the law; but here is an inequality which touches not an individual, but a race. We revolt at the relation of caste; but here is a caste which is established under a Constitution, declaring that all men are born equal.

Condemning caste and inequality before the law, let us now consider more particularly the powers of the School Committee. Here it will be necessary to enter into some details.

VI. The Committee of Boston, charged with the superintendence of the Public Schools, have no *power* under the Constitution and laws of Massachusetts, to make any discrimination on account of color or race, among children in the Public Schools.

It has been already seen that this power is inconsistent with the Constitution and laws of Massachusetts, and with all adjudications of the Supreme Court. The stream cannot rise higher than the fountain-head, and if there be nothing in these elevated sources, from which this power can draw its sanction, it must be considered a nullity.

.   .   .   .   .

But it is said that the Committee, in thus classifying the children, have not violated any principle of Equality, inasmuch as they have provided a school with competent instructors for the colored children, where they have equal advantages of instruction with those enjoyed by the white children. It is said that in excluding the colored children from the Public Schools open to white children, they furnish them an equivalent.

.   .   .   .   .

In point of fact, it is not an equivalent. We have already seen that it is the occasion of inconveniences to the colored children and their parents, to which they would not be exposed, if they had access to the nearest public schools, besides inflicting upon them the stigma of Caste. Still further, and this consideration cannot be neglected, the matters taught in the two schools may be precisely the same; but a school, exclusively devoted to one class, must differ essentially, in its spirit and character, from that public school known to the law, where all classes meet together in equality. It is a mockery to call it an equivalent.

But there is yet another answer. Admitting that it is an equivalent, still the colored children cannot be compelled to take it. Their rights are Equality before the law; nor can they be called upon to renounce one jot of this. They have an equal right with white children to the general public schools. A separate school, though well endowed, would not secure to them that precise Equality, which they would enjoy in the general public schools. The Jews in Rome are confined to a particular district, called the Ghetto. In Frankfort they are condemned to a separate quarter, known as the Jewish quarter. It is possible that the accommodations allotted to them are as good as they would be able to occupy, if left free to choose throughout Rome and Frankfort; but this compulsory segregation from the mass of citizens is of itself an *inequality* which we condemn with our whole souls. It is a vestige of ancient intolerance directed against a despised people. It is of the same character with the separate schools in Boston.

.   .   .   .   .

Who can say, that this does not injure the blacks? Theirs, in its best estate, is an unhappy lot. Shut out by a still lingering prejudice from many social advantages, a despised class, they feel this proscription from the Public Schools as a peculiar brand. Beyond this, it deprives them of those healthful animating influences which would come from a participation in the studies of their white brethren. It adds to their discouragements. It widens their separation from the rest of the community, and postpones that great day of reconciliation which is sure to come.

The whole system of public schools suffers also. It is a narrow perception of their high aim which teaches that they are merely to furnish to all the scholars an equal amount in knowledge, and that, therefore, provided all be taught, it is of little consequence where, and in what company it be done. The law contemplates not only that they shall all be taught, but that they shall be taught *all together*. They are not only to receive equal quantities of knowledge, but all are to receive it in the same way. All are to approach together the same common fountain; nor can there be any exclusive source for any individual or any class. The school is the little world in which the child is trained for the larger world of life. It must, therefore, cherish and develop the virtues and the sympathies which are employed in the larger world. And since, according to our institutions, all classes meet without distinction of color, in the performance of civil duties, so should they all meet, without distinction of color, in the school, beginning there those relations of equality which our Constitution and laws promise to all.

As the State receives strength from the unity and solidarity of its citizens, without distinction of class, so the school receives new strength from the unity and solidarity of all classes beneath its roof. In this way, the poor, the humble, and the neglected, share not only the companionship of their presence, in drawing towards the school a more watchful superintendence. A degraded or neglected class, if left to themselves, will become more degraded or neglected. To him that hath shall be given; and the world, true to these words, turns from the poor and outcast to the rich and fortunate. It is the aim of our system of Public Schools, by the blending of all classes, to draw upon the whole school the attention which is too apt to be given only to the favored few, and thus secure to the poor their portion of the fruitful sunshine. But the colored children, placed apart by themselves, are deprived of this blessing.

Nothing is more clear than that the welfare of classes, as well as of individuals, is promoted by mutual acquaintance. The French and English, for a long time regarded as natural enemies, have at last, from a more intimate communion, found themselves to be natural friends. Prejudice is the child of ignorance. It is sure to prevail where people do not know each other. Society and intercourse are means established by Providence for human improvement. They remove antipathies, promote mutual adaptation and conciliation, and establish relations of reciprocal regard. Whoso sets up barriers to these, thwarts the ways of Provi-

dence, crosses the tendencies of human nature, and directly interferes with the laws of God.

---

6. Chief Justice Lemuel Shaw, speaking for a unanimous Court, holds that Sarah Roberts has not been deprived of her rights by the School Committee

Sarah C. Roberts *v.* City of Boston, 5 Mass. Reports, 206–207, 209–210 (1849).

The great principle, advanced by the learned and eloquent advocate of the plaintiff, is, that by the constitution and laws of Massachusetts, all persons without distinction of age or sex, birth or color, origin or condition, are equal before the law. This, as a broad general principle, such as ought to appear in a declaration of rights, is perfectly sound; it is not only expressed in terms, but pervades and animates the whole spirit of our constitution of free government. But, when this great principle comes to be applied to the actual and various conditions of persons in society, it will not warrant the assertion, that men and women are legally clothed with the same civil and political powers, and that children and adults are legally to have the same functions and be subject to the same treatment; but only that the rights of all, as they are settled and regulated by law, are equally entitled to the paternal consideration and protection of the law, for their maintenance and security. What those rights are, to which individuals, in the infinite variety of circumstances by which they are surrounded in society, are entitled, must depend on laws adapted to their respective relations and conditions.

Conceding, therefore, in the fullest manner, that colored persons, the descendants of Africans, are entitled by law, in this commonwealth, to equal rights, constitutional and political, civil and social, the question then arises, whether the regulation in question, which provides separate schools for colored children, is a violation of any of these rights.

Legal rights must, after all, depend upon the provisions of law; certainly all those rights of individuals which can be asserted and maintained in any judicial tribunal. The proper providence of a declaration of rights and constitution of government, after directing its form, regulating its organization and the distribution of its powers, is to declare great principles and fundamental truths, to influence and direct the judgment and conscience of legislators in making laws, rather than to limit and control them, by directing what precise laws they shall make. The provision, that it shall be the duty of legislatures and magistrates to cherish the interests of literature and the sciences, especially the university at Cambridge, public schools, and grammar schools, in the towns, is precisely of this character. Had the legislature failed to comply with this injunction, and neglected to provide public schools in the towns, or should they so far fail in their duty as to repeal all laws on the subject, and leave all education to depend on private means, strong and explicit as the direction of the constitution is, it would afford no remedy or redress to the thousands of the rising generation, who now depend on these schools to afford them a most valuable education, and an introduction to useful life.

．　．　．　．　．　．

In the absence of special legislation on this subject, the law has vested the power in the committee to regulate the system of distribution and classification; and when this power is reasonably exercised, without being abused or perverted by colorable pretences, the decision of the committee must be deemed conclusive. The committee, apparently upon great deliberation, have come to the conclusion, that the good of both classes of schools will be best promoted, by maintaining the separate primary schools for colored and for white children, and

we can perceive no ground to doubt, that this is the honest result of their experience and judgment.

It is urged, that this maintenance of separate schools tends to deepen and perpetuate the odious distinction of caste, founded in a deep-rooted prejudice in public opinion. This prejudice, if it exists, is not created by law, and probably cannot be changed by law. Whether this distinction and prejudice, existing in the opinion and feelings of the community, would not be as effectually fostered by compelling colored and white children to associate together in the same schools, may well be doubted; at all events, it is a fair and proper question for the committee to consider and decide upon, having in view the best interests of both classes of children placed under their superintendence, and we cannot say, that their decision upon it is not founded on just grounds of reason and experience, and in the results of a discriminating and honest judgment.

The increased distance, to which the plaintiff was obliged to go to school from her father's house, is not such, in our opinion, as to render the regulation in question unreasonable, still less illegal.

---

7. The Massachusetts legislature reverses the Roberts case decision, 1855

"An Act in amendment of 'An Act concerning Public Schools . . . ,' " 1855 — ch. 256, *Massachusetts Acts and Resolves, 1854–1855* (Boston, 1855), pp. 674–675.

In determining the qualifications of scholars to be admitted into any public school or any district school in this Commonwealth, no distinction shall be made on account of the race, color or religious opinions, of the applicant or scholar.

Any child who, on account of his race, color or religious opinions, shall be excluded from any public or district school in this Commonwealth, for admission to which he may be otherwise qualified, shall recover damages therefore in an action of tort, to be brought in the name of said child by his guardian or next friend, in any court of competent jurisdiction to try the same, against the city or town by which such school is supported.

A college proposed in New Haven, Connecticut, for Negro youth, 1831

---

1. Resolutions in favor of the college

Minutes and Proceedings of the First Annual Convention of the [Free] People of Colour, held at Philadelphia, June 1831 (Philadelphia, 1831), pp. 6–7.

The plan proposed is, that a College be established at New-Haven, Connecticut, as soon as $20,000 are obtained, and to be on the Manual Labour System, by which, in connexion with a scientific education, they may also obtain a useful Mechanical or Agricultural profession, and . . . a benevolent individual has offered to subscribe one thousand dollars towards this object, provided, that a farther sum of nineteen thousand dollars can be obtained in one year.

After an interesting discussion, the above report was unanimously adopted; one of the inquiries by the Convention was, in regard to the place of location. On interrogating the gentlemen why New-Haven should be the place of location, they gave the following as their reasons: —

1st. The site is healthy and beautiful.

2d. Its inhabitants are friendly, pious, generous, and humane.

3d. Its laws are salutary and protecting to all, without regard to complexion.

4th. Boarding is cheap and provisions are good.

5th. The situation is as central as any other that can be obtained with the same advantages.

6th. The town of New-Haven carries on an extensive West India trade, and many of the wealthy coloured residents in the Islands, would, no doubt, send their sons there to be educated, and thus a fresh tie of friendship would be formed, which might be productive of much real good in the end.

And last, though not the least, the literary and scientific character of New-Haven, renders it a very desirable place for the location of the College.

The Convention, having received the report of the committee, and being deeply impressed with the importance of such an institution, do hereby resolve, that it is highly expedient to make an effort to carry the same into effect, under due regulations. Therefore, resolved, that this Convention earnestly recommend to our Brethren, to contribute as God has given them the ability, to aid in carrying into operation the proposed institution; and the Convention would wish it to be distinctly understood, that the Trustees of the contemplated Institution, shall a majority of them be coloured persons; the number proposed is seven, three white, and four coloured; who shall be elected by the subscribers, contributors, or their representatives: the elections to be held in the city of New-York, unless ordered otherwise by the Convention.

---

2. Local opposition prevents the founding of the college

Resolutions of a meeting of New Haven freemen, Sept. 10, 1831, in Simeon S. Jocelyn, *College for Colored Youth: An Account*

of the New Haven City Meeting and
Resolutions (New York, 1831),
pp. 4–5.

At a City Meeting, duly warned, and held at the City Hall in the city of New-Haven, on Saturday the 10th day of September, 1831, to take into consideration a project for the establishment in this city of a College for the education of *Colored Youth;* the following preambles and resolutions were by said meeting adopted, viz: —

Whereas endeavors are now making to establish a College in this city for the education of the colored population of the United States, the West Indies, and other countries adjacent; and in connection with this establishment, the immediate abolition of slavery in the United States is not only recommended and encouraged, by the advocates of the proposed College, but demanded as a right; and whereas an omission to notice these measures may be construed as implying either indifference to, or approbation of the same —

Resolved, That it is expedient that the sentiments of our citizens should be expressed on these subjects, and that the calling of this meeting by the Mayor and Aldermen is warmly approved by the citizens of this place.

Resolved, That in as much as slavery does not exist in Connecticut, and wherever permitted in other States depends on the municipal laws of the State which allows it, and over which neither any other State, nor the Congress of the United States has any control, that the propagation of sentiments favorable to the immediate emancipation of slaves in disregard of the civil institutions of the States in which they belong, and as auxiliary thereto the contemporaneous founding of Colleges for educating colored people, is an unwarrantable and dangerous interference with the internal concerns of other States, and ought to be discouraged.

And whereas in the opinion of this meeting, Yale College, the institutions for the education of females, and the other schools, already existing in this city, are important to the community and the general interests of science, and as such have been deservedly patronized by the public, and the establishment of a College in the same place to educate the colored population is incompatible with the prosperity, if not the existence of the present institutions of learning, and will be destructive of the best interests of the city: — And believing as we do, that if the establishment of such a College in any part of the country were deemed expedient, it should never be imposed on any community without their consent. — Therefore, *Resolved,* — by the *Mayor, Aldermen, Common Council and Freemen of the City of New-Haven, in City Meeting assembled,* That we will resist the establishment of the proposed College in this place, by every lawful means.

Dennis Kimberly, Mayor.
Elisha Monson, Clerk.

The decision to admit black students to Oberlin College, 1834–1835

With the College only recently founded and desperately short of funds, its officials discovered that they could recruit both a distinguished faculty and a group of theological students and secure large sums by committing internal management to the faculty and admitting black students on equal terms with white.

---

1. Students should be received "irrespective of color"

Rev. John J. Shipherd from Cincinnati, Ohio, agent of the College, to an official in Oberlin, Dec. 15, 1834, from a copy in the Robert S. Fletcher File, Oberlin College Archives, Oberlin, Ohio.

Dear Br. Fletcher;

. . . I desire you at the first meeting of the Trustees to secure the passage of the following resolution, viz. "Resolved, That students shall be received into this Institution irrespective of color."

This should be passed because it is *right principle,* and God will bless us in doing right. Also because thus doing right we gain the confidences of benevolent and able men who probably will furnish us some thousands. Moreover, Bros. Mahan and Morgan will not accept our invitation unless this principle rule.

Indeed if our Board would violate right so as to reject youth of talent and piety, because they were *black* I should have *no heart* to labor for the upbuilding of our Seminary, believing that the curse of God would come upon us as it has upon Lane Seminary, for its unchristian abuse of the poor Slave.

---

2. The board rejects Shipherd's request — a retrospective account

Letter of N. P. Fletcher to Levi Burnell, 1837, from a copy in the Fletcher File, Oberlin College Archives.

The close of the year 1834 found the Oberlin Institute in debts, without a head or professors, and no funds to sustain appointments which were indispensibly necessary, want of harmony, concert in prayer and action at this Junction would have been criminal and Indeed notwithstanding, the Tardy Labour of Some, the Cruel Indifference of others, and direct and open opposition of a few — God evidently said in his kindness go forward, and the hand of the Lord led bro. Shipherd to the *men* and the *money* on this Information reaching Oberlin — a General panic — and dispair seized the Officers Students and Colonists — P. P. Stewart the Organ of Opposition at once proclaimed Bro. Shipherd

Mad!! crazy etc. etc. and that the School was changed into a Negro School . . . Its founders would be disappointed and hundreds of negroes would be flooding the School — despondency brooded with sable distrust over almost every soul, because the Christian patrons made it a Condition in their donations that Coloured people should stand equal in the privileges of the Institution — many students said they would leave and Br. Stewart sd. he would not stay —

The board refused to recognize the doings of Br. Shipherd their Agent and during the siting of the board at Elyria the same *rancour* and malevolence were exhibited by the Opposition and no notice was taken by the board of the imprudent and wicked conduct of Stewart —

---

3. The board supplied with numerous reasons for admitting black students

Rev. John J. Shipherd, New York City, to the trustees of Oberlin College, Jan. 19, 1835, from a copy in the Fletcher File, Oberlin College Archives.

Soon after receiving this letter, the board reconsidered its earlier decision and voted to admit Negroes.

Here, beloved brethren, I am sensible I touch a delicate subject. I do it with kindest feeling toward any that may differ, and with respect to their opinions. And let me say that I regret the agitation produced by my request respecting the admission of colored students. That agitation was unexpected, and your decision surprising and grievous to my soul. I did not desire you to hang out an abolition flag or fill up with filthy stupid negroes; but I did desire that you should say you would not reject promising youth who desired to prepare for usefulness because God had given them a darker hue than others. I asked that resolution without a doubt but what you would pass it;

and for the purpose of satisfying subscribers and professors elect that we were right on this subject. My reasons for receiving colored youth into our institutions are —

1. *All christians* agree that they ought to be educated and fitted for the full privileges of freemen.

2. There is no school of their own, or for them, where they can be well educated; and they can be sooner qualified, and better fitted to labor for the elevation of their oppressed race in connexion with whites (now comparatively elevated) than in a separate school.

3. We should receive *only* those to whom no objection could be made except by prejudice against a dark skin.

4. This was done by our first institutions till "Abolition" aroused and inflamed prejudice. Dartmouth had a special fund for educating indians, and did educate them, and did not stop because of their color. Rev. br. White of this city was educated at Princeton, and he is *Black* etc. etc.

.   .   .   .   .

7. The prejudice against eating and associating with colored people is like that of the scribes and Pharasees against the publicans and sinners with whom Christ ate to their great displeasure. He ate with those publicans and sinners to do them good; and doubtless would eat with negroes if on earth. Should we reject those whom God receives?

8. There is no more danger of intermarriages among our white and colored youth than there is of fornication among our white sexes, and yet we *wish* that sin among them to gain important ends.

9. We shall not *force* an association with them. The willing minded will be their associates. If they cannot be borne at the Institute's table, I and the Faculty will board any that we would receive.

10. I was brot. up with blacks, and slaves and would choke with thirst before I would drink from the same cup with them; but God has shown me that it was an *unholy pride*

and *sinful prejudice* which I dare not cherish longer through fear of his displeasure.

11. Although we may by receiving colored youth displease the pride of some fellow creatures; by refusing to receive them we must offend God. So I verily believe.

12. If we were colored applicants for admission to the O. C. Inst. what wd. we tell its guardians the law of love to our neighbor requires?

13. If we say we will not permit our professors to decide on the reception of colored youth we lose the best Faculty that can be found; for bros. Mahan and Finney and Morgan will not engage with us unless they can be permitted to instruct colored youth if they please; nor shall we be likely to find others, such as we need in other respects, who would engage without this privilege.

14. The reception of colored students is not wronging old subscribers, for it is a common understanding that they can be admitted to literary institutions if worthy.

15. We injure no one by permitting worthy colored youth to qualify for usefulness at our institution, but by refusing, we do our injured neighbor of color an *unpardonable* injury.

16. I do not believe that God will bless us if we suffer a worldly *expediency* to control us so far as to withold the right of education at our Seminary from our colored brothers. Therefore lastly. If my dear brethren of the Board cannot consent to this, I cannot *conscienciously* consent to labor any longer for the building of the O. C. Institute. If *right, eternal right,* its glory, must forsake it *I* must forsake it too.

Blacks' views of education

1. An appeal to free Negroes to seek education, 1830

[David Walker], *Walker's Appeal, in Four Articles Together with a Preamble, to the Coloured Citizens of the World, but in Particular, and very Expressly, to those of the United States of America* . . . 3d ed. (Boston, 1830), pp. 35–38.

This celebrated call to action was written by a free Negro born in North Carolina and living in Boston when it was published. Walker (1785–1830) surveyed the oppression of Negroes and advocated violence if masters, failing to follow the demands of Christianity, refused to free their slaves. The pamphlet was banned in the South and a price put on Walker's head. The selection is from Article II, "Our Wretchedness in Consequence of Ignorance."

There is a great work for you to do, as trifling as some of you may think of it. You have to prove to the Americans and the world, that we are MEN, and not *brutes,* as we have been represented, and by millions treated. Remember, to let the aim of your labours among your brethren, and particularly the youths, be the dissemination of education and religion. It is lamentable, that many of our children go to school, from four until they are eight or ten, and sometimes fifteen years of age, and leave school knowing but a little more about the grammar of their language than a horse does about handling a musket — and not a few of them are really so ignorant, that they are unable to answer a person correctly, general questions in geography, and to hear them read, would only be to disgust a man who has a taste for reading; which, to do well, as trifling as it may appear to some (to the ignorant in particular), is a great part of learning. Some few of them, may make out to scribble tolerably well, over a half sheet of paper, which I believe has hitherto been a powerful obstacle in our way, to keep us from acquiring knowledge. An ignorant father, who knows no more than what nature has taught him, together with what little he acquires by the senses of hearing and seeing, finding his son able to write a neat hand, sets it down for granted that he has as good learning as any body; the young, ignorant gump, hearing his father or mother, who perhaps may be ten times more ignorant, in point of literature, than himself, extolling his learning, struts about, in the full assurance, that his attainments in literature are sufficient to take him through the world, when, in fact, he has scarcely any learning at all!!!!

I promiscuously fell into conversation once, with an elderly coloured man on the topics of education, and of the great prevalency of ignorance among us: Said he, "I know that our people are very ignorant but my son has a good education: I spent a great deal of money on his education: he can write as well as any white man, and I assure you that no one can fool him," &c. Said I, what else can your son do, besides writing a good hand? Can he post a set of books in a mercantile manner? Can he write a neat piece of composition in prose or in verse? To these interrogations he answered in the negative. Said I, Did your son learn, while he was at school, the width and depth of English Grammar? To which he also replied in the negative, telling me his son did not learn those things. Your son, said I, then, has hardly any learning at all — he is almost as ignorant, and more so, than many of those who never went to school one day in all their lives. My friend got a little put out, and so walking off, said that his son could write as well as any white man. — Most of the coloured people, when they speak of the education of one among us who can write a neat hand, and who perhaps knows nothing but to scribble and puff pretty fair on a small scrap of paper, immaterial whether his words are grammatical, or spelt correctly, or not; if it only looks beautiful, they say he has as good an education as any white man — he can write as well as any white man, &c. The poor, ignorant creature, hearing this, he is ashamed, forever after, to let any person see him humbling himself to another for knowledge but going about trying to deceive those who are more ignorant than himself, he at last falls an ignorant victim to death in wretchedness. I pray that the Lord may undeceive my ignorant brethren, and permit them to throw away pretensions, and seek after the substance of learning. I would crawl on my hands and knees through mud and mire, to the feet of a learned man, where I would sit and humbly supplicate him to instil into me, that which neither devils nor tyrants could remove, only with my life — for coloured people to acquire learning in this country, makes tyrants quake and tremble on their sandy foundation. Why, what is the matter? Why, they know that their infernal deeds of cruelty will be made known to the world. Do you suppose one man of good sense and learning would submit himself, his father, mother, wife and children, to be slaves to a wretched man like himself, who, instead of compensating him for his labours, chains, handcuffs and beats him and family almost to death, leaving life enough in them, however, to work for, and call him master? No! no! he would cut his devilish throat from ear to ear, and well do slave-holders know it. The bare name of educating the coloured people, scares our cruel oppressors almost to death. But if they do not have enough to be frightened for yet, it will be, because they can always keep us ignorant, and because God approbates their cruelties, with which they have been for centuries murdering us. The whites shall have enough of the blacks, yet, as true as God sits on his throne in heaven.

Some of our brethren are so very full of learning, that you cannot mention any thing to them which they do not know better than yourself!! — nothing is strange to them!! — they knew every thing years ago! — if any thing should be mentioned in company where they are, immaterial how important it is respecting us or the world, if they had not divulged it; they make light of it, and affect to have known it long before it was mentioned and try to make all in the room, or wherever you may be, believe that your conversation is nothing!! — not worth hearing! All this is the result of

ignorance and ill-breeding; for a man of good-breeding, sense and penetration, if he had heard a subject told twenty times over, and should happen to be in company where one should commence telling it again, he would wait with patience on its narrator, and see if he would tell it as it was told in his presence before — paying the most strict attention to what is said, to see if any more light will be thrown on the subject: for all men are not gifted alike in telling, or even hearing the most simple narration. These ignorant, vicious, and wretched men, contribute almost as much injury to our body as tyrants themselves, by doing so much for the promotion of ignorance amongst us; for they, making such pretensions to knowledge, such of our youth as are seeking after knowledge, and can get across to them, take them as criterions to go by, who will lead them into a channel, where, unless the Lord blesses them with the privilege of seeing their folly, they will be irretrievably lost forever, while in time!!!

I must close this article by relating the very heartrending fact, that I have examined school-boys and young men of colour in different parts of the country, in the most simple parts of Murray's English Grammar, and not more than one in thirty was able to give a correct answer to my interrogations. If any one contradicts me, let him step out of his door into the streets of Boston, New-York, Philadelphia, or Baltimore (no use to mention any other, for the Christians are too charitable further south or west!) — I say, let him who disputes me, step out of his door into the streets of either of those four cities, and promiscuously collect one hundred school-boys, or young men of colour, *who have been to school,* and who are considered by the coloured people to have received an excellent education, because, perhaps, some of them can write a good hand, but who, notwithstanding their neat writing, may be almost as ignorant, in comparison, as a horse. — And, I say it, he will hardly find (in this enlightened day, and in the midst of this *charitable* people) five in one hundred, who are able to correct the false grammar of their language. — The cause of this almost universal ignorance among us, I appeal to our schoolmasters to declare. Here is a fact, which I this very minute take from the mouth of a young coloured man, who has been to school in this state (Massachusetts) nearly nine years, and who knows grammar this day, *nearly* as well as he did the day he entered the school-house, under a white master. This young man says: "My master would never allow me to study grammar." — I asked him, why? "The school committee," said he, "forbid the coloured children learning grammar — they would not allow any but the white children to study grammar." It is a notorious fact, that the major part of the white Americans, have, ever since we have been among them, tried to keep us ignorant, and make us believe that God made us and our children to be slaves to them and theirs. *Oh! my God, have mercy on Christian Americans!!!*

---

2. Frederick Douglass advises Harriet Beecher Stowe to assist in the foundation of a manual labor school, 1853

Letter dated March 8, 1853, in *Proceedings of the Colored National Convention, Held in Rochester, July 6th, 7th, and 8th, 1853* (Rochester, 1853), pp. 33–38.

My Dear Mrs. Stowe:

You kindly informed me, when at your house, a fortnight ago, that you designed to do something which should permanently contribute to the improvement and elevation of the free colored people in the United States. You especially expressed an interest in such of this class as had become free by their own exertions, and desired most of all to be of service to them.

In what manner, and by what means, you can assist this class most successfully, is the subject upon which you have done me the honor to ask my opinion.

. . . . .

First of all, let me briefly state the nature of the disease, before I undertake to prescribe the remedy. Three things are notoriously true of us, as a people. These are POVERTY, IGNORANCE and DEGRADATION. Of course there are exceptions to this general statement; but these are so few as only to prove its essential truthfulness. I shall not stop here to inquire minutely into the causes which have produced our present condition; nor to denounce those whom I believe to be responsible for those causes. It is enough that we shall agree upon the character of the evil, whose existence we deplore, and upon some plan for its removal.

. . . . .

To deliver them from this triple malady, is to improve and elevate them, by which I mean simply to put them on an equal footing with their white fellow-countrymen in the sacred right to "*Life, Liberty* and the pursuit of happiness." I am for no fancied or artificial elevation, but only ask fair play. How shall this be obtained? I answer, first, not by establishing for our use high schools and colleges. Such institutions are, in my judgment, beyond our immediate occasions, and are not adapted to our present most pressing wants. High schools and colleges are excellent institutions, and will, in due season, be greatly subservient to our progress; but they are the result, as well as they are the demand of a point of progress, which we, as a people, have not yet attained. Accustomed, as we have been, to the rougher and harder modes of living, and of gaining a livelihood, we cannot, and we ought not to hope that, in a single leap from our low condition, we can reach that of *Ministers, Lawyers, Doctors, Editors, Merchants* &c. These will, doubtless, be attained by us; but this will only be, when we have patiently and laboriously, and I may add successfully, mastered and passed through the intermediate gradations of agriculture and the mechanic arts. Besides, there are (and perhaps this is a better reason for my view of the case) numerous institutions of learning in this country, already thrown open to colored youth. To my thinking, there are quite as many facilities now afforded to the colored people, as they can spare the time, from the sterner duties of life, to avail themselves of. In their present condition of poverty, they cannot spare their sons and daughters two or three years at boarding schools or colleges, to say nothing of finding the means to sustain them while at such institutions. I take it, therefore, that we are well provided for in this respect; and that it may be fairly inferred from the past that the facilities for our education, so far as schools and colleges in the Free States are concerned, will increase quite in proportion with our future wants. Colleges have been open to colored youth in this country during the last dozen years. Yet few, comparatively, have acquired a classical education; and even this few have found themselves educated far above a living condition, there being no methods by which they could turn their learning to account. Several of this latter class have entered the ministry; but you need not be told that an educated people is needed to sustain an educated ministry. There must be a certain amount of cultivation among the people to sustain such a ministry. At present, we have not that cultivation amongst us; and therefore, we value, in the preacher, strong lungs, rather than high learning. I do not say that educated ministers are not needed amongst us. — Far from it! I wish there were more of them; but to increase their number is *not* the largest benefit you can bestow upon us.

You, dear Madam, can help the masses. You can do something for the thousands; and by lifting these from the depths of poverty and ignorance, you can make an educated ministry and an educated class possible. In the present circumstances, prejudice is a bar to the edu-cated black minister among the whites; and ignorance is a bar to him among the blacks.

We have now two or three colored lawyers in this country; and I rejoice in the fact; for it affords very gratifying evidence of our progress. Yet it must be confessed that, in point of success, our lawyers are as great failures as are our ministers. White people will not employ them to the obvious embarrassment of their causes, and the blacks, taking their cue from the whites, have not sufficient confidence in their abilities to employ them. Hence, educated colored men, among the colored people, are at a very great discount. It would seem that education and emigration go together with us; for as soon as a man rises amongst us, capable, by his genius and learning, to do us great service, just so soon he finds that he can serve himself better by going elsewhere. In proof of this, I might instance the Russwurms — the Garnetts — the Wards — the Crummells and others — all men of superior ability and attainments, and capable of removing mountains of prejudice against their race, by their simple presence in the country; but these gentlemen, finding themselves embarrassed here by the peculiar disadvantages to which I have referred — disadvantages in part growing out of their education — being repelled by ignorance on the one hand, and prejudice on the other, and having no taste to continue a contest against such odds, they have sought more congenial climes, where they can live more peaceable and quiet lives. I regret their election — but I cannot blame them; for, with an equal amount of education, and the hard lot which was theirs, I might follow their example.

But, again, it has been said that the colored people must become farmers — that they must go on the land, in order to their elevation. Hence, many benevolent people are contributing the necessary funds to purchase land in Canada, and elsewhere, for them. That prince of good men, Gerrit Smith, has given away thousands of acres to colored men in this State, thinking, doubtless, that in so doing he was conferring a blessing upon them. Now, while I do not undervalue the efforts which have been made, and are still being made in this direction, yet I must say that I have far less confidence in such efforts, than I have in the benevolence which prompts them. Agricultural pursuits are not, as I think, suited to our condition. The reason of this is not to be found so much in the occupation (for it is a noble and ennobling one) as in the people themselves. That is only a remedy, which can be applied to the case; and the difficulty in agricultural pursuits, as a remedy for the evils of poverty and ignorance amongst us, is that it cannot, for various reasons, be applied.

We cannot apply it, because it is almost impossible to get colored men to go on the land. From some cause or other (perhaps the adage that misery loves company will explain) colored people will congregate in the large towns and cities; and they will endure any amount of hardship and privation, rather than separate, and go into the country. Again, very few have the means to set up for themselves, or to get where they could do so.

Another consideration against expending energy in this direction is our want of self-reliance. Slavery, more than all things else, robs its victims of self-reliance. To go into the western wilderness, and there to lay the foundation of future society, requires more of that important quality than a life of slavery has left us. This may sound strange to you, coming, as it does, from a colored man; but I am dealing with facts; and these never accommodate themselves to the feelings or wishes of any. They don't ask, but take leave to be. It is a fact then, and not less so because I wish it were otherwise, that the colored people are wanting in self-reliance — too fond of society — too eager for immediate results — and too little skilled in mechanics or husbandry to attempt to overcome the wilderness; at least, until they have overcome obstacles less formidable. Therefore, I look to other means than agricultural pursuits for the elevation and improvement of colored people. Of course, I allege this of the many. There are exceptions. In-

dividuals among us, with commendable zeal, industry, perseverance and self-reliance, have found, and are finding, in agricultural pursuits, the means of supporting, improving and educating their families.

The plan which I contemplate will (if carried into effect) greatly increase the number of this class — since it will prepare others to meet the rugged duties which a pioneer agricultural condition must impose upon all who take it upon them. What I propose is intended simply to prepare men for the work of getting an honest living — not out of dishonest men — but out of an honest earth.

Again, there is little reason to hope that any considerable number of the free colored people will ever be induced to leave this country, even if such a thing were desirable. The black man (un-like the Indian) loves civilization. He does not make very great progress in civilization himself, but he likes to be in the midst of it, and prefers to share its most galling evils, to encountering barbarism. Then the love of country — the dread of isolation — the lack of adventurous spirit — and the thought of seeming to desert their "brethren in bonds," are a powerful and perpetual check upon all schemes of colonization, which look to the removal of the colored people, without the slaves. — The truth is, dear Madam, we are here, and here we are likely to remain. Individuals emigrate — nations never. We have grown up with this Republic; and I see nothing in our character, or even in the character of the American people, as yet, which compels the belief that we must leave the United States. If, then, we are to remain here, the question for the wise and good is precisely that you have submitted to me — and that which I fear I have been, perhaps, too slow in answering — namely, What can be done to improve the condition of the free colored people in the United States? The plan which I humbly submit in answer to this inquiry (and in the hope that it may find favor with you, dear Madam, and with the many friends of humanity who honor, love, and co-operate with you) is the establishment in Rochester, N.Y. — or in some other part of the United States, equally favorable to such an enterprise — of an Industrial College, in which shall be taught several important branches of the mechanic arts. This college to be open to colored youth. I will pass over, for the present, the details of such an institution as that I propose. It is not worth while that I should dwell upon these at all. Once convinced that something of the sort is needed, and the organizing power will be forthcoming. It is the peculiarity of your favored race that they can always do what they think necessary to be done. I can safely trust all details to yourself, and to the wise and good people whom you represent in the interest you take in my oppressed fellow-countrymen.

Never having myself had a day's schooling in all my life, I may not be expected to be able to map out the details of a plan so comprehensive as that involved in the idea of a college. I repeat then, I leave the organization and administration to the superior wisdom of yourself and the friends that second your noble efforts. The argument in favor of an Industrial College (a College to be conducted by the best men, and the best workmen, which the mechanic arts can afford — a College where colored youth can be instructed to use their hands, as well as their heads — where they can be put in possession of the means of getting a living — whether their lot in after life may be cast among civilized or uncivilized men — whether they choose to stay here, or prefer to return to the land of their fathers) is briefly this — prejudice against the free colored people in the United States has shown itself nowhere so invincible as among mechanics. The farmer and the professional man cherish no feeling so bitter as that cherished by these. The latter would starve us out of the country entirely. At this moment, I can more easily get my son into a lawyer's office, to study law, than I can into a blacksmith's shop, to blow the bellows, and to wield the sledge-hammer. Denied the means of learning useful trades, we are pressed into the narrowest limits to

obtain a livelihood. In times past we have been the hewers of wood and the drawers of water for American society, and we once enjoyed a monopoly in menial employments, but this is so no longer — even these employments are rapidly passing away out of our hands. The fact is (every day begins with the lesson, and ends with the lesson) that colored men must learn trades — must find new employments, new modes of usefulness to society — or that they must decay under the pressing wants to which their condition is rapidly bringing them. We must become mechanics — we must build, as well as live in houses — we must make, as well as use furniture — we must construct bridges, as well as pass over them — before we can properly live, or be respected by our fellow men. We need mechanics, as well as ministers. We need workers in iron, wood, clay, and in leather. We have orators, authors, and other professional men; but these reach only a certain class, and get respect for our race in certain select circles. To live here as we ought, we must fasten ourselves to our countrymen through their every day and cardinal wants. We must not only be able to black boots, but to make them. At present, we are unknown in the Northern States, as mechanics. We give no proof of genius or skill at the County, the State, or the National Fairs. We are unknown at any of the great exhibitions of the industry of our fellow-citizens — and being unknown, we are unconsidered.

The fact that we make no show of our ability, is held conclusive of our inability to make any. Hence, all the indifference and contempt, with which incapacity is regarded, fall upon us, and that too, when we have had no means of disproving the injurious opinion of our natural inferiority. I have, during the last dozen years, denied, before the Americans, that we are an inferior race. But this has been done by arguments, based upon admitted principles, rather than by the presentation of facts. Now, firmly believing, as I do, that there are skill, invention, power, industry, and real mechanical genius among the colored people, which will bear favorable testimony for them, and which only need the means to develop them, I am decidedly in favor of the establishment of such a college as I have mentioned. The benefits of such an institution would not be confined to the Northern States, nor to the free colored people: they would extend over the whole Union. The slave, not less than the freeman, would be benefitted by such an institution. It must be confessed that the most powerful argument, now used by the Southern slave-holder — and the one most soothing to his conscience — is, that derived from the low condition of the free colored people at the North. I have long felt that too little attention has been given, by our truest friends, in this country, to removing this stumbling block out of the way of the slave's liberation.

The most telling, the most killing refutation of slavery, is the presentation of an industrious, enterprising, upright, thrifty and intelligent free black population. Such a population, I believe, would rise in the Northern States, under the fostering care of such a College as that supposed.

To show that we are capable of becoming mechanics, I might adduce any amount of testimony; but dear Madam, I need not ring the changes on such a proposition. There is no question in the mind of any unprejudiced person, that the negro is capable of making a good mechanic. Indeed, even those who cherish the bitterest feelings towards us have admitted that the apprehension that negroes might be employed in their stead, dictated the policy of excluding them from trades altogether; but I will not dwell upon this point, as I fear I have already trespassed too long upon your precious time, and written more than I ought to expect you to read. Allow me to say, in conclusion, that I believe every intelligent colored man in America will approve and rejoice at the establishment of some such institution as that now suggested. There are many respectable colored men, fathers of large families, having boys nearly grown up, whose minds are tossed by day and by night, with the anxious enquiry,

what shall I do with my boys? Such an institution would meet the wants of such persons. Then, too, the establishment of such an institution would be in character with the eminently practical philanthropy of your transatlantic friends. America could scarcely object to it, as an attempt to agitate the public mind on the subject of slavery, or to "dissolve the Union." It could not be tortured into a cause for hard words by the American people; but the noble and good of all classes would see in the effort an excellent motive, a benevolent object, temperately, wisely, and practically manifested.

Wishing you, dear Madam, renewed health, a pleasant passage and a safe return to your native land,

I am, most truly, your grateful friend,
Frederick Douglass.

Mrs. H. B. Stowe.

---

3. Reflections of Charlotte Forten, a Salem, Massachusetts, schoolgirl, 1855

Ray A. Billington, ed., *Journal of Charlotte L. Forten* (New York, 1953), pp. 62–63.

Miss Forten, granddaughter of the Philadelphia Negro abolitionist James Forten, came to Salem in 1854 at age sixteen to attend school. Her journal is a unique record of the activities, thoughts, and feelings of a sensitive Negro girl in a white community.

Wednesday, Sept. 12. To-day school commenced. — Most happy am I to return to the companionship of my studies, — ever my most valued friends. It is pleasant to meet the scholars again; most of them greeted me cordially, and were it not for the thought that *will* intrude, of the want of *entire sympathy* even of those I know and like best, I should greatly enjoy their society. There is one young girl and only one — Miss [Sarah] B[rown] who I believe thoroughly and heartily appreciates anti-slavery, — *radical* anti-slavery, and has no prejudice against color. I wonder that every colored person is not a misanthrope. Surely we have everything to make us hate mankind. I have met girls in the schoolroom [—] they have been thoroughly kind and cordial to me, — perhaps the next day met them in the street — they feared to recognize me; these I can but regard now with scorn and contempt, — once I liked them, believing them incapable of such meanness. Others give the most distant recognition possible. — I, of course, acknowledge no such recognitions, and they soon cease entirely. These are but trifles, certainly, to the great, public wrongs which we as a people are obliged to endure. But to those who experience them, these apparent trifles are most wearing and discouraging; even to the child's mind they reveal volumes of deceit and heartlessness, and early teach a lesson of suspicion and distrust. Oh! it is hard to go through life meeting contempt with contempt, hatred with hatred, fearing, with too good reason, to love and trust hardly any one whose skin is white, — however lovable, attractive and congenial in seeming. In the bitter, passionate feelings of my soul again and again there rises the questions "When, oh! when shall this cease?" "Is there no help?" "How long oh! how long must we continue to suffer — to endure?" Conscience answers it is wrong, it is ignoble to despair; let us labor earnestly and faithfully to acquire knowledge, to break down the barriers of prejudice and oppression. Let us take courage; never ceasing to work, — hoping and believing that if not for us, for another generation there is a better, brighter day in store, — when slavery and prejudice shall vanish before the glorious light of Liberty and Truth; when the rights of every colored man shall everywhere be acknowledged and respected, and he shall be treated as a *man* and a *brother!*

September. This evening Miss B[rown] and I joined the Female Anti-Slavery Society. I am glad to have persuaded her to do so. She seems an earnest hearted girl, in whom I cannot help having some confidence. I can only hope and pray that she will be true, and courageous enough to meet the opposition which every friend of freedom must encounter . . .

Government cooperation with private agencies in the education of Indian youth

1. The establishment of the Indian civilization fund, 1819

"An Act making provision for the civilization of the Indian tribes adjoining the frontier settlements," *Annals of Congress,* 15 Cong., 2 Sess. (1819), XXXIV, 2527.

This law was enacted following a recommendation by President James Monroe. The money appropriated was turned over to agents of Protestant missionary societies.

Be it enacted, etc., That, for the purpose of providing against the further decline and final extinction of the Indian tribes, adjoining to the frontier settlements of the United States, and for introducing among them the habits and arts of civilization, the President of the United States shall be, and he is hereby, authorized, in every case where he shall judge improvement in the habits and condition of such Indians practicable, and that the means of instruction can be introduced with their own consent, to employ capable persons, of good moral character, to instruct them in the mode of agriculture suited to their situation; and for teaching their children in reading, writing, and arithmetic, and for performing such other duties as may be enjoined, according to such instructions and rules as the President may give and prescribe for the regulation of their conduct, in the discharge of their duties.

And be it further enacted, That the annual sum of ten thousand dollars be, and the same is hereby, appropriated, for the purpose of carrying into effect the provisions of this act; and an account of the expenditure of the money, and proceedings, in execution of the foregoing provisions, shall be laid annually before Congress.

---

2. A circular issued by the War Department inviting the cooperation of "benevolent associations" in civilizing the Indians, 1819

The Works of John C. Calhoun, V (New York, 1883), 71.

Calhoun was secretary of war in Monroe's cabinet.

Sir, — In order to render the sum of $10,000, annually appropriated at the last session of Congress for the civilization of the Indians, as extensively beneficial as possible, the President is of opinion that it ought to be applied in cooperation with the exertions of benevolent associations, or individuals, who may choose to devote their time or means to effect the object contemplated by the act of Congress. But it will be indispensable, in order to apply any portion of the sum appropriated in the manner proposed, that the plan of education, in addition to reading, writing, and arithmetic, should, in the instruction of the boys, extend to the practical knowledge of the mode of agriculture, and of such of the mechanic arts as are suited to the condition of the Indians; and in that of the girls, to spinning, weaving, and sewing. It is also indispensable that the establishment should be fixed within the limits of those Indian nations who border on our settlements. Such associations or individuals who are already actually engaged in educating the Indians, and who may desire the co-operation of the Government, will report to the Department of

War, to be laid before the President, the location of the institutions under their superintendence, their funds, the number and kind of teachers, the number of youths of both sexes, the objects which are actually embraced in their plan of education, and the extent of the aid which they require; and such institutions as are formed, but have not gone into actual operation, will report the extent of their funds, the places at which they intend to make their establishments, the whole number of youths of both sexes which they intend to educate, the number and kind of teachers to be employed, the plan of education adopted, and the extent of the aid required.

---

3. Additional regulations adopted by the War Department, 1820

John C. Calhoun, "Regulations for the Civilization of the Indians," in *Indian Treaties, and Laws and Regulations Relating to Indian Affairs* (Washington, 1826), pp. 487–488.

The position selected for the establishment, a plan of the buildings contemplated, with an estimate of the costs, to be submitted to the secretary of war, to be laid before the president.

Government will, if it has the means, and approves of the arrangement, pay two-thirds of the expense of erecting the necessary buildings. No part of the money to be advanced until after the buildings are commenced; and one-fourth to be reserved until they are completed. The payment to be made on the certificate of the agent of Indian affairs, for the tribe or nation in which the establishment is located, as to the facts of the commencement and completion of the buildings.

The president of the United States will contribute, out of the annual appropriation, to such institution which may be approved of by him, a sum proportionate to the number of pupils belonging to each, regard being had to the necessary expense of the establishment, and the degree of success which has attended it.

No advance to be made, except for the buildings, till the school is in actual operation; of which fact, and the number of pupils belonging to it, the certificate of the superintendent, or person having the principal control of the institution, will be sufficient evidence.

A report will be annually made for each establishment, on the 1st of October, of the number and names of the teachers, and other persons belonging to it. The number of students; the number which have completed their course, and left the institution, since the first day of October, of the preceding year; the number entered; the amount of disbursements, for the same period, and the value and description of property on hand; which report will be certified by the superintendent or person having the principal control of the establishment.

It is considered to be the duty of all persons who may be employed, or attached to any institution, not only to set a good example of sobriety, industry, and honesty, but as far as practicable, to impress on the minds of the Indians, the friendly and benevolent views of the government towards them, and the advantage to them in yielding to the policy of the government, and co-operating with it, in such measures as it may deem necessary for their civilization and happiness. A contrary course of conduct cannot fail to incur the displeasure of the government, as it is impossible that the object which it has in view can be effected, and peace be habitually preserved, if the distrust of the Indians, as to its benevolent views, should be excited.

---

4. Report on the school at Eliot,
Choctaw Nation, 1822

Rev. Cyrus Kingsbury, superintendent of schools in the Choctaw mission, to John C. Calhoun, Jan. 30, 1822, in Jedidiah Morse, *A Report to the Secretary of War . . . on Indian Affairs* (New Haven, 1822), pp. 188–191.

This school, named in honor of the celebrated Puritan missionary to the Indians, was conducted by the American Board of Commissioners for Foreign Missions, an organization of the Congregationalist churches.

This establishment was commenced in August, 1818. During the past year, it has been strengthened by the arrival of the Rev. Mr. Byington; Captain John Smith, and Mr. Elijah Bradwell, with their families; and a single female. The following is a list of the persons permanently employed at Eliot, with their occupations.

Rev. Cyrus Byington, Missionary and Rector.
Mr. Moses Jewell, Mechanic.
Mrs. Jewell and one child.
Mr. Zechariah Hawes, Farmer and Shoemaker.
Mr. Anson Dyer, Steward.
Mr. Joel Wood, Teacher.
Mrs. Wood.
Capt. John Smith, Farmer, and Manager of Plantation.
Mrs. Smith and five children.
Mr. Elijah Bradwell, Farmer and Teacher.
Mrs. Bradwell and three children.
Miss Hannah Thacher, Teacher.

All these persons, children excepted, have freely offered their services to labor for the support of the school, and have been duly accepted by the Prudential Committee of the A. B. C. F. M. All, whose health will permit, are diligently, and most of them laboriously employed in their respective departments.

Besides the above, from eight to twelve Mechanics, laborers, and domestics, are hired to labor for the establishment.

In the school, there is an annual vacation of six weeks, commencing on the first Wednesday in August. The past vacations have been longer, on account of sickness in the family. From the commencement of the term in October 1820, to August 1821, when it closed, the number of scholars varied from fifty to seventy. During this period, twenty-nine new ones were admitted; one was expelled for obstinate disobedience; and six others were taken home by their parents, who thought that they could no longer spare them to attend school. The latter had all been at school before they came to Eliot, and when they left, could read and write very well.

The boys' school is taught on the Lancasterian plan. During the three last months of the term, the organization and discipline of the school was improved, and the progress of the scholars more rapid. While out of school they labored cheerfully, and with effect. Besides planting and hoeing, and laboring in various other employments, they cleared several acres of land. It is believed that ten to fifteen acres, may in this way be annually added to the plantation. Three of the scholars are learning the blacksmith's trade. They are alternately in the school and shop.

The female scholars have been placed under a female teacher. While out of school they are employed in various domestic labors, under the superintendence of their teacher, and the other ladies. Their improvement has fully equalled our expectations.

Exertions were made to provide, as far as possible, for the support of the school, and family from our own resources. The plantation was cultivated in the best manner — the stock carefully attended to and every department was managed with economy, skill and persevering industry. The prospects of the establishment were never more promising than at the commencement of the vacation.

About that time a distressing and fatal sickness commenced in the family. One after another was attacked with the bilious or intermittent fever. Those who for a time enjoyed health by attending day and night on the sick, soon became the victims of disease. Of twenty-eight persons, including children, who composed the permanent family at that time, not one escaped. Several of the hired people, and three or four scholars, who continued at Eliot through the vacation, were also sick.

Mrs. Judith Williams, after a long and distressing illness, died on the 13th of October. She had taken an active and laborious part in the domestic concerns of the family. Mr. and Mrs. Jewell buried their oldest child. One of the scholars, a promising half breed lad, about thirteen years old, also died. He was kind and affectionate in his deportment, much engaged in learning, and we hope truly pious.

. . . . .

The schools are more flourishing than at any former period. There are in both seventy-five scholars, descendants of the Choctaws, and about twenty of them full blooded natives. Five children belonging to the white families, also attend the school. The natives, especially in the neighborhood of Eliot, are friendly, and highly pleased with the opportunity of educating their children.

The past year, in some respects, has been an expensive one. Sickness obliged us to hire more than would otherwise have been necessary. There has been erected a house ninety feet by forty, two stories high, and calculated for four families. This house is not yet completed. Sixty of the scholars have been entirely supported, as to board and tuition, and many of them clothed. Smithwork and other property, to the amount of more than $300, have been furnished from Eliot, to the school now establishing among the Cherokees, on the Arkansaw.

The whole amount of disbursements from September 30, 1820, to October 1st, 1821, was $8,388,87; And the receipts, during the same period, amounted to $8,191,23.

. . . . .

Much credit is due to Captain Smith, and those who have labored in the several departments, for their unremitting exertions in the midst of sickness, and difficulties. They have labored for this school with more persevering industry and self-denial, than almost any persons exercise for the support of their own families. Mr. Wood and Miss Thacher, have been indefatigable in their attention to the schools. Mr. Byington is an active man, and watches with a vigilant eye over the interests of the institution.

5. The Committee on Indian Affairs of the House of Representatives praises the civilization policy, 1824

American State Papers, Indian Affairs, II (Washington, 1834), 457–459.

The committee have carefully examined the measures which have been adopted for the disbursement of the annual allowance made by this law, and find them very judicious, and such as are best calculated to effectuate the benevolent designs of the Government . . .

From this statement, it will appear that twenty-one schools have been established; all, except three, since the passage of the above law, and principally by the means which it affords. At these schools there are taught more than eight hundred scholars, whose progress in the acquisition of an English education exceeds the most sanguine expectations that had been formed.

Very comfortable school-houses have been erected for the accommodation of the different schools, and, in most cases, convenient dwellings for the teachers.

So far as the committee have been able to ascertain, the plan of education has been very judicious, and no pains seem to have been spared to extend to the Indians the full benefit of the law.

All the schools are increasing; and so urgent is the wish of the Indians to have their children educated, that numerous applications are re-fused, from the limited means which the schools possess. The time of the children is not wholly devoted to their books while at school; the girls are instructed in such arts as are suited to female industry in civilized life, and the boys are required to devote a part of their time in acquiring a knowledge of husbandry. The advances of males and females in these branches are most satisfactory, and have already had no small influence in inducing their parents to become less fond of an erratic life, and more inclined to have fixed residences, and rely for their support on the cultivation of the ground. Such has been the effect of the above circumstances, combined with some others not more influential, that, at many of the places where schools have been established, the Indians have already constructed comfortable dwellings, and now cultivate farms of considerable extent. They have become the owners of property necessary to agricultural pursuits, and for the conveniences of life.

The committee are aware that very considerable aids have been given by different Christian denominations, all of whom feel a deep interest in the paternal views of the Government. But the committee are well persuaded that, had the Government afforded no pecuniary aid, very few, if any, of the benefits which have been conferred, would have been experienced by the Indians. The annual appropriation of ten thousand dollars has encouraged the benevolent and pious, in many parts of the country, to form associations and collect donations, with the view of aiding the humane purposes of the Government. Hundreds of such associations are now in active operation; and they are much cheered in their exertions by the rapid advances to civilization which the Indians have made.

It requires but little research to convince every candid mind that the prospect of civilizing our Indians was never so promising as at this time. Never were means for the accomplishment of this object so judiciously devised, and so faithfully applied, as provided in the above act, and the auxiliary aids which it has encouraged. It is believed to be an essential part of any plan for Indian civilization, that, with the rudiments of education, the males should be taught the arts of husbandry, and the females to perform those domestic duties which peculiarly belong to their stations in civilized life. The attempts which have heretofore been made, many of which have failed, omitted this essential part. Many zealous but enthusiastic persons, who have been most conspicuous in endeavoring to reclaim the Indians, persuaded themselves to believe that, to secure this object, it was only necessary to send missionaries among them to instruct them in the Christian religion. Some of their exertions failed, without producing any salutary effect, because the agents employed were wholly unfitted for the task. Others, though productive of some good effect at first, eventually failed, because to their missionary labors were not added the institutes of education and instruction in agriculture. These are combined in the exertions now making; and, from the good which has been done, the most pleasing anticipations of success are confidently cherished. There are many Indian nations within our boundaries who have experienced no aid from these efforts; being restricted in the means, the benefits are, consequently, limited. But the committee are assured that the continuation of the appropriation, seconded by the liberal and increasing aids which are afforded by voluntary contributions, will gradually, and most effectually, extend the benefits of the law to the remotest tribes who inhabit our extensive domain. This will be a work of time; and, for its accomplishment, great labor and perseverance will be necessary. The progress, however, of this work may be more rapid than any can now venture to anticipate. The instruction and civilization of a few enterprising youths will have an immense influence on the tribes to which they belong. As the means are constantly applied, the numbers reclaimed will increase, and an increase of numbers will insure, in a geometrical proportion, success for the future. It is difficult to

say what may not be accomplished under such circumstances. No one will be bold enough to denounce him as a visionary enthusiast, who, under such auspices, will look with great confidence to the entire accomplishment of the object.

.   .   .   .   .

[The Indians] understand the motive of the Government, and properly appreciate it. So far as the benefits of this policy are extended, will this feeling be cherished; and it affords the safest guaranty against future wars. To say nothing of the valuable lives which have been lost in the Indian conflicts we have had, how much treasure has been expended in our defence! More money was expended, in protecting the exposed parts of our country from Indian depredations, during the late war, than would be required, if judiciously applied, to secure the great plan of Indian civilization.

.   .   .   .   .

The Indians are not now what they once were. They have partaken of our vices more than our virtues. Such is their condition, at present, that they must be civilized or exterminated; no other alternative exists. He must be worse than savage who can view, with cold indifference, an exterminating policy. All desire their prosperity, and wish to see them brought within the pale of civilization. The means which have been adopted, and of which the law in question is the foundation, seem the most likely to obtain the desired result. They should not, therefore, be abandoned. The passage of this law was called for by many of the people in the most populous and influential sections of our country. Their wishes were made known in language that evinced a deep interest — an interest not produced by a momentary excitement, but the result of much reflection and a high sense of moral duty. It may be said, emphatically, that the passage of this law was called for by a religious community. They were convinced of the correctness of the policy in a political point of view, and, as Christians, they felt the full force of the obligations which duty enjoined. Their zeal was tempered by reason. No fanciful schemes of proselytism seem to have been indulged. They formed a correct estimate of the importance of their undertaking, and pointed to the most judicious means for the accomplishment of their wishes. Since the passage of the law, hundreds and thousands have been encouraged to contribute their mite in aid of the wise policy of the Government. However the various denominations of professing Christians may differ in their creeds and

that we feel less for their prosperity than our professions have encouraged them to believe; and such an impression cannot fail to produce the most injurious consequences.

From the various lights in which the committee have viewed the policy of this law, they are convinced that it was founded in justice, and should not be repealed. They therefore submit to the House the following resolution: *Resolved,* That it is inexpedient to repeal the law making an annual appropriation of ten thousand dollars for the civilization of the Indians.

.　　　.　　　.　　　.　　　.

Establishments for civilizing the Indians

Stations	Sponsor	Year	Scholars	Annual tuition from U.S.	Missionary families	Total expense, 1833
School at Cornwall, Conn.	Am. Board of Foreign Missions, Boston	1817	35	$1,438	—	—
Brainard, Cherokee nation, Tenn.	Am. Board of Foreign Missions, Boston	1817	84	1,200	42	$ 7,632
Elliot, Choctaw nation	Am. Board of Foreign Missions, Boston	1818	80	1,200	12	9,735
Newell, Choctaw nation	Am. Board of Foreign Missions, Boston	1821	15	350	—	668
Mayhew, Choctaw nation	Am. Board of Foreign Missions, Boston	1822	66	800	10	15,706
Dwight, Cherokees, Ark.	Am. Board of Foreign Missions, Boston	1820	50	600	9	6,241
Ft. Wayne, Ind. and Mich.	Baptist General Convention	1820	40	200	10	3,000
Valley Towns, Cherokees, Tenn.	Baptist General Convention	1820	50	500	26	3,000
Tensawattee, Cherokees, Tenn.	Baptist General Convention	1821	25	250	—	—
Withington, Creek nation	Baptist General Convention	1823	40	600	7	3,000
Oneida nation	Hamilton Baptist Missionary Society	1820	24	500	—	—
Tuscarora nation, N.Y.	United Foreign Missionary Society, N.Y.	1819	45	450	—	—
Seneca nation, N.Y.	United Foreign Missionary Society, N.Y.	1819	31	450	6	2,451
Union, Osages, Ark.	United Foreign Missionary Society, N.Y.	1820	12	250	30	6,700
Harmony, Osages, Mo.	United Foreign Missionary Society, N.Y.	1822	17	250	41	4,680
Wyandots, near Upper Sandusky	Methodist Ohio Conference	1821	60	500	—	1,950
Spring Place, Cherokees, Tenn.	United Brethren	1801	20	300	—	744
Monroe, Chickasaw nation	Synod of S.C. and Ga.	1821	54	500	12	2,675
Charity Hall, Chickasaw nation	Cumberland Missionary Society	1822	21	400	—	608
Ottawa, Miami of the Lake	Western Missionary Society	1823	—	300	21	—
Florissant, Mo.	Catholic Bishop of New Orleans	1823	—	800	—	—

general doctrines, they all unite in their wishes that our Indians may become civilized. That this feeling almost universally prevails, has been declared in language too unequivocal to admit of doubt. It has been seen in their words and in their actions.

. . . They are taught the first rudiments of education, the duties which appertain a man as a member of civil society, and his accountability as a moral agent. Repeal this law, and these exertions are not only paralyzed, but destroyed. The Indians will see, in such an act,

The establishment of the Choctaw Academy, a secondary school for Indian youth

The academy was founded in 1825 by Colonel Richard M. Johnson (1780–1850), United States senator from Kentucky, in cooperation with the Baptist General Convention. Johnson was vice-president of the United States, 1837–1841.

1. Instructions sent to the principal of the academy, Rev. Thomas Henderson, 1825

U.S. Congress, House, Exec. Doc. 109, *Choctaw Treaty,* 26 Cong., 2 Sess. (Washington, 1841), pp. 23–24.

Dear Sir: You have probably received information that, by the board of managers of the Baptist General Convention, you have been unanimously elected instructor and superintendent of the Choctaw Academy, recently located in your vicinity. I am directed, in behalf of the said board of managers, to present to you an outline of the instructions which they conceive may contribute to the improvement of the Indian youth, to your own comfort and usefulness, and to the consequent prosperity of the whole concern. The board wish you, once in each week (on a Monday or Saturday, as you may find convenient) to review the conduct of the youth, and to offer to them such expressions of approbation or censure as their conduct shall appear to deserve; prohibiting them entirely from the use of ardent spirits, which has, in so many lamentable instances, brought destruction to the health and character of individuals and settlements. They recommend your offering to them frequent and affectionate lectures upon the advantages of temperance, mutual good will, respect for their parents, and upon all other topics which an exalted morality can embrace, especially upon the truth and excellency of the Christian religion, and on the happiness of those who welcome its doctrines, observe its precepts, and live under its blessed influence. It is the desire of the board, and they hereby urge the duty of enjoining a strict observance of the Lord's Day, restraining the pupils from all practices which tend to demoralize the mind, and to produce indifference as to the Divine institutions; to which ends, the requiring of a regular attendance upon the public worship of God on that holy day will be found indispensable.

Convinced of its importance to the success of the institution, the board wishes you to visit the children frequently at their respective dwellings, by night and by day, to prevent any disorders which might arise, and to direct them as to the proper employment of their time; to facilitate which, they request you to see that the buildings be conveniently situated, and sufficiently contiguous to each other. It is wished that you ever exercise especial care in observing that the children are comfortably located, and amply supplied with every thing necessary for their welfare; and, particularly, not to suffer them to be interrupted from their studies by manual labor, excepting making their own fires, and performing such services as may be found necessary to their health, recreation, and improvement. You will consider yourself authorized to receive white children into the school, provided their number shall not exceed that of the Indians, and provided, also, that they shall be subject to the same rules, and be placed in every respect on an equality with them.

2. The superintendent of the Choctaw Academy supports manual training, 1832

Thomas Henderson to Lewis Cass, secretary of war, in U.S. Congress, House, *Choctaw Treaty,* pp. 66–67.

Dear Sir: I have had it in contemplation for several years, to suggest to the honorable Secretary of War the probable advantage that might result to this institution by having attached to the establishment, at some convenient distance from the academy, a few workshops, embracing the most useful and necessary mechanical arts for the promotion of civilized life: say a blacksmith, shoemaker, and wheelright who understood stocking ploughs; or any other which would seem best calculated to suit the present condition of the Indians.

I have been led to these reflections partly from the nature of the case, as it has been presented to my own mind, and partly from having had some boys in the school whose minds appeared to be turned more upon some kind of work than upon their books; and also from the discovery of a considerable mechanical genius among them, together with a desire, manifested by some of the youths themselves, to become mechanics.

It is very certain (were it even practicable to make good scholars of every youth sent to the institution) that, by their education alone, they cannot all hope to get employment, and be supported in the nation, in its present uncultivated condition; and it is equally certain, that nothing will tend more rapidly to promote civilized habits among that unfortunate race of people (in addition to even a moderate English education) than the encouragement of the mechanical arts. Every person is well apprized that it is not every sprightly boy among our white children that is calculated to become a scholar; and although the progress of students in this school has generally far exceeded our most sanguine expectations, yet, while some take learning kindly, manifesting quite a taste for literary attainments, others, like our own children, discover a different turn of mind.

In such cases, it does appear to me that much more good would result to the different tribes by making mechanics of such youths as either cannot or will not take learning freely, and I would not deprive even the most sprightly from the opportunity of acquiring some mechanical art, when it was desired by them. The more I reflect on this subject the more of its benefits, I think, I have been able to discover; and all to whom I have communicated my views have concurred in opinion with me, that, in addition to an education, nothing could possibly be introduced of more real advantage to the Indians than to have their children instructed in some active employment, by which they will be able to support themselves in future life, and benefit their tribes.

My plan would be to erect shops near to the academy, and have professional mechanics entirely under the direction and control of the superintendent of the institution, so that their whole time should be devoted exclusively in learning the boys the respective arts of each trade. I think, by proper management, the greater part of the students, in nearly the same time now devoted at school, would be sent home with good trades, and a sufficient education for mechanics and farmers. Let such as discover a genius and talent for education be permitted to pursue a regular course to the full extent.

---

3. An Indian teacher in the Academy suggests that the students be taught trades, 1833

J. N. Bourassa to Lewis Cass, secretary of war, in U.S. Congress, House, *Choctaw Treaty,* pp. 62–64.

Respected Sir: Knowing that your honor has a great desire to see the time when the *natives* shall live like the *whites,* and knowing, too, full well, that you are accessible, even by children, I would humbly offer a few things relative to this Indian school, in which I have taught nearly a year, and sincerely hope that you may receive these lines as an humble token of regard and friendship.

The plan of this institution would be more beneficial to the scholars and Indians that are sent to this place, were the Department of War to give a view of it to those tribes that are concerned in educating their youth here. For the majority of boys that take a course in this academy would be able amply to learn a trade in the same length of time generally spent in obtaining a mere education, provided there were joined to this institution two or three shops, to enable some of the boys that cannot learn their books, to get a trade, which they could do to great advantage. This would obviate a great disadvantage, under which the different tribes labor, in not having proper persons selected to choose the smartest youths they have among them, to send to this school. For, sir, there are some young men, were they to live as long as the man of 969 years, and study all the time, could not get sufficient learning to teach the Indians.

The plan of the Rev. Thomas Henderson was a one that I like very much. I ask, why do the boys retain their old habits, and play so much? The reason is, because they have no regular employment. But if they had shops to work in, and had a person purposely to teach them, they would find it a great recreation; for it will not do to confine the Indian boys to study too much, for they were never, among their friends, confined. For, if we tie them too close to their books, they will be tired and discouraged; and your honor well knows, that a young man with an education alone can find no business in the tribes as they are now, but a young man with a trade can work for himself, and even for access to some tribes, if not all: especially the blacksmith's trade; for I have no doubt in my mind, that the Department of War would be glad to give a chance to such a young man to be employed for his tribe, by which he would be enabled to provide for himself, family, and nation. But it is not a savage or wandering tribe, that is capable of supporting a school and teacher. It is also evident, most any trade will prove more beneficial than a good education in the first settling of a country. For if we just look on the first settling of this country, we see that it was not by the use of the pen and book, but the use of the axe and plough. So then, if we wish to civilize the Indians, we must take the same course.

This would do away that habit of laziness in the Indian character, for which he has been, and is, more censured than for any other he possesses. And the erection of the shops would be no great expense to the tribes, and not so much to the department, for the boys could do all nearly themselves; and I am confident the profits that would accrue from these shops, both to the pupils and the several tribes, would overbalance what it would cost the nation to hire two or three persons to oversee the shops. This is the only way I can see that this oppressed and poor race of men can rise. It is by the aid of their own young men; and I feel it my duty to state my mind to you, as I am one of the Indians, and I hope you will pardon my freedom. And I say that this colonizing business will either prove the everlasting ruin and fall, or else the rise and elevation, of the Indians; and they never will prosper, unless their own children help them by trades and education; and your honor, I must say, is the only man we can look to for assistance in this thing. It seems to me, that all the friends of the cause would rejoice in supporting such a promising establishment. But presume not that I wish to dictate — no, you are too well acquainted in all these things; but beg your honor to consider these few incorrect lines as my own feelings, and what some of the chiefs suggested to me, last treaty in Indiana. And if this should be granted to this school, I would feel that this nation was about to rise in the estimation of the world.

The superiority of boarding schools for Indian youth

1. An Indian boarding school on the Yakima Reservation, Washington Territory, 1862

A. A. Bancroft, Indian agent,
to Calvin H. Hale, superintendent, in
"Report of the Washington Superintendency,"
in *Report of the Commissioner of Indian Affairs for 1862* (Washington, 1863), pp. 420–421.

The first Indian school organized upon this reservation was in the fall of 1860, Rev. James H. Wilbur having been appointed superintendent of teaching and William Wright, teacher.

At the opening of the school about twenty scholars were in attendance — seventeen boys and three girls. About six of them were from eighteen to twenty-one years old, and the age of the others ranged from nine to eighteen. The scholars were fed and clothed, and, being uniformly dressed, presented quite an interesting appearance. The boys lodged in the upper room of the school-house, and the girls in a part of the house occupied by the teacher's family. The time spent by the teacher in the school-room was from ten to twelve o'clock in the morning, and from one to three o'clock in the afternoon. In the morning, before school time, and in the afternoon, after school hours, the boys were taken into the garden or the field and instructed by the superintendent of teaching how to work in the garden, and how to plough, sow, etc. The scholars were orderly and well-behaved, and advanced rapidly in learning the alphabet, spelling, reading, writing, and arithmetic.

The scholars were allowed to visit their parents occasionally, and after spending a few days with them were contented to return to school and continue their studies.

A school was also taught by Mrs. L. A. Wilbur, where the Indian women were taught how to card wool, spin, knit, and how to cut and make garments for themselves and families. For this school cards and spinning-wheels had been purchased, and a great abundance of wool was on hand to operate upon. I esteem this an important branch of instruction.

These schools were in a flourishing condition when the superintendent of Indian affairs (B. F. Kendall) visited this agency and removed the superintendent of teaching and the two teachers, and the schools were broken up. I was instructed to discontinue the practice of feeding and clothing the school children.

For nearly a year we have tested the plan of having a school without subsisting the scholars, and the experiment has proved almost, if not quite, a failure. There is a desire on the part of many of the Indians to send their children to school, and yet it is impossible for them to do so while their homes are many miles away from the agency, and there is no provision made for their subsistence here. Annual appropriations are made by Congress to "provide for the support of two schools, keeping them in repair, providing suitable books and stationary, and for the employment of one superintendent of teaching and two teachers." Now, unless the helping hand of the government is extended to the Indian children, and they are provided with food and raiment, these liberal appropriations which were intended for their good will fail to reach them, and the amount appropriated for their education will be lost to them. To my mind it is clearly the duty of the government to feed and clothe the school children, and place them under the eye and care of judicious teachers. By this system the children are easily managed, and their prompt and regular attendance at school secured. There are other advantages: it brings together a larger number of children, making it more pleasant for them, and in their studies they advance more rapidly, as they take pride in teaching each other.

Upon the Sabbath the Indians, old and young, usually turn out in large numbers to receive religious instruction. Two rooms are used for this purpose — one in which the Indian children are taught by the employés, and in the other the adult Indians are instructed by Rev. James H. Wilbur, who, assisted by an interpreter, talks to them in a plain and familiar way of the great truths of christianity. An hour or more is thus devoted on the Sabbath exclusively to the Indians. They listen with great attention to what is said to them, and express themselves as being anxious to know and to do that which is right. A change for the better has taken place with many of them, and there is great encouragement here to labor for the spiritual as well as temporal good of the Indians.

---

2. Advocacy of boarding schools for Indians in Oregon, 1867

J. R. Doolittle, *Condition of the Indian Tribes,*
Report of the Joint Special Committee
with Appendix (Washington, 1867), pp. 3–4.

The schools, provided for at both the Siletz and Grande Ronde, seem to result in but little, if any, practical benefit to the Indians, and this remark applies with equal force to all of the tribes, with two or three exceptions, that I have visited.

There is usually incorporated in Indian treaties a provision that a teacher shall be employed and paid by the government; then follows inadequate appropriations for his services, with, occasionally, some slight provision for school books, and here the government terminates its efforts at educating the Indians, without taking into consideration the fact that a poorly paid teacher and a small supply of books furnish but inadequate means for educational purposes. The consequence is, that there is an occasional spasmodic effort made, when some ill adapted and empty building can be obtained for the purpose, in which to teach a few young Indians the alphabet, and usually before that feat is accomplished the teacher leaves, disgusted with the inadequacy of his compensation, or the appropriations become exhausted, and the school is discontinued, to be resumed again at an interval sufficiently remote to give the pupils ample time to forget the lessons but imperfectly learned under the former teacher.

An institution conducted upon such a plan among white people would seldom become famous for its educational advantages. All experience has demonstrated the impossibility of educating Indian children while they are permitted to consort and associate with their ignorant, barbarous, and superstitious parents. It is admitted by all teachers who have ever made the experiment, that the vicious home influences of the Indian lodge or wigwam during the recess of school hours are more than sufficient to counterbalance and destroy all that is taught to the pupil during the period allotted to study.

The only Indian schools which have attained to any degree of success are those where the means have been supplied to feed, clothe, and lodge the children separate and apart from their parents and members of their tribes. Where the Indian youth is left to the alternate struggle between civilization and barbarism the contest is likely to culminate on the side of his savage instincts. To provide for a school for the education of savages in the usual manner which we have adopted is not only a waste of funds, but a mockery.

Where the government has entered into treaty stipulations for the support of Indian schools, it should redeem the pledge by procuring suitable buildings for the purposes of the school remote from the tribe and its influences. It should board, lodge, and clothe the pupils, and employ suitable persons to instruct them in not only what is taught in books, but in other things pertaining to civilization. When this is done, the Indian who parts with his land under the impression that his offspring is to receive an instalment of civilization and intelligence in return, will not be defrauded by a humbug too transparent to deceive any one except a savage. If it is thought that it will require too great an outlay of money to comply in this manner with our treaty stipulations, it would be better to abolish the farce of our annual meagre appropriations for Indian schools, as, under the present system, the most of those appropriations are wasted without doing the Indians or any one else any good.

IV Child Labor

In the mid-nineteenth century child labor, per se, was not a major concern of humanitarian reformers. As in the past, children were expected to work and their labor was deemed socially productive and individually beneficent. Child labor in farming, trade-and-mercantile apprenticeship, seafaring, and domestic service continued to be considered an introduction to useful adult pursuits. Child labor in factories, however, was a different problem because factory work offered child laborers scant opportunity for trade education and left them no time for formal schooling. The first child labor laws, recognizing the value of both work and education, required that children employed in factories attend school for a specified number of months or weeks each year. The Massachusetts statute of 1836, the earliest of the compulsory school attendance laws, declared that children under fifteen could be employed in manufacturing only if they had received three months of schooling in the year preceding their employment. An attempt to make the law apply to agriculture and the mechanical trades as well as to manufacturing failed. Several other states adopted school attendance laws patterned after that of Massachusetts. Prior to the Civil War a few states supplemented school attendance laws with legislation prohibiting the employment of children under twelve in factories and establishing a ten-hour workday for children.[1]

These laws, although few in number and limited in scope, represented an advance in the legal status of the working child. For many years, however, they were either so poorly enforced or so unenforceable that their practical effect in protecting child laborers was negligible. Six years after the passage of Massachusetts' school attendance law Horace Mann asserted: "It is obvious that children of ten, twelve, or fourteen years of age may be steadily worked in our manufactories, without any schooling, and this cruel deprivation may be preserved for six, eight or ten years, and yet during all this period, no very alarming outbreak will occur to rouse the public mind from its guilty slumber." [2] The superintendent of public schools of Providence described the Rhode Island law as a "dead letter." A Connecticut report used identical language.[3] Employers easily found ways of violating the laws. Since they were not required to keep school certificates on file, they could assert without fear of contradiction that the child had been to school. A child might be sent to work in another mill every nine months, and so evade the three months requirement. In the case of ten-hour laws, because an employer was liable only if he "wilfully" and "knowingly" violated the age limit, he could argue that he did not know the child's true age. Out of necessity, timidity, or greed parents cooperated with employers in violating child labor laws. Thus, despite attempts at regulation, children's work continued to be supplied to the factories of the new industrial order.

1. For a summary of child labor legislation prior to 1860 see U.S. Bureau of Labor, *Report on Condition of Woman and Child Wage-Earners in the United States,* 19 vols. (Washington, 1910–1913), VI, 73–128, 207–209

2. Massachusetts, Board of Education, "Third Annual Report of the Secretary, January 1840, Board of Commissioners of Common Schools," *Education and Labor, 1842* (Boston, 1842), p. 45.
3. Quoted in Edith Abbott, *Women in Industry* (New York, 1909), p. 344.

A. THE GOSPEL OF WORK AND THE AMERICAN CHARACTER

Labor and the Promised Land

Augustine J. H. Duganne,
The Gospel of Labor (Boston, 1849),
pp. 9–10.

Augustine J. H. Duganne (1823–1884),
writer and poet in Boston, Philadelphia,
and later New York, produced a quantity of
adventure novels for Erastus Beadle
and other publishers. Success of the Know-
Nothing party in 1855 carried him
into the New York Assembly.

Labor and Liberty are forever one: —
In man's true life their work is jointly done!

Behold! they have descended
Through ages and through centuries,
Since Moses first through parted seas,
Led forth the ransomed Israelites —
And taught the tribes in one great nation
blended,
The Decalogue of Human Rights!
Through the long pilgrimage of forty years —
The cloud by day — the Pillar of Fire by
night —
Leading their trustful sight: —
On to the goal of all their hopes and
fears —
On to their Paradise bright,
The Promised Land!
Wandered that chosen band!

Tocqueville on the differences between
North and South, 1832

Tocqueville, *Democracy in America,*
I, 394–395.[1]

The American of the North sees no slaves
around him in his childhood; he is even un-
attended by free servants, for he is usually
obliged to provide for his own wants. As soon
as he enters the world, the idea of necessity
assails him on every side; he soon learns to
know exactly the natural limits of his power;
he never expects to subdue by force those who
withstand him; and he knows that the surest
means of obtaining the support of his fellow-
creatures is to win their favour. He therefore
becomes patient, reflecting, tolerant, slow to act,
and persevering in his designs.

In the southern states the more pressing
wants of life are always supplied; the inhabitants, therefore, are not occupied with the material cares of life, from which they are always
provided for by others; and their imagination
is diverted to more captivating and less definite
objects. The American of the south is fond of
grandeur, luxury, and renown, of gayety, of
pleasure, and above all of idleness; nothing
obliges him to exert himself in order to subsist;
and as he has no necessary occupations, he gives
way to indolence and does not even attempt
what would be useful.

But the equality of fortunes, and the absence
of slavery in the north, plunge the inhabitants
in those same cares of daily life which are dis-
dained by the white population of the south.
They are taught from infancy to combat want;
and to place comfort above all the pleasures of
the intellect or the heart. The imagination is

1. The British traveler Harriet Martineau visited
the South in 1835 and observed, "Wherever there is
a servile class, work is considered a disgrace, unless
it bears some other name, and is of an exclusive
character. In the free States, labor is more really and
heartily honored than, perhaps, in any other part of
the civilised world." See Martineau, *Society in America,* II (1837), 99.

extinguished by the trivial details of life; and the ideas become less numerous and less general, but far more practical and more precise. As prosperity is the sole aim of exertion, it is excellently well attained; nature and men are turned to the best pecuniary advantage; and society is dexterously made to contribute to the welfare of each of its members, while individual egotism is the source of general happiness.

The American of the North has not only experience but knowledge; yet he values science not as an enjoyment, but as a means of obtaining a certain end, and he is only anxious to seize its useful applications. The citizen of the south is more given to act upon impulse; he is more clever, more frank, more generous, more intellectual, and more brilliant.

"Let not one of your children . . . be from school, or without a regular employment"

Joseph Tuckerman, "A Word to Fathers and Mothers," *Reports, etc. of the Minister to the Poor* (Boston, 1832), pp. 3–4.

Joseph Tuckerman (1778–1840), Unitarian clergyman and early advocate of scientific philanthropy, began his ministry-at-large in Boston in 1819 in service of the poor who were not affiliated with any churches. He continued this service until 1833. From visiting the poor in their homes, he became interested in their living and working conditions and was an early critic of child labor.

Thirdly. *Have you a child between the ages of 14 and 21, who is without a regular employment?* Look at that child, and say, what is his condition? With his present dispositions, and the habits which he is every day and hour forming and confirming, what may be your hopes concerning him? Let me ask you, affectionately, but plainly, is he not in the way

to *destruction?* Have you not every thing to fear concerning him? And why is he not in some regular employment? Why is he not an apprentice, or upon a farm, or in some course of useful labor? Is not your soul chargeable with the misery of his present condition; with the fruit of his present conduct; with the sins and miseries to which idleness, intemperance, and dishonesty, if not immediately corrected, will bring him? Give not sleep to your eyes, till you have begun the work of his salvation. Allow not rest to your soul, till you have done all that you can do, to place him in a condition, and to fix him in employment, which promises at least, with God's blessing, that he may be useful, virtuous and happy.

Parents, a most momentous responsibility rests upon us. God intrusts our children to us, that they may be reared, and instructed, by our care, and our exertions for them. Let us not attempt to throw off our responsibility for them, for God will require it of us. In our free government, the children of the poorest may rise to the highest stations of wealth, honor, trust and usefulness. Let not one of your children, then, between the ages of 4 and 21, be from school, or without a regular employment. Make any sacrifice, but of virtue, and encounter any sufferings, rather than be the instruments of their ignorance, their vice, and their ruin. There are many who will help you, if you need, and seek, their help; and God will help those, who are faithful to themselves, and to his will. But if you permit your child, or your children, with the opportunities which you have in this city, to grow up untaught, and ignorant, and vicious, you will be partakers of their guilt, and sharers of their awful condemnation.

A PARENT.

Horace Greeley on the accumulators, 1850

Horace Greeley, "Emancipation of Labor."

Hints Toward Reforms
(New York, 1850), pp. 15–16.

The story of Greeley's own youth
exemplifies the Gospel of Work.[1]

The man of respectability and property,
whose blocks of houses adorn the busiest streets
of our towns, and whose note goes unquestioned in bank, can you think him distinguished
by no substantial qualities from those who were
his playmates and schoolmates, and who are
now his tenants and hirelings? O rely on it,
there is no such instance of results without a
cause in Nature! The man may be no better,
I readily grant you, than those around him —
perhaps in the truest sense no wiser — but
very different he must be, and for that one
purpose of accumulating property, a vastly superior being.

.   .   .   .   .   .

Nay, I go farther, and insist that a keen eye
would have readily picked him out from among
his schoolmates, and said, "Here is the lad who
will die a Bank President, owning factories and
blocks of stores!" . . . Trace his history
closely, and you will find that in his boyhood he
was provident and frugal — that he shunned
expense and dissipation — that he feasted and
quaffed seldom, unless at others' cost — that
he was rarely seen at balls or frolics — that he
was diligent in study and in business — that he
did not hesitate to do an uncomfortable job,
if it bade fair to be profitable — that he hus-
banded his hours and made each count one,
either in earning or in preparing to work efficiently. He rarely or never stood idle because
the business offered him was esteemed ungenteel
or disagreeable — he laid up a few dollars during his minority, which proved a sensible help
to him on going into business for himself —
he married seasonably, prudently, respectably
— he lived frugally and delved steadily until
it clearly became him to live better, and until

1. See James Parton, *The Life of Horace Greeley*
(Boston, 1872), pp. 48–71.

he could employ his time to better advantage
than at the plow or over the bench. Thus his
first thousand dollars came slowly but surely;
the next more easily and readily by the help of
the former; the next, of course, more easily still;
until now he adds thousands to his hoard with
little apparent effort or care. But the germ of
all this spreading oak was in the tough acorn
whence it sprang. Given the original qualities
of the lad, all beyond was plainly deducible
therefrom, unless prevented by death or some
extreme calamity.

In praise of mechanics

1. The dignity of the mechanic

Mechanics' Free Press (Philadelphia),
Sept. 13, 1828.

The earliest American labor paper
published for any considerable period, the
Mechanics' Free Press first appeared
in Philadelphia in 1828. As the official organ
of the Mechanics' Union of Trade Associations,
it championed the formation of a working
men's party. In the 1831 city elections,
labor men polled only 400 votes,
and with that defeat the party died. The
Mechanics' Free Press then merged with two
other journals, the *Philadelphia Times*
and the *Working Man's Register*. The
combined publication lasted until 1835.

If the dignity of things may be measured by
their importance to mankind, there is nothing,
perhaps, which can rank above the mechanic
arts. In fact they may be called the lever, and
the power which moves the world . . . .
What gives to civil nations their superiority
over the savage? It is chiefly mechanic arts. By
them the beautiful and convenient mansion is
substituted for the rude and uncomfortable hut;
and "scarlet and fine twined linen" supply the

wardrobe, in place of the skins of wild animals. They are the foundation of nearly all the improvements and comforts of life, and further, we may say, of the glory and grandeur of the world. By them the farmer ploughs the land, and by them the mariner ploughs the ocean; by them the monarch is adorned with his crown, and by them the peasant is clad in comfortable garments; by them the triumphal arch is raised to the hero, and by them the temple ascends to the Deity; by them the wealthy roll in chariots and loll on couches; by them the table is spread, the bed is decked, and the parlour is furnished. To them the poet owes the perpetuation of his fame . . .

And much of this is owing to two single arts, that of printing, and the manufacture of paper. By the former learning has been rescued from the gloom of the dark ages; but without the latter, the benefit of the printing would be circumscribed to very narrow bounds. It is by means of the press, chiefly, that so much of christendom owes its escape from the thraldom of superstition.

But in speaking of the dignity of the mechanic arts, we could not confine them to the mere hand that executes, without thinking of the head that plans; for without the latter, but little more credit would be due to the person who exercises these arts than to the automaton Turk, who mechanically astonishes the world at the game of chess. To produce the great effects, we have mentioned above, to do so much to enlighten, to beautify and improve the world, to labour for the glory and happiness of others, and yet be ignorant of the springs by which the important movements are carried on, would ill comport with the dignity of the mechanic. He would be ("if we may compare small things with great") warmth, and comfort to mankind, without itself being conscious thereof.

There is a philanthropy in the mechanic arts . . . The mechanic who perfectly understands his trade, as well as in the principles as the practice of it, gets himself a degree of no inconsiderable rank and honour, and that without the intervention of a college, or the formal vote of a learned corporation. To become an ingenious and enlightened mechanic, it is necessary that the youth who is destined for a trade, should bring to his employment a mind inquisitive, studious, busy, and inclined to mechanic pursuits. Such a mind, with ordinary attention to its cultivation, can scarcely fail of becoming in a very considerable degree enlightened. But to the common sources of information, a good many mechanics add a very laudable attention to books, to the periodical publications of the day, and to the associations for mutual improvement. Mechanics' and apprentices' libraries are established, and mechanics' societies are formed, which, by inducing studious habits, interchange of ideas, and collision of sentiments, must tend to improve the minds of the members in a high degree. There is, in fact, at the present time, a very large share of information and solid practical knowledge among the mechanics of this country.

The life of the mechanic, it is true, is a life of labour; and while he wipes the sweat from his brow, he may perhaps murmur at his fate, and envy what he considers the easy lot of other professions. But where is the business which exempts a man from a life of labour? The life of a judge, and of the first officer under government is a life of labour. But can these "honourable men" build a ship, or raise a spire to heaven, or exercise all or any of the arts which add so much to the comfort and grandeur of the world? These the mechanic can do; and if he duly reflect on the importance of his labours, he can scarcely repine at his lot.

2. Encouragement of choice of mechanical occupations

Mechanics' Magazine, XXVI (December 1836), 287–288.

If we should desire to counteract the pernicious influence of Trades Unions and radicals from abroad, we must teach our sons the Mechanic Arts and bind more of them as apprentices to substantial and profitable employments than we are now in the habit of doing. We are all wrong in underrating the value of mechanical occupations — we are all wrong in making all our sons Doctors, Lawyers, Divines and Merchants. Some branches of the family should be mechanics, and if when they are out of their time, we can give them some money to commence business, with which we at once set them on the road to independence — to solid independence, weight and influence. Employment, labor, healthy, refreshing, constant labor, is the grand secret to keep boys correct and moral, to keep them out of vice in every shape, to make good sons and good citizens of them. There are many poor widows with boys from ten to thirteen years of age, who are not probably aware that if they are good and industrious can earn from one hundred to one hundred and fifty dollars per annum, and have steady employment. This is much more profitable in every respect, than running about the streets after soldiers or fire engines.

We have often wondered that so few sons of gentlemen of fortune, offer as apprentices to some mechanical pursuit to the Printing business — a business which is light and agreeable, and combines so many advantages. It may be asked what are the benefits of this branch of the Mechanical Arts.

.   .   .   .   .

The Printing business includes a knowledge of proof reading, some acquaintance with the art of paper making — and in newspaper office where a boy is intelligent, quick, ambitious to excell, he becomes familiar with editorial pursuits — and when out of his time, becomes proprietor, or part proprietor of a city or country paper, and if prudent, temperate and industrious, may become a conspicuous politician, and fill any of the high offices of the country,

as we see at present in beholding Printers, Senators in Congress and members of the House of Representatives. So much for our profession, but there are many noble mechanical pursuits which should be cultivated by young men of good family and education.

The Builder, which includes the beautiful science of architecture, the ship builder; a first rate and respectable calling. Workers in gold, silver, copper and other metals. Cabinet Making. In short, we could name fifty occupations — more   valuable — more   enduring — more healthy; more positively independent, than the range of professional callings, and the sickly, poverty stricken labor of the midnight lamp.

By this course we shall bring into the line of mechanics an intelligent, well educated, highly respectable class of American citizens, free from radicalism, combinations, unjust extortions or disreputable associations.

The ideology of mobility

1. The independence of the little man, 1832

Frances Trollope, *Domestic Manners of the Americans* (London and New York, 1832), pp. 109–111.

There was one house in the village which was remarkable from its wretchedness. It had an air of *in*decent poverty about it, which long prevented my attempting an entrance; but at length, upon being told that I could get chicken and eggs there whenever I wanted them, I determined upon venturing. The door being opened to my knock, I very nearly abandoned my almost blunted purpose; I never beheld such a den of filth and misery: a woman, the very image of dirt and disease, held a squalid imp of a baby on her hip bone while she kneaded her dough with her right fist only. A great lanky girl, of twelve years old, was sitting on a barrel, gnawing a corn cob; when I made known my business, the woman answered, "No, not I; I got no chickens to sell, nor eggs neither; but my son will, plenty I expect. Here, Nick" (bawling at the bottom of a ladder), "here's an old woman what wants chickens." Half a moment brought Nick to the bottom of the ladder, and I found my merchant was one of a ragged crew, whom I had been used to observe in my daily walk, playing marbles in the dust, and swearing lustily; he looked about ten years old.

"Have you chicken to sell, my boy?"

"Yes, and eggs too, more nor what you'll buy."

Having enquired price, condition, and so on, I recollected that I had been used to give the same price at market, the feathers plucked, and the chicken prepared for the table, and I told him that he ought not to charge the same.

"Oh for that, I expect I can fix 'em as well as ever them was, what you got in market."

"You fix them?"

"Yes to be sure, why not?"

"I thought you were too fond of marbles."

He gave me a keen glance, and said, "You don't know I. — When will you be wanting the chickens?"

He brought them at the time directed, extremely well "fixed," and I often dealt with him afterwards. When I paid him, he always thrust his hand into his breeches pocket, which I presume, as being *the keep,* was fortified more strongly than the dilapidated outworks, and drew from thence rather more dollars, half-dollars, levies, and fips, than his dirty little hand could well hold. My curiosity was excited, and though I felt an involuntary disgust towards the young Jew, I repeatedly conversed with him.

"You are very rich, Nick," I said to him one day, on his making an ostentatious display of change, as he called it; he sneered with a most unchildish expression of countenance, and replied, "I guess 'twould be a bad job for I, if that was all I'd got to shew."

I asked him how he managed his business. He told me that he bought eggs by the hundred, and lean chicken by the score, from the waggons that passed their door on the way to market; that he fatted the latter in coops he had made himself, and could easily double their price, and that his eggs answered well too, when he sold them out by the dozen.

"And do you give the money to your mother?"

"I expect not," was the answer, with another sharp glance of his ugly blue eyes.

"What do you do with it, Nick?"

His look said plainly, what is that to you? but he only answered, quaintly enough, "I takes care of it."

How Nick got his first dollar is very doubtful; I was told that when he entered the village store, the person serving always called in another pair of eyes; but having obtained it, the spirit, activity, and industry, with which he caused it to increase and multiply, would have been delightful in one of Miss Edgeworth's dear little clean bright-looking boys, who could have carried all he got to his mother; but in Nick it was detestable. No human feeling seemed to warm his young heart, not even the love of self-indulgence, for he was not only ragged and dirty, but looked considerably more than half starved, and I doubt not his dinners and suppers half fed his fat chickens.

I by no means give this history of Nick, the chicken merchant, as an anecdote characteristic in all respects of America; the only part of the story which is so, is the independence of the little man, and is one instance out of a thousand, of the hard, dry, calculating character that is the result of it. Probably Nick will be very rich; perhaps he will be President. I once got so heartily scolded for saying, that I did not think all American citizens were equally eligible to that office, that I shall never again venture to doubt it.

2. Honor to the self-reliant, honest newsboy

Elizabeth Oakes Smith, *The Newsboy*
(New York, 1870), pp. 33, 68–71.

Elizabeth Oakes Smith's series of vignettes
of the newsboy is symptomatic of the
sentimental newsboy literature of the period.
It romanticizes him as a heroic and
self-reliant young entrepreneur.

As you look at the Newsboys, one thing will
strike your attention. There is no appearance
of vice amongst them. Nothing skulking, nothing mean, nothing vicious lurks in the aspect
of the true Newsboy. No redness of the eyes,
no bloated face, no pallid debauchery. His
eyes are open and candid, and his air as free
from the braggart as the coward. Honor to
the self-reliant, self-maintained, honest Newsboy.

.   .   .   .   .

He [Jack] had a keen observation, and many
a time the police had got a clue to some outrage
they were trying to trace home to its source,
by some old memory suddenly revived in the
mind of Flashy Jack. He knew all the women
who kept apple stands at the corners of the
streets, and there wasn't one of them that
wouldn't toss him an apple or a cake in return
for his good-natured impudence, and all the
soda women in Fulton street refused his coppers
when he took a glass at their tables. Many's the
time Jack had cried "hot corn" for the little
girls at night, and sent them home with empty
pails. He'd turn match vender any time, if the
child looked weary or disheartened — he was
ready for a fight, always in aid of the weak
party. In truth, the generous instincts of Flashy
Jack were better than other people's virtues.

Of a rainy day he would help the little girls
who swept the crossings — laugh at their dirty
faces, till they learned to "spruce up," because
of "that little devil, Flashy Jack." He knew
them all, and tossed them coppers, "just by

way of *model* to them poor sneaks what go up
and down Broadway, shined up to kill, and all
too deuced mean to give a penny to a slip of a
gal, that hadn't a second rag to her back."
Flashy Jack said this, and things of the like,
in a manner as if it hurt him to not be allowed
"to pitch at once into such folks."

Cold winter mornings Flashy Jack "turned
to" and helped the miserable, shivering women
and children who searched over the coal ash
heaps in vacant lots, and in barrels and tin
kettles left for the dustman to take away, that
they might get something to supply a little heat.
Oh! Jack had funny things to say, and kind
things to say, and ten to one they found pennies in the coal, and then there was a time indeed, and nobody looked more strange about it
than Jack did; and when the women and children went away to cook their scanty breakfast,
they carried home something like a smile, and
the cold morning wasn't half so cold as they
had thought it, and the old hood was warmer
than it had ever been before, and the old brown
shawl, crossed over the breast and tied in a knot
behind, had grown wondrously in comfort. Oh!
they all knew Flashy Jack, "the darling rascal
that he was."

Jack knew all the "sporting men about town."
In his ignorance more than one was quite a
hero in his eyes. Jack, open hearted and generous himself, saw something handsome, and
strong, and brave in this rude aspect of life;
and to be generous, kind, and courageous, was
the sum of Flashy Jack's moral creed. My
readers must decide whether it was a broad or
a narrow creed.

Then there were various games in which
Jack excelled. He was fond of a boat, and fond
of a dog, not as a companion merely, but as
gratifying this proclivity of his to the sporting
line. "I ought to be happy," he would say, "for
I have the smartest and smallest black and tan
terrier in the city." This animal's ears were cut
to the very acme of terrier point, making her
look as keen as a needle, and pert as a fox;
and Jack said, "as to her narrative, it is bit off
till it isn't a circumstance of a narrative." This

dog, named Vic, was the pride and glory of Flashy Jack's life. He would pinch and pull her, and make her fly at him and bark a perfect fury, he all the time laughing like mad; and when he was tired of the sport, he would open his bosom and the little creature would crawl in, and lie buttoned up close to Jack's heart for hours. He made heavy bets upon Vic, sure to win, for "she was death on rats," as he said; his triumph always being wound up with, "Oh! she's game I tell ye, she'll fight like blazes — come here Vic," and he stowed her away in his bosom, bloody as she was from her encounter with the rats.

3. From rags to respectability

Horatio Alger, *Ragged Dick,* ed. Richard Fink (New York: Collier Books 1962), pp. 42–45, 62, 75, 108, 109, 110, 130, 138, 167, 215; first published serially in *Student and Schoolmate* in 1867 and in book form in 1868.

Alger (1832–1899) was graduated from Harvard Divinity School in 1860. In 1866 he resigned from the ministry in order to devote full time to writing. *Ragged Dick* was the first of his books to be published.

Our ragged hero wasn't a model boy in all respects. I am afraid he swore sometimes, and now and then he played tricks upon unsophisticated boys from the country or gave a wrong direction to honest old gentlemen unused to the city.

.   .   .   .   .

Then I am sorry to add that Dick had formed the habit of smoking.

.   .   .   .   .

There was another way in which Dick sometimes lost money. There was a noted gambling-house on Baxter Street, which in the evening was sometimes crowded with these juvenile gamesters, who staked their hard earnings, generally losing of course, and refreshing themselves from time to time with a vile mixture of liquor at two cents a glass. Sometimes Dick strayed in here, and played with the rest.

I have mentioned Dick's faults and defects, because I want it understood, to begin with, that I don't consider him a model boy. But there were some good points about him nevertheless. He was above doing anything mean or dishonorable. He would not steal, or cheat, or impose upon younger boys, but was frank and straight-forward, manly and self-reliant. His nature was a noble one, and had saved him from all mean faults. I hope my young readers will like him as I do, without being blind to his faults. Perhaps, although he was only a boot-black, they may find something in him to imitate.

.   .   .   .   .

"That's where the mayor's office is," said Dick. "Him and me are very good friends. I once blacked his boots by particular appointment. That's the way I pay my city taxes."

.   .   .   .   .

"That's a pretty good story," said Dick, "but I don't believe all the cats in New York will ever make me mayor."

"No, probably not, but you may rise in some other way. A good many distinguished men have once been poor boys. There's hope for you, Dick, if you'll try."

"Nobody ever talked to me so before," said Dick. "They just called me Ragged Dick, and told me I'd grow up to be a vagabond (boys who are better educated need not be surprised at Dick's blunders) and come to the gallows."

"Telling you so won't make it turn out so, Dick. If you'll try to be somebody, and grow up into a respectable member of society, you will. You may not become rich, — it isn't everybody that becomes rich, you know, — but you can obtain a good position, and be respected."

"I'll try," said Dick, earnestly, "I needn't have been Ragged Dick so long if I hadn't spent my money in goin' to the theatre, and treatin' boys to oyster-stews, and bettin' money on cards and such like."

.   .   .   .   .

"I believe he is a good boy," said Mr. Whitney. "I hope, my lad, you will prosper and rise in the world. You know in this free country poverty in early life is no bar to a man's advancement. I haven't risen very high myself," he added, with a smile, "but have met with moderate success in life; yet there was a time when I was as poor as you."

"Were you sir?" asked Dick, eagerly.

"Yes, my boy, I have known the time when I have been obliged to go without my dinner because I didn't have enough money to pay for it."

"How did you get up in the world?" asked Dick, anxiously.

"I entered a printing-office as an apprentice, and worked for some years. Then my eyes gave out and I was obliged to give that up. Not knowing what else to do, I went into the country, and worked on a farm. After a while I was lucky enough to invent a machine, which has brought me in a great deal of money. But there was one thing I got while I was in the printing-office which I value more than money."

"What was that, sir?"

"A taste for reading and study . . ."

.   .   .   .   .

"Good-by, my lad," said Mr. Whitney. "I hope to hear good accounts of you sometime. Don't forget what I have told you. Remember that your future position depends mainly upon yourself, and that it will be high or low as you choose to make it."

.   .   .   .   .

Our hero took his bank-book, and gazed on the entry "Five Dollars" with a new sense of importance. He had been accustomed to joke about Erie shares; but now, for the first time,

he felt himself a capitalist; on a small scale, to be sure, but still it was no small thing for Dick to have five dollars which he could call his own. He firmly determined that he would lay by every cent he could spare from his earnings towards the fund he hoped to accumulate.

But Dick was too sensible not to know that there was something more than money needed to win a respectable position in the world. He felt that he was very ignorant. Of reading and writing he only knew the rudiments, and that, with a slight acquaintance with arithmetic, was all he did know of books. Dick knew he must study hard, and he dreaded it. He looked upon learning as attended with greater difficulties than it really possesses. But Dick had good pluck. He meant to learn, nevertheless, and resolved to buy a book with his first spare earnings.

When Dick went home at night he locked up his bankbook in one of the drawers of the bureau. It was wonderful how much more independent he felt whenever he reflected upon the contents of that drawer, and with what an important air of joint ownership he regarded the bank building in which his small savings were deposited.

.   .   .   .   .

"You didn't learn to read in that time, of course?"

"No," said Dick; "but I was a newsboy a little while; so I learned a little, just so's to find out what the news was. Sometimes I didn't read straight, and called the wrong news. One morning I asked another boy what the paper said, and he told me the King of Africa was dead. I thought it was all right till folks began to laugh."

"Well, Dick, if you'll only study well, you won't be liable to make such mistakes."

"I hope so," said Dick. "My friend Horace Greeley told me the other day that he'd get me to take his place now and then when he was off makin' speeches if my edication hadn't been neglected."

But then the reader must not forget that Dick

was naturally a smart boy. His street education had sharpened his faculties, and taught him to rely upon himself. He knew that it would take him a long time to reach the goal which he had set before him, and he had patience to keep on trying. He knew that he had only himself to depend upon, and he determined to make the most of himself, — a resolution which is the secret of success in nine cases out of ten.

"Dick," said Fosdick, one evening, after they had completed their studies, "I think you'll have to get another teacher soon."

.   .   .   .   .

Dick left the counting-room, hardly knowing whether he stood on his head or his heels, so overjoyed was he at the sudden change in his fortunes. Ten dollars a week was to him a fortune, and three times as much as he had expected to obtain at first. Indeed he would have been glad, only the day before, to get a place at three dollars a week. He reflected that with the stock of clothes which he had now on hand, he could save up at least half of it, and even then live better than he had been accustomed to do; so that his little fund in the savings bank, instead of being diminished, would be steadily increasing. Then he was to be advanced if he deserved it. It was indeed a bright prospect for a boy, who, only a year before, could neither read nor write, and depended for a night's lodging upon the chance hospitality of an alleyway or old wagon. Dick's great ambition to "grow up 'spectable" seemed likely to be accomplished after all.

.   .   .   .   .

"By gracious!" he exclaimed; "somebody's stole my Washington coat and Napolean pants. Maybe it's an agent of Barnum's, who expects to make a fortun' by exhibitin' the valooable wardrobe of a gentleman of fashion."

Dick did not shed many tears over his loss, as, in his present circumstances, he never expected to have any further use for the well-worn garments. It may be stated that he afterwards saw them adorning the figure of Micky Maguire; but whether that estimable young man stole them himself, he never ascertained. As to the loss, Dick was rather pleased that it had occurred . . . it seemed to cut him off from the old vagabond life which he hoped never to resume. Henceforward he meant to press onward, and rise as high as possible.

———————————————

4. Climbing the ladder of wealth and respectability

A. Forbes and J. W. Greene, *The Rich Men of Massachusetts* (Boston, 1851), pp. 10, 16, 17, 18, 35, 43, 56–57, 85, 91, 93, 133, 159, 167.

The professed aim of *The Rich Men of Massachusetts* was "to furnish encouragement to the young, from the contemplation of success resulting from a suitable combination of those sterling qualities, Perserverance, Energy, Carefulness, Economy, Integrity."

———————————————

Adams, Seth   [$]150,000

Came from Rochester, N.H., a poor boy. Machinist in South Boston. At ten years of age he was fatherless, and went into a factory to earn a little something to help his mother support the family. The next three years he and his elder brother worked the farm; then the elder brother left home, leaving Seth to manage alone. He assisted in supporting the family the best way he could. Went into the wood, cut timber, sawed shingles, and put a new face on the old roof. Occasionally went out shoemaking among the neighbors. Had but little time to attend the district school. At seventeen went to learn the cabinet-maker's trade. At the age of twenty-one came to Boston, and worked at his trade six months. The next year worked at pattern-making. Next commenced machine business on his own hook. This is a man of *some* trades and no mistake. In addition to those already named, he worked at sign-painting, chair-making, blacksmithing, and carpentering. At any one of these trades he can "earn his living." Was once a member of the City Council. He is one of the old Adams stock; his great-grandfather was the Rev. Joseph Adams, of Newington, N.H., who was uncle to old John Adams, the elder President of the United States. This industrious scion of a Presidential stock is now about starting a sugar-refinery in Gouch Street. He is, beyond all question, a stirring, go-ahead Yankee; and another thing, he is a man of much benevolence.

.   .   .   .   .

Bowker, Albert   [$]100,000

While a mere youth he was appointed an usher in one of the Boston schools, and subsequently promoted to a mastership. He is one of the very few who have ever *voluntarily* resigned that office. He married the only child of Benjamin Lampson, and the presumptive heiress of a large fortune.

.   .   .   .   .

Brewster, Osmyn   [$]100,000

Of the firm of Crocker & Brewster. A printer; learned his trade in the place where he now keeps, and where, men and boys, he and his partner have been for more than forty years. At first they were apprentices to, then partners with, and subsequently successors of Samuel T. Armstrong. In this establishment fortunes have been made in the sale of religious books, it being the only place in Boston, for many years, denominated a "religious book store." Mr. Brewster has ever been a close applicant to business, and has earned the respect of his fellow-citizens, who have often honored him with their confidence.

Brigham, Peter B.   [$]200,000

The guardian genius of that shrine of Epicurus and temple of Bacchus, Concert Hall . . . He is a native of Vermont; came to the city when young; worked in a grocery store at eight dollars per month; was faithful and dili-

gent in the service of his employer; gained his confidence, had his wages raised; laid up money enough to open an oyster-shop in the basement of the building where he now keeps. In those days, no one ever prepared a better clam-chowder, or was more attentive to those who gave him a call. In due time, however, he was enabled to get *above* that humble situation, and he took possession of the whole of that princely establishment he now occupies.

.   .   .   .   .

Humphrey, Benjamin   [$]750,000

Began poor. Formerly merchant. Born in Weymouth; an only son. At the age of fourteen came to Boston, and obtained a situation with Abraham Wild, a merchant engaged in extensive business. At twenty, with the consent of his master, he commenced business in Fore, now Ann Street, and by close attention and strict integrity, laid the foundation of his present prosperity.

.   .   .   .   .

Merriam, Charles   [$]250,000

Of the firm of Sayles, Merriam & Brewer. He served an apprenticeship with Col. Lampson, of Weston, in a country store, where he early gave promise to all who came in contact with him in trade, that he would be a rich man if he lived. Often, when a hard customer came into the store, would his master find it convenient to be absent, and leave the difficult case with Charles, who seldom failed successfully to meet the exigency. Col. Lampson died, and Mr. Merriam, though a mere youth, succeeded him, and soon made money enough to engage in a more extensive business in the city.

.   .   .   .   .

Sears, Joshua   [$]1,500,000

Came to Boston from Cape Cod a poor boy, with a notion in his head to this purport: "I will make *ten thousand dollars,* then go home satisfied, to provide for father and mother," &c. A very few years sufficed to turn up the wished-for sum. "Now," said he to his partner, "I must go back to Cape Cod; I have made money enough, all I came here to make." "Nonsense, Mr. Sears! How can I spare you now? My health is so poor, you must not think of leaving me yet." Well, he stayed; went on from year to year, till his partner was obliged to give up business, — and still he went on, alone, because there was no stopping-place.

.   .   .   .   .

Rich men of other cities in Massachusetts

Salem

Pingree, David   [$]2,000,000

Unlike most of the wealthy men of Salem, his early education and experience were not upon the great deep, but among the cabbages and potatoes of a country farm. He, however, in early life became engaged in commercial pursuits, in which he was moderately successful. He inherited from his uncle, Thomas Perkins, Esq., one of the merchant-princes of Salem, about $400,000, and from that time his success in life was put beyond a doubt.

.   .   .   .   .

Brighton

Coffin, Jared   [$]300,000

Began his career as a cooper on board a Nantucket Whaler; finally became master and owner of a ship, and acquired large wealth by his enterprise and fact for saving. He is a rough sort of a stick, as might be expected, and things none the less of his dignity because it is backed by a fat purse.

.   .   .   .   .

Cambridge

Douglass, Robert   [$]100,000

Began poor. Confectioner. At the age of sixteen he was left fatherless, with eight brothers and sisters and a mother. *He supported them all;* brought up all the children and provided for them, and still provides for his mother. The ordinary terms expressive of *efficiency,* and *benevolence,* are altogether too tame to be

applied to Robert Douglass. The world has few instances of *such* "great men."

.   .   .   .   .

Lancaster

Henshaw, David   [$]200,000

Born, 1791, in Leicester. Brought up on a farm, and became as expert as any other boys at making the hay fly, the corn-stalks rattle, and the potatoes tumble. His father was a man much respected in his day, and was for a great number of years a magistrate of the county. At the age of sixteen, having received a common education, David was sent to Boston, an apprentice to the druggist's business, with Dix & Brimley. Prosecuted this business so successfully as to have made a fortune in 1829, when he retired from it.

.   .   .   .   .

Pittsfield

Allen, Phineas   [$]60,000

Began poor. Entered as an apprentice at the printer's trade in Southampton, but ran away before his time was up. Came to Pittsfield, and started a Democratic paper (the "Pittsfield Sun") by which he made his money. A man of extremely regular business habits. Always about his business; a correct, go-ahead man, but no speculator. Has been a member of both branches of the Legislature.

.   .   .   .   .

Dorchester

Gleason, Roswell   [$]100,000

Came to Dorchester from the country a poor boy. Commenced business without any other capital than a determination to do *something* and be *somebody*. Went to work; and all the noise he made was in his tinshop, where there was an incessant din, from day-light in the morning to a late hour of the night. He succeeded. Such a man *must* succeed; and it was but a short time before there might daily be seen an army of honest tin-peddlers departing from his factory to furnish the "*real* tin," and to bring back in return "rags" and the "pewter." He gives employment to a large number of laborers, and gives support to many poor persons; is a bank director, enjoys the confidence of the community, and is highly respected as a citizen.

B. APPRENTICESHIP IN THE EARLY INDUSTRIAL ERA

"The institution of long apprenticeship has no tendency to form young people to industry"

Adam Smith, *An Inquiry into the Nature and Causes of the Wealth of Nations,* I (2d ed.; London, 1778), 151–153.

The institution of long apprenticeships can give no security that insufficient workmanship shall not frequently be exposed to publick sale. When this is done it is generally the effect of fraud, and not of inability; and the longest apprenticeship can give no security against fraud. Quite different regulations are necessary to prevent this abuse. The sterling mark upon plate, and the stamps upon linen and woollen cloth, give the purchaser much greater security than any statute of apprenticeship. He generally looks at these, but never thinks it worth while to enquire whether the workman had served a seven years apprenticeship.

The institution of long apprenticeships has no tendency to form young people to industry. A journeyman who works by the piece is likely to be industrious, because he derives a benefit from every exertion of his industry. An apprentice is likely to be idle, and almost always is so, because he has no immediate interest to be otherwise. In the inferior employments, the sweets of labour consist altogether in the recompence of labour. They who are soonest in a condition to enjoy the sweets of it, are likely soonest to conceive a relish for it, and to acquire the early habit of industry. A young man natu-rally conceives an aversion to labour, when for a long time he receives no benefit from it. The boys who are put out apprentices from publick charities are generally bound for more than the usual number of years, and they generally turn out very idle and worthless.

Apprenticeships were altogether unknown to the antients. The reciprocal duties of master and apprentice make a considerable article in every modern code. The Roman law is perfectly silent with regard to them. I know no Greek or Latin word (I might venture, I believe, to assert that there is none) which expresses the idea we now annex to the word Apprentice, a servant bound to work at a particular trade for the benefit of a master, during a term of years, upon condition that the master shall teach him that trade.

Long apprenticeships are altogether unnecessary. The arts, which are much superior to common trades, such as those of making clocks and watches, contain no such mystery as to require a long course of instruction. The first invention of such beautiful machines, indeed, and even that of some of the instruments employed in making them, must, no doubt, have been the work of deep thought and long time, and may justly be considered as among the happiest efforts of human ingenuity. But when both have been fairly invented and are well understood, to explain to any young man, in the compleatest manner, how to apply the instruments and how to construct the machines, cannot well require more than the lessons of a few weeks: perhaps those of a few days might be sufficient. In the common mechanick trades, those of a few days might certainly be sufficient. The dexterity of hand, indeed, even in common trades, cannot be acquired without much practice and experience. But a young man would practice with much more diligence and attention, if from the beginning he wrought as a journeyman, being paid in proportion to the little work which he could execute, and paying in his turn for the materials which he might sometimes spoil through awkwardness and inexperience. His education would generally in this way be more effectual, and always less tedious and expensive. The master, indeed, would be a loser. He would lose all the wages of the apprentice, which he now saves, for seven years together. In the end, perhaps, the apprentice himself would be a loser. In a trade so easily learnt he would have more competitors, and his wages, when he came to be a compleat workman, would be much less than at present. The same increase of competition would reduce the profits of the masters as well as the wages of the workmen. The trades, the crafts, the mysteries, would all be losers. But the public would be a gainer, the work of all artificers coming in this way much cheaper to market.

Abuse of apprenticeship

---

1. Master mechanics accused of employing apprentices instead of journeymen

Mechanics' Free Press, Nov. 23, 1828.

Masters and Apprentices. Messrs. Editors — The practice of many master mechanics in this city [Philadelphia] in employing none but apprentices in their manufacturing establishments, is an evil severely felt by the journeymen of all denominations; for whenever there is a greater number of mechanics than the demand of labour requires, it is evident the surplus must be thrown out of employ. There are men in this city who have from 15 to 20 apprentices, who never or very seldom have a journeyman in their shops; but to supply the place of journeymen, and to monopolize to themselves trade and wealth, as one apprentice becomes free, another is taken to fill up the ranks . . .

When we bind our sons for five, six or seven years, to learn a trade, it is with an idea that when he has faithfully served out the term of his apprenticeship, he will be enabled at least to find employment as a journeyman. This reasonable expectation very often ends in disappointment; for the very moment he assumes his independence his troubles begin: he is thrown out of employment by his parsimonious and ungenerous master, with whom no consideration of past services has any weight, and whose heart can melt at the sight of nothing but money.

. . . He must now either turn his attention to some laborious work, to which he has not been accustomed, and which is at times difficult to obtain, or turn vagabond at once. It is no wonder that so many young men, under such unfavorable circumstances, are ruined in their morals and reputations, and the world is too apt to throw all the blame upon the unfortunate, while they pass over with impunity the causes that produced it.

There are other master mechanics who are less fortunate than the former; they do much injury to society, without enriching or benefiting themselves. These are men who manufacture goods altogether by apprentices, and sell them at so very low a rate, that they can scarcely live by the profits.

One of the above description was selling some hats, some time ago, and another of the trade asked him how he could afford to sell them so very low. His answer was, that if he had not had them manufactured altogether by apprentices, he could not have afforded to have sold them for anything like the price. These men appear to me to injure others without benefiting themselves.

I hope, Messrs. Editors, that some philanthropic spirit will dictate some lawful means to eradicate and destroy such deadly poison, circulated throughout the veins of society, and if it cannot be finally rooted out, let us employ the best antidote we can. Let us do good in our day and generation, by establishing societies for the protection and help of such unfortunate young men as I have already sufficiently spoken of. If all were master mechanics, there would be no more labour performed than there is at present; but there would be a more equal distribution of the profits of that labour among the members of society; and consequently would destroy the powerful influence of monopolists.

---

2. Apprenticeship as a state of bondage, 1829

Mechanics' Free Press, Sept. 26, 1829.

. . . Unless it can be made appear, that apprenticeship is instituted and maintained for the benefit of the apprentice, during the term of his apprenticeship, and also during his subsequent life; the institution must be abolished . . . No benefit, either real or supposed, to capitalists will be sufficient to uphold a state of bondage, during a period equal to one tenth of an extremely long life, unless it shall be fully made to appear that the bondsman comes in for a certain advantage which he could not have obtained without incurring the bondage.

---

3. Half-trained boys replace journeymen printers, 1845

New York Daily Tribune, Sept. 11, 1845.

For the journeyman printers' protest in 1811 see above Part Two, Chap. II, sec. A, The making of a printer, 1809–1826, doc. 2.

Although there is very little, if any, regular apprenticing to the business now, every Print-

ing Office has its quota of boys, ranging in number from one to twenty, or more, according to the method and extent of its operations. These boys receive from $1 50 to $2 00 per week, for one or two years — when, if they become at all skillful in the art of type-setting, they are permitted to work on their *own hook* as *two thirders,* at 18¾ and 20 cents per thousand, and thus oust from their legitimate places regular journeymen. If the boy has become remarkably quick and correct in composition, he can readily obtain a situation at from five to seven dollars per week — in every instance usurping the place of another, and not unfrequently that of a man of family. This is an evil with which the journeymen are forced to contend at odds, as this class of interlopers is constantly accumulating from the surrounding country and by foreign influx.

---

4. Apprenticeship and delinquency, 1846

Boston, Common Council, "Report of the Directors of the House of Industry and Reformation," *City Doc. No. 14* (Boston, 1846), pp. 9–10.

Another embarrassment results from the change in public sentiment and practice, especially in some parts of Massachusetts, in regard to apprenticeship. Formerly mechanic's apprentices served a full term of seven years, resided in the families of their masters, and received moral as well as mechanical instruction. The system produced thorough mechanics, and well disciplined, thrifty young men. At the present time mechanics employ boys and young men, at particular branches of trade, for limited or uncertain periods, allowing them to board where they may, and conduct themselves, when away from their workshops, as they will. This usage must be injurious to the young who are often changing their places, and produces discontent among regular apprentices who are subjected to wholesome restraint.

The Directors have many opportunities to see the favorable effects of judicious apprenticeship. Committees of the Board make occasional visits to apprentices, particularly in neighborhoods where several are located, and they have been pleased to find the majority doing well and in good hands. The effect of these visits is believed to be beneficial both to masters and apprentices. And the Directors are often gratified by visits of former apprentices from both Houses, promising young men, already established in honorable callings, and proving good citizens. In several instances within a few years children have been placed with masters, who were themselves apprenticed by our predecessors.

Delinquents from the New York House of Refuge indentured as apprentices

Society for the Reformation of Juvenile Delinquents, *Eighth Annual Report, 1832* (New York, 1833), p. 44.

The 116 that have been indentured during the past year, have been put to the following trades and business, viz:

Girls — To Housewifery,	37
Boys — To Farmers,	29
Shoe and Boot Makers,	8
Sea Service,	22
Carpenters,	3
Tanners and Tanner and Curriers,	3
Blacksmiths,	4
Tailors,	2
Cabinet Makers,	2
Carriage Maker,	1
Boat Builder,	1
Chocolate Manufacturer,	1
Fancy Weaver,	1
Chair Manufacturers,	2
	116

Decline of apprenticeship

---

1. The impact of technology, 1855

Edward Everett Hale, "The State's Care of Its Children," in Hale, et al., *Prize Essays on Juvenile Delinquency* (Philadelphia, 1855), pp. 13–14.

Modern arrangements of manufacture and commerce, tempt men to abandon the old systems of apprenticeship, and also give children a distaste to them. The simple processes, for which machines can be made available in the arts, are precisely those which once made the early years of young apprenticeship valuable. The introduction of the planing machine, for instance, has fixed a later period in life, than custom formerly fixed, for the beginning of an apprenticeship in carpentry. The machine does what the boys in a shop used to do. On the other hand, a boy, who can earn two or three dollars a week in tending an *envelope* machine, disdains to go to learn a trade, in an apprenticeship which will pay him nothing more than the cost of his food and clothing in its first year. But at the end of a few years, he is nothing but an over-grown boy, fit to tend that machine. He has learned little else. And that want of training has been, in itself, enough to train him as a vagabond, unless counteracted by other influences.

Under the best legislative systems yet attempted, this difficulty is inherent in the arrangements of factory labor which employs children. Under the Massachusetts statutes for instance, all persons who employ children, are obliged to send them to school thirteen weeks, at least, in a year. The statute is generally enforced and obeyed. But although the education of the children in reading, writing and arithmetic, is thus provided for, their gradual training to employments fit for men and women is, in most instances, not provided for. Of the processes of machinery in which children are made of use, there are very few which introduce them to the more complicated processes, such as those which men and women are employed for.

A like misfortune befalls boys or girls, who are engaged in peddling newspapers or other small wares, as so many are, in our larger towns.

It is, in a word, the necessary evil, accompanying every employment, which confines a child to a single duty, without giving him an opportunity to watch and learn more difficult processes connected with it.

It results, as has been said, in training boys and girls, who at last, dissatisfied with their childish industry, turn to dishonest gains for their compensation.

---

2. "Apprenticeship as our fathers knew it is dying," 1870

James Shields Whitney, "Apprenticeship and a Boy's Prospect of a Livelihood," in Social Science Association of Philadelphia, *Papers of 1872* (Philadelphia, 1872), pp. 12–20.

James S. Whitney, member of the Board of Public Education of the First District of Pennsylvania and member of the Central High School Committee, analyzed the apprenticeship problem from an educational point of view.

The number of men and women employed in the manufactories of this city in 1870, as carefully collected by Mr. Lorin Blodget, was 127,590, of which the men are 72 per cent. The total number of "youths" employed was 10,286; and supposing the boys to be in the proportion of 60 per cent., there will be 6,172 of them.

Of these a very large number are children below the age of 16, the lowest age of apprentices, and many are not in any sense apprentices, so that the male "learners of trades" must be expressed by a much smaller number. The census report gives 5,832 as the "total number of apprentices," boys and girls, which no doubt includes many besides apprentices proper, while it is not likely to omit many of them. Taking the boys at 60 per cent., we have 3,500 as the extreme number of male apprentices in this city in 1870. There are about 8,000 establishments in which men and boys are employed, and 92,112 workingmen in shops. The apprentices, therefore, cannot exceed the proportion of 1 to every 2¼ shops, and to every 26 workmen — a proportion not equal to the requirements of the guilds, or the allowance of the trades-unions. As the number of boys between the ages of 16 and 21 must be at least 25,000, of whom not over 3,000 are in school or college, it would seem that the small number of apprentices cannot be due to a deficiency of material.

But why do not the boys learn trades? This question, already answered, generally needs more specific reply. In the first place, boys are human; and in the second place, they are boys. Unfortunately, their parents are human, too, and the natural indisposition to hard work, and the preference for clean hands and clothes, is not always discouraged by parental ambition. The class of whom this may be said, though it may need it more, deserves not so much our sympathy as another, where ambition or necessity obliges the father to forego some of this indulgence, that the son may aid him in the support of the family, or be fitted to maintain another. Perhaps it is a mother, alone but for the boy, who is forced into the unnatural position of his parent's adviser, in deciding the momentous question of a trade. There are long discussions as to whether the family purse can bear the strain of the first two or three years, while the boy earns only his own board; and all choice must often be subordinated to the necessity of taking the trade which pays best and soonest. The first decision is perhaps for that of a machinist, which seems to have a great attraction for most boys. Yes, and our hero finds on the books of the larger establishments to which he first applies forty or fifty names already entered, waiting their turn. He cannot wait six months or a year, besides he finds that in the large shops frequently a boy works during his whole term on a few machines and does not learn the whole "handcraft." He goes to the smaller shops where the applicants are fewer, but the vacancies are fewer still. He asks a neighboring carpenter and builder for a place. But this trade does not take boys. The work is all prepared in mills, by men who have learned carpentering in the old times, or who have learned to attend a single machine, and there is nothing for a boy to do. He may not be strong enough for blacksmithing, and there are few boys wanted in the shops where general work is done, as the steam hammer can be both boy and man.

The bricklayers also seem "not to approve of boys" — as the master can oversee them but little, from the nature of the employment; bad work is a serious thing to remedy; and the contract system of building requires great economy and dispatch. Only boys who can stand hard work, too, need apply. With both bricklayers and plasterers there is a prejudice against boys, as so many unfaithful learners have brought discredit on the name. Our hero asks to be a moulder; there is a better opening here, and the wages are good — beginning with $3.50 or $4.00 per week — but almost anywhere but in this city (and here, too, until a few years ago), the Union tells him that they allow but one apprentice to every ten men in a shop, after the one to which each shop is entitled. He has another rebuff from this source, when he asks to learn the art of printing. A rule of the Union declares that no member shall work in any *newspaper* office employing an apprentice, and allows in other offices only one apprentice to every five men, after the one to which each office is entitled. Repressing his ambition for the constructive arts, and that preservative of all others, our lad would be a tailor, or shoemaker. But scarcely any one will take apprentices at these trades. I am told that it is doubtful whether there is in this city an

apprentice in the former — and that there are probably not over a dozen shops employing them in the latter. The work among tailors is done by men, mostly of foreign birth, each employing a female helper or two. But the best of the "foreign talent" does not immigrate, for of the 3,000 sewing tailors in the city, only about 300 are capable of the finest work. Notwithstanding the lack of learners among shoemakers, however, their Union forbids the employment in the shoe factories (where wages of $25 per week are often made, and the greater part of the shoes for city and country trade) of any but those who have learned the art, at least so as to be able to make in some sort a shoe. Of course, the supply must be kept up by importation, or by half-educated home-learners tempted by the high wages, to work a year or two at the bench as apprentices. The bricklayers' and plasterers' Unions, too, have their restrictive rules, but they are not now enforced. The hatters have their's and enforce them, I believe.

You will be as weary as our hero with further illustrations of this part of my subject. It is sufficient to say that in the majority of cases the boy is forced by necessity, or drawn by the prospect of greater immediate wages, to work in a bolt or umbrella factory, a type foundry or some such establishment, where he is paid "by the piece," and can earn five or six dollars, or more, per week. He becomes a man, but he cannot maintain a family even on wages that allowed him to dress showily when off work; he has learned no trade that will bring him more; and is obliged to give place to another generation of boys glad to take what he has outgrown. He becomes in a small way an adventurer, seeking for pay that represents an education which he has not; and often swells the number of incompetent artisans, a "dangerous class" who do our poor work of various kinds.

We have supposed the case of a boy who wishes, or whose parents wish him, to learn a trade. But what of that large class not above the necessity of labor, and who have no one who will or can procure them places? There are about five thousand of them here, enough to form at least the nucleus of a still more dangerous class. Many of these, through a kind Providence, and some act of their own or their parents, find their way to the House of Refuge, or they are taken into some "Home," whence they are provided with places to learn trades, or at least make a living. But let no boy, disheartened in his efforts to find such a place, look with jealous eye on the graduates of the House of Refuge. Few of them are apprenticed to handicrafts, the wages of which rapidly supply the place of capital. Out of thirty-nine boys indentured in 1870, twenty-seven were placed with farmers and ten were divided among seven trades. Out of forty in 1871, twenty-six went to farmers and eleven to nine trades. The balance in each year went to occupations other than trades.

We have looked at this matter chiefly as regards the boys' interest. But it has a larger, a national aspect. The scarcity of skilled labor is a direct loss of productive power, and so far a national waste.

.   .   .   .   .

In whatever way, therefore, we regard it, the evil is a serious one. No class is more fully sensible of this than workingmen, now employers, who served their apprenticeship twenty or thirty years ago, when indentures were more frequently made and respected. These say that they do not see where the skilled workers of the future are to come from. This is specially true of the trades where manual skill and strength have not been replaced by machinery. The boys who generally offer themselves for these are not such as employers feel safe in accepting. At present *we* obtain a large number of mechanics by immigration. Of 17,857 male immigrants for whom the labor bureau at Castle Garden, New York, found places in 1870, 3,186, say one-sixth, were mechanics. Almost all of these were settled in New York city, or its neighborhood. The trades chiefly represented were: shoemakers, 345; tailors, 315; cabinet-makers, 371; making about one-third of the whole. No doubt, of the large number not helped by this agency, many were also mechanics, and of sufficient means to be able to dispense with aid. But the same causes are at work abroad as here, as we have shown, to lower the standard of good work; and there may come a time when the student of social elegance as well as of social science may have as much reason to complain of the quality as of the price of his coat and his boots.

In what direction shall we look for a remedy for all this? To the laws of supply and demand? But these laws, if any, have superseded during the last fifty years the old apprentice laws, and to this pass are we come . . . To leave this matter to regulate itself is to leave it to the contending interests of employers and employed, which had so large a share in the breaking up of the old system. I do not enlarge upon the laws of the trade unions, because they are only a feature of this struggle. They are the narrow, but natural expression of the supposed interests of one class, in opposition to movements sometimes similar, sometimes supposed to be so, of the other. The boys, for whom I speak to-night, are in the interest of neither party, and of both; they are the children of the employer as well as of the workman, and may grow up interchangeably into either. And in their name I ask, Where is the larger spirit to which they may appeal from the three obstacles — themselves, the workman and the employer — blocking the door to apprenticeship and self-maintenance?

.   .   .   .   .

It may be said that the less Government interferes with labor the better — and why should it concern itself to find work for children rather than any other class? It might be answered, because they *are* children; but I prefer to rest my plea on the broader ground that this is not in itself a question of labor, but of education.

. . . I would have our public schools give to their pupils such a knowledge of tools, and of the simpler processes of the manual arts, that a boy could enter upon these on the same footing that he can obtain a clerkship in a store, receiving wages that will enable him to form at once the habit of accumulation, because he will be of value to his employer from the beginning. Where there should be no necessity for immediate entrance on labor, a taste formed in the rudimentary school could be cultivated in higher technical schools, controlled or aided by government.

The subdivision of old trades into specialties, which grow into new trades, and the increased use of machinery, are arguments even better than Dr. Adam Smith's, a century ago, against long apprenticeship; and the same degree of skill can be gained in less time, where to learn and to teach are the ends, than where the labor is a matter of wages, and learning an incident. This instruction in handicraft would not conflict with that in letters. It is found in England that children employed in factories and receiving school instruction alternately are better scholars as well as better workers. It is well known that our country schools, kept through the winter only, and made up of boys who work on farms during the summer, will compare favorably with city schools, whose only recess is a long holiday. The training of the eye and the hand by drawing, measuring, handling forms and materials, cannot but have a beneficial reaction on the mind; and the learning how to *work,* which is something different from bodily *exercise,* is a most desirable preparation for any position in life.

There was a time when an artisan who could no more than read and write was an exception. To extend the limits of the learning that comes from books among workingmen was the first object of the public school. It has achieved the object; but those whom it reaches do not remain of the class of workingmen. This is not stated as an objection to the system, yet if among the thousands of workmen's children who are its subjects a small minority become skilled artisans, there is certainly a want left unsupplied, if not created; and a fear may be

expressed that the community is being educated away from labor. Out of 52 lads graduating from the Philadelphia Central High School in 1848, but 7 were engaged in mechanical employments some fourteen years afterwards. Out of 38 graduating in 1867, 21 became clerks, 6 salesmen, and 4 mechanics. Of 54 graduating in 1856, 30 became clerks and salesmen, and 11 mechanics. In each case, the total number includes all of whom any record could be made. The usual graduating age is about 17 years. It may be said that the pupils of the High School are not generally from the working class; but employers say that when they served their time, apprentices came very largely from the class corresponding to that whose sons graduate from the High School. The statistics of Girard College may be expected to be different, but of the 221 former pupils who were apprentices on Dec. 31st last, about one-half only, including 26 printers, engravers, etc., were learning mechanical trades. Human progress is always by exaggerated and reactive movements; and it may be that the time has come to revert to the instruction in labor of those who formerly had little other instruction. It is certainly too late to say that government has nothing to do with education. That point has been fixed, and we are passing on to another. It will soon be too late, we hope, to say that government has nothing to do with education, further than parents desire. And certainly education will not need to be any the more "compulsory" when it holds out the prospect of knowledge of a trade as well as of books.

It is too late, too, to say that the teaching of trades in schools is a new and untried notion. Industrial and technical schools, in Germany and France, have shown that it is practicable to instruct youths in this way in the manual arts, as well as polytechnic schools, here and abroad, can teach them the applied sciences. And even at home the principle of combining the study of letters and of handicrafts is illustrated in our reform schools, and in some of our benevolent institutions. Why should the State forbear to do that preventively which she does, to some extent, punitively? Why should not the children who have their natural protectors be, at least, as well provided for as those who have lost them?

I do not propose to dwell upon the details of this suggestion. My object will have been accomplished if it be fairly realized that apprenticeship, as our fathers knew it, is dying, and naturally; that it belongs to a state of society which will probably never return, and that to lament its decay is as absurd as to mourn for the middle ages; yet, that the want which it supplied is more imperative than ever, and that there is no power but the State itself — the true Guild — that can build anew and on broader foundations the complete system of learning — the true Apprenticeship.

---

3. "I do not desire my sons to follow the same trade"

Massachusetts, Senate, "Report on the Statistics of Labor," Doc. 120, *Documents, 1870* (Boston, 1870), pp. 270–271.

APPRENTICESHIP.

74. How did you acquire a knowledge of your present trade or employment? whether by serving an apprenticeship, or by what other means; and do you teach your sons (if any) the same trade, or desire them to follow it?

Office No. 86. An Iron Moulder. "Learnt by apprenticeship. I do not desire my sons to follow the same trade."

Office No. 42. A Woollen Weaver, English. "Learnt my trade from my parents."

Office No. 103. A Carpenter. "I served four years with my father. My own three sons have no desire to learn the trade, nor would I desire them to do so."

Office No. 26. A Shoe Inspector. "Have worked at shoemaking fifteen years; never served an apprenticeship; began on cheapest kind of work, and worked my way up to a skilled workman by my own energy, close ap-

plication, and desire to be as good as anybody. Should not desire my son to learn shoemaking; think it a very poor trade at present *time, owing to the large number of persons unemployed* the greater portion of the year; consider the trade very injurious to health."

Office No. 3. A Bootmaker. "Served an apprenticeship of three months to learn a part of the trade; satisfied that my children will go at it, as I expect that the business will improve; there are too many at it now, and not work enough for eight months in the year and that at miserable wages; when work is plenty, have to work when we should be in bed, or reading, or gaining necessary knowledge, or teaching our children that they may be properly brought up."

REMARKS.

From the above replies, and many similar, it is manifest that as general rule, parents prefer that their trade should not be the trade of their children.

Should people trained in factories be classed as indentured apprentices?

Massachusetts, Senate, "Report on Labor," pp. 356–357.

Office No. 51 says, in reference to question 74: "There don't seem to be any rules in this town, or in fact, in any of the small towns, in regard to apprentices. There is not work enough in winter to guarantee the binding of an apprentice for either one or three years. When I first went to work, my employer said he would pay my board for a few weeks until he could see how I would 'break in;' at the end of a few weeks he agreed to hire me and give me $1.50 per day, as long as he had work. I averaged about $30 a month for seven months, then the work got slack, so I had to look for a factory job for the winter, as I did not have enough earned to keep me the remaining five months. I got work in a factory until the following spring, when I left and began to work for my old employer on my second year, at $2 per day. Things were pretty much the same; I had to find another job in winter, and last spring I came back to my old employer on my third year, for $2.25 per day, with the previous understanding of getting work while he had it. I am now idle, this being a dull winter for factory business.

"For my part, I think it is no worse to get a trade so, than to be regularly indentured for three years; and if the question were asked me by other than the Labor Bureau, if I served an apprenticeship, I should answer yes! But to you, gentlemen, I give the details, for there is many others at this (house painting) as well as other trades, that learn them as above stated. I should like to know if, in your opinion, we that learn trades as I have above stated, should not be worthy of being classed with those who have papers of apprenticeship to show, 'provided we can do as good a job of work' as they can?

"No youth should migrate to a city without a thorough mastery of some good mechanical trade"

Horace Greeley, *Hints Toward Reforms* (New York, 1850), pp. 185–188, 361, 362.

When a poor youth, who has devoted every hour of his time, every farthing of his means, to the acquirement of what is called a Liberal Education, finds himself afloat on the great sea without a haven before him — no call for him in any professional capacity, no influential friends to make a position — no fitness, but rather decided unfitness, for usefulness in any mechanical vocation — and has the simple choice afforded him, to beg, starve, or turn his acquirements to some gainful but infamous use — there is another victim of Social injustice.

. . . . . .

— 'But do you contend that no American youth should *ever* migrate from the country to one of our Cities?' No, Sir, I do not. What I *do* maintain is this — Whoever leaves the country to come hither should feel sure that he has faculties, capacities, powers, for which the Country affords him no scope, and that the City is his proper sphere of usefulness. He should next be sure that he has ability to procure a livelihood while he shall be laboring to attain that sphere which he regards as his ultimate destination. No youth should migrate to a city without a thorough mastery of some good mechanical trade or handicraft such as is prosecuted in cities, although he may not intend to follow it except in case of dire necessity . . .

The young man fit to come to a City does not begin by importuning some relative or friend to find or make a place for him. Having first qualified himself, so far as he may, for usefulness here, he comes understanding that he must begin at the foot of the class and work his way up. Having found a place to stop, he makes himself acquainted with those places where work in his line may be found, sees the advertisements of "wants" in the leading journals at an early hour each morning, notes those which hold out some prospect for him, and accepts the first place offered him which he can take honorably and fill acceptably. He who commences in this way is quite likely to get on.

The importance of general education for apprentices

---

1. Education as "the true road to independence"

M. M. Noah, *Address at the Apprentice's Library, September 23, 1850* (New York, 1850), pp. 7–10, 14, 15.

. . . The time has arrived, when it has become apparent that the destinies of our country are finally to be placed under the control of the Mechanics and Labouring Men of the Union . . .

The President of the United States was a mechanic — an apprentice boy, as many of our hearers have been; true, in after life he studied law, and was a successful practitioner, but he carried into that study, and into that practice, and into that high station which he now adorns, the elements of patient industry, hard study, economical habits, and persevering labour, acquired when he was an apprentice. Should not this important fact stimulate us to aid the apprentice in educating himself, in strengthening his mind, and enlarging his sphere of usefulness . . .

It is our duty, therefore, to place this Mechanics' Society, and this Apprentices' Library, among the great and benevolent institutions of our city . . .

A Library, judiciously selected, is the Garden of Eden, in which is planted the tree of useful knowledge, the fruit of which is life, not death.

I have long urged wealthy parents to throw aside false pride, and make their sons Mechanics instead of Lawyers, Physicians and Divines: the bar is crowded and unprofitable, medicine is also overstocked with practitioners, and the pulpit has many laborious and poorly paid pastors. If we improve hereafter as rapidly as we heretofore have done, these professions and pursuits will be simplified, and we shall find that every man can be his own lawyer, his own doctor, and in his own domestic circle, with that great and good book, the Bible, he can become his, in part, own preacher; but a knowledge of the Mechanical Arts, steadily and industriously carried out, must in this great and increasing country, be for ever the source of profit, and the true road to independence. This Library, therefore, is the great platform on which a high moral and intellectual character may be formed. When the labour of the day is over, instead of the apprentice scouring the streets, visiting bar-rooms or theatres, mingling with idle, vicious companions, he takes his seat in this Library, with a rich intellectual repast

before him, or, being privileged to take a book home with him, he trims his lamp and reads aloud to his little brothers and sisters, scattering the good seeds among them, to take root hereafter. To-night he invites himself to pass the evening with the elegant Addison, to-morrow night he spends with Goldsmith, or Doctor Johnson, or Smollet, or Gibbon, the society of eminent and illustrious men, whom it is his pride to know from the rich emanations of their genius. If he wishes to travel, he sets out with Anson and Captain Cook, and makes a voyage around the world . . .

2. "Many children . . . never received an hour's education"

New York, Select Committee of the Senate Appointed to Visit Charitable Institutions, *Report, 1857* (Albany, 1857), pp. 216–217.

"I have found many children bound out by the superintendents who never received an hour's education during their apprenticeship, and who, at the age of twenty-one were cast loose on the world no better than the heathen. How can children brought up in this way be expected to become anything else than criminals or paupers, and fathers and mothers of criminals and paupers? They have no ambition to acquire property, and if they had, they have no means to acquire it. They cannot enter into trade, because in order to do this with any success they must be able to read, write and cypher, and this they cannot do.

Efficient rules should be adopted to guard against abuses in the apprenticeship of pauper children. Full enquiries should be made as to the character of the proposed master, and the answer should be made a matter of record. The parents or friends of the apprentice should be cited to attend, and their objections, if any, should be recorded and carefully weighed. The master should not be allowed to remove the apprentice from the town where he was originally bound without the consent in writing of the superintendents. The indentures should fully declare the duties of the master and provide for a proper amount of schooling and the provision of the necessary school books."

Samuel Gompers joins a union

Samuel Gompers, *Seventy Years of Life and Labor,* I (New York: E. P. Dutton & Company, 1925), 33, 170.

Samuel Gompers (1850–1924), organizer and president of the American Federation of Labor, started work at age ten as an apprentice for a shoemaker in London. He switched immediately, however, to cigar-

making because of his father's activity in the Cigarmakers' Society. The Gompers family sailed to the United States in 1863. In New York, young Gompers worked with his father, who started to make cigars at home. He was fourteen years old when he joined his first union.

In 1864 I joined the Cigarmakers' Local Union No. 15 which was the English-speaking union of New York City. This organization was not strong. There was also Union No. 90 of German-speaking cigarmakers which was affiliated to the German Labor Union that met in the Tenth Ward Hotel. All my life I had been accustomed to the labor movement and accepted as a matter of course that every wage-earner should belong to the union of his trade. I did not yet have a conscious appreciation of the labor movement. My awakening was to come later. However, I attended union meetings and observed union regulations.

C. BOYS AT SEA

The lure of the sea

1. A boy dreams of seeking his future on the sea

Herman Melville, *Redburn* (London and New York, 1849), pp. 1–11.

Herman Melville (1819–1891) was eighteen years old when he went to sea as a cabin boy on a ship bound for Liverpool. Upon his return to the United States he taught school, and then again shipped out on the schooner *Acushnet,* bound for the South Seas. *Redburn* tells the story of a young boy's trip to England.

I was then but a boy. Some time previous my mother had removed from New York to a pleasant village on the Hudson River, where we lived in a small house, in a quiet way. Sad disappointments in several plans which I had sketched for my future life, the necessity of doing something for myself, united to a naturally roving disposition, had now conspired within me, to send me to sea as a sailor.

Particularly, I remembered standing with my father on the wharf when a large ship was getting under way, and rounding the head of the pier. I remembered the *yo heave ho!* of the sailors, as they just showed their woolen caps above the high bulwarks. I remembered how I thought of their crossing the great ocean; and that that very ship, and those very sailors, so near to me then, would after a time be actually in Europe.

Added to these reminiscences my father, now dead, had several times crossed the Atlantic on business affairs, for he had been an importer in Broad Street. And of winter evenings in New York, by the well-remembered sea-coal fire in old Greenwhich Street, he used to tell my brother and me of the monstrous waves at sea, mountain high; of the masts bending like twigs; and all about Havre, and Liverpool, and about going up into the ball of St. Paul's in London . . .

I frequently fell in long reveries about distant voyages and travels, and thought how fine it would be to be able to talk about remote and barbarous countries; with what reverence and wonder people would regard me, if I had just returned from the coast of Africa or New Zealand; and how dark and romantic my sunburnt cheeks would look; how I would bring home with me foreign clothes of a rich fabric and princely make, and wear them up and down the streets, and how grocers' boys would turn back their heads to look at me as I went by. For I very well remembered staring at a man myself, who was pointed out to me by my aunt one Sunday in church, as the person who had been in Saudi Arabia, and passed through strange adventures there, all of which with my own eyes I had read in the book which he wrote, an arid-looking book in a pale yellow cover.

.   .   .   .   .

In course of time my thoughts became more and more prone to dwell upon foreign things; and in a thousand ways I sought to gratify my tastes . . .

As years passed on, this continual dwelling upon foreign associations bred in me a vague prophetic thought, that I was fated, one day or other, to be a great voyager; and that just as my father used to entertain strange gentlemen over their wine after dinner, I would hereafter be telling my own adventures to an eager auditory. And I have no doubt that this pre-

sentiment had something to do with bringing about my subsequent rovings.

But that which, perhaps more than anything else, converted my vague dreamings and longings into a definite purpose of seeking my fortune on the sea, was an old-fashioned glass ship, about eighteen inches long, and of French manufacture, which my father, some thirty years before, had brought home from Hamburg . . .

.   .   .   .   .

We have her yet in the house, but many of her glass spars and ropes are now sadly shattered and broken, — but I will not have her mended; and her figure-head, a gallant warrior in a cocked hat, lies pitching head-foremost down into the trough of a calamitous sea under the bows, — but I will not have him put on his legs again, till I get on my own; for between him and me there is a secret sympathy; and my sisters tell me, even yet, that he fell from his perch the very day I left home to go to sea on this *my first voyage.*

It was with a heavy heart and full eyes, that my poor mother parted with me; perhaps she thought me an erring and a willful boy, and perhaps I was; but if I was, it had been a hard-hearted world and hard times that had made me so. I had learned to think much and bitterly before my time; all my young mounting dreams of glory had left me; and at that early age I was as unambitious as a man of sixty.

Yes, I will go to sea . . .

"Yes, I will write you, dear mother, as soon as I can," . . .

.   .   .   .   .

So I broke loose from their arms, and not daring to look behind, ran away as fast as I could, till I got to the corner where my brother was waiting. He accompanied me part of the way to the place where the steamboat was to leave for New York; instilling into me much sage advice above his age, for he was but eight years my senior, and warning me again and again to take care of myself . . .

We walked on in silence till I saw that his strength was giving out — he was in ill-health then, — and with a mute grasp of the hand, and a loud thump at the heart, we parted.

---

2. Henry George goes to sea

Henry George, Jr., *The Life of Henry George* (New York, 1900), pp. 19–22.

George (1839–1897), author of *Progress and Poverty* and founder of the Single-Tax movement, developed a passion for the sea in early childhood. He used the wharves of Philadelphia as a playground, and was enchanted by stories about his grandfather, Richard George, a shipmaster. In 1855, at the age of fourteen, George shipped as a foremast boy on the bark *Hindoo,* bound for Melbourne and Calcutta.

The *Hindoo* was to sail from New York Harbour early in April. On Sunday, April 1, after Sunday school, Henry George received a Bible and a copy of "James's Anxious Enquirer"; and the next morning, bidding farewell at the wharf to his father, and uncles Thomas Latimer and Joseph Van Dusen, his cousin George Latimer and his friends Col Walton and Joe Roberts, he and Captain Miller went aboard the steamboat, crossed the Delaware, took train, and four hours afterwards were in New York. Two letters from him, written from the ship before she got away, have been preserved. They are in large, clear, firm hand, with some shading, some flourishes and a number of misspelled words. In the first, under date of April 6, he says:

"I signed the shipping articles at $6 a month and two months' advance, which I got in the morning.

"While we were down town we stopped at the Custom House, and Jim [an ordinary seaman] and I got a protection, for which we paid $1 each to a broker.

"The New York Custom House looks like a cooped up affair along side of the Philadelphia one — there are so many people and so much business and bustle.

"The upper part of New York is a beautiful place — the streets wide, clear and regular; the houses all a brown stone and standing ten or twenty feet from the pavement, with gardens in front."

To the foregoing letter was added this:

April 7, 1855

"I was stopped [writing] suddenly last night by the entrance of the men to haul her [the vessel] to the end of the wharf and was prevented from going on by their laughing and talking. At about twelve o'clock we commenced and by some pretty hard heaving we got her to the end of the wharf. It was then about two o'clock. So we turned in and slept until about half past five. We got our breakfast, and being taken in tow by a steamboat about 7:30 a.m., proceeded down the stream till off the Battery, where we dropped anchor and now lie.

"I ate my first meals sailor style to-day and did not dislike it at all. Working around in the open air gives one such an appetite that he can eat almost anything. We shall go to sea Monday morning early. I should love to see you all again before I go, but that is impossible. I shall write again tomorrow, and if possible get the pilot to take a letter when he leaves, though it is doubtful that I shall be able to write one."

It was in these days preparatory to starting, when there were a lot of odd things to do, that the boatswain, busy with some splicing, sent the boy for some tar; and when the boy stopped to look around for a stick, the sailor in surprise and disgust cried to him to bring the tar in his hand! Another incident of a similar kind appears in his second letter, which is dated April

9 and is addressed to his Aunt Mary, one of his mother's sisters . . .

"We are not at sea, as we expected to be by this time, but still lying off the Battery. The ship could not sail this morning for want of seamen. They are very scarce in New York now and all sorts of men are shipping as sailors. Two Dutch boys shipped as able seamen and came on board yesterday afternoon. The smallest one had been to sea before, but the largest did not know the difference between a yard and a block. The second mate told them to go aloft and slush down the masts. This morning the smallest went up, but the other could not go up at all. So I had to go aloft and do it. The work was a good deal easier than I expected. I don't mind handling grease at all now."

.   .   .   .   .   .

"Captain Miller has been ashore all day trying to get men. There is to be one sent on board in place of the largest Dutchman. I pity the poor fellow, though to be sure he had no business to ship as seaman. He says he has four trades — baker, shoemaker, etc. Another man came aboard this morning as able seaman who could not get into the foretop. They sent him ashore. The captain shipped to-day as ordinary seamen two lads, one a Spaniard and the other English, I believe. They are fine sailor looking fellows. The cook, steward and two of the men are from the West Indies. All sailed in whalers. There are no cleaner looking men in Parkinson's.

"We have better living than I expected — fresh and salt beef, potatoes and rice — and all cooked in the finest style; but I cannot like the coffee as yet.

"They have just brought two men aboard and taken the Dutchmen off. This is the last letter that I shall have a chance to send till we get to Melbourne, where I hope there will be letters awaiting me."

3. A boy on a whaler

William Davis, *Nimrod of the Sea; or, the American Whaleman* (New York, 1874), pp. 17–24.

Boys as young as thirteen, but more commonly fifteen or sixteen, shipped on whaling voyages that lasted at least two years, and sometimes extended to four years. Each vessel usually carried two or three boys in its crew. An ordinary seaman's share was 1/165, that is, one barrel of whale oil out of every 165 barrels extracted. In addition to escape and adventure, the sea promised young boys an opportunity to climb the ladder of responsibility and success. The crew lists at the Free Public Library of New Bedford, Massachusetts, contain many cases of boys who rose on successive voyages to second mate, first mate, and eventually to master.

My journal is used as a cord on which are strung the experiences and adventures of others, such as I have been enabled to pick up in the form of yarns on board the *Chelsea*. Omitting a date to my voyage, I am thus enabled to give the experiences of a quarter of a century. About the internal economy of our ship I write as the boyish sailor; and I ask you old captains, in imagination, to sit barefooted on an old sea-chest as you read my story as I sat to write it.

Is it necessary that I should recount how complaisant the major was before I signed the ship's articles? It appeared that the major was anxious to fill up his crew, that the vessel might not be detained when her fitting was completed; and doubtless, as he regarded the tall, slender, and rather weakly youth before him, he deemed it necessary to throw in an encouraging word to strengthen good resolutions:

"Ah! you're from Pennsylvania. Very good place that: a little too far from salt-water to be wholesome, I guess. Salt air will soon put color in your cheeks. You think you'll like the sea? Of course you will. Nice life—very, if you take to it right. Been aboard the *Chelsea* yet?

Yes; good ship the *Chelsea,* and such a sailer! A regular Baltimore clipper; easy times aboard that ship. You've trade-winds most of the way to Cape Horn: trade-winds, you know, are steady; as fixed, sir, as the needle to the pole, as the poet has it. And then there's the Pacific! Grand sea that; all about Juan Fernandez, Magellan, and the Southern Cross it's as calm and smiling as a mill-dam — so smooth that the illimitable sea seems a boundless oil-tank; where you see reflected in it the belt of Orion and the Pleiades. The thought almost tempts me to run out on a voyage, just to see that whaleman's heaven.

"Do you know that you get fresh beef at sea? Yes, sir, you do. Porpoises are to be had for the catching. Porpoise has muscle in it; you'd stiffen up on porpoise. And albatross too, big as geese; a little oily, but you'll get used to that. It makes a man water-proof to eat albatross."

The good man never dreamed that this moment was the fulfillment of the dreams of my short life. When I was a little boy, I had rigged and sailed my toy boats; and when a few years older, I had devoured Cook and Delano, and was happy in the library of Mavor, looking forward to the time when I too should visit the strange seas and scenes I had pictured in imagination. I took joy in the major's persuasions, as I knew that he would accept me, and allow me to go in his ship. Let me say it was no freak of a child, no sudden whim, which led me to this point. Twice I had been disappointed in going to sea. Once I had shipped in the *Globe,* East Indiaman, when a severe accident kept me confined for weeks after she had been under way. On a bed of sickness my young heart followed that gallant ship on her course, and I found consolation only in the promise of my fatherly brother, that when well another berth should be found me.

Then I shipped on board the saucy little free-trader, *Star,* bound for the coast of British India. She was armed, and carried a very heavy crew. My kit was purchased and taken on board, and one drizzly dark morning I went on board in my gay shirt and spotless ducks. When examined by the surgeon, he pounced on my wrist, left crooked from fracture in the late accident. It was still tender: he gave it an awful wrench; I flinched. "You won't do," was his awful verdict. In vain I told him that it was getting well very fast, and would soon be as sound as the other. He saw my heart was in going, and, being a kindly man, he said, "I can't pass you as sound; but go on shore now, and thank God that a weak wrist stands between you and this voyage." I did not know what he meant, but I went home to the quiet country almost heart-broken; and had no peace of mind until a letter from my friend, Mr. Lorenzo Draper, of New York, brought the glad tidings that he had secured a place for me on the *Chelsea.* And in a few days, with great joy in my heart (for which God forgive me), I kissed the tearful faces which bade me farewell for the long and, to them, fearful voyage which lay before me. Little did the good major know how little I needed the kindly encouragement he was extending; and lest I might again be disappointed, I made haste to append my name to the articles.

"Ah! you've signed. That's a good Bill; there's a captain's berth ahead if you earn it. Now run down to Mr. Strong in the basement; he'll finish your outfit in a jiffy. Take good advice: he is as sharp as he's Strong; make him take off fifteen per cent. for cash: he will get rich faster than you or I at that. Get a good outfit; spend your money for clothes, and not for tobacco, so that you may keep clear of the slop-chest. You have a week before you sail: look about you, and make the most of New London; for a three years' voyage is no trifle, and you won't see a better place the other side of the land. Good-morning."

I did not again speak to the major for forty-five months.

.   .   .   .   .

The crew was composed of a captain; a mate, who headed the larboard watch; a second mate, who, with the third mate, headed the starboard watch; four harpooners, and the trades mentioned before, with greenhorns and old salts, who were known to be, and shipped as, able seamen. The strong force on board a whaleship and the duties in the boats give an importance to the under officers unknown in the merchant service. With us the second mate was the officer of the deck during his watch, and he never left it to furl or reef: he exacted as respectful an "Ay, ay, sir," in answer to his orders as did the captain himself. The harpooners were divided, two in each watch, save when we were on cruising grounds. Then we reefed down every night, and each boat-steerer headed his own boat's crew's watch during the night, and became officer of the deck.

Our outfit consisted of extra sails and rigging, spare spars, and a store of tar, paint, etc., for repairs to ship; cedar boards and light timbers for the boats; a large quantity of admirably made whale line; a store of harpoons made of the softest and toughest iron, with lances of a quality of steel and capacity of cutting edge that might excite the envy of a diplomaed "sawbones;" also cutting-in spades, boat hatchets and knives; casks for the oil, stowed with water, food, or clothing; and all the very many necessaries to cover the wear and tear of long years of arduous service. An important and peculiar feature in the equipment of a whaleship is the "try-work." This consisted in our ship of three large iron pots, built in brick-work, and so supported by iron stanchions, that a body of water was maintained between the hearths and the deck to intercept the heat of the furnaces. For stores we carried as a staple, ship-biscuit, pork, and beef, with coffee, tea, molasses, rice, beans, Indian meal, flour, and pickles. Our worthy major was a professor of religion, and I am quite sure that on the day of final account he may safely call upon the *Chelsea*'s crew to testify to his liberality in our outfit. We might confuse the accountants if we gave our entire list of luxuries, which included "doughboys," "choke-dog," "lobscouse," "dough jehovahs," and "menavellins." Each day of the week some one of the above delicacies accompanied the

inevitable salt-junk; and, believe it who may, we had pork every day, not two or three days a week, as some unfortunates have it. Furthermore, access to the bread cask and the molasses tank was never denied. Perhaps there is no single article, I may say in parenthesis, in which the superiority of the American whaleman's outfit is more manifest, than in the excellent ship-biscuit which all carry, the greatest care being taken to exclude dampness or decaying influences. It will be noticed at once how well we were provided for.

---

4. The adventures of Jack, the virtuous cabin boy

Samuel Griswald Goodrich, *Jack Lawrence; or, the Adventures of a Cabin Boy* (Philadelphia, 1836), pp. 14–17, 144.

This is an example of the success story in popular literature for the generation preceding Horatio Alger. Jack loses his father at the age of eleven. He works diligently to help his mother, but is obsessed by the sea. He finally gets to sea, falls into bad company, reforms, marries the daughter of a wealthy passenger, and settles in Boston.

A few days afterwards, Jack, having completed the planting of his mother's garden, went to work as he had proposed for squire Coffin, a very worthy gentleman of the neighbourhood, who had been a particular friend of his mother since her removing to the cottage. He had also taken a particular fancy to Jack, and treated him with great kindness during the time he remained in his employment.

Jack continued in his service till the fall harvest was completed, when he received seventeen dollars all in hard money, which was a greater sum than he had ever seen before . . .

"What do you intend to do with all that

money, my boy?" "I shall take it home and give it to my mother," replied Jack . . .

". . . Now let me ask you one more question. If you were left to your own choice, what branch of business would you rather follow?"

"I had rather be a seaman, sir," replied Jack, promptly. "A seaman!" said the squire in surprise; "who has put that notion into your head?" "No one, sir." "And why would you wish to be a seaman?" "In the first place, because I should like to see foreign countries; and in the second place, I think that I could be of more service to my mother and sisters in this, than in any other way." "And have you ever mentioned the subject to your mother?"

"No, sir; I know she would be opposed to it, and I therefore never mentioned it for fear of giving her pain." "And do you think of going to sea without the permission of your mother?"

"By no means, sir; I shall stay with her at present, and perhaps when I am older she may be more willing for me to leave her; but I shall never do so without there is a prospect of my doing better for her abroad than by staying at home."

.   .   .   .   .

On the following spring, as Jack and his mother were engaged in removing some rubbish from the garden, she could not help remarking that he stopped from time to time and gazed with a longing look at the various sails that appeared upon the vast expanse of water, spread out before them. "What do you see," she at length inquired, "that engages so much of your attention?" "I was thinking," said Jack . . . "You were thinking how much happier you would be on the water than you are on the land."

Jack blushed deeply, but being bred to scorn any thing like falsehood, he replied, "Some such thoughts were passing in my mind. But tell me, mother, has squire Coffin told you any thing about the conversation that we had on the subject of my going to sea?" "It is not necessary, my son, that another should inform an anxious mother of the leading propensities of her chil-

dren. I have long foreseen your predilections for a seaman's life; but why, my son, have you never before mentioned the subject to me?"

"Because I was fearful of giving you unpleasant feelings, and as there is no prospect of my leaving you at present, I thought it unnecessary to say any thing about it before the time." "That was a kind thought, my good boy; but I hope you do not consider me so selfish as to oppose any measure that may be for your interest, merely to gratify my own wishes."

.   .   .   .   .

Such were the adventures of Jack during the time he served in the capacity of a cabin boy. But notwithstanding the satisfaction he enjoyed by his mother's fire-side, after remaining at home about three years, and prosecuting such studies as were calculated to prepare him for mercantile business, which his mother strongly recommended to him, he felt an unconquerable desire to try his lot again upon the water.

In his nineteenth year, therefore, he shipped as second mate, on board of a ship bound to India, by means of which he was enabled to circumnavigate the earth, which to him had been a primary object. He made two more voyages in the capacity of master, which he executed with success.

The fourth, however, was even more disastrous than the one already mentioned . . . This seemed to cure his predilection for a seafaring life, and having married Emeline Brainard, he settled down in the city of Boston, where he lived many years beloved and respected by all.

Abuse of boys at sea

1. Captain indicted for abuse of a boy aboard ship, 1822

Niles' Weekly Register, Feb. 9, 1822, p. 381.

The master of a vessel has been sentenced at Boston to the payment of 4000 dollars as damages for abuse of a boy, on board his ship, when on a voyage to the East Indies. The boy is now in the lunatic hospital, as is supposed, in consequence of his ill treatment.

---

2. Punishments inflicted on boys by tyrannical captain

Daniel Weston Hall, *Arctic Rovings* (Boston, 1861), pp. 37–38, 43–48, 64–65, 157–158.

Daniel Hall of New Bedford, Massachusetts, was fourteen in 1856 when he went aboard the whale ship *Condor,* Samuel H. Whiteside, master. In October 1858, after having been subjected to a series of abuses, Hall and a companion deserted when the ship was off the coast of Siberia. They were eventually rescued by another whaler and Hall returned to New Bedford to testify in the lawsuit his father had brought against Captain Whiteside.

We arrived at Ayan on the 25th of June: and the work of repairing the ship was immediately commenced. With a single exception, no incident of particular importance occurred during our stay in this port. The exception to which I allude, was a most severe and unmerited punishment inflicted upon me by the captain.

Up to this time, I had endeavored to conduct myself in such a manner as to preclude the possibility of punishment. I had cheerfully, and to the best of my ability, obeyed what I regarded as the most unreasonable commands; I had submitted without a murmur, to what I considered to be most reproachful and abusive language; in short, I had endured, what seemed to me, a life of the most abject slavery that I might not afford the faintest shadow of a pretext for further abuse.

It appears, however, that all my efforts to please my superiors, and save myself from disgraceful punishment, were destined to prove unavailing. On one occasion during our stay at Ayan, as I was standing on deck, engaged in the performance of some trivial duty, the captain approached me, and without any provocation that I am aware of, began to beat and kick me in the most cruel manner; after which he led me aft, and gave me fourteen blows with the end of the main-top-gallant brace! To this day, I am entirely at loss to account for this act: for I am not conscious of having disobeyed a single command, or offended in any manner whatever.

.   .   .   .   .

A few days after the squall, which has been previously described, a young man by the name of Pope, and myself, chanced to be engaged in what is termed by sailors, "skylarking" in the forecastle, during our forenoon watch below.

.   .   .   .   .

On this particular occasion Pope and myself were having a "set to" at sparring, merely for the fun of the thing, and without the slightest ill will or anger upon either side.

While amusing ourselves in this manner, the mate came forward, and ordering us on deck, bade us walk aft and report ourselves to the captain.

.   .   .   .   .

We were at length commanded to come down, and stationed side by side near the mizzen rigging; when the captain informed us that as we had been "making believe fight for our own amusement we should now fight in earnest for his," adding, that whoever got whipped should receive a flogging from him also.

Having no alternative but to obey, we commenced fighting; taking care, however, to strike as lightly as we dared under the circumstances. After a few minutes of this compulsory fighting, Pope gave up, saying that I was too much for him; but this was not sufficient to satisfy the captain, who exclaimed, "That is no fighting at all!" adding, with an oath, "I will show you how to fight and help you myself in the bargain."

He then procured a short whip, having several lashes of small tarred cords, similar to what is known on shipboard as the "Cat," and, to my surprise, ordered me "to strip!" The reader can well imagine, that I obeyed this command most unwillingly: I was completely in his power, however, and neither dared to disobey or even to express my indignation at this picture of injustice. I accordingly removed all my clothing above the waist; after which, the captain bade me "take fast hold of the mizzen belaying pins," and not to let go when he struck unless "I wished to receive a double portion." He then proceeded to give me eighteen blows upon my bare back, with the whip, laying them on with his whole strength, and causing the blood to flow freely at nearly every blow; after which he handed the instrument to Pope, and bade him give me "half a dozen." This was promptly done; the blows which I received from my fellow sufferer, however, being far less painful than those given me by the captain.

As soon as Pope had given me six lashes, he himself, was ordered to strip; and having been placed in the same position as myself, was then flogged in a similar manner; receiving, however, but eighteen blows from the captain, and none from myself.

We were then allowed to resume our clothing, and, with many curses, were ordered to return to the forecastle. We suffered intensely for many days afterwards, from the effects of this flogging, and it was with no little difficulty that we performed our duties: Still, we dared not complain, for we knew too well the temper of our commander; and were well aware that a still more painful punishment would attend a refusal to perform our appropriate labors.

The reader will please to bear in mind the fact that this severe punishment was inflicted upon us, simply, because we ventured to indulge in a little harmless sport, during our watch below, and not in consequence of neglect of duty or a single act of insubordination.

The injustice, as we considered it, of the punishment, however, only rendered it the more unendurable, and many times, while suffering from the painful wounds, inflicted by the cat, I thought of Burns' oft quoted words, —

"Man's inhumanity to man,
    Makes countless thousands mourn, — "

But I forbear. The reader's own sense of justice will enable him to render a just decision in regard to such a case as this, without further comment from me.

.   .   .   .   .

One morning during the season, the cry of "Whales!" was heard from the mast head; and as usual, the boats were hastily manned for the chase. At that time I belonged to the captain's boat and, upon this occasion, while rowing, I accidentally did what many an older and better seaman than myself has occasionally done before me, that is to say, I had the misfortune to "cramp" my oar; whereupon the captain immediately knocked me off my seat. He then proceeded to kick me as I lay in the bottom of the boat, and to strike me several blows with an oak stick, which he found in the stern sheets of the boat. One of these blows inflicted a wound upon my side, from which I never expect to recover; having produced an internal injury of a severe and painful nature.

As the reader may well imagine, this treatment rendered me unfit for the proper performance of my duty; nevertheless, I was compelled to resume my seat, and pull at my oar until the whale of which we were in pursuit of had been overtaken, killed, and towed alongside of the ship.

On the following morning I found myself scarcely able to leave my berth, from the effects of my injuries; still, I dared not complain, or refuse to perform duty. Accordingly, I hobbled on deck, as well as I was able; and, soon afterwards, the cry of "whales" having been raised, was placed in the boat, by the assistance of my shipmates, and, although in great pain, compelled to pull an oar for many hours.

.   .   .   .   .   .

The trial was then held; the attorney of Captain Whiteside, who was then absent at sea, appearing for his client; and after a full investigation of the facts in the case, the jury, admitting my letter as legal testimony, rendered a verdict against Capt. Whiteside, of three hundred dollars damages, as compensation for the time which I had been compelled to lose by leaving the ship.

Thus, not only had Divine Providence permitted me to return in safety to my home and friends; but I had, in a measure, obtained legal redress for my wrongs. In bringing this suit against Captain Whiteside, however, my father had been actuated by a higher motive than the desire to obtain pecuniary redress. He wished to make the case of Captain Whiteside an example to convince other commanders, who might be disposed in future, to tyrannize over their crews, that the laws of America *will protect the seamen from abuse,* or, at least, afford them compensation for their sufferings, and punish the tyrant of the quarter deck.

He hoped in this manner, to perform a service to his fellow men; particularly to those "who go down to the sea in ships"; and the publication of this work has been undertaken, by the author, partly with a view to further this desirable end.

Boys in cod and whale fisheries

Massachusetts, Senate, "Report on Statistics of Labor, 1871," Doc. 150, *Documents, 1871* (Boston, 1871), p. 179.

Cod and whale fishermen do not generally carry any boys under fifteen years old. Mackerel fishermen take two or three, and they are usually paid, on the first voyage, a third line, less a share of expense for the bait. In most cases after the first voyage, they will get a half line. A boy of fifteen will often catch as many fish as a man. Mackerel fishing requires such a degree of activity, expertness and slight of hand, that it can hardly be acquired at all unless one begins when young. Boys generally begin before they are fifteen. Often a smart young man becomes a captain by the time he is twenty-one years old.

Seafaring as penance

Diary of Robert Weir, 1855–1858, G. W. Blunt White Library, The Marine Historical Association, Incorporated, Mystic, Conn.

In August 1855, seventeen-year-old Robert Weir, having assumed the name Wallace, sailed from New Bedford, Massachusetts on the whaler *Clarabelle.* Robert, son of Robert Walter Weir (1803–1889), a well-known painter and professor of art at the U.S. Military Academy, West Point, chose exile at sea because he had fallen into debt and wanted to spare his father disgrace. The diarist later served as an officer in the Union navy and acted as war reporter and illustrator for *Harper's Weekly.*

August 18th, 1855.

Hauled off from the most detestable of places — New Bedford, and here we are anchored about two miles down the stream. Glad to get away from New Bedford. Never spent two such wretched weeks in all my life. True I had a pleasant place to board at Mrs. Doan's, but I could never feel settled no matter how long I might stay there. Read every book and every piece of book that I could find. Tried to smoke plug tobacco in pipes — couldn't enjoy that.

19th Sunday. Oh! if the folk at home knew what a field I am about — to launch upon what would they say — What does dear father think — but I cannot turn back — I may just as well as not begin to cut my way in the world, now, rather than leave it till I am older. Spent this day sacriligeously in climbing about the rigging, didn't venture much — but guess I'll soon get used to it. Hurrah for hard times — at least I'd like to make myself feel so, but I scarcely dare look ahead — it seems rather dark. Have great anticipations of future independence. I shall *never never* call on father again — but I dare not speak his name. I have wronged him too much to be his son.

20th Monday. A day to be remembered. The Captain came aboard a little after 9 o'clock, and we weighed anchor and set sail. Then came the first touch of work, in hauling up the anchor — such a pondrous thing is only fit to be buried at the bottom of the sea. I sincerely hope we shall not have the pleasure of dropping it till we again reach home — the chains were soon stowed between decks or rather in the chain pens — and the anchor's catted and lashed — and now we are on our way rejoicing? The first mate sent me aloft to slush the fore top gallant mast in the afternoon. The crew were divided into two watches, the Larboard and Starboard. I belong to the Mates or Larboard watch.

August 21st [1855] Tuesday, Beginning to get seasick and disgusted. Land out of sight — feel awful. We have to work like horses and live like pigs — eyes beginning to open — rather dearly bought independence — however, get on the sunny side shortly I hope.

22nd Wednesday. We are far very far out of sight of land — of sweet Ameriky. I was sent aloft on the lookout for whales and whatnots — And oh! how dreadfully sick I was. Saw two sharks, one about 12 ft. long and the other 5 or 6 ft. I felt very much tempted to throw myself to them for food. I can truly say I never was disgusted before in my life. The sea presents a cobalt blue appearance — it is beautiful — in the afternoon took my first trick at the

helm — two weary, dreary, desolate hours — can a human being get toughened to all this —

23rd Thursday. Sick as ever if not more so — but for all that have to work like a dog. We have an excellent breeze but our barque pokes her nose under outrageously . . . Captain Robbins gave us a short harangue of which I noticed these few words — he'd give us plenty to eat and plenty to do — if we acted like men he'd treat us like men — no swearing etc. etc. etc. — This afternoon the captain caught an albacore, a fish about 3 ft long — very thick and solid. I *turn in* emphatically speaking, disgusted and thinking of home.

24th Friday. Day commenced with a very stiff breeze, increased so much that we had to take in most of the sails; rained pretty hard in the evening — and I got wet and tired out tending the rigging and sails. Tumbled into my bunk with exhausted body and blistered hands — Romantic.

25th Saturday. The wind still blows pretty hard and the decks are constantly washed by the waves — not quite recovered from sickness yet, but think I am getting better. I am absolutely sick and disgusted with the living and everything.

26th Sunday. Commenced the day at the masthead feeling quite well; while looking about for whales or rather *nothing* (for I did not search the seas much as it was the Sabbath) I had pleasant thoughts of those I left so unkindly and abruptly but I console myself that it will be some relief to dear father, for me to be off his hands. I also amused myself by singing all the psalms and hymns, chants etc. that dear Emma and myself used to sing in our little Church — by that time my patience was pretty well exhausted and seasickness beginning to come on. My relief came very leisurely up the rigging — and now once more I find myself on deck, but am so sick from the rocking of the mast that I cannot read much in my bible as I intended, and can scarcely write. About noon it was a dead calm with heavy swell — the sails make a very loud noise flapping against the masts. — tumble into my bunk in disgust.

27th Monday. Good breeze blowing — another week of toil before one — cheer up — we'll soon get used to hard work and look at it as play; but the feed — awful. The waters have not been quiet enough to allow writing with ease since we started. Often a big lurch of the ship will knock half the ideas out of ones head. I must give up now anyhow —

30th Thursday. For 9 days we have been out of sight of land — and for the last four days nothing has broken the line of the horizon — haven't heard the cry "there she blows" yet — but we are not left idle. Every day since we left home the hold has been overhauled or something otherwise done about the ship — seizing on the chafing gear to prevent the rigging wearing way — and *innumerable* jobs. It gives me great relaxation, when I am on the lookout at the masthead; to sing over those dear old songs that Emma and I used to amuse ourselves with at home — for father's amusement, visitors, and a great many too that could never appreciate them.

2nd. Sunday. . . . passed a most miserable Sabbath — could neither read nor write — had to take my station aloft on the lookout between 2 and 4 p.m. though I did not go higher than the fore-top gallant yard — the weather being bad, I was quite exhausted and faint from holding on — for the vessel tossed about most unmercifully — very little did I see like a whale.

Thursday, November 29, 1855.
Hard at work stowing down the oil — This is slavery — a perfect dogs life — at 4 p.m. raised more whales — lowered & were unsuccessful — at sunset shortened sail — two sails in sight, turned in weary and worn — and sick at heart, if I could get anywhere upon the American coast I'll be happy — however — Cheer up — old boy — "behind the clouds is the sun still shining."

.   .   .   .   .

Saturday, December 13th, 1855.
Stowed the oil (105 lbs.) last Thursday — an awful job — had to break out clean to the keelson — chocked empty casks and ran the oil through a hose into them — this makes way with a great deal of labor. At 4 1/2 p.m. lowered for a whale and chased till sunset — with usual luck. There are quite a number of whales on this ground — and we are most always in sight of one another — four sails in sight, at sunset.

.   .   .   .   .

Sunday, December 30, 1855.
Christmas-day was not noticed on board — it happened to be my midnight trick at the wheel Christmas eve — and if I did not feel bad then I never did and never shall — hard life this, but may get used to it . . .

Monday, September 17, 1858.
Two short weeks have elapsed since I last got a chance to jot any items — it has been all work & no play — and I have not till now felt able to do anything in the writing line — with the exception of a . . . letter to Seymour — and 10 to 1 he never gets it. A great deal has happened during the first night above mentioned. We have laid off two ports — in the Azores — Flores & Fayal.

At Flores we recruited ship — took on board any quantity of potatoes, pumpkins, onions, fowl &c. Plenty of grapes — but to obtain them it is necessary to have plenty of money but with tobacco we made pretty good trades—for apples, peaches, figs, and cheeses — donkey cheese at that — and right good & wholesome they were. I don't know that I ever enjoyed fruit & cheese so much — it seemed as though we had been deprived of them for years instead of a few weeks, it was long enough to make me long for something fresh — as I was so totally disgusted with shipfare — I am now getting more used to saltjunk, coffee & tea? I can't say what the coffee is made of, but it resembles that delicious beverage as much as ink resembles water — there is but little coffee taste about it — still it is a little preferable to the stale water — As for the tea — if I only had some of the currant leaves off the bushes in our front yard, I'd feel grateful — but there is no use crying over spilt milk — get case hardened & go ahead — but I would like some one at home to have a sip of this same tea or coffee.

Sunday, September 23, 1858.

I am getting quite used to work now — and my hands can testify that quite plainly — for they are as hard as horn inside — pulling & hauling on hard ropes — and the outside have a most beautiful . . . brown color — all in the voyage — the handling of ropes & tar has very visible effect on the hands.

I like the sea — and I always thought I would — but it is hard to be separated from the dear ones at home — by such a distance of waters —

The manner in which the Sabbath is spent on board by nearly all — is truly deplorable, there is very little regard paid for the day — if we are not making & taking in sail all the while — and the weather is pleasant — most of the men will be seen squatting about the fore hatch smoking — dozing or growling — some read or wash — sew &c &c — but no thought is given to the welfare of the soul — And our noble 1st mate sets a most beautiful example by lounging on the quarter deck, the picture of idleness & misery — if he could he would like nothing better than to keep the crew hard and work Sundays as well as week days —

I shall indeed be thankful to get settled somewhere on land, where we can have a chance of improving the mind & choice of good companions. *N'il desperandum.*

D. CHILDREN IN FACTORIES

By the 1830's the use of child factory labor was common not only in cotton textile manufacture but also in the printing, dyeing, iron, glass, and shoe industries. Children in factories worked from ten to twelve hours per day for wages ranging from twenty-five to fifty cents.

*Family employment
in the textile industry*

1. Families at the Slater mills

Letters and misc. 1824–1837, XXVI, Slater Papers, Baker Library, Harvard University Graduate School of Business Administration, Boston, Mass.

A m[emorandum] of an agreement made and entered into by and between Jesse S. ——— of Thompson in the County of Windham and State of Connecticut. Labourer on the one part and Slater & Howard of Dudley in the County of Worcester and State of Massachusetts Woolen manufacture on the other part. Witnesseth said S ——— on his part agree to work for said Slater & Howard one year from the first day of April next with his family *viz* my son Joseph at six shilling per week. My son William at ten shillings per week and my son Lyman seventeen shillings per week for myself — four dollars per week the whole amt. . . . to be payable at the expiration of one year. I also agree for myself and family to work faithfully for said Slater & Howard at any branch of business they may think most to their benefit and I also agree for myself and family at all times while in their employ to abide to the order and rules of this said Slater & Howard in their establishment.

Said Slater & Howard agree to pay unto said S   for himself and family the above mentioned sums as above . . . at the expiration of one year that is to say after that rate for all the time the said S   and family may work. The said Slater & Howard agreed to find a dwelling house for said S   and family to dwell in and said S   paying said Slater & Howard the sum of twenty-five dollars at the expiration of this contract as witness our hand dated at Dudley February 18th, A.D. 1823.

A memorandum of an agreement made and concluded by and between Josiah Moutton of Stasford, Connecticut and Slater & Howard of Dudley for the time of one year to commence the first day of April next 1827 — the contract to end the first of April 1828. Said Moutton on his part agrees for himself and six children viz my sons Mark, John, James, Josiah & Othniel and daughter Elizabeth for the consideration of six hundred and twenty dollars for their faithful performance according to the order and regulation. Slater & Howard, Establishment.

Said Slater & Howard agree to pay to Josiah Moutton six hundred and twenty dollars for the faithful performance in discharging this duty in the different branches of Slater & Howard Establishment by said Moutton and six children and that I will for myself and family agree to do everything according to direction of Slater & Howard during one year to commence April 1st, 1827 and end April 1828. Witness our hands, dated at Dudley Feb. — 5th A.D. 1827.

George Smith   Josiah Moutton
Paul Dodge   Slater & Howard

[In a subsequent contract for 1828–29, signed February 23, 1828, the wages were specified for each member of the Moutton family.]

Josiah	$16.00 per month	$192.00 per year
Mark	15.87 " "	182.00 " "
John	8.67 " "	104.00 " "
James	6.50 " "	78.00 " "
Elizabeth	4.70 " "	56.33 " "
Josiah	4.33 " "	52.00 " "
Nathaniel	3.25 " "	39.00 " "
	$58.62 " "	$703.33 " "

2. Wanted: white women, boys, and girls

The Federal Union (Milledgeville, Ga.), Sept. 3, 1834.

NOTICE. The Eatonton Manufacturing Company have now the pleasure of informing the public, that their Cotton and Woollen Manufactory will be ready to commence operations in a few days, and will probably be in full operation by the 20th of next month (September). A large supply of Cotton Yarn, from No. 3 to No. 20, will be constantly for sale; and, as they expect to weave from six to eight hundred yards of Cloth per day, they will be able to sell that quantity of the various qualities. Their Woollen Manufactory will be very complete; and first, in operation, they will card wool, or card and spin wool, or card, spin and weave Woollen Yarn on Cotton Warp, and make an excellent article for Negroes' winter clothing . . . They . . . wish to hire twenty to thirty suitable laborers to work in the Factory. White women, girls and boys are such as will be wanted, aged ten years or upwards. Entire families may find it to their interest to engage in our service. A good house of entertainment will be kept near the Factory. Eatonton, August 22, 1833.

The Lowell factory girls

The cotton textile mills established in Lowell, Massachusetts during the 1820's employed many young women in their late teens and early twenties who had been recruited from rural families to work for "gain" rather than "bread." [1] The Lowell girls, although the most publicized of early nineteenth-century New England factory employees, were not typical textile workers. In dress, deportment,

1. On the Lowell system of factory organization see Caroline Ware, *Early New England Cotton Manufacture* (New York, 1966), p. 60.

and educational aspiration these "ladies of the loom," living in boardinghouses supervised by their employers, constituted a distinct element in the labor force. In the 1840's some of them contributed poems, stories, essays, and sketches of factory life to the *Lowell Offering*.[2]

1. The official picture, 1845

Massachusetts, House, "Report on Hours of Labor, 1845," Doc. 50, *Documents, 1845* (Boston, 1845), p. 10.

In Lowell, but very few (in some mills none at all) enter into the factories under the *age of fifteen*. None under that age can be admitted, unless they bring a certificate from the school teacher, that he or she has attended school at least three months during the preceding twelve. Nine-tenths of the factory population in Lowell come from the country. They are farmers' daughters. Many of them come over a hundred miles to enter the mills. Their education has been attended to in the district schools, which are dotted like diamonds over every square mile of New England. Their moral and religious characters have been formed by pious parents, under the paternal roof. Their bodies have been developed, and their constitutions made strong by pure air, wholesome food, and youthful exercise.

After an absence of a few years, having laid by a few hundred dollars, they depart for their homes, get married, settle down in life, and become the heads of families. Such, we believe, in truth, to be a correct statement of the Lowell operatives, and of the hours of labor.

2. The workers' testimony

Massachusetts, House, "Report on Hours of Labor, 1845," pp. 2–3, 5, 6–9.

The first petitioner who testified was *Eliza R. Hemmingway*. She had worked 2 years and 9 months in the Lowell Factories, 2 years in the Middlesex, and 9 months in the Hamilton Corporations. Her employment is weaving, — works by the piece. The Hamilton Mill manufactures cotton fabrics. The Middlesex, woollen fabrics. She is now at work in the Middlesex Mills, and attends one loom. Her wages average from $16 to $23 a month exclusive of board. She complained of the hours for labor being too many, and the time for meals too limited. In the summer season, the work is commenced at 5 o'clock, A.M., and continued till 7 o'clock, P.M., with half an hour for breakfast and three quarters of an hour for dinner. During eight months of the year, but half an hour is allowed for dinner. The air in the room she considered not to be wholesome. There were 293 small lamps and 61 large lamps lighted in the room in which she worked, when evening work is required. These lamps are also lighted sometimes in the morning. — About 130 females, 11 men, and 12 children (between the ages of 11 and 14) work in the room with her. She thought the children enjoyed about as good health as children generally do. The children work but 9 months out of 12. The other 3 months they must attend school. Thinks that there is no day when there are less than six of the females out of the mill from sickness. Has known as many as thirty. She, herself, is out quite often, on account of sickness. There was more sickness in the Summer than in the Win-

2. The *Lowell Offering: A Repository of Original Articles Written Exclusively by Females Actively Employed in the Mills,* 1841–1845, 5 vols., and the *New England Offering: A Magazine of Industry Written by Females Who are or Who Have Been Factory Operatives,* 1845–1850, 3 vols., edited by Harriet Farley, were preceded by an earlier periodical, *The Operatives' Magazine,* 1840–1841, edited by Lydia S. Hall and Abby A. Goddard. See Lucy Larcom, *A New England Girlhood, Outlined from Memory* (Boston and New York), pp. 209–225.

ter months: though in the Summer, lamps are not lighted.

. . . . .

Miss Olive J. Clark. — She is employed on the Lawrence Corporation; has been there five years; makes about $1.62½ per week, exclusive of board. She has been home to New Hampshire to school. Her health never was good. The work is not laborious; can sit down about a quarter of the time. About fifty girls work in the spinning-room with her, three of whom signed the petition. She is in favor of the ten hour system, and thinks that the long hours had an effect upon her health. She is kindly treated by her employers. There is hardly a week in which there is not some one out on account of sickness. Thinks the air is bad, on account of the small particles of cotton which fly about. She has never spoken with the agent or overseer about working only ten hours.

. . . . .

Mr. Gilman Gale, a member of the city council, and who keeps a provision store, testified that the short time allowed for meals he thought the greatest evil. He spoke highly of the character of the operatives and of the agents; also of the boarding houses and the public schools. He had two children in the mills who enjoyed good health. The mills are kept as clean and as well ventilated as it is possible for them to be.

Mr. Herman Abbott had worked in the Lawrence Corporation 13 years. Never heard much complaint among the girls about the long hours, never heard the subject spoken of in the mills. Does not think it would be satisfactory to the girls to work only ten hours, if their wages were to be reduced in proportion. Forty-two girls work in the room with him. The girls often get back to the gate before the bell rings.

. . . . .

On Saturday the 1st of March, a portion of the Committee went to Lowell to examine the mills, and to observe the general appearance of the operatives therein employed. They arrived at Lowell after an hour's ride upon the railroad. They first proceeded to the Merrimack Cotton Mills, in which are employed usually 1200 females and 300 males. They were permitted to visit every part of the works and to make whatever inquiries they pleased of the persons employed. They found every apartment neat and clean, and the girls, so far as personal appearance went, healthy and robust, as girls are in our country towns.

The Committee also visited the Massachusetts and Boott Mills, both of which manufacture cotton goods. The same spirit of thrift and cleanliness, of personal comfort and contentment, prevailed there. The rooms are large and well lighted, the temperature comfortable, and in most of the window sills were numerous shrubs and plants, such as geraniums, roses, and numerous varieties of the cactus. These were the pets of the factory girls, and they were to the Committee convincing evidence of the elevated moral tone and refined taste of the operatives.

The Committee also visited the Lowell and the Middlesex mills; in the first of which carpets are manufactured, and in the second, broadcloths, cassimeres, &c. These being woollen mills, the Committee did not expect to find that perfect cleanliness which can be and has been attained in cotton mills. It would, however, be difficult to institute a comparison between the mills on this point, or to suggest an improvement. Not only is the interior of the mills kept in the best order, but great regard has been paid by many of the agents to the arrangement of the enclosed grounds. Grass plats have been laid out, trees have been planted, and fine varieties of flowers in their season, are cultivated within the factory grounds. In short, every thing in and about the mills, and the boarding houses appeared, to have for its end, health and comfort. The same remark would apply to the city generally. Your committee returned fully satisfied, that the order, decorum, and general appearance of things in and about the mills, could not be improved by any suggestion of theirs, or by any act of the Legislature.

.   .   .   .   .

From Mr. Clark, the agent of the Merrimack Corporation we obtained the following table of the time which the mills run during the year.

Begin work. — From 1st May to 31st August, at 5 o'clock.

From 1st September to 30th April, as soon as they can see.

Breakfast. — From 1st November to 28th February, before going to work.

From 1st March to 31st of March, at 7½ o'clock.

From 1st April to 19th September, at 7 o'clock.

From 20th Sept. to 31st October, at 7½ o'clock. Return in half an hour.

Dinner. — Through the year at 12½ o'clock.

From 1st May to 31st Aug. return in 45 minutes.

From 1st Sept. to 30th April, return in 30 minutes.

Quit work. — From 1st May to 31st August, at 7 o'clock.

From 1st September to 19th Sept., at dark.

From 20th Sept. to 19th March, at 7½ o'clock.

From 20th March to 30th April, at dark.

Lamps are never lighted on Saturday evenings. The above is the time which is kept in all the mills in Lowell, with a slight difference in the machine shop; and it makes the average daily time throughout the year, of running the mills, to be 12 hours and ten minutes.

There are four days in the year which are observed as holidays, and on which the mills are never put in motion. These are Fast Day, Fourth of July, Thanksgiving Day, and Christmas Day. These make one day more than is

usually devoted to pastime in any other place in New England. The following table shows the average hours of work per day, throughout the year, in the Lowell Mills:

	Hours	Min.
January	11	24
February	12	
March[1]	11	52
April	13	31
May	12	45
June	12	45
July	12	45
August	12	45
September	12	23
October	12	10
November	11	56
December	11	24

3. Regulations for workers in the factories of the Hamilton Manufacturing Company, Lowell, 1848

Hand-book for the Visitor to Lowell (Lowell, 1848), pp. 42–44.

All persons in the employ of the Hamilton Manufacturing Company, are to observe the regulations of the room where they are employed. They are not to be absent from their work without the consent of the overseer, except in cases of sickness, and then they are to send him word of the cause of their absence. They are to board in one of the houses of the company and give information at the counting room, where they board, when they begin, or, whenever they change their boarding place; and are to observe the regulations of their boarding-house.

1. The hours of labor on the 1st of March are less than in February, even though the days are a little longer, because 30 minutes are allowed for breakfast from the 1st of March to the 1st of September. [Note in House "Report."]

Those intending to leave the employment of the company, are to give at least two weeks' notice thereof to their overseer.

All persons entering into the employment of the company, are considered as engaged for twelve months, and those who leave sooner, or do not comply with all these regulations, will not be entitled to a regular discharge.

The company will not employ any one who is habitually absent from public worship on the Sabbath, or known to be guilty of immorality.

A physician will attend once in every month at the counting-room, to vaccinate all who may need it, free of expense.

Any one who shall take from the mills or the yard, any yarn, cloth or other article belonging to the company, will be considered guilty of stealing, and be liable to prosecution.

Payments will be made monthly, including board and wages. The accounts will be made up to the last Saturday but one in every month, and paid in the course of the following week.

These regulations are considered part of the contract, with which all persons entering into the employment of the Hamilton Manufacturing Company, engage to comply.

John Avery, Agent.

Child life in the Lowell mills

1. The memories of an early mill girl

Harriet Robinson, *Loom and Spindle, or Life Among the Early Mill Girls* (Boston, 1898), pp. 25–37, 39, 60–61.

Harriet Jane Hanson Robinson (1825–1911), a fighter for women's rights and one of the organizers of the General Federation of Women's Clubs, was ten years old when she went to work in a Lowell mill.

In attempting to describe the life and times of the early mill-girls, it has seemed best for me to write my story in the first person; not so much because my own experience is of importance, as that it is, in some respects, typical of that of many others who lived and worked with me.

Our home was in Boston, in Leverett Court, now Cotting Street, where I was born the year the corner-stone was laid for the Bunker Hill Monument, as my mother told me always to remember.

.   .   .   .   .

In 1831, under the shadow of a great sorrow, which had made her four children fatherless, — the oldest but seven years of age, — my mother was left to struggle alone; and, although she tried hard to earn bread enough to fill our hungry mouths, she could not do it, even with the help of kind friends. And so it happened that one of her more wealthy neighbors, who had looked with longing eyes on the one little daughter of the family, offered to adopt me. But my mother, who had had a hard experience in her youth in living amongst strangers, said, "No; while I have one meal of victuals a day, I will not part with my children." I always remembered this speech because of the word "victuals," and I wondered for a long time what this good old Bible word meant.

My father was a carpenter, and some of his fellow-workmen helped my mother to open a little shop, where she sold small stores, candy, kindling-wood, and so on, but there was no great income from this, and we soon became poorer than ever.

. . . And so I went to the sewing-school, like any other little girl who was taking lessons in sewing and not as a "charity child"; until a certain day when something was said by one of the teachers, about me, as a "poor little girl," — a thoughtless remark, no doubt, such as may be said to-day in "charity schools." When I went home I told my mother that the teacher said I was *poor*, and she replied in her sententious manner, "You need not go there again."

Shortly after this my mother's widowed sister, Mrs. Angeline Cudworth, who kept a factory boarding-house in Lowell, advised her to come to that city. She secured a house for her, and my mother, with her little brood and her few household belongings, started for the new factory town.

.   .   .   .   .

I had been to school constantly until I was about ten years of age, when my mother, feeling obliged to have help in her work besides what I could give, and also needing the money which I could earn, allowed me, at my urgent request (for I wanted to earn *money* like the other little girls), to go to work in the mill. I worked first in the spinning-room as a "doffer." The doffers were the very youngest girls, whose work was to doff, or take off, the full bobbins, and replace them with the empty ones.

I can see myself now, racing down the alley, between the spinning-frames, carrying in front of me a bobbin-box bigger than I was. These mites had to be very swift in their movements, so as not to keep the spinning-frames stopped long, and they worked only about fifteen minutes in every hour. The rest of the time was their own, and when the overseer was kind they were allowed to read, knit, or even to go outside the mill-yard to play.

Some of us learned to embroider in crewels, and I still have a lamb worked on cloth, a relic of those early days, when I was first taught to improve my time in the good old New England fashion. When not doffing, we were often allowed to go home, for a time, and thus we were able to help our mothers in their housework. We were paid two dollars a week; and how proud I was when my turn came to stand up on the bobbin-box, and write my name in the paymaster's book, and how indignant I was when he asked me if I could "write." "Of course I can," said I, and he smiled as he looked down on me.

The working-hours of all the girls extended from five o'clock in the morning until seven in the evening, with one-half hour for breakfast and for dinner. Even the doffers were forced to be on duty nearly fourteen hours a day, and

this was the greatest hardship in the lives of these children. For it was not until 1842 that the hours of labor for children under twelve years of age were limited to ten per day; but the "ten-hour law" itself was not passed until long after some of these little doffers were old enough to appear before the legislative committee on the subject, and plead, by their presence, for a reduction of the hours of labor.

I do not recall any particular hardship connected with this life, except getting up so early in the morning, and to this habit, I never was, and never shall be, reconciled, for it has taken nearly a lifetime for me to make up the sleep lost at that early age. But in every other respect it was a pleasant life. We were not hurried any more than was for our good, and no more work was required of us than we were able easily to do.

Most of us children lived at home, and we were well fed, drinking both tea and coffee, and eating substantial meals (besides luncheons) three times a day. We had very happy hours with the older girls, many of whom treated us like babies, or talked in a motherly way, and so had a good influence over us. And in the long winter evenings, when we could not run home between the doffings, we gathered in groups and told each other stories, and sung the old-time songs our mothers had sung, such as "Barbara Allen," "Lord Lovell," "Captain Kid," "Hull's Victory," and sometimes a hymn.

.   .   .   .   .

And we told each other of our little hopes and desires, and what we meant to do when we grew up. For we had our aspirations; and one of us, who danced the "shawl dance," as she called it, in the spinning-room alley, for the amusement of her admiring companions, discussed seriously with another little girl the scheme of their running away together, and joining the circus. Fortunately, there was a grain of good sense lurking in the mind of this gay little lassie, with the thought of the mother at home, and the scheme was not carried out.

There was another little girl, whose mother

was suffering with consumption, and who went out of the mill almost every forenoon, to buy and cook oysters, which she brought in hot, for her mother's luncheon. The mother soon went to her rest, and the little daughter, after tasting the first bitter experience of life, followed her. . . . Many pathetic stories might be told of these little fatherless mill-children, who worked near their mothers, and who went hand in hand with them to and from the mill.

·   ·   ·   ·   ·

Holidays came when repairs to the great mill-wheel were going on, or some late spring freshet caused the shutting down of the mill; these were well improved. With what freedom we enjoyed those happy times! My summer playhouse was the woodshed, which my mother always had well filled; how orderly and with what precision the logs were sawed and piled with the smooth ends outwards . . .

The yard which led to the shed was always green, and here many half-holiday duties were performed. We children were expected to scour all the knives and forks used by the forty men-boarders, and my brothers often bought themselves off by giving me some trifle, and I was left alone to do the whole. And what a pile of knives and forks it was! But it was no task, for did I not have the open yard to work in, with the sky over me, and the green grass to stand on, as I scrubbed away at my "stent"? I don't know why I did not think such long tasks a burden, nor of my work in the mill as drudgery. Perhaps it was because I *expected* to do my part towards helping my mother to get our living, and had never heard her complain of the hardships of her life.

On other afternoons I went to walk with a playmate, who, like myself, was full of romantic dreams, along the banks of the Merrimack River, where the Indians had still their tents, or on Sundays, to see the "new converts" baptized. These baptizings in the river were very common, as the tanks in the churches were not considered *apostolic* by the early Baptists of Lowell.

Sometimes we rambled by the "race-way" or mill-race, which carried the water into the flume of the mill, along whose inclining sides grew wild roses, and the "rock-loving columbine"; and we used to listen to see if we could hear the blue-bells ring, — this was long before either of us had read a line of poetry.

·   ·   ·   ·

I was a "little doffer" until I became old enough to earn more money; then I tended a spinning-frame for a little while; and after that I learned, on the Merrimack corporation, to be a drawing-in girl, which was considered one of the most desirable employments, as about only a dozen girls were needed in each mill. We drew in, one by one, the threads of the warp, through the harness and the reed, and so made the beams ready for the weaver's loom. I still have the two hooks I used so long, companions of many a dreaming hour, and preserve them as the "badge of all my tribe" of drawing-in girls.

It may be well to add that, although so many changes have been made in mill-work, during the last fifty years, by the introduction of machinery, this part of it still continues to be done by hand, and the drawing-in girl — I saw her last winter, as in my time — still sits on her high stool, and with her little hook patiently draws in the thousands of threads, one by one.

When I look back into the factory life of fifty or sixty years ago, I do not see what is called "a class" of young men and women going to and from their daily work, like so many ants that cannot be distinguished one from another; I see them as individuals, with personalities of their own. This one has about her the atmosphere of her early home. That one is impelled by a strong and noble purpose. The other, — what she is, has been an influence for good to me and to all womankind.

Yet they were a class of factory operatives, and were spoken of (as the same class is spoken of now) as a set of persons who earned their daily bread, whose condition was fixed, and who must continue to spin and to weave to the end of their natural existence. Nothing but this was expected of them, and they were not supposed to be capable of social or mental improvement. That they could be educated and developed into something more than mere work-people, was an idea that had not yet entered the public mind. So little does one class of persons really know about the thoughts and aspirations of another! It was the good fortune of these early mill-girls to teach the people of that time that this sort of labor is not degrading; that the operative is not only "capable of virtue," but also capable of self-cultivation.

At the time the Lowell cotton-mills were started, the factory girl was the lowest among women. In England, and in France particularly, great injustice had been done to her real character; she was represented as subjected to influences that could not fail to destroy her purity and self-respect. In the eyes of her overseer she was but a brute, a slave, to be beaten, pinched, and pushed about. It was to overcome this prejudice that such high wages had been offered to women that they might be induced to become mill-girls, in spite of the opprobrium that still clung to this "degrading occupation." At first only a few came; for, though tempted by the high wages to be regularly paid in "cash," there were many who still preferred to go on working at some more *genteel* employment at seventy-five cents a week and their board.

---

2. Mrs. Hanson renounces her right to her fifteen-year-old daughter's earnings, 1840

Robinson, *Loom and Spindle*, pp. 67–68.

Be it known that I, Harriet Hanson, of Lowell, in consideration that my minor daughter Harriet J. has taken upon herself the whole burden of her own support, and has undertaken and agreed to maintain herself henceforward without expense to me, do hereby release and quitclaim unto her all profits and wages which she may hereafter earn or acquire by her skill or labor in any occupation, — and do hereby disclaim all right to collect or interfere with the same. And I do give and release unto her the absolute control and disposal of her own time according to her own discretion, without interference from me. It being understood that I am not to be chargeable hereafter with any expense on her account.

(signed) Harriet Hanson

July 2, 1840.

---

3. "It is just like play"

Larcom, *A New England Girlhood*, pp. 153–155.

Lucy Larcom (1824–1893), who later achieved modest fame as a poetess, was one of eight children in a family left destitute by the death of the father. Lucy worked in the Lowell mills for a few years in the 1840's before becoming a schoolteacher in Illinois.

The older members of the family did everything they could, but it was not enough. I heard it said one day, in a distressed tone, "The children will have to leave school and go into the mill."

There were many pros and cons between my mother and sisters before this was positively decided. The mill-agent did not want to take us two little girls, but consented on condition we should be sure to attend school the full number of months prescribed each year. I, the younger one, was then between eleven and twelve years old.

I listened to all that was said about it, very much fearing that I should not be permitted to do the *coveted work*. For the feeling had already frequently come to me, that I was the one too many in the overcrowded family nest. Once, before we left our old home, I had heard a neighbor condoling with my mother because there were so many of us, and her emphatic reply had been a great relief to my mind: —

"There isn't one more than I want. I could not spare a single one of my children."

But her difficulties were increasing, and I thought it would be a pleasure to feel that I was not a trouble or burden or expense to anybody. So I went to my first day's work in the mill with a light heart. The novelty of it made it seem easy, and it really was not hard, just to change the bobbins on the spinning-frames every three quarters of an hour or so, with half a dozen other little girls who were doing the same thing. When I came back at night, the family began to pity me for my long, tiresome day's work, but I laughed and said, —

"Why, it is nothing but fun. It is just like play."

And for a little while it was only a new amusement; I liked it better than going to school and "making believe" I was learning when I was not. And there was a great deal of play mixed with it. We were not occupied more than half the time. The intervals were spent frolicking around among the spinning-frames, teasing and talking to the older girls, or entertaining ourselves with games and stories in a corner, or exploring, with the overseer's permission, the mysteries of the carding-room, the dressing-room, and the weaving-room.

I never cared much for machinery. The buzzing and hissing and whizzing of pulleys and rollers and spindles and flyers around me often grew tiresome. I could not see into their complications, or feel interested in them. But in a room below us we were sometimes allowed to peer in through a sort of blind door at the great waterwheel that carried the works of the whole mill. It was so huge that we could only watch a few of its spokes at a time, and part of its dripping rim, moving with a slow, measured strength through the darkness that shut it in. It impressed me with something of the awe which comes to us in thinking of the great Power which keeps the mechanism of the universe in motion. Even now, the remembrance of its

large, mysterious movement, in which every little motion of every noisy little wheel was involved, brings back to me a verse from one of my favorite hymns: —

Our lives through various scenes are drawn,
    And vexed by trifling cares,
While Thine eternal thought moves on
    Thy undisturbed affairs.

There were compensations for being shut in to daily toil so early. The mill itself had its lessons for us. But it was not, and could not be, the right sort of life for a child, and we were happy in the knowledge that, at the longest, our employment was only to be temporary.

---

4. Conflict between school and mill: "I would go to school again whatever happened"

Larcom, *A New England Girlhood*, pp. 155–159.

When I took my next three months at the grammar school, everything there was changed, and I too was changed. The teachers were kind, and thorough in their instruction; and my mind seemed to have been ploughed up during that year of work, so that knowledge took root in it easily. It was a great delight to me to study, and at the end of the three months the master told me that I was prepared for high school.

But alas! I could not go. The little money I could earn — one dollar a week, besides the price of my board — was needed in the family, and I must return to the mill. It was a severe disappointment to me, though I did not say so at home . . .

.   .   .   .   .

. . . I think the resolution was then formed, inwardly, that I *would* go to school again, some time, whatever happened. I went back to my work, but now without enthusiasm. I had looked through an open door that I was not willing to see shut upon me.

I began to reflect upon life rather seriously for a girl of twelve or thirteen. What was I here for? What could I make of myself? Must I submit to be carried along with the current, and do just what everybody else did? No: I knew I should not do that, for there was a certain Myself who was always starting up with her own original plan or aspiration before me, and who was quite indifferent as to what people generally thought.

Well, I would find out what this Myself was good for, and that she should be!

It was but the presumption of extreme youth . . .

.   .   .   .   .

When I thought what I should best like to do, my first dream — almost a baby's dream — about it was that it would be a fine thing to be a schoolteacher, like Aunt Hannah. Afterward, when I heard that there were artists, I wished I could some time be one. A slate and pencil, to draw pictures, was my first request, whenever a day's ailment kept me at home from school; and I rather enjoyed being a little ill, for the sake of amusing myself in that way. The wish grew up with me; but there were no good drawing-teachers in those days, and if there had been, the cost of instruction would have been beyond the family means. My sister Emilie, however, who saw my taste and shared it herself, did her best to assist me, furnishing me with pencil and paper and paint-box.

If only I could make a rose bloom on paper, I thought I should be happy! or if I could at last succeed in drawing the outline of winter-stripped boughs as I saw them against the sky, it seemed to me that I should be willing to spend years in trying.

.   .   .   .   .

I seldom thought seriously of becoming an author . . . although now and then I thought I could feel ideas growing in my mind that it might be worth while to put into a book, — if I lived and studied until I was forty or fifty years old.

---

5. The factory girl's *alma mater*

Robinson, *Loom and Spindle,* pp. 40–46, 50–51.

As the cotton-factory was the means of the early schooling of so large a number of men and women, who, without the opportunity thus afforded, could not have been mentally so well developed, I love to call it their *Alma Mater.* For, without his incentive to labor, this chance to earn extra money and to use it in their own way, their influence on the times, and also, to a certain extent, on modern civilization, would certainly have been lost.

I had been to school quite constantly until I was nearly eleven years of age, and then, after going into the mill, I went to some of the evening schools that had been established, and which were always well filled with those who desired to improve their scant education, or to supplement what they had learned in the village school or academy. Here might often be seen a little girl puzzling over her sums in Colburn's Arithmetic, and at her side another "girl" of fifty poring over her lesson in Pierpont's National Reader.

.   .   .   .   .

The discipline our work brought us was of great value. We were obliged to be in the mill at just such a minute, in every hour, in order to doff our full bobbins and replace them with empty ones. We went to our meals and returned at the same hour every day. We worked and played at regular intervals, and thus our hands became deft, our fingers nimble, our feet swift, and we were taught daily habits of regularity and of industry; it was, in fact, a sort of manual training or industrial school.

Some of us were fond of reading, and we read all the books we could borrow. One of my mother's boarders, a farmer's daughter from "the State of Maine," had come to Lowell to work, for the express purpose of getting books, usually novels, to read, that she could not find in her native place. She read from two to four volumes a week; and we children used to get them from the circulating library, and return them, for her. In exchange for this, she allowed us to read her books, while she was at work in the mill; and what a scurrying there used to be home from school, to get the first chance at the new book!

It was as good as a fortune to us, and all for six and a quarter cents a week! In this way I read the novels of Richardson, Madame D'Arblay, Fielding, Smollett, Cooper, Scott, Captain Marryatt, and many another old book not included in Mr. Ruskin's list of "one hundred good books."

. . . . . .

I read and studied also at my work; and as this was done by the job, or beam, if I chose to have a book in my lap, and glance at it at intervals, or even write a bit, nothing was lost to the "corporation."

Lucy Larcom, in her "New England Girlhood," speaks of the windows in the mill on whose sides were pasted newspaper clippings, which she calls "window gems." It was very common for the spinners and weavers to do this, as they were not allowed to read books openly in the mill; but they brought their favorite "pieces" of poetry, hymns, and extracts, and pasted them up over their looms or frames, so that they could glance at them, and commit them to memory. We little girls were fond of reading these clippings, and no doubt they were an incentive to our thoughts as well as to those of the older girls, who went to "The Improvement Circle," and wrote compositions.

Bobbin boys

1. In the governor's mill, 1835

Stephen A. Knight, "Reminiscences of Seventy-one years in the Cotton Spinning Industry," *Transactions* of the National Association of Cotton Manufacturers, LXXX (1906), 231–232.

On the first day of April in the year of our Lord one thousand eight hundred and thirty-five the writer of this paper commenced his labors in a cotton mill as bobbin boy, or, as it was termed in those days, back boy. The mill was in the state of Rhode Island being in the town of Coventry. It was owned by a man who was at one time Governor of Rhode Island, a man who was a progressive and intelligent manufacturer. His mill was "up-to-date" and among the most successful in the country at that time.

My work was to put in the roving on a pair of mules containing 256 spindles. It required three hands, — a spinner, a foreside piecer and a back boy, — to keep that pair of mules in operation . . .

The running time for that mill, on an average, was about fourteen hours per day. In the summer months we went in as early as we could see, worked about an hour and a half, and then had a half hour for breakfast. At twelve o'clock we had another half hour for dinner, and then we worked until the stars were out.

From September 20 until March 20, we went to work at five o'clock in the morning and came out at eight o'clock at night, having the same hours for meals as in the summer time.

For my services I was allowed forty-two cents per week, which, being analyzed, was seven cents per day, or one-half cent per hour.

The proprietor of that mill was accustomed to make a contract with his help on the first day of April, for the coming year. That contract was supposed to be sacred and it was looked upon as a disgrace to ignore the contracts thus made. On one of these anniversaries, a mother with several children suggested to the proprietor that the pay seemed small. The proprietor replied "You get enough to eat, don't you?" The mother said, "Just enough to keep the wolf from the door." He then remarked, "You get enough clothes to wear, don't you?" to which she answered, "Barely enough to cover our nakedness." "Well," said the proprietor, "We want the rest." And that proprietor, on the whole, was as kind and considerate to his help as was any other manufacturer at that time.

The opportunities for an education among the factory help were exceedingly limited, as you can well see, both from the standpoint of time and from the standpoint of money.

2. Andrew Carnegie gets his start in life, 1850

Andrew Carnegie, *Autobiography* (Boston and New York: Houghton Mifflin Company, 1920), pp. 31–38.

The great question now was, what could be found for me to do. I had just completed my thirteenth year, and I fairly panted to get to work that I might help the family to a start in the new land. The prospect of want had become to me a frightful nightmare. My thoughts at this period centered in the determination that we should make and save enough of money to produce three hundred dollars a year — twenty-five dollars monthly, which I figured was the sum required to keep us without being dependent upon others. Every necessary thing was very cheap in those days.

The brother of my Uncle Hogan would often ask what my parents meant to do with me, and one day there occurred the most tragic of all scenes I have ever witnessed. Never can I forget it. He said, with the kindest intentions in the world, to my mother, that I was a likely boy and apt to learn; and he believed that if a basket were fitted out for me with knickknacks to sell, I could peddle them around the wharves and make quite a considerable sum. I never knew what an enraged woman meant till then. My mother was sitting sewing at the moment, but she sprang to her feet with outstretched hands and shook them in his face.

"What! my son a peddler and go among rough men upon the wharves! I would rather throw him into the Allegheny River. Leave me!" she cried, pointing to the door, and Mr. Hogan went.

She stood a tragic queen. The next moment she had broken down, but only for a few moments did tears fall and sobs come. Then she took her two boys in her arms and told us not to mind her foolishness. There were many things in the world for us to do and we could be useful men, honored and respected, if we always did what was right.

    ·   ·   ·   ·   ·

Soon after this incident my father found it necessary to give up hand-loom weaving and to enter the cotton factory of Mr. Blackstock, an old Scotsman in Allegheny City, where we lived. In this factory he also obtained for me a position as bobbin boy, and my first work was done there at one dollar and twenty cents per week. It was a hard life. In the winter father and I had to rise and breakfast in the darkness, reach the factory before it was daylight, and, with a short interval for lunch, work till after dark. The hours hung heavily upon me and in the work itself I took no pleasure; but the cloud had a silver lining, as it gave me the feeling that I was doing something for my world — our family.

    ·   ·   ·   ·   ·

Soon after this Mr. John Hay, a fellow-Scotch manufacturer of bobbins in Allegheny City, needed a boy, and asked whether I would not go into his service. I went, and received two dollars per week; but at first the work was even more irksome than the factory. I had to run a small steam-engine and to fire the boiler in the cellar of the bobbin factory. It was too much for me. I found myself night after night, sitting up in bed trying the steam gauges, fearing at one time that the steam was too low and that the workers above would complain that they had not power enough, and at another time that the steam was too high and that the boiler might burst.

But all this it was a matter of honor to conceal from my parents. They had their own troubles and bore them. I must play the man and bear mine. My hopes were high, and I looked every day for some change to take place. What it was to be I knew not, but that it would come I felt certain if I kept on. Besides, at this date I was not beyond asking myself what Wallace would have done and what a Scotsman ought to do. Of one thing I was sure, he ought never to give up.

One day the chance came. Mr. Hay had to make out some bills. He had no clerk, and was himself a poor penman. He asked me what kind of hand I could write, and gave me some writing to do. The result pleased him, and he found it convenient thereafter to let me make out his bills. I was also good at figures; and he soon found it to be to his interest — and besides, dear old man, I believe he was moved by good feeling toward the white-haired boy, for he had a kind heart and was Scotch and wished to relieve me from the engine — to put me at other things, less objectionable except in one feature.

It now became my duty to bathe the newly made spools in vats of oil. Fortunately there was a room reserved for this purpose and I was alone, but not all the resolution I could muster, nor all the indignation I felt at my own weakness, prevented my stomach from behaving in a most perverse way. I never succeeded in overcoming the nausea produced by the smell of the oil. Even Wallace and Bruce proved impotent here. But if I had to lose breakfast, or dinner,

I had all the better appetite for supper, and the allotted work was done. A real disciple of Wallace or Bruce could not give up; he would die first.

My service with Mr. Hay was a distinct advance upon the cotton factory, and I also made the acquaintance of an employer who was very kind to me. Mr. Hay kept his books in single entry, and I was able to handle them for him; but hearing that all great firms kept their books in double entry, and after talking over the matter with my companions, John Phipps, Thomas N. Miller, and William Cowley, we all determined to attend night school during the winter and learn the larger system. So the four of us went to a Mr. Williams in Pittsburgh and learned double-entry bookkeeping.

One evening, early in 1850, when I returned home from work, I was told that Mr. David Brooks, manager of the telegraph office, had asked my Uncle Hogan if he knew where a good boy could be found to act as messenger. Mr. Brooks and my uncle were enthusiastic draught-players, and it was over a game of draughts that this important inquiry was made. Upon such trifles do the most momentous consequences hang. A word, a look, an accent, may affect the destiny not only of individuals, but of nations. He is a bold man who calls anything a trifle. Who was it who, being advised to disregard trifles, said he always would if any one could tell him what a trifle was? The young should remember that upon trifles the best gifts of the gods often hang.

My uncle mentioned my name, and said he would see whether I would take the position. I remember so well the family council that was held. Of course I was wild with delight. No bird that ever was confined in a cage longed for freedom more than I. Mother favored, but father was disposed to deny my wish. It would prove too much for me, he said; I was too young and too small. For the two dollars and a half per week offered it was evident that a much larger boy was expected. Late at night I might be required to run out into the country with a telegram, and there would be dangers to encounter. Upon the whole my father said that it was best that I should remain where I was. He subsequently withdrew his objection, so far as to give me leave to try, and I believe he went to Mr. Hay and consulted with him. Mr. Hay thought it would be for my advantage, and although, as he said, it would be an inconvenience to him, still he advised that I should try, and if I failed he was kind enough to say that my old place would be open for me.

This being decided, I was asked to go over the river to Pittsburgh and call on Mr. Brooks. My father wished to go with me, and it was settled that he should accompany me as far as the telegraph office, on the corner of Fourth and Wood Streets. It was a bright, sunshiny morning and this augured well. Father and I walked over from Allegheny to Pittsburgh, a distance of nearly two miles from our house. Arrived at the door I asked father to wait outside. I insisted upon going alone upstairs to the second or operating floor to see the great man and learn my fate. I was led to this, perhaps, because I had by that time begun to consider myself something of an American. At first boys used to call me "Scotchie! Schotchie!" and I answered, "Yes, I'm Scotch and I am proud of the name." But in speech and in address the broad Scotch had been worn off to a slight extent, and I imagined that I could make a smarter showing if alone with Mr. Brooks than if my good old Scotch father were present, perhaps to smile at my airs.

I was dressed in my one white linen shirt, which was usually kept sacred for the Sabbath day, my blue roundabout, and my whole Sunday suit. I had at that time, and for a few weeks after I entered the telegraph service, but one linen suit of summer clothing; and every Saturday night, no matter if that was my night on duty and I did not return till near midnight, my mother washed those clothes and ironed them, and I put them on fresh on Sabbath morning. There was nothing that heroine did not do in the struggle we were making for elbow room in the western world. Father's long factory hours tried his strength, but he, too, fought the

good fight like a hero and never failed to encourage me.

The interview was successful. I took care to explain that I did not know Pittsburgh, that perhaps I would not do, would not be strong enough; but all I wanted was a trial. He asked me how soon I could come, and I said that I could stay now if wanted. And, looking back over the circumstance, I think that answer might well be pondered by young men. It is a great mistake not to seize the opportunity. The position was offered to me; something might occur, some other boy might be sent for. Having got myself in I proposed to stay there if I could. Mr. Brooks very kindly called the other boy — for it was an additional messenger that was wanted — and asked him to show me about, and let me go with him and learn the business. I soon found opportunity to run down to the corner of the street and tell my father that it was all right, and to go home and tell mother that I had got the situation.

And that is how in 1850 I got my first real start in life. From the dark cellar running a steam-engine at two dollars a week, begrimed with coal dirt, without a trace of the elevating influences of life, I was lifted into paradise, yes, heaven, as it seemed to me, with newspapers, pens, pencils, and sunshine about me. There was scarcely a minute in which I could not learn and how little I knew. I felt that my foot was upon the ladder and that I was bound to climb.

Working girls in New York, 1845

1. Umbrella and parasol makers
New York Daily Tribune, Sept. 17, 1845.

There are many large establishments in the City, some of them giving employment to thirty or forty hands each. The youngest girls employed are about fifteen or sixteen years of age.

Covering Umbrellas or Parasols requires a good deal of strength and skill, which are required to make the work *fit nicely,* and girls younger than fifteen are seldom employed in this business.

The girls who work at this business are mostly Americans. There are a few Germans and Irish; but the Americans are considered the best workers . . . There are some places in the City where the girls are required to furnish their own thread. — This to the uninitiated at first would appear to be no great hardship; but when we take into consideration the large numbers of umbrellas made and the few cents apiece these poor girls are allowed for their work on them, this thread becomes quite an important item.

The girls work about ten hours a day. They bring their dinners with them, as they generally live at such a distance from the establishment that it would take up too much of their time to go home and return again. They are paid for their work by the piece. Some of the girls at the establishment are permitted to take their work to their homes and do it there; but these are good and well-tried hands, who have been long employed . . . At the prices usually paid the girls at this trade can make, some of them twenty shillings, some three dollars and some who are *extraordinarily smart,* four and five dollars a week. There are many who do not earn twenty shillings. These are to be found chiefly among that class who work on the commonest umbrellas made of coarse muslins, cane frames, tin tips, &c. For covering these they get from four to six cents apiece. This is the kind of umbrellas which keep off a shower about as well as a sieve, and generally turn inside out when going round a corner.

---

2. Milliners

New York Daily Tribune, Sept. 16, 1845.

The condition of the Milliner-girls in respect to mental and physical education, moral and social refinement, and all those graces which create an atmosphere of enchantment around the female sex, must, as a general remark, be deplorable. In the keen and bitter competition which pervades every branch of business the price of labor is kept down to the lowest possible point — although one would suppose that the large profits of Millinery bore so magnificent relations to the cost of labor as to avoid the necessity of such a result. But when or where was the price of labor *not* cut down as low and as fast as possible? What branch of employers, as a class, have ever come forward to arrest the downward tendency of wages?

The Milliner-girls mostly go to the business very young and with a most deficient common education. While engaged in their apprenticeship they probably board with some poor relative or friend and have to work over-hours to pay for their homely accommodations and meager fare. They have of course no time for study; and we have never heard that their advantages for moral improvement were conspicuous. At the end of their apprenticeship, if they get work, they make $2.50 or $3 per week. Their board and washing cost at least $2 of this and their clothes must also be provided for somehow. What ought we to look for under these circumstances?

It is generally known that there is a class of pretended "Milliner shops" which are only used as a mask for the most disgraceful practices. The proverbial notoriety of these has served in the minds of some persons to cast a stain upon all women engaged in the Millinery business. But this is cruel and unjust. As a general thing the Milliners are as virtuous as any other class of females exposed to similar trials, hardships and temptations. Let those who look harshly upon the errors and vices of the hard-working classes surround themselves in imagination with poverty, want, weariness, lack of healthful food and sleep, and ponder well on what would be *their* reflections on beholding the gay and joyous life of vice as it appears outwardly, and they will learn to pity while they do not cease to condemn the unfortunate guilty.

Child labor in Utopia

1. Robert Owen on child labor

Robert Owen, *Observations on the Effect of the Manufacturing System,* 2d ed. (London, 1817), pp. 9–11.

Robert Owen (1771–1858), the British reformer and socialist, agitated for child labor laws in Britain. He believed, however, that children over ten ought to work. Thus, in the utopian community which he founded in New Harmony, Indiana, in 1825, children shared the burden of labor.

In the manufacturing districts it is common for parents to send their children of both sexes at seven or eight years of age, in winter as well as summer, at six o'clock in the morning, sometimes of course in the dark, and occasionally amidst frost and snow, to enter the manufactories, which are often heated to a high temperature, and contain an atmosphere far from being the most favourable to human life, and in which all those employed in them very frequently continue until twelve o'clock at noon, when an hour is allowed for dinner, after which they return to remain, in a majority of cases, till eight o'clock at night.

The children now find they must labour incessantly for their bare subsistence: they have not been used to innocent, healthy, and rational amusements; they are not permitted the requisite time, if they had been previously accustomed to enjoy them. They know not what relaxation means, except by the actual cessation from labour. They are surrounded by others similarly circumstanced with themselves; and thus passing on from childhood to youth, they become gradually initiated, the young men in particular, but often the young females also, in the seductive pleasures of the pot-house and inebriation: for which their daily hard labour, want of better habits, and the general vacuity of their minds, tend to prepare them.

. . . The direct object of these observations is to effect the amelioration and avert the danger. The only mode by which these objects can be accomplished is to obtain an Act of Parliament,

1st. To limit the regular hours of labour in mills of machinery to 12 per day, including one hour and a half for meals.

2nd. To prevent children from being employed in mills of machinery until they shall be 10 years old, or that they shall not be employed more than 6 hours per day until they shall be 12 years old.

3rd. That children of either sex shall not be admitted into any manufactory, — after a time to be named, — until they can read and write in an useful manner, understand the first four rules of arithmetic, and the girls be likewise competent to sew their common garments of clothing.

2. Child labor at Brook Farm

Constitution of Brook Farm, in O. B. Frothingham, *Transcendentalism in New England* (Boston, 1903), p. 161.

Brook Farm, founded in 1841, was a product of transcendentalism. Its founder, George Ripley, a Boston Unitarian minister, aimed at creating a society which would afford a wholesome and simple life, free of the pressures of a competitive society.

Children over ten years of age shall be provided with employment in suitable branches of industry; they shall be credited for such portions of each annual dividend, as shall be decided by the Association, and on the completion of their education in the Association at the age of twenty, shall be entitled to a certificate of stock to the amount of credits in their favor, and may be admitted as members of the Association.

E. OPPOSITION TO CHILD LABOR AND EFFORTS AT REGULATION

Protests against child labor, 1830–1836

1. The suffering of children in Philadelphia factories

Mechanics' Free Press, Aug. 21, 1830.

In looking over one of your late numbers, I was rejoiced to find that some friend has noticed the sufferings of people employed in our manufactories; particularly in that of cotton. It is a well known fact, that the principal part of the helps in cotton factories consist of boys and girls, we may safely say from six to seventeen years of age, and are confined to steady employment during the longest days in the year, from daylight until dark, allowing, at the outside, one hour and a half per day. In consequence of this close confinement, it renders it entirely impossible for the parents of such children to obtain for them any education or knowledge, save that of working that machine, which they are compelled to work, and that too with a small sum, that is hardly sufficient to support nature, while they on the other hand are rolling in wealth, of[f] the vitals of these poor children every day. We noticed the observation of our Pawtucket friend in your number of June 19th, 1830, lamenting the grievances of the children employed in those factories. We think his observations very correct, with regard to their being brought up as ignorant as Arabs of the Desert; for we are confident that not more than one-sixth of the boys and girls employed in such factories are capable of reading or writing their own name. We have known many instances

where parents who are capable of giving their children a trifling education one at a time, deprived of that opportunity by their employer's threats, that if they did take one child from their employ (a short time for school), such family must leave the employment — and we have even known these threats put in execution. Now as our friend observes, we may establish schools and academies, and devise every means for the instruction of youth in vain, unless we also give time for application; we have heard it remarked to some employers, that it would be commendable to congress to shorten the hours of labour in factories; the reply was: it would be an infringement on the rights of the people. We know the average number of hands employed by one manufacturer to be, at the lowest estimate, fifty men, women and children. Now the query is: whether this individual, or this number employed by him, is the people.

. . . We think it is high time the public should begin to notice the evil that it begets. We see the evil that follows the system of long labor much better than we can express it; but we hope our weak endeavors may not prove ineffectual.

2. Child labor leads to delinquency

Joseph Tuckerman, *An Essay on the Wages Paid to Females for their Labour* (Philadelphia, 1830), pp. 21–35.

Tuckerman (1778–1840), a Unitarian clergyman, was minister to the poor in Boston, ca. 1825–1830.

. . . Even in a time of prosperity, the number of girls, as well as of boys, who are . . . constantly exposed to moral ruin, is alarmingly great. And if we add to these, who are living with their parents, the large number of boys, who, while they can only, and very imperfectly read and write, and have not begun to cipher, are taken from school to be placed in shops and offices, not as apprentices, but as errand boys, and who will therefore grow up in ignorance, and probably be alone the associates of vicious boys; and of girls who are put to service at twelve, and fourteen years of age, in families in which their education and their virtue are unregarded; — the number of children of the poor, in a large city, demanding the most solemn interest in their dangers, and the most earnest efforts for their rescue, will be considerably enlarged. Some of the children to whom I refer, are truants from our schools. Some are kept at home by their parents, either to gather chips, or to beg, or to be market boys. And some are suffered by their parents to live where they will, and as they will, provided only that they occasion to them as little inconvenience as may be. What, then, in these various families, must be the effects on children, of a time of great and pressing want, when it shall scarcely be practicable, by any honest occupation, to obtain the means of subsistence? Can it be doubted, whether the number of young vagrants, in such a time, will be greatly increased? Or, is it doubted, whether they will be proportionally more dishonest, or more reckless in the sins to which they have become accustomed? This, to my mind, is one of the most affecting of the aspects of a time of great distress among the poor; and unless, at such a time, some strong means shall be used to prevent the evil, it will be found that a few months only of peculiar want and difficulty will be sufficient, to add a large per centage to the amount of future crime, and wretchedness.

There is a view of this subject, which, if it could be brought distinctly before the public, could hardly fail, I think, at once to make a deep and strong impression of the moral dangers of a large class of children in our cities, now but too little regarded by us; and to excite an active sympathy for the families to which they belong. I refer to the disclosures which might be obtained, of the causes of crime, by a careful examination and comparison of the cases of juvenile offences, which are brought before our Police Courts. Ask the magistrates of these courts, from whence come the children who are arraigned before them for pilfering, and whom they are every week sending to the Refuge, or to Prison? They will tell you, that three fourths of them are from families, which have looked to these children *for a part of their means of support.* And if they have looked into these cases, they will tell you also, that some of these children have been kept from school, that they might beg; and others, that by any service they might earn a dollar a week, to be appropriated for the payment of rent, or for the purchase of necessary food. Is it asked, from whence arises the dependence of these parents upon their children? I answer, often, without doubt, from the idleness and intemperance of the parents. But not always. There are cases, and very affecting cases, in which poor mothers, widows, who have three, four, or five children, who must be sheltered, and fed, and clothed, and warmed; and for whom they cannot, by their best labours, provide a home, and the absolute necessaries of existence. These children, to a considerable extent, form a distinct class. They have other associations with life, and form other habits, than the children who are in a regular course of education at school. They have much time, every day, which they know not how to appropriate to any useful purpose; and they are every day at once surrounded by temptations to dishonesty, while passion, and appetite, and all the lower propensities of our nature are developing within them, and maturing under the influences, which are most suited to make them the governing principles in the mind. — I pity the man who can look upon all this evil, and say that these parents alone are accountable for it . . .

3. New England workers take a stand on child labor, 1832

Boston Evening Transcript, March 24, 1832.

The New England Association of Farmers, Mechanics and other Working-men was organized in Providence, Rhode Island, in December 1831 to promote the ten hour labor movement. The association resolved to appoint vigilance committees in each state represented "to collect and publish facts respecting the conditions of labouring men, women, and children." Although advocating the extension of educational privileges to working children, the association did not demand an abolition of child labor.

Report of the Committee appointed by the New England Association of Farmers, Mechanics and other Working-men, to take into consideration the subject of the education of children in manufacturing districts.

The Committee ask leave to report: That from statements of facts made to your committee, from delegates to this body, the number of youth and children of both sexes, under sixteen years of age, employed in Manufactories, constitute about two fifths of the whole number of persons employed. From the returns from a number of manufactories, your committee have made up the following summary, which, with some few exceptions and slight variations, they are fully persuaded will serve as a fair specimen of the general state of things. The regular returns made, include establishments in Massachusetts, New-Hampshire and Rhode Island; which employ altogether something more that four thousand hands.[1] Of these, about sixteen hundred are between the ages of seven and sixteen years. In the return from Hope Factory, R.I., it is stated that the practice is, to ring the first bell in the morning, at ten minutes after

1. In this statement, Lowell and Pawtucket are not included, nor in fact any establishment but those named in the report. [Note in Committee Report.]

the break of day, the second bell ten minutes after the first, and in five minutes after which, or in twenty-five minutes after the break of day, all hands are to be at their labor. The time for shutting the gates at night, as the signal for labor to cease, is eight o'clock, by the *Factory time,* which is from twenty to twenty-five minutes *behind* the *true time.* And the only respite from labor during the day, is twenty-five minutes at breakfast, and the same number at dinner. From the village of Nashua, in the town of Dunstable, N.H. we learn that the time of labor is from the break of day in the morning, until eight o'clock in the evening; and that the *Factory time* is twenty-five minutes *behind* the *true Solar time.*

.   .   .   .   .

From these facts, your committee gather the following conclusions: 1. That on a general average the youth and children that are employed in Cotton Mills, are compelled to labor at least thirteen and a half, perhaps fourteen hours per day, Factory time; and 2. That in addition to this, there are about twenty, to twenty-five minutes added, by reason of that time being so much slower than the true Solar time; thus making a day of labor to consist of at least fourteen hours, winter and summer, and out of which is allowed, on an average, not to exceed one hour, for rest and refreshment. Your committee also learn that in general, no child can be taken from a Cotton Mill, to be placed at School, for a time, however short, without certain loss of employ; as with very few exceptions, no provision is made by manufacturers, to obtain supernumerary help of this description, in order that one class may enjoy the advantages of the school, while the other class is employed in the mill. Nor are parents, having a number of children in a mill, allowed to withdraw one or more, without withdrawing the whole; and for which reason, as such children are generally the offspring of parents, whose poverty has made them entirely dependent on the will of their employers, any are very seldom taken from the mills, to be placed at school.

From all the facts in the case, it is with regret, that your committee are absolutely forced to the conclusion, that the only opportunities allowed to children generally, employed in manufactories, to obtain an education, are on the Sabbath, and after half past eight o'clock, of the evening of other days. To these facts, however, your committee take pleasure in adding two or three others of a more honorable character. It is believed, that in the town of Lowell, no children are admitted to the labors of the mills, under twelve years of age; and that the various corporations provide and support a sufficient number of good schools, for the education of such as have not attained that age. In the Chickopee Factory Village, Springfield, Mass., and also in the town of New Market, N.H., we also learn that schools are provided, and the children actually employed in mills, allowed the privilege of attending school, during a portion, say about one quarter of the year. Your committee mention these facts as honorable exceptions to the general rule, with a desire to do justice to all concerned, and the hope that others may be inspired by their example to go much further still, in their efforts to remove the existing evils. A few more instances of the above character may exist; but if so, they have not come to the knowledge of your Committee, and they have every reason to believe them to be extremely rare.

Your committee cannot therefore, without the violation of a solemn trust, withhold their unanimous opinion, that the opportunities allowed to children and youth employed in manufactories, to obtain an education suitable to the character of American Freemen, and the *wives* and *mothers* of such, are altogether inadequate to the purpose: That the evils complained of are unjust and cruel; and are no less than the sacrifice of the dearest interest of thousands of the rising generation of our country, to the cupidity and avarice of their employers. And they can see no other result in prospect, as likely to eventuate from such practices,

than generation on generation, reared up in profound ignorance, and the final prostration of their liberties at the shrine of a powerful aristocracy. Deeply deploring the existing evils, and deprecating the dreadful evils that may hereafter be practiced, your committee respectfully recommend the adoption of the following resolution:

Resolved, That a Committee of Vigilance be appointed in each State represented in this Convention, whose duty it shall be to collect and publish facts respecting the condition of laboring men, women and children, and abuses practiced on them by their employers; that it shall also be the duty of said committee, as soon as may be, to get up Memorials to the Legislatures of their respective States, praying for the regulation of the hours of labor, according to the standard adopted by this Association, and for some wholesome regulations with regard to the education of children and youth employed in Manufactories; and to make report of their doings at the meeting of this body, on the first Thursday of September next.

Voted, That in accordance with the foregoing resolution, the Delegates constituting this body, also constitute a committee of vigilance for the purposes therein specified; and forward the statements of facts they may obtain from time to time, for publication in the *New England Artisan.*

---

4. Child labor means neglect of education

Seth Luther, *An Address to the Working Men of New England on the State of Education and on the Condition of the Producing Classes in Europe and America . . .* (Boston, 1832), pp. 35–36.

Seth Luther (fl. 1817–1846), a self-educated New England carpenter, was elected secretary of the General Friends Convention in Boston in 1834. As a labor reformer and pamphleteer, he fought for a ten-hour work day and better conditions for women and children in the cotton mills.

―――――――――――――――

. . . Our wish is to show that education is neglected, and that as a matter of course, because if 13 hours actual labour, is required each day, it is *impossible* to attend to education among children, or improvement among adults. With regard to hours of labour in cotton mills, there is a difference here as well as in England. In Manchester 12 hours *only* is the rule, while in some other towns in England many more are required. The mills *generally* in New England, run 13 hours the year round, that is, actual labour for all hands; to which add one hour for two meals, making 14 hours actual labour — for a man, or woman, or child, must labour hard to go a quarter, and sometimes half a mile, and eat his dinner or breakfast in 30 minutes and get back to the mill. At the Eagle mills, Griswold, Connecticut, 15 hours and 10 minutes actual labour in the mill are required; at another mill in the vicinity, 14 hours of actual labour are required. It needs no argument, to prove that education *must* be, and is almost entirely neglected. Facts speak in a voice not to be misunderstood, or misinterpreted. In 8 mills all on one stream, within a distance of two miles, we have 168 persons who can neither read nor write. This is in Rhode Island. A committee of working men in Providence, report "that in Pawtucket there are at least *five hundred children,* who scarcely know what a school is. These facts, say they, are adduced to show the blighting influence of the manufacturing system as at present conducted, on the progress of education; and to add to the darkness of the picture, if blacker shades are necessary to rouse the spirit of indignation, which should glow within our breasts at such disclosures, in all the mills which the enquiries of the committee have been able to reach, books, pamphlets, and newspapers are *absolutely prohibited.* This may serve as a tolerable example for every manufacturing village in Rhode Island." In 12 of the United States, there are 57,000 persons,

male and female, employed in cotton and woollen mills, and other establishments connected with them; about two-fifths of this number, or 31,044 are under 16 years of age, and 6,000 are under the age of 12 years. Of this 31,044, there are in Rhode Island *alone* 3,472 under 16 years of age. The school fund is, in that State, raised in considerable part by lottery. Now we all know, that the poor are generally the persons who support this legalized gambling; for the rich as a general rule, seldom buy tickets. This fund then, said to be raised by the rich, for the education of the poor, is actually drawn from the pockets of the *poor,* to be expended by the rich, on *their own children,* while this large number of children (3,472) are entirely, and totally deprived of all benefit of the school fund, by what is *called* the *American System.* Actually *robbed* of what is *emphatically* their own, by being *compelled* to labour in these *"principalities of the destitute"* and these *"palaces of the poor,"* for 13 hours per diem, the year round. *What must be* the result of this state of things? "We cannot regard even in anticipation, the contamination of moral and political degradation spreading its baleful influence throughout the community, through the medium of the uneducated part of the present generation, promulgated and enhanced in the future, by the increase of posterity, without starting with horror from the scene, as from the clankings of a TYRANT's chain."

.   .   .   .   .

"If education and intelligence is the *only sure* FOUNDATION of public safety," and if we are convinced that there are causes in active operation sapping and mining that foundation, can any man say, "It is nothing to me?" "If the children of the poor ought to be instructed as well as the rich," ought we not to see that it is done? If it depends on education whether we "live in a peaceable, orderly community, free from excess, outrage and crime, can we say it is nothing to us?" Who knows but in the course of events his son or daughter, or sister or brother, will not be driven into a cotton mill by the hard hand of adverse fortune, and be made to suffer the evils we have described. If "without the assistance of the common people a free government cannot exist," and we find that the capability to govern depends on intelligence and learning; is it not a fearful reflection that so many thousands of children are deprived of education, and so many adults of every opportunity for mental improvement? Let us no longer be deceived. Let us not think we are free until working-men no longer trust their affairs in the hands of designing demagogues.

5. The pathos of child labor

"The Free Enquirer," in *New Harmony Gazette,* IV (July 14, 1832), 300–301.

I often think how once we used in summer fields
    to play,
And run about and breathe the air that made
    us glad and gay;
We used to gather buttercups and chase the
    butterfly;
I loved to feel the light breeze lift my hair as
    it went by!

Do you still play in those bright fields? and are
    the flowers still there?
There are no fields where I live now — no
    flowers any where!
But day by day I go and turn a dull and tedious
    wheel;
You cannot think how sad, and tired, and faint
    I often feel.

I hurry home to snatch the meal my mother can
    supply,
Then back I hasten to the task — that not to
    hate I try.
At night my mother kisses me, when she has
    combed my hair,
And laid me in my little bed, but — I'm not
    happy there:

I dream about the factory, the fines that on us
    wait —
I start and ask my father if — I have not lain
    too late?
And once I heard him sob and say — "Oh bet-
    ter were a grave,
Than such a life as this for thee, thou little sin-
    less slave!"

I wonder if I ever shall obtain a holiday?
Oh, if I do, I'll go to you and spend it all in
    play!
And then I'd bring some flowers home, if you
    will give me some,
And at my work I'll think of them and holidays
    to come!

6. Children work longer hours than convicts

New York, Assembly, "Report of the committee on trade and manufactures, on the memorial of sundry inhabitants in the counties of Oneida and Otsego," Doc. 205, *Documents, 1835* (Albany, 1835), III, 1–5.

That the number of hours they [children] are required by the established customs and rules of these incorporations to labor each day, is altogether too great a proportion of their time,

    .   .   .   .

That the persons employed in these manufactories, are required to labor from twelve to fourteen hours each day, being several hours more daily labor than is exacted even from the convicts in our State Prisons; these laborers have thus no opportunity for ordinary and necessary relaxation and recreation, or for mental improvement, and the children among them are necessarily brought up in comparative ignorance, and are unfitted to become valuable citizens.

Your committee, as well from the facts stated in the petition as from other information upon which they can rely, and their own observation, are satisfied that the long and continued confinement at labor in these manufactories, in a hot and somewhat impure atmosphere, is unfavorable to health, and injurious to the constitutions of those who are thus confined, and particularly to children.

.   .   .   .   .   .

Your committee can not conceive of any case where any portion of persons in this country could be placed where they would be more likely, from their peculiar situation, to be improperly operated upon in making their contracts than that of the poor and indigent females and children in these manufactories, who are literally driven there, in many instances, to gain a subsistence, by the death of parents and other misfortunes, and are, of all others that can be imagined, the least able to assert and maintain their rights. In many establishments, where none but stout, healthy men are employed, who are able and competent to understand and maintain their rights when invaded, the case is entirely different.

---

7. A pro-slavery attack on child labor

William J. Grayson, *The Hireling and the Slave,* 2d ed. (Charleston, 1855), pp. 23–46; first published 1836.

William J. Grayson (1788–1863), a lawyer, was a member of the South Carolina House of Representatives and Senate. He wrote *The Hireling and the Slave* while serving as a Whig in the United States House of Representatives.

There, unconcerned, the philanthropic eye
Beholds each phase of human misery;

Sees the worn child compelled in mines to slave
Through narrow seams of coal, a living grave,
Driven from the breezy hill, the sunny glade,
By ruthless hearts, the drudge of labour made,
Unknown the boyish sport, the hours of play,
Stript of the common boon, the light of day,
Harnessed like brutes, like brutes to tug and
    strain
And drag, on hands and knees, the loaded wain:
There crammed in huts, in reeking masses
    thrown,
All moral sense and decency unknown,
With no restraint, but what the felon knows,
With the sole joy, that beer or gin bestows,
To gross excess and brutalizing strife,
The drunken Hireling dedicates his life.
There women prostitute themselves for bread,

.   .   .   .   .   .

Childhood bestows no childish sports or toys,
Age, neither reverence nor repose enjoys,
Labour, with hunger, wages ceaseless strife,
And want and suffering only end with life;
In crowded huts, contagious ills prevail,
Dull typhus lurks and deadlier plagues assail,
Gaunt famine prowls around his pauper prey,
And daily sweeps his ghastly hosts away;
Unburied corpses taint the summer air,
And crime and outrage revel with despair.

.   .   .   .   .   .

Taught by the Master's efforts, by his care,
Fed, clothed, protected, many a patient year,
From trivial numbers now to millions grown,
With all the Whiteman's useful arts their own,
Industrious, docile, skilled in wood and field,
To guide the plough, the sturdy axe to wield,
The Negroes schooled by Slavery embrace
The highest portion of the Negro race;
And none the savage native will compare,
Of barbarous Guinea, with its offspring here.
    If bound to daily labour while he lives,
His is the daily bread that labour gives;
Guarded from want, from beggary secure,
He never feels what Hireling crowds endure,
Nor knows, like them, in hopeless want to
    crave,

For wife and child, the comforts of the slave,
Or the sad thought that, when about to die,
He leaves them to the world's cold charity,
And sees them slowly seek the poor-house
    door —
The last vile hated refuge of the poor.

Compulsory school attendance laws for factory children

Governors, state legislators, and other public officials often called attention to the neglect of education among factory children. Prior to the Civil War, however, only the New England states and Pennsylvania adopted legislation making specified periods of school attendance compulsory for working children. For a summary of such laws see below, doc. 7.

1. Governor of Rhode Island urges legislature to meet educational needs of factory children, 1818

Address of Governor Nehemiah R. Knight of Rhode Island to the Gentlemen of the Senate and Gentlemen of the House of Representatives, *Rhode Island, Acts and Resolves, 1818,* Oct. Sess. (Providence, 1818), pp. 3–4.

While the General Government protects and encourages agriculture, commerce and manufactures, the Legislatures of the several States are the immediate guardians of the public morals and education; to them is more particularly entrusted the duty of providing for the cultivating and enlightening of the mind — a trust so essential in all good societies, and especially so, in a government where all power is vested in the people, and all the acts of the public

functionaries weighed and tested by public opinion. It is true that many persons have done much by establishing Sunday schools in the neighborhood of some of the manufacturing villages of this State; but when we reflect how small a portion of time is appropriated to education by Sunday schools alone, we must be sensible, that the acquirements of the youth who labour in these factories must be extremely limited. And it is a lamentable truth, that too many of the rising generation, who are obliged to labour in those works of almost unceasing application and industry, are growing up without an opportunity of obtaining that education which is necessary for their personal welfare, as well as the welfare of the whole community.

I am well assured a plan can be devised and carried into effect, by the aid of the Legislature, and without any expense to the State, that shall educate them in a manner that will make them not only useful to their country, but also to themselves, and will enable them not only to exercise the privileges of freemen, but be capable of estimating these blessings.

2. Unsuccessful appeal for compulsory school attendance law, New York, 1833

New York, Assembly, "Annual Report of the Superintendent of Common Schools," Doc. 17, *Documents, 1833* (Albany, 1833), I, 23–24.

A strong conviction that something ought to be done to provide the means of instruction for the inmates of the manufacturing establishments, which are building up in various sections of the State, induces the Superintendent again to call the attention of the Legislature to this subject. In many of these establishments children are employed at a very early age; and there is great reason to apprehend, that the necessities or the cupidity of parents and guardians, will, in too many cases, overcome their obligations to their children and to society, and induce them entirely to neglect their education, in order to secure the comparatively miserable stipend which they can earn in these manufactories. Our laws now require the children in the poor-houses to be instructed; and if they are bound out, the law requires a condition in each indenture, that the master will cause such child to be instructed to read and write, and if a male, will cause him to be instructed in the general rules of arithmetic . . .

The policy of all our laws is to secure a good common school education to every child in the State; and the condition of the children who are employed in the manufactories, as to their means of instruction, ought to be carefully inquired into and provided for. The diffusion of education among all classes of our population is deemed of such vital importance to the preservation of our free institutions, that if the obligations which rest upon every good citizen in this particular, are disregarded, the persons having the custody of such children, ought to be visited with such disabilities as will induce them, from interest if not from principle, to cause the children to be instructed, at least in reading, writing and arithmetic.

---

3. Why legislation is needed, Massachusetts, 1836

Massachusetts, House, "Committee Report on the Education of Working Children, 1836," Doc. 49, *Documents, May 17, 1836* (Boston, 1836), pp. 5–14.

The chairman of this committee, James Gordon Carter (1795–1849), was a leading figure in the common school revival in Massachusetts in the 1820's. In 1837 he was appointed the first member of the state Board of Education.

. . . It becomes the solemn and indispensable duty of the representatives of the people to provide seasonably and effectually, that those institutions, which have given to New England her peculiar character for general intelligence and virtue, be not changed with the changing employments of her people.

. . . . . .

It cannot be denied, nor disguised, that the employments, and consequently the condition, of large classes of the population of New England, and especially of Massachusetts, are changed and are rapidly changing . . . The sons and daughters of New England are presented . . . with the alternative of becoming essentially a manufacturing people, or of bidding adieu to their native hills, the land, the home, and the graves of their forefathers, and following the rising glories of the west.

. . . It requires no spirit of prophecy to foresee and to know, that the collection of large masses of children, youth and middle aged persons, of both sexes, into compact villages, is not a circumstance favorable to virtue. Nor is it difficult to understand that a change in occupation, from those diversified employments which characterize a sparse and agricultural population, to the simple operations consequent upon that minute subdivision of labor, upon which the success of manufacturing industry depends, is not a circumstance favorable to intellectual development. By the former, the ingenuity and inventive powers are called into action, in the combination and adaptation of means to ends, and thereby they are developed and strengthened. By the latter employment, the invention having been made by some master spirit, the operative is reduced, in some degree, to the humble sphere of a part of the machinery.

. . . . . .

Two principal causes . . . are in constant operation to frustrate and prevent that universal education which our institutions suppose and require within the sphere of large manufacturing establishments.

1. . . . Labor being dearer in this country, than it is in any other, with which we are brought in competition in manufacturing, operates as a constant inducement to manufacturers to employ female labor, and the labor of children to the exclusion of men's labor, because they can be had cheaper.

2. . . . The families usually collected in our large manufacturing establishments, are either those that have been unfortunate, or from some cause, unsuccessful in agriculture or other employments, and are there collected in despair of obtaining more than a comfortable support, or a bare subsistence; or they are families formed around the establishments, on the strength of the then present prospect of gaining a certain support, by those young people, who depend solely upon their daily wages, and have nothing to expect but what they can obtain from day to day, or week to week. Of course . . . there is a strong interest and an urgent motive to seek *constant* employment for their children, at a very early age, if the wages obtained, can aid them even but little in bearing the burden of their support.

These two causes or principles of interest . . . are operating silently perhaps, but steadily and powerfully to deprive young females particularly, and young children of both sexes, in a large and increasing class in the community, of those means and opportunities of mental and moral development and cultivation, which are essential to their becoming the intelligent mothers and educators of the next generation, and good citizens of the republic.

.   .   .   .   .

. . . In four large manufacturing towns, not, however, including the largest, from which we have no information upon that topic, containing, by the last census, a population of a little less than twenty thousand, there appears to be *eighteen hundred and ninety-five* children, between the ages of 4 and 16, who do not attend the common schools any portion of the year. And from this number there is but a very

slight deduction to be made for those who attend private schools. If full and accurate answers were given by all the towns in the Commonwealth, to the question designed to obtain this information, it is believed there would be developed a state of facts, which would at once arrest the attention of the Legislature, and not only justify, but loudly demand legislative action upon the subject. And this state of facts as appears by the returns, is peculiar in degree and almost in kind to the manufacturing towns.

---

4. The first compulsory school attendance law, Massachusetts, 1836

"An act to provide for the better instruction of youth employed in manufacturing establishment," 1836 — ch. 245, *Laws of Massachusetts, Jan. 1834–Apr. 1836* (Boston, 1836), pp. 950–951.

This law, sponsored by James Gordon Carter (see preceding document), met little legislative opposition. Rhode Island and Connecticut adopted similar legislation in 1840 and 1842 respectively.

Be it enacted by the Senate and House of Representatives, in General Court assembled and by the authority of the same, as follows:

Sec. 1. From and after the first day of April, in the year eighteen hundred and thirty seven, no child under the age of fifteen years shall be employed to labor in any manufacturing establishment, unless such child shall have attended some public or private day school, where instruction is given by a teacher qualified . . . at least three months of the twelve months next preceding any and every year, in which such child shall be so employed.

Sec. 2. The owner, agent or superintendent of any manufacturing establishment, who shall employ any child in such establishment contrary to the provisions of this act, shall forfeit the sum of fifty dollars for each offence, to be recovered by indictment, to the use of common schools in the towns respectively where said establishments may be situated.

---

5. Massachusetts education law evaded by the "cruel and mercenary owners of the children," 1839

Boston Daily Times, July 16, 1839.

In point of education the factory girl who goes young to the mill, and children who grow up in the towns where factories are located, must always be sufferers. The cupidity of parents induces them to place their offspring in one establishment as soon as possible. The law requires that they shall have at least three months schooling in each year, until they arrive at a certain age, and the corporations are liable to punishment if any child is employed by them the whole time. But this law is evaded by the cruel and mercenary owners of the children, who keep them nine months in one factory, and then take them directly to another, with a lie in their mouths, that the children have had three months schooling. Nine months in this factory, fits them to go back to their old situation, and when the mills are short of hands, the superintendents are not very anxious to ascertain the truth: nor do they care much for the welfare of the children or obedience to the law. Here again, is another source from which an ignorant, unhealthy, and permanently unhappy manufacturing population is raised, to swell the numbers of our degraded, enslaved citizens of the country.

---

6. Horace Mann on the implementation of the school attendance law, 1840

Massachusetts, Board of Education, "Third Annual Report of the Secretary, Jan. 1840, Board of Commissioners of Common Schools," *Education and Labor, 1842* (Boston, 1842), pp. 9–13.

The law has now been in operation sufficiently long, to make manifest the intentions of those to whom its provisions apply, and whether those humane provisions are likely to be observed or defeated. From the information obtained, I feel fully authorised to say, that, in the great majority of cases, the law is obeyed. But it is my painful duty also to say, that, in some places, it has been uniformly and systematically disregarded. The law is best observed in the largest manufacturing places. In several of the most extensive manufacturing villages and districts, all practicable measures are taken to prevent a single instance of violation. Some establishments have contributed most generously towards the schools; and, in one case (at Waltham), a corporation, besides paying its proportion of taxes for the support of the public schools in the town, has gratuitously erected three schoolhouses, — the last in 1837, a neat, handsome, modern, stone building, two stories in height, — and maintained schools therein, at a charge, in the whole, upon the corporate funds, of a *principal* sum of more than seven thousand dollars. It would be improper for me here to be more particular than to say, that these generous acts have been done by the *"Boston Manufacturing Company";* though all will regret, that the identity of the individual members who have performed these praise-worthy deeds, should be lost in the generality of the corporate name.

Comparatively speaking, there seems to have been far greater disregard of the law, by private individuals and by small corporations, especially where the premises are rented from year to year, or from term to term, than by the owners or agents of large establishments. Private individuals, renting an establishment for one, or for a few years, — intending to realise from it what profits they can, and then to abandon it and remove from the neighborhood or town where it is situated, — may be supposed to feel less permanent interest in the condition of the people who are growing up around them, and they are less under the control of public opinion in the vicinity. But, without seeking an explanation of the cause, there cannot be a doubt as to the fact.

It is obvious, that the consent of two parties is necessary to the infraction of this law, and to the infliction of this highest species of injustice upon the children whom it was designed to protect . . . Yet, strange to say, there are many parents, not only of our immigrant, but of our native population, so lost to the sacred nature of the relation they sustain towards the children whom they have brought into all the solemn realities of existence, that they go from town to town, seeking opportunities to consign them to unbroken, bodily toil, although it involves the deprivation of all the means of intellectual and moral growth; — thus pandering to their own vicious appetites, by adopting the most efficient measures to make their offspring as vicious as themselves.

If, in a portion of the manufacturing districts in the State, a regular and systematic obedience is paid to the law, while, in other places, it is regularly and systematically disregarded, the inevitable consequences to the latter will be obvious, upon a moment's reflection. The neighborhood or town where the law is broken will soon become the receptacle of the poorest, most vicious, and abandoned parents, who are bringing up their children to be also as poor, vicious, and abandoned as themselves. The whole class of parents, who cannot obtain employment for their children at one place, but are welcomed at another, will circulate through the body politic, until, at last, they will settle down, as permanent residents in the latter; like the vicious humors of the natural body, which being thrown off by every healthy part, at last accumulate and settle upon a diseased spot. Every breach of this law, therefore, inflicts direct and positive injustice, not only upon the children employed, but upon all the industrious and honest communities in which they are employed; because its effect will be to fill those communities with paupers and criminals; — or, at least, with a class of persons, who, without being absolute, technical paupers, draw their subsistence, in a thousand indirect ways, from the neighborhood where they reside; and without being absolute criminals in the eye of the law, still commit a thousand injurious, predatory acts, more harassing and annoying to the peace and security of a village than many classes of positive crimes.

.   .   .   .   .

. . . The children are in their years of minority, and they have no control over their own time or their own actions. The bell is to them what the water-wheel and the main shaft are to the machinery which they superintend. The wheel revolves, and the machinery must go; the bell rings, and the children must assemble. In their hours of work, they are under the police of the establishment; at other times, they are under the police of the neighborhood. Hence this state of things may continue for years, and the peace of the neighborhood remain undisturbed, except perhaps, by a few nocturnal or sabbath-day depredations. The ordinary movements of society may go on without any shocks or collisions, — as, in the human system, a disease may work at the vitals and gain a fatal ascendancy there, before it manifests itself on the surface.

. . . But when the children pass from the condition of restraint to that of freedom, — from years of enforced but impatient servitude to that independence . . . bound, from the political nothingness of a child to the political sovereignty of a man, — then, for that people, who so cruelly neglected and injured them, there will assuredly come a day of retribution. It scarcely needs to be added, on the other hand, that if the wants of the spiritual nature of a child, in the successive stages of its growth, are duly supplied, then a regularity in manual employment is converted from a servitude into a useful habit of diligence, and the child grows up in a daily perception of the wonder-working power of industry, and in the daily realization of the trophies of victorious labor. A majority of the most useful men who have ever lived, were formed under the happy necessity of mingling bodily with mental exertion.

7. Summary of school attendance laws enacted before 1860 (see table below)

Adapted from U.S. Bureau of Labor, *Report on Condition of Woman and Child Wage-Earners in the United States,* VI, 208–209.

Regulation of child labor in factories before the Civil War

1. Massachusetts, 1842

"An act concerning the employment of children in manufacturing establishments," 1842 — ch. 60, *Massachusetts Acts and Resolves, 1839–1842* (Boston, 1842), pp. 561–562.

From and after the passage of this act, no child under the age of twelve years shall be employed in laboring in any manufacturing establishment more than ten hours in any one day.

The owner, agent or superintendent of any manufacturing establishment, who shall know-

School attendance requirements

State	Year	Industries affected	Age group	Required attendance	Enforcement
Massachusetts	1836	Manufacturing	Under 15	3 of 12 months	No provision
	1849	Manufacturing	Under 15	11 weeks	No provision
	1858	Manufacturing	Under 12	18 weeks	No provision
Rhode Island	1840	Manufacturing	Under 12	3 of 12 months	
	1854	Manufacturing	Under 15	3 of 12 months	No provision
Connecticut	1842	All occupations	Under 15	3 of 12 months	School visitors
Vermont	1837	Manufacturing		At discretion of selectman	
New Hampshire	1846	Manufacturing	12 to 15	3 of 12 months	School committies inform on violations
			Under 12	6 of 12 months	
	1848	Manufacturing	12 to 15	12 weeks	No provision
			Under 12	6 of 12 months	
Maine	1847	Cotton and woolen manufacturing	12 to 15	3 of 12 months	No provision
			Under 12	4 of 12 months	
Pennsylvania	1849	Cotton, woolen, silk, paper, bagging, flax	13 to 16	3 of 12 months, consecutively	No provision

New York Street Cry: "Black Your Boots," ca. 1850. Watercolor drawing by A. C. Howland.

New York Street Cry: "Give Me a Penny!" ca. 1850. Watercolor drawing by A. C. Howland.

New York Street Cry: "Extra Sir?" ca. 1850. Watercolor drawing by A. C. Howland.

The Truant Gamblers, 1835. By William S. Mount.

ingly employ any such child under the age of twelve years in such establishment . . . shall forfeit the sum of fifty dollars for each offence, to be recovered in any court of this Commonwealth competent to try the same, to the use of the person prosecuting.

2. Connecticut, 1842

"An act in addition to an act entitled 'An act relating to Masters and Servants,' " 1842 — ch. 28, *Connecticut Public and Private Acts, 1840–1842* (Hartford, 1842), p. 42.

No proprietor or proprietors of any cotton or woolen manufacturing establishment in this State, or person or persons carrying on the business of manufacturing in any such establishment as lessees or in any other manner, or person or persons having charge of the affairs of any such establishment or business, shall employ, or suffer to be employed, or aid or assist in employing in such establishment, any child under fourteen years of age, a greater length of time than ten hours in any one day. And every person who shall violate any of the provisions of this section of this act, shall forfeit and pay for each offence, a penalty of seven dollars.

3. Pennsylvania, 1848

"An act to limit the hours of labor, and to prevent the employment, in factories, of children under twelve years of age," 1848 — ch. 227, *Acts and Laws of Pennsylvania,* 1848 (Philadelphia, 1848), pp. 278–279.

. . . The labor performed during a period of ten hours, on any secular day, of all cotton, woolen, silk, paper, bagging and flax factories, shall be considered a legal day's labor; and that hereafter, no minor or adult engaged in any such factories, shall be holden or required to work more than ten hours on any secular day, or sixty hours in any secular week, and that after the fourth day of July, of the present year, no man shall be admitted as a worker, under the age of twelve years, in any cotton, woolen, silk or flax factory, within this commonwealth; that any owner of or employer in any such factories aforesaid, shall employ any such minor, he shall be adjudged to pay a penalty of fifty dollars one-half thereof to the party so employed, and the other half to the commonwealth, to be recovered in like manner as fines of like amount are now recoverable by law: Provided, That nothing contained in any act shall be construed to prevent minors, above the age of fourteen years, from being employed more than ten hours in any day, if the same be done by special contract with their parents or guardians.

4. Horace Greeley supports a ten-hour law for children under twelve, ca. 1850

Greeley, *Hints Toward Reform,* pp. 30–33.

And while I hold that the State can not properly prescribe that no man shall in any case work more for another than ten hours in any one day . . . it may yet, as the general Protector of the Weak against the Strong, do much, and ought to do much, to mitigate the evils of excessive hours of daily toil. The action I would recommend, and which in one State [New Hampshire] has already in part received the sanction of the Legislature, is substantially as follows:

1. An act forbidding absolutely the employment of children or minors, whether Apprentices or Hired, for more than ten hours per day.

The State has a right to see, and ought to see, that the frames of the rising generations are not shattered nor their constitutions undermined by excessive labor. She should do this for her own sake as well as Humanity's. She has a vital interest in the strength and vigor of those who are to be her future fathers and mothers, her defenders in war, her cultivators and artisans in peace. She may safely make this limitation imperative, since for whatever service it may be necessary to employ labor for a longer term per day there will always be found an abundance of adults, if proper inducements are offered.

sum not less than five, or more than fifty dollars.

§2. That in all engagements to labor in any mechanical or manufacturing business, a day's work, when the contract of labor is silent upon the subject, or where there is no express contract, shall consist of ten hours; and all agreements, contracts, or engagements in reference to such labor, shall be so construed.

§3. That whenever a fine shall be collected, in accordance with the first section of this act, the same shall be paid over to the trustees of the township wherein the trial may be had, and the same shall be by them disbursed for the benefit of common schools.
March 19, 1852.

5. Ohio, 1852

Acts of a General Nature passed by the Fiftieth General Assembly of the State of Ohio, L (Columbus, 1852), 187.

§1. *Be it enacted by the General Assembly of the State of Ohio,* That in all manufactories, workshops and other places used for mechanical or manufacturing purposes, in the state of Ohio, where children under the age of eighteen years, and women, are employed, the time of labor of the persons aforesaid, shall not exceed ten hours for each day; and any owner, stockholder, overseer, employer, clerk or foreman, who shall compel any woman or any child under eighteen years of age, to labor in any day exceeding ten hours, or shall permit any child under the age of fourteen, to labor in any factory, workshop, or other place used for mechanical or manufacturing purposes, for more than ten hours in any one day, where such owner, stockholder, overseer, employer, clerk or foreman has control, such person so offending shall be liable to a prosecution, in the name of the state of Ohio, before any Justice of the Peace or Court of competent jurisdiction of the county, wherein the same shall occur, and upon conviction thereof, be fined in any

6. Rhode Island, 1853

Rhode Island, *Acts and Resolves, January Session, 1853* (Providence, 1853), pp. 245–246.

Unlike preceding acts in Rhode Island and other New England states, this law not only limited the hours of labor but also prohibited employment of children below the age of twelve.

AN ACT to limit the hours of labor and to regulate the employment of children in factories.

It is enacted by the General Assembly as follows:

SECTION 1. From and after the first day of July next, labor performed in any manufacturing establishment and all mechanical labor, during the period of ten hours, in any one day, shall be considered a legal day's work, unless otherwise agreed by the parties, and no minor, under the age of twelve years shall be employed in or about any manufacturing establishment; provided, that the provisions of this section concerning the hours of labor, shall not apply to persons employed solely in packing goods in any warehouse or part of a factory not used for any manufacturing process or for any labor incident to a manufacturing process.

SEC. 2. If any owner of, or employer in, any manufacturing establishment, or his or her agent, shall knowingly and wilfully employ any minor under the age of twelve years as aforesaid, the person so offending, shall pay a penalty of twenty dollars for every such offence, one half thereof shall enure to the complainant and the other half thereof to and for the use of the district school in the district in which such manufacturing establishment is situated.

SEC. 3. Hereafter, no minor who has attained the age of twelve years and is under the age of fifteen years, shall be employed in any manufacturing establishment more than eleven hours in any one day; any owner of, or employer in any manufacturing establishment as aforesaid,

Adapted from U.S. Bureau of Labor, *Report on Condition of Woman and Child Wage-Earners in the United States,* VI, 207–208.

offending against the provisions of this section, shall be liable to a penalty of twenty dollars for every such offence, and one half thereof shall enure to the complainant, and one half thereof to and for the use of the district school in the district in which such manufacturing establishment is situated.

SEC. 4. From and after the first day of July next, if any parent or guardian shall permit or consent to the employment of his or her child or ward under the age of twelve years, in any such manufacturing establishment, or of his or her child or ward, over the age of twelve years and under the age of fifteen, for a longer time than eleven hours in any one day, the person so offending shall forfeit and pay the sum of twenty dollars for every such offence, to be appropriated as provided in the second section of this act.

7. Analysis of child-labor legislation prior to 1860 (see table below)

I. Age of employment

State	Year	Industries affected	Minimum age	Proof of age
Rhode Island	1853	Manufacturing	12	Not required
Connecticut	1855	Manufacturing and mechanical	9	Not required
	1856	Manufacturing and mechanical	10	Not required
Vermont	1837	Manufacturing	At discretion of selectman	Not required
New Jersey	1851	Manufacturing	10	Not required
Pennsylvania	1848	Cotton, woolen, silk, flax	12	Not required
	1849	Cotton, woolen, silk, flax, paper, bagging	13	Not required

II. Limitations on children's work hours

State	Year	Industries affected	Age group	Maximum hours daily	Enforcement
Massachusetts	1842	Manufacturing	Under 12	10	No provision
Rhode Island	1853	Manufacturing	12 to 15	11	No provision
			Under 18	a	No provision
Connecticut	1842	Cotton and woolen	Under 15	10	No provision
	1855	Manufacturing and mechanical	Under 18	11	No provision
	1856	Manufacturing and mechanical	Under 18	12	Violation inquiry by constables and grand jury
Vermont	1837	Manufacturing		At discretion of selectman	
New Hampshire	1847	Manufacturing	Under 15	10, without written consent of parents	No provision
Maine	1848	Manufacturing	Under 16	10	No provision
New Jersey	1851	Manufacturing	Minors	10	No provision
Pennsylvania	1848	Cotton, woolen, silk, paper, bagging, flax	Minors	10	No provision
			Over 14	Over 10 by special contract	
	1849	Cotton, woolen, silk, paper, bagging, flax	13 to 16	10	No provision
	1855	Cotton, woolen, silk, paper, bagging, flax	Minors	10[b]	Constables act on complaint
Ohio	1852	Manufacturing and mechanical	Under 14	10	No provision

[a] The law provided that children under eighteen could not work between the hours of 7:30 P.M. and 5:30 A.M.

[b] The law established a maximum of sixty working hours per week for minors.

Violation of child labor laws in Massachusetts, 1866

Massachusetts, House, "Report of the Special Commission on the Hours of Labor and the Condition and Prospects of the Industrial Classes," Doc. 98, *Documents, 1866* (Boston, 1866), pp. 3–11.

VIOLATION OF THE LAW.

A saddening amount of testimony, by letter and at the hearings, has been brought before the Commission, concerning the frequent and gross violation of this law. We by no means suppose this violation to be universal. We have had cheering testimony from Lowell, in particular, of the faithful observance of the law in that city, and the high regard in which it is held. There may be other places from which we have not heard, where the statute is strictly obeyed.

We present such testimony as we have received.

Erastus Maltby, Esq., of Taunton writes: "I do not think the law of the State, in regard to the working of children in factories, and attending school, is fully and faithfully obeyed in this city."

Henry Jennings, Esq., of New Bedford, writes: "There is a considerable number of cases of children kept away from school. They are employed in almost all kinds of labor. Some girls have been employed as young as seven. One man who has I believe, three sons, aged respectively, eight, ten and twelve, told a gentleman of our city who asked him if it did not go hard with so young a child to rise so early in the morning, 'that it was a very hard thing for the little fellow at the beginning, but that he had got more used to it now, and stood it pretty well.' "

A letter from Sudbury states that at the factory in Assabet, partly in that town, eleven hours are required, and that children are at work there who should be at school.

Charles Durfee, Esq., of Fall River, writes: "Quite a number of children and youth are employed in the common operations of manufacturing. To a limited extent they are kept from school by their parents."

Another letter from Fall River, stated the case more strongly. It says "there are 652 children, of both sexes, from eight to fourteen, working in the mills, most of them unable to read or write, all kept from school. A great number of the *adults* are unable to write their name."

Similar testimony came before the Commission at the hearings. Robert Bowers of Lawrence stated, "there is a great number of children from twelve to fifteen years, who work at night. The majority of those who do night work are under eighteen years of age. The statute prohibiting the employment of children under twelve years of age, is constantly violated in the Lawrence mills."

The following is the

Testimony of T. J. Kidd, of Fall River.

Question. Did you know that there was a statute against the employment of such children?

Answer. There has been some talk about it. Only among a few working men.

Q. You have a school committee. Have you ever made any representations to them?

A. Don't suppose a word was ever said to them about it.

Q. Was there ever any one who tried to cause the children to be sent to school?

A. Not since the old man Robeson died.

Q. Why do not the parents send them to school?

A. Small help is scarce; a great deal of the machinery has been stopped for want of small help, so the overseers have been going round to draw the small children from the schools into the mills; the same as a draft in the army.

Q. Do I understand that agents go about to take children out of the schools, and put them into the mills?

A. They go round to the parents and canvass them. This produces nothing but misery and crime. I have looked into it more the last year than before. The boys and girls are all mixed together, from seven years up to thirteen, and are entirely demoralized. One demoralizes another. They get so that they don't care for their employers or their parents. The next thing they say is, "I won't work." I can go round the streets of Fall River in the night, and pick up boys who are staying away from home, and who won't work because they are so demoralized. It all comes from their not having schooling. You can attribute it to no other cause.

The Testimony of John Wild, also from Fall River.

I don't know as I have any more to say, except that I have two little boys, one eleven and the other about eight and a half. I am no scholar myself, because I have always been working in the mill, and I am sorry for it. I don't want my children to be brought up in the same way. I wish to get them to work a little less hours, so that I can send them to night school. I want, if it is possible, to get a law so that they can go to school, and know how to read and write their names.

Q. Do they work in the mill?

A. I have been forced to send them in. My earnings would not keep the door open. I had to send them in to help me earn a living. They are getting pretty big, and they want a deal of clothing, and I could not get it out of my earnings. I wish to get shorter hours. I am willing to lose the extra hours for the good of my children.

Q. Do the children work by the day?

A. By the day.

Q. How old are the children?

A. Seven and eight.

Q. Have you a child of seven working in the mill?

A. Yes, I have.

Q. You have only two children working in the mill?

A. Only two.

Q. What wages do these children get?

A. $2.30 per week, the smallest one.

Q. Does the other get the same?

A. Yes, sir.

Q. How long has the youngest worked in a mill?

A. About five or six months.

Q. Had he been kept in school up to that time?

A. Yes, sir, but he didn't learn much — not so much as I'd like to have him.

Q. Does he get any schooling now?

A. When he gets done in the mill, he is ready to go to bed? He has to be in the mill ten minutes before we start up, to wind spindles. Then he starts about his own work, and keeps on till dinner time. Then he goes home, starts again at one, and works till *seven.* When he's done, he is tired enough to go to bed. Some days he has to clean and help scour during the dinner hour. We used to scour all dinner hour, but we stopped that some little time ago. It takes us till about half past twelve; some days, all the time. Some days he has to clean spindles. Saturday he's in all day.

Q. Is there any limit on the part of the employers as to the age when they take children?

A. They'll take them at any age when they can get them, if they are old enough to stand.

Q. How young are the youngest?

A. I guess the youngest is about seven. There are some that's younger, but very little.

Q. Do you know that your children are working contrary to law?

A. I didn't know there was any law.

Q. Did you know that if I should go to Fall River and prosecute their employer, he could be compelled to pay a fine for employing your children?

A. No, sir, being no scholar.

V Care of Dependent Children

In the mid-nineteenth century, almshouse and orphan asylum represented the extremes of care for dependent children; the former exhibited the effort and neglect of public bodies, the latter typified the achievement and limitation of private philanthropy.

During the 1820's American poor law reformers like Josiah Quincy of Massachusetts and J. V. N. Yates of New York identified four methods of public assistance. Since children were not yet recognized as constituting a special category of recipients their care came under the same general headings as that of adults:

1. Outdoor relief or assisting needy people in their own homes;

2. Vendue or auctioning off the poor individually to the lowest bidders;

3. Contracting with the lowest bidder for the care of the entire lot of paupers; and

4. Concentrating all the dependent and defective in an almshouse owned and managed by public authority.

Because of the extreme decentralization of responsibility for poor relief all of these systems might be in operation within a single state; adjacent towns or counties might follow different practices, sharing only a disinclination to assist any but their "own" poor; and a city, as was true of New York City, might extend outdoor relief to some of its paupers and send others to the almshouse.

The poor law and charity reformers of the 1820's and 1830's agreed that outdoor relief was the most pernicious form of public assistance because, as they firmly believed, it promoted pauperism by making aid too easy to get and not shameful enough to receive. Disdaining the vendue and contract systems, which

stiff-necked countrymen liked because they were cheap and easy to administer, the reformers advocated indoor or institutional relief. Their name for the almshouse was the "poor farm," where, under judicious management, paupers could engage in wholesome, productive labor and earn their own keep.

With few exceptions, the reformers' dreams that paupers could be made self-supporting on a well-regulated farm were as illusory as those of the founders of the communitarian experiments of the 1840's. Brook Farm evaporated leaving the poorhouse in its stead. By the 1850's the almshouse/poor farm no longer seemed a panacea, except to sensitive people living in communities which still disposed of their poor by contract or vendue. As often as not the almshouse had come to be a symbol of mismanagement, political chicanery and corruption, public apathy, and human wretchedness.

In state after state legislative committees and concerned individuals investigated conditions in almshouses; their reports pronounced some good, many indifferent, some bad, others horrible. The investigators pointed out that even a reasonably well-conducted almshouse was a poor place to raise a child. In strongest language, citing considerations of health, education, citizenship, morality, and humanity they urged removal of children from the almshouse. Unfortunately, the reports lay unnoticed among other legislative documents and have been read more by historians than by those to whom they were addressed. Recommendations that special provision be made for pauper children and that greater care be exercised in apprenticing them went unheeded or were only half-heartedly implemented. The failure and inappropriateness of public efforts for dependent children and the seeming indifference of voters and officeholders to correct those defects eroded confidence in the ability of government to promote social welfare.[1]

The number of children in almshouses rose from year to year but their numbers would have been even greater had it not been for the multiplication, especially after 1830, of private orphan asylums.[2] Some of the institutions were founded for the benefit of children whose parents perished in cholera, yellow fever, and typhus epidemics; others were established to receive orphans whose plight appealed to the compassion of individual philanthropists, ethnic and occupational groups, benevolent associations, and religious sects. Many orphanages, in recognition and encouragement of their services to the community, obtained assistance from public as well as private funds. Between 1847 and 1866 the legislature of the state of New York, to cite one example, contributed lump sum grants totaling more than $600,000 to some sixty private asylums, and in addition made annual appropriations to be distributed among the incorporated orphan asylums in the state on a per capita basis.[3]

1. "Reform came slowly in view of the evidence of the serious conditions in the almshouses, because public funds had been invested in land and buildings and because of the fatal ease with which children and families could be placed in an almshouse. Moreover, as the number of children in almshouses was large, the problem of what to do with them if this form of care were abandoned was one not easily solved." Abbott, *Child and the State*, II, 7.

2. In New York state there were approximately 3,000 children under sixteen years of age in 1847; 5,400 in 1857; 8,000 in 1861; and 26,000 in 1866. New York had only two orphan asylums in 1825, more than sixty in 1866. David M. Schneider, *The History of Public Welfare in New York State, 1609–1866* (Chicago, 1938), pp. 344–345. Of the estimated seventy-one orphanages founded in the United States between 1801 and 1851, sixty-two were founded after 1821 and fifty-six after 1831. Homer Folks, *The Care of Destitute, Neglected, and Delinquent Children* (New York, 1900), p. 36.

3. Schneider, *History of Public Welfare in New York*, p. 339. The annual, per capita appropriations ranged from $35,000 distributed among twenty-six orphan asylums (maintaining 2,800 children) in 1857 to $80,000 awarded to sixty-three private child-care institutions in 1866.

As alternatives to almshouses and vendues the asylums had obvious advantages. The legislative committees which deplored conditions in the public institutions commended the cleanliness and order of the asylums and the good deportment of the children who called them home. The praise showered on orphanages, not only by legislators and journalists, but also by their founders, administrators, and boards of directors of directresses, contributed to the increasing prestige of private benevolence. Lavish praise of the orphanages also contributed to an overoptimistic view of the scope of their work. Operating, even when assisted by the state, on limited budgets, usually directing their charity to particular religious, racial, or ethnic groups, selective in their admission policies, and free to discharge children when they saw fit, the orphanages served only a fraction of the children who needed help. They were valuable supplements to, but no substitute for, better public care.

In the 1850's and for forty years thereafter, the most outspoken critic of both almshouse and asylum care for children was Charles Loring Brace, secretary of the New York Children's Aid Society. Brace's work for the prevention of the dependency and delinquency is treated in Chapter VII, and will be further examined in Volume II. Here it is necessary only to note his opposition to institutional life of any kind, and his insistence that the best place for dependent or needy children was in foster homes, preferably on western farms. Brace's concern was with the vagrant, homeless, street children of New York and with the devising of measures to prevent these children, already outlaws, from growing up to be menaces to society. The final step in his program of "moral disinfection" was to send boys and girls west to be placed (not bound out) in farmers' homes. They were placed without the formality of indenture, so that the placement might be terminated if either party became dissatisfied. Brace called this part of his society's work "emigration." Like seventeenth-century Londoners, Brace, seeking a way to rid *his* city of troublesome youth, looked westward. He envisaged the young emigrants bringing the boon of cheap labor to farmers and, in return, finding opportunities and gaining rewards beyond their reach at home.

A. CHILDREN UNDER THE POOR LAW

Auctioning off versus poor farm

In the 1820's and for several decades thereafter charity reformers recommended substitution of poor farms for the auctioning off or vendue system of poor relief. A well-conducted poor farm, according to its advocates, was the most economical, humane, and scientific method of caring for paupers.

---

1. Methods of caring for the poor in New York, 1823

New York State, State Board of Charities, "Report of the Secretary of State in 1824 on the Relief and Settlement of the Poor," *Thirty-fourth Annual Report, 1900* (Albany, 1901), I, 979–980, 984–987, 998–999, 1006–1007.

Secretary of State J. V. N. Yates prepared this report on the basis of an investigation conducted in 1823. The following are extracts from replies made by supervisors of the poor in the indicated towns to Yates's inquiries about methods employed in caring for the poor.

GHENT

There is no *poor-house,* nor *house of industry* in our town. We have our poor kept by

the week. Children from two to seven years old, from 25 cents to 56 cents per week. Aged paupers, we pay from 50 cents to $1 25, per week, for board and clothing. We are informed that the legislature have it in contemplation, to pass an act to build a *poor house in each county.* To this we are *decidedly opposed* as the plan we have adopted to support our poor, is the best we can devise. We find that our poor tax is reduced annually, and that the sum of $200, will be quite sufficient to support our poor. And we wish to retain our present privilege, that is to support our own poor, in our own way and not to be associated with any other towns, or the county . . .

STAMFORD

The people of Stamford are very well satisfied with the poor laws as they now are. We should be apprehensive that any alteration in the system, might operate injuriously to our interests. Especially we hope that the legislature will not make it *compulsory* on any towns, or grant liberty to counties to erect houses of industry. We think that the legislature went far enough last session, in giving this power, to those towns that should wish to exercise it. It would be a detriment to this town, for instance, to contribute to the expense of erecting a poor house in this county. We should first lose our funds, and then we should be driven to taxation, and at last the poor could not be so cheaply, and I may add, so comfortably supported . . .

WALTON

Our general practice of assisting the poor, is when there is a family needy in order to prevent their being thrown on the town, our poor masters are requested to give them occasional assistance, and find good places for them to put their children to service.

BEEKMAN

Previous to the year 1820, the poor of our town were kept by individuals, one, two or three in a place, by persons who would keep them the lowest, at the average expense of $35 each, and their clothing furnished at the expense of the town. Since the year 1820, we have contracted with one man to keep *all* the paupers, and he to furnish them with clothing, at $32 each, for those over 12 years of age, and those of 12 and under, $16 each.

POUGHKEEPSIE

There have been 144 paupers, supported in this town, during the last year — 76 for the whole year, and 68 partially through the winter — 50 have been kept in our house of industry, and 26 out on small allowances. Those kept in the house have been employed in cooking, washing, spinning, picking oakum,[1] &c. and in husbandry. The value of labor will amount probably to $400. There were 27 males, 23 females, 18 blind, lame, or otherwise disabled by sickness or disease, and 17 children among the number. The average expense of those kept in the house, about $25 *each per year, their labor included.* Our paupers have increased about one-third, but it is calculated that our house of industry affords an opportunitly to economize, and to support our paupers *at least*

1. "Picking oakum" involved loosening hemp or jute fibers in rope; the fibers, after having been impregnated with tar, were used in calking seams in boats.

50 per cent less than formerly, and when they were billetted out.

BROOKLYN

In Brooklyn there are 54 paupers, consisting of 13 men, 21 women, 13 boys and 7 girls employed mostly in picking oakum, to the amount of 31 cwt., sold for $139 50 . . . The town has an alms-house under the management of two overseers and one keeper, having a separate house for an hospital attended by a very respectable physician. The present law for the settlement of the poor, passed April 8, 1813, is very deficient in its provisions, as it does not give any authority to the overseers, to make salutary rules for the good order of the house, nor any discretion to coerce the obstinate or punish the refractory; they having only one remedy in all cases to expel them from the house, which in the severity of winter would be little short of murder. If the overseers could confine the impudent and refractory in solitary places, and keep them on bread and water, it would have a good effect. To prevent, however, any improper severity, it may be made the duty of the justices and supervisor once a year at least, to inspect the whole economy of the house . . . It is indispensable that the children should be educated; but in some alms-houses (as it is in ours at present) there may be none able to teach the children; and on account of disorders, incident to public places, it would be improper and ungenerous to send them to the public district school; the children must remain uneducated, or some provision must be made to hire a teacher. Would it not be right to give the alms-house a particular demand on the school fund?

FLORIDA

We have no poor-house, properly so called, but we advertise for proposals, and allow one month to receive them. The lowest bidder takes the poor, if in all respects qualified to take care of them. They are all in one room, and taken care of by the family. Seven are thus provided for, and three children, were taken care of in the town of Knox, at one place for $35, and the seven were taken care of for $270 last year. This year we have adopted the same plan. Six persons are at one place, for $230 — the three children are taken care of in Knox for $35 — two old persons, have been taken by their relations this spring, for $55, rather than go with the rest of the poor — they are very troublesome, and the contractor would not keep them, for the average sum he kept the rest. In answer to your eighth question, I observe, that the town of Florida, are satisfied, that they cannot do better than by the present mode of keeping the poor. If a poor-house is to be built, they must go to the expense of building. Now the contractor looks out for his own convenience in keeping them — if we help to build a county poor-house, we will have to do it at an expense.

JOHNSTOWN

The poor may, with propriety, be divided into three classes, the aged, the sick, lame and blind, and the infant: These are the proper objects for the care of our law, and the only ones that perhaps, strictly speaking, should receive its bounty. To these there may be added, a fourth class, composed of the idle, vicious and intemperate; and this class I fear, on examination, will be found to receive more of public and private charity, than all the other three combined. The support of the poor, is in all countries a burthen, and the object of the legislature, is to make that burthen as little felt by the industrious citizen as possible. There are three modes in practice of supporting paupers. 1. By selling them at public auction, to the lowest bidder. 2. By hiring one individual to keep all the poor belonging to a town. 3. Establishing a poor-house or house of industry for the county. Of these modes, I am decidedly of opinion, the last is much to be preferred. First,

on account of its cheapness: The support of the poor in this town varies from 50 cents, to $2, per week; and the average amount may be stated at 90 cents; this is treble the amount that it would cost in a house of industry. Second — Many of the poor in the house of industry, can nearly support themselves by their labor. Third — The aged and decrepit, and the children, the care of whom forms an important item of expense, can be watched and attended to by those who are more healthy and capable. Fourth — It will lessen the number of paupers at least one half, and destroy the trade of *street-beggars*. There are many persons who now receive sums from the overseers of the poor, whose pride, and the pride of whose connexions, would not permit them to go to a poorhouse. And the idle vagabond, when he finds that work he must, at least would certainly prefer working for himself. The only objection to this mode is, the expense of transporting them to the house of industry (which ought always to be as near the centre of the county as convenient), and this would be but trifling, compared with the saving effected . . .

The second plan above alluded to, of having one man, for a stipulated sum to support all the poor of a town, is, in miniature, the same as the above, and of course, must be more expensive. But this plan had been found to be more economical than the first one, of selling the poor; and has, in those towns which have entered into it, lessened the expense more, than fifty per cent. The poor themselves, would be better clothed and dieted, in a poor-house than they now are, inasmuch as those, who purchase, are themselves generally poor and unable to afford to keep them well.

---

2. Auction system breaks up a family: annual town meeting, Manchester, New Hampshire, March 8, 1825

"Early Records of the Town of Manchester, 1817–1828," *Collections* of the Manchester Historical Association, XI (1909), 218.

Voted Marjory Boyes and her child may be put to separate places — Marjory Boyes was struck off to Israel Merrill at 16 cents per week Mary Boyes was struck off to Nathaniel Baker at 37 cents per week Elenor Boyes was struck off to Reuben Sawyer at 48 per week Jonathan Boyes was struck off to Peter Young at 42 cents per week.[1]

---

3. Defense of vendue system, 1827

Niles' Weekly Register, XXXII (1827), 312.

PAUPERISM. Gov. Plumer, of New Hampshire, who is writing in the Portsmouth Journal, in one of his numbers, treats of pauperism. He says:

"In some towns the project has been adopted to purchase a house and farm, and appoint an agent to superintend the labor of the paupers in cultivating and improving it. In nine times out of ten, this mode, instead of diminishing, increases the expense of supporting the poor. The most eligible and cheapest method I have known for country towns is annually to vendue the board, clothing, and taking care of the poor to the lowest bidder, whom the selectmen consider suitable for that purpose. This will place the poor of a town in one or more families where they will be well treated, and where the interest of the undertakers will require the paupers to labor and be industrious, and in some measure support themselves. If we except sickness and old age, all assistance to the poor which does not promote industry, is rather a

1. The Boyes case plus many other instances of the operation of the vendue system are examined in Benjamin J. Klebaner, "Pauper Auctions: The 'New England' Method of Public Poor Relief," *Essex Institute Historical Collections*, XCI (1955), 195–210.

premium to idleness and improvidence, than acts of charity and benevolence. The food of the poor, should be wholesome, but cheap; and their clothing plain, but sufficient to protect them against the inclemency of the seasons."

---

4. Care of pauper children under the vendue system, Rhode Island, 1850

Thomas R. Hazard, *Report on the Poor and Insane in Rhode Island* (Providence, 1851), pp. 49–51.

In 1850 Thomas Hazard (1797–1886), a Quaker farmer, textile manufacturer, and social reformer, conducted an investigation of poor relief practices in Rhode Island and reported his findings and recommendations to the state legislature. In one town, Coventry, he found that a contractor received $594 a year to care for sixteen paupers, seven of whom were under twelve years of age.

Visited the poor of this town, on the 5th of 9th month last, and found them in the most deplorable condition imaginable. The house in which they were huddled, was old and dilapidated — and the furniture was absolutely unfit for the use of the most degraded of savages. This, I understood the keeper to say, that the town was to furnish. The mattresses and bed clothing were filthy and ragged. Not a sheet nor a pillow case was to be seen, and I afterwards understood that the town did not deem such articles necessary, and therefore were not in the practice of furnishing them. The chairs were all more or less broken or worn out, and there was but one in the house that had both back and bottom. A poor helpless, palsied female, who had not stood for years, was braced in the skeleton of one of these, by its being stuffed with rags. An insane woman who had been recently removed by the town from the Butler Hospital, was ordered from her filthy lair (where she was confined by the corner of a bedstead being pushed against the door) in a tone of voice such as keepers of wild beasts use in colloquy with Tigers. At the stern summons, she came forth and stood silent and motionless, to be gazed at — a caricature of dispair clothed in filth and rags. No sign, look or token, indicated that she noticed ought that was said, until at her keeper's bidding, she quietly retired to her den. I happened to visit this house when the poor inmates were engaged at what was intended for dinner. A few hours before I had witnessed the poor in the town of Scituate, partaking of a plentiful breakfast of good and wholesome food. This, perhaps, rendered the appearance of the repast before me, the more striking. On the table I now beheld, a dish of unripe, watery potatoes, was all the food to be seen, or that was visible in the house, save a mouthful of indian bread which a woman held in her hand. The supply of these miserable potatoes was evidently scanty, as they were soon all devoured, and the children lingered about the table evidently hungry still. As I was about leaving the premises, I observed two of these children going towards a pond with sticks in their hands. Supposing that they were going to fish, I was curious to inspect their tackle, and called them to me. I found that their poles were taken from a pile of brush near by, and that their lines were made of short strips of worn and faded cotton cloth tied together. They had no hooks of any description, and I question whether even a pin could be found in the poor-house for that purpose. This was a trifling incident to be sure, but associated as it was with the desolateness of every thing around me, I do not remember of ever having witnessed one that impressed me with a more heart sickening sense of utter and helpless destitution.

I would gladly have been spared the pain of this narration, especially as the friends of humanity in the town of Coventry, have recently succeeded in their efforts to induce their fellow townsmen to take decided steps to do away most of the abuses it discloses. But it should be remembered that these abuses grow in a great measure out of the system of venduing the poor, which, though now abandoned in Coventry, is still adhered to by many other towns in the State; and whose paupers may be consigned by the next chance fall of the auctioneer's hammer, to the same wretched fate that those in Coventry have just been rescued from. And it seems but fair to infer that if these disclosures have tended to awaken the people of Coventry to a proper sense of the injustice of venduing their poor to the lowest bidder, and to the necessity of its abandonment, that their perusal may also incite the citizens of other towns who still practice the same system, to abandon it also.

---

5. Hazard's criticism of the vendue system in Rhode Island, 1851

Hazard, *The Poor and Insane in Rhode Island,* pp. 85–89.

Hazard's report was ignored by the state legislature.

. . . Four different modes are pursued by the towns in maintaining their poor.

1st. By venduing them to the lowest bidder.

2d. By contracting for their maintenance, with an individual, or individuals, through the agency of a committee or otherwise.

3d. By placing all the poor in one Asylum, owned by the town.

4th. By placing all such in an Asylum as are bereft of home and friends, and administering out-door relief to such as have.

The cruelty and injustice of the first mentioned of these systems — that of venduing the poor, and compelling them to live with the man who will take them off the town for the least sum — is so obvious, that it seems almost insulting to the understanding, to attempt to prove it wrong. We are all more or less, creatures of habit. By becoming familiar with the most hideous objects, they lose in our eyes, half their deformity. And this tendency in our nature is, perhaps, all that can be offered in palliation of this wretched system. When stripped of all disguise, selling the poor to the lowest bidder, is simply offering a reward for the most cruel and avaricious man that can be found to abuse them. Without making continual sacrifices from year to year, it is impossible under such a system, that a conscientious man should long continue to be their care-taker. Supposing that by accident or otherwise, a humane man should become their purchaser — he would feel it to be his duty not only to lodge and feed them well, but likewise to *clothe* them well. As the annual sale draws near, the avaricious eye of an unprincipled townsman has inventoried their apparel. With scarcely the addition of a patch it can be made, in his estimation, to cover the nakedness of his intended victims another whole year. His bidding in town meeting is graduated accordingly, against that of their present keeper, whose conscience would compel him to keep the clothing of the poor constantly good — and thus, unless he is both able and willing to submit to annual sacrifices, he must surrender the poor into the hands of one who buys them to obtain a reward by their oppression. But, say the advocates of the system (perhaps), we allow none but good men to bid them off — we appoint committees to visit the poor, and we take bonds of their keeper that they *shall* be well treated. This may all sound very well to an inexperienced ear — but really it is but adding the sin of mockery to the still more heinous sin of oppressing and selling the poor. Bad men are not unfrequently good politicians. Such often hold the balance of power in small towns; and who, especially when party spirit runs high, let me ask, is to throw themselves between such men and their prey, should they resolve to purchase the poor themselves — or confer them on a partisan of dubious politics but of undisputed depravity. The very man, in all probability, through whose influence the poor have thus been sold to secure

a wavering vote, becomes both the surety and overseer of their keeper. This system is mainly practiced in agricultural towns — and let me ask, is there a man in any one of these, who aspires to the name of a farmer, who would in any contingency, offer his cattle at auction to be kept by the lowest bidder, and depend solely for their good treatment on such security as is taken for that of their pauper, poor? . . . It is high time that this miserable system of venduing the poor, revolting alike to common humanity and to every precept of the christian religion, was abolished in our land. Out of it have grown some of the most dreadful abuses that have ever been perpetrated by man on his fellow man . . .

The 4th named system, adopted by some towns, viz: to own an Asylum to which all persons who are destitute of a home and friends are sent, and to administer out-door relief to such as *have*, is probably the most humane and christian-like plan that in the present state of society, can be pursued. It is urged by some, against this plan, that, by adopting it, the public is liable to be subjected to imposition. To meet this it might be said, that other plans subject the *poor* to impositions, which they are quite as unable to bear as the public. It is a maxim I believe, in law, that it is better that nine guilty persons should escape, than that one innocent person should be condemned . . . No individual or community was ever yet made poor by the practice of a liberal, discriminating charity — carried out in good faith — void of any selfish motives lurking at heart, and founded solely on love to God and his creatures . . .

I feel great confidence in recommending this mixed plan of granting relief to their poor, to every town in the State which has not yet adopted it. In building an Asylum, I would recommend that it should be placed on a public road, and on good land if it is to be procured — such as is suited to garden and fruit culture, that the inmates of the house should not be obliged to go far to their work, and expose themselves to the vicissitudes of the weather, far from any shelter. Being situated on a road renders the house easy of access to the public, and brings its affairs more or less before the people who pass it — this operates as a safeguard in some measure for the good treatment of the poor. Besides these advantages, the passing and little incidents that occur on the road tend not a little to dissipate the tediousness that often connects itself with the monotonous life the old and decrepid are forced to lead. There may be counter advantages in some instances, that would render a situation off the road, and perhaps near the water, preferable; but I believe that such will not often occur. Every citizen of the town should take an interest in their Asylum and occasionally visit it — which they will not be liable to do so often if it be located in a place difficult of access, as they would if situated on a road that they necessarily pass in attending to their daily concerns.

Children in almshouses

1. New York law authorizing magistrates to send neglected children to almshouses, 1821

Laws of the State of New York passed at the Forty-second, Forty-third and Forty-fourth Session of the Legislature from January 1819 to April 1821 (Albany, 1821), V, 182–183.

. . . If any child or children, shall hereafter be found begging for alms, in any of the cities in this state, and whose Parent or Parents, is or are not a charge to such City, as a pauper or paupers, it shall and may be lawful for any magistrate of such city to take up and send such child or children to the almshouse, or other place for the support of the public poor of such city, there to be detained and supported until such child or children shall become of sufficient age to be bound out, or until some fit

and proper person or persons shall be found to take such child or children, when it shall be the duty of the overseers of the poor of such city, to bind out such child or children, in the same manner as is prescribed in the Act, entitled "an Act concerning apprentices and servants."

2. Poorhouses in New York, Baltimore, Boston, and Providence, 1827

Niles' Weekly Register, XXXII (1827), 383–384.

Pauper establishments. — In a former paper we gave an extract from the report of the Philadelphia committee who were appointed to examine some of the principal pauper establishments in the United States. We have since been furnished by the committee with a copy of their report, and are enabled to exhibit a comparative view of all the establishments which they visited in their tour. The first in order was the Baltimore alms house.

This belongs to the city and county, and is under the care of seven trustees, four in the city annually appointed by the mayor and council, and their residents of the county appointed by the governor and council. They meet weekly and are allowed two dollars per day for their services. The house is situated on a farm of more than 300 acres. It consists of a centre building and wings, capable of accommodating 8 or 900 paupers. It contains an infirmary, a lying hospital, work house for the employment of vagrants, an asylum for destitute children, a lunatic hospital, and a medical and chirurgical school. The officers of the establishment are, a master who is paid $600 per annum, a matron $200, a physician $400 who is allowed students who pay him $200 each, a superintendent of the farm $400 — clerk to the steward, schoolmaster, nurses and assistant cooks, and those not receiving salary are paupers. An account is opened with every male over 15 years of age, and every female over 12, who are credited with any work done towards their maintenance, the charge of which is not to exceed 30 cents per day. The average number in the house is about 400 . . . The amount expended on account of the poor of the city, including every expense, except the interest of the purchase money of the farm, averages about $18,000. The population of Baltimore exceeds 70,000.

New York. — The next which they visited, was the almshouse in New York, distant from the city about two and a half miles. It is within an enclosure of 26 acres, surrounded by a stone wall. It is 325 feet long and consists of a centre with the wings. The centre building is 4 stories high including the basement, the wings three stories. The inmates are lodged in 42 rooms, each about 22 by 45 feet. — There are from 20 to 24 persons in each room, and are classed according to sex, nation, and habits. — The different wards are under inspection of persons selected from the most exemplary of the paupers. The house is warmed by the funnels of stoves in the basement story. By the use of anthracite coal, about $3000 was saved last year. The average number of paupers in the house is 1949, of whom 425 are children. About 150 are employed in picking wool, spinning, gardening, &c. There is attached to the establishment a farm of 100 acres, which is at present unproductive. There are within the enclosure, besides this building, a penitentiary, a hospital for the sick and insane, containing about 280 patients: a large building for the manufacturers, in the upper story of which is a school room, where are taught about 258 children. The committee saw specimens of writing, which were of superior elegance. There are two detached buildings where the children are kept separate from the paupers . . . The expenses of the institution are about $58,500. The relief out doors, last year, was distributed among 1500 families. Part of it was eight thousand dollars in cash. The relief is either in money, wood, or provisions. The whole expenses of the poor establishment are $72,190. The district contains 175,000 inhabitants.

Providence, R.I. — In Providence, the whole of the concerns of the poor is directed by one overseer, who has a salary of $700, and a keeper of the almshouse, salary $150. The inmates of the house are boarded by the keeper for $1 25 per head, children half price. — . . . No labor has been introduced except the picking of oakum. One physician with a salary of $75 per ann. is employed for the paupers . . .

Boston. The almshouse is about two miles from the city, and on a farm of 60 acres. The buildings are of stone, 220 feet long by 40 deep, four stories high. The rooms are 15 by 13, and contain from 3 to 5 persons. — On the first floor are apartments used as hospitals. — There is a detached building for the blacks, and another for the insane. The average number in the house annually about 450 . . .

. . . The expense in Philadelphia, in case of bastardy, excited surprise, say the committee, in every place which they visited. In New York the cases of this kind are between 80 and 90. Boston 9 and 10. Salem 2 or 3. — Baltimore none. Philadelphia 269!! The committee were much pleased with the house of refuge in New York. They recommend the establishment of an asylum for the intemperate, the directors of which should be authorised to arrest and imprison every person guilty of this vice.

---

3. Children in New York City pauper institutions, 1838

George Combe, *Notes on the United States of North America During a Phrenological Visit in 1838–9–40*, I (Philadelphia, 1841), 140–141.

George Combe (1788–1858), British lecturer and phrenologist, was particularly interested in and observant of American charitable, correctional, and eleemosynary institutions. The Farm Schools he visited had been established in 1831 as a temporary shelter for children removed from the Bellevue almshouse during a severe epidemic of ophthalmia (see below, Chap. VII, sec. B, Health problems of dependent children in institutions, 1831–1832). In 1848 the city opened a new institution for pauper children on Randall's Island.

November 29, 1838. . . . This is "Thanksgiving Day" in New York. Service is performed in all the churches, in which gratitude is expressed to God for his mercies, and the evening is spent in domestic festivities . . .

I availed myself of the leisure which the day afforded, to visit the Alms-House, Lunatic Asylum, and Penitentiary at Bellevue, about three miles from New York, on the East River; also the Criminal Prison, and the new Lunatic Asylum on Blackwell Island; and the school for charity orphan and destitute children on Long Island, called the Farm Schools. All these institutions are under the management of the civic corporation of the city. Some of the buildings at Bellevue are old, ill-adapted to their purposes, and crowded, and, in consequence, the inmates are not properly accommodated . . . The children in the Farm Schools presented a melancholy aspect. The weather was cold, and as the cold had come suddenly, many of them had not yet received their winter supply of stockings and shoes. They were crowding round the stoves with an expression of suffering and discomfort, which was distressing to behold. The buildings in which they live are frame or wooden houses, divided into moderate-sized rooms, low in the ceilings, and without any means of ventilation except the doors and the windows. They sleep crowded together in these apartments; the beds stand so close to the windows, and the air is so cold, that they are not open during the night, and the air is excessively vitiated before the morning. The consequences are visible in the appearance of the children; many of them are suffering under ophthalmia, and they present generally that sunken, inanimate, and unhappy aspect which betokens blood in a bad condition from imperfect nutrition and impure air. There is, I believe, no stinting of food; but the digestive functions suffer from the confinement in an unwholesome atmosphere, and hence the nutrition is imperfect.

On my return to the city, I made inquiries of several persons how it happened that these institutions are in a condition so unworthy of a great city, and various reasons were assigned. They lie upwards of three miles from the town, and so many pressing public duties are imposed on the members of the civic council, that they have not adequate time to visit them. One excellent person, whose attention was particularly directed to them, saw and proclaimed their imperfections to the council, but he could not succeed in drawing sufficient attention to their condition. Again; most of the buildings are old, and money is indispensable for their improvement. In New York, the whigs and democrats are nearly equally balanced, and each party makes "political capital" out of every increase of expenditure and taxation proposed by the other, and hence the party which should improve these institutions too rapidly at the expense of the citizens would lose their places. Economy there, as everywhere else, is the watchword of opposition; and in New York the people are disposed to place the advocates of it in power. Farther: In this city vast improvements, partly for the introduction of water, are actually in progress; many more are wanted; and the rulers are compelled to accomplish those works first which are advocated by the most influential persons. The poor, the insane, and the criminal have few, and these not noisy, advocates, and their interests are postponed. Lastly, it is an *unpopular duty* to expose the imperfections of any American institutions, and hence the actual condition of some of these establishments is really unknown to the great body of the upper classes of the city, who would otherwise be well disposed towards their improvement.

---

4. Charles Dickens on children in Boston almshouse, 1842

Charles Dickens, *American Notes for General Circulation* (London, 1842), I, 113–117.

The orphans and young children are in an adjoining building; separate from this, but a part of the same Institution [House of Industry]. Some are such little creatures, that the stairs are of lilliputian measurement, fitted to their tiny strides. The same consideration for their years and weakness is expressed in their very seats, which are perfect curiosities, and look like articles of furniture for a pauper doll's-house. I can imagine the glee of our Poor Law Commissioners at the notion of these seats having arms and backs; but small spines being of older date than their occupation of the Board-room at Somerset House, I thought even this provision very merciful and kind.

Here again, I was greatly pleased with the inscriptions on the wall, which were scraps of plain morality, easily remembered and understood: such as "Love one another" — "God remembers the smallest creature in his creation": and straightforward advice of that nature. The books and tasks of these smallest of scholars, were adapted, in the same judicious manner, to their childish powers. When we had examined these lessons, four morsels of girls (of whom one was blind) sang a little song, about the merry month of May, which I thought (being extremely dismal) would have suited an English November better. That done, we went to see their sleeping-rooms on the floor above, in which the arrangements were no less excellent and gentle than those we had seen below. And after observing that the teachers were of a class and character well suited to the spirit of

the place, I took leave of the infants with a lighter heart than ever I have taken leave of pauper infants yet.

---

5. "Easy, happy life in an almshouse"

Massachusetts, General Court, "Report on Public Charitable Institutions, 1858," Doc. 2, *Documents of the Senate, 1859* (Boston, 1859), p. 69.

Lastly, and the greatest evil of all [sending needy children to almshouses], *creates* and perpetuates *paupers*, by accustoming all the children in them to an easy, happy life in an almshouse, where they are well fed, clothed and instructed, so that the inducement for them to labor for their own support — and that of their parents — is completely lost sight of; for as is said by one who for twenty years was governor of an English workhouse, "when children are brought up in a workhouse they never have a disposition to shun it."

Education and apprenticeship of pauper children, New York, 1853

"Franklin" to Hon. Elias W. Leavenworth, secretary of state-elect of the state of New York, Senate, Doc. 72, *Documents, 1855*, III (Albany, 1855), 85–87, 121–122.

Apprenticeship was the standard method of disposing of older poorhouse children. Seven- or eight-year-old children were sometimes apprenticed, but the usual age was twelve to fifteen. Boys were occasionally apprenticed to craftsmen, but in most cases they were bound to farmers; girls were bound out as household servants.

The following is one of twenty-three letters from "Franklin" originally published in the *Columbia Record* (Hudson, New York) in 1853. Franklin's identity is unknown.

. . . — Another cause of the increase of pauperism arises from the neglect of the proper officers to give a suitable education to the children born and brought up in our poor-houses.

The number of children under 16 years in the poor-houses of the State was, in

	Females	Males	Total.	No. instructed during the year.	Time of instruction.
1849	1,120	1,755	2,875	2,639	8 months.
1850	1,275	1,960	3,235	2,635	7½ do
1851	1,152	1,976	3,128	2,849	8½ do
1852	1,155	1,992	3,147	3,147	8 do

The returns look fair enough on their face, with respect to instruction; it would seem that the children in these establishments enjoy better educational privileges than the children of farmers in most of the rural districts of the State.

I have ascertained, however, from personal investigation, that there is no reality in all this, as you may also ascertain, if you will take the trouble to examine for yourself. I really don't know what meaning the county superintendents of the poor attach to the word *Education;* I know they sometimes use words in a sense not warranted by any Dictionary that ever I consulted. But if they mean anything which elevates the mind — anything which ministers to the moral feelings or the intellectual powers — anything which will help to get a living, or to discharge intelligently the duties incident to citizenship — there is no such thing given to the youth in our county houses. I have visited many of the poor-houses myself, and have obtained authentic information by correspondence, from many others, and from all this I think I am warranted in saying that out of the 3,000 children sheltered in them, only a very small fraction, a mere drop in the bucket, obtain an education that will be of the slightest use to them in getting a living or making useful members of society. In many cases the teacher is a pauper, generally an old drunkard, whose temper is soured and whose intellect is debased, and who spends the school hours in tormenting, rather than in teaching his pupils. In many of these schools there is no book except the Testament to be found, no slates, pens or paper. In some counties not a dollar has been expended in text books or stationery since the county system has been adopted. Under such circumstances the name of school is a mere farce.[1]

There are between five and six hundred children bound out every year from the poor-houses under the authority of the superintendents of the poor.

		No. bound out.
In the year 1848,		306
do	1849,	601
do	1850,	848
do	1851,	972
do	1852,	873

There is always a stipulation in the indentures for a certain amount of education for each

1. Dorothea Dix, in *Memorial to the . . . Legislature of the State of New York* (Albany, 1844), wrote of the Seneca County poorhouse: "There was no school for the children; they were at one time sent to the district school in the immediate vicinity, but parents objected to having their children associate 'with the children of the paupers,' and these were sent home. The county provided no teacher, and the house afforded no person supposed competent to teach. The children took their education therefore into their own hands, and were acquiring a sort of knowledge which years of careful instruction will fail to eradicate."

child, or, more properly, that the child should have a certain number of months' schooling during each year of its apprenticeship. It is of course impossible for a private person like myself to acquire accurate information in relation to the fidelity with which this stipulation is fulfilled. What I could do I have done. I have made personal inquiries of the superintendents of many counties, and have sought information extensively by correspondence. I do not recollect more than two or three who had ever made a single inquiry on the subject, or who knew whether the children so bound out were sent to school or not, and in these few cases there was no pretence that the inquiries had been systematic or thorough. I have found many children bound out by the superintendents who never received one hour's education during their apprenticeship, and who, at the age of twenty one, were cast loose on the world no better than the heathen. How can children brought up in this way be expected to become anything else than criminals or paupers? They have no ambition to acquire property, and if they had, they have no means to acquire it. They cannot enter into trade, because in order to do this with any success they must be able to read, write, and cypher, and this they cannot do . . . A single seed of Canada thistle planted in a field will bear a full sized plant, which, in its turn will bear seeds from which new plants will spring, and thus a field, once fertile, will become filled with these noxious plants. Just so with the 3,000 children in our poor-houses, and with the 600 who are annually bound out. Each of these is a seed of pauperism, which will bear plants that will again bear seed, and in time will overrun the State with a burden of pauperism and crime, which it will be unable to bear.

.   .   .   .   .

Efficient rules should be adopted to guard against abuses in the apprenticeship of pauper children. Full enquiries should be made as to the character of the proposed master, and the answer should be made a matter of record.

The parents or friends of the apprentice should be cited to attend, and their objections, if any, should be recorded and carefully weighted. The master should not be allowed to remove the apprentice from the town where he was originally bound without the consent in writing of the superintendents. The indentures should fully declare the duties of the master and provide for a proper amount of schooling and the provision of the necessary school books. A list of pauper apprentices in each town should be furnished on the last day of October in each year to the town superintendent of common schools, as to the manner in which the stipulations with regard to education in the indentures have been complied with. This plan would . . . greatly tend to elevate the character of the State and the condition of the poor.

The schools in our county houses should be made district schools. No teacher should be employed who has not received a full certificate from the town superintendent, and such schools should be allowed to participate in the public money, so far, at least, as to receive its distributive share of *library money*. The superintendents should be required to furnish them with suitable seats, desks, books, stationery and apparatus. If these be removed from the character of our State, and I am confident, it will dry up a very considerable tributary to the broad stream of pauperism.

"State pauper" children in Massachusetts

Massachusetts, unlike most states, provided relief for the "unsettled" poor, that is, the poor who could claim no legal settlement in any town or city. Prior to 1852 state paupers were supported in the towns where they fell into distress, the state reimbursing local authorities at a rate fixed by law.

1. No able-bodied male between ages of twelve and sixty to be supported by state funds

Laws of the Commonwealth of Massachusetts (Boston, 1823), p. 126.

. . . After the first day of June next, no male person, over the age of sixteen years, and under the age of sixty years, while of competent health to labor, shall be considered as a State Pauper, and entitled to support as such.

. . . Whatever the Overseers of the Poor, in any town or city within this Commonwealth, shall exhibit an account against the same, for the support of the paupers . . . they shall certify that no part of such account is for the support of any male person, over the age of twelve, and under the age of sixty years, while of competent health to labor.

2. Ten cents a day

Laws of the Commonwealth of Massachusetts (Boston, 1831), p. 672.

. . . All accounts against the Commonwealth, for the support of paupers, shall be made out and charged at a fixed price per day, and . . . the allowance shall not exceed ten cents per day for the support of paupers over twelve years of age, and six cents per day for the support of paupers under twelve years of age, and five dollars for the funeral expenses of each pauper deceased over twelve years, and two dollars and fifty cents for the funeral expenses of each pauper under twelve years of age.

3. A state institution for pauper children

Franklin B. Sanborn, "The Monson Almshouse," in Massachusetts, State Board of Charities, *First Annual Report, 1864* (Boston, 1865), pp. 272–277.

In 1852 Massachusetts undertook to care for state paupers in its own institutions. Three state almshouses were established, each of which received both adults and children. Persistent efforts were made — and staunchly resisted — to send all the children to Monson and to convert that institution into a school for pauper children.

. . . Very early in the history of this institution it was marked out as a receptacle and school for the pauper children. An Act of the General Court, passed May 19, 1855, established a compulsory classification of the State paupers for this purpose, and directed that the children fit for school should be sent to Monson. The Inspectors say, in their report for 1855: —

"By this Act it is expressly set apart for the purpose of a State Pauper School, in which all the State Pauper children between five and sixteen years of age, so long as they are dependent upon public charity, or are not indentured, are to be supported and educated, to the exclusion of all others, except in a few cases which are designated in the Act.

"The Act went into practical operation in the month of June (between the 13th and 16th of the month), when an interchange of paupers took place between the Monson State Almshouse and the other State Almshouses, agreeably to the provision of the Act. The change made in the institution by the new law of classification is much greater than would be supposed, on a superficial view of the matter. Prior to the time of the change, the inmates included State paupers of every description, all necessarily mingled together indiscriminately, to an extent that could not be otherwise than deleterious. Now, for the most part, only the young and the comparatively healthy and robust are brought together in this institution. It is now emphatically, as denominated in the statute, a State Pauper School, whose primary object is to take care of and educate those children of the State who have none beside the State to care for them."

. . . . .

The Inspectors and officers of the other Almshouses did not consider this classification expedient, and protested against it so forcibly that the law was repealed in 1856. It will be well to quote what was said on both sides of a question which is not yet settled. The Inspectors at Tewksbury said in 1855: — ". . . May it not be advisable to allow some degree of latitude, as to such children as have parents, who will probably soon call for them, and relieve the State entirely of the burden of their support? As the law now stands it is imperative that *all* children, between the ages of five and fifteen, with the exception of idiots, shall be sent to Monson."

The Superintendent of Tewksbury said in the same report: —

". . . By having them all in one place it lessens the opportunities in procuring them good homes and relieving the State of their support. Would it not be better to have a building erected at each of the State almshouses capable of accommodating two hundred children, the first story for a school-room and the upper story for sleeping; the building to be near the main house, but disconnected — that all their work, cooking, washing, making, mending, &c., may be done by the inmates, while the children will be removed from all the bad influences of the adults, and under the charge of their teachers?"

. . . . .

The Superintendent at Bridgewater, Mr. Goodspeed, said in the same report: —

"The expense and inconvenience attending the practical operation of the statute referred to,

are, such as to render the policy thereof somewhat questionable . . . I have thought it proper to suggest the plan of having a cheap and convenient building provided, at a small expense, for the special accommodation of the children and youth, apart from the adult department, where they may be permanently furnished with a home and the necessary means of instruction. The only additional expense attending such a plan would be the cost of the building."

After the repeal of the law in 1856, the Monson Inspectors gave the following account of its workings there, and deprecated the policy of mingling the children with the adult paupers. They said: —

. . . . .

"The salutary effects of the system of classification are strikingly manifested in reference to the children, both physically and morally. A large proportion of the children come here suffering from bodily disease and previous destitution, and from causes also of a moral and social nature. But here they are placed under better treatment and more genial influences, and, as far as possible, are kept separate from all vicious associations. By such means, and with the kind care and supervision of those who have the charge of them, they soon undergo a thorough change in appearance, manners and habits, and are so transformed as hardly to be recognized as the same children. Any one who will visit this institution, and survey the happy and well-trained group of children here assembled, and witness their exercises in the week-day school, and the Sabbath school, cannot but see a striking contrast between them and the children of the foreign population in our cities and large places, living with parents whose habits of life are low, grovelling and vicious. When children of this description mingle indiscriminately with adult persons of the same class, whether in the community at large or in almshouses, jails, &c., it is impossible to protect them effectually against bodily disease and moral pollution. In the best regulated establish-ments, where this association of the young and the old takes place, there is great danger of such contamination; and the moral are more to be dreaded than the physical evils. There is another consideration on this point, which ought not to be overlooked. Children of foreign par-entage, by being constantly and exclusively as-sociated with Americans in the relation of ma-trons, teachers, &c., generally soon lose, in a great degree, their early habits, peculiarities and associations as *foreigners,* and become assimi-lated to those under whose influence and in-struction they are placed. Thus they grow to maturity, like the children of our own citizens, educated in the spirit and principles of our insti-tutions, and prepared to take their positions, at full age, as intelligent and worthy members of our community."

. . . . .

There has been no further legislation on the subject of classifying the inmates of our alms-houses. For a year or two after the repeal of the law of 1855, few or no children were trans-ferred to Monson from the other houses; but since then, the power vested in the Governor, the Alien Commissioners, and more recently in the Board of State Charities, has been exer-cised to make Monson, as far as possible, a school for the pauper children. During the pres-ent year, upwards of two hundred children have been transferred from Bridgewater, Tewksbury, Rainsford and Lancaster.

Proposed reforms in New York poor law, 1857

Deplorable conditions in county poorhouses prompted a state legislative committee to recommend return to outdoor relief and removal of children from almshouses.

1. The situation in 1856

New York State, Senate, "Report of Select Committee Appointed to Visit Charitable Institutions Supported by the State," Doc. 8, *Documents, 1857* (Albany, 1857), I, 2–10.

The poor houses throughout the State may be generally described as badly constructed, ill-arranged, ill-warmed, and ill-ventilated. The rooms are crowded with inmates; and the air, particularly in the sleeping apartments, is very noxious, and to casual visitors, almost insuffer-able. In some cases, as many as forty-five in-mates occupy a single dormitory, with low ceilings, and sleeping boxes arranged in three tiers one above another. Good health is incom-patible with such arrangements. They make it an impossibility.

The want of suitable hospital accommoda-tions is severely felt in most of the poor houses. The sick, considering their physical condition, are even worse cared for than the healthy. The arrangements for medical attendance are quite inadequate to secure that which is suitable; the physician is poorly paid, and consequently gives only such general attention as his remuneration seems to require. In some cases, the inmates sicken and die without any medical attendance whatever. In one county almshouse, averaging 137 inmates, there were 36 deaths during the past year, and yet none of them from epidemic or contagious disease. Such a proportion of mortality indicates most inexcusable negligence.

A proper classification of the inmates is al-most wholly neglected. It is either impossible, or when possible, it is disregarded. Many of the births occurring during the year are doubtless, the offspring of illicit connections. During the last year, the whole number of births was 292. The indiscriminate association of the sexes gen-erally allowed strongly favors this assumption. By day, their intercourse is common and un-restricted; and there is often no sufficient safe-guard against a promiscuous intercourse by night. In one case, the only pretence of a separation of the sexes consisted in the circumstance of separate stairs being provided at each end of a common dormitory; and a police regulation, requiring one sex to reach it by one flight, and the other sex by another, appeared to be deemed a sufficient preventive of all subsequent intercourse.

In two counties, the committee found that the poor houses were supplied by contract, the contractor being allowed to profit by all the labor which he could extort from the paupers. In *both* counties, the contractor was a *superintendent of the poor;* and in *one,* he was *also keeper of the poor house.* In one, the keeper received his compensation from the contractor; and in this case, the food supplied was not only insufficient in quantity, but consisted partly of tainted meat and fish. The inmates were consequently almost starved. They were also deprived of a sufficiency of fuel and bedding, and suffered severely from cold . . .

A still more efficient and economical auxiliary in supporting the poor, and in the prevention of absolute pauperism, consists, in the opinion of the committee, in the proper and systematic distribution of *out door* relief. Worthy indigent persons should, if possible, be kept from the degradation of the poor house, by reasonable supplies of provisions, bedding, and other absolute necessaries, at their own homes. Half the sum requisite for their maintenance in the poor house would often save them from destitution, and enable them to work in their households and their vicinity, sufficiently to earn the remainder of their support during the inclement season when indigence suffers the most, and when it is most likely to be forced into the common receptacles of pauperism, whence it rarely emerges without a loss of self-respect and a sense of degradation. The committee are confirmed in their opinion by the success of the system of *out door* relief practised in the city of New York; and they see no good reason why a similar system might not be adopted throughout the State, with great benefit to the several counties, as well as to

those indigent persons who require only occasional assistance. The present provisions of law seem to be inadequate and ill-suited to the purpose . . .

The most important point in the whole subject confided to the committee, is that which concerns the care and education of the children of paupers. There are at least thirteen hundred of these now inmates of the various poor houses, exclusive of those in New-York and Kings county; enough, in these nurseries, if not properly cared for, to fill some day all the houses of refuge and prisons in the State. As receptacles for adult paupers, the committee do not hesitate to record their deliberate opinion that the great mass of the poor houses which they have inspected, are most disgraceful memorials of public charity. Common domestic animals are usually more humanely provided for than the paupers in some of these institutions; where the misfortune of poverty is visited with greater deprivations of comfortable food, lodging, clothing, warmth and ventilation than constitute the usual penalty of crime. The evidence taken by the committee exhibits such a record of filth, nakedness, licentiousness, general bad morals, and disregard of religion and the most common religious observances, as well as of gross neglect of the most ordinary comforts and decencies of life, as if published in detail would disgrace the State and shock humanity. The committee hesitate to record in the pages of their report the particular instances which would amply justify their general condemnation of these misnamed charitable provisions for the *adult* poor. But with respect to *children,* the case is far worse; and the committee are forced to say that it is a great public reproach that they should ever be suffered to enter or remain in the poor houses as they are now mismanaged. They are for the young, notwithstanding the legal provisions for their education, the worst possible nurseries; contributing an annual accession to our population of three hundred infants, whose present destiny is to pass their most impressible years in the midst of such vicious associations as will stamp them for a life of future infamy and crime. From such associations they should be promptly severed; and provision should be made for them either in asylums devoted to their special use, or in such orphan asylums as would consent to take charge of them for a fair compensation to be provided by the State, or by the several towns and counties properly chargeable with the expense.

Although pauperism is not in itself a crime, yet the kind of poverty which ends in a poor house, unless it is the result of disease, infirmity, or age, producing a positive inability to earn a livelihood, is not unusually the result of such self-indulgence, unthrift, excess, or idleness, as is next of kind to criminality. With such pauperism as that it is certain that the young should not be associated and trained to maturity for it is an association with discomfort, evil maners, profanity, and licentiousness. The education which the statutes provide for them is not suited to their particular case. In-door instruction is often confided to unfit and vicious teachers, and the attendance of pauper children at schools in the vicinity of the almshouse is accompanied by a sort of disgrace attaching to their position which has a most unfavorable influence. Orphanage is not subject to the like stigma; and therefore to go from an orphan asylum to a public school does not expose the orphan to the same taunts and inconsiderateness that follow the pauper child who is the inmate of a poor house which is generally reputed, in its vicinity, as a habitation for vice and degradation, so low has it fallen from its original purpose.

If adequate provision cannot be made in the various existing orphan asylums, and such as may be hereafter founded, for the support and education of these unfortunate children of poverty . . . then the committee most earnestly recommend the establishment of special institutions for the purpose of maintaining and educating them by themselves, apart from the contaminations which now surround and vitiate them. It would, in the end, prove a most useful and economical public charity, and one which the present state of the almshouses seems to

demand very urgently, if the welfare of succeeding generations is worthy of the care of the present one.

Before passing from the subject of poor houses, the committee may be allowed to say that it is much to be regretted that our citizens generally manifest so little interest in the condition even of those in their immediate neighborhood. Individuals who take great interest in human suffering whenever it is brought to their notice, never visit them, and are entirely uninformed, that in a county house almost at their own doors, may be found the lunatic suffering for years in a dark and suffocating cell, in summer, and almost freezing in the winter, — where a score of children are poorly fed, poorly clothed, and quite untaught, — where the poor idiot is half starved and beaten with rods because he is too dull to do his master's bidding, — where the lunatic, and that lunatic too, a *woman,* is made to feel the lash in the hands of a brutal under-keeper — yet these are all to be found — *they all exist in our State.* And the committee are quite convinced that to this apparent indifference on the part of the citizens, may be attributed in a great degree, the miserable state to which these houses have fallen; and they would urge upon the benevolent in all parts of the State to look into their condition, and thus assist to make them comfortable abodes for the indigent and the unfortunate.

2. The Committee recommends removal of children from almshouses

New York State, Senate, "Report of Select Committee," pp. 22–23.

The general result of the examinations made by the committee, is a conviction of the necessity of providing by law:

1st. For a more efficient and constant supervision of all the charitable and reformatory institutions which participate in the public bounty, or are supported by the Governor and Senate, with such arrangement of the terms of service as will constantly secure experience, appears to be the best mode of effecting the purpose.

2d. For the better regulation of poor houses, so as to make fit for asylums for the worthy indigent; for which purpose better structures than now commonly exist, should be legally required, with such arrangements for warmth, ventilation, bathing, classification of the inmates, separation of the sexes, labor, medical attendance, instruction, and religious exercises, as decency, health, and sound morals demand.

3d. For the better maintenance, and education of pauper children, either in the orphan asylums, or in such local institutions as may be established in the several judicial districts by special provisions of law.

4th. For the establishment of two or more asylums for the insane, in addition to the existing asylums, and to be under similar control and management with the State asylum.

5th. For the establishment of an asylum for *insane* convicts in the prisons grounds at Auburn.

6th. For the more efficient regulation of county jails in regard to their structure, and most of the particulars requisite for the better of poor houses as above specified.

7th. For a revision of the poor laws.

Respectfully submitted.

MARK SPENCER
GEO. W. BRADFORD.
M. LINDLEY LEE.

---

3. New York law encouraging removal of children from almshouses, 1857 [1]

1. For the more stringent law of 1875 see Volume II, Part Three, Chap. I, sec. A, Children in almshouses, doc. 5.

"An Act in relation to orphan and destitute children," 1857 — ch. 61, *Laws of the State of New York* (Albany,1857), I, 94.

It shall be lawful for the superintendents of the poor, in counties in which there shall be no orphan asylum, and the overseers of the poor of towns in such counties, to place the children, chargeable to and supported at the expense of such counties or towns, in any incorporated orphan asylum in any county of the state, upon such terms as shall be agreed upon with the managers or trustees of said asylum, at the proper expense of the counties or towns to which they are properly chargeable.

It shall be the duty of the managers of every orphan asylum or other institution authorised to receive and bind out orphan or destitute children, to provide and keep always open for the inspection of all desiring to examine it, a book, in which shall be registered the names, age and parentage, as near as the same can be ascertained, of all children committed to their care or received into such institution, in which book or register shall also be written the time such child left the institution, and if bound out or otherwise, place out at service, or on trial, the name and occupation of the person with whom it is so placed and his or her place of residence. The managers shall have no power to bind out any person mentioned in the first section.

Poor relief in a southern state, 1839–1856

---

1. A removal case, North Carolina, 1839

Archibald A. T. Smith Papers, Southern Historical Collection, University of North Carolina Library, Chapel Hill, N.C.

Whether in South or North, counties and towns refused to support any but their own poor and went to considerable trouble and no little expense to remove persons likely to become public charges to the localities in which they had legal settlement. In the following case the removal of two poor families from one North Carolina county to another proceeded without the complications and litigation which sometimes occurred.

State of North Carolina
Cumberland County   to the Sheriff or any Lawful Office for Said County

Forasmuch as the Warden of the Poor for the county of Cumberland have complained before Mr. Gordon Deming one of the Justices of the Peace in and for the said county that Matthew Runnels, wife and several children, poor persons, hath come into the said county of Cumberland to inhabit and reside from and out of the county of Columbus in which the said Matthew Runnels, wife & children hath gained a legal settlement by being actually resident therein one whole year, and is likely to become chargeable to the said county of Cumberland and the said warden for the County of Cumberland have made before me due proof of the premises, I do therefore command you the said constable to convey the said Matthew Runnels, wife & children from and out of the said county of Cumberland and then deliver to the wardens of the poor for the said county of Columbus or to some or one of them together with a true copy of this precept at the same time showing to them the original given under my hand & seal this 19 March 1839.

G. Deming

I hereby constitute and appoint Thos. H. Massey to serve the above warrant.

G. Deming

State of North Carolina.
I John W. Lamin, Jr. Clerk of the Court of Pleas & Quarter Session of Cumberland County do certify that the name and signature of G. Deming Esq. which appears to the annexed

warrant is in the proper hand writing of the said G. Deming and that he is an acting Justice of the Peace for said County duly commissioned and sworn, and that full faith and credit is due to his official acts —

In testimony whereof I have hereunto set my hand and affixed the county seal at Fayetteville, this 19th day of March A.D. 1839

Mr. W. Lamin Jr.

I delivered the within named persons and a copy of the within to Mr. Lott Williamson, Warden of Columbus County N.C. this 22nd day of March 1839

Thos. H. Massey Constable

Received from Thos. H. Massey Constable for the Wardens of Cumberland County, N.C. two families James Runnels, wife and children also Mathew Runnels, wife & children. This 22nd day of March, 1839.

Lott Williamson, Warden
for Columbus County, N.C.

The Wardens of the Poor of Cumberland County, 1839.
To Tho. H. Massey Dr.

March 22 to 6 day hire of wagon & driver
         to carrying 2 families to Columbus
         County   30.00
         to 6 days services as Constable   6.00
                                                            $36.00

Cr. by deducting from the bill   3.00
                                                            $33.00

Provisions for the two families   6.25
                                                            $39.25

---

2. Outdoor relief for defective children, North Carolina, 1845–1846

Orange County (North Carolina), Records of

the Court of Wardens, 1832–1856, North Carolina State Department of Archives and History, Raleigh, N.C.

July 7, 1845: Ordered that John Owen be allowed $10 for the support of his deformed child and that the treasurer pay the same to Henry Edwards, Jr. who will disburse the same for his benefit.

.   .   .   .   .

A memorial in favor of Nelly Brown and her blind son having been laid before the wardens it was ordered that the Treasurer pay to George W. Rhodes $10 to be applied by him towards their support.

November 24, 1846: Ordered that Nancy Carroll be allowed Five dollars for the support of her idiot child to 1st April next and that the superintendant pay the same.

Ordered that Nelly Brown be allowed Five dollars for the support of her blind son to 1st April next and that the superintendant furnish the same.

3. Care of an infant orphan, North Carolina, 1846–1848

Orange County, Records of the Court of Wardens.

September 7, 1846: Ordered that the Treasurer pay to Mrs. Kendall W. Wait thirty Dollars for taking care of Elizabeth Truelove for six months.

Ordered that the Treasurer pay to Mrs. Wait Four dollars per month for taking care of Elizabeth Truelove, an infant, for two months and twenty Dollars for the next six months.

Ordered that the Treasurer pay to Howel Gilliam five dollars for taking care of Lucy Truelove [mother of Elizabeth].

Ordered that the Treasurer pay to John W. Carr four dollars for finding coffin & burying clothes of Lucy Truelove.

September 6, 1847: Ordered that the Superintendant pay to Mrs. Price twenty dollars semiannual allowance the support of Elizabeth Truelove from 1st April last & fifteen dollars for the next six months up to 1st April 1848.

April 5, 1848: Ordered that the Superintendant pay to Mrs. Price fifteen dollars semi-annual allowance for the support of Elizabeth Truelove to 1st Oct. next.

September 4, 1848: Ordered that the Superintendant receive Elizabeth Truelove, an infant, as a pauper at the Poor House.

4. Relief for children of Mexican War soldiers, 1847–1848

Orange County, Records of the Court of Wardens.

September 6, 1847: Ordered that the Superintendant bring the children of Young Barbee to the poor House.

November 23, 1847: Ordered that the sum of twelve dollars & fifty cents ($12.50) be paid to C. W. Johnston, Esq. for the support of the children of Young Barbee who is at present a volunteer in the N.C. Regiment in Mexico.

April 5, 1848: Ordered that the Superintendant pay to Murrell Chisenhall twenty dollars for taking care of the children of Young Barbee before they were brought to the poor House . . .

Ordered that Superintendant be directed to bring the children of Calvin Bacon (who is now a Soldier in Mexico) to the poor House.

---

5. Binding out of poorhouse boys

Orange County, Records of the Court of Wardens.

November 24, 1846: Ordered that the Superintendent bring Andrew Jackson, a free boy of color, raised at the Poor House . . . to the present Term of the Court of Pleas and Quarter Sessions for the purpose of being bound out.

September 2, 1856: Ordered that this Court recommend to the next County Court to be bound to D. D. Phillips a free boy of color by the name of William James Stowers aged
years who is to learn him the art and mystery of a *coarse harness maker* and shop work generally and when he arrives at the full age of twenty-one years to give him a set of tools suitable for his work and twenty-five dollars in cash or its equivalent.

B. SPECIAL INSTITUTIONS FOR DEPENDENT CHILDREN

Orphan asylum disasters, 1822, 1863

---

1. Philadelphia, 1822

Niles' Weekly Register, Feb. 2, 1822, p. 367; Feb. 9, 1822, p. 381.

The Orphan Society of Philadelphia was founded in 1814 "to rescue from ignorance, idleness, and vice, unprotected and helpless children, and to provide for them, that support and instruction which may eventually render them valuable members of the community."

Terrible fire. Among the institutions which manifested the zeal of the citizens of Philadelphia in works of benevolence and charity, the Orphan Asylum stood conspicuous. This fine building, located at the corner of Schuykill, Sixth and Cherry streets, was the happy home of about one hundred little orphan girls, in which they were brought up and instructed to become useful members of society. But in the dead hour of the night of the 23d ult. one of the coldest that we have had this season, all that was combustible of this building was consumed by fire — and, horrible to relate, twenty-three of the litle innocents perished in the flames! The children slept in the third story, the fire broke out below, and those rescued were snatched out of their beds, at great personal hazard, chiefly by two neighboring watchmen, named *Butcher* and *Miller*. The remote situation of the building from the body of the population of the city, prevented the usual assistance of the firemen and others, until the whole of the interior was on fire; and then the great effort was to save the Widow's Asylum adjoining, which was effected. The cost of the edifice was $20,299, and the value of the bedding, clothes and furniture destroyed, is estimated at $3,000; the property was insured at $6,000 only. But the sympathies of the people have been excited, and liberal contributions are tendering — and the prospect is, that all will soon be restored to what it was, save the little sufferers; who, to use the language of the editor of the Democratic Press, "we humbly trust are taken to the bosom of their Father and their God." The legislature of Pennsylvania has *unanimously* passed a bill appropriating 5,000 dollars to re-build the edifice.

.   .   .   .

Orphan Asylum, Philadelphia. Individually and by companies, &c. money is pouring in to re-establish this institution. The legislature of the state granted 5000 dollars, unanimously — a member said, "let us pass the bill 'ere the embers of the building become cold and the tears of the orphans dry." A masonic lodge gave 100 dollars, and several other associations from 50 to 100. Messrs. Warren and Wood, of the theatre, gave a night for the benefit of the establishment — the whole receipts were 1745 dollars, net amount, deducting expenses, 1403, which were immediately paid over. The amount already received considerably exceeds the loss of *property* sustained.[1]

---

2. Burning of the Colored Orphan Asylum, New York City, 1863

The New York Times, July 14, 1863.

The Colored Orphan Asylum was founded in 1836. The 233 occupants, ranging in age from two to twelve, escaped from the burning building unharmed and found shelter, first in a police station, and later in the almshouse. The burning of the asylum was an episode in the New York draft riots.

The Orphan Asylum for Colored Children was visited by the mob about four o'clock. This Institution is situated on Fifth Avenue, and the building, with the grounds and gardens adjoining, extended from Forty-third to Forty-fourth Street. Hundreds, and perhaps thousands of the rioters, the majority of whom were women and children, entered the premises, and in the most excited and violent manner they ransacked and plundered the building from cellar to garret. The building was located in the most pleasant and healthy portion of the city. It was purely a charitable institution. In it there are on an average 600 or 800 homeless colored orphans. The building was a large four-story one, with two wings of three stories each.

When it became evident that the crowd designed to destroy it, a flag of truce appeared on the walk opposite, and the principals of the establishment made an appeal to the excited populace, but in vain.

Here it was that Chief-Engineer Decker showed himself one of the bravest among the brave. After the entire building had been ransacked, and every article deemed worth carrying away had been taken — and this included even the little garments for the orphans, which were contributed by the benevolent ladies of this city — the premises were fired on the first floor. Mr. Decker did all he could to prevent the flames from being kindled, but when he was overpowered by superior numbers, with his own hands he scattered the brands, and effectually extinguished the flames. A second attempt was made, and this time in three different parts of the house. Again he succeeded, with the aid of half a dozen of his men, in defeating the incendiaries. The mob became highly exasperated at his conduct, and threatened to take his life if he repeated the act. On the front steps of the building he stood up amidst an infuriated and half-drunken mob of two thousand, and begged of them to do nothing so disgraceful to humanity as to burn a benevolent institution, which had for its object nothing but good. He said it would be a lasting disgrace to them and to the city of New York.

These remarks seemed to have no good effect upon them, and meantime the premises were again fired — this time in all parts of the

---

1. On December 13, 1822, two of the orphans tried to set fire to the temporary asylum. The attempt failed and, according to a contemporary observer, "the little culprits were judiciously disposed of." The new asylum opened in January 1823. Thomas Wilson, *Picture of Philadelphia for 1824* (Philadelphia, 1823), p. 65.

house. Mr. Decker, with his few brave men, again extinguished the flames. This last act brought down upon him the vengeance of all who were bent on the destruction of the asylum, and but for the fact that some firemen surrounded him, and boldly said that Mr. Decker could not be taken except over their bodies, he would have been dispatched on the spot. The institution was destined to be burned, and after an hour and a half of labor on the part of the mob it was in flames in all parts. Three or four persons were horribly bruised by the falling walls, but the names we could not ascertain. There is now scarcely one brick left upon another of the Orphan Asylum.

Orphanage philanthropy, 1830–1865

In the two decades after 1830 benevolent individuals and religious and ethnic groups founded fifty-six orphanages and other institutions for children. The spread of such institutions reflected sympathy for children, social need, and the strength of sectarian feelings.

---

1. New York: the Leake and Watts Asylum, 1830–1831

Dorothy C. Barck, ed., *Letters from John Pintard to His Daughter . . . 1816–1833,* III (New York, 1941), 134–135, 152–153, 219, 241.

John Pintard (1759–1844), a humanitarian reformer, was one of the organizers of the New York House of Refuge and a founder of the New York Historical Society.

March 25, 1830 . . . I believe that I have not mentioned to you the prospect of a great act of Charity in favour of Orphans, without distinction of religion or country that is about to take place in this city. John G. Leake Esq. a wealthy Bachelor, died last year, leaving a Will drawn by himself, but not executed, in favour of Robert Watts, son of John Watts Esq. of N Rochelle, in your time, on condition of taking the name of Leake. The Will, after legal investigation was adjudicated to be valid, but before the condition could be fulfilled by an Act of the Legislature, young Watts, the only remaining son of his Father died. In case of such decease or non compliance, the whole Estate of Mr. Leake, a few legacies excepted, was devised to the Rector of Trinity Church, the senior Ministers of the Dutch & Presbyterian Churches, the Mayor & Recorder of this City in Trust, the income & profits of both Real & Personal Estate to be applied to building & supporting an Orphan Assylum, in the suburbs of the city. The Real Estate becomes escheated to the State, about $100,000, the personal between 200 & 300,000 Dollars goes to the Trustees who are applying to the Legislature for an Act of Incorporation. It is contemplated to merge our present Orphan Assylum in this new *Leake* O. A., whereby it can go into immediate operation & support forthwith 300 Orphans. It is to be hoped that the Legislature will release their claim, & thus carry the benevolent intention of Mr. Leake into full effect. The Real Estate may be worth $100,000, making altogether $400,000 by far the largest benefaction ever bequeathed in this city.

.   .   .   .   .

June 11, 1830 . . . There is no end to collections in this city. I only wish that my purse were adequate. Had it not been for this circumstance I should have taken Sister & my namesake to St. Patricks Cathedral next Sunday morning where a collection is to be made for the benefit of their Orphan Assylum. I can however give my mite, but I should have been gratified to hear the superb music usual on these occasions which attracts great numbers of other denominations & they generally get about $12,000. This Assylum, being strictly Roman Catholic, derives no benefit from our State School Fund, which is applied to public schools that are not sectarian. Such is our Orphan Assylum, where no distinction is made. The R. Catholics are overwhelmed with orphans, so many poor Irish die after a short residence in this city, martyrs, men & women, to intemperance. Ardent spirits are so cheap, that poor Pat & his wife Shelah cannot withstand the temptation. Of course a large supply of orphan children are annually cast on the benevolence of the Catholics & tho generally humble the Irish are very charitable & share their last potato with a famished fellow creature. It is the duty therefore of every Protestant citizen to assist them.

.   .   .   .   .   .

February 5, 1831 . . . Died yesterday AE. 46 John Watts, Jr. M.D. President of the College of Physicians, a manager of the A.B.S.[1] & a useful member of several of our humane & benevolent Institutions. I mentioned something a year ago about a large legacy left by the late John G. Leake Esq. to Robert, son of John Watts, uncle to the Doctor. The will, after being carried up to the court of errors was adjudged in favour of Robert, who had just come of age & shortly after died, whereby his Father became heir at law to Mr. Leakes estate valued at $300,000. It was a condition of the Will, that in case Robert should die, without heirs, & before he came of age, that the whole of the estate should go towards founding an assylum for Orphans, without distinction of denomination. Mr. J. Watts has most honourably relinquished his legal right to this large estate to carry into effect the intention of Mr. Leake, and a Bill is now before our Legislator, to incorporate Trustees to take charge of the Estate & fulfil the intentions of the munificent Testator. The Building will probably be designated, the Leake & Watts Orphan House. This probably the largest single legacy ever bequeathed to a

1. American Bible Society.

single object in the U States. Few, very few would be found to act the liberal & generous part of Mr. Watts. The higher praise be his.

.   .   .   .   .   .

April 14, 1831 . . . Yesterday Sister attended in the City Hotel the ann[iversar]y meeting of the Orphan Assylum. The exhibition of the children was most interesting. She paid her own & mothers subs[cription]s $2 each with great satisfaction. The duties of the Seamans Bk occurring at the same hour, 12, prevented me the pleasure of complimenting the good ladies who interest themselves in this important institution. Among the children were 3 orphan daughters of Mr. Duff formerly a wine merchant in this city. His wife was a daughter of Dr. Tillary a respectable physician of the best practice, who lived at the corner of Broadway and Wall Street when Grandma lived in 72 Broadway. She was a very pretty little woman, but unfortunately became, from her husbands misfortunes intemperate. They both died in early [life] leaving their 3 children a charge on the Assylum. It makes one shrink when we regard such instances & ask whose children may in process of time become subjects of the Assylum, to be bound out to service after the decease of parents, who spent their all in profuse extravagance, which was literally the case with Mr. Duff, who was one of poor Uncle Lewis' boon companions.

---

2. Endowment of Girard College, Philadelphia, 1830

The will of Stephen Girard in Edgar W. Knight and Clifton L. Hall, *Readings in American Educational History* (New York: Appleton-Century-Crofts, 1951), pp. 247–254.

Stephen Girard (1750–1831), a childless widower, left a fortune estimated at about six million dollars to found a "college" for "poor male white orphans." Girard College, the largest endowed institution for children in the United States, opened on January 1, 1848. During the 1960's the racial restrictions in the Girard will became the subject of extensive litigation. They were nullified by a federal appeals court in 1967 and the first male black orphans were admitted to the institution in 1968.

And, whereas, I have been for a long time impressed with the importance of educating the poor, and of placing them, by the early cultivation of their minds and the development of their moral principles, above the many temptations to which, through poverty and ignorance, they are exposed; and I am particularly desirous to provide for such a number of poor male white orphan children, as can be trained in one institution, a better education, as well as a more comfortable maintenance, than they usually receive from the application of the public funds: . . . Now, I do give, devise and bequeath, *all the residue and remainder of my real and personal estate of* every sort and kind wheresoever situate (the real estate in Pennsylvania charged as aforesaid) unto "the Mayor, Aldermen and Citizens of Philadelphia, their successors and assigns, in trust, to and for the several uses, intents and purposes hereinafter mentioned of and concerning the same, that is to say; so far as regards my real estate in Pennsylvania, in trust, that no part thereof shall be ever sold or alienated by the said Mayor, Aldermen and Citizens of Philadelphia, or their successors, but the same shall forever thereafter be let from time to time, to good tenants, at yearly or other rents, and upon leases in possession not exceeding five years from the commencement thereof, and that the rents, issues and profits arising therefrom, shall be applied towards keeping that part of the said real estate situate in the City and Liberties of Philadelphia constantly in good repair (parts elsewhere situate to be kept in repair by the tenants thereof respectively), and towards improving the same,

whenever necessary, by erecting new buildings; and that the net residue (after paying the several annuities herein before provided for) be applied to the same uses and purposes as are herein declared of and concerning the residue of my personal estate: and so far as regards my real estate in Kentucky, now under the care of Messrs. Triplett & Brumley, in trust, to sell and dispose of the same, whenever it may be expedient to do so, and to apply the proceeds of such sale to the same uses and purposes as . . .

And so far as regards the residue of my personal estate . . . to apply and expend so much of that sum as may be necessary, in erecting, as soon as practicably may be, in the centre of my square of ground between High and Chestnut streets, and Eleventh and Twelfth streets, in the City of Philadelphia (which square of ground I hereby devote for the purposes hereinafter stated, and for no other, forever) a permanent College, with suitable out-buildings, sufficiently spacious for the residence and accommodation of at least three hundred scholars, and the requisite teachers and other persons necessary in such an institution as I direct to be established, and in supplying the said College and out-buildings with decent and suitable furniture, as well as books and all things needful to carry into effect my general design.

.   .   .   .   .

. . . When the College and appurtenances shall have been constructed, and supplied with plain and suitable furniture and books, philosophical and experimental instruments and apparatus, and all other matters needful to carry my general design into execution; the income, issues and profits of so much of the said sum of two millions of dollars as shall remain unexpended, shall be applied to maintain the said College according to my directions.

1. The Institution shall be organized as soon as practicable, and to accomplish the purpose more effectually, due public notice of the intended opening of the College shall be given — so that there may be an opportunity to make

selections of competent instructors, and other agents, and those who may have the charge of orphans, may be aware of the provisions intended for them.

2. A competent number of instructors, teachers, assistants, and other necessary agents shall be selected, and when needful, their places from time to time, supplied; they shall receive adequate compensation for their services: but no person shall be employed, who shall not be of tried skill in his or her proper department, of established moral character, and in all cases persons shall be chosen on account of their merit, and not through favour or intrigue.

3. As many poor male white orphans, between the age of six and ten years, as the said income shall be adequate to maintain, shall be introduced into the College as soon as possible; and from time to time, as there may be vacancies, or as increased ability from income may warrant, others shall be introduced.

4. On the application for admission, an accurate statement should be taken in a book, prepared for the purpose, of the name, birthplace, age, health, condition as to relatives, and other particulars useful to be known of each orphan.

5. No orphan should be admitted until the guardians or directors of the poor, or a proper guardian or other competent authority, shall have given by indenture, relinquishment or otherwise, adequate power to the Mayor, Aldermen and Citizens of Philadelphia, or to directors or others by them appointed, to enforce in relation to each orphan every proper restraint, and to prevent relatives or others from interfering with or withdrawing such orphan from the Institution.

6. Those orphans, for whose admission application shall first be made, shall be first introduced, all other things concurring — and at all times priority of application shall entitle the applicant to preference in admission, all other things concurring; but if there shall be at any time, more applicants than vacancies, and the applying orphans shall have been born in different places, a preference shall be given —

first to orphans born in the City of Philadelphia; *secondly,* to those born in any other part of Pennsylvania; *thirdly,* to those born in the City of New York (that being the first port on the continent of North America at which I arrived) and *lastly* to those born in the City of New Orleans, being the first port on the said continent at which I first traded.

7. The orphans admitted into the College, shall be there fed with plain but wholesome food, clothed with plain but decent apparel (no distinctive dress ever to be worn), and lodged in a plain but safe manner; Due regard shall be paid to their health, and to this end their persons and clothes shall be kept clean, and they shall have suitable and rational exercise and recreation. They shall be instructed in the various branches of a sound education: comprehending Reading, Writing, Grammar, Arithmetic, Geography, Navigation, Surveying, Practical Mathematics, Astronomy, Natural, Chemical and Experimental Philosophy, the French and Spanish languages (I do not forbid, but I do not recommend the Greek and Latin languages), and such other learning and science as the capacities of the several scholars may merit or warrant. I would have them taught facts and things, rather than words and signs; and especially, I desire that by every proper means a pure attachment to our republican institutions, and to the sacred rights of conscience, as guaranteed by our happy constitutions shall be formed and fostered in the minds of the scholars.

8. Should it unfortunately happen, that any of the orphans admitted into the College, shall, from malconduct, have become unfit companions for the rest, and mild means of reformation prove abortive, they should no longer remain therein.

9. These scholars, who shall merit it shall remain in the College until they shall respectively arrive at between fourteen and eighteen years of age; they shall then be bound out by the Mayor, Aldermen and Citizens of Philadelphia, or under their direction, to suitable occupations, as those of agriculture, navigation,

arts, mechanical trades, and manufactures, according to the capacities and acquirements of the scholars respectively, consulting, as far as prudence shall justify it, the inclination of the several scholars, as to the occupation, art or trade, to be learned.

. . . . . .

I enjoin and require that *no ecclesiastic, missionary, or minister of any sect whatsoever, shall ever hold or exercise any station or duty whatever in the said College; nor shall any such person ever be admitted for any purpose, or as a visitor, within the premises appropriated to the purposes of the said College.* In making this restriction, I do not mean to cast any reflection upon any sect or person whatsoever; but, as there is such a multitude of sects, and such a diversity of opinion amongst them, I desire to keep the tender minds of the orphans, who are to derive advantage from this bequest, free from the excitement which clashing doctrines and sectarian controversy are so apt to produce; my desire is, that all the instructors and teachers in the College, shall take pains to instill into the minds of the scholars the *purest principles of morality,* so that, on their entrance into active life, they may, *from inclination and habit,* evince *benevolence towards* their fellow creatures, and *a love of truth, sobriety, and industry,* adopting at the same time such religious tenets as their *matured reason* may enable them to prefer.

---

3. Founding of St. Vincent's Orphan Asylum, Louisville, Kentucky, 1832

Sister Columba Fox, *The Life of the Right Reverend John Baptist Mary David, 1761–1841* (New York: United States Catholic Historical Society, 1925), pp. 131–132.

J. B. M. David was bishop of Louisville in 1832. "Mother Catherine" was Catherine Spalding (1793–1858), founder and mother superior of the Sisters of Charity of Nazareth. In 1831, with the assistance of Bishop David, she established the first Roman Catholic school in Louisville and during the cholera epidemic of 1832 she and the nuns at the school nursed the sick poor of the city.

While laboring to promote the interests of education, it was always Mother Catherine's noble ambition to find a means for harboring the homeless little ones, an ambition which her spiritual father, Bishop David, gladly fostered and pointed to as a worthy goal of her endeavors. Among the pupils of the Louisville school there were some much in need of food and raiment. These were promptly cared for, but to give shelter to those in need of it, did not seem possible, because of the limited quarters of the Sisters.

One evening late in the autumn of 1832, a messenger came to tell Mother Catherine that a family of non-Catholics, by the name of Jenkins, had lately arrived from Pennsylvania, and were in such a destitute condition that any assistance would be a great charity. She, taking a Sister companion, went to the place designated and there found lying lifeless on a cot, a mother with a babe of a few months, near her a daughter of sixteen sick of heart disease, and another of five or six years of age. The father was helpless. A son of eighteen had gone to Indiana to purchase a farm.

Mother Catherine's practical mind and ready hand found means for relieving the sad situation. She called on kind neighbors who promptly responded. The deceased was given suitable burial and she offered to take the sick girl and the two little ones home with her, but the girl refused and nobly insisted that she would be able to keep the family together, and her brother, on returning, sustained her in her resolution. After two weeks, however, worn out and over-weary she lay down at the close of the day to rest, as her brother thought, but when morning came he found she had passed away.

The father and brother were now willing to let Mother Catherine take the two little girls to the Sisters' home. These formed the nucleus of St. Vincent's Orphan Asylum, an institution which has since sheltered thousands, saving many from ruin here and hereafter. Bishop Flaget's desire for such an institution in his diocese had been frustrated by the want of means. He thanked Providence for opening now this opportunity for its establishment, and blessed the woman of indomitable will whose zeal, energy, and ingenuity could effect it. Before the close of the year four more little girls were received. Nazareth sent Sisters to care for them and purchased a lot near St. Louis' Church on which an orphanage might be built.

The Catholic ladies of the city became interested, and held a meeting under the direction of Father Abell, to devise means for raising funds. A Fair was planned, and so much enthusiasm awakened that the sum of eleven hundred and fifty dollars was realized. When the new house was completed in the spring of 1833, Mother Catherine and four Sisters moved into it with twenty-five or thirty orphans.

From the beginning a well-regulated household was established with hours for every duty and work allotted according to the capacity of each member. It was financed by occasional small donations, by the sale of articles which the industry and skill of the Sisters and the children furnished, and by the generosity of the merchants and farmers who soon learned to appreciate the value of the great work.

---

4. "The Howards," New Orleans, 1853

Report of the Howard Association: Epidemic of 1853 (New Orleans, 1854), pp. 24–28.

Sympathizers throughout the nation contributed $228,000 to "the Howards," a voluntary association which provided nurses, physicians, medicine, food, and shelter to victims of the yellow fever epidemic in New Orleans and other parishes of Louisiana.

The total number of cases of yellow fever attended to in this city, as per returns of the members, is 11,088, to which we might add several thousands of cases in the surrounding country, where the offices of the association have been extended, and where, in many instances, in addition to the means forwarded, our members have attended in person.

It will also be borne in mind that we have given special relief in this city, to the indigent whose sufferings either directly or indirectly grew out of the fell pestilence that stalked among us, and thus, whilst our expenditures may seem large at the first glance, they will appear moderate when compared with the number to whom we have afforded comfort during their sickness — sustenance in their convalescence. The Stranger, the Poor, the Widow and the Orphan have all been cared for. In practice, the association ever since its formation in 1837 has adopted as its Motto, the noble sentiment, "I am a man; — whatever concerns mankind concerns me."

.   .   .   .   .

It may interest our friends at a distance and those of our citizens who were not eyewitnesses of the manner in which the Association worked during the late Epidemic, to know that we had in operation during the season, in various Districts of the City, two Convalescent Infirmaries, in which were received persons just recovered from the fever, and yet too weak to enter upon their ordinary pursuits. In addition to these, which were for the most part used as auxilliaries to our own and the City Hospitals, we also established three Orphan Asylums, in which were received 241 children left totally destitute by the death of their parents.

We had also . . . in charge of wet-nurses throughout the city under our daily supervision, 97 babies at the breast; some of whom, as well as many of the Orphans above alluded to — when we determined to dispose of them, and after using every possible means to ascertain if they had any relations living, were adopted by our citizens.

At the close of the Epidemic, all the Orphans remaining on our hands were transferred from our own temporary Asylums to those regularly established in this city; and in this transfer, the sectarian views of the parents of these little unfortunates were our only guide in deciding to the care of which of these Institutions, each Orphan should be entrusted.

It is deemed proper to remark that we transmitted the sum of one hundred dollars with each and every child that we thus disposed of, to the various Orphan Asylums; and these facts will account for the amounts charged up under the several headings, in the specified list of expenditures in the foregoing report.[1]

It is scarcely necessary to add that in every instance, in and out of our Asylums, Hospitals and Infirmaries, that as far as lay in our power, every attention was paid to the food, clothing, cleanliness and general comfort of all those who were the recipients of the offices of the Association; and that the establishments above named were scarcely ever without the personal attendance of some one or more of our members, although carefully provided at the same time with the best superintendents that could be secured.

---

5. The Jewish Foster Home, Philadelphia, 1855–1860

Letters of Rebecca Gratz, Philadelphia, to relatives in Savannah, Georgia, in Miriam G. Moses Papers, Southern Historical Collection, University of North Carolina.

The philanthropic career of Rebecca Gratz (1781–1869) extended over almost sixty-five

1. The Howard Association donated a total of $17,500 to four orphanages.

years and included service for the Female Association for Relief of Women and Children in Reduced Circumstances, Philadelphia Orphan Society, and the Hebrew Sunday School Society, as well as the Jewish Foster Home.

April 15, 1855

. . . The children in our new foster home are still more remarkable, having now a very happy home, under an amiable matron, they improve in every respect. I wish you could see & become interested in this society which we hope will not only shelter destitute children, either orphans, or those whose parents are unable to take care of them, but by instruction render them capable of getting their own living in a more reputable way than is usually resorted to by poor Jews. [Education] has long appeared to me, the one thing needful to elevate the character of our poor. They come in great numbers from foreign countries where they are oppressed and have no prospect of doing more than sustaining life, and these children are ill clothed, ill fed & left to pick up bad habits in the streets while [the parents] having no trade, go peddling about the country. There are twelve children in the foster home who have been there nearly a year. Most of them have one parent living who are permitted to visit them once a fortnight and if able pay 25 cents per week to the society.

It is astonishing to see the change in the manners, conduct and character of these little beings. They can all read & write, behave with the utmost decorum at meals where they repeat grace in the Jew and English, have all the comforts of cleanliness, order, and good treatment and are taught religious & social duties. With God's blessing I trust this may be the beginning of a new era in the history of Jewish charity and that in every town namely where there are destitute children such provision may be made for them. Funds are wanted to increase the accommodations of our Foster home. We require a larger house for the many applications made for admission. At present we have not room for more than sixteen or eighteen children. Do you think you can procure us any aid among the rich & charitable in your congregation?

.   .   .   .   .

October 11, 1855

. . . I am not quite sure that I sent you the constitution of the Jewish foster home. If not I will send one — it is getting on very well, we have twelve half orphan children well provided for. Our Matron gives us some care, because we never feel sure of keeping her. She is a young woman, who has been many years in this country, an excellent housekeeper, very neat, and is fond of teaching the children, and is moreover a strict Jewess but her *temper* is so ragged that we are continually troubled by her complaints. She calls her outbreaks *nervousness,* which does not signify anything but an apology, too often repeated to be satisfactory. Her salary is $156 per annum and a comfortable home — Is there any one in your Jewish community that you could recommend to such a situation? You know exactly what are requisite for a Matron of such an institution. She has a domestic woman, and with careful instruction may soon teach the little girls to be useful. It is necessary the matron should be able to read & write English, the one we have knows Hebrew & German & French, but as we do not expect any occasion for many tongues, enough Hebrew to teach the blessings & prayers in that language will satisfy us.

.   .   .   .   .

[1860]

I have this day received your affectionate letter concerning your liberal donation to the Foster home of $25 . . . Encouragement from such a source, makes labour light. We have now 33 little destitute children under tuition, who are in full health and appear very happy . . . I must tell you, that two boys after attaining the age of 13, have been provided with good places, one with a Tobacconist, to be taken care of until he reaches the age of 21. The other in Mr.

Henry Cohen's Stationery establishment for the same term of years, so that we hope they will become good Jewish citizens capable of filling a respectable station in the community. We bless you for your benevolent wishes, and pray God may grant them, and reward you.

Public subsidies for private institutions

In the nineteenth century the philanthropic economy was a mixture of public and private effort, and the practice of public support for private institutions was well established.

---

1. Dickens on state support of charities

Dickens, *American Notes,* I, 64–65.

It is a great and pleasant feature of all such institutions in America, that they are either supported by the State or assisted by the State; or (in the event of their not needing its helping hand) that they act in concert with it, and are emphatically the people's. I cannot but think, with a view to the principle and its tendency to elevate or depress the character of the industrious classes, that a Public Charity is immeasurably better than a Private Foundation, no matter how munificently the latter may be endowed. In our own country, where it has not, until within these later days, been a very popular fashion with governments to display any extraordinary regard for the great mass of the people or to recognise their existence as improveable creatures, private charities, unexampled in the history of the earth, have arisen, to do an incalculable amount of good among the destitute and afflicted. But the government of the country, having neither act nor part in them, is not in the receipt of any portion of the gratitude they inspire; and, offering very little shelter or relief but that which is to be found in the workhouse and the jail, has come, not unnaturally, to be looked upon by the poor rather as a stern master, quick to correct and punish, than a kind protector, merciful and vigilant in their need.

---

2. Justification for the subsidy system, 1857

New York State, Senate, "Report of the Select Committee to Visit Charitable Institutions," Doc. 8, *Documents* (Albany, 1857), 10–11, 21–22.

The Committee recommended the course which New York subsequently (in 1875) adopted: removal of children from county almshouses to privately managed but publicly subsidized orphan asylums.

It is agreeable to turn from the consideration of poor houses and their mismanagement, to the examination of the Orphan Asylums to which the benefactions of the State are contributed. The committee visited them all. Whether it be that the principal charge of these is confided to females, or whatever be the cause, it is certain that with less comparative expenditure of the public moneys an incomparably greater amount of comfort, cleanliness, kind treatment, health, and good education is secured to the inmates, than happens to be the lot of the paupers in our poor houses.

To a cordial expression of praise respecting the general management and good condition of the Orphan Asylums, the committee most cheerfully add a recommendation of them to the liberal support of the State government; and especially if additional benefactions can be made the means of relieving the poor houses of their young inmates, by providing for their support and education in the Orphan Asylums as heretofore suggested by the committee. Children, whose parents are paupers in the legal sense, and actual residents in pauper asylums, are generally to all practical intents as much orphans as those who are deprived by death of their natural protectors; and their actual condition is much more pitiable. An association with their destitute parents, and their necessary poor house companions, is not only a deprivation of the attention and comforts which they ought to enjoy during their tender years, but it is a fatal exposure to examples of most evil tendency. Their chance to become virtuous and exemplary citizens is the most desperate of all human chances; and upon a future generation is inflicted the necessary consequence of supporting them as criminals in our jails and prisons.

The Orphan Asylums are twenty-six in number and contain 2816 children, of whom 2224 are of foreign parentage; to whose support the State appropriates the annual sum of thirty-five thousand dollars.

In connection with this fact the committee desire to state that the cost to the public of supporting 678 prisoners confined in the *jails,* is eighty thousand seven hundred and thirty dollars. The inference is, that to educate one orphan to usefulness, the public treasury expends less than one-tenth as much as it does to maintain one useless convict in jail.

At suitable ages, orphan children are placed in respectable families (by which they are frequently adopted as children) or they are indentured, the boys to farmers and mechanics, the girls to learn housekeeping and needle work. The care of the managers still follows them beyond the precincts of the asylum, until they become of age, and if they are unsatisfactorily provided for, or are ill-treated, new situations are obtained for them. The committee in all cases made strict inquiry as to the standing and reputation of the inmates who had left the asylums, and it was ascertained that, with few exceptions, they became good and useful citizens.

. . . . .

There are various associations in the state, and particularly in the cities and larger towns, for charity, reform and education, which not receiving aid from the state, do not fall within the terms of the resolution of the Senate under which the committee have pursued their investigations. Many of them, however, have been visited by the committee for purposes of information and of comparison with other institutions of a kindred character which were the legitimate subjects of visitation. They are generally supported by private endowments and contributions, with occasional aid, perhaps, from the local authorities. Homes for the friendless, and industrial and other schools are of this class; charities devoted to the maintenance or training of vagrant and destitute children, to the care and protection of young females out of employment or in reduced circumstances, as well as of aged or decrepid women. They deserve to be favorably regarded when the Legislature is considering any general and economical plan of charity or reform. Those, more particularly, which have for their object the support and training of destitute children, and their salvation from the evils of vagrancy, idle habits, and vicious examples, are worthy of attention and encouragement. The management of such charitable enterprises happens fortunately to be confided mainly to benevolent women, whose thrift, economy of expenditure, skill in management, and tenderness of feeling, enable them to produce greater results with less means than is the usual fortune of the other sex. The public bounty bestowed on such institutions, under such management, goes farther and is more certain of producing a suitable return, than the usual application of it. It gives the committee great pleasure to commend such charities to approval and support, as no insignificant part of the great scheme of benevolence and reformation which it is the duty of every good government to maintain.

---

3. Institutions aided by state subsidy, 1857

Louisiana, "Special Report of Legislative Committee on Charitable Institutions," *Legislative Documents, 1857* (New Orleans, 1857), pp. 10–17.

The institutions discussed were among the approximately twenty homes and asylums to which the state of Louisiana contributed a total of $42,600 in 1857.

ORPHAN'S HOME

This Institution is situated on the corner of Constance and Seventh streets, Fourth District of New Orleans. In its organization it was the result of the great epidemic of 1853. That almost unparalleled calamity, in its direful consequences, left large numbers of children deprived of their parents and friends, thrown upon the community as objects of their best charity. Under these circumstances was this Home provided, where the brother and sister could live together as they did ere the pestilence came which so ruthlessly sundered the holiest and dearest relations.

The rooms are sufficiently large and well ventilated, with spacious gallery or hall for play room. The entire building will now comfortably accommodate one hundred and thirty children, and is furnished neatly and substantially. Few similar Institutions exhibit a more cheerful interior, evincing everywhere comfort and neatness.

. . . . .

The number of children admitted during this year has been — 36
Died — 11
Placed out and given to relatives — 34
At present remaining in the Asylum — 103

The whole number of children who have been relieved from want and supplied with necessary care and comforts since the opening of the Institution, has been two hundred and ninety-eight. Of those, ninety-three have died, and about one hundred have been given to their relatives or placed out in good situations.

The full supply of their physical wants, the cleanliness of their apartments, the employment of those of a suitable age in household labors, the indulgence in healthful play, and the intellectual, moral, and religious education which they receive, have combined in the formation of a happy and orderly family, the members of which are training for a useful and happy future.

The receipts into the treasury during the year were derived as follows:

From donations, etc.	$5,089	42
Annual appropriation by the State Legislature	3,000	00
Proceeds of entertainment given at Odd Fellows' Hall on the evening of 22d, 23d, and 24th April	3,101	25
Annual subscription of 160 members	800	00
Life-membership fees	150	00
Interest allowed by the Bank of New Orleans on money deposited with it at 4 per cent. per annum	161	00
Sundry sources, being for board of children, sale of plated ware, etc.	154	00
	$12,455	67

Your Committee recommend an appropriation of $3,000.

CAMP STREET FEMALE ORPHAN ASYLUM

This Institution your Committee found in the best condition, so far as the carrying out its benevolent objects is concerned, although greatly in need of assistance.

Your Committee deem it almost unnecessary to descant upon the merits and eminent usefulness of this Institution; as the orphans cared for in helpless infancy, educated in youth, and trained for a future life of benefit to themselves and society, have published the facts to the world. Sister Regis, under whose kind and self-sacrificing watchfulness the Asylum has for so many years continued to extend its benevolence and fostering care to the houseless and friendless, is still untiring in her mission of love, and asking no boon for herself, seeks only the aid of our wealthy and prosperous State in behalf of the destitute little ones under her charge. Over three hundred children are now dependent upon the Asylum for a home, and look to Sister Regis as their only earthly protector; and taking into consideration the fact that the augmentation of this family of helpless ones, has been greater than usual within the last year, thus entailing heavy and unprovided for expenses, your Committee think that the State is justly called upon to act promptly and liberally . . .

On numerous occasions within the past six months, the treasury of the Asylum has been entirely empty, there not being a dollar wherewith to purchase provisions for the next meal; but amidst all these embarrassing circumstances, the zeal of Sister Regis has never faltered, and by sacrifices and exertions worthy of the noble cause in which she is engaged, she has provided for the wants of her charge.

From a statement furnished to your Committee, it appears that the expenses of the Institution for the year ending on the 1st of January last were $18,594.79, of which the Legislature furnished $5,000.

An appropriation of $5,000 is recommended.

ST. ELIZABETH'S (FORMERLY ST. ANNA'S) HOUSE OF INDUSTRY

This Institution for destitute orphan girls, is situated on the corner of Magazine and Josephine streets. It is conducted by the Sisters of Charity, for the purpose of training up to trades destitute orphan girls, giving them the opportunity of learning that which will render them useful members of society, and enable them to obtain their living hereafter in a respectable manner. Formerly these orphans were obliged to leave the Asylum at the age of twelve and fourteen years — the very period they needed the most protection — and they were thus exposed to most alarming dangers. This Institution is designed to prevent such a necessity.

The building is at present in a very unfinished condition, and claims the aid of the Legislature in covering its naked walls and finishing the flooring — essentials to the proper comfort and regularity of the inmates. The Institution contains now within its unfinished walls, eighty-three destitute orphans from the age of ten to sixteen years. The debt upon the buildings amounts to $4,000; to aid in the payment of which, a portion of the annual distribution is prayed for by the directors. It is to be presumed that this Institution will in course of time be a self-sustaining concern; but being now in its infancy, is unable to support itself. Your committee suggest a liberal consideration in its behalf, and would recommend an appropriation of $5,000.

.   .   .   .   .

ST. JOSEPH'S GERMAN ORPHAN ASYLUM
Is situated in the Fourth District, city of New Orleans. It was established for both male and female German orphans, who are mainly the children of unacclimated German parents, who perished in the terrible pestilence of 1853, leaving their children houseless and homeless. Never was there such a mortality amongst the destitute German population in New Orleans, and orphanage in its accumulated forms and most pitiable aspect was seen in every direction. The German Catholic people of the Fourth District, moved by their duty towards the city of their adoption, and the cause of humanity, though with limited means, resolved to furnish out of their own resources, and such others as they could command, a home and support to those little unfortunates. Hence originated the Institution. A house was rented, and for one year one hundred children were provided for. The present site was purchased two years since by the Directors, and a building erected in

which these orphans reside. Their number has been as high as 125; at present it is 113, being 72 males and 41 females.

The amount expended for ground and building was $13,700. There has been a grave-yard purchased on account of the Asylum, for $4,000, of which there has been paid $2,300, and about $1,000 for fencing. The Institution is now about $5,000 in debt. The first and only Legislative aid received by the Asylum, was an appropriation of $3,000, at the last session. It has no regular income, and its only reliance in meeting its current expenses is the hand of private charity, which is at all times heavily taxed in New Orleans. No salaries or wages are paid to the attendants in the Asylum — all the duties having been assumed by females, who have devoted their life to the cause of charity. An appropriation of $3,000 is recommended.

"On arriving at suitable ages they are bound out to such pursuits as offer"

Although policies varied from institution to institution, orphanages generally received children between the ages of three and ten and tried to bind them out by the age of fourteen.

1. Changes in indenture procedure for orphan girls, Boston, 1842

Abby L. Wade, *Reminiscences of the Boston Female Asylum* (Boston, 1844), pp. 58–62.

The greatest care is always taken in selecting places for those who are old enough to go into families. And this it might seem easy to do, as applications for the children always greatly exceed the number to be placed out. Yet it cannot be denied that the most difficult duties of the managers in regard to them often occur after they leave the Asylum. It is true that instances of mutual satisfaction — of good treatment on the one side, and good conduct on the other greatly preponderate. But cases of an opposite character were presented often enough to induce the managers to consider, whether they did not in part arise from some cause that might be removed.

In the "olden time," when the regulations for binding out the children were adopted, it was very much the custom for the mistress of a family to take from poor, though often respectable parents, a young girl to clothe and instruct until she should be eighteen years old, in return for her services. Sometimes this was done by indenture, and sometimes by simple verbal agreement; and from such agreements faithfully observed, have arisen many connexions productive of mutual advantage through life. The Asylum children then, were placed out on conditions perfectly according with prevailing customs. And nothing more was required in their indentures, than kind treatment, suitable clothing and instruction, and when they should be eighteen years old, "two suits of clothes, one proper for Sunday, the other for domestic business."

But "times are changed." The increase of wealth and variations in the forms of society, have at the same time increased the demand for service, and removed the mistress of a family farther from that direct supervision of those who perform it, which is so especially important to the young. Now a girl, long before she is eighteen, can obtain wages, which enable her to indulge that love of dress, which is a prevailing folly, and give a feeling of that independence, the desire for which, is often most strong in those who least know how to use it. It was not then perhaps strange that the girls should, during the last years of their apprenticeship, feel dissatisfied, at seeing others possess apparently greater advantages than themselves.

And that some forgetting the destitution of their early childhood, the advantages of a permanent home, thorough instruction in domestic affairs, and the power of securing friends who may be of incalculable benefit to them through life, should be tempted by the precarious, and often delusive good of having an earlier command of wages, and imagine that mere food and clothing and teaching, are insufficient compensation for the work for which they see others obtaining a recompense which seems larger.

It is true that domestic labor commands a larger remuneration than formerly; and it seems but just that these girls should have their share in the advantage. It is true that some who apply for them may have little other purpose than that of obtaining a selfish convenience; the most service at the least price at which it can be procured; that in the idea of the *servant* some may lose sight of the *child,* of one needing all the instruction, forbearance, encouragement and restraint that youth always requires. That disappointed in their expectation of finding at once an obedient and useful domestic, some become impatient and unmindful of their obligations.

These considerations led the managers in 1842, to review their form of indenture, and the following additional requisitions were inserted in it. First, that a written report should be required once in each year, relative to the health, character and well-being of the apprentice.

This condition would, it was hoped be a security for kind treatment toward the girl, and at the same time a restraint and incitement to her.

Secondly, that the sum of fifty dollars should be substituted for the clothing formerly required at the expiration of apprenticeship; this sum to be paid "unless the apprentice shall have been guilty of such gross misconduct that the Board of Managers shall be of opinion that she has forfeited her claim to it."

This alteration secures a more equal and definite recompense to those who merit it, and threatens certain loss to those who abuse their privileges, or leave their places without being regularly discharged.

It has been suggested that the payment of so considerable a sum at one time, might be an inconvenience to some persons whose families might, nevertheless, be excellent places for the protection and good training of our children. It may be answered, that by laying aside from time to time during the one or two last years of their service, a sum much smaller than would pay the wages of hired domestics, the inconvenience might be avoided — that justice to the apprentice should be considered as well as the convenience of the employer; and that, after all, the sum is hardly more than the former requirement of clothing, if faithfully fulfilled, would amount to. But it has been well known, that while the letter of the obligation has been answered, as to the prescribed *quantity* of clothing, its *value* has so varied, as to make the recompense very unequal to many who have been equally deserving.

The third, and last alteration is, that a penalty of one hundred dollars is incurred by neglect in fulfilling the conditions of the indenture. This will be readily perceived to be a necessary guard to the Institution.

---

2. A "missing link in the chain of benevolent enterprise," Boston, 1862

Boston Children's Friend Society, *Twenty-Ninth Annual Report* (Boston, 1862), pp. 10–12.

Before closing, we would call your attention to the statement . . . that eleven children have been removed to Monson during the past year. The Institution to which they have been taken is an Almshouse, and this is the only way of disposing of our boys, after they reach the age of seven years. It seems of importance that this fact should be distinctly understood, that we may consider whether a better disposition of them cannot be effected. Our rules admit children, of both sexes, at the age of three years. The girls are kept here at school, unless adopted, until they are twelve years old, when they are sent out to homes at service, excepting those who are retained as help in the house. But for the boys, the period of continuance with us is comparatively brief. At seven, they are supposed to require so much governing, and need so much more room to expand, that our limits are too strait for them, and we are obliged to send them away.

For the last two and a half years there has been but a single application for a boy, and that one was brought about by the mother, and the home to which the child was sent was obtained through her efforts. In the majority of cases it is quite as difficult to provide for them at seven, as it was at three. They are not large enough to be of any service, and few wish to adopt a boy. Now if the years immediately following the seventh are not quite so important to sound physical development as those that preceded it, they certainly are more so in determining the moral and intellectual status of the future man; and after we have furnished a comfortable home, moral and religious instruction, and all the advantages which our children enjoy, it seems a stern necessity which compels us to send them to the Almshouse. Not that we would depreciate that Institution, and particularly the one to which we send our children. These charities and the liberal spirit in which they are sustained, are an honor to our State; but can we not do better for our boys? Could we not have a separate department, or building, into which we could transfer them, when they outgrow our limits, and into which others, between the ages of seven and ten, could be received, to whom we are now obliged to say, No, you are too old, we can do nothing for you? . . . The Farm School is now the only one to which we can apply, and that receives but a limited number; and when we make application, they tell us our boys are too small, so that, if a vacancy should occur, we could not be benefited by it.

When we speak to friends, of this missing

link in the chain of benevolent enterprise, and ask if something cannot be done, we are told that it must not be thought of in these war times; all that can be spared must go to the soldier. True, our soldiers are, and should be, objects of earnest and anxious solicitude, but have we no duty to their children? What is to become of many of the sons of soldiers killed in battle? How many of them are to be exposed to poverty, want and crime. How many, in early life, are to become inmates of houses of correction and reformation; and how blest our privilege, if by timely effort we may rescue some, if we may be instrumental in shielding and saving them from the sins and sorrows of a wicked life, and guiding their feet in the paths of integrity and righteousness, that they may obtain good hope of life everlasting.

3. Finding homes for war orphans and other distressed children, Boston, 1865

The Little Wanderers' Advocate, I (1865), 69.

F.A., a boy aged nine; father killed in the war; mother a cripple; sent to a home in Ohio, and adopted by a wealthy Christian gentleman who has no child. His sister, seven years of age, is still with us.

. . . . .

Thomas B., three years old; father killed at the battle of Bull Run; mother unable to care for him. Who will be a father to the child of one who fell in defence of his country?

. . . . .

A little brother and sister, forsaken by their mother, and their father a disabled soldier. They have been adopted by a wealthy gentleman in Chicago.

. . . . .

Three Portuguese children, whose father died on the voyage to this country. Will some one whose heart pants to go to the isles of the sea and preach Christ take these fatherless children and train them for life and immortality?

. . . . .

The wife of a soldier who sleeps in a Southern grave, where he fell, comes to us with health ruined by excessive toil in her efforts to support her five children. She could not support them, and she could not give them up; but a little effort persuaded her relatives to aid her, and thus save a mother's feelings.

. . . . .

A smart, intelligent contraband comes to us from the sunny South. Once a slave, but now free, he has more than ordinary intellect, and will make a good boy for some gentleman to take and teach the principles of freedom. He is twelve years old, and was brought here by an officer in the army.

"Asylum-life is a bad preparation for practical life"

Charles Loring Brace, *The Dangerous Classes of New York* (New York, 1880), pp. 235–236; first published in 1872.

The "we" of the document is the Children's Aid Society of New York of which Brace was secretary. The specific asylum he was criticizing was the New York Juvenile Asylum. For additional information on these organizations see below, Chap. VII, sec. C.

We . . . took the ground that, as our children were not criminals, but simply destitute and homeless boys and girls, usually with some ostensible occupation, they could not easily, on any legal grounds, be inclosed within Asylums; that, if they were, the expense of their maintenance would be enormous, while the cost of a temporary care of them in our Schools and Lodging-houses, and their transferrence to the West, was only trifling — in the proportion of fifteen dollars to one hundred and fifty dollars, reckoning the latter as a year's cost for a child's support in an Asylum. Furthermore, we held and stoutly maintained that an asylum-life is a bad preparation for practical life. The child, most of all, needs individual care and sympathy. In an Asylum, he is "Letter B, of Class 3," or "No. 2, of Cell 426," and that is all that is known of him. As a poor boy, who must live in a small house, he ought to learn to draw his own water, to split his wood, kindle his fires, and light his candle; as an "institutional child," he is lighted, warmed, and watered by machinery. He has a child's imitation, a desire to please his superiors, and readiness to be in-fluenced by his companions. In a great cara-vansary he soon learns the external virtues which secure him a good bed and meal — decorum and apparent piety and discipline — while he practices the vices and unnamable habits which masses of boys of any class nearly always teach one another. His virtue seems to have an alms-house flavor; even his vices do not present the frank character of a thorough street boy; he is found to lie easily, and to be very weak under temptation; somewhat given to hypocrisy, and something of a sneak. And, what is very natural, *the longer he is in the Asylum, the less likely he is to do well in outside life*. I hope I do no injustice to the unfortunate graduates of our Asylums; but that was and continues to be my strong impression of the institutional effect on an ordinary street boy or girl.

VI Juvenile Delinquency

By 1820 larger urban communities considered juvenile delinquency a threat to public order, but they depended mainly upon private citizens to establish the first institutions intended specifically for young offenders. Boston's City Council founded and controlled the city's House of Reformation (1826). In New York City (1825) and Philadelphia (1828), however, local philanthropists established and managed the two Houses of Refuge which became the country's best known juvenile reformatories. City and state governments in New York and Pennsylvania expressed their concern and gratitude by providing the Refuges with public funds while at the same time exercising minimal supervision over their management.

This flurry of activity resulted from the belief that the prevailing system of criminal justice treated delinquent children cruelly and corrected them unsatisfactorily. A New York Refuge report stated the dilemma: "If acquitted, they were returned destitute, to the same haunts of vice from which they had been taken, more emboldened to the commission of crime, by their escape from present punishment. If convicted, they were cast into a common prison with older culprits to mingle in conversation and intercourse with them, acquire their habits, and by their instruction to be made acquainted with the most artful methods of perpetrating crime."[1] The children's family life supposedly amplified this injustice. "Their faults are not their own," wrote a visitor to the Boston House of Reformation. "They have never been taught the laws of God or man, or if they have, it has been only that they may despise them."[2]

The founders of the first juvenile reformatories — men such as Pennsylvania Congressman John Sergeant, Roberts Vaux of the Philadelphia Society for Alleviating the Miseries of Public Prisons, and, in New York City, Mayor Cadwallader D. Colden and John Griscom, the noted philanthropist and educator — conceded that childhood diminished responsibility for crime; nevertheless, pity and sympathy for the young were secondary considerations in their institutional plans. They aimed instead to train youths to become independent moral agents by inculcating them with workshop habits, Protestant pieties, and common school skills. They believed that their mandate was broad enough to cover vagrant and neglected children as well as delinquents. Juvenile reformation assumed, therefore, the proportion of a root and branch operation which implied that these youths needed a long period of confinement in order that respectable values might be inculcated in them.

To undertake a task of such magnitude, the refuges required legal as well as financial aid from the state. They particularly needed protection against the claims of parents who regarded reform schools as usurpers of family government. State courts provided this help by rejecting the pleas of parents whose children had been taken from them. The Supreme Court of Pennsylvania asked the self-answered question: "May not the natural parents, when unequal to the task of education, or unworthy of

---

1. New York Society for the Reformation of Juvenile Delinquents, *Annual Report, 1826* (New York, 1827), p. 4.

2. Boston Prison Discipline Society, *Third Annual Report, 1828* (Boston, 1828), p. 25.

it, be superseded by the *parens patriae* or common guardian of the community?" [3]

To carry out "the task of education," the refuges established and supervised large workshops where the boys, whose labor was contracted to local entrepreneurs, made brass nails, cane chairs, and cheap shoes; delinquent girls were occupied with domestic chores in a separate part of the building. The children labored approximately eight hours a day and spent most of the remainder of their waking hours in the refuge classroom learning how to read, write, and cipher. After delinquents had been trained "for usefulness," the institutions often apprenticed them to local artisans and farmers. Girls were bound out as housemaids and older, more intractable boys were indentured to ship captains in the whaling or merchant service. Those who rebelled against the authority of their foster family were either returned to the refuge or sent to jail.

The rapid proliferation of both municipal refuges and state reform schools at mid-century suggests that the original institutions were considered successful. Enoch C. Wines and Theodore W. Dwight, in their comprehensive survey, *Report on the Prisons and Reformatories of the United States and Canada* (1867), noted seven state reform schools outside of New York and local reform schools in Providence, Cincinnati, Louisville, Baltimore, St. Louis, and Chicago. The first state reform schools, like the refuges, resulted from a mixture of public and private efforts. The State Reform School for Boys at Westborough, Massachusetts (1847) owed its existence to the donations of former Boston Mayor Theodore Lyman. Other state schools were also aided by private citizens although, in time, public institutions had to depend upon revenue derived primarily from contract labor and legislative appropriations. In physical features, such as large congregate dormitories and workshops, most state reform schools resembled the refuges.

Despite or perhaps because of the spread of traditional reform schools, organizations such as the New York Children's Aid Society (1853) were founded to prevent juvenile delinquency rather than to correct juvenile delinquents. Charles Loring Brace, secretary of the Society, reflected its anti-institutional bias when he warned, "We have crowded asylums and reformatories with young paupers and vagrants and petty criminals not yet inured in crime." [4] Brace disparaged the "institutional child" as one who "is lighted, warmed and watered by machinery . . . he is found to lie easily, and to be very weak under temptation . . . and . . . *the longer he is in the asylum, the less likely he is to do well in outside life.*" [5] Regarding the chaotic urban environment itself as the major cause of delinquency, the Children's Aid Society collected destitute and delinquent street waifs and railroaded them west in wholesale lots to "the best of all asylums . . . *the farmer's home.*" The Society distributed children to individual farms where they supposedly were reformed by receiving affectionate familial care and by learning the agrarian routine.

The New York Juvenile Asylum (1851) and the Boston Children's Aid Society (1864) also believed that the essence of juvenile reformation lay in rural placement. Prior to transportation, however, these institutions trained children in a manner similar to that of the reform schools. Like the refuges, preventive societies were incorporated by private citizens who cooperated with state and local governments in return for financial and legal assistance. The Juvenile Asylum received public money while the Boston Children's Aid Society admitted children to its farm from Suffolk county court through a rudimentary system of probation.

Two state reform schools, the Massachusetts State Industrial School for Girls (1856) and

---

3. *Ex parte* Crouse, 4 Wharton (Pa.) 9 (1838).

4. Charles Loring Brace, *The Best Method of Disposing of Our Pauper and Vagrant Children* (New York, 1859), pp. 5–6.

5. Charles Loring Brace, *The Dangerous Classes of New York* (New York, 1880), p. 235.

the Ohio Reform School (1857), internalized the ideal of family placement by dividing their inmates into physically separated "cottage families." In Ohio boys lived on a farm with "elder brothers" chosen specially for their ability to inspire good behavior and love of the country. "Habituate him [the delinquent] to the life and labor of the farm," advised the commissioners of the Ohio School, "and he will, in nearly every case, continue so to live and labor when restored to society." [6]

The cottage and agrarian concepts of juvenile reform never lacked opponents. Leaders of congregate reform schools resented the accusation that their institutions corrupted innocent children by confining them indiscriminately with older, presumably hardened offenders. Orlando Hastings of the Western House of Refuge in Rochester, New York, spoke for the schools when he said, "you may divide these boys into classes, and the vicious will grow more vicious . . . but when mixed with the rest, and when they see a public opinion in favor of reform, they will reflect, improve, and in the end be reformed." [7] The liberal placement policy of the New York Children's Aid Society was condemned both by reform schools and other preventive agencies. "Shall we take these children as they are brought to us, thieves, liars, profane swearers, licentious, polluted in body and soul, and put them into your families in that condition?" asked R. N. Havens of the New York Juvenile Asylum. [8]

Under all reformatory schemes, delinquent children of Catholics or free Negroes suffered added discrimination because of their religious faith or race. Catholic youths were subjected to the proselytizing of Protestant ministers who dominated both the reform schools and the child-saving societies while Negro children, when they were accepted at all, were rigidly segregated. "It would be degrading to the white children to associate them with beings given up to public scorn," said the director of the Philadelphia Refuge.[9] By the time of the Civil War, Catholic philanthropists and religious orders were forming institutions to reform and protect the vagrant and delinquent children of their faith.

The war revealed and contributed to the inadequacy of existing reformatory efforts. Public and private investigations discovered numerous children, many of whom had fathers in the army, suffering degradation and cruelty in local jails. Reform schools and preventive societies sent many older boys to fight for the Union, but received even more of their younger brothers and sisters than they could care for. Wines and Dwight recommended more public nurseries and preventive agencies for "unfallen street children," but they proposed no new solution to the problem of juvenile reformation. In 1865 few could foresee the full impact of urbanization and industrialization which would transform America in the late nineteenth century and force state governments into an increasingly active role in devising new methods of social control.

6. Ohio, Commissioners of the Ohio Reform School, *Annual Report, 1856* (Columbus, 1857), p. 619.

7. *Proceedings* of the First Convention of Managers and Superintendents of Houses of Refuge and Schools of Reform, 1857 (1858), p. 29

8. *Proceedings* of the Second Convention of Managers and Superintendents of Houses of Refuge and Schools of Reform, 1859 (1860), p. 29.

9. Quoted in George Wilson Pierson, *Tocqueville and Beaumont in America* (New York, 1938), p. 512.

A. THE REFUGE MOVEMENT

Edward Livingston proposes a "School of Reform" for juvenile delinquents, Louisiana, 1824

Edward Livingston, *A System of Penal Law for the State of Louisiana* (Philadelphia, 1833), pp. 714–722.

The school of reform was part of the revised code of penal law which Edward Livingston (1764–1836), a follower of Jeremy Bentham, prepared for the legislature of Louisiana. The "Livingston code," although not adopted in Louisiana, was widely discussed in Europe and America and exercised strong influence on the reform of criminal and penal law. See William B. Hatcher, *Edward Livingston* (Baton Rouge, 1940), pp. 245–288.

Of the School of Reform.
Of the persons to be admitted into the school of reform.

Art. 191. All persons under the age of eighteen sentenced to imprisonment and labour (unless for life), and all vagrants under that age and above six years, shall be sent to the School of Reform.

Art. 192. All minors above six and under eighteen years of age, who have no visible means of honest subsistence and are not supported by any friend or relation; all common beggars within the said age of eighteen; all females under seventeen years of age, who live by prostitution in a disorderly house, shall be considered as vagrants under the last article, and may, by order of the mayor of New Orleans, or the parish judge and two other magistrates, be committed to the School of Reform.

Art. 193. All minors above nine and under the age of fifteen, who shall commit an offence of which they shall be acquitted on account of the want of sufficient discretion to know the nature of the offence, may, at the discretion of the court, be committed to the School of Reform.

Art. 194. In like manner a minor, who being accused of a crime and shall be acquitted by showing that at the time of the commission thereof he was under the age of nine years, may, at the discretion of the court, be sent to the School of Reform.

Art. 195. In cases of misdemeanor, committed by a minor under eighteen years of age, and punishable by simple imprisonment in close custody, the court may also, at their discretion, send the defendant to the School of Reform.

Art. 196. In exercising the discretion given by the three last preceding articles, the court must consider that the object of the School of Reform is not only to punish by restraint, but to separate the juvenile offender from the association of vice, to afford him the means of education, religious and moral instruction, and instruction in some mechanic art, so as to make him a useful member of society; and that where, from the circumstances of the case, these objects will probably be attained without committing the defendant to the School of Reform, that this public institution ought not to be so burthened.

.   .   .   .   .

Of the instruction in the School of Reform.

Art. 201. The time of school instruction shall be one hour, to commence at sunrise, and one hour after labour in the afternoon.

Art. 202. The children shall be taught reading and writing in the French and English language, and arithmetic; and such of the boys as show an aptitude for learning, in the opinion of the teacher and warden, shall be taught geography, land surveying, and navigation.

Art. 203. Before the instruction begins, select

portions of the scriptures shall be read morning and evening.

Art. 204. Premiums of books and badges of merit shall be given to the scholars by the warden, on the recommendation of the teachers, to the children who shall show the most diligence and be distinguished for orderly conduct.

Art. 205. A small collection of entertaining and instructive books shall also be provided for the use of those who have badges of merit.

Art. 206. The teacher has no greater power of correction than is given by law in ordinary schools, and it extends only to faults committed in relation to the literary instruction.

Art. 207. No punishment shall be inflicted on any of the females for faults committed in school but by the matron, or in her presence.

Art. 208. The boys and girls shall be taught separately, and the matron, or her assistant, shall always be present during the instruction of the girls.

Art. 209. Examinations of the scholars shall be had once every three months, in the presence of the inspectors and such of the visitors as choose to attend.

Art. 210. The teacher shall use the system of mutual instruction, and shall endeavour to qualify such of the children, of both sexes, as show a particular aptitude, to be themselves teachers according to the same method.

Of employment in the School of Reform.

Art. 211. All the hours between sunrise and sunset that are not hereby appropriated to instruction, to meals, or to relaxation and exercise, must be employed in labour.

Art. 212. The labour to be performed shall be such as, in the opinion of the inspectors, shall be best calculated to procure a subsistence for the prisoners when they shall be restored to liberty.

Art. 213. Each of the boys shall be taught a mechanic art, and for this purpose the warden shall, with the approbation of the inspectors, contract with mechanics to find materials, to send foremen to the prison to superintend their work and teach them the different trades, pay-ing a reasonable sum for the value of their labour. The necessary tools and implements shall be provided by the institution.

Art. 214. The foremen so employed by the mechanics shall be men of good characters, approved by the inspectors; they shall remain in their respective workshops during the hours of labour, preserve order therein, and keep the boys at work, teaching them carefully all the branches of the trade; but they shall inflict no punishment, unless by direction of the warden and in his presence, and such punishment shall be such moderate correction as a master is authorized by law to inflict on an apprentice.

Art. 215. The foremen shall make daily reports to the warden of each boy under his care, for which purpose he shall keep a calendar containing the names of each of them, on which he shall make marks, denoting offences, or extraordinary diligence, or good conduct, which shall be shown daily to the warden.

Art. 216. Great care shall be taken to suit the employment to the physical force and constitution of each boy; and the warden shall frequently visit the workshops, and see that unreasonable tasks are not imposed by the foremen.

Art. 217. If no such contract should be offered for the labour of the boys as the warden and inspectors shall deem advantageous, proper persons may be employed by the inspectors to instruct them in some mechanic art.

Art. 218. Besides the mechanic arts the boys shall be exercised for two periods in each day (not exceeding half an hour each time) in some laborious employment, that shall require as much as possible the exercise of all the muscular powers, to strengthen and fit them for any hard labour to which they may afterwards be called; for this purpose a hydraulic or other machine, to be moved by manual labour, shall be constructed in the enclosure of the School of Reform, and a mast, with yards and standing and running rigging, shall be erected, on which they shall be taught to climb, and prepare themselves for a seafaring life.

Art. 219. The tread-mill shall not be introduced into this or any other of the places of confinement established by this Code.

Art. 220. The girls shall be taught needle-work, and be employed in washing, ironing, baking, and other works of housewifery; and they may also be taught such trades as women are usually employed in, at the time and place in which they are confined. The matron shall superintend this part of their employment, and none but female instructors in any branch, except the school-master, shall be admitted into their department.

Art. 221. The children of both sexes shall, by turns, be employed in the menial service of the establishment to which they belong — wait-ing at the table, cleaning the workshops and eating-rooms, and other places for the common resort of the persons confined; but each one is bound to sweep and clean his own cell.

.   .   .   .   .

Of the discharge from the School of Reform.

Art. 247. Discharges from the School of Re-form may be either by the expiration of the term of service or by apprenticeship.

Art. 248. Whatever may be the term of im-prisonment designated by law for the offence of which the party sent to the School of Reform is convicted, such party cannot be discharged (unless by apprenticeship), if a female, before she has attained the age of nineteen, or if a male, before twenty-one.

Art. 249. Those who are sentenced for a term that will not expire until after they have respectively attained the ages mentioned in the last preceding article, and whose conduct has not entitled them to the recommendation here-inafter mentioned for apprenticeship, shall, within six months after attaining the ages afore-said, be transferred to the Penitentiary to serve out the remainder of the term.

Art. 250. Those who are entitled to the rec-ommendation, and who have not been appren-ticed for some other cause, shall be discharged after having attained the age of twenty-two if a male, or twenty if a female, although the term of imprisonment in the sentence be for a longer time.

Art. 251. The warden is authorized to bind out, by indentures of apprenticeship, such of the prisoners confined as come within the de-scription contained in the next succeeding arti-cle; and the indentures shall impose the same obligations and give the same rights and reme-dies as indentures of apprenticeship made by a parent or guardian, with the assent of the minors, under the civil law of the state.

Art. 252. In order to be legally bound, pur-suant to the last article, the apprentice must have been two years in the School of Reform; he must have learned to read, write, and un-derstand the first three rules in arithmetic; and must have obtained a certificate signed by the warden (and if a female by the matron), ap-proved by the inspectors, declaring that the moral conduct and diligence of the party has evinced such a reformation as, in their opinion, will render it safe to receive him as an ap-prentice.

Art. 253. The duration of the apprenticeship shall be until the party bound shall attain the age of twenty-one if a male, or nineteen if a female, unless, at the time of making the in-denture, the male apprentice shall have attained nineteen years of age, or the female seventeen; in which case the indenture may be for three years, if the term of the sentence does not ex-pire before; but if the term should expire be-fore, the apprentice cannot be bound for a longer term than the attainment of twenty-one years for a male, or nineteen for a female, without his or her consent, and then only for the said term of three years.

Art. 254. The male apprentices shall be put out, if possible, to mechanics of the same trade they have been taught in the School of Reform; if no mechanic pursuing the same profession offers, some other demanding, as near as may be the same species of labour, shall be pre-ferred; but whatever trade may have been taught to the apprentice, he may, by his own consent, be apprenticed to a farmer or a mariner.

Art. 255. The conditions of the articles of apprenticeship shall be, on the part of the apprentice, obedience to lawful commands, and diligence, sobriety, and honesty; on the part of the master, that he will perfect the apprentice in the trade he has been taught, or teach him the new business if such be the case, that he will continue his schooling at least one day in the week, that he will provide him necessary food, clothing, lodging, medical assistance, and that, at the end of the period, he will give him new clothing and a sum of money to be specified in the indenture, and such as the warden and the master shall think reasonable.

Art. 256. No one shall be apprenticed to any one residing out of the state, nor shall the indenture be assignable without the assent of the apprentice.

Art. 257. The clause relating to the teaching and perfecting in a trade or business, is not indispensable in the indenture of a female.

Art. 258. No female shall be indented to an unmarried man, or to a married man living apart from his wife.

Art. 259. It shall be a condition in the indenture between the warden and the master, that a report shall be made once in every year of the conduct of the apprentice to the warden; and if he has reason to believe that his reformation is complete, that he will permit him, if within the city of New Orleans or its suburbs, to visit the school and converse with the others still there.

Art. 260. The convict at the time of his discharge, whether apprenticed or not, shall be comfortably clad, and the inspectors, at their discretion, may make him an allowance in money, or deliver him books or tools, if they are satisfied with his conduct.

Children in jail

1. Boy offenders in the Bellevue prison, 1822

New York Society for the Reformation of . . Juvenile Delinquents, *Memorial to the Legis-*

lature of New York . . . with an abstract from a report of a committee appointed by the Society for the Prevention of Pauperism . . . on the subject of erecting a House of Refuge, for Vagrant and Depraved Young People (New York, 1824), pp. 16–18.

The New York Society for the Reformation of Juvenile Delinquents was a more specialized successor institution to the Society for the Prevention of Pauperism. Both groups were guided by such distinguished philanthropists as Thomas Eddy, John Griscom, and John Pintard.

The most important facts relative to the Bellevue prison, as connected with the objects of this report, will be best understood from the following answers of Arthur Burtis, Esq., superintendent of that extensive establishment, to questions sent to him from this committee.

Ques. 1. What number of boys are sent to the Penitentiary in the course of a year, and of what ages; and what is the average number at one time in the prison?

Ans. The average number of boys sent to the Penitentiary for the last three years, has been seventy-five per year, from twelve to sixteen years old. The average at one time in the house is about thirty-five.

Ques. 2. For what offences generally are they imprisoned?

Ans. Most generally for petit larceny and vagrancy.

Ques. 3. What proportion of them are sent there for the second or third time?

Ans. About one-half are in for the second and third time; but it is impossible to be exact, as the same boys come in by so many different names.

Ques. 4. How far are the boys instructed?

Ans. They are taught the catechism, and to read and write.

Ques. 5. How far are they put to labour, in the Penitentiary?

Ans. We have not put them to labour, except a part in the Pin Factory.

Ques. 6. What effect has the present treatment upon them, in reference to their reformation and future usefulness?

Ans. The effect of their present condition is deplorable. Instead of reformation, they must become worse, as we are compelled to put a boy for his first, perhaps small crime, with the old offender, if not in years, in crime, in the same room.

Ques. 7. What proportion of them are destitute of parents, or other persons to take charge of them?

Ans. About two-thirds have one or more parents, but in almost every case their parents have taken very little or no care of them.

.   .   .   .   .

Ques. 9. What proportion of them can read and write, at the time of their committal?

Ans. About one in eight.

Ques. 10. How far are the boys separate from old offenders by day and by night?

Ans. They are kept entirely separate, except a few who are in the Pin Factory, and they are under the care of a keeper.

2. Children in jail, Boston, 1827

Boston Prison Discipline Society, *Second Annual Report, 1827* (Boston, 1827), pp. 28–29.

The Society, established in 1825 under the leadership of Reverend Louis Dwight (1793–1854), became the leading advocate of the Auburn or congregate system of prison discipline.

Imprisonment of Youth and Children. — The following table shows the proportion in different Prisons, under 21 years of age.

	Whole No.	No. under 21 years.	Proportion.
In Maine,	116	22	1 to 5
" New Hampshire,	253	47	1 to 5
" Vermont,	534	75	1 to 7
" Connecticut,	117	39	1 to 3
At Auburn, whole term,	997	148	1 to 6
In Richmond, Vir.	201	30	1 to 7

From the above table it appears, that the proportion of those committed to Prison under 21 years of age, in all the prisons mentioned, is one-seventh part at least, and in some much more. It is sufficiently apparent, from the disclosure of the vices existing in Prisons, how great is the evil of bringing so great a proportion of young offenders within the corrupting influence of this wretched community. About three hundred youth are continually in a course of education in these high schools of iniquity.

The evil is not only apparent from the great proportion under 21 years of age; but from the tender years of a considerable proportion of this number. Children have been found in some of our Prisons under twelve years of age, who have been many months, and some of them more than a year, intimately associated with the most profligate and vile of the human race. The loathsome skin, the distorted features, the unnatural eyes of some of these boys, indicate, with a clearness not to be misapprehended, the existence of unutterable abominations, which it were better for the world if they had been foreseen and avoided. The greatness of the evil, if there is no injustice and criminality in it, of placing a child, and confining him there with strong bolts and bars, among a den of thieves, where he may be subject to any violence, and not be permitted to enter a complaint without the hazard of his life, has surely not been sufficiently contemplated.

Establishment of the houses of refuge

1. Proposal for the creation of the first house of refuge, New York, 1824

New York Society for the Reformation of Juvenile Delinquents, *Memorial to the Legislature of New York . . . on the subject of erecting a House of Refuge*, pp. 22–26.

The design of the proposed institution is, to furnish, in the *first place*, an asylum, in which boys under a certain age, who become subject to the notice of our Police, either as vagrants, or houseless, or charged with petty crimes, may be received, judiciously classed according to their degrees of depravity or innocence, put to work at such employments as will tend to encourage industry and ingenuity, taught reading, writing, and arithmetic, and most carefully instructed in the nature of their moral and religious obligations, while at the same time, they are subjected to a course of treatment, that will afford a prompt and energetic corrective of their vicious propensities, and hold out every possible inducement to reformation and good conduct. It will undoubtedly happen, that among boys collected from such sources, there will be some, whose habits and propensities are of the most unpromising description. Such boys, when left to run at large in the city, become the pests of society, and spread corruption wherever they go. To expect the reformation of such, by the ordinary chances of Sunday schools, churches, or admonitions from Magistrates, would be vain and fruitless. There may be some, who, in the best regulated institution, would prove altogether incorrigible. But if placed in a situation in which their dress, their food, their labour, their privations, and enjoyments, are all made to depend on their conduct; and in which every important step in the prog-

ress of improvements, advances them into a better class, and greater comforts, — when they learn to know that a daily register is made of their conduct, that this register is inspected by the governors of the institution, and by respectable visitors, — that the public eye is thus fixed upon them, and their future welfare has become the subject of public concern — is it not probable that in a majority of cases, the latent sparks of emulation may be elicited, and fanned into a goodly desire that they may yet live to honour their country, and to reward the assiduity which thus labours to save them? Such an institution would, in time, exhibit scarcely any other than the character of a decent school and manufactory. It need not be invested with the insignia of a prison. It should be surrounded only with a high fence, like many factories in the neighbourhood of cities, and carefully closed in front. *Second.* — In addition to the class of boys just mentioned, the committee have no doubt that were such an institution once well established, and put under good regulation, the Magistrates would very often deem it expedient to place offenders in the hands of its Managers, rather than to sentence them to the City Penitentiary. The gradations of crime are almost infinite; and so minute are the shades of guilt, so remote, or so intimate the connexion between legal criminality, and previous character, it would often be judged reasonable to use all the discretion which the law would possibly admit, in deciding upon the offence and the destination of juvenile delinquents; and every principle of justice and mercy, would point, in numerous cases of conviction for crime to such a refuge and reformatory, rather than to the Bridewell or City Prison.

A third class which it might be very proper to transplant to such an establishment, and to distribute through its better divisions, are boys (some of whom are of tender age) whose parents, either from vice or indolence, are careless of their minds and morals, and leave them exposed in rags and filth, to miserable and scanty fare, destitute of education, and liable to become the prey of criminal associates. Many of such parents would probably be willing to indenture their children to the managers of a House of Refuge; and far better would it be for these juvenile sufferers, that they should be thus rescued from impending ruin. The laws of this state, do not, as in Massachusetts and some other places, authorize magistrates to use compulsory measures with parents who thus grossly abuse their charge, and, at the same time, absolutely refuse to resign their children to the hands of the guardians of the poor; but it is surely presumable, that were suitable provision made for the economical support and instruction of such children, a law for this purpose might readily be obtained.

. . . . . .

There remains to be noticed but one more class, for whom a House of Industry and Correction, under the management we contemplate, would be an appropriate place for reformation and improvement. We allude to that class of delinquent females, who are either too young to have acquired habits of fixed depravity, or those whose lives have in general been virtuous, but who, having yielded to the seductive influence of corrupt associates, have suddenly to endure the bitterness of lost reputation, and are cast forlorn and destitute upon a cold and unfeeling public, full of compunction for their errors, and anxious to be restored to the paths of innocence and usefulness. That there are many females of tender age just in those predicaments in this city, none can doubt who surveys the list of last year's culprits, furnished by the District Attorney. In this list, are the names of thirteen females, of 14 years of age, fourteen others of 15 and 16, and about forty of 17 and 18. The ages of a considerable number in this appalling catalogue have not been inserted, and it is by no means to be supposed that even a majority of those unhappy females who are in the predicament we have alluded to, have become the subjects of police investigation.

It is very far from the intention of the Com-

mittee, to propose, that the contemplated Refuge should become the receptacle of females whose ages and habitudes in the paths of guilt, render their restoration to society a question of dubious result. However desirable it may be, that an institution should be formed for the special purpose of affording the means of reformation, to those who are sincerely desirous to abandon a life of such debasement and wretchedness, we have no hesitation in expressing the belief, that it ought to be altogether detached from every other concern, and conducted by a separate association, and with the most prudent attention to delicacy and retirement. But within the ages and under the circumstances we have alluded to, it is our decided opinion, — an opinion founded not only upon the reasonableness of the proposition, but upon the result of similar institutions in Europe, that destitute females might form one department of the establishment, with the greatest benefit to themselves, and with advantage to the institution. Occupying apartments entirely distinct from those of the other sex and separated from them by impassable barriers, the females might contribute, by their labour, to promote the interests of the establishment, and at the same time, derive from it their full and appropriate share of benefit. On this point, however, the Committee only mean to express their opinion, without urging it as an indispensable part of the concern.

---

2. The establishment of the Boston House of Reformation, 1826

"An Act Concerning Juvenile Offenders in the City of Boston," 1826 — ch. 30, Boston, Common Council, *Charter and Ordinances* (Boston, 1827), pp. 195–197.

This was the first strictly public institution for juvenile delinquents. The houses of refuge in New York (1824) and Philadelphia (1826) were private corporations which received public funds.

The City Council of the City of Boston . . . are authorized to erect a building in said city, for the reception, instruction, employment and reformation of such Juvenile Offenders, as are hereinafter named; or to use for these purposes the House of Industry, or Correction, at South Boston, or any other House or building belonging to said city, that the City Council may appropriate to these uses.

The Directors of the said House of Industry, or such other persons as said City Council shall appoint Directors of said house, for the employment and reformation of Juvenile Offenders, shall have power, at their discretion, to receive and take into said house all such children who shall be convicted of criminal offences or taken up and committed under and by virtue of an act of this Commonwealth, "for suppressing and punishing of rogues, vagabonds, common beggars, and other idle, disorderly and lewd persons," and who may, in the judgment of any Justice of the Supreme Judicial Court, sitting within and for the County of Suffolk, or of the Judge of the Municipal Court of the City of Boston, or of any Justice of the Police Court, within and for the City of Boston, be proper objects therefore; and upon the conviction or commitment aforesaid, of any child, in the judgment of such Judge or Justice a proper object for the said house of employment and reformation, the said Judge or Justice, previous to declaring the sentence of the law on such child, shall cause notice to be given to the Directors of the said house; and in case the said Directors shall declare their assent to the admission of such child into said house, the said Judge or Justice shall sentence him or her to be committed to said house of employment and reformation . . .

Any Justice or Judge of either of the said Courts respectively, on the application of the Mayor, or of any Alderman of the City of Boston, or of any Director of the House of Industry, or house of Reformation, or of any Overseer of the Poor, of said city, shall have power to sentence to said house of employment and reformation all children who live an idle or dissolute life, whose parents are dead, or if living, from drunkenness, or other vices, neglect to provide any suitable employment, or exercise any salutary control over said children. And the persons thus committed, shall be kept governed and disposed of, as hereinafter provided, the males till they are of the age of twenty-one years, and the females of eighteen years.

The Directors of said House of Industry, or such other persons as said City Council shall appoint Directors of the institution, authorized by this act, may receive the persons sentenced and committed as aforesaid, into said institution; and they shall have power to place the persons committed to their care, the males until they arrive at the age of twenty-one years, and the females until they arrive at the age of eighteen years, at such employments, and to cause them to be instructed in such branches of useful knowledge, as shall be suitable to their years and capacity; and they shall have power to bind out said minors as apprentices or servants, until they arrive at the ages aforesaid, to such persons, and at such places, to learn such arts, trades, and employments, as in their judgment will be most for the reformation, amendment, and future benefit and advantage of such minor . . .

Whenever said Directors, Overseers, or Managers, shall deem it expedient to discharge any minor, committed to their charge as aforesaid, and not bound out as a servant or apprentice, and shall recommend the same in writing to the court by whom such minor was committed, said court shall have power to discharge him or her from the imprisonment or custody aforesaid.

The said Judge or either of the said Justices . . . shall have power to order the transfer of any child committed to the common gaol, or the House of Correction, and inmates of the same at the time of passing this act, to the said house for the employment and reformation of

Juvenile Offenders, to be received, kept, or bound out by the Directors thereof in conformity with the provisions of this act.

---

3. Private philanthropists and public officials share control and support of the Baltimore House of Refuge, 1830

"An Act to establish a House of Refuge for Juvenile Delinquents," 1830 — ch. 64, *Laws Made and Passed by the General Assembly of the State of Maryland, 1830* (Annapolis, 1831), pp. 61–64.

Because the managers of the Baltimore Refuge were unable to raise sufficient funds, the institution did not open until 1851. According to article 78 of the *Maryland Code of 1860* (I, 548–549), only white children could be committed to the House of Refuge.

The estate and concerns of said corporation [House of Refuge] shall be managed and conducted by twenty-four managers, of whom sixteen shall be residents of the city of Baltimore, and who shall be annually appointed in the month of February in the following manner, viz.: eight by the governor and council of this state, eight by the members of the association, and eight by the mayor and city council of Baltimore, seven of which said managers shall constitute a quorum for the transaction of business; and the said managers shall appoint from their own body a president, a secretary and a treasurer, and prescribe the duties of each;

. . . . . .

The managers of the House of Refuge, under this act, may from time to time make by-laws, ordinances and regulations, relative to the management, government, instruction, discipline, employment and disposition of the said minors, while in the said House of Refuge, not contrary to law, as they may deem proper, and may appoint such officers, agents, and servants, as they may deem necessary to transact the business of the said corporation, and may designate their duties; and further, that the said managers shall make annual report to the legislature of Maryland, of the number of minors received by them into the House of Refuge, the disposition which shall be made of the said children, by instructing or employing them in the said House of Refuge, or by binding them out as apprentices, the receipts and expenditures of the said managers, and generally all such facts and particulars as may tend to exhibit the effects, whether beneficial or otherwise, of the said association.

The ground and the buildings which may be erected thereon for said House of Refuge shall be free of tax.

And, as the means of said association are insufficient, without legislative assistance, to carry its benevolent and useful objects and intentions into efficient operation, and as the diminution of crime, and the reformation of juvenile delinquents are subjects of paramount importance, therefore, Be it enacted, That in addition to the funds to be furnished by the members of the association hereby incorporated, the whole net balance of the annual profit accruing from the state penitentiary, after payment of all expenses and appropriations for interest, and in aid of the sinking fund, shall be and the same is hereby appropriated for the next five years to the use of the said House of Refuge; Provided, they shall not exceed five thousand dollars in any one year, nor in the whole exceed the sum of twenty thousand dollars; and it shall be the duty of the directors of the penitentiary annually in the month of December to cause a statement of the said profits to be made out and delivered to the president of the House of Refuge, and within thirty days thereafter to pay the amount of the net profits to the treasurer of the said House of Refuge.

*Foreign visitors view
American institutions for
juvenile delinquents*

1. The Duke of Saxe-Weimar visits the New
York Refuge

Bernhard, Duke of Saxe-Weimar Eisenach,
*Travels through North America during the
years of 1825 and 1826* (Philadelphia, 1828),
I, 131.

The institution for juvenile offenders is situated out of town; it is for children condemned
by the court to imprisonment, and are thus confined in a separate prison to improve their principles by education. When they are improved,
and have some education, they are then bound
out to a farmer in the country, but if they are
of an untameable disposition, and need stronger
control, they are then disposed of as sailors.
The girls are bound out as servants in the country. In order to have a good location for this
institution, the society bought, of the United
States government, a building, heretofore used
as an arsenal, but become useless to the government on account of its distance from the
water. It has existed but one year, and has at
present forty-four juvenile delinquents. The
sexes are separated, and each child occupies
a distinct chamber. During the day they are
mostly employed in learning, and in domestic
occupations. As the building was not sufficiently
large to receive all the offenders, a new one
was built in the rear of the first, which the boys
were employed in erecting. One of the boys who
had escaped twice, walked about with an iron
chain and heavy iron ball secured to his leg. A
young man of respectable family, sixteen years
old, who was imprisoned for his great propensity to stealing, was employed as a sub-instruc-
tor, account-keeper, and sub-overseer of the
institution. Hopes are still entertained that he
may be reclaimed.

2. Beaumont and Tocqueville appraise early
American refuges

Gustave de Beaumont and Alexis de
Tocqueville, *On the Penitentiary System in the
United States and its Application in France;
with an Appendix on Penal Colonies and also
Statistical Notes,* trans. Francis Lieber
(Philadelphia, 1833), pp. 111, 117–119, 122.

Three refuges — New York in 1825, Boston
in 1826, and Philadelphia in 1828 — had
been established at the time of this famous
investigation. No other institutions strictly for
juvenile delinquents were opened until 1847.

The houses of refuge are composed of two
distinct elements: there are received into them
young people of both sexes under the age of
twenty, condemned for crime; and also those
who are sent there by way of precaution, not
having incurred any condemnation or judgment.

Nobody contests the necessity of houses of
refuge for young convicts. In all ages and in all
countries, the disadvantage has been acknowledged which results from placing in the same
room, and submitting to the same discipline, the
young delinquents and the guilty offenders
whom age has hardened in crime: the prisoner,
yet of tender age, has often committed but a
slight offence: how can we justly make him the
associate in prison of another, who is doomed
to expiate heavy crimes? This defect is so serious, that magistrates hesitate to pursue young
delinquents, and the jury to condemn them. But
there another danger presents itself. Encouraged
by impunity, they give themselves up to new
disorders, which a punishment proportionate
to their offence would perhaps have prevented
them from committing.

The house of refuge, the discipline of which
is neither too severe for youth, nor too mild for
the guilty, has therefore for its object both the
withdrawal of the young delinquent from a too
rigorous punishment and from the dangers of
impunity.

The individuals, who are sent to the houses

of refuge without having been convicted of some offence, are boys and girls who are in a position dangerous to society and to themselves: orphans, who have been led by misery to vagrancy; children, abandoned by their parents and who lead a disordered life; all those, in one word, who, by their own fault or that of their parents, have fallen into a state so bordering on crime, that they would become infallibly guilty were they to retain their liberty.

.   .   .   .   .

Though, on the whole, the subsistence of the young prisoners is expensive, every thing seems to be calculated to avoid unnecessary expense. The houses of refuge contain both boys and girls, who, though under the same roof, are perfectly separated from each other. But this circumstance permits some labour to be done by the girls, which, if it were performed by others, would be a charge to the house. Thus they do the washing, mend the clothes, and make the greater part of their own dresses, and those worn by the boys; they also do all business in the kitchen for the whole house; thus they are employed in a way useful for themselves, and for the house, whilst it would be difficult to give them any other productive work.

This order of things is established and maintained by disciplinary means, which we ought to examine. Two principal means are employed: punishments and rewards; but we must make a distinction upon this point, between the houses of refuge of New York and Philadelphia, and that of Boston.

In the two first establishments, the punishments inflicted for disobeying the discipline, are:

1. Privation of recreation;
2. Solitary confinement in a cell;
3. Reduction of food to bread and water;
4. In important cases, corporal punishment — that is to say, stripes.

In New York, the house is expressly authorized to apply stripes. In Philadelphia, the regulations do not permit them expressly, but merely do not prohibit them. The distribution of punishments belongs to the superintendent, who

has a discretionary power in the establishment.

Whilst the refractory children are subjected to these various punishments, according to the character of their offence, distinctions of honour are accorded to the children whose conduct is good. Besides the honour of belonging to the first class, those who distinguish themselves in this, wear badges of honour; lastly, the superintendent designates among the best, a certain number of monitors, to whom he confides part of the *surveillance* with which he is charged himself: and this testimony of confidence is for those whom he has chosen — a distinction to which they attach great value.

In Boston, corporal chastisements are excluded from the house of refuge; the discipline of this establishment is entirely of a moral character, and rests on principles which belong to the highest philosophy.

Every thing there tends to elevate the soul of the young prisoners, and to render them jealous of their own esteem and that of their comrades: to arrive at this end, they are treated as if they were men and members of a free society.

We treat of this theory with reference to discipline, because it has appeared to us, that the high opinion instilled into the child, of his own morality and social condition, is not only fit to effect his reformation, but also, the best means to obtain from him entire submission.

.   .   .   .   .

We have seen how the youth enters the house of refuge, and what discipline he is subjected to.

Let us at present examine by what means he may obtain the restoration of liberty, and let us follow him into the society which he re-enters.

The principle above laid down, that the inmate of a house of refuge does not undergo a punishment, finds here, again, its application. As he has been sent to the house for his own interest only, he is allowed to leave it as soon as his interest requires it.

. . . Yet absolute and complete liberty is not restored to him; because, what would become of him in the world, alone, without support, unknown by any body? — He would find himself precisely in the same situation in which he was, before he entered the house. This great danger is avoided: the superindendent waits for a good opportunity to bind him out as apprentice with some mechanic, or to place him as a servant in some respectable family; he avoids sending him into a city, where he would relapse into his bad habits, and find again the companions of his disorderly life; and every time an opportunity offers, employment for him, with farmers, is preferred. At the moment he leaves the establishment, a writing is given to him, which, in kind words, contains advice for his future conduct; the present of a Bible is added.

In general, it has been found inconvenient to restore liberty to these juvenile offenders, before they have been in the house at least one year, in order to acquire habits of order.

---

3. Charles Dickens comments on two Boston institutions, one for neglected boys, the other for delinquents

Dickens, *American Notes,* pp. 58–59.

There are two establishments for boys . . . One is called the Boylston school, and is an asylum for neglected and indigent boys who have committed no crime, but who in the ordinary course of things would very soon be purged of that distinction if they were not taken from the hungry streets and sent here. The other is a House of Reformation for Juvenile Offenders. They are both under the same roof, but the two classes of boys never come in contact.

The Boylston boys, as may be readily supposed, have very much the advantage of the others in point of personal appearance. They were in their school-room when I came upon them, and answered correctly, without book, such questions as where was England; how far

was it; what was its population; its capital city; its form of government; and so forth. They sang a song too, about a farmer sowing his seed: with corresponding action at such parts as " 'tis thus he sows," "he turns him round," "he claps his hands"; which gave it greater interest for them, and accustomed them to act together, in an orderly manner. They appeared exceedingly well taught, and not better taught than fed; for a more chubby-looking, full-waist-coated set of boys, I never saw.

The juvenile offenders had not such pleasant faces by a great deal, and in this establishment there were many boys of colour. I saw them first at their work (basket-making, and the manufacture of palm-leaf hats), afterwards in their school, where they sang a chorus in praise of Liberty: an odd, one would think, rather aggravating, theme for prisoners. These boys are divided into four classes, each denoted by a numeral, worn on a badge upon the arm. On the arrival of a newcomer, he is put into the fourth or lowest class, and left, by good behaviour, to work his way up into the first. The design and object of this Institution is to reclaim the youthful criminal by firm but kind and judicious treatment; to make his prison a place of purification and improvement, not of demoralisation and corruption; to impress upon him that there is but one path, and that one sober industry, which can ever lead him to happiness; to teach him how it may be trodden, if his footsteps have never yet been led that way; and to lure him back to it if they have strayed: in a word, to snatch him from destruction, and restore him to society a penitent and useful member.

Life and problems in the houses of refuge

---

1. Joseph Curtis, the first superintendent of the New York House of Refuge, records the case histories of the first refuge children, 1825

New York Society for the Reformation of
Juvenile Delinquents, *Examination of Subjects
who are in the House of Refuge in the City
of New York* (Albany, 1825), pp. 3, 5, 11,
15–17.

M.A.P., aged 14 years 28th August, 1824.
Her father has been dead two years. He put
her to live with a Mr. Ayres, near Goshen, who
in July, 1823, removed from there to the new
countries. She then returned to the city, and
lived one year with her aunt Coddington, on
the corner of Broome and Thompson-streets.
She kept boarders — had two female one's at
the time, who were not good characters. Mr.
Hunter (at the request of her mother, who
lived out at service) had her sent to the alms-
house about the 1st July, 1824, where she remained till about the 30th October following,
when, at the request of Mr. A. Burtis, she was
taken in my kitchen. She is large for her age —
has the appearance of a woman; unacquainted
with house-work; quite sluttish, and wanting
of ambition. She was seduced one month before
she went to the alms-house. 1825, January 1st.
— She has improved; has some ambition; think
the prospects are flattering. She reads well, and
much. She enters 5th [lowest] class.[1]

·   ·   ·   ·   ·

M.S., from the police, aged 13 years — born
in New-York. Her father has been dead seven
years. Her mother has since married a Mr.
Smith, who left her mother last spring . . .
Her mother now lives in Banker-street; has
lived there nearly two years; takes in washing,
and goes out to work. Margaret has lived with
Caleb Coggeshall five years; left there more
than a year since, because they were not able
to keep two persons, and she was too small
to do all their work. She then lived seven

---

1. Refuge and reformatory children were classified
according to their behavior. By staying out of trouble,
the child gained not only minor privileges within the
institution, but also opportunity for early placement or
release. Children who misbehaved repeatedly were
often sent to jail or to the almshouse.

months with Capt. Morgan, when they gave up
house-keeping, and she then returned to her
mother. She used to pick chips, and play in the
streets; — was taken up at the theatre, with
others. She has been at school to Mrs. Coggeshall. Enters 5th class.

·   ·   ·   ·

J.B., aged 15 years July, 1824 — born in
New-York. His father, John, lives in Pike-street;
is ship-rigger. His mother died nine years since.
Father married twice since. He was put to live
with Mr. Bull at Newburgh, where he stayed
two weeks; then on board the sloop Sportsman
two months; then through part of Pennsylvania;
to Baltimore, to Harrisburgh, to Carlisle, to
Philadelphia, Trenton, New-Brunswick, to New-
York; all of which places he worked some
time. He had no particular home; strayed about
the streets; was taken up for stealing a pistol,
and sent here. He has been in the alms-house;
was bound out from there, but did not stay over
four months; has been to school; enters the 3d
class.

Joseph   , mulatto, aged 13 years 4th
July, 1824 — born at Mount Pleasant, where
he lived with Mr. Jacob Arthur, Mr. Williamson and Aaron Ward, who he left last spring,
and came to New-York in the stage, and run
about the streets, and slept under stoops for
about one week, when he was sent to the alms-
house, where he stayed two or three weeks,
when he was put to live with Mr. Pell in Broadway, where he stayed one month; then about
the streets for a few days; then with J. Brooks
in Greenwich-street, two months; then about
the streets; then out of town to Davis Mertan's,
three months; then again about the streets, until
taken up by the watch, and sent here. He enters
the 3d class. He never knew his father; his
mother, Diana, is in the alms-house.

·   ·   ·   ·

S.S., from the police, aged 16 years 9th May,
1824 — born at Fishkill; moved to New-York
quite young. Father has been dead ten years.
His mother has been dead five years. He has

lived with Richard Whittemore, at Manhattan Island, seven months; then with Israel Hunt, at East-Chester, eighteen months; then with his brother James, in this neighborhood, seven months; then about the streets, having no particular place of residence, for three months; then to the alms-house; from there to a Mr. Thompson's, where he stayed two weeks; then to the alms-house; then to his brother's, who took him away; then ran about the streets for three weeks, when he was taken up and sent to the penitentiary for six months; which time expired four weeks ago this day; has been to school about two years . . . He played truant most of the time. He enters 3d class.

J.M., from the police, aged 14 years 17th March, 1824 — born in Philadelphia. Father has been dead four years. His mother since married to Moses Isaacs, who has gone to London. His mother lives in North Fourth-street, Philadelphia . . . his mother put him to live with Peter Snyder, a tailor, where he lived from six to eight months, and then returned home. A few weeks after, he went to live with Mr. Duncan, an iron-monger, where he lived about six weeks, when he ran away and came to New-York about two months since; has been in prison in Philadelphia twice, for, as they say, stealing shoes, which he says he did not take. His motive in coming to New York was to get a situation to go to sea. On his arrival, he took lodgings wherever they might be found. The first money that he got in New York was at the theatre, when he picked a gentleman's pockets of $27. He says that was the only theft he committed in New-York. He continued to walk about the streets, boarded at any tavern, had no particular one; was taken up by Mr. Hays without any cause, and sent to Bridewell, where he was three or four days before he was sent here. He enters 5th class.

2. Segregation of Negroes in New York House of Refuge, 1834

Nathaniel C. Hart to Stephen Allen, Dec. 17, 1834, Allen Papers, New York Historical Society.

The board of Managers have heretofore called the attention of the Legislature and the Public, to the unprovided state of the delinquent coloured children, found in great numbers in our city — the proportion of delinquent children among the blacks being much greater than in our white population. This disparity arises in part, from the broad line of separation between the whites and the blacks, being so strikingly drawn, as often to deprive the latter of many employments which are open to the whites. And the number has also been increased by the Policy of several of the Southern States which forbids the free blacks from continuing to reside among them.

Our prisons and alms-houses, from this and other causes are crowded with this description of persons; their children being in numerous cases left unprovided for, soon become delinquent, and proper subjects for the Refuge; but our arrangements have not enabled us to receive them, except by placing them with the white children, which it is apprehended would be injurious to our institution. Under such circumstances we applied to the corporation of our city, which promptly tendered us the permanent use of a lot of ground, and also a donation of $3000 — which amount, with our other resources, and the expectation that the Manumission Society of the City of New York, would furnish us with from 5,000 to 10,000 dollars, would have enabled us to have gone on with, and completed a building adjoining our present enclosure, sufficient to have accommodated from 150 to 200 coloured children.

The Manumission Society, have the resources & are enabled to transfer the same to us, having no longer to support their African Schools; their Schools having been received by the Trustees of the Public School Society . . .

The building is in a good state of forwardness, the roof is on, the rooms on the first floor are studded off, lathed and the first coat of plastering on — the carpenters are now at work preparing for the dormitories, — there is a good dry cellar under the whole building, which is 150 feet long & 200 wide; and the wall which is to enclose I should judge 1/2 acres of ground has been commenced, and we anticipate occupying it, by the first of May next.

3. A routine day in the New York House of Refuge, 1835

New York Society for the Reformation of Juvenile Delinquents, *Tenth Annual Report* (New York, 1835), pp. 6–7.

At sunrise, the children are warned, by the ringing of a bell, to rise from their beds. Each child makes his own bed, and steps forth, on a signal, into the Hall. They then proceed, in perfect order, to the Wash Room. Thence they are marched to parade in the yard, and undergo an examination as to their dress and cleanliness; after which, they attend morning prayer. The morning school then commences, where they are occupied in summer, until 7 o'clock. A short intermission is allowed, when the bell rings for breakfast; after which, they proceed to their respective workshops, where they labor until 12 o'clock, when they are called from work, and one hour allowed them for washing and eating their dinner. At one, they again commence work, and continue at it until five in the afternoon, when the labors of the day terminates. Half an hour is allowed for washing and eating their supper, and at half-past five, they are conducted to the school room, where they continue at their studies until 8 o'clock. Evening Prayer is performed by the Superintendent; after which, the children are conducted to their dormitories, which they enter, and are locked up for the night, when perfect silence reigns throughout the establishment. The foregoing is the history of a single day, and will answer for

every day in the year, except Sundays, with slight variations during stormy weather, and the short days in winter.

4. Superintendent's report on discipline in the Boston House of Reformation, 1841

Boston, Doc. 18, *City Documents* (Boston, 1841), pp. 39–41.

The system of discipline, as to punishments and privileges for moral effect, is substantially, as last reported, slightly modified, as I have further matured it. Each Officer and monitor is required to keep an account daily of the conduct and particularly of the faults of the boys, falling under their notice in the discharge of duty. A Court is held every night by the Superintendent, the officers all being present. All the faults recorded, during the day, are called, and the cases are silently admitted, or investigated and settled. If the fault be aggravated and such, as indicates, that the boy is in a bad state of feeling and dangerous to the good order of the other boys, his punishment is awarded on the spot at the time. For such cases the solitary is used. The boy is locked up, that he may not injure the others, and to give him time for reflection and penitence. I seldom assign any definite period of solitude, at the time of locking up; but attending on him daily, once at least, to see how he feels, and to cut him off from all sympathy from others. He is never taken out, until he asks to be taken out. I have, in one instance, kept a boy thus, seven days, and in another, six days; often, three days. They are, however, led out to be washed, &c. if necessary. They, in such cases, know, that they can be sooner released, if they manifest the proper feelings and wishes. I sometimes apply the shower bath, effectually. This mode of punishment is objected to by some, and much applauded by others. I find it of little use, if frequently resorted to. But, as a mode of punishment to adopt for variety, and to be used with discretion, with those, not of the most stubborn character, I find it very useful. It is a severe punishment, in cold weather, and much dreaded. But nothing subdues, humbles and leads to penitent reflection, those of a quiet, stubborn, sullen cast of mind so effectually, as a solitary cell. Yet this I regard, as injurious to health, especially in the warm season. I am not so entirely modern, as to lay aside, entirely and under all circumstances, the use of stripes. Nor will I shun the responsibility of so doing, by avoiding to report the fact. But I do mean carefully to avoid the frequent or severe use of this punishment. And when I resort to it, I endeavor to do it after cool deliberation and with the expression of regret. If its effects be not favorable and only excite temper, I desist and substitute solitude. Slight faults, occurring daily, are entered in a book, kept and settled at the end of the week. In the same book, meritorious conduct is recorded; adopting numerals to designate degrees of each, one being the smallest. For the weekly settlement of this class of cases, a system of punishment, consisting of restraint and deprivation of play, is adopted. Those sentenced to it are required to stand during play hours in line, in charge of an officer. If they are in need of exercise for health, they are required to run, under the restraint of perfect regularity of movement, distance, &c. In addition to all this, I have, for moral effect, adopted a system awarding written testimonials of character every three months. I make the giving out of them a matter of some ceremony. Those deserving full bills being arranged in line in Chapel in front of the others, and being addressed on the subject. Those, the records against whom are such, as that they cannot get a full clean bill, are allowed as good characters, as they deserved; the rest being erased by black lines. If they decline such an one, they can wait and try for a clean bill at the end of the next three months. The effect of this is further increased, in several ways. Their clean character bill is to be presented to their friends, at the quarterly visit. As all through life a good character is a necessary passport to preferment, so I make their character bill a passport to preferment at the house. Those, who have clean characters, are to be preferred for monitorships, and may ask to be allowed to visit their friend on their parole of honor. They are also to be shewn to gentlemen, who visit to select boys for places. Here we see, that on good conduct and the regular certified evidence of it, almost all they most think of and value depends. One of the leading defects of this class of children is, that they have not had opportunities to learn nor been made to regard the value of character, nor have they any proper conceptions, of what particular traits a good character is constituted. The system works beautifully. It is simple, certain, practical and efficient.

---

5. A dissenting view on the benefits of refuge life

Elijah Devoe, *The Refuge System, or Prison Discipline Applied to Juvenile Delinquents* (New York, 1848), pp. 24–28.

Elijah Devoe was the assistant superintendent of the New York House of Refuge from 1845 to 1848.

Children are committed to the House of Refuge to be dealt with according to law. They are not sent for any specified term. They are subject to the control and disposition of the managers. But, as the managers seldom remain any length of time in the house, and never participate in the government of its inmates, it is impossible for them to have the requisite knowledge of the merits of any particular child or his fitness for egress. They must therefore depend wholly upon the superintendent for information upon this subject. It is, then, for the superintendent to determine the time, in a large majority of cases, that the children are to remain in the institution.

But the superintendent himself has little to do with the immediate supervision and training of the boys. He, in turn, must rely chiefly upon the assistant, who, in fact, really makes the greatest number of selections. This is well, perhaps, in the main, but where a difference of opinion arises in regard to the qualifications of any particular boy, the superintendent, who, in the nature of things, must be supposed to know the least about it, governs the case. The error here is not that the superintendent should control the selections, but that being superintendent he should be least qualified to judge.

By many it is considered a fine feature in the Refuge system, that the disposition of the children sent to the institution is left entirely in the hands of the managers.[1] Aside from the extraordinary power vested in the society, the plan of indefinite commitments is productive of mischievous results. The state of suspense and uncertainty in which every boy is held, keeps his mind in constant agitation and disquiet, and however judicious may be the selections, they never fail to give dissatisfaction to many who remain.

In a conversation with a boy who made one of the most desperate attempts to escape that occurred while I was in the institution, he told me that if he knew how long he had to remain, he could reconcile himself to his punishment; but, that he could not endure to have his mind constantly racked by uncertainty and suspense. He would rather by far be in State Prison, he said, for then he would know how long he should have to remain.

My own observation convinced me in numberless instances, that neither positive nor relative justice was the controlling motive in the selection of subjects for apprenticeship.

I remember at this moment an instance of a boy who had been in the Institution nearly three years (the average time that boys are kept in the House is about fourteen months). For upwards of two years he had worn No. 1 badge, was a faithful boy to work, and had at no time been corrected for any offence of a worse character than that of having tobacco. Yet this boy was kept in the House on the pretext that he was corrupt, — as if that were an uncommon case; or as if the *rights* of a corrupt boy should not be held sacred. If he were very corrupt, his influence would be so much the worse among other inmates; and this fact itself becomes another reason why he should not be detained beyond the average time for those boys whose *Refuge character* was no better than his.

Physical defects in children otherwise well qualified and desirable, become a bar to their obtaining good places. The consequence is, they sometimes remain much longer than they ought, exposed to the corrupting influences of the Institution. A fair face or fine form not unfrequently gives one boy an advantage over others, to whom nature has been less lavish of her gifts. A boy of very repulsive appearance came to me on one occasion, and said in a pathetic manner, "Mr. D., won't you get me a place in the country? I have no father nor mother, nor any friends to look after me. I have been here a long time, and think I ought to go out." "But they say you are a bad boy," I replied. "I am not so bad as they think me," said he, "but I am pock-marked, and every body thinks I am bad. When I 'get a sight to go out,'[2] no body will take me I am so ugly-looking. If I was handsome, I should not be thought so bad, and plenty of farmers would take me." I was struck by the character of his reply, and resolved to study his disposition,

1. The paternity of the inmates is assumed by the managers of the society. They bind the children to farmers and mechanics; and, as a general thing, parents are not allowed to know where their children are sent. Many mothers have I seen leave the house with streaming eyes, because this information had been withheld from them. In this way there is no doubt that some children are separated from their parents and friends for life; for not unfrequently children are sent to a distance of several hundred miles from the city. [Devoe's note.]

2. This term describes the displaying of eligible children before prospective employers.

which I found to be generous, forgiving, and grateful.

No treatment, however kind or generous, will serve to make children contented in the Refuge after a certain period has elapsed. A wall is around them. Every moment they are under strict *surveillance*. The severity of discipline to which every boy, however well-disposed, is subjected — the unceasing and unvaried repetition of duties, fare and employment — breed disgust which degenerates into melancholy and despair. When from careless or purposed neglect, a boy has been suffered to remain longer in the House than the average time in such cases, he grows restless and unhappy — a state of feeling succeeded by that kind of sickness of the heart which comes from "hope deferred." He mopes about, and takes no part nor interest in the sports of the playground. When hope flies, nature relaxes in a degree her firm hold upon the principle of life. The functions of the body are performed with less energy. He droops, and if Liberty do not come to him, Death will. Well do I remember the case of poor J.S. After repeated but fruitless attempts to escape, he fell into a state of hopeless dejection, from which he never revived — for, a few months after, Death sent him a reprieve.

Are children happy in the Refuge? There is scarcely any conceivable position in life that would render human beings entirely and uninterruptedly wretched. Complete misery destroys; — elasticity of human nature is so great that any state which is endurable, becomes daily more tolerable, until at length it affords intervals of pleasure. Although to children, life in the Refuge is dark and stormy, still, in general they know how to avail themselves of all facilities that afford present enjoyment; and do not fail to bask in those rays of sunshine which occasionally light up and warm their dreary path. But, nothing short of excessive ignorance can entertain for a moment the idea that the inmates of the Refuge are contented. In summer, they are about fourteen hours under orders daily. On parade, at table, at their work, and in school, they are not allowed to converse. They rise at five o'clock in summer — are hurried into the yard — hurried into the dining-room — hurried at their work and at their studies. For every trifling commission or omission which it is deemed wrong to do or to omit to do, they are "cut" with ratan. Every day they experience a series of painful excitements. The endurance of the whip, or the loss of a meal — deprivation of play or the solitary cell. On every hand their walk is bounded; while Restriction and Constraint are their most intimate companions. Are they contented?

The detention of delinquent children: the state versus the parent

1. "The right of parental control is a natural, but not an unalienable one"

Ex parte Crouse, 4 Wharton (Pa.) 9 (1838).

This was a *habeas corpus* directed to the keeper and managers of the "House of Refuge," in the county of Philadelphia, requiring them to produce before the Court one Mary Ann Crouse, an infant, detained in that institution. The petition for the *habeas corpus* was in the name of her father.

By the return to the writ it appeared, that the girl had been committed to the custody of the managers by virtue of a warrant under the hand and seal of Morton M'Michael, Esq., a justice of the peace of the county of Philadelphia, which recited that complaint and due proof had been made before him by Mary Crouse, the mother of the said Mary Ann Crouse, "that the said infant by reason of vicious conduct, has rendered her control beyond the power of the said complainant, and made it manifestly requisite that from regard to the moral and future welfare of the said infant she should be placed under the guardianship of the managers of the House of Refuge"; and the said alderman certified that in his opinion the said infant was "a proper subject for the said House of Refuge." Appended to the warrant of commitment were the names and places of residence of the witnesses examined, and the substance of the testimony given by them respectively, upon which the adjudication of the magistrate was founded.

The House of Refuge was established in pursuance of an act of assembly passed on the 23rd day of March, 1826. The 6th section of that act declared that the managers should, "at their discretion, receive into the said House of Refuge, such children who shall be taken up or committed as vagrants, or upon any criminal charge, or duly convicted of criminal offences, as may be in the judgment of the Court of Oyer and Terminer, or of the Court of Quarter Sessions of the peace of the county, or of the Mayor's Court of the city of Philadelphia, or of any alderman or justice of the peace, or of the managers of the Alms-house and house of employment, be deemed proper objects." By a supplement to the act passed on the 10th day of April 1835, it was declared, that in lieu of the provisions of the act of 1826, it should be lawful for the managers of the House of Refuge "at their discretion, to receive into their care and guardianship, infants, males under the age of twenty-one years, and females under the age of eighteen years, committed to their custody in either of the following modes, viz. First: infants committed by an alderman or justice of the peace on the complaint and due proof made to him by the parent, guardian or next friend of such infant, that by reason of incorrigible or vicious conduct such infant has rendered his or her control beyond the power of such parent, guardian or next friend, and made it manifestly requisite that from regard for the morals and future welfare of such infant, he or she should be placed under the guardianship of the managers of the House of Refuge. Second: infants

committed by the authority aforesaid, where complaint and due proof have been made that such infant is a proper subject for the guardianship of the managers of the House of Refuge, in consequence of vagrancy, or incorrigible or vicious conduct, and that from the moral depravity or otherwise of the parent or next friend in whose custody such infant may be, such parent or next friend is incapable or unwilling to exercise the proper care and discipline over such incorrigible or vicious infant. Third: infants committed by the Courts of this commonwealth in the mode provided by the act to which this is a supplement."

Mr. *W. L. Hirst,* for the petitioner, now contended, that these provisions so far as they authorised the committal and detention of an infant without a trial by jury, were unconstitutional. He referred to the sixth and ninth sections of the Bill of Rights . . .

Mr. *Barclay* and Mr. *J. R. Ingersoll,* for the managers of the House of Refuge.

PER CURIAM. — The House of Refuge is not a prison, but a school. Where reformation, and not punishment, is the end, it may indeed be used as a prison for juvenile convicts who would else be committed to a common gaol; and in respect to these, the constitutionality of the act which incorporated it, stands clear of controversy. It is only in respect of the application of its discipline to subjects admitted on the order of a court, a magistrate, or the managers of the Alms-house, that a doubt is entertained. The object of the charity is reformation, by training its inmates to industry; by imbuing their minds with principles of morality and religion; by furnishing them with means to earn a living; and, above all, by separating them from the corrupting influence of improper associates. To this end, may not the natural parents, when unequal to the task of education, or unworthy of it, be superseded by the *parens patria,* or common guardian of the community? It is to be remembered that the public has a paramount interest in the virtue and knowledge of its members, and that, of strict right, the business of education belongs to it. That parents are ordinarily entrusted with it, is because it can seldom be put into better hands; but where they are incompetent or corrupt, what is there to prevent the public from withdrawing their faculties, held, as they obviously are, at its sufferance? The right of parental control is a natural, but not an unalienable one. It is not excepted by the declaration of rights out of the subjects of ordinary legislation; and it consequently remains subject to the ordinary legislative power, which, if wantonly or inconveniently used, would soon be constitutionally restricted, but the competency of which, as the government is constituted, cannot be doubted. As to abridgment of indefeasible rights by confinement of the person, it is no more than what is borne, to a greater or less extent, in every school; and we know of no natural right to exemption from restraints which conduce to an infant's welfare. Nor is there a doubt of the propriety of their application in the particular instance. The infant has been snatched from a course which must have ended in confirmed depravity; and, not only is the restraint of her person lawful, but it would be an act of extreme cruelty to release her from it.

---

2. "The injudicious interference of the parents was prevented"

Proceedings of the First Convention of Managers and Superintendents of Houses of Refuge and Schools of Reform, 1857, pp. 60–61.

Mr. McCobb, of the Maine State Reform School:

We have had great trouble in the State of Maine on account of short commitments, and I fear we are destined to have more. The law of the State allows commitments for a term not less than a year. Our difficulty is with the Legislature and the magistrates. We have not hitherto been able to prevail upon the former to take action upon this subject . . .

Dr. Graves, of the Baltimore House of Refuge:

There is a decision in relation to this matter. Judge Gibson refused an application of *habeas corpus* to take a child from the Institution, on the ground that the institution stood in *loco parentis* to the child [see above, *Ex parte* Crouse]. Profiting by this decision, I drew the amended charter of our House so that the commitments should be during minority, and we have found the advantage of it. Only two weeks ago there were three applications for the discharge of children. We refused it upon this ground; we did not think it proper, under the charter, that the parents should obtain the committal of their children, and after two or three months, upon the application of the same individual who made the commitment, the child should be given up. We had no guarantee that they would not be sent back to us in a month or two. You cannot expect reform under two years. The managers must have complete power over the child until he has attained the age of twenty-one. He finds that there is no hope of speedy discharge, submits to the discipline, and improves. A case recently occurred which may serve to illustrate the advantage of guardianship till majority. Two very interesting children, a girl and a boy, were sent to us last winter. Being extremely destitute, they were committed as vagrants, and we took charge of them. After we had found a home for the little girl, the mother made an application for her, which we refused. She succeeded in finding where the child was, and demanded it. The man with whom we had placed her was quite firm, and refused to surrender her, but told the mother that if she conducted herself well, and he thought it would do her good, the mother might visit her. She threatened legal proceedings, but our power over the child was superior to hers, and thus the injudicious interference of the parents was prevented. I think it would be judicious to take a vote upon this question. It has been decided, in all cases in our courts, in Maryland, that these Institutions shall stand in the place of the parents during minority . . .

Disposition of delinquent children

1. Binding out — the hope of reformation

New York Society for the Reformation of Juvenile Delinquents, *Annual Report, 1828* (New York, 1829), pp. 48–50.

In the period 1825–1850 most of the children were indentured to farmers or ship captains; girls were usually bound to families as domestics. A few boys were indentured to skilled tradesmen — carpenters, coopers, saddlemakers, shoemakers — or were bound to business firms. Ship service was the common means of disposing of older boys.

LETTER TO THE MASTERS

Sir,

We have consented to bind   one of the children under our care in the House of Refuge, to you as an apprentice, pursuant to powers given to us by an act of the Legislature of this state.

We should not have done this, had not our inquiries, as to your character, induced us to believe, that your example, and your treatment of this young person will be such as may tend to perfect the moral reformation, we have reason to hope, he has experienced since he has been in the asylum under our charge.

Great pains are taken to impress on the children, committed to the House of Refuge, a love of truth, to give them religious instruction, habits of order and industry, and to teach them to be respectful and obedient. We have found from experience, that this may be done by a

steady and firm conduct, not incompatible with great kindness. We are persuaded that most children may be more easily, and more effectually, governed by proper appeals to their mental feelings, than by corporal punishments, and that where these are inflicted frequently and with severity, it oftener marks a want of sense or humanity, on the one part, than demerit, on the other.

We hope the system we pursue, will have had an effect on the child you will receive from us, which will render him useful to you, and contribute to make him a worthy member of society, when his connection with you shall cease. But this can not be expected, unless you, to whose care he will now be committed, interest yourself in his welfare.

It has not been concealed from you, and ought not to be forgotten, that this child has been a delinquent. We beg, therefore, to remind you that   conduct may require more attention than might be thought necessary to one who had never been led from the paths of virtue. Should your kindness and care redeem this child, and make   religious, moral, and industrious, you will participate with us in those feelings, which must result from the reflection that we may have contributed to the temporal and eternal happiness of a fellow-being.

It will be very satisfactory to us, to receive from you, from time to time, an account of the conduct of this young person. This is desirable not only as respects the individual, but should   behave, as we hope   will, your favorable report will be serviceable to our Institution. We wish you would encourage   to write occasionally to our superintendent. We are happy to say, that the accounts we have had of, and from the children, we have bound out, have been, except in a very few instances, highly satisfactory. When the child's service has expired, it is desirable that should receive from you a certificate, which may express your opinion of   conduct while   was under your care.

With a hope that you may find in your apprentice a worthy and useful servant, and he in you an able instructor and kind master, and with our best wishes for   and your happiness and prosperity, we commit   to your care.

By order and in behalf of the Board of Managers,

Superintendent.

LETTER TO THE APPRENTICE

You are about to leave the House of Refuge. You will be bound as an apprentice to a person, who, the Managers believe, will provide for you, instruct you, and if you behave well, treat you with kindness.

We should not have consented to part with you at this time, had not your conduct given us reason to hope that the religious and moral instruction you have received since you have been under our care, have disposed you to lead an honest, industrious, and sober life . . .

Do not be discouraged by what has happened from striving to raise yourself to a respectable station in the world. If your life be hereafter exemplary, the errors of your infancy will be forgiven or forgotten. In our happy country, every honest man may claim the rewards he merits. Many of our most distinguished citizens have been the makers of their own fortunes, and in their childhood were as poor and unprotected as you have been.

.   .   .   .   .

You well know the evil consequences of bad company: there is nothing as to which you ought to be more on your guard. You ought particularly to avoid those with whom you associated before you was placed in the House of Refuge. That you may not be again tempted by these, you should not be too anxious to return to this city, and put yourself in a situation where you may meet with them. When your time of service is out, and you become your own master you may have a better chance of success in the world, if you will establish yourself where you will have no friends but those

you may hereafter make by your good conduct, and where the history of your early life is unknown.

It will always be gratifying to us to hear of your welfare. We shall be pleased to learn that you preserve and often read this letter. We wish you occasionally to write to our superintendent; you will always find in him, and in us, friends ready to advise and to serve you.

Committing you to the protection of Providence, and to the care of your master, and repeating our admonition to you, to be religious, to love the truth, to be sober and industrious, and to avoid bad company, we bid you farewell.

By order and on behalf of the Board of Managers,

Superintendent.

---

2. Maryland authorizes binding out in lieu of imprisonment for juvenile offenders, 1831

"An act relating to crime and punishments," 1831 — ch. 208, Clement Dorsey, comp., *The General Public Statutory Law and Public Law of the State of Maryland, 1692–1839,* II (Baltimore, 1840), 1025.

. . . When any infant under the age of fifteen years, shall be convicted of any indictable offence, other than some malicious felony, the court before whom such conviction shall take place, shall have full power and authority to suspend sentence upon such convicted party, and bind the same to a master or mistress, whether resident within or without this state, or to procure other employment for the same, in or out of this state, and to compel such infant to comply with the terms of their judgment in the premises: *Provided however,* that no binding as aforesaid, shall be for a term extending beyond the age of sixteen years in females and twenty-one years in males, and that the infant be not bound to any service in the county within which he or she shall have been convicted.

B. THE GROWTH OF STATE INSTITUTIONS

*The first state institution
for juvenile delinquents,
Massachusetts, 1847* [1]

---

1. Children in Massachusetts jails, 1845

Massachusetts, Senate, "Report of the Joint Special Committee to investigate the establishment of a State Institution for the reformatories of Juvenile Offenders," Doc. 86, *Documents, 1846* (Boston, 1846), pp. 2–3.

From the information collected by this Committee, it appears that *ninety-seven children,* between the ages of six and sixteen years, were convicted and sentenced to the Houses of Correction in this Commonwealth, in the year 1845 . . . Ninety-seven children in one year, placed in a school which will infallibly make them accomplished knaves and villains, who might have been rescued by the strong arm of the Commonwealth, and educated in such manner as to have made honest and useful citizens. Ninety-seven children in one year, placed on the highroad — and a rail-road, too — which ends at the State Prison, almost without a hope that one of them may ever be turned back!

Is there no remedy for this alarming and ever increasing evil? Will the Legislature of Massachusetts, year after year, turn a deaf ear to the cries of these poor children? refuse to stretch forth a hand for their succor; *compel* them to travel the downward path of sin and infamy; to become vagabonds, thieves, drunkards, — a band of Ishmaelites, preying upon ourselves? This Committee are of opinion that a remedy may be found — that the Commonwealth may increase her high renown for good

deeds, by adding one more to the number of her charitable institutions, which shall be as fruitful in good results as any now existing.

---

2. A magistrate explains his reluctance to convict juvenile delinquents

Letter from William Sawyer to E. Rockwood Hoar, Feb. 26, 1846, in Massachusetts, Senate, "Report of the Joint Special Committee," pp. 7–8.

Sir, — I have received your circular of the 20th, and am happy to learn that public attention is called to the laws touching juvenile offenders. I have long been under the impression that a revision of those laws would be a public benefit, and that future enactments are required to meet the wants of society . . . It seems to me that public policy requires that the State should take charge of these unfortunate ones; and, when they are found thus neglected, instead of meting out punishment for them, should provide means for their relief.

During the past nine years, I have been frequently called upon to issue warrants against juvenile offenders. The complaints are for petty thefts, pilfering from gardens and orchards, malicious or thoughtless mischief — Sabbath-breaking, gambling for money, for being runaways, stubborn children, idlers and vagabonds; sometimes against boys under ten years of age, but mostly between the age of ten and sixteen. But there is seldom a case of a juvenile offender, in which I am not well satisfied that the parents, or person having the child in charge, is most blamable — they take no pains to make him attend school — they suffer him to be out nights without knowing or caring where; and,

---

1. The Western House of Refuge, Rochester, New York, was a state institution incorporated in 1846 but not opened until 1849.

in many instances, they are incapable of taking care of themselves, much less their children; they have no home fit for a child; their residence is a grog-shop; their companions drunkards and gamblers or worse; they bestow no thought upon their child, until he falls into the hands of an officer and is brought before a court. If there was an institution where such boys might be sent at the outset, not for six months, but during the discretion of a competent board of overseers, I doubt not many would be saved who are now lost, and society would be the gainer.

With these views, I need not inform you that I issue warrants with great reluctance against juveniles, and enforce laws which lock them up among old offenders, and seem to me to make and increase the very evil they propose to remedy. I know officers serve such warrants with reluctance. I know public sympathy, awakened by the youth, or neglected and friendless condition of such offenders, often breaks out in harsh language against the law, and sometimes its indignation falls most unfairly upon the magistrate who is compelled to administer it.

P.S. I wish it to be distinctly understood, that the number of boys arrested on warrants in 1845, is, by no means all who have been complained of to me; for want of some suitable place or means to reform such, I have declined issuing legal process in a far greater number of cases.

3. The remedial legislation

"An Act to establish the State Reform Schools," 1847 — ch. 185, Massachusetts, *Acts and Resolves, 1847* (Boston, 1847), pp. 405–407.

Section 1. There shall be established, in the town of Westborough, in the county of Worcester, on the land conveyed to the Commonwealth for the purpose, a school, for the in-

struction, employment, and reformation, of juvenile offenders, to be called the State Reform School; and the government of said school shall be vested in a board of seven trustees, to be appointed and commissioned by the Governor, by and with the advice of the council.

. . . . .

Section 3. As soon as the governor shall have been notified, by the commissioners to be appointed under a resolve "for erecting the State Reform School Buildings," that said buildings are prepared for occupancy, he shall, forthwith, issue his proclamation, giving public notice of the fact.

Section 4. After proclamation shall have been made, as provided in the third section of this act, when any boy, under the age of sixteen years, shall be convicted of any offence, known to the laws of this Commonwealth, and punishable by imprisonment, other than such as may be punished by imprisonment for life, the court, or justice, as the case may be, before whom such conviction shall be had, may, at their discretion, sentence such boy to the State Reform School, or to such punishment as is now provided by law for the same offence. And if the sentence shall be to the Reform School, then it shall be in the alternative, to the State Reform School, or to such punishment as would have been awarded if this act had not been passed.

Section 5. Any boy, so convicted and sent to said school, shall there be kept, disciplined, instructed, employed, and governed, under the direction of said board of trustees, until he shall be either reformed and discharged, or shall be bound out by said trustees, according to their by-laws, or shall be remanded to prison, under the sentence of the court, as incorrigible, upon information of the trustees, as hereinafter provided.

Section 6. If any boy shall, upon any conviction, be sentenced to said school, and the trustees, or any two of them in the absence of the others, shall deem it inexpedient to receive him, or if he shall be found incorrigible, or his continuance in the school shall be deemed prejudicial to the management and discipline thereof, they shall certify the same upon the mittimus by virtue of which he is held, which mittimus, together with the boy, shall be delivered to the sheriff of any county or his deputy, or to the constable of any town, who shall, forthwith, commit said boy to the jail, house of correction, or state prison, as the case may be, in pursuance of the alternative sentence provided for in the preceding section of this act.

Section 7. All commitments, to this institution, of boys, of whatever age when committed, shall be for a term not longer than during their minority, nor less than one year, unless sooner discharged by order of the trustees, as hereinbefore provided; and whenever any boy shall be discharged therefrom, by the expiration of his term of commitment, or as reformed, or as having arrived at the age of twenty-one years, such discharge shall be a full and complete release from all penalties and disabilities which may have been created by such sentence.

Section 8. The trustees of this school shall have power to bind out all boys committed to their charge, for any term of time during the period for which they shall have been committed, as apprentices or servants, to any inhabitants of this Commonwealth; and the said trustees, and master or mistress, apprentice or servant, shall, respectively, have all the rights and privileges, and be subject to all the duties, set forth in the eightieth chapter of the Revised Statutes, in the same manner as if said binding or apprenticing were made by overseers of the poor.

Section 9. The trustees shall cause the boys under their charge to be instructed in piety and morality, and in such branches of useful knowledge as shall be adapted to their age and capacity; they shall also be instructed in some regular course of labor, either mechanical, manufacturing, agricultural, or horticultural, or a combination of these, as shall be best suited to their age and strength, disposition and capacity; also such other arts and trades, as may

seem to them best adapted to secure the reformation, amendment, and future benefit, of the boys; and, in binding out the inmates, the trustees shall have scrupulous regard to the religious and moral character of those to whom they are to be bound, to the end that they may secure to the boys the benefit of a good example, and wholesome instruction, and the sure means of improvement in virtue and knowledge, and, thus, the opportunity of becoming intelligent, moral, useful, and happy citizens of this Commonwealth.

---

4. A comment on the new institution

Theodore Lyman to Alfred Dwight Foster, Nov. 26, 1847, in Massachusetts, Senate, "Report on Public Charitable Institutions, 1858," Doc. 2, *Documents, 1859* (Boston, 1859), pp. 112–116.

Lyman (1792–1849), mayor of Boston, 1831–1835, eventually contributed $22,500 to help establish the State Reform School and bequeathed the institution an additional $50,000. Foster was a commissioner of the School.

My Dear Sir . . . I am very glad to learn that the interior will be adapted to the management of the boys on the social plan.[1] That this is the best system for persons of the age and character of those that will go to the school, I am well persuaded. The object of this institution, as I understand it, is not so much that of punishment as of reform, for I suppose it never would have been established except on the ground and expectation that many of the inmates would be reformed. When out of the

1. By the "social plan" Lyman meant the Auburn or congregate system of prison discipline as opposed to the Pennsylvania or solitary system.

school they must live and associate with other boys and with men. I think that they will be more likely to do that without risk and peril to themselves, if while in the school, they are trained to the habits of social life. Young persons stand extremely in need of sympathy, and I think that they can only really find it by being mingled under some restrictions with others of the same age and condition. It strikes me that if it were possible to see a human being dazzled, bewildered, lost, it would be a lad that should be kept in separate confinement two or three years in the school at Westborough, and then all at once turned out into the hurry and noise and bustle of the world, particularly such a very driving, go-ahead world as we have in these parts. And here let me say a word on a subject, in regard to which I have some practical knowledge.

It is sometimes said by those who vindicate the principle of separate confinement and labor, that a sufficient number of persons can be found to visit, gratuitously and voluntarily, prisoners in their cells, talk with them, read to them, and in other ways break up the dreadful solitude to which, in a separate confinement, they are condemned. But, truly, I greatly doubt if a sufficient number of suitable persons can be procured for any length of time. In Boston, it is now difficult to obtain the services of a sufficient number of suitable persons to attend to our charities and other institutions, and yet there are very many benevolent, enlightened individuals there, well qualified for such a work. It is not difficult to get plenty of money for these institutions, or to induce persons in high positions in life to be present on stated anniversaries for the purpose of making or hearing addresses, or to get speeches delivered on public occasions, or to have reports written and printed for a wide distribution. Such a sacrifice of a man's time or interruption of his usual habits is, at the worst, periodically made and at long intervals, in the presence of an audience, or in some shape, that of the public. But this is a very different sort of a business from going quietly and all by one's self two

or three times a week, for a year or more to the same man in a solitary cell. There is no audience there, and after the first visits, no excitement.

Some individuals, I know are ready for and equal to a labor so entirely obscure, so long continued and both voluntary and gratuitous. But as I have seen men, the greater part require that what they do frequently, periodically, through a series of months and without notice and compensation, shall be made of more stimulating stuff. Besides in the different communities of this country most persons are too much occupied with their private affairs, to be able to undertake a work that not only requires a strong effort of philanthropy, but also a large share of leisure . . .

Being tolerably well acquainted with the general subject of juvenile delinquency, with the condition of the truant or idle or profligate boys in large towns; being also persuaded that the quickest, surest, mildest, cheapest, and therefore, on all accounts, the wisest mode of diminishing suffering, vice and crime, was by beginning with the young, I confess I felt the strongest desire that a reform school should be established under the authority and auspices of the State. And after carefully considering in my own mind, the nature and cost of the enterprise, particularly the novelty of it and the uncertainty of any good results, as some might think, proceeding from it, I determined to offer, in the first place, ten thousand dollars towards it and afterwards as it is known to you, I added a similar amount for the general purpose, in both cases, of giving the work a strong and early start or push, and of securing for it, as far as such a step on the part of an individual could do it, the public attention and favor. I was then very solicitous as I still am, that the institution should be made a model one, not only for the great good it would do Massachusetts, but in order, also, that other States might be induced to establish schools similar both in plan and principle; for in my opinion they will gain in proportion just as much as we shall by beginning with the young . . .

Considerations leading to the establishment of the first state institution for delinquent girls, Massachusetts, 1851–1856: placing out versus institutional care

---

1. "The great object being to prevent crimes rather than to punish them"

Massachusetts, House, "Report of the Commissioners appointed to consider the subject of the Reform School for Girls," Doc. 85, *Documents, 1851* (Boston, 1851), pp. 7–10.

There are two distinct grounds, on which children may be confined in such an institution. First: — simply as a punishment, on conviction of some offence known to the law, in which case, it would seem that the term of confinement should bear some relation to the gravity of the offence, and the prisoner at the end of that term be discharged: or secondly: — by virtue of the right of the State to assume the guardianship of minors, whose natural or actual guardians encourage or permit them to pursue a course of life detrimental or dangerous to society, in which case, the managers of the institution should have the complete power of guardians over the inmates, including that of binding them as apprentices, during minority.

So great is the reluctance among us to prosecute young girls for a first offence, or for any but very grave offences, that commitments on the first ground would probably be very few, and those of the most incorrigible character. But it is estimated that in Boston alone, there are three hundred girls, under seventeen years of age, who on the latter ground would be fit subjects for such an establishment, and twelve hundred boys.

The commissioners have above submitted all the information, they have procured, which seems to them to have a bearing on the subject referred to them.

·   ·   ·   ·   ·

It is their opinion, that if any such institution for female children be established, it should not be confined to those convicted or accused of crimes, but should be based on the right of the State to appoint guardians for all children, so destitute of efficient guardianship and control as to endanger their own morals and the safety of society; the great object being to prevent crimes rather than to punish them. The managers of such an institution, therefore, should in effect, be guardians of all such children as should be committed to their charge during their minority or until eighteen years of age, proper securities being provided . . . against any abuse of their power, or the subjection of any one to unlawful or improper restraint.

It follows from this view, that the inmates should not be regarded, either as criminals to be punished, or as pupils to be educated, but solely as children to be provided for; and for whom the best provision would be to place them at once in some respectable family. The sooner this is done, the better for the individuals, and the more extensive the benefits of the institution.

Many fit objects of such guardianship might undoubtedly, without a week's delay, be placed in some private family, where they would be as free from temptation, and under as beneficent influences as in any public institution. It is needless to say how much such an arrangement would tend to anticipate and prevent criminality, and to extend the benefits of this public charity in the most economical manner.

It is therefore the impression of your commissioners, that, if any such action over female children be assumed, it should be understood to be a mere guardianship, or agency, to place them in reputable families and under private domestic protectors, as soon as possible. They are aware that these views differ from any which have been hitherto acted on, either in Europe or America; but they are not therefore the less adapted to our state of society, the less worthy of Massachusetts, nor the less likely to promote the usefulness and the happiness of her native or adopted children.

---

2. A practical plan for reforming girls

Samuel Gridley Howe, *A Letter to the Commissioners for the State Reformatory for Girls* (Boston, 1854), pp. 26–29.

I think a plan can be pointed out, by which, taking advantage of the *natural reform schools* existing in the Commonwealth, a fair trial of the capacity of the girls for reformation may be made, without the outlay of such a vast capital as will be necessary for the proposed great central establishment; a plan too, which, while it holds out great promise of success, cannot occasion great loss or harm by its failure.

Facts and experience, though ever so homely, are what the good people of Massachusetts value more than theories and speculations, though ever so fair; let me hold out a fact then, as a sort of lure to make them attend a little to what may be said afterwards in way of theory. When I was a Director in the House of Reformation in Boston, it used to be the practice to keep the boys a long time, many years even, in the House, and then apprentice them out to mechanics, farmers and others. At first, these persons were required to obligate themselves to fit out the lad with a suit of clothes on his becoming of age, and to give him a sum of money.

I think there was a great fundamental error in the principle upon which the establishment was managed — that of trusting too much to the machinery of reformation in the House, and of keeping the boys a long time under its operation, until it was supposed they had become fit for apprentices. But the important fact to be noted is, that some of the most satisfactory cases of reformation that I knew, were those effected out of the House, and in families, after the machinery of the Institution had failed to do them any good. They were incorrigible while in it.

But besides these cases occurring in public establishments, every person who has had much practical knowledge of society, can recall cases of wayward and apparently vicious youth who have been reformed by kind and wise treatment, and by being thrown into a circle of virtuous acquaintances, especially by being brought under the saving influence of the society of virtuous women.

Proceeding, then, upon the principle above alluded to, and encouraged by the facts mentioned, I would propose that an institution for the reform of girls be upon the following plan.

Suppose we are to begin with one hundred girls, who are not to be admitted all at once, but at first about twelve each month. Let us find an intelligent, benevolent, active and practical man, who has a wife of the like character, and let them be appointed Superintendent, and Matron, with liberal salaries. Give them ample power and discretion. Let them select and nominate their assistants, who of course would be women, and such noble specimen of womankind as Massachusetts yields, — her richest produce. Make the Superintendent responsible to a Board for the general *result,* but not for his daily doings; let him be the *head* and not the servant of the establishment; tell him what he is to do, and let him do it in his own way; if he cannot do well, exchange him for one who can.

Let there be a common house hired and furnished for him; or a contract made with some good family, to board him and his officers, and as many girls (not over twelve years of age) as may be sent to him. They should, however, be sent a few at a time, at first, and only as fast as he gives notice of his readiness, so that he might not have many at a time upon his hands. These arrangements made, the Institution would be ready to go into operation. It might commence indeed in one month after the passage of the act creating it.

The first business of the Superintendent would be to procure places in suitable families for the girls as fast as they should be sent to him. He would not, however, follow the old plan; he would not count upon people paying for keeping the girls as domestics; or taking them in the expectation of grinding as much work out of them as possible; — on the contrary, he would offer *to pay the families for taking them!* He would issue a stirring circular, setting forth the necessity of the case, and calling on the women of the Commonwealth, to come to his aid in the attempt to save these perishing girls. To any respectable and suitable family, that would take one of them, bring her up properly for two, three, or more years, give her instruction in needle-work and house-work, and teach her at home, or send her to town school in winter, he would offer not only the advantage of her services as a domestic or an apprentice, but furnish her clothing, and guaranty to them the sum, say of fifty dollars a year, to be paid at the expiration of her time, provided they faithfully performed their duty to her.

As soon as a number of places was provided, the Superintendent would give notice of his readiness, and the magistrate would send the girls to Worcester, where they would be taken in charge by the Superintendent's wife, and watched over, studied and cared for. The Superintendent would get all possible information about each girl's case, her peculiarities and her wants. He would select the proper family from among his applicants and send her to them at once, under charge of one of his assistants. The assistant would perhaps tarry a little with the girl in her new home, to give and receive all necessary information, and then return to Worcester, to go out again upon the same errand. The hundred would be soon placed. The Institution would be in full operation, and yet there would be *no pupils to be seen.* The business of the assistants would then be, to go from place to place, each one in her circuit, and visit the girls as often, and tarry with them as long as might be necessary. They would learn from the families how the girl was behaving, and from the girl, how she was treated. Each case would be rigidly inspected, noted down, and the details sent to Worcester. There might be as many girls thus placed out, as there are boys in the State Reform School. They might be vigilantly watched and under constant control; the Institution might be in all respects, as powerful and as efficient as that is, and yet there would be no great building, no great congregation of girls, and no display. The machinery would be out of sight, but working silently and smoothly, and its influence be felt from Cape Cod to Berkshire. Besides its immediate officers, it would find every where earnest and able assistants in its work of love. It would not have to depend alone upon the family in which the girls were placed, but in every town would enlist one or more benevolent women, and thus secure sympathy and friendship for them.

Can one doubt that, with the authority of law, the aid of the State, the countenance of the public, the labors of zealous and efficient assistants, the co-operation of families in which these girls were placed, and the support of several earnest and religious women in each town, a Superintendent could not reform more out of three hundred girls, than if he had them shut up altogether in one building with ever so efficient corps of officers about him?

Can any one whose creed is, and whose practice should be, — Do unto others as you would they should do to you, — can he hesitate which situation he would prefer, for his own perverse child, a residence in the bosom of a private family, or in a community of vicious girls, though ever so well regulated, where she would be exposed to public gaze, and necessarily get for life the name and character of a "House of Reformation Girl?" Surely not!

---

3. The state must care for neglected children

Edward Everett Hale, "The State's Care of Its Children," in Hale et al., *Prize Essays on*

Juvenile Delinquency (Philadelphia, 1855), pp. 22–26.

Hale (1822–1909) wrote this article when he was a Unitarian minister in Worcester, Massachusetts. In 1856 he became the minister of the South Congregational Church in Boston and commenced his career as a famous spokesman for humanitarian causes.

The American theory has generally stopped short, when it has provided for the intellectual education of all its children. It leaves their moral training, their religious training, and also their training to work or business, entirely to private care. The system is founded on a judicious regard for the rights of families, and for the natural affection of parents for their children.

It is all the while very evident, that in many instances, the State is a great sufferer, by leaving children for these three most important fields of discipline, to persons wholly incompetent. It is more agreeable to a father and mother, to have their children left to their own care; but when they bring them up fit for nothing; — intemperate, irreligious, or vagabonds; — the State sustains a great loss from that consideration, which has treated so delicately the parents' rights. The child sustains a like loss.

E.F. is a girl twelve years old, the only daughter of intemperate and unhealthy parents, who are beggars by profession. She is an interesting, wholly uneducated child. They move from place to place through New England, too indolent, intemperate, and sick, indeed, to work; and trust themselves to the care and charity of their neighbors. When this charity presumes to go beyond a provision for their own physical wants and her's, they move away from the town. When, two years since, they thus encamped for six months in this town, those interested in them, attempted in different ways, to separate their child from them, that she might be trained in better habits of life. But the parents were not willing she should go. And it proved impossible then, as it almost always does, to find any public officer willing to undertake the responsible and unpopular duty of separating by legal process, a child from her parents. I suppose the child is with them still, though in this broad free-will, left them by society, they have taken her to other fields for gleaning. It is almost impossible that she should grow up fit for any useful life. It would have been a great gain to her, and to the community, if any system had been in force, by which those debauched parents could have been deprived of the care, which, morally, they had forfeited.

However seriously then we may regret the crime of children, we have this compensation, when the State is able to educate its young criminals. In those cases it gains a power, which for its own sake, if that were all, it should be glad to exercise in every case. If, of a thousand vagabond boys in a large town, five hundred fall under the hand of the State in any way, there ought to be no doubt whatever, that from that very fact, they shall prove to be the citizens who will cost the State much less, in money and in reputation, than the five hundred who kept out of its care.

This consideration readily extends itself farther. And it shows, that, wherever there are parents, incompetent to make their homes fit training places for their children, the State should be glad, should be eager to undertake their care. Nay more, its own means for training those children, must not be merely such as will suffice for the waifs and strays whom no one else shall care for. They must be so thorough, and so successful, that parents shall not themselves regret the care which is given to their children; and that, as often as possible, selfish and incompetent parents, too poor to educate their children well, may be willing to give them up to care which is so much better. The arrangements should be so wide, that the State should never refuse the care of children who may be offered to it by those who have them in charge.

This proposal is not so Utopian, as to those unused to the subject, it may appear. As soon as, in any community, really good arrangements are made for young vagrants, or young criminals, it is evident that they are better off than many boys who were never vagrant nor criminals. And so there directly comes up this question: —

"Do you want to restrict the number of boys you care for, to the number who have been previously dealt with by law?"

The Massachusetts "Reform School" has made itself popular among the very class of people whose children are most apt to fill it. For one instance — where I could easily collect twenty — G.H. is a boy thirteen years old, who has been there for a year past. His father is not now living. He outgrew his mother's control, was disobedient at home, a truant from school, and finding him so, she turned to her friends, that she might get him "a place in the State School." I have known many mothers do the same thing, with the same sort of feeling with which other mothers, in another walk of life, apply for positions in West Point for their sons. It is a government school; and therefore they rely on it as the best. When G.H.'s mother made this request, the school was full. Some months afterward we heard there were a few vacancies, and I found that she still desired to send him there. He had not pilfered any thing; he was not a criminal, in the ordinary sense of the word; but he was idle, disobedient and growing up to vice. A police officer brought him quietly to the justice, sent as quietly for his poor mother, made the formal complaint, that the boy was disobedient; she testified that he was, and the justice committed him to the care which she desired for him; stricter and more effective than she pretended to be able to maintain. She did this with pain, undoubtedly. But she had no other sense of disgrace, than has a mother in the highest walks of life, who sends her boy away from home to a boarding school, when she finds that he is too wayward or headstrong for her control.

.   .   .   .   .   .

The State ought to rejoice at such a disposition on the part of incompetent parents to entrust their wayward children to its disposal. If it have taken effective means to train well the children whom it receives, every such surrender of parental authority is a gain to it rather than an evil.

---

4. "One affectionate, motherly ear"

Massachusetts, Trustees of the State Industrial School for Girls, *First Annual Report, 1857* (Boston, 1857), p. 6.

The school utilized the cottage or "family plan," a compromise between the congregate system and the placement of girls in private homes. On the cottage plan see also the following document.

. . . It [the Massachusetts State Industrial School for Girls] is . . . designed for those who are wayward, obstinate, or who from the poverty, ignorance, neglect or abuse of parents, are exposed to, or have become, vagrants, or have taken the initiatory steps in crime, and to save them from inevitable ruin, and from becoming a nuisance to society. It is to stand between the criminal courts and the prison, and also to snatch from the thoughtless, incompetent, vicious or brutal parent, his offspring, and save it, by performing those duties which he has ignorantly or criminally neglected. It is to be a *home*. Each house is to be a *family,* under the sole direction and control of the matron, who is the *mother* of the family. The government and discipline are strictly parental. It is the design to give a home interest, a home feeling and attachment, to the whole family; to make these homeless, parentless, or worse than parentless, wanderers and outcasts, feel that there is, at least, one place on earth in which they have an interest, and which has an interest in them; that there is one affectionate, motherly ear, into which they can whisper their wants and afflictions, with confidence of sympathy; one heart which beats in unison with their own, and to which they can appeal for kindness, for guidance and support, and around which their affections may cluster, with the assurance of a kind and affectionate response. It is to educate, to teach them industry, economy, self-reliance, morality and religion, and prepare them to go forth qualified to become useful and respectable members of society . . .

The Ohio Reform School, 1856–1858

1. Recommendation for a state farm school based upon the cottage or family plan, 1856

Ohio, Commissioners of the Ohio Reform School, *Annual Report, 1856,* pp. 618–619, 622–623.

In 1856, Charles Reemelin, one of the commissioners, visited a number of European institutions for delinquent children including the reform school at Mettray, France, the most fully developed and often copied cottage institution. Like Mettray, the Ohio institution contained separate and semiautonomous cottages within a rural estate — an arrangement which had the supposed advantages of segregating the more accomplished offenders from their younger colleagues and of providing more personalized, better trained supervision than was possible in the larger congregate institutions. Although the cottage plan was first adopted in the United States by the Massachusetts State Industrial School for Girls in 1856, the Ohio School with its farm was the fullest expression of the idea of rural reform.

[The Commissioners recommend that . . . the State] . . . provide an institution, such as

all experience and the joint testimony of all, who have examined into this interesting subject, demonstrate to be the right one, we mean a *State Reform Farm,* where the mass of these unfortunate youths may be employed in agricultural, horticultural, and concomitant mechanical labors, — an institution without any semblance of a prison, and upon a system of labor, education and discipline, for which, life *as it is,* and not as *life should not be,* forms the model.

Such a farm should consist of, at least, 2,000 acres. The land should be selected more with regard to health than its richness. The first cost of it should not exceed $20,000. Upon this farm the State should establish its principal reformatory school, under the system now in successful operation in Mettray, in France, modified according to the habits of life and domestic economy of this country. That system is called "the *family system,*" as contradistinguished from the *big house cell* or *prison system.* Its main differences are — 1st, That instead of one large building there are several detached ones, and each constituting one family, or household of 40 inmates, with a chief or *"father,"* and two sub-chiefs, or *"elder brothers,"* for each. 2nd, That all the various kinds of agricultural and a few of the more simple and more generally diffused mechanical trades form the source of employment. 3d, The establishment grows gradually and chiefly through the labor of the inmates, 4th, Its discipline is that of a family whose subsistence springs from labor, and officers as well as inmates are employed and work with each other; and, 5th, In its simplicity and studied adhesion to the kind of life led by the mass of the community, avoiding all experimenting in food, dress, lodgings, etc.

Such an institution, based upon the quantity of land suggested, might be started with one family of 40 boys; the building (and any common good farm house, or Swiss cottage, suits for it) being either already on the land, or to be erected at a cost not to exceed $2,000, — and this one family taken from the Cincinnati institution, of the most able bodied and better disposed boys could build the houses for the second and so on, until the whole farm would gradually grow to be the *model farm* of the State. The labor to be under the charge of the State Board of Agriculture. Such an institution appears to be just the thing wanted, for the following reasons.

The first and most prominent is, that divine law indicates the *family,* and its discipline dictated as it is by parental duty and enforced by parental love, as the institution where youth is best taken care of. Few, not more than one half per cent. of the population, happily ever require any other. The other should be as near the heaven-appointed institution as the nature of the case will admit of. Prisons are never of much use for educational and reformatory purposes, even for adults. To obviate the dire necessity of other existence, or, at least, to mitigate and diminish their extent, in other words to "stop the supplies" for crimes and prisons is the avowed and chief object of reform schools, houses of refuge and such like establishments, and, in view of this, it certainly seems to us a proposition too clear for argument, that the true way to accomplish this object is not a prison, but rather, an institution as much unlike it as possible. There are some boys and girls who are unfit for any other than prison life, but they are exceptions, and for them, and them only, prisons should be erected with most rigid discipline. And in this connection may we be allowed to state the well known fact, that nine-tenths of all the inmates of such establishments came there, because they either never enjoyed the sweet of a good family home, or the family influences surrounding them were bad. Does not that fact teach the unmistakable lesson, that the State, to reform such youths, must, in the means employed, come as near the idea of a well regulated, honest family, as is possible under the circumstances? Employment on a farm and instruction in its agricultural and simple mechanical labors, is universally admitted to be the best adapted for the purpose. Every in-

stitution we visited admitted this, and all of them used the land they could use, however little, with avidity. It affords variety of labors, and thereby the means to employ nearly every inmate usefully. "Boys are nearer to the ground than men," says a French proverb, whence may be argued with propriety, the general adaption of boys to the greater part of agricultural and horticultural labor.

The experience of all houses of refuge and similar institutions, teaches that the mass of the inmates of such establishments come from cities, and very frequently their mere removal is a reform in itself. Must not this fact at once suggest the idea, that the instruction and employment should be such as not to lead the youth after discharge right back to his haunts of vice? Confine him to mere mechanical or manufacturing employment, and he must after his discharge seek the cities to earn his livelihood. Habituate him to the life and labor of a farm, and he will, in nearly every case, continue so to live and labor when restored to society, and so the good influences commenced in the State institution will not be effaced.

.   .   .   .   .

. . . Let us remark upon an invariable characteristic difference between the family and the big house system. In the first, the inmates are always more mannerly, more cleanly and more cheerful. Manners, neatness, and all those so called outer qualities of men, are almost invariably neglected in the big houses. The inmates sleep, eat, walk, dress and play slovenly, and sore hands and eyes, and torn clothes are frequently seen. The reason for this is obvious — it is always a part of the cell system, which is generally a part of the prison system. We regard these matters of the greatest moment. The reformation of the outer man should be as much the care of such an institution, as the inner. Religion and morality should form the great basis of all systems for the formation of human character; they should be, to use a familiar expression, its citadel; but its out-posts are those qualities through which industry, routine, order, good manners, cleanliness and proper rules in eating, drinking and sleeping, become fixed habits, and without them, human character, however deep may be its religious foundations, cannot be safely trusted to bear up amidst the vicissitudes of life. This is especially true of juveniles, such as we have to deal with, and next to the development of a fine sense of right and wrong, they need as a chief protection against a relapse, good manners and fixed and regular habits. The morals and religion of a habitually clean and well mannered boy are much safer than those of him whose early training in these matters is neglected. Everything depends upon such a training of these poor inmates, as to make them proof against the approach of vice, and to make them loathe their former haunts of infamy. These poor unfortunate juveniles are without those passports into life which parental and other family influences afford to the more fortunate children of society. How necessary, then, that the institution should supply them with those other passports to the favors of the world — polite manners, clean habits, and a capability to adapt themselves easily to each new family — such a demeanor, in short, as will turn away the finger of scorn, which the rude world is apt to point at such persons. The institution itself is much benefited by these matters, as it gives a tone of propriety, such as facilitates vastly the general discipline.

We feel bound to insist that, in all institutions of this character, a strict account should be kept between the State and the inmates. The "costs" for each inmate, before entrance and afterward, for food, clothing, etc., should be carefully entered, and the inmate be duly credited for all his labor. This account should, if at all possible, be duplicated by each inmate himself, and pains be taken to instruct him in it. And if the inmate should be unable to liquidate all that may be set down against him, before discharge, let it go with him into life, as a debt of honor. An opportunity should also be given to each inmate to earn small extra wages, with which to purchase, without re-

straint, books, ornaments for his person, and even a few specific luxuries, at certain fixed rates, within the institution, so as to teach him the use of money. Such a system of accounting might be troublesome for officers to get up, but once got up, it works with ease, and is at the same time, a self-operating check upon the expenditures of the institution. Nor can it fail to impress the youth with many good feelings, among which that of impressing him with a sense of the punctilious justice of the State will not be the least beneficent; and that it will be a most excellent preparation for life after discharge, is a self-evident proposition. Any and every appliance should thus be used, to prepare the boy for life outside; and a most essential point in his education, is to teach him "self-control and self-regulation."

Gymnastics and Music should be cultivated, as a part of a well-regulated system of recreation. To teach a person how to employ his *idle* time, is a most important item in all education, and particularly with the *"children of idleness,"* such as the inmates of such establishments generally were. Instead of bells and gongs use horns, with a few hearty blasts to some simple piece of music. And in this connection we would say that bathing and swimming, and, if possible, in open air, and in a running stream, should not be omitted.

---

2. Staffing Ohio's "Log Cabin" reform school

Ohio, Board of Commissioners for Reform Schools, *Second Annual Report, 1857* (Columbus, 1858), pp. 608–609.

The "First Family" log cabin is, at the transmission of this report, not quite finished, but sufficient has been done to enable us, to announce to you, that it will be ready before the expiration of this year, unless the early setting in of the winter disappoints us, for the reception of such youth as may be sent there under the laws of the State. When this report shall go before the General Assembly, we hope to have the ranks of our first family on the Farm, fully filled up; and thus having fairly got started, during the year 1857, we shall be ready to make further progress during the year 1858.

It is our purpose to name each "Family" building after the several rivers of this State (the Indian names of most of which have been preserved), and the first one we have named "The Hocking Family," this being the nearest river to the Farm.

The selection and appointment of the Steward, Farmer, and especially of the Elder Brothers, was a matter of much solicitude with us. We were anxious to steer clear of that peculiar class of people styled "applicants for office," and we succeeded better than we expected. We let it be known, on all proper occasions, that the places, or situations to be filled by our appointment, subject to the advice and consent of the Governor, were not "offices," in the ordinary acceptation of that term, but that hard work at common wages was expected . . .

Wm. H. Jaeger, of Columbus, was appointed Steward, on the 20th of September, and by you confirmed on the 1st of October. He and his wife receive, jointly, $750 per annum. The rules and regulations explain their duties; they have no children. Mrs. Jaeger attends to the general household duties. Mr. Jaeger has been well and thoroughly educated in good schools, both in this country and in Europe. He was raised on a farm, under a father who, from his military habits, is a most rigid disciplinarian. He is proficient in the exact sciences; has served as an officer in the Mexican war; and was, at the time of his appointment, an Engineer on the Marietta Railroad. He speaks, reads and writes both English and German. We made no inquiry as to his sectarian views, and still less as to his political opinions; our examination was mainly directed as to whether he possessed the qualifications requisite for the place, and whether he regarded it as his religious duty to devote his entire energies to the ob-

jects contemplated by the State in establishing the "State Reform Farm." He and his wife have been very useful on the farm ever since they have been on it. The fruit has been gathered and housed, and in the erection of the building the Steward has rendered faithful service. Both are well able and willing to undertake any and all labor that may properly be required of them. The Steward gave bond and security in the sum of $1,000.

New Jersey looks out for her children

New Jersey, *Report of Commissioners on Reform of Juvenile Offenders* (Jersey City, 1865), p. 3.

New Jersey, as a long living parent, has a deep interest in every child she rears. And if from penury, or orphanage, or neglect, or the direct evil training of parents, any of her youth are in danger of becoming criminals, it is her *right* — it is her *duty* — to take care of *her own* and of *their* future, to remove them from evil influences and to provide them with virtuous instructions. Thus by a wise and economic foresight, will she bless herself and them.

A state institution in trouble

1. The fire at Westborough, 1859

Massachusetts, State Reform School at Westborough, *Thirteenth Annual Report, 1859* (Boston, 1859), pp. 3–4.

On the thirteenth of August, a large part of the building was destroyed by fire. Daniel Credan, a boy who had already assaulted one of the officers, set fire to a wooden ventilating flue in the north-eastern part of the building. The flames were at once carried, by the strong draught, to the main flue, and thus to the dry woodwork of the roof. The fire spread with great rapidity and destroyed about three-fourths of the building, before it could be stopped. By dint of hard work on the part of the officers, the boys, and the fire departments from neighboring towns, the towers, west wing, and a portion of the workshops were saved. Most of the furniture, also, was got out with little hurt. The whole loss has been estimated at not over $50,000.

Of the boys thus left without shelter, 240 were sent to the new jail at Fitchburg; 26 of the less trusty ones to Concord jail, and the rest, about 300, were housed in the dormitory which had not been burnt.

. . . Credan and five other boys, his accomplices, have been committed for trial.[1]

---

2. Proposed reforms

Massachusetts, House, "Report of Committee, with Bills and Resolves concerning State Reform School," Doc. 285, *Documents (extra session)*, 1859 (Boston, 1859), pp. 1–6.

The Committee soon after their appointment visited the school at Westborough, for the purpose of observing the actual condition of the buildings and the accommodation provided for the boys since the occurrence of the fire; and they have every reason to think that the disposition of the inmates made by the trustees,

with the sanction of the governor, was the best that could have been made under the circumstances. They subsequently invited the trustees and the superintendent to communicate fully their views on the reorganization of the school; and they desire to express their obligations to those gentlemen for the readiness with which they furnished all the information that was requested, and for many valuable suggestions.

The Committee do not think it necessary to recapitulate the history and details of the system heretofore established at the school, nor to inquire precisely how far that system was a success or a failure. But they have endeavored to ascertain what defects in it are traceable to imperfect legislation, and how far legislation can remedy them. Those defects they believe to be substantially these: —

1. That the power given to all courts and trial justices to commit boys to the school is often exercised without due consideration, and offers too great facilities for sending to the institution those who are not fit subjects for it.

2. That the laws requiring towns and parents or kindred to contribute to the support of the boys furnish no check upon those facilities being practically inoperative.

3. That boys may be committed up to the age of sixteen. Since the foundation of the school more than forty per cent., and during the past year precisely fifty per cent. of the whole number committed were fourteen years of age or upwards. And experience confirms the opinion of the founder of the school, that boys committed at that age are generally hardened offenders, whose influence on their companions is injurious, and who can themselves rarely be reclaimed.

4. That boys may be committed for periods so short that they look upon the school only as a place of brief imprisonment; the trustees being thereby deprived of their legitimate influence as guardians of the boys, and of the power of binding them out.

5. That every boy is committed with an alternative sentence to a jail, a house of correction or the prison; and when as is frequently

---

1. *Worcester Daily Spy,* Dec. 19, 1860, reported: "Daniel Credan, the boy who set fire to the State Reform School buildings at Westboro died at the jail in this city yesterday of consumption. While at the jail he had been a very well disposed and obedient boy, and had won the affection of those to whose care he was consigned. His mother, by his desire, was with him during the last few days of his illness."

the case, the term of commitment to the school is a long one, and that to prison a short one, the boy has an inducement to be so refractory as to be sent to prison by the trustees, that he may obtain a more speedy release.

6. That the number of six hundred, which the school could and did contain, was too large to admit of suitable employment being readily obtained for all of them, and would have been unwieldy and unmanageable under any system.

7. That that number was especially unwieldy and unmanageable under a system which congregated them all in one mass, and by which the most cunning and depraved were able to exercise their evil influence over the largest body of juvenile offenders that could be collected together within the Commonwealth.

The Committee propose that these defects should be removed as far as possible, by providing: —

That boys shall be committed to the Reform School only by justices of the supreme and superior courts, and by judges of probate.

That the town in which a boy resides at the time of his commitment shall contribute fifty cents a week towards his support, and may recover that amount from parents or kindred legally bound to maintain him.

That no boy over fourteen years of age shall be committed to the school.

That all boys shall be committed during their minority.

That alternative sentences to jails, &c., shall be abolished, and that a correctional department shall be established in the institution itself, for the most refractory and incorrigible.

And to overcome the difficulties which have arisen from the size of the school and the aggregation of the boys, the Committee propose its reorganization upon a diminished scale and a different plan. The larger part of the building, as it existed before the enlargement, is uninjured by the fire. The Committee recommend that the injured portions of that original building be reconstructed, and the internal arrangement of it remodelled, so that it shall accom-

modate not more than two hundred boys; and that the building be so arranged as to divide this number into, 1st. A correctional department, to contain 25 or 30; 2d. A receiving department, to contain 40 or 50, in which boys should be placed upon their arrival at the school, and until it is ascertained into what other class they ought to be admitted; and 3d. Three other departments, each to contain from 40 to 50 of those boys who can least safely be trusted outside the walls. Each department should be under its own sub-master, who would be responsible for the discipline within it; and the boys in each should be entirely separated from those in the other departments, whether in the dormitories, at meals, at school, at work, or at play. In remodelling the building, means should be taken to prevent the spreading of a fire, by erecting brick partition walls, and by other precautions. The Committee are aware that a re-arrangement of the old building upon a new plan, will be attended with considerable expense, but they would prefer to see it wholly demolished rather than retained upon the old plan.

They further propose the erection upon the farm of three or four buildings, to be as distant as possible from each other, and to accommodate thirty boys each. These houses should contain one or two dormitories, a dining-room, kitchen, rooms for the farmer's family, &c.; in a word, they should be plain farmhouses, which could be erected at small expense, by using the bricks now on the ground or in the injured walls of the enlargement that are still standing. There are three or four farm buildings now on the place, some of which could be fitted for the same purpose at little expense, though in only one of them could as many as thirty boys be lodged. Each of these houses should be under the charge of a sub-master, who should be a practical farmer, and share as well as direct the labor of the inmates of his family; and if he needed assistance in his duty, the Committee are of opinion that he should receive it from monitors selected for good character and conduct among the older boys, rather than from a salaried assistant. They also consider that the boys in each house should be entirely separated from those in the other houses and in the main building, and that the number in all the detached houses should not exceed one hundred and fifty. They would thus limit the whole number in the institution to three hundred and fifty at the utmost; and they desire to express their unanimous opinion, that if, now or hereafter, more need to be provided for, it should be done elsewhere than at Westborough.

.   .   .   .   .

Even with the proposed restrictions upon commitments, it is believed that the number of juvenile offenders to be provided for must considerably exceed three hundred and fifty. And the Committee earnestly recommend that further provision be made for them by the establishment of a Nautical School. Such an institution would offer to many active and adventurous boys an occupation with which they would be far better contented than with farming or a trade, and in which, for that reason, they would be more likely to conduct themselves well. From the advantages of knowledge and training which could there be given, they could, when the trustees considered them fit, easily be placed with captains competent to take charge and care of them; and they would enter the merchant service with a fair prospect of advancement in it, if they had any aptitude for the sea. In the case of boys who had not, power should be given to the trustees to apprentice them in other employments.

The Committee propose that an old ship should be obtained and fitted up for the accommodation of one hundred and fifty boys: that the discipline established among them should be that of a well ordered man-of-war: that they should be instructed in all the duties of seamen, and in such knowledge as would be useful to them in any pursuit, as making and mending their own clothes and shoes, and preparing their food: and that they should be taught the ordinary branches of education, and, as far as possible, navigation. It is supposed that they

could, in these ways, be sufficiently employed; but if not, other means of occupying them could easily be devised.

It is supposed that some boys between fourteen and sixteen years old may well be admitted to the Nautical School, and it might therefore be left in the discretion of the courts to commit to it boys of that age considered to be fitted for seamen. In other respects, the laws regulating commitments would be the same for the schoolship as for Westborough; and boys should be transferable from one to the other by consent of both boards of trustees, or by order of the governor. It is obviously necessary for the success of the Nautical Branch that it should have the favor and support of the merchants and shipmasters; and in order to invite their aid in placing the boys and in the management of the school, it is proposed that one of the five trustees should be appointed by the Board of Trade, and another by the Boston Marine Society, both appointments to be subject to the approval of the governor and council.

_____

Resolutions presented for debate at First Convention of reformatory officials, 1857

Proceedings of the First Convention of Managers and Superintendents of Houses of Refuge and Schools of Reform, 1857, pp. 16, 46.

_____

The following resolutions were read . . . and laid on the table . . .

1. That separate institutions ought to be organized for the reformation of juvenile offenders of each sex, and be placed under the care of different officers and distinct Boards of Managers.

2. That while it may not be expedient nor practicable to classify the delinquents in these institutions according to character, except in

a restricted sense, the buildings for their accommodation should be so constructed and arranged as to enable the officers to prevent all intimate communion between the younger and less corrupt portion of them with the older and more vicious.

3. That this Convention are favorably impressed with the utility of the "Family System" of government in these Institutions, as distinguished from the "Congregated System," and deem it matter for grateful thanksgiving to God, that experiments are being made which will soon test the applicability of it to the state of society in this country, and its practicability.

4. That the government of these Institutions should be strictly parental — as nearly conformed as possible to that of a well-regulated family.

5. That as the statistics of these Institutions show that a large portion of the delinquents, at their entrance, are unable to read or write, it is of highest importance that a sufficient number of competent, kind-hearted teachers should be employed to instruct them, and that at least four hours of each day should be devoted to that object, and that all the branches should be taught which are pursued in our best common schools.

6. That, recognizing the truth, "that the fear of the Lord is the beginning of wisdom," as fundamental, the Convention deem it indispensable that efficient religious instruction should be provided for the delinquents, not only upon the Sabbath, but that their responsibility to God for their conduct should be constantly kept before their minds; that the practical duties of religion, as taught in the Bible, should be foremost in all instruction of this character, and that instruction, properly denominated as sectarian, should be avoided.

7. That the Convention are of the opinion that rewards may be resorted to as incentives to virtuous action, but that they should be used with great caution, lest a mercenary spirit should thereby be promoted.

8. That an appeal to the sense of honor may be employed, with advantage, as an incentive to right action, if judiciously used.

. . . . .

9. That in reformatories, the first requisite from all inmates should be a strict obedience to the rules of the institution; and, where moral suasion fails to produce the desired result, the more severe punishments of deprivation of meals, in part, and of recreation and the infliction of corporal punishment should be resorted to: the latter only, however, in extreme cases.

10. That committals to Houses of Reformation should always be until the children are of age, to be released only at the option of the managers of such Reformatories. That the object of such committals is not punishment, but reformation, and that no delinquent should be discharged until satisfactory evidence of reformation be given.

11. That the employments of the delinquents should, if practicable, be analogous to the employments common in the community, in order that, when discharged, they need not be idle; that the Convention is of the opinion that the inculcation of industrious habits is one of the chief means of permanent reform, and that from seven to eight hours ought to be devoted to labor.

12. That the delinquents should be allowed a time for recreation on each day, and that it may, to some extent, be proportioned to the diligence applied by them to their tasks, and that provision should be made for this purpose at all seasons, and in all conditions of the weather.

13. That delinquents ought in all cases, to be discharged to the care of their parents, where they are of good character and capable of taking care of them; in other cases it may be advisable to obtain the consent of parents to their being indentured or put to service, but, where the parents are morally disqualified for sustaining the parental relation, it is proper entirely to disregard their wishes.

14. That we regard parental neglect and in-

dulgence as the general and prolific causes of youthful crime — the neglect to impart suitable religious and moral instruction, to secure submission to authority, to inculcate habits of industry, to improve the mind by education, and, more than all, to set before them a good example and to secure for them suitable companionship.

The impact of the Civil War on delinquency

1. Massachusetts Nautical Reform School accepts wayward boys

M. L. Elbridge, "History of the Massachusetts Nautical Reform School," in Enoch C. Wines, ed., *Transactions* of the National Congress on Penitentiary and Reformatory Discipline, Cincinnati, 1870 (Albany, 1871), pp. 352–353.

The school was hardly in good working order when the war commenced. The absence of fathers and older brothers in the army and navy removed the restraints which had held in check many wayward boys; and it was soon seen that the tide of disobedience and incipient crime was sweeping an unusually large number of youth into our reformatories. During the four years ending October 1, 1865, the nautical school received, by commitment from the courts, 713 boys, and 84 by transfer from the Westborough school, making 797 boys in all, while the school of Westborough received by commitments above 496 boys; making a total of more than 1,200 received into our two reformatories in four years. It was found necessary, during this period, to repeatedly notify the courts that our institutions were full, and that no more could be received. Still the pressure continued; and in 1865 an additional ship was purchased for

the use of the nautical school, of sufficient capacity to accommodate 180 boys . . . But if the war contributed to increase the number committed to our school, it also made a demand for the services of such as were qualified to serve the country in the army and navy; and, during the four years to which I have referred, not less than 162 enlisted from our school in these two arms of the public service. The demands of our navy for more men left the merchant service but scantily supplied; and the nautical school furnished about 300 boys for our commercial marine.

2. Soldiers' children fill Massachusetts jails

Massachusetts, Senate, "Special Report on Prisons and Prison Discipline," Doc. 74, *Documents* (Boston, 1865), pp. 66–67.

This report was made by Frederick B. Sanborn, secretary of the Massachusetts Board of State Charities.

Since the first of March last, 239 boys and girls, under fifteen, have been committed to our Jails, and 95 to our Houses of Correction. Of these 334, probably thirty appeared both in Jail and in the House of Correction, so that 300 would be about the number imprisoned in seven months, or at the rate of 500 a year. Of all these, if we can trust the opinion of the prison officers, scarcely one is morally benefited by his imprisonment, while the great majority are made worse by it. Among them are mere infants, almost, such as one whom I found in the Plymouth House of Correction, sentenced to thirty days imprisonment, — and he only *six years old.*

To show how our prison discipline corrects these boys, let me cite the case of one at Dedham. I visited the House of Correction there on Friday, the 30th of September last. The Tuesday noon before, this lad had been discharged from a first imprisonment of thirty days, and on Wednesday night he was brought back under a sentence of six months for stealing. This is, perhaps, a strong instance, but there are many pointing the same way; the House of Correction, as a rule, ruins more children than it reforms. Among the older criminals, there are some, no doubt, who are reformed, at least temporarily, but not enough, I am convinced, to balance the mischief done to young offenders.

. . . . .

The proportion of minors to adults among the prisoners has . . . increased considerably, but, perhaps, no more than might be expected from the fact that the war has drawn off so many of the adult proportion.

There is one fact, however, not appearing in the statistics, which deserves to be considered by the Legislature and people of Massachusetts. I have learned by my visits to the prisons in the past year, that a great number of these minors are the children, or the brothers and sisters, of soldiers in our army. The boy of six years old, already mentioned as imprisoned for thirty days at Plymouth, was the son of a Massachusetts cavalry soldier, who shortly before his son's imprisonment was killed in General Grant's May campaign against Richmond; and I have talked with many boys in Jails and Houses of Correction, who were either the sons or the brothers of soldiers or sailors in the service. It may not be extravagant to say that one in four of the many children committed to our prisons have near relatives in the army.

___

3. Massachusetts soldiers' sons in trouble

History of Boys, Bound Manuscript Records, Lyman School for Boys, Westboro, Massachusetts.

___

Case 2969. John J. B.
Committed 8th of February 1863 for being stubborn and disobedient. He was born in 1852. His father is in the army.

He was committed for breaking into a schoolhouse and stealing some money. It appears that the boy in the absence of his father has been unmanageable by his mother and at length, getting into bad company, has been guilty of some petty offences which make him accountable to the criminal jurisdiction of the courts. He is smart and good hearted. Has turned out well and been sent to the farm house.

1 December 1864. Indented to his father, E.B., to be instructed in the art of morocco dressing and to attend school — father has been in army. John is easily influenced by other boys.

Case 2999. William F.
Committed May 6, 1863 for being a stubborn boy. Born September 1852 in Salem. Father in army.

General character: He is committed for truancy and not minding mother. He seems to have been led away by bad boys into things to which he is not naturally inclined. He is good dispositioned and has ability and will do well if only controlled which has not been the case since his father has been in the army . . .

October 22, 1864. Placed with his father Samuel F. of Salem. His father has recently returned from the army and it is thought he can take proper care of him. Has improved with us and has generally been a good boy.

12 January 1865. Father writes that he has been a good boy — attends school every day.

Former delinquents serve their country

___

1. Philadelphia, 1865

Board of Managers of the Philadelphia House of Refuge, *Thirty-Seventh Annual Report, 1865* (Philadelphia, 1865), p. 10.

Many of the gallant *élèves* of the Institution have perilled their lives in defence of their country, and not a few have sealed their devotion to her with their lives.

---

2. New York, 1862

New York Juvenile Asylum, *Eleventh Annual Report, 1862* (New York, 1863), pp. 46–47.

Sixty-four boys have joined the army and are now in the field. Eleven are members of a company recruited by their pastor, Rev. Mr. Todd, of Washington County [Illinois], mostly from his own church and nearly all have been regular attendants for years. This company, known in the Regiment as the "psalm singing company," went into one of the recent battles in Missouri, chanting the beautiful words of the 23d Psalm. Not a man in the company was injured though many fell around them.

Though our boys have participated in nearly all of the principal battles in the south-west, we have so far heard of but two deaths, — one at Fort Donelson and the other at Shiloh. Several others have been wounded.

The letters received from these boys all breathe the sentiments of patriotism. Some of them are sending their money as they receive it, to the Treasurer of the Asylum, to be held in trust for themselves or their friends. One boy, Henry Alberts, has thus sent $53.00. As he has no relatives living, he wishes the money to go to the Asylum in case of his death. Thomas Green drew $51.00 on account of bounty money. Of this he sent $50.00 to his destitute mother in New York, reserving but $1.00 for himself. As winter was coming on, I tried to induce him to reserve in addition a small sum for his own use, but he insisted upon sending it all, adding, "she took care of me when I was small, and I want to help her now." John Turell, one of our boys, who went West six

years ago, being intelligent, took a leading position among the young men of the neighborhood, and was elected Secretary of a Temperance Society. He enlisted one year ago, and has since risen to the rank of Lieutenant. Theodore Reeves, another of our boys, also enlisted early in the war, and is now a bearer of dispatches for General Rosecrans. Eight of these boys, members of different regiments now in Tennessee, arranged among themselves to spend Thanksgiving Day together in Nashville. Their meeting was a joyful one, and though it is six years since they left us, they still cherish towards each other the sentiments of brotherly regard and affection, learned by them in the Asylum.

Treatment of juvenile delinquents, ca. 1865

---

1. The best and worst institutions

Enoch C. Wines and Theodore W. Dwight, *Report on the Prisons and Reformatories of the United States and Canada* (Albany, 1867), pp. 354–355.

This report, prepared by commissioners of the Prison Association of New York, provides a comprehensive and authoritative review of conditions in penal institutions in the northern and border states at the end of the Civil War.

. . . If we might venture, among so many excellent institutions, to single out any that seem to us to possess an excellence superior to the others, we could not hesitate to name the reform schools of Massachusetts; and of these we should feel as little hesitation in pronouncing first among its peers the Industrial School for Girls at Lancaster. At the same time, truth compels us to state that there is one reformatory in the old Bay State, more open to criticism than any we met with elsewhere in the whole course of our visitation — we refer to the House of Reformation on Deer Island. We append a brief extract from our note book, being a memorandum made at the time of our visit: "September 28. — Visited the city institution on Deer Island. Here we found, under the same roof, a city almshouse; a house of industry, which is a city prison for persons convicted of minor offenses, not unlike, in its general features, the county houses of correction; and the boys' department of the house of reformation, which was for a long time a general reformatory for juvenile delinquents, but has become, of late years, a mere receptacle for truant children from the Boston schools. The girls' department is in a separate building near at hand. All these different institutions are under one superintendent, who happened, unfortunately, to be away from the island at the time of our visit. The whole establishment is clean and orderly, but in other respects is much inferior to the reform schools at Westborough and Lancaster. It has, to our minds, a number of objectionable features. 1. The mixing up, in one concern, of criminals, paupers and truant children, is more than an incongruity; it is a monstrosity. 2. Meals are served to the prisoners in the kitchen, where all the food is prepared; and males and females eat at the same time, simply occupying different sides of the apartment, and sitting with their backs to each other. 3. The male criminals and the boys of the reformatory, work on the same farm (180 acres); not indeed, we were told, in company, but they must, necessarily, often meet each other and hold more or less intercourse, which can hardly fail to be corrupting to the boys."

---

2. The situation in Ohio

Cyrus Mendenhall to Enoch C. Wines, Dec. 6, 1866, in Wines and Dwight, *Report on the Prisons,* pp. 388–390.

The prison system of Ohio embraces the reform school, the penitentiary at Columbus and the county jails. The latter are almost solely left to the charge of the county sheriffs, without any control as to internal regulation by the state. The judges of the court, at long periods, give their "instructions" to the sheriffs, and but little further attention is paid to the matter, and those instructions are seldom obeyed . . . Since the receipt of your letter, I had occasion to visit St. Clairsville, our county seat, and was kindly shown through our jail by the sheriff. I found it to contain three cells and two upper rooms. (The population of the county is about 40,000.) The cells were on a level with the ground — were poorly ventilated, or rather not ventilated at all — were damp, and not occupied. The rooms over them were about fifteen by eighteen feet, with two small windows on one side, and a small hole in the door opening into a hall, on the other — one of these rooms was unoccupied, and in the other were four men and a boy twelve years of age — the men had just been sentenced to the penitentiary for terms of from one to five years, and the boy was to go to the reform school. They had all, boy included, been confined in this manner for several months! or during a long vacation of the court. No other care had been extended to them than to prevent their escape, and to feed and keep them tolerably clean.

.   .   .   .   .

It is the practice for prisoners of the same sex to associate promiscuously in our county jails, except such as are confined, for greater security, in cells. As to the influence of such associations, my own observation at home, and a somewhat extensive enquiry of prisoners in the Ohio penitentiary, as to their experience, would pronounce it decidedly bad, and our jails, in many cases, as crime producers instead of crime repressers. So fully [am I] convinced of this, that I have often to rejoice when I see a young man, and especially a boy, escape a con-

New York House of Refuge on Randall's Island, 1871.

Girls' Dormitory, New York House of Refuge, 1871.

Laundry, New York House of Refuge, 1871.

Little Boys at Skirt-Making, New York House of Refuge, 1871.

Dining-Hall, New York House of Refuge, 1871.

Boys' Washing Room, New York House of Refuge, 1871.

finement there when he was clearly liable to it by law.

3. A general survey

Wines and Dwight, *Report on the Prisons,* pp. 399–431.

Wines and Dwight sent this questionnaire to superintendents of reform schools outside of New York state.

When was your institution established?
Connecticut — In 1854.
Illinois — In 1855.
Maine — In 1850.
Maryland — Incorporated in 1849; opened in 1855.
Massachusetts — State reform school opened Nov. 1, 1848; nautical branch established in 1859; state industrial school for girls, founded Aug. 27, 1856.
Michigan — Opened September 2, 1856.
Missouri — Founded in 1854; incorporated in 1856.
Ohio — Opened in 1850.
Pennsylvania — Eastern house of refuge (white), in 1826; colored, 1850.
Rhode Island — In 1850.
Wisconsin — Incorporated in 1857 and completed in 1860.
Was the institution founded by the authorities of the state or city, or by private benevolence?
Connecticut — Partly by private benevolence ($10,000), but mostly by state funds.
Illinois — By the city authorities of Chicago.
Maine — By the state authorities.
Maryland — By private benevolence and city of Baltimore.
Massachusetts — State reform school, by the authorities of the state, aided by gifts from Hon. Theo. Lyman, to the amount of $72,500;

nautical branch by the state; state industrial school for girls, $20,000 furnished by private benevolence, and $20,000 by the state, for the original buildings; two additional buildings have since been erected by state appropriation.
Michigan — By the authorities of the state.
Missouri — The act of incorporation provides that the board of managers shall be appointed in the following manner: The mayor of the city is a member *ex officio;* the city council elect *four* from their own body; the mayor appoints *two* from the citizens at large; the county court of St. Louis appoints *two* — total 9.
Ohio — It was founded under the authority of the state, by the city of Cincinnati, and by private subscription.
Pennsylvania — White department, private benevolence and appropriations from the state legislature and city councils, were the means relied upon for its establishment. Colored department was founded by private benevolence, legacy, and small appropriations by the city and state.
Rhode Island — By the city authorities of Providence.
Wisconsin — By the state authorities.
How are the funds for its support obtained?
Connecticut. — From the state, from the earnings of inmates, from use of the farm, and from boarding pupils.
Illinois. — By city tax.
Maine. — The funds are obtained by annual appropriations by the state; from taxes levied upon cities and towns for subsistence and clothing; from the products of the farm, and from the earnings of the boys.
Maryland. — They are obtained chiefly from the city and state, and from the labor of inmates.
Massachusetts. — For State Reform School, they are obtained from the state, interest on the Lyman and Mary Lamb funds, and from earnings. For the Nautical Branch and the Girls' Industrial School, from appropriations by the Legislature.
Michigan. — It is sustained by an appropria-

tion from the state treasury, and by the labor of the boys.

Missouri. — The expenses of the institution are paid by the *city*, with the exception of a comparatively small amount paid by the county for board of subjects committed by courts of St. Louis county.

Ohio. — This institution is sustained by taxation upon the property of the city, and incidental receipts for the labor of inmates, and for the board of inmates not otherwise entitled to admission to the Refuge.

Pennsylvania. — Both departments, from appropriations of money by the city and state, together with the earnings of the inmates.

Rhode Island. — The funds are derived from the city authorities.

Wisconsin. — By legislative appropriation, and a tax of one dollar per week for "incorrigibles" and "vagrants," imposed on the several counties from whence sent.

.   .   .   .   .

How many inmates will the institution accommodate?

Connecticut. — Two hundred inmates can be accommodated.

Illinois. — This institution can receive two hundred and fifty inmates.

Maine. — Can accommodate two hundred and forty pupils.

Maryland. — The boys' building is calculated for three hundred and fifty — girls, seventy five.

Massachusetts. — State Reform School — from three hundred to three hundred and twenty-five; Nautical Branch, three hundred and fifty boys (two ships); Girls' Industrial School — the five buildings, each containing thirty, accommodate one hundred and fifty.

Michigan. — The institution was originally designed to accommodate one hundred and fifty-two boys, but there are in the house two hundred and sixty-two.

Missouri. — The buildings of the female department will accommodate well about one hundred inmates; those of the male department about one hundred and seventy.

Ohio. — The buildings will accommodate 350 inmates.

Pennsylvania. — There are separate rooms in the white department for 432 children — 304 boys and 128 girls; in the colored department, for 198 children — 122 boys and 76 girls; 630 children, in all, can be comfortably accommodated.

Rhode Island. — 200 inmates can be accommodated.

Wisconsin. — The large building has 78 rooms for boys, and about 20 for girls. The family building will accommodate forty boys.

.   .   .   .   .

Are children of both sexes received? If so, are they kept entirely separate?

Connecticut. — Only males are received.

Illinois. — Only males at present. Are about ready to take girls, who will have separate apartments.

Maine. — Only males are received.

Maryland. — Both sexes are received and kept separate?

Massachusetts. — Only boys are received into the State Reform School and Nautical Branch of same; only girls in the State Industrial School for Girls.

Missouri. — Several small boys are kept in the female department. With that exception, the sexes are kept about forty rods apart.

Michigan. — Only boys.

Ohio. — Both sexes. Kept entirely separate.

Pennsylvania. — Both sexes are received and are kept entirely separate, both in white and colored departments.

Rhode Island. — Both sexes are received and kept separate.

Wisconsin. — Both sexes received and kept separate, except in school houses.

Between what ages are they admissible?

Connecticut. — Between the ages of 10 and 16 years.

Illinois. — From 12 to 16 years of age.

Maine. — Between 3 and 16 years of age.

Maryland. — Boys from 9 to 16; girls from 8 to 12.

Massachusetts. — State Reform School — between 7 and 14 years of age. Nautical Branch — between 12 and 18. Girls' Industrial, — from 7 to 16.

Michigan. — Between 7 and 16.

Missouri. — From 2 or 3 to 16.

Ohio. — Boys under 16 years, and girls under 14.

Pennsylvania. — White department. The law specified no limit as to age. At present inmates range from 8 to 19 years of age. Colored department — between 9 and 16 years. A special resolution of the board is necessary to admit any over 16, and under 21, sent from Philadelphia county. If sent from other counties by the courts, they are received.

Rhode Island. — Children received from 7 years old to 18.

Wisconsin. — Boys received between 8 and 15; girls heretofore between 7 and 10. The ages of girls was changed from 10 to 14 last winter, owing to want of sufficient accommodations.

For what causes may children be received?

Connecticut. — Children may be committed for any crime known to the law, and for which punishment may be jail or state prison.

Illinois. — In this institution, the only commitment is for want of parental care. Every child deemed a fit subject for the school, is sent before a commissioner appointed by the city for the purpose, who thoroughly examines the case, has power to call witnesses, &c., &c. Whatever may be the offence of the boy, he is only committed for want of proper parental care.

Maine. — Children may be received for any offence, punishable by imprisonment not for life.

Maryland. — Children may be received for criminal offences, incorrigible and vicious conduct and vagrancy, and as boarders.

Massachusetts. — State Reform School and Nautical Branch — for "any offence which may be punished by imprisonment, other than imprisonment for life." Girls' Industrial School —

for committing any offence known to the laws of this commonwealth, punishable by fine or imprisonment, other than such as may be punished by imprisonment for life; also for leading an idle, vagrant, or vicious life, or being found in any street, highway or public place, within this commonwealth, in circumstances of want and suffering, or of neglect, exposure, abandonment, or beggary.

Michigan. — For all prison offences, except those of which the punishment according to law, is imprisonment for life.

Wisconsin. — For violations of state laws; for crimes such as larceny, arson, burglary, &c., and for being found abandoned, or dangerously exposed, or in lewd houses, or for incorrigibility.

Ohio. — Vagrancy, incorrigibility, and such crimes as are punishable by imprisonment in the county jail or the state prison.

Pennsylvania. — Received for incorrigible or vicious conduct, for vagrancy, and on complaint of parent, guardian, or nearest friend.

Rhode Island. — For vagrancy and being disorderly or criminal.

Wisconsin. — For vagrancy, incorrigibility, and any crime or misdemeanor.

Are they committed for a specific time, or indefinitely?

Connecticut. — They are committed for a definite period of time.

Illinois. — They are committed till 21 years of age, or till they become good boys.

Maine. — They are committed during minority.

Maryland. — For an indefinite period; but in case of boarders, never less than six months.

Massachusetts. — During minority in all.

Michigan. — During minority.

Missouri. — During minority.

Ohio. — They are committed, subject to the laws and rules governing the institution, till of legal age.

Pennsylvania. — Both departments, the law with respect to boys, contemplates their commitment during minority, with power to bind. Girls under 16, are committed until 18, and those 16 and upward, till 21, with power to indenture.

Rhode Island. — For not less than two years, nor beyond minority.

Wisconsin. — In all cases during minority.

If indefinitely, when does the right of guardianship expire?

The uniform reply to this question is in substance: "It expires with minority, unless the governing board sooner grant an absolute discharge."

Who judges whether the child is fit to leave the place before the time has expired, to which the right of guardianship extends?

The general response is: The governing board, on the recommendation of the superintendent.

What are the different modes of release?

Connecticut. — The modes of release are: 1st, expiration of sentence; 2d, discharge to friends; and 3d, discharge on parole of honor.

Illinois. — On good conduct; being 21 years old; and sometimes discharged to the care of parents.

Maine. — Unconditional discharge; and discharge upon trial; and on indenture.

Maryland. — By discharge to parents or friends, and by indenture.

Massachusetts. — State Reformed School and Nautical Branch. — Pardoned by governor; by order of the court, and by trustees. Girls' Industrial School. — Indentured till 18; or unconditionally discharged at 18; or discharged for good reason prior to that age.

Michigan. — By discharge; by leave of absence, and by indenture.

Missouri. — The power of discharging inmates who have been legally admitted, resides *only* in the board of managers. The following courts of St. Louis county have exclusive jurisdiction of all writs of *habeas corpus* for the discharge of any minor confined in the house of refuge, to wit: Circuit court, court of common pleas, land court, county court, and the criminal court of St. Louis county, or the judges of any of the said courts in vacation.

Ohio. — Discharged by indenture; to the care of friends, and to their own care, mostly upon the evidence of reform indicated by a system of merits and demerits.

Pennsylvania. — By indenture; return to friends, and by order of court and examining judges.

Rhode Island. — By placing out at trades, with or without indentures; by discharge as reformed; or upon expiration of sentence.

Wisconsin. — 1, On trial, with "ticket-of-leave," subject to be recalled for misbehavior; 2, full discharge to the care of parents or guardians. None have ever been indentured.

.   .   .   .   .

Have the children committed to this institution any right of protection against the decision of the functionaries who sent them here, and if so, what is it, and is it ever exercised?

Connecticut. — By writ of *habeas corpus.* Recourse is not unfrequently had to it; about thirty boys have been discharged in this way within a year.

Maine. — We think they have the same right of protection against the functionaries who sentence them here, as criminals have against the magistrates who sentence them; but it has never been exercised.

Maryland. — Their cases can be brought before the courts by writ of *habeas corpus,* and this is sometimes done.

Massachusetts. — State Ref. School and Nautical Branch — Yes, such a right exists, and is sometimes exercised, but there never has been any trouble in this State. Industrial School for Girls — The following is an extract from the statute: "Any girl who shall be ordered to be committed to said school, under the provisions of this act, may appeal from such order, in the same manner and upon the same terms as is now provided in respect to appeals in criminal cases; and the appeal shall be entered, tried and finally determined in the court to which the same shall be made, in like manner as if it had been commenced there originally." There has never been any such appeal.

Michigan. — No doubt the legality of the

commitment might be tested by *habeas corpus,* but I have never known an instance where it has been done.

Missouri. — Yes, either the children or their parents may test the legality of their commitment by *habeas corpus.* No inmate has ever made such a request, but the right is often exercised by parents and guardians.

Maryland. — They have such right, and it is sometimes used.

Pennsylvania. — Every commitment of a child sent here is carefully examined by a committee of the managers, specially appointed for this purpose; their action is then reviewed by the entire board; and even then, the commitment is not absolute in its character until examined by one of the judges of our courts. All this is done to see that the child is properly and legally committed. If after all this the parent is not satisfied, he can have the case reviewed by writ of *habeas corpus.* The right is occasionally exercised.

Rhode Island. — They have, by *habeas corpus,* but the right has been used in only one case.

Wisconsin. — The writ of *habeas corpus* could be granted upon proper application, but has never been asked for. The power to pardon rests with the Governor, but cannot be exercised without a certificate of good behavior from the superintendent. This power has been exercised two or three times, but *always to the injury of the inmate.*

.   .   .   .   .

Are they all taught a trade?

The replies are all substantially the same. It is not an object to teach the children a trade; but they all have regular work, and are trained to habits of industry. The girls are instructed in household labor and in plain sewing. Some boys acquire a trade.

What are the different handicrafts carried on in the institution?

Connecticut. — Mostly on cane seat chairs; about 20 on the farm and 30 in the sewing shop.

Illinois. — Shoemaking, tailoring, basket-making, cane seating chairs and farming.

Maine. — Shoemaking, chair seating, sewing and knitting, farming, and brick and tile making.

Maryland. — Shoemaking, combing and assorting bristles, tailoring, box making, farming and gardening.

Massachusetts. — State Reform School: Chair-seating, sewing and knitting, washing, domestic work, shoemaking, farming and gardening. They are taught to be industrious, and prepared to learn a trade. Nautical Branch — Practical seamanship. Girls' school — They are taught housework, knitting, braiding and plain sewing.

Michigan. — Tailoring, shoemaking, matting and weaving chair seats, farming, gardening, and braiding palm leaf hats.

Missouri. — At present shoemaking, to a limited extent tailoring, and knitting stockings for the use of the institution. The cooking, washing, ironing &c., are done by inmates. A limited number are also employed in gardening.

Ohio. — All the boys, not employed in performing the necessary work of the institution, are engaged in manufacturing shoes. The females are employed in the laundry, sewing room, kitchen, knitting room, hall and chamber work.

Pennsylvania. — Brushmaking, shoemaking, boxmaking, chairmaking, blacksmithing, the manufacture of umbrella wires, match boxes, and shoes for the inmates of both the white and colored departments.

Rhode Island. — Shoemaking.

Wisconsin. — Shoemaking and tailoring.

Is the labor of the children let out on the contract principle, or do they work for the institution?

Connecticut. — They work for the institution; none on contract.

Illinois. — They work for the institution.

Maine. — They work for the institution.

Maryland. — About one-half are let out on contract.

Massachusetts. — The officers of the institution have entire charge of the work and discipline of the boys. Girls' Industrial School: They work for the institution, a small portion of the profit being allowed the girls, to be spent at the discretion of the matron.

Michigan. — The children work for the institution or for others, by the piece, under the direction of the officers of the institution. We think contract labor pernicious to the best interests of the school.

Missouri. — They work for the institution. In the tailor shop work is done for the clothing stores by the piece.

Ohio. — All the boys, with the exception of those doing work for the institution, are contracted for by a Cincinnati firm, engaged in the manufacture of shoes.

Pennsylvania. — They are hired at so much a day to contractors. As 7½ hours of the day are devoted to active labor in the shops, and this portion of the time constitutes about one-half of the days' exercise, it is important that the supervision of the boys should be entrusted only to those whose moral habits and kindly dispositions qualify them for so important a charge.

The system of labor, as at present administered, is radically defective. The children are hired to contractors at so much *per diem,* and it is reasonable to suppose that a pecuniary advantage to them is the only motive for the contract. Those immediately entrusted with the government of the boys are generally but illy qualified for so responsible a position. The amount of labor they exact is the *sine qua non* of their exertions. If the work be well done and a reasonable amount of it, they are satisfied. These seven and a half hours of labor are spent without one moral lesson taught the boys, at least so far as the workmen of the shops are concerned.

With respect to the enforcement of the discipline, as the overseers act merely in a monitorial capacity, and are not properly officers of the institution, frequent complaints on the part of the boys are heard, and in many cases it is difficult to determine which is the aggrieved party; but as it would be destructive to discipline, unless in a well attested case, to condemn the action of the overseers, it necessarily follows that their complaints must generally be received as truthful.

If the labor of the boys is profitable to those who employ them, it certainly ought to be as profitable to the institution, and so far as the mere profit is concerned ought to inure to its benefit, producing an important addition to its receipts, besides the accession of a number of officers, who would not only be serviceable in the work shops, but in many other respects. Those entrusted with the management of the boys in the shops would be selected, not merely with reference to their mechanical skill, but a capacity for imparting instruction, a kindly disposition, and correct moral habits, would be indispensable qualifications.

If a reformatory institution availed itself of the entire profit of the labor of the boys, its receipts would be materially increased; there would be the enforcement of better discipline in the shops, and the opportunity afforded to those constantly with the boys to inculcate wholesome, moral truths connected with their avocations.

Rhode Island. — The labor of the children is let out on the contract principle.

Wisconsin. — All work for the institution under the supervision of our own officers.

C. PREVENTION OF DELINQUENCY AND DEPENDENCY

An institution for boys needing "protection, assistance, and discipline," Boston, 1832

1. The Farm School, Thompson's Island

Charles Jackson et al., *Report on the Establishment of a Farm School* (Boston, 1832), pp. 3–8.

The Farm School, established in 1833, is still in existence and is now known as Thompson Island Academy.

. . . All who have considered the state of the poor among us are aware, that there is a considerable body of children in this city between the ages of seven and fourteen, who are growing up in idleness and hastening to crime; and for whose rescue no adequate or appropriate means are yet provided. These children are generally recognized and easily detected as truants from our public schools, and are such as we meet constantly in our streets and on our wharves, where they pass a large part of their time in stubborn vagrancy. Some of them are orphans, in whom little interest is felt by the poor and miserable connexions, on whom they hang as a heavy burthen. Some are the children of widows, whose time is so filled with labor to procure a mere subsistence, that their sons still more than their daughters are unavoidably neglected, and at seven, or even six years old, become unmanageable. Some, having lost their mothers, are left to the care of fathers, whose means and opportunities for domestic control are yet less effectual than those of widows. Some have intemperate or profligate parents, and suffer, of course, from the disorder and misery to which they were born. And some are children of the ignorant, inefficient and helpless, who seem, almost from nature, incapable of fulfilling discreetly the commonest duties of life. But *all* of them, from these and other causes, are daily and hourly exposed to the contagion of vice, and growing up in idle and ruinous habits, from which, perhaps a few may, by fortunate circumstances, be reclaimed before they arrive at manhood, while by far the greater part will be hurried to an early death, the victims of intemperance and want, or live on only to prey upon the community, fill our Alms-houses and Prisons, and increase the burthens and crimes of the State.

But, for this whole class, there are now no means of safety and restoration provided. For while, on the one hand, the Boy's Asylum rarely receives any so old, and never any tainted with the faults which are already beginning to be developed in this unhappy class; — on the other hand, the House of Reformation for Juvenile Offenders is closed against them, since none are received there, who have not been convicted of some offence before a Court of Justice. So that, singular as it may seem, it is nevertheless true, that the very class most needing protection, assistance, and discipline, and who will best reward them; — the class, we mean, of the quite young, who in poverty and neglect are just beginning to yield to the temptations of guilt, — is precisely the class for which no provision is made among us, either by the institutions of the Commonwealth and the city, or by those of private benevolence.

For this class of children, then, who are growing up to become the natural enemies and great burthen of the community, it is proposed to provide the asylum their peculiar situation needs, and to prepare them, while there, for lives of industry and usefulness. That the expense of such an asylum would ultimately prove a great economy, none can doubt; since it would take an evil yet small and eradicate it, instead of waiting till it has grown formidable and perhaps unmanageable, and then attempt to alleviate, without hoping to cure it, by the costly apparatus of Alms-houses, Houses of Correction, and Prisons, which already press with such an unwelcome and portentous weight on the resources of society. The plan for doing this, which is suggested in the preceding resolution and was more fully developed in the discussion, by which it was originally accompanied, is very simple, and, as the committee think, in all respects, well suited to its purpose. It is proposed to form the school of such *boys between the ages of seven and fourteen* as their parents or legal guardians may surrender during the remainder of their minority, or the directors of the school may think fit to receive; — those who are younger than seven, being thought to require a more personal and tender care than could well be given in such an institution, besides being incompetent to the labor it requires;

while those who are older than fourteen, might bring with them habits and opinions injurious to their associates, and demanding a more rigorous discipline than it would be desirable to introduce. — It is proposed to remove these boys from the city, and, therefore, from all their usual temptations, haunts and companions; and to place them on a *Farm, where some of the more common mechanic trades may be practised;* so that the labors, in which they will be daily instructed and engaged, either in gardening, agriculture or the useful arts will contribute to their health and support, and tend, at the same time, to form in them habits of industry and order, and prepare them to earn their own livelihood. It is proposed to fill up the time not needed for manual labor, rest and recreation, with instruction in the *elementary knowledge usually communicated in our common schools,* so as to fit them for the occupations, to which they will probably be afterwards called. And finally, when they shall be found to have gone through the discipline and education intended by this school, it is proposed to *bind out at an age not younger than fourteen,* those who may have been surrendered to the directors; generally indenting them to farmers, but sometimes to mechanics and others, under whom they may be qualified to enter with advantage on the labors of life as honest and useful men.

It is proposed, that the whole establishment, as far as its *external government,* the making of rules and orders for its management, and the appointment of its master and his assistants, are concerned, should be placed under a Board of Directors to be annually chosen by the shareholders; and that it should be situated so near the town as to enable the Directors easily to oversee it, and yet so far off as to discourage the visits of the connexions and former associates of its pupils. As far as its *internal management* and discipline are concerned, it is proposed to place it under a head master and such assistants as experience may show to be needful, who shall supply, as far as possible,

that parental and domestic control, which the children committed to their care may before have failed to receive; and who shall endeavor to form and cultivate in them those religious and moral principles, and those habits of industry, order, and fidelity to duty, which shall fit them to become good and useful men and citizens.

It is believed, that such a school, while it would be a great benefit to the children educated in it, and to the community from which they would be taken, would, out of the labor of its own pupils, furnish a large part of the means for its own support. It is believed, that we can thus take those unfortunate children of our city, who are without the protection of efficient and faithful parents, and give them the best substitute for it; — that we can take those who are growing up in ignorance and all its evils, and give them instruction; — and, finally, that we can take those, who are now in the midst of temptation and vice, and destined soon to spread mischief around them; and prepare them for the duties and labors to which they will be called as men and as Christians. And if this can be done, — as we believe it can, — not only will the children themselves receive a great benefit, but we shall directly promote the chief ends of society, by the prevention of evil, misery and crime, and by increasing the security of life and property.

CHARLES JACKSON, *Chairman,*
WILLIAM PRESCOTT,   GEORGE BOND,
J. TUCKERMAN,   GEORGE TICKNOR,
P. T. JACKSON,   JAMES BOWDOIN,
JOHN TAPPAN,   W. C. WOODBRIDGE,
S. T. ARMSTRONG,   E. M. P. WELLS.
MOSES GRANT,

2. Nathaniel Hawthorne visits the Farm School, 1837

Nathaniel Hawthorne, *Passages from the American Notebooks* (Boston, 1884), II, 89–90

Monday, August 27th. — Went to Boston last Wednesday . . . — An excursion aboard a steamboat to Thompson's Island, to visit the Manual Labor School for boys . . . Examination and exhibition of the boys, little tanned agriculturists. After examination, a stroll around the island, examining the products, as wheat in sheaves on the stubble-field; oats, somewhat blighted and spoiled; great pumpkins elsewhere; pastures; mowing ground; — all cultivated by the boys. Their residence, a great brick building, painted green, and standing on the summit of a rising ground, exposed to the winds of the bay. Vessels flitting past; great ships, with intricacy of rigging and various sails; schooners, sloops, with their one or two broad sheets of canvas: going on different tacks, so that the spectator might think that there was a different wind for each vessel, or that they scudded across the sea spontaneously, whither their own wills led them. The farm boys remain insulated, looking at the passing show, within sight of the city, yet having nothing to do with it; beholding their fellow-creatures skimming by them in winged machines, and steamboats snorting and puffing through the waves. Methinks an island would be the most desirable of all landed property, for it seems like a little world by itself; and the water may answer instead of the atmosphere that surrounds planets. The boys swinging, two together, standing up, and almost causing the ropes and their bodies to stretch out horizontally. On our departure, they ranged themselves on the rails of the fence, and, being dressed in blue, looked not unlike a flock of pigeons

A child placement agency, Boston, 1849–1856

Unpublished records of the Children's Mission to the Children of the Destitute, now Parents' and Children's Services of Children's Mission, Office of the Mission, Boston.

In 1849 Unitarian clergymen and superintendents and teachers of Sunday schools organized a mission for "destitute and morally exposed children" to be supported in part by contributions of children in the Unitarian Sunday schools of Boston. The mission maintained a temporary home from which children were passed on to jobs and foster homes. John E. Williams, first president of the mission, later moved to New York City and helped organize the New York Children's Aid Society. Joseph E. Barry, whose title was children's missionary, served the mission for fifty years. The following are extracts from Barry's abbreviated case records and an undated advertisement placed by the Children's Mission.

William B. 13 years, American. Mother a widow very poor. This lad is very active intelligent boy. Jonathan Brown & Son, Marblehead, Mass. has taken the lad to learn the shoe business. Both parties are well satisfied. I have seen him once since his going to Mass. he seems much attached to his new home. April 2, 1851.

Patrick B., 13 years. Parents very worthy — has a brother in state prison for robbery. Patrick has been idle around the streets for months, and his parents fear that he would get into trouble. Mr. George Emerson of South Hanson, has taken him to learn the shoe business. This boy was associated with a large number of very bad boys — some of them have been arrested for theft. Mr. Emerson says he is a smart boy to work with. June 1851.

Richard B., 15 years — has been absent from school several months, his mother represented him to be a very disobedient boy. I called at his home in Sullivan place and had some conversation with him. I called to see Mr. Brown, a printer and he took him into his employ November 28, 1851.

Blackwell E., 15 yrs. of age, American, residing in C Street. His parents were very poor — the father intemperate. They kept a small shop in one corner of the room. They had four children — a girl of 14, and one of 10 and a boy of 4 yrs. May — 14 yrs. of age, was reported to the Marshall as a very unruly girl. I got the children into my Sabbath School where they remained several months. I then saw that the children could not be benefited as long as they remained on C Street. I urged the parents to go to the country, assisted them to get to Wareham, Mass. where they now remain, 1849; They were [still] there Jan. 20, 1852.

William B., 14 yrs. found him living in C Street with his mother and stepfather, who was very sick; visited them several times until they died. The mother and husband had been very intemperate. The mother kept a milliner shop on Wash Street. They were in good circumstances but a life of dissipation brought her into extreme poverty. They lived in one room in an attic in C Street. They kept two sons. William was a very bad boy, would stay out nights pilfer etc. Mr. Cox of Lynnfield has him — he is a good boy — 1850.

John B., 13 years, Irish. Dr. Bigelow sent him in the country, to a place. The name is forgotten. 1851.

Thomas B., American 13 yr. of age — a good boy; parents poor, sent him to Mr. Joseph Russell, West Needham, to work on shoes part of the time, and on the farm, June 20, 1851.

John C., 15 yrs. — orphan from Nova Scotia, has been in Boston for a few weeks. Mr. Poole of Milton has taken him to learn the Carriage Smith business July 8, 1850.

Phillip C., 13 yrs., American, to learn farming and shoemaking with Joseph Russell of West Needham. April 12, 1851.

Sarah R., 10 years of age — American, orphan — found in the street begging for work, her parents were both intemperate, a very bright girl — sent her to the home from which she has been adopted. May 1854.

A girl seven years — C — Mother a Prostitute living in Ann Street — has been in the house of correction several times — a woman acquainted with her says she has no affection for her offspring; the girl is very intelligent —

took her to the home — she has been adopted into a very worthy family. May 1854.

Miss A.W., 15 — parents have ill-used her very much; father forbid her to come to his house. Mrs. Joyce, Boylston Square, has taken her into her family; she gives a good character of the girl.

David N., guilty of stealing; sent him a voyage to California and Calcutta. *One year's voyage.* (1854)

Henry S. 12 years of age — stopping with his uncle 8 Charter Street — this boy's mother died a few weeks ago and left four children with a very worthy father who is in feeble health to look after him. Rev. Jas. F. Clarke has known the family for years and recommends them very highly. Mr. Charles Hood of Dorchester has taken Henry to bring up — a very good home for him. (1854)

A rich farmer in Pittsfield, N.H. took a boy and girl from the poorhouse on Deer Island. I spent some time in urging him to take these children — the girl had been sentenced by the court. They will have a good home. June 25, 1854.

Ellen T. 12 years of age — father a very worthy man, who died a few weeks ago leaving seven children. The mother a very indifferent woman. The children were very unruly, and it is expedient that they should be separated. Mrs. Butts, Carter Farm, Chelsea has taken her until she is 18 years of age. September 2, 1854.

Charles D. 17 yrs. — from jail — bailed out by Rev. A. Bigelow — offense stealing. May & Co. Westbrookfield, Mass. has taken him to learn the printing business, Oct. 17, 1854. Doing finely in 1856.

George Austin Smith, age 11 years, American. Father separated from his wife. George is a very unruly boy. Played truant from school several times — after visiting the father several times I obtained his consent to have him go to Farm school. November 20, 1854.

George K. American, mother residing in Cambridgeport. George has been provided with a number of places, but his waywardness was such that he did not remain but a short time.

He has been idling away his time for several months and it was feared he would get into bad company. After seeing Mrs. K. several times she was finally induced to send him to sea. He sailed today in a ship *Oceaniaca* for South America. He called at the office to take his leave and I gave him some tracts and a testament. April 6, 1855.

Simon P. and Melinda M., age 7 years and 9 years — Father in the house of correction where he has spent several terms. The mother is one of the most depraved women I have ever visited — intemperate and licencious has frequently sent her children to purchase rum, and had intercourse with men in her own house. The eldest son 13 yrs. left his mother a few weeks ago in consequence of her treatment to him — has thrown an axe at him, sticks of wood, and cruelly beaten him. He came to us for protection; Mrs. Barry very gladly complied with his request. He was sent to a place in B. — His last word to Mrs. Barry were take my brother and sister from Mother. After calling on the mother more than twenty-five times I prevailed upon her to give me the children. The mother exchanged the rice that I gave her for rum. The children are in the home at Kneeland Street and appeared very happy. February 23, 1856.

George M. English, orphan — has been living with Mr. DeWitt, a blind man, who beat him most unmercifully. Called to see him but did not get much satisfaction. The lad has an only sister, a poor girl who has paid his board for four weeks. I clothed him up, and sent him to D. Chickerings in Dover. Farmer Mr. C. has brought up two boys of mine. February 7, 1856.

James M., 12 years of age — Father dead, Mother residing at Bartlett Street. She has five children, very poor. This is a very promising boy good disposition. And will make useful young man. Mr. Elisha Hopkins of Orleans, — Mass. has taken him until he is 21 years of age. This same gentleman took a lad from me seven years ago who was an orphan and without any home. He was obliged to sleep out nights. He came up to me in the street and represented his condition saying that he had attended my Sunday school. He was a pitiful looking object. Mr. Hopkins said he never had occasion to speak a cross word to him. David C. was the boy's name. He has proved very studious and is a promising young man. Mr. Hopkins will do well by James. May 15, 1856.

James G. age 10 years. (Irish) orphan without any home, playing about the streets. An Irishwoman took him into her house in Madison Place who sent him to get coal in a Providence transportation yard. He stole some coal. I took him to my home fed and clothed him and sent him to Miss N. A. Drew, Newington, N.H. September 16, 1856.

Joseph M. aged 13 years. American orphan, parents died of intemperance. Mr. Willett, overseer of the poor sent this lad to my office. His nakedness was scarcely covered by his overcoat and he exhibited a very wretched appearance. Took him to my house and kept him ten days. Mr. Roland G. Paine of Marshfield, Mass. has taken him in; this is a bitter cold day. January 10, 1856.

William Wilcot wife and two children sent to Dover, Mass. Mr. Wilcot has been intemperate for years not truthful and a very lazy man. He has permanent work. It is a great blessing to remove such a family from our midst. I begged $2 from Mr. Berry, overseer of the poor, also a pair of stockings from wife.

Newspaper advertisement
of Children's Mission, ca. 1855

Places wanted for orphan and destitute boys and girls. Is there any kind and good farmer or mechanic or any good man or woman who'll give a place to a deserving orphan or destitute boy, — one willing to work and anxious to find a position where he can be taught some trade by which he can earn a living and make his way in the world?

The Children's Mission has now under its care boys from seven to fourteen years old wanting places, — good boys who can be recommended, all healthy and active; also one boy strong and well but *lame,* a good boy who must be taught some trade.

Also for adoption three nice healthy boys, one four and two seven years of age.

No better deed can be done by any man or woman than to give a home to one of these little ones, or a place to one of these boys where he can be assisted to grow up capable of taking care of himself and filling his proper position in the community.

Whoever reads this will please consider it a *personal appeal* to take an interest in one of these cases, and if not in a position to take one of the boys themselves, then to try and induce some neighbor or friend to do so.

Any friend who aids one of these destitute children will have the lifelong satisfaction of having helped to save a child, and of having done a great service to the community at large. Any person interested in the above, and willing to aid in any manner, is requested to call at the office of the Children's Mission, or to address by mail, William Crosby, Superintendent of the Children's Mission to the Children of the Destitute. No. 277 Tremont Street, Boston.

The probation movement in Boston, 1846–1865

1. John Augustus describes his efforts to keep children out of Boston's jails, 1846–1850

John Augustus, *A Report of the Labors of John Augustus, for the Last Ten Years, in Aid of the Unfortunate* (Boston, 1852), pp. 33–35, 95–96.

Augustus (1785–1859), a shoemaker by trade, often called the first probation officer, had no official position with the Boston courts. He began parole work with adults in 1841.

During the year 1846 I became bail to the amount of about $3000, in the Police Court, having bailed between sixty and seventy persons. That year I became surety for eleven boys, who were arrested for larceny; they were young, being from nine to thirteen years old. I also bailed ten other boys, from thirteen to sixteen years of age, and also nine girls, from fourteen to eighteen years old, who were arraigned for various offences, chiefly for larceny. By a decision of the Court upon my motion, the cases of these children were to be continued, but the question of the term of continuance caused considerable discussion. I always urged a protracted continuance, but Mr. Parker [District Attorney for Suffolk County] was extremely anxious to have the cases disposed of as early as possible. I wished ample time to test the promises of these youth to behave well in the future. Judge Cushing was disposed to allow such cases to stand continued from term to term, and if at the expiration of a certain period, a good report was given of their behavior during the time they had been on probation, their sentences were very light.

This year my labor was extremely arduous and every moment of my time was occupied. In addition to the calls upon my attention at court, and in procuring suitable places of employment for the females whom I bailed, a new avenue seemed to be opened; a great many females, young and old, whom I had not seen at court, called upon me to ask assistance in some form or other. Of this class I was called upon, and provided temporary homes for forty females during the year. The whole number of persons bailed in both courts was one hundred and forty-four.

The girls whom I bailed were with one exception, all discharged at the expiration of their term of probation, by the payment of a nominal fine; the girl who was not discharged, was sentenced to the House of Correction. The boys were all discharged in the same way.

In 1847, I bailed nineteen boys, from seven to fifteen years of age, and in bailing them it was understood, and agreed by the court, that their cases should be continued from term to term for several months, as a season of probation;

thus each month at the calling of the docket, I would appear in court, make my report, and thus the cases would pass on for five or six months. At the expiration of this term, twelve of the boys were brought into court at one time, and the scene formed a striking and highly pleasing contrast with their appearance when first arraigned. The judge expressed much pleasure as well as surprise, at their appearance, and remarked, that the object of the law had been accomplished, and expressed his cordial approval of my plan to save and reform. Seven of the number were too poor to pay a fine, although the court fixed the amount at *ten cents* each, and of course I paid it for them; the parents of the other boys were able to pay the cost, and thus the penalty of the law was answered. The sequel thus far shows, that not one of this number has proved false to the promises of reform they made while on probation. This incident proved conclusively, that this class of boys could be saved from crime and punishment, by the plan which I had marked out, and this was admitted by the judges in both courts.

Great care was observed of course, to ascertain whether the prisoners were promising subjects for probation, and to this end it was necessary to take into consideration the previous character of the person, his age and the influences by which he would in future be likely to be surrounded, and although these points were not rigidly adhered to, still they were the circumstances which usually determined my action. In such cases of probation it was agreed on my part, that I would note their general conduct, see that they were sent to school or supplied with some honest employment, and that I should make an impartial report to the court, whenever they should desire it.

This course adopted by the court I hailed as one extremely favorable to the success of my efforts, and I soon found, that it spared me an immense amount of labor which I should otherwise have been compelled to perform; I was pleased too, to observe that the opposition on the part of the District Attorney was gradually and rapidly giving way. But the toil thus saved

was required in another manner, for I had frequent occasion to provide indigent girls with suitable places, and often young females were brought to my house, sometimes late at night, who required a shelter, and frequently these cases were extremely urgent; although by no means situated in a manner suited to open an asylum of this kind, I accommodated them as well as my humble means would allow. That year I took seven young girls from houses of ill-fame; these girls were from ten to thirteen years of age, the most of whom had been placed there by applications at *intelligence* offices. For these children I was obliged to incur considerable expense, in providing them with a temporary home. Sometimes young girls were brought to my house by express-men and cab-men, who felt a kind interest in their welfare.

.   .   .   .   .

In August, 1850, as I was walking around in Leveret street jail, I found a small boy who was crying. I asked him why he was there, and he said he did not know. I inquired of the officers and they informed me that he was there on charge of committing a rape; at first, I paid no attention to the reply, thinking of course, that the statement was false, but I afterwards learned, that such was the fact. He was but *seven* years old. I proceeded directly to court, and informed his Honor, Judge Hoar, who was then presiding, of the fact. The judge immediately issued a *capias* and the child was brought into court. By advice, he pleaded not guilty. A jury was impanneled in the case, and though the presumption was that the judge's instruction to the jury would result in the boy's acquittal, just as the trial was about to proceed, I told the judge that I thought it a shame and a disgrace to all present to proceed with the case; his Honor asked what could be done; I replied, "let him be sent to his mother and placed in her lap"; I stated that I would bail him, and to this the court readily assented. I bailed him, then moved to have the indictment placed on file, which was done, and I carried the child to his home in Chelsea. This is the only case where I became bail when the indictment was laid on file on a plea of not guilty, except perhaps, when parties have died. The Grand Jury were not aware that the charge which they investigated was against so young a child. The girl upon whom the assault was alleged to have been committed was but ten years old.

I have bailed persons charged with all sorts of crimes bailable on the Statute book, but only now and then a case like the above. Some people will insist that I do more harm than good in bailing so many. They say it is of no use to complain of boys or girls, or women, for I manage to get them discharged; that all sorts of crimes, even rape and highway robbery, may be committed with impunity, and I will bail them. But this representation is false. I have indeed bailed a party charged with the crime of rape, and also in a case of highway robbery, and as I have related the former, I will briefly give the other.

Sometime during the year 1847, two boys were at play on the Tremont road, and finally got to quarreling; one seized the other's cap, and the other in return took six cents from the first; they then separated. Soon after, the first returned with the cap, and claimed the six cents, but the boy who had taken the money was not disposed to give it up, and a prosecution at the Police Court was the consequence of the refusal. The boy was arrested on a charge of committing highway robbery, and was confined in jail. His father applied to me to bail him, and I did so; afterwards the parents of the boys, by consent of the court, settled the matter satisfactorily to themselves; and here ended the great highway robbery case. One of the boys was nine, and the other ten years old. In former times a birch rod would have been law and gospel to them both.

2. Saving children from jail in Boston during the Civil War

Boston Children's Aid Society, *First Report of the Executive Committee* (Boston, 1865), pp. 5–8, 12–16.

A year has nearly passed since we first collected our family at Pine Farm; and we feel that some account of its condition is due to those who take an interest in it, and have contributed to its support.

Its purpose — as is well known to the subscribers — is to take from the streets, boys, from seven to twelve years of age, who are living in such exposed and neglected circumstances, as to be likely to fall into vicious habits, or those who have already taken the first step into crime; and, in place of the wild life they have been leading, to train them for a while, as in a family, with love and religious care; to place them, if possible, in better circumstances, and to maintain an oversight and influence upon them after they leave us.

These boys are brought to us, by Mr. Rufus R. Cook, usually from the Police Court, or the custody of the Truant Officers. Mr. Cook is Chaplain of Suffolk County Jail, and also agent of our Association. He is a most kind friend to the poor stray children whom he picks up, and his good influence is felt throughout our little household.

．　．　．　．　．

Some of our boys had fathers or protectors in the service of the Government. Many children will be left fatherless and uncared for, after the losses and destruction of the war; and to whom does the country owe so deep a debt as to these?

We hope, that, before costly and permanent asylums are built for them, it will be considered whether their welfare is not best secured in temporary institutions like . . . our Farm, from which they can be distributed in private families.

．　．　．　．　．

We add a short account of Mr. Cook's labors in connection with the society.

When the Association was first organized, Mr. Cook consented to act as its agent in behalf of boys confined in the jail. By his desire, and with Sheriff Clark's permission, some members of the Association visited the jail weekly, to distribute books from the library to the boys; to talk with them, and to gain their confidence, in the hope of helping them to a better course when they left the jail.

The assistance of a regular visitor was found necessary; and we engaged the services . . . of Miss Burnham. It has been a large part of Miss Burnham's work to inquire about the previous character and the homes of the boys who are brought up for trial. Mr. Cook is in daily attendance at the Police Court, and at the monthly sittings of the Superior Court. His opinion is usually consulted, and has great influence as to the disposition to be made of young offenders; and his judgment is much guided by the accounts furnished him by Miss Burnham. This, with the visiting in jail, which has of late fallen mainly upon her, and visiting the boys whom Mr. Cook has put on probation, or any children whom he wishes her to inquire about, comprise the duties which Miss Burnham performs, with much energy and excellent judgment.

Mr. Cook's labors have a much larger scope. He is, as has been said, in Court every day, and present at the trials of all children brought there. He studies their cases; and when he thinks that there is good hope of their amendment, without further punishment, he gives bail for them, or gets the judge to put them on probation. He has thus bailed many boys, saving them from the injurious effect of an imprisonment in jail.

It may not be generally understood, that there are two classes of boys in jail. One class consists of those children who have been tried and sentenced in the Police Court, and who, in consequence of non-payment of fines, are held in jail for various periods of time, from a few days to several months. Boys of the other class are charged with offences that must be tried in the Superior Court. They are detained in the jail from the time of their arrest till the next sitting of the Court. They are often very young, but eight or nine years old, and may have to wait some weeks for trial.

Mr. Cook's kindness embraces all of these boys, and not these alone, but every stray child that reaches his hand. Many friendless and destitute children are brought to him by the Police and Truant Officers, of whom he disposes in various ways. He has within a year sent fifty-seven such children to the Catholic Home, which has been lately opened at 19, High Street.

The New York Juvenile Asylum, 1851–1860

1. Public-private cooperation for the care of vagrant and neglected children

New York Juvenile Asylum, *Eleventh Annual Report* (New York, 1863), pp. 50–63.

The Juvenile Asylum was intended for beggars, truants, and waifs formerly — for want of more suitable institutions — sent to the almshouses or House of Refuge. The Association for Improving the Condition of the Poor (A.I.C.P.) was instrumental in organizing the Juvenile Asylum; the incorporators included persons active in the A.I.C.P. and the New York Prison Association. The charter, granted in June 1851, was amended in 1854, 1856, and 1857.

Sec. 1. Robert B. Minturn . . . [and 23 others] and their associates, are hereby constituted a body corporate, by the name of "New York Juvenile Asylum" . . .

Sec. 2 . . . The objects of this corporation are to receive and take charge of such children, between the ages of seven and fourteen years, as may be voluntarily entrusted to them by their parents or guardians, or committed to their care by competent authority, and provide for their support, and to afford them the means of moral, intellectual and industrial education.

. . . . .

Sec. 6. The corporation hereby created may, so soon as may be practicable, procure suitable building sites and lands, and erect and maintain thereon an asylum for such children as . . . may be entrusted or committed to the care and management of the said corporation.

. . . . .

Sec. 18. The said corporation shall have power, in its discretion, to bind out or indenture, as clerks or apprentices, to some profession, trade, or employment, the children entrusted or committed to its charge, and for a shorter or longer period, not exceeding, however, in the case of girls, the age of eighteen years; and, in that of boys, the age of twenty-one years.

. . . . .

Sec. 25. . . . The board of directors of the said corporation shall, on or before the fourth Monday of January, in each and every year, make a detailed report to the Legislature of the state and to the common council of the city of New York, of the whole number of children received into the asylum during the year, specifying their sex, place of nativity, age, residence, health at the time of admission, state of education, religious instruction, whether their parents are living or dead, temperate or intemperate, the time devoted to instruction, the nature and amount of punishment, the cases of disease, the number apprenticed or who shall have escaped, died, or, been restored to parents or guardians, or returned to the committing magistrate during the year, and also such information as they may have received of those who have been bound out or apprenticed, as well as the facts generally in relation to the performance of their duties, also their industrial occupations, with their results, the receipt and expenditures and financial condition of the corporation and its general operations, with their results.

Sec. 26. It shall be the duty of the Common Council of the city of New York, by committee or otherwise in its discretion, to visit and inspect the said New York Juvenile Asylum twice at least in each year.

Sec. 27. To provide the pecuniary means for the establishment and support of the said New York Juvenile Asylum, whenever it shall be proved to the board of supervisors of the city and county of New York, by the affidavit or affirmation of the president and secretary of the said asylum, that fifty thousand dollars in money or approved securities, have, by voluntary subscription or otherwise, been raised for the purposes of such asylum, and deposited to the credit of that corporation in one of the incorporated banks of the city of New York, or of the banks formed under the general banking law, the said board of supervisors may, in their discretion, raise and collect a like amount of fifty thousand dollars by tax upon the real and personal property of the said city and county, to be so levied and collected at the same time and in the same manner as the contingent charges and expenses of the said city and county are levied and collected. Such moneys so raised by this corporation, and the said board of supervisors, to be together expended by said corporation in procuring the necessary buildings, sites and lands, in erecting and furnishing the necessary buildings, and in defraying the current expenses of the said asylum, until its permanent buildings shall be completed.[1]

Sec. 28. . . . In each and every year thereafter, the said board of supervisors shall, in the same manner, levy and collect by tax, and pay over to the said New York Juvenile Asylum, for the uses and purposes thereof, a sum not exceeding seventy-five dollars per annum,[2] and

---

1. The legislature authorized additional grants of $20,000 in 1856 and 1858 on condition that the corporation raise a like amount through voluntary contributions.

2. The figure was originally set at forty dollars per annum.

proportionally for any fraction of a year, for each child which, by virtue and in pursuance of the provisions of this act, shall be entrusted or committed to the said asylum from the city and county of New York, and shall be supported and instructed therein; but the sum to be collected and paid by the said board of supervisors for each child so received, supported and taught, in said asylum, shall, in no case, exceed the lowest cost of support and government of a child of the same age in any of the public institutions at present under the care of the ten governors of the alms-house and prison department of the said city; the moneys so to be received from the said board of supervisors, together with all other moneys raised by the said New York Juvenile Asylum, to be applied to the payment of the current expenses, and for the perfect establishment and general support of the said asylum.

Sec. 29. . . . Whenever any child, properly chargeable upon the fund placed by law at the disposal of the commissioners of emigration, shall, agreeably to the provisions of this act, be received, supported and instructed in the said New York Juvenile Asylum, the said corporation shall be entitled to receive therefore, from that fund, sixty dollars per annum, and proportionally for any fraction of a year, for every such child so received, supported and instructed in said asylum, but in no case shall the sum so received exceed the lowest expense to the city and county of New York, of a child of the same age in any of the public institutions under the charge of the ten governors of the alms-house and prison departments of the said city and county.

Sec. 30. The schools established and maintained by the New York Juvenile Asylum, shall participate in the distribution of the common school fund, in the same manner and degree as the common schools of the city and county of New York.

2. The rules of the house, 1853

New York Juvenile Asylum, *First Annual Report* (New York, 1853), pp. 19–22.

The Asylum commenced operations in January 1853. Its object, according to a later (1856) report was "not the establishment of a Juvenile Prison, or the subjection of unruly children to a merely punitive discipline; but . . . to found an Asylum, where the friendless child might find friends, the wayward child might be taught the great lesson of self-government, and all coming to it might be placed under kindly home influences, and be provided for well acting their part in the great drama of life."

1. All pupils when received shall be placed, as soon thereafter as the Superintendent shall direct, in the Probationary grade, and afterwards divided according to character and conduct, into four grades. The most exemplary being placed in the first grade; those who are less worthy, in the second; those who stand still lower, in the third; and the least tractable, in the fourth. Any pupil who may be proved guilty of profaneness, lying, stealing, attempting to escape from the Asylum, or any other grossly bad conduct may be expelled from the grades, for a longer or shorter period, according to the aggravation of the offence. Pupils under expulsion shall not be allowed any play or conversation, their food shall be bread and water, and when not at work or in school, they shall be confined in solitude. Pupils in the fourth grade shall be deprived of play and conversation. Those in the third grade may play and converse with each other, but not with the pupils in the other grades. Pupils in the second and first grades may converse and play together, and have the privilege of using the books in the library. From these two grades pupils may be selected as monitors, and for other places of confidence and honor. Pupils in the first grade may be distinguished by an appropriate badge, and be indulged with other privileges at the discretion of the Superintendent, under the general direction of the Board,

2. The punishment allowed in the Institution shall consist chiefly in bad marks, loss of grade, deprivation of play, and confinement in solitude. A regular account shall be opened with each pupil, in which he shall be charged with bad marks that he may have incurred for his faults, and credited with good marks that may be awarded him for meritorious conduct. The bad marks shall be settled for by good marks, or the infliction of such punishment as their number may require; and the good marks may be rewarded at the discretion of the Superintendent.

3. When a child is received into the Asylum, he shall, if necessary, be thoroughly washed, and decently clothed. If thought expedient, he may be kept apart from the other pupils, for a longer or shorter time, according to his age and habits of life. When a pupil is dismissed from the Asylum, with the approbation of the Board, he shall be furnished with a suit of decent and comfortable clothing, a Bible, and such good advice as he may be thought to stand most in need of.

.   .   .   .   .

5. The work of the boys may consist of gardening, tailoring, shoe-making, the plaiting of straw and palm leaf, the manufacture of brass nails, and such other kinds of labor as may be approved by the Board of Directors. The girls shall be employed in cooking, washing, ironing, scouring, sewing, knitting, and such other kinds of work as may be suitable to their sex, and directed by the Board.

6. No play or conversation shall be allowed among the children, while engaged at their work, on parade, at meals, or after they have retired to their sleeping rooms.

7. The food of the children may consist of beef, mutton, fish, bread, rice, potatoes, hasty-pudding, milk, milk-porridge, and cocoa; subject to such additions and alterations as the Board may from time to time direct. On Christmas, New-Year's, and Thanks-giving days, and on the Fourth of July, the children may be allowed food of a better kind than usual, and be exempt for their ordinary occupations.

8. The children shall be required to wash their faces and hands, and have their heads combed, at least once a day. As often as once a week they shall wash their necks and feet, and change their shirts and socks; and, whenever the season will permit, they shall have the benefit of bathing. Personal cleanliness shall be rewarded, and the want of it punished, at the discretion of the Superintendent.

9. Every part of the house shall be swept daily, except on the Sabbath, and the floors scoured once a week, or oftener, if required. The beds and bed-clothing shall be kept clean, and nothing offensive shall be allowed to remain in any part of the house or yards.

10. No communication whatever shall be allowed between the boys and girls, nor shall they ever be permitted to pass into the apartments or yards of each other, unless directed to do so by an officer.

11. Permission may be obtained by citizens to visit the Asylum on Fridays only, between three and six o'clock in the afternoon, in summer; and from two to four o'clock, in winter. This rule shall be varied only for the accommodation of strangers temporarily in the city. And in all cases, a permit from one of the Directors shall be required for admission.

The last Thursday in January, April, July, and October, from one o'clock until five o'clock in the afternoon, shall be especially appropriated to the visits of the parents and friends of the children, under such restrictions as may be prescribed by the Superintendent. No conversation respecting the discipline of the Institution shall be allowed in the presence of the children, and no visitor shall be allowed to speak to a child without permission of an officer.

12. No boy not sent by public authority, shall be admitted into the Asylum, unless by the consent of two Directors; and unless the parent or guardian, if any there be, shall have surrendered him to the Institution, and shall also have entered into an obligation to receive him back, if after a trial of three months, the Direc-

tors shall choose to return him, and also not to interfere in the management of the child and not to visit him without the consent of a Director, nor ask or receive any compensation for his services, nor induce or attempt to induce any child to leave the Asylum, or the family, or station in which the Directors may place him. No pupil shall be retained in the Asylum who, from his character or other cause, is likely to interfere with the improvement of the pupils, or otherwise injuriously affect them.

13. When any parent or guardian shall desire to place a boy in the Asylum, and pay in whole or in part for his maintenance and education, the Board of Directors may in their discretion admit him on such terms and conditions as they shall think proper.

14. No relative or acquaintance of any pupil shall interfere in the management of the pupil, or be permitted to visit him except in presence of the Superintendent, unless by special permission of the Visiting Committee.

---

3. Indenture practices, 1860

New York Juvenile Asylum, *Ninth Annual Report* (New York, 1861), pp. 39–46.

The policy of the Juvenile Asylum was to keep children in the institution for a substantial period — six months to five years — before placing them in farm homes in the West.

New York, December 31, 1860.
To the Chairman of the Indenturing Committee of the New York Juvenile Asylum:

During the last eighteen months, I have occupied the position of Indenturing Agent in your Institution, and have accompanied, in that capacity, eight companies of children to the West. The whole number of children was 290, of whom 210 were boys. One hundred and thirteen children have been provided with homes, mostly among the farmers of Champaign Co., Illinois, and the remaining 177 have been settled in Washington Co. and vicinity, about one hundred miles south of the first-named locality, in the same State.

The course generally pursued to provide homes for the children is as follows: A locality is visited, a Local Agent appointed, and notices posted in public places inviting farmers to make application for children, from three to six months previous to the time the company is ready to leave New York. These applications are received by the Local Agent, who, from time to time, advises us as to the progress of the list, and when a sufficient number of applications are received, a company is sent, varying in number from 25 to 45 children. On our arrival, a list is placed in my hands, and the merits of the applicants are thoroughly canvassed. To those who appear worthy, the children are intrusted for two to three days on trial, the object being to give the farmer a chance to judge more fully as to the disposition and character of the child, and also to let the child see the family, as well as the surroundings of the farm. It also gives an opportunity for further investigation as to the character of the applicant, should it be deemed necessary. On the day appointed, the farmer returns with the child, and if both are well pleased with each other, and the farmer is well recommended, the child is indentured. In all cases the children are consulted as to their preferences, and often show considerable shrewdness in the selection of their future homes.

The placing of several successive companies in neighboring counties has a number of advantages, prominent among which are the perpetuation of the friendships among the children formed under good influences at the Asylum and developed in their new homes, the opportunities afforded for finding homes for brothers or sisters of children sent out in previous companies, who, by this means, can be settled in the same neighborhood, and the facilities which it affords for frequently hearing from and visiting them in their new homes. In this way, our children in the State of Illinois can be looked after and visited in one-third of the time that would be required to visit an equal number in the State of New York, where they would be more scattered. Often, while settling a company, visits are received from boys of former companies living from ten to twenty miles distant, whose employers readily grant them a holiday on the occasion. They generally come into town on horseback, and seem very much to enjoy their visit among their old friends. The little girls, also, are often brought in by their kind foster-parents. Nearly all the children are improved in health and personal appearance.

About two hundred of the children have been visited personally in their homes. This, though a work of great difficulty in a country where there are few guide-boards, and bad roads most of the year, has been an exceedingly interesting one. They are always glad to see me, and lead me over the farm, talking of wheat, corn, horses, and cattle with the air of old farmers. Sometimes the boys point out to me with pride their own horses, presented as a reward for good conduct by their foster-parents. One boy, of the company of February 1860, has two horses acquired in this way. Many of the little girls have received presents of lambs and calves, of which they seem equally proud.

.   .   .   .   .

Report of . . . Children Indentured in Illinois, in February, 1860.

No.	Condition when Admitted	Condition, August, 1860.
1	Was arrested for theft; in the Asylum three years.	Has an excellent home on a farm; is doing very well, and is much liked by his employer.
2	Was arrested for sleeping out; was in the Asylum nearly two years; his mother dead.	No better boy in the county; is peaceable and quiet; his new foster-parents regard him with much affection, and speak of him with great interest. They are wealthy people.
3	Small boy; his mother dead, and his father intemperate; he was arrested for pilfering; in the Asylum two years.	Have not heard from this boy recently, but as there is no complaint to our Agent, he is undoubtedly doing well.
4	Was surrendered by his father as a bad boy; was in the Asylum six months.	Very good boy; is obedient. Saw him at his home. He has a fine place with a good farmer on a large farm; he likes the West very much, and means to remain and make a man.
5	Parents both dead; got into the company of bad boys, and his brother could not manage him; he brought him to the Asylum as a bad boy; remained in the Asylum three and a half years.	Lives with a farmer who is very much pleased with him; boy has learned to ride; does not study as diligently as his employer would like, but is more fond of out-door work; he is not required to work in the hot weather, but his employer is anxious to have him frequent his library and improve his mind. He is quite wealthy, and has no children of his own.

No.	Condition when Admitted	Condition, August, 1860.
16	Parents both dead; had no home; gave himself up; his habits were good; was in Asylum six months.	Heard from a neighbor that he is still in his place. He is well and doing well.
17	Brought in by his mother as a bad boy; his father is dead.	Met his employer, who says that he is all right; he made no complaint. A neighbor told me that the boy has a strong temper.
18	Parents both dead; his father was of intemperate habits; was placed in the Asylum by his aunt, who could not care for him; remained thirty-three months.	Visited him at his home in August. His employer says that there is not one boy in fifty who would please them so much. He has two horses of his own.
		At the time his name was proposed for the West, one of the Asylum Officers expressed a doubt as to whether his behavior had been sufficiently good to enable him to recommend him. The boy hearing of this, resolved to try doubly hard; and that he has so far succeeded, is manifest in the report.
19	Father intemperate; no home for the boy.	Saw employer. Very smart boy, but is not truthful; this is the only complaint. Boy is nine years of age.
20	Father dead, and mother unable to support him; intellect dull; in Asylum five years.	Saw employer, Boy doing pretty well; is slow to learn; generally well behaved.
21	Orphan; had no home; in Asylum two years.	Has an excellent home with a farmer, an unusually good place; he is in the vicinity of several other Asylum boys. His employer is pleased with him.
22	Orphan boy; had no home; was in Asylum seven months.	Too much indulged; has been dishonest and disobedient; he is still in his place, and his employer promised to forgive him and educate him, if he will reform. Saw him several times. Advised a more rigid discipline in the future.
23	Parents both in the Tombs for intemperance; boy had no one to care for him; remained in the Asylum one year.	Saw his employer. Boy is very much liked, and he made no complaint; he appears to have quite an affection for the boy, who is only eight years of age.
24	Father intemperate, and mother dead; boy had no home; was in the Asylum four years.	Quite a young farmer. Heard of him several times. He is still in his place, and doing finely. The neighbors consider him a good boy. Employer says he is "all right."

The Children's Aid Society, New York, 1853–1860

---

1. Objectives of the Children's Aid Society, 1853

Brace, *The Dangerous Classes of New York,* pp. 90–93.

After a period of service as a missionary in the Five Points District of New York City, Brace (1826–1890) helped organize the Children's Aid Society. He was the institution's general secretary from the time of its founding until his death.

This society has taken its origin in the deeply settled feelings of our citizens, that something must be done to meet the increasing crime and poverty among the destitute children of New York. Its objects are to help this class by opening Sunday Meetings and Industrial Schools, and, gradually as means shall be furnished, by forming Lodging-houses and Reading-rooms for children, and by employing paid agents whose sole business shall be to care for them.

. . . Thus far, alms-houses and prisons have done little to affect the evil. But a small part of the vagrant population can be shut up in our asylums, and judges and magistrates are reluctant to convict children so young and ignorant that they hardly seem able to distinguish good and evil. The class increases. Immigration is pouring in its multitude of poor foreigners, who leave these young outcasts everywhere abandoned in our midst. For the most part, the boys grow up utterly by themselves: No one cares for them, and they care for no one. Some live by begging, by petty pilfering, by bold robbery; some earn an honest support by peddling matches, or apples, or newspapers; others gather bones and rags in the street to sell. They sleep on steps, in cellars, in old barns, and in markets, or they hire a bed in filthy and low lodging-houses. They cannot read; they do not go to school or attend a church. Many of them have never seen the Bible. Every cunning faculty is intensely stimulated. They are shrewd and old in vice, when other children are in leading-strings. Few influences which are kind and good ever reach the vagrant boy. And, yet, among themselves they show generous and honest traits. Kindness can always touch them.

The girls, too often, grow up even more pitiable and deserted. Till of late no one has ever cared for them. They are the crosswalk sweepers, the little apple-peddlers, and candy-sellers of our city; or, by more questionable means, they earn their scanty bread. They traverse the low, vile streets alone, and live without mother or friends, or any share in what we should call a *home.* They also know little of God or Christ, except by name. They grow up passionate, ungoverned, with no love or kindness ever to soften the heart. We all know their short wild life — and the sad end.

These boys and girls, it should be remembered, will soon form the great lower class of our city. They will influence elections; they may shape the policy of the city; they will, assuredly, if unreclaimed, poison society all around them. They will help to form the great multitude of robbers, thieves, vagrants, and prostitutes who are now such a burden upon the law-respecting community.

In one ward alone of the city, the Eleventh, there were, in 1852, out of 12,000 children between the ages of five and sixteen, only 7,000 who attended school, and only 2,500 who went to Sabbath School; leaving 5,000 without the common privileges of education, and about 9,000 destitute of public religious influence.

In view of these evils we have formed an Association which shall devote itself entirely to this class of vagrant children. We do not propose in any way to conflict with existing asylums and institutions, but to render them a hearty co-operation, and, at the same time, to fill a gap, which, of necessity, they all have left. A large multitude of children live in the city who cannot be placed in asylums, and yet who are uncared for and ignorant and vagrant. We propose to give to these work, and to bring them under religious influence. As means shall come in, it is designed to district the city, so that hereafter every Ward may have its agent, who shall be a friend to the vagrant child. "Boys' Sunday Meetings" have already been formed, which we hope to see extended until every quarter has its place of preaching to boys. With these we intend to connect "Industrial Schools," where the great temptations to this class arising from want of work may be removed, and where they can learn an honest trade. Arrangements have been made with manufacturers, by which, if we have the requisite funds to begin, five hundred boys in different localities can be supplied with paying work. We hope, too, especially to be the means of draining the city of these children, by communicating with farmers, manufacturers, or families in the country, who may have need of such for employment. When homeless boys are found by our agents, we mean to get them homes in the families of respectable, needy persons in the city, and put them in the way of an honest living. We design, in a word, to bring humane and kindly influences to bear on this forsaken class — to preach in various modes the gospel of Christ to the vagrant children of New York.

Numbers of our citizens have long felt the evils we would remedy, but few have the leisure or the means to devote themselves personally to this work with the thoroughness which it requires. This society, as we propose, shall be a medium through which all can, in their measure, practically help the poor children of the city.

We call upon all who recognize that these are the little ones of Christ; all who believe that crime is best averted by sowing good influences in childhood; all who are the friends of the helpless, to aid us in our enterprise. We confidently hope this wide and practical movement will have its full share of Christian liberality. And we earnestly ask the contributions of those able to give, to help us in carrying forward the work.

March, 1853.

---

2. Brace urges placing out rather than institutional care for destitute and vagrant children, 1859

Proceedings of the Second Convention of Managers and Superintendents of Houses of Refuge and Schools of Reform (New York, 1860), pp. 46–49.

The Children's Aid Society and the Juvenile Asylum each relied on "placing out" as the best method of dealing with destitute and vagrant children. The Children's Aid Society advocated moving the children west as rapidly as possible; the Juvenile Asylum, as noted above, believed that a period of training and taming in the institution must precede placement.

Mr. President: As one of the Committee who drew up the first topic under discussion — viz.: The distinction which should be observed between vagrancy and destitution, on the one hand, and crime, on the other — I would say, we had in view that there was everywhere a narrow line of distinction between these two sides. We felt that, with every poor boy and girl in a city like this, there is a certain line, beyond which if he proceeds, he is a criminal, and on this side of which he is peculiarly susceptible of reformatory and preventive influences. I suppose that this Convention, in considering that topic, will feel that our different institutions represented here are really concerned with different sides of this question. The House of Refuge is more especially concerned with the children who have passed that line; while the preventive societies are more interested in those who have not reached that vague shadowy line of distinction. Therefore, the great question with us who represent the preventive institutions is, What are the principles of treatment of children who have not become criminal — who have not come under the legal authority? I hope, on this occasion, to present a few facts which may have been overlooked by parties interested in this subject, and which, it seems to me, are often disregarded. I think, sir, that if we act with force upon the question of juvenile vagrancy, poverty, and crime, we must, in the first place, act in coincidence with the great laws of God. It will not do, even with the most complete theoretic system of reform, to go against what are natural principles — natural laws . . . We must consider that the Creator has established, for instance, the family institution. He has arranged it so that every human being is influenced more for good in the family than by any other influence in social life; and, therefore, no organization which deals with the young can hope to produce the best effect without using that institution in some form or other . . . In addition to considering these laws of God, we must also, in a country like this, consider the particular influences of our situation. America is very different from England or the Old World, in the influences it can bring to bear upon the poor. The whole question of reform here is a different one from what it is in the Old Country. I fear that our institutions are often copied too closely from the plans in use in the Old World. You know that in England, when a boy is brought into a public institution, and is trained there and reformed, the question is, what to do with him. They do not know where to put him, every branch of labor is so crowded. In this country we have an immense advantage, though it is not an advantage of which we should be too proud — that of having plenty of room. We have room enough for a vast population, and, in addition, we have an unlimited demand for labor all through this country. There is everywhere a demand for labor, juvenile and adult. In any grand system of reform which would

act upon the juvenile poor, we must consider that peculiarity of this country.

In addition to these characteristics of our country, throughout the Eastern and Western portions of the United States, there can be discerned a peculiarly deep religious principle, the old Puritan principle of New England, that every Christian family is bound to deny itself in some respects for the sake of doing good to others. We can, in this country, appeal to this principle more than in any other country in the world. Therefore, that must be considered in any plan for the improvement and reform of the juvenile population.

.   .   .   .

Our object is, to relieve and aid destitute children of New York. Our plan is based upon the principles I have mentioned. We feel that if we cannot influence these children to the best purpose, we must get them into the best families. There is a line beyond which we do not attempt to influence them. It is a line that cannot always be recognized by legislation; but by practical experience and humane men, it may, to a certain degree, be discerned; and on this side of that vague line we attempt to take the children and place them where their labor is in demand, and under the influences that we can find in the West. We believe that in doing that, we act in harmony with the great divine principle of the family system, and in the next with the peculiarly fortunate characteristics of this country — the great demand for labor from our rural district. If there is a good family in the West, that is willing to take in a poor boy from the city, to give him social and Christian instruction, why, in God's name, should they not do it? What if the boy is bad, they know his character and his associations. If they are willing, from Christian and business motives (because his labor is useful), to take that child in and train him, why should they not be permitted to do so? If enough families can be found to serve as reformatory institutions, is it not the best and most practical and economical method of reforming these children to put them under the charge of such families? This plan has been used with great effect in Europe. I had the pleasure of witnessing it in Norway, Sweden, and parts of Germany. It was done under legal power. Government is often injurious in such operations; we merely want it to support them to a certain extent. The voluntary power is the best — leaving to the boy and the employer whether he will remain — and the peculiar influences we can get to bear upon him seem the best of all influences. We hope that this system will spread through the various parts of this country. We are rejoiced to hear, from Ohio and Massachusetts, that operations on a similar principle are being carried on in both those States, with great success; and I do believe that many gentlemen here might find it for the interest of their respective communities to introduce operations of this nature into their cities and communities for a class which is not treated by the houses of refuge, that is, for the class who have not passed the criminal line. One great argument and reason for this is, the peculiar economy of this system. An organization like the Children's Aid Society can send *six, seven, or eight* children over the country (of whom a large proportion do well), at an expense of from $10 to $11. But take any other large institution, like the Juvenile Asylum, or the Home of the Friendless, and you will find that the proportion which their expenses bear to each individual child will range from $80 to $100: and it may be that the advantage is not materially greater than in the other case. That is, supposing them to treat children who have not passed the line I have mentioned.

---

3. Placing children in the West, 1857

"The Children's Exodus," *The Five Points Monthly* (June 1857), pp. 66–67.

Brace's society sent its first band of child emigrants to the West in 1855. By two years later the organization had found homes for approximately six hundred city children. C. C. Tracy was the emigration agent of the Children's Aid Society.

The latest expedition which has reported its result . . . was taken out by Mr. TRACY, accompanied by Rev. J. P. ROOT of the Brooklyn Children's Aid Society, on the last day of March. There were about sixty of them, mostly boys from nine to thirteen years of age.

.   .   .   .   .

All the way was wonderful and glorious — such glorious riding, by water and rail, so many wonderful sights, and above all, such a wonderful succession of meals, three every day, wonderful to them and wonderful to all beholders! At Albany they went up to the State-house and lionized the Legislature: at Niagara they honored the Falls with pure, spontaneous, unbounded admiration; such homage as few tourists are able to pay. So we believe, at least; for in no human beings have we ever witnessed so keen a susceptibility to beauty in Nature, as in her lost and forgotten children.

As they enter Canada, we begin already to realize the welcome of the new world to the sturdy little emigrants. Dense forests now skirt the track, to the awe of the company, and rude pioneer dwellings are scattered between the remote villages. One of the boys, a humorous and grotesque looking fellow, with a coat reaching downward nearly to his heels, and a surplus half foot of trowsers turned upward to meet it, seemed rather taken with this wild scenery, and observed that "he'd like to get off, some place or other, and take lodgins in one o' them log-cabins." Hardly sooner said than done! An old Canadian settler just then passed along, and after a scrutiny of the line of faces, fixed upon Joe as the lad for him. Poor Joe was flattered by the hardy old man's preference, and at the next station, a new but thriving village, with the consent of Mr. TRACY he slipped off and followed his new friend home with much careless satisfaction. In a few hours more, the rest of the company stopped in the center of Michigan, at Battle Creek, where the best citizens of the place kindly welcomed them, and in the course of a week they were all dispersed among the comfortable farmers of that fertile region. We were touched by the simple reply of a kind-hearted old Dutchman, familiarly known there as "Uncle John," who on taking with him an interesting little boy named Willie ———, was entreated by Mr. TRACY to be a father to the young stranger. "Yes," replied Uncle John: "de Lord has been good to me, and I will be good to de boy."

Mr. TRACY had not only to dispose of his fresh lot, but to look after the last, and to full-fil some engagements relating to them. Among others, on his last trip, a good couple by the name of M——— childless themselves, had come in some distance from the country, de-sirous to confer and perhaps to realize in turn, some benefit, by taking in a street-boy to their comfortable home. Unfortunately, as they were rather late, the lot was already closely culled, and presented a somewhat dismal remainder for their choice. Among the "leavings" was a poor fellow from the sheds and lanes of Brook-lyn, who was a picture of conscious misery. Moody and downcast, he glowered upon every-body and every thing, past, present and future, with the same sullen discontent. He didn't want to stay out here: — did he want to go back to Brooklyn? — no, that suited him still less. In short, he didn't know what he did want. But Mr. TRACY knew; and as poor John was really the only one left who would do at all for Mr. and Mrs. M———, he led or rather pulled him up to them, and recommended a fair trial of what kindness and a good home would do for *that* boy: giving as his opinion that it would not unpleasantly disappoint them. They stared at the unhappy young loafer in dismay. He reciprocated the compliment with rueful and dissatisfied glances. Mr. TRACY plead his cause, and promised that if he did not suit, he himself would come, at his next trip, within a month or two, and remove him to some other place. Persuasion finally prevailed, and the good folks

consented, much against their minds, and quite as much against John's mind, to take him home, and away they went, all hands disgusted with their luck; though for John that was no more than an habitual frame of mind.

For some time, John and his luck never seemed to improve. Nothing suited him. His work always seemed to be the very thing he would rather not do; his food, whatever it was, might have been something else; and his clothes whether new or old, were invariably susceptible of criticism. Kindness, he had not yet learned to understand, especially when not very dis-tinctly labelled as such. John had not yet found his element. At length he ran away, and came down to the village. Here a friend of the good work, who had readily agreed to Mr. TRACY's request that he would keep a little lookout for the boys, found him, and at once inquired what he was about. Getting no very satisfactory ac-count, he took John into his back office, and set so plainly before him the blessings of his situation and the ingratitude of his conduct, that it made him ashamed of himself. "Now," said he, "do you go home to Mrs. M———, and tell her you are sorry, and have come back to try and do better; and if I ever catch you running away again, I'll take you into this back room, and I'll" ——— completing the sentence with certain energetic gestures which left John in no doubt of the nature or the sincerity of his intentions. He went back, with his faculties somewhat quickened, and told his errand faith-fully. Mrs. M——— was unexpectedly pleased and encouraged, and that encouraged John. He went to work, tried to please, and the first he knew, he was pleased himself. To cut the story short, in a little time there was not a happier or better boy than John in the town. When Mr. TRACY arrived out this time, there were Mrs. M——— and her favorite on hand to greet the new company: the latter so transformed in face and garb and bearing as to be quite beyond rec-ognition. No words could express for the good lady her satisfaction with her involuntary choice. John was equally pleased. "Did he wish to change his place?" "O, no, Mr. Tracy! I'll never leave there, as long as they'll let me stay."

The New York Catholic Protectory

The Protectory was founded by Catholic laymen in 1863 and administered by the Christian Brothers. By 1884 this institution held thirteen hundred children.

---

1. "An impulse of true charity"

Levi Silliman Ives, "The Protection of Destitute Catholic Children," in New York Catholic Protectory, *First Annual Report, 1864* (New York, 1864), pp. 71–72, 74, 80–81.

Levi Silliman Ives (1797–1867), Episcopalian bishop of North Carolina, was converted to Catholicism during a visit to Rome in 1852. Upon his return to the United States he joined the faculty of St. John's College, Fordham, New York, and became a leading spokesman for Catholic philanthropy. He was the first president of the Society for the Protection of Destitute Roman Catholic Children of the City of New York — the corporation that managed the Protectory.

For the last ten years I have been a close observer of what has passed among the rising generation in this great metropolis, and I cannot suppress the humiliating conviction that even pagan Rome, in the corrupt age of Augustus, never witnessed a more rapid and frightful declension in morals, never witnessed, among certain classes of the young, a more utter disregard of honor, of truth and purity, and even the commonest decencies of life.

Extraordinary as this statement may seem, it is, nevertheless, a statement of fact; and I think it not difficult to define the cause. Some persons refer it to the rapid influx of foreign population; but I trace it to the spirit of infidelity, of insubordination to Almighty God, that is cherished among us. I admit that to a certain degree, and in a certain sense, this foreign immigration may have contributed to increased immorality, because it has furnished a considerable portion of the material out of which such immorality has been produced. But the active principle or busy agent in the work is quite another thing, and attributable to quite another cause.

You will say, perhaps, that, under the promptings of charity, much has been done to check this evil. I reply that, in addition, much, under the name of charity, has been done to foster and increase this evil. Efforts well meant, efforts flowing from a desire to do good, often actually do harm — sometimes from ignorance, sometimes from false zeal, sometimes from false principles. An impulse of true charity may sometimes be perverted or misdirected by some other predominating impulse. A work may commence with a view to a most useful and desirable end, which, in its progress, may be made to subserve a very different one. Let us illustrate: A number of destitute families land upon our shores, seeking protection and subsistence in our city. They are strangers, and know little of the hardships and difficulties to be encountered in their new situation. Their extravagant expectations are not realized. Where they had been assured of ready employment, high wages, and encouraging sympathy, they experience only cold looks, hard labor, and scanty remuneration. Sickness overtakes them, debt turns them out of doors; or intemperance, perhaps, brings upon them its deadly swarm of miseries. Their small earnings are consumed. Their children cry for bread, and are turned as beggars into the streets. They rehearse from door to door their piteous tale. Frequent repulse hardens them, drives them to exaggeration, to falsehood, to theft, sometimes to the most wretched haunts of vice, to save them from starvation. Public sympathy is excited. Measures are adopted to rescue these unfortunates from their deplorable condition. Here, then, may be the promptings of charity — the enlistment of the heart in a good and praiseworthy enterprise. But, suppose these children differ from their benefactors in religion. Here a temptation arises to wean them from the faith of their parents. The temptation prevails. Steps are taken, in effecting this purpose, to place a bar between these children and their parents; to sever the precious tie which binds them to the parental heart and the parental influence. Concealment is first resorted to, a veil of secrecy is drawn over the proceedings, parental inquiries are baffled, the yearnings of the mother are stilled by tales of wonderful advantages to her children, and promises of their speedy restoration to her arms. Yet all this while they are undergoing a secret process by which, it is hoped, that every trace of their early faith and filial attachment will be rooted out; and, finally, that their transportation to that indefinite region, "the far West," with changed names and lost parentage, will effectually destroy every association which might revive in their hearts a love for the religion of which they had been robbed, — the religion of their parents. Here, then, a new principle has been at work. What charity commenced, fanaticism has grossly perverted; or what we had supposed charity, turns out to be only sectarian zeal. We had looked for a great benefit, and behold a great wrong, a foul injustice, has been practised.

. . . . .

That was a sad day for the civilization of this country when a false philanthropy attempted, for its own selfish ends, to lower in the eyes of children the standard of duty to their parents, or the sacredness of parental authority — as it was a fatal blow, aimed at the very foundations of the social structure. Teach children to put a low estimate upon the parental

claim to their obedience, and you give them the most effective lesson of insubordination to all rule and all government. Take away from them proper reverence for those who are the instruments of their being, and who nourish their infancy, and whom Almighty God has made their first and essential spiritual guides, and you take from them a vital principle, a controlling power, which can never be restored. You deprive them, in the very beginning of their race, of that subordinating spirit which will be found so needful in every step of their progress through life.

. . . . .

. . . We have here been speaking of children who are supposed to remain for years in the institution; and hence of that class who are either wholly destitute of proper protection, or have become reprobate from want of discipline . . . The idea of sending them out into life after a few months' training, and expecting that they will be contented and grow up to be good members of society, is, as a general thing, perfectly preposterous. Their condition, as well as their very natures, forbids the possibility. With all the influence of good parental guidance and strong social ties, it is no easy task in this age to keep children in the right way: what, then, must the prospect be, when children are deprived of these and sent into a strange land, and made subject to the will of strangers? What moral and mental fitness have they to meet the requirements of a hard and untried life in our new settlements of the West? In such settlements where society is only in progress of formation, and every social, every moral bond is more or less relaxed, does it not follow, almost as an axiom, that children of the character we are considering, — children roving in their dispositions, lawless in their habits, will, as a general rule, find no restraint adequate to their condition, and hence must, in a little time, sink into a moral state even worse than that in which they were found in our streets?

But what in itself seems so inevitable, is

abundantly confirmed by sad experience. Some years previous to the establishment of our Reformatory, I had been in the practice of securing good homes in the country for untrained and destitute Catholic children; and although I succeeded in finding places for many, I can call to mind only a single instance where the child either did not abscond or prove utterly ungovernable and worthless. Our experience has been substantially the same since the commencement of our work in the institution. We have apprenticed a considerable number of orphans to good Catholic masters, selected with great care, and we are pained to say that a majority of these orphans have proved to be wholly unmanageable. Besides, in many instances where after a few months' discipline and good behavior, children had been discharged, they have in a short time been returned to us from the courts, and for the same causes which led to the first commitment. Now, from these facts, it seems to me quite manifest that the system which is flooding our Western country with undisciplined, vicious children, is much to be deprecated — is simply a system to rid ourselves of them while we make them a pest to our neighbors; and that, by the laws of society, these neighbors would do perfectly right in returning them upon our hands.

---

2. The Catholic argument for public funds

New York Catholic Protectory, *Second Annual Report, 1865* (New York, 1865), pp. 61–63.

It is admitted by all that the largest and most afflicted portion of poor children in this city is of Catholic parentage. Now it ought, in this free country, where the liberty of conscience in matters of religion is justly the boast, to be equally manifest that the only institution, except in the case of orphans, which makes a suitable and equitable provision for training these Catholic children, is "The Society for the Protection of Destitute Roman Catholic Children in the City of New York." All other institutions organized for the protection of destitute children are Protestant, having Protestant directors, Protestant superintendents, Protestant teachers, Protestant worship, and Protestant instruction and training. Under such circumstances, can it be thought surprising or unreasonable that poor Catholic parents should have a settled aversion to these Protestant institutions as the Christian home of their children — where these children are to receive instructions hostile to the faith which is given them in holy baptism, and which their parents solemnly bound themselves to inculcate? Suppose the Legislature had taken under its care some large Catholic institution, or some institution under Catholic direction, and had, by virtue of the promise that no particular religion should be taught, required that poor Protestants should allow their children to be trained there, and that rich Protestants should quietly consent to be heavily taxed to keep up the establishment, would it be considered unreasonable for Protestants to object, and ask relief of the Legislature to enable them to establish and to support an institution of their own? And suppose, when they asked for an appropriation of money or land, that Catholics in the Legislature should reply — "We have no objection to your having an institution, but you must support it yourselves. You must continue to pay your taxes to keep up our liberal institution, but we cannot allow you to have any portion of the State or city money, because you might have your children trained by us!" In plainer words, "We want both your money and your children; but, if you will persist in holding on to your children, we must at least have your money: keep your children, but pay your taxes to us." This is the exact logic of the argument — the unmistakable English of the objection to our appeal. Let Protestants take the place of Catholics before your honorable body; and would they be able to suppress a feeling of righteous indignation at such an objection?

Take another view. Suppose you grant an appropriation adequate to the wants of the Catholic institution, do you increase the expenses of the city or State? The managers maintain that you would lessen them. Take the data furnished in this report. By an examination of the record, it will be seen that the managers have supported and trained on an average about 450 children during the year. Suppose these children had been sent, for example, to the "Juvenile Asylum:" what would have been the expense to the State? $40,500, according to the per capita allowance of $90, which that institution receives. Now, what has it cost the Catholic institution of the managers? $38,176, including rents and furnishing houses. Now, how much of this sum have the city and State contributed? $17,000! What, then, have the city and State gained in the reduction of taxes by the corporate existence of "The Society for the Protection of Destitute Roman Catholic Children"? Just $23,500! Catholics, then, instead of having received any real benefit from the State, have actually kept in its treasury the $23,500 which would have gone to the Juvenile Asylum, had the Catholic children been sent there, instead of being sent to the Catholic House of Protection.

towards the erection of the buildings necessary for the purpose of its corporation, and also yearly the sum of fifty dollars per capita on average of persons annually maintained in its institution; and the board of supervisors of the county of New York are hereby authorized and directed to levy the said sum of fifty thousand dollars and the said annual amounts yearly, and the Comptroller of the City of New York to draw his warrant for the said several amounts to the said society. The average number of persons thus maintained shall be ascertained by the examination and testimony, under oath, of the president or secretary of said society.

2. The said society may locate its buildings within any part of the Metropolitan Police District of this State, provided always that it shall keep and maintain a House of Reception in the City of New York; and any lands within said district which such society may heretofore have purchased, shall be vested in and belong to said society, in the same manner and with the same effect, to all intents and purposes, as though the same had been purchased by and conveyed to said society after the passage of this act.

3. The real and personal estate belonging to and used for the charitable purposes of said association shall be exempt from taxation.

---

3. State financial aid for the Protectory

"An Act for the relief of The Society for the Protection of Destitute Roman Catholic Children in the City of New York," ch. 647 — 1866, *Laws of the State of New York* (New York, 1866), pp. 27–28.

1. "The Society for the Protection of Destitute Roman Catholic Children in the City of New York" shall be entitled to receive the sum of fifty thousand dollars,[1] provided a like amount is contributed by private contribution,

1. The society received the full amount.

Recommendations for preventing delinquency and reforming juvenile delinquents, 1867

Wines and Dwight, *Report on the Prisons*, pp. 62–67.

Having given in this section a bird's eye view of the prison systems of the United States and Canada, and having stated the opinion that they are all, to a greater or less extent, deficient in their principles and methods, it may be proper, at this point, briefly to sketch the system which, after the best thought we have been able to give to the subject, appears to us most wisely adapted to the ends of a just and true prison discipline.

As a preparatory step, we would have a law enacted, by which the education of all the children of the state should be made compulsory. Every child should be compelled, within a certain range of years, to attend regularly some school, either public or private; or, if parents desire a more select education for their offspring, they should be required to show that they are receiving, during the legal age, adequate instruction at home. No half-way measures, no patchwork legislation will meet the necessities of the case. It is far better to force education upon the people than to force them into prisons to expiate crimes, of which neglect or ignorance has been the occasion. Deep and broad foundations of moral and religious, no less than of intellectual character must be laid in our common schools, despite the obstacles that bigotry and sectarian jealousy may throw in the way; and the children of the state must be there, even by compulsion, if need be, to be so trained.

This essential preliminary aid being thus secured, the first in our series of establishments, looking to the repression of crime, should be institutions of a preventive character. Here, indeed, to our view, is the real field of promise. The problem is to stay the current of crime, to turn it back upon itself, and to dry up its fountain-heads. In studying this question, the mind turns instinctively to childhood as the true field of effort for the accomplishment of the desired end.

Two classes of institutions, it appears to us, are needed and are sufficient at this stage of the work — public nurseries and industrial schools.

Public nurseries for children of two or three to five or six years old, of pauper parents, and perhaps of some others, are the first link, the earliest agency in the prevention of crime in youth and manhood. The importance of this class of institution will appear evident when it is considered that the first impressions made upon the mind, whether good or evil, are the most lasting and the most difficult to eradicate. All experience shows that such impressions received in early childhood, and the habits formed at that tender age, usually exercise a controlling influence throughout the period of youth. Accordingly, it is from the class of children who receive their impressions and form their habits in the streets, from the age of four to ten years, that our reformatories, jails, houses of correction and state prisons are mainly peopled. Is it possible, then, to exaggerate the importance to society of institutions such as those here proposed? Ought not systematic and energetic measures to be directed by legislators, as well as philanthropists, to this department of prevention? Can any system of legislation which aims at the suppression and extinction of crime overlook so potent an agency to that end as the one here recommended, and yet lay claim to the attributes of sagacity and humanity? Here the serpent may be crushed in the egg, the hydra strangled in the birth, the harvest of evil nipped in its first sprouting. A fact bearing on this subject, at once instructive and encouraging, is mentioned in a Government Report on Prisons in France. It is worth repeating here. A vast number of abandoned children in that country are received, almost from birth, into foundling asylums, where they are cared for and educated, till they are of a suitable age to put out; yet the number of children reared in these asylums, who have subsequently found their way into prison, is quite significant — a striking proof of the almost omnipotent power of early (the very earliest) moral, religious, intellectual and industrial training, as a security against the commission of crime.

The industrial school, whether called by that name or some other — truant, ragged, or whatever it may be — is the next link, the second agency in the preventive part of the system. The children of parents who neglect their offspring, either because they are vicious or indifferent to their welfare — children who roam the streets and prowl about docks and wharves, and are almost sure in the end to take up crime as a trade — should be gathered into institutions of this class, where they would receive that mental, moral and industrial training which their own homes would never afford them, and from which they would at length be sent out to good situations in the country, or elsewhere, where they would grow into virtuous and useful citizens, adding to, instead of preying upon, the productive industry of the country. A few schools of this sort have been established with the best results; but nothing has been done by them in rescuing vagrant children and youth of both sexes from vice and crime, at all commensurate with the good that might be effected in this direction through their agency. These schools should be open to the voluntary resort of neglected children, whose parents, regardless of their future character and condition, leave them to do for themselves, battling with their hard lot as best they may be able.

The discipline in these industrial schools should be strictly of the family character. All the arrangements should be such as to cultivate industrious habits, and prepare their inmates for the stations they are afterwards to fill. The kitchen, the wash-tub, the sewing and knitting room, the work shop, the farm, and, above all, the school room, together with such recreation as may be suitable to their years, should occupy the time of those who find their home there; and this home should be, though tidy and attractive, yet of the plainest character, partaking as nearly as may be of the nature of the domestic departments of families in moderate circumstances. Criminal and vicious habits should be the only bar to reception here; and children, tainted with such practices, should in no case be permitted to come in contact with the destitute but yet unfallen street children, for whom alone the industrial school is designed. Should any such, by mistake, ever be admitted, when discovered, they should be at once transferred to institutions, whose distinctive character is reformatory rather than preventive.

It is confidently believed that if these two classes of institutions — public nurseries and industrial schools — were sufficiently multiplied and placed under judicious control and management, and proper care taken to keep them free from those who have reached the point of crime, thousands of young victims of parental indifference or vice would be kept from idle and vicious habits, and from the ruin they bring in their train; the most prolific fountain of crime would be cut off; and the numbers confined in reformatories and prisons would be materially diminished, perhaps brought down almost to zero.

We have spoken of the need of judicious management in these institutions. Probably a union of private and public effort would best secure the requisite wisdom and efficiency; but, in any case, liberal pecuniary aid must be supplied by municipal and legislative grants.

Is the expense of such institutions made a point of objection? Let it be considered — for of this we are fully persuaded — that a judicious and effective system of prevention in behalf of this class of juveniles would be an arrangement the most economical to the public, as well as the most merciful to themselves which could be made. To save them — and the plan we propose would no doubt be the salvation of almost the entire class — would be to cut off one of the most copious sources of adult crime, and of course to dry up an incessant and tremendous drain upon the wealth of the state, through their depredations, when arrived at manhood, on the property of the citizens.

Vagrant, neglected, and "dangerous" children, 1821–1865

---

1. Josiah Quincy on the poor, idle, and vicious children of Boston, 1821

Boston, *Report of the Committee on the Subject of Pauperism and a House of Industry in the Town of Boston* (Boston, 1821), pp. 8–9.

Quincy was chairman of the committee.

. . . Those who are poor, and in infancy or childhood . . . have a right to require from society a distinct attention and more scrupulous and precise supervision. Their career of existence is but just commenced. They may be rendered blessings, or scourges to society. Their course may be happy or miserable, honourable or disgraceful, according to the specific nature of the provision, made for their support and education. It follows that the charitable establishments of every wise and virtuous community ought to be such as to enable it to effect these interesting objects, in the most perfect and satisfactory manner.

The present condition of the Boston Alms House, precludes all possibility of extending that free air, exercise, and healthful labour, and of attaining that separation from the contamination of vicious language and example, which is requisite and due to this class. Intimately connected with this topic is that of providing for those idle and vicious children, of both sexes and different ages, which often under the command, and always with the permission of thoughtless and abandoned parents, are found begging in our streets, or haunting our wharves, market places, sometimes under the pretence of employment, at others for the purpose of watching occasions to pilfer small articles, and thus beginning a system of petty stealing; which terminates often in the gaol; often in the penitentiary; and not seldom, at the gallows.

Power enough already exists, in the hands of the constituted authorities, and if it do not, might easily be obtained, to rid ourselves of this nuisance, and to place these unfortunate children under either a system of discipline, or of restraint; or of useful labour. At present, however, this is absolutely impracticable. There is no place, suitable for their reception. The present Alms House is insufficient for its present tenants; more it is impossible to accommodate. A work house, or house of industry, is, therefore, absolutely essential, previously to taking any steps for the improvement of this unhappy, and abandoned class, of children. On this point, your committee do not apprehend that any thing more forcible can be added, to make the essential nature of such an establishment as that, which they recommend, apparent and unquestionable.

2. Child beggars, Baltimore, 1821

Niles' Weekly Register, Dec. 15, 1821, p. 256.

Several of our cities suffer exceedingly from the impositions of little boys and girls, who lie, and cheat and steal to an alarming extent — generally assuming the character of great distress, to excite sympathy or excuse a vagabond life. It appears as if there was a gang of them at Philadelphia, and there are some of the same class in Baltimore. The best way to correct this abuse, is to pay no attention to the applicants, or else to propose to go home with the little storytellers, and witness the misery about which they are so eloquent. On manifesting a resolution to do this, the little wretches uniformly run away, or otherwise avoid an investigation. There is, no doubt, a great deal of real distress, and all should be prompt to relieve it — but it must be an extreme case indeed, that can justify a parent in giving his or her child a *patent* to become a vagabond or strumpet; as ninety-nine hundredths of the children thus turned out upon the public eventually arrive at.

3. Characteristics of street boys, 1839

John H. B. Latrobe, *Address on the Subject*

of a Manual Labour School (Baltimore, 1840), pp. 5–7.

Latrobe (1803–1891), son of the architect, Benjamin Henry Latrobe, was legal counsel for the Baltimore and Ohio Railroad, and advocate of the colonization of free Negroes in Africa.

I appear before you this evening as the advocate of a manual labour school for indigent boys, which it is proposed to establish in the vicinity of Baltimore.

.   .   .   .   .

The manual labour school . . . may be defined to be an institution for the education of those boys, belonging to the city, whose extraordinary exposure to moral evil requires peculiar provision to be made for forming their character, and promoting and securing the happiness of their lives; which is proposed to be effected by separating them from vicious associations, placing them under the care of proper instructors, and employing them in labour, as their strength and years permit, not only for the purpose of teaching them to obtain their future livelihood, but also as a means of making them contribute to their own present support.

The class of boys for whom the manual labour school is intended is a numerous one, and forms a distinct portion of the population of all large communities. It has its peculiar and strongly marked characteristics, the most prominent of which is recklessness. It ranks among its members the half-grown, half-fed, half-clothed, hard-worked children of the very indigent, as well as the apparently purposeless idlers, who seek in winter the most sheltered spots, to bask where the sun shines warmest, and who lounge through the long days of summer about the suburbs, where the trees spread the coolest shadows. It is a class which has its oracles and its leaders, who want not for energy or talent, and who exhibit their first promise of future power for good or evil, in directing and controlling with despotic authority the pranks and mischief of their boyish associates. Accustomed, as this class is from infancy, to all the shifts of poverty, made useful as soon as they can walk, their intellects become sharpened to a degree unnatural to their years, and they learn to comprehend the business and the feelings of men, before they have passed the first periods of childhood. Unfortunately too, the knowledge thus acquired is imbibed in a foul and unwholesome moral atmosphere, and it is with the vices, not the virtues of more advanced years, that the class of children, of which I am speaking, become thus prematurely familiar. The master spirits of this class, whose will sways the less resolute and gives its laws to the young community, are easily distinguished. If you watch them you will seldom find them engaged in games of mere amusement. Tops and marbles they sometimes patronize when the play is not, in boyish dialect, "for fun," but "for good"; because the winnings may be disposed of for the money, whose value and whose uses they are already well acquainted with; but hoops and kites, hide-and-seek, and bandy, they generally eschew, for these require exertion, and they are profitless. Their favourite amusements are pitch-and-toss, and the penny sweat-cloth, and the low gambling which is to be found in the precincts of the race-course, and in the yards of tippling-houses. They aim much at what they esteem a knowing carriage; and we have often seen a fine, bright-eyed, intelligent little fellow belonging to this class, with his cap set jauntily on one side of his head, his arms akimbo, his hands in his pockets, his feet apart, and, with a cigar in his mouth, bandying oaths and obscene jests with full-grown men, as though their equal in years and vice. If a quarrel takes place among their young associates, they form the ring, they place the chip on the shoulder, they encourage the timid combatant, and act as arbiters of the battle. If there is a tumult of any kind in the street, they swarm like bees around the spot, coming from we know not where, as though some bond of union existed among them, which vibrated throughout the Ishmaelite fraternity to all sounds of violence and misrule. If a fire takes place, there is always one or more of them certain to be in the vicinity; and their wild and elfish shrieks are echoed by the whole tribe throughout the streets until the entire city is alarmed. They seize the ropes of the engines, they crowd around the flames, they dare danger with the boldness of older spirits, and when the fire is extinguished they are to be seen prowling among the blackened ruins, turning over the smouldering fragments of beams and rafters and seeking among them for the spoils that the conflagration may have spared. They jostle and fight, too, for their plunder, like the foul birds whose feasts are made of the leavings of decay and death. And when the demon spirit of the mob is roused, these boys form the nucleus upon which gather all the malignant elements of incendiary violence; theirs is the loudest shout; their hands are the first to hurl the missile and apply the firebrand; and nameless and irresponsible, but numerous and bold, they often succeed in giving to the suggestions of a few discontented spirits the character of a general outbreak, which, though subversive of the laws, is made by the means I have described to appear to have the sanction of the people.

---

4. Child vagrancy in New York City, 1849

George W. Matsell, chief of police, to Hon. Caleb S. Woodhull, mayor of the city of New York [Oct. 31, 1849] in New York City, Police Department, *Semi-Annual Report, May 31–October 31, 1849* (New York, 1849), Appendix.

In the *First Annual Report* of the Children's Aid Society, Charles Loring Brace stated that Matsell's 1849 report first revealed the full extent of child vagrancy in New York.

Sir: I herewith transmit to you the Semi-Annual Report of the Police Department, commencing with the 1st of May, and ending with the 31st of October, 1849.

In connection with this report I deem it to be my duty to call the attention of your Honor to a deplorable and growing evil which exists amid this community, and which is spread over the principal business parts of the city. It is an evil and a reproach to our municipality, for which the laws and ordinances afford no adequate remedy.

I allude to the constantly increasing numbers of vagrant, idle and vicious children of both sexes, who infest our public thoroughfares, hotels, docks, &c. Children who are growing up in ignorance and profligacy, only destined to a life of misery, shame and crime, and ultimately to a felon's doom. Their numbers are almost incredible, and to those whose business and habits do not permit them a searching scrutiny, the degrading and disgusting practices of these almost infants in the schools of vice, prostitution and rowdyism, would certainly be beyond belief. The offspring of always careless, generally intemperate, and oftentimes immoral and dishonest parents, they never see the inside of a school-room, and so far as our excellent system of public education is concerned (and which may be truly said to be the foundation stone of our free institutions), it is to them an entire nullity. Left, in many instances, to roam day and night wherever their inclination leads them, a large proportion of these juvenile vagrants are in the daily practice of pilfering wherever opportunity offers, and begging where they cannot steal. In addition to which, the female portion of the youngest class, those who have only seen some eight or twelve summers, are addicted to immoralities of the most loathsome description. Each year makes fearful additions to the ranks of these prospective recruits of infamy and sin, and from this corrupt and festering fountain flows on a ceaseless stream to our lowest brothels — to the Penitentiary and the State Prison!

Reports have been made to me from the Captains of the 1st, 2d, 3d, 4th, 5th, 6th, 7th, 8th, 10th, 11th and 13th Patrol Districts — from which it appears that the enormous number of 2,955 children are engaged as above described in these Wards alone. And of these *two thirds are females between eight and sixteen years of age!* This estimate I believe to be far short of the number actually engaged.

. . . . .

. . . Many of them are the children of respectable parents, but through a mistaken leniency or a criminal carelessness, they are suffered to spend their evenings and Sabbath in small gatherings on the corners of the streets, annoying the neighborhood and passers by with their wrangling and fighting practices, and with the most reckless oaths and blasphemies. They will often steal, and many of them absent themselves from the roof of their parents or guardians for weeks together, sleeping in market wagons and other places of shelter; consorting with the vilest of both sexes, and forming habits of vice and dissipation which cling to them through all their after years. Frequent complaints are made by citizens in regard to the practices of these juvenile rowdies, but under existing regulations the efforts of the police are found inadequate to the suppression of the nuisance. The number of these is estimated at between 1,600 and 1,700. Besides these, there are reported to me from the above named districts, 2,383 children that do not attend school.

In presenting these disagreeable facts for the consideration of your Honor, I trust that I may be pardoned for the suggestion, in conclusion, that in my opinion some method by which these children could be compelled to attend our schools regularly, or be apprenticed to some suitable occupation, would tend in time more to improve the morals of the community, prevent crime, and relieve the City from its onerous burden of expenses for the Alms-House and Penitentiary, than any other conservative or philanthropic movement with which I am at present acquainted.

5. Street girls in New York City, 1851

Allan Nevins and Milton Halsey Thomas, *The Diary of George Templeton Strong*, 4 vols. (New York: Macmillan, 1952), II, 56.

Strong's entry for July 7, 1851, noted that New York City did not yet have social problems as acute as those of London and Manchester.

Yet we have our Five Points, our emigrant quarters, our swarms of seamstresses to whom their utmost toil in monotonous daily drudgery gives only bare subsistence, a life barren of hope and of enjoyment; our hordes of dock thieves, and of children who live in the streets and by them. No one can walk the length of Broadway without meeting some hideous troop of ragged girls, from twelve years old down, brutalized already almost beyond redemption by premature vice, clad in the filthy refuse of the rag-picker's collections, obscene of speech, the stamp of childhood gone from their faces, hurrying along with harsh laughter and foulness on their lips that some of them have learned by rote, yet too young to understand it; with thief written in their cunning eyes and whore on their depraved faces, though so unnatural, foul, and repulsive in every look and gesture, that that last profession seems utterly beyond their aspirations. On a rainy day such crews may be seen by dozens. They haunt every other crossing and skulk away together, when the sun comes out and the mud is dry again. And such a group I think the most revolting object that the social diseases of a great city can produce. A gang of blackguard boys is lovely by the side of it.

6. Boys as leaders of the mob in the New York draft riots, July 1863

Harper's Weekly, July 25, 1863, p. 466.

The affair of Monday last bore a closer resemblance to a European riot than any thing we have ever had here. The leaders and principal actors in the affair were boys — beardless youths of fifteen to eighteen. Behind these, and seemingly operating as a mere reserve force, was a body of men — operatives in foundries and factories, laborers, stablemen, etc. — who did the murdering of policemen, the gutting of houses, the firing of dwellings, etc., after the boys had opened the battle with volleys of stones. In all the crowds there was a fair sprinkling of women, not young, but married women, who were probably roused to fury by the fear of having their husbands taken from them by the draft. This kind of mixed crowd, though often good-humored and apt to be easily managed by a skillful leader, is likewise prone to the wildest excesses of passion and brutality. The boys and men invariably get drunk at an early stage of the proceedings; the women appear to become equally intoxicated with excitement; and all together commit crimes from which every individual in the crowd would probably shrink if he were alone. Such crowds are so cowardly that a handful of disciplined troops will scatter them like chaff; and so bloodthirsty that they will tear in pieces an individual against whom their fury happens to be directed, or burn a building in which women and children are situated without chance of escape.

7. Beware the "dangerous classes," 1854, 1863

Charles Loring Brace in New York Children's Aid Society, *Eleventh Annual Report* (New York, 1864), p. 4.

Brace, recalling the warning he had issued a decade earlier in the *First Annual Report* of the Children's Aid Society, maintained that the rioters were "merely *street-children* grown up."

. . . It should be remembered, that there are no dangers to the value of property or to the permanency of our institutions, so great as those from the existence of such a class of vagabond, ignorant, ungoverned children. This "dangerous class" has not begun to show itself, as it will in eight or ten years, when these boys and girls are matured. Those who were too negligent or too selfish to notice them as children, will be fully aware of them as men. They will vote. They will have the same rights as we ourselves, though they have grown up ignorant of moral principle, as any savage or Indian. They will poison society. They will perhaps be embittered at the wealth, and the luxuries, they never share. Then let society beware, when the outcast, vicious, reckless multitude of New-York boys, swarming now in every foul alley and low street, come to know their power and *use it!*

VII Child Health

In matters relating to health, the children benefiting most from the welfare movements of the early nineteenth century were the deaf-mute, the blind, and the feeble-minded. The relationship of the modern concept of health to advancements made with deaf and blind children, and to a lesser degree with the mentally ill, must, however, be interpreted only in the broadest sense. Helping handicapped children had more in common with the general movement of humanitarianism and the growing concern with education than with the medical aspects of health.

Proposals for education of the deaf were by no means accepted with assurance and certainty. The idea that young people with such physical handicaps could be educated to assume a normal place in society was considered strange and unlikely. Nevertheless, some Americans were aware of and interested in European experiments in education of the deaf. In 1815 friends of Alice Cogswell, a young deaf girl living in Hartford, Connecticut, provided funds to permit Thomas H. Gallaudet, a theology student, to visit England and France to observe methods of instructing the deaf. On Gallaudet's return to America he initiated efforts to open a school for the deaf. In 1816 the legislature of Connecticut incorporated the institution and appropriated an initial sum of five thousand dollars.

Admission to the American Asylum at Hartford for the Education and Instruction of the Deaf and Dumb was not limited to residents of Connecticut. Students came from neighboring states whose legislatures appropriated funds to help defray the costs of their instruction. In 1819 the Massachusetts legislature allocated

funds for its students at the Asylum. New Hampshire did the same in 1821, and Vermont and Maine in 1825. Beginning in 1834, Georgia and South Carolina, neither having institutions for the education of the deaf, provided funds to send some of their children to out-of-state institutions. The practice of supplying funds to send young people to out-of-state institutions continued until each state provided facilities to care for its own indigent handicapped. This policy applied not only to the deaf but also to the blind.

The first formal attempt to educate the blind did not occur until 1832, when the New England Asylum for the Blind in Boston, under the direction of Samuel Gridley Howe, received its first six pupils. Like Gallaudet, Howe first traveled to Europe and visited schools to learn methods of teaching the handicapped. Shortly after Howe's venture, institutions opened in New York and Philadelphia. In 1837 Ohio founded a state school for the blind and in 1839 Virginia established an institution for the blind and the deaf.

Funds for the support of institutions for the deaf and blind were not limited to state appropriations. The federal government made sizeable grants of land to the Connecticut and Kentucky institutions for the deaf. Philanthropy added large sums toward the maintenance of the institutions and the support of their students. Money was also acquired from subscriptions, fairs, and from exhibitions at which pupils were displayed. In 1833 the Massachusetts legislature offered the New England Asylum an appropriation of ten thousand dollars if twice the sum could be secured from private sources. The money was raised in a short time.

758

Howe's work with children was not limited to the blind. His interest in feeble-minded children inspired him to bring several of them to the Perkins Institution for the Blind.[1] Howe's campaign to provide an institution for the feeble-minded of Massachusetts resulted in the appointment of a committee in 1846, "to consider the expediency of appointing commissioners to inquire into the condition of the idiots of the commonwealth, to ascertain their number and whether anything can be done for their relief." [2] Within two years the Massachusetts legislature appropriated seventy-five hundred dollars for an experiment in the teaching and training of ten idiot children. By 1851 New York had opened a state asylum for the feeble-minded, and in 1853 the legislature of Pennsylvania incorporated a training school for feeble-minded children.

The hygiene and medical care of children received more attention during the first half of the nineteenth century than ever before. In 1825 William P. Dewees, lecturer on midwifery at the University of Pennsylvania, published a paper on the physical and medical treatment of children which may be considered the first comprehensive American work to treat the subject of child health in a scientific manner. Joseph Parrish, William E. Horner, J. Forsyth Meigs, and Charles D. Meigs also wrote significant works on diseases of children. Pediatrics was not yet a defined subject, but changes taking place in the medical world would have a direct bearing on the development of specialized medical care for children. The number of medical institutions of all types, especially hospitals, schools, and professional societies, increased greatly. The American Medical Association was established in 1847. During the 1850's the first two American hospitals intended exclusively for children were founded in Philadelphia and New York. Clinical medicine developed significantly as observation replaced theory in the treatment of sickness and the old practices of bleeding and purging declined in popularity.[3]

If there was progress toward a recognition of child health problems in American cities the same was not the case on the frontier. The opportunity to acquire medical care was at a minimum among the pioneers in the West and South; home remedies, superstitions, and quackery were common. Whooping cough, diphtheria, and epidemics of other contagious diseases, as well as the hard life, kept the mortality rate high among children. Nevertheless, early marriages and large families were the rule and the population continued to grow. "Why sir, you may visit the humblest cottage in our country, and you will find everything to admire," said a Kentucky congressman in 1824. "You would have the singular felicity of beholding a most delightful spectacle — about twelve or thirteen fine, ruddy, well-formed, hearty-looking young *Democrats*, would run out to see the stranger; and upon entering the house, you would be met by a very plain unaffected woman, to all appearances about thirty years old, whose countenance would at once tell you to make yourself easy; you would meet with kindness, and, in casting your eyes around, you would see two more little fellows, who were too small to run out at the first alarm." [4]

About 1820 the United States entered a new epidemic period in which yellow fever, smallpox, typhoid fever, and especially cholera swept through cities and rural communities. Tuberculosis was also responsible for increasing mortality; among children diarrhea and enteritis were the chief causes of death. In 1850 statistics of mortality indicated no improvement since

1. Formerly the New England Asylum, the institution was renamed in honor of its early benefactor, Thomas Handasyd Perkins.

2. Quoted in Leo Kanner, *A History of the Care and Study of the Mentally Retarded* (Springfield, Ill., 1964), p. 41.

3. Physician John B. Beck supported the bloodletting of adults but opposed practicing it on children because, "important peculiarities . . . [showed] a difference in the effects produced in the young subject, from those in the adult." John B. Beck, *Effects of Bloodletting on the Young Subject* [New York, 184?], p. 1.

4. Quoted in Madge E. Pickard and R. Carlyle Buley, *The Midwest Pioneer; His Ills, Cures and Doctors* (Crawfordsville, Ind., 1945), p. 31.

1790. Proportionately as many children under five years of age died in 1850 as in 1789 and the percentage of total deaths for all age groups showed that more children and youths between the ages of five and nineteen died in the mid-nineteenth century than at the end of the eighteenth century.[5]

Progress in medical treatment of children was accompanied by growing interest in public

5. James A. Doull, "The Bacteriological Era (1876–1920)," in Franklin H. Top, *The History of American Epidemiology* (St. Louis, 1952), pp. 68–69.

health and growing awareness of the relationship between child health and sanitary conditions. Initial investigative and legislative works included John Griscom's study of tenement conditions in New York City (1845), Lemuel Shattuck's survey of sanitation in Massachusetts (1850), and Stephen Smith's authorship of the New York City Metropolitan Health Law (1866). These efforts prepared the groundwork for the public health movement of the later nineteenth century.

A. AFFLICTED CHILDREN

The deaf

During the half century before 1815 two different methods of educating the deaf came into use in Europe. In England and Scotland members of the Braidwood family and persons licensed by them taught lip reading and articulation; in France the prevailing system was the sign language developed by Charles Michel, Abbé de l'Epée and Roche-Ambroise, Abbé Sicard. Most of the early American institutions for the deaf adopted the sign language system.

1. Founding of the first free school for the deaf in the United States, Hartford, Connecticut, 1815–1817

Connecticut Asylum for the Education and Instruction of Deaf and Dumb Persons, [*First Annual*] *Report, 1817* (Hartford, 1817), pp. 5–7.

The Connecticut Asylum was a private institution, incorporated and subsidized by the

state of Connecticut, which was intended for both charity and tuition-paying students. Massachusetts, beginning in 1819, New Hampshire in 1821, and Vermont and Maine in 1825, made annual appropriation to the Asylum for the education of deaf children from those states.

About two years since, seven persons met in this city, and appointed a committee to solicit funds to enable Mr. Gallaudet[1] to visit Europe, for the purpose of qualifying himself to become an instructor of the deaf and dumb. The generous promptitude with which means were furnished, put it in his power to embark soon after for England. Not meeting with a satisfactory reception at the London Asylum, he went to Edinburgh. Here new obstacles arose from an obligation which had been imposed upon the institution in that city, not to instruct teachers in the art for a term of years; thus rendering unavailing the friendly desires of its benevolent instructor, and the kind wishes of its generous patrons. After these repeated disappointments and discouragements, in which,

1. Thomas Hopkins Gallaudet (1787–1851), the principal founder of the Connecticut Asylum and superintendent of the institution from 1817 until 1830.

however, let us behold a providential hand, Mr. Gallaudet departed for Paris, where he met with a very courteous and favourable reception from the Abbé Sicard, and soon commenced his course of lessons in the establishment over which that celebrated instructor presides. An arrangement made with Mr. Laurent Clerc, himself deaf and dumb, one of the professors in the institution of Paris, and well known in Europe as a most intelligent pupil of his illustrious master, enabled Mr. Gallaudet to return to his native country, with this valuable assistant, much sooner than had been expected. By this circumstance, a new zeal in the cause was excited, in some measure commensurate with the more favourable auspices under which the interests of our Asylum now appeared. They arrived in this place in August last, and soon after visited some of our large cities, for the purpose of soliciting funds for the establishment . . . Many instances of individual munificence will be found recorded in the list of donations. The patrons of this institution need not our thanks: they have a higher gratification in the reflection, that they have contributed to the means which are now using, for shedding light upon many an immortal mind which, but for their munificence, might otherwise have remained in darkness. We solicit their prayers that the means they have furnished may be so blessed as to promote the cause of Christ, and the eternal welfare of those who are here benefited by their bounty.

In May, 1816, the legislature of this state passed an act incorporating this institution; and in October last made a grant of five thousand dollars in aid of its funds.

The establishment was opened on the 15th April, and it already contains upwards of twenty pupils . . . A number of them are of full age, some of whom have expressed much interest at the attempts which have been made, as yet in a very imperfect manner, to explain to them some of the simplest doctrines of revelation.

When we look back we have surely cause for abundant gratitude to God for what has already been accomplished; and although we have to lament that our means are altogether inadequate to the support and instruction of those pupils who are in indigent circumstances, let us look forward with humble confidence that HE, by the word of whose power the dumb spake, can prepare the way before us, and will, if he see fit, make use of this Asylum as an instrument, not only to increase the temporal happiness of those who may become the objects of its care, but to communicate to them a knowledge of himself, as their only Saviour, and of those mansions of rest, where all will equally rejoice in the participation of happiness without imperfection, and without end.

---

2. "There are chains more galling than those of the dungeon"

Thomas H. Gallaudet, *A Sermon Delivered at the Opening of the Connecticut Asylum for the Education and Instruction of Deaf and Dumb Persons* (Hartford, 1817), pp. 6–8.

The instruction of the deaf and dumb, if properly conducted, has a tendency to give important aid to many researches of the philanthropist, the philosopher, and the divine. — The philanthropist and the philosopher are deeply interested in the business of education. The cultivation of the human mind is paramount to all other pursuits; inasmuch as spirit is superior to matter, and eternity to time. Youth, is the season in which the powers of the mind begin to develope themselves, and *language,* the grand instrument by which this developement is to take place. Now it is beyond all doubt, that great improvement has been made in the mode of instructing children in the use and power of language. To what extent these improvements may *yet* be carried, time alone can determine. The very singular condition in which the minds of the deaf and dumb are placed, and the peculiar means which are necessarily employed in their instruction, may furnish opportunities for observation and experiment, and the establishment of principles, with regard to the education of youth, which will not be without essential service in their general application. How much light also, may in this way, be thrown upon what are supposed to be the *original truths,* felt and recognised to be such by the mind, without any *reasoning process.* Many speculations, too, which now are obscure and unsettled, respecting the faculties of the human mind, may be rendered more clear and satisfactory. How many questions, also, may be solved, concerning the capability of man to originate *of himself,* the notion of a God and of a future state, or, admitting his capacity to do this, whether, as a *matter of fact,* he ever would do it. What discoveries may be made respecting the *original notions* of right and wrong, the obligations of conscience, and, indeed, most of the similar topics connected with the moral sense. These hints are sufficient to show, that aside from the leading and more important uses of giving instruction to the deaf and dumb, their education might be made to subserve the general cause of humanity, and of correct Philosophy and Theology.

.   .   .   .   .

But there is a *sickness* more dreadful than that of the body; there are *chains* more galling than those of the dungeon — *the immortal mind preying upon itself,* and so imprisoned as not to be able to unfold its intellectual and moral powers, and to attain to the comprehension and enjoyment of those objects, which the Creator has designed as the sources of its highest expectations and hopes. Such must often be the condition of the uninstructed deaf and dumb! What mysterious darkness must sadden their souls! How imperfectly can they account for the wonders that surround them. Must not each one of them, in the language of thought, sometimes say, "What is it that makes me differ from my fellow men? Why are they so much my superiors? What is that strange mode of com-

municating, by which they understand each other with the rapidity of lightning, and which enlivens their faces with the brightest expressions of joy? Why do I not possess it, or why can it not be communicated to me? What are those mysterious characters, over which they pore with such incessant delight, and which seem to gladden the hours that pass by me so sad and cheerless! What mean the ten thousand customs, which I witness in the private circles and the public assemblies, and which possess such mighty influence over the conduct and feelings of those around me? And that termination of life; that placing in the cold bosom of the earth, those whom I have loved so long and so tenderly; how it makes me shudder! — What is death? — Why are my friends thus laid by and forgotten? — Will they never revive from this strange slumber? — Shall the grass always grow over them? — Shall I see their faces no more forever? — And must *I* also thus cease to move and fall into an eternal sleep!

---

3. The Kentucky institution for the deaf and dumb, 1822

"An act to endow an asylum for the tuition of the deaf and dumb," 1822 — ch. 481, *Acts of the General Assembly, Commonwealth of Kentucky* (Frankfort, 1822), pp. 179–180.

Contrary to Gallaudet's hope that the country's resources for the deaf would be concentrated in one establishment, the Connecticut Asylum, additional institutions for the deaf were established in New York (1818), Pennsylvania (1820), and Kentucky (1822). Southern states sent their deaf children to the Kentucky institution just as the New England states sent theirs to the Connecticut Asylum.

Whereas, It is desirable to promote the education of that portion of the community, who, by the mysterious dispensation of Providence, are born deaf and of course dumb, and experience in other countries having evinced the practicability of reclaiming them to the rank of their species, by a judicious and well adapted course of education — it is represented that many of our philanthropic citizens would contribute to promote an object so benevolent and humane, if this legislature would co-operate, by affording pecuniary aid, and designating a mode by which the gratuities devoted thereto could be effectually applied. Therefore,

SECTION 1. *Be it enacted by the General Assembly of the Commonwealth of Kentucky,* That the trustees and their successors of the Central College at Danville, shall be, and they are hereby authorised and empowered to receive by legacies, conveyances or otherwise, lands, slaves, money and other property, and the same to retain, use and apply to the education of the deaf and dumb within this commonwealth, to any amount, the interest, profits or proceeds of which, shall not exceed the sum of thirty thousand dollars per annum.

The institution shall be located at Danville, in Mercer county, and supported by the donations and legacies of the charitable, by such aid as the legislature may be pleased to afford and by the money to be received for the education of children whose parents, guardians or friends are of ability to pay.

. . . . . .

Indigent children resident any where within the state, shall be received into the asylum, maintained and educated gratuitously, so far as the funds of the institution will admit: *Provided,* that where more children shall be offered for the benefit of this institution than can be received at any one time, the trustees shall so apportion their number among the several counties of this commonwealth, according to their representation, when application shall be made, that every county may equally receive the benefits of the same.

SEC. 2. That in order to aid the funds of the said asylum, the governor is hereby authorised and required to draw his warrant on the auditor of public accounts in favor of said trustees, for the further sum of one hundred dollars for every indigent pupil taught in said asylum . . . *Provided,* That no one scholar shall be taught at the expense of the state more than three years; and *Provided also,* That the sum so to be drawn from the treasury, for such tuition shall, in no one year, exceed the sum of two thousand five hundred dollars.

---

4. State pupils in New York

New York Institution for the Instruction of the Deaf and Dumb, *Eighth Annual Report, 1826* (New York, 1827), pp. 4–8.

The New York Institution was a private charity which, after 1822, admitted a limited number of "state pupils" — poor children who received three years of instruction at the expense of the state.

Several of the pupils now in the school have expressed to their teachers the impropriety of their former conduct towards their friends and parents, in telling lies, stealing, and misbehaving in a variety of ways, the evil of which they were not aware before instruction. One of these, from Saugerties in Ulster County, is a most promising young man, about 19 years of age; kind, obedient, and well disposed, and will do credit to himself and the Institution. He has fifteen months yet to remain in school under the state laws.

Another about the same age, from Salina in Onondaga County, will also afford a bright example of moral as well as intellectual improvement. His time as a state pupil expires on the 10th January, inst. and the Directors have determined to retain him till spring at the expense of the Institution.

Among the moral effects of instruction may be mentioned a number of the former pupils of this school, whose ability to communicate and understand, has enabled them to acquire trades and obtain a living by their industry. Some of these are in the city of New York working at their trades, and others have been reported as residing in different parts of the country, much respected and esteemed.

A female pupil (whose surviving parent was reduced by misfortune), was patronized by this Institution, brought up and instructed here, until nearly nineteen years old, when she was married to the young gentleman who is now the Principal Teacher in the Central School at Canajoharie, and who obtained his first information of the method of instructing the Deaf and Dumb in the school of this Institution.

Under this head of *moral and intellectual improvement,* we cannot omit to mention the young man who for several years past has acted as an Assistant Teacher. He was one of the Deaf Mutes who came to this Institution as a State Pupil from Otsego County, and after completing the period of three years under the first state law, he was retained as an Assistant in the school, and has been provided with board and clothing for his services, and at convenient intervals received instruction as a pupil. His improvement has been so creditable that the Directors have now struck his name from the list of pupils and engaged him as a teacher at a salary; thus enabling him to provide for himself in a useful and creditable manner. When first received in this Institution, he gave no indication of capacity, and there was no appearance in his countenance of intelligence or quickness of intellect. He was, upon the whole, rather a coarse and rough boy, and was considered as a dull pupil. It was some time before his abilities began to develop themselves, and then when internal light began to shine, its effect was manifest in his countenance and manner, and he has since continued to improve, and is also cautious and circumspect in his moral deportment. The Directors hope to continue him in the Institution, and that he will be an example for other Deaf Mutes to imitate, and do honour to the Institution, himself, and his friends.

.   .   .   .   .   .

Sources of revenue to the Institution . . . have arisen last year from *pay pupils, donations and subscriptions, Corporation annuity, the sale of books and pamphlets, from interest on asylum fund, and the amount received for pupils of the Female Association.*

The Directors cannot pass over this opportunity of expressing a sense of their obligations to a Society of Ladies in New York, who have associated under the title of the *"New York Female Association to aid in giving support and instruction to the indigent Deaf and Dumb."* They have selected seven pupils, placed them in the Institution, and paid for their board and tuition from resources collected in this city, thus adding to the income of the parent Society.

More than half the income of this Institution is derived from means collected in the city of New-York; and of the State Pupils, one only belongs to the city. Thus the Directors have endeavoured to appropriate the income derived from the State, almost wholly to other counties than their own.

———————————

5. Principal of the Pennsylvania Institution for Education of the Deaf and Dumb urges federal support, 1828

Lewis Weld, *An Address Delivered in the Capitol, in Washington City . . . at an Exhibition of Three of the Pupils of the Pennsylvania Institution for the Education of the Deaf and Dumb* (Washington, 1828), pp. 3–9.

In 1819 Congress granted the Connecticut Asylum 23,000 acres — roughly a township — of public lands from the sale of which the institution ultimately realized $300,000. In 1826 the Kentucky Asylum received a grant for a similar amount of public land. During the 1830's and 1840's Congress considered but did not enact several bills which would have endowed all schools for the deaf then in existence with land grants. The subject of federal aid is discussed in Harry Best, *Deafness and the Deaf* (New York, 1943), pp. 423–424, 595–596.

In this age of enterprise and of effort, when genius is enlarging the boundaries of knowledge, when literature, science and art are immeasurably multiplying their resources, and with them the conveniences and enjoyments of life, benevolence too is expanding her energies, and in harmony with her sister-agents, is actively promoting the happiness of man. But I come not here to portray the beauties of benevolence. I would rather call your attention to a few plain facts, on a subject, which from the necessity of the case, is but imperfectly understood, even by the most enlightened in any country.

.   .   .   .   .

In the year 1820 the number of deaf-mutes was ascertained in forty-one counties of the state of Pennsylvania. The result was, that among the whole white population of twenty-five of these counties, the proportion of the Deaf and Dumb, was precisely one to every two thousand, and in regard to the whole population of the state, this proportion holds very nearly.

Similar enumerations have been made in other states, and in foreign countries, and the results tend to establish the same position.

Assuming it then as proved, that this is the true proportion in our country generally, we may easily ascertain not only the whole number of Deaf and Dumb persons, but those who are proper subjects for instruction. To this end I have referred to the census of 1820, as published under the direction of the government, and have ascertained the free white population of the several states and territories of the Union, and also that portion of this population between the ages of ten and twenty-six years; knowing that the proper period for educating the Deaf and Dumb, is between those ages. Indeed the best period is generally between twelve and eighteen years. The result of calculations made on these data is, that among the whole free white population of the United States in 1820, there were three thousand nine hundred and thirty-five deaf-mutes of all ages: among that portion of this population between ten and twenty-six years of age, there were probably one thousand three hundred and eighty-eight. Most of these we may suppose were at that time capable of receiving an education.

.   .   .   .   .

The experience of the best institutions goes to show, that one which is well supported, is able to keep constantly under instruction from one hundred and fifty to two hundred pupils. This is important on various accounts, but principally, perhaps, from motives of economy. The expenses of qualifying and supporting teachers, procuring suitable buildings, furniture, &c. are necessarily great. But an institution fairly established, can receive and educate a pretty large number at a rate much less in proportion than a small one, and be quite as likely or more so, to give them the best advantages. Such an institution can readily furnish mechanical and other proper employments for the poor among its pupils; and thus by giving them industrious habits, and a knowledge of some proper occupation, may prepare them for usefulness immediately upon leaving it.

.   .   .   .   .

Let us suppose that six institutions were endowed, properly located and provided with instructors; and also, that the whole number of deaf-mutes which probably existed among the whites of the United States in the year 1820, namely, three thousand nine hundred and thirty-five, should in the course of *ten* successive years be offered to them. There would be about three hundred and ninety-four for them all, or about sixty-six for each, annually. If the course of instruction continued five years, the whole number of pupils in each institution, would be three hundred and thirty;

but all the facts we can collect, tend to prove, that this estimate is by far too large, for deductions are to be made for disease, idiocy, accident and death; to each of which evils, this class of people are no less liable than others. Age too, at the present time, would make another deduction, though this will eventually cease to operate, because all may be received at the proper age.

.   .   .   .   .

The New England states all unite in patronizing one institution; and it is capable of demonstration, that it is much cheaper for the state of Maine, for example, to send her pupils to Connecticut for education, than to establish a school of her own. Maine, Massachusetts, New Hampshire, and Vermont, have for some years made appropriations for the education of their indigent deaf-mutes at the Asylum in Connecticut . . . If one institution is sufficient for the New England states at this time, when there are, so to speak, two or three generations to be educated, it will surely remain so when the annual increase only is to be taught. The same remark may be made of the other divisions of the country.

We ought in this connexion to recollect, that the population of our country is rapidly increasing, and hence, the proportion of deaf-mutes continuing the same, we may reasonably suppose, that six institutions would be supplied with a respectable number of pupils, notwithstanding the numerous necessary deductions to which we have alluded.

There are many reasons why it seems proper, that aid for the support of this object should be asked of the general government. Public institutions having from necessity, if prosperous, to derive their pupils from a considerable extent of country, including several states, cannot expect to be permanently endowed by any individual state. If they are not prosperous, in other words, if they cannot have a pretty large number of pupils, they obviously will not long exist. Another reason is, that a great majority of these people are in indigent circumstances.

If educated at all, the expense to their friends, must therefore be small.

---

6. The National Deaf-Mute College, Washington, D.C., 1864

Edward M. Gallaudet, "Inaugural Address," in Columbia Institution for the Deaf and Dumb and the Blind, *Seventh Annual Report, 1864* (Washington, 1864), pp. 15–25.

Edward M. Gallaudet (1837–1917), son of Thomas Hopkins Gallaudet, was appointed president of the Columbia Institution in 1864. The collegiate department of the institution was renamed Gallaudet College in 1894.

Our institution, by the provisions of its organic law, is not limited as to the extent to which it may carry forward the education of those placed under its fostering care by the United States. It is authorized to receive and instruct deaf-mutes from any of the States or Territories of the United States, on such terms as may be agreed upon by their parents, guardians, or trustees, and the proper authorities of the institution. By a recent act of Congress the institution is authorized to confer degrees in the arts and sciences after the manner pursued in colleges. It thus appears that this institution has power to open a collegiate department of study, and to offer to such deaf-mutes as may avail themselves of its privileges, academic honors equal in rank to those conferred on hearing and speaking persons by the highest literary schools in the land.

To fulfill these important trusts is the earnest desire of those to whom the direction of the institution has been committed, and it is their intention to spare no efforts, that here, at the nation's capital, may be successfully established a seat of learning which may extend its benefits to deaf-mutes from every State of our Union.

There are cogent reasons why the college for

deaf-mutes — and I say *the* college, since many years must elapse before the wants of the deaf and dumb in this country will require more than one — should be built up at Washington; one of the most weighty of which is that it has already, by the highest authority in the nation, been ushered into life here with its functions complete, although they may not yet possess that power and endurance that the accretions of maturity alone can give.

Appropriations of public money as well as the benefactions of private munificence will be needed in the development of the National Deaf-Mute College, and while it would not be right to ask the representatives in any State legislature to tax their constituents for the support of an institution for the benefit of citizens of other States, it is eminently proper to solicit the aid of the national legislators, representing as they do the people of every State, in behalf of an institution that shall extend its humane and elevating influences throughout the entire national domain. Undoubtedly the assistance of the Federal Government would be most important in the establishment and perfection of a national institution for the deaf and dumb; and where would that aid be more likely to be afforded than to a school already established and supported by the United States, under the very eaves, as it were, of its Capitol.

While our institution confined its operations to residents of the District of Columbia, Congress accorded a ready support; when its scope was extended to embrace the children of our soldiers and seamen, the Government promptly increased its appropriations; and now that we propose to enlarge our sphere of operations so as to offer to deaf-mute citizens of every State and Territory advantages which they cannot obtain elsewhere, the law-makers of the nation have set their seal of approbation on our undertaking by the appropriation of larger sums than ever before, supplying the needs of the institution incident to the establishment of the college, and giving an earnest of their intention to aid in its extension hereafter.

It is a question that may very naturally arise in the minds of those interested in the various State institutions, whether the proposed development of the Columbia Institution into a college will interfere in any way with the operations of its sister schools. To answer such queries in advance, it may be stated that our collegiate department is not designed to conflict, nor need it do so, with any existing organization for the instruction of the deaf and dumb.

It is no part of our plan to attempt to supersede or interrupt the most excellent and useful "high classes" now in operation. On the contrary, we desire the speedy advent of that day when every institution shall have its high class.

In no institution for the deaf and dumb have degrees in the arts and sciences been conferred upon graduates. In no institution does the course of study come up to the standard which would warrant such graduation. We propose to leave untouched in their operations the high classes, and bidding them God-speed in their good work, and urging their multiplication, to occupy a field of usefulness hitherto wholly uncultivated.

The time is not distant when the United States will contain a population of a hundred million souls. There will then be a deaf and dumb community in the country of fifty thousand. At least ten thousand of these would be undergoing instruction at the same time, requiring the employment of five hundred well-educated instructors.

The existing opportunities for mental culture are only enough to fit deaf-mutes to teach classes of low grades, and, as a consequence, they must receive relatively low rates of compensation, while the higher classes in our institutions demand the service of liberally-educated men at relatively high salaries.

It is admitted that deaf-mutes could be employed to a much greater extent than now, as instructors of their fellows in misfortune, and would make much more valuable teachers could they enjoy the advantages of a classical education. One of the designs of our college is to furnish deaf-mutes the means of obtaining that mental training and those academic honors which may entitle them to consideration in the world of letters, and allow them to gain positions of much greater usefulness and higher emolument than they can now aspire to.

We propose at least to test the question whether what is valued so highly by hearing and speaking persons, as a preparation for entering the more elevated spheres of usefulness in life, may not in like manner result in opening to deaf-mutes positions and pursuits from which they have been hitherto debarred.

If education to a high degree is important to a man possessed of all his faculties, is it not of even more consequence that those who make their way through the world in the face of difficulties which but a few years since seemed almost insurmountable, should, now that their aptitude for learning is proved beyond a question, have every advantage that the ingenuity or liberality of their more favored fellow-mortals can furnish?

The work of deaf-mute instruction in America may not inappropriately be compared to the erection of a stately building. Fifty years ago its foundations were laid broad and deep among the granite hills of New England, and a shaft of rare beauty and strength was reared thereon. Year by year the noble work has proceeded until but the pinnacle-stone is lacking to complete the structure; and, though it must be small in size and may escape notice amid the massive and beautiful pillars and arches on which it must of necessity rest, yet it is needed to perfect the work, and the founders of the Columbia Institution would fain essay to place it in position.

And so to-day, in this solemn and public manner, they inaugurate the "College for the Deaf and Dumb"; looking to Congress for a continuance of its favor, to a benevolent public for its approbation, to sister institutions for their countenance and sympathy, and to Him who "doth not willingly afflict or grieve the children of men" for His sustaining Providence to bear up the enterprise to a successful consummation.

The blind

In the United States education for the blind began in 1832 when Samuel Gridley Howe (1801–1876) founded the New England Asylum for the Blind, renamed in 1839 the Perkins Institution in honor of its patron, Thomas Handasyd Perkins (1764–1854). Other schools for the blind opened in New York in 1832 and in Philadelphia in 1833. During the next twenty years the number of such institutions increased to twenty.

---

1. Funds for the New England Asylum for the Blind, 1833

"Resolve in behalf of the trustees of the New England Asylum for the Blind," *Resolves of the General Court of the Commonwealth of Massachusetts, 1833* (Boston, 1833), pp. 338–339.

Most schools for the blind received state funds but they also solicited gifts from private donors and raised money by subscriptions, fairs, and exhibitions of students. In 1833 the Massachusetts legislature offered the New England Asylum a grant of $10,000 on condition that double that amount be secured from private sources. The sum was promptly obtained.

Resolved by the Senate and House of Representatives, in General Court assembled, That there be paid out of the Treasury of the Commonwealth to the Trustees of New England Asylum for the Blind the sum of six thousand dollars annually, in quarterly payments, the first payment to be made on the first day of April next, and the subsequent payments upon the first day of each successive quarter; and the whole to continue during the pleasure of the

Legislature and no longer. *Provided*, that in consideration of said sum of six thousand dollars the said New England Asylum shall receive, board, lodge and educate twenty poor persons belonging to the State, to be placed there under the direction of the Governor and Council; and to be dismissed from the Asylum by the same authority; *and provided further*, that no individual under the age of six years nor over the age of twenty-four years shall be placed in said Asylum by said authority, nor any person who shall be excluded by the standing by-laws of the Asylum.

2. Samuel Gridley Howe describes the cases of Abby and Sophia Carter and Laura Bridgman

Perkins Institution and Massachusetts School for the Blind, *Forty-third Annual Report, 1874* (Boston, 1875), pp. 73–89.

Before becoming a teacher of the blind, Howe participated in the Greek War of Independence and administered relief to Greek civilians. Among his many contributions to the education of the blind was the invention of the "Boston Letter," an improved type for printing books for the blind. Laura Bridgman (1829–1889), Howe's most famous pupil, spent her life at the Perkins Institution where she helped teach sewing in the workroom.

In the year 1832, while inquiring for blind children suitable for instruction in our projected school, I heard of a family in Andover in which there were several such, and immediately drove out thither with my friend and co-worker, Dr. John D. Fisher. As we approached the toll-house, and halted to pay the toll, I saw by the roadside two pretty little girls, one about six, the other about eight years old, tidily dressed, and standing hand in hand hard by the toll-house. They had come from their home, near

by, doubtless to listen, as was their wont, to gossip between the toll-gatherer and the passers-by. On looking more closely, I saw that they were both totally blind. It was a touching and interesting scene — that of two pretty, graceful, attractive little girls, standing hand in hand, and, though evidently blind, with uplifted faces and listening ears, as if brought providentially to meet messengers sent of God, to deliver them out of darkness. If there were depth of soil enough in my mind to nourish superstition, the idea of a providential arrangement of this meeting would have taken deep root. It would, indeed, be hard to find, among a thousand children, two better adapted, irrespective of their blindness, for the purpose of commencing our experiment. They were shy of us at first; but we gained their confidence with some difficulty; after which they led the way to their home in a neighboring farm-house. They were two of a numerous family, the parents of which were substantial, respectable people, and particularly good samples of the farming class of New England. The mother was especially intelligent, and devoted to her children; and much concerned about the barrier which blindness placed in the way of educating the five who were blind. She was much interested in the novel plan for educating the blind, which we explained to her. She had never thought of instructing children through any sense but that of sight; but she soon saw the practicability of the thing, and, being satisfied about our honesty, she consented with joy and hope to our proposition of beginning with her two girls, ABBY and SOPHIA CARTER. In a few days they were brought to Boston, and received into my father's house, as the first pupils of the first American School for the Blind.

The children were naturally so bright, and docile, and apt at learning, that they easily comprehended our purpose in making them feel of strange signs or types, representing the letters of the alphabet, and tried eagerly to learn. These metal types each bore, upon one end, the raised outlines of a letter, or of an arithmetical or geometrical figure. The children soon learned that, by being placed in certain relative positions, these types represented an apple, or a chair, or some other substantive thing. They soon comprehended that these signs were twenty-six in number. They learned to set them upright in a metal frame perforated with square holes, so that the sign upon the end protrudes above the surface of the frame, and can be felt above it by the finger.

They then learned that there were ten other types, with differently shaped tangible lines upon them, and that they represented the ten arithmetical digits, or figures, one, two, three, etc. Also, four others, representing the stops, and others for marks of interrogation and exclamation; so that, by forty-six different types, placed in horizontal lines upon the plate, and in various juxtapositions, they could spell out the names of things, ask questions, and express their thoughts concerning the qualities and quantities of all things, for they had learned their native language as other children do, by the ear.

They soon understood that sheets of stiff pasteboard, marked by certain crooked lines, represented the boundaries of countries; rough raised dots represented mountains; pins' heads, sticking out here and there, showed the location of towns; or, on a smaller scale, the boundaries of their own town, the location of the meeting-house, of their own and of the neighboring houses, and the like; and they were delighted and eager to go on with tireless curiosity. And they did go on until they matured in years, and became themselves teachers, first in our school, afterwards in a private school opened by themselves in their own town. They have continued, up to this day, maintaining excellent characters, supporting themselves comfortably, and helping support their parents as they declined in strength.

.   .   .   .   .

Children totally blind and totally deaf, and for a time deprived of the sense of smell, are very rare: but such exist . . .

,   ,   ,   ,   ,

The question has been discussed by writers on the philosophy of education, whether beings in human form, but so closely shorn of those senses requisite for communing with the outer world, could be taught any systematic language for such communion. The renowned Abbé Sicard, of France, naturally proud of his success, and of his eminent authority in matters connected with the education of deaf-mutes, formed the opinion, in his learned speculations, that they might be, and he made some rough observations about his mode of procedure, should such a case ever come to his knowledge. But none ever came to his knowledge, or to that of any other regular teacher, in any language with which I am acquainted. It was, therefore, considered as an open question whether such a person, if found, could be taught any system of signs which would serve for a language . . . I often, while reading or thinking of the matter, had asked myself the same question, soon after becoming familiar with the usual methods of teaching the blind and the deaf-mutes, and I resolved to make the attempt to teach the first one I should hear of. When, therefore, I read in a country paper an account . . . of a girl in New Hampshire said to be devoid of sight, hearing and smell, I started forthwith to ascertain the facts of the case.

I found in a little village in the mountains, a pretty and lively girl, about six years old, who was totally blind and deaf, and who had only a very indistinct sense of smell; so indistinct that, unlike other young deaf-mutes, who are continually smelling at things, she did not smell even at her food. This sense afterwards developed itself a little, but was never much used or relied upon by her. She lost her senses by scarlet fever so early that she has no recollection of any exercise of them. Her father was a substantial farmer; and his wife a very intelligent woman. My proposal to try to give regular instruction to the child seemed to be a very wild one. But the mother, a woman of considerable natural ability, animated by warm love for her daughter, eagerly assented to my proposal, and in a few days little Laura was brought to my house in Boston, and placed under regular instruction by lessons improvised for the occasion.

I shall not here anticipate what I intend to write about her, further than to say that I required her by signs, which she soon came to understand, to devote several hours a day to learning to use her hands, and to acquiring command of her muscles and limbs. But my principal aim and hope was to enable her to recognize the twenty-six signs which represent the letters of the alphabet. She submitted to the process patiently, though without understanding its purpose.

I will here give a rough sketch of the means which I contrived for her mental development. I first selected short monosyllables, so that the sign which she was to learn might be as simple as possible. I placed before her, on the table, a pen and a pin, and then, making her take notice of the fingers of one of my hands, I placed them in the three positions used as signs of the manual alphabet of deaf-mutes, for the letters *p e n* and made her feel of them, over and over again, many times, so that they might be associated together in her mind. I did the same with the pin, and repeated it scores of times. She at last perceived that the signs were complex, and that the middle sign of the one, that is, the *e*, differed from the middle sign of the other, that is, *i*. This was the first step gained. This process was repeated over and over, hundreds of times, until, finally, the association was established in her mind between the sign composed of three signs, and expressed by three positions of my fingers, and the article itself, so that when I held up the pen to her she would herself make the complex sign; and when I made the complex sign on my fingers, she would triumphantly pick up the pen, and hold it up before me, as much as to say, "This is what you want."

Then the same process was gone over with the pin, until the association in her mind was intimate and complete between the two articles, and the complex positions of the fingers. She had thus learned two arbitrary signs, or the names of the two different things. She seemed conscious of having understood and done what I wanted, for she smiled, while I exclaimed, inwardly and triumphantly, "εὑρῆχα! εὑρῆχα!" I now felt that the first step had been taken successfully, and that this was the only really difficult one, because by continuing the same process by which she had become enabled to distinguish two articles, by two arbitrary signs, she could go on and learn to express in signs two thousand, and, finally, the forty and odd thousand signs, or words in the English language.

Having learned that the sign for these two articles, *pin* and *pen*, was composed of three signs, she would perceive that in order to learn the names for other things, she had got to learn other signs. I went on with monosyllables, as being the simplest, and she learned gradually one sign of a letter from another, until she knew all the arbitrary, tangible twenty-six letters of the alphabet, and how to arrange them to express various objects: knife, fork, spoon, thread, and the like. Afterwards she learned the names of the ten numerals or digits; of the punctuation and exclamation and interrogation points, some forty-six in all. With these she could express the name of everything, of every thought, of every feeling, and all the numberless shades thereof. She had thus got the "open sesame" to the whole treasury of the English language. She seemed aware of the importance of the process; and worked at it eagerly and incessantly, taking up various articles, and inquiring by gestures and looks what signs upon her fingers were to be put together in order to express their names. At times she was too radiant with delight to be able to conceal her emotions.

It sometimes occurred to me that she was like a person alone and helpless in a deep, dark, still pit, and that I was letting down a cord and dangling it about, in hopes she might find it; and that finally she would seize it by chance and, clinging to it, be drawn up by it into the light of day, and into human society. And it did so happen; and thus she, instinctively and unconsciously, aided in her happy deliverance.

---

3. Daily routine at the Ohio Institution for the Instruction of the Blind, Columbus, 1841

Ohio, Institution for the Instruction of the Blind, *Fifth Annual Report, 1841* (Columbus, 1842), pp. 6–13.

At the date of our last report, the number of pupils was *thirty-six*. Since which, *three* have been discharged; *eighteen* have been admitted, and *one* has not returned — making the present number in the Institution, *fifty*.

There has been no death during the year, and no case of dangerous illness.

Of the three who were discharged, one was a young girl, a recent pupil, not of sound mind. Another, a female, could receive no further benefit in the Institution. And, the third, a boy, was subject to frequent convulsions, which rendered his further continuance inconvenient to the Institution, and of no utility to himself.

During the past vacation, another tour was made with several pupils, to Cincinnati, and other towns, in the south and west parts of the state, embracing a circuit of about 400 miles, which was attended with the usual success, of a considerable addition to our number. A portion of these would, otherwise, probably never have reached the Institution; some of them being entirely ignorant, even, of its existence. Further experience confirms the truth, of the great reluctance of most of the blind to leaving home, and of their parents to parting with them—a difficulty of so formidable a kind as to be removed only by a personal application from the Institution. In all parts of the state that were visited by us, this noble work of state beneficence was regarded with universal favor.

.   .   .   .   .   .

The order of studies, and the branches taught, are substantially the same as they were last year — embracing spelling, and definitions, with the latin roots; reading, writing, geography, including maps and statistics; arithmetic, mental, and on slate frames; and algebra. Also, daily lectures on moral and natural philosophy, logic, belleslettres, political economy, general and natural history, &c., which all the pupils attend.

The hour of rising is half past 5. The exercises commence at one quarter past 6, and continue, with a short recess between each lesson, until 1 o'clock, P.M. The lessons are one hour long, each. The singing and band exercises intervene between 10½ and 12. The afternoon, from 2 to 5, is spent, by nearly all the pupils, at work. One hour of each evening is occupied in reading history, biography, &c., to all the pupils. The Matron also reads one hour, every afternoon, to the girls, while at their work. Scientific discoveries, important events, and the leading current news of the day, are communicated to the pupils, from time to time.

The religious privileges of the pupils continue to be respected, and secured to them. They are required to attend church on the Sabbath, at places of their own choice, without the least restraint. And, if the weather is unpleasant, appropriate exercises are held in the Institution.

.   .   .   .   .   .

When it is understood how great a source of enjoyment this delightful science (music) ever proves to the Blind, it will not, we hope, be thought that too much attention is bestowed upon it here. It occupies a prominent place in all other institutions for the Blind. No lessons are crowded out by it — no time is taken up that would otherwise be profitably employed. On the contrary, it affords an agreeable and necessary relaxation to the other teachers, as well as the pupils; and, its influence, regarded in that light alone, is entirely salutary.

The mechanical department is entitled to your continued care. In its practical operation, of giving useful trades to the Blind, at a very moderate expense, it is decidedly successful. And we are still encouraged to hope that the time is not far distant when it will defray all its expenses, including the teacher's salary. This, however, cannot be expected until the proportion of advanced pupils, to beginners, shall be greater. This department is still in the infancy of its operations.

The beauty and durability of the work done by the pupils, prove their skill and capacity in the various manufactures. *Eighteen* are daily engaged, who are distributed as follows, viz: *twelve* at brushmaking; *three* at willow baskets; *one* at carpet weaving; *one* at shoemaking; and *one* at manilla door mats. Their teacher is constantly engaged in his faithful labors, of advancing the pupils, and elevating the condition of his department. The new work shop, erected for their better accommodation, has but lately been occupied, and proves to be, in all respects, convenient and comfortable.

The work department of the female pupils is equally interesting. In addition to knitting and plain sewing, they are taught to make worsted baskets and flowers, lamp mats, silk purses, reticules, watch guards, &c., &c. These specimens of delicate skill are justly the admiration of numerous visitors.

It is but doing justice to the Blind to say, that, with all their privations and discouragements, a more industrious class of persons can nowhere be found. This interesting fact is much overlooked by indulgent parents, and by the community, generally. Before the existence of these institutions, the Blind were looked upon as entirely helpless and dependant; and, the thought that they must ever remain so, only increased this dependance to degradation and effeminacy — the only real misfortune of blindness.

· · · · ·

With intellectual faculties equal, in every respect, to those of seeing persons, and as capable of acquiring a knowledge of the useful and liberal sciences, and the mechanic arts,

they stand forth, with the rest of the human family, rational, intelligent, and responsible beings. Blindness has not darkened their souls. The devices of modern art have discovered means by which another sense has wonderfully supplied the loss of sight. And, now they ask — not the chilling voice of pity — not the pittance of cold charity, which is but a badge of pauperism — but, that their present opportunities may be continued to them, in a spirit of high and rational benevolence; of cultivating the powers which God has given them; of maintaining their independence by their own talents and industry; and thus, by a full and proper developement of all their energies, moral, mental, and physical, of enabling them to take an equal station in life, on the same platform with their fellow beings.

The ease with which most of the Blind learn to read, and the proficiency which some of them make in their general studies, have frequently led to reports concerning them highly exaggerated, and bordering on the marvellous. These give rise to unreasonable expectations, which are unfavorable to them. No pretensions are made to extraordinary proficiency; nor do they invite the apology, so often made for them, that they do well *for blind persons*. They desire to be judged simply on their merits as scholars — not *as the blind* — and with no more indulgence than is awarded to seeing pupils.

· · · · ·

With a strong desire to keep our expenses within the smallest practical limit, I cannot hesitate respectfully to suggest, for your consideration, the expediency of purchasing an organ for the Institution, at an early day. With funds already received, and in expectation, it is believed an appropriation to an amount of one half the cost would be sufficient. This instrument furnishes an important branch of musical instruction in every other institution, which is in full operation; and this is all that is now needed to make our own system complete. Such an improvement would not only add much to the gratification of our pupils, but it would give to some of them a respectable means of support hereafter. Other institutions have already sent forth pupils, who are now profitably employed as organists in churches, and teachers on the piano forte. It should be added, that some of our pupils, of promising musical talent, have but a limited time to stay; and it must forever prove a misfortune to them if they should be deprived of this valuable accomplishment.

There are now four institutions for the instruction of the blind in the United States, besides ours — situated in Boston, New York, Philadelphia, and Staunton, Virginia. The first three have existed from eight to ten years. The last was commenced since our own. In Boston and Philadelphia only, have printing presses for the blind been established. It has been through the enterprize of those institutions, and the generous contributions of societies and individuals, to their printing fund, that we have thus far been supplied, at a moderate cost, with books of a beautifully embossed letter. It can never be the policy of this, or any other institution, to commence printing, so long as these presses are kept in action. One printing press would be sufficient to supply all the blind in the United States with books. But, while we are thus relieved from a burden which would otherwise be necessary, it will be a just and liberal course, to make such free purchases of new publications, as may give further encouragement to their being printed.

The insane and feeble-minded

---

1. Insane in county poorhouses, New York, 1844

Dorothea L. Dix, *Memorial, to the Honorable the Legislature of the State of New York* (Albany, 1844), pp. 3–51.

Miss Dix (1802–1887) was a strong-willed gentlewoman who was at once high-minded and practical. Formerly a school mistress and tutor of the children of her friend and pastor, William Ellery Channing, she began her investigation of the care, or rather the neglect, of the pauper and indigent insane in her native state, Massachusetts, in 1841. For more than forty years thereafter — with time out for service as superintendent of nurses for the Union forces in the Civil War — she traveled from state to state visiting jails, poorhouses, and other public institutions, reporting her findings in articles, addresses, and *Memorials* to state legislatures and Congress, and lobbying for improved and expanded facilities for the insane.

Your attention is solicited to the condition of many indigent and pauper insane persons in the county-houses of this State . . . Your petitioner asks to present their wants and their claims . . . not as being properly the charge of those towns and counties where their lot may have fallen, but as Wards of the State, made so by the most terrible calamity that can assail human nature — a shattered intellect, a total incapacity for self-care and self-government.

Notwithstanding the liberal appropriations for the relief of this class by the establishment of the State curative asylum at Utica, large numbers are yet unprovided for. Many whose cases offer every hope of recovery, if brought under remedial treatment, are sinking in the prime of life into irrecoverable insanity; others, whose condition exhibits nothing to encourage hope of benefit from being placed in a curative asylum, are permitted to fall into states of the most shocking and brutalizing degradation — pitiable objects, at once sources of greatest discomfort to all brought within their vicinity, and exposed to exciting irritation from the reckless sports of the idle and vicious. But this is is not the darkest view of their condition; these most unfriended and wretched beings are often subject to more horrible circumstances. Fidelity to my cause compels me, however revolting the topic, to speak more explicitly. I state, therefore, that both idiots and insane women are exposed to the basest vice, and become mothers without consciousness of maternity, and without capacity in any way to provide for their offspring, or to exercise those cares which are instinctive with the lowest brute animals. Is this a condition of things to be tolerated in a christian land, in the very heart of a community claiming to take rank for elevation of moral principles and high-minded justice? . . .

I will not consume time by narrating individual histories, which, however they might rouse your indignation, or awaken your sensibilities, will, I believe, not be needed to strengthen a cause so evidently claiming your very serious consideration and efficient action. I shall, as briefly as possible, refer to those institutions in the State, where are found both sufficient and defective provision for all classes of the insane, that from such statements you may determine what additional establishments are required.

The Asylums at Utica and at Bloomingdale afford insufficient accommodations for the reception of even the curable insane; large numbers of both classes are accumulated in the county alms-houses, and in private dwellings. Of the condition, generally, of such as are retained by their own families, I am unprepared to speak; were it proper to visit these as a stranger, time would not have afforded opportunity. Ten weeks of uninterrupted travelling has barely sufficed to ascertain the general condition of those in county-houses; but inquiry in towns through which I have passed, has been met by information of one or several cases in each neighborhood; sometimes these have been represented as hopelessly insane, returned from hospitals; but oftener such as have received no skilful care or remedial medical treatment; and in not few instances subject to the application of a severe discipline, almost too terrible to be described. The cases are not many where this has appeared to be the result of wilful brutality, so much as a consequent of ignorance and great

perplexity under unaccustomed trials. Few persons, however well-disposed and patient of trouble, have tact and discretion in managing a raving madman, or a perverse maniac.

I am spared the pain of describing the jails of New-York as containing, like those of Massachusetts, receptacles for the insane, or dungeons occupied not by criminals, but by those whom misfortune, not guilt, has brought low. Against that monstrous abuse, your just laws have effectually guarded; nearly every county-house however, has its "crazy-house," its "crazy-cells," or its "crazy-dungeons" and "crazy-cellar," as that of Albany, for example.

.   .   .   .   .

Albany County Alms-House, at Albany, as I saw it in November, 1842, presented scenes of horrible neglect and misery, which even now I shudder to recall, and I rejoice, that a late visit in December, 1843, afforded evidence of many favorable changes, especially in the "dungeons" so called, and the "crazy-cellar"; yet there even now, one finds many friendless creatures whose condition urges a sufficient and early provision, by the State, for their relief.

It was on the afternoon of a severely cold day in November of 1842, that I visited the alms-house at Albany. Inquiring of the master who held charge of the establishment, the number of the insane then in close confinement, I was answered, "There are plenty of them; somewhere about twenty." "Will you let me see them?" "No, you can't, they're naked, in the crazy-cellar." "Are all in the same apartment then?" "No, not all, but you can't see them." "Excuse me, but I must see the women's apartment. It is to learn the condition of the insane here, that I have come." At length a direction was given, and I was conducted by the mistress of the house into a court-yard, and the person holding charge over the insane women was summoned to attend me. Ascending a flight of stairs, conducting from without, to the second story of a large building, I entered an apartment not clean, not ventilated, and over-heated: here were several females chiefly in a state of dementia; they were decently dressed, but otherwise exhibited personal neglect; the beds were sufficiently comfortable; the hot air, foul with noisome vapors, produced a sense of suffocation and sickness impossible to be long endured by one unaccustomed to such an atmosphere. I delayed here but few moments, and asked to be conducted to the dungeons: "dungeons," repeated the attendant, eyeing me closely. "Yes, the dungeons, I have heard there are dungeons here; I am in haste, oblige me by losing no time." She still hesitated, when speaking more decidedly I said, "I must go, friend, and that immediately": whereupon she led the way over the outer staircase, across the common court-yard, and descending into a spacious cellar kitchen, crowded by a most disorderly and profane set of men, women, and children, emerged on the opposite side upon a yard enclosed by a high board fence, and opening on the left upon still another enclosed space, surrounding a wooden building. We here encountered the man who kept the keys of this place, and who appeared to have charge of the building. I do not hesitate to say that he was unfit for the office. I was told both these persons were "paupers from Canada," and their phraseology did not contradict the information. A noisy altercation ensued, made up of coarse oaths and expletives, unmatched except in Newgate or on Blackwell's island. I again interposed, and at length induced the turnkey to produce his keys. Detaining my first companion, I followed through the opened doors, and ascending a flight of steps found myself in a passage not very narrow, on each side of which were "the dungeons" or cells. These were totally dark and unventilated, and there was then no provision for drying or warming them. To describe the scenes which were revealed as these loathsome dens were successively thrown open is impossible . . . The keeper unlocking the first door on the left, vociferated to the poor wretch there confined, to "come out to the light and be seen." The horrible stench emitted from this dreadful place compelled me repeatedly to retreat to the outer air to recover from over-

powering sickness. When I could so far command myself as to observe this dungeon and its occupant, God forgive me (if it was sinful) the vehement indignation that rose towards the inhabitants of a city and county, who could suffer such abominations as these to exist; — towards all official persons holding direct or indirect responsibility, who could permit these brutalizing conditions of the most helpless of human beings, and towards a country ever vain-glorious of its liberty, and of its civil, social, and religious institutions. I affirm that the dungeons of Spielberg and of Chillon, and the prisons of the Court of the Inquisition before their destruction, afforded no more heart-rending spectacles than the dungeons (not subterranean) of the Albany alms-house, at the time referred to. Language is feeble to represent them, and the mind shudders with disgust and horror in the act of recalling the state of the unfortunate insane there incarcerated.

. . . . . .

I revisited this county house a few weeks since; there had been a change of masters. The present overseer evidently has qualifications which enable him to secure a very improved order of things throughout the establishment; he has to contend against the great defects of the present system, and prominent evils must of course exist. Five hundred paupers of every age and various conditions (a large proportion of these able-bodied foreigners, who here are idle for want of work, which the county does not provide, as well as idle in many cases from choice) compose this family or rather community. Considering the very crowded state of the house, and all the difficulties to be encountered, a surprising degree of order and cleanliness are now secured. But inevitably this is a soil where the vices will take root and flourish. I visited "the dungeons," and found but two females in confinement there; by comparison only could they be called comfortable. A stove is now placed in the passage, I cannot say it seemed to afford any great advantage to the insane in the cells; in these apartments were bunks, beds and bed-clothing. The apparel was slight and required attention; but the fact is, the inmates ought to be transferred to a hospital where they can receive appropriate care. In the crowded "crazy-cellar" I found improved accommodations, better beds, &c. One man "poor George," had just deceased, and his coffin was borne past as I stood at the entrance of this dreary place; surely the angel of death here performed a most blessed ministration. Several men were chained to the beds or the floor; a general quiet prevailed. I noticed that the master "our boss" was welcomed as a friend, and no doubt, so far as he had the power, the condition of these friendless insane was made comfortable. The time has past, however, for society to sanction such provision for this class of the poor.

.   .   .   .   .

Clinton County House at Plattsburgh, is not a good building, and much out of repair; it is not large enough for the numbers thronging to it in the winter. It is distinguished by a remarkable neatness throughout. I visited this place on a stormy day, at an unexpected and unseasonable hour; it was doubly gratifying to notice a place of so much comfort and quiet, made so by the uncommon care and capability of the master and mistress of the house. Here the sick were in well arranged apartments, and well attended; the household suitably and neatly clothed; garments well made, and in good repair; clean beds, bed-steads, and bed-clothing; clean tables, chairs and floors; clean walls and clean windows, showing that neither the application of white-wash, or water and the scrubbing brush were spared. The kitchen in good order.

.   .   .   .   .

Compassion was deeply moved at seeing a little girl, about nine or ten years of age, who suffered the fourfold calamity of being blind, deaf, dumb, and insane. I can conceive no condition so pitiable as that of this unfortunate

little creature, the chief movements of whose broken mind, were exhibited in restlessness, and violent efforts to escape, and unnatural screams of terror. No gentleness or kindness seemed to sooth her, or to inspire confidence. Various methods had been tried to promote her comfort, but with little success. She would rend her garments and bed-clothing to pieces, and seemed most content when she could bury herself in a heap of straw; when food was presented, she swallowed it with avidity, and seemed indifferent to its kind or quality. It was necessary to watch her with great care. To promote her comfort at one time, she was removed from the cells and placed with other persons in a large room, fastened by a small chain to the floor, to prevent her from falling upon the heated stove. She resists control, and perpetually struggles to escape. If left at large in mild weather, for a few minutes, she gropes her way, or rather rushes off avoiding by some invisible instinct violent falls, and conceals herself beneath a bush or fence: when brought back she resists violently, and utters the most vehement outcries. I took her hand gently, but she fell into the wildest paroxysm, which passed by, only when she had concealed herself in the straw in her cell. The utmost care was taken to keep her clean, and to do all for her comfort that her unhappy condition permitted.

There is at this house no provision for the insane who are at any time too violent to be permitted at large, except low, dismal cells, fit for no use, and which should never be employed for any persons of this class. The true remedy will be found in State asylums, on a cheap, but comfortable plan for the uncurables.

.   .   .   .   .

Wayne County-House at Lyons, is at the present time under excellent administration, good discipline, kind care, and neatness being secured to a considerable degree. The master of this establishment was a sensible well-informed man, having a clear comprehension of his duties, and understanding in the discharge of them. So complex are the arrangements in alms-houses which are made to serve so many purposes opposite in object and result, that one must be rather singularly endowed to meet every emergency . . . The cells for the insane were to some extent rendered comfortable — that is to say — though not by any means fit for crazy men and women . . . One circumstance especially pained me; it was the situation of an insane girl, who though placed in a comfortable apartment and decently dressed, was attended by a woman whose ill-temper was apologized for from the fact of her probably having been disturbed through the night by the restlessness and cries of the young woman. She was represented as being a good nurse, and no doubt had some excellent qualifications, but she was not a good nurse for a creature like this poor girl, placed so much in her power. "This is no house for such rich folks as her's to send their children to; it is for the poor, and they may take care of her for themselves." "She is more ugly than crazy, and knows well enough what she is about." I pointed to a large bruise on the temple of the weeping girl; the nurse did not deny that she had inflicted a blow, but persisted that the girl was "ugly and wouldn't be still!"

.   .   .   .   .

Permit me, briefly, to refer to the prominent defects of the present county-house system throughout the State.

These institutions are compound and complex in their plans and objects. They are at one and the same time, alms-houses, or retreats for the aged, the invalid, and helpless poor: houses of correction for the vicious and abandoned; asylums for orphaned and neglected children; receptacles for the insane and imbecile; extensive farming, and more limited manufacturing establishments. Beside, in addition to being mixed establishments, they are not, one in ten or twenty counties, built in reference to these various objects. They are not planned to secure division and classification of the inmates. They afford insufficient accommodations, both in "the day rooms," and in the lodging apartments; not being constructed with a view to securing

convenient arrangement or sound health. They are almost universally deficient in hospitals, or rooms especially appropriated to the sick, and to invalids. They do not guard against the indiscriminate association of the children with the adult poor. The education of these children, with rare exceptions, is conducted on a very defective plan. The alms-house schools, so far as I have learnt from frequent inquiries, are not inspected by official persons, who visit and examine the other schools of the county.

The moral and religious instruction of the poor at large, in these institutions is either attended to at remote and uncertain intervals, or entirely neglected. The scriptural text, that to "the poor the gospel is preached," that "good news of glad tidings," appears to have failed in its application to alms-houses. "We cannot afford it," says one; "our subscriptions and donations are even now burthensome in the support of foreign missions to Asia and the South Sea islands." "We have not time," say others, "we have in our town been wholly engaged, for the last six months, by a revival." "Why do you not visit those degraded beings at your alms-house, and try to reclaim them to goodness and virtue?" "Oh, I have no time for such things. I am an active member and secretary of the Moral Reform Society." "How can you refrain from interposing in behalf of those poor fettered maniacs, wearing out a terrible life in chains, shut out from the light of the beautiful sky, and pining in friendless neglect?" "I assure you I have quite as much as I can do to work for the Anti-Slavery Fair. I detest all abuses and oppressions, and have devoted myself to the cause of emancipation in the slaveholding States." "And I," said another, "must lecture on freedom, and justice, and human rights. We at the north must be zealous to rouse the citizens of the southern States from their apathy to the claims of suffering humanity." These, and such like answers, to often renewed questionings, are given continually; and to me they are evidence of our proneness to overlook the discharge of duties "nigh at hand"; and to forget that "the good example" is better than the "reiterated precept." Here at home, for a long time, have we ample fields of labor: to teach the gospel of the blessed Jesus by word and life; to enlighten ignorance; to stay the tide of vicious pauperism; to succor the friendless, support the feeble; to visit the afflicted; to raise the depressed; to lessen human suffering, and elevate human aims; to redress wrongs; rectify abuses; unloose the chains of the maniac and bring release to those who pine in dark cells and dreary dungeons: having plucked the beam from our own eye, we can with a less pharisaical spirit, direct our efforts to clearing the mental vision of neighbor.

2. Twenty-five years of progress in education of idiots, 1848–1873

Walter E. Fernald, "The History of the Treatment of the Feeble-Minded," in *Proceedings* of the Twentieth National Conference of Charities and Corrections, 1893 (1893), pp. 203–209.

Walter E. Fernald (1859–1924) was appointed superintendent of the Massachusetts School for the Feebleminded in 1887. He was a professor of mental diseases at Tufts College, lectured on the mental diseases of children at the Harvard Graduate School of Education, and wrote extensively on the education of mentally deficient children.

The first recorded attempt to educate an idiot was made about the year 1800, by Itard, the celebrated physician-in-chief to the National Institution for the Deaf and Dumb at Paris, upon a boy found wild in a forest in the centre of France, and known as the "savage of Avey-ron." "This boy could not speak any human tongue, and was devoid of all understanding and knowledge." Believing him to be a savage, for five years Itard endeavored with great skill and perseverance to develop at the same time

the intelligence of his pupil and the theories of the materialistic school of philosophy. Itard finally became convinced that this boy was an idiot, and abandoned the attempt to educate him.

In the year 1818 and for a few years afterward, several idiotic children were received and given instruction at the American Asylum for the Deaf and Dumb at Hartford, and a fair degree of improvement in physical condition, habits, and speech was obtained.

In the year 1828 Dr. Ferret, physician at the Bicêtre in Paris, attempted to teach a few of the more intelligent idiots who were confined in this hospital to read and write and to train them to habits of cleanliness and order. In 1831 Dr. Fabret attempted the same work at the Salpetrière; and in 1833 Dr. Voisin opened his private school for idiots in Paris. None of these attempts was successful enough to insure its continuance.

In 1837 Dr. E. Seguin, a pupil of Itard and Esquirol, began the private instruction of idiots at his own expense. In 1842 he was made the instructor of the school at the Bicêtre, which had been reopened by Dr. Voisin in 1839. Dr. Seguin remained at the Bicêtre only one year, retiring to continue the work in his private school in the Hospice des Incurables. After seven years of patient work and experiments and the publication of two or three pamphlets describing the work, a committee from the Academy of Sciences at Paris in 1844 examined critically and thoroughly his methods of training and educating idiot children, and reported to the Academy, giving it the highest commenda-tion and declaring that, up to the time he com-menced his labors in 1837, idiots could not be educated by any means previously known or practised, but that he had solved the problem. His work thus approved by the highest author-ity, Dr. Seguin continued his private school in Paris until the Revolution in 1848, when he came to America, where he was instrumental in establishing schools for idiots in various States.

In 1846 Dr. Seguin published his classical

and comprehensive "Treatise on Idiocy," which was crowned by the Academy and has continued to be the standard text-book for all interested in the education of idiots up to the present time. His elaborate system of teaching and training idiots consisted in the careful "adaptation of the principles of physiology, through physiological means and instruments, to the development of the dynamic, perceptive, reflective, and spontaneous functions of youth." This physiological education of defective brains as a result of systematic training of the special senses, the functions, and the muscular system, was looked upon as a visionary theory, but has been verified and confirmed by modern experiments and researches in physiological psychology.

Dr. Seguin's school was visited by scientists and philanthropists from nearly every part of the civilized world, and, his methods bearing the test of experience, other schools were soon established in other countries, based upon these methods.

In 1842 Dr. Guggenbuhl established a school upon the slope of the Abendenberg in Switzerland, for the care and training of cretins, so many of whom are found in the dark, damp valleys of the Alps. This school was very successful in its results, and attracted much attention throughout Europe. At Berlin, in 1842, a school for the instruction of idiots was opened by Dr. Saegert. In England the publication of the results of the work of Drs. Seguin, Guggenbuhl, and Saegert, and the efforts of Drs. Connolly and Reed, led to the establishment of a private school at Bath in 1846, and later to the finely appointed establishments at Colchester and Earlswood.

The published description of the methods and results of these European schools attracted much interest and attention in America. In this country the necessity and humanity of caring for and scientifically treating the insane, the deaf and dumb, and the blind had become the policy of many of our most progressive States. The class of helpless and neglected idiots who had no homes, as a rule were cared for in jails and poorhouses. A few idiots who had been received at the special schools for the deaf and dumb and the blind showed considerable improvement after a period of training. Other cases who were especially troublesome had been sent to the insane hospitals, where it was shown that the habits and behavior of this class could be changed very much for the better. In their reports for 1845 Drs. Woodward and Brigham, superintendents of the State Insane Hospitals in Massachusetts and New York respectively, urged the necessity of making public provision for the education of idiots in those States. On the 13th of January, 1846, Dr. F. P. Backus, a member of the New York Senate, made the first step toward any legislative action in this country in behalf of idiots, by moving that the portion of the last State census relating to idiots be referred to the committee on medical societies of which he was chairman. On the following day he made an able report, giving the number of idiots in the State, a brief history of the European schools, with a description of their methods and results, and showed conclusively that schools for idiots were a want of the age. On the 25th of March following he introduced a bill providing for the establishment of an asylum for idiots. The bill passed the Senate, but was defeated in the Assembly.

In Massachusetts, on the 23d of January in the same year, 1846, Judge Byington, a member of the House of Representatives, moved an order providing for the appointment of a committee to "consider the expediency of appointing commissioners to inquire into the condition of idiots in the Commonwealth, to ascertain their number, and whether anything can be done for their relief." This order was passed, and, as a result, a board of three commissioners was appointed, of which Dr. S. G. Howe was chairman. This commission made a report in part in 1847, which included a letter from Hon. G. S. [sic] Sumner, in which he described in glowing terms the methods and results of the school of Dr. Seguin in Paris. In March, 1848, the commission made a complete and exhaustive report, with statistical tables and minute details, and recommended the opening of an experimental school. This report was widely circulated and read throughout America and Europe, and furnishes to-day the basis of cyclopedic literature on this topic.

By a resolve passed on the 8th of May, 1848, the legislature appropriated $2,500 annually for the purpose of establishing an experimental school, with the proviso that ten indigent idiots from different parts of the State should be selected for instruction. This act founded the first State institution in America. The first pupil was received on the 1st of October, 1848. The direction of the school was undertaken by Dr. Howe, and for several years was carried on in connection with the Perkins Institution for the Blind, of which he was the director. Mr. J. B. Richards, an able instructor, was engaged as teacher, and went to Europe to study the methods of the foreign schools. The school was considered so successful that, at the end of three years, the legislature doubled the annual appropriation, and by incorporation converted the experimental school into a permanent one under the name of "The Massachusetts School for Idiotic and Feeble-minded Youth."

Two months after the legislature had authorized the establishment of the Massachusetts School, a private school was opened at Barre, Mass., by Dr. H. B. Wilbur, the first pupil being received in July, 1848. In the modest announcement of the project Dr. Wilbur says, "This institution is designed for the education and management of all children who by reason of mental infirmity are not fit subjects for ordinary school instruction." The school was organized on the family plan. The pupils all sat at the same table with the principal, and were constantly under the supervision of some member of the family in the hours of recreation and rest as well as of training. This private school has been continued on the same plan, and has been very successful and prosperous under the administration of Dr. Wilbur and that of his able successor, the late Dr. George Brown.

In the State of New York the legislative attempt defeated in 1846 was renewed in 1847, and this bill also passed the Senate, to be again defeated in the Assembly. The necessity for action was urged in the governor's annual messages in the years 1848, 1850, and 1851. Finally, in July, 1851, an act was passed appropriating $6,000 annually for two years, for the purpose of maintaining an experimental school for idiots. A suitable building, near Albany, was rented and the school opened in October, 1851. The trustees selected for superintendent Dr. H. B. Wilbur, who had so successfully organized and conducted the private school at Barre, Mass., for more than three years previously. In the first annual report of the trustees, published in 1851, the aims and purposes of the proposed school were summed up as follows: —

We do not propose to create or supply faculties absolutely wanting; nor to bring all grades of idiocy to the same standard of development or discipline; nor to make them all capable of sustaining creditably all the relations of a social and moral life; but rather to give to dormant faculties the greatest possible development, and to apply these awakened faculties to a useful purpose under the control of an aroused and disciplined will. At the base of all our efforts lies the principle that, as a rule, none of the faculties are absolutely wanting, but dormant, undeveloped, and imperfect.

This school attracted much attention from educators and others, and was frequently and critically inspected by the members of the legislature and other State officials. On the 11th of April, 1853, the legislature authorized the erection of new buildings. The citizens of Syracuse donated the land, and the corner-stone of the first structure in this country built expressly for the purpose of caring for and training idiots was laid Sept. 8, 1854. The school at Syracuse continued under Dr. Wilbur's direction until his death in 1883. In this school the physiological method of education has been most thoroughly and scientifically carried out, and a high degree of success attained.

Pennsylvania was the third State to take up the work. In the winter of 1852 a private school for idiots was opened in Germantown, by Mr. J. B. Richards, the first teacher in the school at South Boston. This school was incorporated April 7, 1853, as the Pennsylvania Training School for Idiotic and Feeble-minded Children. The first money received for its support was raised by private subscription, and the State contributed an equal sum. In 1855 the present site at Elwyn was secured, and the foundations laid for the present magnificent institution village with nearly a thousand inmates.

The Ohio Institution at Columbus was established April 17, 1857, and pupils were received the same year. The State of Ohio has from the beginning provided for her feeble-minded children on a more liberal and generous scale than any other State. The Columbus Institution, with its substantial buildings and splendid equipment, its admirably conducted school and industrial departments, has been made one of the best institutions in the world devoted to the care and training of this special class.

In Connecticut, in 1855, a State commission was appointed to investigate the conditions of the idiotic population, and to consider the advisability of making suitable provision for the education of this class. The report of this commission resulted in the establishment of the Connecticut School for Imbeciles at Lakeville, in 1858, under the superintendency of Dr. H. M. Knight. This school, although aided by the State, has been largely supported by private benevolence and payments from private pupils.

The Kentucky Institution at Frankfort was opened in 1860. For many years previously the State had granted an allowance of $50 per annum to each needy family afflicted with the burden of a feeble-minded child. In Illinois an experimental school for idiots and feeble-minded children was opened in 1865 as an offshoot of the school for deaf-mutes at Jacksonville. In the course of a few years this school obtained a separate organization, and new institution buildings were constructed at Lincoln and occupied in 1873. The Hillside Home, a private school, was opened at Fayville, Mass., in 1870.

·   ·   ·   ·

The early history of these pioneer State institutions in many respects was very similar. They were practically all begun as tentative experiments in the face of great public distrust and doubt as to the value of the results to be obtained. In Connecticut the commissioners found a "settled conviction of a large majority of the citizens of the Commonwealth that idiots were a class so utterly helpless that it was a waste of time even to collect any statistics regarding them." Very little was known of the causes, frequency, nature, or varieties of idiocy, or of the principles and methods to be employed in successfully training and caring for this class of persons. The annual reports of the early superintendents, Drs. Howe, Wilbur, Brown, Parrish, and Knight, exhaustively considered the subject in all relations, and graphically presented to legislators and the public convincing and unanswerable reasons as to the feasibility and necessity of granting to feeble-minded children according to their ability the same opportunities for education that were given to their more fortunate brothers and sisters in the public schools.

All of these schools were organized as strictly educational institutions. In one of his earlier reports Dr. Howe says, "It is a link in the chain of common schools, — the last indeed, but still a necessary link in order to embrace all the children in the State." Again he says, "This institution, being intended for a school, should not be converted into an asylum for incurables." Dr. Wilbur, in his seventh annual report, says, "A new institution in a new field of education has the double mission of securing the best possible results, and at the same time of making that impression upon the public mind as will give faith in its object." With the limited capacity of these schools as established, it seemed best to advocate the policy of admitting only the higher-grade cases, where the resulting improvement and development could be compared with that of normal children.

It was hoped and believed that a large proportion of this higher-grade or "improvable" class of idiots could be so developed and educated that they would be capable of supporting themselves and of creditably maintaining an independent position in the community. It was maintained that the State should not assume the permanent care of these defectives, but that they should be returned to their homes after they had been trained and educated. It was the belief of the managers that only a relatively small number of inmates could be successfully cared for in one institution. It was deemed unwise to congregate a large number of persons suffering under any common infirmity.

Nearly every one of these early institutions was opened at or near the capitals of their various States, in order that the members of the legislature might closely watch their operations and personally see their need and the results of the instruction and training of these idiots. No institution was ever abandoned or given up after having been established. In all of the institutions the applications for admission were far in excess of their capacity.

---

3. Helping idiots an "imperative duty," 1848

Samuel G. Howe, *Report Made to the Legislature of Massachusetts, Upon Idiocy* (Boston, 1848), pp. 8–17, 51–53.

In 1846 Howe was appointed to a commission charged with investigating the number and condition of idiots in Massachusetts and ascertaining whether anything could be done for their relief. After considering Howe's report the Massachusetts legislature appropriated $2,500 per annum for an experiment in teaching ten idiots. In 1850 the legislature issued to Howe and his associates a charter of incorporation for the Massachusetts School for Idiotic and Feeble-minded Youth.

Our commission is to examine into the condition of idiots. What is an idiot? — A being in the human form, but utterly devoid of sense and understanding? If so, then our report would be brief. Very few such have been found. Creatures are sometimes born of women, who are utterly wanting in the corporeal instruments by which understanding is most immediately manifested, — monsters without heads; but Nature lets none such cumber the earth; they come into life only to die; they take one short step from birth to death. A few seem to possess a brain and nervous system, but in such an abnormal condition as will not suffice even for command of muscular motion. Such creatures have only organic life. All other beings in human shape, manifest some sense and understanding.

Take the case No. 349 . . . an instance of the lowest kind of idiocy.

William ——— has the form and name of a human being, but not much else. He is at the age of early manhood, when some have gained victories in fields of war or science; but William has not yet learned enough to go alone, to feed himself, or know his own name. An intelligent dog knows more than he; and a child of two years old would be a prodigy of talent and knowledge compared with him. He lies most of the day upon a mat on the floor, rolling his lack-lustre eyes, and tossing his limbs. Sometimes they put him into a chair, and fasten him, as they do an infant, to prevent him from pitching forward. This change and approach to the human posture pleases him, but he soon slips down, and then moans and cries until they put him up again.

His natural desire for action manifests itself by his continual motions and by his cries, for he is seldom quiet when awake. He cannot feed himself, and observes not the decencies of life as well as a trained dog or cat.

Surely, it will be said, this man is an idiot; and yet he is not devoid of sense and understanding.

He knows no arbitrary language; words are to him of less import than to a horse; and yet he has a natural language that tells you he has consciousness, memory, hope, fear, and even judgment and discrimination, feeble though it be. This language, too, tells imperfectly the story of his experience; it tells what kind of treatment he has received; it tells of kindness and cruelty, of gentle and harsh tones, of curses and blows.

When he is first approached abruptly, he shows signs of fear, which you cannot mistake; he shrinks from your raised hand, and manifests signs of resistance and defence; but if you draw near to him gently, he does not shrink away; if you speak kindly to him, he smiles; if you caress him he is pleased; and if you continue your gentle attentions, you may make him yield obedience to your wishes, as far as he can understand them. He has a yet higher faculty, the sense of music; the poor creature loves sweet sounds, and, in his most uneasy moments, all his contortions of body and all his wild cries are soothed into calm, and hushed into silence, by any music.

. . . . .

It may be supposed, from the tenor of our remarks, that we are not much disposed to draw any sharp line of distinction between idiots and other human beings, and still less disposed to deny them the attributes of humanity and sink them to a level with the brutes. Indeed, if they have not even the germs of the peculiarly human faculties, then are they, though made in God's image, far lower than the brutes; for many brutes have more intelligence, and indeed more reasoning power, than the idiots of the lowest grade. We agree with Esquirol,[1] that idiocy is not a disease. We go farther, and maintain that it is impossible to fix the point at which idiocy ends and reason begins. The truth is, that extreme cases only are considered in general classifications, and lead to the popular belief, that distinctions do exist between them, which really differ only as more and less. When a man's skin begins to feel a

1. Jean Etienne Dominique Esquirol (1772–1840) was chief physician of the asylum at Charenton, France.

little dry, and he is rather thirsty, and his pulse is a very little quickened, and he feels rather ill at ease, we say he is somewhat unwell, but has no disease; — but when all these symptoms have increased in severity, until his skin is as dry as a drum-head, and his tongue rattles like a bit of baked leather in his parched mouth, and his hot blood is jerked rapidly through his tense and turgid arteries, then we say he has a fever; but no one can fix the point at which the indisposition ends, and the fever begins.

So it is with the imperfect development of intelligence of idiots. They all manifest some degree of sense and understanding; and the difference between their intelligence and that of other men, is a difference in degree, and not in kind. The light of a candle strikes the eye of the most stupid idiot, and causes sensation, perhaps thought, as of his supper; the light of a star strikes the eye of a scholar, and produces sensation, perhaps thought, as of a parallax. From the most stupid idiot up to the most brilliant genius, the distance is immense; but every step of that distance is occupied. We have names to mark the idiot, the fool, the simpleton, the weak-minded, the man of common sense, the strong-minded man, the man of talent, and the man of genius; but for the thousand intermediate grades we have no name, though we admit their existence.

Now, we claim for idiots a place in the human family. We maintain that they have the germs of the human faculties and sentiments, which in most cases may be developed. Indeed, the number of persons left by any society in a state of idiocy, is one test of the degree of advancement of that society in true and Christian civilization.

. . . . .

No systematic efforts have yet been made in this country to teach a class of these sorely bereaved creatures, but individual efforts have not been wanting in Massachusetts. The success here obtained, for the first time, in the education of persons who, by the English law, are considered to be necessarily idiots, as "wanting all those senses which furnish the human mind with ideas," has encouraged attempts to educate idiots. The results thus far are most satisfactory. In view of all these circumstances, therefore, we most earnestly recommend, that measures be at once taken to rescue this most unfortunate class from the dreadful degradation in which they now grovel.

The reasons for this are manifold, and strong, and hardly need to be repeated. In the first place, it would be an economical measure. This class of persons is always a burden upon the public. It is true, that the load is equally divided; it falls partly upon the treasury of the different towns; partly upon the state treasury, and partly upon individuals; so that the weight is not sensibly felt; but still it is not a whit the less heavy for that. There are at least a thousand persons of this class who not only contribute nothing to the commons stock, but who are ravenous consumers; who are idle and often mischievous, and who are dead weights upon the material prosperity of the State. But this is not all; they are even worse than useless; they generally require a good deal of watching to prevent their doing mischief, and they occupy considerable part of the time of more industrious and valuable persons. Now it is made certain, by what has been done in other countries, that almost every one of these men and women, if not beyond middle age, may be made to observe all the decencies of life; to be tidy in their dress, cleanly in their habits, industrious at work, and even familiar with the simple elements of knowledge. If they were all made to earn something instead of spending, wasting, and destroying, the difference would be considerable. It would be an economy to some towns to send a young idiot across the ocean if he could be trained to such habits of industry as to support himself, instead of dragging out a life of two or three score years in the almshouse, and becoming every year more stupid, degraded, and disgusting. Many a town is now paying an extra price for the support of a drivelling idiot, who, if he had been properly trained, would be earning his own livelihood,

under the care of discreet persons who would gladly board and clothe him for the sake of the work he could do.

The moral evils resulting from the existence of a thousand and more of such persons in the community are still greater than the physical ones. The spectacle of human beings reduced to a state of brutishness, and given up to the indulgence of animal appetites and passions, is not only painful, but demoralizing in the last degree. Not only young children, but "children of an older growth" are most injuriously affected by it. What virtuous parent could endure the thought of a beloved child living within the influence of an idiotic man or woman who knows none of the laws of conscience and morality, and none even of the requirements of decency? And yet, most of the idiots in our Commonwealth, unless absolutely caged up (as a few are) have, within their narrow range, some children who may mock them indeed, and tease them, but upon whom they in return inflict a more serious and lasting evil. Every such person is like an Upas tree, that poisons the whole moral atmosphere about him.

But the immediate adoption of proper means for training and teaching idiots, may be urged upon higher grounds than that of expediency, or even of charity; it may be urged upon the ground of imperative duty. It has been shown, that the number of this wretched class is fearfully great; that a large part of them are directly at the public charge; that the whole of them are at the charge of the community in one way or another, because they cannot help themselves. It has been shown, that they are not only neglected, but that, through ignorance, they are often badly treated, and cruelly wronged; that, for want of proper means of training, some of them sink from mere weakness of mind, into entire idiocy; so that, though born with a spark of intellect which might be nurtured into a flame, it is gradually extinguished, and they go down darkling to the grave, like the beasts that perish. Other countries are beginning to save such persons from their dreadful fate; and it must not longer be, that here, in the home of the Pilgrims, human beings, born with some sense, are allowed to sink into hopeless idiocy, for want of a helping hand.

Massachusetts admits the right of all her citizens to a share in the blessings of education, and she provides it liberally for all her more favored children. If some be blind or deaf, she still continues to furnish them with special instruction at great cost; and will she longer neglect the poor idiot, — the most wretched of all who are born to her, — those who are usually abandoned by their fellows, — who can never, of themselves, step up upon the platform of humanity, — will she leave them to their dreadful fate, to a life of brutishness, without an effort in their behalf?

---

4. Methods and results of instruction at New York Asylum for Idiots, 1852

New York Asylum for Idiots, *Second Annual Report, 1852* (Albany, 1853), pp. 21–30.

Dr. Hervey Backus Wilbur (1820–1883) was superintendent of the New York Asylum from its founding in 1851 until his death. His career was marked by controversy over asylum management and the care of inmates, but his own institution became a model for similar institutions in the United States, Canada, and many European countries.

The apparatus we employ is of the simplest character; a series of ladders in various positions; wooden and iron dumb-bells; a treadmill; simple blocks; boards with depressions of various shapes and sizes, with blocks to fit the depressions, to teach distinctions of form and size; cups and balls of various colors; pictures; the simpler forms of common school apparatus; black boards everywhere; special contrivances for individual cases; and last though not least, the extensive apparatus of ordinary childish sports.

With this imperfect statement of some matters that have occurred to me as aiding any one to comprehend our general plan of instruction, I will proceed to some particulars.

A certain portion of the younger and more backward pupils are placed in what may be termed the nursery department, coming into the school room only for a few moments at a time, at the opening and close of school sessions, when there is singing or other general exercises. These children are watched carefully with reference to their habits of body and mind, to the best mode of commencing our course of instruction with them — the most appropriate first steps in their pupilage. Every means that can be thought of are attempted to attract their attention to exercise their senses, to awaken perceptions, to excite the curiosity and encourage their imitative faculty.

. . . Properly belonging to these preliminary measures is the imparting an idea of language; they learn their names; they learn to obey a few simple commands, at first aided by appropriate gestures; they learn the names of different objects, names of form, of color and other properties of matter, and finally of pictures.

Arrived at this point, we may commence with exercises more resembling those of ordinary schools. We have cards with the names of familiar objects printed upon them which are learned by the pupil. Before learning the names of the letters of the alphabet they are taught to distinguish their differences of shape and even to form them into the words previously learned. With such preparation, the step is not a difficult one to learning to read by the ordinary word method. They can receive instruction in drawing on the black board, gradually passing into exercises in writing; they can receive oral lessons in geography with exercises upon the outline maps; they can be taught the simple relations of numbers.

· · · · ·

The children rise early, the older ones taking a walk in the open air or active exercises within

doors in addition to their preparation for breakfast. Considerable time is spent with the
younger and lower grades of pupils in teaching
them step by step, and little by little in the
matter of dressing themselves, from barely holding out an arm for the reception of a sleeve up
to all the mysteries of buttons, hooks and eyes
and shoe-ties.

After breakfast, the older ones make their
beds and assist in other simple household duties. All take as much exercise as possible, till
nine, the hour of school. At eleven there is a
recess of half an hour with a slight lunch.
School ends at 1/2 past 12 for the forenoon
session. Dinner is at one, consuming some
time, as we regard it of great importance to
inculcate habits of decorum, of moderation, and
general propriety. Each is required to wait till
all are helped, and then to eat slowly.

After dinner they are occupied in plays of
various sorts, till 3, when school begins again.
At 1/2 past four school closes for the day.
Then follow, with a short interval for supper,
under the supervision of intelligent persons, a
great variety of exercises and amusements. We
have military exercises for the boys; gymnastic
exercises for the girls; dancing, singing, games
of various sorts. These all deserve as high a
place in any system of education for idiots as
the more customary matters of instruction, and
they are carried on here under as much supervision as the school exercises. It is in these out
of school employments that the pupils acquire
that little every day knowledge and judgment,
that they are so entirely destitute of when they
come to us.

On the Sabbath, they are divided into smaller
companies and scattered through the house, to
encourage a more quiet deportment than on
other days. We are compelled, however, to have
systematic exercises on that day. In the afternoon, the older children have a Sunday-school,
in which they are taught simple moral duties,
scripture history in its simplest form, and children's songs.

In the evening they spend an hour listening
to the reading of such stories as are adapted to
their comprehension, manifesting much interest
and pleasure.

Were we at a more convenient access from
any house of religious worship, we have quite
a class that would conduct themselves with
propriety in attending it, and would certainly
receive one benefit from it, that of increased
reverence.

From a residence of a longer or shorter period under the circumstance and influences I
have mentioned, the results have been as described in the following cases.

.   .   .   .   .

Case No. 1.

A lad of 10 years old, well formed, healthy
and cleanly in his habits, though of rather irritable temper, and quite mischievous; he came
October 29th, 1851; he did not speak at all till
five years old; could not tell his age; did not
know a single letter; could not count or distinguish colors; was excessively timid.

Cause — had severe convulsions when a year
old, lasting for ten days.

He is now much less mischievous; less irritable and nervous; he knows two-thirds of the
letters of the alphabet; can spell quite a number
of words; can count 15; has quite an idea of
forms and colors; can form some letters on the
black-board, and is in a class in drawing, and
also in Webb's First Reader.

Case No. 2.

A boy of 10 years old, idiotic from birth;
well formed, healthy, good tempered, though
somewhat passionate; he feeds himself with his
fingers, not stopping to masticate his food; he
is inattentive to the calls of nature; came October 29th, 1852; could not speak a word; had
no idea of language, not even knowing his own
name when called; would not hold anything
in his hands except food; was excessively timid;
he now feeds himself very well with a fork;

knows his own name; will obey some simple commands; holds anything in his hands; will sit or stand still when required; can assist himself more in dressing or undressing; will pick up blocks and place them in a wheelbarrow, when commanded; will go up and down ladders when told, and takes pleasure in marching.

His father wrote, after seeing him at the end of his first three months with us: "I can truly say there was more of a change in him than I expected to see in so short a time."

CASE No. 3.

A boy of 8 years old; well formed, though walking badly; healthy, and excessively irritable; feeds himself with his fingers, and has no idea of cleanliness; has a constant habit of biting his hands, and is always covered with saliva to the waist; he came October 30th, 1852; he did not speak a word, and knew the meaning of but few words, if any.

Cause — the idiocy is ascribed by the parents to the sudden appearance of a cutaneous disease of the scalp, when one year old.

This boy was so entirely unmanageable, when first received, that we were compelled, for awhile, to forego any attempts to govern. He had not been accustomed to wearing shoes and stockings, and he resisted all our efforts to keep them on him. He would pull them off as often as they were put on, and when his hands were confined, he would stoop down and tear them off with his teeth; he screamed regularly every day, till nearly noon; in an attempt to conquer him by holding him, I was compelled to retire from the conquest vanquished, carrying the marks of his teeth in my hands for some time; I then thought I would trust to time, and the influence of the discipline of the school, to acquire control over him, taking care never to require anything of him but what I could compel him by main force to do. This course of proceeding is beginning to have the desired effect; he now obeys many little commands; is very much under the control of my will; though

one of our lowest pupils, he still manifests a very decided improvement in all respects; such was the gratifying testimony of his father who lately visited him.

CASE No. 4.

A boy of 11 years old; well formed, healthy, good tempered, and cleanly in his habits; came Nov. 7th, 1851. He speaks with occasional stammering; he was slightly mischievous in his propensities; could not be taught to read or write, or count, or distinguish colors by ordinary methods of instruction; he is now reading in a class in Webb's Reader; is in our first class in arithmetic, adding simple numbers; he is in a class in geography, and quite familiar with all the leading features of several of our series of outline maps; he is in a class in drawing on the black-board, and can also make any of the letters of the alphabet; he has much more confidence in himself; takes the lead in all the sports of childhood, and will unquestionably finish his education in a common school.

CASE No. 5.

A girl of 11 years old; peculiar from birth; now healthy. There is a peculiar form of the head in her case, and a slight deformity of the limbs; she came November 27th, 1851; she was quite mischievous, with a propensity to hide herself; could not be left alone with children, from a propensity to hurt them; very frank to confess her offences, and very penitent after committing them; she was excessively nervous and talked very indistinctly; she knew many of her letters, but could not read or write.

She has now been with us thirteen months; she is steadily improving in mental condition, as in all her habits; she is much less nervous; articulates much better; she has gone through nearly all of Webb's First Reader, and reads well what she does read; she is learning to form the letters in writing; is studying geography and arithmetic, and I think no one who should now see her, would doubt her ability eventually to master all the common school studies of children.

Her wayward propensities have almost entirely disappeared under the influence of the constant occupation of her time; she now sews very well; assists in many little domestic matters, and will in time be capable of performing all customary household duties.

CASE NO. 6.

A boy of 12 years old; very small of his age, but with an old looking face; peculiar from birth; has always been healthy.

Came May 5th, 1852; he did not speak but a few words; could not distinguish colors; had no idea of numbers, and did not know a letter. He was, in general, good tempered, though very obstinate at times.

We began with teaching him to notice distinctions of forms; then of colors. He very soon began to improve in all respects, and has been jumping from one class to another, so that he will soon be in our first class in all branches.

---

5. President Pierce's veto of the "Twelve Million Acre Bill," 1854

James O. Richardson, comp., *Messages and Papers of the Presidents, 1789–1897,* V (Washington, 1897), 247–256.

In 1848 Dorothea Dix sent a *Memorial* to Congress noting that existing hospitals and asylums could accommodate only one-twelfth of the insane population of the country and proposing federal land grants to the states to assist in caring for the insane. In 1854, after eight years of lobbying by Miss Dix, Congress passed an act apportioning 12,225,000 acres of public land among the states for the support of institutions for the insane and the deaf. President Pierce vetoed the bill on constitutional grounds and because he feared federal aid would dry up state and local "fountains of charity."

Washington, May 3, 1854.
To the Senate of the United States:

The bill entitled "An act making a grant of public lands to the several States for the benefit of indigent insane persons," which was presented to me on the 27th ultimo, has been maturely considered, and is returned to the Senate, the House in which it originated, with a statement of the objections which have required me to withhold from it my approval.

.   .   .   .   .   .

This bill . . . proposes that the Federal Government shall make provision to the amount of the value of 10,000,000 acres of land for an eleemosynary object within the several States, to be administered by the political authority of the same; and it presents at the threshold the question whether any such act on the part of the Federal Government is warranted and sanctioned by the Constitution, the provisions and principles of which are to be protected and sustained as a first and paramount duty.

It can not be questioned that if Congress has power to make provision for the indigent insane without the limits of this District it has the same power to provide for the indigent who are not insane, and thus to transfer to the Federal Government the charge of all the poor in all the States. It has the same power to provide hospitals and other local establishments for the care and cure of every species of human infirmity, and thus to assume all that duty of either public philanthropy or public necessity to the dependent, the orphan, the sick, or the needy which is now discharged by the States themselves or by corporate institutions or private endowments existing under the legislation of the States. The whole field of public beneficence is thrown open to the care and culture of the Federal Government. Generous impulses no longer encounter the limitations and control of our imperious fundamental law; for however worthy may be the present object in itself, it is only one of a class. It is not exclusively worthy of benevolent regard. Whatever considerations dictate sympathy for this particular object apply in like manner, if not in the same degree, to idiocy, to physical disease, to extreme destitution. If Congress may and ought to provide for any one of these objects, it may and ought to provide for them all. And if it be done in this case, what answer shall be given when Congress shall be called upon, as it doubtless will be, to pursue a similar course of legislation in the others? It will obviously be vain to reply that the object is worthy, but that the application has taken a wrong direction. The power will have been deliberately assumed, the general obligation will by this act have been acknowledged, and the question of means and expediency will alone be left for consideration. The decision upon the principle in any one case determines it for the whole class. The question presented, therefore, clearly is upon the constitutionality and propriety of the Federal Government assuming to enter into a novel and vast field of legislation, namely, that of providing for the care and support of all those among the people of the United States who by any form of calamity become fit objects of public philanthropy.

I readily and, I trust, feelingly acknowledge the duty incumbent on us all as men and citizens, and as among the highest and holiest of our duties, to provide for those who, in the mysterious order of Providence, are subject to want and to disease of body or mind; but I can not find any authority in the Constitution for making the Federal Government the great almoner of public charity throughout the United States. To do so would, in my judgment, be contrary to the letter and spirit of the Constitution and subversive of the whole theory upon which the Union of these States is founded. And if it were admissible to contemplate the exercise of this power for any object whatever, I can not avoid the belief that it would in the end be prejudicial rather than beneficial in the noble offices of charity to have the charge of them transferred from the States to the Federal Government . . . Can it be controverted that the great mass of the business of Government — that involved in the social relations, the internal arrangements of the body politic, the mental and moral culture of men, the development of local resources of wealth, the punishment of crimes in general, the preservation of order, the relief of the needy or otherwise unfortunate members of society — did in practice remain with the States; that none of these objects of local concern are by the Constitution expressly or impliedly prohibited to the States, and that none of them are by any express language of the Constitution transferred to the United States? Can it be claimed that any of these functions of local administration and legislation are vested in the Federal Government by any implication? I have never found anything in the Constitution which is susceptible of such a construction. No one of the enumerated powers touches the subject or has even a remote analogy to it. The powers conferred upon the United States have reference to federal relations, or to the means of accomplishing or executing things of federal relation. So also of the same character are the powers taken away from the States by enumeration. In either case the powers granted and the powers restricted were so granted or so restricted only where it was requisite for the maintenance of peace and harmony between the States or for the purpose of protecting their common interests and defending their common sovereignty against aggression from abroad or insurrection at home.

.   .   .   .   .

I can not but repeat what I have before expressed, that if the several States, many of which have already laid the foundation of munificent establishments of local beneficence, and nearly all of which are proceeding to establish them, shall be led to suppose, as, should this bill become a law, they will be, that Congress is to make provision for such objects, the fountains of charity will be dried up at home, and the several States, instead of bestowing their own means on the social wants of their own people, may themselves, through the strong temptation which appeals to states as to individuals, become humble suppliants for the bounty of the Federal Government, reversing their true relations to this Union.

.　　.　　.　　.　　.

After the most careful examination I find but two examples in the acts of Congress which furnish any precedent for the present bill, and those examples will, in my opinion, serve rather as a warning than as an inducement to tread in the same path.

The first is the act of March 3, 1819, granting a township of land to the Connecticut asylum for the education of the deaf and dumb; the second, that of April 5, 1826, making a similar grant of land to the Kentucky asylum for teaching the deaf and dumb — the first more than thirty years after the adoption of the Constitution and the second more than a quarter of a century ago. These acts were unimportant as to the amount appropriated, and so far as I can ascertain were passed on two grounds: First, that the object was a charitable one, and, secondly, that it was national. To say that it was a charitable object is only to say that it was an object of expenditure proper for the competent authority; but it no more tended to show that it was a proper object of expenditure by the United States than is any other purely local object appealing to the best sympathies of the human heart in any of the States. And the suggestion that a school for the mental culture of the deaf and dumb in Con-

necticut or Kentucky is a national object only shows how loosely this expression has been used when the purpose was to procure appropriations by Congress. It is not perceived how a school of this character is otherwise national than is any establishment of religious or moral instruction. All the pursuits of industry, everything which promotes the material or intellectual well-being of the race, every ear of corn or boll of cotton which grows, is national in the same sense, for each one of these things goes to swell the aggregate of national prosperity and happiness of the United States; but it confounds all meaning of language to say that these things are "national," as equivalent to "Federal," so as to come within any of the classes of appropriation for which Congress is authorized by the Constitution to legislate.[1]

.　　.　　.　　.　　.

The general result at which I have arrived is the necessary consequence of those views of the relative rights, powers, and duties of the States and of the Federal Government which I have long entertained and often expressed and in reference to which my convictions do but increase in force with time and experience.

I have thus discharged the unwelcome duty of respectfully stating my objections to this bill, with which I cheerfully submit the whole subject to the wisdom of Congress.

Franklin Pierce.

1. Thirty-five to fifty years after Pierce's veto, Congress, in admitting new states from the Great Plains and far West, regularly made grants to the states for charitable, educational, penal, and reformatory institutions. On this point see Best, *Deafness and the Deaf,* pp. 595–596.

B. RECOGNITION OF SPECIAL HEALTH PROBLEMS OF CHILDREN

"The American practice" in the diseases of children, 1825

William P. Dewees, *A Treatise on the Physical and Medical Treatment of Children* (Philadelphia, 1825), II, i–iv.

Dewees (1768–1841) was lecturer on midwifery at the University of Pennsylvania. His *Treatise* was the first comprehensive work by an American to approach child health in a scientific manner.

The diseases of childhood have never until lately, sufficiently engaged the attention of physicians, however strongly they have claimed it. It would be difficult to explain satisfactorily, the causes of this indifference; it may however, chiefly be ascribed to the following; 1st. To the practice of midwifery being confined almost exclusively to women, until within the last fifty or sixty years; thereby preventing the physician from seeing much of the diseases of children. 2d. In Great Britain especially, to a by-law of the Royal College of Physicians, "by which its fellows are compelled to exclude themselves from practising midwifery," thereby operating like the first cause. 3d. To a belief, that the diseases of childhood are obscure, or even unintelligible. 4th. To parents supposing that nurses and old women are more conversant with these diseases than the most enlightened physician; whereby he is deprived of the opportunity of studying them with as much diligence and accuracy, as they deserve.

But fortunately for the little sufferers, an almost entire change has been made within the years just stated, by the practice of midwifery becoming almost entirely confided to the physician; and by the public mind inclining to the belief, that the diseases of infancy may be understood, by due attention and study; and

that, there is rather more safety in the prescriptions of the physician, than in those of the nurse.

In consequence of the changes in public sentiment, the care of the diseases of childhood, has been committed to the physician; who now has the opportunity of watching them through all their changes, from the moment of birth, to that of puberty. Hence, we have within the last few years, some valuable treatises upon this subject; so many, they may appear to some, as to lead to the belief, that it is exhausted. Under this impression, the present undertaking may be thought to be unnecessary, or to require apology.

In our defence, however, we shall merely observe, that the profession of medicine must necessarily be a progressive one; and that its advancement must mainly depend upon the improvements its respective followers may make, in the exercise of its various departments; consequently, each one is bound to contribute his mite towards the general benefit . . .

.   .   .   .   .

We may urge another inducement to this undertaking; namely, that hitherto, no one on this side the Atlantic, has thought proper to give to the public at one view, the American practice in the diseases of children. This supineness of our physicians, is no less surprising than reprehensible; especially as many are so well qualified for the task by their talents, and experience, and moreover as such strong inducement was held out, by the peculiar character of our diseases, and in many instances, by the novelty and boldness, of the mode of treatment.

Hitherto, we have almost exclusively depended upon European publications for information upon almost every subject connected with medical science; and we acknowledge to have received much advantage from them; especially from their elementary works: but it must not be disguised, that the same advantage has not been derived from their practical works. This has not arisen from a deficiency either of opportunity, or of talent; for we confess both, in many instances, to have been great; but to the want of proper adaptation of their remedies, to the state, force, and peculiarity of our diseases. For it cannot escape the observation of any intelligent practitioner who may have visited both countries, how essentially our diseases are modified by climate, soil, manners, and habits; and that these modifications require corresponding changes of treatment.

Most of the diseases of this country, have a peculiarity of character, an intensity of force, and a rapidity of march, altogether unknown to European climates; and were reliance to be placed upon the feeble practice of that portion of the globe, however well suited to the state of their diseases, we should but too often have the mortification to see our patients hurried to an untimely tomb.

The diseases of childhood in this country, like those of adult age, require to be met with promptitude, and with adequate force; a temporising treatment suits not the character of their diseases; and if adopted, is almost sure to end in defeat.

.   .   .   .   .

In our account of the diseases of childhood, we shall endeavour to separate the accidental, from the characteristic, or permanent symptoms; and only detail such, as are known to accompany the disease in this country. This determination will almost necessarily confine us, to the history and treatment of such diseases only as exist in this country; and especially to those, in this part of our continent. For the history of the diseases to which children in Philadelphia, and its neighbourhood are liable, will be, we are of opinion, a pretty faithful account of almost all in this country; since the heat of our summers will have nearly as decided an influence upon their constitutions, as the sun of the Carolinas or Georgia; while

the cold of our winters, will produce consequences analogous to those of more northern latitudes.

At all events, very little mischief can arise from this mode of treating our subject; and none, which cannot be immediately repaired by any well instructed practitioner; for it will entirely consist in the proper adaptation of remedy, to the force of disease; taking it for granted, he understands its character; and in this country this is generally so uniform, as not to make him liable to much error.

Indeed, we may safely add, that the general simplicity of the diseases of children, renders their management more easy, as well as more certain than those of adults; their complaints are almost always acute, and of the sthenic kind . . .

Health problems of dependent children in institutions, 1831–1858

---

1. Ophthalmia in New York City

"Petition of the commissioners of almshouses [to the Common Council] for the accommodation of certain children affected with sore eyes, May 18, 1831," New York City Municipal Archives and Record Center, New York.

Purulent ophthalmia was a constant problem in nineteenth-century institutions for children. A serious outbreak occurred in 1831 in the children's department at Bellevue, the New York City hospital and almshouse.

The . . . commissioners of the almshouse respectfully report that they have accompanied Doctor Wood in an examination of the children at Bellevue. The whole number in the establishment is about 600 — say 400 boys and

200 girls from infants up to ten years old. About 140 of this number are affected with various degrees of contagious purulent ophthalmia or inflammation of the eyes — many are slightly affected while a great many others (principally boys) present the painful spectacle of total blindness and most appalling swellings, and redness. 25 eyes are seriously injured. Five children [are] totally blind and many [others] in . . . one eye.

This contagious inflammation was introduced from some unknown quarters about three years since. At times it has been reduced to a few cases, especially last year by separating them from the well children.

The [Commissioners] have been empowered by your predecessors to procure or erect a temporary place for these unfortunate children but have not been able to hire any suitable place, and as considerable time will be necessary to erect a permanent establishment for the children, they are of opinion that it is expedient and adviseable to erect forthwith temporary accommodations whence to remove the children who are affected with the contagion and thereby prevent the continued spread of the disease amongst those who are taken in at Bellevue and also to afford a prospect of speedy restoration to those little objects whose very appearances make an irresistible appeal to the sympathy of every beholder.[1]

2. Efforts to control ophthalmia in orphan asylums

"Report of the Board of Assistants to the Committee on Charity and Almshouses, September 24, 1832," New York City Municipal Archives and Record Center.

1. The Common Council acted favorably upon the proposal to erect separate lodgings for ophthalmia victims and purchased a property on Long Island, known later as the Long Island Farms. All the children at the Bellevue establishment were subsequently removed to the Farms.

The 1832 cholera epidemic took more than 3,500 lives in New York City during the months of July and August. One result of the epidemic was that many children were orphaned and sent to asylums.

The committee on charity and almshouse to whom was referred the annexed resolution from the Board of Aldermen's appropriation of $1,-000 to the orphan asylums in this city to aid in the support of the orphans who have been received into these institutions during the prevalence of the present epidemic, respectfully report . . .

In the Asylum at Greenwich were some 159 orphans, including both sexes — 56 of whom have been received during the existence of the cholera, some are refused admittance.

The ophthalmia still exists in this institution but this condition in this respect is much improved since May last. There are now probably fifteen or twenty in all whose eyes are affected in a greater or lesser degree.

The children are taught in the rudiments of an English education and when of proper age are bound to suitable persons. They were, at the time, at school and appeared cleanly and in good order. Their sleeping rooms were also cleanly and well ventilated.

Your Committee, however, beg leave to offer some remarks which they deem important in the preservation of health among so large a congregation of children and more particularly to prevent the introduction and spread of the ophthalmia. Children should never be permitted, whether sick or well, to sleep, work or rise in common.

Each child should be furnished with a separate bed, a separate basin of clean water and a separate napkin. In no other way can we fortify these poor children against the inroads of this distressing and hitherto obstinate disease.

The expense of napkins will be very inconsiderable inasmuch as a square yard of linen or diaper will make twelve napkins sufficiently large for all the uses necessary.

The children when this disease exists should then be divided into three classes, the healthy, the sick, and the convalescing which should never be permitted to intermingle.

The sleeping rooms should also be divided into wards and one of the nurses or superintendents should sleep in each ward with the children and always in readiness to attend to their wants during the nights.

Of the Catholic Asylum in Prince Street your committee can only speak in terms of the warmest approbation. It is an institution alike honourable to its benevolent supporters and highly creditable to the city.

The sisters of charity who have . . . the superintendance certainly merit the greatest praise for their unwearied attention to the education and wants of these helpless orphans. Their improvements in many . . . fine and ornamental branches of education would do honor to our most reputable boarding schools.

They have now in the institution 141 children including males and females — 32 of whom have been received during the existence of the present epidemic and they can accommodate 18 or 20 more when their rooms will be all filled.

They have it in contemplation to enlarge this establishment by erecting a building on the adjoining lot, where they will probably be enabled to receive all who may be offered.

The above institutions are both supported by private individual charity and are certainly deserving an encouragement from the public authority.

In recommending a concurrence with the Board of Aldermen in the adoption of the resolution, your committee are of opinion that the public moneys cannot be applied to a more charitable purpose.

---

3. "The smell of the almshouse will cling to them still," Philadelphia, 1836

Alfred Stillé, "Reminiscences of the Philadelphia Hospital" and "Additional Reminiscences of the Philadelphia Hospital" in D. Hayes Agnew et al., *History and Reminiscences of the Philadelphia Almshouse and Philadelphia Hospital* (Philadelphia, 1890), pp. 56–57, 58–59, 65–66.

Stillé (1813–1900), author of *Elements of General Pathology* (Philadelphia, 1848), was professor of the theory and practice of medicine at the University of Pennsylvania, 1864–1883.

In 1836, the buildings composing the almshouse, except the additions to the southernmost one, were substantially the same as now, but the uses of some of them were different. The southern building was then entirely occupied by the hospital — its eastern half by the male, its western half by female patients — while in the centre was the lecturing and operating amphitheatre. The east return wing was filled with insane males, and the west with insane females . . . The lying-in wards were in the west end of the building forming the northern side of the quadrangle, and the children's asylum in the corresponding part of the east end.

I lived in the children's asylum, of which I had special charge, although I had also charge of medical and surgical wards in the hospital itself. If I were asked what half-year in my professional life was the happiest, I should reply the period that I lived in that asylum. I occupied a vast chamber that looked out upon green fields and a fair river, with a view of the city beyond them. I had no companions to disturb me; I was aflame with the desire of knowledge, and all my time was eagerly devoted to the study of disease and of books.

.   .   .   .   .

. . . It was a very interesting field for me from a humanitarian as well as a medical point of view. A hundred or more children were sheltered there on their way to the early grave to which most of them were destined: Illegitimate and other outcasts formed the majority, and ophthalmia, that curse of children's asylums, made of them a blear-eyed, puny crowd, most pitiable to see. I soon became convinced of the causes that produced the crippling and mortality of these outcasts and waifs. I pointed out to the committee of the board how the disease was disseminated by the children washing in the same basins and using the same towels, and how it was maintained by their having no shaded places for exercise in the open air, and also by the insufficient food permitted them; for if the soup which they received one day was nutritious, the meat of which the soup had been made, and which formed their dinner on the following day, must necessarily be nearly devoid of nutriment. But, of course, the committee on the children's asylum and the guardians knew better than I, and at the time, at least, nothing was done to correct this wrong.

. . . . .

It seems to me that the almshouse smell must be immortal, or can only "by annhilation die." It is, or was, a smell *sui generis,* for every hospital has its specific smell. Certainly it has no resemblance to the smell of rose, or violet, or lily, nor, on the other hand, is it borrowed of asafoetida or cacodyl. It is a smell that one may recognize as a familiar acquaintance in the prisons of Naples or in the Edinburg infirmary. The smell of a civil or military hospital has its characteristics, but the effluvium of a pauper almshouse hospital has a much intenser quality. It is compounded of the exhalations of the habitually great unwashed; of effluvia generated by the decay of the sick, and the decomposition of their excretions; of the stale or rotting food that has been accumulated surreptitiously and hidden away; of steam from the meat caldron and emanations from the bakehouse or the fresh bread; from the heaps of musty old boots and festering garments thrust out of sight and fermenting in unopened closets; and then, mingling with and overlaying all of these, a certain medicinal odor which may be traced to the accumulation of tinctures, and mixtures, and unguents, and plasters, upon the

bedside tables of many patients. It is not what perfumers call a bouquet, which plays a gamut of delight upon the olfactory sense, but an acrid, foetid, sickening, musty, fusty, and above all, frowsy smell, more complex in its combination than the most ingenious compound of the perfumer's art. It is the pervading *genius loci,* and never is to be encountered outside of the walls of a pauper hospital. You cannot sweeten it; you cannot altogether expel it.

"You may scrub, you may ventilate wards as you will,
But the smell of the almshouse will cling to them still."

It can "only by annihilation die," by a fire that should consume the whole building. But the remedy is too costly.

. . . . .

As everybody knows, one gets used to foul smells, and at last ceases to notice them. Indeed, some persons seem rather to thrive in a contaminated atmosphere. So it is said that scavengers and night-soil workers acquire an immunity to certain diseases. In like manner, the inhabitants of the Nile and the Mississippi basins are said to prefer the muddy water of those streams to clear and sparkling mountain brooks. But it does not follow that the ignorant and stupid and careless should be allowed to sacrifice either themselves or those who are under their care. I cannot doubt that the day will come when it shall no longer be thought any more consistent with humanity and benevolence that almshouse paupers and hospital patients and their physicians and attendants should breathe a noisome and pestilent air, than it now is to chain maniacs to their cell walls, or strap them in "tranquillizing chairs," as was not long ago the custom.

---

4. Foundlings at Massachusetts state almshouses, 1858

Massachusetts, General Court. "Report on Public Charitable Institutions, 1858," p. 66.

One other objection to the State almshouses may be here urged, and that is the inducement they offer for mothers to have their little ones in them, or else close to them, when they . . . find their way there. Dr. Brown, of Tewksbury, thus alludes to this evil: —

The other subject to which I would refer is the mortality of our motherless infants. Most of these, no doubt, have mothers living, who have sent them to the almshouse by some one of the following expedients: — The mother may have abandoned her infant in the street, or left it with some family, without providing for its board; or, through the assistance of some friend, or *would be* benevolent individual, she may have obtained a situation at service, while the child, in such case, is sent to the almshouse, to almost certain death. Or she may have absconded from the institution, leaving her infant to its fate. No less than forty of these almshouse orphans, as they may properly be termed, have died the past year; thirty-two of which were less than one year of age, the others between one and two. No recorded statistics are at hand, but probably not more than three per cent. of these orphans, of an age less than one year when they enter the almshouse, live.

Dr. Coggswell, of Bridgewater, in remarking upon the death of children, says: —

A large number of "foundlings" and orphans are sent here during the year, from two or three days old, up to six months or a year of age. Some have lain in the streets through one night, and have gone without nourishment, no one can tell how long. They are mostly illegitimate and diseased. By the time they get here they are almost dead, and soon die; it is almost an impossibility to bring one up in one of these institutions, as the statistics too truly show. Some thirty of our deaths have been amongst this class.

Hospitals for children

1. Needed: a permanent hospital for sick children of the poor, 1852

Philopedos, pseud. ("An Ex-Dispensary Doctor"), *A Few Remarks about Sick Children in New York, and the Necessity of a Hospital for Them* (New York, 1852), pp. 11–13.

"Philopedos" has not been identified, but it is safe to assume that he was instrumental in establishing the Nursery and Child's Hospital which was organized in New York on March 1, 1854.

The sick children of the poor are so numerous — and with almost a never-ending pestilence among them — that it is proposed to establish a permanent hospital as one of the necessary measures for their relief.

For the children of the poor abundant provision is made for the peculiar wants attendant upon their condition in life. The juvenile criminal is sought that he may be reclaimed ere the habit of vice shall render him incapable of moral renovation. Schools are freely opened for the reception of all children, and in such numbers that no one, however poor, need grow up to adult age ignorant of the rudiments of knowledge; and instruction, extending even to literary and scientific accomplishment, is offered to all. Asylums for the utterly destitute offer their protection to multitudes of the helpless offspring of the city pauper, while thousands of parentless children are tenderly carried through that period of life when their very ignorance of a parent's care adds a touching interest to their claims for nurture, for protection and for guidance. Under all circumstances of ordinary destitution is the child cared for by some special method adapted to his needs, with the single exception of sickness.

. . . . .

It must be evident to all who will reflect upon the large amount of sickness there is among the children of the poor in our city, that hospital accommodations for them are among its most urgent wants. In the dwellings of the very poor there is almost always more or less absence of everything necessary for the ordinary relief of the sick, and especially of the unremitting attention that is needed by them. The necessity of constant occupation to obtain the means of existence, precludes the possibility, in a large number of instances, of devoting any time to the requirements of the sick; and it is from this want of attendance, next to want of pure air, that children suffer most. Often too, all the care and watchfulness bestowed may be rendered useless by the absence of the most necessary accommodations. This may be tolerated during health, but in sickness it is not only distressing, but positively injurious. For those who have the necessary comforts for the sick, or who have time that they may bestow upon their families, when they most require it, dispensary attendance is sufficient for their wants in sickness; but when it is known that many children are absolutely destitute of all these — indispensable as they are — the necessity of providing well-ventilated accommodations is evident; a place where all the wants of the sick may be supplied, and especially when personal care must form an essential part of the arrangement: — a need only to be supplied by the establishment of a well-organized hospital.

If it is thought by any that such children as may require removal from their homes could be accommodated in the hospitals already established, it will be necessary to state that there are not hospitals enough for the ordinary wants of our city, now containing more than half a million of inhabitants. Among so large a number of people, many more hospitals than now exist could be filled with distinct classes, either of people or of diseases. Where sickness among children exceeds to so great a degree sickness among adults . . . there will always be a sufficient number of applicants to fill any number of hospitals that will be established for their exclusive use.

The need, also, of a special hospital for children, is evident when it is considered that a large number is to be provided for, and that there should be an adaptation to the wants of a particular class of patients, who require a peculiar mode of management, and attendants *adapted* exclusively to them.

.   .   .   .   .

After a careful consideration of the truths here presented, surely no one can hesitate to do what is in his power to assist in the establishment and support of a Child's Hospital in New York.

---

2. Children's Hospital, Philadelphia, 1855

Children's Hospital of Philadelphia, *Constitution and By-laws* (Philadelphia, 1856), pp. 5–6.

"THE CHILDREN'S HOSPITAL OF PHILADELPHIA" owes its establishment to a conviction on the part of a few individuals that much of the mortality which prevails among the children of the poorer classes is owing to the want of careful medical attendance and nursing, and to the deprivation of pure and wholesome air in the narrow and densely crowded courts and houses, in which those of limited means are compelled to live. The bills of mortality of our city will show a large proportion of the deaths to have been of children under fifteen years. This will, of course, vary with the season. In winter it amounts to about one-half, while in summer, when diseases peculiar to our hot weather are so prevalent, the proportion rises to fifty-five to sixty per cent.

Most of these deaths must occur in the families of those unable to provide the necessary appliances for relieving pain and disease; and is it an unfounded supposition that some of them, at least, would have been prevented if prompt medical advice, careful nursing, and a healthy atmosphere could have been obtained?

The "Children's Hospital" was established to meet this want. It aims to supply to the children of the poor in sickness, a portion of the care and comforts which are enjoyed by the more favored classes — to surround them with circumstances favorable to recovery.

.   .   .   .   .

When the effort to establish the Hospital in this city was first made, funds were solicited to the extent of $1,800, — a sum amply sufficient, it was thought, to meet all the expenses of organization and support for the first year. This was promptly granted, and sufficient interest shown in the undertaking to warrant its projectors in starting the institution on a permanent basis, and in expecting the continued support of the benevolent.

A building has been rented and furnished, located in a central and accessible part of the city. It is not as well adapted to the purpose of a hospital as one built for the object, but it can be made to answer until our means will enable us to secure a larger and more convenient one.

It was a question among the founders of the Institution and its friends, whether the natural unwillingness of parents to intrust their offspring to the care of strangers, peculiarly strong in some classes of our poor, might not at first affect its influence, and check, to some extent, its career of usefulness. But this doubt is removed. The Institution is already, in two months from its opening, filled to its fair capacity, and with every reasonable prospect that each succeeding week will bring an increased demand on its accommodations.

If this is the fact at this comparatively healthy season of the year, what must be the case in summer, when the diseases peculiar to this climate, dysentery, diarrhea, and cholera infantum, are attacking the young, and sweeping them off by hundreds?

Many of these cases, we firmly believe, might be saved by the application of relief such as this Hospital would afford, and we earnestly desire to extend the benefit of the charity to all who need it. But to do this, we must add to our accommodations. The funds already collected will carry it on its present scale through the current year, but after that time we have no certainty of its continuance beyond a confidence that the benevolence of the community will not suffer a charity so deserving to fail for want of pecuniary support.

---

3. The children's hospital in New York City, 1857

New York State, Senate, "Report of Select Committee Appointed to Visit Charitable Institutions Supported by the State and All City and County Poor and Work-houses and Jails of the State of New York," Doc. 8, *Documents, 1857* (Albany, 1857), I, 133–134.

Under the act for the incorporation of charitable and religious societies, a number of benevolent ladies associated about three years ago for the purpose of taking charge of the children of poor women, who were compelled to leave their homes during the day to seek employment to enable them to support themselves and those dependant upon them. Children, whose mothers had died in giving them birth, were also received and provided for by nurses in the institution, and thus saved from the alms house.[1] A greater number than the society were able to accommodate asked for admission; and last year two hundred and sixty-seven children and one hundred and twenty-two women were benefited by this charity, nearly all of whom, during their residence there, required medical

---

1. On page 164 of the *Report* the Select Committee noted that children between the ages of two and five made up 74 per cent of all those who died at the children's department of the almshouse.

treatment. Mothers with infants, without a home, of good character, were received and places provided for most of them, and their children kept here at a small charge while the mother was enabled to obtain high wages in other parts of the city. Destitute, neglected and deformed children, far gone for want of proper care, were never refused admission, and often raised from an almost hopeless condition to a healthy state. It was soon found desirable to establish a hospital for the treatment of the sick children apart from those in health, and a small one was provided for the purpose, the benefits of which have been apparent the last summer, when a large number were attacked with scarlet fever; every one of whom recovered, and by this separation the others escaped the disease. The hospital is found quite too limited in its accommodations, and it is in contemplation to build one of suitable dimensions, where the society may be enabled to receive all destitute children who need hospital treatment, and which it is not to be supposed this class can find elsewhere.

The mortality in this institution is found to be about twenty per cent., which is less than in the foundling hospitals of Paris and other cities in France. The managers of this charity are assisted in their work by a board of eight distinguished physicians, some of whom are in daily attendance at the hospital, and all are serving without compensation.

It is understood the corporation of the city will give the grounds required as soon as the means are provided for the erection of the hospital; and they have already shown their estimation of the institution, by appropriating two hundred and fifty dollars towards its support. The Howard Association, of New Orleans, upon being acquainted with its objects, also sent a liberal donation for its encouragement and assistance. Large donations have been made by the citizens for the support of the institution, and upon these it must depend for current expenses hereafter; and it is supposed for this purpose they will be continued; but for carrying out the objects of the association, and providing a suitable Children's Hospital, larger means are required than the managers can at present command.

----

4. The impact of the Civil War on a children's hospital

New York City, Nursery and Child's Hospital, *Eleventh Annual Report, 1865* (New York, 1865), pp. 3–4, 9–10.

The war has imposed upon "The Nursery," as upon all other public or charitable institutions, new and unusual trials. While the burdens of the war have diminished our income, by compelling many persons to retrench all their expenditures, including their usual annual outlay in the way of charity, it has seriously enhanced the price of all the supplies necessary to maintain our institution. But while it has thus curtailed our powers for good, the war has also multiplied the calls upon us for succor. By withdrawing the men of the laboring classes from civil life into the army, it has increased the number of women of those classes who are compelled to seek our sheltering wards, or leave with us their helpless children, while they devote themselves with unremitting toil to procure a bare subsistence from day to day.

The appropriations from the State Hospital Fund and the Common Council of the city, which from time to time have been made in aid of our institution, we cannot include in our estimate of this year. We do not by any means despair, however, of this source of revenue; but we should be unfaithful to our sacred trust, and to the mute appeals of the helplessness which looks to us alone for aid under heaven, if we forbore to press upon individual benevolence the necessity of putting beyond all chance or change our ability to discharge this trust.

Mothers! fathers! come with us to our Hospital wards, lean with us over the cribs of our patient little sufferers —

"Think what pain
Makes a young child patient."

Remember the happy homes left behind us;

remember the joyous, healthful faces there, and let us endeavor, with God's help, to bring to these poor waifs on life's shore something of life's sunshine.

C. HEALTH EDUCATION AND SCHOOL HYGIENE

Teaching hygiene in the schools

1. Horace Mann on schools and children as the medium for health education of the community, 1842

Horace Mann, "The Study of Physiology in the Schools — Dissertation Upon the Subject; Report for 1842," *Annual Reports on Education* (Boston, 1868), pp. 131–144.

The study of human physiology . . . by which I mean both the laws of life and hygiene, or the rules and observances by which health can be preserved and promoted, — has claims so superior to every other, and, at the same time, so little regarded or understood by the community, that I shall ask the indulgence of the Board while I attempt to vindicate its title to the first rank in our schools, after the elementary branches.

In civilized communities, where the rates of mortality have become a statistical science, it is found that more than one fifth, almost a fourth part, of the human race die before attaining the age of one year. Instead of filling the number of threescore years and ten, — the period spoken of by the Psalmist as the allotted life of man, — almost one-quarter part of the race perish before attaining one-seventieth part of their natural term of existence. And, before the age of five years, more than a third part of all who are born have died.

After the age of two or three years, however, the annual proportion of deaths rapidly diminishes. Those children who have inherited feeble constitutions from their parents have been thinned off, and the rest have escaped the terrible slaughtering of that ignorance which presides over the nursery. Nature then seems to take them under her care; she prompts them to activity, and even counsels disobedience and stratagem to secure for them the oft-prohibited boon of exercise and outdoor air. Still a vast majority of mankind die before attaining *one-half* of that age at which the faculties of body and mind reach their fullest development and vigor. Before the age of twenty years . . . one-half of the human race are supposed to have died. Nor is this all, or the worst; for a vast portion of those who survive suffer pains which it is frightful to think upon. The sick and valetudinary, instead of being here and there an individual, are a countless host; and it is rare to find any person entirely free from all ailments, organic and functional. Instead of contributing their share to those productions and improvements by which life is sustained, and the arts of life and the resources of well-being supplied, these classes are grievous burdens upon their friends or upon society. The worldly prosperity of thousands of families is destroyed by the diseases or infirmities of one, if not both, of their heads. Children are made orphans, or mainly deprived of parental nurture and supervision; or, on the other hand, parents are bereaved of their children. And further, although it is most true that the calamity of sickness, or even of death itself, is nothing, compared with crime, yet it is also true that sickness induces poverty, which is one of the tempters to crime; and that a deranged condition of the physical system often urges to vicious and destructive indulgences by the unnatural appetites which it creates, and thus ill health becomes the parent of guilt as well as of bodily pains.

Should any one think that this view of the subject refers too much of human suffering and delinquency to an ignorance or disregard of the *physical laws*, let him learn what the most obvious and palpable of those laws enjoin; and then let him go through society, and see how systematically and flagrantly they are violated, and he will be in haste to retract his former opinion. I have the concurrent authority of many of our most eminent physicians for saying that *one-half* of all human disability, of the suffering and early death inflicted upon mankind, proceeds from ignorance, from sheer ignorance, of facts and principles which every parent, *by virtue of his parental relation*, is as much bound to know as a judge is bound to know the civil or criminal law which he undertakes to administer, or as a juror, in a case of life and death, is bound to understand the evidence on which his verdict is to be rendered. When we reflect that every child in the community, before he arrives at the age of twenty years, might and should become acquainted with those organic laws upon which the Creator of the body has made its health and vigor to depend, how worthless in the comparison becomes a knowledge of algebra, of ancient mythology or history, or of all the Grecian and Latin lore which has come down to us from author or commentator!

.   .   .   .   .

I see no way in which this knowledge can ever be universally, or even very extensively, diffused over the land, except it be through the medium of our Common Schools. All other instrumentalities for instructing mankind reach but a small part of them, and, of course, must fail extensively in accomplishing any general purpose. Only a comparatively small portion of our youth attend the higher seminaries of learning; and, while this species of knowledge is every way as important to females as to males, the latter only enjoy the benefits of our colleges or universities. Besides, the course of studies in these higher seminaries is already so full as almost to forbid the introduction of more; and those branches which have general usage and prescription in their favor will not readily yield to others, however much more intrinsically important. And hence it is that students are instructed in languages, and in the recondite truths of mathematics and astronomy; they are taught all the motions of the planets, and even the librations of the moon, as carefully as though those mighty orbs would fly from their paths or lose their balance if their course and equipoise were not prescribed anew from year to year, and to class after class; while the structure of their own bodies, and the simple and beautiful laws on which life and all our capabilities of usefulness are dependent, are almost universally neglected.

.   .   .   .   .

There is a frightful extent of ignorance on the subject of the physical laws, as they appertain to the human constitution (and in this sense only I use the phrase), pervading the whole community. Even educated men, who are not physicians, are rare exceptions to this remark. The graduated of colleges and of theological seminaries, who would be ashamed if they did not know that Alexander's horse was named Bucephalus, or had not read Middleton's octavo volume upon the Greek article, are often profoundly ignorant of the great laws which God has impressed upon their physical frame, and which, under penalty of forfeiting life and usefulness, he has commanded them to know and obey.

.   .   .   .   .

An accurate knowledge of a few great physiological principles, together with a sound judgement or discretion in applying them, will suffice to ward off an inconceivable amount of human suffering, and to confer an ability to make great additions to the public welfare, instead of subtracting from it. The Creator assures us that "he doth not afflict willingly nor grieve the children of men;" and if, in all things, the race should obey the physical laws of God, they would no more suffer physical pain, than they would suffer remorse, or moral pain, if in all things they would obey the moral laws of God.

This subject has its merits, which should command the attention of the statesman and political economist. All investments to preserve or increase the public health would be reimbursed many fold, in an increased capacity for production. One of the most important items in a nation's wealth consists in the healthfulness and vigor enjoyed by its people. All agriculturists and manufacturers must feel the force of this remark in regard to their own workmen; and they would feel it still more if they were obliged, at their own expense, to support those workmen during all periods of sickness or incapacity to labor; and this is the relation in which the State stands to its citizens . . . Omitting all considerations of personal and domestic suffering, of the extinction of intellectual power, and of those moral aberrations which originate in physical derangement and disease, — and considering the race under the mere aspect of a money-making power, — in this respect it is clear, that the health and strength of one community, if set in opposition to the debility or infirmity of another, would be sufficient, not only to determine the balance of trade, but to settle all other points of relative superiority. Let such information be diffused through the public as all the children in our schools might easily acquire, and a single generation would not pass away, without the transfer of immense sums to the other side of the profit-and-loss account in the national ledger . . .

2. Massachusetts recommends the teaching of physiology and hygiene in public schools, 1850

"An act requiring physiology and hygiene to be taught in public schools," 1850 — ch. 229, *Acts and Resolves Passed by the General Court of Massachusetts, 1850* (Boston, 1850), p. 419.

Physiology and hygiene shall hereafter be taught in all the public schools of this Commonwealth in all cases in which the school committee shall deem it expedient.

All school teachers shall hereafter be examined in their knowledge of the elementary principles of physiology and hygiene, and their ability to give instructions in the same.

This act shall take effect on and after the first day of October, one thousand eight hundred fifty-one.

3. Sanitary science as a branch of education, 1850

Massachusetts, Sanitary Commission, *Report of a General Plan for the Promotion of Public and Personal Health, Devised, Prepared and Recommended by the Commissioners Appointed Under a Resolve of the Legislature of Massachusetts, Relating to a Sanitary Survey of the State* (Boston, 1850), pp. 178–179.

This report, prepared by Lemuel Shattuck (1793–1859) and two other commissioners, and usually known as the Shattuck Report, included fifty specific recommendations for promotion of public and personal health.

We recommend that measures be taken to ascertain the amount of sickness suffered, among the scholars who attend the public schools and other seminaries of learning in the Commonwealth.

It has recently been recommended that the science of physiology be taught in the public schools; and the recommendation should be universally approved and carried into effect as soon as persons can be found capable of teaching it. Sanitary science is intimately connected with physiology, and deserves equal and even greater commendation as a branch of education. Every child should be taught, early in life, that, to preserve his own life and his own health and the lives and health of others, is one of his most important and constantly abiding duties. By obeying certain laws, or performing certain acts, his life and health may be preserved; by disobedience, or performing certain other acts, they will both be destroyed. By knowing and avoiding the causes of disease, disease itself will be avoided, and he may enjoy health and live; by ignorance of these causes and exposure to them, he may contract disease, ruin his health, and die. Every thing connected with wealth, happiness and long life depend upon health; and even the great duties of morals and religion are performed more acceptably in a healthy than in a sickly condition.

Health conditions in schools

---

1. Poor ventilation in public schools, 1845

John H. Griscom, *The Sanitary Condition of the Laboring Population of New York* (New York, 1845), pp. 11–12.

The necessity for breathing space was among the cardinal tenets of mid-nineteenth-century "sanitary science." John H. Griscom (1809–1874), a pioneer sanitarian of New York City, found overcrowding of rooms and inadequate ventilation as characteristic of schools as of tenements, factories, reformatories, and jails.

An inquiry into the amount of air allowed to children in schools, to the inmates of prisons, and to laborers in work-shops, will exhibit a degree of neglect, or ignorance, in relation to this vitality important subject, in individuals having the training and guardianship of these classes, truly lamentable, as well as surprising. For examples.

One of the Public Infant Schools of this city, having an average attendance the year round, of 200 children, was for a long time, and until recently, kept in the basement of a church, the dimensions of which were 46 × 30 × 8½ feet, equal to 11730 cubic feet. The proximity of the adjoining buildings rendered it so dark in a sunny day, it was difficult to see to write on a slate a short distance from the windows. A large stove warmed the room in winter. These children had about sixty cubic feet each, for the six school hours, equal to ten cubic feet per hour, when each child should have ten cubic feet per minute. Ventilation was unthought of, until recently, and now in consequence of the position and arrangement of the building, it is very imperfect.

The dormitories of the House of Refuge have each an area of less than 200 cubic feet. When the door is closed on the inmate, his bed, which is about eighteen inches from the floor, is extended nearly across the cell, diminishing by so much its atmospheric area, and intercepting almost wholly the communication between a very small opening at the bottom, and another at the top, and one in the middle, of the door. Those openings were intended, but are wholly inadequate, for ventilation, even if no bed were there. For the perfect decarbonization of the blood, the air in each dormitory, at the lowest proper estimate, will remain sufficiently pure for the space of thirty minutes only, yet the youthful inmates are locked in from 8 P.M. till 5 A.M. nine hours, with no other ventilation than what I have described. Their work-shops cannot be said to be much better supplied with air. The effects of this privation are plainly marked upon the countenances, and general physical development, of the children.

The general arrangement of the cells in the City Prison is but little if any better. Besides the small window near the ceiling on one side, air is admitted only through five auger holes in the door on the opposite side, and these latter are of no service at night, when the inner door is closed.

this evil will not be so sorely felt as it would be in cities less happily constructed. Broadway, when graded and set with trees, according to the plan which has been commenced, will afford a promenade as beautiful as could be desired.

2. Public schools in Louisville, Kentucky, 1849

L. P. Yandell, "Sanitary Condition of Louisville, Kentucky," *Transactions* of the American Medical Association, II (1849), 615.

Early public schools often met in converted houses, hotels, or stores rather than in buildings specially designed and constructed as schoolhouses.

The public schools, twenty-four in number, are open to children at the age of six years, and all are crowded. The system is one which calls for reform in several particulars. Too many scholars are congregated in a room, either for health, or for mental or moral improvement. In some, there are as many as 130; and in none, less than 60. The largest rooms are not forty feet square, and many are of much smaller size. The children are kept in them from three to four hours in the morning, and two and a half to three hours in the afternoon. The long vacation is in summer, and lasts six or seven weeks. The health of the children is good. The number of teachers in the several schools is too small. It is not possible for the children to take exercise in the small yards connected with the schools, and they are consequently forced into the streets to enjoy it. Louisville, by a fatal oversight, neglected to provide grounds, when she might, for the exercise and recreation of her children, and now the opportunity has passed away. Fortunately, her streets are so wide that, planted as they are with fine trees,

3. "Are our public schools injuring the bodies of our children?" 1855

The American Medical Monthly, IV (1855), 411–412.

There is not a more important interest in the State than the Common School. Occupying the exclusive attention of those who are to be the men and women of the next generation, for many hours of each day, its influence upon society can scarcely be overrated, and any error of physical training that by implication or by constitution it circulates becomes a serious wrong.

We have often queried whether there were not something decidedly wrong in the amount of time that the Common School demands of our children for study, and in the still greater amount that it spoils for recreation.

Our city schools require — and it amounts to about the same thing throughout the State — that the scholar shall be on hand from 9 o'clock to 12, and from 12½ to 3. Now 5½ hours would not be too much for any healthful child, if with the ringing of the dismissal bell there came a season of relaxation until nine of the next day. But when we meet our boy of ten years old returning from school, we find him always loaded down with books — geography, astronomy, physiology, and half a score of the sort beside — in several of which he assures us that he must get a lesson before morning. And upon further inquiry, we find that except exercises in arithmetic, reading, spelling, and writing, all his studying is to be done out of school hours! Of course, if he is bright, he soon learns how to make short work of his lessons, and by hurried or stolen reviews in school to "stuff" for recitation. But if he is dull, he has a harder lot. Coming home from school he is jaded and weary. He loathes the sight of a book. He longs to put his old "trowsers" on and kneel in the gutter or on the crossing to have one good game of marbles, or he agonizes for a game at ball, or "tag." He wants to expand his lungs and stretch his legs, and shake himself unhampered by a nice coat and out of the sight of grumbling teachers or guardians.

The prudent parent may consent to this in the summer time, but in winter there is no larger margin for play between the last hour of school and the first of night than a supper of proper length should entirely occupy, and none like to have their children out rioting after dark. Then, with the coming dark, the lad must sit down to his books. Under the most favorable circumstances he shares a light with the other members of the family, and while they talk of new dresses and gossip of the day's affairs, he must keep his attention on problems that he abominates, or strive perpetually to commit to memory dates, names, figures, in which he can have no mortal interest. He is three times as long about it as if he had learned the same lesson in school; has acquired a habit of studying lazily, or rather has fallen into a habit of "mocking" over books and calling it study, besides finding his temper soured, and his spirits broken by the constant repetition of rebukes that really kind parents and sisters inflict upon him for listening to their conversation rather than attending to his business. But with the end of his labors it is bed-time, and with the end of breakfast it is school-time again. So whatever of recreation, whatever of physical training, whatever of development of muscle or

exercise of body he gets, is stolen during the week or lumped together upon Saturday, when there is no school.

Our Board of Education and excellent corps of teachers could scarcely adopt a more ingenious device to secure a generation of puny people. They inject great quantities of elementary knowledge into the mind, and surfeit it where they should feed it with the greatest care. The body is ignored — its organs recognized only as things to be mortified. They struggle vigorously to crowd boys into the Free Academy, but take very feeble measures to prepare them to face the world and take part in its stern conflicts. Our own impression is — perhaps it may be a crude and undigested one — that the five and a half or six hours a day are an ample time to detain young children upon any intellectual exercise that is not positively alluring to them. We are not alarmed lest our children should study too much — they and nature conspire to prevent any such evil. But nature and the child together are incompetent to prevent the wrong that our system imposes in abbreviating the hours of physical exercise.

We are aware that some of the order and fine show of the school-room must be sacrificed if this doctrine is adopted. But, we think, neither the health of the scholar nor the convenience of families can afford to construe our school-rooms into mere recitation-rooms, or halls in which to parade the military precision of classes. Let the school hours be divided between recitation and study, and the scholar will have time enough for necessary exercise. The body will be encouraged to keep pace with the growing intellect. The winter evenings will come to be envied seasons of rest, of and for pleasant reading. What is now a drudgery and a bore to so many — the Common School — would become a pleasure, and of course a most certain profit.

D. HEALTH HAZARDS OF URBAN CHILDREN

Bad housing

1. Human costs of urbanization and civilization, 1845

Griscom, *Sanitary Condition of the Laboring Population of New York City*, pp. 4–5, 21.

Griscom's study was inspired by Edward Chadwick's *Sanitary Condition of the Labouring Population of Great Britain* (1842) and was intended to promote a similarly comprehensive investigation of sanitary conditions in New York. For a summary of Griscom's efforts on behalf of sanitary reform a decade and a half after the 1845 study, see his *Sanitary Legislation, Past and Future: The Value of Sanitary Reform, and the True Principles for Its Attainment* (New York, 1861).

At all seasons of the year, there is an amount of sickness and death in this, as in all large cities, far beyond those of less densely peopled, more airy and open places, such as country residences. Even in villages of small size, there is an observable difference over the isolated country dwelling, in the proportionate amount of disease prevailing; proving conclusively that the congregation of animal and vegetable matters, with their constant effluvia, which has less chance of escape from the premises, in proportion to the absence of free circulation of air, is detrimental to the health of the inhabitants.

These circumstances have never yet been investigated in this city, as they should be. Our people, especially the more destitute, have been allowed to live out their brief lives in tainted and unwholesome atmospheres, and be subject to the silent and invisible encroachments of destructive agencies from every direction, with-

out one warning voice being raised to point to them their danger, and without an effort to rescue them from their impending fate . . .

It is of course among the poorer labouring classes that such knowledge is most wanted. The rich, though they may be equally ignorant of the laws of life, and of the best means of its preservation, live in larger houses, with freer ventilation, and upon food better adapted to support health and life. Their means of obtaining greater comforts and more luxuries, are to them, though perhaps unconsciously, the very reason of their prolonged lives. Besides this, they are less harassed by the fears and uncertainty of obtaining for themselves and families a sufficiency of food and clothing. They are thus relieved of some of the most depressing influences, which tend to reduce the energy of mind and body in the poor, and render the latter more susceptible to the inroads of disease.

Sanitary regulations affect the pauper class of the population more directly than any other, because they live in situations and circumstances which expose them more to attacks of disease. They are more crowded, they live more in cellars, their apartments are less ventilated, and more exposed to vapours and other emanations, &c., hence, ventilation, sewerage, and all other sanitary regulations, are more necessary for them, and would produce a greater comparative change in their condition.

.   .   .   .   .

It is ascertained that in civilized communities, one-fourth part of all the human race who are born, die before attaining their first year; more than one-third before arriving at five years of age, and before the age of twenty, one half the human race, it is supposed, cease to exist. On referring to the last two annual reports of the mortality of this city, I observe that of the persons who *have died*, about the same proportion as is above stated, of all who are *born*, that is, about one-fourth died in the first year, about one-third before five years, *but more than one half* before twenty years of age.

No facts would speak in louder tones of the injurious operations of the circumstances of civilized life. That one-half should die before arriving fairly upon the broad platform of strength, usefulness, and hope in the world, is the significant finger pointing with unerring certainty to the sins of ignorance, and abuse of the bountiful and unfailing means of life and comfort lavished upon us by Providence, which lie at our doors. Can this ignorance of the laws of health be excused, or can this abuse of Heaven's bounties be defended? There can be no justification for either in the eye of the Creator and Giver of all things.

The savages who live in the caves of the earth, because they have neither the knowledge, nor means, to build houses, are pardonable; yet their natural instincts teach them the uses and necessity of fresh air and exercise. Yet we, who claim to be intelligent and civilized, who are taught the minutest particulars of nature's laws, suffer our numbers and strength, the bones, and sinews, and hearts of our people, to waste and die away in narrow and gloomy caverns of our own construction, with a rapidity surpassing that of the combined torrents of pestilence and war. Our sin is the greater that we permit these things in the midst of the light of science, and under the inspiring dictates of a religion, whose most prominent features are charity and love.

---

2. "This crowded mode of living," 1852

Philopedos, *Sick Children in New York*, pp. 3–10.

The population of the city of New York in the year 1850, was 515,392, and the number of deaths was *one* in *thirty-three*. The same census gives *one* in *sixty-seven* as the proportion of the deaths to the living population in the other parts of the State. This difference in the rate of mortality, in the city and country, appears to indicate the prevalence of more health, and a far better prospect of longevity among the inhabitants of the rural parts of the State; and the difference between the two is a matter of surprise, and, by many, can scarcely be credited. It is, however, perfectly accurate, and, so far as the city is concerned, received its corroboration from the report of the City Inspector for that year . . . [The report] also supplies another species of information of considerable importance, in explanation of the difference, and which can be obtained by referring to the table containing the *ages* of the deceased. It will there be seen that 8,052, or 61 per cent. of these deaths, were children under the age of ten years. In the year 1851 there were 22,024 deaths reported; of which number 11,856, or 54 per cent., were children at the same ages. During the seven weeks of the present year (1852) ending on the 28th of August, there were reported 3,712 deaths, of which number there were 2,480, or 66.81 per cent. children under the age of ten years. On examining also these records for a number of years past, the fact of the immense mortality among them, is one of the most prominent there mentioned; 49 per cent. being the average number for a period of sixteen years. It is evident, therefore, that the excess in the number of deaths for the city, is made up exclusively of young children, to an extent that is truly alarming.

Not only is this mortality excessive, but it appears also to have been upon the increase. This will appear, by comparing the number of deaths with the population at the different census periods; thus, in 1835, the deaths were as 1 in 46.87; in 1840, 1 in 39.74; in 1845, 1 in 37.55, and in 1850, 1 in 33.52.

The causes of this fatality among the younger portion of the population, must be referred to the peculiar condition in which people live in cities, acting especially upon such as are most liable to receive physical impressions. This condition is that of crowding a vast number of people in comparatively a small space, and the effect is the deterioration of the air that they breathe.

.   .   .   .   .

In a city like ours, the air, in over-crowded houses, must . . . become exceedingly impure. In summer, such a state of living becomes almost insupportable, and in some of the poorer parts, the doors, windows and steps may be seen in the evening crowded with people endeavoring instinctively to obtain a little fresh air.

As was just remarked, children suffer most from this crowded mode of living, and it is the children of the extremely poor that die in such frightful numbers and swell so enormously our city bills of mortality.

Many persons are ignorant of the large number of people that are in one house among the poor. The average number in an ordinary sized house is about fifty; and it is by no means unusual to find six permanent occupants of one room, and it is known to have reached the number of twenty.

All this is bad enough where the houses stand side by side fronting the street with some space in the rear; but it is inconceivably worse where every available spot of ground is occupied by some kind of building, and where double or treble the proper number are crowded together with barely space enough among them to reach the different entrances.

.   .   .   .   .

A more particular sketch, however, may be necessary to give the reader some idea of the needs of those who suffer most in such habitations, and for whom all must feel some interest.

Go with me, therefore, kind reader, on a visit to some of my dispensary patients. The scenes will of necessity be for you but the pictures of the imagination; for me they will be the strong reminiscences of the truthful scenes of years now long past.

Here is my memorandum. In addition to the name and number of the street, it has this ob-servation, "*Chd.* 3 *f. f.*," which, translated into English, means "child, 3d floor, front." Here it is: an old house, the "3 *f. f.*," proves to be the upper floor of the building, next to the roof. There is no plastering, and the sun's rays streaming upon it, produces a great intensity of heat, which rarifies the air beneath it, while from the construction of the house, and from its situation, closely surrounded by others, there can be no direct passage of air from without; what little arrives, there comes through the midst of a score or two of people below. Both these causes so affect the air as to make it impossible to receive at each inspiration a sufficiency of oxygen to satisfy the hungry lungs; we feel that we are on an allowance, and are suffering lassitude and even faintness, and that if such a state of prostration should continue, we could not retain vital energy enough to resist the invasion of disease.

There are three little people sweltering in this air, for whom I am expected to prescribe. To direct any kind of medicine to be given to them is positively absurd; it is disheartening to visit such a place, and to be required to relieve physical suffering when the first and indispensible pabulum of life is wanting. We must leave them for the present, and endeavor, before our next visit, to devise something that, professionally speaking, "will fulfil the indication."

Let us change the scene from the heat of our tropical summer to the intensity of our winter's cold. "3*r. row b.*," which means "3d house, rotten row-basement." Every city has its "rotten row," and doubtless dozens of them. It is a favorite term, and a highly expressive one. The one I now refer to, stood — if that term is a suitable one — precisely where the building of the Northern Dispensary now stands. It was a row of very old houses which cannot be better described than it is by the name that was given to it.

When it rained hard, the cellars were over-flowed with water. The numerous crevices and openings caused but little difference in the winter's temperature outside or inside of some inhabited parts of "Rotten Row." One of these is the cellar which we are now to visit. There, upon a pile of shavings gathered for fuel, portions of which adhere in hard frozen lumps, lies the mother of the child I am to prescribe for. She is dead drunk. One of the children is clambering over the mother, making vain attempts to awake her. The sick child, a neighbor informs me, has been taken into temporary charge by her, as it appeared to be perishing with cold. The natural instinct to render assistance to the helpless, or perhaps the exercise of the Christian principal of benevolence, has been exerted to relieve this little child from present suffering.

.　　.　　.　　.　　.

Let us visit "Rotten Row" in summer. We will enter again one of these dilapidated cellars. Why, the floor is covered with water! True, it rained hard last night, and these places are generally so after a hard rain: the water is only about half an inch in depth, and you observe that bricks are placed at convenient distances for stepping to the bedside, that the feet may not get wet. It is of very little importance to know what form of disease it is that we see in the bed, or what description of person lies prostrated by it; whether the robust man or feeble woman — the aged, whose day is rapidly closing, or the young child, whose morning has but just dawned — all present a hopeless task for him who would relieve them by the resources of the medical art.

I once knew a pool of water, that was in an area, burst through the foundation of a house, and empty itself into a room where people were sleeping, carrying with it a quantity of mud and sand; it is even said that some have in this way been drowned. Besides the heavy rains that overflow these places, the water not unfrequently gets into them by the tide rising, and people living in them have barely escaped with their lives. In one instance, on the extraordinary rise of the tide in a cellar in Washington street, it disturbed *thirteen* people, four adults, and nine children, during their sleep.

With or without excessive rains or unusually high tides, these places are always damp, and are thereby a continued source of various inflammatory diseases, rendered more complicated and unmanageable by the positive deterioration of the air from want of ventilation; indeed, the occupants of cellars are always sick in a never-ending rotation. Sickness among the poor is always great, and in these damp and badly-ventilated places is more protracted, besides being more fatal, especially among children, than above ground. More than two-thirds suffer some lingering disease, existing among such as are almost constantly exposed to the causes that are always in action in such places, as women and children. They pass most of their time, both day and night, in the confined air of their abodes, while the men pass the day at their usual out-door work, and are under "*home influences*" only at night. In many of these places the floors are rotten, and impart an odor peculiar to decaying wood, while the whole has a chilly feeling, and yields a damp earthly odor, strongly suggestive of the odor of a vault. It cannot, therefore, be a subject for wonder that, in proportion to the number of inhabitants, the demands for medical services should be much more numerous by the inhabitants of cellars than by others.

Another memorandum indicates that I have been desired to call at No. — ———— street, "*ch'd. f. b.*," which means "child, front basement." Here is the house. The door is locked. Knock. No response. Knock again. Still no notice is taken of us; it is evident that we can not gain admittance. We will not go away yet. I have had some experience in these matters before. Sick people are not in the habit of being removed when the doctor is sent for. Yonder is a little window through which we may look, and perhaps learn something of the state of things within, and of the reason wherefore we could not be admitted. Let us look into the apartment. Every thing is rather obscure, but as the eye becomes accustomed to the gloom, objects gradually appear with more distinctness. There are evidently two children in that room; one lying on a bed, and the other sitting on the floor amusing itself with some uncouth play-things. Now the condition of things is better understood. The mother has left these children alone, while she has gone to earn a trifle by a day's work. This is the reason also that a request, of which I took no memorandum, was left that I would call at a designated hour, at which time she doubtless left her work, and went home to see her little ones and meet the doctor. My engagements not permitting me to call at the time desired, she had again locked them in and had gone to finish her day's work. We can see things in the room a little more clearly; the little one on the bed has a highly flushed cheek, and is, no doubt, burning with fever, while there is no one — nor will there be for many hours — even to give it a drink of water. God help you, my poor little creature, in your loneliness and suffering!

Still another memorandum to visit a cellar. This one is in a rear building. The house is one of those that has been built on the rear of a lot of ground, even after it would appear that every spot on it had already its house. It is completely hemmed in, and as we descend, observe how extremely dark it is. In addition to the want of ventilation so common to all such places, there is a remarkable absence of light. From the position of the room the rays of the sun have never reached it, and it appears doomed to un-interrupted murkiness and gloom. Notice the inmates, how pale they are! what a waxen, cadaverous complexion these children have! the very lips are pale and the whole face is puffy and destitute of expression. The father and one child died about a month since, and the entire family appear to have been always sick.

.   .   .   .   .

Go with me now, after the lapse of a fort-night, to the New York Hospital, whither these children with their mother were sent. I must repeat the remark that this is no picture drawn by the imagination, but a simple truth. They begin to look as children should look. The first tinges of the ruddy hue of health have already appeared. They are cheerful and play-ful. What has brought about all this change? Not a particle of medicine has been given, but they have been placed in a large, light, and well-ventilated ward, while they have been sup-plied with ordinary healthy nourishment.

We may form an idea from this sketch of the causes of some of the sufferings of the poor, and learn also that those who have the least to do with the production of these causes and with any arrangement necessary for their physi-cal comfort — such as can have no thought whatever upon the subject — are the principal victims.

It is certainly a remarkable fact, that those who could have had no agency whatever in causing the evils they suffer, should be among those that are first and the most grievously punished . . .

---

3. Tenements and health, ca. 1866

Stephen Smith, *The City That Was* (New York 1911), pp. 18–21.

Stephen Smith (1823–1922), surgeon and pioneer in public health, was principal author of New York City's Metropolitan Health Law of 1866 and commissioner of the Board of Health, 1868–1875. *The City That Was* de-scribes the sanitary condition of New York before 1866.

From the year 1622 to the year 1866, a period of two hundred and forty-four years, the people elected that the city should be unhealthy. The land was practically undrained; the drink-ing water was from shallow wells, befouled by street, stable, privy, and other filth; there were no adequate sewers to remove the accumulating waste; the streets were the receptacles of gar-bage; offensive trades were located among the dwellings; the natural water courses and springs were obstructed in the construction of streets and dwellings, thus causing soakage of large areas of land, and stagnant pools of polluted water.

Later, in these centuries of neglect of sanitary precautions, came the immigrants from every nation of the world, representing for the most part the poorest and most ignorant class of their respective nationalities. This influx of people led to the construction of the tenement house by landowners, whose aim was to build so as to incur the least possible expense and accommodate the greatest possible number. In dark, unventilated, uninhabitable structures these wretched, persecuted people were herded together, in cellars and garrets, as well as in the body of the building, until New York had the largest population to a square acre of any civilized city.

The people had not only chosen to conserve all the natural conditions unfavorable to health, but had steadily added unhygienic factors in their methods of developing the city.

The result was inevitable. New York gradually became the natural home of every variety of contagious disease, and the favorite resort of foreign pestilences. Smallpox, scarlet fever, measles, diphtheria, were domestic pestilences with which the people were so familiar that they regarded them as necessary features of childhood. Malarial fevers, caused by the mosquitoes bred in the marshes, which were perfect culturebeds, were regularly announced in the autumnal months as having appeared with their "usual severity." The "White Plague," or consumption, was the common inheritance of the poor and rich alike.

With the immigrant, came typhus and typhoid fevers, which resistlessly swept through the tenement houses, decimating the poverty-stricken tenants. At intervals, the great oriental plague, Asiatic cholera, swooped down upon the city with fatal energy and gathered its enormous harvest of dead. Even "Yellow Fever," the great pestilence of the tropics, made occasional incursions and found a most congenial field for its operations.

Failure to improve the unhealthy conditions of the city, and the tendency to aggravate them by a large increase of the tenement-house population, offensive trades, accumulations of domestic waste, and the filth of streets, stables, and privy pits, then universal, caused an enormous sacrifice of life, especially among children. This fact is strikingly illustrated by the following comparison of figures taken from the official records.

The standard ratio of deaths to the total living in a community, where the death-rate is normal under proper sanitary conditions, has been fixed by competent authority at about 15 in 1,000 of population. The death-rate in New York, in the five years preceding 1866, averaged 38 in 1,000 population, which is 23 in excess of the normal standard of 15 in the 1,000. In a city with a population of 1,000,000, the estimated population of New York in 1865, a death-rate of 38 in the 1,000 means 23,000 deaths annually from preventable diseases.

. . . The lesson which these figures teach should be engraven on the memory of every man, woman, and child.

Impure milk

1. Dairies and distilleries, 1842

Robert M. Hartley, *An Historical, Scientific, and Practical Essay on Milk, as an Article of Human Sustenance; with a Consideration of the Effects Consequent upon the Present Unnatural Methods of Producing it for the Supply of Large Cities* (New York, 1842), pp. 139–143.

Hartley (1796–1881) was one of the founders (1843), and for many years secretary, of the New York Association for Improving the Condition of the Poor.

Is any one . . . still skeptical as to the pernicious quality of the milk with which he is supplied, or as to the patronage he is indirectly giving the distiller, though he uses not a drop of alcohol in any form as a beverage, let him accompany his milkman to his dairy, and, nineteen chances out of twenty, his doubts will be removed by a full demonstration of the facts insisted upon. If the wind is in the right quarter, he will smell the dairy a mile off; and on reaching it, his visual and nasal organs will, without any affectation of squeamishness, be so offended at the filth and effluvia which abounds, that still-slop milk will probably become the object of his unutterable loathing the remainder of his life. His attention will probably be first drawn to a huge distillery, sending out its tartarian fumes, and, blackened with age and smoke, casting a sombre air all around. Contiguous thereto, he will see numerous low, flat pens in which many hundreds of cows, owned by different persons, are closely huddled together, amid confined air, and the stench of their own excrements. He will also see the various appendages and troughs to conduct and receive the hot slush from the still with which to gorge the stomachs of these unfortunate animals, and all within an area of a few hundred yards. He will discern, moreover, numerous slush-carts in waiting and in motion, for the supply of distant dairies; empty milk-wagons returning, and others with replenished cans, as constantly departing. Moored off in the distance, he will, perhaps, discover a schooner discharging her freight of golden grain into huge carts, each drawn by four oxen, employed to convey it to the distillery mill, which, grinding at the rate of one hundred bushels per hour, rapidly converts the nutritious substance into slop and whisky, to "scatter firebrands, arrows and death," through the community.

This sketch, though drawn from actual observation, very inadequately represents one of the still-slop milk and whisky manufactories, in the vicinity of New-York. Description, to be effective, must be more minute . . .

The situation of Johnson's distilleries, and the manner of feeding the cattle with hot slop by means of gutters, etc., has already been given. The dairies have been formed around the distilleries, for the purpose of consuming on the spot the slop refuse of this extensive concern, which, as we were informed, distills about *one thousand* bushels of grain daily. The cowpens are rude, unsightly wooden buildings, varying from fifty to two hundred feet in length, and about thirty feet in breadth. They are very irregularly arranged, so as to cover the entire ground, excepting narrow avenues between; and appear to have been temporarily constructed, as the arrival of new dairies required enlargements for their accommodation. It is said they will contain about two thousand head of cattle, but this estimate, we would judge, is an exaggeration. The stalls are rented by the proprietor of the distilleries to the different cow owners, at from four to five dollars a year per each head of cattle, while the slop is furnished at nine cents a barrel. Slop constituting both food and drink, water and hay or other solid or gramineous fodder, supply no part of the wants to these abused animals. The fluid element, indeed, appears not to be in request for purifying purposes. Fountains of pure water, extensive hay-ricks, capacious out-houses, and similar conveniences, which are ordinarily deemed so important for the feeding and watering so large a stock, are here dispensed with as unnecessary appendages to a city dairy.

The interior of the pens corresponds with the general bad arrangement and repulsive appearance of the exterior. Most of the cattle stand in rows of from seven to ten across the building, head to head and tail to tail alternately. There is a passage in the rear for cleaning, and another in front which gives access to the heads of the cattle. The floor is gently inclined, but no litter is allowed. The stalls are three feet wide, with a partition between each, and a ceiling about seven feet high overhead. But the chief and most inexusable defects are the want of ventilation and cleanliness, though in the latter respect, since public attention has been called to their vile condition, they are somewhat improved. There appears, however, no contrivance for washing the pens, or by which a circulation of air can be produced.

.   .   .   .   .

Such, then, as described, is the barbarous and unnatural treatment of this docile, inoffensive and unfortunate animal, that is destined to supply us with nutriment, both when living and dead, and which is one of the most valuable gifts of Providence to ungrateful men. Here, in a stagnant and empoisoned atmosphere that is saturated with the hot steam of whisky slop, and loaded with carbonic acid gas, and other impurities arising from the breath, the perspiration, and excrements of hundreds of sickly cattle, they are condemned to live, or rather to die on rum-slush. For the space of *nine months,* they are usually tied to the same spot, from which, if they live so long, they are not permitted to stir, excepting, indeed they become so diseased as to be utterly useless for the dairy. They are, in a word, *never unloosed while they are retained as milkers.* In some few cases the cattle have stood in the same stalls for fifteen or eighteen months; but so rapid is the progress of disease under this barbarous treatment, that such instances are exceptions to the general rule, and of very rare occurrence. Facts show that all the conditions necessary to the maintenance of health and life, are recklessly violated to an extent which, if not well authenticated, might appear incredible in a Christian community. Of course, by a law of physical nature, the digestion of the animals becomes impaired, the secretions vitiated, loathsome and fatal diseases are engendered, and if not seasonably slaughtered, and eaten by our citizens, the abused creatures die, and their flayed carcases are thrown into the river.

---

2. Effects of swill-milk diet on child health, 1858

Letter from Dr. John H. Griscom in New York City, Board of Health, *Majority and Minority*

Reports of the Select Committee of the Board of Health Appointed to Investigate the Character and Condition of the Source from which Cow's Milk is Derived for Sale in the City of New York . . . (New York, 1858), pp. 294–297.

In 1862 the New York state legislature passed an act making it a misdemeanor to "keep cows for the production of milk for market, or for sale or exchange, in a crowded unhealthy condition, or feed the same on food that produces impure, diseased, or unwholesome milk." See David T. Valentine, comp., *A Compilation of the Laws of the State of New York Relating Particularly to the City of New York* (New York, 1862), p. 965.

It seems scarcely necessary to reiterate the opinion which has been so often expressed by myself and others as to the value of good milk as an article of diet, and the disastrous effects of the impure substances which are called milk, and which are in great quantities supplied to our citizens, possessing scarcely any of the attributes of that important article of consumption. Medical books contain abundant evidence of the deleterious effects of an imperfect diet in children, and that swill milk is an article of that description is indisputable . . . That swill milk *will not coagulate* as readily or as perfectly as pure milk, shows that it is not milk in the proper sense of that word, though it may have been drawn from the source whence milk is taken. The microscope reveals the fact that the butter globules of this villainous stuff are essentially different from those of pure milk; and it is a well established law that any change in the mechanical organization of a compound body is an indication of a change in its physiological and chemical constitution. Pure milk, whose butter globules are always the same under the microscope, is the most wholesome food that can be given to a child; but swill milk is exactly the reverse. The property of coagulation of the milk is essential to its digestion. In the case of pure milk the gastric juice effects that process in *a few minutes* in the stomach, and the process of digestion and nutrition goes rapidly on. But with swill milk, coagulation requires sometimes as many hours as the other requires minutes. Without this coagulation in the stomach there can be no digestion, and no nutrition, and the mass of impure substance either remains in the stomach undigested, producing distressing symptoms of various kinds, or passes into the bowels, resulting in diarrhea, dysentery, cholera morbus, and many other direct diseases, besides numerous secondary ills not so apparent to the common observer, but which may be traced by the eye of the physician to the influence of impure or insufficient food.

If, in addition to the statements and illustrations already made upon this subject, any argument is needed by our fellow-citizens to prove the influence, direct and indirect, of impure diet, and examination of our necrological records will furnish it. For example, the total number of deaths of persons under five years of age in 1856 was 13,373. Of this number the deaths from diseases attributable, more or less directly, to defective diet and bad air, amounted to nearly one-half, viz, 6,558 . . .

In considering this dark catalogue of infants slaughtered, we are not to overlook the important fact that it is often owing to the debilitated condition of the body, arising from insufficient nutrition, that great havoc is made by several other diseases. It is not difficult to understand how a child, whose veins were filled with good blood, the result of nutritious diet and pure air, may withstand the shock of scarlet fever, or measles, or inflammation of the brain or lungs, or any other of the numerous ills which infant flesh is heir to, to which the victim of swill milk must almost certainly succumb. In this view we must add another thousand to this holocaust of children in that single year.

Chronology   Events Relating to the History of the Health, Education, and Welfare of Children and Youth, 1535-1865

1535   Under Henry VIII a statute is enacted for apprenticing poor children

1562   The Elizabethan Statute of Artificers legalizes and regulates apprenticeship

1587   Virginia Dare (1587–?) is first white child born in English colonies. She disappears with other members of the "Lost Colony"

1601   Elizabethan Poor Law and Statute of Charitable Uses enacted by Parliament

1609   Virginia Company officials are authorized to kidnap Indian children in order to bring them up Christians

1619   A London philanthropist gives £500 for the education of Indian children in Virginia

1619   First Negroes land at Virginia

1619   Shipment of poor children from England to Virginia is regularized

1620   Privy Council grants Virginia Company authority to coerce children to ship out to Virginia

1620   One-third of *Mayflower* passengers are children. Peregrine White is born on the ship as it lies in Plymouth harbor. He lives until 1704

1621   English brides arrive in Virginia to be sold to planters

1634   Benjamin Syms of Virginia endows first free school in the colonies

1635   Boston Latin School, modeled after English grammar school, founded

1636   Harvard founded

1636   Lord Baltimore promises fifty-acre land grants to every immigrant child under the age of sixteen

1636   Massachusetts requires single persons to live in families

1637   Connecticut requires single young men to live with families unless the town consents otherwise

1638
–1639   Maryland law establishes length of service owed by imported servants

1639   Salem, Massachusetts, court acquits master arraigned for death of his apprentice

1641   Massachusetts defines inheritance for children whose parents die intestate

1641   In Plymouth children of relief recipients must work

1641   Three Massachusetts clergymen—Hugh Peter, Thomas Weld, and William Hibben—are sent to England to raise money for Harvard, missionaries to the Indians, and the transportation of poor children

1642   Massachusetts statute requires parents and masters to teach their children to read and to learn a trade

1642
–1643   Virginia law establishes length of service of servants imported without indentures

1645   Directors of West India Company urge importation of poor and orphaned children from the Netherlands

1646   John Eliot in Massachusetts catechizes Indian children

1646   Massachusetts courts assume responsibility for poor and idle children

1647   Massachusetts General Court requires towns to maintain schoolmasters

1651   New Haven court upholds binding out of children without father's consent

1654   Shipment of poor Dutch children arrives at Fort New Amsterdam

1660   Massachusetts holds men proved to be fathers of bastards liable for the children's support

1661   Maryland court binds brother and sister to different masters

1661
–1662   Virginia preserves orphans' estates for their education and binds out poor orphans as apprentices

1662   Virginia establishes inheritance of slave status through the mother

1664   Carolina promises land to freemen and their families

1664   Council for Foreign Plantations recommends to Privy Council that compulsory shipping of children to Virginia be halted

1668   Counties in Virginia take responsibility for binding out and training poor children in useful occupations and trades

ca.
1670   Massachusetts assigns tithingmen to assist selectmen and constables in supervising family government

1671   Bill to halt involuntary shipping of children to Virginia fails to pass Parliament

1672   Boston orders poor families to bind out their children as servants

1672   In Virginia poor children must be apprenticed until twenty-one (boys) or eighteen (girls) years of age

1674   Salem, Massachusetts, court awards damages to father of boy abused by his master

1675   Suffolk County (Massachusetts) Court removes children from unsuitable homes

1675   Massachusetts General Court legislates against unconventional hair styles

1676   Laws of the Duke of York establish corporal punishment for stubborn children

1676   Connecticut requires single persons to submit to authority of family with whom they are living

1682   Pennsylvania rules that parents, masters, and guardians must see that their children are educated and trained. The Crown disallows the law

1682   Massachusetts tithingmen extend responsibilities to include investigation of idle persons who fail to support their families

1683   New York court cautions master against abusing his apprentice

ca.
1690   *The New England Primer* published

1690   John Locke publishes *Some Thoughts Concerning Education,* classic expression of faith in reason and common sense as guides to the good life

1692   Witch trials in Salem

1693   College of William and Mary chartered. Robert Boyle leaves the residue of his estate to the College for the education of young Indians

1699   North Carolina binds out poor orphans

1700   Connecticut General Court requires towns to establish grammar schools and threatens fines to ensure compliance

1701   Society for the Propagation of the Gospel in Foreign Parts chartered in England and begins sending schoolmasters and missionaries to the southern and middle-Atlantic colonies

1701   Yale founded

1705   Virginia requires children of white women and Negroes to serve thirty-one years

1709
–1710   Three thousand poor and sick Palatine Germans arrive at New York

1711   South Carolina legislates that baptism of slaves does not affect their slave status

1721   Cotton Mather persuades Dr. Zabdiel Boylston to experiment with smallpox inoculation. The practice remains controversial for many years

1729   Orphan home established at Ursuline Convent, New Orleans, first in present boundaries of United States

1734
–1742   Great Awakening

1738   German settlers establish Georgia's first orphanage, at Ebenezer

1739
–1740   George Whitefield raises funds for an orphan house in Georgia

1740   South Carolina prohibits teaching slaves to write. This is the earliest statutory prohibition of education for slaves

1746   College of New Jersey founded. It later becomes Princeton University

1749   Benjamin Franklin publishes his influential *Proposals Relating to the Education of Youth in Pennsilvania*

1751 The Academy, Benjamin Franklin's brainchild, opens in Philadelphia. It later becomes the University of Pennsylvania

1752 Pennsylvania Hospital, Philadelphia, opened

1754 Eleazar Wheelock founds school for Indians in Connecticut. In 1769 he moves school to New Hampshire where it becomes Dartmouth College

1754 Kings College (Columbia) founded

1764 Brown University founded

1765 First medical school founded in Philadelphia by John Morgan; later becomes the Medical Department of University of Pennsylvania

1766 Queens University founded. It later becomes Rutgers

1767 Kings College starts medical school

1776 North Carolina Constitution authorizes establishment of public schools

1777 Vermont constitution establishes public schools

1778 Phillips Academy, Andover, founded

1779 Thomas Jefferson proposes a comprehensive system of public schools in Virginia

1780 Pennsylvania legislature passes an act for the gradual abolition of slavery

1784 Rhode Island enacts law authorizing gradual abolition of slavery

1785 United States Land Ordinance reserves a lot within every township "for the maintenance of public schools"

1785 In Virginia overseers of the poor replace churchwardens in administration of poor relief

1787 Northwest Ordinance includes phrase "schools and the means of education shall forever be encouraged" in the Northwest Territory

1788 Slaveowners in New Jersey required to teach their slaves to read

1789 Massachusetts law creates new educational jurisdiction, the school district

1789 University of North Carolina founded

1789 Samuel Slater introduces Arkwright machinery and the family employment system to the American textile industry

1790 Charleston, South Carolina, establishes country's first public orphanage

1791 Alexander Hamilton recommends employment of women and children in manufacturing

1793 Respublica *v.* Keppele, 2 Dallas (Penna.) 197, rules parents and guardians cannot bind out their children except as apprentices

1793 Maryland act regulates apprenticing of poor children

1793 Yellow fever epidemic in Philadelphia

1795 New York state law authorizes the use of New York City funds to support charity schools. State funds match these city funds

1796 President Washington recommends establishment of a national university

1796 Charles Caldwell submits first medical monograph relating to children for doctor of medicine degree

1797 Society for the Relief of Poor Widows with Small Children founded in New York

ca.
1800 Female charitable orphan asylums established in Savanna, Baltimore, Salem, Boston, Philadelphia, and New York

1800 Dr. Benjamin Waterhouse tests smallpox vaccination on his own family

1800 South Carolina punishes "unlawful assemblage of persons of colour" including schoolroom gatherings

1802 Pennsylvania legislature provides for establishment of free schools for the poor

1805 Public School Society of New York City is founded to educate poor children not attending parochial charity schools

1806 Orphan Asylum Society established in New York, an outgrowth of the Society for the relief of Poor Widows with Small Children

1809 South Carolina court decision equates children of slaves with offspring of animals (M'Vaughters, Administrator of M'Lain *v.* Elder, 2 Brevard 307)

1809 New York state legislature awards Orphan Asylum Society five thousand dollars from the proceeds of a lottery

1809 Public School Society of New York introduces Lancastrian system of instruction in its schools

1811 New York state grants annual subsidy of

five hundred dollars to Orphan Asylum Society

1813   Connecticut passes country's first law providing for education of factory children

1813   Federal law encourages vaccination

1817   American Asylum for the Education and Instruction of the Deaf and Dumb, Hartford, Connecticut, opens with Thomas Hopkins Gallaudet as the first principal. Asylums for deaf children established in Philadelphia and New York, 1818–1822

1818   American Board of Commissioners for Foreign Missions (Congregational) establishes Indian school at Eliot, Choctaw Nation

1818
–1819   New York philanthropist John Griscom visits Europe to learn of various efforts to help destitute and incorrigible children

1819   Congress appropriates funds for Indian education

1819   Louisiana grants annual subsidy to Female Orphan Society. This program subsequently expands to other homes and asylums

1819   Dartmouth College Case

1821   New York law authorizes magistrates to send neglected children to almshouses

1821   English High School founded in Boston

1825   House of Refuge, first institution for juvenile delinquents in United States, founded in New York. Similar institutions founded in Boston (1826) and Philadelphia (1828)

1827   Massachusetts legislature makes compulsory the support of schools by taxation

1830
–1831   Leake and Watts Asylum for orphans founded in New York City

1832   Samuel G. Howe opens New England Asylum for the Blind in Boston. It later becomes Perkins Institution

1833   Beaumont and Toqueville visit American juvenile reformatories

1834   Pennsylvania makes public education general instead of confining it to the children of the indigent; entire system becomes tax supported

1836   Colored Orphan Asylum opened in New York City

1836   Massachusetts adopts compulsory school attendance law, the country's first

1836   Mt. Holyoke Seminary founded, first women's college

1837   Appointment of Horace Mann as secretary of Massachusetts State Board of Education

1837   Instruction of Laura Bridgman, blind and deaf girl, is begun by Samuel G. Howe at Perkins Institution

1838   Pennsylvania court upholds right of magistrates to commit children to house of refuge over parental opposition (*Ex parte Crouse*, 4 Wharton 9)

1840
–1842   Rhode Island (1840) and Connecticut (1842) adopt compulsory school attendance laws

1841   Dorothea L. Dix opens crusade for better care of insane; submits her first *Memorial* to Massachusetts legislature in 1843

1842   Massachusetts and Connecticut limit working day for children under twelve to ten hours

1842   John Augustus saves children from jail in Boston by going bail for them

1847   New York State Board of Commissioners of Emigration created, the first permanent state agency for the protection and relief of immigrants

1847   State Reform School for Boys established in Westborough, Massachusetts, the first state institution for juvenile delinquents

1848   Pennsylvania bars children under twelve from factory work

1848   Girard College opens in Philadelphia

1848   Samuel G. Howe reports to the Massachusetts legislature on education of idiots

1849   Western House of Refuge, a state institution for juvenile delinquents, opens in Rochester, New York

1850   Lemuel Shattuck issues *Report* on sanitary survey of Massachusetts

1850   Teaching of physiology and hygiene recommended in all public schools in Massachusetts

1850   Massachusetts incorporates school for idiotic and feeble-minded youth

1850   House of Refuge for Negro children opens in Philadelphia

1851 New York Juvenile Asylum founded for para-delinquent children

1851 New York State Asylum for the feeble-minded founded

1852 Massachusetts undertakes care of state paupers in state institutions

1852 Ohio limits working day of children under eighteen to ten hours

1853 New Orleans yellow fever epidemic makes orphans of many children

1853 New York Children's Aid Society founded

1853 Rhode Island prohibits factory employment of children under twelve

1854 President Pierce vetoes Dix bill proposing land grants to states for support of institutions for the insane and the deaf

1855 Immigrant landing depot established in Castle Garden, New York, to protect immigrants from unscrupulous transportation agents and boarding house runners

1855 Children's Hospital of Philadelphia founded, first institution designed exclusively for children

1855 New York Children's Aid Society sends its first band of child emigrants to the West

1856 Massachusetts State Industrial School for Girls, the first United States reform school to adopt the cottage plan, founded at Lancaster

1857 New York legislature urges superintendents of poor to remove poor children from almshouses and place them in orphanages

1857 The Columbia Institution for the Deaf, Dumb and Blind incorporated by act of Congress. In 1894 it is renamed Gallaudet College

1857 Ohio Reform School for boys, a cottage school, established

1860 Dr. Abraham Jacobi, at the New York Medical College, is appointed to the first special chair of diseases of children

1860 Indian boarding school founded on the Yakima Reservation, Washington Territory

1861 –1866 Number of children in New York almshouses increases 300 per cent as Civil War makes orphans of many children and intensifies problems of dependency

1862 Morrill Act grants land for colleges

1863 Emancipation Proclamation

1863 New York draft rioters burn Colored Orphan Asylum

1863 New York Catholic Protectory founded

1863 Massachusetts State Board of Charities organized

1864 Congress passes legislation authorizing the Columbia Institution for the Deaf and Dumb to present college degrees. Edward M. Gallaudet elected president

1865 Thirteenth Amendment abolishes slavery

Appendix   The Child and the State Project, 1965-1970

DIRECTOR

Martha M. Eliot, M.D.

ASSOCIATE DIRECTOR

William M. Schmidt, M.D.

EDITOR

Robert H. Bremner

ASSOCIATE EDITORS

John Barnard
Tamara K. Hareven
Robert M. Mennel (1969–1970)

EXECUTIVE COMMITTEE

Martha M. Eliot, M.D.
William M. Schmidt, M.D.
Thomas R. Hood, M.D.
Oscar Handlin
Robert H. Bremner

EDITORIAL ASSISTANTS

Paula Cronin
Robert S. Demorest

SENIOR RESEARCH ASSISTANTS

Robert Mennel (Delinquency, 1966–1968)
Susanna Adams (Child labor, education, and
    welfare)
Leslie Rosenfeld (Education)
Manfred Waserman (Health)

RESEARCH ASSISTANTS

Dwight Allen
Joan P. Barnard
Marc Blackman
Marcia Brubeck
Peter Buchsbaum

Timothy Burke
Marcia Hovey Chessman
John Driscoll
Richard M. Friedman
Allan Gerschenson
Robert Hanson
George Hayward
Ellen Kerstedter
Gultekin Ludden
Steven Marrone
Nicholas D. Nelson
Helen Olney
Phyllis Palmer
John P. Resch
Max Richtman
Donald B. Schewe
Roger Schnapp
Linford Smith
Mindy Winslow
Roy Wortman
Donald Zelman
Patricia Grace Zelman

SECRETARIAL ASSISTANTS

Elaine Bialczak
Claudia Crispin
Gisela G. Mennel
Esther Pepple
Sara Rollins
Marie-Dolores Solano
Mary Stroud
Jack Weitz
Cheryl Wilson

CONSULTANTS

Winifred Bell
Jessie M. Bierman, M.D.
John Blake
Clarke Chambers
Robert Church
John Demos

823

Jeremy Felt
Daniel Fox
Alfred Kadushin
Kenneth Keniston
Marvin Lazarson
James Leiby
Lloyd Ohlin
Leonard Schneiderman
Vladimir Steffel
Arthur E. Sutherland
John Te Paske
Stephan Thernstrom
John D. Thompson
David Tyack
Stephen Wood

ADVISORY PANEL

Dr. James E. Allen, Jr., United States
Commissioner of Education

Jessie M. Bierman, M.D., Director,
MCH Research Unit, University of
California at Berkeley

Dr. Eveline M. Burns, Professor of Social
Work, Columbia University School of
Social Work

Professor Clarke Chambers, Department of
History, University of Minnesota

Dr. Kenneth B. Clark, Director, Northside
Center for Child Development, New York City

Eli E. Cohen, Executive Secretary, National
Committee on Employment of Youth

Dr. Lawrence A. Cremin, Professor of
Education and Head, Department of Social and
Philosophical Foundations of Education,
Columbia University

Arthur J. Lesser, M.D., Deputy Chief,
Children's Bureau, Department of Health,
Education, and Welfare

Alton A. Linford, Dean, School of Social
Service Administration, University of Chicago

Milton G. Rector, Director, National Council
on Crime and Delinquency

Joseph Reid, Executive Director, Child
Welfare League of America

Julius B. Richmond, M.D., Dean, State
University of New York, Upstate Medical
Center, College of Medicine

William M. Schmidt, M.D., Professor of Maternal
and Child Health, Harvard School of Public
Health

Arthur E. Sutherland, L.L.B., Bussey Professor
of Law, Faculty of Public Administration,
Harvard Law School

John D. Thompson, M.D., Professor and
Chairman, Department of Gynecology and
Obstetrics, Emory University, School of Medicine

Selected Bibliography

GENERAL

Abbott, Grace. *The Child and the State*. 2 volumes. Chicago: The University of Chicago Press, 1938.

Adams, James Truslow. *Provincial Society, 1690–1763*. New York: The Macmillan Company, 1927.

Andrews, Charles M. *Colonial Folkways: A Chronicle of American Life in the Reign of the Georges*. New Haven: Yale University Press, 1919.

———— *The Colonial Period of American History*. 4 volumes. New Haven: Yale University Press, 1934–1938.

Ariès, Philippe. *Centuries of Childhood*. New York: Alfred A. Knopf, 1962.

Bremner, Robert H. *American Philanthropy*. Chicago: University of Chicago Press, 1960.

Bridenbaugh, Carl. *Cities in Revolt: Urban Life in America, 1743–1776*. New York: Alfred A. Knopf, 1955.

———— *Cities in the Wilderness: The First Century of Urban Life in America, 1625–1742*. New York: Alfred A. Knopf, 1964.

———— *Vexed and Troubled Englishmen*. New York: Oxford University Press, 1968.

Brown, Alexander. *The Genesis of the United States*. 2 volumes. Boston and New York: Houghton, Mifflin and Company, 1890.

Bruce, Philip Alexander. *Economic History of Virginia in the Seventeenth Century*. 2 volumes. New York: The Macmillan Company, 1896.

Buley, Roscoe Carlyle. *The Old Northwest Pioneer Period, 1815–1840*. 2 volumes. Bloomington: Indiana University Press, 1951.

Calhoun, Arthur. *A Social History of the American Family*. 3 volumes. New York: Barnes and Noble, 1960.

Crane, Verner W. *The Southern Frontier, 1670–1732*. Ann Arbor: The University of Michigan Press, 1956.

Earle, Alice M. *Child Life in Colonial Days*. New York: The Macmillan Company, 1899.

———— *Home Life in Colonial Days*. New York: The Macmillan Company, 1910.

Greene, Evarts Boutell, and Virginia D. Harrington. *American Population Before the Federal Census of 1790*. Gloucester, Mass.: Peter Smith, 1966.

———— *Provincial America, 1690–1740*. New York: Harper and Brothers, 1905.

Heimert, Alan. *Religion and the American Mind, from the Great Awakening to the Revolution*. Cambridge, Mass.: Harvard University Press, 1966.

Jameson, J. Franklin. *The American Revolution Considered as a Social Movement*. Princeton, N.J.: Princeton University Press, 1926.

Kirkland, Edward C. *Men, Cities and Transportation: A Study in New England History, 1820–1900*. 2 volumes. Cambridge, Mass.: Harvard University Press, 1948.

Laslett, Peter. *The World We Have Lost*. New York: Charles Scribner's Sons, 1966.

Main, Jackson Turner. *The Social Structure of Revolutionary America*. Princeton, N.J.: Princeton University Press, 1965.

Morgan, Edmund S. *The Puritan Family: Essays on Religion and Domestic Relations in Seventeenth-Century New England*. Boston, Mass.: The Trustees of the Public Library, 1944.

———— *Virginians at Home: Family Life in the Eighteenth Century*. Williamsburg: Colonial Williamsburg, Inc., 1952.

Morison, Samuel Eliot. *The Story of the Old Colony of New Plymouth, 1620–1692*. New York: Alfred A. Knopf, 1956.

Neill, Edward D. *Virginia Carolorum: The Colony under the Rule of Charles the First and Second . . . 1625–1685*. Albany: J. Munsell's Sons, 1886.

Nettles, Curtis P. *The Emergence of A National Economy, 1775–1815*. New York: Holt, Rinehart and Winston, 1962.

Oberholzer, Emil, Jr. *Delinquent Saints: Disciplinary Action in the Early Congregational Churches of Massachusetts*. New York: Columbia University Press, 1956.

Olmsted, Frederick Law. *The Cotton Kingdom*. 2 volumes. New York: Mason Brothers, 1861–1862.

Rossiter, W. S. *A Century of Population Growth from the First Census of the United States, to the Twelfth, 1790–1900*. Washington, D.C.: Government Printing Office, 1909.

Thernstrom, Stephan. *Poverty and Progress: Social Mobility in a Nineteenth Century City*. Cambridge, Mass.: Harvard University Press, 1964.

Ver Steeg, Clarence. *The Formative Years, 1607–1763*. New York: Hill and Wang, 1964.

Weeden, William B. *Economic and Social History of*

New England, 1620–1789. 2 volumes. New York: Hillary House Publishers, Ltd., 1963.

Wertenbaker, Thomas Jefferson. *The First Americans, 1607–1690.* New York: The Macmillan Company, 1927.

CHILD HEALTH

Best, Harry. *Deafness and the Deaf.* New York: The Macmillan Company, 1943.

Blake, John B. *Public Health in the Town of Boston, 1630–1822.* Cambridge, Mass.: Harvard University Press, 1959.

Caulfield, Ernest. *A True History of the Terrible Epidemic Vulgarly Called the Throat Distemper.* New Haven: Yale Journal of Biology and Medicine, 1939.

Deutsch, Albert. *The Mentally Ill in America.* 2d edition. New York: Columbia University Press, 1949.

———— "The Sick Poor in Colonial Times." *American Historical Review,* XLVI (April 1941), 560–579.

Duffy, John. *Epidemics in Colonial America.* Baton Rouge: Louisiana State University Press, 1953.

Garrison, Fielding H. *History of Pediatrics; with New Chapters on the History of Pediatrics in Recent Times by Arthur F. Abt.* Philadelphia: W. B. Saunders Co., 1965.

Kett, Joseph F. *The Formation of the American Medical Profession: The Role of Institutions, 1780–1860.* New Haven: Yale University Press, 1968.

Morton, Thomas G. *The History of the Pennsylvania Hospital, 1751–1895.* Philadelphia: Times Printing House, 1897.

Postell, William D. *The Health of Slaves on Southern Plantations.* Baton Rouge: Louisiana State University Press, 1951.

Ramsay, David. *A Review of the Improvements, Progress, and State of Medicine in the XVIIIth Century.* Charleston, S.C.: W. P. Young, 1801.

Shryock, Richard H. "Changing Outlooks in American Medicine over Three Centuries," in Joseph H. Kiefer, comp., *Essays in the History of Medicine.* Urbana: University of Illinois Press, 1965.

———— *The History of Nursing.* Philadelphia: W. B. Saunders Company, 1959.

———— *Medicine and Society in America, 1660–1860.* New York: New York University Press, 1960.

Waring, Joseph Ioor. *A History of Medicine in South Carolina, 1670–1825.* Charleston: South Carolina Medical Association, 1964.

———— "St. Philip's Hospital in Charlestown: Medical Care of the Poor in Colonial Times." *Annals of Medical History,* IV (May 1932), 283–289.

Wisner, Elizabeth. *Public Welfare Administration in Louisiana.* Chicago: University of Chicago Press, 1930.

CHILD LABOR

Abbott, Edith. "A Study of the Early History of Child Labor in America." *The American Journal of Sociology,* XIV (July 1908), 15–37.

———— "The Wages of Unskilled Labor in the United States, 1850–1900." *Journal of Political Economy,* XIII (1905), 321–367.

———— *Women in Industry.* New York and London: D. Appleton and Co., 1909.

Bagnall, William R. *Textile Industries of the United States.* Cambridge, Mass.: The Riverside Press, 1893.

Ballagh, James Curtis. *White Servitude in the Colony of Virginia.* Baltimore: The Johns Hopkins Press, 1895.

Batchelder, Samuel. *Introduction and Early Progress of the Cotton Manufacture in the United States.* Boston: Little, Brown and Company, 1863.

Bishop, J. Leander. *A History of American Manufactures from 1608–1860* . . . 3 volumes. Philadelphia: Edward Young & Co., 1861–1866.

Bridenbaugh, Carl. *The Colonial Craftsman.* New York: New York University Press, 1950.

Cole, Arthur Harrison. *The American Wool Manufacture.* 2 volumes. Cambridge, Mass.: Harvard University Press, 1926.

Commons, John R. et al., eds. *A Documentary History of American Industrial Society.* 10 volumes. Cleveland: Arthur H. Clark Company, 1910–1911.

———— *History of Labor in the United States.* 4 volumes. New York: The Macmillan Company, 1918–1935.

Coolidge, John P. *Mill and Mansion: A Study of Architecture and Society in Lowell, Mass., 1820–1865.* New York: Columbia University Press, 1942.

Douglas, Paul H. *American Apprenticeship and Industrial Education.* New York: Columbia University, 1921.

Dunlop, O. Jocelyn, and Richard D. Denman. *English Apprenticeship and Child Labour: A History.* New York: The Macmillan Company, 1912.

Fite, Emerson D. *Social and Industrial Conditions in the North During the Civil War.* New York: The Macmillan Company, 1910.

Geiser, Karl F. *Redemptioners and Indentured Servants in the Colony and Commonwealth of Pennsylvania.* New Haven: The Tuttle, Morehouse and Taylor Company, 1901.

Gitelman, H. H. "The Labor Force at Waltham Watch during the Civil War Era." *The Journal of Economic History,* XXV (June 1965), 214–243.

Herrick, C. A. *White Servitude in Pennsylvania: Indentured and Redemption Labor in Colony and Commonwealth.* Philadelphia: John Joseph McVey, 1926.

Hohman, Elmo Paul. *The American Whaleman: A Study of Life and Labor in the Whaling Industry.*

New York: Longmans, Green and Company, 1928.

Jernegan, Marcus Wilson. *Laboring and Dependent Classes in Colonial America, 1607–1783.* Chicago: The University of Chicago Press, 1931.

Kingsbury, Susan M., ed. *Labor Laws and their Enforcement.* New York: Longmans, Green and Company, 1911.

Kirkland, Edward C. *A History of American Economic Life.* 3d edition. New York: Appleton-Century-Crofts, 1951.

Morris, Richard B. *Government and Labor in Early America.* New York: Columbia University Press, 1946.

Morison, Samuel Eliot. *The Maritime History of Massachusetts, 1783–1860.* Boston and New York: Houghton Mifflin Company, 1961.

Otey, Elizabeth Lewis. "Employment of Children in the Colonies." *Report on Condition of Woman and Child Wage-Earners in the United States*, VI, 10–23. Washington, D.C.: U.S. Government Printing Office, 1910.

Salmon, Lucy Maynard. *Domestic Service.* New York: The Macmillan Company, 1897.

Seybolt, Robert F. *Apprenticeship and Apprenticeship Education in Colonial New England and New York.* New York: Teachers College, Columbia University, 1917.

Smith, Abbot Emerson. *Colonists in Bondage: White Servitude and Convict Labor in America, 1607–1776.* Chapel Hill: University of North Carolina Press, 1947.

Smith, Warren B. *White Servitude in Colonial South Carolina.* Columbia: University of South Carolina Press, 1961.

Spruill, Julia Cherry. *Women's Life and Work in the Southern Colonies.* Chapel Hill: University of North Carolina Press, 1938.

Thernstrom, Stephan. *Poverty and Progress: Social Mobility in a Nineteenth Century City.* Cambridge, Mass.: Harvard University Press, 1964.

Tryon, Rolla Milton. *Household Manufactures in the United States, 1640–1860.* Chicago: The University of Chicago Press, 1917.

United States Bureau of Labor. *Report on Condition of Woman and Child Wage-Earners in the United States.* 19 volumes. Washington, D.C.: Government Printing Office, 1910–1913.

Ware, Caroline F. *The Early New England Cotton Manufacture: A Study in Industrial Beginnings.* Boston and New York: Houghton Mifflin Company, 1931.

White, George S. *Memoir of Samuel Slater, the Father of American Manufacturers.* 2d edition. New York: A. M. Kelley Publishers, 1967.

DELINQUENCY

Barnes, Harry Elmer. *The Evolution of Penology in Pennsylvania.* Indianapolis: The Bobbs-Merrill Company, 1927.

Brace, Charles Loring. *The Dangerous Classes of New York, and Twenty Years' Work Among Them.* New York: Wynkoop and Hallenbeck, 1872.

Erikson, Kai T. *Wayward Puritans: A Study in the Sociology of Deviance.* New York: John Wiley and Sons, Inc., 1966.

Fairchild, Byron. "Reefs and Shoals of Colonial Justice." *New England Quarterly*, XXIII (September 1950), 339–350.

Folks, Homer. *The Care of Destitute, Neglected and Delinquent Children.* New York: The Macmillan Company, 1902.

Hale, Edward Everett, T. V. Moore and A. H. Grimshaw. *Prize Essays on Juvenile Delinquency.* Philadelphia: Edward and John Biddle, 1855.

Jacoby, George Paul. *Catholic Child Care in Nineteenth Century New York.* Washington, D.C.: The Catholic University of America Press, 1941.

Katz, Michael B. *The Irony of Early School Reform: Educational Innovation in Mid-Nineteenth Century Massachusetts.* Cambridge, Mass.: Harvard University Press, 1968.

Lane, Francis E. *American Charities and the Child of the Immigrant.* Washington, D.C.: The Catholic University of America, 1932.

Lane, Roger D. *Policing the City: Boston, 1822–1855.* Cambridge, Mass.: Harvard University Press, 1967.

Langsam, Miriam Z. *Children West: A History of the Placing Out System of the New York Children's Aid Society, 1853–1890.* Madison: State Historical Society of Wisconsin, 1964.

Leiby, James. *Charities and Correction in New Jersey: A History of State Welfare Institutions.* New Brunswick, N.J.: Rutgers University Press, 1967.

Lewis, Orlando F. *The Development of American Prisons and Prison Customs, 1776–1845.* Albany: The Prison Association of New York, 1922.

McKelvey, Blake. *American Prisons: A Study in American Social History Prior to 1915.* Chicago: The University of Chicago Press, 1936.

Mohl, Raymond A., Jr. "Poverty, Public Relief and Private Charity in New York City, 1784–1825." Unpublished Ph.D. dissertation, New York University, 1967.

O'Grady, John. *Levi Silliman Ives, Pioneer Leader in Catholic Charities.* New York: P. J. Kenedy and Sons, 1933.

Peirce, Bradford K. *A Half Century With Juvenile Delinquents.* New York: D. Appleton and Company, 1869.

Pierson, George Wilson. *Tocqueville and Beaumont in America.* New York: Oxford University Press, 1938.

Powers, Edwin. *Crime and Punishment in Early Massachusetts.* Boston: Beacon Press Incorporated, 1966.

Schneider, David M. *The History of Public Welfare in New York State, 1609–1866.* Chicago: The University of Chicago Press, 1938.

Schwartz, Harold. *Samuel Gridley Howe: Social Reformer, 1801–1876.* Cambridge, Mass.: Harvard University Press, 1956.

Stewart, William R. *The Philanthropic Work of Josephine Shaw Lowell.* New York: The Macmillan Company, 1911.

Thurston, Henry W. *Concerning Juvenile Delinquency: Progressive Changes in Our Perspectives.* New York: Columbia University Press, 1942.

Williams, Jack Kenny. *Vogues in Villainy: Crime and Retribution in Antebellum South Carolina.* Columbia: University of South Carolina Press, 1959.

DEPENDENCY

Brace, Charles Loring. *The Dangerous Classes of New York and Twenty Years' Work Among Them.* New York: Wynkoop & Hallenbeck, 1872.

Breckinridge, Sophonisba P. *The Illinois Poor Law and Its Administration.* Chicago: The University of Chicago Press, 1939.

Brown, Roy M. *Public Poor Relief in North Carolina.* Chapel Hill: University of North Carolina Press, 1929.

Buckingham, Clyde. "Early American Orphanages: Ebenezer & Bethesda." *Social Forces,* XXVI (March 1948), 311–322.

Butler, James D. "British Convicts Shipped to America." *American Historical Review,* II (October 1896), 12–33.

Campbell, Mildred. "English Emigration on the Eve of the American Revolution." *American Historical Review,* LXI (October 1955), 1–20.

Creech, Margaret D. *Three Centuries of Poor Law Administration; A Study of Legislation in Rhode Island.* Chicago: University of Chicago Press, 1936.

Cruzot, Heloise Hulse. "The Ursulines of Louisiana." *Louisiana Historical Quarterly,* II (January 1919), 5–23.

Folks, Homer. *The Care of Destitute, Neglected, and Delinquent Children.* New York: The Macmillan Company, 1902.

Haviland, Thomas P. "Of Franklin, Whitefield, and the Orphans." *Georgia Historical Quarterly,* XXIX (September 1945), 211–216.

Heffner, William C. *History of Poor Relief Legislation in Pennsylvania, 1682–1913.* Cleona, Pa.: Holzapfel Publishing Company, 1913.

James, Arthur W. "Foster Care in Virginia — 1679–1796." *Public Welfare,* VIII (March 1950), 60–64.

Jernegan, Marcus Wilson. *Laboring and Dependent Classes in Colonial America, 1607–1783.* Chicago: University of Chicago Press, 1931.

Kelso, Robert W. *History of Public Poor Relief in Massachusetts, 1620–1920.* New York: Houghton Mifflin Company, 1922.

Klebaner, Benjamin J. "Pauper Auctions: The 'New England' Method of Public Poor Relief." *Essex Institute Historical Collections,* XCI (July 1955), 195–210.

——— "Public Poor Relief in America, 1790–1860." Unpublished Ph.D. dissertation, Columbia University, 1952.

Leiby, James. *Charities and Correction in New Jersey: A History of State Welfare Institutions.* New Brunswick: Rutgers University Press, 1967.

McEntegart, Bryan J. "How Seventeenth Century New York Cared for Its Poor: The English Period, 1664–1700." *Thought,* II (December 1927), 403–429

Mackey, Howard. "The Operation of the English Old Poor Law in Colonial Virginia." *Virginia Magazine of History and Biography,* LXXIII (April 1965), 29–40

Melder, Keith. "Ladies Bountiful: Organized Women's Benevolence in Early 19th-Century America." *New York History,* XLVIII (1967), 231–254.

Mencher, Samuel. *Poor Law to Poverty Program: Economic Security Policy in Britain and the United States.* Pittsburgh: University of Pittsburgh Press, 1967.

Mohl, Raymond A., Jr. "Poverty, Public Relief, and Private Charity in New York City, 1784–1825." Unpublished Ph.D. dissertation, New York University, 1967.

O'Brien, Edward J. *Child Welfare Legislation in Maryland, 1634–1936.* Washington, D.C.: The Catholic University of America Press, 1937.

Schneider, David M. *The History of Public Welfare in New York State, 1609–1866.* Chicago: The University of Chicago Press, 1938.

Semple, Henry C. *Ursulines in New Orleans . . . A Record of Two Centuries, 1727–1925.* New York: P. J. Kenedy & Sons, 1925.

Surrency, Erwin C. "Whitefield, Habersham, and the Bethesda Orphanage." *Georgia Historical Quarterly,* XXXIV (September 1950), 87–105.

Thurston, Henry W. *The Dependent Child: The Story of Changing Aims and Methods in the Care of Dependent Children.* New York: Columbia University Press, 1930.

Wisner, Elizabeth. *Public Welfare Administration in Louisiana.* Chicago: University of Chicago Press, 1930.

Zietz, Dorothy. *Child Welfare: Services and Perspectives.* 2d edition. New York: John Wiley & Sons, Inc., 1969.

EDUCATION

Andrews, Charles C. *History of the New York African Free Schools.* New York: M. Day, 1830.

Bailyn, Bernard. *Education in the Forming of American Society.* Chapel Hill: University of North Carolina Press, 1960.

Billington, Ray A. *The Protestant Crusade, 1800–1860: A Study of the Origins of American*

Nativism. New York: The Macmillan Company, 1938.

Bourne, William O. *History of the Public School Society of New York*. New York: W. Wood & Company, 1870.

Brookes, George. *Friend Anthony Benezet*. Philadelphia: University of Pennsylvania Press, 1937.

Carlton, Frank T. *Economic Influences upon Educational Progress in the United States, 1820–1850*. Madison, Wis.: The University of Wisconsin, 1908.

Coon, Charles L. *The Beginnings of Public Education in North Carolina: A Documentary History, 1790–1840*. Raleigh: Edwards and Broughton Printing Company, 1908.

Cremin, Lawrence. *The American Common School: An Historic Conception*. New York: Bureau of Publications, Teachers College, Columbia University, 1951.

Culver, Raymond B. *Horace Mann and Religion in the Massachusetts Public Schools*. New Haven: Yale University Press, 1929.

Elson, Ruth M. *Guardians of Tradition: American Schoolbooks of the Nineteenth Century*. Lincoln, Nebr.: University of Nebraska Press, 1964.

Finegan, Thomas E. *Free Schools: A Documentary History of the Free School Movement in New York State*. Albany: The University of the State of New York, 1921.

Fleming, Sandford. *Children and Puritanism: The Place of Children in the Life and Thought of the New England Churches, 1620–1847*. New Haven: Yale University Press, 1933.

Hofstadter, Richard and Wilson Smith, eds. *American Higher Education*. 2 volumes. Chicago: University of Chicago Press, 1961.

Honeywell, Roy J. *The Educational Work of Thomas Jefferson*. Cambridge, Mass.: Harvard University Press, 1931.

Johnson, Clifton. *Old-Time Schools and School-Books*. New York: The Macmillan Company, 1904.

Katz, Michael B. *The Irony of Early School Reform: Educational Innovation in Mid-Nineteenth Century Massachusetts*. Cambridge, Mass.: Harvard University Press, 1968.

Kiefer, Monica. *American Children Through Their Books, 1700–1835*. Philadelphia: University of Pennsylvania Press, 1948.

Knight, Edgar W., ed. *A Documentary History of Education in the South before 1860*. 5 volumes. Chapel Hill: University of North Carolina Press, 1949–1953.

Kuhn, Anne L. *The Mother's Role in Childhood Education: New England Concepts, 1830–1860*. New Haven: Yale University Press, 1947.

Livingston, Helen E. "Thomas Morritt, Schoolmaster at the Charleston Free School, 1723–1728." *Historical Magazine of the Protestant Episcopal Church*, XIV (1945), 151–167.

McCadden, Joseph J. "Bishop Hughes Versus the Public School Society of New York." *Catholic Historical Review*, L (September 1965), 188–208.

Messerli, Jonathan C. "Localism and State Control in Horace Mann's Reform of the Common Schools." *American Quarterly*, XVII (Spring 1965), 104–118.

Middlekauff, Robert. *Ancients and Axioms: Secondary Education in Eighteenth-Century New England*. New Haven: Yale University Press, 1963.

Morison, Samuel Eliot. *The Founding of Harvard College*. Cambridge, Mass.: Harvard University Press, 1935.

———— *Harvard College in the Seventeenth Century*. 2 volumes. Cambridge, Mass.: Harvard University Press, 1936.

———— *The Puritan Pronaos*. New York: New York University Press, 1936.

Murdock, Kenneth B. "The Teaching of Latin and Greek at the Boston Latin School in 1712." *Publications of the Colonial Society of Massachusetts*, XXVII (1927–1930), 21–29.

Pinchbeck, Joy. "The State and the Child in Sixteenth Century England." *British Journal of Sociology*, VII (1956), 273–285; VIII (1957), 59–74.

Rudolph, Frederick. *The American College and University*. New York: Alfred A. Knopf, 1962.

Seybolt, Robert F. *The Evening School in Colonial America*. Urbana: University of Illinois, 1925.

———— *The Private Schools of Colonial Boston*. Cambridge, Mass.: Harvard University Press, 1935.

———— *The Public Schoolmasters of Colonial Boston*. Cambridge, Mass.: Privately printed at the Harvard University Press, 1939.

———— *The Public Schools of Colonial Boston, 1635–1775*. Cambridge, Mass.: Harvard University Press, 1935.

Shipton, Clifford K. "Secondary Education in the Puritan Colonies." *New England Quarterly*, VII (December 1934), 646–661.

Welter, Rush. *Popular Education and Democratic Thought in America*. New York: Columbia University Press, 1962.

Woodson, Carter G. *The Education of the Negro Prior to 1861*. 2d edition. Washington, D.C.: Associated Publishers, Inc., 1919.

IMMIGRATION

Abbott, Edith. *Historical Aspects of the Immigration Problem*. Chicago: The University of Chicago Press, 1926.

———— *Immigration: Select Documents*. Chicago: The University of Chicago Press, 1924.

Adams, W. F. *Ireland and the Irish Emigration to the New World, from 1815 to the Famine*. New Haven: Yale University Press, 1932.

Berthoff, Rowland T. *British Immigrants in Industrial America, 1790–1950*. New York: Russell & Russell Publishers, 1953.

Blegen, Theodore C. "Immigrant Women and the

American Frontier." *Norwegian-American Studies and Records.* Northfield, Minn., 1930.

———, ed. *Land of Their Choice: The Immigrants Write Home.* Minneapolis: University of Minnesota Press, 1955.

——— *Norwegian Migration to America, 1825–1860.* Northfield, Minn.: The Norwegian-American Historical Association, 1931.

Bromwell, William J. *History of Immigration to the United States.* New York: Redfield, 1856.

Campbell, Mildred. "English Emigration on the Eve of the American Revolution." *American Historical Review,* LXI (October 1955), 1–20.

Cullen, James Bernard. *The Story of the Irish in Boston.* Boston: J. B. Cullen & Company, 1889.

Ernst, Robert. *Immigrant Life in New York City, 1825–1863.* New York: Columbia University Press, 1949.

Handlin, Oscar. *Boston's Immigrants, 1790–1865: A Study in Acculturation.* Rev. and enl. ed. Cambridge, Mass.: Harvard University Press, 1959.

——— *The Uprooted.* Boston: Little, Brown & Co., 1951.

Hansen, Marcus Lee. *The Atlantic Migration, 1607–1860.* Cambridge, Mass.: Harvard University Press, 1940.

Johnson, Stanley C. *A History of Emigration from the United Kingdom to North America, 1763–1912.* New York: E. P. Dutton & Company, 1914.

Kapp, Friedrich. *Immigration and the Commissioners of Emigration of the State of New York.* New York: The Nation Press, 1870.

Knittle, Walter A. *Early Eighteenth Century Palatine Emigration.* Philadelphia: Dorrance & Company, 1937.

Kuhns, Oscar. *The German and Swiss Settlements of Colonial Pennsylvania.* New York: Henry Holt & Company, 1901.

Lane, Francis E. *American Charities and the Child of the Immigrant.* Washington, D.C.: The Catholic University of America, 1932.

McGhee, Thomas D'Arcy. *A History of the Irish Settlers in North America.* Boston: Office of the "American Celt," 1851.

Maguire, John F. *The Irish in America.* London: Longman's, Green and Company, 1868.

Schrier, Arnold. *Ireland and the American Emigration, 1850–1900.* Minneapolis: University of Minnesota Press, 1958.

Stephensen, George M. *A History of American Immigration, 1820–1924.* New York: Ginn and Company, 1926.

Wittke, Carl. *We Who Built America . . .* Cleveland: Press of Western Reserve University, 1939.

NEGROES AND INDIANS

Franklin, John Hope. *The Free Negro in North Carolina, 1790–1860.* Chapel Hill: The University of North Carolina Press, 1943.

Greene, Lorenzo J. *The Negro in Colonial New England, 1620–1776.* New York, Columbia University Press, 1942.

Hagan, William T. *American Indians.* Chicago: University of Chicago Press, 1961.

Jordan, Winthrop D. *White Over Black: American Attitudes toward the Negro, 1550–1812.* Chapel Hill: The University of North Carolina Press, 1968.

Klingberg, Frank J. *An Appraisal of the Negro in Colonial South Carolina.* Washington, D.C.: Associated Publishers, Inc., 1941.

Litwack, Leon F. *North of Slavery: The Negro in the Free States, 1790–1860.* Chicago: University of Chicago Press, 1961.

Phillips, Ulrich B. *American Negro Slavery.* New York: D. Appleton & Company, 1918.

——— *Life and Labor in the Old South.* Boston: Little, Brown & Company, 1929.

Russell, John H. *The Free Negro in Virginia, 1619–1865.* Baltimore: Johns Hopkins Press, 1913.

Stampp, Kenneth. *The Peculiar Institution.* New York: Alfred A. Knopf, 1956.

Wade, Richard. *Slavery in the Cities: The South, 1820–1860.* New York: Oxford University Press, 1964.

Wiley, Bell Irvin. *Southern Negroes, 1861–1865.* New Haven: Yale University Press, 1938.

Woodson, Carter G. *The History of the Negro Church.* 2d edition. Washington, D.C.: Associated Publishers, Inc., 1921.

Index